Ecology and Management of the Mourning Dove

ECOLOGY AND MANAGEMENT
of the

MOURNING DOVE

A Wildlife Management Institute Book

Compiled and edited by

**Thomas S. Baskett, Mark W. Sayre
Roy E. Tomlinson and Ralph E. Mirarchi**

Technical editor **Richard E. McCabe**

Text illustrations by **Harold W. Irby**

Dustjacket illustration by **Francis E. Sweet**

Published by STACKPOLE BOOKS, Harrisburg, PA, USA

The *WILDLIFE MANAGEMENT INSTITUTE* is a private, nonprofit, scientific and educational organization based in Washington, D.C. The Institute's sole objective, since its founding in 1911, has been to help advance restoration and proper management of North America's natural resources, especially wildlife. As a part of the Institute's program, scientific information generated through research and management experiences is consolidated, published and used to strengthen resource decision making and management. *Ecology and Management of the Mourning Dove* is one of more than twenty-five wildlife books produced by WMI, including the award-winning *Ducks, Geese and Swans of North America*, *Big Game of North America*, *Mule and Black-tailed Deer of North America*, *Elk of North America*, and *White-tailed Deer*. For additional information about the Institute, its programs and publications, write to: Wildlife Management Institute, Suite 725, 1101 Fourteenth Street, N.W., Washington, D.C. 20005.

Copyright © 1993 by the **Wildlife Management Institute**

Published by STACKPOLE BOOKS
Cameron and Kelker Streets
Harrisburg, Pennsylvania 17105

Design and layout by REM/WMI

Printed in the U.S.A.

10 9 8 7 6 5 4 3 2 1

First edition

Library of Congress Cataloging-in-Publication Data

Ecology and management of the mourning dove / compiled and edited by
    Thomas S. Baskett . . . [et al.] : text illustrations by Harold W.
    Irby. — 1st ed.
        p.   cm.
    "A Wildlife Management Institute book."
    Includes bibliographical references (p.   ) and index.
    ISBN 0-8117-1940-5
    1. Mourning dove. 2. Bird populations. 3. Wildlife management.
    4. Mourning dove shooting. I. Baskett, Thomas S.
    QL696.C63E36   1993
    639.9'7865—dc20   92-28155
                                                          CIP

This book is dedicated to the memories of
Howard M. Wight and Mark W. Sayre.
Each, in his own time and his own way, provided
much of the impetus for the book.

Howard M. Wight
1923–1975

Mark W. Sayre
1951–1990

Foreword

The Voice of the Turtle was the title of a play that enjoyed a run of almost 1,600 stage performances in New York City in the 1940s, capped off by a hundred more performances in London in 1947. The play's name was drawn from the Old Testament, Song of Solomon, Chapter 2: "The flowers appear on the earth; the time of the singing of the birds is come, and the voice of the turtle is heard in our land."

This biblical "turtle" is an Old World dove, celebrated by the ancients as a harbinger of spring. It shares with most doves and pigeons worldwide the habit of extending and retracting its neck when walking, suggestive of a turtle pulling its head in and out of its shell.

The voice of our New World "turtle" — the mourning dove — has utility to wildlife biologists and managers far exceeding the pleasant news that winter is ending. The mourning dove Call-count Survey, based on systematic annual tallies of singing males, provides one of the most carefully organized and analyzed data sets for population trend assessment of any single North American gamebird species.

We can argue that, despite widespread participation in or support of annual Call-count Surveys, wildlife researchers, managers and their administrative supervisors have not given the mourning dove the attention it deserves. Consider that the annual harvest of this dove in the United States is about 45 million birds — far more than any other species of gamebird. Furthermore, it is a familiar and much-appreciated bird in some cities and in many suburban and rural settings in southern Canada, the entire United States, and northern Mexico.

It is paradoxical that we question the attention given the mourning dove, when this book contains citations of more than 1,300 references germane to the biology and management of the species. Many of these publications were ultimate products of a surge of interest in mourning doves from the late 1940s through the mid-1960s. Solid research and management programs emerged during that period, and important research papers and bulletins resulted.

It is significant, however, that this is the only comprehensive book dealing with basic biology, ecology and management of the mourning dove. Its relatively late appearance is symptomatic of the generally subsiding research and management thrusts for the species in recent years. (Fortunately, there are a few vigorous exceptions to the waning trend.)

Much remains to be done. We still lack a uniform nationwide framework for collecting and analyzing harvest data for the most shot-at gamebird in the United States. We no longer have a comprehensive nationwide banding program that enables us to check mortality/survival rates or changes thereof with the precision needed to adjust harvest regulations appropriately for this dove. This lack of continuous banding data is particularly unfortunate at a time when there is clear evidence of population declines in parts of the mourning dove's range. Also, we lack definitive knowledge about quantitative effects of ongoing, readily discernible environmental changes on both the production and survival of mourning doves. Finally, we are too often puzzled about effective procedures to provide better nesting habitat for increased production of this extremely adaptable bird, even on lands we control.

But prospects are certainly not all gloomy, and successes are documented in several chapters of the book. Besides, the mourning dove is noted for its resilience. The twenty-three authors and editors of this book join in the hope that the information brought together herein will contribute to a long and successful run of the voice of our "turtle," *Zenaida macroura*, on the North American stage.

Thomas S. Baskett

Acknowledgments

Certain costs of organizing and illustrating this book were defrayed by a grant from the U.S. Fish and Wildlife Service through the Missouri Cooperative Fish and Wildlife Research Unit to the University of Missouri, Columbia. Preparation of final figures in this work was contributed by the U.S. Fish and Wildlife Service's Office of Migratory Bird Management and coordinated by David D. Dolton.

Any multiauthored work such as this requires extensive handling of manuscripts, tabular matter and other components. It also involves careful management of schedules, correspondence and numerous other essential administrative details. Without such quality-control investments, this book could not have been attempted and would not have been completed. For their thousands of hours of work, patience with the editors and authors, and dedication to the objectives of this book, the following individuals deserve special recognition:

Sandy Clark, *Missouri Cooperative Fish and Wildlife Research Unit, Columbia*

Kelly Glidden, *Wildlife Management Institute (WMI), Washington, D.C.*

Carol Griner, *U.S. Fish and Wildlife Service, Albuquerque, New Mexico*

Kathy Mitchell, *Auburn University, Auburn, Alabama*

Julie O'Donnell, *WMI, Washington, D.C.*

Donna Wood, *Southeastern Cooperative Wildlife Disease Study, University of Georgia, Athens*

The authors and editors acknowledge with gratitude important advice and other contributions to portions of this book made by the following:

H. Lloyd Alexander, Jr., *Delaware Division of Fish and Wildlife, Dover*

Charles C. Allin, *Rhode Island Division of Fish and Wildlife, West Kingston*

Claudia Angle, *U.S. Fish and Wildlife Service, Washington, D.C.*

James B. Armstrong, *Auburn University, Auburn, Alabama*

Richard C. Banks, *U.S. Fish and Wildlife Service, Washington, D.C.*

Richard J. Barker, *U.S. Fish and Wildlife Service, Gainesville, Florida*

John C. Barron, *Texas Parks and Wildlife Department, Austin*

Marjorie K. Baskett, *Columbia, Missouri*

Hugh A. Bateman, *Louisiana Department of Wildlife and Fisheries, Baton Rouge*

Troy L. Best, *Auburn University, Auburn, Alabama*

Carl W. Betsill, *North Carolina Wildlife Resources Commission, Elm City*

Craig Bihrle, *North Dakota Game and Fish Department, Bismarck*

Albert E. Bivings IV, *University of Arkansas, Little Rock*

Daniel D. Blatt, *Washington Department of Wildlife, Olympia*

Eric G. Bolen, *University of North Carolina, Wilmington*

Karen S. Bollinger, *U.S. Fish and Wildlife Service, Anchorage, Alaska*

Joyce Bond, *Collegeville, Pennsylvania*

Theodore T. Buerger, *Clemson University, Clemson, South Carolina*

R. Wayne Campbell, *British Columbia Provincial Museum, Victoria*

Mary E. Carrington, *University of Florida, Gainesville*

Elizabeth Carroll-Horrocks, *American Philosophical Society, Philadelphia*

Glenn D. Chambers, *Missouri Department of Conservation, Jefferson City*

Edward C. Channing, *Turlock, California*

Ted L. Clark, *Texas Parks and Wildlife Department, Austin*

Dale A. Coleman, *Auburn University, Auburn, Alabama*

John Cominsky, *Stackpole Books, Harrisburg, Pennsylvania*

Mark C. Conner, *Remington Farms, Chestertown, Maryland*

Michael J. Conroy, *U.S. Fish and Wildlife Service, Athens, Georgia*

Kathryn A. Converse, *U.S. Fish and Wildlife Service, Madison, Wisconsin*

Stephen E. Cornelius, *World Wildlife Fund, Washington, D.C.*

Glenna J. Dean, *University of New Mexico, Albuquerque*

Charley Dickey, *Tallahassee, Florida*

James L. Dobie, *Auburn University, Auburn, Alabama*

Tom Dotson, *West Virginia Department of Natural Resources, Point Pleasant*

Ronald D. Drobney, *U.S. Fish and Wildlife Service, Columbia, Missouri*

Samuel W. Droege, *U.S. Fish and Wildlife Service, Laurel, Maryland*

x • *Acknowledgments*

Robert W. Duncan, *Virginia Game and Inland Fisheries Commission, Richmond*

Ken Durbin, *Oregon Department of Fish and Wildlife, Portland*

Julian L. Dusi, *Auburn University, Auburn, Alabama*

Bonita Eliason, *University of Minnesota, Minneapolis*

Ronald W. Engel-Wilson, *Arizona Game and Fish Department, Phoenix*

Silvia O. Estrada, *Departamento de Vida Silvestre, Managua, Nicaragua*

John R. Faaborg, *University of Missouri, Columbia*

Anne Fairbrother, *Environmental Protection Agency, Corvallis, Oregon*

George W. Folkerts, *Auburn University, Auburn, Alabama*

Donald J. Forrester, *College of Veterinary Medicine, University of Florida, Gainesville*

Ron M. Fowler, *South Dakota Department of Game, Fish and Parks, Pierre*

Curtis H. Freese, *World Wildlife Fund, Washington, D.C.*

Erik K. Fritzell, *University of Missouri, Columbia*

Howard D. Funk, *Colorado Division of Wildlife, Fort Collins*

Alan E. Fusonie, *National Agricultural Library, Beltsville, Maryland*

Kenneth E. Gamble, *U.S. Fish and Wildlife Service, Columbia, Missouri*

Lynda J. Garrett, *U.S. Fish and Wildlife Service, Laurel, Maryland*

Paul H. Geissler, *U.S. Fish and Wildlife Service, Laurel, Maryland*

Fred Giese, *U.S. Fish and Wildlife Service, Upham, North Dakota*

W. Reid Goforth, *U.S. Fish and Wildlife Service, Washington, D.C.*

James B. Grand, *U.S. Fish and Wildlife Service, Anchorage, Alaska*

Bette S. Gutierrez, *WMI, Washington, D.C.*

Craig Guyer, *Auburn University, Auburn, Alabama*

Cheryl Gwinn, *Illinois Department of Conservation, Springfield*

Ed Hackett, *Mississippi Department of Wildlife Conservation, Jackson*

Mark W. Hall, *South Carolina Wildlife and Marine Resources, Columbia*

Greg Hallen, *Wyoming Game and Fish Department, Cheyenne*

Diana L. Hallett, *Missouri Department of Conservation, Columbia*

Curtis H. Halvorson, *U.S. Fish and Wildlife Service, Fort Collins, Colorado*

Jimmy D. Hamilton, *Texas A&M University, College Station*

Jeff S. Hatfield, *U.S. Fish and Wildlife Service, Laurel, Maryland*

Charles J. Henny, *U.S. Fish and Wildlife Service, Corvallis, Oregon*

Gary R. Hepp, *Auburn University, Auburn, Alabama*

Jeff T. Herbert, *Montana Department of Fish, Wildlife and Parks, Helena*

Joe L. Herring, *Louisiana Department of Wildlife and Fisheries, Baton Rouge*

Larry J. Hindman, *Maryland Forest, Park and Wildlife Service, Wye Mills*

James E. Hines, *U.S. Fish and Wildlife Service, Laurel, Maryland*

Ronald R. Hitchcock, *Northwestern College, Powell, Wyoming*

Judy Ho, *National Agricultural Library, Beltsville, Maryland*

Gerald J. Horak, *Kansas Fish and Game Commission, Emporia*

Marshall A. Howe, *U.S. Fish and Wildlife Service, Laurel, Maryland*

Stephanie L. Hubacek, *Texas A&M University, College Station*

Dale D. Humburg, *Missouri Department of Conservation, Columbia*

Tim Ivey, *South Carolina Wildlife and Marine Resources Department, Columbia*

Laurence R. Jahn, *WMI, Washington, D.C.*

Carla S. Jensen, *University of Missouri, Columbia*

Ken Johnson, *Nebraska Game and Parks Commission, Lincoln*

Kenneth G. Johnson, *Alabama Department of Conservation and Natural Resources, Andalusia*

John R. Jones, *University of Missouri, Columbia*

Malcolm T. Jones, *University of Maine, Orono*

Charles D. Kelley, *Alabama Department of Conservation and Natural Resources, Montgomery*

Yulac H. Kindell, *Auburn University, Auburn, Alabama*

J. Richard King, *Harrisburg, Pennsylvania*

M. Kathleen Klimkiewicz, *U.S. Fish and Wildlife Service, Laurel, Maryland*

Stanley C. Kohn, *North Dakota Game and Fish Department, Bismarck*

David G. Krementz, *U.S. Fish and Wildlife Service, Athens, Georgia*

Anthony P. Krenzer, *Columbia Graphics Corporation, Beltsville, Maryland*

Floyd Kringer, *Illinois Department of Conservation, Vandalia*

Joe C. Kurz, *Georgia Game and Fish Division, Atlanta*

William P. Kuvlesky, Jr., *Texas A&M University, College Station*

Regent (Ray) Lalonde, *Canadian Wildlife Service, Ottawa, Ontario*

Jeffrey S. Lawrence, *Minnesota Department of Natural Resources, Bemidgi*

Marisa K. Lee, *Auburn University, Auburn, Alabama*

Martin L. Levitt, *American Philosophical Society, Philadelphia, Pennsylvania*

Robert S. Lishak, *Auburn University, Auburn, Alabama*

Louis N. Locke, *U.S. Fish and Wildlife Service, Madison, Wisconsin*

Kenneth J. Lord, *Chambers Group, Inc., Albuquerque, New Mexico*

Michael P. Losito, *State University of New York, Syracuse*

Martin J. Marchello, *North Dakota State University, Fargo*

Carolyn M. Marn, *Oregon State University, Corvallis*

Worth Mathewson, *Salem, Oregon*

Bob Matthews, *Kansas Department of Wildlife and Parks, Topeka*

Jimmy May, *Kentucky Department of Fish and Wildlife, Frankfort*

Robert A. McCabe, *University of Wisconsin, Madison*

Don M. McCarty, *Texas Parks and Wildlife Department, Austin*

Mary McGinnis, *Ambler, Pennsylvania*

Larry McKibben, *California Department of Fish and Game, Sacramento*

D. Frank McKinney, *University of Minnesota, Minneapolis*

Cathy McNassor, *Natural History Museum of Los Angeles County, Los Angeles, California*

Wyman Meinzer, *Benjamin, Texas*

E. Charles Meslow, *U.S. Fish and Wildlife Service, Corvallis, Oregon*

Cynthia F. Mirarchi, *Opelika, Alabama*

Margaret R. Mitchell, *University of Missouri, Columbia*

Robert A. Montgomery, *Max McGraw Wildlife Foundation, Dundee, Illinois*

Michael E. Morrow, *U.S. Fish and Wildlife Service, Eagle Lake, Texas*

Robert H. Mount, *Auburn University, Auburn, Alabama*

James W. Mullan, *U.S. Fish and Wildlife Service, Wenatchee, Washington*

Lynn N. Neher, *University of Missouri, Columbia*

John D. Newsom, *U.S. Fish and Wildlife Service, Baton Rouge, Louisiana*

Sammy Nooner, *Hondo, Texas*

Mike Olinde, *Louisiana Department of Wildlife and Fisheries, Baton Rouge*

Michael E. O'Meilia, *Oklahoma Department of Wildlife Conservation, Oklahoma City*

Leslie Overstreet, *Smithsonian Institution, Washington, D.C.*

Francis B. Parnell, *Wilmington, North Carolina*

Carol Jean Peddicord, *WMI, Washington D.C.*

Jeff Pederson, *New Mexico Department of Game and Fish, Santa Fe*

Doris Peterson, *Wilmington, North Carolina*

C. (Red) Pittack, *Wenatchee, Washington*

Daniel A. Poole, *WMI, Washington, D.C.*

John F. Pritchett, *Auburn University, Auburn, Alabama*

Charles F. Rabeni, *U.S. Fish and Wildlife Service, Columbia, Missouri*

Irene Radkey, *University of California, Berkeley*

Herbert A. Raffaele, *U.S. Fish and Wildlife Service, Washington, D.C.*

Ellen Reeves, *Auburn University, Auburn, Alabama*

Mark C. Reiter, *Indiana Division of Fish and Wildlife, Indianapolis*

Josef A. Renden, *Auburn University, Auburn, Alabama*

Terry E. Retterer, *Nevada Department of Wildlife, Reno*

Archey Roach, *FTE Enterprises, New York City*

Jay A. Roberson, *Utah Division of Wildlife Resources, Salt Lake City*

John T. Roberson, *Texas Parks and Wildlife Department, Austin*

Randy D. Rodgers, *Kansas Department of Wildlife and Parks, Hays*

Mark R. Ryan, *University of Missouri, Columbia*

James L. Sartin, *Auburn University, Auburn, Alabama*

Rose M. Scheidt, *Missouri Department of Conservation, Columbia*

Eric W. Schenck, *Kansas Department of Wildlife and Parks, Pratt*

Judith Schnell, *Harrisburg, Pennsylvania*

John H. Schultz, *Missouri Department of Conservation, Columbia*

Charles W. Schwartz, *Coeur d'Alene, Idaho*

Elizabeth Schwartz, *Coeur d'Alene, Idaho*

George Seketa, *Indiana Department of Natural Resources, Indianapolis*

Leonard Serdiuk, *Wyoming Game and Fish Department, Lander*

Alfonso Sermeño, *Direccion General de Recursos Naturales Renovables, San Salvador, El Salvador*

Francisco C. Serrano, *Direccion General de Recursos Naturales Renovables, San Salvador, El Salvador*

Brian E. Sharp, *U.S. Fish and Wildlife Service, Portland, Oregon*

Dale E. Sheffer, *Pennsylvania Game Commission, Harrisburg*

Steven L. Sheriff, *Missouri Department of Conservation, Columbia*

Fred D. Singer, *University of Minnesota, Minneapolis*

Donald B. Siniff, *University of Minnesota, Minneapolis*

Alan R. Smith, *Canadian Wildlife Service, Saskatoon, Saskatchewan*

Bruce D. Smith, *Smithsonian Institution, Washington, D.C.*

Carey S. Smith, *U.S. Fish and Wildlife Service, Portland, Oregon*

Philip M. Smith, *Arizona Game and Fish Department, Phoenix*

Robert H. Smith, *U.S. Fish and Wildlife Service, Medford, Oregon*

Larry Soileau, *Louisiana Department of Wildlife and Fisheries, Opelousas*

Edward C. Soutiere, *Tudor Farms, Inc., Cambridge, Maryland*

Gordon Spratt, *Florida Game and Fresh Water Fish Commission, Ocala*

James O. Stevenson, *U.S. Fish and Wildlife Service, West Bethesda, Maryland*

H. Lee Stribling, *Auburn University, Auburn, Alabama*

Petra A. Stubbs, *Provincial Museum of Alberta, Edmonton*

Timothy M. Sutterfield, *Hawaii Department of Land and Natural Resources, Honolulu*

David R. Synatzske, *Texas Parks and Wildlife Department, Artesia Wells*

Robert G. Tonkin, *Valley Freedom Newspapers, Brownsville, Texas*

Harrison B. Tordoff, *University of Minnesota, Minneapolis*

Lowell True, *Agricultural Extension Service, Phoenix, Arizona*

David Uhler, *Stackpole Books, Harrisburg, Pennsylvania*

Harold Umber, *North Dakota Game and Fish Department, Bismarck*

Marilyn M. Wade, *Aberdeen, South Dakota*

Ron Wages, *Collector's Covey, Dallas, Texas*

Gary L. Waggerman, *Texas Parks and Wildlife Department, Edinburg*

Darold R. Walls, *U.S. Fish and Wildlife Service, Upham, North Dakota*

Jannel Ward, *New Mexico Department of Game and Fish, Albuquerque*

Ed L. Warr, *Tennessee Wildlife Resources Agency, Nashville*

Ellen Wells, *Smithsonian Institution, Washington, D.C.*

Lisa M. White, *University of Georgia, Athens*

Beth Wiel, *University of California, Berkeley*

Charles R. Wilkins, *Texas Parks and Wildlife Department, San Antonio*

Gary C. Will, *Idaho Department of Fish and Game, Boise*

Larry O. Williams, *Auburn University, Auburn, Alabama*

T. Monique Williamson, *U.S. Fish and Wildlife Service, Washington, D.C.*

Robert J. Wilson, *University of Missouri, Columbia*

Steve Wilson, *Hondo, Texas*

David B. Wingate, *Bermuda Department of Agriculture and Fisheries, Hamilton*

Lawrence C. Wit, *Auburn University, Auburn, Alabama*

Marie W. Wooten, *Auburn University, Auburn, Alabama*

Scott C. Yaich, *Arkansas Game and Fish Commission, Little Rock*

Heather Young, *U.S. Fish and Wildlife Service, Washington, D.C.*

Harold D. Irby, of Austin, Texas, is a Ph.D. wildlife biologist—a dove biologist. Retired from distinguished careers with the U.S. Fish and Wildlife Service, Texas A&M University, and the Texas Parks and Wildlife Department, Hal was invited to illustrate this book because he also is an accomplished artist. His artwork features a pointillism technique.

Francis E. Sweet, of Bowie, Maryland, is one of the foremost professional wildlife artists in North America. He has earned numerous awards and honors for his artwork principally in oil and scratchboard. His exceptional talent is featured in a variety of Wildlife Management Institute publications. The dustjacket art for this book is a scratchboard medium.

Contents

List of Tables

List of Figures

I.

Introducing the Mourning Dove

Chapter 1

Characteristics and Importance

Thomas S. Baskett
Cooperative Fish and Wildlife Research Unit
U.S. Fish and Wildlife Service
The School of Natural Resources
University of Missouri
Columbia, Missouri

Mark W. Sayre
Department of Forestry and Wildlife Management
University of Massachusetts
Amherst, Massachussetts

The mourning dove (*Zenaida macroura*) is the most abundant and widespread North American gamebird (Grue et al. 1983) and one of the continent's most adaptable and plentiful bird species. In the 1989 North American Breeding Bird Survey—a standardized procedure to assess continental bird resources—mourning doves occurred on 1,254 of 1,344 routes analyzed, ranking second behind red-winged blackbirds (on 1,256 routes). Mourning doves showed a relative abundance of 30.0 birds per route over their range, ranking eleventh among the 251 species analyzed (Droege and Sauer 1990).

Mourning doves, like their three hundred or so cousins in the family of doves and pigeons (Columbidae), lay a small number of eggs—usually two per nest—and the parents share incubating duties. Both parents feed the rapidly growing young, at first on a highly nutritious material known as "crop milk," later supplemented by seeds. Nesting cycles are short, and repeated nestings are necessary to maintain population levels. Mortality rates of mourning doves are high, reaching 58 percent per year for adults and 69 percent for immatures in the eastern part of the continent (see chapter 17).

Most mourning doves are migratory; those nesting in northern parts of the breeding range may migrate great distances. Level-flight speeds up to 55 miles per hour (89 km/h) have been witnessed from an automobile (Bastin 1952) and 37 to 40 miles per hour (60 to 64.5 km/h) have been registered by radar (Schnell and Hellack 1978). Migration and "normal" speeds probably are near the lower end of the range.

Life spans of mourning doves banded in the United States average about 1.0 year for immatures and 1.5 years for adults, but there is a longevity record of 19.3 years for a free-living dove (Clapp et al. 1983). Other noteworthy records are of mourning doves between 7.5 and 12.8 years of age, including a dove banded in Wisconsin and shot in Texas 12.2 years later (R. R. George personal communication: 1984).

Due to its widespread range, numerical abundance and adaptation to human habitats, the mourning dove easily is one of the most recognized birds in North America. Its attractiveness, gentle song, speed aflight and appeal as table fare ensure *Zenaida macroura*'s popularity among hunters and nonhunters alike. *Photo by Ed Bry; courtesy of the North Dakota Game and Fish Department.*

SIGNIFICANCE AS A GAME SPECIES

The mourning dove is the leading gamebird species in North America, with numbers harvested easily exceeding all other migratory gamebirds combined. During the 1972–73 hunting season, the estimated harvest in the United States was 49.4 million doves (Keeler 1977). It increased to 51 million in 1982 and declined to an average of 44.8 million per year during 1983 through 1987 (see chapter 24). According to the *1985 National Survey of Fishing, Hunting and Wildlife Associated Recreation* (U.S. Fish and Wildlife Service 1988), "dove" hunting (species not named) provided more than 19 million recreational trips for about 3.1 million hunters in 1985. Assuming that dove hunters spend less than other migrating-bird hunters do for their respective trips— say, $175 versus $216—dove hunters in 1985 may have expended more than $540 million in pursuit of doves.

In a South Carolina field study, mourning dove hunters fired 8.6 shots per retrieved bird (Haas 1977). If this figure is broadly applicable to the average harvest of 44.8 million doves in the United

The mourning dove is North America's number one gamebird, providing a hunter harvest of approximately 40 to 50 million birds annually in recent decades. According to a 1985 survey, more hunters (3.1 million) pursued doves that year than hunted ducks (2.5 million), geese (1.5 million), wild turkey (1.9 million), and grouse and prairie chicken (2.2 million). *Photo by Ron George; courtesy of the Texas Parks and Wildlife Department.*

States from 1983 to 1987, the average number of shells fired for dove hunting was more than 385 million per year. At $4.50 per box of shells (25 shells per box), nearly $70 million were spent on shells alone for mourning dove hunting. This provided about $7.6 million per year—through an 11-percent federal excise tax via the Federal Aid in Wildlife Restoration (or Pittman-Robertson) Program—to the states for wildlife conservation programs. This estimate is based on untested assumptions and may be too low; Williams (1985), for example, estimated $14 million. At any rate, as a direct result of dove hunting, millions of dollars are made available for state research and management programs for nonhunted wildlife as well as hunted species.

A strong tradition for hunting mourning doves is ingrained in some northern states, many midlatitude states, and in the Southwest and Southeast. This tradition grew more slowly for doves than for many other American gamebirds, owing in part to the early preeminence of the passenger pigeon. But grow it did. As Madson (1978) wrote, dove hunting is both a tradition and an institution in the South, where migratory populations build up and good hunting lasts longest. Opening week in the southeastern states "is a blend of family reunion, lodge picnic, an old-style barbecue, and a Juarez election" (Madson 1978: 46).

The flavor of the old-time dove shoot in the South is preserved by Russell (1974: 95), who wrote that the big shoots were lengthy "shootin', pickin', and partyin'" affairs. Because of the expense of food, drink and ammunition, they were an institution for the country gentleman, the banker and other well-heeled participants. A broader group of hunters now participates because of increased affluence of other people, the advent of public hunting areas and other factors.

In Madson's (1978) view, the nation's most intensive pass shooting begins when the dove season opens each autumn. Pass shooting at mourning doves is far from easy and requires special skills.

Mourning dove hunting tradition developed first and is most ingrained in the South, but the species' "formidable reputation of being the hardest gamebird on the North American continent to bring down consistently" (Dickey 1976: 5) has made it a favorite quarry in all states where ecological conditions and political reality enable regulated dove hunting seasons. Mourning dove hunting contributes many millions of dollars annually to local economics in the United States and, through a federal excise tax on sporting firearms and ammunition, more than $7.6 million per year to state wildlife agencies for programs that benefit all wildlife. *Illustration by A. Lassell Ripley; courtesy of the Library of Congress.*

The devotee finds dove hunting very exciting and certainly not just a "warm-up" for more serious hunting later on, as is sometimes claimed. A friend in central Missouri spends at least $100 for gasoline alone to find where the doves are and to firm up permission to hunt, before each hunting season starts. He may be exceptionally thorough, but he is not unique in making such preparations.

By any measure, whether numbers of doves harvested, hunter hours spent, income invested, shells expended, traditions met or fulfillment afforded the hunter, the mourning dove is clearly one of the most important gamebirds in the world.

SYMBOLIC AND OTHER VALUES

The value of this species as game is far from the entire story. The mourning dove is intimately known to suburbanites, many city dwellers and countless others who are not hunters. Its widespread occurrence, its nesting in trees of yards and farmsteads, and its appearance at winter bird feeders, even in middle latitudes, all contribute to this familiarity and interest.

The mourning dove is sometimes associated with biblical references to doves, even though it is strictly a New World bird (now introduced elsewhere, as in Hawaii). In fact, records of many ancient religions of the Old World are replete with references to doves or pigeons, whose symbolic importance was tremendous. This matter, and the dove's broad "constituency" in America, deserve special attention here. First, however, some basic facts about this entire family of birds must be recognized.

ATTRIBUTES OF THE COLUMBIDAE

Columbids are distributed worldwide and number three hundred species (Goodwin 1983), give or take a few according to the authority consulted. There is no ornithological distinction between doves and pigeons, but in English and American usage, the larger species usually (though not always) are called "pigeons" and the smaller ones are referred to as "doves." *Columba livia*—still wild and free in parts of Eurasia and Africa—gave rise to all domestic and feral pigeons. The parent species is known to some ornithologists as "rock dove" and to others as "rock pigeon," illustrating the confusion. Difficulties inherent in translation may further jumble the identities of doves/pigeons mentioned in ancient writings.

Except for a few aberrant forms, columbids are remarkably similar to one another throughout the world. Goodwin (1983) noted that exotic columbid species at zoos are quickly recognized by the public as doves/pigeons. Behavioral traits and general appearance (apart from color and size) are giveaways. These likenesses doubtless underlie frequent similarities in symbolisms of doves from one human culture to another and help explain the transfer of imagery across the ocean in the case of the American mourning dove.

The best *biological* perspective on defenselessness and similar purported attributes of doves and pigeons that have contributed to their symbolism was provided by Goodwin (1983) in *Pigeons and Doves of the World*. Goodwin noted that, at first, it appears surprising that pigeons are so successful, being highly edible and sought after by all kinds of predators, including man. Though they can give a good cuff with the carpal joint of the wing, columbids are not able to do serious damage to attackers. These characteristics, plus their small clutches of eggs, helpless nestlings, weak beaks and restricted foods all seem to make them out-pointed by parrots, for example. Members of that family also are strong fliers, mostly arboreal and eat mainly seeds and fruits, but they have strong, formidable beaks that can "deal with food or foe" (Goodwin 1983: 9). Yet pigeons not only thrive in all lands inhabited by parrots but also have a much more extensive distribution. Thus, pigeons are at least biological equals of parrots and most other birds. They owe their success to being physically and biologically "tough" despite their fragile appearance and timidity. If things do not go well, Goodwin noted, the eggs and young are expendable; they can be replaced quickly, owing to short incubation and fledgling periods. The tragedy of the passenger pigeon notwithstanding, most pigeons and doves are hardy and adaptable birds, and not defenseless biologically.

RELIGIOUS IMPORTANCE AND SYMBOLISM OF DOVES AND PIGEONS

Inscriptions found by archeologists prove that, thousands of years before recorded history, some doves or pigeons were considered holy (Levi 1977). In early historic times, the Semitic peoples regarded one or another species with reverence. At least six different species were possibilities, according to the "Biblical Natural History" section of a Bible published in the late 1800s by W. L. Richardson and Company, Boston. The dove was sacred among Phoenicians and Philistines as well as Assyrians and Egyptians. The early Greeks revered the doves that drew Venus' chariot (Armstrong 1975, Rowland 1978).

From the first, symbolism was complex and sometimes contradictory. In several ancient civilizations the dove symbolized fertility and the soil. In early Hindu writings it was a messenger of death yet served as a steed for the god of love. In China it represented longevity, faithfulness and filial piety. Among the ancient Hebrews, the dove was the symbol of purity and the image of the spirit of God. To early Christians, the white dove (turtledove?) was the symbol of the Holy Ghost, the Virgin, spiritual love, innocence, defenselessness and sorrow. No other bird(s) had such importance in the Christian faith (Rowland 1978), for there the sentiments about the dove/pigeon of the parental Hebraic religion were sublimated (Levi 1977).

It follows that no other bird group is so frequently referred to in the Bible, both Old and New Testaments. Many of the allusions are to the dove as a standard for comeliness—especially the soft eyes (Song of Solomon) and plaintive voice (Isaiah)—quick flight (Psalms) and dependability (bringing good news of land to Noah), and as a harbinger of spring—"the voice of the turtle" (Song of Solomon). Hosea, however, considered the dove "silly and without sense."

The gentle symbolism hardly fits the eyes of some columbids. Rowland (1978: 41) invited the reader to confront a feral pigeon face-on: "You will be surprised at what you see: hard, mean-looking eyes." She added that this larger version of the dove of peace has an expression as cold, shrewd and secretive as that of a world-class secret agent, but she conceded that the mourning dove has "soft black-pearl eyes."

Doves and pigeons have not always profited from their religious connections. Domestic or feral pigeons and turtledoves frequently were sacrificed in temples in both Old and New Testament times (Armstrong 1975).

All members of the family are highly palatable, and although some religions forbade their use as food (as in ancient Syria), they have often been important as table fare. Pigeons were domesticated and used for food in Egypt at least as early as 3000 B.C. (Levi 1977). Monasteries and manors had their dovecotes in medieval Europe. One English monastery had a dovecote that accommodated fourteen hundred birds, "the medieval equivalent of our large-scale chicken 'factories'" (Armstrong 1975: 132). In nineteenth-century Syria, the wealth of village sheiks was judged by the size of their dovecotes.

SIGNIFICANCE OF THE MOURNING DOVE TO NONHUNTERS

Contradictory human attitudes hang over the mourning dove, as with its relatives the world over. Some ambiguity of spirit exists even in the origin of the mourning dove's scientific name. Charles Lucien Bonaparte, a French ornithologist, brought his nineteen-year-old bride to Philadelphia in 1822. They returned to Europe six years later, with both his scientific reputation and their family healthy and growing. Among his many lifetime accomplishments, he described a New World columbid, the zenaida dove. The bird's name was later appropriated for the genus *Zenaida*, now including the mourning dove. We suppose that the name honored the dovelike gentleness of his wife, Zénaïde. Husband and wife were cousins (Millikin 1955, Markham 1975); their fathers were brothers of Napoleon I. Thus, a tender love story was told through scientific nomenclature by members of a family best known for making war.

In the early 1800s, Charles Lucien Bonaparte, nephew of Napoleon I, visited America for several years to study the New World's bird life. Among his many contributions to the field of ornithology was naming a new dove of the West Indies the zenaida dove (*Columba zenaida*) in honor of his wife, Zénaïde (right). *Zenaida* ultimately was accepted by taxonomists as the genus for the mourning dove and close relatives. Seated to the left of Zénaïde is her sister Charlotte, also daughter of Joseph Bonaparte and niece of Emperor Napoleon. Portrait by Jacques Louis David. *Photo courtesy of the Library of Congress.*

Whether the mourning dove should be hunted has long been a point of contention. Although it is easier to quantify evidence of interest in mourning doves among hunters than among nonhunters, it is by no means difficult to find proof of the latter's intense concerns. During her twelve years (1972–84) as a state senator in North Dakota, Stella Fritzell received a single death threat, and that came as a result of her espousal of a measure to permit dove hunting in North Dakota (E. K. Fritzell personal communication: 1987).

In Indiana, the status of the mourning dove was changed from songbird to gamebird in 1984 after years of discussion. (It had been a gamebird earlier.) In March 1985, *Audubon* magazine ran an article entitled "The quick metamorphosis of Indiana's doves." The author explored both the pros and cons of dove hunting and concluded that doves ought to be hunted "because lots of people enjoy hunting them, because there is nothing wrong with hunting them, and because hunting does not affect dove numbers" (Williams 1985: 44).

The response, as reflected in the "Dialogue" department of subsequent issues of *Audubon*, was rapid, vigorous and even rancorous, and it continued until, three issues later, the editors declared a "final round" for dove letters. (Even so, there was a reprise.) Many of the letter writers, incensed by Indiana's dove season and by Williams' article, clearly were writing from an antihunting bias, and the mourning dove was mainly a convenient centerpiece. But many were specifically opposed to dove hunting. One letter writer (Godish 1985: 98) succinctly wrote: "Is the mourning dove just another gamebird? Not in suburbia! Doves are family to many people. One man cannot hunt another man's family and expect acceptance."

The diversity of feelings brought to the fore in the Indiana circumstance points up the necessity for fish and wildlife agencies to view the mourning dove as a species of outstanding importance for a very broad constituency that includes both hunters and dove watchers.

Our purpose in this book is to make available a comprehensive coverage of research findings about the mourning dove, both for the sake of knowledge itself and in the hope that this information and the perspectives provided will be useful in the wise management of the species.

In 1990, the South Carolina Wildlife and Marine Resources Department first sponsored and promoted a parent/child mourning dove hunt. The effort was prompted to encourage family members to share and enjoy the outdoors and to discourage youngsters from using drugs. The 1991 hunt, featuring the slogan "Shoot for the Future—Don't Use Drugs," was targeted for protest by antihunters and animal rightists. The hunt detractors campaigned to ban the hunt, arguing variously that hunting was cruel, shooting doves was not a "healthy substitute" to using drugs, and the killing of doves for any reason was "unnecessary and senseless." A small group (about twenty) of individuals picketed in Columbia prior to the one-day event; others vowed to demonstrate at the hunt sites (about twelve did at one site). Neither tactic succeeded in banning or disrupting the hunts, which the participants (176 youngsters plus adults) declared worthwhile and successful (T. Ivey personal communication: 1992). Such protest, however successful, reflects a social phenomenon of opposition to the traditions and management role of recreational hunting. Due to the drift of human society away from nature and natural processes, there appears to be less public understanding and tolerance of hunting wildlife for recreation. While such concern and sensitivity frequently defy or ignore the biological, economic, recreational, educational and other values attendant to hunting, the manifestations tend to make "good press." Media coverage of impassioned antihunting messages or events sometimes misleads otherwise unconcerned nonhunters to question the legitimacy of wildlife management in general. Certain traditional symbolism of doves makes hunting of mourning doves especially vulnerable to emotional or moralistic challenges by nonhunters. *Photo by Jim Arnold; courtesy of the Columbia (S.C.) State Newspaper.*

Chapter 2

Historical Perspective

Henry M. Reeves
Office of Migratory Bird Management
U.S. Fish and Wildlife Service
Washington, D.C.

Richard E. McCabe
Wildlife Management Institute
Washington, D.C.

In biology, as in other fields, history is the genesis of the present and precursor of the future. It serves as the canon against which prevailing events, circumstances, standards and thoughts are measured and judged. History is perspective.

PRE-COLUMBIAN TIME

Fossil Records

Mourning dove remains have been found in early Pleistocene deposits. The Pleistocene epoch, which commenced about 1.8 million years ago, was characterized by the sprawl and recession of continental ice sheets and the appearance of *Homo sapiens*. Evidence of mourning doves has been found at natural sites predating the emergence of mankind, as well as in middens and at other sites occupied by prehistoric people.

Natural sites. Fossilized remains of mourning doves have been identified from at least eleven sites in six U.S. states and from other sites in Mexico and the Caribbean. None of the sites showed evidence of concurrent human occupation. In general, mourning dove fossils are associated with limestone formations of Florida, caves of the semiarid and arid Southwest, and asphalt pits of southern California.

Mourning dove fossils have been recovered from at least four Florida localities. At Seminole Field near St. Petersburg, Wetmore (1931) identified the mourning dove among an extensive series of fossil bird bones. Brodkorb (1957) found both the mourning dove and passenger pigeon among fifty-two species of bird fossils excavated at Reddick in Marion County. Associates of the mourning dove at Arredondo included a number of extinct mammals—the short-faced bear, dire wolf, ground sloth, mammoth, horse, tapir and a species of camel (Brodkorb 1959).

Perhaps the northernmost mourning dove fossil was found by Downs (1954) at Jones Sink in Meade County, Kansas. A single bone documents the mourning dove among fifteen avian species at Miller's Cave, Llano County, Texas (Weigel 1967). Also, a single fossil recovered at Smith Creek Cave in White Pine County, Nevada, establishes the species there. The cave lies some 6,200 feet (1,890 m) above the great desert basin of Utah, near an arm of ancient Lake Bonneville. Other fossils at the site represented the remains of forty-nine other avian species, extinct goats, camels, horses and sheep, and a huge raptor classified as *Teratornis incredibilis* (Howard 1952).

The richest Pleistocene deposits in North America are three tar pools or asphalt pits in southern California. They are the Rancho La Brea, now on Wilshire Boulevard in metropolitan Los Angeles, and the McKittrick and Carpinteria pits in Kern and Santa Barbara counties, respectively. More than a million fossil bones—their date estimated at 10,000 to 40,000 B.C.—have been retrieved from La Brea alone since 1901 (Stock 1972).

The La Brea deposits are characterized by a great preponderance of predators that apparently were drawn into the tarry morass by mired prey. La Brea victims include the American mastodon, ground sloth, western horse, dwarf pronghorn, bison, American lion, saber-toothed cat and many avian species. Despite the astounding number and variety of fossil remains at La Brea, only twenty-nine specimens representing seventeen mourning doves have been documented (Howard 1937).

McKittrick differs markedly from La Brea by largely containing remains of nonpredatory species. But of thirty-four avian species there, the mourning dove is represented by only three bones (Miller 1925). And at Carpinteria, only a single mourning dove fossil has been reported (DeMay 1941).

A solitary specimen also documents the mourning dove's presence at Barranco Seco in Veracruz State, Mexico (Brodkorb 1963). Another Mexican fossil record is for San Josecito Cavern, located in a limestone scarp flanking the Sierra Oriental in Nuevo Leon State. Mourning dove and band-tailed pigeon fossils were among the remains of forty avian species and are thought to have been brought into the cave as prey or carrion (Miller 1943).

In the Caribbean, mourning dove fossils have been found in the Cerro de San Francisco of the Dominican Republic (Brodkorb 1971).

Evidence of the mourning dove at some archeological sites is limited to one or a few fossils, so it is fortunate that a single fragment often is sufficient for species identification. The scarcity of mourning dove remains in Pleistocene deposits has puzzled paleontologists (Miller and DeMay 1942). However, complex mechanisms influenced the presence of live animals at potential fossilization sites and whether identifiable fossils ensued. Thus, fossil deposits do not accurately represent the numbers and prevalence over time of animals that once frequented the site vicinity.

Human-occupied sites. Evidence of human occupation may take many forms, including human skeletal remains, artifacts, broken bones of known food animals, shells and hearths. Mourning dove remains were found in Shelter Cave in Dona Ana County, New Mexico, but evidence of the Basket Maker culture there casts doubt on whether those remains were of late Pleistocene or early Recent age (±9000 B.C.). They were among the re-

mains of fifty-eight avian species identified from two caves located on opposite sides of Pyramid Peak (Howard and Miller 1933).

Seven mourning dove specimens were found at Turkey Tank Caves, Winona Village and Wupatki Pueblo sites in the San Francisco Mountain region near Flagstaff, Arizona (Hargrave 1939). These Indian dwellings date from about 700 to 1300 A.D. Although Hargrave clearly associated the doves with Indian culture, he did not speculate on their use by Indians.

In the mid-1930s DeMay (1942) excavated over three thousand bird bones from two Indian middens on the shores of former Buena Vista Lake in Kern County, California. Water birds dominated the more than fifty-six species identified, and the mourning dove was represented by a single bone. The middens were thought to be less than five hundred years old and representative of species taken for food.

Mourning dove bones in coprolites (fossilized human feces) were excavated from Hinds Cave in West Texas during studies of stratified deposits in rock shelters near the lower Pecos River (Williams-Dean 1978). The deposits were aged by the radio-carbon dating process to before 7000 B.C. and evidently reflect the earliest known use of mourning doves by prehistoric man. These ancient cave dwellers are informally known as the "Pecos People."

At the same site, mourning dove bones of shoulder and pelvic girdles, limbs, feet and claws were identified (Lord 1984). These remains, and those of rodents and other birds, suggest that the bones—some as long as 1.2 inches (3 cm)—had been only lightly chewed or had been swallowed unchewed, either covered with meat or after having been scraped or boiled clean. Since no marks were indicative of scraping or of pitting from extensive boiling, the bones were probably ingested with meat.

At a much later time, Indians of the Arroyo Hondo, situated between the Rio Grande and Pecos rivers of northcentral New Mexico, occasionally used doves as a minor food supply (Lang and Harris 1984). In one midden sample, dated to about 1330 to 1340 A.D., 7 bones representing six individual mourning doves were identified among 849 bird bones. Lang and Harris, extrapolating from bone remnants, estimated that birds provided only about 23 percent of the usable meat in the diet of these Indians; bones of wild turkey were most numerous among the identified avian remains. However, other researchers have cautioned that bird bones, particularly from small birds, often are not preserved as well as bones from mammals and larger birds. Also, birds may have been more important, in terms of frequency of consumption, in Indian diets prior to the advent of agriculture.

Indian Hunting

Evidence from Hinds Cave (Lord 1984) indicates that mourning doves were taken and consumed by a nomadic hunting and gathering people who subsisted principally on rodents and a few species of cacti. Apparently, deer were then uncommon in comparison with their current abundance in the locale. Archeological evidence further suggests that these aborigines took small game by means of the dart and atlatl (spear thrower) as well as with nets of knotted cords.

Remains of two doves in Hinds Cave predate 7170 B.C.; six were dated by radiocarbon between about 7170 and 4800 B.C.; two were from between 3040 and 2460 B.C.; one probably from 3000 to 1800 B.C.; and one from between 350 B.C. and 100 A.D. Though mourning doves probably were not a major food item or used on a regular or continuous basis, the Pecos People hunted and consumed them over a span of seven millennia.

Early chroniclers of the New World frequently wrote of the innovation and remarkable skills of the Indians in hunting with primitive weaponry. Weapons and hunting technologies varied somewhat from region to region and from tribe to tribe. Nonetheless, there was widespread use of deadfall and pit traps, nets, snares, hand-thrown or atlatl-projected missiles (sticks, stones, rocks, darts, spears), bows and arrows, and even blowguns and bolas in some locales. For small birds such as the mourning dove, arrows shot from blinds placed near water or food (including bait), baited deadfall traps, nets and snares probably were among the most commonly employed means. To improve the efficiency of arrows for killing birds, crosspieces sometimes were fixed on the arrow shaft to enlarge the impact area (Luomala 1978).

The Papagos, in southern Arizona, caught mourning doves in cage traps constructed of split giant cactus ribs and, more often, shot roosting doves with arrows at dusk (Castetter and Opler 1936). These Indians reportedly never consumed bird eggs. Corbusier (1886: 328), on the other hand, writing of the Yavopai of westcentral Arizona, noted: "Doves, ducks, geese and swan are rarely eaten, but their eggs are relished when boiled."

Hinds Cave is an archeological site nestled in cliffs overlooking the lower Pecos River in Valverde County, Texas. Findings at the cave, sporadically occupied by the nomadic Pecos Peoples (Williams-Dean 1978, Lord 1983), establish the earliest known association between the mourning dove and humans. Bones from two doves apparently eaten by these aborigines were radiocarbon dated to 7170 B.C. A single coprolite (fossilized human feces) containing dove bones as long as 1.2 inches (3 cm) suggests that they had been ingested along with meat. Other bones indicate that mourning doves were a minor food of the Pecos Peoples until about 100 A.D.—a span exceeding seventy-two centuries. *Photo courtesy of Glenna Dean.*

Hopi Indian youths used baited deadfall traps and snares made of twisted horsehair to take all sorts of birds (Beaglehole 1936). Mourning doves were taken for food by several California tribes, including the Costanoan (Levy 1978), Tipai and Ipai (Luomala 1978), all of whom lived along the southern coast. However, the Luiseño Indians, who also lived in southern coastal California, initially did not eat doves or wild pigeons, apparently because of superstitious or totemic beliefs (Sparkman 1908).

Fisher (1893: 33), of the U.S. Bureau of Biological Survey's Death Valley Expedition, provided one of the few firsthand accounts of southwestern Indians hunting mourning doves for food: "Mourning doves furnish a large amount of food to the Indians during the spring and summer. Before migration commences the Indians build crude huts of brush, grass, and weeds, in which to secrete themselves, near the springs and streams. Loopholes are made on the sides toward the water, through which arrows are shot at the birds as they alight to drink."

Buskirk (1986) observed that doves were hunted and eaten by all western Apaches. These birds frequently were hunted at night while roosting. The hunters sometimes used torches to blind or "stupefy" the birds. On occasion, White Mountain Apache girls built fires under dove roosts while boys shot the birds.

Cibecue Indians of central Arizona were similarly reported to hunt mourning doves from blinds (Gifford 1940). The hunters selected a tree or erected an old dry tree near a spring and piled up brush at the base in the general fashion of a modern duck blind. The hunters then positioned themselves inside the brush and shot birds that alighted in the tree branches above.

Mourning doves also were taken for food by the Tarahumara, an Indian tribe living in Chihuahua, Mexico. They called the dove the "uli"—a name apparently derived through imitation of the bird's vocalizations (Bennett and Zingg 1976).

A review of a number of key ethnological references failed to uncover evidence that the mourning dove was a significant food item for any pre-Columbian Indians. Certainly, it was hunted at times for its meat or eggs (see Corbusier 1886), but no indication has been found that dove in any form was a regular aspect of the Indian diet. Except in the arid Southwest, Great Basin, and parts of California and Mexico, Indians' subsistence energies tended to be directed toward animals and plants whose procurement produced maximum return for relatively minimum investment. Wherever more prevalent, easily secured and substantive food sources were available, the dove seems to have

been virtually ignored. Even among the most destitute tribes of the Southwest, taking doves appears to have been more a matter of providence than a concerted food quest. Its harvest often was a recreational/educational exercise and contribution by children but was not likely worth the regular or frequent attention of the adult providers.

Indian Culture and Folklore

Nearly all animals contributed materially and spiritually to Indian culture, and the mourning dove was no exception. And because their economies depended greatly and sometimes exclusively on wildlife, Indians were especially aware of distinctions among species. Merriam and Heizer (1979), for example, documented "mourning dove" in the lexicons of 105 Indian tribes or subgroups from California and adjoining areas.

In the voluminous literature about Indians, there is frequent reference to the mourning dove, particularly with respect to spiritualism. Observing that doves customarily drink at rain pools and springs in the morning and evening, certain Pueblo Indians associated the bird's vocalization as an invocation for these sources of water and as indication of places where people might slake their thirst (Tyler 1979). Also, since doves feed on seeds, the product of flowers, and plants need rain to bloom and produce seeds, the calls of doves were thought of as "rain songs" (Tyler 1979).

The mourning dove was known to the early Delaware Indians as "mowi-teo" and to tribal members who later located in Oklahoma as "mamendhakema"—"one prays (or pleads) earnestly" (Speck 1946). These Indians held the bird in high sentimental esteem, unlike the Canadian Munsee-Mahican (of Ontario) and others who had no sentimental or spiritually restrictive compunction about killing and eating doves.

The mourning dove occurs frequently in Pueblo Indian mythology. Its roles include supplicant for rain, indicator of water, mourner, winnower of seeds and teller of falsehoods (presumably as a foreteller of water when none was available). Tyler (1979: 130) presents one such myth: "The Shongopovi were living in their village and south of the village there was a hill called Kwakchome. There was a great deal of this grass called *kwakwi* there. A Turtle-dove one time was rubbing out seeds from the tassels of this grass, and while doing so cut her hand with the sharp edge of one blade. It bled profusely, and the turtle-dove was moaning as follows: 'Hoohoo, hoo, hooho, hoo, hooho, hoo Ho-ho-ho.' While she was moaning, Coyote came along and heard somebody singing, as he believed. So he approached the place. When he arrived he saw the Turtle-dove sitting and leaning forward in great distress. 'Are you singing?' he asked the Dove. 'Are you thus singing?' 'No,' she said, 'I am crying.'"

Tyler (1979) noted that the significance of the dove may have extended, as in this myth, to sympathy for the Indian women harvesting wild grain. However, the basic theme among Puebloans was that the seed-eating dove calls out above all for water and for rain; rain does not always come, so the bird sorrows.

Doves also figured in various clans and societies within Pueblo culture (Tyler 1979). Their feathers could be used on masks but not on prayer-stick (paho) offerings, perhaps in recognition of a myth in which the "War Twins" killed two Navajo girls whose spirits became doves, and the ensuing belief that scalps of Navajo maidens were potent rain makers. The Zunis, however, did make ritual-

istic use of the six partially white tail feathers from the male mourning dove as part of the sacred corn-ear fetish, the mi-li. The La'lakontu, one of the three Hopi women's societies, used the standard consisting of the white corn ear, sumac and dove feathers. Also, Tyler (1979: 129) wrote: "A Dove lineage in the Hopi Snake clan keeps the tiponi or fetish of the Antelope Society, one of the participants in the complex Snake-Antelope ceremony involving rain, seed germination and growth, ripening of corn, and some degree of Sun ritual."

Actually, there was a Dove clan, or "huwi," that was a unit of the Snake society or phratry (Hodge 1907c: 562). The basic purpose of the Hopi clan, other than for social organization, spiritual identity and fraternity, was to protect, preserve and enhance the society's symbolic and ceremonial values and those of the phratry under whose umbrella it existed. Also, two northern Plains Blackfeet Indian divisions, the Piegan and Blood, both had Dove bands (Grinnell 1962).

The top scene reportedly features the sacred sun dance of the Dove Society of Blood Indians, secretly photographed in 1907 by missionary C. Van Wagen (Brandon 1982). Below, the photographer has been detected and one of the Indians is racing toward Van Wagen to send him away. Despite notation that the Indians were of the Dove Society, that affiliation is in doubt. Grinnell (1962: 222) observed that certain groups, such as the Doves, were societies among the boys and young men "that imitated the secret societies of adult males and were of comparatively recent origin" (circa 1870). Given that most of the ceremony participants shown are adults, and because the Doves are not known to have had sacred rituals, the scenes most likely represent the All Comrades' Horn Society. *Photos courtesy of the Glenbow Museum.*

The mourning dove also constituted part of the folklore of other American Indians. In the Great Lakes region, the following explanation of why the mourning dove builds such a flimsy nest reportedly was told by Pottawatomie mothers to their children (Brigham 1943: 55): "A long time ago when birds came to live in the world they were all called together by a teacher who was going to tell them many of the things which birds need to know. So all of the different kinds of birds gathered around the teacher. They were told how to fly, how to sing and gather food. Finally the teacher began to tell the birds how to build nests—what materials they could use and how they could shape and fasten them together. Most of the birds listened carefully and when the lesson was over they knew how to build good nests of various materials in different places. But the little Mourning Dove became sleepy shortly after the teacher began the lesson. She heard how to gather a few sticks and place them in a tree as a foundation for the nest, but before the teacher had told the rest of the story the Mourning Dove was fast asleep. She missed most of the lesson and never learned how to build more than a foundation for her nest."

Some western Indians were named or characterized, often pejoratively by other Indians, according to certain habits or traits. For example, according to Hultkrantz (1974: 200): "Haivodika [a subunit of the Fort Bridger Shoshone in extreme southwestern Wyoming, also known as the Black's Fork Shoshone] split away from the buffalo-hunting Shoshones . . . in 1842. 'Dove-eaters' . . . their derogatory nickname, [was] applied to them by the buffalo hunting Shoshones, because from the viewpoint of the latter they seemed to behave timidly and passively."

EXPLORATION AND SETTLEMENT

Early Accounts

A varied assemblage of people are responsible for early knowledge about the mourning dove of North America. The cast includes the "Admiral of the Ocean Seas," several Spanish conquistadors, a Franciscan missionary in New Spain, various explorers and settlers, a propagandizer of the New World who never visited it, an English naturalist/artist who first made the mourning dove known to science, a wandering Quaker and his son, King George II's personal physician, a Swedish scientist who created chaos while seeking order, the "Father of American Natural History," the third president of the United States, the nephew and niece of Napo-

leon Bonaparte, the son of a Scottish smuggler, America's most renowned ornithologist/artist, two captains of the Corps of Discovery, several surgeon/naturalists attached to the many western surveys, and the founder of scientific studies of North American bird migration.

Columbus. Did the mourning dove contribute to the success of Christopher Columbus' voyage in 1492? Perhaps the most scholarly examination of records of the "Admiral of the Ocean Sea" is that of the eminent historian Samuel Eliot Morison (1963), who relied on ornithologist Ludlow Griscom to interpret Columbus' numerous references to birds.

On the forenoon of Thursday, September 6, 1492, Columbus departed the harbor of Gomera, in the Canary Islands, aboard the *Santa María*, accompanied by the smaller *Pinta* and *Niña*, to find a more direct route to Cathay (China) via Cipangu (Japan). As the three small ships penetrated farther into the unknown western sea, the crews' anxieties heightened to near mutiny. Columbus allayed their fears by asserting that the presence of birds demonstrated that land was near.

On Sunday, September 23, a *"tortola"* and several other birds were seen. Griscom interpreted tortola as being "any small ground dove," the first terrestrial species seen (Morison 1963: 56). Increasing numbers of birds appeared and Columbus, well aware that Portuguese explorers had found many islands by following birds' flight lines, altered his course on October 6 to west-southwest. Finally, on October 11, a watchman made landfall. The following morning, Friday, October 12, Columbus set foot on the island now believed to be Samana Cay in the Bahamas (Marsden 1986).

In discussing Columbus' tortola sighting on September 23, Morison (1963: 56) referred to a voyage of his own: "On 7 September 1939, a mourning dove flew about our *Capitana* when in about lat. 38° 15' N, long. 55° W, and lit on the weather fore brace, and stayed aboard several hours. She was probably migrating from Newfoundland to the West Indies. Although Columbus was considerably to the E and S of that position, he may have sighted a mourning dove blown off its course, or he may have mistaken one of the phalaropes or petrels for a dove." Morison's speculation about the origin and destination of the bird must be regarded with caution. Although the mourning dove has been reported from Newfoundland, it is quite scarce there (Peters and Burleigh 1951). According to his navigational fix, Morison's observation was approximately 810 nautical miles (1,500 km) east of New York City. The date of his observation, as well as that of Columbus, does coincide with the southward migration of mourning doves.

Others have reported the mourning dove at sea. Gross (1958) saw a mourning dove land aboard ship approximately 175 miles (282 km) out of New York on November 10, 1957. On November 1, 1954, Lamm (1956) saw a mourning dove alight on his ocean steamer, following gale force winds, about 850 nautical miles (1,575 km) east of New York. On the west coast, Roest (1947) wrote that a mourning dove alighted on his ship some 60 miles (111 km) west of Ensenada, Baja California, Mexico, the nearest land being about 50 miles (93 km) distant. Finally, Stevenson (1957), in his study of trans-Gulf and circum-Gulf bird migration, concluded that some mourning doves flew northward across the Gulf of Mexico during their spring migration. Another consideration is the successful and apparently natural establishment in the mid-1950s of a thriving population of mourning doves on Bermuda—approximately 550 nautical miles (1,020 km) east of North America (Wingate 1973).

The mourning dove occurs throughout the Bahamas and Greater Antilles (Bond 1971). However, other columbids, including the similar Zenaida dove and the white-crowned pigeon (noted for its oversea flights) also are present. Although Columbus was intelligent and well trained in nautical matters, he surely was not a naturalist. Consequently, he may have seen any of several species of columbids indigenous to the region—including the mourning dove.

Spanish and French explorers and missionaries. Ingersoll (1923: 138) wrote: "In the first [1519] voyage for [Spaniard] Hernando Cortez [captor of Montezuma II and Tenochtitlán (the ancient Mexico City) and subjugator of the Aztec Empire] to America water and food were almost exhausted and everybody in the vessel was discouraged and mutinous, when 'came a Dove flying to the Shippe, being Good Friday at Sunsett; and sat him on the Shippe-top; whereat they were all comforted; and tooke it for a miracle and good token . . . and all gave heartie thanks to God, directing their course be the way the Dove flew.' Any sort of bird would have been welcome as an indication of nearness of land, but a *dove* meant to them a heavenly pilot. No wonder they were comforted! And when they had landed they found in abundance a flower (the orchid *Peristera elata*) which they at once named La Flor del Espiritu Santu—Flower of the Holy Ghost. Why? Because in its center the consolidated pistil and stamens form an unmistakable image of a dove."

Again, the species of dove reported is not known. Early conquistadors, explorers and settlers of the New World were ill prepared or disinclined to describe the natural history of the "new" land in detail. As Allen (1951: 449) noted of English settlers: "It is not surprising therefore that in the early days of colonization the settlers showed no interest in birds, beasts, or plants except as they served to provide them with, or deprive them of, the necessities for life. . . . Little can be learned of birds from these meager lists but it is obvious that the writers viewed them with . . . [foreign] eyes and had no understanding that American birds could be entirely different from those of Europe."

Perhaps more conclusive was identification of "tortolas" among the wildlife of New Spain, as cited in a letter from Cortez to Spanish emperor Carlos (Charles) V, written on July 10, 1519, from Vera Cruz (de Gayangos 1866: 22, McNutt 1908: 161).

Ponce de Léon, the first European known to have set foot on the mainland of the southeastern United States (in 1513), undoubtedly observed the mourning dove, but there is no documentation that he did. Alvar Nuñez Cabeça de Vaca, in describing birds seen during his long journey (1528–36) along the Gulf Coast and through present-day Texas, listed geese, ducks, flycatchers, night herons and several species of raptors as abundant (Hodge 1907a). Again, no specific mention was made of doves, although the mourning dove surely was present if not abundant along the Spaniard's lengthy route.

Likewise, for Hernando de Soto's exploration of the Gulf Coast and Lower Mississippi River Valley during 1539–42, the chronicles mention the numerous and varied bird life but without specific reference to mourning doves (Lewis 1907).

In 1540, Francisco Vasquez de Coronado marched north from Mexico on a three-year journey that took his expedition to the "buffalo plains" of present-day Kansas. Little mention was made of birds save occasional notice of wild turkeys and eagles. In writing of the buffalo plains, chronicler Pedro de Casteñeda noted the presence of "every sort of game and fowl there" (Hodge 1907b: 344), but he failed to describe them. Today, some of the highest concentrations of breeding mourning doves occur in the region.

Within a half century of Spain's conquest of Montezuma's empire in 1519, Franciscan Fray Bernardino de Sahagún, regarded as the "Father of American Ethnohistory," began a thirteen-volume opus, written in Nahuatl (modified Aztecan) and eventually titled *General History of the Things of New Spain* (Sahagún 1963–1982). In Book XI, *Early Things*, Sahagún and his specially educated Indian colleagues attempted to describe the natural resources of New Spain (the part now comprising Mexico). Among them was the "uilotl," or mourning dove: "It has a slender, pointed bill . . . is chalky-ashen [in overall coloration] . . . its tail is long . . . its food is of grains, maize, *chia*, amaranth, *argemone, lepidium* seed. . . . Its nest is only sticks. . . . They are very attentive to their mates . . . the one [remaining, if one dies] always lives in mourning . . . it seems constantly to weep . . . [and] it makes [the sound] *uilo-o-o*." (Sahagún 1963: 50–51).

Father Joseph De Acosta, a learned Jesuit, spent considerable time traveling in New Spain in the late 1500s and reported his observations of "partridges, turtles, pigeons, stock doves, quails, and many sorts of falcons" (Allen 1951: 428). At that time, the Old World turtledove was frequently referred to as a "turtle." However, inasmuch as De Acosta did not visit the North American mainland portion of New Spain, it appears that his "turtles" probably were one or more kinds of the many columbids native to Central or South America or the West Indies.

If not Columbus, Cortez or Sahagún, French explorer Jacques Cartier may have been the first European to report seeing the mourning dove in North America. He reported spotting "Turtles" and "wilde pigeons" on his second voyage up the St. Lawrence River in 1535 (Burrage 1906: 71). The latter surely were passenger pigeons, while the former apparently were mourning doves, the only other columbid conceivably frequenting the region, albeit in much smaller numbers. Cartier's observation, if valid, must have been near the northernmost range of the species, or else the sighting was of an accidental occurrence.

English explorers and settlers. Thomas Hariot, the first trained naturalist in America, accompanied Sir Walter Raleigh when he landed at Roanoke Island, in present-day North Carolina, in August 1585. In his *A Briefe and True Report of the New Found Land of Virginia* . . . (1590), Hariot presented the names of eighty-six birds "in the countrie language" and had pictures drawn of twenty-five (Goode 1897: 361). Among them was the "stockdove"—a species native to England, about the size of the common "city or barnyard pigeon." Although the stock dove lacks the long tail of either the passenger pigeon or mourning dove, likely one of these was the species to which Hariot referred.

John White, who made four voyages to the New World, was the first to draw American birds extensively, and it was he who illustrated Hariot's (1590) work. According to Feduccia (1985), White depicted thirty-two birds, of which twenty-six were endemic to the colony, but did not include either the mourning dove or passenger pigeon.

Twenty years elapsed after the abandonment of the Roanoke Colony before Captain John Smith brought his contingent of settlers to the New World in 1607 and established Jamestown, in present-day Virginia. In 1615, Ralphe Hamor the Younger, secretary of the Jamestown Colony, published *True Discourse of the Present Estate of Virginia*. Hamor was the first to detail the great flights of wild (passenger) pigeons, but his list of birds lacked the turtledove. William Strachey, another Jamestown colonist, also described the passenger pigeon and other Virginia birds in 1612 and likewise failed to mention any resembling the mourning dove (see Bryant 1934). Captain John Smith published *The Generall Historie of Virginia, New England & The Summer Isles* (1624: 57), in which he listed natural resources of the area, including birds. "Pigeons" were included, and he recognized that there were "some other strange kinds [of birds] to us unknown by name." Presumably, Smith was acquainted with the common turtledove from his native England, thus its omission is puzzling—as it is for the Hamor and Strachey accounts.

Sir Richard Hakluyt never visited North America but gathered and published early accounts of explorations of the New World. In 1582, he published *Divers Voyages Touching the Discoverie of America* . . . , which summarized observations made in the New World. His compilation of birds included "Pigeons" and "Turtles," the latter apparently being mourning doves.

Possibly the first English visitation to New England was the 1602 voyage by Captain Bartholomew Gosnold (though he was preceded by the Italian Verrazano and the Portuguese Gomez). In an account of Gosnold's voyage, M. J. Brereton (1602: 40) listed "pigeons, ringdoves, turtles . . ." among the native species. These surely were the passenger pigeon and mourning dove, but the ring dove reference is perplexing.

Captain George Waymouth, in 1605, was among the earliest Englishmen to explore coastal New England. James Rosier (1605), chronicler of the expedition, described the region's resources and listed "turtle-doves" and eleven other species of birds, plus "Many birds of sundrie colours" and "Many other fowles in flocks, unknowen." Thus, Rosier evidently reported the mourning dove but not the passenger pigeon—unless he did not distinguish between the two.

William Wood described the natural resources of New England in *New Englands Prospect* . . . (1634: 27) and embellished his narrative with poetry, including:

"The harmonious Thrush, Swift Pigeon, Turtle-dove,
Who to her mate doth ever constant prove . . ."

Surely, Wood's "Turtle-dove" referred to the mourning dove.

Thomas Morton listed birds in his *New English Canaan . . .* (1637), but neither the passenger pigeon nor mourning dove was among them.

John Lawson's *A New Voyage to Carolina . . .* (1709) was the most complete natural history of the Carolinas to that time; it included Lawson's observations on a 550-mile (885 km) trek during 1700–1701 through present-day North and South Carolina. Lawson reported seeing "turtle doves" and noted that they were destructive to "pease" (peas) and therefore trapped by settlers.

Mark Catesby. Mark Catesby must be credited for making the mourning dove of continental North America known to science. Catesby came to America in 1712 and became so engrossed in the natural history of the new land that he remained for seven years (Allen 1951). Principally a collector of botanical specimens for European patrons, he also had a strong interest in birds. His observations and drawings led to *Natural History of Carolina, Florida, and the Bahama Islands . . .* (1731–1743), issued in four sections. A highlight of this ornithological opus is the depiction of 109 species of birds with descriptions in English and French. Catesby set his birds in lifelike manner against some associated vegetation, thus initiating the bird illustration pattern to be followed by George Edwards, Alexander Wilson, John James Audubon and others. It is puzzling, however, why Catesby chose the mayapple as the setting for his mourning dove rendering.

Naming the many birds posed a problem, and Catesby (1731–1743: xii) wrote: "Very few of the Birds having Names assign't them in the Country, except some which had *Indian* Names; I have call'd them after *European* birds of the same Genus, with an additional Epithet to distinguish them. As the Males of the Feather'd Kind (except a very few) are more elegantly colour'd than the Females, I have throughout exhibited the Cocks only, except two or three; and have added a short Description of the Hens, wherein they differ in colour from the Cock, the want of which Method has caused great Confusion in works of this Nature." Accordingly, Catesby called the mourning dove "The Turtle of Carolina" and gave it the Latin name *Turtur carolinensis*. For ensuing decades, the mourning dove was to be known as the "turtle" or "turtle dove," for its European namesake. Of the one hundred species illustrated and described in Volume 1, seventy-one (including the mourning dove) were to be used by Linnaeus (1758) in his *Systema Naturae*.

Father and son naturalists. John Bartram, a Quaker plant collector from Philadelphia, is best known for *Observations on the Inhabitants, Climate,*

Mark Catesby's "Turtur Caroliniensis," or "The Turtle of Carolina," is believed to be the first scientific illustration of the mourning dove. This illustration and the following text by Catesby (1731: 24) were not used by Linnaeus (1758) in naming and classifying the species nearly twenty years later: "This is somewhat less than a Dove house Pigeon: the Eyes black, compassed with a blew skin: the Bill black: the upper part of the Head, Neck, Back, and upper part of the Wings brown: the small feathers of the Wing, next the Back, have large black spots: the lower part of the Wing and Quill-feathers of a lead colour. Three or four of the longest being almost black: The Breast and Belly of a pale Carnation colour. On each side of the Neck, the breadth of a Man's Thumb, are two spots of the colour of burnished Gold, with a tincture of crimson and green; between which and its Eye is a black spot. The Wings are long, the Tail much longer, reaching almost five Inches beyond them, and hath fourteen feathers, the two middle longest, and of equal length, and all brown; the rest are gradually shorter, having their upper part lead colour, the middle black, and the end white. The Legs and Feet are red. They breed in *Carolina*, and abide there always. They feed much on the Berries of Poke, i.e. *Blitum Virginianum*, which are Poison. They likewise feed on the Seeds of this Plant; and they are accounted good Meat." *Photo courtesy of the Smithsonian Institution.*

Soil, Rivers, Productions, Animals, and Other Matters Worthy of Notice . . . (Kalm 1751), which reported on natural phenomena seen by Bartram during a 1743 journey from Pennsylvania to southern Canada. Although Bartram saw passenger pigeons, he either did not observe mourning doves (a virtual impossibility), did not recognize them as different from passenger pigeons (also unlikely) or else did not think them worthy of note.

John Bartram's son, William, accompanied his father on some expeditions and later traveled independently. In his *Travels . . .* (1791: 288), the younger Bartram listed the mourning dove as "*Columba Carolinensis*, the turtle dove" and footnoted: "These arrive in Pennsylvania in the spring season from the South, which after building nests, and rearing their young, return again Southerly in the autumn."

A surgeon and a Swede. During much of the 1700s, George Edwards was the focal point of ornithology in England, and travelers and correspondents supplied him with information and specimens of newly found, rare and often undescribed birds. Edwards, also first physician to King George II, is best known for *A Natural History of Uncommon Birds* (1743–1751). Like Catesby's earlier work, Edwards' featured lifelike, full-page, watercolor illustrations of birds, each accompanied by a page of text. Edwards was particularly impressed with the length of the mourning dove's tail, leading him to give it the name "Long-tail'd Dove" (*Columba macroura*). His mourning dove illustration exaggerated the tail length and reportedly was based on a captive bird held by a Mr. John Warner of Rotherhith, who secured it from the West Indies. Thus, Edwards' figure and description are of the form that later came to be regarded as the nominate subspecies of the mourning dove.

Carolus Linnaeus, a Swedish academician, was the central figure among eighteenth century naturalists. It was he who conceived and implemented the present system for identifying, describing, classifying and cataloging new animal and plant species. The tenth edition of his *Systema Naturae* (1758) introduced the comprehensive Latin binomial classification system. Although Linnaeus never visited the New World, European visitors, settlers and emerging American naturalists supplied him with countless new specimens of plants and animals to be named and classified.

George Edwards' "Long-tail'd Dove" (left) is believed to be the second scientific illustration of the mourning dove. Edwards' (1742: 15) art and accompanying description were used by Linnaeus (1758) to classify the species: "The Figure of this Bird shews it of its natural Bigness; it hath but a small Head in proportion to the Body; the neck of a middling Length; the Body pretty long; the Tail longer than the whole Body; the Wings of middling Length; the Bill is straight, not very thick, a little bend downwards at the Point, of a Horn-colour, light about the Nostrils, and a little Rising, darker towards the Point; the Iris of the Eye is of a dark Colour; from the Corner of the Bill to the Eye, is drawn a white Line, which incircleth the Eye; the Fore-part of the Head, above and beneath the Bill, is of a yellowish or Clay-colour, the hinder Part is of a *Pigeon* Blue, pretty light; these Colours lose themselves in each other, where they unite; where these two Colours meet on the Sides of the Head, just under the Ear-holes, are situate on each Side a round black Spot of the bigness of a Tare; the Fort-part of the Neck and Breast are of a bluish or Blossom-colour, more intense above, changing gradually towards the Belly into a Clay-colour; the lower Part of the Belly, Thighs, and Coverts under the Tail, being Clay-colour, with a little mixture of Cinerious; the upper Side of the Neck, Back, and upper Side of the Wings, is of a dark, dirty Brown, the Quills being darker than the Covert-feathers, though the Edges of the Webs of the Quill-feathers are a little lighter colour'd than the rest of the Wing; the Scapular-feathers between the Back and Wing, as also some of the Quills and Coverts next the Back, are marked at their Ends with oval black Spots of different Magnitudes, about 10 or 12 in Number on each Side; the Rump, and Feathers covering the Tail, are more inclining to Ash-colour than the Back and Wings; the middle Feathers of the Tail are very long and black, the side Feathers gradually grow shorter, so that the outer-most on each Side, little exceed half the Length of the middlemost; the outer Feathers are of a bluish or Ash-colour, having Bars of Black near their Tips, the Tips themselves being White; the Legs and Feet Red, as in other *Doves*; it hath four Toes standing after the usual Manner; the Claws are Brown. What is most singular in this Bird, is the Length of the Tail, which is shap'd like a *Magpye's*, no Bird of the *Dove* or *Pigeon*-kind, what I have met with, having the like. This Bird hardly differs at all from some others in the *West-Indies*, save in the Tail. . . . I drew this Bird at Mr. *John Warner's* of *Rotherhith*; who had it of a Person that brought it from the *West Indies*." *Photo courtesy of the Smithsonian Institution.*

Despite his best intentions to make order of chaos, Linnaeus badly muddled the taxonomy of the mourning dove. The problem would persist for nearly two centuries. He erroneously listed Catesby's *Palumbus migratorious* (the Latin name Catesby had given "The Pigeon of Passage," or passenger pigeon) synonymously with Edwards' *Columba macroura*, the Long-tail'd Dove (mourning dove). The later scientific name was accepted by Linnaeus even though it followed by more than a decade Catesby's initial description and naming of the mourning dove. It also accounts for the later-discovered West Indian form being the nominate subspecies instead of the continental form. It fell to Wetmore and Swales (discussed later) to finally set the taxonomic record straight.

Early American naturalists. Physician Benjamin Smith Barton, credited by some as being the "Father of American Natural History" (Goode 1897: 419), was a keen observer of the occurrence and migration of birds in the Philadelphia area around 1800. Barton (1799) believed that most species, including the "turtle-dove," were "birds of passage," or migratory birds. He observed, however, that during mild winters, some "turtle doves" remained year-round. In a list of birds frequenting the Philadelphia area, including their average date of spring arrival, Barton noted that the "Carolina-Pigeon" (mourning dove) arrived about April 18, coincident with the passenger pigeon and "Summer Duck" (wood duck) and at the same time as five local violets were in flower and "the Bull-Frog begins its amours."

Natural history was among Thomas Jefferson's varied interests and talents. In 1781 his *Notes on the State of Virginia* appeared. Although now regarded as possibly the most scientific work published in America to that time, it had not been written for publication. Using Catesby's, Buffon's and Linnaeus' works, Jefferson compiled a list of ninety-three Virginia birds, adding thirty-three species not previously listed by them. In his list, Jefferson referred to the "Turtle" or "Turtle Dove" as *Turtur carolinensis* according to Catesby and *Columba carolinensis* according to Linnaeus.

Two captains west. In 1803, President Jefferson dispatched the famed Corps of Discovery westward to find a route to the Pacific and gather scientific information about the recent Louisiana Purchase and unclaimed lands lying to the west. Jefferson also instructed the expeditioners to observe and record information on "The animals of the country generally, and especially those not known in the United States" (Coues 1893: xxviii). The expedition, launched under the leadership of Captain Meriwether Lewis, was ably assisted by Captain William Clark. Both, like Jefferson, were quite familiar with the mourning dove. On at least eight occasions in their lengthy journals (Thwaites 1905), Lewis and Clark mentioned the mourning dove (as "turtle doves," "doves" or "Dovs"). Most of their notes (and maps) indicate when and approximately where the species was seen (e.g., Sun River in Montana, Salmon River in Idaho and Fort Clatsop in Oregon). Although they reported taking passenger pigeons for food, no such use of the mourning dove was reported. Also, on May 27, 1806, Lewis reported doves cooing, "which is the signal as the Indians [Nez Percé] inform us of the approach of the salmon" (Coues 1893: 1,296).

Thomas Nuttall, an Englishman, who lived most of his life in the United States, traveled extensively in North America studying birds. In *A Manual of Ornithology of the United States and Canada* (1832: 627), Nuttall provided interesting though romanticized descriptions of the call and courtship flight of the male "Carolina Turtle Dove": "Commencing as it were with a low plaintive sigh, a'gh ćoo ćoo còo, repeated at impressive intervals of half a minute, and heard distinctly to a considerable distance through the still and balmy air of the reviving season." And on the courtship call of the male, Nuttall elaborated: "In the nuptial period, the wide circling flight of the male is often repeated, around his mate, towards whom he glides with wings and tail expanded, and gracefully alights on the same or some adjoining tree, where she receives his attentions or fosters her eggs and infant brood."

Napoleon's nephew and niece. Unlike many members of the Bonaparte family, Charles Lucien Jules Laurent Bonaparte, Prince of Canino and of Musignano, was more of a scientist than a politician or military leader. A nephew of Napoleon I, he married his cousin Princess Zénaïde Bonaparte in 1822. Charles and his wife soon sailed for America, and he immediately immersed himself in the ornithology of the young nation. At age twenty-two, he began publishing *American Ornithology . . .* (1825–1833), destined to become a major contribution to knowledge of new or theretofore incorrectly described avian species. Although he ignored the mourning dove in his four-volume opus (because it had already been described by Catesby and Edwards), Bonaparte did describe a new dove from the West Indies. He gave it the common name Zenaida dove, honoring his wife (see chapter 1). Through the deliberations of avian taxonomists, the given name of Charles' wife, Napoleon's niece, is not only perpetuated in the name of the Zenaida dove but also in the generic name, *Zenaida*, later applied to the mourning dove and its close relatives.

A Scotsman. Alexander Wilson moved to America in 1794, where he traveled widely in the eastern United States and recorded by pen and brush all that interested him (Cantwell 1961). His nine-volume *American Ornithology* (1808–1814) and abridgments of that original work were eagerly purchased by the public as guides to local bird life. In one such edition, *Wilson's American Ornithology* (Brewer 1840: 388), the calling behavior of the mourning dove is anthropomorphically described: "Its notes are four; the first is somewhat the highest, and preparatory, seeming to be uttered with an inspiration of the breath, as if the afflicted creature were just recovering its voice from the last convulsive sobs of distress; this is followed by three long, deep, and mournful moanings, that no person of sensibility can listen to without sympathy. A pause of a few minutes ensues, and again the solemn voice of sorrow is renewed as before."

America's premiere ornithologist-painter. John James Audubon (1785–1851) probably is America's best known ornithologist, past or present. Many are familiar with his artistic renditions of birds (Audubon 1827–1838), but few are aware of the copious notes he prepared to accompany the illustrations (Audubon 1840–1844).

At social gatherings in England, Audubon frequently was asked to imitate songs of North American birds, and those of the mourning dove and wild turkey were among his favorites (Durant and Harwood 1980). Audubon died in 1851. In 1893 a Celtic cross monument was placed on his grave at Trinity Chapel of the Intercession, New York City, by the New York Academy of Sciences, and fittingly, the dove was among the dozen endemic North American birds selected to decorate the monument's shaft (Durant and Harwood 1980).

Alexander Wilson's *American Ornithology* (1808–1814) featured a colored engraving "drawn from Nature" of a "Turtle Dove" (along with, counterclockwise, a hermit thrush, "tawney thrush" [veery] and "pine-swamp warbler" [black-throated blue warbler]). Despite the public popularity of this multivolume "guide" book and its revised editions, the Scotsman's illustrations generally were recognized as inferior to those done by his contemporary John James Audubon. *Photo courtesy of the Library of Congress.*

John James Audubon depicted the mourning dove ("Carolina Turtle-dove") in Plate CCLXXXVI of his famous elephant folio collection and wrote: "I have tried, kind reader, to give you a faithful representation of two as gentle pairs of Turtles as ever cooed their loves in the green woods. I have placed them on a branch of Stuartia, which you see ornamented with a profusion of white blossoms, emblematic of purity and chastity. . . . Look at the female as she assiduously sits on her eggs, embosomed among the thick foliage, receiving food from the bill of her mate, and listening with delight to his assurances of devoted affection. . . ." (Audubon 1840–1844[v]: 36). *Photo courtesy of the Library of Congress.*

Usually, a medical officer with some biological interests and sometimes zoological training was assigned to each of the subsequent six (four railroad and two boundary) survey expeditions. These surgeon/naturalists often had ample time between their medical obligations to study local natural history. In so doing, they contributed much to knowledge of the mourning dove in the West.

The finding and describing to science of the western subspecies of mourning dove (*Z. m. marginella*) is credited to Dr. Samuel W. Woodhouse, surgeon/naturalist of U.S. Army Lieutenant Lorenzo Sitgreave's 1851 expedition in the Southwest. Woodhouse (1854) proposed the new bird—based on but one specimen collected along the north fork of the Canadian River—as a full species under the genus *Ectopistes*. The collection of only a single specimen is puzzling inasmuch as Baird et al. (1874 [3]: 383) wrote: "Dr. Woodhouse mentions that the mournful notes of these birds [mourning doves] were to be heard continually throughout the Indian Territory and the greater part of Texas and New Mexico, in which countries it breeds." Nonetheless, Woodhouse's description of the western subspecies still stands.

The Audubon Monument in Trinity Church Cemetery, New York City. Erected by the New York Academy of Sciences in 1893 to mark the burial site of John James Audubon (1785–1851), America's best-known ornithologist, the Celtic cross shaft features thirteen birds, of which the dove is uppermost. *Photo by F. E. Parshley; courtesy of American Museum of Natural History, Department of Library Services (neg. #337359).*

Surveyors and surgeons. The western U.S. survey expeditions of the nineteenth century may be divided into two phases, interrupted by the Civil War. In general, those of the first period were conducted by the military; those of the second period were directed initially by the military but later by civilian agencies, chiefly the U.S. Geological Survey.

In 1853 Congress appropriated funds to survey various routes along which railroads might be constructed from the Mississippi River to the Pacific Ocean (Hume 1942). Spencer Baird (1855: 9), Assistant Secretary of the Smithsonian Institution, instructed the survey parties: "As the expedition will travel through the breeding-ground of many species of birds whose nidification and eggs are not known, attention should be paid to securing abundant specimens of nests and eggs. As far as possible the skin of the bird to which each set of eggs may belong should be secured, and have a mark common to it and the egg."

As an Acting Assistant Surgeon, U.S. Army, Dr. Samuel W. Woodhouse provided both medical and naturalist support to various military surveying expeditions. In 1851 he accompanied the expedition led by U.S. Army First Lieutenant Lorenzo Sitgreaves to the Southwest in search of a better route to California. While passing through present-day Oklahoma, Woodhouse collected a single immature male mourning dove, and this specimen and his description of it were the basis for recognition of the western subspecies, *Zenaida macroura marginella.* Woodhouse described its general form as similar to the eastern subspecies "but much more delicate" (Sitgreaves 1854: 93). *Photo courtesy of the Library of Congress.*

James G. Cooper and George Suckley were attached as naturalists to the survey of the Northern Pacific Railroad Route in 1853. Their ornithological observations were reported in *The Natural History of Washington Territory . . .* (Cooper and Suckley 1859: 219). Regarding the mourning dove, Cooper wrote: "The Carolina dove is common about prairies and farms of the interior, and probably some remain all winter in the Territory, though none were at Vancouver [Washington] in the snowy winter of 1853. They rarely appear along the coast border, but doubtless extend east to the Rocky Mountains." Suckley added: "Very abundant throughout both Territories [Washington and Oregon]. At Fort Steilacoom [near present-day Tacoma] this species arrives and departs about the same time as the *Columba fasciata* [band-tailed pigeon]." Both naturalists evidently failed to recognize the western mourning dove as differing from the eastern form.

After the Civil War, the nation's interest in its West returned with heightened fervor. Bartlett (1962: xii) wrote: "The results of this quest for knowledge about the American West after the Civil War were four great geographical and geological surveys conducted over large areas of the West from 1867 until 1879, when the United States Geological Survey . . . took over." Although the main purposes of the surveys were to establish basic measurements and reference points and to map the unexplored domain, naturalists were assigned to each major survey party.

C. Hart Merriam, at age sixteen, accompanied the 1872 Ferdinand V. Hayden Expedition into the remote region destined to become Yellowstone National Park. While in Utah, Merriam (1873: 710) observed: "Mourning or ground doves were very numerous in the Salt Lake Valley. . . . They lay two white eggs, either in a slight excavation in the ground lined with a few pieces of straw or dry grass laid loosely together, or in a nest of fibrous roots, which is placed on a bush from two to five feet above the ground."

Ornithologist Elliott Coues accompanied Hayden's U.S. Geological Survey of the Territories during 1876 through 1880 in present-day Colorado and Wyoming. Even before this, Coues (1874: 389) had reported on the mourning dove in previous avian collections of the Survey: "I note but a single instance of its occurrence in the British Provinces [Canada]. The parallel of 49° is probably about its normal northern limit. . . . I have found it alike abundant in all kinds of country I have visited even in the terrible alkaline deserts of the southwest, where its presence is cheering evidence that water may be found not far off . . . while in Arizona reptiles of the most venomous character abound,

the bird seeks safety for its eggs by placing the nest on bushes. The principal bushes of some parts of the Territory are cacti and other thorny growths, so terribly prickly that snakes can scarcely climb through them."

During 1871–74, Henry W. Henshaw was attached to Lieutenant George Wheeler's expedition through parts of Nevada, Utah, California, Colorado, New Mexico and Arizona. His fieldwork culminated in *Report upon the Ornithological Collections* (1875: 432), in which Henshaw wrote of the mourning dove: "In Utah, common everywhere on the plains; occurs sparingly in mountains. . . . In very large numbers in the cottonwood groves along the banks of the Platte, and elsewhere abundant. The first nest seen was found on the ground May 7, contained a freshly laid egg. The species is not particular in the choice of a location for its nests. A favorite site is the thick undergrowth which clothes the trunks of cottonwoods. But nests are often placed on the ground, not infrequently in an open place. . . . Abundant throughout Eastern Arizona."

Father of North American bird migration study. The earliest detailed study of bird migration over a substantial part of the United States was that of Wells W. Cooke, a biologist assigned to the fledgling U.S. Division of Economic Ornithology. In discussing the mourning dove, Cooke (1888) wrote that it was a common breeder throughout the Mississippi Valley. He observed that the dove was abundant year-round from latitude 36 degrees south (level of Knoxville, Tennessee) and that it wintered regularly between 36 and 38 degrees (latitude of Evansville, Indiana).

THE MOURNING DOVE AND THE PASSENGER PIGEON

The passenger pigeon's demise (see Schorger 1955) has sometimes been seen as a reason to be concerned about the status of the mourning dove and particularly about hunting of the species.

The two birds were superficially similar and, at one time, assigned to the same genus, *Ectopistes*. Goodwin (1983) considered the two forms, though of different genera, as stemming from the same branch of his columbid family tree.

As Roberts (1932 [1]: 572) noted, even experienced ornithologists sometimes confused the two species in the field: "A word of caution should be given in regard to the still frequent mistake of reporting the Mourning Dove as the now extinct Passenger Pigeon. An exceptionally well-developed and highly colored Dove may suggest a Wild Pigeon, and even trained observers may for a moment be startled by the resemblance. Even men who knew the Pigeon well in its day are deceived, and many positive reports of seeing Passenger Pigeons here and there during the past twenty years have appeared in print."

Schorger (1955: 286), who noted that sight observations carry interest but little weight, reinforced Roberts' observation: "Persons with wide experience with the passenger pigeon have been deceived by the mourning dove under certain conditions."

As with the mourning dove now in many locales, the passenger pigeon was an extremely abundant species in its preferred habitat. Beyond that, the similarities between the two species lessened or vanished *(Table 1)*.

Table 1. Comparisons of the passenger pigeon and the mourning dove.

Characteristic	Passenger pigeon[a]	Mourning dove[b]
Present status	Extinct; last of the species died in 1914, in captivity	Generally thriving except recently in parts of the Western and Central management units
Length	16.6 inches (423 mm)	11–13 inches (280–330 mm)[c]
Wing span	23–25 inches (584–635 mm)[d]	17–19 inches (423–483 mm)[c]
Weight	9–12 ounces (256–342 g)	4.4 ounces (124 g)[e]
Range	Forested eastern U.S. and southern Canada, casual or accidental in western states and provinces	All 48 contiguous United States, southeastern Alaska, southern Canada, Bahamas, West Indies, Mexico, Central America south to Panama; established in Hawaii and Bermuda
Abundance	Estimated at 3–5 billion at time of settlement	Autumn flights of 350–600 million in conterminous United States
Preferred habitat	Climax deciduous forests, particularly of mast-bearing species	Nearly cosmopolitan
Chief foods	Acorns, beechnuts, fruits, occasionally cultivated grains	Wide variety of seeds, including cultivated seeds and grains
Sociability	Extremely gregarious throughout year	Usually solitary or in pairs and small flocks, becoming gregarious at choice feeding or watering sites especially during autumn and winter
Fidelity to natal nest areas	Little if any; major nesting areas usually shifted annually, evidently in response to available food	Adults usually return to previous nesting area; some yearlings also return, while others pioneer new areas
Nesting locations	Huge roosts in climax forests, usually in remote locales	Wide array of sites including trees, shrubs and structures, and on the ground in rural, suburban and urban locales
Overall reproductive potential	Limited	Very high
Roosts	Huge concentrations in climax forests	Scattered, in trees, bushes, or on the ground
Flight	Noiseless[f]	Whistling
Vocalization	Generally very noisy while feeding, roosting and flying	Generally quiet except for "perch coo" (advertising song)
Vulnerability to exploitation and local calamity	Very high because of extreme gregariousness even when breeding	Low because birds are usually widely dispersed, especially during breeding season
Wariness	Unwary at all times	Somewhat responsive to danger
Adaptability	Highly specialized and rigid	Remarkably flexible and adaptive
Interspecific association	Generally, the two species did not intermingle, but as passenger pigeons neared extinction, individuals were observed to accompany mourning doves	

[a] Summarized from Schorger (1955).
[b] Many of these characteristics are treated in depth and documented elsewhere in this book.
[c] From Edminster (1954).
[d] From Coues (1903).
[e] From Hanson and Kossack (1963).
[f] From Chapman (1939) and Forbush (1927).

The passenger pigeon was considerably larger than the mourning dove and more highly colored, with a bluish back and reddish underparts. However, it was their distinctive behaviors, particularly the passenger pigeon's colony nesting, that readily set the two similar species apart. *Artwork by Owen J. Gromme; photo courtesy of the Milwaukee Public Museum.*

The most conspicuous characteristic of the passenger pigeon was its extreme gregariousness throughout the year. Swedish naturalist Pehr Kalm (1911 [1759]: 409), for example, noted huge flights in Pennsylvania and New Jersey in mid-March, 1740: "Their number, while in flight, extended 3 or 4 English miles in length, and more than 1 such mile in breadth, and they flew so closely together that the sky and sun were obscured by them, the daylight becoming sensibly diminished by their shadow."

Also commenting on the abundance and gregariousness of passenger pigeons, Audubon (1831: 322) wrote: "Let us take a column 1 mile in breadth, which is far below the average size, and suppose it passing over us without interruption for three hours, at the rate mentioned above of 1 mile in the minute. This will give us a parallelogram of 180 miles by 1, covering 180 square miles allowing 2 pigeons to the square yard, we have 1,115,136,000 pigeons in one flock." Similarly, Wilson (1808–1814) calculated that one flock he observed contained 2,230,272,000 birds.

One may dispute the precision of these estimates, but they and those of other reputable observers suggest that the passenger pigeon populations at times of settlement were prodigious, perhaps numbering 3 to 5 billion birds (Schorger 1955). (Interestingly, Audubon's number is precisely half of Wilson's. It would seem that Audubon, who was not particularly friendly toward Wilson, may have based his calculation on Wilson's observation *and* previously published estimate.)

Roger Tory Peterson (1941) estimated that the population of all breeding birds in the United States in the early 1940s was around 6 billion. The total avian population of the United States in the nineteenth century was probably even higher, leading Schorger (1955) to speculate that the passenger pigeon may have once formed 25 to 40 percent of the total bird population of the United States.

The extreme gregariousness of the species subjected it to prodigious risks of local calamity such as severe weather, habitat destruction, predation and disease. Further, the astonishing concentrations of passenger pigeons rendered the birds susceptible to unsustainable human exploitation. Countless millions were trapped, clubbed, shot and otherwise pillaged from roosts for a variety of reasons, including "sport," food, commerce and to protect against damage caused by the birds' feeding and waste.

As early as 1869, French sportsman Bénédict Henri Révoil (1874) had predicted that the passenger pigeon would be exterminated by the end of the century; however, in captivity, the species endured until 1914. What may have been the greatest biomass of a single avian species in historic times had vanished.

Aldo Leopold (1947: 3), in delivering the eulogy at the dedication of a monument in Wisconsin commemorating the extinction of the passenger pigeon, eloquently declared in what is one of the most moving passages in the wildlife literature: "The passenger pigeon was no mere bird, he was a biological storm. He was the lightning that played between the biotic poles of intolerable intensity: the fat of the land and his own zest for living. Yearly the feathered tempest roared up, down, and across the continent, sucking up the laden fruits of the forest and prairie, burning them in a traveling blast of life. Like any other chain-reaction, the pigeon could survive no diminution of his own furious intensity. Once the pigeoners had subtracted from his numbers, and once the settlers had chopped gaps in the continuity of his fuel, his flame guttered out with hardly a sputter or even a wisp of smoke."

In contrast, the mourning dove, never afflicted with the remarkable gregariousness of its cousin, is now among the most populous and widely distributed North American birds. In the cooperative Breeding Bird Survey conducted in the United States and Canada during 1987, mourning doves were observed on 1,721 (86.7 percent) of 1,984 possible routes and totaled 54,980 individuals along routes, ranking sixth among all species (W. R. Peeples personal communication: 1988). The mourning dove is an extraordinarily adaptable and widely distributed species and, over large areas, is quite abundant. It also is the number one gamebird in the United States in terms of number harvested annually. Where hunting is permitted, under definitive regulatory guidelines, the species generally continues to thrive.

COMMERCIALIZATION

The mourning dove apparently was not an important commodity in the early game markets. Edminster (1954: 430) noted that the dove was not specially sought by market hunters during the "era of game commercialization." This is not surprising in view of the abundance of larger birds, mammals, fish and shellfish readily available near most metropolitan markets in the eighteenth and early nineteenth centuries.

De Voe (1862) discussed the various kinds of game marketed in New York City in early years, including their local abundance, and no specific mention was made of the mourning dove (although the passenger pigeon was noted). Nonetheless, it is probable that small numbers of mourning doves were occasionally offered. As early as 1763, the New York City Common Council set pricing standards for marketed wildlife, and mourning doves would have fallen within the following category: "For *snipes* of the smaller sort, and other small birds, by the dozen, *sixpence*; and after that rate for a greater or smaller number" (De Voe 1862: 143).

Oldys (1911) identified the principal game markets of the United States at the time as Chicago, New York, Philadelphia and Boston. The large marketplace in St. Louis had closed the previous year (1910), and those in Detroit, Milwaukee, St. Paul, Minneapolis and Omaha had closed earlier. Smaller markets still existed in Baltimore, Washington, New Orleans and Denver. Although Oldys specifically mentioned various gamebirds offered for sale (including quail, ruffed grouse, pigeons, wild turkeys, woodcock, snipe, and several species of ducks and geese), he wrote nothing of the mourning dove.

The only published reference found concerning doves being sold for food is in Grinnell et al. (1918:

601): "In 1895–96, when doves were yet permitted to be sold in the markets, the records of the California Fish and Game Commission . . . show that 5,160 birds were received in San Francisco and Los Angeles from October to February, inclusive. Their value was quoted as slightly less than five cents apiece." It seems probable that these were mourning doves, because white-winged doves (which also breed in southern California) would have emigrated by then. If the "doves" had been band-tailed pigeons, they probably would have been identified as "pigeons."

Thus, the mourning dove escaped the brunt of unregulated market gunning that contributed to the decimation of many game species during the 1800s and early 1900s.

Bird feathers, skins, eggs and nests had considerable economic value during the latter part of the nineteenth century and early part of the twentieth century until federal and state laws abolished commercialization of migratory birds. Amateur collectors and traders, as well as professional ornithologists, avidly purchased, sold and exchanged bird skins, eggs and nests. Societies were formed, periodicals printed and price guidelines published, much as they are today for other collectibles. In one such guide (Anonymous 1890), a prepared mourning dove skin was valued at $0.25 to $0.75, depending on its condition. At the same time, single passenger pigeon skins were bringing $1.50 to $3.00. Mourning dove eggs were priced at $0.03 each, compared with the handsome sum of $2.00 for a passenger pigeon egg (Anonymous 1889). Considering the dollar's worth then, these prices were sufficient to support a vigorous and lucrative business in collection and trade of bird skins, eggs and nests.

Aside from their commercial values, mourning doves often provided welcome nourishment to travelers when and where larger game was unavailable or when a change of diet was sought. Maximilian, Prince of Wied-Neuwied, a German naturalist and traveler, noted in his journal for May 27, 1833 (Thwaites 1906 [XXII]: 312) that "The Carolina pigeon was frequent here [along the Missouri River in present-day South Dakota], and was sought after by our people for dinner." Although the identity of the "Carolina pigeon" is questionable, accounts elsewhere about the passenger pigeon suggest that this reference was to the mourning dove.

In his journal of an 1899 paleontological expedition led by John C. Merriam of the University of California to the fossil beds of the John Day Basin of central Oregon, Loye Miller reported that doves sometimes were shot for food. For example, on May

The mourning dove was never hunted intensively for commercial purposes and only seldom for recreation or subsistence in the 1800s, principally because shooting at doves—relative to other game and given the firearms of the day, a dearth of shotgun ammunition, and the species' elusive flight characteristics—was too expensive an investment of time and resources. Hunters had little reason to chance squandering shots at mourning doves, considering that even successful shots provided nominal return. This scene from the eastcentral Plains about the turn of the century may be all the more remarkable if the two birds on the left side of the "trophy line"—between a greater yellowlegs and what appear to be four passenger pigeons—are mourning doves, as suspected. The plumage of the waterfowl indicates the season is late summer or early autumn. *Photo courtesy of the Kansas Historical Society.*

29, Miller wrote, "Dr. [Merriam] shot three doves and I a rabbit with our pistols so we had game dinner," and on May 30 the party had a "Fine supper of doves" (Shotwell 1972: 5,6).

SPORT HUNTING AND REGULATIONS

The mourning dove clearly is the most abundantly harvested gamebird in the United States today, including all waterfowl species combined. But its popularity as a gamebird is a comparatively recent phenomenon.

As previously noted, the mourning dove was seldom mentioned, if at all, in accounts of early explorers, travelers and settlers, and it was not an important commodity in early game markets. However, in the few references to the dove as a food item, the mention usually emphasized its delicacy.

For example, Audubon (1840–1844[V]: 38) proclaimed: "The flesh of these birds is remarkably fine, when they are obtained in the proper season. Such birds become extremely fat, are tender and juicy, and in flavour equal in the estimation of some of my friends, as well as in my own, to that of the Snipe or even Woodcock; but as taste in such matters depends much on the circumstances, and perhaps on the whim of individuals, I would advise you, reader, to try for yourself."

The several hunting and sporting books published shortly before or following the Civil War tended to ignore the mourning dove as a sporting species. No attention was given the species in *Krider's Sporting Anecdotes* (Klapp 1853). H. S. Herbert, who used the pseudonym "Frank Forester" and wrote widely of hunting, paid little if any attention to the mourning dove. It was totally ignored in his *Frank Forester's Field Sports of the United States and British Provinces of North America* (1858). R. B. Roosevelt published *The Gamebird of the Coasts and*

Lakes of the Northern States of America (1866) and discussed quail, grouse and turkeys but failed to mention the mourning dove. French sportsman Bénédict Henri Révoil ignored the species in his *Chasses dans l'Amerique du Nord* (1869), though he wrote at length of pigeon hunting. Similarly, the species was either overlooked or ignored in *Sport with Gun and Rod* (Mayer 1883), *Names and Portraits of Birds Which Interest Gunners . . .* (Trumbull 1888), *Shooting on Upland, Marsh, and Stream* (Leffingwell 1890), and *Game Birds at Home* (Van Dyke 1895).

Palmer (1912: 7–8) traced the evolution of the term "game" in the United States. He wrote that Frank Forester had declared in 1848 that, although "game" was an arbitrary term, it applied in its first and most correct sense to "those animals whether of fur or feather, which are the natural pursuit of certain high breeds of dogs." Palmer added, "I can not lend my humble sanction to the shooting of . . . pigeons . . . [or] calling them game."

The appropriateness of regarding various birds and mammals as game was discussed in an early Division of Biological Survey bulletin (Palmer and Olds [sic] 1900: 11): "Certain mammals and birds which are sometimes classed as game should, for various reasons, be otherwise regarded. Among such . . . may be . . . cranes, wild pigeons, doves. . . . Cranes, pigeons, and doves are ordinarily considered legitimate game, but are now so rare that in most States they have been practically removed from the game list." The authors' rationale for grouping the dove with the then nearly extinct passenger pigeon is unclear. However, at that time, the American Ornithologists' Union's (AOU) definition of gamebirds still excluded the Columbidae (see Palmer 1900).

The ambiguous—if not ambivalent—attitude toward the mourning dove as a gamebird at the turn of the century also is evident in yet another passage in Palmer and Olds [sic] (1900: 15). Under the heading "Species Erroneously Considered Game Birds," they listed the passenger pigeon, band-tailed pigeon and mourning dove, then hastened to assure readers that "Where it [the mourning dove] is abundant, as in southern California and some parts of the Southwest, it is perhaps in no immediate danger of extermination if the slaughter is kept within reasonable bounds."

Palmer (1900) noted that twelve states then protected the mourning dove throughout the year and nineteen only at certain times of the year, while the remainder afforded it no protection whatsoever. Among the nineteen dove-hunting states, seasons varied in length from two to nine months, beginning on June 1 in Arizona, July 1 in Utah, July 4 in Ohio, and July 15 in California and Colorado—all

well within the species' peak nesting season.

Model legislation developed in 1886 by the AOU's Committee on the Protection of Birds, titled "An Act for the Protection of Birds and Their Nests and Eggs," was included in Palmer's (1900) comprehensive review of protective legislation for birds. Section 1 of the Act listed the natural avian families proposed for inclusion; the Columbidae did not appear. However, it was noted that "In many States doves are universally classed as game birds, and where the game laws cover their protection during a closed season they may be so classed in section 1 if necessary" (Palmer 1900: 48–49). Many states adopted this option when they incorporated the AOU model legislation into their laws or regulations.

This ambiguity about the sporting status of the mourning dove probably existed because preoccupation with the enormous flights of passenger pigeons simply drew attention from the smaller, less conspicuous but more widely distributed mourning dove. Also, some areas of the country still had a relative abundance of big game and larger gamebirds. Wild game was a food staple in rural areas, and hunters logically directed their efforts to species that could be taken efficiently and economically and that supplied relatively large quantities of meat per unit of hunting effort. Enormous quantities of game were being shipped to metropolitan areas by wagon and rail, and harvesting efficiency was an important consideration. Furthermore, most firearms in use through the mid-nineteenth century were muzzleloaders and, later, single-shot breechloaders. Considerable time and effort were required to prepare each charge. Clearly, such firearms were not conducive to rapid, repetitive shooting, such as the mourning dove often provides. Also, given the cost and availability of ammunition, shooting of doves likely was viewed as a poor investment. Finally, it seems probable that the mourning dove populations of that period were not as large or widely distributed as they are today.

The enigma of the mourning dove as a sporting species persisted long after the turn of the century. In some instances, the feeling can be clearly explained on grounds of moral or other personal beliefs. This position is well exemplified by William T. Hornaday, an influential conservation persona of the early twentieth century. A once avid hunter, Hornaday was one of the most vocal, uncompromising, controversial members of an emerging group of staunch wildlife preservationists. He adamantly opposed dove hunting: "I do not approve the new game-bird status of the mourning dove. . . . It is another thorn in my flesh. That lovely and lovable bird is a farm and family ornament. Where

I was brought up, any man killing doves as game would have been jeered at . . ." (Hornaday 1931: 74). In an earlier publication, Hornaday (1904: 238) acknowledged that his aversion to recognizing the mourning dove as a gamebird was inspired by an injunction from his mother, "a charge as binding as one of the ten commandments."

Grinnell et al. (1918: 590) included the mourning dove in *The Game Birds of California*, but, as others before and after, they waffled on declaring the dove a "proper" game species: "The birds have been hunted in California for many years, and still are; but in many of the eastern states they are now classed as nongame birds and protected by law. In California the nesting period of the dove has been found to include almost every month of the year, and on the basis of the argument that no shooting should be allowed when it is nesting, the arrangement of a proper hunting season has presented considerable difficulty. Indeed, this and other considerations, particularly its service as a destroyer of weed seeds, have quite properly raised the question whether we should continue to allow the dove to be shot as a game bird."

Oddly, a disregard of the mourning dove as a gamebird spilled over into later professional wildlife literature. Aldo Leopold, "Father of American Wildlife Management," did not mention the species in *Report on a Game Survey of the North-Central States* (1931), even though the dove then was being hunted in Illinois, Minnesota and Missouri—all within Leopold's study area. A decade earlier, Leopold (1921) had published "A Hunter's Notes on Doves in the Rio Grande Valley" in the *Condor*, a leading ornithological journal. Although Leopold's *Game Management* (1933) contained a brief discussion of the population dynamics of the mourning dove, far more attention was given to the exotic ring-necked pheasant and gray (Hungarian) partridge and to the native northern bobwhite, wild turkey and ruffed grouse (Leopold 1933).

The mourning dove was not noted in the wildlife textbook *Wildlife Management: Upland Game and General Principles* (Trippensee 1948). Nor was there mention of the species in Durward Allen's *Our Wildlife Legacy* (1962), although considerable attention was given several exotic gamebirds.

Even more perplexing is the following definition of "waterfowl and other game birds" in *Wildlife Conservation* (Gabrielson 1941: 134): "This group of migratory game birds includes ducks, geese, coots, gallinules, and rails, which together have constituted one of America's greatest sources of huntable game." Gabrielson wrote his book while serving as Director of the U.S. Fish and Wildlife Service, the very agency charged with administering interna-tional migratory bird treaties and the Migratory Bird Treaty Act, which list the mourning dove as a migratory gamebird. It appears its omission was an oversight, for in a photograph caption (verso page 172), Gabrielson noted, "the mourning dove, a game bird as well as a songbird raises its young . . . in solitary nesting places; doves are now protected under the Migratory Bird Treaty Act." In fact, they had been under federal protection during the preceding twenty-three years.

In 1945, F. C. Lincoln, Chief of the U.S. Fish and Wildlife Service's migratory gamebird program, authored a leaflet titled *The Mourning Dove as a Game Bird*. Albert M. Day, then Assistant Director of the Service, observed in the foreword that better public understanding—including the need to delay dove hunting seasons in some southern areas until October 1 or even later—was the most pressing need in mourning dove management. Lincoln noted that, in 1921, the federal court in Athens, Georgia had decided that the species was migratory and entitled to federal protection even though some individuals may remain year-round within the borders of certain states. After reviewing pertinent biological data, Lincoln concluded that, in the region lying south of the northern boundaries of North Carolina, Tennessee, Arkansas and Oklahoma, sport shooting should not be permitted before October 1. That statement was to fuel a controversy over dove hunting in general, and September dove hunting in particular, for decades to come.

On the question of hunting mourning doves, Swift and Lawrence (1966: 475) provided a rationale: "Mourning doves are the most abundant and widely distributed game birds in our country. Of all the doves frequenting our country in August, 70 percent will die before spring because of disease, accident, predation, or at the hand of the hunter. Of the millions of doves that die each year of all causes, hunters harvest only 20 percent. In view of the present status of the resource, the lack of evidence that hunting has an adverse effect on dove populations, and the great amount of recreation afforded by hunting, prohibiting dove hunting is not only unnecessary but is not in the public interest."

HABITATS AND ADAPTATIONS

A National Research Council study in 1970 noted that any review of habitat requirements of North American birds and mammals demonstrates that relatively few species are characteristic of climax vegetation and that most species of major interest to people depend on a stage of vegetation below the climax, or make use of several successional stages, or migrate from one vegetational zone to another. The mourning dove utilizes all three vegetational situations. The study concluded that pre-Columbian environments in the eastern half of North America were characterized by great variety in vegetative patterns and a corresponding wide distribution of wildlife species depending on edges and several stages of vegetation. One of these species was and is the mourning dove.

The mourning dove is adapted to a wide variety of habitat conditions but depends particularly on edge cover and mixed successional stages throughout its range. *Top photo (Georgia) by Daniel O. Todd; courtesy of the USDA Forest Service. Center photo (Oklahoma) by Robert E. Rolley; courtesy of the Oklahoma Cooperative Wildlife Research Unit. Bottom photo (Arizona) by S. C. Martin; courtesy of the USDA Forest Service.*

Pre-Columbian Habitat Influences

There is a common misconception that eastern North America was, at its rediscovery, an unbroken climax forest (see McCabe and McCabe 1984). There were extensive forests but also numerous openings, parklands and forested tracts in early successional stages—all the result of varying soil types, periodic wildfires, Indian incendiarism, wind-throw, disease and other factors. In fact, Florentine explorer Giovanni da Verrazano, who investigated the Atlantic coast in 1524, reported: "We often went five or six leagues [12 to 15 miles: 19 to 24 km] into the interior and found the country as pleasant as it is possible to conceive, open plains twenty-five or thirty leagues [62 to 75 miles: 100 to 121 km] in extent entirely free from trees" (Russell 1976: 4).

Natural influences. Natural forces evidently created or helped maintain habitat suitable for mourning doves. Then, as now, lightning fires were extremely important natural agents. Forty to eighty lightning strikes per year may occur within an average square mile (15 to 31/km²) of the United States (Komarek 1964). Where fuel is available, lightning may ignite fires that can burn for weeks or months until they are extinguished by rain, consume all available fuel or reach a barrier—such as a large body of water—and burn out. In the extreme, lightning fires can alter habitats for decades and even centuries.

Wind, the agent that drives fires, often is overlooked as an important habitat influence. Fire weakens trees, rendering them more susceptible to wind-throw; in turn, windstorms produce the tangled mass of brush and fallen timber necessary to fuel severe burns. Also, the threat of wind-throw increases as a forest stand matures, the trees grow taller and the soil becomes more moist. Wind often is cited as the most common cause of death of over-mature trees (National Research Council 1970).

Some species of wildlife were—and are—so abundant as to have a marked and enduring influence on their environment. Local destruction of hardwood forests by nesting and roosting passenger pigeons is well documented (Schorger 1955). Big game species, notably bison, drastically influenced vegetation throughout their range, particularly on the Great Plains. Their grazing, wallowing and trailing not only helped maintain native grasses but exposed soil for the invasion of forbs and certain grasses. And a host of rodents, particularly prairie dogs and ground squirrels, influenced grassland communities.

In one way or another, natural forces and factors set the stage for habitat alterations by Indians and later by European invaders, further affecting the amount and suitability of habitat for mourning doves.

Indian-induced influences. Numerous authorities concur that the Indian had a profound—even if sometimes local—effect on the North American environment encountered by European explorers and settlers (Day 1953). Fires set by Indians were perhaps even more significant from the standpoint of wildlife habitat alteration than were those set by lightning (National Research Council 1970). Thomas Morton, in his *New English Canaan* (1637: 52), wrote of Indian incendiarism: "The Salvages are accusted, to set fire of the Country in all places where they come; and to burne it, twize a yeare, vize at the Spring, and the fall of the leafe."

Stewart (1951) found more than two hundred references to Indians setting fire to vegetation in aboriginal times, and these burns occurred in all major geographic and cultural areas. Indians used fires to clear forests for agriculture, fell trees for firewood, facilitate travel, assist in hunting and warfare, encourage nut, fruit and berry production and harvest, drive away insects and reptiles, and even to improve habitat for wildlife (particularly deer). Plains Indians intentionally fired grasslands to benefit bison, elk and other big game (McCabe 1982).

Nearly all the woodland Indians of the Northeast and elsewhere along the Atlantic coast lived in villages that varied in size and permanence (Day 1953). They cleared forests for village sites and foraged considerable distances for foods (including game), fibers, medicines, wood and bark for utensils, weapons, canoes and shelters, and particularly for firewood, which was consumed in substantial quantities. Roger Williams (1643) wrote that firewood was so important that the Narrangansetts of Rhode Island thought that the English had come to North America because they lacked firewood at home. Village sites often covered 100 to 150 acres (40 to 61 ha), and one Virginia village reportedly had 3,000 acres (1,214 ha) of cleared land, mostly planted to corn (Shannon 1934). Trees were killed by girdling and felled intentionally by repeated fires or by stone axes.

The relatively sedentary existence of many tribes was made possible by agriculture, particularly by the staple food, maize. Because corn could be grown in "hills" planted a considerable distance apart, land did not need to be totally cleared. Thus, it was planted among stumps and downed timber, and even among trees killed by girdling. Corn thus planted and other cultivated and gathered products grown or encouraged by Indians— such as by fertilization and annual burning—directly benefited some wildlife, including mourning doves, or did so indirectly by retarding overgrowth of forests and promoting growth of seral stage plant foods.

Certain Indians, particularly in the Southwest, developed irrigation systems to permit sustainable agriculture, thus increasing to some extent available water and plant foods in otherwise relatively poor, arid habitats. There is evidence that as early as 300 B.C. Hohokam Indians irrigated croplands in what is now Arizona (Ebling 1979). In the dry but fertile bottomlands of the Salt and Gila rivers, they excavated irrigation ditches 30 feet (9.1 m) wide and 10 feet (3 m) deep. In the Salt Valley alone, at least 150 miles (241 km) of such ditches were dug. The Hohokams mysteriously disappeared shortly after 1400 A.D., leaving their huge ditches abandoned.

When the Spanish explorer Fray Marcos de Niza first entered the Pima Indian country of southern Arizona in 1534, he found that both sides of the Gila River Valley were being farmed and irrigated by water diverted from the river and directed through hand-dug ditches to the fields (Ebling 1979). Also, in 1776, Fray Silvestre Escalante recorded in his diary that, on the Pilar River (now Ash Creek), 25 miles (40 km) south of Zion Canyon, he found fields being watered by Indians with very well-made irrigation ditches (Ebling 1979).

The activities of Indians represent the first artificial impacts in a progression of many that altered pristine North America. Their fires often swept vast forested areas soon pioneered by seed-producing forbs and grasses valuable as dove foods. On a more limited scale, Indian cultivation of crops, tree girdling and felling, and development of water supplies very likely were beneficial to local dove populations. Thus, the Indians set the stage for enormous changes to occur with the coming of Europeans.

Historic Habitat Influences

Colonial agriculture. As Sauer (1941: 161) wrote, "The fact that any group of overseas colonists needed above all else to sustain themselves by products of their agriculture was understood very slowly." Many early English settlements in Newfoundland, Maine, North Carolina and even the tropics failed simply because the suitability of climate and soil for farming was ignored.

Successful colonization often depended on assistance from Indians to teach the newcomers how to plant crops that could provide a subsistence food supply. Colonists who received such help were quick to accept the knowledge and adopt the unfamiliar practices, augmenting them with seeds

and farming implements from the Old World.

The impact of colonization on mourning dove populations was incalculable. Settlers further cleared and burned the forest and introduced new plants—weeds as well as desired species—many of which provided new foods for doves. The grazing and trampling by pastured livestock promoted an increase of seed-producing forbs and coarse grasses also useful to doves. The net effect was an enriched and diversified habitat to which the mourning dove readily adapted.

Westward expansion and public lands. The first stage for westward movement was set in part by acquisition and incorporation of lands into the public domain. Altogether, the original states ceded 233 million acres (94.3 million ha) of their western lands to the federal government between 1781 and 1802. In the next sixty-four years, many additional acquisitions were made totaling nearly 1.5 billion acres (605 million ha) *(Table 2)*.

The second stage preparatory to westward expansion was the federal government's decision of which lands to open to private appropriation and what requirements would be imposed on settlers of these new lands. In 1796 and subsequently, congressional actions regulated the size of land units to be sold to settlers and the prices for those lands. In the Homestead Act of 1862, the primary objective became provision of homesites for settlers. It was realized that larger units were required to support family farms farther west. The standard 160 acres (64.8 ha) allotted to each settler in the eastern plains equated to 2,560 acres (1,036 ha) in some parts of the arid West to meet the same subsistence level of productivity (Webb 1931). Therefore, it was inevitable that the original provisions of the Act be changed as settlers swept westward and knowledge of land capabilities and limitations became better understood.

Table 2. United States federal land acquisitions, 1803–67.

Purchase or action (and source)	Area		Date
	Acres[a]	Hectares[a]	
Louisiana Purchase (from France)	552	223.4	1803
Florida Cession (from Spain)	43	17.4	1819
Oregon Compromise (with Great Britain)	181	73.2	1846
Mexican Cession	335	135.6	1848
Gadsden Purchase (from Mexico)	19	7.7	1853
Alaskan Purchase (from Russia)	365	147.7	1867
Total	1,495	605	

[a] In millions.

The Timber Culture Act of 1873 permitted a homesteader to apply for an additional 160 acres (64.8 ha), which would be deeded to him if he planted and cared for trees. Under the Morrill Land Grant Act of 1862, states were granted 140 million acres (56.66 million ha) of land that they could sell, provided that the proceeds were used to educate settlers to become farmers. The Desert Land Act of 1877, promoted by stockmen's associations, permitted settlers to obtain 640 acres (259 ha) of grassland, provided that water could be delivered to the land within three years. The Grazing Homestead Act of 1916 also provided 640 acres (259 ha) to settlers who met certain irrigation requirements.

Yet another impetus for easterners to broach the uncertainties and trepidations of the West was the lure of minerals, particularly gold. Discoveries of gold in California, the Black Hills of the Dakota Territory and other areas triggered emigrant waves of argonauts across the continent. "California or bust" was not the only popular refrain of those in the initial wave, who faced a long and arduous overland trek in the mid-1800s to goldfields in the Sacramento Valley. "Oh! That I had the wings of a dove" reportedly was a common lament of "forty-niners" invariably ill prepared for the ordeal of *journados*, fatigue, danger and demoralization en route (Robrock 1892:3).

The western movement itself was the implementation of the popular Manifest Destiny credo. The significance of movement from the forested East into western grasslands was described by Trewartha (1941: 167): "This is a region of most unusual natural potential. No other region of the earth of equal size is so well endowed physically—in surface configuration, soil, and climate—for agricultural use. . . . Never had white settlers entered into such a 'promised land,' and never can they again, for no such frontiers remain."

The transfer of vast arable lands from the public domain to private ownership and the subsequent occupation of those lands unleashed new economic and social forces of the still fledgling democracy. Decisions on use of the private holdings became individualistic rather than bureaucratic. Settlers had a living or, in some cases, a fortune to make, dependent on the sorts of decisions they made in using—or misusing—the virgin lands. Those decisions ultimately diversified midwestern and western landscapes and the habitats of virtually all native wildlife. For many species, the flood of human migration and enterprise had a seriously deleterious impact. For others, including the mourning dove, the changes were quite favorable.

Homesteaders and speculators line up for the September 16, 1893 land rush into the 6.5 million-acre (2.6 million ha) Cherokee Outlet in present-day Oklahoma. The lure of free or inexpensive land opened by the federal government—in an effort to expand the national dominion and economy—forever changed the face of the Great Plains. For most indigenous wildlife, the introduction of agriculture was a negative impact. However, some species, such as the mourning dove, benefited in the short term from the introduction of grain crops and irrigation practices. *Photo courtesy of the U.S. Bureau of Land Management.*

Settlement agriculture. New agricultural problems were encountered in the subhumid region (Trewartha 1941), on the Great Plains (Thornwaite 1941), in the arid West (Bailey 1941) and in the summer-dry region (Leighly 1941). Also, new farming implements and practices were required for the prairies. These needs spurred the invention and production of machinery suited to prairie conditions. As summarized by Smith (1979), the most notable technological innovations between 1830 and 1870 were the grain reaper, horse-drawn reaper, grain combine, "clean-scouring" plow, threshing machine, double-row horse-drawn corn planter, improved grain drill, grain elevator, revolving disc harrow and spring-toothed harrow. Eventually, the reaper-combine, or simply combine, displaced the reaper, harvester, binder and threshing machine and the various engines required to drive each. One combine and operator could perform the work of 145 skilled farm laborers. Where corn was grown, the mechanical corn picker/sheller similarly reduced manpower needs.

Finally, the advance of the railroads onto and across the prairies provided the practical means to ship produce to eastern and overseas markets. The trains delivered more settlers, machines and other products from the mechanized East. During 1880–90 alone, 71,000 miles (11,452 km) of railroad track were laid (see McCabe and McCabe 1984).

Late-arriving pioneers found that farming practices profitable on eastern prairies were unsuitable or marginal west of about 100 degrees longitude because of inadequate precipitation. In 1863, Mormon farmers in Utah began dryland farming where irrigation was not possible or feasible. Under this system, half the available cropland is planted annually to small grain and the remainder cultivated to deter weeds. The pattern is alternated annually. In this manner, more than one year's moisture supply can be accumulated for a single year's crop. Dryland farming is widely practiced in the West where soils and topography allow and precipitation necessitates. As grasslands had been earlier, the arid lands became the new frontier.

The impact of settlement on the heartland's prairies and plains—insofar as the mourning dove is concerned—probably was even greater than on the eastern seaboard. This land was well suited to the production of cereal grains, an astoundingly plentiful new food supply readily accepted by mourning doves. The general scarcity of surface water forced the building of dams, excavation of impoundments to capture runoff, drilling of wells and installation of windmills. Water to quench doves' thirst became plentiful in areas of former scarcity. Shelterbelts planted over vast expanses of formerly treeless grassland provided choice new nesting sites. Waste grain at livestock feedyards, at grain-storage facilities and along rail lines and roadways ensured a virtual year-round supply. Many of these same developments were similarly beneficial to doves breeding even farther west, where new water supplies resulting from irrigation were especially important.

Agriculture diversified the American West, providing mourning doves with new nesting habitats, more sources of food in the form of cereal grains, and reduced predation and intraspecific competition. The extent to which the opening of the grasslands and the West to settlement influenced mourning dove populations is uncertain, but it surely expanded the species' range and probably its numbers. *Top photo from the Solomon D. Butcher Collection; courtesy of the Nebraska State Historical Society. Bottom scene courtesy of the U.S. Soil Conservation Service.*

Grazing. The earliest settlers along the eastern seaboard brought a variety of livestock, including horses, cattle, sheep, goats and swine. In the forested East, livestock were either herded or confined by fences. Lands worn out by overtillage and then abandoned to weedy fallow made for poor pastures but probably good mourning dove feeding fields.

An entirely different situation prevailed west of about the hundredth meridian, where moisture might be sufficient one year but not the next. Some would-be farmers turned to ranching, probably taking cue from the long-established livestock ranching economy developed under the Spanish influence in Texas and the Southwest. With virtual extirpation of the plains bison and the subjugation and relocation of the Indians on reservations, a bewilderingly large pasturage of unfenced public domain became available to both cattlemen and sheepmen, who often feuded for space, grass and water.

In the treeless West and prairie parts of the Midwest, conventional fencing material was often unavailable and too costly to be shipped from the East. Planted fences of native Osage-orange furnished attractive nesting habitat for mourning doves (see chapter 5). The thorn hedge, not altogether stockproof, inspired invention of barbed wire in 1873. Barbed wire enabled farmers to protect their crops where open range was the policy. Elsewhere, ranchers could confine their stock to their own holdings and, with interior fencing, shift stock among pastures to better distribute grazing intensity. In 1875, 600,000 pounds (272,160 kg) of barbed wire were produced, and by 1901, output had soared to nearly 300 million pounds (136 million kg). Its price fell from $20.00 to $1.80 per hundred pounds ($44.00 to $4.00/100 kg), making it the least expensive form of fencing. Range warfare among the cattlemen, sheepmen and farmers now assumed a new dimension—"fence men" versus "no-fence men"—and fence-cutting wars ensued.

In the 1870s, Major John Wesley Powell, explorer of the Colorado River and mapper of the Southwest, and others recognized the threat to the western public lands from unbridled competition between cattlemen and sheepmen. By the time Powell began his campaign to save the West from destruction, exploiters already had obtained more than 500 million acres (202 million ha) of public domain; the railroads, 181 million acres (73 million ha); and the states, 140 million acres (56.6 million ha). The General Land Office had sold more than 100 million acres (40.5 million ha), and nearly that much land had been returned to Indians, much of it to be claimed by or sold to speculators.

Livestock grazing and even overgrazing in the early West probably improved conditions temporarily for mourning doves. The trampling and removal of grasses, resultant erosion, supplemental feeding of livestock, and development of surface water sources all contributed to essential habitat elements for doves. *Top photo from the F. M. Steele Collection; courtesy of the Library of Congress. Bottom photo from the Wittemann Collection; courtesy of the Library of Congress.*

Powell urged that the remaining public lands be classified and disposed of in accordance with their capabilities. Despite bitter opposition by stockmen, Congress directed the Public Lands Commission in 1879 to investigate the whole land system and propose general reforms. Little came of Powell's recommendation, however, and the controversy over the public lands still seethes without full resolution.

In his overview of the livestock industry, Wagner (1978) reported that sheep numbers (including lambs) in the West peaked at 40 million between 1890 and 1900, and cattle (including calves) reached 15 million by the 1920s. Grazing pressures declined on national forests after 1920 and on Bureau of Land Management lands after 1940 (Wagner 1978). But by then, incalculable damage had been inflicted on the public range, and decades would be required to restore its productivity markedly for grazing livestock and wildlife.

Finally, in 1934 Congress passed the Taylor Grazing Act, which sought "To stop injury to the public grazing lands by preventing overgrazing and soil deterioration; to provide for their orderly use, improvement, and development; to stabilize the livestock industry dependent upon the public range. . . ."

Despite the long-term detrimental effects of overgrazing to pastures and rangelands, the mourning dove probably benefited, at least in the short term. Overgrazing, trampling and resultant soil erosion permitted the invasion of forbs and coarse grasses whose seeds augmented foods already present. Wells and impoundments provided additional, better distributed and more reliable sources of water. Supplemental livestock feeding on the range and subsistence feeding in feedlots also improved dove food supplies, particularly during periods of severe weather.

Forest clearing. As settlement progressed in the 1800s, the need for lumber increased, and attention turned to the northern forests. As had been the case for farming, new machinery and practices contributed to timbering efficiency and profitability. Major tool improvements included the circular saw, gang-saw, replaceable tooth saw, crosscut saw, double-bladed "Yankee axe" and peavey. Lumbering leapfrogged westward from Maine through the northern coniferous forests. New York became the premier lumbering state after Maine forests had been cut. It, in turn, was replaced by Pennsylvania, and then by Great Lakes states. After the dominance of Michigan during 1869–85, attention shifted to native southern forests of the Gulf Coast, only to focus, after 1920, on the Pacific Northwest and, most recently, on southeastern pine plantations.

In its early days in particular, lumbering often was accompanied by major forest fires, which sometimes consumed more timber than was productively logged. For example, the Tillamook fire of 1933 in Oregon consumed timber on 311,000 acres (125,910 ha) during a twenty-hour "blow-up." The loss of 12.5 billion board feet during that single fire was nearly equivalent to the current lumber demands of the nation for one year (Holbrook 1960: 140). And the remaining Tillamook and adjoining forests were to burn twice more at seven-year intervals with fires of nearly the same magnitude.

Several observers have commented on the response of the mourning dove to forest clearings. Bennitt and Nagel (1937: 70) wrote: "A bird of the open country and one that has profited by the clearing of forest lands for agriculture and grazing, the mourning dove is increasing in Missouri. In the early days, when three-fourths of Missouri was woodland, there were not nearly so many doves as there are now." Of his investigations in Ohio in the 1930s, Trautman (1940: 269) speculated that the eastern mourning dove may have been more numerous at the time than ever before and added: "Environmental conditions were more favorable than in early historic time when the area was largely wooded and when there was possible food competition with the Passenger Pigeon."

Dawson (1909) noted that, in the state of Washington, mourning doves did not deeply penetrate the timber, preferring instead to spend their time in open fields. Similarly, Kitchen (1949: 115, 135) wrote: "As our coastal lands [in Washington] are being cleared and open fields appear the doves show a tendency to move in to our new country. West of Tacoma . . . the birds have established themselves in a logged-off burnt over country and breed there."

Evidence suggests that forest clearing and lumbering, and associated burning, facilitated the northward expansion of the mourning dove, a subject to be discussed later, and made otherwise unattractive forest tracts hospitable for the species.

Tree planting. To settlers from the eastern seaboard and Europe, the treeless prairies and plains appeared stark and foreboding (Pike 1810, see also DeVoto 1947). As early as 1866, Joseph S. Wilson, then Commissioner of the General Land Office, proposed to Congress that a tree-planting program be established: "If one-third the surface of the Great Plains were covered with forest, there is every reason to believe the climate would be greatly improved, the value of the whole area as a grazing country would be wonderfully enhanced, the greater portion of the soil would be susceptible of a high degree of cultivation" (Hatton 1935: 51).

The rapacious clearing of forests during the late 1800s severely scarred the American landscape but opened vast areas to seral-stage vegetation and edge that often was well-suited to the needs of mourning doves. *Left photo by A. G. Varela; courtesy of the USDA Forest Service. Right photo courtesy of Ralph I. Blouch.*

As early as 1865, some Plains states offered an incentive of $0.50 per acre ($1.24/ha) for a period of twenty-five years to settlers planting five acres (two ha) or more in trees; the payment was later increased to $2.00 per acre ($4.94/ha) (Griffith 1976). In 1902 President Theodore Roosevelt, by proclamation, established the Nebraska National Forest in the treeless sandhills of northern Nebraska. There a forest was to be created by tree planting. By the mid-1930s, approximately 12,000 acres (4,856 ha) of conifers had been established in an essentially treeless region, demonstrating the feasibility of such planting.

In 1924 the landmark Clark-McNary Act was passed. It provided for state and federal cooperation with landowners in protecting forest lands from fire, devising tax laws conducive to forest con-servation, procuring and distributing seeds and planting stock, establishing shelterbelts and wood-lots, and developing and improving denuded forest lands by means of federal acquisition and control.

In the 1930s, searing winds on the parched Great Plains swept away vast expanses of unprotected topsoils and created dust storms observable hundreds of miles away. Tree planting fitted nicely into the soil conservation program launched in the "Dirty Thirties" to combat effects of drought and soil erosion. The federal government proposed designating a "shelterbelt zone" extending from the Canadian border in eastern North Dakota southward to Abilene, Texas (Olson 1935, Davis 1976). Within the zone, three types of tree plantings were proposed: field shelterbelts; farmstead windbreaks; and block plantings in selected areas.

The greatest concerted effort to plant trees in the United States took place in the Plains states between 1935 and 1942 under the auspices of the Prairie States Forestry Project. During that period, approximately 20,000 miles (32,186 km) of shelterbelts were planted on 31,000 farms, and 218 million trees were planted (Griffith 1976). The popularity of tree planting continued after the project was terminated. As in the development of livestock water, the U.S. Soil Conservation Service often provided technical assistance to participating farmers, and the Agricultural Stabilization and Conservation Service provided financial inducements on a cost-share basis. A similar program was initiated in Canada.

Dozens of nesting studies document the extremely high use of field shelterbelts and farmstead windbreaks by nesting doves. On a per-acre basis, tree plantings surely rank among the mourning dove's most favored nesting sites. The spate of tree planting since the 1930s, particularly in areas broken by agriculture and where woody vegetation formerly was sparse, undoubtedly had a favorable influence on the abundance and distribution of mourning doves.

The so-called "Dust Bowl Era" on the Great Plains in the 1930s was brought on by drought and exacerbated by overgrazing, cutting of riparian timber, farming of marginal soils, and other crop-production practices that left soils too exposed to erosion. The impact was devastating to people and wildlife alike. Ensuing massive tree-planting programs, especially shelterbelts, helped to retard erosion, stabilize soils and provide shelter and nesting habitat for wildlife, including the mourning dove. *Top photo by B. C. McLean; courtesy of the U.S. Conservation Service. Bottom left photo by E. S. Shipp; courtesy of the USDA Forest Service. Bottom right scene by D. E. Hutchinson; courtesy of the U.S. Soil Conservation Service.*

Irrigation. Surface water is a central component of mourning dove habitat. It is required on a frequent basis by doves, and their range is expanded or contracted by the availability of such supplies. Historic irrigation practices in seasonally or permanently arid regions not only provided accessible water but also enhanced the other vital dove habitat components of food and shelter.

Besides finding cropland irrigation practiced by some southwestern Indians, early Spanish missionaries furthered its application elsewhere (Ferris 1968). Franciscans constructed the Espada Aqueduct near present-day San Antonio, Texas, during 1731–45 to irrigate crops associated with five missions. Similarly, irrigation was established at several missions in California.

But it was the Latter Day Saints—or Mormons—who developed and applied irrigation on a grand scale in the arid West. They entered the Great Salt Lake Valley of Utah in July 1847 and, before the end of that month, flooded some land for farming (Ebling 1979). Principally by ditching, Mormons rapidly harnessed the many streams and rivers issuing from the west flank of the Wasatch Mountains. During the next several decades, they carried irrigation into portions of western Wyoming, southern Idaho, northern Nevada and northern Arizona. By 1865, there were more than 1,000 miles (1,600 km) of irrigation canals in Utah, and by 1946, some 8,750 miles (14,000 km). Mormon irrigation engineering also provided the foundation for dozens of irrigation projects cooperatively constructed in the West by Mormon and non-Mormon settlers and the U.S. Bureau of Reclamation.

By 1964, irrigated farmlands throughout the United States totaled more than 37 million acres (15 million ha), with seventeen western states accounting for 33 million acres (13.35 million ha) of the total (National Research Council 1970). By 1970, 40 million acres (16.2 million ha) were under irrigation, and nearly 780,000 new acres (315,660 ha) were being added annually.

Following World War II, sprinkler irrigation quickly came into prominence. It became feasible because of advanced well-drilling technology, improved pumps and sprinkler heads, availability of relatively inexpensive aluminum pipe and affordable power. Advantages of sprinkler irrigation include: (1) usefulness where gravity irrigation is impossible or infeasible; (2) more efficient delivery of water to the sprinkler head; (3) more even application of water over the field; and (4) much reduced manpower requirements for maintenance and operation.

In 1949, a Colorado wheat farmer developed center-pivot sprinkler irrigation. Such a system

Center-pivot irrigation has proven to be a boon to agricultural production in many arid and semiarid parts of the West, and grain crops mean food for mourning doves. On the other hand, center-pivots require removal of shelterbelts and other vegetation—vital to doves—that interfere with the irrigation pattern. Furthermore, the drawdown of watertables in such areas may have long-term negative consequences for the land and eventually for its wildlife. *Photo courtesy of the U.S. Soil Conservation Service.*

typically irrigates 133 acres (53.8 ha), or 83 percent of the standard quarter section. In the prairie and Plains regions, center-pivot irrigation facilitated corn production on land that previously could grow only small grains. Farther west, livestock forage crops consequently could be grown where only grazing had been feasible. On the other hand, this technology requires unimpeded movement of irrigation pipes and sprinklers. Thus, farmers have been compelled to remove such obstacles as shelterbelts and other niches of wildlife habitat by clearing and grading the land to be irrigated. To date, there has been no extensive replacement of lost woody cover in the nonirrigated corners of the irrigated blocks.

Other new types of irrigation are now in use. Some motorized systems simply move across fields rather than around them. Portable pipe systems are now replacing or expanding fields once ditch irrigated. In many western orchards, water is sprayed from overhead sprinkler systems. And in parts of the country with normally sufficient annual precipitation and groundwater supplies, supplemental irrigation systems are employed to assure or increase crop production.

It is uncertain how much longer pump irrigation can continue to draw from aquifers that clearly are showing signs of depletion. Most of the non-mountainous West is being subjected to moderate-to-critical overdrafts of groundwater, particularly in California's Central Valley, southern Arizona and the Ogallala Aquifer of the southern High Plains (El-Ashry and Gibbons 1987). Water supplies, new water policies and economics will determine the future of irrigation and of the agriculture and associated habitats it supports. The impacts on dove populations may be substantial.

Since its initial use in the 1800s, and particularly in the arid West, irrigation has provided doves with new sources of cereal foods, ensured food availability even during times of drought and supplied additional drinking water.

Other surface water resources. Dependable sources of water were of vital importance to settlers in arid and semiarid regions. Where surface water was scarce, some were able to dam small watercourses to create impoundments, but more often they had to dig wells by hand. Eventually, means were developed to drill wells mechanically, and windmills were erected and put into common use to power water pumps. The combination of wells, pumps and windmills supplied water for both domestic needs and livestock. On the range, windmills enabled ranchers to distribute livestock more widely and over longer periods of time.

Webb (1931) considered the historic evolution of western rangeland to consist of four stages: (1) open range; (2) fenced range without windmills; (3) fenced range with windmills; and (4) fenced farms with windmills. Since about 1850, more than 6 million windmills have been installed (Ebling 1979),

although many have been dismantled or are no longer functional. They still are very important in many agricultural areas and contribute to sustained populations of certain wildlife, including mourning doves.

Since the 1930s, much emphasis has been placed on constructing stock ponds and dugouts to provide water, primarily for livestock. During 1956–70, approximately 2 million ponds were built, and new ones were being added at the rate of about 60,000 per year. The farm and ranch ponds existing in the mid-1960s had a total water surface approaching that of Lake Ontario (7,540 square miles: 19,529 km²).

Windmills and stock ponds have provided important and well-dispersed sources of surface water for mourning doves in areas where otherwise limited supply would preclude the presence or abundance of doves. *Top photo by Ron George; courtesy of the Texas Parks and Wildlife Department. Bottom photo by Col. J. P. Barney; courtesy of the U.S. Department of Defense.*

In addition to the small farm and ranch ponds, larger reservoirs were built by federal and state agencies for irrigation, power domestic water supplies, flood abatement and transportation. By 1970, the surface area of these reservoirs—more than 23,000 square miles (59,570 km²)—was nearly double that of all large natural lakes in the continental U.S., exclusive of the Great Lakes (see U.S. Geological Survey 1984). These important water sources, however, submerged a vast but unquantified amount of riparian habitat of value to doves.

There is little question that improved distribution of surface water throughout much of the United States and southern Canada has been of great benefit to wildlife in general, including some populations of mourning doves. Inasmuch as mourning doves may fly several miles daily to water, the only areas where water may now be a limiting factor are the most arid deserts of the Southwest. Even in these locations, water catchment basins and small reservoirs have been constructed by wildlife agencies (Wright 1959). Moreover, mourning doves do not have to drink daily and can survive on mildly saline water (see chapter 9). Stock ponds also often support trees and bushes around their peripheries and on downstream seepages. Such woody growth is sometimes all that is locally available, and it is used by mourning doves.

City Dwellers

Mourning doves prosper and reproduce prolifically in urban and suburban environments. Some evidence suggests, however, that the mourning dove's use of residential habitat may be a relatively recent phenomenon. Woolfenden and Rohwer (1969), for example, noted that, had the species been a conspicuous part of suburban avifauna four decades ago, it surely would not have gone without notice by ornithologists. They also cited findings by Graber and Graber (1963) of mourning dove densities of 14.3 pairs per hundred acres (35.3/100 ha) in Illinois during 1957–58, compared with only 0.9 pairs per 100 acres (2.2/100 ha) in 1907–09 in urban and rural Illinois. Woolfenden and Rohwer (1969) hypothesized, citing differences in flushing behavior observed, that the mourning dove may have become more tolerant of man in urban situations. They also believed that the absence of hunting in suburban areas may have been a factor.

The attraction of doves to urbanizing America also has been prompted by ornamental plantings of shrubs, bushes and trees used for nesting, perching, roosting and feeding. Surface water in bird baths, roadways, cooling water basins, etc., is readily used by mourning doves, as are bird feeders and urban/suburban gardens.

Other Influences

Several other historical land description and use decisions indirectly influenced mourning doves. For example, habitat types, shapes and sizes—and the edges between them—often are predetermined largely by the basic land-survey system employed. In the United States, three basic systems are used: (1) maps or plats of tracts; (2) metes and bounds; and (3) government subdivisions. In the East, early surveys often were influenced by natural features of land, thus necessitating use of the first two systems. The rectangular government survey system is used in all or portions of thirty midwestern and western states. Regardless of the system used, it set the base for ownership boundaries and, to a considerable degree, their subdivision into fields, forests, woodlots, pastures and other land-use units. In turn, this determined placement of fences, hedgerows, shelterbelts, water supplies, roads, utility lines, buildings and other human developments.

Since the mourning dove is a bird of the ecological edge, or ecotone, the survey schemes, together with topography and watercourses, almost certainly have had a profound effect on dove habitat. Artificial demarcations of ownership boundaries, such as fences, roadways and buffer strips, have permitted the growth of plants useful to doves. Zoning in some areas has allowed for "greenbelts" and parks that diversify the landscape and flora in human-concentration areas. Golf courses, cemeteries, playgrounds, schoolyards, campuses and other open expanses with interior or peripheral plantings frequently are used extensively and often intensively by doves. And the basic sprawl of suburbia into agricultural areas, while perhaps detrimental to most wildlife in the long run, invariably affords most—including doves—with access to a wider variety of valuable habitats.

The introduction of some exotic plants into North America has been beneficial to the dove. Also, many important agricultural crops, notably the small grains, stem from introductions. Many of the inadvertently introduced weed species also have provided additional food for mourning doves (see chapter 11). And many species of commercial fruit and nut trees support substantial densities of nesting mourning doves.

However, not all introduced plants beneficial to doves are useful to or wanted by people. One of the most notable examples is saltcedar, or tamarisk—

Where urban growth and suburban sprawl have been accompanied by residences, plantings, parks, greenways, cemeteries, golf courses and other open areas, doves can habituate themselves quickly, easily and sometimes in large numbers. *Photo by Hugo Bryan; courtesy of the U.S. Soil Conservation Service.*

a phreatophyte (from the Greek, meaning "well plant" because of its dependence on the water table for its moisture). The saltcedar first appeared in 1910 south of Mesilla Park, New Mexico, along the Rio Grande; it spread with such rapidity that, by 1960, it and related phreatophytes had invaded 7 million acres (2.83 million ha) of the Southwest (Bowser 1957). The phreatophyte problem has been widely studied, discussed and debated (e.g., Phreatophyte Subcommittee 1958, U.S. Senate Select Committee 1960, R. C. Culler 1970). Mechanical removal and herbicidal programs have been undertaken to eradicate the offending invaders. On the other hand, phreatophytes provide important nesting and wintering habitat for many avian species, including mourning doves (see Wells et al. 1979). Their continued eradication can only affect doves adversely.

The advent of grain farming in North America had incidental effects beneficial to morning doves. Grain storage and transportation facilities constitute important feeding sites, where doves frequently gather to feed on waste grain. Also, much grain is spilled along railroads and highways—favored feeding areas that have a secondary value as sources of grit. Ligon (1961) observed that, in the arid and semiarid Southwest, runoff from paved roads often allows seed-producing weeds to grow along the shoulders where they otherwise could not exist. Nearly every railroad and highway is flanked by power and telephone lines, and these, along with field fences, provide much-used perching sites for doves.

Some programs of mechanical and chemical eradication of certain "pest" plants to accommodate agricultural interests and diversify wildlife use actually can reduce or eliminate valuable dove nesting and wintering habitat. *Photo by George E. Glendening; courtesy of the USDA Forest Service.*

Dove Range Expansion and Increase Since Settlement

As noted earlier, most of the few North American explorers and settlers who thought the dove worthy of mention in their journals typically failed to distinguish it from similar species known in the Old World. As Edminster (1954: 430) explained: "The mourning dove was not particularly prominent in the affairs of the early settlers; it was not uncommon around the forest edge, but neither was it abundant. Its small size, rather drab colors, and quiet habits obscured it in comparison with the large, more noisy turkey, grouse, and waterfowl. In its own group, the pigeons and doves, the vastly more abundant passenger pigeon drew attention away from its smaller relative." Similarly, Tyler stated that, "well known and widely distributed as the bird is, it is not a conspicuous bird of the country at all. It is quiet in voice, neutral in color, and so unobtrusive in deportment that it seems little more than a part of its background; a quiet, pastoral bird . . ." (Bent 1932: 402).

Early naturalists in North America concentrated on finding new species and collecting information chiefly on nesting, plumage, food habits and behavior. Determinations of absolute or relative population sizes, migrations and ecological relationships were not then of particular interest. Observers seldom tried to judge numbers of birds or populations they beheld. Wilson, however, recorded that, "On the 2nd of February, in the neighborhood of Newbern [New Bern], North Carolina, I saw a flock of Turtle Doves of many hundreds; in other places, as I advanced further south, particularly near the Savannah River, Georgia, the woods were swarming with them, and the whistling of their wings was heard in every direction" (Brewer 1840: 339).

Even later, when ornithologists began to comment on the relative abundance of various species, they resorted to such vague adjectives as "abundant," "common," "tolerably numerous," "not uncommon" and even "present." Indeed, it was not until about the mid-1930s, shortly after Aldo Leopold's (1933) pronouncement of essential wildlife management principles—including the need to inventory populations—that any serious attempt was made to estimate mourning dove numbers.

Bennitt and Nagel (1937) appear to have been the first to develop a population estimate for an area as large as a state. Extrapolating from data provided by hunters, they estimated the early autumn population of Missouri mourning doves during 1934 to be 3 million.

No information suggests that the two subspecies of mourning doves native to North America have extended their ranges farther south. On the other hand, a northward extension of the mourning dove's range was repeatedly reported. Minot (1895: 402), at the end of the nineteenth century, flatly stated: "They do not occur to the northward of southern New England, where they are summer residents of great rarity in many places, though common . . . on Cape Cod."

Allen (1909: 94) provided more specific information for certain states: Connecticut—"Uncommon summer and rare winter resident"; Rhode Island—"Uncommon summer resident in northern and western parts"; Massachusetts—"Uncommon migrant and summer resident—rare winter resident"; Vermont—"Rare summer resident"; New Hampshire—"Rare migrant and summer resident in southern part"; and Maine—"Rare migrant and summer resident in southern part . . . accidental in winter."

Bent (1932: 409) added: "In eastern Massachusetts, where since 1910 the birds have become well established, they frequent the dry, sandy, sparsely wooded hillsides characteristic of the glaciated country, and retire to nest in the near-by pine woods."

Kennard and Kennard (1967) reported that, in New Hampshire, the mourning dove had greatly extended its range northward during the previous half century.

Of mourning doves in Maine, Palmer (1949: 298) wrote: "By the early 1920's, the species was common in York and Cumberland Counties, and, by 1930, flocks of 35 to 50 were seen occasionally in August. The population continues to increase slowly, and the bird is extending its breeding range in the state." Forbes (1959) stated that the mourning dove had recently increased markedly in Maine and that it had extended its range northward except in forested, mountainous country.

The northward range extension was confirmed by information from Canada. Squires (1960) reported that old records of the mourning dove in New Brunswick described it as "rare," "very rare" or "accidental," and generally were sightings of individual birds. Since 1950, however, observations have been so numerous as to be no longer noteworthy. Tufts (1961) believed the mourning dove to be increasing in Nova Scotia.

Since 1922, in the vicinity of Montréal, Québec, the eastern mourning dove reportedly has become more common, nests locally and is extending its range northward (Cayouette 1947). Ouellet (1970) concluded that the species had moved into southern Québec about the turn of the century and became fairly numerous in suitable habitats near Montréal.

Allin (1959) reported that mourning doves were gradually increasing in the Thunder Bay region of Ontario and that the species was extending its range northward. Later, Allin (1959: 174) noted: "In recent years, reports indicating substantial numbers of wintering Mourning Doves . . . in southern Ontario have increased significantly, particularly since about 1960. . . . Since 1968 the winter range has expanded further and the birds winter regularly in Kenora District and at Thunder Bay." Alison (1976) wrote that doves rarely wintered in southern Ontario until about 1940. They increased greatly between the 1945–49 and 1970–74 periods. However, dove numbers appeared to decline in late January and February, presumably because of emigration or mortality.

Houston (1986: 86) published an extensive assessment of the mourning dove in Manitoba, Saskatchewan and Alberta and wrote: "Prior to settlement, the Mourning Dove was absent or extremely rare throughout what were then the Canadian North West Territories. After white men had established fur-trading posts, careful pre-settlement studies at Fort Carlton and Cumberland House by John Richardson and Thomas Drummond in the 1820's (listing 173 species), and at Carlton House by Thomas Blakiston in 1857–58 (listing 129 species), failed to record a single Mourning Dove. . . . John Macoun failed to observe this species in his journeys across the Canadian plains in 1872, 1879, 1880 and 1881, and it was absent from his first published list of 235 species. . . . Historical evidence from Manitoba, Saskatchewan and Alberta consistently supports the hypothesis that the mourning dove advanced and increased as the area became settled."

Regarding the United States, Hatch (1892: 173) wrote of mourning doves in Minnesota: "I have neither visited any parts of the state nor corresponded with persons residing in different sections, where this species has not been found fairly common." Also, with reference to Minnesota, Roberts (1932 [I]: 574) reported: "The Mourning Dove is one of the few birds that have increased greatly in numbers in recent years. It was always common but is now abundant and getting more so each year. With the clearing and settling of the northern forests it has appeared in many localities where it was formerly absent."

In Washington, the species evidently has enjoyed a steady increase of late years. Slipp (1941: 59) reported them "common in parts of Pierce County, but not to be compared in numbers with those east of the Cascades." Alcorn (1949) reported a dove nest in the Tacoma area and speculated that it was probably the first such record. He further noted

that the mourning dove was becoming more common in western Washington during summer.

Gabrielson and Lincoln (1959) summarized early records of mourning doves in Alaska and stated that there were no positive records of the species breeding there. Two decades later, the status and distribution of the mourning dove in the state was updated by Kessel and Gibson (1978), who wrote their opinion that, in south coastal Alaska and in central Alaska south of the Alaska Range, the dove was a rare autumn visitant from late September through October and a very rare spring migrant and summer visitor. They described it as a casual autumn visitor and very rare spring migrant and summer visitor in central Alaska north of the Alaska Range. Most Alaskan observations have been of single birds seen in autumn, although a flock of eight mourning doves was seen at the mouth of the Stikine River, in southeastern Alaska, in September 1976 (Kessel and Gibson 1978). The sixth edition of the *Check-list of North American Birds* (American Ornithologists' Union 1983: 257) recorded that the mourning dove occurs casually in summer and "possibly breeding" in southeastern Alaska.

The foregoing records strongly indicate that the mourning dove has extended its range—both breeding and wintering—northward during the period for which information is available. This phenomenon is best documented for northern New England, southern Canada west through the prairies, Washington and Alaska. Many of these records, plus others discussed later, suggest that mourning dove numbers also have increased.

Nevertheless, a few reports suggested local, sporadic and short-term population declines, usually related speculatively to unregulated shooting. Forbush (1927: 84), for example, wrote: "Formerly this gentle dove was abundant in that part of southern New England best suited to its needs, but it had decreased so much in numbers in the early part of the twentieth century that Massachusetts led the way in 1908 by giving it perpetual protection under the law, to save it from extirpation. Soon its numbers began slowly to increase." Todd (1940: 263) observed: "More than forty years ago this dove was one of the most abundant birds in western Pennsylvania, but where there may once have been fifty pairs there is probably not one now. Shooting the species for game in the southern states has very likely been the main cause of the decrease." And, specific to California, Grinnell et al. (1918: 600) wrote: "Excessive shooting does undoubtedly have its effect, for in Los Angeles County . . . the birds have been greatly reduced, and the same report comes from Solano County." Also in California, interspecific competition was thought to have been detrimental to mourning dove numbers: "McClure . . . says that there is definite conflict between the mourning dove and the introduced Chinese spotted dove in parts of California; in the Bakersfield area, wherever the one species is nesting, the other will not be found" (Edminster 1954: 436).

Of primary importance to the general population increase and range expansion of the mourning dove during and since human settlement has been the species' innate adaptability to a wide array of altered habitats. According to Dodson, mourning dove populations in Oklahoma were thought to have adapted significantly to land-use changes resulting from particular agricultural practices: "The salvation of the mourning dove in central and western Oklahoma has apparently been its ability to become adapted to an ever-changing environment. Fifteen years ago the dove population in this area was very high. A sudden change to summer fallowing of wheat land reflected a rapid population decline. Most doves formerly nested on the ground in those fields, but summer fallowing disrupted such activity throughout the summer months. Now a sizable population nests in trees and shrubs" (Edminster 1954: 436).

The apparent natural establishment of the mourning dove in Bermuda already has been noted, and successful introduction to the island of Hawaii also has been achieved.

More expansively, with respect to the mourning dove's range, Edminster (1954: 430) wrote: "The settlers encountered the mourning dove wherever they went—even to the Far West, Mexico and much of southern Canada. But it was not a bird of the forest, nor of the open plain, but rather of the open woodland edge. As the forests were opened up for agriculture the amount of suitable habitat was increased; the dove moved into these new areas, but not in large numbers. In time they became common to abundant over much of the geographical range, and remain so today."

Leopold et al. (1981: 80) also claimed: "General farming and the introduction of exotic weeds and agriculture crops has greatly improved the habitat for mourning doves, and there doubtless are many more of these birds in North America now than there were before settlement. Unlike the passenger pigeon, the mourning dove is fully compatible with man and his modern environments. High populations of doves are characteristic of urban and suburban areas as well as farmlands. Many doves have learned to use bird feeders. Also, their strong power of flight enables them to exploit food resources some distance from the nest. Heavy hunting has not caused any general decrease in the species. All in all, the mourning dove is one of the most successful and persistent game birds."

Goodwin (1983: 178) wrote of the mourning dove: "Unless very intensely persecuted it generally increases in range and numbers where man destroys the original vegetation and replaces it with cultivation and secondary growth and pasture."

THE MOURNING DOVE IN AMERICAN CULTURE

In the Old World, columbids occupied an unusually prominent and generally revered position in ancient culture and religion, and such belief widely persists even now. Doves were historically important in both Protestant and Catholic religions, to which most early North American explorers, visitors and settlers professed. So it is not surprising that those adventurers brought such perspective and values to the New World and transferred them to the dove species found there. The mourning dove's appearance and behavior were especially reminiscent of the Old World turtledove. Consequently, the species inherited more than its share of ancient traditions and beliefs.

Place Names

North American explorers and settlers sometimes named physical features and places of inhabitation for endemic animals. According to Ristow (1966), who studied such toponyms in the United States, pigeon and dove place names were outnumbered only by those derived from eagles, turkeys, swans and geese. However, an early gazetteer for the United States (Baldwin and Thomas 1854) listed no entries for either "dove" or "turtledove," while eleven entries appeared for pigeon and seventeen for "turkey"—most being ascribed to hamlets or waterways. A later gazetteer (Anonymous 1883) listed one "dove" entry—for Dove, a rural post office (now abandoned) in Pike County, Ohio—and eighteen entries for "pigeon" and thirty-two for "turkey." Thus, Ristow's (1966) assessment appears to have rested on the early popularity of the passenger pigeon rather than the mourning dove. Nevertheless, the hamlet of Dove Creek exists in a remote area of southwestern Colorado, where, presumably, the only dove is the mourning dove.

The Spanish word "paloma" includes both doves and pigeons. Thus, place names containing "paloma" cannot be assigned to any particular columbid. It seems likely, however, that those men-

Not all dove watering holes or oases are frequented by their namesakes. *Photo by Ron George; courtesy of the Texas Parks and Wildlife Department.*

tioned by Ristow (1966)—Palomar Mountain and Palomar State Park, both in southern California—are associated with the band-tailed pigeon.

Arts and Literature

The mourning dove has been a subject for artistic expression in American painting, sculpture, literature and music. For example, despite its rather drab plumage and retiring nature, the mourning dove is frequently chosen as a subject by many of North America's leading wildlife artists. It periodically is represented, for example, in the prestigious and critically judged "Birds in Art" exhibition held annually at the Leigh Yawkey Woodson Art Museum in Wausau, Wisconsin. During the 1980s, the mourning dove was featured in 1980 by David Hagerbaumer (watercolor), in 1982 by Martin Murk (acrylic), in 1983 by Ahmad Sakhavorz (watercolor), in 1984 by Wilhelm J. Goebel (acrylic) and Lindsay B. Scott (pencil), in 1985 by M. A. Glassford (wood/acrylic sculpture) and John S. Scheeler (painted wood sculpture), in 1987 by Tom Ruddy (watercolor), in 1988 by Francis E. Sweet (scratchboard) and in 1989 by Neal Anderson (gouache). J. Joseph Sweet's oil on canvas of mourning doves was juried into the 1991 exhibit.

The popularity of the mourning dove is evidenced by the fact that, in the 1980s, ten mourning dove artworks were juried into the prestigious Lee Yawkey Woodson "Birds in Art Exhibition," including Francis E. Sweet's scratchboard art in 1988. *Photo by Peter Bruning; courtesy of the Lee Yawkey Woodson Museum.*

A marble bas-relief of doves forms the background to an exterior staircase landing at William Randolph Hearst's "Castle" at San Simeon, California. A dove symbolizes peace in a lifelike bronze statue of the late Samantha Smith, the Maine schoolgirl who befriended Soviet leader Andropov in 1983.

A dove is featured on a weathervane atop the cupola of George Washington's mansion at Mount Vernon in Virginia. In 1783, Washington requested: "I should like to have a bird . . . with an olive branch in its mouth. The bird need not be large (for I do not expect that it will traverse with the wind and therefore may receive the real shape of a bird, with spread wings)" (Fitzgerald 1967: 25). Although the weathervane's wings are faithful to the mourning dove, the tail is not. Possibly this was an alteration by Washington's artisans to improve the vane's aerodynamics.

A bas-relief panel entitled "The Doves" was sculpted by Gilbert Privat in the early 1920s and purchased by William Randolph Hearst in 1929. The marble sculpture is displayed at the Hearst "Castle" in San Simeon, California. *Photo courtesy of the Hearst San Simeon Historical Monument, California Department of Parks and Recreation.*

A weathervane atop George Washington's Mount Vernon mansion in Virginia, just south of Washington, D.C., features a dove in flight bearing an olive branch (top), as specifically requested by General Washington in 1783. The dove weathervane is clearly visible from the mansion's east front, overlooking the Potomac River (bottom). The dove's tail was forged anatomically incorrectly, but this probably was intentional, to maximize the vane's aerodynamic properties. *Photos courtesy of the Mount Vernon Ladies' Association.*

Mourning doves are also mentioned in classic American literature. Ralph Waldo Emerson noted them in his essay *Natural History of Intellect*, using the obsolete name "Turtle." Naturalist/philosopher Henry David Thoreau occasionally mentioned mourning doves in his writings. And Edgar Allan Poe wrote in *The Bells*:

"What a liquid ditty floats
To the turtle-dove that listens, while she gloats
On the moon."

Larry McMurtry's Pulitzer Prize-winning novel *Lonesome Dove* (1985) is set initially in a fictitious town of the title name.

References to the "turtledove" and "turtle-doving" appear in American popular music, particularly that of the "Big Band Era" in ballads such as *I Want to Be Loved* and *I Don't Want a Ricochet Romance*, and in country/western tunes such as *My Dixieland Love*.

Regardless of these examples, the mourning dove often has been slighted. For example, despite its abundance and wide distribution, it was not chosen as an official state bird—five states selected the same bird (the northern cardinal), and five species in total represent twenty-four states. Two states even have designated breeds of chickens. Nor has the mourning dove been chosen to appear on a U.S. postage stamp, even though dozens of other birds—wild, introduced and domestic—are.

Superstition and Symbolism

Although many beliefs about doves and pigeons originated in the Old World, others arose in the New World. In the Old World—specifically, the Middle East—the dove became a symbol of peace, love and virility about 4500 B.C. (Johnson 1990). Old World doves and pigeons, recognized as prolific breeders and for lengthy pair bonding, eventually became associated with such fertility goddesses as Astarte, Venus and Aphrodite.

Such symbolic links were well-established by biblical times, and the dove frequently was represented in the period art and rituals of early Christianity. Researchers believe that this was about the time when white became the dove's symbolic color. Folklorist Boria Sax reported that, according to legend: "Noah sent out a raven that didn't come back and later a dove that returned with the olive branch, a sign of peace. The colors were assigned in connection with performance. Doves, which were blessed, became white, and ravens, which were damned, became black" (Johnson 1990: 19).

Except for biologists, taxonomists, sportsmen and hobbyists, most people do not distinguish greatly among congeneric wildlife, particularly those with overtly similar physical characteristics (e.g., the moose of North America and the elk of Europe, the elk of North America and the red deer of Eurasia, the reindeer of Scandinavia and the caribou of North America, the American and Eurasian wigeons, plus eagles, woodcock, falcons, deer, hummingbirds, grouse and many others). This certainly was true, as discussed earlier, for Old and New World doves and pigeons. Consequently, the trans-Atlantic abridgment of wildlife-associated symbolism was as prevalent as was the tendency to lump together by name many continentally endemic species. Thus, through the prisms of history, biology and human culture, the mourning dove inherited the stature of bird of peace and love that originated thousands of years ago with its Old World counterparts. In 1990, for example, the Hallmark Company expected to sell to Americans nearly 1.5 million Christmas cards featuring the dove of peace.

De Lys (1948: 13) summarized some New World superstitions: "The cooing of a strange dove at the window is a sign of sad news. If turtle-doves live near a house, they are believed to banish rheumatism. It is unlucky to eat the eggs of a dove. For a dove to coo in the doorway foretells a death. A dead dove, placed on the chest of a person suffering from pneumonia, is supposed to insure prompt recovery."

Ingersoll (1923: 8–9) described the following superstition: "When a Georgia girl first hears in the spring the plaintive call of returning doves she must first immediately attend to it if she is curious as to her future partner in life. She must at once take nine steps forward and nine backward, then take off her right shoe; in it she will discover a hair of the man she is to marry—but how to find the owner is not explained!" Ingersoll also reported on the dove as an augury: if a farmer hears the first mourning dove of the year above him, supposedly he will prosper; if from below him, his own course henceforth will be downhill.

In earlier times, the dove was conspicuous in beliefs among black Americans. Missouri blacks, for example, reportedly swallowed a raw dove's heart, point down, to inspire love in a beloved (Leach 1949).

The folk belief that the constant cooing of a dove foretells rain is quite general through the southern United States. Likewise, the sound of a mourning dove in the vicinity of a house has been thought to foretell death in the homeowner's family within a few days.

In an episode of the award-winning television series "The Civil War," aired in 1990, narrators reported that the wife of a Confederate soldier heard a dove call at her window one evening. She feared it was a death omen. The next day she was informed that her husband had been killed.

In *Birds in Legend, Fable and Folklore* (1923), Ingersoll devoted much attention to doves and pigeons. His research disclosed a dichotomous symbolism in religion, customs and art, running almost continuously from the beginning of history to the present. He reported that the dove serves as an emblem of purity and conjugal affection in one association, yet also has been linked with things "soiled." Evidence of the latter is that, in nineteenth-century mining camps in the American West, prostitutes were frequently referred to as "soiled doves" or merely "doves" (Fisher and Holmes 1968).

SUMMARY

The mourning dove undoubtedly is more abundant and widely distributed now than it was historically and in pre-Columbian time. Its increase is linked to human alteration of the temperate North American environment, which perhaps began even before European colonization. Along with incendiarism, the introduction and cultivation of maize, which provided the foundation of sustained agriculture, thus enabling some Indians to abandon nomadic lifestyles, may have provided a start. European and other immigrants greatly accelerated environmental change with agriculture, livestock, homesteading, introduction of exotic plants, irrigation, urbanization and in myriad other ways.

The mourning dove has adapted to—indeed, usually prospered from—human uses and abuses of land. Its habitats range from virtual wilderness to highly urbanized areas, and its range has expanded northward, particularly in New England and southern Canada. By virtue of its adaptability and consequent population growth, the mourning dove may be more important to people—as North America's most sought-after gamebird, as a symbol of human growth and simply as a popular feature of the continental fauna—than ever before. It has a rich historical tradition and, assuming humans do not unreasonably impinge upon the limits of its adaptability to habitat change or inflict mortality beyond its reproductive capabilities, the mourning dove's future should be bright.

Chapter 3

Classification and Distribution

John W. Aldrich
Division of Wildlife Research
U.S. Fish and Wildlife Service
and
National Museum of Natural History
Smithsonian Institution
Washington, D.C.

Practically all parts of the world, outside the polar regions, are inhabited by some kind of pigeon or dove. Together, they comprise the family Columbidae, which numbers more than three hundred species (Peters 1961). They occur in many environments—from the high alpine zone of the Himalayas, where the snow pigeon *(Columba leuconota)* breeds, to the tropics, inhabited by a multitude of species.

Doves and pigeons range in color from the bright-hued fruit doves *(Ptilinopus* spp.) of southwestern Pacific islands to the more characteristically subdued kinds in many parts of the world. They vary in size from the chicken-sized crowned pigeons *(Goura* spp.) of New Guinea to the minute ground doves *(Columbina* spp.) of tropical America.

With exceptions among only a few species, bills of the Columbidae are rather weak—adapted in general to feed only on seeds and fruit or other items small enough to be swallowed whole. Doves and pigeons are relatively defenseless, although they are capable of striking rather sharp blows with the bony joints of their wings. The wings of most doves and pigeons are relatively strong and capable of rapid and extended flight. Most members of the Columbidae family are relatively short-legged, but exceptions to this rule are the pheasant pigeon *(Otidiphaps nobilis)* and the thick-billed ground pigeon *(Trugon terrestris)* which, with their relatively long legs, superficially resemble gallinaceous birds (Goodwin 1983).

Many species of doves and pigeons have proved remarkably adaptable, and as a family they are very successful in reproduction and survival, as indicated by their extensive worldwide range. The production of crop milk, an efficient way of feeding their young, is one reason given for that success, although flight speed and maneuverability as mechanisms of escaping predators may be equally or more important in survival (Goodwin 1983).

Distinction between pigeons and doves is arbitrary and usually based on size, with "pigeon" commonly referring to the larger species. However, this usage is not followed consistently, as the relatively large ancestor of the common domestic pigeon *(Columba livia)* is referred to as "rock dove" in ornithological literature (Goodwin 1983).

MOURNING DOVE CHARACTERIZATION AND TAXONOMY

The mourning dove *(Zenaida macroura)* is a medium-sized member of the Columbidae with a delicate bill, long, graduated (pointed), white-tipped tail, and rather soft, grayish brown and buff coloration. There are black spots on the wing coverts and near the ears. Tail and wing feathers are gray except for the black-bordered white tips on the tail. Eyes are brown, bordered by light blue bare skin. Its legs and feet are dull red. Males, in addition to averaging larger than females, are slightly more brightly colored, with a more pinkish wash on the breast and brighter blue-gray coloration on the top of the head and hind neck. Juveniles have light buff tips to their feathers, giving a scaly appearance.

By direct comparison of specimens in the National Museum of Natural History collection, I have noted the most important characteristics that distinguish the mourning dove from other members of the genus *Zenaida*. The mourning dove differs from the eared dove (*Z. auriculata*) of South America, which it resembles in general appearance including coloration, in having a much more graduated tail, a stouter bill and much less purplish underparts. The mourning dove differs from the zenaida dove (*Z. aurita*) of the West Indies in its much longer and more graduated tail, less stocky build and absence of white in the wings (present on the tips of the secondaries of *aurita*). The mourning dove also lacks the *aurita*'s yellowish brown coloration of the neck and upper breast and iridescent purple patches on the sides of the neck. The mourning dove differs from the white-winged dove (*Z. asiatica*) of the southwestern United States, West Indies, Mexico and Central America in its smaller size, much more pointed tail and absence of broad white bands present on the wings of *asiatica*. White-winged doves also lack the black spots present on the wing coverts of mourning doves. From the very different Galapagos dove (*Z. galapagoensis*) of the Galapagos Islands, the mourning dove differs in larger size, much longer and more graduated tail, shorter legs and less decurved bill. The Galapagos dove also differs from the mourning dove markedly in having distinct black facial stripes below and behind its eyes, enclosing whitish areas, and in having many more black markings, together with white patches on its wing coverts.

The mourning dove is one of forty-three species of Columbidae indigenous to North and Central America, including the West Indies, and one of fourteen species occurring in North America north of Mexico, of which one (the passenger pigeon) is extinct and three (rock dove, ringed turtledove [*Streptopelia risoria*] and spotted dove [*S. chinensis*]) are introduced foreign species (American Ornithologists' Union 1983).

The taxonomy of this species was confused for many years because of the original composite description of *macroura* by Linnaeus (1758)—based on the long-tailed dove (*Columba macroura*) of Edwards (1743), which is the mourning dove of the West Indies—and Catesby's (1731) *Palumbus migratorius*, which is the passenger pigeon. Linnaeus obviously was much confused in his descriptions, considering the passenger pigeon (*migratorius*) the same as the mourning dove (*macroura*), and later considering *carolinensis* of Catesby (1731) as different from either one in his twelfth edition (Linnaeus 1766). Ridgway (1916) may have been the first reviser to use the name *macroura* strictly for the mourning doves of the West Indies and distinct from *carolinensis*, which he applied to the birds of mainland North America. This is the usage followed by Wetmore and Swales (1931), who gave a detailed description of the confused nomenclatural history of the mourning dove and who were responsible for allocating the type locality of *macroura* as Cuba. The same arrangement was followed by Peters (1961) and the American Ornithologists' Union (1983) and is used in this chapter.

Zenaidura Bonaparte (1855), the generic name adopted and commonly used for the mourning dove through the fifth edition of the AOU Checklist (American Ornithologists' Union 1957), was based on relative length of wing, tail, tarsus, bill and toes, compared with the genus *Zenaida* Bonaparte (1838). However, all of these supposed differences are so variable and overlapping that they now are not considered of generic distinctiveness and *Zenaidura* has been synonymized with the older name *Zenaida* by the American Ornithologists' Union (1983).

MOURNING DOVE DISTRIBUTION

Mourning doves breed from southwestern and eastcentral British Columbia, central Alberta, central Saskatchewan, southern Manitoba, southern Ontario, southern Quebec, New Brunswick, Prince Edward Island and Nova Scotia to southcentral Baja California, Sonora (in the Pacific lowlands), the interior mountains and central plateau of Mexico to Oaxaca and Puebla, northern Tamaulipas (in the Caribbean lowlands), Texas, the Gulf of Mexico coast and southern Florida. Their breeding range also includes Bermuda, the Bahamas and Greater Antilles (east to Puerto Rico and Culebra and Vieques islands), the Revillagigedo (Clarión) and Tres Marías islands off western Mexico, Costa Rica and Panama east to the savannahs of the Pacific slope of western Panama (Wetmore 1968), and probably elsewhere in northern Central America *(Figure 1)*. They occur casually in summer (and possibly breeding) in southeastern Alaska (American Ornithologists' Union 1983, Dunks et al. 1982, D. Bystrak personal communications: 1986).

Mourning doves winter *(Figure 1)* primarily in northern California, across the central United States to Iowa, southern Michigan, southern Ontario, New York and New England (uncommonly to

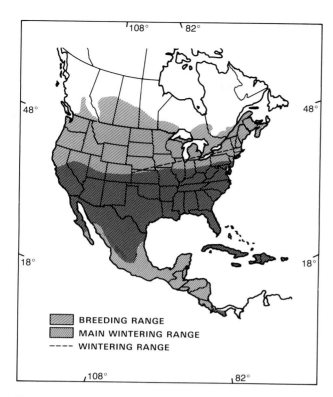

Figure 1. Breeding and wintering ranges of the mourning dove. Breeding range information from Aldrich and Duvall (1958), Godfrey (1966), Lack (1976), Leopold (1972), Salt and Salt (1976), Armstrong (1977), Cadman et al. (1987), Campbell et al. (1990), Smith and Adam (in press), Semenchuk (in preparation) and Breeding Bird Survey files. Winter range information from Keeler (1977) and American Ornithologists' Union (1983).

the northern limits of their breeding range), and south throughout the breeding range and over most of Mexico and Central America to the Pacific slope of western Panama (Wetmore 1968, American Ornithologists' Union 1983).

The species is found occasionally in western and central Alaska, southern Yukon, southern Mackenzie, northern Manitoba, northern Ontario and central Quebec, Labrador and Newfoundland. It is accidental in Greenland and Colombia (Wetmore 1968, American Ornithologists' Union 1983).

Mourning doves are migratory in the northern part of their range but may be sedentary in some localities from about the middle United States southward (Leopold and Dedon 1983, see also chapter 4). Doves that breed farther north winter farthest south, apparently leapfrogging the wintering range of the more southern breeders (Dunks et al. 1982).

The species was introduced in the Hawaiian Islands (on Hawaii) in 1963 and has established a small population in the North Kona region (American Ornithologists' Union 1983, Scott et al. 1986).

There are fossil records of mourning doves from the upper Pleistocene in California, Nuevo Leon, Kansas and Florida (American Ornithologists' Union 1957, see also chapter 2).

GEOGRAPHICAL VARIATION

There are three geographical trends in morphological variation of mourning dove populations on the North American continent: (1) tone of plumage coloration varies from dark in the East to pale in the West, with a broad area of intergradation in the transition between eastern forest and western grasslands *(Figure 2)*; (2) length of wing changes gradually from shorter in southern to longer in northern areas; and (3) toe length decreases from east to west (Aldrich and Duvall 1958).

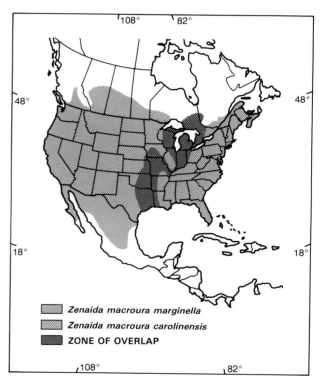

Figure 2. Breeding ranges of the eastern *(Zenaida macroura carolinensis)* and western *(Z. m. marginella)* subspecies of the mourning dove.

Recent analyses (J. W. Aldrich personal files) of the same measurements of mourning dove males used by Aldrich and Duvall (1958) for the North American continent, grouping them by the ecoregion provinces of Bailey and Cushwa (1981) and Bailey (1983) (see *Table 3* and *Figure 3*), indicated a similar geographical distribution of the morphological differences noted in the previous study, except

Table 3. Mean measurements, in millimeters, of male mourning doves[a] for ecoregion provinces in order of decreasing values.

Structure		Ecoregion province[b]	n	Mean	SD
Wing	241	Willamette-Puget Forest	5	150.60	3.90
	M241	Pacific Forest	3	150.00	2.29
	M311	Rocky Mountain Forest	7	148.21	4.31
	311	Short-grass Prairie	8	147.38	3.59
	312	Palouse Grassland	4	146.63	5.50
	211	Laurentian Mixed Forest	9	146.17	3.18
	313	Intermountain Sagebrush	7	145.64	0.94
	221	Eastern Deciduous Forest	35	145.36	3.90
	231	Outer Coastal Plain Forest	15	145.00	3.76
	—	Bermuda Island	6	144.32	1.30
	232	Southeastern Mixed Forest	12	144.17	3.42
	251	Prairie Parkland	63	143.33	2.91
	253	Tall-grass Prairie	40	143.15	3.51
	252	Prairie Brushland	15	142.50	2.68
Bill	—	Bermuda Island	6	14.53	1.01
	312	Palouse Grassland	3	14.27	0.38
	252	Prairie Brushland	15	13.97	0.56
	M311	Rocky Mountain Forest	7	13.77	1.00
	313	Intermountain Sagebrush	7	13.77	0.87
	221	Eastern Deciduous Forest	33	13.72	0.70
	211	Laurentian Mixed Forest	9	13.67	0.79
	253	Tall-grass Prairie	35	13.58	0.80
	241	Willamette-Puget Forest	5	13.50	0.61
	251	Prairie Parkland	53	13.41	0.58
	M241	Pacific Forest	3	13.40	0.36
	231	Outer Coastal Plain Forest	15	13.17	0.45
	311	Short-grass Prairie	7	13.14	0.99
	232	Southeastern Mixed Forest	12	12.83	0.97
Tarsus	M241	Pacific Forest	3	21.83	0.29
	232	Southeastern Mixed Forest	12	21.75	0.97
	241	Willamette-Puget Forest	5	21.70	0.57
	253	Tall-grass Prairie	38	21.43	0.74
	221	Eastern Deciduous Forest	34	21.41	0.74
	252	Prairie Brushland	15	21.23	0.84
	231	Outer Coastal Plain Forest	15	21.20	0.94
	M311	Rocky Mountain Forest	5	21.20	1.15
	313	Intermountain Sagebrush	7	21.14	0.90
	251	Prairie Parkland	63	21.01	1.66
	311	Short-grass Prairie	8	20.94	0.50
	211	Laurentian Mixed Forest	9	20.72	0.71
	—	Bermuda Island	6	20.57	1.30
	312	Palouse Grassland	4	20.38	0.48
Middle toe	—	Bermuda Island	6	20.72	1.01
	232	Southeastern Mixed Forest	12	20.50	1.37
	231	Outer Coastal Plain Forest	15	20.43	0.98
	251	Prairie Parkland	64	20.07	0.75
	252	Prairie Brushland	15	20.07	0.94
	253	Tall-grass Prairie	39	20.05	0.96
	221	Eastern Deciduous Forest	34	20.04	0.87
	311	Short-grass Prairie	8	19.81	0.46
	M311	Rocky Mountain Forest	6	19.80	0.84
	313	Intermountain Sagebrush	7	19.61	0.40
	312	Palouse Grassland	4	19.45	0.80
	211	Laurentian Mixed Forest	9	19.28	0.83
	M241	Pacific Forest	3	19.17	1.61
	241	Willamette-Puget Forest	5	18.90	0.82

[a] From J. W. Aldrich (personal files).
[b] From Bailey and Cushwa (1981).

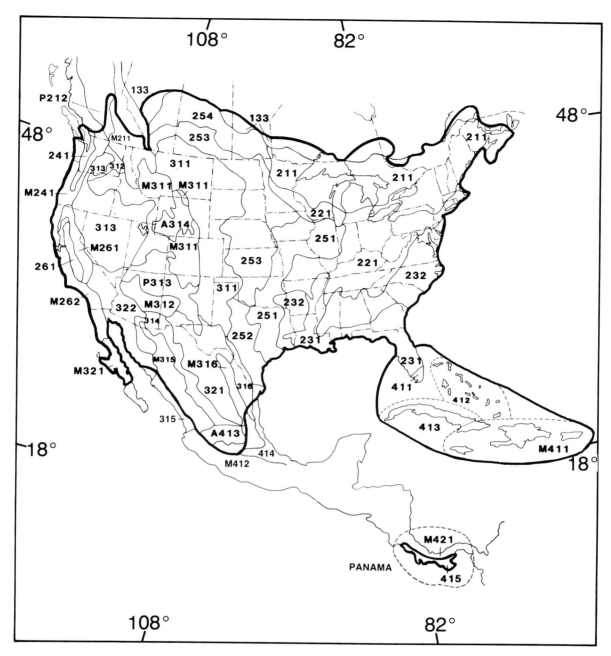

Figure 3. Ecogeographic distribution of breeding mourning doves. Ecoregion province designations from Bailey and Cushwa (1981). Breeding range boundary based on American Ornithologists' Union (1983), Dunks et al. (1982), Cadman et al. (1987), Campbell et al. (1990), Smith and Adam (in press), Semenchuk (in preparation) and D. Bystrak (personal communication: 1986). Ecoregion provinces:

133 Boreal Forest	254 Aspen Parkland	M315 Sierra Madre Occidental
211 Laurentian Mixed Forest	261 California Grassland	316 Rio Grande Shrub Steppe
M211 Columbia Forest	M261 Sierran Forest	M316 Sierra Madre Oriental
P212 Fraser-Nechaco Plateau	M262 California Chaparral	321 Chihuahuan Desert
221 Eastern Deciduous Forest	311 Great Plains Short-grass Prairie	M321 Baja California
231 Outer Coastal Plain Forest	M311 Rocky Mountain Forest	322 American Desert
232 Southeastern Mixed Forest	312 Palouse Grassland	411 Everglades
241 Willamette-Puget Forest	M312 Upper Gila Mountains Forest	M411 Greater Antillean Islands
M241 Pacific Forest	313 Intermountain Sagebrush	412 Bahamas
251 Prairie Parkland	P313 Colorado Plateau	413 Cuban Savanna
252 Prairie Brushland	314 Mexican Highland Shrub Steppe	A413 Central Mexico
253 Tall-grass Prairie	A314 Wyoming Basin	415 Pacific Savanna Woodland
		M421 Central American Ranges

for bill and tarsus lengths. In the recent analysis, I found that the mean wing length is significantly longer in the northern and western ecoregion provinces, such as Willamette-Puget Forest and Rocky Mountain Forest provinces, than in the more southern and eastern ones, such as Southeastern Mixed Forest and Prairie Brushland provinces. Both wing and toe lengths seem to be related to geographical distribution without obvious ecological relationships. On the other hand, tarsus lengths are greater in ecoregion provinces characterized by more forested or closed vegetation situations, such as Pacific Forest and Southeastern Mixed Forest provinces. Shorter tarsi occur in more open grassland areas such as the Short-grass Prairie and Palouse Grassland provinces. Conversely, longer bills, although not as obvious, tend to occur in the more open ecoregion provinces, such as Palouse Grassland and Prairie Brushland, and shorter bills tend to prevail in the more forested areas, such as Pacific Forest and Southeastern Mixed Forest. The inverse correlation between tarsus and bill length of males is significant ($r = 0.63$, $P < 0.01$). Such statistically significant differences between bill and tarsus length seem to follow this pattern and be independent of geographical location. This would seem to be contrary to the original conclusion regarding geographical distribution of tarsus and bill measurements (Aldrich and Duvall 1958). However, a greater amount of open country in the western ecoregion provinces and more forest in the eastern ones may account for the previous conclusion that bills average longer in the West and tarsi longer in the East.

The marked differences in the way that morphological variation of characters responds to environmental factors are a warning not to generalize in describing morphological variation of bird populations strictly on geographical grounds. In some cases, such as longer wings and toes of mourning doves, the variation seems to be more directly related to northern or western climates, whereas in other characteristics, such as bill and tarsus lengths, the differences may respond to vegetation types (which are indirectly related to climates) that may affect the feeding and other habits of doves sufficiently to be significant in adaptive morphological variation. See chapter 8 for discussion of subspecific weight variation.

In addition to the mensural characters recently analyzed and the previously noted east-to-west gradation of increasingly pale coloration of mourning doves in North America, there is a slight trend toward a more brownish tint to the plumage in the South and a more grayish cast in the North. This appears to be due to slightly different color phases present to some extent in all areas, with the grayish phase occurring more frequently in the North and the brownish phase occurring more frequently in the South, particularly the arid Southwest.

In addition to those North American variations, other differences in other populations are: (1) dark buff underparts associated with small size of doves in the West Indies and Florida Keys; (2) deep brownish coloration associated with relatively long bills and toes on Clarion Island of the Revillagigedo Islands off the western coast of Mexico; (3) short wings and legs and long bills, together with pale grayish coloration, in Panama and possibly other parts of Central America (Aldrich and Duvall 1958, Wetmore 1968).

SUBSPECIFIC CLASSIFICATION

These combinations of geographically related morphological characters have led to the classification of mourning dove populations into five subspecies (Ridgway 1916, Aldrich and Duvall 1958) *(tables 3 and 4)*:

1. The long-winged, long-toed, short-billed, dark population of the eastern United States east of the prairie grasslands, Bermuda and the Bahama Islands—*Zenaida macroura carolinensis* (Linnaeus 1766) or eastern mourning dove *(Figure 2)*.

2. The long-winged, long-billed, short-toed, pale population of the western United States from prairie grasslands westward, southern Canada and temperate Mexico—*Z. m. marginella* (Woodhouse 1852) or western mourning dove *(Figure 2)*.

3. The short-winged, short-legged, long-billed, pale grayish population of western Panama and possibly other parts of Central America—*Z. m. turturilla* (Wetmore 1956) or Panamanian mourning dove.

4. The short-winged, dark-to-medium-toned, deep buff-bellied population of the western West Indies and Florida Keys—*Z. m. macroura* (Linnaeus 1758) or West Indian mourning dove.

5. The relatively large-footed, large-billed, very dark brownish population of Clarion Island of the Revillagigedo group off the western coast of Mexico—*Z. m. clarionensis* (Townsend 1890) or Clarion Island mourning dove.

Zenaida graysoni (Lawrence 1871), formerly a resident of Socorro Island off western Mexico but now extirpated from the wild, has been considered by the American Ornithologists' Union (1983) as a species distinct from the mourning dove. This status has been reinforced by recent studies of behavior and vocalizations as well as morpho-

Table 4. Measurements, in millimeters, of subspecies of *Zenaida macroura*, based on breeding specimens only.[a]

Subspecies	Sex	Wing			Culmen		
		Sample	Mean	SE	Sample	Mean	SE
marginella	M	118	144.3	0.34	107	13.5	0.08
	F	36	141.7	0.79	34	13.5	0.01
carolinensis	M	34	144.8	0.73	32	13.3	0.13
	F	17	137.9	0.97	17	12.9	0.23
macroura	M	11	137.8	0.52	11	12.8	0.14
	F	10	132.4	1.04	10	12.8	0.32
turturilla	M	6	137.3[b]		4	13.9[b]	
	F	3	127.0[b]		2	13.2[b]	
clarionensis	M	4	139.9	2.12	4	15.1	0.13
	F	3	136.7	2.70	4	14.9	0.69

[a] From Aldrich and Duvall (1958).
[b] From Wetmore (1968).

Subspecific identification of the mourning doves shown above is based primarily on geographical location of breeding range. Without information on breeding range association, identification of the five mourning dove subspecies can be made only by careful measurements and by critical analysis of colors compared in the hand with properly identified specimens. *Left photo of* Zenaida macroura carolinensis *courtesy of the U.S. National Archives. Right photo of Z. m.* marginella *by Ed Bry; courtesy of the North Dakota Game and Fish Department.*

logical differences of surviving captive individuals (Baptista et al. 1983).

It has been impossible to verify Ridgway's (1916) characterization of a morphologically distinct population in the Cape San Lucas district of Baja California. Aldrich and Duvall (1958) were unable to locate any breeding specimens from there nor, indeed, did Ridgway mention any. In fact, no mourning doves are thought to breed that far south in Baja California (Friedmann et al. 1950). As noted previously, the brown coloration, thought by Ridgway to characterize that population, is now believed to be a color phase that is somewhat more prevalent in the arid Southwest and may have been noted by Ridgway on nonbreeding doves from southern Baja California.

Likewise, it has been impossible to verify con-

clusively the existence of a dark-colored subspecies native to the humid Pacific Northwest, *Z. m. caurina* (Ridgway 1916), although additional supporting evidence in the form of a specimen has come to light since a previous report (Aldrich and Duvall 1958). This specimen, unsexed but considered by its plumage to be a male, was collected at Fort Steilacoom, Puget Sound, Washington by Dr. George Suckley during the 1850s. Cooper (1860) reported on the birds he collected together with Suckley on that survey and mentioned taking many specimens of mourning doves at Fort Steilacoom in the 1850s. However, only two of these, both collected by Suckley, were cataloged in the U.S. National Museum (#8755 and #8756). The latter reportedly was destroyed in 1881. Thus, Ridgway (1916) did not have access to it in his description of *caurina*. The other

Suckley specimen from Steilacoom (#8755) probably was one of the two specimens, in addition to the type, used by Ridgway in his original description of *caurina*. The whereabouts of a supposed third specimen still is unknown. The two specimens that are extant—the type from the Peale Collection, probably taken along the lower Columbia River (Aldrich and Duvall 1958), and the Suckley specimen from Fort Steilacoom—are as Ridgway said, very dark and are quite different from both an 1860 specimen taken by Kennerly in eastern Washington and the more recent specimens, one collected September 1, 1924 by Ira Gabrielson at Portland, Oregon, two from Tacoma taken June 14, 1918 and now in the University of Washington museum, and five collected in late May 1954 by T. D. Burleigh in the southern Puget Sound region near Fort Steilacoom. With the addition of the Suckley specimen taken in that area in the 1850s, which matches the type of *caurina* in color, it appears more likely that there may have been a small population of dark mourning doves in the humid northwest coastal area that became extinct sometime after the 1850s and was replaced by the population of typical *Z. m. marginella* that exists there today, as suggested originally by Jewett et al. (1953). If this did happen, it must have been at a very early date, since a male specimen (#20731) in the Carnegie Museum taken June 7, 1884 at Beaverton, Oregon is pale and similar to more recently collected specimens from that area identified as *Z. m. marginella*.

The subspecies *Z. m. tresmariae*, described by Ridgway (1915), from Maria Madre Island of the Tres Marías group off the Pacific coast of Mexico, is thought to be based on a migrant specimen from some unknown breeding population, since no mourning doves are known to breed on those islands (Aldrich and Duvall 1958).

The single specimen seen in the Bahama Islands and taken July 16, 1903 appears to be typical *Z. m. carolinensis* (Aldrich and Duvall 1958). A series of breeding specimens taken in Bermuda by David Wingate on June 12, 1967 were identified as typical *Z. m. carolinensis* (J. W. Aldrich personal files).

Wetmore and Swales (1931), who definitely ascribed the name *Z. m. macroura* to the West Indian population with type locality Cuba, noted that mourning doves from western Cuba and Tortue Island, Haiti were darker than those from other West Indian areas. However, they considered the differences as individual variation. They considered *Z. m. bella* (Palmer and Riley 1902) from Mariel, Cuba, the type specimen of which is a dark-colored bird, as *macroura*. Aldrich and Duvall (1958) agreed with Wetmore and Swales (1931), although with reservations, in not recognizing more than one sub-

species in the West Indies and the Florida Keys.

Z. m. peninsulari (Bailey 1923), based on February-taken specimens from Miami Beach, Florida, was determined to be referable to *Z. m. macroura* by Hubbard and Banks (1970). The locality is slightly north of the known breeding range of *macroura* in the Florida Keys, and Bailey's specimens may have been winter wanderers from there.

MIGRATION DETERMINED FROM MORPHOLOGICAL CHARACTERISTICS

Analysis of morphological characters of collected specimens is one method of determining (1) the breeding areas of migrant and wintering populations and (2) the relative numerical importance of certain breeding areas to the various migrant aggregations. By this method, it was determined that early migratory flights of doves to southern Florida come chiefly from more northern parts of the eastern United States rather than from the West Indies, as had been assumed previously (Aldrich 1952). It also was determined by examination of specimens that doves shot by hunters during an early autumn season in Georgia were chiefly of the eastern race, *carolinensis*, while those shot in a later winter season were chiefly of the western population, *marginella* (Aldrich et al. 1958). Studies in Texas (Aldrich et al. 1958) showed differences in population migrations similar to those noted in Georgia, with doves shot early in the hunting season coming primarily from the East and those taken later in the season coming from more western populations. Another result of the specimen examination studies was the discovery that early migratory flights are composed mostly of young of the year, while later flights contain relatively more adults.

Thus, critical analyses of morphological variation in breeding populations of mourning doves may be considered an adjunct to the study of migration by means of banded individuals. Findings from specimens supplement band recoveries to the extent that they include representatives of some dove populations that have not been banded. These facts demonstrate the need for more critical analyses of geographical variation in morphological characters so that a greater number of different breeding sources of migrants can be identified. Particularly needed are studies of ecogeographical variation, which relate morphological variation with the major ecological zones or ecoregions where the birds breed. Such information not only aids in locating more exactly the breeding areas of particular morphological variants but also suggests the adaptive function of the variant characters.

II.

Life History and Biology

Chapter 4

Migration

Roy E. Tomlinson
Office of Migratory Bird Management
U.S. Fish and Wildlife Service
Albuquerque, New Mexico

The word "migration" may be used to describe any movements of animals, with or without return trips. Many mammals, fish and insects migrate, but the phenomenon is more prevalent among birds (Griffin 1964). Migration by birds usually is regarded as an annual, two-phased cycle during which a population from a defined breeding area makes a large-scale shift to and from a restricted wintering area (Lack 1954; see also Gauthreaux 1982, Ketterson and Nolan 1983, Faaborg 1988). Most migratory nearctic breeders move south to the neotropics for about six months during autumn and winter (September through February) and return to breed during spring and summer (March through August).

BIOLOGICAL ASPECTS OF MIGRATION

In North America, there is a tendency to regard migratory birds as originating on the breeding grounds and migrating to southern areas to escape harsh winters (Gauthreaux 1982). This view, however, presents several paradoxes, discussed by Rappole et al. (1983). Migrants usually leave breeding areas *before* inclement weather sets in and there are food shortages. They sometimes fly thousands of miles over hostile environments to arrive at areas that may differ substantially from those that they left. Once there, they must compete with endemic species and other migrants for food and cover. They then must survive their winter stay before undertaking the hazardous trip north. A contemporary explanation for these paradoxes is that many migrants from the north that winter in the neotropics actually are neotropical species that happen to breed in the temperate zone (Keast 1980, Rappole et al. 1983, Sinclair 1983). This hypothesis appears appropriate to the Columbidae in general.

The vast majority of columbid species inhabits the tropics or subtropics and "in fact this group is a characteristic tropical family" (Chadwick 1983: 1). Columbids are poorly adapted for survival in the nearctic winter because of feeding habits, water requirements and body structure. Large numbers of mourning doves, for instance, may die when food supplies are covered by snow or ice and temperatures are below freezing for extended periods (Hennessy and Van Camp 1963, Armstrong 1977). In addition, their fleshy feet often are frozen and digits (even entire feet) frequently are lost by overwintering birds (see chapter 13).

Whatever their geographic origin, many birds apparently have adopted migration as an evolutionary mechanism to enhance survival. Lack (1954) postulated that birds migrate from wintering grounds when breeding is, on the average, more successful elsewhere, and that this increased success outweighs any costs associated with migration. Conversely, they migrate from breeding grounds to winter elsewhere because survival is more successful among those that depart than among those that remain. For those species in which one segment migrates and the other does not, the dangers of migration and winter residence are about equal; otherwise, one or the other trait would have been eliminated by natural selection (see Fretwell 1980).

The stimuli initiating annual bird migrations commonly are grouped as "ultimate" and "proximate" factors (Farner 1955, Berthold 1975, Gauthreaux 1982). Ultimate factors are those that affect survival and reproduction and therefore influence the evolution of migration, such as food availability and climatic conditions. Proximate factors are those that twice annually bring birds into actual migration, such as day length. For typical migrants, the proximate factors operate to initiate migration in advance of the seasonal occurrence of the ultimate factors (Berthold 1975). However, certain meteorological phenomena, and sometimes food availability, may act as proximate factors in the timing of migration, even when the act itself seems to precede the need for it.

Although trapping and banding of migrants have produced much information on migratory physiology, studies of caged migratory birds in the laboratory have yielded more detailed data on the mechanisms that control the migratory condition (Gauthreaux 1985). Migratory restlessness, or *Zugunruhe*, is measured quantitatively in pens equipped with microswitches on perches located at various compass points around the circumference of the cage.

As a result of these and other studies, migratory condition for most nearctic/neotropical migrants is generally held to be initiated by genetically determined response to photoperiod, which in turn is regulated by internal hormonal changes (Faaborg 1988).

During late summer when migratory birds are completing molt, their metabolism changes drastically. Probably as the result of decreasing daylight length, the pituitary gland is stimulated to produce the hormones prolactin and corticosterone. These hormones control fat (lipid) retention and cause *Zugunruhe* (von Haartman 1949, Gauthreaux 1982). When sufficient lipids have been accumulated to allow long flights, migratory behavior may be initiated by onset of rainfall, decreased temperature and/or southerly winds. A similar sequence of events occurs on the wintering grounds. Increasing photoperiod causes recrudescence of gonads; warmer weather stimulates nightly unrest and, with increased feeding beyond needs of existence, lipid deposition occurs. All three factors serve to place the birds in physiological and psychological

readiness for migration (Van Tyne and Berger 1976). The triggering stimulus probably is continued warm temperature and/or northerly winds.

Migratory flights among nearctic species are nocturnal or diurnal or both. Nocturnal migrants usually are secretive birds and include such species as rails, cuckoos and wood warblers. Examples of diurnal migrants are hawks, swallows, hummingbirds, crows and jays. Representative birds that migrate both during the day and at night are ducks, geese, shorebirds and most doves, including the mourning dove (Van Tyne and Berger 1976).

Radar studies reviewed by Gauthreaux (1985) showed that most songbirds migrate at night at altitudes below 1,300 to 2,300 feet (400 to 700 m). Maximum altitudes reported in nine studies were between 9,800 and 20,700 feet (3,000 to 6,300 m). Migratory waterfowl fly from a few feet above sea level to more than 20,000 feet (6,100 m) (Bellrose 1976). Waterfowl and sandhill cranes have been known to reach 15,000 feet (4,500 m) and higher when crossing the Rocky Mountains (Bellrose 1976, Terres 1980), but Bellrose (1976) also has witnessed lesser snow geese migrating at altitudes as high as 10,000 feet (3,050 m) over Mississippi River lowland terrain.

Mourning doves normally migrate at low altitudes. I have seen thousands of early morning migrating mourning doves in flocks of 5 to 50 birds flying just over the tops of mixed mesquite, ironwood and paloverde trees in Sonora, Mexico, during late August and September. Similar observations have been made in Texas (H. M. Reeves personal communication: 1986) and Colorado (C. E. Braun personal communication: 1986). However, doves also have been seen crossing Tioga and Mammoth passes at more than 9,800 feet (3,000 m) in the Sierra Madres of California (McLean 1959).

Many migrant bird populations return to the same general breeding or wintering areas, or both, year after year. As an example, breeding mourning doves banded in South Dakota migrate south through Texas to westcentral Mexico (Dunks et al. 1982) and presumably return to South Dakota the following spring. As with all facets of migration, the means by which birds determine where to migrate and how to find their way (navigate) are complex. Lincoln et al. (1979) speculated that these are inherited traits (see also Gauthreaux 1982, Baker 1984). Although it can be argued that adult and more experienced birds lead the way, many species migrate in flocks segregated by age or sex. The young of many shorebird species breeding in the Arctic depart after the adults and may fly in segregated groups (Faaborg 1988). For mourning doves, immatures usually precede adults in migration,

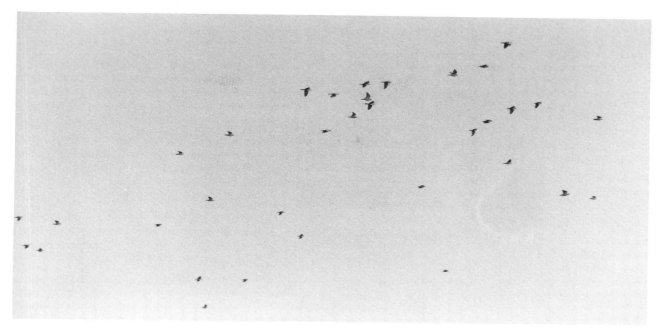

Mourning doves migrate at night as well as during the day. Typically, they fly in small flocks of less than fifty, though flocks of fifty to one hundred are not uncommon. While migrating they fly at fairly low levels (generally not more than a few hundred feet above the ground). Average flight speeds and daily distance data show that mourning doves tend to migrate for less than a few hours each day, usually in early morning, and make frequent stops en route to loaf and feed. *Photo by Ron George; courtesy of the Texas Parks and Wildlife Department.*

suggesting that they must have some kind of innate faculty to accomplish the trip unguided.

Several hypotheses have been proposed on the means by which birds find their directions during flight (see Matthews 1968, Ketterson and Nolan 1976, Baker 1978). Cues employed by migratory species for navigation may include topography, winds aloft, position of the sun and stars, and geomagnetism (Emlen 1975). Recent evidence suggests that olfactory stimuli may be used by domestic pigeons in homing experiments (Baldiccini et al. 1982). However, as emphasized by Walcott and Lednor (1983), results of the pigeon experiments may not apply to twice-yearly migration by wild birds. Many researchers have studied the possibility that birds are acutely sensitive to the earth's magnetism (Keeton 1972, Keeton 1974, Baker 1978). Although some authorities still have reservations, the general consensus is that there is now enough evidence to accept that birds have a magnetic compass and use it during migration (Baker 1984).

Navigation by birds indeed is quite complex. Keeton (1972) stressed that bird navigation is not accomplished through any single factor; birds accumulate a variety of orientation information, and one or all means may be used. Chief among the cues for true migrants are orientation to the sun and stars, topography of the land, and magnetism of the earth.

BANDING TO DETERMINE MIGRATORY PATTERNS

Although both Aristotle (Barnes 1984) and Pliny the Elder (Rackham 1947) recognized migratory behavior in birds, many early naturalists believed that winter disappearance of birds was the result of their hibernation in caves, under the bark of trees and even in the sea (see Baker 1984). By the late 1700s, however, some learned individuals were contradicting this notion. Barton (1799: xii) stated: "Some ingenious gentlemen, with whom I have conversed on the subject, are even of the opinion, that but a very few of our birds are, strictly speaking, birds of passage . . . that our birds hiemate [sic], or take up their winter-quarters among us, and that they do not migrate to a distance. Still, however, I cannot but adopt the latter notion."

Knowledge of avian migratory behavior slowly was accumulated during the nineteenth century. The phenology of spring migrations in the United States was first documented in 1884 and 1885 by Cooke (1888). He enlisted the aid of helpers to report arrivals of migrating birds at several geographical points throughout the Mississippi River Valley. Mourning doves, for example, were reported during a "fifth wave" that occurred on March 22, 1884 at St. Louis, Missouri, and later that spring at more northern locations.

Since the turn of this century, researchers have placed serially numbered bands on the legs of birds to gather information about individual birds and the populations they represent (U.S. Fish and Wildlife Service 1972). Within the past twenty-five years, coincident with the development of computer technology, analyses of banding data have become a sophisticated tool to estimate various parameters of bird population dynamics. These parameters include kill rates, annual survival rates and indirect population estimates, all of which are discussed in chapter 16. However, the original reason for banding birds was to learn more about migratory patterns, areas of origin and wintering areas. In this chapter, discussion is directed to these aspects of dove biology.

Mourning doves, being nonsecretive and widely distributed in the breeding range, are relatively easy to locate and observe. The use of mist nets, cannon nets and simple bait traps in areas of abundance usually results in capturing large numbers of doves for banding. Because doves are hunted over a large portion of their range, the rate of recovery is fairly high, at least for purposes of determining migratory tendencies.

A national banding program and the subsequent recovery of bands, mostly submitted by hunters to the U.S. Fish and Wildlife Service, has been the primary mechanism for researchers to determine mourning dove population dynamics, particularly the species' seasonal and home range movements. Accordingly, species management is emphasized on a geographic (management) unit basis, similar to the flyway concept for waterfowl. *Photo by Ron George; courtesy of the Texas Parks and Wildlife Department.*

During the past fifty years, more than a million mourning doves have been captured and banded, either as the result of efforts by individual banders or through active regional and national banding programs. Subsequent analyses have yielded excellent information on the migrational routes of doves from virtually every breeding area of the United States. The following discussion summarizes these studies in chronological order within eastern, central and western sections of the United States. All references to "Latin America" in this chapter refer collectively to Mexico and the five Central American countries of Guatemala, El Salvador, Honduras, Nicaragua and Costa Rica. See chapter 16 for definitions of banding analysis terminology (e.g., age class, cohort, direct and indirect recovery, distribution and derivation of the harvest, and pre- and postseason periods).

Eastern United States

Perhaps the first attempt at analysis of mourning dove bandings with emphasis on migrational routes was undertaken by Taber (1930). He reported on all recoveries (49) of doves received by the U.S. Bureau of Biological Survey up to March 1928. Most of the bandings had been made in Illinois and other northcentral states. He suggested that there were three areas of winter concentration for doves—in southern Georgia/northern Florida, southern Louisiana and northeastern Texas. The Wabash River Valley was seen to be the boundary between areas where doves migrated to either the southwest or southeast. Moore and Pearson (1941) reported on recoveries of 15 doves banded in Alabama and recovered elsewhere and 8 doves from other states recovered in Alabama. These recoveries indicated that doves wintering in Alabama came from northcentral and northeastern states. Austin (1951) added considerably to the knowledge of dove migration in the East with his study of 2,690 doves banded at Cape Cod, Massachusetts, between 1930 and 1950. He demonstrated that breeding doves from Cape Cod generally wintered along the southern coastal plain from Virginia to Florida, although a few birds were reported from as far as Louisiana and Texas. Aldrich (1952) examined band recoveries in Florida and concluded that the doves originated from an extensive area of the eastern United States but that a substantial segment came from the upper midwestern states. Quay (1954) obtained similar results from an analysis of banded doves recovered in North Carolina.

A major mourning dove banding effort was undertaken between 1948 and 1956, mainly in southeastern states but including areas of the Northeast and Midwest (Southeastern Association of Game and Fish Commissioners 1957). The final analysis included 145,000 dove bandings in the United States from 1920 to 1955 that yielded nearly 5,500 recoveries. This study confirmed results of earlier work: most doves banded east of the Mississippi River tend to migrate southward into southeastern states during winter, thus remaining east of the Mississippi. It further suggested that there were three major dove flyways in the United States that generally consisted of the (1) eleven western states, (2) states east of the Mississippi and (3) states between.

In a comprehensive study of mourning doves in Illinois, Hanson and Kossack (1963) discussed migratory routes of doves banded between 1920 and 1958. They concluded that southward movement of doves banded in Illinois tended to be channeled within the Mississippi River Valley until the birds reached the Gulf Coast region. From there, flights spread both eastward and westward. Although 22 percent of 140 recoveries of doves banded in Illinois and recovered elsewhere were reported from Texas and Latin America, most recoveries (78 percent) were reported from areas to the south or southeast. This finding was consistent with that of the Southeastern Association (1957).

J. M. Allen (no date) delineated the distribution of 78 recoveries from mourning doves banded in Indiana during 1950 to 1965. Two pathways were apparent: the main path was southeastward into Florida (24 percent), Georgia (18 percent) and Alabama (13 percent); the other was southwestward to Louisiana (14 percent) and east Texas (6 percent). Four recoveries (5 percent) were reported from Mexico. Nearly 90 percent of the recoveries were east of the Mississippi River.

In an analysis of banding data for the period 1949 to 1962, Watts (1969) computed the weighted derivation of the mourning dove harvest in Louisiana. Approximately 62 percent of the harvest was composed of birds originating in that state; 25 percent originated in other states east of the Mississippi River; and 13 percent originated west of the Mississippi. Of birds banded in Louisiana, 86 percent of the recoveries were taken in Louisiana, 10 percent in Texas and Latin America, and only 4 percent in other southeastern states.

In a recent analysis of the derivation of 1,625 mourning dove recoveries in Florida between 1931 and 1978, Marion et al. (1981) determined that 57 percent of Florida's dove harvest was composed of immigrant doves. Of birds with out-of-state origin, more than 60 percent came from a nine-state area of the mid- and northcentral United States (Minne-

sota, Wisconsin, Michigan, Iowa, Illinois, Indiana, Ohio, Missouri and Kentucky). Eastern seaboard states contributed 20 percent of the harvest and Gulf Coast states about 10 percent. In contrast, nearly 99 percent of Florida's summer resident doves remained within the state during winter; the few birds that left emigrated to the nearby states of Alabama, Georgia and South Carolina.

Hayne and Geissler (1977) provided a series of miniprint tables with "Importance Values" that can be used to identify migratory patterns among mourning doves throughout the United States. No analysis of the resulting statistics was attempted, however. Later in this chapter, data extracted from Hayne and Geissler are used to illustrate migratory patterns of doves banded in the eastern United States.

Central United States

In addition to Taber's (1930) study of banding recoveries in Illinois, McClure (1943) conducted an intensive study of doves in Iowa from 1938 to 1940. McClure banded 1,643 doves, from which 22 recoveries (1.3 percent) were recorded in areas outside of Iowa. All of these recoveries were obtained from areas west of the Mississippi River, mainly in Texas and Latin America.

Tomlinson (1959) obtained similar results from a study of doves banded in northern Missouri during 1953 through 1958. Of 73 recoveries, 69 (95 percent) were obtained west of the Mississippi River and 43 (58 percent) were in Texas and Latin America.

Rice and Lovrien (1974) reported that recoveries of most doves banded in South Dakota occured in Texas and Latin America. Less than 3 percent of all recoveries of birds banded during this study were taken east of the Mississippi River.

Citing information derived from dove band recoveries in the midwest, Wight (1954) showed that flyways developed for waterfowl regulation were unsuitable for dove management. Specifically, the Mississippi Flyway appeared to contain separate population segments that had affinities either to the east or west of the Mississippi River. Wight urged that an analysis of mourning dove banding data be conducted to delineate more functional units for this species.

Largely in response to this suggestion, a nestling banding program was conducted by the U.S. Fish and Wildlife Service, cooperating state agencies, and private banders throughout the United States between 1955 and 1960. Although only nestlings were sought because their exact origins could be established, it was later determined that adults and free-flying young banded in the same locations during May through August had identical recovery patterns. The U.S. Fish and Wildlife Service then published an analysis of all bandings (113,978) accomplished between 1954 and 1957 and the resulting recoveries (3,543) (Kiel 1959). It was concluded that there were three clearly defined areas within the country containing mourning dove populations that were largely independent of each other. This work also suggested the three zones be considered as separate management units. As a result, the Eastern (EMU), Central (CMU) and Western (WMU) management units *(Figure 4)* were established as operational entities in 1960 (Kiel 1961). Management decisions have been made within these boundaries since then.

Blankenship and Reeves (1970) first pointed out the importance of Mexico as a harvest area for mourning doves, especially from the CMU and WMU. They estimated that, during the late 1960s, 2.85 million mourning doves produced in the United States were harvested annually in Mexico, in comparison with 40.8 million doves taken in the forty-eight conterminous U.S. states during that time. This information suggested that a significant segment of the United States' population winters in Mexico.

An important analysis of dove banding and recovery data in Texas was published by Dunks (1977). Based on more than 900,000 doves banded in the United States between 1967 and 1974 and nearly 2,000 recoveries in Texas, Dunks reported that 58 percent of the direct recoveries originated in Texas, 40 percent from other CMU states and only 2 percent from the EMU. An insignificant number of recoveries (7) originated from the WMU. It also was determined from 1,168 direct recoveries of birds banded in Texas that the breeding population does not significantly contribute to the harvest of any areas other than Texas (94 percent) and Latin America (4 percent). Dunks concluded that four mourning dove population segments related to Texas: those birds that nest in and do not leave Texas; those that nest in Texas and migrate south; birds that nest in states to the north and terminate migration in Texas; and doves that nest to the north and migrate through Texas to Latin American wintering areas.

Braun (1979) examined the integrity of the boundary between the CMU and WMU by analyzing mourning dove banding data from those portions of Montana, Wyoming, Colorado and New Mexico west of the Continental Divide. Although the doves from this area exhibited a definite tendency to migrate westward and to the south, Braun

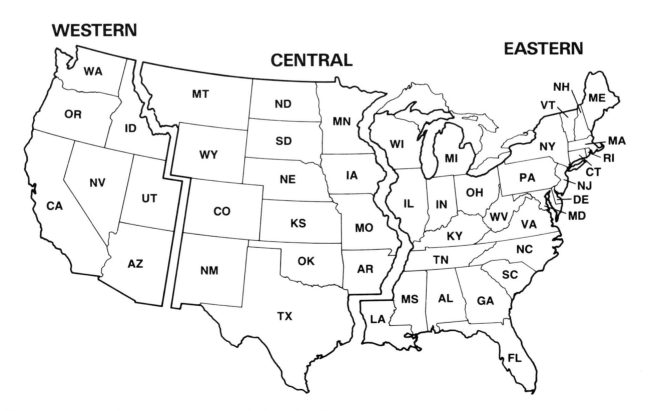

Figure 4. Mourning dove management units in the United States.

concluded that the available data did not strongly support alteration of the present boundary between the two units.

Biologists in Missouri conducted a mourning dove banding program between 1953 and 1976. Analyses of early data were reported by Tomlinson (1959), Tomlinson et al. (1960) and Henry (1970). The most recent and comprehensive analysis was by Atkinson et al. (1982), with banding data obtained from 1968 through 1976.

Mourning doves banded in Missouri were harvested along two main pathways. Doves from eastern Missouri generally moved south-southeast into Mississippi, Louisiana, Alabama, South Carolina and Florida. Most doves from the central and western parts of Missouri migrated southwestward across Kansas and Oklahoma into Texas and Mexico. Thus, although there were exceptions to the rule, doves from the eastern part of the state showed migratory tendencies similar to those from the EMU, whereas central and western Missouri doves had affinities like those from the CMU.

In 1966, the U.S. Fish and Wildlife Service, in conjunction with the respective Management Unit Dove Technical Committees, embarked on a comprehensive nationwide mourning dove banding program to provide larger and better distributed banded samples. Initially scheduled as a five-year program, the study was delayed and extended and eventually covered a period of nine years, from 1967 through 1975. Annual banding quotas (Martinson 1969, 1971) were set for the United States at about 175,000, and each state was to contribute 3,000 to 5,000 each year (smaller states had quotas of 250 bandings; California and Texas each had highs of 8,000). Instructions to states stressed the need for wide distribution of banding effort according to physiographic divisions in each state. More than 868,000 mourning doves ultimately were banded in the United States during the preseason banding period of June through August.

Using data obtained from this source, Dunks et al. (1982) made a thorough analysis encompassing the CMU. Of 5,266 direct recoveries from doves banded in the CMU, 4,134 (79 percent) were taken in the unit, 722 (15 percent) in Latin America, 292 (6 percent) in the EMU and 48 (1 percent) in the WMU. The pattern of migration was generally southward and fan shaped. Doves originating in northern latitudes and states adjacent to the EMU and WMU exhibited greater probability of being recovered in the other units than did doves originating in southern latitudes. Of the total dove harvest in the CMU, nearly 98 percent originated within the CMU and less than 3 percent from the WMU and EMU combined.

Western United States

Although there has been an extensive banding effort in the WMU during the past thirty to forty years, it has been inconsistent in time, area covered and cohorts sampled. Furthermore, much of the collected information has not been analyzed and few publications have resulted to date.

McLean (1959) summarized mourning dove migration routes for the WMU from existing banding records. Doves from Washington, Oregon and northern California generally migrated south through Nevada and California into southern California, Arizona and Mexico. Three main wintering areas were evident: the Imperial Valley of California, southcentral Arizona and the Jalisco-Michoacan-Nayarit region of westcentral Mexico. Doves from Idaho and Utah also moved south and southwestward into California and Arizona; some continued into Mexico.

Channing (1979) conducted a mourning dove banding study in the San Joaquin Valley near Turlock, California from 1961 to 1968 and analyzed the resulting data, as well as those from doves banded in Yakima, Washington within the same period. Recoveries from the Yakima bandings confirmed the conclusions of McLean (1959)—most doves migrated through California, Nevada and Arizona into Mexico, but one bird was reported from Central America. All 56 recovery records of doves banded as nestlings at Turlock were reported within the Central Valley and most within a short radius of Turlock. This prompted Channing (1979) to conclude that locally produced doves were basically nonmigratory. Birds banded as adults and free-flying immatures yielded similar results. Of 100 recoveries, 82 were within 25 miles (40 km) of the banding site. Most of the rest were recovered south of Turlock, including 7 in Mexico. Channing theorized that some northern doves were already southbound in July and August when trapping occurred and these birds were sampled at that time.

Further evidence of nonmigratory dove populations in California was supplied by Leopold and Dedon (1983). Of 1,184 birds banded in the urban environment of Berkeley, 42 recoveries (3.5 percent) were reported. Of these, only one bird was recovered outside the San Francisco Bay area, near Yuma, Arizona. It was concluded that the Berkeley population is locally resident and probably does not migrate.

For Arizona, Kufeld (1963) presented information on 886 recoveries of doves banded in that state and 35 recoveries in Arizona of birds banded elsewhere. As one might expect, most of the Arizona-banded recoveries (826: 94 percent) were taken in-state. Of the remaining 60 recoveries, 55 percent were taken in Mexico, 30 percent in California and 15 percent in other nearby states (except for 1 in Washington). Arizona derived most foreign recoveries from Oregon, California, Nevada and Utah, but a few recoveries originated in Colorado and New Mexico.

Braun's (1979) analysis of recoveries from doves banded west of the Continental Divide in New Mexico, Colorado, Wyoming and Montana illustrated the fact that most doves from the WMU remain in the unit or migrate into Mexico.

The nationwide banding program of 1967–75 also provided data for the WMU, analyzed by Tomlinson et al. (1988). Of the 88,540 bands placed on doves in the WMU during the study period, 2,859 direct recoveries were obtained. Of these, 2,668 (93 percent) were taken in the WMU, 13 (0.5 percent) in the CMU and 0 in the EMU. Latin America accounted for 178 recoveries (6.7 percent), most of which (176) were from Mexico. Doves banded in Washington and Oregon were several times more likely to be recovered in California than were doves banded in Idaho, Utah and Nevada. Similarly, doves from Utah and Nevada were at least twice as likely to be recovered in Arizona as were doves from any other WMU state. This suggested that most mourning doves from the WMU migrate straight south or slightly southeastward. Tomlinson et al. (1988) also estimated that an individual dove banded in the WMU had about the same chance of being recovered in Mexico as one banded in the CMU, but a dove banded in the CMU was thirteen times more likely to be recovered in Central America than was one banded in the WMU.

Alaska

No mourning doves have been banded in Alaska, but Cottam (1948) published records of seventeen sightings in the state to that date. All but one of these sightings were made during July through November, causing speculation that the birds were vagrants from more southern populations.

MIGRATORY PATTERNS REEXAMINED

Although the information reviewed in the preceding section provides substantial insight into mourning dove migration, an updated general analysis of banding data was needed to clarify migratory patterns and wintering areas throughout the range of the species. Accordingly, data from three publications—Hayne and Geissler (1977), Dunks et al. (1982), and Tomlinson et al. (1988)—were reanalyzed. Discussions in this section and the next incorporate results of that analysis.

Mourning dove breeding populations are widespread throughout North America and exhibit highly diversified migratory movements according to origin. To aid in describing their migratory patterns, I have adopted several distinctive reference areas of the United States and Latin America. Major regions of the United States are the three management units described by Kiel (1959)—Eastern, Central and Western (*Figure 4*). Emulating Dunks et al. (1982), I further subdivided the management units into groups of states that contained doves with similar migrational patterns. This resulted in division of the EMU into six regions, the CMU into three north-south tiers and the WMU into two north-south tiers. Mexico and Central America were divided into eight geographical regions with similar physiographic features and band-recovery patterns (*Figure 5*).

The information provided is derived from direct recoveries of mourning doves banded in each management unit as follows: 396,510 bandings in the EMU during 1966–71 (Hayne and Geissler 1977); 332,314 bandings in the CMU during 1967–74 (Dunks et al. 1982); and 88,590 bandings in the WMU during 1967–75 (Tomlinson et al. 1988). These data were examined in two ways: (1) distribution of recoveries from specific points of origin; and (2) derivation of recoveries in specific harvest areas. These data signify only patterns of hunting harvest, because all recoveries were from hunters or hunting activity. However, because hunting was allowed rather uniformly throughout the migration corridors, the pattern of direct recoveries generally should reflect migratory patterns as well.

Eastern Management Unit

Doves from the EMU generally migrate south and southeasterly and winter within the unit (*Figure 6*). Only 2 percent of the recoveries originating within the EMU were reported from outside the unit (*Table 5*). The major recovery areas were: the Carolinas for doves from the New England and mid-Atlantic states; Alabama, Georgia and Florida for doves from northcentral states; and Louisiana and Texas also for doves from northcentral states.

New England. Most doves from this region move through the mid-Atlantic states into the Carolinas and Georgia where they apparently winter (*Table 5*). Some birds continue into Alabama and

WESTERN   CENTRAL   EASTERN

Coastal WMU
Interior WMU
West CMU
Mid-CMU
East CMU
North-central
New England
Mid-Atlantic
Mid-central
Carolinas
South

1
2
3
4 5
6
7
8

1 NORTHWEST COAST
2 NORTHERN HIGHLANDS
3 NORTHEAST COAST
4 WESTERN HIGHLANDS
5 CENTRAL HIGHLANDS
6 SOUTHERN
7 YUCATAN PENINSULA
8 CENTRAL AMERICA

Figure 5. Reference areas used to describe distribution and derivation of mourning dove recoveries.

Florida and even to Mississippi and Louisiana, but no emigrating doves were recovered outside the EMU.

Northcentral. Emigration from the northcentral states is two-pronged—one segment migrates into Alabama, Georgia and Florida and the other into Louisiana and Texas *(Table 5)*. Doves from these upper Midwest states are particularly important to the harvest in Florida.

Although most recoveries of doves banded in northcentral states are confined to the EMU, doves from Wisconsin and Illinois also show a tendency to migrate into the CMU (particularly Texas) and Mexico.

Mid-Atlantic. Emigration from this region follows the pattern of that from New England. Most doves not recovered within state of banding were recovered in the Carolinas and Georgia *(Table 5)*. This suggests that their southern terminus is in that area. No doves were recovered outside of the EMU.

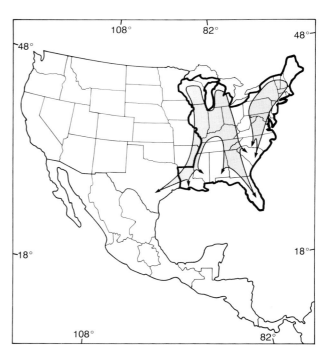

Figure 6. General migrational distribution of mourning doves banded in the Eastern Management Unit.

Table 5. Percentage distribution of direct recoveries of all mourning doves banded preseason in the Eastern Management Unit, 1966–71.[a]

Area of recovery	Eastern Management Unit area where banded			
	New England	Northcentral	Mid-Atlantic	Midcentral
Eastern Management Unit				
Rhode Island	13.1 (6.3)			
Pennsylvania	58.3 (6.3)	0.1 (0.2)	0.6 (4.8)	
New England	71.4 (12.6)	0.1 (0.2)	0.6 (4.8)	
Illinois		35.6 (1.6)		0.8 (7.5)
Northcentral		35.6 (1.6)		0.8 (7.5)
Delaware	1.5 (4.6)		0.5 (2.1)	
Maryland	3.6 (11.0)	0.1 (0.2)	34.6 (0.5)	
Virginia	3.4 (10.5)	0.4 (0.6)	52.1 (4.8)	
West Virginia			1.4 (0.0)	
Mid-Atlantic	8.5 (26.1)	0.5 (0.8)	88.6 (7.4)	
Kentucky		3.1 (4.7)		17.9 (13.4)
Tennessee	0.3 (0.8)	1.4 (2.2)	0.2 (1.6)	73.4 (5.9)
Midcentral	0.3 (0.8)	4.5 (6.9)	0.1 (1.6)	91.3 (19.3)
North Carolina	4.8 (14.8)	1.2 (1.8)	3.5 (28.6)	0.2 (2.1)
South Carolina	5.1 (15.6)	1.9 (2.9)	2.5 (20.1)	0.2 (1.6)
Carolinas	9.9 (30.4)	3.1 (4.7)	6.0 (48.7)	0.4 (3.7)
Georgia	4.6 (13.9)	7.1 (10.8)	2.7 (21.7)	0.5 (4.8)
Florida	2.5 (7.6)	14.9 (22.7)	1.4 (11.1)	1.4 (13.4)
Alabama	1.7 (12.2)	8.0 (12.2)	0.4 (3.2)	1.0 (9.1)
Mississippi	0.4 (1.3)	3.2 (4.9)	0.1 (1.1)	2.0 (20.3)
Louisiana	0.7 (2.1)	11.0 (16.9)	0.1 (0.5)	1.2 (11.2)
South	9.9 (37.1)	44.2 (67.5)	4.7 (37.6)	6.1 (58.8)
Subtotal	100.0 (99.9)	87.9 (81.6)	100.1 (100.1)	98.9 (89.3)
Central Management Unit				
Missouri		1.9 (2.9)		0.6 (5.3)
Kansas		0.4 (0.6)		
Oklahoma		0.1 (0.2)		
Arkansas		0.1 (0.2)		0.3 (3.2)
Texas		6.7 (10.2)		0.2 (2.1)
Subtotal	0.0 (0.0)	9.2 (14.1)	0.0 (0.0)	1.1 (10.7)
Mexico				
Northwest Coast		0.1 (0.2)		
Northeast Coast		0.1 (0.2)		
Western Highlands		1.9 (2.9)		
Central Highlands		0.3 (0.4)		
Southern		0.1 (0.2)		
Unknown		0.1 (0.2)		
Subtotal	0.0 (0.0)	2.7 (4.1)	0.0 (0.0)	0.0 (0.0)
Central America subtotal	0.0 (0.0)	0.1 (0.2)	0.0 (0.0)	0.0 (0.0)
Total	100.0 (99.9)	99.9 (100.0)	100.0 (100.0)	100.0 (100.0)
Number of recoveries	725 (237)	779 (510)	1,536 (189)	1,750 (187)

[a]Percentages in parentheses represent data from which in-banding-state recoveries are excluded.

Midcentral. Doves emigrating from Kentucky and Tennessee fan into the five southern states of Louisiana, Mississippi, Alabama, Georgia and Florida (*Table 5*). In addition, a few birds (11 percent of out-of-state recoveries) were reported from the CMU. Because more than 90 percent of the recoveries of doves originating within this region were taken in the region, some population segments may be nonmigratory.

Carolinas. Recoveries of doves banded in the

Table 5. (continued)

Carolinas		South		Total EMU	
				0.7	(0.7)
				3.0	(1.2)
				3.7	(1.9)
		Tr	(0.3)	2.0	(1.2)
		Tr	(0.3)	2.0	(1.2)
				0.1	(0.7)
		Tr	(0.1)	3.9	(1.4)
0.5	(5.5)	Tr	(0.3)	5.9	(2.5)
				0.2	(0.0)
0.5	(5.5)	Tr	(0.4)	10.1	(4.6)
				2.4	(2.4)
		0.7	(7.5)	9.4	(3.9)
		0.7	(7.5)	11.8	(6.3)
40.5	(40.5)	0.1	(0.7)	7.1	(9.3)
55.2	(11.0)	0.1	(0.7)	9.3	(5.9)
95.7	(51.5)	0.2	(1.4)	16.4	(15.2)
2.6	(29.5)	21.9	(24.3)	12.3	(18.2)
1.0	(11.0)	11.9	(16.2)	7.5	(15.6)
0.2	(2.5)	22.4	(9.4)	12.1	(8.3)
		11.5	(5.1)	6.3	(5.1)
		29.0	(10.9)	15.6	(9.4)
3.8	(43.0)	96.7	(65.9)	53.8	(56.6)
100.0	(100.0)	97.6	(75.5)	98.0	(85.8)
		Tr	(0.3)	0.2	(1.3)
		Tr	(0.1)	Tr	(0.2)
				Tr	(Tr)
		0.5	(4.8)	0.3	(2.0)
		1.8	(18.1)	1.3	(9.1)
0.0	(0.0)	2.3	(23.3)	1.8	(12.6)
				Tr	(Tr)
				Tr	(Tr)
		0.1	(0.8)	0.1	(1.0)
				Tr	(0.1)
		Tr	(0.1)	Tr	(0.1)
				Tr	(Tr)
0.0	(0.0)	0.1	(1.0)	0.2	(1.4)
0.0	(0.0)	Tr	(0.3)	Tr	(0.1)
100.0	(100.0)	100.0	(100.1)	100.0	(99.9)
3,245	(200)	7,306	(709)	14,341	(2,032)

Carolinas indicate that these populations are relatively sedentary and do not migrate to other areas. Ninety-six percent of the recoveries of Carolina-banded birds were taken within the region and about 4 percent in Georgia and Florida, immediately south *(Table 5).*

South. This region is a major winter recipient of migrating mourning doves from the EMU and adjacent states of the CMU *(tables 5 and 6).* Doves banded in Florida are essentially nonmigratory, whereas birds from the other southern states evinced some migratory tendencies despite the states' desirability as wintering areas *(Table 5).* Most out-of-state recoveries of doves banded in Georgia were reported from the adjoining states of Alabama and Florida. Migrating Alabama doves moved mainly into Georgia and Florida, but doves emigrating from Mississippi and Louisiana moved westward and southward into Arkansas, Texas and Mexico.

Central Management Unit

The migratory pattern of doves banded in the CMU can be characterized as a giant fan (Dunks et al. 1982), with doves moving generally south into Texas, Mexico and Central America but with a sizable segment moving southeast into the EMU and a smaller group southwest into or through the WMU *(Figure 7).* The major recovery areas appear to be Texas and the Western Highlands of Mexico for most CMU breeding populations, Florida and Louisiana for birds from certain sections of the East CMU, and Central America *(Table 6).*

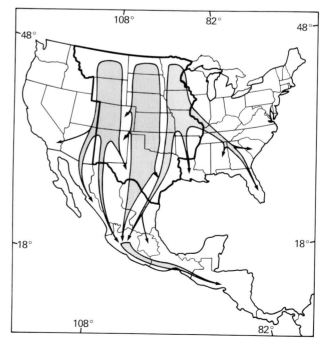

Figure 7. General migrational distribution of mourning doves banded in the Central Management Unit, according to East, Mid and West tiers.

Table 6. Percentage distribution of direct recoveries of all mourning doves banded preseason in the Central and Western management units, 1967–75.[a]

Area of recovery	Management unit area where banded							
	East CMU		Mid-CMU		West CMU		Total CMU	
Central Management Unit								
Missouri	31.4	(0.8)	0.1	(0.4)			9.4	(0.5)
Arkansas	23.7	(1.1)					7.0	(0.4)
East CMU	55.1	(1.9)	0.1	(0.4)			16.4	(0.9)
South Dakota	0.2	(0.4)	18.4	(0.4)	0.2	(0.3)	10.9	(0.4)
Kansas	1.1	(2.4)	8.5	(1.6)	0.2	(0.3)	5.3	(1.6)
Oklahoma	1.6	(3.5)	6.4	(1.9)	0.5	(0.9)	4.3	(2.3)
Texas	16.0	(34.9)	49.0	(42.4)	7.1	(12.9)	34.3	(35.0)
Mid-CMU	18.9	(41.2)	82.3	(46.3)	8.0	(14.4)	54.8	(39.3)
Wyoming					0.6	(0.0)	0.1	(0.0)
Colorado	0.1	(0.3)	0.4	(1.2)	27.7	(7.6)	3.5	(1.9)
New Mexico	0.1	(0.3)	0.9	(2.7)	26.9	(10.9)	3.7	(3.2)
West CMU	0.2	(0.6)	1.3	(3.9)	55.2	(18.5)	7.3	(5.1)
Subtotal	74.2	(43.7)	83.8	(50.5)	63.1	(32.8)	78.5	(45.3)
Eastern Management Unit								
Northcentral	1.3	(2.8)			0.3	(0.6)	0.4	(1.1)
Mid-Atlantic	0.1	(0.1)					Tr	(Tr)
Midcentral	0.3	(0.7)	Tr	(0.1)			0.1	(0.3)
Carolinas	0.6	(1.4)					0.2	(0.5)
South	13.8	(30.1)	1.2	(3.7)			4.8	(12.2)
Subtotal	16.1	(35.2)	1.2	(3.8)	0.3	(0.6)	5.5	(14.2)
Western Management Unit								
Idaho					0.3	(0.6)	Tr	(0.1)
Utah					0.3	(0.6)	Tr	(0.1)
Arizona	0.1	(0.1)	0.2	(0.7)	3.1	(5.6)	0.5	(1.3)
Interior WMU	0.1	(0.1)	0.2	(0.7)	3.7	(6.8)	0.6	(1.5)
Washington							0.0	(0.0)
Oregon							0.0	(0.0)
Nevada							0.0	(0.0)
California	0.3	(0.6)	Tr	(0.1)	1.9	(3.5)	0.3	(0.8)
Coastal WMU	0.3	(0.6)	Tr	(0.1)	1.9	(3.5)	0.3	(0.8)
Subtotal	0.3	(0.7)	0.3	(0.8)	5.6	(10.3)	0.9	(2.3)
Mexico								
Northwest Coast	0.3	(0.6)	0.6	(2.0)	3.5	(6.5)	0.9	(2.2)
Northern Highlands	0.3	(0.6)	0.2	(0.5)	1.1	(2.1)	0.3	(0.8)
Northeast Coast	0.1	(0.3)	0.2	(0.6)	0.2	(0.3)	0.2	(0.4)
Western Highlands	5.7	(12.4)	10.0	(30.5)	24.2	(44.0)	10.4	(26.5)
Central Highlands	0.6	(1.3)	1.0	(3.0)	0.8	(1.5)	0.8	(2.1)
Southern	0.4	(1.0)	0.4	(1.1)			0.3	(0.9)
Unknown	0.2	(0.4)	0.3	(0.9)	0.5	(0.9)	0.3	(0.7)
Subtotal	7.5	(16.5)	12.6	(38.5)	30.3	(55.1)	13.2	(33.6)
Central America subtotal	1.8	(3.9)	2.1	(6.4)	0.6	(1.2)	1.8	(4.5)
Total	99.9	(100.0)	100.0	(100.0)	99.9	(100.0)	99.9	(99.9)
Number of recoveries	1,564	(716)	3,081	(1,011)	621	(341)	5,266	(2,068)

[a] Percentages in parentheses represent data from which in-banding-state recoveries are excluded.

East CMU. Emigration from this tier of states appears to be directed mainly south and southwest into Louisiana, Texas and the Western Highlands of Mexico *(Table 6 and Figure 7)*. Some birds continue into Central America as far south as Nicaragua. However, those birds from the eastern edge of the tier evidence a tendency to move southeasterly into Alabama, Georgia and Florida. The states of Min-

Table 6. (continued)

Interior WMU		Coastal WMU		Total WMU	
				0.0	(0.0)
				0.0	(0.0)
				0.0	(0.0)
				0.0	(0.0)
				0.0	(0.0)
				0.0	(0.0)
0.4	(3.0)	0.2	(1.4)	0.3	(1.9)
0.4	(3.0)	0.2	(1.4)	0.3	(1.9)
				0.0	(0.0)
		0.1	(0.7)	0.1	(0.5)
0.3	(2.3)			0.1	(0.7)
0.3	(2.3)	0.1	(0.7)	0.2	(1.2)
0.7	(5.3)	0.3	(2.1)	0.5	(3.1)
				0.0	(0.0)
				0.0	(0.0)
				0.0	(0.0)
				0.0	(0.0)
				0.0	(0.0)
0.0	(0.0)	0.0	(0.0)	0.0	(0.0)
1.0	(0.0)	0.1	(0.3)	0.4	(0.2)
7.9	(0.0)	0.1	(0.7)	2.9	(0.5)
81.7	(28.0)	3.4	(22.0)	31.1	(23.9)
90.6	(28.0)	3.6	(23.0)	34.4	(24.6)
0.2	(1.5)	19.0	(0.3)	12.3	(0.7)
		8.6	(0.0)	5.5	(0.0)
0.1	(0.8)	3.6	(1.7)	2.4	(1.4)
2.7	(20.5)	58.4	(31.0)	38.7	(27.7)
3.0	(22.8)	89.6	(33.1)	58.9	(29.8)
93.6	(50.8)	93.2	(56.1)	93.3	(54.4)
1.2	(9.1)	1.5	(9.4)	1.4	(9.3)
0.3	(2.3)	0.1	(0.7)	0.2	(1.2)
0.1	(0.8)			Tr	(0.2)
3.6	(27.3)	4.9	(31.4)	4.4	(30.1)
0.1	(0.8)	0.1	(0.3)	0.1	(0.5)
				0.0	(0.0)
0.3	(2.3)			0.0	(0.7)
5.5	(42.4)	6.5	(41.8)	6.2	(42.0)
0.2	(1.5)	0.0	(0.0)	0.1	(0.5)
100.0	(100.0)	100.0	(100.0)	100.1	(100.0)
1,012	(132)	1,847	(287)	2,859	(419)

nesota, Iowa and Missouri, as in the northcentral region of the EMU, contribute a significant number of doves to the EMU harvest (Dunks et al. 1982).

Mid-CMU. This tier of states encompasses "America's breadbasket" and, according to Call-

count estimates, contains more than 35 percent of all mourning doves in the United States (Dunks et al. 1982). The migratory pathway for birds from this tier runs south into Texas and Mexico, then bends southeastward into Central America *(Table 6 and Figure 7)*. The main recovery areas for emigrating populations are Texas, the Western and Central highlands of Mexico, and Central America as far south as Costa Rica. Although a few birds have been recovered in the EMU, particularly Louisiana, they comprise a statistically insignificant part of the total.

Doves from breeding populations of Texas, especially south Texas, appear to be relatively sedentary. Less than 8 percent of recoveries from Texas-banded doves are reported outside of Texas, and most of those are in Mexico (Dunks et al. 1982).

West CMU. Doves from this group of states also generally migrate straight south through the tier into Mexico *(Table 6 and Figure 7)*. Nevertheless, some birds move southeastward into Texas and others follow a path into and through California and Arizona to northwestern Mexico. The main recovery area appears to be the Western Highlands of Mexico, with a few birds traveling as far south as Guatemala and El Salvador in Central America.

Western Management Unit

Doves from the WMU migrate south and southeast *(Figure 8)*. Few doves were recovered

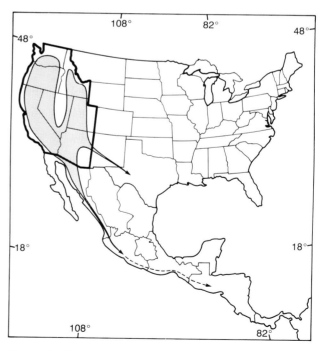

Figure 8. General migrational distribution of mourning doves banded in the Western Management Unit.

Table 7. Weighted derivation (in percentage) of the mourning dove harvest in selected wintering areas of southeastern states, direct recoveries, 1966–71.[a]

Contributing area	Eastern Management Unit recovery area			
	Louisiana	Mississippi	Alabama	Georgia
Eastern Management Unit				
New York	0.3 (0.6)	0.1 (0.4)	0.4 (1.4)	0.9 (3.2)
Massachusetts			Tr (0.1)	0.1 (0.3)
Rhode Island				0.1 (0.3)
New Jersey				0.2 (0.6)
Pennsylvania		0.2 (1.8)	0.4 (1.3)	0.4 (1.4)
New England	0.3 (0.6)	0.3 (2.2)	0.8 (2.8)	1.6 (5.8)
Wisconsin	5.8 (10.5)	1.4 (10.4)	4.1 (14.4)	1.8 (6.4)
Michigan	3.7 (6.7)	3.2 (24.0)	2.7 (9.4)	2.3 (8.3)
Ohio	1.2 (2.2)	0.4 (3.1)	0.8 (2.7)	0.7 (2.6)
Indiana	0.6 (1.0)	0.1 (1.0)	0.9 (3.3)	0.4 (1.5)
Illinois	5.1 (9.2)	0.9 (6.7)	3.0 (10.6)	2.8 (10.0)
Northcentral	16.3 (29.6)	5.9 (45.2)	11.5 (40.4)	8.1 (28.8)
Delaware				0.1 (0.3)
Maryland			Tr (0.1)	0.2 (0.8)
Virginia	0.1 (0.1)	0.2 (1.7)	0.4 (1.3)	2.0 (7.0)
West Virginia			0.1 (0.5)	0.2 (0.6)
Mid-Atlantic	0.1 (0.1)	0.2 (1.7)	0.5 (1.9)	2.4 (8.7)
Kentucky	2.6 (4.8)	0.3 (2.2)	0.4 (1.3)	0.6 (2.2)
Tennessee	0.6 (1.2)	1.6 (12.1)	0.8 (2.9)	0.3 (1.1)
Midcentral	3.3 (6.0)	1.9 (14.3)	1.2 (4.2)	0.9 (3.3)
North Carolina			0.4 (1.3)	0.2 (0.9)
South Carolina			0.1 (0.2)	3.1 (11.1)
Carolinas	0.0 (0.0)	0.0 (0.0)	0.4 (1.5)	3.4 (12.0)
Georgia		Tr (0.4)	3.3 (11.4)	72.0 (−)
Florida			Tr (Tr)	0.2 (0.7)
Alabama	0.7 (1.3)	0.5 (3.7)	71.5 (−)	6.5 (23.2)
Mississippi	7.8 (14.1)	86.8 (−)	0.4 (1.3)	
Louisiana	45.0 (−)	0.4 (3.2)	0.2 (0.6)	0.1 (0.2)
South	53.5 (15.4)	87.8 (7.3)	75.3 (13.3)	78.7 (24.1)
Subtotal	73.5 (51.7)	96.1 (70.7)	89.8 (64.1)	95.1 (82.7)
Central Management Unit				
Minnesota	3.8 (7.0)	1.0 (7.9)	1.0 (3.6)	0.9 (3.4)
Iowa	4.8 (8.7)	0.1 (0.7)	2.6 (9.2)	1.4 (5.0)
Missouri	7.3 (13.2)	1.2 (9.2)	2.8 (10.0)	2.3 (8.1)
Arkansas	2.4 (4.3)	0.3 (2.2)	1.7 (5.9)	0.3 (0.9)
East CMU	18.2 (33.2)	2.6 (20.0)	8.2 (28.7)	4.9 (17.4)
North Dakota	1.6 (2.8)		1.1 (3.8)	
South Dakota	2.0 (3.6)	0.3 (1.9)	0.5 (1.6)	
Nebraska	0.6 (1.2)	0.6 (4.5)		
Oklahoma	1.4 (2.6)			
Texas	2.7 (4.8)	0.4 (3.1)	0.5 (1.7)	
Mid-CMU	8.3 (15.0)	1.3 (9.5)	2.0 (7.1)	0.0 (0.0)
Subtotal	26.5 (48.2)	3.9 (29.5)	10.2 (35.8)	4.9 (17.4)
Total	100.0 (99.9)	100.0 (100.2)	100.0 (99.9)	100.0 (100.1)
Number of recoveries	2,330 (285)	924 (122)	1,777 (206)	1,816 (391)

[a]Percentages in parentheses represent data from which in-banding-state recoveries are excluded; (−) indicates state or region from which in-banding-state data were omitted.

south of Mexico's Western Highlands, and 70 percent of the unit's recoveries were reported from California and Arizona, suggesting that those two states are important as wintering areas *(Table 6)*.

Interior WMU. The migrational pattern of doves from this tier of states appears to be straight

Table 7. (continued)

Eastern Management Unit recovery area					
Florida		South EMU		Carolinas	
0.8	(1.1)	0.6	(1.7)	1.3	(12.6)
0.1	(0.1)	0.1	(0.2)	0.1	(1.0)
0.1	(0.2)	Tr	(0.1)	0.2	(1.5)
0.1	(0.1)	0.1	(0.2)	0.2	(1.7)
0.2	(0.3)	0.3	(0.8)	0.6	(5.5)
1.3	(1.8)	1.0	(3.0)	2.3	(22.3)
8.4	(12.1)	4.2	(12.9)	0.7	(6.7)
8.9	(12.7)	4.1	(12.5)	0.6	(5.9)
1.2	(1.8)	0.9	(2.6)	0.3	(2.5)
1.9	(2.8)	0.8	(2.6)		
8.3	(11.9)	4.0	(12.4)	0.7	(6.7)
28.7	(41.3)	14.0	(43.0)	2.3	(21.9)
		Tr	(0.1)	0.1	(1.0)
0.2	(0.3)	0.1	(0.3)	0.3	(2.8)
1.5	(2.1)	1.0	(3.0)	3.0	(29.2)
		0.1	(0.2)	0.4	(3.7)
1.7	(2.4)	1.2	(3.7)	3.8	(36.7)
4.9	(7.1)	1.7	(5.2)	0.2	(2.3)
0.9	(1.3)	0.8	(2.4)	0.2	(1.6)
5.9	(8.4)	2.5	(7.6)	0.4	(3.9)
0.8	(1.2)	0.3	(1.0)	46.9	
1.3	(1.8)	1.2	(3.5)	42.7	
2.1	(3.0)	1.5	(4.6)	89.6	(—)
3.1	(4.5)	21.6		0.3	(3.1)
30.2	(—)	6.4			
2.5	(3.6)	19.4			
2.5	(3.6)	13.7			
0.3	(0.5)	6.3			
38.7	(12.2)	67.4	(—)	0.3	(3.1)
78.3	(69.1)	87.6	(61.9)	98.8	(87.9)
3.2	(4.5)	1.8	(5.6)	0.1	(1.0)
4.4	(6.3)	2.6	(7.9)	0.4	(3.7)
10.9	(15.6)	4.7	(14.5)	0.6	(5.9)
1.9	(2.7)	1.2	(3.8)	0.1	(1.4)
20.3	(29.1)	10.4	(31.8)	1.3	(12.1)
		0.5	(1.4)	0.0	(0.0)
1.3	(1.9)	0.7	(2.1)	0.0	(0.0)
		0.2	(0.5)	0.0	(0.0)
		0.2	(0.6)	0.0	(0.0)
		0.5	(1.6)	0.0	(0.0)
1.3	(1.9)	2.1	(6.3)	0.0	(0.0)
21.7	(31.0)	12.4	(38.1)	1.3	(12.1)
100.0	(100.1)	100.0	(100.0)	100.0	(100.0)
1,136	(382)	7,983	(919)	2,361	(213)

south into southern California and Arizona and along the west coast of Mexico to the Western Highlands (*Table 6 and Figure 8*). A small contingent moves southeastward into Texas and New Mexico. Judging from the high proportion of recoveries in California and Arizona, many doves probably winter there (*Table 6*). However, a sizable contingent also moves into the Western Highlands. Only 2 doves were recovered south of there—both in Central America. The large numbers of doves produced and recovered in Arizona indicate a strong nonmigratory tendency.

Coastal WMU. Migrating doves from the coastal states of the WMU tend to stay within this tier and then bend into Arizona and Mexico, although a segment from Washington appears to move southeastward through Idaho and Utah to Texas (*Figure 8*). Principal recovery areas are in southern California and Arizona and the Western Highlands of Mexico (*Table 6*). No recoveries were recorded south of the Western Highlands.

WINTERING AREAS REEXAMINED

It is difficult to pinpoint wintering areas of doves from recovery records because many birds may have been in transit when harvested or may have arrived in a wintering area that was preconceived as a way station. Despite this drawback, there appear to be six general areas to which breeding mourning doves of the United States migrate and overwinter. These are: (1) the Carolinas; (2) the South EMU, including Louisiana, Mississippi, Alabama, Georgia and Florida; (3) Texas; (4) California and Arizona; (5) Mexico; and (6) Central America. Each receives doves from divergent breeding locations of the U.S. For better understanding of migration, the derivation of harvest in each area is considered below (data from Hayne and Geissler 1977, Dunks et al. 1982, Tomlinson et al. 1988). Derivation data were weighted to adjust for differences in banding efforts among origination states, as well as for the varying sizes of the areas and density of breeding doves within them (Kiel 1959, Dunks et al. 1982).

Carolinas

Although about 90 percent of mourning doves harvested in the Carolinas originate within the two states (*Table 7*), harvested doves in the Carolinas from other source areas probably exceed 600,000 (Hayne and Geissler 1977). Of that portion of the harvest that comes from other areas, New England and mid-Atlantic states are the most important contributors (59 percent). Doves from the Northcentral EMU and East CMU states comprise 22 percent and 12 percent, respectively. Doves from the CMU, however, largely bypass North Carolina and move into South Carolina. Modest numbers of birds also come from Kentucky and Tennessee (4 percent) and

Georgia (3 percent). The relatively mild climate and abundant food supply of the Carolinas undoubtedly make this region ideal to support its own production of doves as well as that of most of the eastern seaboard.

South EMU

The southern states of Louisiana, Mississippi, Alabama, Georgia and Florida are winter hosts for most of the migrating mourning doves of the eastern and midcentral United States *(Table 7)*. Although the proportion of the dove harvest that originates from outside each state varies considerably—Louisiana 55 percent, Mississippi 13 percent, Alabama 28 percent, Georgia 28 percent, Florida 70 percent—all states harvest large numbers of doves from other areas. The most important out-of-state contributors to the South EMU harvest are the Northcentral EMU (43 percent) and the East CMU (32 percent). Depending on the state of harvest, 46 to 78 percent of the immigrants originate from these two areas. The midcentral states of Kentucky and Tennessee contribute about 8 percent of the South EMU harvest.

As might be expected, nearly 50 percent of mourning dove immigrants to Louisiana come from the CMU and less than 1 percent from the eastern seaboard *(Table 7)*. Thirty percent of Louisiana's out-of-state harvest comes from northcentral states, 6 percent from midcentral states and 15 percent from other South EMU states.

Mississippi, Alabama and Florida demonstrate nearly identical immigration patterns. Of doves migrating to these states, 40 to 45 percent originated from the Northcentral EMU, 30 to 36 percent from the CMU and 17 to 20 percent from Midcentral EMU states and other South EMU states *(Table 7)*. Of the harvest originating from outside these states, only 4 to 7 percent came from New England, the Carolinas and the mid-Atlantic states combined.

Georgia exhibits a closer immigration affinity with the Carolinas than do other South EMU states *(Table 7)*. Nearly 27 percent of immigrating doves originate from New England and mid-Atlantic states and the Carolinas. However, northcentral states (29 percent) and CMU states (17 percent) also are important contributors to the Georgia harvest.

Texas

Because about 92 percent of the recoveries of mourning doves banded in Texas are recovered in the state (Dunks et al. 1982), it is assumed that many of them winter in the state. If this assumption is correct, Texas probably also is a major wintering area for doves migrating from the north. However, this state undoubtedly serves as a resting area for doves that eventually migrate farther south. In either case, Texas appears to be important as a reservoir for migrating doves.

Approximately 41 percent of the harvest in Texas consists of immigrant mourning doves *(Table 8)*. Of this segment, by far the most important contributing area is the Mid-CMU, accounting for 70 percent of the total. Proportional contributions to Texas from this tier increase by state from north to south, leading one to speculate that doves from the far north rapidly migrate through Texas into Mexico, whereas birds from Kansas and Oklahoma initially move into Texas and then linger before continuing south. The only other contributing area of importance is the East CMU (20 percent). The EMU, mainly northcentral states, contributes about 5 percent of the total, the West CMU 4 percent and the WMU less than 2 percent. Dunks (1977) and Dunks et al. (1982) separated Texas into north and south zones corresponding to hunting areas in existence during the analysis period. Both harvest zones had similar derivation patterns, but the south zone tended to receive a larger proportion of its harvest from the EMU than did the north zone, and the north zone had a relatively larger proportion from the West CMU.

California and Arizona

Southern portions of California and Arizona contain excellent winter habitats with sufficient food and water for mourning doves. As in Texas, most direct recoveries (more than 90 percent) of doves banded in these two states were taken within the state of banding (Tomlinson et al. 1988). This suggests that many doves produced in the states also winter there.

Of all direct recoveries in Arizona and California, 11 to 19 percent, respectively, are of doves originating outside of those states *(Table 8)*. Of California recoveries with out-of-state origin, 66 percent came from other Coastal WMU states (mainly Oregon—41 percent), 25 percent from Interior WMU states and less than 10 percent from the CMU. Arizona received 80 percent of its out-of-state recoveries from the WMU (45 percent, Coastal WMU; 35 percent, Interior WMU) and about 20 percent from the CMU, mainly the West CMU.

Whether doves banded in more northern areas actually winter in Arizona and California or are

Migration • 73

Table 8. Weighted derivation (in percentage) of the mourning dove harvest in selected wintering areas of southwestern United States, Mexico and Central America, direct recoveries, 1967–75.[a]

Contributing area	California		Arizona		Texas		Mexico	Central America
Western Management Unit								
Washington	2.9	(15.4)	0.2	(2.1)	0.1	(0.2)	2.0	
Oregon	7.9	(41.4)	0.8	(7.0)			3.6	
Nevada	1.8	(9.5)	1.9	(17.4)	0.1	(0.3)	2.4	
California	81.0	(—)	2.1	(18.7)	Tr	(0.1)	5.2	
Coastal WMU	93.6	(66.3)	5.0	(45.2)	0.2	(0.5)	13.2	0.0
Idaho	1.9	(10.2)	1.2	(11.1)			1.8	2.9
Utah	1.0	(5.3)	2.6	(23.6)	0.1	(0.1)	1.5	0.6
Arizona	1.7	(9.0)	88.9	(—)	0.2	(0.5)	6.6	
Interior WMU	4.6	(24.5)	92.8	(34.7)	0.3	(0.7)	9.9	3.5
Subtotal	98.2	(90.8)	97.8	(79.9)	0.5	(1.2)	23.1	3.5
Central Management Unit								
Montana	1.0	(5.2)	0.7	(6.1)	0.3	(0.8)	5.3	1.0
Wyoming	0.2	(0.9)	0.4	(3.6)	0.2	(0.5)	2.8	
Colorado	0.2	(1.3)	0.5	(4.8)	0.5	(1.2)	4.3	1.0
New Mexico					0.5	(1.2)	3.7	0.6
West CMU	1.4	(7.4)	1.6	(14.5)	1.6	(3.8)	16.1	2.6
North Dakota			0.2	(1.9)	3.2	(7.7)	4.7	14.2
South Dakota	0.1	(0.4)	0.2	(2.0)	4.0	(9.7)	6.8	7.5
Nebraska					4.3	(10.5)	10.0	10.9
Kansas					7.2	(17.6)	9.0	24.3
Oklahoma					9.9	(24.4)	12.8	9.1
Texas			0.1	(0.9)	59.2	(—)	8.5	10.0
Mid-CMU	0.1	(0.4)	0.5	(4.9)	87.7	(69.9)	51.8	76.0
Minnesota	0.2	(0.8)	0.1	(0.8)	2.0	(5.0)	2.9	3.5
Iowa					3.1	(7.7)	2.3	7.8
Missouri	0.1	(0.6)			2.1	(5.1)	2.0	4.2
Arkansas					0.8	(2.1)	0.4	1.7
East CMU	0.3	(1.4)	0.1	(0.8)	8.1	(19.8)	7.6	17.2
Subtotal	1.7	(9.2)	2.2	(20.1)	97.4	(93.6)	75.5	95.8
Eastern Management Unit	0.0	(0.0)	0.0	(0.0)	2.1	(5.3)	1.5	0.6
Total	99.9	(100.0)	100.0	(100.0)	100.0	(100.1)	100.1	99.9
Number of recoveries	1,123	(133)	919	(129)	1,978	(901)	902	102

[a] Percentages in parentheses represent data from which in-banding-state recoveries are excluded; (—) indicates state or region from which in-banding-state data were omitted.

migrating through the states to Mexico when harvested is not known. It is probable that both situations occur.

Mexico

Many areas of northern Mexico support breeding populations of mourning doves. During autumn and winter, these birds are joined by emigrating doves from the north. Because little banding of doves has been accomplished in Mexico, the following discussion of derivation pertains only to doves banded in the United States.

Of the 902 direct recoveries in Mexico of doves banded in the United States during 1967 through 1975, 76 percent originated in CMU states, 23 percent in WMU states and less than 2 percent in the EMU (Table 8). The greatest contributor to the harvest in Mexico was the Mid-CMU (52 percent). Next in importance were the West CMU (16 percent), the Coastal WMU (13 percent), the Interior WMU (10 percent) and the East CMU (8 percent).

Although Mexico is a large country with varied terrain, apparently relatively few locations are favored by migrating doves. The most important harvest area is the Western Highlands—a region comprising the five states of Jalisco, Michoacan,

Guanajuato, Colima and Guerrero along Mexico's west coast. More than 78 percent of the recoveries in Mexico were reported from this region *(Table 9)*. Because the Western Highlands contains extensive agricultural land and water sources, it provides excellent habitat for wintering doves.

The Northwest Coast region of Mexico is the next most important harvest area with 10 percent of the immigrating doves *(Table 9)*. However, most of the doves reported from this region probably were in the process of migrating farther south into the Western Highlands when harvested. Southern Sinaloa, with a predominantly irrigated farmland economy, probably is the only location where doves winter in the region.

The Central Highlands, which surround Mexico City, provided a moderate proportion of the Mexican harvest (6 percent), mainly from the two eastern tiers of the CMU and the EMU *(Table 9)*. Few doves are recovered in the huge expanse of the Northern Highlands and Northeast Coast regions. Evidently, doves either bypass or overfly these areas on their way to the Western Highlands. No birds were recovered in the Yucatan Peninsula, which suggests that they neither fly through nor winter there. Likewise, the relatively small number of recoveries in the Southern Mexico region suggests that doves fly through that region and stop only briefly on their way to Central American wintering grounds.

Central America

Of the mourning doves banded in the United States between 1967 and 1975 and recovered south of its border, 11 percent were reported from Central America *(Table 9)*. All five countries reported recoveries, most of which came from Guatemala (46 percent) and El Salvador (28 percent). The wintering area is concentrated along the southern Pacific coast, where extensive clearing of thorn-scrub vegetation has created an agricultural environment geared toward small grains.

Recovery records indicate that the southern terminus for emigrating doves from the United States is Costa Rica (Hayne and Geissler 1977, Dunks et al. 1982, Tomlinson et al. 1988). Nevertheless, a bird banded as a nestling in Iowa on June 1, 1956 was reported recovered in Cartago Valle in Colombia, South America on May 4, 1957 (Maltby 1958). The original record at the Bird Banding Laboratory was checked carefully (D. Dolton personal communication: 1986), and enough inconsistencies were found to question its validity. Even if accurate, the record probably represents a unique occurrence. Mourn-

ing doves generally winter no farther south than northwestern Costa Rica.

Ninety-six percent of the Central American harvest originated in the CMU (76 percent from the Mid-CMU, 17 percent from the East CMU and 3 percent from the West CMU) *(Table 8)*. Most doves from the EMU and WMU apparently stopped far short of Central America, although both areas were represented—EMU 1 percent and WMU 4 percent. Tomlinson et al. (1988) estimated that a dove banded in the CMU was thirteen times as likely to be recovered in Central America as was a dove banded in the WMU. Thus, it appears that a sizable segment of doves from the CMU annually makes the long journey to Central America, whereas birds from other sections of the country winter in the southern United States and Mexico.

DIFFERENCES IN MIGRATION BY AGE AND SEX

Examination of mourning dove band recoveries has revealed that migrational patterns are similar among all age and sex categories (Dunks et al. 1982, Tomlinson et al. 1988). Thus immatures, adult males and adult females from a specific area of origin would be expected to migrate to the same general wintering areas. However, there are differences in the proportions of each cohort that are recovered in the state of banding. For example, in the CMU, the proportion of immature doves taken within the state of banding versus out of state was substantially lower than that of adult males and generally lower than that of adult females (Dunks et al. 1982). Similarly, adult males had a higher probability of being recovered in-state than did adult females. This information indicates that proportionally more immatures had moved to other areas by the time hunting seasons had opened in early September. This led Dunks at al. (1982) to conclude that immature mourning doves are the first population segment to begin southward migration, followed by adult females and finally by adult males. A similar conclusion for doves banded in the WMU was reached by Tomlinson et al. (1988).

Tomlinson et al. (1960) and Truett (1966) color-marked doves during summer in Missouri and Arizona, respectively, to determine chronology of migration. Immatures in Missouri disappeared within two weeks of initial capture and marking, whereas some marked adults were observed throughout the rest of the summer. In Arizona, immatures congregated in feeding flocks until mid-July, after which they left the general area where marked. Both studies concluded that immature doves wan-

Table 9. Weighted distribution of the Latin American mourning dove harvest by Mexican state and Central American country, 1967–75. All doves, direct recoveries.

Harvest region	Number of recoveries	Weighted recoveries	Mexican or Central American harvest (percentage)	Latin American harvest (percentage)
Mexico				
Baja California	13	121.76	2.0	1.8
Nayarit	12	76.16	1.3	1.1
Sinaloa	56	367.58	6.2	5.5
Sonora	6	45.23	0.8	0.7
Northwest Coast	87	610.73	10.2	9.1
Aguascalientes	0			
Chihuahua	3	11.84	0.2	0.2
Durango	3	14.59	0.2	0.2
Zacatecas	15	107.14	1.8	1.6
Northern Highlands	21	133.57	2.2	2.0
Coahuila	2	12.84	0.2	0.2
Nuevo Leon	3	18.44	0.3	0.3
San Luis Potosi	3	13.16	0.2	0.2
Tamaulipas	3	13.87	0.2	0.2
Northeast Coast	11	58.31	1.0	0.9
Colima	16	83.33	1.4	1.2
Guanajuato	125	894.71	15.0	13.3
Guerrero	35	217.31	3.6	3.2
Jalisco	265	1,832.80	30.7	27.3
Michoacan	253	1,640.00	27.5	24.5
Western Highlands	694	4,668.15	78.2	69.6
Hidalgo	5	43.21	0.7	0.6
Mexico	7	59.28	1.0	0.9
Mexico, D.F.	2	7.37	0.1	0.1
Morelos	19	144.64	2.4	2.2
Puebla	10	61.74	1.0	0.9
Queretaro	5	39.84	0.7	0.6
Tlaxcala	1	6.98	0.1	0.1
Central Highlands	49	363.06	6.1	5.4
Chiapas	2	10.49	0.2	0.2
Oaxaca	6	44.96	0.8	0.7
Veracruz	12	82.36	1.4	1.2
Southern Mexico	20	137.81	2.3	2.1
Belize[a]	0			
Campeche	0			
Quintana Roo	0			
Tabasco	0			
Yucatan	0			
Yucatan Peninsula	0			
Subtotal[b]	882	5,971.63	100.0	89.0
Central America				
Guatemala	45	338.63	46.1	5.1
El Salvador	30	204.10	27.8	3.0
Honduras	12	67.78	9.2	1.0
Nicaragua	13	103.91	14.1	1.5
Costa Rica	2	20.06	2.7	0.3
Subtotal	102	734.53	100.0	11.0
Total Latin America[b]	984	6,706.16		100.0

[a] The Central American country of Belize is included in the Yucatan Peninsula for convenience.
[b] Excludes 20 direct recoveries in Mexico of unknown harvest location.

der randomly during summer, with interchange of individuals among flocks, and then begin migration in late summer.

In another Arizona study, Blankenship et al. (1967) compared the probable September ages of immatures banded in summer with ages of birds collected from September hunting samples. Their data, based on wing-aging techniques, suggested that a sizable percentage (16 to 29) of banded birds should have molted the tenth primary by September 1. In the wing collection, however, fewer than 4 percent of the sample had completed molt. They concluded that many early hatched young doves had migrated from the study area by early September and were unavailable to be harvested locally. A low age ratio (0.79:1) of recovered doves from Arizona supported that conclusion. Thus, it is probable that immatures initiate migration in August, followed by adult females and then adult males, although mixing by individuals of each cohort may occur during any part of the process.

CHRONOLOGY

Spring Migration

Timing of the mourning dove spring migration is not completely understood because the presence of overwintering populations in many areas masks the return phenomenon. When the annual Call-count Survey technique was being developed, researchers conducted weekly counts to identify the most suitable period to conduct the operational surveys. The counts—from such diverse areas as Wisconsin, Tennessee, Ohio and Georgia—indicated that calling activity peaked in late April and early May and then plateaued from late May to mid-July (McGowan 1952, Duvall and Robbins 1952, Southeastern Association of Game and Fish Commissioners 1957). Researchers recommended that the survey be conducted during May 20 to June 10—the plateau period thought to be after all migrants had returned to breeding areas.

Hanson and Kossack (1963) stated that the principal movements of doves into Illinois took place during the last half of April but that migratory flocks had been observed as late as mid-May. Ginn (1950) documented that the first influx of doves into Indiana also occurred in April. In a study of breeding doves in Minnesota, Harris et al. (1963) noted that a few doves appeared near breeding areas in late March and began cooing. Additional birds arrived during April, and nesting began. By June 3, nesting was in full swing and 200 adults were estimated on the 160-acre (65 ha) study area.

It is concluded that spring migration probably begins in March, progresses slowly during April and terminates in mid- to late May for most areas of the United States. Perhaps the northward movement ends earlier in the south and later in the north; however, the time disparity does not appear to be great—possibly no more than two weeks.

Autumn Migration

Once immature doves become independent of their parents, they begin to flock with other young birds (Hanson and Kossack 1963). Color-marking and banding studies have shown that few young birds remain in natal areas longer than two or three weeks (Tomlinson et al. 1960, Truett 1966, P. Smith personal communication: 1984). These flocks, which have been seen as early as mid-June (Rensel 1952), apparently wander in quest of food sources, sometimes north of the natal areas.

As summer progresses, flocks grow larger and are composed of both young and adults that have finished nesting. Random movements continue until mid-August when sharp declines in flock numbers are noticed (Miles 1976, Funk 1977) and migration begins in earnest. Staging behavior and uniform initiation of migration from year to year suggest that migration is influenced more by internal mechanisms than by external stimuli (Miles 1976). In some years, however, sudden climatic changes may trigger the impulse.

The rate of the autumn mourning dove migration has been described as leisurely (Jenkins 1955, Hanson and Kossack 1963). Although doves are known to fly at speeds of 45 to 55 miles (72 to 89 km) per hour (Brooks 1943, Bastin 1952), they apparently do not sustain such speeds during migration and frequently stop to feed and loaf.

A search of recovery records for birds banded during August in the CMU and WMU from 1967 to 1975 revealed that a few birds averaged 62 to 78 miles (100 to 125 km) per day but most averaged 19 to 34 miles (30 to 55 km) per day (see also Low 1935). For example, an immature dove banded in Washington and recovered in Colorado twelve days later averaged 73 miles (117 km) per day. Another immature went from Wyoming to California in nine days, averaging 70 miles (113 km) per day. Three immatures banded in South Dakota migrated 1,800 to 2,500 miles (2,900 to 4,000 km) to Colima and Jalisco, Mexico, and to El Salvador, averaging 28, 30 and 22 miles (45, 48 and 35 km) per day, respectively. These records have to be considered as minimum speeds because the actual times of departure from the origination areas and the arrival times at

In most areas mourning doves become increasingly gregarious prior to the onset of autumn migration. Not all apparent stagings of doves are for migratory purposes, since evidence indicates that not all mourning doves migrate. Some gatherings may be more the result of concentrated food availability during and after agricultural crop harvests. *Left photo courtesy of the Illinois Department of Conservation. Right photo by Ron George; courtesy of the Texas Parks and Wildlife Department.*

their destinations are unknown. It seems safe to conclude that most migrating mourning doves fly only short distances each day, probably no more than 50 to 100 miles (80 to 160 km).

Arrival times for autumn-migrating mourning doves can be determined by examining dates when birds are recovered in southern areas. In Texas, doves from northern states began to arrive in September and increased in numbers through October (Dunks et al. 1982). The peak recovery period for Mexico was mid-October (Dunks et al. 1982) and for Central America from late October to early November (Purdy 1978b). Thus, autumn migration begins before September and ends at the farthest locations in November.

OVERLAND VERSUS OVERWATER MIGRATION ROUTES

Mourning doves need not travel over large bodies of water along most migratory routes. For birds originating from most areas of the CMU and WMU, overland routes are the logical means of travel, even for those doves traveling to Central America. Indeed, mourning doves are regularly observed migrating over land. In the EMU, most migrating doves winter in southeastern states *(tables 5 and 7)* and therefore are not required to migrate over water. However, mourning doves have been identified as trans-Gulf migrants during both spring and autumn (Bullis and Lincoln 1952, Siebanaler

1954, Stevenson 1957). The shortest distance across the Gulf of Mexico from Louisiana to the Yucatan Peninsula is about 540 miles (870 km), which would represent a nonstop flight of ten hours at 55 miles (89 km) per hour. This is dubious behavior for a bird that apparently travels no more than 100 miles (160 km) a day on the average during migration.

Furthermore, expected points of arrival along the east coast of Mexico and in the Yucatan Peninsula have recorded so few dove recoveries as to cast doubt on a theory of widespread overwater migration by mourning doves. A more logical explanation is that some doves may take shortcuts over the Gulf but remain in sight of land and that others become lost or travel over water only in emergency situations.

Early reports suggested that mourning doves from the eastern United States regularly migrated to Cuba and other Greater Antilles islands (Lincoln 1933, 1937, 1941). Winston (1954) reported that 8 recoveries from Florida, 1 from Illinois and 1 from Mississippi had been reported in Cuba up to that time. However, Marion et al. (1981) analyzed recoveries in and from Florida between 1931 and 1978 and reported no direct recoveries from Cuba or the West Indies. A search of the recovery records at the Bird Banding Laboratory (D. Dolton personal communication: 1986) uncovered 13 total recoveries in Cuba of birds banded in the United States. Of these, 9 were from Florida, 2 from Indiana, 1 from Mississippi and 1 from Wisconsin. All but 2 of the recoveries from Florida were from birds banded in September through November—outside the normal preseason banding period of June through August—so the Florida origin of these birds is questionable. Of the 2 recoveries of birds banded during the preseason period, neither was considered to be direct. These factors explain why Marion et al. (1981) did not recognize the Cuban recoveries. All but 2 of the 13 Cuban records were recovered between 1936 and 1959. The 2 Indiana doves were recovered in the 1970s.

Since Cuba is only about 80 to 100 miles (129 to 160 km) from Key West, Florida, it is well within reach of migrating doves. The lack of reported recent recoveries in Cuba could be the result of political differences between the two countries, small banded samples or a combination of both. That some interchange of individual doves occurs between Florida and Cuba is undeniable. Nevertheless, because of the relatively few recoveries (6) in Cuba during early years of heavy EMU banding effort (1948–56), it is concluded that migration between the United States and islands of the Greater Antilles is not a regular occurrence (see also Aldrich 1952).

OVERWINTERING POPULATIONS AND NONMIGRATION

Most mourning doves from northern parts of the breeding range migrate south each year. Often, however, small segments of these populations will remain over winter. This behavior has been noted in Washington and Oregon (Booth 1945), Wisconsin (Thompson 1950), Pennsylvania (Rensel 1952), Ohio (Hennessy and Van Camp 1963), Ontario (Alison 1976), Massachusetts (Heusmann 1979), and other locations. An increasing winter food supply (e.g., waste or stored corn) has been suggested as responsible for this relatively recent behavior (Chambers 1963, Armstrong and Noakes 1983). The overwintering doves, however, are subjected to frequent below-freezing temperatures and snow- or ice-covered food sources. This combination of factors can be lethal and doves often succumb (Errington 1935, Thompson 1950, Hennessy and Van Camp 1963).

In a Missouri study, Chambers et al. (1962) demonstrated that overwintering mourning dove flocks were composed largely of adult males, which prompted the authors to conclude that male doves winter farther north than females. Hanson and Kossack (1963) theorized that a difference in basal metabolism between male and female doves may be a contributing factor to the differential migrational patterns. The metabolic rate of male mourning doves is 3.8 percent higher per unit of body weight than that of females (Riddle et al. 1932).

The phenomenon of males wintering farther north than females has been noted in many migratory species (see Nice 1933, Lack 1944, Selander 1966, Ketterson and Nolan 1976). Nichols and Haramis (1980) and others have made the assumption that differences in winter distribution of migratory birds reflect sex-specific differences in evolutionary costs and benefits associated with wintering at specific latitudes. Thus, there must be some cost associated with this dimorphic behavior or one would expect males to winter as far south as females do. Armstrong and Noakes (1983) hypothesized that, in the case of mourning doves, a successfully overwintering population could contribute substantially to local recruitment, i.e., wintering doves would avoid the hazards of migration and hunting (in Ontario) and be able to compete more successfully for mates and possibly increase the length of the breeding season. That only a small proportion of northern breeding populations overwinters each year is testimony to the fact that, by and large, migration from upper latitudes is less hazardous than overwintering.

The winter range of mourning doves is generally considered to be south of the thirty-ninth parallel, a line that extends from Washington, D.C. through Kansas City, Missouri and Carson City, Nevada (see *Figure 1*) (Keeler 1977, Dunks et al. 1982). Doves are presumed to have less migratory inclination in the southern part of their breeding range, where it overlaps winter range. Recent evidence suggests that certain discrete breeding populations within this area are completely nonmigratory. Channing (1979) and Leopold and Dedon (1983) demonstrated that local dove populations near Turlock and Berkeley, California, respectively, did not migrate. Similar nonmigratory populations were noted at College Station, Texas (Bivings 1980) and in Florida (Marion et al. 1981). Indirect evidence indicates that many if not most doves from breeding populations in Kentucky (Russell 1955), Tennessee (Orr 1973), Louisiana (Watts 1969), southern Arizona (Brown and Smith 1976), Texas (Dunks 1977), South EMU states and the Carolinas (Quay 1951b) are also nonmigratory. The winter climate in each of these areas is mild and food supplies are generally plentiful year-round. In areas such as northern Arizona, New Mexico and the panhandle of Texas, where climate has been modified by altitude or other factors, mourning doves migrate in a manner similar to doves from the north. Thus, winter temperatures probably are important in determining the migratory behavior of dove populations throughout their breeding range.

MIGRATIONAL HOMING AND RATE OF RETURN

The natural movement of wild birds in returning to natal or nesting areas is called migrational homing or faithfulness to home (see Hickey 1943, Austin 1951). Rowan (1931) stated that, of the many facts brought to light by bird banding, none is more striking than the return of individuals to the same nesting site each year, in some cases having traveled thousands of miles between times. Breeding site tenacity has been noted for many species, such as swallows (Thompson 1936), song sparrows (Nice 1937), house wrens (Kendeigh 1941b), robins (Farner 1945), pied flycatchers (von Haartman 1949), sandpipers (Oring and Lank 1984), and red-winged blackbirds (Picman 1987), as well as mourning doves (Nice 1922, 1923, Barkalow 1936).

Homing Accuracy

Several authors have reported mourning doves nesting in the same nest as in previous years. Stew-art and Mackey (1953) and Mackey (1965) observed two pairs of doves that used the same nests two consecutive years in Ohio. Wood (1951) reported on a nest that, before being destroyed, was used by one or more pairs of doves for nine successive years. In South Carolina, a nest was used by the same pair of doves for four years (Cutts 1954). Whether these birds migrated and then returned to nest is not known. If so, they demonstrated remarkable homing accuracy.

Tomlinson et al. (1960) and Harris (1961) independently studied migratory homing behavior of mourning doves in Missouri and Minnesota, respectively. In Missouri, 87 percent of 211 mourning doves returning to the banding area one or more years later were recaptured within 1 mile (1.6 km) of the original point of capture; more than 25 percent returned to the exact spot of original capture. In Minnesota, 80 percent of the nest sites of returning adult mourning doves were located within 200 feet (61 m) of sites used the previous year and nearly 50 percent were within 50 feet (15 m). Furthermore, doves found nesting two years after initial capture had moved only an average 300 feet (91 m) from original nest sites. Because most mourning doves from these relatively northern areas do migrate south each year, it is concluded that birds returning from wintering areas are faithful to specific nesting locations.

Return Rate

Austin's (1951: 160) banding studies during 1930 to 1950 on Cape Cod provided the first solid evidence of site tenacity for mourning doves. Allowing for annual mortality, he estimated that "considerably more than half the surviving doves must return to the trapping area each summer season." Tomlinson et al. (1960: 264) corrected for annual mortality and trapping inefficiency and concluded that "virtually all surviving adult males return to nest in the area of previous nesting." Although there was a smaller percentage of surviving adult females that returned (92 percent), the difference was considered inconsequential. However, because few immatures returned (13 of 411 banded: 3.2 percent) during the six-year study period, it was assumed that homing occurred principally to first nest sites and rarely to natal sites. Harris (1961) obtained similar results. Ninety-five percent of surviving adult males and 60 percent of surviving adult females were estimated to return to previous nesting areas in Minnesota. Of birds banded as nestlings, only 2 percent were estimated to return in later years.

In a review of homing tendencies, von Haartman (1949) concluded that immatures of most songbird species are not as faithful to home as are adults and that adult males generally disperse over a smaller area than do females. It appears that mourning doves conform to this behavior. The odds are high that an adult dove will return to the area of previous nesting and select a nest site near a previous site, possibly at the exact location. Adult female doves may be somewhat less site-tenacious than adult males. Immature doves, however, disperse over a wider area and may not return to the general natal area.

Chapter 5

Nesting and Production

Mark W. Sayre
Department of Forestry and Wildlife Management
University of Massachusetts
Amherst, Massachusetts

Nova J. Silvy
Department of Wildlife and Fisheries Sciences
Texas A&M University
College Station, Texas

NESTING SEASON

The mourning dove breeds throughout the forty-eight contiguous states, the southern portions of the Canadian provinces, the Greater Antilles and Mexico (Keeler 1977). Its breeding season is among the longest of all North American birds, and active dove nests have been found in every month of the year in the southernmost parts of the breeding range (Peters 1961). Most nesting studies *(Table 10)* indicate a definite temporal pattern, with a peak of nesting activity occurring sometime in late spring or early summer and a decline sometime before September. However, the extent of the nesting season and patterns of peak nesting vary considerably throughout the species' vast breeding range.

The most ambitious and extensive study of seasonal nesting patterns was the cooperative nationwide mourning dove nesting survey undertaken in 1979 and 1980 (Geissler et al. 1987). During those two years, weekly nest searches were conducted from February through October on 106 study areas in twenty-seven states within the Eastern (EMU), Central (CMU) and Western (WMU) management units *(Figure 9)*. Based on 6,950 active nests found during the course of the study, temporal patterns of nesting activity differed by geographic region, with shorter nesting periods to the north *(Figure 10)*. Doves in the South EMU began nesting in February and continued into October. In contrast, doves in the North CMU and WMU (Utah and California) had a nesting season that extended from mid-March through September. Nationwide, more than 83 percent of the nests found were present from May through August. Fewer than 3 percent of the annual total nests found were present in September and October *(Table 11)*.

Table 10. Peak and extent of the mourning dove nesting season as reported from various locations in the United States (updated from Hanson and Kossack 1963).

Location[a]	Peak of nesting season	End of nesting season	Reference
North EMU			
Illinois	Late April–early May	Late September	Hanson and Kossack (1963)
	Late May–early June	September 14	Putera et al. (1985)
Michigan		August	Lund (1952)
		September	Davey (1953)
	April 21–June 20	Late September	Caldwell (1964)
		August 31	Calhoun (1948)
Ohio		Mid-October	Webb (1949)
	March–April	September 30	Mackey (1954)
Pennsylvania		September	Sheldon (1957)
Virginia	July	September	Semmes (1907)
	June	October	Sprunt (1951)
South EMU			
Alabama	Mid-June	October	Pearson and Rosene (1938)
	Early June	October	Pearson and Moore (1939)
	Mid-May	October	Moore and Pearson (1941)
	April–May	October	Mirarchi and Hudson (1981)
Georgia	April–May	September	Hopkins and Odum (1953)
	May–June	August 12	Lowe (1956)
Florida	March–July	November	Marion and Schnoes (1982)
Louisiana	May–July	September	Soileau (1960)
Mississippi	July–August	September	Handley and Edwards (1958)
North Carolina	May	October	Taylor (1941)
	May	October	Quay (1951)
Tennessee	May	October	Monk (1949)
North CMU			
Colorado	June–August	Mid-September	Olson and Braun (1984)
Iowa	May	September	McClure (1942)
		October 15	McClure (1950)
	May	September	George and Wooley (1980)
Minnesota	Early June	Early October	Harris et al. (1963)
Nebraska		September 23	McClure (1950)
	June 6	September 15	LaPointe (1958)
	June 20	September	Frates (1963)
South Dakota	Late May–early June	September	Drewien and Sparrowe (1966)
North Dakota	August 13–19	September 25	Boldt and Hendrickson (1952)
	June–August	September 21	Randall (1955)
South CMU			
Kansas	May	July 18	Linsdale (1933)
	June to mid-July	September 11	Schroeder (1970)
Missouri	Mid-April	Early September	Armbruster (1973)
	Early June		
Oklahoma	May	October 1	Nice (1923)
	Late July–early August	September 15	Dodson (1955)
	May 24–June 29		Carpenter (1970)
Texas	July	September 25	Jackson (1940)
	July	October	Swank (1955)
	June	October	Morrow and Silvy (1982)
	May–June	October	Morrow and Silvy (1983)
	May 18	October 5	George (1986)
WMU			
California	July	September 24	McClure (1950)
		September	Cowan (1952)

Table 10. (continued)

Location[a]	Peak of nesting season	End of nesting season	Reference
WMU (continued)			
Idaho	Late July	Early September	Fichter (1959)
Utah	June–July Mid-June– late July		Howe and Flake (1989) Dahlgren (1955)
Washington	July	August	Knight et al. (1984)
United States	Late May– mid-June	October	Geissler et al. (1987)

[a] EMU = Eastern Management Unit; CMU = Central Management Unit; WMU = Western Management Unit.

For the vast majority of temperate zone bird species, increasing day length after the winter solstice is the most important signal for gonadal development (Immelman 1971). Cole (1933), in a controlled-lighting experiment, concluded that increasing light triggered the onset of reproduction in the mourning dove. However, many subsidiary environmental factors may help determine the actual inception of breeding once a gonadal threshold has been reached. The vital role of these subsidiary factors in adjusting timing of nesting to birds' environmental resources was illustrated by Linsdale (1933). He pointed out an apparent correlation between availability of food for young birds of many species and the timing of nesting. In turn, the availability of both plant and animal food is directly dependent on local weather.

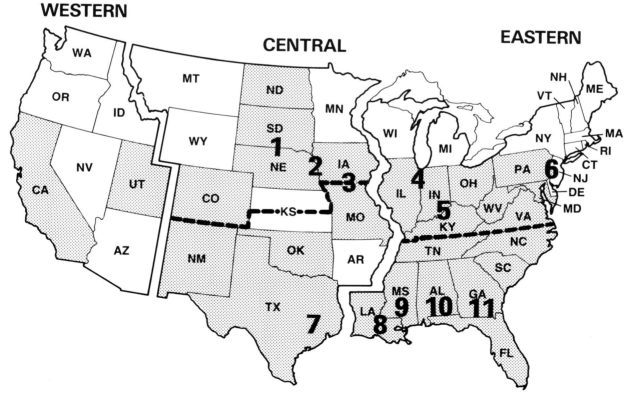

Figure 9. Study area (numbered) locations for nationwide cooperative dove nesting study (from Geissler et al. 1987). Shaded states contained study areas used to determine annual patterns of nesting activity. Heavy dash lines show north and south subdivisions of the Eastern and Central management units.

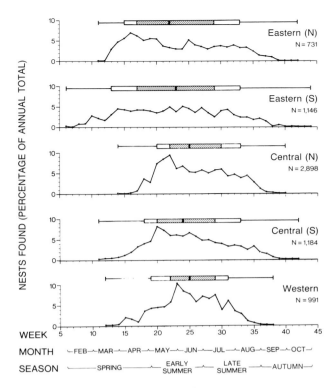

Figure 10. Seasonal patterns of nesting activity: nests first found each week shown as percentages of an annual total from combined 1979 and 1980 data for mourning dove management unit subdivisions. End points of horizontal lines on boxes represent maximum and minimum dates. Each entire box plot shows 80 percent of the total, with the shaded area representing 50 percent of the total about the median (from Geissler et al. 1987).

For mourning doves, Lund (1952) stated that the nesting season in southern Michigan varied from year to year and seemed contingent upon prevailing weather. Hanson and Kossack (1963) perceived a correlation between temperature in spring (April and May) and the phenology of dove nest initiation over a nine-year period in northeastern Illinois *(Table 12)*. Generally, unseasonably cold temperatures delayed nesting attempts, whereas unusually warm temperatures accelerated them.

In summary, although increasing day length stimulates the mourning dove's readiness to breed, there also appears to be a more subtle relationship between latitude and regional or local weather regimes (particularly temperature) regarding the actual commencement and duration of mourning dove nesting.

NESTING CYCLE

Courtship and Pairing

Mourning doves are monogamous and form strong bonds that persist at least during one nesting season. Some indirect evidence suggests doves may remain paired throughout the winter. Mackey (1965) noted three pairs of marked doves that remained mated during two successive nesting seasons, although he did not observe these pairs during the intervening winter. Taylor (1941) observed wintering flocks of doves in North Carolina and noted that alarmed birds flushed both singly and in pairs. Cowan (1952) believed that wintering flocks of doves in California were composed primarily of paired adults. However, Leopold (1943) noted a tendency toward sexual segregation among wintering doves in Missouri, with males composing sampled flocks. In another Missouri study, Chambers et al. (1962) concluded that male doves tended to winter farther north than females and that at least some males did not migrate from their nesting range. Leopold and Dedon (1983) presented evidence that some local populations of mourning doves (including both males and females) in the central and southern portions of the range are nonmigratory, but they did not discuss whether pair bonds were maintained through the winter.

Even though some adults may remain paired during winter, most doves probably are unpaired at the onset of the breeding season. Unmated male doves typically are aggressive toward other doves in the vicinity of their display perches, but they do

Table 11. Estimated proportions of active mourning dove nests[a] by season in selected areas of the United States.

Season[b]	Area[c]					
	North EMU	South EMU	North CMU	South CMU	WMU	United States
Spring	25.5	30.2	2.4	9.8	6.3	11.0
Summer	67.1	63.7	93.6	84.2	93.1	84.5
Autumn	7.4	6.1	4.0	6.0	0.6	4.5
Total nests	3,424	4,556	12,644	4,676	4,560	29,860

[a] Derived from weekly counts of nests with individual eggs or nestlings present (Geissler et al. 1987).
[b] Spring = February–April; Summer = May–August; Autumn = September–October.
[c] EMU = Eastern Management Unit; CMU = Central Management Unit; WMU = Western Management Unit.

Table 12. Relationship of temperatures during April and May to mourning dove nest initiation in northeastern Illinois, 1950–58 (from Hanson and Kossack 1963).

	Temperature conditions		Dove nesting initiation
Year	April	May	
1950	Much below normal; coldest in 43 years	Early part unseasonably cold, rising to 80°F (26.7°C) on May 4 and 5	Very late
1951	Near normal; latter part considerably above normal	Normal during first week; above normal second and third weeks; fourth week normal	Normal
1952	First half largely below normal; second half largely above normal	May 1–6 much above normal; remainder of month considerably below normal	Early
1953	Averaged below normal	Slightly above normal	Normal
1954	Warmest in 29 years; more persistent warm spell April 18–27	Cool and dry; 3.7°F below normal, coolest since 1945; eighth coolest on record	Early
1955	Second hottest on record; average 59.2°F (15.1°C), nearly equaling all-time high	Month averaged 2.5°F above normal; first few days averaged 12° above normal; 22° above normal on May 3 and 4	Very early
1956	Mostly cool and dry; generally 1–3°F below normal	Pleasant; above normal	Late
1957	First half cold, subnormal; second half warm	Near normal	Very late
1958	Warm; a record high of 84°F (28.9°C) on April 17, but a record low of 31°F (−1°C) on April 29	Above normal	Normal

not establish well-defined territories before pairing (Jackson and Baskett 1964, Irby 1964, Sayre et al. 1980). Swank (1955a) noted that a male dove did not tolerate intrusion by other doves into areas near its cooing perch nor into the area where it was searching for nest materials. After the nest was established, however, defense of territory near it was virtually eliminated. This is emphasized by frequent presence of two or more active dove nests in the same tree. Swank noted that in no instance were nests in the same stage of development found close together, indicating that territorial tendencies prevent two pairs from building closely adjacent nests simultaneously.

Unpaired males devote considerable time to perch cooing and other displays. The perch coo is a vocalization consisting of "five to seven notes; one note, then a higher one, and finally three to five notes held at greater length" (McClure 1939:323). Perch cooing serves to identify a territorial male and to attract and court the female (Stone 1966). Since the rate of perch cooing decreases considerably after pairing (Baskett et al. 1978), mate attraction may be the more important function of the dove's song. Unmated males have been observed perch cooing and performing their flapping/gliding display flight (see chapter 10) at various times throughout the day, but displaying activity is most intense in the early morning and evening (Sayre et al. 1980).

Behavior leading to formation of the pair bond (see chapter 10) has been described from observations of penned doves (Whitman 1919, Frankel 1961, Goforth and Baskett 1971b, Armbruster 1983) and wild doves (Jackson and Baskett 1964). According to Jackson and Baskett (1964), a female may respond to a courting male in at least three different ways: (1) she may fly away, in which case a pursuit chase occurs; (2) she may ignore the male and continue feeding or preening; or (3) she may permit copulation and formation of the pair bond. After establishing a pair bond, the male and female loaf together for a few days before initiating nest building.

The proportions of doves in a population that eventually pair and nest cannot be accurately determined. Intensive studies of color-marked or radio-tagged doves have demonstrated that unmated males are present in the population throughout the nesting season (Jackson and Baskett 1964, Irby 1964, Sayre et al. 1978, Sayre et al. 1980).

Site Selection and Nest Building

There are many recorded observations of mourning dove behavior associated with nest site selection and nest building (Gifford 1909, Nice 1922, 1938, Mackey 1954, Jackson and Baskett 1964, Goforth and Baskett 1971b, Armbruster 1983). The male takes the initiative in nest site selection and may begin searching for a new site before the young of the previous nesting have fledged. After the nest site has been selected, the pair proceeds with building the nest. During nest building the male selects small twigs and delivers them individually to the

While the female of a mated pair of mourning doves waits at the nest site (usually selected by the male), the male makes thirty to forty trips to the site, bringing single twigs or other ground debris for the female to fashion into a nest. The nest-building process takes seven to ten hours, often over the course of two to four days. *Photo by Charles W. Schwartz.*

female, who arranges them into the nesting platform (Nice 1922). The male may make thirty to forty trips to the nest site in a given bout of nest building and may repeat the sequence later in the day (Jackson and Baskett 1964). Nest construction takes a total of seven to ten hours and may be spread over a period of two to four days (Blockstein 1986a). Time required for courtship, nest site selection and nest construction varies from three to seven days (Cowan 1952, Mackey 1954).

The availability of nest material is important in determining the territorial boundaries of mourning doves (Goforth and Baskett 1971b). Swank (1955a) noted that mourning doves prefer to collect nest materials from areas with sparse cover. Soutiere and Bolen (1972, 1976) noted that, although burning of rangelands reduced the total amount of available litter, it added to the suitability of habitat by increasing the amount of open space where doves eventually might collect nest materials.

Mourning doves are opportunistic nesters, exhibiting willingness to nest wherever there is a flat substrate and usually some protection from disturbance. *Top left photo (dove nesting on the head of a mop hung on a wall) by James B. Grand; courtesy of the Auburn University Department of Zoology and Wildlife Science and the Alabama Agricultural Experiment Station. Bottom left photo (nest on a windowsill) by David Dolton. Top right photo (dove nesting on the side of an automobile) by Albert E. Bivings. Bottom right photo (nesting on a mangled car bumper in an auto junkyard) by David Dolton.*

Egg Laying and Clutch Size

Mourning doves are determinate layers with a genetically controlled clutch size of two eggs; nevertheless, reports of dove nests containing more than two eggs are not uncommon (Moore and Pearson 1941, Quay 1951). Nice (1922b) found three nests that contained three eggs and cited eight reports of four-egg clutches and forty observations of three-egg clutches. Weeks (1980) noted that, in almost all reported instances of three-egg clutches, the third egg was deposited substantially later than the first two. Based on this fact and observations of adventitious laying (deposition of eggs with no nest) by mourning doves, he concluded that three-egg nests result from the addition of an egg by a second bird ("dump nesting") rather than an individual female laying a three-egg clutch.

Blockstein (1986a) showed, through manipulation of clutch size, that mourning dove pairs can incubate three eggs. When a third nestling was added during and after the period of complete dependence on crop milk, growth rates were significantly reduced for crop milk-dependent young in broods of three. Westmoreland and Best (1987), in a similar study, observed that parents incubating three eggs and brooding three nestlings produced broods that grew more slowly, took longer to fledge and weighed less than their control counterparts.

Parents of enlarged broods fledged 30 percent more offspring than those with two young. However, the low survival rate of the young fledglings in the enlarged broods probably negated the positive effect on reproductive success.

Mourning doves are unusual because they lay white eggs in open nests. To determine whether this depressed reproductive success, Westmoreland and Best (1986) compared the survival of white clutches to that of clutches spattered with brown paint, simulating cryptic coloration. These treatments were compared under constant incubation typical of mourning doves and interrupted incubation in which the attending adult was flushed from the nest once every three days. Cryptic clutches had greater survival when incubation was interrupted, but did not have greater survival when incubated constantly. Westmoreland and Best argued that white egg coloration in doves may have been a selective factor for development of constant incubation (see chapter 6).

Hanson and Kossack (1963) recorded linear and volumetric measurements of mourning dove eggs. In almost all cases, the first egg laid was more oval in shape and easily distinguishable from the longer, more pointed second egg. The first egg of twenty-eight clutches averaged 1.08 by 0.84 inches (27.5 by 21.4 mm); the second egg averaged 1.11 by 0.84 inches (28.3 by 21.4 mm). The difference between the first and second egg was limited to shape; volumetric measurements of first and second eggs in ten clutches did not differ and averaged 0.22

Mourning doves produce two eggs per clutch but are capable of incubating artificially enlarged three-egg clutches. Because of occasional "dump nesting" (a female laying in another's nest), nests can be found with three or four eggs; the young of all eggs may hatch, but the viability of the young is probably compromised. *Left photo by Charles W. Schwartz. Right photo (mourning dove egg in a robin's nest) by Ron George; courtesy of the Iowa Conservation Commission.*

ounces (6.6 ml). The largest egg recorded by Hanson and Kossack measured 1.57 by 0.80 inches (40.0 by 20.2 mm).

Pearson and Moore (1939) noted that female doves laid eggs on successive days in twenty-six nests under observation. Hanson and Kossack (1963) reported egg-laying intervals for twenty-seven clutches of captive doves. The eggs of seventeen clutches (63 percent) were laid on alternate days (twenty-four to forty-eight hours apart), and the eggs of ten clutches (37 percent) were laid on consecutive days (twelve to twenty-four hours apart).

Incubation and Brooding

Hanson and Kossack (1963) presented evidence that mourning doves initiate incubation either after the first egg has been laid or after the second egg has been laid, depending on interval of deposition. For those clutches laid on alternate days, generally little incubation took place until the second egg was laid. But eggs laid on the same day or successive days hatched at a rate of fourteen days each, suggesting that incubation began immediately after the first egg was laid.

Unlike many other bird species, both the male and the female mourning dove share in incubation and brooding. Male doves typically incubate the eggs from midmorning until late afternoon, although time of nest exchange between the male and female is variable *(Table 13)*. Incubation nor-

Table 13. Number of morning and afternoon observations of nest exchange times during incubation and brooding of mourning doves (from Sayre et al. 1980).

Nest exchange times	Position in nesting cycle	
	Incubation	Brooding (1–9 days)
Morning		
8:00–9:00	0	2
9:00–10:00	17	26
10:00–11:00	22	10
11:00–12:00	6	0
After 12:00 Noon	1	0
Afternoon		
4:00–5:00	2	1
5:00–6:00	13	7
6:00–7:00	15	19
After 7:00	1	2

mally requires fourteen to fifteen days; based on observations of sixteen clutches of captive pairs, Hanson and Kossack (1963) noted that: in four clutches (25 percent), both eggs hatched on the same day; in eleven clutches (70 percent), eggs hatched on successive days (twelve to twenty-four hours apart); and in one clutch (5 percent), the eggs hatched on alternate days (twenty-four to forty-eight hours apart).

Walsberg and Voss-Roberts (1983) noted that for desert-nesting mourning doves, thermal stress may be most critical during reproduction. They noted that during the reproductive period adult doves were restricted to the nest for large portions of the

Mourning dove eggs are white. The first-laid egg typically is oval shaped, and the second is slightly longer and more elliptical. Incubation (from laying of the second egg to pipping) is about fourteen days. Nests and eggs of white-winged doves can be confused with those of mourning doves in areas of nesting overlap. Only slightly larger, whitewing eggs usually are cream-colored rather than white. *Ground nest (left) photo by Don Wooldridge; courtesy of the Missouri Department of Conservation. Shrub (mesquite) nest photo by Robert M. Kral; courtesy of the U.S. Soil Conservation Service.*

day. They concluded that mourning doves nesting in the Sonoran Desert maintained their eggs at viable temperatures despite higher environmental temperatures. Egg cooling was accomplished by contact with the adult's body, which was held at a relatively low core temperature (mean = 100 degrees Fahrenheit: 38.3° C) (see chapter 9).

After hatching, young mourning doves (squabs) are brooded by both parents for differing lengths of time depending on the sex of the parent (Hitchcock and Mirarchi 1984). Hanson and Kossack (1957) presented a detailed description of nestling growth, discussed in more depth in chapter 8. Mourning doves nourish their young with "crop milk," or "pigeon milk," a milklike substance consisting of epithelial cells sloughed from the crop wall. The crops of both male and female doves undergo remarkable anatomical and physiological changes during the course of a nesting cycle (see chapter 7). As nestlings grow older, the amount of crop milk regurgitated by the adults decreases and is gradually supplemented by seeds. At the time of fledging, there is little difference in the diets of fledgling and adult birds. Nestlings generally fledge from the nest at eleven to fifteen days of age (Nice 1922, 1923, Pearson and Moore 1939, Austin 1951, Cowan 1952, Mackey 1954, Swank 1955a).

Young doves remain dependent on parental care for several days after fledging. Mirarchi and Scanlon (1981) observed that *captive* fledglings that had access to food became independent of parental care at approximately eighteen days of age (five to nine days after fledging) and that survival of fledglings was reduced markedly when both parents were killed before that time. Hitchcock and Mirarchi (1984) used radio telemetry to study the duration of dependence of mourning dove fledglings *in the wild*. For ten to twelve days after fledging, young doves usually stayed within 110 yards (100 m) of the nest tree, and the frequency of feedings by the male parent remained relatively high and constant. Fledglings began feeding themselves at seventeen days of age and were feeding entirely independently by thirty days of age. Hitchcock and Mirarchi (1986) observed that fledglings used about three "reference areas" (specific areas in which they interacted with the male parent) and loafed within 148 feet (45 m) of the former nest site during their period of dependence on male parents (fifteen to twenty-seven days of age). The maximum distance moved each day and distances to the roost site increased with age. When deprived of parental care, fledglings less than twenty-one days of age moved as far as 1,148 feet (350 m) to feed. However, fledglings usually did not abandon reference areas until twenty-seven to thirty days old, at which time they

Both mourning dove parents feed and brood their offspring until they fledge at twelve to fifteen days of age. The male parent continues to feed the fledglings for ten to fifteen days. At about thirty days of age, the young become entirely independent. *Photo by Charles W. Schwartz.*

joined juvenile flocks. Remaining in reference areas and responding preferentially to the vocalizations of male parents may lower predation rates on nestling and fledgling doves and ensure favorable parental feeding rates throughout the juvenile dependency period (Hitchcock et al. 1989).

Interval between Nestings

On average a pair of mourning doves requires about thirty-two days (plus or minus five) to complete a nesting cycle—three to seven days for courtship and nest building, fourteen to fifteen days for incubation, and eleven to fifteen days for brooding. Adults, particularly the male, feed the fledged young for ten to twelve days but normally begin renesting within two to five days of the fledging date. Occasionally, eggs are laid in the same nest before the previous clutch has fledged. Early reports of the interval between successive nestings vary considerably (Lincoln 1945, Cowan 1952, Webb 1949, Harris et al. 1963) and were based on observations of the elapsed time between fledging (often difficult to determine precisely) and initiation of a new nesting. Swank (1955a) noted that the period between laying of a successful clutch and the start of a second clutch ranged from twenty-five to thirty-five days with a mean of thirty-two days. He also observed that when three nests were destroyed, the pairs resumed nesting (egg laying) within two to five days, even though the initial nests were in different stages of development.

Hanson and Kossack (1963) also emphasized that the interval between completion of one clutch (laying of the second egg) and initiation of the next clutch clearly was dependent on the fate of the first clutch. Thirty days was the most frequent interval between initiation of a successful clutch and initiation of a subsequent clutch.

The most frequent interval between an unsuccessful nesting and initiation of a new clutch was six days, according to Hanson and Kossack (1963). The shortest intervals between nesting attempts following an unsuccessful nesting occurred when the nesting was disrupted during incubation. The longest interval between an unsuccessful nesting and the next clutch occurred in instances when nesting was disrupted during brooding. In two instances when nestlings died at seven and eight days of age, a period of twenty-four days elapsed before initiation of a new nesting cycle. A total of thirty-one days elapsed between the disruption of one nest at hatching and renesting by the same

The mourning dove's nesting cycle is thirty-two days (plus or minus five days), including three to seven days for courtship and nest building, fourteen to fifteen days for incubation, and twelve to fifteen days for brooding. On occasion an adult pair will produce a second clutch in the same nest before their first nestlings have fully fledged. *Photo courtesy of the Alabama Cooperative Wildlife Research Unit.*

pair. Hanson and Kossack (1963) concluded that hormonal condition of the adults associated with brooding and crop gland development were antagonistic to a rapid "recycling" of the ovary. By the time the nestlings were eight or more days old, crop gland activity diminished and the female was more physiologically prepared for the next cycle.

As discussed in chapter 6, mourning doves have several adaptations that promote multiple brooding. Both males and females produce crop milk for nestlings and feed older nestlings a diverse granivorous diet. This allows an extended breeding season. By constructing small nests and reusing old nests, they initiate nesting cycles quickly. Small clutch size, constant incubation, fast nestling growth and early fledging serve to shorten the nesting cycle. Crop milk evidently is a key element in rapid recycling because it allows rapid growth in nestlings and probably, in the long term, limits clutch size (see chapter 6).

NESTING

Nesting Habitat

Nesting habitat is difficult to define for a highly adaptable species such as the mourning dove. The dove has a breeding distribution that extends throughout the contiguous United States, Mexico and southern portions of the Canadian provinces extending into southern Alaska (Keeler 1977). Within this broad range, doves utilize an array of ecological types for nesting, and the highest densities of breeding doves occur in the agricultural areas of the Midwest, Southeast and Southwest (*Figure 11*).

Although the dove is perhaps best adapted to and most closely associated with agricultural habitats, it will nest in many other habitat types. Eng (1986) concluded that the wide breeding distribution of the mourning dove almost precludes describing habitat features with precision. He noted that it is primarily an inhabitant of woodland/grassland edge. Thus, both clearing of large areas of forest in the eastern United States and planting of shelterbelts in the plains states has enhanced mourning dove habitat. Eng further noted that, although tree nesting is most common, doves readily nest on the ground in the absence of trees or shrubs. In the Great Plains, conversion of large tracts of treeless prairie to domestic grains and farmsteads (trees) has created an excellent combination of food (waste grain) and nesting cover for doves. Call-count Survey information from 1966 to 1989 demonstrated that the prairie states of North

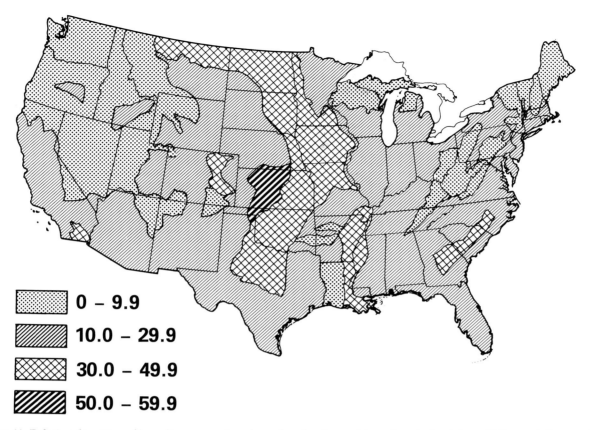

0 – 9.9

10.0 – 29.9

30.0 – 49.9

50.0 – 59.9

Figure 11. Relative densities of breeding mourning doves by physiographic region derived from Call-count Survey data, 1965–73.

Dakota, South Dakota, Nebraska and Kansas contain some of the most abundant dove breeding populations in the country (Dolton 1989). Intensive grazing on many ranges has encouraged invader plant species that often produce more seeds than native grasses. Grazing management also includes stock dams that provide water in areas where it is otherwise scarce.

Grue et al. (1983) correlated habitat variables on lands surrounding mourning dove Call-count routes in Texas with numbers of mourning doves heard calling along the routes. Whether or not a particular habitat variable was correlated with Call-counts depended on the abundance and distribution of the other habitat types and structural features present. If one or more of the requisites for dove survival and reproduction (food, water, cover and nest sites) was limited, habitat types and structural features that provided them usually were positively correlated with Call-counts. Conversely, abundant habitat types that did not provide all of these requisites usually were negatively correlated with Call-counts. Grue et al. also found that, in Texas habitats similar to those found in the southeastern United States, variables associated with the presence of edges and clearings and the absence of

understory within continuous forests appeared to be selected by calling doves. In Texas areas representative of the Great Plains, habitat variables associated with cropland were negatively correlated with Call-counts, but those associated with rangeland and the presence of woody vegetation were positively correlated. In Texas areas representative of the southwestern United States, Call-counts were correlated with habitat variables associated with breaks (croplands and fields) within the shrub and brushlands. Grue et al. concluded that, because mourning doves can fly long distances for food and water, management to improve breeding habitat should be considered only for relatively large areas. It would be unnecessary and economically infeasible to provide all of the requisites for dove survival and reproduction within small areas. Management should provide adequate food, water, cover, nest sites and song posts within the normal daily flight range of the bird. Different habitat types and structural features that provide these requisites appear to be needed to improve nesting habitat within several parts of the United States. In particular, extensive areas of single habitat types should be diversified to provide all of the requirements of breeding doves.

An examination of agricultural practices failed to positively isolate any that were directly responsible for the long-term decline of mourning dove populations in the WMU (Tomlinson and Dolton 1987). In a similar examination of the effects of agricultural changes on declining dove populations in the eastern tier of the CMU, George et al. (1987) found that trends in numbers of mourning doves heard appeared to be correlated most closely with numbers of farms (positive) or size of farms (negative). Additionally, the numbers of farms and acres of soybeans, oats and sorghum were identified as positive predictors to the number of doves heard.

Amend (1969) noted that, although pine trees are considered by many biologists to be desirable as dove nesting habitat in the Carolina Sandhills, the premise is true only with mixed-age natural stands. An increase in large, single-aged stands, Amend predicted, would cause dove nesting densities to drop, since doves preferred nesting near some sort of edge (Hopkins and Odum 1953).

The dramatic increase in the numbers of mourning doves on the Canadian prairies during this century (Houston 1986) has been attributed to planting of trees in shelterbelts, the advent of agriculture with plentiful grain and weed seeds as a stable food supply, creation of small water supplies for livestock, and the erection of telephone and later power lines, used by the doves for perching. However, Houston (1986) cautioned that the conclusion, so evident in Canada, does not hold true for North Dakota, as mourning doves are "abundant" everywhere along the Missouri and Yellowstone rivers and on the Plains, where their nests frequently are found, always on the ground.

Downing (1959) found that nesting mourning doves in Oklahoma seemed to prefer trees to ground sites, although ground nesting was common. However, doves did not nest in trees until the trees leafed out fully. He also speculated that doves raised in ground nests may prefer to nest on the ground. Downing estimated that 71 percent of the mourning dove population in northwestern Oklahoma nested on the ground and concluded that tree nesting was less important than ground nesting only because the area occupied by trees was so limited. Also working in northwestern Oklahoma, Carpenter (1970) conversely observed ground nesting to be uncommon, and where it occurred, the nests frequently were destroyed by agricultural activities.

Fichter (1959) observed a "considerable" proportion of ground nesting on the Snake River Plain in Idaho. He further noted that ground nesting probably was more important than tree nesting for much of the "Intermountain West." Howe and Flake (1989a), also working on the Snake River Plain, observed all nests to be ground nests. Olson et al. (1991) found, in eastern Colorado, that dove nesting densities and production were greater in shelterbelt trees than in ground nests of the surrounding prairies, particularly in agricultural areas. They concluded that the continued removal of shelterbelts and the conversion of native prairies to cropland will substantially reduce high-quality nesting habitat and ultimately result in decreased mourning dove production on a regionwide basis.

Downing (1959) stated that overhead cover did not appear to be essential to ground-nesting mourning doves in Oklahoma, but Hon (1956) observed that 93 percent of the ground nests in North Carolina had at least partial overhead cover. All ground nests observed by Howe and Flake (1989a) were located in shrubs, primarily big sagebrush.

Nest Construction

Mourning doves are notoriously poor nest builders. Most dove nests are scarcely more than mere platforms of sticks, and the eggs often are visible from below because of the loose construction (Stockard 1905). Nests are constructed of small twigs, grasses, pine needles or other similar materials located in the vicinity of the nest site. Construction of the nest, in which both sexes participate, usually requires about two to four days for completion.

Although dove nests are less substantial than those of most other birds and seem more vulnerable to destruction by weather and other disturbances, they suffice for the dove. Frail nests take relatively less time to construct and may be one of the time-conserving adaptations evolved by doves related to the reproductive strategy of multiple brooding (Westmoreland et al. 1986).

Secondary Use of Nests

Doves frequently use previously constructed dove nests or nests of other species. They have been recorded nesting in the abandoned nests of American robins, northern mockingbirds, house sparrows, common grackles, blue jays, black-crowned night-herons and several other avian species (McClure 1943, Swank 1952, Hanson and Kossack 1963, Blockstein 1986a). Doves also have been reported to use nests of fox squirrels (McClure 1943) and gray squirrels (Monk 1949). Reported percentages of mourning dove clutches that are laid in pre-existing nests range from 20 to 40 percent (Mc-

Some mourning doves (20 to 40 percent) save time and energy by occupying nests built and vacated by other birds, and merely adding small amounts of new nest material. The dove shown here has taken up residence in an abandoned robin's nest. *Photo by Ralph E. Mirarchi; courtesy of Virginia Polytechnic Institute and State University Department of Fisheries and Wildlife Science.*

Clure 1950a, Cowan 1952, Hanson and Kossack 1963, Blockstein 1986a).

Pairs of doves sometimes may reuse their own nests. Stewart and Mackey (1953) reported that a pair of marked doves used a nest in two consecutive years. Blockstein (1986a) observed that some nests are occupied by the same individual (with different mates) for two to four years. Most observations indicated that a pair of doves is much more likely to reuse a previously successful nest than one that was unsuccessful in fledging young (Jackson 1963). Blockstein (1986a) found that the percentage of nest reuse by successful nesters (30 percent) was considerably higher than that for unsuccessful nesters (10 percent) and that successful nesters usually renested closer to their previous nest site. Whether reuse is made of their own nests or nests of other birds, a layer of fresh nesting material usually is added before egg laying (Hanson and Kossack 1963).

Swank (1955a) observed a marked pair to nest three times during one summer in a nest on which they were captured. This nest contained a clutch of eggs destroyed prior to capture of the pair, and Swank believed the eggs belonged to this pair. Swank also noted that several nestings in the same nest were not always made by a single pair but that there was a tendency for a pair to return to a nest previously used. Walkinshaw (1962) observed a nest in Michigan that was used four times during summer 1960; it produced eight young. Four more nestings were attempted in this nest during 1961, from which six young were produced. Walkinshaw was not able to determine if the nesting adults were the same or different individuals throughout the two years.

Number of Nesting Attempts Per Pair

Adult females may nest as often as five or six times in a single season in warm southern climates but average only two or three attempts per season in northern states (George 1988). Lincoln (1945) noted that, in the most northern parts of the breeding range, two broods were common; in southern parts, there were as many as five or six broods per year.

Dunks et al. (1982) and Tomlinson et al. (1988) calculated the annual production required by each pair of doves to balance mortality and maintain stable breeding populations in the CMU and WMU, respectively. Although production requirements varied by state, the number of fledglings needed annually per pair of nesting adults averaged 2.2 in the CMU and 2.8 in the WMU. Given a 30-percent fledging rate (Geissler et al. 1987), a pair of mourning doves would have to average 3.7 and 4.7 annual nesting attempts in the CMU and WMU, respectively, just to maintain populations.

In Iowa, McClure (1943) observed an average 5.4 and 5.1 nesting attempts, respectively, in 1938 and 1939. Webb (1949) found that doves nested about four times per year in Ohio. Swank (1955a) observed six known nesting attempts by two marked pairs in Texas. In addition, he observed five attempts by another pair, four attempts by two additional pairs and three attempts by two additional pairs for an average of 4.4 attempts per pair.

Literature sources suggest that an average of 3.6 young are fledged annually per breeding pair nationwide *(Table 14)*. The CMU averaged 3.8 young fledged per breeding pair, whereas the WMU averaged 4.4. Thus, available evidence suggests that mourning doves, at least during 1950–80, have been successful in balancing mortality through production.

Table 14. Densities of nests and production estimate for mourning doves by region (updated from Hanson and Kossack 1963).

Location[a]	Dates	Nest density[b]	Production estimate[c]	Reference
North EMU				
Illinois	1950–58		2.4	Hanson and Kossack (1963)
Kentucky	1949–53		6.0	Russell (1954)
Maryland	1917–23	0.27 (0.67)		Andrews (1925)
Michigan	1954	0.08 (0.20)	2.2	Caldwell (1964)
Ohio campus	1946	0.74 (1.83)		Calhoun (1948)
Pennsylvania	1944–45	0.14 (0.35)		Preston and Norris (1947)
	1954		4.0	Howarth (1954)
	1956		7.0	Sheldon (1957)
Wisconsin park	1947	1.00 (2.47)	0.8	Young (1948)
Mean		0.37 (0.91)	3.7	
South EMU				
Georgia	1950–51	0.03 (0.07)	2.1	Hopkins and Odum (1953)
	1954	0.03 (0.07)	2.0	Lowe (1956)
Mississippi orchard	1957	1.56 (3.85)	1.4	Handley and Edwards (1958)
North Carolina		0.15 (0.37)		Hon (1956)
Mean		0.44 (1.09)	1.8	
North CMU				
Iowa	1938–39		5.3	McClure (1943)
	1941	0.34 (0.84)		McClure (1946)
Ground	1974–77	0.03 (0.07)		George et al. (1979)
Kansas hedgerow	1962	17.30 (42.75)	4.5	Schroeder (1970)
Ground	1980–81	0.05 (0.12)		Rodgers (1983)
Missouri	1971–72	0.04 (0.10)		Armbruster et al. (1978)
Nebraska	1957	16.15 (39.90)	2.2	LaPointe (1958)
Shelterbelt	1962	40.00 (98.84)	2.4	Frates (1963)
North Dakota coulee	1952	12.11 (29.92)	4.6	Randall (1955)
Shelterbelt		6.47 (15.99)	4.4	
Shelterbelt	1950		3.2	Boldt and Hendrickson (1952)
South Dakota shelterbelt	1965	1.94 (4.79)	2.2	Drewien and Sparrowe (1966)
Mean		9.44 (23.33)	3.8	
South CMU				
Oklahoma campus	1920	7.50 (18.53)		Nice (1923)
Campus	1921	0.80 (1.98)	3.7	
Farmstead	1956	4.91 (12.13)		Downing (1959)
Groves		2.35 (5.81)		
Shelterbelt		0.64 (1.58)		
Natural tree		0.98 (2.42)		
Ground		0.03 (0.07)		
	1968	0.05 (0.12)		Carpenter (1970)
Texas trees	1939	0.03 (0.07)		Jackson (1940)
Campus	1950	1.10 (2.72)		
Campus	1951	0.32 (0.79)	6.7	Swank (1952)
Ground	1970–71	0.06–0.28 (0.15–0.69)		
Tree		0.03–0.31 (0.07–0.77)		Soutiere and Bolen (1976)
Campus	1978	0.67 (1.66)	3.0	Bivings (1980)
Campus	1979	1.52 (3.76)	1.9	
Mean		1.27 (3.14)	3.8	
WMU				
California	1948–50	0.01 (0.02)	6.2	Cowan (1952)
Idaho orchard	1953	7.46 (18.43)	3.2	Fichter (1959)
Ground	1983–85	0.01 (0.02)		Howe and Flake (1989)
Utah orchard	1952	7.82 (19.32)	3.9	Dahlgren (1955)
Washington	1975		2.0	Knight et al. (1975)
Mean		3.83 (9.46)	4.4	
United States		3.45 (8.53)	3.6	

[a] EMU = Eastern Management Unit; CMU = Central Management Unit; WMU = Western Management Unit.
[b] Maximum number of active nests or estimated number of nesting pairs per acre (ha).
[c] Young fledged per breeding pair.

Densities of nests (maximum number of active nests per acre or estimated number of pairs per acre) varied from an average of 0.37 active nests per acre (0.91/ha) in the North EMU to 9.44 per acre (23.33/ha) in the North CMU. Nest densities for many studies reported in the literature were from such limited areas as shelterbelts, hedgerows and orchards that had high densities and were not the normal densities, as evidenced by Cowan's (1952) data from California. The overall density of nests in Cowan's study was 0.01 nests per acre (0.25/ha); however, he observed areas of willow with nest densities of more than 4 per acre (9.9/ha).

Nest Site Characteristics

Nest site characteristics and preferences of mourning doves are as varied as the number of habitat types utilized for nesting. Doves nest in a variety of both coniferous and deciduous tree species, shrubs, vines, building ledges, chimneys, and commonly on the ground in some parts of their range. Heavy use is made of conifers and orchard trees in the EMU, shelterbelt trees (elms, Osage-orange, Russian olive, wild plum and various conifers), mesquite and on-ground sites in the CMU, and cottonwoods, mesquite, saltcedar, fruit orchards, grapevines, palms and on-ground sites in the WMU *(Table 15)*.

Working in the Ozark foothills of Missouri, Armbruster (1973) noted the importance of interspersion of vegetative types in nest site selection by mourning doves. For example, one 150-acre (61 ha) study area had thirty-five active dove nests in 1970. Another area with similar topography and plant species had only three active nests that year. Removal of trees with large, dense canopies in the second area created openings with scattered eastern red cedar and hawthorn. In 1972, the second area was as attractive to nesting doves (thirty-nine active nests) as was the first area (thirty-eight nests). The presence of bare or nearly bare ground near potential nest trees or shrubs also seemed important in nest site selection (Armbruster 1973). Heavy grazing and other agricultural practices that resulted in bare ground or sparse, low vegetation therefore seemed to be favorable factors for nesting doves.

Location of the nest within the tree and other nest site characteristics are extremely variable, as documented in the descriptions of mourning dove nests and nest sites provided by Nice (1922, 1923). McClure (1946) recorded several nest site characteristics for a large sample of dove nests in Nebraska. He reported an average diameter of 10.2 inches (25.9 cm) for nest trees, an average nest height of 9.3 feet (2.8 m) and nest locations an average of 5 feet (1.5 m) from the center of the tree. Carpenter (1970), in Oklahoma, noted that the majority of nests found were in trees and situated 3 to 6 feet (0.9 to 1.8 m) above the ground; ground nesting was uncommon. Harris et al. (1963) evaluated factors influencing selection of nest sites in Minnesota. Considered important were density of cover provided by the nest trees, availability of horizontal limbs or crotches, proximity of relatively open perches for cooing, and proximity of the nest tree to an open view and flight path on at least one side.

Swank (1955a) observed that live oak trees in Texas provide excellent support and protection for mourning dove nests. The horizontal limbs and numerous diverging small twigs of this species serve to anchor the nests in place. Swank also noted that live oaks contain leaves year-round, which provides protection for early nests constructed before leaves develop on such species as hackberry, chinaberry and pecan.

Conifer nesting. In the North, South and certain parts of the mountainous West, mourning doves appear to prefer coniferous to deciduous trees for nesting sites. Moore and Pearson (1941) noted that of 680 nests observed in Alabama, approximately 84 percent were located in pine trees—mainly shortleaf and loblolly. In North Carolina, Quay (1951b) found dove nests in fifty-five species of trees and shrubs; however, 67 percent of 771 nests were located in seven species of conifers. Although pines appeared to be preferred in Alabama, the differences in overall tree use by doves may have resulted from the relatively high abundance of pines in the area (Pearson and Moore 1939).

Nest site and nest tree preferences may shift throughout the nesting season in many areas. Coniferous or other evergreen trees in Alabama appeared to be used more frequently by doves during spring before leaves had emerged on deciduous species (Moore and Pearson 1941). Similarly, early-nesting (March and April) doves in Missouri nested exclusively in eastern red cedar (Armbruster 1973).

In a southern Michigan study, doves preferred red pine and Norway spruce. White pine and Scotch pine, although present in the study area, were not used by nesting doves (Caldwell 1964). Hanson and Kossack (1963) stated that doves showed a strong preference for blue spruce over other coniferous plantings on their Illinois study areas. Norway and blue spruce also were important nest trees in Iowa (McClure 1943). In New Jersey, doves selected coniferous (Austrian pine and Norway spruce) nest sites (93.3 percent) over other cover types (Castelli 1988).

Table 15. Nest substrate (primary and secondary) for mourning doves by region.

Location[a]	Dates	Nest substrate[b]		Reference
		Primary	Secondary	
North EMU				
Illinois	1950–58	Blue spruce	Norway spruce	Hanson and Kossack (1963)
	1982–83	Standard apple	Semidwarf apple	Putera et al. (1985)
Indiana	1950–51	Austrian pine	White spruce	Hosford (1955)
Maryland	1917–23	Grape	Rose	Andrews (1925)
Michigan	1954	Red pine	Norway spruce	Caldwell (1964)
South EMU				
Alabama	1936–38	Shortleaf pine	Longleaf pine	Pearson and Moore (1939)
Mississippi				
Central	1956–57	Oak	Pine	Handley and Edwards (1958)
Prairie		Osage-orange	Cedar	
Delta		Peach	Pecan	
North CMU				
Iowa				
Town	1938–40	Elms	Boxelder	McClure (1942)
Country		Red pine	Apple	
	1955	American elm	Boxelder	Jumber et al. (1956)
Ground	1974–77	Switchgrass	Indiangrass	George et al. (1979)
	1983	Jack pine	Multiflora rose	Westmoreland and Best (1985)
Kansas	1961	Osage-orange	Ground	Shroeder (1970)
Ground	1980–81	Wheat stubble		Rodgers (1983)
Minnesota	1978–79	White spruce	Colorado blue spruce	Yahner (1982)
	1974	White spruce	Blue spruce	Nelson (1976)
Nebraska	1941–43	American elm	White spruce	McClure (1946)
	1957	American elm	Ponderosa pine	LaPointe (1958)
	1962	Eastern redcedar	Red mulberry	Frates (1963)
North Dakota	1950	Elm	Russian olive	Boldt and Hendrickson (1950)
	1952	Oak	Green (red) ash	Randall (1955)
South Dakota				
University farm	1965	Honeysuckle	Apple	Drewien and Sparrowe (1960)
Shelterbelt		Wild plum	Russian olive	
South CMU				
Oklahoma	1919–21	Elms	Locusts	Nice (1922)
	1925	Hackberries	Elms	Nice (1926)
	1968	Mesquite	Osage-orange	Carpenter (1970)
Texas	1950	Live oak	Eastern redcedar	Swank (1952)
	1970–71	Ground	Mesquite	Soutiere and Bolen (1976)
	1978–80	Mesquite	Colima	Passmore (1981)
	1982–84	Mesquite	Huisache	George (1986)
WMU				
California	1944	Palms	California pepper-tree	McClure (1946)
	1967–74	Grapevines		Channing (1979)
Idaho	1983–85	Ground under big sagebrush	Ground under rabbitbrush	Howe and Flake (1989)
Southwest	1980s	Saltcedar, mesquite	Riparian	Kerpez and Smith (1987)
Washington	1975	Apple, standard	Apple, dwarf	Knight et al. (1984)
WMU	1967–75	Cottonwood, mesquite, saltcedar, fruit orchards		Tomlinson et al. (1988)

[a] EMU = Eastern Management Unit; CMU = Central Management Unit; WMU = Western Management Unit.

[b] Substrates are those in which the greatest number of nests was found, but may not reflect "preference"—defined as substrate used divided by substrate availability.

Conifers commonly are planted in rural and urban cemeteries throughout the United States. The cemeteries provide excellent nesting cover for mourning doves, and disturbance factors are at a minimum. At least during spring, before leaves develop on deciduous trees, cemetery nesting is important to local dove production.

Shelterbelt nesting. Hedgerows or shelterbelts, planted to provide protection from the wind in midwestern and plains states, are popular dove nesting areas. In South Dakota, Russian olive and wild plum trees located at the edge of shelterbelts were observed to be preferred by nesting doves (Drewien and Sparrowe 1966). Elm and Russian olive were reported to be the preferred nesting trees of doves in North Dakota shelterbelts (Boldt and Hendrickson 1952).

Osage-orange hedgerows were planted widely throughout the Midwest during the early 1900s. These trees provide excellent platform structure for dove nests. Carpenter (1970) found that Osage-

orange, elm, mesquite and orchard trees were preferred nest tree species in Oklahoma, whereas blackjack oak, eastern red cedar, locust, mulberry, cottonwood, hackberry and saltcedar supported fewer nests. Osage-orange trees were preferred by nesting doves over other tree species in northern Missouri during 1955–59 (R. E. Tomlinson personal communication: 1990). Hanson and Kossack (1963) reported that American elm and boxelder were important nesting trees in northern Illinois and that Osage-orange hedgerows were heavily used by nesting doves in some parts of Illinois.

Unfortunately, shelterbelts in many areas are being removed to provide easier access for large-scale agricultural practices and to conserve water. The elimination of these coverts is a serious detriment to dove production, particularly in the Great Plains (Olson et al. 1991).

Orchard nesting. Fruit orchards commonly are used by nesting doves in various parts of the country. Fichter (1959) observed successful nesting

In many parts of their nesting range, mourning doves prefer to nest in conifers (left). In such areas, some doves that choose to nest on the ground (right) will make their nests partly or entirely of conifer needles—pine in this case. *Left photo courtesy of the Alabama Cooperative Wildlife Research Unit. Right photo by Ed Bry; courtesy of the North Dakota Game and Fish Department.*

in apple, pear and cherry orchards of Idaho. In central Washington, where apple orchards are primary nesting habitat (Zeigler 1977), doves preferred to nest in old (twenty-five to thirty-five years), spreading trees. Furthermore, they selected regular over semidwarf varieties because of the more suitable branching structure of the former (Knight et al. 1984). Drewien and Sparrowe (1966) also reported that mature orchards were preferred over younger orchards on a South Dakota study area. Doves nesting in Illinois orchards showed a definite preference for standard varieties over semidwarf varieties of apple trees (Putera et al. 1985).

Nesting of mourning doves in citrus groves is a common occurrence in southern Texas, Florida and Arizona (R. E. Tomlinson personal communication: 1990). Although white-winged doves apparently adapt more readily to (and probably compete more successfully in) citrus nesting, mourning doves also make use of this habitat. Because the citrus belt is restricted to the extreme southern part of the country, however, dove production there is no doubt of little overall significance.

Urban and farm nesting. Nesting mourning doves commonly are seen around human habitations, either in cities and towns or on farms. Wherever trees and shrubs become mature in suburban subdivisions, dove nesting populations gradually increase in those areas. The use of shrubbery and trees surrounding buildings by nesting doves is well documented (see Jackson 1940, McClure 1941b, Moore and Pearson 1941, Hanson and Kossack 1963). DeGraaf and Stihler (1979) found that doves in a suburban study area of New York preferred to nest in ornamental shrubs. McClure (1943) listed a variety of trees used by doves in Lewis, Iowa, including white (American) and red (slippery) elms, box elder, and silver maple. However, he also found dove nests in eave troughs, grapevines, rose arbors, and even on light poles and electrical signs. We have seen pictures of doves on nests located in a traffic signal light and on the side-view mirror of an automobile. Using radio-fixes on nesting doves, Fuemmeler (1992) found 28.5 percent (1990) and 16 percent (1991) of the nesters using "atypical" sites (agricultural fields, open pastures, tree limbs in forest interiors) in northcentral Missouri. Clearly, mourning doves are highly adaptable to a wide variety of nesting situations.

Ground nesting. Ground nesting by mourning doves is most common in the prairie regions of the Midwest and Great Plains states, Intermountain West, and certain portions of the Southwest. However, there are scattered reports of ground-nesting mourning doves in all parts of the species' breeding range.

George et al. (1979) recorded ground nest densities of 1 per 29.2 acres (11.8 ha) in active prairie grass pastures in Iowa. Ground-nesting doves showed a marked preference for panicum switchgrass and yellow Indiangrass over big bluestem and little bluestem. Doves nesting in yellow Indiangrass or panicum switchgrass selected short grass or open areas of bare ground between clumps as nesting sites. Downing (1959) found an overall ground-nesting density of 0.03 nests per acre (0.07/ha) on nineteen study areas totaling 1,184 acres (479 ha) in northwestern Oklahoma. In the same region, he estimated a tree-nesting density of 1.78 nests per acre (4.4/ha), although trees occupied less than 1 percent of the study area. Olson et al. (1991) reported that during a three-year study (1978–80) in Colorado, mourning dove ground-nesting densities never exceeded 0.04 nests per acre (0.1/ha). Nesting densities in nearby shelterbelts, on the other hand, ranged from 9 to 25 nests per acre (22 to 62/ha). Howe and Flake (1989a) found 0.05 ground nests per acre (0.12/ha) in Idaho and suggested that overhead shading and cover, especially from big sagebrush, was important to these ground-nesting doves. Hon (1956) reported 0.2 ground nests per acre (0.49/ha) on coastal islands of North Carolina. Cowan (1952) estimated that, in some areas in southern California, 70 percent of all dove nests were ground nests. He further observed that doves commonly nested on the ground in cotton fields even though adequate tree-nesting sites were available in nearby willow groves.

In the tobosa grass/mesquite rangelands of Texas, ground nesting of mourning doves increased substantially following spraying or prescribed burning (Soutiere and Bolen 1976). Although doves more commonly nested in mesquite in undisturbed areas, the incidence of ground nesting was not due only to absence of mesquite. Ground nests were never more than 200 feet (61 m) from a tree, and most ground-nesting doves selected sites in burned areas that provided vertical cover (e.g., pricklypear pads, mesquite sprouts or fallen mesquite branches) on at least one side of the nest (Soutiere and Bolen 1972).

Reports from the Midwest also support observations that ground nesting is not restricted to areas without suitable nest trees. In central Missouri, M. W. Sayre (file data) found ground nests in both fallow and cultivated fields in close proximity to woody hedgerows and field borders. In the Kansas Flinthills, ground nests were common even though draws and drainages contained suitable trees for nesting (N. J. Silvy file data). Hanson and Kossack (1963) cited numerous reports by others of ground nests throughout most of Illinois.

Ground nesting by mourning doves is common, even in areas where there are trees, shrubs and other suitable sites for nest perches. Ground nests tend to be in patches of bare ground with some protective vegetation. Although such nests seem to be highly conspicuous, they are not when a parent is on the nest (which is almost continuously), insomuch as the adult's coloration blends with open patches of dry soil. *Left photo by William B. Brooks; courtesy of the U.S. Soil Conservation Service. Right photo by Charles W. Schwartz.*

NEST SUCCESS AND PRODUCTIVITY

Factors Affecting Nest Success

Nest success rates reported from nesting studies conducted throughout the range of the dove varied from 0 ($n = 23$) to 82 ($n = 39$) percent and averaged 48 percent *(Table 16)*. Nest loss may be attributable to many different factors, such as weather, predation or disturbance. The relative importance of each of these factors may vary throughout the nesting range and even among years on the same area.

Many observers have noted that the bulk of the nest loss occurs during the incubation stages of the nesting cycle (McClure 1942, Fichter 1959, Harris et al. 1963). Most likely, this occurs because adults brooding young are more attentive and less likely to flush or abandon the nest, and because nestling doves are less apt to fall out of the nest than eggs are (McClure 1942).

Coon et al. (1981) demonstrated that the probability of a nest succeeding is affected by its structural stability. Structural stability was considered a function of both the choice of nest site and the quality of construction. Nice (1923) noted that dove nests in crotches of trees were nearly twice as successful as nests on branches. In Iowa, doves that nested in old robin nests had greater nesting success than those in nests constructed by doves (McClure 1943). Nice (1922) made similar observations and suggested that the chief advantage of building on another nest lies in a larger, stronger place for holding young. Ground-nesting doves in Oklahoma had lower nest success (29 percent) than did tree-nesting doves (49 percent) on the same area (Downing 1959). However, Soutiere and Bolen (1976) reported that ground-nesting doves were more successful than doves nesting in trees on their study area in Texas.

Table 16. Nest success (the percentage of nests that fledged at least one young) reported in mourning dove nesting studies.

Location[a]	Dates	Number of nesting attempts	Percentage of nests successful	Reference
North EMU				
Illinois	1921–39	62	50	Kendeigh (1942)
	1950–58	940	64	Hanson and Kossack (1963)
	1982–83	121	42	Putera et al. (1985)
Indiana	1950–51	152	44	Hosford (1955)
Kentucky	1949–53	606	49	Russell (1954)
Maryland	1979–80	119	44	Nichols et al. (1984)
Michigan	1952	30	50	Davey (1953)
	1954	164	35	Caldwell (1964)
New Jersey	1981–83	258	50	Castelli (1988)
Ohio, artificial	1946	31	39	Calhoun (1948)
Pennsylvania	1956	118	70	Sheldon (1957)
Wisconsin	1947	11	18	Young (1948)
	1950	110	65	Mathiak (1953)
Total/weighted mean		2,741	53	
South EMU				
Alabama	1936–38	592	47	Pearson and Moore (1939)
	1949–50	135	53	Keeler (1953)
Florida	1979–80	120	30	Marion and Schnoes (1982)
Georgia	1950–51	66	48	Hopkins and Odum (1953)
	1954	23	61	Lowe (1956)
Louisiana	1956	120	66	Henson (1956)
North Carolina	1939–42	771	45–50	Quay (1951)
Tennessee	1946–48	235	52	Monk (1949)
Total/weighted mean		2,062	48	
North CMU				
Colorado	1978–80	479	44	Olson and Braun (1984)
Iowa	1938–40	3,878	48	McClure (1946)
	1936	45	44	Rosene (1950)
	1955	203	61	Jumber et al. (1956)
	1963	50	70	
	1969–70	23	0	LaPerriere and Haugen (1972)
Ground nests	1973–77	7	71	George et al. (1979)
Windbreak		150	25	Westmoreland and Best (1985)
Kansas	1962	389	57	Schroeder (1970)
	1980–81	18	61	Rodgers (1983)
Minnesota	1957–58	505	65	Harris et al. (1963)
Natural	1974	224	44	Nelson (1976)
Artificial		69	61	
Missouri	1970–72	161	46	Armbruster (1973)
Nebraska	1941–43	385	47	McClure (1946)
	1957	98	26	LaPointe (1958)
	1962	46	59	Frates (1963)
North Dakota	1950	43	58	Boldt and Hendrickson (1950)
	1952	156	70	Randall (1955)
		31	77	
	1981–84	1,540	28	Blockstein (1986)
South Dakota	1965	50	56	Drewien and Sparrowe (1966)
Total/weighted mean		8,107	46	
South CMU				
Oklahoma	1919–21	141	43	Nice (1923)
	1925	39	82	Nice (1926)
Ground nests	1956	130	29	Downing (1959)
Tree nests		167	49	
Texas	1949–51	656	62	Swank (1955)
Ground nests	1970–71	170	23	
Tree nests		113	16	Soutiere and Bolen (1976)
	1978–79	236	29	Bivings and Silvy (1981)
	1982–84	476	32	George (1986)
Total/weighted mean		2,128	42	

Table 16. (continued)

Location[a]	Dates	Number of nesting attempts	Percentage of nests successful	Reference
WMU				
California	1944,46–49	335	55	McClure (1950)
	1948–52	220	65	Cowan (1952)
Idaho				
Orchard	1953	266	67	Fichter (1959)
Ground	1983–85	24	75	Howe and Flake (1989)
Utah	1951–52	417	58	Dahlgren (1955)
Washington				
Orchard	1975	123	40	Knight et al. (1984)
Total/weighted mean		1,262	61	
United States		16,300	48	

[a] EMU = Eastern Management Unit; CMU = Central Management Unit; WMU = Western Management Unit.

Weather. Weather is thought to be an important source of nest loss (Nice 1922, 1923, McClure 1942, Hanson and Kossack 1963). It is not uncommon to find broken dove eggs on the ground under nests after thunderstorms or periods of high winds. In Texas, Morrow and Silvy (1982) found significant correlations between monthly estimates of nest mortality and the number of days in which wind speed exceeded 15 knots per hour (27.6 km/hr). Mean monthly temperature also was positively correlated with nest success, indicating that below-normal temperatures may adversely affect nesting success. Yahner (1983) found that 7 percent of nest loss in a Minnesota shelterbelt could be attributable to weather conditions.

Predation. Predation on eggs or nestlings is a major factor affecting nesting success. Blue jays have been observed attacking dove nests and stealing eggs or killing nestlings (Nice 1923, Pearson and Moore 1939, Swank 1955a). On their Texas study area, Morrow and Silvy (1982) found a significant correlation between blue jay abundance and dove nest loss. Common grackles, American crows and house cats have been implicated as important nest predators (Hosford 1955, Grau 1979, Harris et al. 1963). Drewien and Sparrowe (1966) observed that a large influx of common grackles into their South Dakota study area in early July coincided with a sharp drop in dove nesting success.

More than 80 percent of the nest loss in a Minnesota shelterbelt could be attributed to predation (Yahner 1983). Red squirrels were considered the major nest predators in this area. Predation accounted for the majority of the nest losses on the mesquite/tobosa grass rangelands in Texas (Soutiere and Bolen 1976). The western coachwhip snake was common on the area and thought to be a major predator of both tree and ground nests.

Other predators common on the study area included rattlesnake, striped skunk, raccoon, ground squirrel and wood rat. The importance of predation as a source of nesting mortality is further supported by the fact that one of the highest rates of nest success (77 percent) was reported for a population of doves nesting in a North Dakota shelterbelt devoid of predators (Randall 1955).

Human disturbance. Disturbance by man or his activities can be a significant source of nest loss in some habitat types. Drewien and Sparrowe (1966) observed substantial nest loss after spraying activities in an orchard on their study area. Putera et al. (1985) reported nest success rates ranging from 24 to 80 percent in three Illinois apple orchards. During the course of the study, fourteen active dove nests were observed during spraying operations. Four of seven adults that were brooding nestlings remained on the nest during the spraying, but only one of seven incubating adults remained on the nest; all adults that had been flushed returned to the nest within thirty minutes. Although 89 percent of the nests containing eggs at the time of spraying eventually were unsuccessful, most nest failures occurred four or more days after spraying.

Soutiere and Bolen (1976) observed that abandonment was the cause of nest failure for 18 percent of the ground nestings and 9 percent of the tree nestings. They indicated that about half of these losses could be attributed to the activities of the investigators. Four (14 percent) of twenty-eight ground nests located by Howe and Flake (1989a) were abandoned due to the investigators' initial disturbance. The effects of human visitation on nest success was experimentally studied by Nichols et al. (1984), who concluded that success rates of mourning dove nests visited at daily and weekly

Agricultural practices generally enhance nesting habitat for mourning doves but also can destroy nests in close proximity to cultivated fields. In this instance, a farmer plowed around a mourning dove nest—an unusual situation, since such nests are not easily detected from modern farm machinery. *Photo courtesy of the Alabama Cooperative Wildlife Research Unit.*

Nesting mourning doves occasionally can be approached very closely before they flush from the nest. However, human disturbance may reduce nest success, especially if the adult is flushed while incubating. *Photo courtesy of the U.S. National Archives.*

intervals were similar. However, they did not study undisturbed nests. Westmoreland and Best (1985) looked at disturbed and undisturbed mourning dove nests and compared them for differences in daily survival probabilities. They concluded that standard nest-checking procedures influenced nesting success and confounded interpretation of nesting outcome.

Hunting. In their nationwide nesting study, Geissler et al. (1987) examined the effects of September hunting on nesting mourning doves. During 1979 and 1980, 6,950 active nests were monitored to obtain data on nesting patterns. The nationwide percentages of total annual nests that were initiated in September and October were 1.0 percent based on back-dating from hatch dates and 2.7 percent based on nests found for the first time.

Nesting activity was measured by numbers of eggs and nestlings present in weekly counts. Nationally, 4.5 percent of the annual nesting activity occurred in September and October. The measure of production used in this study was numbers of young fledged. Nationally, 10.3 percent of all observed fledging occurred in September and October. Because an observed decline in nests found in the latter half of the nesting season preceded the September 1 start of hunting, Geissler et al. concluded that the reduction in nesting activity at the end of the season was a natural phenomenon and not caused by hunting disturbance.

In a separate part of this study, the authors estimated survival rates in adjacent hunted and nonhunted zones from data on 668 nests. The estimated daily survival rates for individual eggs and nestlings were 95.8 percent for nonhunted areas and 95.0 percent for hunted areas. The corresponding fledging rates were 33 and 26 percent, respectively. Neither differences in survival nor fledging rates between nonhunted and hunted zones were statistically significant ($P > 0.05$). Geissler et al. concluded that dove hunting under current regulations had no substantial effect on recruitment of fledglings into the mourning dove population, even though there have been emotional (McClure 1991) rather than scientific pleas to the contrary. This important subject also is addressed in chapters 7 and 16.

Other studies in local areas have shown differing results of hunting on survival of mourning dove nests. Even though the impact of September hunting on annual recruitment may be small, some nest abandonment and nestling mortality undoubtedly occur. Lincoln (1945) noted that late breeding by mourning doves was the main factor complicating dove management and that it would be a mistake to permit hunting during a period when two young may die in the nest from starvation after a nesting adult is killed. However, not all young may die from starvation; Hitchcock and Mirarchi (1985) noted a 6.5 percent surrogate feeding rate of orphans.

McClure (1950a) noted in California that only 48.8 percent of nests active on the day before hunting started were successful, as compared with 56.5 percent success of nests active prior to the season. Loss of young was even greater, as only 64 percent were fledged from nests active after September 1, while 80 percent were fledged from earlier nests. No new nests were built after the opening of the season.

In Kansas, Schroeder (1970) noted that the opening of autumn hunting seasons discouraged further nesting attempts by mourning doves. Doves were still in the process of nest building and incubation when the season began, but no new nests were started after that time. In 1961, a search of his study area on August 31 revealed thirty-two active nests. Twelve of these contained eggs and twenty contained thirty-two young. On September 7, when the area was searched again, five of the twelve nests containing eggs had successfully hatched nine young, six of which were dead when found. Squabs were found dead in eight of the twenty nests that had contained living young. A search of Schroeder's study area on August 30, 1962, yielded forty-eight active nests. Twenty nests

contained thirty-nine nestlings, and twenty-eight contained fifty-six eggs. Thirty-seven nests failed during the first eleven days of September. On September 5, all of the nests with eggs were found inactive and the eggs broken. Only eleven nests were successful in fledging one or more nestlings. Young in successful nests averaged eight days of age at the start of the hunting season, and those in unsuccessful nests averaged five days of age.

Bivings (1980) concluded that, although the removal of one parent from nests with eggs or young less then seven days old resulted in a significant reduction in nesting success, some young would reach fledging stage. Haas (1980) reported that nests losing one parent prior to eight days posthatching were less successful than were two-parent nests. Mirarchi and Scanlon (1981) believed that to maximize fledgling survival, parental care by at least one adult was needed for eighteen days posthatching (five to nine days postfledging).

Observing penned birds, Laub (1956) reported that, following the removal of one of an adult pair, the remaining adult was unable to fledge young that were less than six days of age at the time of removal. Goforth (1964) observed a captive male successfully hatch and fledge two young after the female had been removed on the fourth day of incubation. However, males from four other captive pairs failed to complete incubation after females had been removed.

Age-related Effects on Productivity

Contribution of immatures to annual production. Moore (1940) observed that juvenile mourning doves hatched in captivity sometimes laid eggs in late summer. In Arizona, immature (young of the year) mourning doves were observed vocalizing, copulating and nesting (Irby and Blankenship 1966). Brown (1967) reported that 8.2 percent of juvenile mourning doves were breeding during June in southern Arizona. Males and females were equally capable of breeding, and some immatures began nesting at the age of ninety days. Mirarchi et al. (1980) examined testes weights and follicular development in captive and hunter-harvested immatures in Virginia and concluded that immature doves reached puberty and were capable of breeding at ninety days of age. In harvest samples collected in September, 16.7 percent of the juvenile males showed evidence of a developed crop, indicative of nesting behavior. Brown (1967) felt that immature breeders had the potential to increase annual production by 4 percent but that this potential was not realized because of such behavioral circumstances as nest desertion and poorly constructed nests.

Reproductive performance. Limited observations suggest that although some immature doves will attempt nesting in their natal year (Moore 1940, Irby and Blankenship 1966, Brown 1967, Mirarchi 1978), nest success of hatching-year breeders is poor.

Armbruster (1983) investigated the influence of age on the chronology of pair formation and nest initiation, and the success of first and subsequent nesting attempts in captive doves. Nesting success (defined as at least one young fledged) of first-year females (less than two years of age) was significantly lower (15.6 percent) than that of older females (83.3 percent). The poor nesting success exhibited by first-year females was attributed to their failure to incubate the clutches they laid. First-year females began incubation but then deserted their nests after two or three days. Because of the implications of reduced reproductive performance of first-year females to the population, this subject warrants further study in wild populations.

Seasonal Patterns of Nest Success and Production

Most seasonal nesting studies indicate that nest success increases as the season progresses (see Nice 1926, Lund 1952, Hanson and Kossack 1963, Harris et al. 1963, Bivings and Silvy 1981, Olson and Braun 1984). Lowered nest success in the early months of the breeding season has been attributed to weather conditions and a greater likelihood of nest desertion. Harris et al. (1963) reported that nest losses to weather, desertion and predation were all greater in the early part of the nesting season (before July 31) on their study area in Minnesota. They attributed this to June thunderstorms and the large number of nesting common grackles present in June and early July.

Morrow and Silvy (1982) obtained data from 1,556 nests from February through October and estimated that 22 percent of eggs laid survived to fledging, with the greatest mortality occurring during the first week after laying. Higher mortality was observed for eggs (56 percent) than for nestlings (45 percent), but there were seasonal differences. Early in the nesting season, mortality for eggs was higher

than mortality for nestlings; this was reversed during July and September with nestling mortality being higher. Total mortality also was found to differ among months. Except for February, which showed a 68-percent nesting cycle mortality, total mortality was high (82 to 85 percent) from March through June, declined to 64 to 70 percent from July to September, and then increased to 82 percent in October.

Geissler et al. (1987) compared seasonal patterns of productivity for mourning doves within different regions of the United States (*Figure 12*). On a nationwide basis, 83.1 percent of the annual total of doves fledged were produced in summer (May through August), 6.6 percent were produced from successful nests initiated in spring (February through April), and 10.2 percent of the total annual production occurred in September and October.

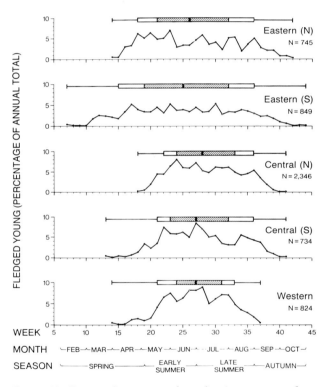

Figure 12. Seasonal patterns of production expressed as young fledged each week as percentages of an annual total from combined 1979 and 1980 data for mourning dove management unit subdivisions (from Geissler et al. 1987).

Chapter 6

Reproductive Strategy

David E. Blockstein
Committee for the National Institutes for the Environment
Washington, D.C.

David Westmoreland
Department of Biology
Emory University
Atlanta, Georgia

The various attributes of a species—size and shape, physiology, and behavioral characteristics— have all been molded by natural selection. Consideration of a species' evolutionary history and the forces that have affected it helps in the understanding of that species as it exists and is seen today. This chapter describes how various reproductive traits of the mourning dove (e.g., number of eggs and nestlings, nestling growth, and parental behavior) are related. It describes a set of morphological, physiological and behavioral characteristics encompassing a "reproductive strategy" that has evolved to maximize the reproductive success of individual mourning doves. Information on a number of other columbid species has been incorporated because many of the attributes of mourning doves seem to have arisen in their ancestors and are shared by most members of the family.

OVERVIEW OF THE COLUMBID REPRODUCTIVE STRATEGY

Mourning doves are among the best-studied members of family Columbidae. Their reproductive traits are unusual among birds but typical of the family *(Table 17)*. Group characteristics include small fixed clutch sizes, small eggs, multiple nestings in a single season, and production of crop milk by both sexes. The reproductive behavior of the mourning dove and all other well-known dove species is remarkably consistent (Kendeigh 1952, Frith 1982, Goodwin 1983, Rowan 1983). For example, all living columbids have a protracted and essentially exclusive (monogamous) pairing relationship and a highly synchronized and stereotyped pattern of parental behavior that involves approximately equal contributions by both sexes—in other words, biparental care (Blockstein 1986a).

EFFECT OF DIET ON THE STRATEGY

Much of the columbid reproductive strategy can be attributed to an unusual diet: columbids are among the strictest vegetarians of all avian orders (Lack 1968). Seeds and fruit constitute the vast majority of food items eaten by all columbids that have been studied, although a few species occasionally eat ground-dwelling invertebrates (Goodwin 1983). Seeds comprise more than 99 percent of the diet of mourning doves (Knappen 1938, Cummings and Quay 1953, Korschgen 1958, Beckwith 1959, Browning 1959, 1962, Chambers 1963, see also chapter 11).

Table 17. Uniformity of reproductive traits in family Columbidae.[a]

Feature	Frequency of occurrence[b]
Clutch of one or two eggs, depending on species	178/178
Unmarked eggs	153/153
Crop milk production	[c]
Small eggs	37/37[d]
Rapid growth of nestlings	57/63
Constant incubation	66/66
Stereotyped pattern of biparental nest attendance	66/66
Monogamy	[e]
Male and female parental investment fairly equal	[e]
Small, loosely constructed nests	106/121
Considerable reuse of nests	22/25
Nesting season more than four months long	31/32
Season-long pair bonds	[e]
Overlap of fledgling care and initiation of next clutch	[e]
Short nesting cycle	51/61
Rapid renesting	[e]
Early sexual maturity	[e]

[a] All are exhibited by mourning doves.
[b] Number of species having trait/number studied; data from Frith (1982), Rowan (1982) and Goodwin (1983).
[c] Apparently occurs in all columbids, but has been reported for only a few.
[d] Data from Lack (1968).
[e] Data from a few, mostly captive species, with no known exceptions.

Crop Milk

Few altricial birds (those whose hatchlings require parental care) raise their young on a vegetarian diet. Fruit contains little protein per unit volume (Ricklefs 1974), and nestlings fed fruit have slower growth rates than those fed animal food (Morton 1973). Seeds are hard to digest, and rock doves and mourning doves less than four days old cannot digest them (Vandeputte-Poma 1980, Blockstein et al. 1987). The protein requirements of a growing bird are better met by animal matter (see Newton 1972, Ricklefs 1974). To compensate, most granivorous birds (grain and seed eaters) eat insects while young. Mourning doves and other granivorous columbids, however, rarely capture insects. These dietary limitations, plus having a large crop in which to store grain, have favored the evolution of crop milk—a feature unique to columbids *(Figure 13)*.

Columbids of both sexes produce crop milk composed of fat-laden cells that slough off the germinal epithelium of the crop (Beams and Meyer

1931, Patel 1936, see also chapter 7). Crop milk is very rich in proteins and lipids (Davies 1939, Desmeth 1980, Desmeth and Vandeputte-Poma 1980) and apparently contains growth-promoting factors (Pace et al. 1952, Hegde 1972). It is the exclusive food of nestlings for the first few days of life, then is gradually replaced by regurgitated seeds (Moore 1940, Mirarchi and Scanlon 1980, Vandeputte-Poma 1980, Blockstein 1986a). Similar to mammalian milk, crop milk is a "reliable, digestible and highly nutritious food which can support very rapid growth even under suboptimal conditions" (Pond 1977: 189). Constraints on its production, however, probably limit clutch size in columbids, as discussed later.

Two other groups of avian vegetarians show traits that may be precursors of a habit similar to crop milk production. Psittaciformes (parrots) regurgitate a "green mush" (Tarboten 1976) that might contain a secretion from the proventriculus (stomach) (Forshaw 1978). Some cardueline finches have enlarged buccal (throat) pouches for seed storage during the breeding season (Miller 1941, French 1954, Newton 1972). They feed their nestlings regurgitated but undigested seeds wrapped in mucus that may contain protein (Newton 1972).

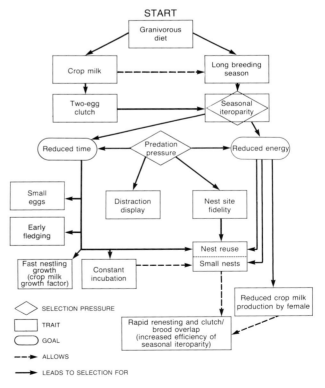

Figure 13. Flow diagram outlining the proposed evolution of traits associated with the granivorous diet of columbids.

Extended Breeding Seasons

Granivorous birds have the potential for long breeding seasons *(Figure 13)* (see also Lack 1968) because an ample supply of seeds to feed nestlings is available for much of the year. Crop milk production allows columbids to raise their young without a change in foraging behavior and to do so when only dry seeds are available. It also is relatively inexpensive; adult ring doves increase their daily energy intake by about 30 percent when producing crop milk (see Brisbin 1969). This low cost may be attributed to production being spread over a large part of the nesting cycle. The crop enlarges throughout the latter half of the incubation phase, and cells that form the initial crop milk are sloughed off in the last few days of incubation (Beams and Meyer 1931, Mirarchi and Scanlon 1980, 1982). Essentially, adults provide nestlings with energy from seeds gathered before the eggs hatch.

The nesting season of mourning doves is one of the longest among North American birds (Peters 1961, see chapter 5). Active nests have been found every month except November and December in Arizona (Irby and Blankenship 1966) and in Texas where seven marked pairs averaged 3.4 known successful broods in a year (Swank 1955a). In North Dakota, near the northern edge of their breeding range, mourning doves lay eggs from late April to early September (Blockstein 1986a). Marked pairs raised as many as three broods in a season from a maximum of five known nesting attempts. In Iowa, a marked pair raised four broods in five attempts (Westmoreland and Best 1987). Production of more than one brood during a long breeding season is characteristic of most if not all columbid species.

Early sexual maturity. A long nesting season favors early sexual maturity, allowing some individuals to breed in the year of their birth. In Virginia and Alabama, 9 and 6 percent, respectively, of the hatching-year female mourning doves collected in late summer to early autumn were capable of breeding (Mirarchi et al. 1980, White et al. 1987). Some males reached reproductive maturity at eighty days of age and some females at ninety-three days (White et al. 1987). In southern Arizona, some hatching-year doves (males and females) began breeding when ninety days old (Brown 1967) and raised at least five young in ten observed nestings (Irby and Blankenship 1966). Even as far north as Ontario, a hatching-year mourning dove was collected with enlarged testes and mature spermatozoa (Armstrong and Noakes 1977b). Reproduction by hatching-year birds probably is common in other tropical columbids that have extended breeding seasons, but few species are well studied.

Diet and Clutch Size

Clutch size is strongly related to diet in columbids. Ninety-three percent (sixty-five of seventy species studied) of granivorous columbids lay two-egg clutches (Blockstein 1986a, tabulated from Goodwin 1983). Notable exceptions with one-egg clutches include the band-tailed pigeon and extinct passenger pigeon, both of which specialize(d) on crops of nuts (Schorger 1955, Smith 1968, Gutierrez et al. 1975, Blockstein and Tordoff 1985).

Seventy-one percent (forty-eight of sixty-eight species studied) of frugivorous (fruit-eating) columbids lay single eggs (Blockstein 1986a, tabulated from Goodwin 1983), probably because the nutritional quality of fruit is much lower than that of grain (Ricklefs 1974). Green pigeons, which include eleven of the thirteen frugivorous columbid species that have two-egg clutches, are the exception that "proves the rule." They are fig specialists (Goodwin 1983, Rowan 1983) with a muscular gizzard and long intestines similar to those of granivorous columbids. Green pigeons grind and digest fig seeds along with the flesh (Cowles and Goodwin 1959). These "granivorous frugivores" have two-egg clutches. In contrast, fruit pigeons, which digest only the pulp of figs (Cadow 1933), have one-egg clutches. Frugivorous pigeons may produce a lower quality or quantity of crop milk than do the granivores (see Cowles and Goodwin 1959), or perhaps the number of nestlings that can be raised is limited by nutrition after the nestlings are weaned from crop milk and are fed fruit. Little is known about the quality of food provided by frugivorous columbids to their nestlings.

Pattern of Constant Incubation and Brooding

Granivorous columbids such as the mourning dove have powerful gizzards and large crops that can store many seeds (Murton et al. 1963). Feeding on seeds that can be stored for hours in the crop and digested slowly (Schmid 1965, Sayre et al. 1980) allows the adults to sit on the nest for long intervals *(Figure 13)*. This is a prerequisite for the pattern of constant incubation and brooding in which each parent replaces the other once a day so the eggs and young squabs always are attended (Harris et al. 1963, Blockstein 1982, 1986a) *(Table 17)*. Constant incubation, in turn, may allow mourning doves and other columbids to have white or otherwise unmarked eggs. Nevertheless, there is some evidence that a cryptic egg coloration would be advantageous even for continuously incubating columbids (Westmoreland and Best 1986).

Continual incubation by one parent or the other may allow mourning doves and other columbids to have white or unmarked eggs, since no camouflage other than the parent in attendance is needed. *Photo by Jim Rathbert; courtesy of the Missouri Department of Conservation.*

Potential for Coloniality

Columbids do not have feeding territories. Instead they feed away from the nest site and must travel to obtain water (Schmid 1965). Seeds are widely distributed (as compared with insect availability), so feeding territories probably would have to be large and, thus, difficult to defend. In the absence of territoriality, some columbids have evolved to breed colonially—passenger pigeon (Schorger 1955, Blockstein and Tordoff 1985), flock pigeon (Morse 1922), white-winged dove (Cottam and Trefethen 1968) and other species (see Lack 1968, Goodwin 1983). Colonial breeding with extreme synchrony but perhaps fewer nestings per year may be an antipredator strategy. Mourning doves show little tendency for colonial nesting, perhaps because their nesting habitat does not occur in the large homogeneous patches that are typical of colonial species. A similar relationship between granivorous diets and coloniality is found among cardueline finches (Lack 1968, Newton 1972).

SELECTION PRESSURE AND REPRODUCTIVE ECOLOGY

Constraints Due to Evolutionary History

Although crop milk production allows columbids to have more than one brood per breeding season (seasonal iteroparity), it also imposes some constraints. Granivorous columbids apparently cannot raise more than two young per nest without significantly reduced growth and survival of the nestlings (Murton et al. 1974a, Burley 1980, Westmoreland and Best 1987, Blockstein 1989). Slow growth seems to result from limits on the rate of crop milk production (Westmoreland and Best 1987, Blockstein 1989), and raising more than two young may be difficult because of the way nestlings are fed. They feed two at a time from the corners of the parent's mouth. This may prevent adults from dividing food equally among three nestlings.

The constraints on clutch size imposed by crop milk production have limited the reproductive options of columbids. Though able to rear only two offspring at a time, mourning doves and other columbids increase their reproductive potential by attempting to raise more than one brood in a season. Many columbid traits can be interpreted as adaptations that increase the efficiency of seasonal iteroparity.

Reduction of Time and Energy

As discussed in chapter 5, a complete nesting cycle for mourning doves takes three to seven days for courtship and nest building, fourteen to fifteen days for egg laying and incubation, eleven to fifteen days for nestling development and ten to twelve days for postfledging parental care (Swank 1955a, Hitchcock and Mirarchi 1984a, Blockstein 1986a). Nesting cycles (from the onset of incubation through fledging) of columbids are 22 percent shorter than would be predicted by their body weight (Westmoreland et al. 1986) *(Figure 14)*.

Columbids have shortened their nesting cycles by having a suite of adaptations (coadapted traits) that save time during the incubation and nestling stages. These traits include small eggs, small nests, reuse of nests, fast-growing nestlings, reduced production of crop milk by females, early fledging and clutch/brood overlap.

Nestling mourning doves are fed crop milk by inserting their bills into the sides of the parent's mouth. More than two young could not feed simultaneously in this manner, which therefore is a constraint on brood size. The reduced strain of feeding only two young may account for the ability of mourning doves to produce more than one successful brood per breeding season. *Photo courtesy of the U.S. National Archives.*

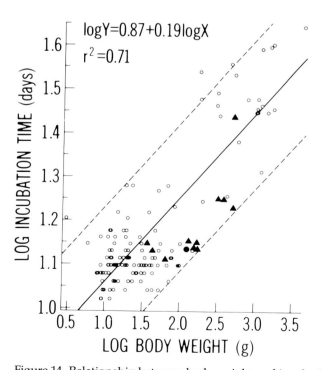

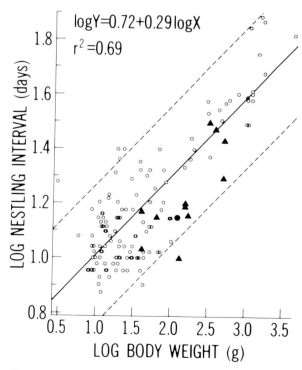

Figure 14. Relationship between body weight and incubation or nestling periods for 128 species of altricial, open-nesting land birds. The solid line was fitted for noncolumbids (open circles). Triangles represent columbids, and the closed circle represents the mourning dove. Dash lines are 95-percent confidence intervals.

Small eggs. On average, columbid eggs are half the weight of those produced by other altricial birds of comparable size (Rahn et al. 1975). They are rich in caloric content (Carey et al. 1980), however, so their small size may not be an energy-saving feature. One advantage of small eggs is that they require shorter incubation periods (Rahn and Ar 1974). Eggs receive nutrients only from the female, while nestlings receive nutrients from both parents. The subsequent rapid growth of columbid squabs may make it beneficial for eggs to hatch early. Murton et al. (1974b) showed that, in wood pigeons, there was no correlation between weight at hatching and weight of nestlings that survived to six days of age. Therefore, larger eggs did not increase the survival prospects of nestlings.

As a result of small clutch size, columbids have a small ratio of clutch weight to body weight—11 percent (Rahn et al. 1975, Murton and Westwood 1977, Walsberg 1983). Thus, early failure during a nesting attempt results in a relatively small waste of reproductive energy. This may explain why mourning doves often abandon their eggs when disturbed shortly after laying, and also why females can initiate new clutches quickly when previous ones have failed (Westmoreland et al. 1986).

Eggs and hatchlings of mourning doves and other columbids are smaller than would be predicted by adult body size. The small eggs require relatively brief incubation time, which is beneficial to altricial birds such as mourning doves that produce more than one clutch per breeding season. *Photo by David E. Blockstein.*

Small nests. Mourning dove nests are small and loosely constructed. Small nests may be advantageous because they save time and energy during nest construction *(Figure 15)*. Nest construction takes seven to ten hours and is spread over two to four days (Blockstein 1986a). On each trip the male carries one piece of nesting material gathered nearby (Cowan 1952, Sayre et al. 1980, Blockstein 1986a) to the female waiting at the nest site (see chapters 5 and 10). The female remains on the nest throughout the nest-building session, thereby minimizing her energy expenditures. A more substantial nest probably is unnecessary because (1) the clutch is small, (2) adults incubate and brood constantly, and (3) the feces of nestlings accumulate on the nest, reinforcing the nest structure (Woolfenden and Rohwer 1969, Blockstein et al. 1987). Blockstein (1986a) found no relation between nest structure and daily survival rates, although in some cases small, thin nests led to nesting failures (Blockstein unpublished data, Coon et al. 1981).

Reuse of nests. Twenty to 40 percent of mourning dove clutches are laid in pre-existing nests of mourning doves and other birds (McClure 1950a, Cowan 1952, Hosford 1955, Hanson and Kossack 1963, Harris et al. 1963, Blockstein 1986a). Other columbids also reuse nests of their own and of other species (Goodwin 1983). Doves usually add a small amount of material to these nests, but

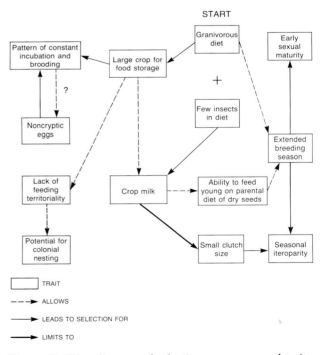

Figure 15. Flow diagram of selection pressures and traits related to production of several broods per season (seasonal iteroparity) in mourning doves.

never as much as would be necessary for a new nest (McClure 1943, Blockstein unpublished data).

Sometimes mourning dove pairs reuse their own nests, which probably is part of a general tendency toward site fidelity (Blockstein 1986a). Successful pairs reuse their nests (30 percent nest reuse) or renest closer to their previous sites more often than do unsuccessful pairs (10 percent) (Blockstein 1986a). Stewart and Mackey (1953) reported that a banded pair of mourning doves used a nest in two consecutive years, and Blockstein (1986a) found that some nests were occupied by the same individual with several different mates for two to four years.

Doves often use nests that they did not build. Such use may increase the likelihood of nest success, but present findings are contradictory. McClure (1943) and Nelson (1976) found that mourning doves using old nests of common grackles and American robins had better success than did those using dove nests. However, others (Woolfenden and Rohwer 1969, Westmoreland and Best 1985) reported that the use of other species' nests did not increase nesting success. In North Dakota, Blockstein (1986a) found that clutches laid in nests of other species had higher probabilities of success than did clutches laid in new mourning dove nests and that clutches in old dove nests had the lowest survival probabilities.

Use of old nests, in general, may have evolved to shorten the nesting cycle and reduce the energy costs of nest building. Successful pairs that reuse their own nests lay a new clutch sooner than do such pairs that change nest sites (Blockstein 1986a). Pairs that use nests they did not build probably also save time and energy, but data are not available to test this hypothesis.

Fast growth of nestlings. Mourning dove nestlings grow rapidly from approximately 0.175 ounces (5 g) at hatching to 2.1 ounces (60 g) at ten days of age (Holcomb and Jaeger 1978, Blockstein 1989, see also chapter 8). Nestlings of most other columbids also grow rapidly (Riddle 1928, Murton et al. 1963, Brisbin 1969) *(Table 17)*. Rapid growth, in addition to early fledging, shortens the nestling phase relative to that of other altricial, open-nesting birds (Westmoreland et al. 1986) *(Figure 14)*.

Rapid growth is a result not only of the high lipid and protein content of crop milk (Davies 1939, Desmeth 1980, Desmeth and Vandeputte-Poma 1980) but also of an unidentified growth-promoting element in crop milk. Hatchling chickens whose initial diet was supplemented with rock dove crop milk grew faster than control groups and continued to do so even after they were no longer being given crop milk (Pace et al. 1952, Hegde 1972).

Mourning dove nestlings grow rapidly on a rich diet of crop milk produced and fed by both parents. Crop milk has high lipid and protein content, plus an unidentified element that promotes growth. Nestlings experience a twelvefold weight increase from hatching to ten days of age. *Photo of nestlings (two to three days old on right, eight to nine days old on left) by David E. Blockstein.*

Reduced crop milk production by females. Studies of mourning dove crop glands indicate that crop milk production regresses four to six days sooner in females than in males (Mirarchi and Scanlon 1980, Books-Blenden et al. 1984a). The hormone prolactin, which stimulates crop milk production, also seems to retard the activity of gonads. In females, an early end to crop milk production may allow the antigonadal effect of prolactin to wane so that production of the next clutch can begin (see Hanson and Kossack 1963, Mirarchi et al. 1982). Small broods require less crop milk and may reduce the amount of prolactin so the ovary can "recycle" soon after the crop milk phase.

Early fledging. Mourning doves fledge at 63 percent of adult weight (McClure 1943), a percentage similar to that of other columbids (Westmoreland et al. 1986) but at the lower end of the range for ninety-four noncolumbid species (Ricklefs 1968). Although early fledging shortens time spent in the nest, parental care does not end at fledging (Hitchcock and Mirarchi 1984a, 1984b, Blockstein 1986a).

Early fledging probably has two advantages. First, it reduces losses to predation. Mourning doves have higher survival rates as fledglings than as nestlings (Grand et al. 1984). After fledging, a single predation event is unlikely to result in death of both young from a nest. Second, early fledging allows the young to start meeting their own energy demands at an early age (five to nine days postfledging) (Hitchcock and Mirarchi 1984a, Blockstein unpublished data). Another effect of early fledging is that the parents are free to start another nesting attempt, possibly in the same nest.

Clutch/brood overlap. Mourning doves often initiate a new clutch before terminating care for the previous fledglings, thus raising two sets of offspring simultaneously. Mourning doves usually begin a new clutch within two to five days after the young fledge (Cowan 1952, Swank 1955a, Harris et al. 1963, Blockstein 1986a, see also chapter 5). At least one parent (usually the male) feeds the fledglings until they are twenty-seven to thirty days old, or up to ten to twelve days postfledging (Hitchcock and Mirarchi 1984a, Blockstein 1986a), while both parents maintain the usual pattern of incubating their new clutch. Radio-tagged males have been observed to feed fledglings in the evening after incubating a clutch in the afternoon (Blockstein 1986a). Fledglings tend to stay in the vicinity of the nest (Hitchcock and Mirarchi 1984a) and recognize the coo of the male that raised them (Hitchcock et al. 1989). This may reduce search time when the male cares for them.

Clutch/brood overlap does not reduce the length of a nesting cycle, but it allows mourning doves to have more nesting attempts in a single breeding season. Overlap is possible because of traits that reduce energy expenditures in the early part of each nesting cycle and because the female plays a smaller role in feeding fledglings. The peak energy demand on columbid parents is in the middle of the nesting cycle (Burley 1980); this differs from most other birds, which experience peak demand just before the nestlings fledge.

Principal Selection Pressures

Mourning doves became efficient at producing multiple broods in a single breeding season by reducing the time and energy invested in each nesting attempt. Time- and energy-saving adaptations carry two advantages. The first is related to predation; predation evidently has a strong influence on reproduction, because mourning doves have evolved a distraction display that usually is exhibited after the eggs hatch (Blockstein 1982, see chapter 10). By minimizing the length of the nesting cycle, mourning doves shorten the period of exposure to potential predation for eggs and nestlings (see Ricklefs 1969). Westmoreland and Best (1985) used Mayfield's (1975) method to calculate a daily survival rate of 0.956 for undisturbed mourning dove nests. Over a twenty-eight-day nesting cycle, a nest would have a 28-percent chance of success. If the nesting cycle were thirty-nine days long, as predicted by adult body weight *(Figure 14)*, a nest would have only a 17-percent chance of success. Energy-saving adaptations are important in minimizing the waste of reproductive energy if a clutch is lost to predators. The importance of predation pressure as a selective factor was underestimated previously (Westmoreland et al. 1986).

Time- and energy-saving adaptations also increase the number of broods that can be produced in a nesting season (Westmoreland et al. 1986). Many reproductive traits of mourning doves could have evolved in response to predation pressure or selection for efficient seasonal iteroparity *(Figure 15)*. However, several traits (clutch/brood overlap, male-biased care of fledglings, reduced crop milk production by females and use of nests built by other birds) are more easily explained by the latter evolutionary force.

MATING SYSTEM

The term "monogamy" is used here to mean a prolonged and essentially exclusive pairing relationship between two individuals (Lack 1968, Wittenberger and Tilson 1980). Because the true (gametic) mating status of mourning doves and other columbids rarely is known, monogamy is defined behaviorally—"apparent monogamy" (Gowaty 1985).

Mourning doves are almost invariably monogamous (Stewart and Mackey 1954, Laub 1956, Jackson 1963, Blockstein 1986a). The only known exceptions are the three trios of two males and one female found by Blockstein (1986b) and a trio of one male and two females found by Laub (1956). Mourning doves usually maintain pair bonds throughout a season (Mackey 1954, Swank 1955a, Laub 1956, Blockstein 1986a) and sometimes in successive seasons (Stewart and Mackey 1954, Brackbill 1970, Blockstein 1986a). Monogamy and biparental care are the rule for all columbids that have been studied (*Table 17*).

In mourning doves and all other columbids, both parents make major contributions to parental care, although the sex roles differ throughout the nesting cycle (Blockstein 1986a). The male always carries the nesting material to the female, who waits at the nest site, as previously noted. Incubation and brooding are shared, with males on the nest for about eight hours in the middle of the day and females on the nest the rest of the time (Harris et al. 1963, Blockstein 1982, 1986a). Roles of the sexes in feeding nestlings are not well known but appear to be fairly equal in mourning doves (Luther 1979, Blockstein 1982, 1986a). Male mourning doves provide most of the food for fledglings, especially the older ones (Hitchcock and Mirarchi 1984a, Blockstein 1986a). Additionally, Hitchcock and Mirarchi (1984a) found that males begin to increase their care of offspring before the young fledge. Although mourning doves have been observed to feed fledglings that are not their own (Hitchcock and Mirarchi 1985, Blockstein unpublished data), this behavior cannot be considered advantageous to adults; it probably results from a limited ability of parents to recognize their offspring visually.

Reproductive behavior and parental roles of males and females appear to be highly stereotyped, with little flexibility in comparison with other birds. An intricate coordination between the parents seems to result from the interactive effects of social and environmental stimuli and hormonal cycles (Silver 1978, 1983, Cheng 1979, 1983). There is considerable experimental evidence of cyclic changes in behavior and in hormonal secretions of male and female ring doves during the nesting cycle. Several mechanisms appear to be operating to achieve breeding synchrony: (1) hormonal synchrony within the pair; (2) association of hormonal states and certain environmental stimuli; and (3) behavioral interactions between pair members, mediated by experience (Cheng 1979, Armbruster 1983, Cheng et al. 1988, see also chapters 7, 9 and 10).

Parental care by mourning doves during the nesting cycle seems to be shared equally by the male and female. During incubation and brooding, the eggs or squabs typically are attended by the adult male during the middle third of the day. Also, males assume a greater role in feeding shortly before the nestlings fledge and during the postfledging period before the young are completely independent. *Photo of male mourning dove feeding two near-fledglings by R. Bennett; courtesy of the U.S. Soil Conservation Service.*

Factors Favoring Monogamy

Evolutionary factors. Wittenberger (1979) and Wittenberger and Tilson (1980) presented five hypotheses for the evolution of monogamy. The hypothesis most relevant to mourning doves is that monogamy will evolve when two parents are necessary to raise one offspring. Lack (1968) proposed a similar hypothesis but implied that monogamy must be advantageous to both sexes.

Although mourning doves (and other granivorous columbids) raise two offspring at a time, biparental care probably is necessary for any offspring to survive. The only case of a single mourning dove raising an offspring from the early egg stage was in a captive situation where food was provided *ad libitum,* and the fledgling still was underweight (Goforth 1964). In single-parent broods of captive rock doves provided food *ad libitum,* the mean fledging rate for nonabandoned clutches was less than one young per nest, and nestlings fledged at low weight (Burley 1980).

Other evidence for obligate monogamy in mourning doves comes from studies in which one parent died or was removed by researchers, leaving a lone adult to rear offspring. When a mourning dove parent dies or deserts during incubation, the remaining adult usually abandons the eggs within a few days (Laub 1956, Goforth 1964, Bivings 1980, Blockstein 1982). During the nestling stage, mourning doves generally cannot rear young unaided unless the nestlings are at least four to five days old when one parent is removed (Haas 1980, Blockstein 1982, 1986a, cf. Bivings 1980). After the nestlings

reach this age, single parents sometimes rear young but with lower fledging success or a prolonged nesting cycle (Laub 1956, Haas 1980). Apparently, the same result occurs whether the male or female is removed. In two cases where a female raised fledglings alone, parental feedings were reduced in number and duration during the first week after fledging (Hitchcock and Mirarchi 1984b).

Present-day factors. The inability of single columbid parents to raise offspring is related to the stereotyped pattern of shared parental attendance at the nest. Under biparental care, brooding is constant until at least eight to ten days after hatching (Nice 1922, Blockstein 1986a). Wild mourning doves extend their incubation and brooding periods when the mate is late in returning, but there is no evidence that males incubate or brood at night (Blockstein 1982, 1986a). Eggs left unattended not only are likely to be chilled but also are more likely to be taken by predators (Murton and Isaacson 1962, Westmoreland and Best 1985, 1986).

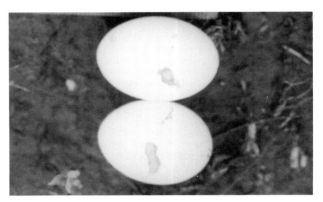

Nest predation appears to have been an important influence on the mourning dove's reproductive strategy, including nest cycle duration, nest building, constant biparental care and brood size. Eggs left unattended (top) are subject to chilling and predation (these eggs were destroyed by the pecking of an avian predator). A drawback to the adults' instinct to incubate and brood continuously is their usual reluctance to leave the nest even under threat of predation, sometimes with fatal results (bottom). *Photos by David E. Blockstein.*

Nestling deaths under conditions of uniparental care occur because of predation, chilling or starvation. Contour feathers cover a nestling's body at about seven to nine days of age (Hanson and Kossack 1963), but nestlings do not thermoregulate completely until nine to twelve days old (Breitenbach and Baskett 1967). Nestlings found dead with full or partly full crops, following abandonment (Blockstein 1986a) or experimental removal (Bivings 1980) of one parent, probably died of hypothermia. Nestlings that die with empty crops during uniparental care may have starved or died of hypothermia (see Burley 1980, Laub 1956). All of these causes of death under uniparental care result from the inability of one parent to maintain incubation or greatly extend the period of brooding in the absence of its mate. Thus, stereotyped parental behavior seems to prevent deviations from monogamy.

Consequences of Obligate Monogamy

Large paternal investment. Male mourning doves have little chance of achieving reproductive success unless they assist the female in rearing young. To the extent that paternal care will increase survival of offspring, natural selection should favor greater parental investment by males. It has been argued that, when male parental investment is high, males should evolve mechanisms to ensure that they are the fathers of the offspring for whom they provide care (Trivers 1972). In contrast, Kurland and Gaulain (1984) argued that high confidence that the male is the genetic father of the offspring in his nest is a prerequisite for paternal care. It is likely that there is a feedback loop where initial high confidence of paternity allows large paternal investment, which in turn selects for mate guarding and thereby limits the female's opportunity to copulate with males other than her mate (*Figure 16*).

High confidence of paternity. The only attempts at extra-pair copulation reported for wild mourning doves involved paired males courting and copulating with hatching-year females (Irby and Blankenship 1966) and an attempted extra-pair copulation that was thwarted by a mate-guarding male (Bruggers unpublished data). Opportunities for extra-pair copulations probably are limited because the pair members are in close proximity prior to incubation. The male's habit of collecting nesting material close to the nest (Cowan 1952, Sayre et al. 1980, Blockstein 1986a) has been interpreted as mate surveillance (Lumpkin et al. 1982). Nest-building males chase other males from the area

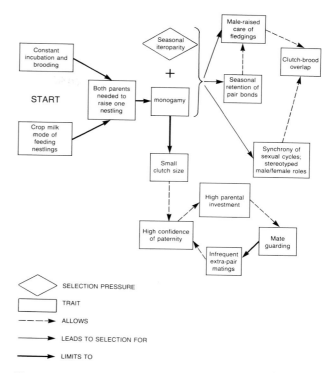

Figure 16. Flow diagram of the proposed evolution of monogamy and associated traits in mourning doves.

(Goforth and Baskett 1971b, Blockstein unpublished data). After paternity is established (i.e., incubation begins), territorial defense seems to wane, or at least the size of the defended area decreases (Lund 1952, Swank 1955a, Jackson and Baskett 1964, Sayre et al. 1980).

Small clutch size also leads to increased confidence of paternity because males must guard their mates for only a short time. In ring doves, the viability of sperm stored by females decreases sharply after three days (Riddle and Behre 1921), although fertile eggs have resulted from copulations that occurred six days before ovulation (Riddle and Behre 1921, Zenone et al. 1979, Cheng et al. 1981). In controlled experiments, the second male to mate with a female always fathers the offspring if ovulation occurs more than two days after he was placed with the female (Sims et al. 1987). This suggests that a paired male can avoid raising offspring fathered by another male (cuckoldry) by copulating with his mate after she has copulated with another male.

Female ring doves solicit copulations from their mate prior to their fertile period (Cheng et al. 1981, Lumpkin 1983), which may force the male to make a time commitment to ensure paternity as well as synchronize his hormonal state with his mate's (Cheng et al. 1981). Under experimental circumstances, male ring doves exhibited several behaviors that were interpreted as reducing the probability that they would be forced to care for offspring that were not their own (Erickson and Zenone 1976, Zenone et al. 1979, Lumpkin et al. 1982, Lumpkin 1983). Taken together, these observations on wild mourning doves and captive ring doves are evidence that males have high confidence of paternity at nests where they provide care.

Pair bond maintenance. The retention of pair bonds throughout the season is a vital part of seasonal iteroparity for mourning doves and is favored by the synchrony between the male and female. Among captive ring doves, pairs that have experience breeding together have more stable incubation and brooding patterns (Wallman et al. 1979) and higher hatching success than do newly paired birds (Erickson and Morris 1972).

Pair bond retention also enables doves to exhibit clutch/brood overlap. The male provides most of the care for the fledglings as well as taking his normal role in the new nesting attempt (Hitchcock and Mirarchi 1984a, Blockstein 1986a). This allows the female to retain a mate with whom she had achieved reproductive success and is behaviorally synchronized, rather than searching for a new mate. The system of pair bond retention also appears to be advantageous to the male, who gets the benefits of a familiar and previously successful and synchronized mate at the cost of caring for his fledged offspring.

SUMMARY

The strict granivorous or frugivorous diets of columbids probably favored the evolution of crop milk production. Present-day finches that feed seeds to their young usually predigest or at least wet them to facilitate digestion by the nestlings. Presumably, any added nutrients would be favored by selection. During their evolution, columbids evidently added nutrients until young nestlings were fed only the fat-laden cells (i.e., crop milk) that sloughed off the crop lining.

Crop milk production has the advantage of allowing extended breeding seasons, but it also restricts columbids to a small clutch size. These factors interact to place a premium on efficient pro-

duction of more than one brood per season. Mourning doves have responded by evolving a suite of adaptations that conserve time and energy during nesting cycles, thus increasing the number of nesting cycles possible per season. Most of these adaptations also reduce the likelihood of nest predation or at least minimize the waste of reproductive energy when predation occurs.

Crop milk production probably is responsible for obligate monogamy among columbids. Such a mating system favors high paternal investment, mate guarding, well-defined male and female roles and, under a system of seasonal iteroparity, the retention of pair bonds.

Most of the hypotheses presented in this chapter need to be tested in the field. In addition, not all features of the reproductive biology of mourning doves fit nicely into the strategy presented. For example, it is not clear why mourning doves use more types of nest sites than other birds do (see Cowan 1952, Downing 1959), why they produce eggs that are smaller relative to body weight (Lack 1968, Rahn et al. 1975, Murton and Westwood 1977) but have a greater energy content per gram than do those of most other altricial birds (Carey et al. 1980), or why the eggs lack a waterproofing cuticle (Board 1974).

Also unclear is the relationship between constant incubation and the color of columbid eggs. Did white eggs evolve as a consequence of constant incubation, or did columbids evolve constant incubation to cover their white eggs? Westmoreland and Best (1986) have shown that mourning dove eggs painted to be cryptic have somewhat better survival than do normal white eggs. This suggests that white eggs may be a nonadaptive evolutionary constraint.

Finally, we assumed in this chapter that the evolution of crop milk imposed a limit to clutch size for columbids. This is not necessarily true. Murray (1979) suggested that small, constant clutch size is an adaptation to the reproductive strategy, not the result of physiological constraints. To determine which approach better explains the reproductive traits of mourning doves, we need to know if columbids could produce more crop milk than they presently do. Studies on the energetics and rate of crop milk production would shed light on this question.

Chapter 7

The Crop Gland

Ralph E. Mirarchi
Department of Zoology and Wildlife Science
and
Alabama Agricultural Experiment Station
Auburn University, Alabama

Mourning dove parents, like other columbids, produce and feed their young (squabs) a curdlike material called "crop milk" during their first days of life. A complete understanding of the distinctive anatomical and morphological changes that occur in the mourning dove crop to accommodate this unique feeding process is essential to biologists who regularly work with the species, or to those who make management decisions that directly impact it. Indeed, because of its potential as an indicator of breeding activity, the crop gland has become an integral part of the process that continues to stimulate the controversy between wildlife biologists and animal rightists over the advisability of hunting mourning doves during September.

THE CROP AND THE CROP GLAND

The crop is part of the mourning dove digestive tract and is situated at the base of the neck in front of the breastbone. Food grasped by the bill passes through the digestive tract in the following sequence: buccal cavity (mouth); pharynx (throat); esophagus; crop; proventriculus (glandular stomach); gizzard (grinding stomach); intestines; cloaca; anus.

The columbid crop is a special adaptation of the esophagus. It is bilobed (a double sac extending sideways) and very distensible and has several functions (Griminger 1983). It is a storage chamber where food can be held and softened prior to mechanical (gizzard) and chemical (proventriculus and intestine) digestion, or prior to being regurgitated and fed to older nestlings and fledglings. A unique feature of the crop is that, at certain times during the reproductive cycle, it becomes a gland that actually produces food (crop milk) for young squabs. The crop gland extracts specific substances (e.g., nutrients) from the blood and concentrates (or alters) them for subsequent secretion into the lumen (chamber) of the crop where they then can be regurgitated and fed to squabs.

The avian crop is a diverticulum of the esophagus and, as such, is similar to it in histological structure. Books-Blenden et al. (1984a) provided a summary of the histology of the mourning dove crop in both breeding and nonbreeding birds of both sexes. Its cellular structure is ideally suited for its role as storage organ and gland. The crop wall is composed of several layers containing a variety of cell types. Together, they provide the blood vessels, connective and muscle tissues, and a lining that allow the crop to be distensible for food storage and also to change rapidly into a food-producing organ. Blood vessels that normally provide nourishment to and remove waste from the crops of nonbreeding doves become more numerous during breeding in order to carry nutrients to the crop gland for crop milk production. Connective and muscle tissues that constitute the crop wall in nonbreeding doves become more important in breeding doves because

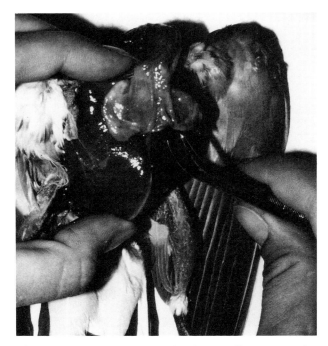

The mourning dove's crop gland normally is a translucent, bilobed storage organ located at the base of the neck in front of the breast bone. The extraction of nutrients from the blood, chemical alteration of these nutrients and secretion into the crop produces a rich food known as crop milk, which is regurgitated and fed by both parents to their young. *Photo by Theodore T. Buerger; courtesy of the Auburn University Department of Zoology and Wildlife Science and the Alabama Agricultural Experiment Station.*

they provide support and contractile capabilities necessary for regurgitation of the crop milk. Finally, the crop lining that normally protects and provides lubrication for the crop interior of nonbreeding doves becomes the nutritious crop milk that is fed to the squabs.

CROP MILK

Formation and the Feeding Process

Although gross morphological and histological changes associated with crop milk production are similar among columbids, variations occur in the timing of these changes. Formation of crop milk is confined to the two lateral lobes in the crop of both parents and is accompanied by changes in the crop wall that are readily observed in dissected specimens. The whole process has been described as a holocrine secretion (Chadwick 1983), i.e., entire cells are discharged during the secretory process and must be renewed for further secretion. During this time, the interior lining (epithelium) of the crop becomes thickened and highly folded. As these folds fuse, the epithelial cells that have become engorged with nutrients are pushed farther and farther away from their source of nutrition (blood vessels), where they degenerate and are sloughed off into the lumen of the crop (Patel 1936). These desquamated cells form the crop milk that is regurgitated to feed the young.

In columbids, the feeding of newly hatched squabs is an innate behavior performed normally even by inexperienced parents (Klinghammer and Hess 1964). A parent often will take the newly hatched squab's soft bill into its mouth to initiate the first feedings (Goodwin 1983). When feeding, mourning dove squabs, either singly or together, insert their open bills into the buccal cavity of the parent in order to receive the regurgitated crop milk. The vigorous pumping action associated with feeding bouts is indicative of active regurgitation. Apparently, any uneaten crop milk is swallowed and digested by the parent.

Mourning dove parents can feed crop milk to both squabs at the same time. The young insert their bills into the parent's mouth to catch the regurgitated food, which is rich in the water, protein, fat and minerals essential to nestling survival. *Photo by Charles W. Schwartz.*

Composition

No publications are available on the composition of mourning dove crop milk. However, several early studies (Carr and James 1931, Reed et al. 1932, Davies 1939) determined the basic constituents of the crop milk of domestic pigeons, and later studies (Vandeputte-Poma 1968, Ferrando et al. 1971, Desmeth 1980, Desmeth and Vandeputte-Poma 1980) have more accurately quantified these constituents and others. Although the constituents of mourning dove crop milk may not be identical to that of the pigeon, they probably are quite similar.

Pigeon crop milk contains 75 to 77 percent water, 11 to 13 percent protein, 5 to 7 percent fat and 1.2 to 1.8 percent mineral matter (Ferrando et al. 1971). Carbohydrates essentially are nonexistent. Approximately 90 percent of the protein content of crop milk is considered to be low-phosphorous casein (Vandeputte-Poma 1968), with 17 percent of the total nitrogen present in free amino acid form (Vandeputte-Poma and van Grembergen 1959). Crop milk fat is primarily (80 percent) in the form of triglycerides, with phospholipids comprising a smaller portion (12 percent) (Desmeth and Vandeputte-Poma 1980). Cholesterol and its esters—monoglycerides and diglycerides—and the free fatty acids make up the remainder. The mineral matter is composed of 0.14 to 0.17 percent phosphorus, 0.12 to 0.32 percent calcium, 0.11 to 0.15 percent sodium and 0.13 to 0.15 percent potassium (Ferrando et al. 1971). Pigeon crop milk also contains vitamin A, thiamine, ascorbic acid and riboflavin. In comparison with mammalian milk, crop milk contains no lactose (carbohydrate) and has less vitamin A, thiamine, ascorbic acid, phosphorus and calcium, but it has more protein and similar concentrations of riboflavin and fat (Griminger 1983). The nutrition provided by crop milk favors muscular development, blood volume increase and bone development (Davies 1939, Pace et al. 1952, Hegde 1972).

Duration of Feeding

Crop milk usually is present in the crop lumen of mourning doves by the eighth day of incubation, reaches maximum production at hatching and is produced at this level until the squabs are five to six days old (Laub 1956). The feedings at this time consist almost entirely of crop milk (Moore 1940, Moore and Pearson 1941, Taylor 1941, Lund 1952, Hammond 1956). The latest stage at which any free milk is conspicuous in adult mourning dove crops is nine days posthatching, but it usually is incon-

spicuous six to eight days posthatching (Laub 1956). Seeds become more prevalent in the diet as crop milk production subsides, and by the time of fledging, there is little difference between the diets of fledglings and adult doves (Moore 1940).

The changeover in the nestling diet from crop milk to seeds is primarily the result of crop gland regression (Patel 1936, Taylor 1941, Laub 1956). As mourning dove squabs mature, their digestive tracts apparently can accommodate more complex foodstuffs. Although nothing is known about changes in the nutritional content of mourning dove squab foods during the brooding period, it is logical to assume that the various nutritional constituents would change as crop milk is replaced by natural foods. Water, protein and fat content decrease dramatically (from 70, 46 and 27 percent to 27, 17 and 3 percent, respectively), and carbohydrates increase substantially (from 21 to 74 percent) from one to twenty-seven days posthatching in the crop contents of pigeon squabs (Leash et al. 1971). The changes begin when crop milk production ends.

CROP GLAND CYCLES

The columbid crop gland undergoes marked cyclic changes during the breeding season, according to the bird's position in the nesting cycle. Additionally, changes occur in gross morphology and histology of the crop within each day, particularly during the brooding period.

Nesting Stages and the Crop Gland

Gross morphology. Mirarchi and Scanlon (1982) provided a detailed summary of the criteria used to evaluate the morphological changes associated with crop gland development in both sexes of mourning doves. Crop gland development can be divided into four distinct phases; the duration of the total process differs with sex of the parent.

1. *Inactive*—externally, the crop lobes are translucent with no thickening or hyperemia (increase in blood vessels); light cream in color; internally, lobes may or may not be slightly stippled, with no crop milk present; fresh weight range = 0.7 to 2.22 grams.
2. *Developing*—externally, lobes are opaque and slightly thickened with slight hyperemia; yellow-rose hue; internally, lobes have folds of medium height and width, with some fold fusion and crop milk present; fresh weight range = 1.2 to 3.4 grams.

3. *Active*—externally, lobes are opaque and very thick with extensive hyperemia; rose red color cast; internally, lobes have folds of great height and width, fold fusion and copious amounts of crop milk; fresh weight range = 2.9 to 6.7 grams.

4. *Regressing*—externally, lobes still are opaque and thickened, but characteristics are not as pronounced as in active crops; hyperemia is reduced, and lobes are pinkish cream; internally, folds have shrunk, little fold fusion occurs and small amounts of crop milk are present; fresh weight range = 1.6 to 4.1 grams.

Crops of nonbreeding mourning doves have the same characteristics outlined for breeding doves with inactive crops. The gross morphology of developing and regressing crop glands differs little, and the two cannot be accurately separated by gross visual examination. If the stage of incubation or brooding were unknown, these crop glands would have to be classified using histological examination.

Histology. Specific details of the histology of the mourning dove crop, presented by Books-Blenden et al. (1984a), are summarized here. Earlier studies of the histology of columbid crop glands were conducted on domestic pigeons (Litwer 1926, Beams and Meyer 1931, Patel 1936, Dumont 1965) and band-tailed pigeons (March and Sadlier 1970, Zeigler 1971), and should be consulted prior to conducting research in this area.

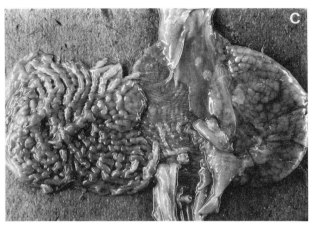

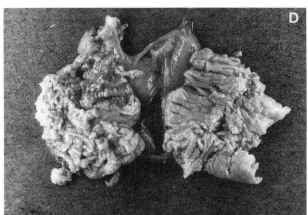

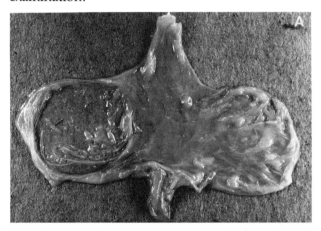

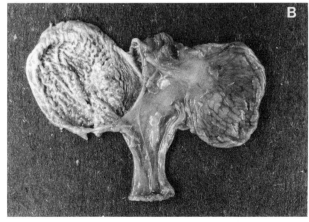

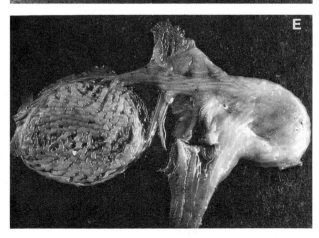

Crop gland development in mourning doves has four distinct phases: inactive (A); developing (B); active (C) and active with crop milk (D); and regressing (E). *Photos by Ralph E. Mirarchi; courtesy of the Virginia Polytechnic Institute and State University Department of Fisheries and Wildlife Sciences.*

The mourning dove crop consists of several layers. The outer layer (tunica adventitia) is composed of connective tissue, blood vessels and nerves. It envelops the crop and attaches it to the dove's body. The next layer (tunica muscularis) consists of outer longitudinal and inner circular muscle layers separated by a thin band of connective tissue. Next is a thin band of muscle (lamina muscularis), more connective tissue and blood vessels (lamina propria), and finally, a stratified squamous epithelium (nutritive epithelium) with a prominent basal layer (stratum basale). The epithelium is provided with a rich supply of blood from nearby capillary loops.

Histological development of the crop, like the gross morphology, can be divided into four different phases, the duration of which may differ with the sex of the parent. The subtle histological changes that occur with crop development precede the gross changes by two or three days. These phases of histological development are:

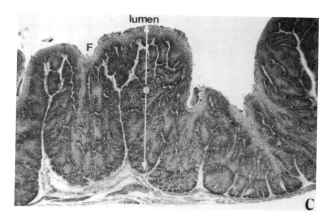

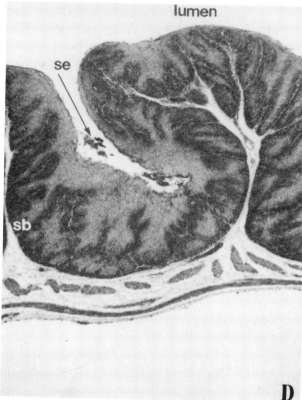

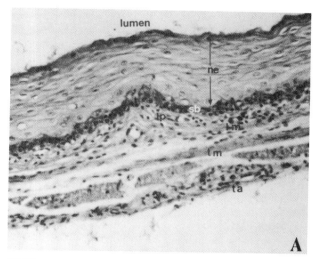

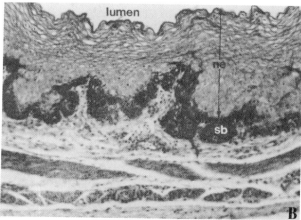

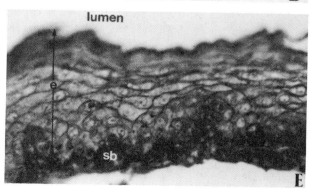

Magnified cross sections of mourning dove crop glands showing histological development phases: inactive, x 380 (A); developing, x 145 (B); developing, x 48 (C); active, x 48 (D); and regressing, x 620 (E). Principal tissues are designated as: e = epithelium; f = fold fusion; ne = nutritive epithelium; se = sloughed epithelium; sb = stratum basale; lp = lamina propria; and lm = lamina muscularis. *Photos from Books-Blendon et al. (1984a).*

1. *Inactive*—entire crop wall thin, little vascularity; stratum basale dark and distinct; cells free of lipid droplets; little epithelial folding.
2. *Developing*—thickness of epithelium noticeably increased; primary and secondary folds develop and fusion of folds begins; nutritive epithelium takes on a "foamy" appearance indicative of lipid deposition; many epithelial cells have large vacuoles; vascularization increases in lamina propria; stratum basale is thick and well defined initially but later lacks definition; some sloughing of epithelium.
3. *Active*—thickness of epithelium is reduced but folds reach maximal height; fusion complete; "foamy" appearance of epithelium continues; sloughing of epithelium apparent; vascularization is great; stratum basale becomes ill defined.
4. *Regressing*—thickness of epithelium decreased; occasional fusion present; folds reduced in size; some sloughing still occurs; vascularization is high; stratum basale begins regaining definition.

The most obvious histological indicators of the various crop phases are changes in the appearance of the epithelium and stratum basale. Again, crops of nonbreeding mourning doves have the characteristics outlined for breeding doves with inactive crops. Although Books-Blenden et al. (1984a) did not specifically outline the differences between developing and regressing crops in mourning doves, the differences appear to be the same as those outlined for the band-tailed pigeon by Zeigler (1971). In Zeigler's study, the two crop phases could be differentiated on the basis of three criteria: (1) the epithelial layers in developing crops were much thicker than in regressing crops; (2) the germinal layers of the stratified epithelium were less prominent in developing crops than in regressing crops; and (3) developing crops contained much larger quantities of lipid droplets in the stratified epithelium than did regressing crops.

Daily Time and the Crop Gland

A daily cycle of crop gland activity has not been reported for the mourning dove. However, such a cycle does exist in the band-tailed pigeon (Zeigler 1971) and appears to exist in the wood pigeon (Murton 1965). These cycles apparently are timed to allow the crop milk (epithelial lining) to be sloughed off en masse when the nestlings are due to be fed (Murton 1965, Zeigler 1971).

The five phases of the daily crop milk production cycle in band-tailed pigeons (Zeigler 1971) are:

Phase I—lobes heavily folded, rosy red in color; small bits of crop milk may be present in lumen and on lobes.
Phase II—lobes thicker, folds partially fused, mottled pinkish white; small bits of crop milk may be present in lumen and on lobes.
Phase III—lobes even thicker, folds completely fused with surface nearly smooth, off-white.
Phase IV—lobes reach maximum thickness; surface is smooth layer of pale yellow crop milk.
Phase V—crop milk is sloughed into lumen; heavily folded lobes visible under crop milk.

Daily cycles of crop milk production by band-tailed pigeons in Zeigler's study differed between sexes, indicating an asynchrony that provides crop milk to squabs at regularly spaced intervals during the day.

Mourning doves feed their young squabs (to six days old) crop milk only at certain regular times each day (Luther 1979), so they too may have marked daily crop gland cycles. Based on the scheduling of the squabs' feeding bouts, sexual asynchrony in daily crop milk production apparently also occurs (Luther 1979).

EXTERNAL AND INTERNAL INFLUENCES

Mourning dove crop gland activity is influenced by external and internal factors that are intimately related. Specific visual, tactile and olfactory cues that impact parent birds trigger production and secretion of certain hormones by glands in various parts of the body. These hormones are carried by the blood to other parts of the body where they cause systemic changes by acting on specific tissues and organs. These seemingly subtle interactions between external and internal stimuli become dramatically apparent when one notes the visible changes in the crop gland during the nesting cycle. The mechanisms of interaction between these stimuli have not been well researched in the mourning dove, but they have been and continue to be intensively studied in other closely related columbids, particularly the ringed turtledove (ring dove). Consequently, the discussion that follows should serve as a sound model that can be used to understand the interaction of external and internal stimuli on the mourning dove crop gland.

Interaction of External and Internal Stimuli

A particular sequence of external and internal events must occur after a pair bond has formed and before crop development begins. These include suitable behavioral interactions between mates (Silver 1977), the presence of nest material (Goforth and Baskett 1971b) and a nest (White 1975) so that incubation can be properly established, and the presence of eggs in a nest so that squabs will be accepted (Moore 1976a). Different hormones may stimulate or mediate transitions in and maintenance of these behaviors so that the cyclic breeding sequence occurs in proper order. Nevertheless, there is evidence that precise hormonal conditions are not always solely responsible for various parental behaviors (Young 1964, Silver and Buntin 1973, Silver and Gibson 1980) and that previous nesting experience (Lehrman 1955, Lehrman and Wortis 1960, Moore 1976a, Armbruster 1983) and cues from the nest, eggs, offspring and mates (Silver and Gibson 1980, Armbruster 1983, Lea et al. 1986) are important components of behavioral responses made by doves during a nesting cycle.

Estrogen (Cheng 1973a, 1973b, Korenbrot et al. 1974) and progesterone (Silver et al. 1974, Cheng and Silver 1975) in the female ring dove and testosterone (Feder et al. 1977) and possibly progesterone (Silver et al. 1974, Cheng 1979) in the male ring dove appear to mediate courtship behaviors and the transition from courtship to incubation. However, cues from one mate profoundly affect the occurrence, type and strength of behavioral response from the other mate (Silver 1978). Similarly, the pituitary polypeptide hormone—prolactin—long has been implicated as the stimulus for crop gland development (Riddle et al. 1933) and is important in the maintenance of incubation behavior or broodiness (Lehrman and Brody 1961, Lea et al. 1986). Most recently it has been verified as the agent responsible for crop gland growth during the normal columbid breeding cycle (Buntin and Forsyth 1979, Goldsmith et al. 1981, Cheng and Burke 1983) and implicated in nest-defense behaviors of both parents (Lea and Vowles 1985). Specific, saturable binding sites for prolactin in the dove brain apparently mediate the effects of prolactin on most behaviors and gonadal functions (Buntin and Ruzycki 1987). However, incubation behavior may involve a peripheral site of prolactin action (Buntin and Tesch 1985). Binding sites in the brain are concentrated in specific loci within the preoptic/hypothalamic continuum (Fechner and Buntin 1989).

After secretion from the pituitary, prolactin apparently moves quite rapidly through the bloodstream and across the crop gland via the intercellular spaces (Shani et al. 1977), where it exerts its influence by binding to the outer surfaces of cells (Roth and Grunfeld 1981). Prolactin's promotion of crop gland development occurs through at least two mechanisms (Anderson et al. 1984). One is a direct sensitization of the epithelium to the mitogenic action of a somatomedinlike growth factor ("synlactin"). The second mechanism increases production and/or secretion of synlactin, which then acts together with prolactin to promote development of the crop gland epithelium.

Prolactin's secretion is intimately related to external stimuli as well. The presence of eggs in the nest and the resultant tactile stimulation influences its initial secretion (Buntin 1977, Lea and Vowles 1985). Additional tactile (Buntin et al. 1977, Buntin and Forsyth 1979), visual (Lea et al. 1986) and even olfactory stimuli (Cohen 1981) from the eggs and squabs appear to be important in maintenance of prolactin secretion and crop gland development. Thus, crop gland growth, maintenance and regression involve hormonal (primarily prolactin) and behavioral events that are intricately interrelated during the nesting cycle.

Other hormones are involved in crop milk production. Calcitonin and parathyroid hormone interact to control calcium mobilization and utilization during crop gland activity (March and McKeown 1977) in the pigeon, whereas growth hormone appears to be responsible for the circadian (twenty-four-hour) rhythm in availability of free fatty acids necessary for increased energy demands during crop milk production (March and McKeown 1978).

DURATION OF CROP GLAND ACTIVITY

The duration of crop gland activity in mourning doves during a "typical" nesting cycle (i.e., one followed by a renesting attempt) has been described in detail by Mirarchi and Scanlon (1980) and is summarized here. This time interval also may be affected by various internal and external stimuli, such as differences in sex, stage of the breeding season, impending migration and/or tactile stimulation.

Sexual Differences (Typical Nesting Cycles)

Gross changes in crop development occur rapidly in both sexes between the tenth and fourteenth day of incubation. Both sexes have active crop glands during the first five to six days posthatching, but the crop glands of male and female parents begin regressing at different rates by nine days posthatching. Some female doves actually have inactive crop glands by that time. The rate of regression of male crop glands is slower and lags behind the female by approximately four to six days. All female doves have inactive crop glands by sixteen to eighteen days posthatching, but only about 40 percent of male dove crops are inactive by that time. New nesting and crop gland cycles are started (indicated by new clutches of eggs and/or inactive, developing or active crop glands in both sexes) by twenty-three to twenty-five days posthatching. Consequently, maximum duration of macroscopic crop gland persistence (posthatching) during a typical nesting cycle in female and male mourning doves is approximately fifteen and twenty days, respectively.

The active crop gland phase in both parents occurs as long as pure crop milk is fed to the squabs (Moore 1940, Laub 1956). Additionally, the duration of the active and regressing crop gland phases shown by the parents (particularly the male) corresponds with the duration of absolute dependence of fledglings on parental care (Mirarchi and Scanlon 1981, Hitchcock and Mirarchi 1984a). The differential regression pattern between sexes coincides with differences in the division of parental responsibilities (female laying new clutch; male care of fledglings) that have been demonstrated in captive and wild mourning doves (Mirarchi and Scanlon 1980, Hitchcock and Mirarchi 1984a). Crop gland activity in female mourning doves is inversely related to ovarian and hormonal activity associated with ovulation (Mirarchi et al. 1982). Female doves, as in other columbids (Riddle and Reinhart 1926, March and Sadleir 1970), may have to shunt mineral and/or energy resources from crop gland development and crop milk production to gonadal development and egg production to maintain the prolific nesting typical of the species. Indeed, crop milk production apparently is an important reason why clutch size of columbids is limited to two eggs (Blockstein 1989). Male doves, on the other hand, divert time and energy to feeding fledglings from the last nest (Hitchcock and Mirarchi 1984a) while still maintaining nest building and incubation responsibilities at a new nest (Sayre et al. 1980).

Experimental manipulation of wild mourning dove clutches provides information on the relationship of crop milk production and clutch size. When a third nestling is added to nests with crop milk-dependent squabs, fledging success is comparable to that of nests with two young. Growth rates are retarded, however, and one squab (top)—not necessarily the introduced bird—is likely to become a runt. When a third nestling is added after the squabs are at least five days old (bottom) and no longer entirely dependent on crop milk, their rate of growth is intermediate between normal and experimentally enlarged broods of crop milk-dependent young. *Top photo by David E. Blockstein. Bottom photo by James Nelson.*

Sexual Differences (Last Nesting Cycle)

Different crop gland regression patterns in both parents could occur during the final nesting cycle of the breeding season, because the hormonal activity associated with subsequent laying cycles would be altered. Theoretically, female mourning dove crop gland cycles could be prolonged because they would not need to shunt mineral and/or energy resources from crop gland development to egg-laying needs. Similarly, male crop gland cycles could be prolonged because the males could spend more time and energy with the last fledglings. Available data on this subject are limited and somewhat conflicting. Books-Blenden et al. (1984b) compared crop gland weights from small samples of mid-season and late-season nesters and suggested that the crop continues to cycle in a typical manner late in the nesting season. On the other hand, Hitchcock and Mirarchi (1984a) observed that the net duration of parental feeding (particularly in the male) of fledglings was longer in late-season nestings, probably as a result of fewer nest-tending and territorial-defense responsibilities at that time. No clear-cut answer to this question exists presently.

Effects of Impending Migration

Prolactin—responsible for crop gland activity in columbids—also has been implicated in regulation of migratory behavior (Meier et al. 1965, 1968), hyperphagia or premigratory fattening (Meier and Farner 1964), and increased liver lipogenesis (Goodridge and Ball 1967) in certain migratory species.

Could elevated levels of prolactin secreted to stimulate migratory and associated behaviors in mourning doves prolong crop gland regression patterns of late nesters? Theoretically, yes, but no direct evidence to support that hypothesis exists in the literature on migratory columbids. Indeed, the limited evidence available tends to contradict the concept. It appears that the crop gland continues to cycle in a typical manner late in the nesting season (Books-Blenden et al. 1984b). Also, little crop gland activity occurs in hatching-year mourning doves during September hunting seasons (Mirarchi 1978). Presumably, prolactin secretions great enough to stimulate migratory behavior and extend crop gland regression patterns in adult mourning doves should do the same in hatching-year doves if the target organ is receptive. Obviously, additional research is needed in this area before a definitive judgment on the effect of impending migration on crop gland regression patterns can be made.

Effects of Tactile Stimulation

As previously noted, visual, tactile and olfactory stimuli are implicated in prolactin secretion and crop gland development in columbids. Additionally, parent/fledgling feeding interactions in mourning doves are prolonged during late-season nesting (Hitchcock and Mirarchi 1984a). Could prolonged parent/fledgling feeding interactions in mourning doves during late-season nestings delay crop gland regression? Evidence in the literature supports this hypothesis. Tactile stimuli associated with regurgitation behavior in ring doves promotes crop gland development, particularly in the male parent (Buntin et al. 1977). Furthermore, differential regression patterns between sexes in ring doves (Silver 1978) and mourning doves (Mirarchi and Scanlon 1980) indicate hormonal and/or physical reasons (i.e., tactile stimulation) for prolonged regression patterns in males of both species. Although evidence that supports the concept that crop gland regression patterns can be prolonged by tactile stimulation is much stronger than that available for the prolactin/migration-delayed regression scenario, it would be premature to make a definitive judgment on this hypothesis now.

CROP GLAND ACTIVITY EVALUATION TECHNIQUES

Development of techniques useful for detection and evaluation of crop gland activity in mourning doves has become necessary in recent years because of the increased use of crop gland activity as an indicator of breeding activity. Several techniques that can be used on live or dead mourning doves have been developed for field and laboratory use. For crop gland research, samples should be collected at the same time each day because of differences in the appearance of the crop gland during its daily cycle. Males and females should be collected at the nest just prior to or immediately after the squabs have been fed (males 9:00 to 11:30 A.M. and 1:00 to 2:00 P.M.; females 5:30 to 7:00 A.M. and 5:00 to 6:00 P.M.) to ensure that crop gland activity is maximized.

Dead Birds

Gross morphology. Wildlife field or research personnel who have had little experience with crop gland activity often have difficulty accurately classifying the various phases by gross morphological traits. A technical bulletin (Mirarchi and Scanlon 1982) that combines photographs (full frontal views of entire crop and close-ups of exposed crop lobes), descriptions and weight ranges of mourning dove crop gland phases during the crop gland cycle was summarized earlier in this chapter and should be consulted by persons conducting research in this area. Developing and regressing crop glands must be distinguished from each other by histological examination if the stage of incubation or brooding is unknown, so the two phases cannot be divided into two different categories based on normal visual examination.

Histology. Preparation of mourning dove crops for microscopic examination is time-consuming and expensive. Such costs probably are not warranted for most research conducted on mourning doves. However, histological study of developing and regressing crop glands is necessary if the research is directed toward classification and quantification of each of the four crop phases and if the stage of the nesting cycle is unknown. Researchers should consult various reports on the subject summarized earlier for mourning doves (Books-Blenden et al. 1984a), domestic pigeons (Litwer 1926, Beams and Meyer 1931, Patel 1936, Dumont 1965) and band-tailed pigeons (Zeigler 1971, March and Sadleir 1970).

Weights. Conservation and/or research organizations that lack the time, personnel, finances or expertise to identify visually or quantify large numbers of crop glands from hunter-harvested doves can evaluate these data in a different manner. Using discriminant function analysis, Mirarchi et al. (1986) developed a series of equations that can be used to classify three different crop gland phases (inactive, active and developing/regressing) of adult and juvenile male and female mourning doves. Researchers can decide which set of equations is most appropriate for their data. Observations from new data sets (crop weights) can be introduced into an appropriate (male or female) three-equation series and the scores compared. Each crop observed then can be classified into the crop gland phase associated with the smallest score. In addition, either precollection sampling or access to computer facilities that generate Statistical Analysis System (SAS) programs is necessary to calculate prior probabilities of specific crop phases being present.

Live Birds

Crop examination and palpation. Techniques that can be used in the field for detection and evaluation of crop gland activity in living columbids also have become necessary for various research projects. Zeigler (1971) used a cystoscope to establish the existence of a daily crop cycle in breeding band-tailed pigeons, but the equipment was too expensive for widespread use. However, palpation of crop lobes in conjunction with use of an inexpensive, commercially produced crop-examination device or "inspection light" has been successfully used to classify crop gland phases in live mourning doves (Mirarchi et al. 1978). Prior to testing wild

To field inspect a live mourning dove for crop gland activity using a crop-examination device, the subject should be defeathered in the lower neck and uppermost breast region to reveal translucent skin. The crop then can be viewed effectively and palpated. Careful plucking of these feathers will not stress a firmly held bird, and new feathers will grow. *Photo by Ralph E. Mirarchi; courtesy of Virginia Polytechnic Institute and State University Department of Fisheries and Wildlife Sciences.*

doves, a captive nonbreeding dove with an inactive crop is palpated and examined in order to provide a reference standard to judge subsequent examinations. Examination of the wild birds consists of holding them for twenty-four hours to allow digestion of crop contents, feather removal from the crop lobe area, palpation of the empty crop lobes for thickening, and insertion of the lighted lamp into the crop interior.

Different crop activity phases present characteristic illumination patterns and light transmittance *(Figure 17)*. Active, inactive and developing/regressing crops were classified correctly 100, 96.5 and 77.8 percent of the time, respectively, using palpation and the crop-examination device together. The crop-examination device performs best when used in dim light. Also, it should be disinfected after field examination of each bird to prevent spread of such diseases as trichomoniasis

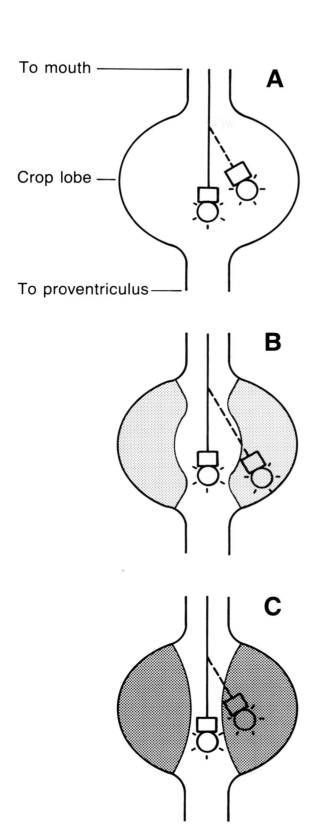

To mouth —————

Crop lobe —

To proventriculus ——

A

B

C

Figure 17. Typical illumination patterns and light transmittance of inactive (A), developing or regressing (B), and active (C) crops when a crop-examination device is used to identify and analyze the crop development phase of a live mourning dove (from Mirarchi 1978).

or avian pox. Proper use of a holding device (Fredrickson 1970, Zeigler 1971, Bolen et al. 1977) and emetics (Tomback 1975) could facilitate the entire procedure.

CROP GLAND ACTIVITY AS AN INDICATOR OF BREEDING ACTIVITY

Proper management of mourning doves involves maximizing consumptive and nonconsumptive uses of the species without adversely impacting it. This is accomplished by setting hunting seasons before most doves have migrated from breeding areas, before natural mortality reduces the population and at a time that does not conflict with the principal nesting season. The fifty-year controversy over the hunting of mourning doves during September has been fueled by the high proportion of hunter-harvested adults that shows signs of crop gland activity at that time (see Mirarchi 1978, Books-Blenden et al. 1984b) and the high nesting success of late summer breeders (Books-Blenden et al. 1984b). The controversy still simmers (primarily because of ethical implications) despite recent indications that only a small proportion of total seasonal nesting occurs during September and that no differences occur in daily survival rates of eggs and squabs or in fledging rates between hunted and nonhunted areas (Geissler et al. 1987).

The significance of crop gland activity during the hunting season must be resolved, because time, energy and money that could be used for better management of the species is wasted in legal disputes between biologists and animal rightist groups. To do this, answers to two outwardly similar but distinctly different questions (one primarily biological, the other primarily ecological) are needed.

First, is crop gland activity a reliable indication that mourning doves have eggs in the nest or dependent young? Yes. Studies of crop gland activity that are properly designed, analyzed and interpreted can be used as very reliable indicators of active or recent nesting. Although various factors may influence the persistence of crop gland activity in mourning doves, particularly males (as previously discussed), the overwhelming evidence (Mirarchi and Scanlon 1980, 1981, Haas 1980, Hitchcock and Mirarchi 1984a) indicates that any mourning dove that has a visibly active crop gland capable of producing crop milk (i.e., from one to six days posthatching) has dependent nestlings that will die if either parent is lost (Haas 1980). Similarly, mourning doves with crops that show signs of developing or regressing represent doves in either the late stages of incubation (nine to twelve days post-laying) or the early stages of fledgling dependency (four to six days postfledging), respectively. The probability of confusing nesting doves in early stages of incubation with nonbreeding doves having inactive crop glands should be minimal because of the lateness of the breeding season. Crop activity studies should strive to separate crop glands into active and developing/regressing or "stimulated" (Olson and Braun 1984) categories so that the option exists to analyze, discuss and interpret the data conservatively (using only active crop glands) or liberally (using all three crop activity phases). Ideally, such studies should concentrate efforts on only one sex to minimize the possibility of double-counting parents from the same nest, particularly in areas where all-day shooting is permitted.

The choice of sex can be made on the basis of whether a conservative or liberal estimate of nesting activity is desired. A conservative estimate of nesting activity would be obtained by concentrating the research effort on the female segment of the population. The relatively rapid regression pattern of the female mourning dove crop gland (Mirarchi and Scanlon 1980) would reduce the likelihood of prolonged crop gland activity, perhaps through a self-reinforcing mechanism. Less tactile stimulation of the crops of female parents by fledglings (Hitchcock and Mirarchi 1984a) and a normally weaker crop gland response to tactile stimulation by female parents (Buntin et al. 1977) would help offset any stimulatory effects of prolactin provided "out of context," as for premigratory readiness. A more liberal estimate of nesting activity would be obtained by concentrating the effort on the male segment of the population for reasons opposite to these.

Second, does the proportion of harvested adult doves with crop gland activity provide a reliable estimate of the proportion of the mourning dove population actually nesting at that time? Not necessarily. Seasonal nesting studies (Geissler et al. 1978, see also Mirarchi 1978, Books-Blenden et al. 1984b) indicate mourning dove nesting activity is low during September, but proportions of adults in harvest

samples that have crop gland activity suggest much higher levels of September nesting activity. This discrepancy is troublesome and indicates potential biases associated with collection of crop gland activity data from hunters. Differential vulnerability of nesting and non-nesting doves to harvest appears to be the most logical explanation for the great disparity in direct (nesting studies) and indirect (crop gland activity in hunter samples) estimates of nesting during September (Books-Blenden et al. 1984b, Olson and Braun 1984). This differential vulnerability to harvest may result from differences in migrational periods (non-nesters may migrate earlier than late nesters), possible differences in breeding patterns of migratory and nonmigratory doves, differences in daily activity patterns of nesting and non-nesting doves (Sayre et al. 1980) or a combination of these factors. Obviously, these potential sources of bias must be resolved before percentages of mourning doves with crop gland activity in harvested samples can be considered as a reliable index of late-season nesting activity.

In summary, recent research has answered the basic biological question about the relationship between crop gland activity and nesting activity of individuals but has only partially answered the ecological question relative to using crop gland activity data from harvest samples to estimate late-season nesting activity of a population. Until the ecological question is answered satisfactorily, crop gland activity collected from hunter check stations should be interpreted carefully. Nevertheless, the wildlife agencies of states that offer mourning dove hunting seasons would be wise to collect statewide data on crop gland and nesting activity during the hunting seasons and relative to the peak of dove migration (Funk 1965, Olson and Braun 1984). Such data can provide a sound base for setting hunting seasons and lead, in turn, to maximum consumptive use of the resource with little adverse effect on it. In the process, a positive public image of the agency as steward may be enhanced, and potential conflicts with animal rightist groups concerning the ethics of hunting may be minimized.

Chapter 8

Growth, Maturation and Molt

Ralph E. Mirarchi
*Department of Zoology and Wildlife Science
and
Alabama Agricultural Experiment Station
Auburn University, Alabama*

Mourning doves grow and develop rapidly during their first year of life. Their growth and maturation, the factors that regulate them, and the selective advantages doves accrue as a result of these processes provide valuable insights for biologists and other people involved with the species' conservation. Many aspects of mourning dove biology bearing on growth, development and wing molt have been well researched; others, including body molt and hormonal regulation of these processes, have not and require additional study.

EGGS AND THE EMBRYONIC STAGE

Egg Measurements

Mourning dove eggs are 1.08 to 1.14 inches (2.75 to 2.90 cm) long and 0.84 to 0.85 inches (2.14 to 2.17 cm) wide. Eggshells are 0.0043 to 0.0067 inches (0.11 to 0.17 mm) thick (Kreitzer 1971). The second egg of each clutch is longer and wider than the first egg, and measurements of both eggs of the second clutch average slightly larger than those of the first clutch (Hanson and Kossack 1963, Mirarchi and Scanlon 1978). Oddly, volumes of first and second eggs—0.223 fluid ounces (6.6 ml) per egg—of each clutch do not appear to differ, nor do volumes in consecutive clutches, despite differences in the

egg measurements (Hanson and Kossack 1963). Differences in egg measurements theoretically could occur without noticeable changes in volume if only *maximal* lengths and widths of eggs are considered and the shape of the egg is not. Eggs weigh approximately 0.21 to 0.25 ounces (6 to 7 g) at laying (Ricklefs 1977, Holcomb and Jaeger 1978, Buerger et al. 1986), and the weight of both eggs tends to increase with each clutch during the breeding season (Holcomb and Jaeger 1978). The water content of some columbid eggs decreases from spring to autumn, while the ratio of yolk to the relatively less dense albumen increases (Riddle 1916b). This could explain how weight changes occur without volume changes.

Embryo Development

Mourning dove embryos grow slowly during the first three days of incubation and develop rapidly thereafter until hatching at fourteen to fifteen days—a pattern typical of birds of all developmental modes (O'Connor 1984). The embryological development of mourning doves is well documented, and aging of embryos can be accomplished either in the field by candling (Hanson and Kossack 1963, see also chapter 21) or in the laboratory through use of photographs, gross descrip-

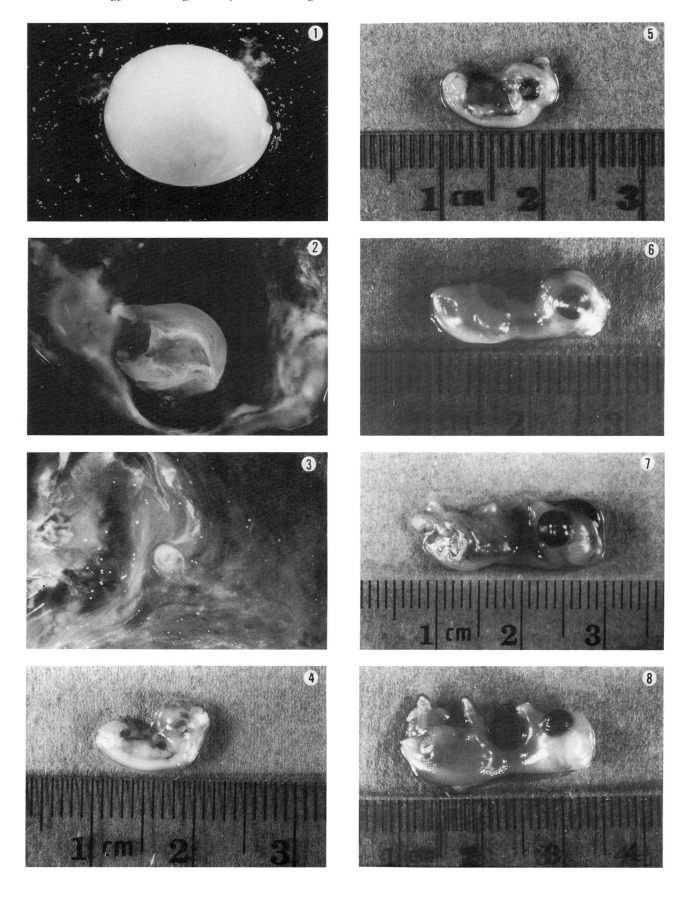

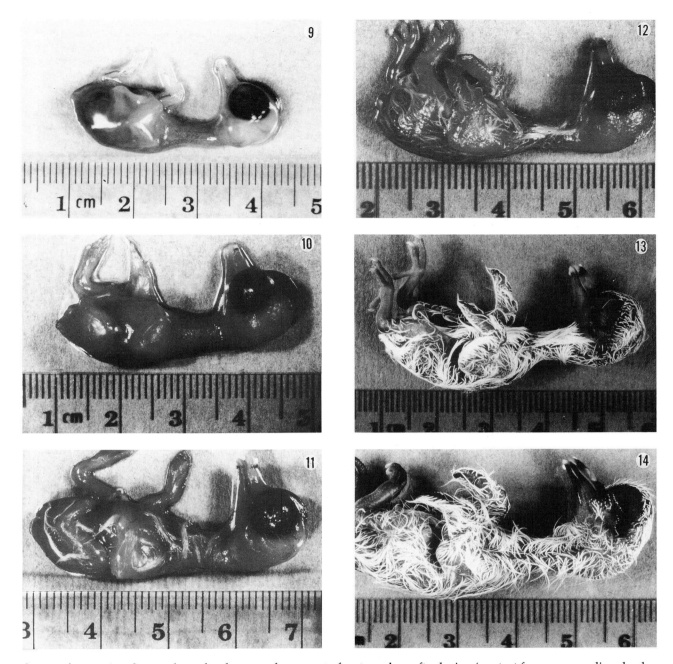

Stages of mourning dove embryo development from one to fourteen days after laying (see text for corresponding day-by-day descriptions). Changes in embryo size and developmental stages of the limbs, mandibles, eyes and feather tracts are useful in determining age. *Photos by Theodore T. Buerger; courtesy of the Auburn University Department of Zoology and Wildlife Science and the Alabama Agricultural Experiment Station.*

tions and measurements (Muller et al. 1984). The following is a brief descriptive chronology of the stages of embryonic development in the mourning dove (after Muller et al. 1984).

Day 1. Yolk remains intact after egg is opened. Chalazae extend from the yolk into the albumen at both poles. A protoplasmic disc is visible on the yolk.

Day 2. Embryo is white to translucent and is distinguishable with the naked eye as a slight vascularization on the yolk. Yolk breaks readily when egg is opened. Amnion (fluid-filled sac around the embryo) is obvious and persistent. Cephalic flexion is noticeable after careful dissection of extra-embryonic membranes. Brain region is bent to side of vertical spinal cord.

Day 3. Yolk sac is extremely fragile. Embryo is C-shaped. Caudal flexion is present and tail appears curled. Spinal cord has noticeable somites and is visible from hindbrain to tail. Differentiation is present in visceral region. Three bulges of the brain are evident and mid-brain is prominent. Optic cup is pigmented (dark gray). Wing and leg buds are distinguishable (10X power).

Day 4. Yolk sac is clearly vascularized. Allantois is visible at ventral-caudal end of the body. Embryo is strongly flexed and pointed tail almost touches head. Flexion is persistent. Embryo has color. Dorsal line and tail region are cream tinted. Eyes are pigmented. Abdominal region is red. Edges of the embryo are translucent. Spinal cord extends from neck to tail, with somites present predominantly at caudal end. Lens inside optic cup is easily seen. Midbrain is conspicuous. Wing and leg buds appear.

Day 5. Vascularization is visible around yolk and allantois. Embryo has marked cephalic, cervical and caudal flexion, but is not as compact as on Day 4. Embryo is predominantly cream colored with distinct translucent midbrain bulge. Abdominal region is red and easily seen through clear skin. Spinal cord extends from hindbrain to tail and somites appear in neck and tail region. Tail is pointed but curls along body. Early differentiation of maxilla and mandible occurs. Maxilla protrudes slightly (10X power), and wing and leg buds are evident. Vascularization to extremities is visible.

Day 6. Embryo is C-shaped and head is bent slightly to side. Tail is pointed and projects beyond body. Legs extend slightly beyond tail. Ends of legs are paddle shaped and claw divisions are visible (10X power). Wings are distinct and have three visible segments. Maxilla appears as small protuberance. Eyelids cover a portion of the eyeballs. Midbrain is prominent as a translucent bulge.

Day 7. Yolk sac is heavily vascularized but resists tearing. Head is flexed sideways and touches wing. Wing and leg buds are distinct. Egg tooth is evident as tiny white spot on maxilla. Mandible is well defined.

Day 8. Claws are distinct. Three segments of wings are visible, with alulae obvious as projections from manus. Maxilla is slightly longer than mandible, and egg teeth are visible. Eyelids cover about half of each eyeball. Embryo is cream colored. Midbrain bulge is prominent but no longer translucent. Down tracts form on body and wings.

Day 9. Embryo has pronounced cervical and slight caudal flexion. Neck is sharply bent at junction with body; segments are visible on metatarsus. Alulae are distinct. Maxilla is solid cream color with white tip. Egg teeth are prominent. Two raised oval areas on maxilla are developing into nares. Eyelids cover about three-fourths of each eyeball, leaving an opening around the lens. Body has pink tint, but extremities are cream colored. Skin over abdominal region is translucent; distinct organs and soft keel are visible there. Auditory opening is presaged by subtle indentation in skin.

Day 10. Embryonic waste appears as long white strands in allantois. Embryo has pronounced bend at neck. Bill is facing side and almost reaches tail. There is slight caudal flexion. Keratin tips on toe digits appear white. Maxilla is cream colored with faint black stripe and white distal end. Egg teeth are obvious. Eyelids form an oval opening over lens. Auditory opening is clearly visible. Down tracts are differentiating, giving embryo a rough texture. Down papillae are forming (10X power).

Day 11. Yolk sac is smaller. Embryo is sharply bent at neck with bill directed to side of body. Tips of claws are distinctly white. Scale ridges are seen on legs (10X power). Oval ridges of nares are visible. Dark stripe is present in front of nares. Eyelids cover most of the eyeballs. Openings over lenses of eyes range from a crescent to a slit. Down papillae are evident, especially on neck and back. Down is shorter on head and dorsal surface of skin over eyes.

Day 12. Significant absorption of yolk is evident. Slight caudal flexion present. Scales are evident on legs. Eyelids close to a small slit and in some specimens appear totally closed. Although skin is translucent, the back, neck and head are cream to purple in color. Keel and some internal organs visible on ventral side of embryo. Down covers most of the body.

Day 13. Some eggs show no signs of being pipped; others do. Embryo appears bent in half at base of neck. The head is strongly flexed to side and reaches tail. Yolk is mostly absorbed, and edges of the yolk sac are viscous. Most of egg is fairly dry. Scales on legs appear as ridges. Bill is dusky purple with a dark stripe beyond the nares. White egg teeth are prominent. Eyeballs are not distinct bulges. Eyelids are closed. Embryo is dark purple. Keel is visible and rigid. Brain is distinguishable as cream-colored lobe. Down is long and covers most of body.

Days 14 to 15. Embryo is ready to hatch or, in some cases, already free from egg. There is little fluid in egg; yolk sac is mostly withdrawn into body cavity. Embryo is curled, just fitting inside egg. Pipping around the shell creates a definite crack. Scales are easily seen on legs. Eyelids are closed. Embryo is dark gray and covered by long down.

Thyroid glands of columbid embryos are present at the same age as those of Japanese quail but develop more slowly, are much smaller and produce less thyroid hormone at hatching (McNabb and McNabb 1977, McNabb et al. 1984a, 1984b). While the prehatching and hatching behaviors of mourning doves have not been described, they probably are typical of other altricial birds, as described by Oppenheim (1972).

NESTLING STAGE
(1 to 15 days posthatching)

Sex Ratios

Data from past studies on sex ratios of nestling mourning doves are contradictory. Some studies indicated a sex ratio skewed in favor of males (Kossack and Hanson 1953, Hanson and Kossack 1963), but Macgregor (1958) indicated a 50:50 ratio overall and the expected 1:2:1 (males only/mixed sexes/females only) clutch ratios (as found in domestic pigeons). Differences in the way these data were collected also confounded results.

Genetic sex determination is not absolute in birds, and many instances of sex reversal have been reported in the avian literature (see Abbott and Yee 1975). Substantial data also indicate that certain metabolic factors, through unknown mechanisms, affect the expression of sex determination that normally is genetically programmed in domesticated doves and pigeons. Oxidation rates, oxygen pressures, yolk size, water and energy content of yolks, and seasonal changes in these variables during incubation have been linked to sexual determination in these species (Riddle 1916a, 1916b, 1917a, 1917b, 1920, 1931). Some recent studies also indicate that a nonrandom determination of sex occurs in other birds (e.g., Ankney 1982, Ryder 1983, Weatherhead 1985) and that environmental conditions may override genetic sex determination (Ankney 1982) in birds in a manner similar to certain reptiles (see Bull 1970). The controlling mechanisms involved in such sex determination remain unknown.

The most complete study to date of sex ratios of hatchling mourning doves (306 squabs from 153 two-egg clutches) provides some interesting findings (Edmunds and Ankney 1987). In that study, there were no statistical differences in overall sex

ratio (although there were 169 males to 137 females), seasonal changes in sex ratio, divergence from the expected 1:2:1 clutch ratios, relationship between egg size and offspring sex, or relationship between sex of offspring and egg sequence over the entire breeding season. However, a seasonal effect on the sex-versus-egg sequence pattern, particularly in broods with both sexes, did occur. Males predominated in first eggs and females in second eggs during the middle of the breeding season, but the pattern was reversed later in the season. While this study goes far in resolving some conflicting information from earlier studies, more rigorously controlled research is needed. More research is warranted as well on the mechanism of sex determination in doves and pigeons.

Mourning dove hatchling sex ratio appears to be about 1:1, but little is known yet about genetic, metabolic and other factors that influence gender determination. There is evidence that males predominate in first eggs and females in second eggs of initial clutches of a breeding season and that the reverse is true for subsequent clutches. *Photo by Charles W. Schwartz.*

Morphological Development

Hormonal changes. Mourning dove squabs remain in the nest for approximately fifteen days posthatching, during which time they undergo rapid development as a result of being fed crop milk by both parents (see chapter 7). Little is known about the hormonal regulation of growth in mourning doves, but ring dove squabs have high blood concentrations of a pituitary growth-regulating hormone during their twelve days of maximum growth (Scanes and Balthazart 1981). They also have increasing concentrations of thyroid hormones (thyroxine and triiodothyronine) in the blood serum for the first eight days posthatching (McNabb and Cheng 1985). These concentrations stabilize by the time the nestlings are fifteen days old and presumably are involved with thermoregulatory capabilities (see chapter 9). Little else is known about glandular involvement and hormonal regulation of columbid squabs during this growth phase.

Physical changes. The growth and development of mourning dove nestlings have been well described and pictured (see Hanson and Kossack 1963, Cheney and Cheney 1967, Holcomb and Jaeger 1978). Bills, legs and feet, wings, and feathers of the nestlings all grow and develop rapidly during this stage, with some characters showing more dramatic differences than others (Holcomb and Jaeger 1978). Squabs increase in total length (tip of bill to tip of tail) from approximately 2.6 to 5.9 inches (65 to 150 mm) and in average weight from about 0.2 to 2.8 ounces (6 to 80 g) during the first fifteen days posthatching (Cheney and Cheney 1967, Holcomb and Jaeger 1978). Growth and development are fastest for first-hatched and single squabs. Nestlings raised during early and late portions of the nesting season grow more slowly than do those raised in the middle period (Holcomb and Jaeger 1978).

Changes in plumage during the nestling period are dramatic and have been well documented (Hanson and Kossack 1957a). Squabs are covered with cream-colored down at hatching. Primary feather sheaths begin to emerge at two days of age, and tail feather sheaths appear at three days. Sheathed body feathers and those on the crown of the head begin to emerge at five and six days, respectively. Tips of primaries and wing coverts begin to "feather out" at seven days, and feathering out of the crown occurs at nine days. Feathers of the head and back are out of sheaths by ten days of age, and feathers of the ventral tract of the belly become unsheathed at eleven days. Feather development from the twelfth to fourteenth day "is that of a refinement, with the completion of feather coverage under the wings and belly and with the development of a fine feather bloom" (McClure 1943: 388).

By fifteen days of age, the nestlings are ready to fledge and have a full complement of feathers differing in appearance from that of adults only in color (slightly darker) and the presence of buff-tipped wing coverts (Petrides 1950). This darkly mottled coloration pattern strongly resembles that of tree structures or fallen debris (e.g., branches, bark, pine cones) and may be an adaptation to avian predation pressure. Recently fledged doves spend much time in densely vegetated reference areas on the ground or in trees, which lends support to that hypothesis (Hitchcock and Mirarchi 1986, Grand and Mirarchi 1988).

The rapid feather development of nestling mourning doves aids in thermoregulation, flight and early independence. Most nestlings fledge at about 15 days of age, which enhances predator avoidance and allows parents to initiate another clutch about a month after starting the previous one. Feather development of nestlings has a stereotyped pattern, so nestling age is fairly easy to determine. Days 0–1 (opposite left): squab approximately the size of the egg and down-covered; eyes closed; egg teeth present on both mandibles *(photo courtesy of the National Archives)*. Days 2–3 (opposite right): eyes still closed; egg teeth still present; primary feather sheaths developing on wings *(photo by Howard Carleton, Jr.; courtesy of the USDA Forest Service)*. Days 4–5 (top left): eyes partially open; egg teeth still present; sheaths of secondary wing feathers becoming prominent *(photo by Charles W. Schwartz)*. Days 6–7 (top right): eyes fully open; egg teeth fading; tips of feathers emerging from primary sheaths; squabs can crawl and/or raise wings over their backs in a defensive posture *(photo courtesy of the National Archives)*. Days 8–9 (bottom left): egg tooth still present at least on lower mandible; upper portion of breast well feathered; crown feathers beginning to appear; older nestling may leave nest when alarmed *(photo courtesy of the National Archives)*. Days 10–11 (bottom right): feathers at the junction of the neck and back remain sheathed at 10 days, and belly feathers begin to unsheath on day 11; nestlings readily leave nest when alarmed; aging henceforth difficult to assess and consists of completion of feather coverage over entire body *(photo courtesy of the National Archives)*.

Mourning dove young may fledge anytime from twelve to fifteen days of age. Young fledglings can be identified by short tails, somewhat mottled appearance and unstable flight patterns. *Photo by Charles W. Schwartz.*

The mottled coloration of recently fledged mourning doves matches tree structures and debris on the ground and camouflages these birds when they are in reference areas awaiting feeding by the male parent. Such camouflage may reduce avian predation during a particularly vulnerable stage of development. The left scene, a detail of the right photo taken at only a few meters distance, illustrates the undetectability of nestlings (see arrows) while on the ground. *Photo by Ralph E. Mirarchi; courtesy of the Auburn University Department of Zoology and Wildlife Science and the Alabama Agricultural Experiment Station.*

IMMATURE OR
HATCHING-YEAR STAGE
(16 to ca. 160 days posthatching)

Sex Ratios

Limited data are available on sex ratios of hatching-year mourning doves. However, for unknown reasons, the ratios apparently skew more in favor of males during this period. The most comprehensive studies indicate sex ratios (males per one hundred females) favoring males in both Missouri—142:100 (Chambers et al. 1962)—and Illinois—113:100 (Hanson and Kossack 1963). Sex ratios vary by month (Chambers et al. 1962), year and locale (Hanson and Kossack 1963). Biases in sampling techniques and age-related physiological differences may affect sex ratios perceived in different locales and should be kept in mind, as discussed later.

Morphological Development

Hormonal changes. Other than hormonal secretions involved with reproduction (see chapter 9), little is known about hormonal regulation of mourning doves, or closely related columbids, during this period of development.

Body weight and lipid deposition. Weight and lipid deposition in hatching-year mourning doves vary greatly as a result of preparation for migration, but there also is a decided increase in weight with age in both sexes (Hanson and Kossack 1957b, Mirarchi 1978). Body weights of males average 3.35 ounces (95 g) at 30 days of age, when they become totally independent of parental care, and 4.59 ounces (130 g) at approximately 160 days (Jenkins 1955, Hanson and Kossack 1957b). Body weights of females average 3.07 ounces (87 g) at 30 days of age and 4.23 ounces (120 g) at 160 days. In every age category, hatching-year males average 5.8 to 10.7 percent heavier than females; the overall average for males is 8.5 percent heavier than for hatching-year females (Hanson and Kossack 1957b). Depending on the amount of lipid deposition, hatching-year doves often attain body weights equal to those of adults about midway between the replacement of the sixth and seventh primary (Hanson and Kossack 1957b).

Lipid reserves in mourning doves generally are higher in winter than in summer, both in wild and captive birds (Jenkins 1955). A distinctive rise in lipid reserves occurs during the last two weeks in September and may signal premigratory preparation. Hatching-year doves have a greater propensity for migration than do adults and are more nu-

merous. Thus, the majority of wild birds sampled in early autumn show an increase in lipid reserves. After the early surge in migration, lipid reserves drop to a low in October and November, then rise to a winter peak in January (Jenkins 1955).

Plumage and molt. The terminology used to describe plumage succession in birds has varied considerably and led to much confusion. A unified treatment of terminology regarding plumages and molts was suggested by Humphrey and Parkes (1959) and is used as the basis for this discussion.

Juvenile plumage (the first covering of true contour feathers) in mourning doves is attained by one month of age (Taylor 1941). The first prebasic molt apparently is a gradual process beginning with the first primary wing feathers and continuing sequentially through the remaining primaries over a period of approximately 130 to 160 days (see chapter 21). It is not known when the body feathers begin to be replaced, but three studies (Moore and Pearson 1941, Taylor 1941, Quay 1951a) and an examination of the body molt of six (three male, three female) hatching-year mourning dove specimens of different ages (J. W. Aldrich personal communication: 1986) indicate that it is a gradual process that occurs between 30 and 160 days of age, until the adult plumage is attained. The entire body molt appears to take eleven to twenty weeks, with an average of sixteen weeks (Pearson and Moore 1940, Taylor 1941, Quay 1951a). Interestingly, doves hatched before June 1 usually attain what appears to be the breeding (first alternate) plumage at 75 days of age (when replacing the sixth primary [Reeves et al. 1968]) as they reach puberty (White et al. 1987). The type of plumage adorning 75-day-old doves hatched after June 1 is unknown. They may molt directly into what appears to be the winter (first basic) plumage. Obviously, little is known about the specifics of body molt in hatching-year doves, particularly relative to hatching date. Additional research is needed in this area.

Timing of primary feather molt in hatching-year mourning doves is related to their hatching date and is variable (Cannell 1984), but the sequence of this molt provides a good estimate of the birds' age (see chapter 21). This primary molt often slows (Thompson 1950, Ault et al. 1976) or is suspended during winter (Armstrong and Noakes 1983). Suspended molt may occur because of severe environmental conditions (Armstrong and Noakes 1983). This situation would be advantageous for hatching-year doves because of their high metabolic expenditures (Ivacic and Labisky 1973), especially for late-hatched doves that most likely overwinter locally, often under rigorous climatic conditions (Hennessy and Van Camp 1963).

The juvenal plumage (first covering of true contour feathers) in hatching-year mourning doves has a mottled or scaled appearance because of the buff-colored tips. *Photo by Charles W. Schwartz.*

ADULT STAGE
(ca. 160 days and older)

Sex Ratios

Reported sex ratios (males per one hundred females) of adult mourning doves range widely from approximately 100:100 (Pearson and Moore 1941, Jenkins 1955) to a preponderance of males. Examples of skewed sex ratios include 125:100 to 159:100 in Illinois (Hanson and Kossack 1963), 145:100 to 433:100 in Arkansas (Booth et al. 1975, 1976), 156:100 to 247:100 in Missouri (Chambers et al. 1962, Henry et al. 1976), 162:100 in North Carolina (Quay 1951a), 170:100 from 118 specimens collected throughout North and Central America for the Chicago Natural History Museum (Hanson and Kossack 1963), and 376:100 in Minnesota (Thomforde 1972). Sex ratios of adults also vary monthly, seasonally and with locality (Quay 1951a, Chambers et al. 1962, Hanson and Kossack 1963), although preponderances of males were evident in all samples. Seasonal and local differences may be due to sexual differences in migratory movements (Chambers et al. 1962) that may have evolved in mourning doves as a result of sexual differences in basal metabolic rate (Riddle et al. 1932, Ivacic and Labisky 1973) and the less favorable surface area to body weight ratio in the smaller females. It is apparent that, whatever the causes (differential hatch-

ing rates, differential mortality rates, sex-selective advantages, etc.), a preponderance of males occurs in the adult mourning dove population of North America. This skewing of the sex ratio in favor of males appears to increase from hatching through adulthood. The only question that still clouds these data involves the randomness of the samples involved. It is possible that the sampling schemes used (samples were collected by shooting or trapping) in some of the studies may have caused some biases. It is known that trap placement does affect the sex composition of the sample (Henry et al. 1976), and placement of shooters certainly may have a similar effect. Also, sampling at certain hours during the breeding season and at certain locales in the winter can affect how sex ratios are perceived.

Morphological and Physiological Characteristics

Hormonal patterns. No data exist on secretory patterns of the nonreproductive hormones of adult mourning doves. However, Lea et al. (1986) found that ring doves show seasonal variations in plasma concentrations of thyroxine, corticosterone and growth hormone associated with molts (increased thyroxine and growth hormone, decreased corticosterone) and with heat production (thermogenesis) during the winter (increased thyroxine).

They theorized that growth hormone and corticosterone may have promoted lipid metabolism to provide the energy necessary during molts. Similar seasonal variations in these hormones also were observed in common pigeons (Saarela et al. 1986), although plasma concentrations varied considerably during the day (Rintamäki et al. 1986). Occurrence of free fatty acids, which also are involved in avian thermogenesis, appeared to be more related to photoperiod than to ambient temperature (Rintamäki et al. 1986). High prolactin levels during autumn appeared to be related to lipid metabolism, supporting the contention that prolactin and corticosterone are important in increasing body weights and fat stores in columbids (Miller and Riddle 1943, Meier and Burns 1976). Additional research is needed to address the relationship between hormonal patterns and body weight changes, lipid cycles, and molts of mourning doves.

Length, body weight and lipid deposition.
Generally, total lengths and body weights of adult mourning doves differ according to race and sex; the eastern race (*Zenaida macroura carolinensis*) tends to be larger and is slightly heavier than the western race (*Z. m. marginella*) and males consistently are larger and weigh more than females in both populations. For *carolinensis*, adult male lengths (dried skins measured from tip of bill to tip of tail) average about 12.6 inches (32.1 cm) and range from 10.7 to 13.4 inches (27.1 to 34.1 cm); adult female lengths (skins) average 10.8 inches (27.3 cm) with a range of 8.9 to 11.7 inches (22.5 to 29.7 cm) (Ridgway 1916). Adult *marginella* male lengths (skins) average 11.7 inches (29.8 cm) and range from 10.4 to 13.3 inches (26.4 to 34.1 cm), whereas adult female lengths (skins) average 11.1 inches (28.1 cm) and range from 9.9 to 12.2 inches (25.1 to 31.0 cm) (Ridgway 1916). For *carolinensis*, adult male weights average about 4.6 ounces (130 g) during the year and range from 3.9 to 6.0 ounces (110 to 170 g); adult female weights average 4.3 ounces (123 g) during the year with a range of 3.5 to 5.5 ounces (100 to 156 g) (Nelson and Martin 1953, Jenkins 1955). Adult *marginella* male weights from May through October average 4.1 ounces (116 g) and range from 3.4 to 5.1 ounces (96 to 143 g), whereas adult female weights average 3.8 ounces (108 g) and range from 3.0 to 5.0 ounces (86 to 142 g) (average of unpublished data from New Mexico [T. L. Best 1988] and Arizona [L. H. Blankenship 1964]).

These length data should be used only to provide a general idea of the size of the bird, because a skin measurement differs considerably from measurement of a live bird and also varies according to how and by whom a skin is prepared. The weight data also should be used with caution, because it is possible that crop contents were included at the time of weighing. Weights of crop contents can add as much as 8 to 10 percent to the body weight of a mourning dove (Hanson and Kossack 1957b). Additionally, it is not always clear if body weight data of adults included birds with any indications of crop gland development. Male doves with crop development weigh 1.6 percent more than do males with no crop development, whereas females with crop development weigh 5.4 percent more than do females with no crop development (Hanson and Kossack 1957b). Differences in body weights of breeding males and females probably are partially the result of increased development of the ovary and oviduct in the breeding female (Hanson and Kossack 1957b).

During the annual cycle, the lightest body weights for both sexes occur during September and October, and the heaviest weights occur during November and December (Jenkins 1955). Body weights gradually decline from the winter peak to the yearly low in the latter half of September and early October. Much of this ebb and flow in body weights apparently can be attributed to changes in lipid reserves, as discussed earlier with hatching-year birds. According to Jenkins (1955), lipid reserves generally are greater in winter than in summer but also are related to migrational status and recent nesting history of the individual. Adult doves apparently have heavy lipid reserves during the spring and autumn just prior to migration. In addition, captive doves that recently have nested lack lipid reserves and are thin.

Obviously, there is a great deal of variability in body weights and lipid reserves among adult mourning doves, particularly during early spring and early autumn when early and late nesters, respectively, are mixed with doves preparing to migrate. No data are available on weekly or daily changes in mourning dove body weights or lipid reserves associated with breeding activity and crop gland cycles. In ring dove pairs, there is a significant increase in total body weight during incubation (6 to 8 percent more than preincubation weight), which peaks at the time of hatching (Riddle and Braucher 1934, Brisbin 1969). This increase in body weight is lost during the period when nestlings are being fed, and body weights return to preincubation levels within twenty days after the young hatch (Brisbin 1969). Interestingly, fat indices (grams of fat per gram lean dry weight) of breeding ring doves are extremely variable, with no definite trends detectable during the breeding cycle; however, these fat indices (range = 0.226–0.453) are considerably lower than fat indices (range = 0.479–0.720, $\bar{x}$ = 0.604) of nonbreeding doves sacrificed during winter months. Most importantly, water indices (grams of water per gram lean dry weight) are lowest during the courting phase and increase to a peak at hatching (Brisbin 1969). By the time the fledglings are eighteen days old, water indices decline to their low preincubation values.

The increase in body weight of ring doves during incubation differs from the weight regime observed in passerines. Although the increase in body weight appears to be associated with growth of the crop gland, only a portion of the weight change can be attributed directly to enlargement of the crop itself (Brisbin 1969). Crop weights of ring dove pairs are about 4 percent of the pair's body weight (Lehrman 1964), yet the observed increase in body weight during incubation is 6 to 8 percent. The difference apparently is due to a general hydration of the body tissues, as indicated by the increase in water index at this time. Similarly, the loss of body weight after the young hatch is a reversal of this process, the main factor being a general dehydration of body tissues (Brisbin 1969).

The lack of change in fat indices is surprising considering that most birds store fat for periods of high energy demand, such as raising nestlings. Apparently it is more advantageous for ring dove adults to store water than fat before squabs hatch, perhaps because of the nutritional components of crop milk (Brisbin 1969). Crop milk is composed of approximately 13 to 19 percent protein, 7 to 13 percent fat, 1 to 2 percent ash and 65 to 81 percent water. Since the body tissues of adult ring doves average 10 to 12 percent fat and 60 to 65 percent water, the loss of 0.035 ounces (1 g) of adult body weight in the form of crop milk would not cause any proportionately heavy drain on body fat stores, but it would put a relatively heavy drain on body water reserves (Brisbin 1969). Both field-oriented and controlled laboratory research on mourning doves needs to be conducted before there is complete understanding of their body weight and lipid dynamics.

Plumage and molt. The adult feather coat of the majority of mourning doves normally is attained after the first prebasic molt. It consists of approximately 2,600 feathers (Hutt and Ball 1938). The timing of the first prebasic molt varies with latitude and among individuals, but it generally occurs at the end of the breeding season in August or September.

No study of the sequence of body molt in mourning doves has yet been published. Such a study would be difficult because the density of the body plumage makes it hard to find pinfeathers (J. W. Aldrich personal communication: 1987). Consequently, what happens during or after the first prebasic molt is not known exactly.

Early studies indicate that mourning doves "have a complete molt in the fall" (Bent 1932: 408), but this may be far too simplistic an explanation. According to J. W. Aldrich (personal communication: 1987), the molt in adults appears to begin "with the termination of their breeding and the reduction in sex hormone production" and "varies greatly with individual birds from late spring to fall." He also believed that an "annual molt . . . of most parts of the body can take place at most any time during the postbreeding season until the last one is complete in late fall." This type of molt might explain the drabber coloration of males and females in autumn and winter, as first described by Ridgway (1916) and observed by biologists and lay persons since. However, it does not explain how the bright colors of the breeding (alternate) plumage reappear in late winter and early spring. This could entail another molt, either complete or partial.

Excessive feather loss and feather accumulations indicative of molts have been noticed in autumn and again in late winter in flocks of captive mourning doves. If this represents a true molt, adult doves evidently renew their feather coats twice yearly during the prealternate molt (December–January) and prebasic molt (August–September). Thus, the normal molt and plumage sequence after the first prebasic molt would be winter (first basic) plumage, first prealternate molt, breeding (first alternate) plumage, second prebasic molt, winter (second basic) plumage, etc. (after Pettingill 1985). If only one molt takes place, the darker or drabber basic plumage of winter could give way to the lighter or paler breeding (alternate) plumage of spring as the result of abrasion or fading, as in many passerine species (Pettingill 1985). In that event, the normal molt and plumage sequence after the first prebasic molt would be winter (first basic) plumage, fading or abrasion, breeding (first alternate) plumage, etc.

Obviously, additional research is needed to determine conclusively how the plumage changes in adult mourning doves. In the process, a semantic problem must be recognized. The word "molt" has been used ambiguously in the mourning dove literature. As explained clearly by Cannell (1984), its definition should include feather loss *and* replacement to be consistent with modern ornithological usage. The simple loss of feathers should be indicated by terms such as "dropped," "shed" or "lost."

The plumage of adult mourning doves is definitive (Humphrey and Parkes 1959) in nature—i.e., the basic colors and patterns in both sexes are the

The adult mourning dove's feather coat is basically grayish brown, with black spots behind the eyes and on the wings. There are grayish white tips and edges on the outer tail feathers and pink or green iridescent feathers on the neck. *Photo by Leonard Lee Rue III.*

same each year and normally do not change with age (see chapters 3 and 21).

The primary, secondary and tertiary wing feathers (remiges) of adult mourning doves are shed and replaced yearly in an orderly sequence, so flight is possible during molt. The innermost primary is shed first; when it has been partially replaced, the next primary is lost. This sequence continues until all of the primaries are replaced. The greater primary coverts tend to be shed slightly before the primary feathers, and by the time the ninth and tenth primaries are shed, the primary coverts have been replaced completely. Little is known about the shedding sequence of the secondary or tertiary feathers or the related coverts. If it is similar to that of passerines, however, loss of the outermost tertiary feather occurs coincident with loss of the fifth or sixth primary (Pettingill 1985). The molt then would continue sequentially until the last or innermost tertiary was shed and replaced.

Similarly, molt of the secondaries would begin with the outermost feather and loss of the innermost tertiary (Pettingill 1985). This molt also would occur sequentially, with the innermost secondary

being the last to be shed and replaced. Molt of the greater secondary coverts also would occur successively and in the same direction as the secondaries. However, the molt would occur much more quickly, and all the greater secondary coverts normally would be replaced before molt of the secondaries ended (Pettingill 1985).

Generally, the primary feather molt of adult mourning doves occurs from May through September, but timing of this molt varies geographically. For example, adult mourning doves complete primary feather loss in the Carolinas (Haas and Amend 1979) earlier than do adult doves in Missouri (Sadler et al. 1970). Unfortunately, timings of primary loss at additional geographic sites are not recorded, so no consistency in pattern can be established nor any definitive conclusions made regarding the reasons for these differences.

Aberrant feather coats. Mourning doves sometimes exhibit different forms of albinism (reduction or absence of melanin [brown-black] pigments in the feathers). The four degrees of albinism in birds (Mueller and Hutt 1941, Pettingill 1985) are: (1) total—all melanin pigments completely missing from the feathers, irises (colored portion of eye) and skin; (2) incomplete—melanin pigments completely absent from feathers, irises or skin, but not from all three; (3) imperfect—all the pigments "diluted" or at least one of the pigments absent in any or all three areas; and (4) partial—pigments reduced or one or more absent from the *parts* of any or all three areas.

Any form of albinism in mourning doves is rare, and all forms appear to be considerably more rare in columbids than in other families of birds (Gross 1965). No specimen exhibiting total albinism has been reported for the mourning dove. However, incomplete (Graefe and Hollander 1945, Braun 1979), imperfect (Ross 1963, Braun 1979, R. E. Mirarchi unpublished data) and partial (Braun 1979, Armstrong and Noakes 1977a, R. E. Mirarchi unpublished data) specimens have been reported. Incompletely albinistic specimens have white bodies, red-pink eyes and "dirty" white and/or spotted wings. Imperfectly albinistic specimens tend to have dark eyes and bill and pale feet; they are either gray-white or "fawn" (brown) in color. Gray specimens are termed nonphaeomelonic forms (Harrison 1963), because there is a loss of brown pigments resulting in some shade of gray or black. Fawn-colored specimens are termed non-

eumelanistic forms (Harrison 1963) because the black or gray pigments are absent, resulting in some shade of brown. In both cases, the plumage tends to show signs of rapid wear and abrasion, and feather tips and edges are worn away, leaving only the shaft (Harrison 1963). Apparently, when these black or gray pigments are present, the amount of keratin present also increases, and this hardens and strengthens the feathers (Voitkevich 1966). Partial albinism in mourning doves generally involves the feathers. Usually the primaries are affected, often symmetrically, with each side of the dove being affected in the same way (see Braun 1979). Occasionally, a few individual feathers on the head or other parts of the body may be involved (R. E. Mirarchi unpublished data).

Little is known about sexual differences in albinism frequencies for mourning doves, although certain forms of albinism in birds appear to be related to sex (Mueller and Hutt 1941). Albinism occurs in both hatching-year and adult mourning doves, but little is known about frequency of occurrence relative to age. Certainly, whenever any form of albinism in mourning doves is reported, an effort should be made to collect the specimens, record all sex and age information, and determine the form of albinism involved.

Fawn-colored or noneumelanistic (left) mourning doves lack black or gray pigments, which represents a form of albinism. They appear brown and white. True albinism in mourning doves is unreported; partial albinism is exceedingly rare, given the annual production of these doves. In noneumelanistic doves, plumage wear is rapid (right), particularly at the wing tips and edges, because the lack of dark pigment prevents keratinization, or hardening, of the feathers. *Specimen donated by Jim Coble, Arab, Alabama; photos by George W. Folkerts; courtesy of the Auburn University Department of Zoology and Wildlife Science and the Alabama Agricultural Experiment Station.*

Chapter 9

Energetics, Metabolism and Reproductive Physiology

Ralph E. Mirarchi
Department of Zoology and Wildlife Science
and
Alabama Agricultural Experiment Station
Auburn University, Alabama

Traditionally, mourning dove biologists have been concerned primarily with preventing conflicts between breeding and hunting seasons, reducing disease and contaminant risks, monitoring population sizes and recommending harvest regulations. As demands for both consumptive and nonconsumptive uses of mourning doves continue to grow, wildlife researchers must find ways to help manage this resource more intensively.

Research on bioenergetics and metabolism of a species provides basic biological information and allows analyses of how and where energy is expended. With such information, the when and where of energy shortfalls can be determined, and biologists can focus on alleviating those shortfalls through proper habitat management. Similarly, intimate knowledge of the reproductive physiology facilitates understanding of why the mourning dove is so prolific and, simultaneously, permits refinement of harvest bag limits and lengths of hunting seasons. Unfortunately, many of these areas of mourning dove research have received little attention. Consequently, most information is gained from research and other experiences with related columbids.

EGGS AND THE EMBRYONIC STAGE

Egg Content

Newly hatched mourning doves are termed "altricial," or "nidicolous" (nest-dwelling), rather than "precocial," or "nidifugous" (nest-fleeing). They are poorly developed at hatching—blind, essentially naked and incapable of self-care for at least their first two weeks. This lack of development at hatching in altricial species is due to a lack of prior provisioning of the egg by the adult (O'Connor 1984) and is reflected in differences in egg weight (Carey et al. 1980, Rahn et al. 1975) and egg composition (Carey et al. 1980, Roca et al. 1982). Because less yolk matter is present in eggs of altricial species such as the mourning dove, the eggs weigh less, contain relatively more water but less lipid and nonlipid, and are less energy-loaded (content per unit weight) than eggs of precocial species (O'Connor 1984). Composition of the major egg components (shell, yolk, albumen) and energy content ($\bar{x} \pm SD = 1.24 \pm 0.07$ kilocalories per gram fresh weight, including shell) of mourning dove eggs are typical of altricial birds (Ricklefs 1977).

Incubation

In ten (37.5 percent) of twenty-seven mourning dove clutches, Hanson and Kossack (1963) found that the second egg was laid within twenty-four hours of the first. In seventeen clutches, the second egg was laid twenty-four to forty-eight hours after the first.

Incubation begins immediately after the first egg is laid (cf. chapters 5 and 6). Mourning doves exhibit a primitive pattern of incubation behavior in that both parents share incubation responsibilities (O'Connor 1984). The natural incubation (egg) temperature of the mourning dove is approximately 98.6 degrees Fahrenheit (37° C) (Huggins 1941, Graber 1955), which is within the optimal incubation temperature range (98.6 to 102.2° F: 37 to 39° C) typical of birds of this size (Franks 1967, O'Connor 1984). Egg temperatures vary by several degrees, depending on nest attentiveness, ambient temperature, wind, sunlight, egg size and possibly embryonic metabolic rate (Huggins 1941). Mourning dove eggs normally are exposed only during parental exchanges, and this incubation pattern may serve both to maintain necessary incubation temperatures (Westmoreland et al. 1986) and avoid heavy predation that could occur in birds having noncryptic (white) eggs (Westmoreland and Best 1986). Also, the flimsy nest of the mourning dove (see chapters 5 and 6) provides relatively little insulation, so constant coverage probably is necessary to maintain suitable egg temperatures.

Actual incubation involves keeping the eggs in contact with the parent's body surface, but mourning doves do not develop a conspicuous brood patch (Maridon and Holcomb 1971) as do many other birds. Constant incubation probably eliminated the need for vascularized incubation patches in mourning doves and other columbids (Westmoreland et al. 1986). Columbids have prominent bare spaces (apteria) between the feathers of the breast (Westmoreland et al. 1986), and the immediate reaction of columbid parents to abnormal egg temperatures is to adjust the contact between the eggs and their skin. Parental body temperatures obviously are affected by changes in egg temperature. Columbid parents pant after exposure to several minutes of abnormally high egg temperatures, and shiver and elevate feathers after exposure to several minutes of abnormally low egg temperatures (Franks 1967). In desert regions, where mourning doves cannot keep the eggs cool enough by using shade from vegetation or their bodies, they rely on transfer of excess heat from the egg to the adult's body, where it is subsequently dissipated by evaporative cooling (panting) (Walsberg and Voss-Roberts 1983) in a manner similar to that of birds with brood patches (Franks 1967). Such increased reliance on evaporative cooling may subject attending parents to substantial dehydration (Walsberg and Voss-Roberts 1983) and probably increases the heavy dependence of doves on water in semiarid and arid areas. Mourning doves (females, at least) apparently do not regulate potential dehydration of their eggs in response to environmental changes. Eggshell conductance is not adjusted to cope with humidity shifts, nor is egg dehydration prevented by parental control of nest humidity (Walsberg 1985).

NESTLING STAGE
(1 to 15 days posthatching)

Energetics of Growth

Metabolism and development of temperature regulation. Nestlings of altricial bird species such as the mourning dove are ectothermic (thermally dependent on their parents) for varying lengths of time after they hatch (O'Connor 1984). Early studies of mourning dove nestlings indicate that their rectal body temperatures range from 94 to 108 degrees Fahrenheit (34.4 to 42.2° C) and vary with age of nestling, time of day and physical activity (Gardner 1930). Body temperatures of nestlings rise as they grow older, during warmer portions of the day and with increases in physical activity. These data correspond with current knowledge of differences between ectothermy and homeothermy (thermal independence) in altricial species. Nestlings become homeothermic as they develop the ability to produce heat through metabolism and retain it due to an insulative layer of feathers. Thyroid hormones play a major role in the control of the metabolism of homeothermic vertebrates. These hormone concentrations are low when ring dove nestlings hatch, but increase steadily and rapidly during the first eight days posthatching when the squabs are ectothermic and dependent on parental brooding. The rate of increase of blood thyroid hormone concentrations slows and stabilizes when the nestlings are fifteen days old and have grown feathers (McNabb and Cheng 1985).

The pattern of temperature regulation for mourning dove squabs resembles that of ring doves. Mourning dove squabs less than six days old are ectothermic, and homeothermy still is incomplete by twelve days of age. Mourning dove nestlings apparently do not achieve complete homeothermy until a favorable body surface/volume ratio and an insulative feather coat are attained just

Mourning dove hatchlings are altricial (dependent on parental care) and ectothermic (dependent on parents to regulate temperature) until they fledge, but progressively less so after they are six days old. Note the matlike growth of pin feathers on these nestlings four and five days old. The feathers not only are necessary for postfledging mobility but are also the principal mechanism of thermoregulation. *Photo courtesy of the Alabama Cooperative Fish and Wildlife Research Unit.*

before fledging at fifteen days of age (Breitenbach and Baskett 1967).

Total energy requirements. Knowledge of the basal metabolism, growth rate and energy content of tissues allows estimation of the total energy requirements of young birds (excluding temperature regulation and activity) during development (Ricklefs 1974). Data on basal metabolism and growth rates of nestling mourning doves are available (Breitenbach and Baskett 1967, Riddle et al. 1932, Cheney and Cheney 1967, Holcomb and Jaeger 1978), but there are no published data on the energy content of tissues of these nestlings. Consequently, their total energy requirements cannot be calculated exactly.

Changes in body composition and total energy requirements of nestling ring doves have been determined (Brisbin 1969) and are described briefly here to give a rough approximation of potential changes in body composition and energetic needs of mourning dove nestlings. Fat indices (grams of fat per gram lean dry weight) of nestling ring doves do not change with age, while water indices (grams of water per gram lean dry weight) decrease significantly with age. Water indices (5.57 to 8.62) of one-day-old ring dove squabs are among the highest reported for whole birds (Brisbin 1969). Lack of

change in fat indices with age indicates that no energy reserves exist in ring dove squabs for periods when food is scarce or unavailable. Of course, the use of crop milk (rich in protein, fat and water) by columbids to feed nestlings probably is adaptive and precludes a need for reserves. Additionally, the wide variety of seeds used as food by columbids probably minimizes prolonged scarcity or unavailability of foods. The high water indices of nestling ring doves also probably reflect the high water content of crop milk during this time. This too may be adaptive, because water stored in tissues at early ages can be used later during nestling dependency as crop milk production slows and dry seeds are fed to nestlings (see chapter 7).

No significant changes in the caloric value of lean dry weight of nestling ring doves (average = 4.9 kilocalories per gram) occur throughout the growth period, but the caloric value of nestling live weights increases (from 1 kilocalorie per gram live weight at hatching to about 2.26 kilocalories per gram live weight at forty-three days of age) as a highly significant linear function of age (Brisbin 1969). This function can be described as: $C = 0.910 + 0.31t$, where $C = Kcal/g$ live weight and t = age in days. Basically, nestling ring doves reach the caloric value (2.26 kilocalories per gram live weight) of adults when they attain adult body size and growth ceases at approximately forty-three days old.

The total number of calories required to raise ring dove squabs from hatching to independence (at the age of twenty-eight days), over and above the standard caloric intake for nonbreeding adults, is 1,134.9 and 922.5 kilocalories for squabs raised one and two per nest, respectively (Brisbin 1969). Total caloric cost of raising ring dove squabs from hatching to maturity is lower for two squabs per nest than for one, probably because the more favorable thermodynamic situation that exists for each individual squab as a result of huddling reduces the caloric costs of maintaining body temperature (Royama 1966).

The degree to which ring dove data apply to wild mourning doves is not known precisely. The two species are very similar in size, and their nestling and fledgling dependency periods are comparable, but rigors associated with living in the wild that mourning dove nestlings and their parents experience certainly must affect metabolic rate, caloric intake, etc. Also, little is known about the insulative quality of mourning dove nests and their ability to conserve heat of nestlings. It is generally acknowledged, though not scientifically proven, that the flimsy mourning dove nests have little insulative capability (Ricklefs 1974).

Energy dependence and parental feeding. After mourning dove eggs hatch, the shell parts are disposed of by the parents, primarily the female. Two trips are made per egg, the parent flying out of sight of the nest while carrying each half in the bill (Luther 1979). There is no evidence that either parent consistently ingests the shells to obtain nutrients or energy.

Both mourning dove parents feed and brood their squabs until they fledge (Taylor 1941). The female parent generally is the first to feed the young after hatching (Luther 1979), probably because she is most often on the nest at the time. The male parent usually broods the young for as little as sixteen minutes (squabs more than three days old) to as much as two to six hours (one-day-old squabs) before feeding them (Luther 1979). This may allow the male to clear the crop of ingested foods prior to crop milk formation (Murton 1964). According to Luther (1979), the greatest number of feedings and longest period of time devoted to feeding the young occur during the first four days posthatching.

The number and duration of feedings by both parents decrease between four and fifteen days after hatching. From four to approximately twelve days posthatching, the female parent spends the most time feeding the squabs, and a shift in feeding responsibilities to the male occurs between the twelfth and fifteenth day (Luther 1979, Hitchcock and Mirarchi 1984a). This shift in feeding responsibility apparently allows the female to shunt mineral and/or energy resources of the body from crop gland development and crop milk production to gonadal development and egg production for the next laying cycle (Mirarchi and Scanlon 1980).

Beginning about the fifth day of brooding, the female and, to a much greater degree, the male parent may perch coo to the nestlings immediately before feeding them (Luther 1979). This behavior continues even after the young leave the nest (Hitchcock 1986). Although the cooing activity may be used to quiet the young to allow easier feeding (Luther 1979), it is more likely that such activity is conditioning the nestlings to recognize the perch coo of the male parent. Subsequently, the young vocalize and wing-solicit when he perch coos near their reference area, aiding him to locate them for feeding interactions. These behaviors could reduce energy expenditures and possibly predation rates of young fledglings (Hitchcock et al. 1989).

Both parents keep the nest free of nestlings' droppings for the first few days after the young hatch, but nest care lags by the time the young are seven to eight days old. Nest sanitation is achieved by the parents swallowing droppings as soon as they appear. Defecation actually may be stimulated by the parents at times (Luther 1979). The significance of nest sanitation in this species is not known, but it generally has been viewed as a means of predator avoidance. Because of the tremendous amount of nutritional and energetic investment by the parents in terms of crop milk production, however, the potential nutritional and energy value of these droppings should not be overlooked. It is interesting, and perhaps not coincidental, that nest sanitation lags about the time crop milk production slows considerably. In at least some species of passerines, young nestlings have low digestive efficiency and the adult probably recovers substantial quantities of nutrients when consuming fecal sacs (O'Connor 1984).

Successful single-parent mourning dove nests have been reported in wild and captive populations (see chapter 5). In the wild, two squabs can be raised to fledging by a single parent if the squabs are five to eight days old when the parent is lost. However, for single-parent nest success to equal two-parent nest success, squabs have to be nine to ten days old when a parent is lost. Sex of the parent removed apparently does not influence fledging success (Haas 1980). Unfortunately, no published data exist on the seasonal effects on such success rates. A great deal of variability may exist during the early and late months of the breeding season

Shells of hatched mourning dove eggs are removed by the parents, usually the female. Shell halves are carried away individually in the adult's bill and usually discarded out of sight of the nest. *Photo by Charles W. Schwartz.*

because of increased energetic demands on nestlings and parents as a result of cooler temperatures.

In captivity, a single male parent has successfully incubated (starting four days postlaying) a normal clutch of two eggs and then raised the two squabs until they fledged (Goforth 1964). Obviously, energetic demands placed on captive single parents are less than on their wild counterparts because of the availability and proximity of food, less rigorous environmental stressors and lack of interaction with conspecifics and predators. Similarly, nestlings of captive single parents would be more likely to survive because of more attentive parents and lack of predation pressures. Consequently, success of single-parent nests containing eggs in wild populations seems highly unlikely.

Conspecific "helpers at the nest" have been reported for the mourning dove during the nestling stage (Blockstein 1986b), and such behavior has been reported between mourning doves and other species of doves in both wild and captive situations (Neff 1945).

Energy dependence and parental brooding. Squabs are brooded constantly until they are four to five days old, after which the adults first leave the nest unattended. By the time squabs are six or seven days old, constant brooding is unusual and the squabs sometimes are left unattended for long periods during suitable weather (Luther 1979). Night brooding normally is discontinued when the young reach nine to ten days of age. Parents also can respond to early fledging (prior to thirteen days posthatching) by brooding on the ground if necessary (Willoughby and Krebs 1986). The female parent contributes the most brooding time through fifteen days posthatching, but there is a dramatic drop in brooding behavior in both parents between twelve and fifteen days (Hitchcock and Mirarchi 1984a). These changes in brooding behavior correspond roughly with what is known about development of temperature regulation in columbids and demonstrate the great importance of interaction among the thermoregulatory capability of the squabs, brooding behavior of the parents and climatic conditions. Unfortunately, none of the energetic expenditures associated with brooding behavior in the mourning dove has been quantified.

Nestling behaviors and energetic considerations. Being altricial, mourning dove nestlings probably closely follow the recognized stages of postembryonic development described by Nice (1962). Theoretically, the presence of a brood mate in the nest should allow the squabs to huddle together and reduce the proportion of brood surface exposed to the air, thereby reducing the amount of heat needed to maintain stable body temperatures

Hatchlings huddled together may provide reduced surface exposure to air temperature for the short periods when they are not being brooded and even when brooded in flimsy nests. Note that the just-hatched squab on the top is smaller than its day-old brood mate, yet neither has its eyes open (squabs' eyes begin to open at four days of age and are completely open by day six). Also, its eggshell has not yet been removed from the nest by a parent, usually the female. *Photo by Charles W. Schwartz; courtesy of the Missouri Department of Conservation.*

(O'Connor 1984). Unfortunately, no information on heat production in one- versus two-squab mourning dove nests is available, so energetic considerations at this level are unknown. Certainly, for the first four days posthatching, the squabs' primary activities are begging, feeding, sleeping and converting ingested food into biomass. Movements and activities are kept to a minimum, with the squabs five to eight days old being just able to crawl and assume a defensive attitude with wings raised over the back (Hanson and Kossack 1963). Comfort movements such as preening also begin at this time. By nine to twelve days, maturation of comfort movements (stretching, exploratory pecking, etc.) occurs and the nestlings are capable of leaving the nest when disturbed. Coincidentally, nestlings nine to twelve days old also are able to recognize the voice of their male parent (Hitchcock et al. 1989). As explained earlier, this allows them to respond to his vocalizations by calling and wing-soliciting, thereby facilitating interactions with him. Just before leaving the nest permanently under their own locomotion (fledging) at thirteen to sixteen days of age (normally), the nestlings begin exploring the immediate vicinity of the nest (usually on foot) and begin exercising their wings (Luther 1979, R. E. Mirarchi unpublished data).

In summary, energy expenditures by nestling mourning doves are kept to a minimum during the time they are wholly or partially ectothermic (one to twelve days posthatching). Thereafter, some energy is expended on exploratory activity and exercising their wings. Unfortunately, none of the energy expenditures associated with these behaviors of nestling mourning doves has been quantified.

IMMATURE OR HATCHING-YEAR STAGE (16 to ca. 160 days posthatching)

Energetics of Growth and Development

Metabolism. Under experimental conditions hatching-year mourning doves tend to have higher metabolic rates (based on oxygen consumption) than adults do, and hatching-year females tend to have higher metabolic rates than do hatching-year males (Ivacic and Labisky 1973). Mean oxygen consumption (cc $O_2 \cdot g^{-1} hr^{-1}$) for hatching-year males ranges from 1.29 at 50 degrees Fahrenheit (10° C) to 2.50 at −0.4° F (−18° C), while that of females ranges from 2.01 at 50° F (10° C) to 3.39 at 14° F (−10° C). Metabolic expenditures of hatching-year birds are due more to changes in ambient temperature than to light or darkness, although increasing light does tend to increase metabolic expenditures. This may indicate that hatching-year doves possess less ability than adults do to thermoregulate under conditions of alternately decreasing or increasing ambient temperatures. It also may partly explain the changes in sex and age structure that occur among flocks of doves wintering in northern parts of their range. The increasing preponderance of males and adults among wintering flocks of mourning doves may be due, in part, to physiological differences in survival ability among doves of different sex and age (Ivacic and Labisky 1973).

Total energy requirements. Although data exist on metabolic rates of hatching-year mourning doves at various ambient temperatures (Ivacic and Labisky 1973), no standardized information is available on growth rates or on the energy content of tissues of hatching-year mourning doves 16 to 160 days of age. Data on the energy requirements of ring doves 16 to 43 days of age (Brisbin 1969) were discussed previously. These data may be helpful in obtaining a general idea of the energy requirements of hatching-year mourning doves of that age class, but they should be used cautiously until data are obtained on hatching-year mourning doves of all age classes.

Energy dependence and parental feeding. Wild mourning dove fledglings depend totally on their parent(s) for food and water until eighteen days of age, and loss of both parents prior to that time jeopardizes their survival (Mirarchi and Scanlon 1981, Hitchcock and Mirarchi 1984a). By the time fledglings are sixteen days old, the females' feeding interactions with them decrease to below 50 percent (of the days observed) and differ dramatically from male parent/fledgling feeding interactions during the same period. Female parent/fledgling feeding interactions decrease steadily after sixteen days and cease by about twenty days posthatching. This pattern coincides with the female's increased responsibilities at a new nest. However, single-parent females can and will feed their young beyond this time if the male parent is lost or does not fulfill his responsibilities (Hitchcock and Mirarchi 1984b). The number and duration of female feedings are not as great as those of males. Thus, single-female-parent fledglings may experience relatively slow development and increased mortality.

Male parents feed nestlings at twelve days posthatching less often than do female parents but are primarily responsible for feeding the young after they fledge. They feed fledglings consistently through twenty-four days of age and in many cases through twenty-seven days of age. It is assumed that during this time fledglings are brought water as well as food, but this has not been confirmed.

Parent/fledgling feeding interactions normally occur in "reference areas" within 145 feet (45 m) of the nest tree through twenty-seven days posthatching. Reference areas approximately 30 feet square (2.78 m²) are located on the ground and in trees (often on specific limbs) and are characterized by dense overhead cover interspersed with openings that facilitate parent/young feeding interactions (*Figure 18*) (Grand and Mirarchi 1988).

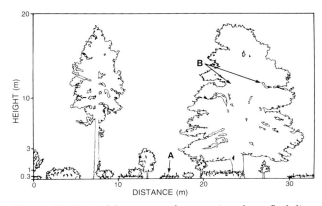

Figure 18. Typical locations of mourning dove fledgling reference areas on the ground (A) and in a tree (B). The nest typically would have been located in the tall pine on the left.

A mourning dove fledgling (arrow) perched and loafing on an eastern red cedar in a typical reference area. Reference areas are sites of fledgling/parent (usually the male) feeding interactions from the time of fledging until the squab is about twenty-seven days old. Such areas tend to be in a tree or on the ground within 145 feet (45 m) of the vacated nest and in areas of dense vegetation interspersed with openings. *Photo by Ronald R. Hitchcock; courtesy of the Auburn University Department of Zoology and Wildlife Science and the Alabama Agricultural Experiment Station.*

Fledglings use more than one reference area ($\bar{x}$ = 3.1) during the period of dependence on parental care and establish new reference areas farther from the nest tree as they grow older (Hitchcock and Mirarchi 1986).

Surrogate feeding (adults performing intra- or interspecific feeding of juveniles other than or in addition to their own) and adoptive behavior also occur in mourning doves (Hitchcock and Mirarchi 1985). Of all feeding interactions observed ($n = 417$) in that study, 6.5 percent involved surrogates. The incidence and proportion of surrogate feedings increase as fledglings grow older. Surrogate feedings usually involve a male parent and fledglings older than his own, as well as his fledglings. Occasionally female parents also adopt and feed fledglings other than their own. Surrogate feedings typically occur where reference areas of two or more sibling pairs are in close proximity or abut juvenile congregation sites. The low frequency of surrogate feedings seems to indicate that these interactions occur incidental to normal feeding interactions. This seemingly "helpful" behavior is perhaps a result of misdirected parental behavior rather than a reproductive "strategy." However, since all fledglings are dependent on parental care until eighteen days of age and captive orphans (ten to seventeen days old) have low survival rates (Mirarchi and Scanlon 1981), adopted orphans are potential beneficiaries of surrogate feedings. Unfortunately, energy costs or benefits associated with these behaviors have not been determined.

Energy dependence and parental brooding. The frequency of parental brooding drops dramatically between twelve and fifteen days posthatching and continues to do so after fledging (Hitchcock and Mirarchi 1984a). Fledglings sixteen to twenty days old occasionally return to the nest to be brooded at night (Grand and Mirarchi 1988), when the female parent most often is involved in brooding. No brooding has been reported after twenty days posthatching in mourning doves. These behavioral interactions correspond well with what little is known about thermoregulatory capabilities of fledglings of this age range. Energetic expenditures associated with brooding behaviors of parents and fledglings have not been determined.

Energy dependence and parental roosting interactions. Fledglings roost with parents most often between fifteen and seventeen days of age, although these interactions occur intermittently until the young are about twenty-seven days old (Hitchcock and Mirarchi 1984a). Females roost with fledglings more often early in the fledgling period than do males, but males roost with fledglings more often later in the period. Siblings consistently roost together until they are about twenty-four days old. Most of the roosting associations with male parents occur when fledglings between twenty-three and twenty-seven days of age follow them to the roost after being fed. It may be that after the fledglings are capable of sustained flight (twenty-one days old) the energy expended flying to the roost with the male parent is a worthwhile investment, because the fledglings then can follow the male from roost to feeding areas early the next morning. Marked fledglings have been observed feeding at times with what appeared to be their male parents (R. R. Hitchcock and R. E. Mirarchi personal observations), which lends support to this hypothesis. No data have been reported on the energetics of roosting interactions of parents and fledglings.

Energy independence. Fledgling mourning doves begin feeding themselves at seventeen days of age and increase this activity markedly by eighteen to nineteen days of age (Hitchcock and Mirarchi 1984a). By twenty-four days, fledglings feed themselves 60 percent of the time, and by thirty days of age, they feed independently. Although fledglings begin feeding themselves at a relatively early age, feeding efficiency is low. They appear to improve feeding techniques daily, and by twenty-one days of age, they feed very much like adults. Predictably, the availability of food also appears to affect fledgling feeding self-sufficiency. If food is available within about 655 feet (200 m) of the nest tree, fledglings can become independent of parental care by eighteen to twenty-one days of age.

Puberty Attainment

For mourning doves to breed in their first year, they must obtain enough energy to meet not only the energy drains of reproduction but also those of growth and feather molt (Muller 1984). In areas with a lengthy period of food abundance in the early portion of the breeding season, it theoretically should be possible for hatching-year mourning doves to develop early enough in the breeding season to reproduce later that same season. Indeed, hatching-year mourning doves fledged early in the breeding season do reproduce later that same year, particularly in the regions of North America with long breeding seasons. Hatching-year mourning doves of both sexes have demonstrated reproductive capabilities in Alabama (Moore 1940, White et al. 1987), Arizona (Irby and Blankenship 1966, Brown 1967), Canada (Armstrong and Noakes 1977b) and Virginia (Mirarchi et al. 1980). Puberty in hatching-year mourning doves generally occurs at about eighty days of age in males and approximately ninety days of age in females (Mirarchi et al. 1980, White et al. 1987).

Factors affecting puberty attainment. The proportion of the hatching-year mourning dove population capable of breeding varies by sex and geographic region, and probably from year to year. However, approximately 5 to 10 percent of hatching-year females and 15 to 20 percent of hatching-year males reach puberty in any given breeding season. Puberty occurs at an early age, but a variety of factors (e.g., body weight, selection pressures, etc.) influence puberty attainment in mourning doves and other columbids (Muller 1984).

Such factors as photoperiodism, temperature, weather, food supply and others affect initiation and termination of reproduction in seasonally breeding birds (Murton and Westwood 1977). In concert, photoperiodism, age and weather probably have the most dramatic effect on puberty attainment in mourning doves. Although puberty is achievable at an early age in mourning doves, that critical age must be reached while day length is still sufficient (approximately 750 to 775 minutes) to stimulate a reproductive response (White et al. 1987). It is unlikely that doves hatched after mid to late June in the southeastern United States reach puberty their first summer, because physiological maturation would have to occur during decreasing day lengths (Mirarchi et al. 1980, White et al. 1987). This emphasizes the importance of nesting success during turbulent spring weather in determining the proportion of hatching-year mourning doves that reach puberty. In a given year, this proportion should roughly approximate nesting success rates of adult doves from February through mid-June in any given area (White et al. 1987).

Some doves hatched during spring and early summer and surviving until late summer may not attain puberty or breed because of other factors such as temperature, food supply, behavioral traits (Lofts and Murton 1968), body weight (Rana 1975) and selection pressures (Murton and Westwood 1977). Body weight rather than age may be critical to puberty attainment. Male and female Indian ring doves attain sexual maturity when they reach 4.6 ounces (130 g) in body weight, at approximately two months old (Rana 1975). No conclusive studies of this relationship have been conducted on mourning doves, although in at least one study for each sex, body weight did correlate significantly with gonadal variables (Mirarchi 1978, Mirarchi et al. 1980). Ultimately, the age of puberty attainment may depend on "a balance of survival probabilities between breeding and increasing the risk of adult death, or not breeding and leaving no progeny" (Murton and Westwood 1977: 888). Theoretically, metabolic changes associated with reproduction and care of the young should require more foraging time, which in turn should increase chances of accidental death. However, the gene pool of birds that did not produce offspring would be eliminated through natural selection. Thus, a compromise is struck between possible evolutionary advantages of breeding at an early age and increasing risks of death as a result of doing so.

Sexual differences in puberty attainment. Generally more male than female hatching-year mourning doves reach puberty in any given year (Mirarchi et al. 1980, White et al. 1987). From an energy standpoint, these males probably can best afford the chance of reproductive activity if there is any likelihood of success, because little energy is invested in testicular growth and maturation even if they do not nest successfully (Kendeigh 1941a). Also, testes of males may increase in size as a result of day length alone (Lofts and Murton 1968, Murton and Westwood 1977). However, reproduction by inexperienced, immature female birds requires large energy investments for egg production and oviduct development (Kendeigh 1941a, King 1973), and female columbids require specific visual and auditory stimuli before breeding (Lehrman et al. 1961, Lott et al. 1967, Lofts and Murton 1968, Lehrman and Friedman 1969, Cheng 1974, Murton and Westwood 1977, Cheng 1986). Male hatching-year mourning doves normally reach puberty earlier than hatching-year females do (Mirarchi et al. 1980, White et al. 1987), which is similar to findings in band-tailed pigeons (March and Sadleir 1970) and wood pigeons (Lofts et al. 1966).

Puberty attainment versus successful nesting. Relatively high rates of reproductive activity, as reflected by gonadal development, do not necessarily reflect high rates of nesting success in hatching-year doves. Courtship, nest building and egg laying in female yearling mourning doves occur later than in their older counterparts (Armbruster 1983). In fact, hatching-year and yearling mourning doves are not as successful in raising young to the fledging stage as are older birds (Irby and Blankenship 1966, Armbruster 1983, White et al. 1987). They also desert nests more readily and have higher nestling mortality rates than adults do (Brown 1967, Armbruster 1983). The lack of nesting success exhibited by yearling females is due primarily to their failure to incubate their clutches (Armbruster 1983). Experience in finding food and nesting material also may be necessary for their successful reproductive efforts (Muller 1984). These tendencies are true for other columbids. For example, the efficiency of reproductive behavior, as well as survival of the young, improves with breeding experience in ringed turtledoves (Lehrman and Wortis 1967, Cheng et al. 1986).

Reproductive hormones. Traditionally, concentrations of reproductive hormones in the blood have been investigated as indicators of breeding activity in birds because of their involvement in development of the gonads. Although blood concentrations of androgens, estrogens and progestins have been compared to crop and gonadal activity in hatching-year and adult mourning doves, no differences between patterns of breeding and non-breeding birds have been clearly delineated (Mirarchi 1978, Mirarchi et al. 1980, 1982). These reproductive hormones show great variability because of pulsatile secretion patterns and their occurrence in small concentrations. Although

changes in gonadal hormone levels may indicate reproductive activity, levels are difficult to sample at the correct times. Therefore, these hormones are not consistently diagnostic of reproductive activity.

Only one study of reproductive hormonal activity in male hatching-year mourning doves has been conducted (Mirarchi 1978). Androgen concentrations in these males tended to increase at ninety days of age, but the data were difficult to interpret because of small sample sizes and the great variability in androgen concentrations in later age classes. There appeared to be no differences among age classes for either androgens or progestins, although androgen concentrations appeared to increase and progestin concentrations appeared to decrease as birds aged. Androgen concentrations in hatching-year birds were inversely correlated with progestin concentrations, while testicular weights were directly correlated with testicular spermatozoan numbers and androgen concentrations. Testicular spermatozoan numbers also covaried positively with androgen concentrations.

Correlations of mourning dove body weights with gonadal variables reflect the anabolic (tissue-building) activities caused by growth of the gonads and subsequent androgen secretions (Sturkie and Opel 1976, Mirarchi 1978). The role of the testes in spermatozoan and androgen production in hatching-year male mourning doves is illustrated by strong correlations between testicular weights and spermatozoan numbers and between testicular weights and androgen concentrations (Mirarchi 1978). Direct correlations between spermatozoan numbers and androgen concentrations and a strong inverse relationship between progestin and androgen concentrations in hatching-year males are reflective of normal reproductive and metabolic processes in birds (Kumaran and Turner 1949a, 1949b, Sturkie and Opel 1976).

No significant differences in mean estradiol and progestin concentrations among age classes of hatching-year female mourning doves have been observed (Mirarchi et al. 1980). Hormone concentrations, particularly estradiol, apparently were extremely variable even among doves of the same age. No strong correlations occurred between estradiol and progestin concentrations, body weights and gonadal variables. The interrelationships of ovary and oviduct weights and follicular development with each other were illustrated by the strong correlations between these variables in hatching-year females. These interrelationships are essentially the same in other birds (Sturkie and Mueller 1976). Relatively high concentrations of estradiol were observed in hatching-year female mourning doves at seventy days of age, which supports the premise of puberty attainment at approximately ninety days (Wineland and Wentworth 1975, White et al. 1987). The lack of correlations between hormone concentrations and gonadal variables in hatching-year females probably reflects the pulsatile secretion patterns of these hormones.

Hormonal control of other blood variables. Gonadal hormones involved in reproduction are difficult to measure directly, but they often alter other blood variables that can be quantified more easily. For example, estrogen production in female ring doves is elevated during the breeding season (Korenbrot et al. 1974), and changes in estrogen concentrations also cause increases in plasma concentrations of lipids, protein, calcium and cholesterol (see Muller 1984).

Understanding the interaction of steroid hormones (e.g., testosterone and estrogen) with the previously mentioned blood constituents and the effects these constituents have on the reproductive physiology of mourning doves is important to biologists because of their potential diagnostic value. Cholesterol is a precursor of many steroid hormones (Lehninger 1982), and cholesterol levels increase in wild female birds engaged in egg laying (Lisano and Kennamer 1977). Increases in total protein levels in laying female birds may result from their use in transporting ions and nutrients to the egg yolks (Schjeide and Urist 1956, Muller 1984). Calcium is involved in many aspects of reproduction in birds. Although constant calcium levels usually are reported for male birds during the breeding season (e.g., Mori and George 1978), dramatic changes occur in females during ovulation and egg laying. The increase in blood calcium concentrations in breeding female birds is the result of intestinal absorption and mobilization from medullary bone (Clark and Simkiss 1980). This additional calcium is necessary for ovulation and egg laying because it is involved in transport of yolk proteins to the ovum (McDonald and Riddle 1945, Schjeide and Urist 1956, Simkiss 1961), eggshell formation (Simkiss 1961) and possibly crop milk production in pigeons and doves (March and Sadleir 1975).

In hatching-year male mourning doves, no differences in cholesterol concentrations occur according to breeding categories, and no correlation exists between cholesterol and total protein, calcium, age, body weight, testicular weights or spermatozoan numbers (White et al. 1987). Thus, cholesterol is not considered to be diagnostic of puberty attainment in male hatching-year mourning doves. In hatching-year females, however, differences in cholesterol concentrations do occur according to breeding categories (White et al. 1987). Cholesterol is higher in imminent egg layers than

in successful nesters, potential breeders or nonbreeders and is correlated with ovary weight, oviduct weight and follicular development. Changes in cholesterol apparently are closely associated with ovarian changes, and the estrogens involved in growth and development of the ovary and oviduct are responsible for increases in cholesterol (White et al. 1987). These results should be viewed with caution because of the small sample sizes. Nevertheless, cholesterol concentrations in the blood do show promise as indicators of puberty attainment in hatching-year female mourning doves.

No differences in plasma total protein concentrations occur among hatching-year male or female mourning doves of different breeding categories, nor are there significant correlations between total protein and other blood variables, age, body weight or other gonadal variables. Thus, levels of total protein in the blood do not appear to be diagnostic of puberty attainment in male or female hatching-year mourning doves (White et al. 1987).

No differences in calcium concentrations occur according to breeding categories in male hatching-year mourning doves, and no correlation occurs between calcium, cholesterol, total protein, age, body weight, testicular weights or spermatozoan numbers. Consequently, calcium is not considered to be indicative of reproductive activity in male hatching-year mourning doves (White et al. 1987). In female hatching-year mourning doves, however, calcium concentrations are higher for potential breeders and imminent egg layers than for successful nesters and nonbreeders, and they increase with ovulation and egg laying in many columbids (Muller 1984, White et al. 1987). Calcium concentrations also are correlated with ovary weight, oviduct weight and follicular development. Lower calcium levels might be expected in successful nesters because depletion of blood calcium could be a reflection of its utilization for development of the ovum, eggshell and crop milk. These findings are similar to those for other columbids (e.g., Riddle and Reinhart 1926, Sendroy et al. 1961). Although some researchers have reported elevated blood calcium concentrations during crop gland development in other columbids (Sendroy et al. 1961, March and Sadleir 1975), no blood calcium increase was observed in hatching-year male mourning doves with crop gland development (White et al. 1987). Consequently, calcium concentrations appear associated more with maturation of the ovary and oviduct in female hatching-year mourning doves (White et al. 1987). Once again, because of small sample sizes involved with this research, results must be viewed with caution. However, blood calcium concentrations also show promise as an indicator of puberty attainment in hatching-year female mourning doves.

ADULT STAGE
(ca. 160 days and older)

Gonadal Changes During Reproduction

The urogenital tracts of adult mourning doves are shown in *Figure 19*.

Testes. Testicular measurements (length and width), weights and histological sections have been used to delineate the initiation, peaks and termination of breeding activity in adult male mourning doves (Pearson and Rosene 1938, Taylor 1941, Quay 1951a, Jenkins 1955, Mirarchi et al. 1982). Breeding activity is controlled by day length and varies with latitude (Cole 1933). Although nesting can be found all year in certain areas (see chapter 5), there is little gonadal activity in male mourning doves of North America from October to mid-December. Gonadal recrudescence normally begins in late December to early January, peaks in May and June, and ends by early October. Generally, male mourning doves with testicular weights of 150 milligrams or more are in reproductive condition (Mirarchi 1978, White et al. 1987).

As one would expect, testicular weights and spermatozoan numbers of breeding male mourning doves are greater than those of nonbreeding males (Mirarchi et al. 1982). However, no differences in testicular weights occur among breeding males during different stages of the nesting cycle.

Additionally, there are no differences between right and left testis weights and numbers of spermatozoa from the right and left testis during the breeding cycle. There is a strong and direct correlation between testis weights and testicular spermatozoan numbers (Mirarchi et al. 1982).

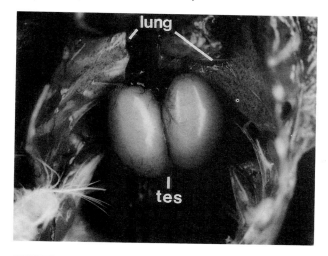

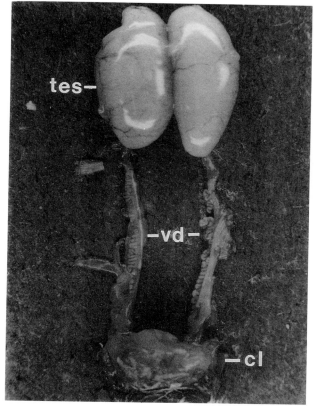

Top: the male mourning dove's testes (tes) are located on the dorsal wall of the body cavity close to the lungs. Bottom: a dissected male reproductive tract featuring enlarged testes (tes), vasa deferentia (vd) and the cloaca (cl). *Photos by Ralph E. Mirarchi; courtesy of the Virginia Polytechnic Institute and State University Department of Fisheries and Wildlife Sciences.*

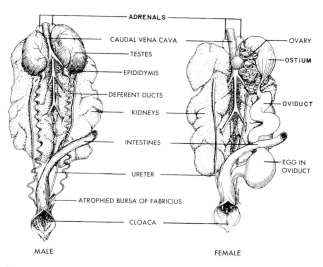

Figure 19. Excised urogenital systems of breeding mourning doves (from Godin 1960, Larson and Taber 1980). *Illustration by A. J. Godin.*

Ovaries, oviducts and follicular development. The gonads of female mourning doves apparently develop more slowly in spring than do those of the males (Jenkins 1955). Ovarian growth and regression in mourning doves are less distinct than are testicular growth and regression (Taylor 1941). Females with ovaries exceeding 100 milligrams in weight generally have sufficient follicular development to be in breeding condition. The average diameter of quiescent ova in the mourning dove is less than 0.04 inches (1 mm), and the average diameter during the breeding season is 0.23 inches (5.8 mm) in adult birds (Irby and Blankenship 1966). Adult or hatching-year mourning doves whose three largest follicle diameters are 0.39 inches (10 mm) or more in sum, or those with one ovarian follicle measuring 0.39 inches (10 mm) or larger, are in breeding condition (Mirarchi 1978, White et al. 1987). Postovulatory follicles disappear rapidly following laying in mourning doves, so egg-laying history cannot be determined by counting ruptured follicles.

In the southeastern states, most mourning dove ovaries are regressing by the first week of September—about two weeks earlier than the testes (Anonymous 1957). However, some ovarian activity is evident during the first two to three weeks of September, particularly in the southeastern United States, where 4 to 6 percent of the females examined have eggs in the oviduct (Guynn and Scanlon 1973, Mirarchi 1978). Additionally, some doves have been collected with follicles 0.39 inches (10 mm) or more in diameter, which they might have ovulated had the birds survived. Usually, few eggs are in the oviduct, and few large follicles are present on the ovaries in doves collected between October and January.

Although little is known about the ovarian cycle in mourning doves, it probably generally follows that of other columbids, as described for the ring dove by Cuthbert (1945). During incubation and squab raising, ovaries of ring doves normally contain small, third-phase ova approximately 0.20 inches (5 mm) in diameter. These third-phase ova remain small throughout the period and are classified as latent. They undergo rapid growth from 0.20 inches (5 mm) in diameter at the beginning of the period to 0.63 inches (16 mm) at dehiscence during courtship and nesting. Approximately six to ten second-phase ova, about 0.04 to 0.20 inches (1 to 5 mm) in diameter, are present in the ovary of the breeding adult at all times. In ring doves, the length of time until laying can be predicted from the stage of ovarian development, as defined by the diameter of the largest follicle, degree of yolk deposition and follicle vascularity (Cheng 1974). Generally, the larger the follicle, the shorter the time until laying.

Ovary weights of breeding adult females at one, three and nine days postlaying and seventeen days posthatching differ from ovary weights of nonbreeding females (Mirarchi et al. 1982). Oviduct

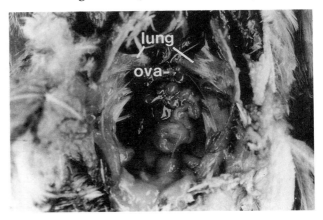

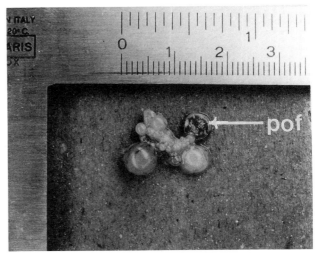

Top: the female mourning dove's ovaries (ova), like the male's testes, are located on the dorsal wall of the body cavity close to the lungs. Center: the ovaries with collapsed postovulatory follicle (pof). Bottom: a dissected female reproductive tract featuring the ovaries (ova), oviduct (ovi) and cloaca (egg). *Photos by Ralph E. Mirarchi; courtesy of the Virginia Polytechnic Institute and State University Department of Fisheries and Wildlife Sciences.*

weights and follicular development generally follow the same pattern as ovary weights during the nesting cycle. All of these variables tend to be highest at oviposition and at nine to seventeen days posthatching. The intimate relationships among ovary weight, follicular size and oviduct weight are demonstrated by strong and direct correlations between ovary weight and follicular development, ovary weight and oviduct weight, and oviduct weight and follicular development (Mirarchi et al. 1982).

Hormonal Changes During Reproduction

Androgens. Plasma androgen concentrations of adult male mourning doves have been quantified during a typical nesting cycle (Mirarchi et al. 1982). No statistical differences were found (probably because of small sample sizes) between nonbreeding and breeding adults, even though androgen concentrations tended to be higher in the breeding birds. Moreover, no distinct cyclic pattern was observed in androgen concentrations among breeding males during a typical nesting cycle, although large fluctuations did occur in androgen concentrations during that time. Androgen concentrations tended to be highest ($\bar{x} > 1{,}700$ picograms per milliliter) during the early stages (three days postlaying) of the nesting cycle, tapered off ($\bar{x} < 100$ picograms per milliliter) during early brooding (five days posthatching), and then rose again ($\bar{x} > 1{,}500$ picograms per milliliter) during the latter (seven to seventeen days posthatching) stages of brooding (about the time a new nesting cycle would begin). The concentrations and patterns of androgens secreted by adult male mourning doves during the nesting cycle correspond closely with those observed in ring doves (Feder et al. 1977). Apparently, elevated androgen concentrations in male ring doves and probably in mourning doves are necessary for courtship, nest soliciting and nest building behaviors (Hutchison 1970, Barfield 1971, Erickson and Morris 1972, Martinez-Vargas 1973) and are influenced by behavior and stimuli presented by the female partner (O'Connell et al. 1981). Thus, androgen concentrations in male mourning doves probably fluctuate most and have the most marked effect on behavior during the courtship/nest soliciting/nest building phase of the nesting cycle. The role of androgens in the maintenance of spermatogenesis and maturation of spermatozoa in mourning doves is supported by strong positive correlations among androgen concentrations, testicular weights and testicular spermatozoan numbers (Mirarchi et al. 1982).

Additional research is needed in this area of mourning dove biology because small sample sizes and the great variability in the data may mask significant changes in androgen concentrations during the nesting cycle. Thus, the relationship between androgen concentrations and male behavior is not possible to interpret adequately.

No studies of androgen concentrations in female mourning doves have been reported. Androgens are detectable in female ring doves, and highest concentrations occur during the courtship phase of the nesting cycle (Feder et al. 1977). Nevertheless, androgen concentrations in female ring doves are lower than those of males during all phases of the nesting cycle.

Estrogens. Estradiol 17β concentrations in the plasma of adult female mourning doves have been quantified during a typical nesting cycle (Mirarchi et al. 1982). No significant differences in estradiol concentrations were observed between nonbreeding and breeding females or among females at different stages of the nesting cycle. Concentrations of estradiol in female mourning doves tended to be highest ($\bar{x} = 900$ to $1{,}500$ picograms per milliliter) before courtship and oviposition (thirteen to sixteen days after hatching of the previous clutch) and just after courtship and oviposition (one to three days postlaying). This same pattern of secretory activity occurs in female ring doves, even though the concentrations of estradiol in female mourning doves are considerably higher (Korenbrot et al. 1974). The differences between the two species in estradiol concentrations may be a reflection of differences between seasonal and nonseasonal breeders. Estradiol concentrations in mourning doves appear to be related intimately to courtship, nest building and egg laying activities, as in ring doves (Korenbrot et al. 1974). The role of estradiol in the growth of mourning dove oviducts is demonstrated by strong positive correlations between oviduct weight and ovary weight and between oviduct weight and follicular development (Mirarchi et al. 1982). The granulosa and theca cells of avian ova have been implicated as major sources of estrogens (Lofts and Murton 1973).

No studies of estrogen concentrations in male mourning doves have been conducted. No detectable estradiol levels are found in male ring dove plasma, and apparently estradiol plays no role in courtship and nest building in male ring doves (Korenbrot et al. 1974).

Progestins. Blood plasma progestin concentrations in breeding and nonbreeding adult male and female mourning doves also have been quantified (Mirarchi et al. 1982). No significant differences in progestin concentrations of nonbreeding and breeding male or female mourning doves were found. No distinct cyclic pattern of progestin concentrations was observed among breeding males or females during a typical nesting cycle, although peaks in progestin concentrations of male mourning doves tended to be highest ($\bar{x} = 650$ to 800 picograms per milliliter) during the late stages of brooding (nine to thirteen days posthatching) when courtship and nest soliciting behaviors would be expected to increase. Concentrations of progestins in female mourning doves tended to be highest (500 to 850 picograms per milliliter) after oviposition (one to three and sixteen to seventeen days postlaying), or about the time of incubation (Mirarchi et al. 1982). Progestin concentrations of adult mourning doves compare favorably with those found in ring doves (Silver et al. 1974). Apparently, progestin levels, in concert with androgens and estrogens, induce incubation behavior in male and female ring doves (Silver et al. 1974, Cheng 1975, Cheng and Silver 1975, Cheng 1979), with nesting experience also being an important contributor to the effectiveness of progesterone in inducing incubation behavior (Michel and Moore 1985). This may also be true in mourning doves, but additional research in this area is needed before definitive conclusions can be drawn regarding that species.

Prolactin and crop gland activity. Serum prolactin concentrations rise markedly during crop gland development in columbids. Changes in prolactin concentrations during nesting cycles and the effect prolactin has on crop glands of columbids have been discussed previously (see chapter 7).

Prolactin versus testicular function. In columbids, the purported antigonadal effect of prolactin on testicular function is clouded by varied and often contradictory data. In domestic pigeons, a decrease in the size of the testes begins with hypertrophy of the crop and reaches a maximum about the middle of the incubation period (Champy and Colle 1919). Retrogression of the testes was characterized by the absence of spermatogenesis and a decrease in the apparent number (as seen in cross section) of seminiferous tubules. Spermatogenesis was reestablished five to six days after the young hatched. Changes in testicular condition during the nesting cycle differed from what normally occurs during the winter regression period. Regression of pigeon testes during winter usually was accompanied by an increase in interstitial tissue, but this was not the case during the nesting cycle. In another study, sizes of pigeon testes were reduced 90 percent by exogenous prolactin injections lasting ten days (Riddle and Bates 1939). A rapid involution of the mature testes in ring doves also was induced by exogenous prolactin injections (Riddle

and Bates 1939). Other studies have contradicted these findings, however. No significant changes in testicular weights, no reduction in the number of seminiferous tubules, and no suppression of spermatogenesis during incubation occurred in another study of domestic pigeons (Patel 1936). Also, no antigonadal response to increased levels of prolactin has been observed in male band-tailed pigeons (March and McKeown 1973). All testes sectioned during the breeding season show active spermatogenesis.

In male mourning doves, analysis of reproductive variables by stage of crop gland activity indicated an inverse relationship between gonadal and crop gland activity (Mirarchi et al. 1982). However, these may be coincidental (if valid) relationships. More research is needed in this area.

Prolactin and ovarian function. The gonads of female domestic pigeons have been reported to regress during the nesting cycle (Champy and Colle 1919). A marked atresia of large oocytes occurs during incubation with the process reaching its peak about the middle of the incubation period. Oocyte atresia takes place during the winter but not to the degree characteristic of the incubation period. Small degenerating ova approximately 0.12 to 0.20 inches (3 to 5 mm) in diameter also are found in some ovaries taken from incubating ring doves (Cuthbert 1945), and oviduct weight and crop weight are inversely related to each other in the species (Lehrman 1964). Oviduct weights are highest after courtship and at ovulation, when crop weights are lowest. Crop weights peak shortly after hatching, when oviduct weights are lowest. Prolactin also may have an antigonadal effect in female band-tailed pigeons, since that species lays only one egg per clutch and because there usually is a second enlarged follicle that rapidly regresses following ovulation (March and McKeown 1973).

In female mourning doves with fully developed crop glands, ovaries approximate closely in volume those of hatching-year females (Taylor 1941). Inverse relationships between other reproductive variables and crop gland activity of female mourning doves also are indicated (Mirarchi et al. 1982). However, these also may be coincidental relationships.

Energetics

Metabolism. Birds generally are assumed to maintain a relatively constant body temperature by increasing their metabolic expenditures as ambient temperature decreases (e.g., Kendeigh 1944). Rising or falling temperature gradients have a greater effect on metabolic rates of mourning doves than do actual ambient temperatures or the presence of light or darkness (Ivacic and Labisky 1973). However, mourning doves do not show the usual straight-line dependency between metabolic rates and decreasing ambient temperatures (Ivacic and Labisky 1973), as reported for other small birds (e.g., Kendeigh 1944a). Mourning doves appear to reduce metabolic rate, body temperature and heart rates when subjected to decreasing ambient temperatures below their lower critical temperature of 86 degrees Fahrenheit (30° C) (Hudson and Brush 1964, Ivacic and Labisky 1973). Essentially, this means mourning doves appear to become torpid (characterized by reduced body temperature and sluggishness) when subjected to decreasing ambient temperatures and food restrictions. In this way, they appear to meet the stressors of low ambient temperatures and the absence of food during winter (Ivacic and Labisky 1973). This capability would have positive survival benefits to a migratory species such as the mourning dove that is exposed to winter's adversities, at least in the northern portions of its range. Mourning doves do not participate in unusual energy-saving behaviors, such as the pyramiding (huddling in tiers) of Inca doves (Robertson and Schnapf 1987), during cold weather. As indicated earlier, adult doves (particularly males), because of the influence of age, superior weight or both, seem better equipped physiologically than hatching-year doves (particularly females) to withstand the rigors of northern winters (Ivacic and Labisky 1973).

Total energy requirements. The total energy requirements of adult mourning doves have not been determined, mainly because of the difficulty in obtaining data on metabolic rates associated with the various activities (e.g., flying, comfort movements, aggressive activities) in which mourning doves engage. Some important energy information on adult mourning and ring doves has been collected, however, and is presented here to provide some insight into the energy requirements of the mourning dove.

The lean dry biomass of a few (*n* = 6) adult mourning doves has been determined to have an energy content of 5.14 kilocalories per gram and an average caloric density (live weight caloric density) of 2.61 kilocalories per gram (Brisbin 1968). Both of these values are higher than those observed in several species of passerines (Odum et al. 1965) but are close to the caloric values (5.00 kilocalories per gram energy content and 2.26 kilocalories per gram caloric density) of adult ring doves (Brisbin 1969). The six mourning doves—two males and four females—sampled during the previously described

study were collected in October (*n* = 4), September (*n* = 1) and April (*n* = 1), without regard to breeding condition. Possible differences in lean dry biomass and average caloric density due to sex, breeding condition or season may have been missed because the samples were pooled. Differences in lipid reserves of mourning doves do change with season (Jenkins 1955). In ring doves, no significant changes occur in the caloric value of either lean dry weight or live weight of adults throughout the breeding cycle (Brisbin 1969), and no sexual differences in body weight occur throughout the breeding cycle (Riddle and Braucher 1934). It is obvious that additional investigation is needed for the mourning dove concerning potential changes in lean dry biomass and average caloric density with sex, breeding condition and season.

A unique way of determining the daily energy intake of adult mourning doves was reported by Schmid (1965). Samples of food taken from full crops of wild adult mourning doves shot over water holes during early autumn were analyzed to determine the energy equivalents of the most prominent seed species present. Nine species comprised 98.4 percent by weight of the 18.76 ounces (531.8 g) of crop material examined. The overall energy equivalents were obtained by weighting the caloric value of each seed species with the proportion of occurrence of each (by weight) in the following formula:

$$\sum_{i=1}^{9} (\text{Kcal/g})_i \times (g_i/\text{total g}) = \text{Kcal/g crop contents,}$$

where i = energy equivalent for each seed sample. The daily caloric intake of the adults was obtained by multiplying the seed intake of 0.57 ounces per day (16.09 g/day) (sum of average weight of seeds taken from crops after morning [7.86 ± 0.32 g] and evening [8.23 ± 0.37 g] feedings) by caloric value of crop contents (4.41 kilocalories per gram) to yield an estimated average intake of 71 kilocalories per day per bird. Metabolic efficiencies of mourning doves vary considerably depending on their diet, and diets differ considerably in their metabolizable energy value to doves (Shuman et al. 1988). This information is important because it allows dove managers to plant foods high in digestible energy. Such foods help doves to maintain body weight during cold periods, resist disease, and spend less time feeding and thereby avoid exposure to predation (Shuman et al. 1988).

Additional work such as this should be undertaken to elucidate possible age and sex differences and, in association with various seasons, variations in environmental conditions (e.g., extremes of cold, heat, rain, snow) and during breeding seasons and breeding cycles. Together with research on activity budgets of mourning doves (e.g., Losito et al. 1990), these methods will allow the opportunity to analyze energy budgets (how and where energy is expended) of wild mourning dove populations. With these data, energy "bottlenecks" can be located and alleviated through proper land-use management. For example, hatching-year mourning doves spend most of the daytime resting and engaged in comfort activities (Losito et al. 1990). Such activities conserve energy and allow doves to keep plumage in good condition for the sometimes long, energetically expensive flights to feeding fields and watering holes. By placing feeding fields and loafing areas in close proximity, energy shortfalls may be alleviated and more doves concentrated into smaller areas.

Special energetic demands. In addition to the energy demands of routine maintenance, birds may experience specific large energy needs for reproduction, molt, seasonal or diurnal fat storage, and migration. These body functions must be partitioned adaptively according to the energy resources provided by the environment. Energy partitioning strategies used by different birds have been previously reviewed (Murton and Westwood 1977).

The molt is one special need that requires energy partitioning. In certain columbids of the temperate zone, it extends over nine or more months, including (but not confined to) the spring and summer, when food is abundant. For example, mourning doves in Missouri molt primary feathers from early June to late October (Sadler et al. 1970). Doves in Georgia begin their wing molt in the summer and continue until autumn (Jenkins 1955). In Alabama, the wing molt occurs from May to October (R. E. Mirarchi unpublished data). Eared doves in Argentina spread their molt over approximately ten months (Murton et al. 1974).

The special energy demands relating to reproduction in columbids have been reviewed by Muller (1984). Reproduction generally occurs at the same time as molt in columbids. Columbid species satisfy these peaks in energy demand by taking advantage of seasonally abundant food, spreading the molt over an extended period and using energy efficient adaptations in reproductive strategies. Many columbids reduce energy demands during reproduction by producing only one or two small eggs, resulting in low clutch weight relative to body weight. The resultant small size of the hatchlings then is compensated for by parents that feed the young highly nutritious crop milk (see chapter 7). This adaptation has been described extensively for

the wood pigeon (Murton et al. 1974). More specifically, mourning doves have a "suite of adaptations that promotes multiple brooding," which is time conserving (Westmoreland et al. 1986: 196, see also chapter 6) and probably energy conserving. These include the production of crop milk, feeding of a diverse granivorous diet to fledglings, constant incubation, fast nestling growth and fledging at low weight (Westmoreland et al. 1986).

Timing of the annual initiation of reproductive activity differs by sex in some columbids. Although very little research in this area has been conducted on mourning doves, their activities probably are very similar to those of the other columbids discussed by Muller (1984) and condensed here. Male columbids generally reach breeding condition first, often becoming reproductively active as a result of photoperiod changes. They then stimulate females to breed through appropriate courtship behavior and by selecting nest sites. Females respond to photoperiodism, but the full reproductive state is finally achieved through complementary proximate factors (Lofts and Murton 1968, Murton and Westwood 1977). For example, the presence of a mate and nesting material is necessary to stimulate complete reproductive capability in female ring doves (Lehrman et al. 1961), and stimuli from the mate and the surrounding breeding colony combine to produce maximum ovarian development in that species (Lott et al. 1967).

The effect of male behavior on ovulation in female ring doves also has been investigated (Cheng 1974). When females in different stages of ovarian development are confined with intact or with castrated males, those paired with intact males lay eggs within five weeks, but those kept with castrated males ovulate only if they had large ovarian follicles before pairing. Castrated males are not effective in stimulating females with smaller follicles to ovulate. Castrated and intact males differ in behavior toward the females. Castrated males, in contrast to intact males, do not display courtship patterns such as bow cooing, preening or copulation (Cheng 1974, Lehrman 1964). Auditory signals from males during courtship also are important in stimulating females (Lehrman and Friedman 1969).

Although male columbids may attain breeding condition as a result of photostimulation alone, the female helps in maintaining the male's reproductive state by adding necessary stimulation during the breeding season. For example, the female is important in stimulating androgen production in male ring doves (Feder et al. 1977, O'Connell et al. 1981). Testicular development also is accelerated in domestic pigeons that are paired with a mate (Haase et al. 1976).

Pigeons and doves coordinate their breeding activity through the previously described interactions. Coordination of breeding efforts in both males and females is energetically essential. It is more efficient for males to initiate the reproductive cycle because the energy requirements for testicular maturation constitute a small percentage of their total energy requirements (Kendeigh 1941a). In contrast, initial gonadal development in the female requires little energy, but egg production is an extremely costly energy investment (Kendeigh 1941a, King 1973). Consequently, the male can afford to be physiologically capable of reproduction ahead of the optimal time dictated by ultimate factors. Reproductive readiness in the male then can be used to stimulate the partially developed female exactly when environmental conditions are at a peak. In this way, overall energetic requirements of the parents for reproduction are handled more efficiently.

Water Requirements and Metabolism

Mourning doves are found throughout North America, inhabiting even its most arid regions. Because they do not eat succulent vegetation, they require surface drinking water but can survive up to seven days on average (eleven days at most) when deprived of water (Bartholomew and Mac-Millen 1960). On dry seed diets, without drinking water, they lose up to 4.8 percent of their initial body weight per day (Bartholomew and MacMillen 1960); the minimum water ration required for maintenance of body weight averages 2.8 percent of their body weight per day (MacMillen 1962). They also lose weight if they drink solutions of salt water (NaCl) more concentrated than 0.19 molar (Bartholomew and MacMillen 1960, MacMillen 1962). They do not use sea water or strongly saline spring water but will use any saline source (up to 0.15 molar saltwater solution) that allows them to maintain a positive water balance. This permits use of many saline desert springs (Bartholomew and MacMillen 1960).

Weight losses of mourning doves deprived of water are due only partially to a loss of body water; the remainder of weight loss apparently is due to a cessation of feeding during water deprivation (Mac-Millen 1962). Although not yet verified for mourning doves, food intake is an important stimulus for water intake in certain situations in the domestic pigeon (Normile and Barraco 1984). The cessation of feeding when deprived of water may partially explain the inability of mourning doves to subsist on metabolic water alone, as the relationship between theoretical metabolic water production and respiratory water loss suggests (Bartholomew and Dawson 1953, MacMillen 1962).

When mourning doves are deprived of water for a few days, their plasma concentrations of sodium cations and chlorine anions increase as body weights decrease. When dehydrated birds are allowed to drink, their osmotic concentrations fall to below normal values within thirty minutes (Smyth and Bartholomew 1966). Thus, the chlorine cation concentrating capacity of mourning doves is comparable to that of other terrestrial bird species that have been studied (Smyth and Bartholomew 1966) and indicates that they have no unusual capacities for tolerance of dehydration, utilization of salt water or salt excretion (Bartholomew and MacMillen 1960). Their need for water also is increased by high temperatures, although doves can endure elevated body temperatures for short periods (Bartholomew and Dawson 1954).

Mildly dehydrated mourning doves can drink in one minute, and in one or two draughts, an amount of water equivalent to about 157 percent of their daily ad libitum intake and about 386 percent of their minimum daily requirement (MacMillen 1962). This ability is consistent with field observations indicating they can slake their thirst in one draught (Cowan 1952). Thus, mourning doves need to visit surface water only a few minutes every day or so to maintain or regain a positive water balance (MacMillen 1962, Howe and Flake 1989a).

Mourning doves require surface drinking water because they do not obtain much water from foods. Although doves can survive up to eleven days without water (less where high temperatures heighten physiological demands), optimal health is predicated on a water balance provided by daily drinking of water that is not highly saline. *Photo courtesy of the National Archives.*

Mourning doves and many other birds use panting and gular flutter to help regulate hyperthermia (Bartholomew et al. 1968). However, cutaneous evaporation (water lost by evaporation from the skin) is now known to comprise as much as 75 percent of total evaporative water loss in most avian species studied so far (Webster and Bernstein 1987). In mourning doves, augmented cutaneous evaporation is utilized as a means of heat defense; 15 to 49 percent of the metabolic heat in resting mourning doves is dissipated in this manner (Webster and Bernstein 1987). Increases in cutaneous evaporation as the temperature rises are due to temperature-dependent reductions in the skin resistance to water loss. Water losses from the skin are highest from the dorsum (back) of a dove. These findings support the concept previously suggested by Marder and Ben-Asher (1983) that columbids utilize cutaneous evaporation as a heat dissipation mechanism more than do other birds.

Mourning doves do not have any special mechanisms for water conservation or salt excretion. However, they do appear to possess a greater capacity for cooling by cutaneous evaporation than other birds do. Additionally, they can use mildly saline solutions, endure elevated body temperatures and extensive dehydration for short periods and make up water deficits quickly. All of these things, combined with their ability to travel long distances to obtain potable water, allow them to meet their water demands even in the deserts of North America.

Chapter 10

Behavior

Mark W. Sayre
Department of Forestry and Wildlife
University of Massachusetts
Amherst, Massachusetts

Thomas S. Baskett
Cooperative Fish and Wildlife Research Unit
U.S. Fish and Wildlife Service
The School of Natural Resources
University of Missouri
Columbia, Missouri

Ralph E. Mirarchi
Department of Zoology and Wildlife Science
and
Alabama Agricultural Experiment Station
Auburn University, Alabama

Doves and pigeons not only have been prominent in humans' cultural history and spiritualism, but also, comparatively recently, they have received the attention of the scientific community. An example is the study of bird behavior. C. O. Whitman was an American pioneer in comparative ethology whose published contributions in this field dealt mostly with columbids. His landmark publication, *The Behavior of Pigeons*, was published posthumously in 1919; it included several descriptions of mourning dove behavior.

The best-studied doves and pigeons have considerable similarity in displays, vocalizations and other behavioral traits. In the early 1900s, Whitman's work evidently was pointed toward the use of behavior in determining phylogenetic (natural evolutionary) relationships among columbids. Unfortunately, his death in 1910 cut short such a synthesis (see W. Craig and O. Riddle in Whitman 1919). This approach has been used extensively by Goodwin (1983) and by Frith (1977) for some Australian columbids. More recently, Baptista et al. (1983) relied heavily on some consistent differences in homologous vocalizations and displays of the mourning dove and the Socorro or Grayson's dove to propose that the latter be recognized as a separate species. However, Johnston (1961) concluded that behavior was not useful in discerning relationships of American ground doves at the generic level.

Despite the early interest in columbid behavior, the "value of behavioral information in illuminating the relationships of pigeons has not been thoroughly explored" (Frith 1977: 167). Progress has been limited by the lack of detailed behavioral information for a great many species, poor understanding of function of several well-described displays, some confusion in terminology and perhaps failure to identify homologous behaviors accurately.

For the mourning dove, the best early descriptions of displays and vocalizations were provided by Craig (1911), a student of Professor Whitman's. In the material to follow, Craig's terminology is employed whenever possible. The main purpose of this chapter is to consolidate published descriptions of mourning dove behaviors and to emphasize their functions for better understanding of mourning dove biology. Perhaps this also will be a convenient source for later studies of taxonomy of this and closely related species.

DISPLAYS AND VOCALIZATIONS

Advertising Behavior

Mourning doves are monogamous and form strong pair bonds that last at least for the duration of the nesting season. Some mourning doves may remain paired throughout the winter (Taylor 1941, Cowan 1952, Mackey 1965) but most probably are unpaired at the onset of the nesting season. Although unmated males typically are aggressive toward other doves in the vicinity of their display perches, they do not establish well-defined territories before pairing (Jackson and Baskett 1964, Irby 1964, Sayre et al. 1980). Unmated male doves have been observed displaying from cooing perches scattered over areas ranging from 15 to 865 acres (6 to 350 ha) (Jackson and Baskett 1964, Sayre et al. 1980).

The perch coo. For many reasons, the "perch coo" (technically, the song) of the male mourning dove deserves special attention. It is the best-known vocalization of the species and is the basis for audio census (Call-count Survey) of this dove (see chapters 14 and 15). Unpaired males devote considerable time to perch cooing and other displays. The perch coo consists of a series of "three (sometimes four) notes on one pitch, preceded by an introductory note which begins below the sustained pitch, glides up above it, and then down to it" (Craig 1911: 401). McClure (1939: 323) described the perch coo as consisting of "five to seven notes; one note, then a higher one, and finally three to five notes held at greater length." Goodwin (1983: 179) described it as a disyllabic coo followed by two or three louder coos, or "Coo-oo, OO, OO, OO!" In giving the song, "the male arches his neck, puffs out the throat, stiffens the body and bobs the tail at each note" *(Figure 20).*

Female mourning doves occasionally utter a faint version of the perch coo (Frankel and Baskett 1961); its behavioral significance, if any, is not known.

Figure 20. The perch coo is the most characteristic and best known of mourning dove vocalizations. Because of its structure and function, the perch coo is technically considered to be the mourning dove's song. It is believed to be an advertising vocalization—to attract a mate—but may have other functions as well. *Illustration by Charles W. Schwartz.*

The male mourning dove's perch coo is equivalent to Goodwin's (1983) "advertising coo," a term he preferred because several columbids issue this vocalization from locations other than perches. Goodwin noted that this utterance is functionally equivalent to the "song" of many passerines (see also Welty 1983). He believed the advertising coo of columbids to be uttered in a wide variety of situations in which the cooing male usually is prevented from reproductive activity—typically, by an unpaired male in breeding condition and holding territory or by a male whose mate was incubating or out of sight for any other reason. In part, these conditions hold for issuance of the perch coo of the mourning dove.

In the mourning dove, the perch coo, or at least a vocalization not distinguishable from it by the human ear, is given in at least three different contexts: (1) in the familiar advertising (sexual) function (Stone 1966); (2) after a charging display, with or without bowing (Jackson and Baskett 1964); and (3) to elicit behaviors in fledglings away from the nest that seem to help the father find and feed them

Figure 21. The male mourning dove's flapping/gliding flight is thought to be an advertising display primarily to attract a mate. The flapping is exaggerated wingbeats upon takeoff. The gliding is a long and rapid spiral descent, with wings motionless and on a plane slightly below the body. The bird in the right-to-left sequence above is just beginning a downward glide. *Illustration by Charles W. Schwartz.*

(Hitchcock et al. 1989). Are these vocalizations really identical, or are there subtle differences that the birds recognize when humans cannot? There is a need to study characteristics of these vocalizations quantitatively, as would be possible through careful sonographic analyses. Since the rate of perch cooing decreases considerably after pairing (see Baskett et al. 1978), mate attraction may be the most important function of mourning dove song.

Flapping/gliding flight. Male mourning doves frequently are observed performing an aerial display known as the "flapping/gliding flight" from cooing perches during the breeding season. In this display, "the male leaves his cooing perch with a vigorous and noisy flapping of wings. The wing beats are exaggerated and the tips of the wings touch beneath the body. The bird may rise to a height of 100 feet (30.5 m) or more. He then extends his wings and carries them motionless on a plane somewhat below that of the body and begins a long spiraling glide *[Figure 21]*. He may make a complete circle before alighting at the original or a different perch. Often he makes a series of flaps and glides before alighting" (Jackson and Baskett 1964: 297). Unpaired mourning dove males perform the flapping/gliding display more frequently than do paired males (Lund 1952); Jackson and Baskett (1964) recorded a rate of 263 flights per one thousand three-minute observations for unpaired males versus only 3.2 flights per thousand such observations for paired males. The diminished frequency of the flapping/gliding display after pairing suggests that the primary function of this display is to attract a female.

Pair Formation

The actual behavioral sequences involved in formation of the pair bond have been described for captive doves by Craig (1911), Whitman (1919) and Frankel (1961). Jackson and Baskett (1964: 299) described what they believed to be the behavioral sequence during the initial stages of pairing of free-flying doves. Courtship begins when a female alights near a displaying male. In most observations, the initial approach of the male is the charge followed by a "bow coo." A female may respond to a courting male in at least three different ways: (1) she may fly away, in which case a long chase ensues; (2) she may ignore the male and continue feeding or preening; or (3) she may permit copulation and formation of the pair bond. After the bond has been established, the pair loaf together for a few days before initiating nest building. The formation of the bond is further confirmed by the dramatic decrease in the frequency of perch cooing and flapping/gliding flights by the male.

The charge and bow coo. Two important displays associated with pair formation in mourning doves are the charge and bow coo. The mourning dove shares with other members of the pigeon family a behavior of charging other individuals with the head held horizontally forward, the tail pointed horizontally back and the whole body raised (Craig 1911). In giving the bow coo, "the male first bows with his head and body until the head nearly touches the ground *[Figure 22]*. He may bow as many as ten times in rapid succession. He then rises to a very erect position, holds his head forward, and utters a loud coo" (Jackson and Baskett 1964: 298). The coo sounds very similar to the perch coo. The charge and bow coo usually are associated, and the sequence described above may be repeated several times. This behavioral sequence always is directed at another bird; it was considered by Jackson and Baskett to be a normal part of the male dove's courtship display.

Jackson and Baskett (1964) observed males using the charge and coo component of this display when defending territory against other doves and when trying to drive a female away from another male. In these incidents, the males did not bow prior to cooing but did coo from an erect position directly at the other bird. Bowing is used by male wood pigeons both as a courtship display and in territorial disputes (Murton and Isaacson 1962). In the mourning dove, the charge and coo seem to be expressions of dominance over other birds during both courtship and defense (Jackson and Baskett 1964).

It is curious that the mourning dove's bow component of this display was not mentioned by either Craig (1911) or Whitman (1919). Goodwin (1983: 179) described the "homologue" of the bowing display in the mourning dove. This description closely parallels what Craig (1911) termed "the charge." Afterward, according to Goodwin (1983: 179), the male stops just behind the female with lifted head and thickened neck, "stands quite still and coos. The neck is inflated. . . . But there is no bowing movement." Goodwin (1983: 30) also noted that the term "bow coo" can be misleading "because in some forms, such as the Mourning Dove . . . no

actual bowing movement occurs in the homologue of the bowing display."

The bow in this display of the mourning dove has been carefully documented by Jackson (1963), reported by Jackson and Baskett (1964) and seen repeatedly in separate studies by M. W. Sayre (personal communication: 1988) and R. E. Mirarchi (personal communication: 1988). M. J. Armbruster (personal communication: 1988) provided carefully taken (unpublished) notes on several occurrences of the bow. Clearly, it is a regular component of courtship display in the mourning dove, but it is not usually employed when a male challenges another male or drives a female away from rival males.

Allopreening. Mourning doves exhibit allopreening during pair formation. It entails the preening of one mourning dove by another and usually occurs between mates. Allopreening consists of gentle caresses or nibbling of the feathers and feather shafts with the beak and generally is concentrated in the head and neck regions *(Figure 23)*. It has been observed between mates during nest site selection activities, during nest building, prior to copulation and occasionally during nest exchanges. Parents also caress their squabs during brooding (R. E. Mirarchi personal files). Allopreening is thought to serve as a method of ectoparasite removal from portions of the body normally difficult to reach and as a display of "affectionate tenderness in which overt sexual and aggressive tendencies have been sublimated" (Goodwin 1983: 38). Ethologists generally refer to this as "appeasement behavior."

Figure 22. The male mourning dove's bow coo (shown here in sequence) is associated with pair formation as part of the mating courtship ritual. It is issued by the male following a stylized "charge" toward a female. *Illustration by Charles W. Schwartz.*

Figure 23. Allopreening, or caressing, strengthens pair bonds among adult mated or mating mourning doves. It also is a mechanism of removing ectoparasites that adults or young cannot remove themselves. *Illustration by Charles W. Schwartz.*

Displacement preening. A member of a mourning dove pair may exhibit "displacement preening"—a behavior also called "ritual preening"—when close to its mate. The preening bird, usually the male, turns its head quickly to the rear, thrusts the bill between the body and the scapular feathers, then may move its bill rapidly along the side of its lower neck and breast. It also may quickly shake its wings at the partner. It may be quickly followed by "billing" and subsequently by copulation (R. E. Mirarchi personal files). Goodwin (1983: 37) asserted that in the domestic pigeon this behavior "is used whenever an impulse to bill or copulate is being frustrated." He further stated that this act appears to provide autoerotic stimulation, to signal "sexual and peaceful intentions and to arouse a similar mood in the mate."

Billing. In mourning doves, billing usually begins with the male offering his open beak to the female after brief bouts of allopreening and displacement preening *(Figure 24)*. The female inserts her bill into his and they briefly pump their heads up and down one to three times in a manner similar to the regurgitating movements performed when feeding the young. Billing is not as intensive a display as seen in the feral pigeon, nor is there any evidence that food is transferred to either member of the pair. In mourning doves, billing functions as part of the copulation ceremony and inevitably is followed by the female crouching as an invitation to the male to mount her (R. E. Mirarchi personal files).

Driving. As in other columbids, male mourning doves occasionally "drive" their mates. This display consists of the male closely following the female everywhere she walks or flies and pecking at her whenever she stops moving. During the display, the male is very intent in his purpose, usually walks in a very erect and stiff-legged manner and seems oblivious to other individuals and to other stimuli.

The function of driving in the feral pigeon has been described as removing "the female from the immediate neighborhood of possible sexual rivals" rather than the male "trying to force the female to go to the nest site" (Goodwin 1983: 39). However, in mourning doves the behavior may serve both functions. Wild male mourning doves drive wild females while in the vicinity of other males, but captive males also drive captive females while they are in separate cages out of view of rival males (R. E. Mirarchi personal files). In the latter case, driving ceases when the female returns to her incubation duties.

Figure 24. Billing in mourning doves usually follows allopreening or displacement preening and is a prelude to copulation. The female inserts her bill into the male's bill in much the same manner that young obtain crop milk from either parent. *Illustration by Charles W. Schwartz.*

Nest Site Selection and Nest Building

Male nest call. The male "nest call" is "much shorter than the song [perch coo], and much fainter. . . . Its typical form is of three notes, a low, a high, and a low, thus somewhat resembling the first bar of the song" (Craig 1911: 402–403). The nest call is highly inflected and each note distinct. Goodwin (1983) described it as a fairly loud "Coo-oo." The call lasts slightly more than one second and, for the mourning dove, ranges in frequency from approximately 400 to 750 hertz (Baptista et al. 1983). The male gives the nest call most frequently during nest site selection and nest building. He calls from a potential nest site (flat limb, crotch or fork in a tree, or on the ground). The male may begin giving the call while standing, but as the intensity of calling increases he seats himself at the actual or potential site of the nest. In giving the call, the male holds his head forward and arches his neck so that the head may at times be lowered enough to touch the limb on which he is sitting. He also begins to flutter his wing tips very slightly and may elevate his tail to a 45-degree angle (Jackson and Baskett 1964).

After the nest is built, the frequency of nest calling decreases dramatically. Males may give the nest call when the pair exchange duties (Frankel 1961). Males sometimes nest call during courtship and occasionally following territorial disputes (Jackson and Baskett 1964). However, the nest call functions primarily to call the female to the male at the nest or potential nest site.

Nest site selection. Most observations suggest that the male takes the initiative in selection of the nest site (Gifford 1909, Craig 1911, Nice 1938, Mackey 1954, Jackson and Baskett 1964). The male flies to a potential nest site and gives the nest call. If the female does not respond, the male may move to a new location and repeat the sequence or may stop calling and begin feeding or some other activity (Jackson and Baskett 1964). This sequence may be repeated over several days until the female eventually responds by flying to the male at the potential nest site. The pair may then begin allopreening and uttering soft nest calls. This mutual preening may establish the attachment to a particular site. The female then replaces the male at the site.

Nest building. Once the nest site has been selected, the pair proceed with building the nest. Building has been described in detail by Nice (1922, 1938) and Jackson and Baskett (1964). The male selects small twigs or other materials on the ground and delivers them individually to the female. Normally, the male stands on the back of the female, who then places the twig in the nest *(Figure 25)*.

Figure 25. The nest-building behavior of mourning doves is characterized by the female remaining on the nest or at the site while the male collects nesting material. The material is positioned by the female after receiving it from the male, who usually stands on her back when he returns with each object. *Illustration by Charles W. Schwartz.*

The male may make thirty to forty trips to the nest site during a bout of nest building, and the pair may repeat the sequence later in the day (Jackson and Baskett 1964). Nest construction takes a total of seven to ten hours and may occur over a period of two to four days (Blockstein 1986, see chapters 5 and 6).

Female nest call. Baptista et al. (1983) described a call of female Grayson's doves as sounding like "oohr-oor" or "ohr-ohr-ohr," lasting approximately 1.5 seconds, and ranging in frequency from 312 to 750 hertz. This call was given periodically by incubating females and sometimes was followed by the approach of the male and a nest exchange. Baptista et al. believed the call was used to call the male to the nest and might be homologous to the "growl" described for white-crowned pigeons (Wiley and Wiley 1979).

Baptista et al. (1983) did not report a comparable call given by female mourning doves, but according to R. R. Hitchcock (personal communication: 1988), there is such a vocalization. He noted that female mourning doves on the nest issue a call sounding quite similar to that of Grayson's dove, as described by Baptista et. al. (1983). It is given under similar circumstances and results in a similar response by the male.

Nest-distraction display. This display, sometimes called the "broken-wing feign," occurs when mourning doves incubating eggs or brooding squabs are flushed from the nest *(Figure 26).* Although briefly described by others (e.g., Hanson and Kossack 1963, Goodwin 1983), it was first described in detail by Nice (1923: 37–38) when she outlined its three different forms. In the most intense form, the parents "throw themselves on the ground near the intruder and flutter about as if seriously injured." In the second form, the dove leaves the nest, "flies some distance, perhaps 10 to 30 yards [9.1 to 27.4 m], flutters a little on the ground, stops and waves its wings, then walks along waving its wings, making little flights into the air . . . in these cases, the pretence of injury has degenerated into a mere form." The final form of the display involves the bird flying "near the ground as if intending to make a demonstration, but instead it flies up again and alights on a tree." Of course, doves may "merely fly to another tree without showing any trace of this 'broken wing' instinct" when flushed from the nest.

Researchers have observed differences in the frequency and/or intensity of the display relative to the stage of the nesting cycle (Nice 1923, Breitenbach and Baskett 1961, Westmoreland 1989). Despite differences in methodology among the studies, the researchers consistently found that frequency and intensity of the display increased after egg laying and reached a peak when squabs were being brooded. The stage of the nesting cycle could not be consistently predicted by the form or intensity of the display, however, because a sizable proportion (approximately 30 percent) of doves never displayed (Nice 1923) and because of the variability in the display among birds during the nesting cycle (Nice 1923, Westmoreland 1989).

Available data on sexual differences in the distraction display are somewhat limited. Breitenbach and Baskett (1961) pooled sex-related data during collection, and Westmoreland (1989) could discern no differences between sexes because of a sampling bias toward males. However, Nice (1923) collected some limited data on sex-related displays and concluded that, if one member of the pair showed the behavior, the other usually did.

Data on the effects of flushing distance (observer to nest; a coarse measurement of broodiness) and habituation on mourning dove distraction displays are available but somewhat conflicting. Breitenbach and Baskett (1961) found that flushing distance and distance flown to perch or ground appeared to decrease as nesting progressed. For example, mean flushing distance (ninety-eight contacts) of mourning dove adults

Figure 26. The nest-distraction display, or broken-wing feign, has a number of variations, but its intent when performed by either bird of a mourning dove pair may be to attract a predator away from a nest, or it may represent conflict between the parent's impulse to escape and the impulse to remain with the nest. *Illustration by Charles W. Schwartz.*

brooding nestlings six to fifteen days old was only one-third as great as that of adults (fifty-eight contacts) flushed from nests in the nest-building or egg-laying stage. However, Westmoreland (1989) found no direct relationship between mourning dove flushing distance and offspring age. Results from both studies indicated that flushing distances for first and subsequent contacts at the same nests were quite similar, indicating that doves were not habituated appreciably by having been flushed. On the other hand, J. B. Grand and R. E. Mirarchi (personal files) believed that mourning doves did become habituated to flushing disturbance and were less likely to display and displayed with less intensity the more they were disturbed.

While the distraction display generally has been considered a behavior that has evolved to lure potential predators away from the nest (see Burger et al. 1989, Hailman 1989), it may be a much more complex phenomenon called "simultaneous-ambivalent behavior." Many ethologists believe, as did Goodwin (1983: 52), that it "is probably usually due, or at least mainly due, to intense conflict between the impulse to escape and to remain with the eggs or young. This is no doubt why it is most often shown by birds with hatching eggs or newly hatched young. At such times the parental impulses are very strong." Some ethologists believe that the distraction display probably started as simultaneous-ambivalent behavior but became more pronounced and ritualized in certain species over time because it had strong survival advantages (R. S. Lishak personal communication: 1988).

Burger et al. (1989) felt that increased distraction displays in zenaida doves during the nesting cycle were related more to the vulnerability of the nestlings after they hatched (see Skutch 1949, Andersson et al. 1980) than to the cumulative parental investment involved (see Trivers 1972). Inconsistency in the intensity of mourning dove distraction displays within (Westmoreland 1989) and among (Nice 1922) mourning dove pairs during the nesting cycle may itself be adaptive. Adult survival could be reduced by consistent responses to predators that learn from repeated encounters with adults (Westmoreland 1989).

Goodwin (1983: 52) offered an alternative suggestion to the motivation behind the distraction display in "that extreme terror may at times result in uncoordinated movements and that the more intense forms of distraction display may result from the fact that the bird has 'stayed till the last minute' on the nest and so is in a state of great fear when it leaves." To support this hypothesis, Goodwin mentioned that three of thirty-two wood pigeons that he captured away from any nest showed an elaborate distraction display. He mentioned that this also occurs in other bird species.

The mechanism mediating the distraction display response to the flushing stimulus also remains open to conjecture. Hormonal secretions and various behaviors affect each other (Manning 1972). Some interaction between the nest distraction display and hormonal secretion would seem to be a certainty, but little research has been conducted in this area. Breitenbach and Baskett (1961) postulated that broken-wing feigns and erratic flight may be stimulated by rising prolactin levels because they coincide with increased broodiness in mourning doves. Nest-defense behaviors in other columbids are related to hormonal secretions. These behaviors (feather erection, wing raising, pecking and wing slapping) in female ring doves peak at egg laying and seem to be related to estrogen and progesterone secretion, while the same behaviors in the male peak later, at hatching and during brooding, and are related to prolactin secretion (Lea and Vowles 1985).

Parental Care

For descriptions of other parental behaviors, see chapters 5 through 9.

MISCELLANEOUS VOCALIZATIONS, BEHAVIORS AND SOCIAL DISPLAYS

Mourning doves exhibit other vocalizations, individual behaviors and social displays (interspecific or intraspecific interactions between two or more individuals), some very subtle, that merit further discussion. They are described in the following or referenced to other chapters where they are described in more detail.

Vocalizations

Greeting call. The "greeting call" usually is given by the male of all *Zenaida* species when rejoining his mate after a period of separation (Baptista et al. 1983). It also may be given by either sex after copulation (Craig 1911, Whitman 1919, Baptista et al. 1983) and is the only instance in which the bill is held wide open while giving a call (Craig 1911). In the mourning dove, the call sounds like a soft "ork," lasts 0.26 to 0.28 seconds and ranges from 375 to 750 hertz (Baptista et al. 1983).

Alarm call. The "alarm call" may be given by either sex during fearful situations (Baptista et al.

1983). It sounds like "rooo-oo" and lasts about 0.78 seconds. The "rooo" portion ranges from 500 to 750 hertz, whereas the "oo" portion ranges from about 125 to 312 hertz (Baptista et al. 1983).

Effect of sex hormones. Many vocalizations of adult mourning doves have sexual implications, as probably is true for most columbids. Not surprisingly, therefore, development of the vocal apparatus, with consequent marked lowering in pitch of vocalizations, can be advanced in juvenile domestic pigeons by application of androgens, delayed by castration or inhibited by hypophysectomy (Abs 1983). Although no research in this area has been conducted on mourning doves, it seems likely that a similar anatomical/physiological relationship exists in this species.

Individual Behaviors

Feeding. Mourning doves are primarily ground feeders, although they occasionally feed on seeds or berries in trees (Losito 1988). They do not scratch for food, but they will use their feet and bodies to bend plants to reach seeds or seedheads (Losito 1988). Recently fledged mourning doves apparently learn to feed by trial and error while in reference areas (Hitchcock and Mirarchi 1984). Typically, they experiment with different-sized objects by pecking at them and grasping them with the tip of the bill. Food items may be picked up and dropped several times before being swallowed. Siblings may peck at the same objects and attempt to take food from each other's bills. Final refinement of the feeding process probably occurs when fledglings follow their fathers from reference areas to foraging areas and observe them and other doves feeding.

Little is known about how doves and pigeons recognize their food or how they learn to eat new items. They are made ill by (and regurgitate) foods that disagree with them and learn to avoid those foods in the future (Goodwin 1983). Conversely, they learn what foods are palatable and develop preferences for certain ones.

Losito et al. (1990) observed that, during summer months, hatching-year mourning doves spent 20 percent of their daily budget feeding (this included searching, procuring and handling food and grit, drinking, and pecking at bark). Most feeding time was spent in searching (42 percent) and procuring/handling (53 percent) activities. Feeding activity was greatest during morning and late afternoon and occurred primarily in upland fields and residential areas (see chapters 7, 9 and 11).

Drinking. Mourning doves regularly drink from free-standing water sources. Unlike most bird species, they drink by inserting the bill into water and drawing liquid up in a continuous draught. They usually lift the head and expand the gape when through, presumably to take a deep breath. Drinking in this manner may be an adaptation to enable liquid to be taken quickly to minimize predation risks (Cade 1965, Goodwin 1983), although they often remain near water sources for extended periods after drinking (Elder 1956, Howe and Flake 1989b). In any event, only a small amount (less than 1 percent) of the daily activity budget of hatching-year mourning doves during the summer actually is spent drinking (Losito et al. 1990). Doves need reasonable access to the water but do not appear to favor ponds of particular size or slope or those with extensive bare shorelines (Howe and Flake 1989b). For more information on water requirements, water metabolism and drinking habits of mourning doves, see chapters 9 and 11.

Mourning doves seek water once or twice a day. Flying to a source of fresh or slightly saline water, they often land on a nearby perch, then fly to the ground within several meters of the water's edge and walk to the drinking site. They may be exposed to avian predators while drinking, and their ability to drink their fill in one or two "pumping" draughts probably evolved as an antipredator strategy. Depending on time of year, breeding status and locality, doves often congregate when drinking. *Photo by Charles W. Schwartz.*

Travel. Mourning doves primarily are aerial travelers, capable of swift direct flights and rapid changes of pace and altitude. They fly as singles or in flocks of two or more. At least two of their flight patterns have specific social connotations, discussed elsewhere in this chapter. While on the ground, mourning doves usually walk and run rather than hop. They use open ground while foraging, searching for nest material, etc., and avoid dense ground covers.

Losito et al. (1990) found that hatching-year mourning doves spent 13 percent of their budget traveling during the summer months. Of that time, 61.5 percent was spent flying, 32 percent was spent walking, 4 percent was spent running and 2.5 percent was spent jumping. Practically all of those activities were movements related to feeding, roosting and loafing.

Preening. As in other birds, mourning doves maintain the plumage on all parts of the body, except the head, with their bills. Head scratching and bill cleaning are accomplished with the feet. The bill also is maintained by whetting it on a branch or other surface. Shaking the head vigorously, blinking the nictitating membranes and rubbing the eyes on the shoulders usually keep them free of debris.

Mourning doves do not have a functional preen gland, or at least do not use it to maintain the plumage (Goodwin 1983). Instead, they grow "powder down"—a type of feather—throughout the plumage. The barbs at the tips of these feathers "disintegrate into a fine, talc-like, water-resistant powder whose particles measure about a micron [0.00004 inches: 0.000001 mm] in thickness" (Welty 1983: 37). The powder is scattered throughout the feathers by preening and ruffling the feathers and gives the plumage its luster and waterproofing qualities.

Preening may be a very important aspect of the mourning dove's daily activities. Losito et al. (1990) found that preening behavior (which included bathing and other comfort movements) comprised the second highest proportion (23 percent) of the daily activity budget of hatching-year mourning doves during summer months. The wings, breast and back were the parts of the body most often preened, followed by the tail, neck, flanks, rump and feet. Losito et al. believed that the high percentage of time spent preening on a daily basis was necessary to maintain a clean, functional plumage that maximized flight efficiency, insulation and water repellency.

Water-bathing. Mourning doves bathe during rains or when they have access to shallow pools of water. The movements and postures associated with both types of bathing are as described in detail by Goodwin (1983) for other types of doves and pigeons.

Mourning doves bathe during hot weather that is punctuated by occasional thunderstorms or rain showers (R. E. Mirarchi personal files). While rain-bathing, they usually lean over to allow the rain to fall under an extended wing and onto the flanks. The plumage often is elevated, allowing penetration by the rain. They may remain in this position for up to twenty minutes (Hanson and Kossack 1963). Occasionally they may elevate a wing perpendicular to the body to take advantage of wind-blown rain (R. S. Lishak personal communication: 1989). Once the bath is over, excess water is shaken off and they often preen the plumage, particularly when the sun reappears. They also behave similarly when bathing in the spray of lawn sprinklers during high (93 to 100° F: 34 to 38° C) temperatures (Hanson and Kossack 1963). Conversely, when mourning doves are exposed to rain and do not want to bathe, they usually will perch in an erect posture with the feathers flattened tight to the body and the neck tucked in. This allows water to drain off the body quickly and with little saturation or penetration effect.

Mourning doves occasionally pool-bathe during prolonged periods of dry, sunny weather (R. E. Mirarchi personal files). This may allow them to soak and clean the plumage more thoroughly than by rain-bathing yet assure that they will have an opportunity for the plumage to dry completely. While pool-bathing, mourning doves walk into the shallow water, crouch slightly, elevate the feathers over the entire body, partially open the wings, and dip and shake the wings and the body vigorously. This effectively splashes water onto most of the plumage. Occasionally they also peck at the water as if trying to toss additional water onto their breasts and flanks. Following bathing, they typically walk out of the pool, shake the plumage free of excess water and fly to a sunny perch where they can preen. They may spread one wing at a time, or partially crouch and elevate the feathers to facilitate drying.

Sunbathing. Mourning doves sunbathe by assuming a posture similar to that for rain-bathing, alternately spreading the wing and tail on each side of the body (*Figure 27*). This normally takes place on a flat substrate, such as on a large tree limb.

Kennedy (1969) summarized the various reasons given for sunbathing behavior of birds: heat absorption; increasing the movement of ectoparasites to facilitate removal by preening (unproven); drying the plumage; aiding the molt (untested); increasing secretions of the preen gland; and producing vitamin D via the preen gland. The last two

Figure 27. Sunbathing by mourning doves enhances heat absorption and drying. It also may aid in molting and, by causing ectoparasites to move, help in their removal. *Illustration by Charles W. Schwartz.*

Other bathing. Mourning doves engage in two other types of bathing behavior. Dust-bathing—the practice of distributing loosened soil throughout the plumage by scratching the soil and simultaneously shaking/ruffling the feathers—is common (Hanson and Kossack 1963). Presumably, it is used to help control ectoparasites. "Air-cooling baths," taken during periods of high temperatures of 90 to 100° F (32 to 38° C), consist of individual doves lying on the grass or soil in the shade where a breeze is present, and alternately tilting the body and stretching each wing (Hanson and Kossack 1963). This behavior presumably is used as a cooling method.

Other comfort movements. Mourning doves frequently stretch by raising their folded wings directly over their backs while simultaneously lowering the head and tail. Following this, one leg often is stretched backward coincident with the wing and the tail on the same side being spread toward and over the leg. In some Australian columbids, wing stretching often displays plumage characters that are distinctive to that species and "has prompted the suggestion that the posture is related to sexual activity" (Frith 1982: 24). In those instances, the term "mantling" to describe the movement has been borrowed from terminology usually associated with falconry. However, there is no indication that the movement serves such a function in the mourning dove.

explanations probably are not valid for mourning doves because of species' seemingly nonfunctional preen gland.

Sunbathing by mourning doves, as well as many other birds, is presumed to be principally a comfort movement. The splaying of feathers assuredly facilitates drying and absorption of heat. *Photo by Glenn D. Chambers; courtesy of the Missouri Department of Conservation.*

Mourning doves often ruffle and shake the feathers, particularly after preening. Generally, all of the feathers are raised, the wings remain partially folded but away from the body, and both the wings and the body are vigorously shaken; then the tail often is shaken laterally. These movements probably aid in realignment of the feathers after preening and help distribute powder down throughout the plumage. This behavior also may have some function in courtship, as it sometimes is observed during allopreening and billing.

Mourning doves also perform a comfort movement that can best be described as a yawnlike stretching of the neck and opening of the gape. It generally occurs while the birds are loafing.

Losito et al. (1990) found that the most frequent comfort movements of hatching-year doves during summer months were body shifting, scratching, stretching, feather shaking and wing flapping.

Resting. Resting also is an important aspect of the daytime and nocturnal activity budgets of mourning doves. It generally consists of roosting at night and loafing during the day. While roosting or loafing, mourning doves draw the head in close to the body rather than tucking it under the wing (Losito et al. 1990). They generally squat on a branch in a dense tree or tree clump, though occasionally they will loaf or roost on the ground (Hitchcock and Mirarchi 1984, Grand and Mirarchi 1988, Losito et al. 1990).

Losito et al. (1990) observed that hatching-year

mourning doves spent 21 percent of their diurnal time resting during summer months. Resting generally peaked during the midafternoon, with loafing (97 percent) being the most common sub-behavior, followed by sleeping (3 percent) and catnapping (less than 1 percent). While on roost, hatching-year mourning doves did not sleep for long periods (35 percent), choosing instead to loaf (35 percent) and catnap (17 percent) (Losito 1988). Diurnal resting was greatest in hedgerows, lone trees and tree clumps. Hatching-year doves rested more on perch than on ground sites and more in noncanopy than in canopy sites. The relatively high proportion of the daily activity budget of hatching-year mourning doves spent resting probably was necessary to conserve energy needed for flight to feeding, watering and roosting areas.

Vigilance. Mourning doves engage in numerous vigilant (alert) activities, including: assumption of the alert posture; extending and twitching the neck; bobbing, pumping and tilting the head; pausing; and preflight crouching. These activities facilitate potential interspecific and intraspecific social interactions as well as predator detection and avoidance.

Losito et al. (1990) found that, during summer months, vigilant activities made up the greatest proportion (24 percent) of the diurnal time budget of hatching-year mourning doves. They also spent 7 percent of the nocturnal time budget in vigilant activities. Diurnal vigilant activities consisted

During summer, hatching-year mourning doves spend about one-fifth of daylight hours loafing in a squatting posture with head drawn in. They prefer to rest (loaf, sleep or catnap) on elevated perches but occasionally do so on the ground. *Photo courtesy of the Florida Game and Fresh Water Fish Commission.*

mostly of neck twitching, assuming alert postures, pausing and neck stretching, followed by head tilting, head pumping, head bobbing and preflight crouching. Hatching-year doves spent similar amounts of time being vigilant at all times of the day and in all habitats. The large proportion of the daily time budget used in vigilant activities probably was reflective of the heavy predation pressure on the species.

Tail tipping. The morning dove "throws up the tail after alighting and as a flight-intention movement" (Goodwin 1983: 178).

Whistling flight. "The mourning dove flight is swift and darting, the wings make a characteristic whistling sound" (Goodwin 1983: 178). Brief mention of this readily heard whistling sound has been made in many descriptive sources. For example, Chapman (1937: 326) noted, "Doves resemble wild [passenger] pigeons . . . [but] their rapid flight is accompanied by the whistling sound of wings while the flight of the [passenger] pigeon is said to have been noiseless." The difference between mourning doves and passenger pigeons was also noted by Forbush (1927: 55 and 83) (see also *Table 1*). Goodwin (1983: 30) indicated that some other species of columbids make "distinctive whistling, creaking sounds with the wings in normal flight." In some, one or more of the primary feathers are especially modified, producing the flight sounds.

The precise means by which mourning doves' wings produce the whistling sounds has not to our knowledge been determined. No behavioral function of the sounds has been identified, but Good-

The mourning dove's defensive-threat display is an attempt to intimidate an intruder into leaving the dove's nesting territory, its food source or a reference area by appearing large and aggressive. *Photo by Irene Vandermolen.*

win (1983) suggested that the sounds may help maintain contact between individuals in flight.

Social Displays

Agonistic. Mourning doves exhibit a variety of agonistic behaviors, including "attack-charge" and "attack-flight" displays, physical contact and the "defensive-threat" display.

The attack-charge and attack-flight displays consist of rapid wing (singly or together) thrusts and beak thrusts (without contact) directed at an intruder. They differ only in that the former takes place on the ground while the latter occurs in short flights, usually 30 feet (9.1 m) or less. Physical contact consists primarily of wing strikes but also may include pecking.

Mourning doves also use the defensive-threat display described by Goodwin (1983), or slight modifications of it, in a variety of situations. In nestlings, the display most commonly occurs at six to seven days of age and entails tucking in the neck, slightly elevating the body and raising both wings above the back (Hanson and Kossack 1963). Hatching-year and adult doves crouch, tuck in the neck and orient the head toward the intruder, erect the plumage, lift and spread the wing farthest from the threat toward the vertical, and spread the tail in the direction of the threat while defending the nest or a food source (R. E. Mirarchi personal files). They also may give an alarm call, peck and snap with the beak, and/or strike out with the wing nearest to the intruder. This display apparently is "simultaneously activated by conflicting impulses to attack and to escape and is commonly shown at highest intensity towards potential nest predators" (Goodwin 1983: 31).

Losito et al. (1990) found that agonistic activities comprised less than 1 percent of the daily time budget of hatching-year doves during summer months. Agonistic activities were highest in the morning and generally were associated with foraging in upland field habitats. Most of the agonistic activities consisted of defensive-threat or attack-charge displays. Physical contact rarely occurred.

The three-bird chase. Multiple-bird flights or chases usually involving three doves were mentioned by Stone (1937) and discussed in some detail by Jackson and Baskett (1964) and Goforth (1971). The authors of the last two papers were able to identify the sex of the three birds involved in many of the observed flights. In three-bird chases in which the sex of all three doves could be identified, the flights involved two males and one female *(Figure 28)*. According to Goforth (1971), the most

Figure 28. The three-bird chase is an agonistic behavior of mourning doves. It usually features an unmated male chasing a mated pair but may occur when a mated male, with mated female following, chases another dove that has intruded on the pair's nesting "territory." *Illustration by Charles W. Schwartz.*

common chases originate when an unmated male gives chase to a pair of doves that flies close to him. Other chases originate when an intruding dove flies close to a pair in their nesting territory. The male of the pair then flies after the intruder and the female flies after her mate.

Goforth (1971) described two basic flight patterns—"straight" and "twisting"—for three-bird chases. In straight patterns, the three birds fly a line with relatively consistent spacing. The flight path of the chase usually is level, with few sharp turns to either side. This is the most common flight pattern in chases originating when an intruding male is chased by a pair and the female occupies the last position. In contrast, the twisting flight form is very irregular, with rapid changes in altitude and many sharp turns to the side. The spacing of the three birds relative to each other also is more irregular than in straight flights. The flight pattern is twisting when the female occupies the lead or middle position. This type of chase most often originates when a pair of doves fly close to the cooing perch of an unmated male; it suggests an effort on the part of the unmated male to gain the attention of the female. Goforth (1971) further hypothesized that this common type of chase could have the effect of preventing a pair from selecting a nest area close to an area already claimed by another male.

MOBILITY

The long-distance migrational movements of mourning doves are described in chapter 4. Until recently, most research on local movements of mourning doves was based on recaptures of banded birds (Tomlinson et al. 1960, Channing 1979, Leopold and Dedon 1983) or resightings of color-marked birds (Webb 1949, Mackey 1954, Jackson 1963, Armbruster 1973). Although valuable, these studies usually were limited by the inability to locate individual mourning doves at will and by the lack of relatively constant contact necessary to identify distinct movement and behavioral patterns of individual mourning doves relative to habitats, seasons, environmental conditions, times of day, etc. These problems were greatly reduced with the development of radio transmitters of a size conducive to use on mourning doves (see chapter 20). Much of the following information has been learned through the use of radio telemetry, but it has been obtained from a limited number of locales. Consequently, much research of a similar nature is needed on a seasonal basis throughout North America for better understanding of the mourning dove mobility and how it relates to the species' ecology.

Local Movements of Fledgling Doves

The most intensive study of mobility of fledgling (fifteen to thirty days old) mourning doves was conducted in eastcentral Alabama by Hitchcock and Mirarchi (1984, 1986). In that habitat type (mixed pine/upland hardwood), mourning dove fledglings left the nest and loafed in reference areas within 148 feet (45 m) of their nest tree until they were twenty-seven days old (Hitchcock and Mirarchi 1986, see chapter 8). Reference areas approximately 32 feet square (3 m²) were located in trees (often on particular limbs) and on the ground and consisted of dense overhead cover interspersed with openings that facilitated parent/young feeding interactions (Grand and Mirarchi 1988). Fledglings established new reference areas farther from the nest tree as they grew older and their flight capabilities improved (Hitchcock and Mirarchi 1986).

Fledglings less than twenty-one days old rarely moved more than 230 feet (70 m) unless disturbed; the maximum distance moved at this age was about 853 feet (260 m) (Hitchcock and Mirarchi 1986). Movements of greater than 230 feet (70 m) were achieved by several short flights. If fledglings were driven from reference areas at this age, they always returned within twenty-four hours. By twenty-four

After mourning doves fledge and until they are about twenty-seven to thirty days old, they remain close to the nest, where they use "reference areas" for feeding interaction with a parent (usually the male). *Photo by Ronald R. Hitchcock; courtesy of the Auburn University Department of Zoology and Wildlife Science and the Alabama Agricultural Experiment Station.*

days of age some fledglings left reference areas and centered their daily activities around abundant food supplies (Hitchcock and Mirarchi 1984). At that age, fledglings moved as much as 1,132 feet (345 m) at one time, though they still were unable to keep pace with adults or older juveniles in flocks (Hitchcock and Mirarchi 1986). Fledglings moved even greater distances at twenty-seven to thirty days of age, at which time they abandoned reference areas and began to associate with flocks of juveniles at distances up to 0.93 miles (1,500 m) from the nest site.

During the period of fledgling dependency on parental care (fifteen to twenty-seven days of age), the maximum movements by fledglings each day usually were to roost sites (Hitchcock and Mirarchi 1986). Roost sites were changed frequently, possibly to avoid nocturnal predators. The greatest amount of movement activity during the dependency period occurred during early morning and late afternoon hours and usually was associated with movements to and from the roost site.

Local Movements of Juvenile Doves

Little information is available about the mobility of juvenile (30 to 130 days old) mourning doves. Using data collected from more than seventy-five radio-tagged juveniles during the summer months in northern Alabama, Losito and Mirarchi (1991) found that daily home range and maximum distance traveled between any two locations by these birds did not vary between sexes, older and younger juveniles, or hunting and nonhunting seasons. On a daily basis, home ranges varied from 124 to 2,965 acres (50 to 1,200 ha) and averaged 539 acres (218 ha). The maximum distance traveled between any two locations varied from 0.6 to 5.0 miles (1 to 8 km) and averaged 2.1 miles (3.4 km), and the total linear distance traveled by five doves followed continuously for a day varied from 2.9 to 11.1 miles (4.7 to 17.8 km) and averaged 5.5 miles (8.9 km).

Data collected for more than thirty days on seasonal movements of individual juvenile doves in Alabama showed that daily home ranges varied dramatically within the seasonal home range over time (Losito and Mirarchi 1991). Daily home ranges (average = 539 acres: 218 ha) were only about one-fourth the size of seasonal home ranges (see *Figure 29* for an example of seasonal and daily home ranges of a single juvenile [Losito 1988]). Similarly, the maximum distance traveled between any two points on a daily basis (average = 2.1 miles: 3.4 km) was considerably shorter than that observed over the longer term (average = 2.8 miles: 4.5 km).

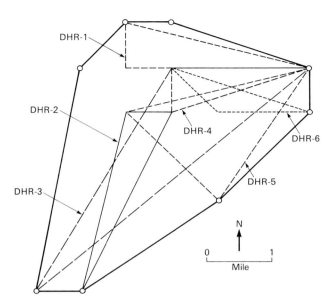

Figure 29. Seasonal home range (6,178 acres: 2,500 ha) and six daily home ranges of a juvenile mourning dove over a six-week period during late summer in northern Alabama (from Losito 1988). Seasonal home range is indicated by outermost solid line. Daily home ranges (DHR 1–6) are indicated by arrows at different line patterns: 1 = 494 acres (200 ha); 2 = 494 acres (200 ha); 3 = 1,853 acres (750 ha); 4 = 247 acres (100 ha); 5 = 1,236 acres (500 ha); and 6 = 247 acres (100 ha).

Additional information collected from banded juveniles in Alabama showed that only one of fifty-three banded doves shot during exposure to their first hunting season was killed farther than 5.3 miles (8.5 km) from the banding site (Losito and Mirarchi 1991). Thus, many juvenile doves in Alabama usually seem to stay within a few miles of their banding sites throughout the summer and early autumn. These findings are similar to those of Channing (1979) and Leopold and Dedon (1983) in midlatitude California but differ from those of Tomlinson et al. (1960) in northern Missouri, where juvenile mourning doves apparently disperse quickly from the vicinity of their banding sites. These studies suggest differences in migrational tendencies among juvenile mourning doves at different latitudes and possibly variations associated with different habitat types.

All these data, together with what is known about habitat use (Losito and Mirarchi 1991) and activity budgets (Losito et al. 1990), provide certain suggestions about juvenile dove mobility in the southeastern United States during late summer months. Prior to any type of migrational movements, juvenile doves will range only as far as necessary to find food, water and shelter. These needs appear to be satisfied in as little as 500 acres (200 ha) on a daily basis and about 6,178 acres (2,500 ha)

over a one- to two-month period. Juveniles will fly as much as 11.2 miles (18 km) in a day and 2.5 to 3.1 miles (4 to 5 km) in one flight to satisfy these needs.

Local Movements of Adult Doves

Sayre et al. (1980) provided some of the most comprehensive information on the mobility of adult mourning doves during the nesting season in Missouri. Using radio telemetry, they determined that their birds had feeding and resting areas located considerable distances from nest sites (Sayre et al. 1980). Males ranged 0.5 to 4.8 miles (0.8 to 7.8 km) from the nest daily. Nesting females sometimes were located as far as 3.3 miles (5.3 km) from the nest site.

In Idaho, Howe and Flake (1988) conducted a study of adult doves to determine how their daily movements related to watering and nesting sites in a cold desert ecosystem. Their radio telemetry results indicated that forty adult doves generally fed, on average, within 1.9 miles (3.1 km) of their watering sites. Maximum distances tallied for twelve doves from their feeding and loafing sites to their nests averaged 2.3 miles (3.7 km). Interestingly, Howe and Flake's (1988) movement data for nesting adults in a cold desert ecosystem did not differ greatly from those of Sayre et al. (1980) in farmlands in northern Missouri, despite distinct difference in latitude and habitat types. Related information about dependence on and diurnal use of man-made ponds in a cold desert ecosystem was presented by Howe and Flake (1989b).

Evidently adult mourning doves, like juveniles, will fly considerable distances to satisfy their daily needs. However, they apparently remain reasonably close to their chosen nesting areas throughout the breeding season despite having sufficient mobility to move into other areas. Tomlinson et al. (1960: 261) accurately summarized that, despite "a few long local flights . . . adult [nesting] doves were remarkably sedentary during the summer."

TERRITORIAL BEHAVIOR

Territoriality and social organization are important aspects of any avian species' breeding biology. "Territory" has been defined as "an area occupied by one male of a species which it defends against intrusions of other males of the same species and in which it makes itself conspicuous" (Mayr 1935). Nice (1941) listed several types of avian territories: mating, nesting and feeding area; mating and nesting, but not feeding; mating area only; and nesting area restricted to the immediate surroundings of the nest site.

Nice (1943) stated that one of the important functions of territory is to prevent interference in nesting and rearing of young. Association with a familiar area makes a male virtually invulnerable to defeat in the vicinity of his nest site. Others believe "that territory is primarily of importance in pair-formation, and perhaps in the maintenance of the pair" (Lack 1953: 147). Females of the species are drawn to an area by display or song; thus, the territorial system reduces both time and energy spent in locating a mate.

Territorial Behavior of Unmated Males

Some early studies implied that male mourning doves established territories before pairing (Edminster 1954, Swank 1955a); others indicated that unpaired males showed little evidence of well-defined territories before pairing (Jackson and Baskett 1964, Irby 1964, Sayre et al. 1980).

Unmated males appear to defend individual cooing perches and are aggressive toward other males in the vicinity of the cooing perch. Sayre et al. (1980) recorded seventy-three intraspecific interactions during forty-two mornings of observation of five radio-tagged unpaired males. Aggressive behavior was provoked by doves flying over or alighting near an occupied cooing perch. Aggressive behavior appeared to be restricted to a relatively small area immediately surrounding the cooing perch. Few aggressive interactions were recorded during numerous observations of unpaired males on feeding or loafing areas.

Jackson and Baskett (1964) noted that cooing perches of unmated males were scattered over relatively large areas of 15 to 20 acres (6.1 to 8.1 ha) and that several males often used different parts of the area simultaneously. Based on locations of all cooing perches used by individual radio-tagged males, Sayre et al. (1980) reported that unmated males displayed over areas ranging from 124 to 865 acres (50 to 350 ha). The cooing perches used by one unmated male for approximately a month are illustrated in *Figure 30*.

Hinde (1964) pointed out that the term "territory" usually is restricted to a topographically localized defended area. However, Dice (1955) used the term "moving territory" to include such concepts as "individual distance" and "mated-female distance." The territory of unmated male doves is perhaps best described as a "moving display territory," with the defended area being defined by the location of individual cooing perches (Sayre et al. 1980).

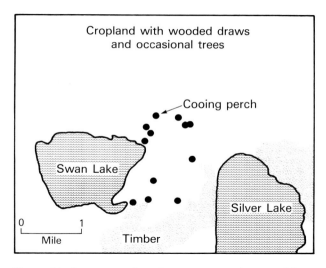

Figure 30. Locations of twelve cooing perches used by a single unmated male mourning dove from May 26 through June 22, 1977, on a study area in northcentral Missouri (from Sayre et al. 1980). The perches shown in cropland actually were in field border trees and shrubs (not shown).

Mate Selection and Establishment of Territory

The territory is established sometime after pairing, with the male taking the initiative in selecting the nest site. Most observers agree that male doves defend discrete nesting territories after pairing. The defended area includes the nest site and cooing perches (Webb 1949, Mackey 1954, Jackson and Baskett 1964). The source of nesting material may be an important aspect in the establishment of territorial boundaries around the nest site (Swank 1955a, Goforth and Baskett 1971b). Territorial defense is accomplished primarily by physical means, with the territorial male chasing intruding male doves from the defended area. Nesting males also are aggressive toward other avian species, especially potential nest predators such as the blue jay (Jackson and Baskett 1964). Mackey (1954) observed male doves attacking robins in the vicinity of the nest site.

There is some disagreement among biologists concerning the type of territory established by a pair of doves, as well as changes in territory size and territorial behavior as the nesting cycle progresses. Territorial defense by the male is most evident during early phases of the nesting cycle (nest site selection and nest building). Swank (1955a) believed that territories were not defended after the nest was established. Jackson and Baskett (1964) suggested that male doves defend their nesting territories throughout the nesting cycle, although males appear to be less aggressive in the later phases of the cycle. Similar observations were reported by Sayre et al. (1980), who found that the number of aggressive interactions decreases markedly as the nesting cycle progresses *(Figure 31)*.

Information about sizes of nesting territories is available from two separate Missouri studies. In the study by Jackson and Baskett (1964) on a university campus, nesting territories ranged in size from 0.7

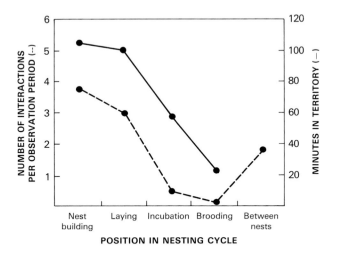

Figure 31. Mean number of intraspecific aggressive interactions and mean number of minutes spent in the territory by nesting male mourning doves during a two-hour morning observation period, related to position in the nesting cycle (from Sayre et al. 1980).

to 1.7 acres (0.3 to 0.7 ha) *(figures 32 and 33)*. Sayre et al. (1980) mapped the nesting territories of six radio-tagged males; these territories ranged from 1.0 to 3.2 acres (0.4 to 1.3 ha). In the latter study, territorial boundaries were determined from (1) sites of territorial disputes and aggressive encounters with other doves and (2) locations of cooing perches used by each male. Territorial boundaries could only be delineated during the early phases of the nesting cycle (nest site selection through laying); observations of territorial defense were too infrequent to permit accurate determination of boundaries during incubation and brooding.

The importance of nest material availability in determining territorial boundaries early in the nesting cycle has been alluded to by several investigators. Irby (1964) noted that males defended a territory the size and shape of the area in which they gathered nest material. After nest building, territory size was reduced to a small area surrounding the nest site.

In a study of captive doves, Goforth and Baskett (1971b) observed that territorial boundaries could be manipulated by changing the location of suitable nest material. Territory size in penned doves was reduced considerably early in incubation when nest materials were no longer rigorously defended. Sayre et al. (1980) stated that the source of nest material was included within the boundaries

This scene, an active robin's nest within 7 inches (17.8 cm) of an active mourning dove nest in a white spruce tree, is unusual. Typically, male doves are antagonistic toward rival males or birds of other species in the "territory" or proximity of a nest site, particularly during the stages of nest site selection, nest construction and early incubation. However, the nest of these doves had to have been fashioned after the robin's nest was built. This exceptional case demonstrates that latitude is needed in interpretation of virtually all aspects of animal behavior and biology. *Photo by Robert A. McCabe; courtesy of the University of Wisconsin-Madison Department of Wildlife Ecology.*

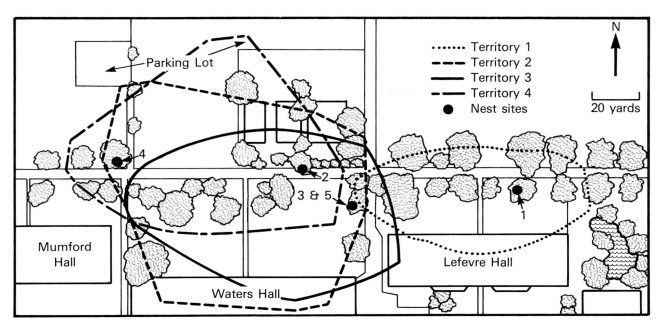

Figure 32. Territory of a pair of mourning doves during a single nesting cycle on the University of Missouri campus, 1962 (from Jackson and Baskett 1964).

of five of six mapped territories. One male gathered nest material in an adjacent disced field at distances of up to 394 feet (120 m) from the nest site and occasionally used parts of the field outside the observed boundaries of his territory. In all other observations, nest material was located within a 164-foot (50 m) radius of the nest.

The presence of nest material has been shown to be an important stimulus in the reproductive cycle of the dove, which may explain the apparent significance of the nest material to establishment of the territory. When suitable nest material is not available, reproductive cycles of penned doves will not progress beyond the courtship stage (Goforth and Baskett 1971b). Lehrman (1958) and Lehrman et al. (1961) demonstrated that the presence of nest material stimulates hormonal changes and incubation behavior in ring doves.

Based on observations of radio-tagged doves, Sayre et al. (1980) related the decline in territorial behavior to shifts in daily activity patterns of nesting males as the nesting cycle progressed. During early phases of the cycle, males spend most of the morning with the female in the nesting territory. With onset of incubation, males spend increasing amounts of time feeding and loafing away from the nest site. Feeding activity increases substantially just before hatching, presumably in anticipation of increased energetic demands of feeding young and production of crop milk. During brooding, males may spend the entire morning and evening periods away from the nest site.

Nesting doves do not feed within their terri-

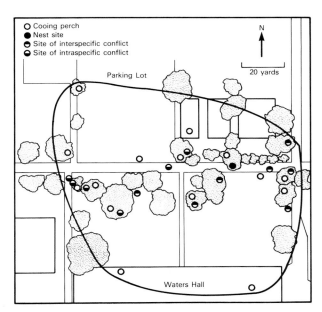

Figure 33. Nest sites and territories used by one pair of mourning doves in successive nestings during one breeding season on the University of Missouri campus, 1962 (from Jackson and Baskett 1964).

tory, and feeding areas may be located considerable distances from the nest site (Sayre et al. 1980). Radio-tagged nesting males were observed feeding and gathering grit in close proximity to other doves with no display of aggression.

During the interval between nestings, mated pairs are not attached to any particular site (Sayre et al. 1980). During this variable period preceding the initiation of a new nest, the male remains with the female at all times. The pair roost, feed and loaf together. Males may be very aggressive toward other male doves in the vicinity of the female. Conder (1949) termed this type of territorial behavior "mated-female distance," with the defended area being defined by location of the female.

Type and Function of Dove Territory

Jackson and Baskett (1964) categorized mourning dove territory as "Type B," or mating-and-nesting territory (see Nice 1941). However, Sayre et al. (1980) frequently observed mourning dove copulation occurring away from a territory, particularly during the interval between nestings. Similar observations were reported by Irby (1964), who studied a semicolonial nesting population of doves in Arizona. Based on these observations, mourning dove territory seems to fit more closely the description of a "Type D," or nesting-station-only, territory.

At least during the early phase of the nesting cycle, territory most likely functions to (1) reduce interference in reproductive activities, especially nest building, and (2) ensure an adequate supply of nest material (Sayre et al. 1980).

SOCIAL ORGANIZATION DURING THE NONBREEDING SEASON

Mourning doves exhibit marked social behavior throughout the annual cycle. They often concentrate in large flocks in autumn and winter, and occasionally nest in densities suggestive of colonial nesting (Irby 1964, Schroeder 1970). Social hierarchies within these assemblages may influence reproductive behavior.

Over a four-year period, Goforth and Baskett (1971b) evaluated relationships among social status, territories and reproductive behavior in penned doves. Their findings are the basis of the following discussion.

Winter Dominance Hierarchies

When nesting activity ceased in September, birds in the pens formed a single unit resembling a flock. A simple hierarchy was established by the six birds. The social structure was maintained by a system called "peck dominance" (Masure and Allee 1934), which is the result of win-or-lose relationships in which the bird retreating fewest times is considered dominant. The authors noted that this type of social structure is not a straight-line hierarchy ("peck right") but one in which, in some instances, bird A dominates bird B and B dominates bird C, which actually may dominate A.

Occasional changes in social position occurred throughout winter, and sex of the bird was not related to dominance rank. Middle rankings were less stable than top and bottom rankings. Individual resting sites were usually not challenged by subordinate doves.

Prebreeding Social Behavior

At the onset of the breeding season, the winter hierarchy broke down and split into two unisexual social orders. The groups remained separate and intermingled only at the feeding station. "Peck dominance" hierarchies were established within each unisexual group.

Mate Selection and Establishment of Territory

All males, regardless of rank, were attracted to dominant females at the onset of mating season. In all cases, dominant males became paired with dominant females. The dominant pair was the first to form a pair bond, establish a territory and initiate nesting. It also was the most successful in subsequent reproductive efforts.

Location of suitable nest material was an important factor determining territorial boundaries in the early phases of nesting. Nesting attempts of subordinate pairs were arrested when all available nest material was defended by the dominant male. The lowest ranking pairs did not initiate nesting.

CONCLUSION

Although much valuable information on mourning dove behavior has been collected, a great deal of investigation and interpretation remains to be done. Recent advances in radio telemetry and other areas have exposed new possibilities for behavioral research on this species. Researchers need to attack behavioral questions that have both applied and basic aspects. Much can be learned about mourning doves simply by initiating experiments similar to those already conducted on other, more domesticated, varieties of doves and pigeons. Additionally, much can be gained in overall understanding of columbid behavior by interacting with amateur dove and pigeon fanciers, who often have valuable insights and knowledge, whether or not formally analyzed and recorded.

Chapter 11

Foods and Feeding Ecology

James C. Lewis
Division of Endangered Species
U.S. Fish and Wildlife Service
Albuquerque, New Mexico

Mourning doves are primarily seed-eating (granivorous) ground feeders. Many studies indicate their diet is more than 99 percent seeds or plant parts. Doves feed on seeds in the size range between field corn and smartweed, eating what is visible or readily accessible in light ground cover. They eat insignificant amounts of animal matter and green forage, and only in specific locales do they utilize significant amounts of tubers, fruits and nuts. Principal food items in the diet vary by region, as discussed later.

The doves' small body size, light weight and short stature help determine where they can feed. They avoid rank, tall vegetation that they cannot force their way through or see over to detect predators. They seldom feed where heavy ground litter makes finding seeds difficult. Doves locate food by sight or by observing other birds feeding; they often return repeatedly to feeding sites until the food is exhausted.

As their delicate feet suggest, mourning doves do not locate food by scratching in ground litter, as do chickens and pheasants. Nor do they probe in the ground with the bill. Doves will move some light ground cover with a sweep of the bill, but most feeding action is by pecking ripe seeds from plant stalks or where seeds have fallen to the ground. Occasionally doves are seen perching on erect plants while feeding on seedheads.

FOOD PREFERENCES

Griffing and Davis (1978) noted that the crop (a pocket in the esophagus wall used for food storage) of an individual dove often contained seeds of only one plant food species. They theorized a search pattern in which the dove samples an area, determines that a palatable food item is present in sufficient density, and proceeds to eat that item to the virtual exclusion of other palatable seeds. The highest number of seeds reported in a single dove crop was 17,200 seeds of annual bluegrass (Rosene 1939).

Davison and Sullivan (1963) reported that doves choose their foods on the basis of taste. Browntop millet—a favored dove food—was colored with odorless and tasteless food coloring. The doves ate groups of seeds of blue, light green, dark green, red, yellow, orange and natural colors without showing any selectivity.

However, Goforth and Baskett (1971a) expressed belief that visual cues play a significant role in food selection by mourning doves. In three laboratory experiments, doves were offered uniform mixtures of natural grains (1) on colored masonite board backgrounds, (2) on window-glass platforms illuminated from beneath through colored filters and (3) accessible only through openings in colored panels. Colors were blue, red, green and yellow. In all experiments, food consumption by the doves was greatest when the color tested was blue and least when it was yellow. Consumption was nearly as low in tests of green as of yellow; red ranked between blue and green.

"Experimental results reinforced other indications that mourning doves have an aversion to wavelengths in the yellow range when encountered outside the usual places in their environment" (Goforth and Baskett 1971a: 262). Studies by Kalmbach and Welch (1946) indicated green and yellow had the most deterrent effect on bird species. As Goforth and Baskett (1971a) noted, Davison and Sullivan's (1963) conclusion that doves choose their foods by taste, not by color, shape or surface texture, may be considerably oversimplified.

Food habits of mourning doves usually have been studied by collecting the birds in their natural habitats and identifying food contents within the birds' crops. The crop is used for temporary storage of recently ingested food and has only a minor role in digestion. Food moves from the crop to the glandular stomach (proventriculus), where digestive juices are prevalent, and then to the adjoining muscular stomach (gizzard), where the food is macerated.

Collections of birds for food habits analysis are made at various seasons and locations until the researcher believes a sufficiently representative sample is available. The food contents then are identified, weighed and counted and the volume measured. Scientific and common plant names used in this chapter have been standardized; the names and their sources are given in Appendix A.

The mourning dove's crop is a thin-walled pocket in the esophagus. Located in the lower foreneck region, it serves to store ingested foods and can hold thousands of small weed seeds. A crop permits a bird to secure considerable food at a minimal number of sites and, with consumption of grit, to digest the food efficiently. Food preferences exhibited by doves are influenced by several factors in addition to the nutritive value of seeds. *Photo by James C. Lewis; courtesy of the U.S. Fish and Wildlife Service.*

The crop contents of three mourning doves taken after early morning feeding feature (top) mainly grit, (middle) mainly wheat, and (bottom) wheat, cracked corn and seeds of several nonagricultural plant species. The tendency of mourning doves to concentrate on one or a few plant foods per feeding is influenced by the variety and abundance of available foods, preference, and feeding efficiency. *Photos by James C. Lewis; courtesy of the U.S. Fish and Wildlife Service.*

Food items that occur in the greatest number of dove crops, and those that comprise the highest percentage of total food volume, are assumed to be the favored dietary items. Such a conclusion may be valid, but researchers seldom have simultaneously collected data on food availability. Consequently, the volume and frequency of food items in bird stomachs reflect the ease with which the seed can be found (availability), seed size and the birds' relative preference for that food item.

Doves are very selective in what they eat (Browning 1959). To determine doves' true preference for various seeds, Davison and Sullivan (1963) offered two hundred species of seed to doves during a three-year study. Wild doves were offered a selection of seeds cafeteria style in Georgia and Mississippi. Ten to twenty types of seeds were placed on the ground at a given location. Each seed species was in a pile, and the piles were spaced 2 to 4 feet (0.6 to 1.2 m) apart. Then the doves' responses were observed. Typically, a dove ate one or two seeds. Then, if it appeared to find the food

acceptable, it "crouched closer to the ground and fed rapidly" (Davison and Sullivan 1963: 381). If, after testing the first one or two seeds, the doves moved on to ingest seeds in other piles, the observer assumed that the food item was low on the preference scale.

Davison and Sullivan (1963) ranked the foods as choice, fair or unimportant. Choice foods were those eaten readily when encountered *(Table 18)*. Fair foods were seldom eaten by mourning doves when choice foods were present, but consumed in abundance when choice foods were unavailable. Foods uneaten or only sampled were ranked as unimportant. Rankings of common cowpea, cultivated peanut, cultivated rice, oriental sesame and common soybean as fair or unimportant foods were in contrast to the earlier concept of some who considered them choice foods. These data provide a guideline for persons desiring to (1) recognize feeding areas where mourning doves might be found or (2) plant food plots for dove hunting, banding or general management.

Sesame seeds are a "good" mourning dove food but less so, nutritionally, than previously believed. *Photos by Ron George; courtesy of the Texas Parks and Wildlife Department.*

Table 18. Choice and fair mourning dove food plants, and those uneaten or only tasted by doves, with listing of names in alphabetical order.[a]

Choice food plants	Fair food plants	Unimportant food plants
American sweetgum	Bahiagrass paspalum	Acorns
Barnyardgrass	Beaked panicum	Alyce clover
Bent euphorbia	Chicken corn	American beech
Bird's-eye caperonia	Common buckwheat	American upland cotton (cottonseed meal)
Blue panicum	Common cowpea	Bicolor lupine
Bread wheat	Common lespedeza	Black locust
Broadleaf croton	Common oat (in hull)	Black medic
Broomcorn panicum	Common redweed	Burnet
Browntop millet	Common rye	California brome
Bull paspalum	Common soybean	Carolina indigo
California poppy	Common sunflower (commercial)	Chufa flatsedge
Canarygrass	Cultivated rice	Common castorbean
Carolina geranium	Hairy crabgrass	Common crownvetch
Chickweed starwort	Johnsongrass	Common flax
Common oat (pieces)	Korean lespedeza	Common orange
Common pokeberry	Lyre-leaf sage	Common safflower
Common ragweed	Oriental sesame	Common tallowtree
Common sorghum	Pennsylvania smartweed	Common vetch
Common sunflower	Ragimillet goosegrass	Creeping wildrye
Cupped euphorbia	Sixrow barley	Crimson clover
Deertongue panicum		Cultivated peanut
Dominican panicum		Dallisgrass paspalum
Faber bristlegrass		Dalmatian ryegrass
Fall panicum		Eastern gama grass
Foxtail bristlegrass		Garden pea
Giant paspalum		Giant ragweed
Glaucous bristlegrass		Grapefruit
Harding grass		Hairy indigo
Hemp		Hairy vetch
Indian corn		Hickory pecan
Japanese millet		Horned beakrush

Davison and Sullivan (1963) noted no seasonal preferences in the doves' selection of these foods. They suggested that tasting behavior of doves probably was the reason that many items occurred in only small (trace) amounts in stomach analyses. Their study was not all-inclusive. They suggested that other seeds also should be evaluated, including amaranth, croton, rushfoil, euphorbia, sunflower, panicum, paspalum, pine and noseburn. A ranking similar to that of Davison and Sullivan (1963) is not available for dove foods in geographic locations outside the Southeast.

In interpreting Davison and Sullivan's (1963) results *(Table 18)*, it should be kept in mind that all seeds were made available on ground that was bare or lightly covered with vegetative material. Dense ground cover discourages dove use of bahiagrass paspalum, hardinggrass, Johnsongrass and several panicums (such as switchgrass panicum), as does unburned ground cover in pine woods. Row cultivation and normal harvest methods suffice to make accessible to mourning doves some seeds that would not be easily accessible if plants were in natural stands.

Stickney (1967) evaluated the preference of doves for nineteen grain and forage crops in Alabama. The foods listed in declining order of preference were Indian corn, bread wheat, common sorghum, common rye, Sudangrass, common soybean, vetch, common cowpea, browntop millet, pearlmillet pennisetum, rough peavine, common oat, crimson clover, Johnsongrass, cultivated peanut and dallisgrass paspalum. Alyce clover, bahiagrass paspalum and common ryegrass were not eaten by doves.

PLANT FOODS

The grass family is an important food producer for doves *(Table 18)*. Knappen (1938) also noted its importance when she compared mourning dove foods nationwide and in the Southeast *(Table 19)*. Grasses are the principal food source (more than 50 percent) in various regions and in most states *(tables 20 to 23)*. Other families important in one or more regions include spurge, composite, buckwheat, pulse, pokeweed, goosefoot and amaranth.

Table 18. (continued)

Choice food plants	Fair food plants	Unimportant food plants
Loblolly pine		Italian ryegrass
Lodgepole pine		Long-pod sesbania
Longleaf pine		Milkvetch
Mexican pricklypoppy		Mung bean
Painted euphorbia		Narbonne vetch
Pearlmillet pennisetum		Narrowleaf vetch
Ponderosa pine		Okra
Prairie sunflower		Oriental arborvitae
Prairie-tea croton		Perennial teosinte
Red euphorbia		Rescue brome
Redroot amaranth		Reseeding soybean
Reed canarygrass		Ribbed paspalum
Rough pricklypoppy		Rough peavine
Shoredune panicum		Saltmarsh bulrush
Shortleaf pine		Senna partridgepea
Slash pine		Sheep sorrel
Slim amaranth		Showy vetch
Sorghum almum		Shrub lespedeza
Sorgo		Smooth sumac
Stiff pokeberry		Soft brome
Sudangrass		Southern waxmyrtle
Sudangrass (wild)		Soybean (pellets)
Switchgrass panicum		Spanishclover deervetch
Texas croton		Spiny beeplant
Texas panicum		Tall fescue
Turkey-mullein		Tennessee black bean
Virginia pine		Trailing wildbean
White pine		Woollypod vetch
White pricklypoppy		Yellow vetch
Winter rape		
Woolly croton		
Yellow bristlegrass		

[a] Adapted from Davison and Sullivan (1963).

Table 19. Principal plant families represented year-round in mourning dove foods in the United States, the Southeast, Alabama, Louisiana and North Carolina.[a]

Plant family	United States n = about 1,000	Southeast n = 219	Alabama n = 287	Louisiana n = 141	North Carolina n = 553
Grass	53.01	54.68	55.6	35.42	59.5
Pulse	11.82	11.47	15.8	2.29	11.2
Spurge	5.41	4.97	6.0	30.50	3.3
Composite	5.02	4.71	1.6	6.73	4.5
Buckwheat	2.97	3.78			
Eveningprimrose			1.6		
Pokeweed	2.12	3.35			4.4
Geranium	1.61	3.33	2.6	1.19	
Amaranth	1.51	1.54			
Pine	1.30		1.9		
Martynia			1.2		
Sedge	1.15	0.94	2.4		2.5
Cocoa				15.14	
Pink	0.65		2.3		
Spiderwort			2.8	5.06	

[a] Column values are volume percentages for the United States and the Southeast (Knappen 1938), Alabama (Rosene 1939), Louisiana (Murry 1952), and North Carolina (Cummings and Quay 1953). The table includes only those items comprising 1 percent or more (volume) of the diet.

Table 20. Principal plant families represented monthly or seasonally in mourning dove foods in Florida, Missouri and Virginia.[a]

Plant family	Florida (October) n = 137	Florida (October) n = 90	Northwestern Missouri (Nov–Mar) n = 73	Missouri (May–Sept) n = 1,959	Virginia (Sept–Nov) n = 238
Grass	5.8	47.3	93.8	83.8	66.0
Pulse		40.3		1.8	
Spurge	13.2	5.7		3.0	15.0
Poppy	42.0				
Pokeweed	1.4	2.7			7.3
Composite	36.0	1.0		1.4	6.2
Agricultural crops[b]	0.9	81.0	49.9	70.3	55.5

[a] Column values are volume percentages for two Florida sites (Beckwith 1959), northwestern Missouri (Crawford 1969), statewide Missouri (Korschgen 1958) and Virginia (Chamberlain 1965). The table includes only those items comprising 1 percent or more (volume) of the diet.

[b] Agricultural crops include bread wheat, Indian corn, common buckwheat, common oats, common sorghum, millet, common rye, cultivated peanut, watermelon and soybeans.

Agricultural Foods

Anyone familiar with the habits of mourning doves is aware of their attraction to agricultural crops, particularly cereal grains (Indian corn, bread wheat, common sorghum, millets, common rye, sixrow barley and common oats). Other agricultural seed crops eaten by doves are cultivated peanuts, watermelon, lespedezas, Sudangrass, soybeans, crotons and common cowpea. Common cowpeas were important in Alabama (Rosene 1939) and North Carolina (Cummings and Quay 1953). When agricultural foods are available, they comprise a large part of the diet—more than 50 percent of the food volume in thirteen of twenty-four studies *(tables 20 to 23)*. Davison and Sullivan (1963) ranked Indian corn, bread wheat, browntop millet,

common sorghum, common oat (pieces), Japanese millet and Sudangrass as choice foods. Common buckwheat, common oat (in hull), common soybean and sixrow barley were ranked as fair foods *(Table 18)*.

Some seeds, such as Johnsongrass, croton and sunflower, are primarily produced in the wild but are agricultural crops in localized areas. Hickory pecan fragments are available where harvest activities break some thin-shelled varieties (Davis and Anderson 1973). Cultivated peanuts and tubers become available during harvest or feeding activities by hogs or wildlife (Rosene 1939, Beckwith 1959).

The ingestion of agricultural foods by mourning doves generally corresponded to the preference rankings of Davison and Sullivan (1963). Examples of the importance of agricultural crops include the

Table 21. Principal plant families represented in mourning dove foods in the Northeast and Midwest.[a]

Plant food	Maine (May–June) n = 120	New York (Mar–Oct) n = 181	North Dakota (Aug–Sept) n = 120	Ohio (Jan–Dec) n = 74	Ontario (Jan–Dec) n = 158	Pennsylvania (Sept–Oct) n = 136
Grass	26.5	69.5	88.5	85.3	86.8	84.0
Spurge				1.0		
Pine	50.7					3.8
Goosefoot	8.1		1.2		1.4	
Amaranth	1.9					
Buckwheat		3.9	5.1	1.4		
Mustard		2.4	1.6			
Composite	1.5	3.2		3.6	2.2	3.1
Flax			2.0			
Agricultural crops[b]	27.7	76.0	24.3	77.6	88.7	55.4

[a] Column values are volume percentages for Maine (Schemnitz 1975), New York (Lehner 1964), Ohio (Webb 1949), Ontario (Armstrong and Noakes 1981) and Pennsylvania (Zilker 1976). North Dakota data are percentage occurrence by weight (Schmid 1965). The table includes only those items comprising 1 percent or more (volume) of the diet.

[b] Agricultural crops include bread wheat, Indian corn, common rye, common sorghum, common buckwheat, Sudan grass and common oats.

Table 22. Principal plant families represented in mourning dove foods in the Great Plains.[a]

Plant family	Eastern Colorado (May–Oct) n = 247	Illinois (mostly Sept) n = 1,142	Iowa (Apr–Oct) n = 157	Oklahoma (June–Oct) n = 546	Oklahoma (Sept) n = 75	Oklahoma (Sept–June) n = 451	Texas (Sept–Oct) n = 651
Grass	21.4	84.9	39.6	63.7	86.7	64.3	36.0
Spurge	5.6	8.5	13.2	15.8	7.4		36.7
Violet	1.1			2.0			
Caper	2.2						
Composite	61.6		3.2	6.6	3.6	4.8	14.8
Amaranth	4.8	5.1	1.2	1.7		6.6	4.1
Buckwheat			16.4				
Pulse				2.7		1.8	
Hemp			34.0				
Eveningprimrose				1.4			
Poppy						8.6	
Rue							1.2
Agricultural crops[b]	17.0	60.7	20.7	62.1	82.2	56.5	26.6

[a] Column values are volume percentages for eastern Colorado (Ward 1964), Illinois (Oberheu and Klimstra 1961), Iowa (McClure 1943), Oklahoma from June to October (Carpenter 1971), Oklahoma in September (Tyler and Jenkins 1979), and 43 counties in Texas (Dillon 1961), and weight percentages for Oklahoma from September to June (Morrison and Lewis 1975). The table includes only those items comprising 1 percent or more (volume) of the diet.
[b] Agricultural crops include Indian corn, bread wheat, millet, common sorghum, Sudan grass, six-rowed barley, common rye and common oats.

autumn diet in Illinois—60.7 percent (Oberheu and Klimstra 1961); spring through autumn in New York—76 percent (Lehner 1964); winter in Ontario—88.7 percent (Armstrong and Noakes 1981); Oklahoma—62 to 82 percent (Carpenter 1971, Tyler and Jenkins 1979, Morrison and Lewis 1975); spring through autumn in Missouri—70.3 percent (Korschgen 1958); Florida in winter—92.7 percent (Beckwith 1959); and Missouri in winter—99 percent (Chambers 1963).

Table 23. Principal plant families represented in mourning dove foods in the western United States.[a]

Plant family	Arizona (May–Aug) n = 80	California (Apr–Sept) n = 275	Idaho (June–Sept) n = 223	New Mexico (1967–68) n = 161	New Mexico (1971) n = 113	Northern Utah (Sept) n = 146	Utah (Apr–Sept) n = 60
Grass	70.0	7.8	44.7	74.3	68.0	27.3	36.6
Composite	1.2	4.6		1.8	1.5	67.1	24.0
Goosefoot	8.9		22.0				
Mustard	1.1						
Buckwheat	18.8						
Spurge		45.0					
Purslane		31.5					
Pink		3.8					
Borage		1.9					
Amaranth			3.9	1.9	4.1	4.5	2.4
Pulse			4.1				
Polemonium			6.7				
Willow			1.6				
Aizoaceae				12.9	2.3		
Sedge				4.9	4.6		
Walnut					11.8		
Plantain					5.0		
Caper							33.4
Agricultural crops[b]	68.2	7.8	19.2	65.6	48.5	27.3	36.6

[a] Column values are volume percentages for the lower Gila River of Arizona (Cunningham 1986), near Sacramento, California (Browning 1959), irrigated farmland along the Rio Grande in southcentral New Mexico in 1967–68 (Davis and Anderson 1973) and 1971 (Davis and Anderson 1973), northern Utah (Slade 1969), and near Fillmore, Utah (Dahlgren 1955). Data for Idaho are weight percentages (Markham and Trost 1986). The table includes only those items comprising 1 percent or more (volume) of the diet.
[b] Agricultural crops include bread wheat, six-rowed barley, common sorghum, common rye, Indian corn, common oats and cultivated peanuts.

Identification of important foods in Texas indicated that mourning doves were feeding mainly in or near agricultural fields (Dillon 1961). Five of the most important foods were agricultural crops, twelve were weeds found in croplands, seven were weeds in cropland and pastures or rangeland, two were characteristic of pasture and rangeland, and two were in field borders or hedgerows. Seeds of the twenty-eight plants comprised 99 percent of the doves' diet (Dillon 1961). Doves in California obtained most of their foods from lands disturbed by man, either by cultivation, grazing, ditch and road-bed maintenance, or similar practices that encourage weedy annuals and cultivated plants (Browning 1962).

Mechanical harvest practices for cereal grains leave an abundant supply of seeds shattered on the ground and available for bird use. Indian corn and bread wheat are the most important agricultural crops utilized by doves (*tables 24 to 27*). Following autumn harvest of corn in Nebraska, 6 to 7 percent of the production remained on the ground as parts

Table 24. Principal mourning dove foods in the southeastern United States, recorded as percentages from crop analyses.[a]

Food item	Florida (October) n = 137	Florida (October) n = 90	Louisiana (Jan–Dec) n = 141	Northern Missouri (Nov–Mar) n = 132	Missouri (May–Sept) n = 1,959	North Carolina (Jan–Dec) n = 553	Virginia (Sept–Nov) n = 238
Grass family						17.2	2.1
Hairy crabgrass		39.8	14.2	95.1	35.0	12.2	54.3
Indian corn		5.3	1.9	14.8	10.9	2.6	
Bristlegrass	1.6	1.2				9.8	2.3
Paspalum	3.1					9.4	1.1
Bread wheat					34.0		3.6
Common sorghum			1.2	3.9			
Carpetgrass	1.1						
Panicum		1.0					
Cultivated rice			1.3				
Barnyardgrass			2.8				
Broadleaf signalgrass			9.9				
Sedge family							
Sedge						2.5	
Pulse family							
Smooth-seeded wildbean					1.8		
Common cowpea						5.0	
Cultivated peanut		40.3	1.7				
Common soybean						6.2	
Spurge family							
Bullnettle		1.0					1.6
Copperleaf							13.4
Spotted euphorbia							
Croton	13.2	4.7			3.0	3.3	
Woolly croton			8.3				
Gulf croton			1.8				
Toothed euphorbia			17.6				
Spurge			2.2				
Poppy family							
Pricklypoppy	42.0						
Pokeweed family							
Common pokeberry	1.4	2.7				4.4	7.3
Composite family							
Common ragweed	36.0	1.0	2.2	1.4	4.5	6.2	
Rough sumpweed			4.6				
Cocoa family							
Common redweed			15.1				
Geranium family							
Geranium			1.2				
Spiderwort family							
Dayflower			5.1				

[a] Column values are weight percentages for two Florida sites (Beckwith 1959) and volume percentages for Louisiana (Murry 1952), northern Missouri (Chambers 1963), statewide Missouri (Korschgen 1958), statewide North Carolina (Cummings and Quay 1953) and central Virginia (Chamberlain 1965). The table includes only those items comprising 1 percent or more (volume) of the diet.

Table 25. Principal mourning dove foods in the northern Great Plains, northeastern United States and southern Ontario.[a]

Food item	Illinois (mostly Sept) n = 1,142	Iowa (Apr–Oct) n = 157	Maine (May–June) n = 120	New York (Mar–Oct) n = 181	North Dakota (Aug–Sept) n = 120	Ontario (Jan–Dec) n = 158	Pennsylvania (Sept–Oct) n = 136
Grass family							
Bread wheat	46.4	14.0	1.2	35.6	19.6	19.7	11.5
Indian corn	13.7	4.5	22.8	22.1	4.7	65.1	42.9
Bristlegrass	23.5	17.5		9.9	61.2	2.0	29.6
Common oat				1.9			
Hairy crabgrass	1.3						1.4
Common sorghum			2.5				1.0
Sudangrass		2.2					
Hegari		1.4					
Broomcorn panicum					3.0		
Pine family							
Red pine			24.9				
White pine			12.7				
Scotch pine			5.7				3.8
Austrian pine			3.0				
White spruce			1.4				
Norway spruce			3.0				
Spurge family							
Red euphorbia		7.7					
Spotted euphorbia	3.6	3.5					
Painted euphorbia		2.0					
Broadleaf croton	3.5						
Hophornbeam copperleaf	1.4						
Goosefoot family							
Lambsquarters goosefoot				8.1		1.2	1.4
Mustard family							
Black mustard				1.4			
Charlock				1.0	1.6		
Amaranth family							
Pigweed		1.6	1.9				
Redroot amaranth				1.2			
Tumbleweed amaranth		3.5					
Buckwheat family							
Common buckwheat				16.4			
Dullseed cornbind					5.1	3.9	
Gourd family							
Muskmelon			1.0				
Hemp family							
Hemp		34.0					
Wood-sorrel family							
Common yellow oxalis		2.0					
Crowfoot family							
Buttercup		1.0					
Pulse family							
Clover				1.4			
Yew family							
Yew			3.9				
Composite family							
Common ragweed		3.2	1.5	3.2		2.2	3.1
Flax family							
Common flax					2.0		
Pigeon milk			2.5				

[a] Column values are weight percentages in North Dakota (Schmid 1965) and volume percentages for Illinois (Oberheu and Klimstra 1961), Cass County, Iowa (McClure 1943), the western Maine Forest Nursery (Schemnitz 1975), Tompkins County, New York (Lehner 1964), the shore of Lake Erie in Ontario (Armstrong and Noakes 1981) and York County, Pennsylvania (Zilker 1976). The table includes only those items comprising 1 percent or more (volume) of the diet.

Table 26. Principal mourning dove foods in the southern Great Plains.[a]

Food item	Eastern Colorado (May–Oct) n = 247	Oklahoma (June–Oct) n = 546	Oklahoma (Sept) n = 75	Oklahoma (Sept–June) n = 451	Texas (Sept–Oct) n = 651
Grass family					
Bread wheat	10.2	55.7	41.5	12.4	2.9
Bristlegrass	1.6	4.0	38.3		
Common oat					2.1
Common rye					1.5
Common sorghum	3.1	2.6	2.1	7.5	19.4
Hairy crabgrass		1.4			
Haygrazer				36.6	
Indian corn	3.5				
Johnsongrass			2.2		3.6
Panicum	3.0			7.8	6.5
Sand dropseed			2.6		
Spurge family					
Bullnettle			2.3		
Carolina leaf flower			5.1		
Croton	3.8	14.0			30.5
Euphorbia	1.8	1.8		5.1	1.6
Noseburn					1.3
Stillingia					3.3
Rue family					
Pricklyash					1.2
Eveningprimrose family					
Cutleaf					
Eveningprimrose		1.4			
Pulse family					
Smooth-seeded wild-bean		2.7		1.8	
Violet family					
Violet	1.1	2.0			
Caper family					
Spider-flower	2.2				
Composite family					
Sunflower	61.6	6.6	3.6	4.8	14.8
Amaranth family					
Pigweed	4.8	1.7		6.6	4.1
Poppy family					
Pricklypoppy				8.6	

[a] Column values are weight percentages for Oklahoma from September through June (Morrison and Lewis 1975) and volume percentages for eastern Colorado (Ward 1964), Oklahoma in June through October (Carpenter 1971) and in September (Tyler and Jenkins 1979), and 43 counties in Texas (Dillon 1961). The table includes only those items comprising 1 percent or more (volume) of the diet.

of ears or kernels (U.S. Fish and Wildlife Service 1981); spilled corn amounted to 357 pounds per acre (400 kg/ha). Many fields were grazed by cattle, which removed much of the ear corn during winter but did not affect kernel corn. By early March, there were 183 pounds per acre (205 kg/ha) remaining for large concentrations of waterfowl, cranes, doves and other birds to utilize. In April, there were still 114 pounds per acre (128 kg/ha) (U.S. Fish and Wildlife Service 1981).

Waste corn averaged 384 pounds per acre (430 kg/ha) in untilled fields in late autumn in central Illinois (Warner et al. 1985). Seed availability declined as intensity of tillage increased and in conjunction with bird use and seed decay throughout winter. Some agricultural seeds deteriorate more rapidly than wild plant seeds, which tend to be durable and slow to germinate (Dillon 1961). Old weathered seeds of common sorghum, bread wheat, common oats and annual sunflower rarely were found in dove crops (Dillon 1961). Agricultural crops were most prevalent in the diet just after harvest when availability was highest or in winter when few other foods were available.

Table 27. Principal mourning dove foods in the West.[a]

Food item	Arizona (May–Aug) n = 80	California (Apr–Sept) n = 275	Southeastern Idaho (June–Sept) n = 223	New Mexico (1967–68) n = 161	New Mexico (1971) n = 113	Utah (Sept) n = 146	Utah (Apr–Sept) n = 60
Grass family							
Barnyardgrass				3.2	3.1		
Bread wheat		7.8	13.2	3.1		27.3	36.6
Canarygrass	4.6						
Common rye				3.0			
Common sorghum	4.3			51.2	42.1		
Cupgrass				1.9	5.7		
Indian corn				1.5			
Indian ricegrass			26.1				
Johnsongrass				2.5	9.5		
Sixrow barley	61.1		5.4	6.8	5.3		
Sudangrass				1.1	2.3		
Spurge family							
Eyed euphorbia		2.2					
Turkey-mullein		42.8					
Goosefoot family							
Common halogeton			22.0				
Fourwing saltbush	1.7						
Lambsquarters goosefoot	3.0						
Patata	4.2						
Composite family							
Sunflower						67.1	21.3
Common sunflower	1.2			1.8	1.5		
Milk thistle		4.6					
Thistle							2.7
Mustard family							
Mustard	1.1						
Pulse family							
Vetch			4.1				
Willow family							
Cottonwood			1.6				
Sedge family							
Nutgrass				4.9	4.6		
Borage family							
Buckthorn weed		1.9					
Purslane family							
Redmaids rockpurslane		31.5					
Walnut family							
Pecan hickory					11.8		
Polemonium family							
Collomia			6.7				
Buckwheat family							
Common buckwheat	18.8						
Plantain family							
Plantain					5.0		
Amaranth family							
Pigweed			3.9	1.9	4.1	4.5	
Amaranth spp.							2.4
Pink family							
Windmill pink		3.8					
Aizoaceae family							
Desert horsepurslane				12.9	2.3		
Caper family							
Spider-flower							33.4

[a] Column values are weight percentages for southeastern Idaho (Markham and Trost 1986), and volume percentages for the lower Gila River of Arizona (Cunningham 1986), near Sacramento, California (Browning 1959), irrigated farmland along the Rio Grande in southcentral New Mexico (Davis and Anderson 1973) in 2 time periods, northern Utah in September (Slade 1969), and Utah from April through September (Dahlgren 1955). The table includes only those items comprising 1 percent or more (volume) of the diet.

Grain sorghum fields and nearby brushy fencerows represent attractive feeding sites to mourning doves, particularly where standing water is available in close proximity. *Photo by Ron George; courtesy of the Texas Parks and Wildlife Department.*

Waste and spilled grains represent a significant source of nutritious food for mourning doves, especially in autumn and winter months when natural seed plant production is relatively limited in most areas. Cereal crop farming has greatly enhanced mourning dove habitat in the Plains and prairie states. *Courtesy of the South Dakota Game, Fish and Parks Department.*

Nonagricultural Foods

Many of the most favored dove foods are seeds produced on herbaceous plants found in early successional stages. They are plants that volunteer on unvegetated soils recently disturbed by man or nature. They typically fall in the broad plant category often referred to as weeds. Availability of such seeds has been studied seasonally and in various habitats (see Bookhout 1958, Robel and Slade 1965, Preacher 1978, Tobler and Lewis 1981).

Grass family. Barnyardgrass, also known as wild millet and watergrass, grows in a number of habitats. Most abundant on mud flats from which water has receded, it is a serious weed in rice fields (Fredrickson and Taylor 1982, U.S. Department of Agriculture 1961). The barnyardgrass group includes annuals found on waste and cultivated lands, as well as wetlands. ("Waste lands," as used in this chapter, refers to areas not cultivated because they are unsuitable for agriculture. They often provide the best habitat for wildlife and include fencerows, ditches, ravines, stone piles and soils too wet or sandy for cropping.) Barnyardgrass is a choice food plant of mourning doves in the Southeast *(Table 18)* and was utilized during summer and autumn in New Mexico (Davis and Anderson 1973).

Thirteen species of bristlegrass were listed by Martin et al. (1961) as occurring in the United States, and several were ranked as choice dove foods *(Table 18)*. Bristlegrasses also are commonly called foxtails or pigeongrass. Yellow bristlegrass and green bristlegrass are among the more abundant and important to mourning doves. About half the species are annuals and all have many seeds. Bristlegrasses occur where the ground has been disturbed, as in grain and clover fields and similar open places and roadsides. German millet and similar cultivated varieties are developed from foxtail bristlegrass (Robinson 1972). Glaucous, Faber and knotroot bristlegrasses also appear in dove diets. Seeds on individual plants ripen unevenly and are therefore available over a longer time interval (U.S. Department of Agriculture 1961).

Although reed canarygrass ranked as a choice mourning dove food in the Southeast, only western species of canarygrass have significant food value for wildlife. Canarygrass comprised 4.6 percent by volume of the summer diet of doves in Arizona (Cunningham 1986).

Crabgrasses are most abundant in the East, especially the Southeast (Martin et al. 1961.) The common name comes from their creeping habit. The common species are many-seeded annuals that pioneer on disturbed ground and often occur on sterile or sandy soils. The small, soft seeds of hairy crabgrass provide mourning dove food that Davison and Sullivan (1963) ranked as fair. In North Carolina, it was the most important dove food—17.2 volume percent of the annual diet (Cummings and Quay 1953) *(Table 24)*—and also was used frequently in Alabama (Rosene 1939).

Species of dropseed grasses are found throughout the United States and are especially important in the prairie region. The seed has a hard coat that makes it slow to deteriorate or sprout, so it is available to birds for long periods. Sand dropseed comprised 2.6 percent of the September diet of mourning doves in Oklahoma (Tyler and Jenkins 1979).

Johnsongrass is a tall perennial introduced and naturalized from Eurasia (Fernald 1970). It persists in dense stands in old fields and other sites where disturbance has set back succession. Considered a fair dove food *(Table 18)*, it is specified as a noxious weed in the Federal Seed Act (U.S. Department of Agriculture 1961). Doves fed on it in Alabama (Rosene 1939), New Mexico and Texas (Dillon 1961). In New Mexico it made up 9.5 percent by volume of the annual diet (Davis and Anderson 1973), with maximum use occurring from August through October.

Panicums, 160 species of which are found in the United States (Martin et al. 1961), are annuals most abundant in the Southeast. Their principal importance as a dove food is in the southern Great Plains, where they occur in fields and upland waste places. Witchgrass panicum is one of the most abundant species and was found in 26 percent of doves examined in Oklahoma (Carpenter 1971). Most panicums and millets were ranked as choice foods *(Table 18)*.

Paspalums are most abundant in the Southeast and important to doves only in that region *(Table 24)*. Bull paspalum, the most important native food in Alabama, provided food in every month and was found in cultivated fields (Rosene 1939). It begins fruiting in early spring and continues until the first heavy frost. Thin paspalum and fringeleaf paspalum, both perennials, also are noted in dove crops. Fringeleaf paspalum is found in dry or moist open places of thin woods (Fernald 1970). Davison and Sullivan (1963) did not test thin or fringeleaf paspalums in their dove food-ranking experiments.

A dozen species of ricegrass are present in the United States but plentiful only in the West. Indian ricegrass, the most abundant, is found on sandy soils and rocky slopes (Fernald 1970). It constituted 26 percent of the mourning dove diet in Idaho (Markham and Trost 1986).

Spurge family. Crotons, also known as doveweed, are found mainly in the Southeast and southern Great Plains in fields, pastures, railroad embankments and other open places in dry soils and waste places. The rather oily seeds are choice food plants *(Table 18)*. Croton is particularly important to dove diets in Florida, Louisiana, Oklahoma and Texas *(tables 24 and 26)*, and is a common volunteer crop after spring harvest of bread wheat, common rye and common oats in Texas (Dillon 1961).

Woolly croton, a summer annual, is managed for bobwhite quail and mourning dove food. Seed production starts during August and the seed shatters gradually as it matures. Seed production can range from 307 to 461 pounds per acre (344 to 517 kg/ha) (Fessler 1960). It is one of the choice bird foods not eaten by cattle and therefore is commonly found in overgrazed pastures. Croton is a plant of early succession stages, particularly on disturbed soils or pastured sites. In the absence of disturbance, it disappears in about three years (Fessler 1960).

There are three seeds in each seed capsule of euphorbia. Painted euphorbia is found in damp, sandy soil and is sometimes a weed of waste places and railroad banks. Spotted euphorbia is found in dry and open soil, waste places, cultivated fields and roadsides. Snow-on-the-mountain euphorbia is common in waste places. These spurges are utilized by doves throughout the central and eastern United States *(tables 24 to 26)*. Leafy spurge is a perennial weed that infests 2.5 million acres (1 million ha) in the United States. The Federal Seed Act classified it as a noxious weed (U.S. Department of Agriculture 1961). Blockstein et al. (1987) noted that mourning doves rarely are dispersal agents for leafy spurge despite the fact it is a common dove food. Euphorbias are choice food plants *(Table 18)* and constituted 14 percent of the mourning dove diet in Virginia (Chamberlain 1965).

Turkey-mullein is a low-growing summer annual occurring mainly in California and adjoining areas. Sometimes called "doveweed" by hunters in California, it commonly grows on disturbed land. It is most prevalent in sparsely vegetated fallow fields, around abandoned homesteads, on roadsides and in firebreaks (Browning 1959). It is closely related to the crotons and has medium to large oily seeds. The seeds drop from late June to early autumn. This choice food *(Table 18)* was 43 percent of the mourning dove diet in California and occurred in 63 percent of the birds (Browning 1959). Turkey-mullein seeds made up 17 percent of the spring diet even though weather-beaten and insect-chewed by then.

Goosefoot family. About twenty species of goosefoot occur in the United States. Lambsquarters goosefoot probably is the most abundant.

These plants are common weeds found in rich soils of gardens, near barns or fields, and along roadsides; nearly seventy-five thousand seeds have been counted on a single plant (Martin et al. 1961). It is a dove food in the Great Plains and West. Lambsquarters goosefoot was in 21 percent of the doves collected in Colorado (Ward 1964) and made up 8 percent of the May and June diet in Maine (Schemnitz 1975). Seeds persist on the plant late in the year and are a valuable winter food.

Saltbushes are western shrubs found in fine, moderately alkaline soils (Martin et al. 1961). Fourwing saltbush, one of the most common, is found from South Dakota to Texas and westward. Good seed crops are borne almost annually (U.S. Forest Service 1948). The seeds are borne in bracts and were utilized by doves in Arizona (Cunningham 1986).

Composite family. About sixty species of sunflowers occur in the United States (Martin et al. 1961). They grow in sunny locations and are most abundant in the Great Plains. Plants are found in cultivated fields, along roadsides and in waste places where the sod has been broken, such as along fences or near ditches and streams. Sunflower has many relatively large, nutritious seeds in the flower head. Common sunflower and prairie sunflower are choice dove foods (Davison and Sullivan 1963). Sunflowers were 61 percent of the May to October mourning dove diet in Colorado (Ward 1964) and 15 percent for doves in Texas during that period (Dillon 1961).

Six ragweed species occur in the United States (Martin et al. 1961). Ragweed often is one of the first plants to invade ground recently disturbed by discing. These annuals mature seed in late summer. Seeds are rich in oil, and seed production per plant is high. Some seeds remain attached to the plant in winter and are above snow cover, where they are available to doves and other birds. Common ragweed is an important dove food in the East *(tables 24 and 25)*. This choice dove food *(Table 18)* was 36 percent of the mourning dove diet by weight in Florida (Beckwith 1959).

Croton (left) and native sunflower (right) are preferred and "choice" natural (nonagricultural) mourning dove foods. Crotons are commonly referred to as "doveweed," and their seeds are particularly important in the dove diet in the South and southern Great Plains. Sunflowers "volunteer" in many disturbed, sunny sites, especially in the Great Plains. The nutritious seeds of most varieties are readily consumed by mourning doves. Both croton and sunflower are native plants but are grown as agricultural crops in some areas. Both also are cultivated in food plots for mourning doves. *Photos by Ron George; courtesy of the Texas Parks and Wildlife Department.*

Pokeweed family. Common pokeberry is one of the most common large weeds. It grows 4 to 12 feet (1.2 to 3.7 m) tall in garbage dumps, roadsides, wood edges, mine spoilbanks, recent clearings, sites disturbed by logging and in rich moist soil (Martin et al. 1961). The dark purple berries are popular with mourning doves in the Southeast *(Table 24)*. This choice food *(Table 18)* was 7 percent of the dove diet in central Virginia (Chamberlain 1965).

Poppy family. Pricklypoppies are most prevalent in the West and Southwest in sandy and gravelly prairies, shores and waste places. However, pricklypoppy comprised 42 percent of the mourning doves' October diet in Florida (Beckwith 1959). Four species ranked as choice foods *(Table 18)*.

Amaranth family. Species of pigweed are found throughout the country in gardens, cultivated fields and waste places in good to fair soil. These annuals produce a large number of small, shiny, circular seeds. On one plant 129,000 seeds were counted (Martin et al. 1961). Seeds persist on the plant into winter months and remain available above the snow. Other species of the genus *Amaranthus* eaten by doves are tumbleweed amaranth

and redroot amaranth. Slim amaranth and redroot amaranth ranked as choice foods (Davison and Sullivan 1963). Pigweed and amaranth made up 1 to 5 percent of the dove diet in Iowa, New York, Maine, Colorado, Oklahoma, Texas, Idaho and New Mexico *(tables 25 to 27)*. In Idaho, pigweed was found only on limited areas disturbed by man or overgrazed by livestock, yet the seeds were almost 4 percent of the mourning dove diet (Markham and Trost 1986). It was found in 21 percent of the doves in Oklahoma in September (Tyler and Jenkins 1979).

Sedge family. About ninety species of these moist soil plants with triangular stems are found in the United States. They are annual or perennial weeds in many fields and gardens in sandy or light loam soils. The tubers of nutgrass—a sedge—were eaten by mourning doves in New Mexico, primarily from March through May (Davis and Anderson 1973), but made up 5 percent of the annual diet. Sedges were part of the dove diet in every month in Alabama (Rosene 1939).

Wood sorrel family. Common yellow oxalis was utilized in the Midwest (McClure 1943) and

Western ragweed is one of six ragweed species in the United States, the seeds of all of which are consumed by mourning doves. A bane to people with respiratory problems, these plants quickly invade disturbed sites, and their seeds often remain available on the plants in winter, even in snow-covered areas. It is a preferred mourning dove food throughout the species' range. *Photo by Ron George; courtesy of the Texas Parks and Wildlife Department.*

Each pigweed plant contains thousands of seeds sought and consumed by mourning doves. The availability of the seeds on the plant into winter makes it an important dove food source during that season, as well as others. Pigweed commonly invades disturbed sites, such as gardens and crop fields, throughout the United States. *Photo by Ron George; courtesy of the Texas Parks and Wildlife Department.*

East (Martin et al. 1961). These plants, found in dry open soil, have minute seeds 0.04 to 0.05 inches (1.0 to 1.3 mm) long. When the seed capsule is mature, it explodes when touched, scattering its seeds.

Buckwheat family. Also known as knotweed, birdweed and false buckwheat, these are the more upland species of the genus *Polygonum*. Common buckwheat and Pennsylvania smartweed ranked as fair dove foods and sheep sorrel as an unimportant one in the Southeast *(Table 18)*. Dullseed cornbind is common in cultivated areas and grainfields and comprised 4 percent of the dove food in winter in Ontario (Armstrong and Noakes 1981). Buckwheats were particularly important in the mourning dove diet in Arizona and New York.

Hemp family. Hemp (marijuana) was a common annual found on waste grounds and roadsides (Fernald 1970) before it came into demand for the illegal drug market. It is a choice dove food *(Table 18)* and grows in gullies, roadsides, bottomland pastures and uncultivated areas. The large, oily fruits ripen in autumn and can influence the population and distribution of wintering doves (McClure 1943). Hemp comprised one-third of the mourning dove diet in southeastern Iowa (McClure 1943) but was less than 1 percent of the diet in Illinois (Hanson and Kossack 1963) and Missouri (Korschgen 1955). The extensive use in Iowa is believed to have been related to plant availability.

Purslane family. Redmaids rockpurslane is a low-growing, semisucculent herb of the Pacific Coast states and the Southwest. Plants are abundant in cultivated and fallow fields. It is one of the earliest maturing spring annuals. In California, it made up 90 percent of the food volume by May and was present in all doves sampled. Its small black seeds constituted almost one-third of the annual diet in that state (Browning 1959).

Mustard family. Mustards are common weeds of cultivated fields and waste places (Fernald 1970). Martin et al. (1961) reported that mustard was an important mourning dove food in Washington, Oregon and California. Winter rape also was ranked as a choice dove food *(Table 18)*. Lehner (1964) reported use of oily seeds of black mustard and charlock by doves in New York.

Pine family. Natural dispersal of seeds of most species of pines in North America begins in autumn and extends into winter. Mourning doves as well as many other birds eat pine seeds readily; Davison and Sullivan (1963) ranked eight pine species as choice dove food plants *(Table 18)*. Mourning doves were the most consistent eaters of longleaf pine seeds in southern Mississippi where, according to Burleigh (1938), birds were mainly responsible for the disappearance of naturally provided and artificially sown longleaf pine seeds. Knappen (1938) ranked pine seed (loblolly and longleaf) as the fifth most important dove food in the Southeast, ranging from 13.7 percent in November to 2.8 percent in April in the monthly diet. When a good seed crop was available, doves frequented white pine stands in Massachusetts (Abbott 1966). Pine seeds formed about 2 percent of the dove diet in Alabama and included slash pine and loblolly pine (Rosene 1939).

Seeds of Austrian, red, white and Scotch pine and of white and Norway spruce were common (comprising 51 percent by volume) in dove food samples from Maine (Schemnitz 1975). The study area was a tree nursery where doves also ate yew seeds. In a similar circumstance, ninety-nine doves were collected during April and May at a nursery in central Louisiana. Seeds of slash pine and longleaf pine formed 75 percent by volume of their diet (Gresham 1950).

ANIMAL FOODS

Foods of animal origin are a relatively insignificant part of the total mourning dove diet, comprising less than 1 percent by volume or weight (range = 0.1 to 0.7 percent). Items eaten in various locales include grasshopper eggs, ants, scale insects, beetles, sow bugs, clover seed chalcids and chewing lice. The most common animal items found in the diet throughout the dove's range are snails (Cummings and Quay 1953, Lehner 1964, Ward 1964, Carpenter 1971, Griffing and Davis 1974, Tyler and Jenkins 1979). Seventeen species of land and aquatic snails were found in the food of doves in Illinois (Oberheu 1956), twenty-three species in Iowa (McClure 1943) and ten species in Missouri (Korschgen 1955). In Korschgen's study, one bird had ingested 58 snails of three species, and another ate 46 snails of a single species. McClure (1943) examined one dove that had ingested 125 snails.

Several studies indicate snails are ingested most frequently during the nesting season (Korschgen 1958, Browning 1962, Armstrong 1977). Adults fed snails to their nestlings, and McClure (1941a, 1943) and Korschgen (1958) thought that the shells fulfilled a calcium requirement for the rapidly growing young. Both dead and live snails were ingested, suggesting the main attraction was the shell material.

Mourning doves also ingest bone material from the skeletal remains of a variety of small vertebrate organisms (e.g., birds and mice), which perhaps serve to meet the same calcium needs for bone growth and eggshell formation.

FOODS OF NESTLINGS

Nestling mourning doves begin accepting food from both parents within a few hours after hatching. The first food is primarily crop milk mixed with a few small seeds. This so-called milk, a yellow curdlike substance, is produced by glands in lateral lobes of the crop of each parent. It is rich in fats and proteins. Crop milk is formed by desquamation of the proliferating epithelium of the crop wall (Levi 1977, see also chapter 7).

Food is regurgitated by the parent while the nestling has its beak inserted in the parent's open mouth. A parent may feed two chicks simultaneously while the young have their beaks inserted in opposite sides of the parent's open mouth. An individual feeding period may last ten minutes (Moore and Pearson 1941) to one hour (Webb 1949), during which the chicks receive food at periodic intervals as it is regurgitated. Nestlings also are fed at night (Webb 1949).

The amount of milk ingested by nestlings diminishes the first few days after hatching. Seed sizes and volumes increase and replace milk in the diet as the nestling grows. The parents feed relatively large seeds (common cowpeas, common soybeans, Indian corn) when nestlings are only four days old (Moore and Pearson 1941). Browning (1959) examined one- to three-day-old nestlings (n = 4) and found their crops contained 75 to 90 percent milk and 10 to 25 percent seeds. Sixty crops from four- to twelve-day-old birds averaged 25 percent dove milk; the remainder was seeds and some snail fragments.

Food volumes found in young ranged from 0.15 cubic inches (2.5 cm³) in one-day-old birds to 0.92 cubic inches (15 cm³) in seven-day-old birds (McClure 1943). Seeds within the crops of nestlings increased from about 0.01 ounces (0.3 g) in one-day-old birds to 0.28 ounce (8 g) in twelve-day-old birds. The number of seed species was smallest in day-old nestlings, but eighteen to twenty-four species could be found when squabs were only two or three days old (McClure 1943).

Crop glands develop rapidly from the tenth to the fourteenth day of incubation and are very active through the first five days posthatching. Glands of both parents begin regressing by nine days posthatching, and some females have inactive glands by then. Glands of males regress more slowly (four to six days later) than those of females. Both sexes generally have inactive glands by eighteen to twenty days posthatching (Mirarchi and Scanlon 1980).

By the time fledglings are sixteen days old, feeding them becomes mainly the duty of the male parent, and this often continues through twenty-seven days after hatching (Hitchcock and Mirarchi 1984). Fledglings begin feeding themselves to some extent by age seventeen days and can gain independence by about twenty-one days. Occasionally fledglings are fed by the parents of other doves (Hitchcock and Mirarchi 1985). By the time the young begin flying, their diet is not noticeably different from that of their parents.

WATER REQUIREMENTS

Mourning doves require surface fresh water for drinking on a regular basis (Elder 1956). They fly to water to drink in morning and evening after feeding (McClure 1943, Slade 1969). Puddles, ponds and stream edges are suitable places for doves to drink in habitats where surface water is abundant. They seem to prefer to alight on unvegetated or lightly vegetated spots where visibility is good, where there is not much nearby vegetation in which predators can hide and from which they can walk easily to the water's edge. Sandbars, gravel bars and mud flats provide such drinking sites. The desired quantity of water may be taken in a single draught (Moore and Pearson 1941, Elder 1956, see also chapter 10).

Doves occupy desert habitats, but only where they can fly to surface water every few days. At a temperature of 73 degrees Fahrenheit (23° C), mourning doves can function for four or five days without water or succulent foods and suffer no permanent ill effect (Bartholomew and Dawson 1954). At 102° F (39° C), however, doves drank four times as much as at 73° F (23° C), and after twenty-four hours without water they experienced a 15-percent loss in body weight. They have little ability to drink brackish water and lose weight if they drink salt solutions more concentrated than 0.19 molar (Bartholomew and MacMillen 1960, Smyth and Bartholomew 1966). However, the ability to drink some saltwater solutions of up to 0.15 molar sodium chloride permits them to utilize saline springs in desert areas.

The minimum daily water ration required by mourning doves averages 2.8 percent of their body weight (MacMillen 1962). Doves under moderate heat stress drink twice as much water as is required to maintain their weight. Dehydrated doves, with losses up to 15 percent of their body weights, replaced this weight in a matter of minutes when water became available (Bartholomew and Dawson 1954). In laboratory studies, dehydrated doves provided with water were able to drink in one or two draughts, within sixty seconds, an amount of water

Mourning doves require water on a regular basis, and they secure it mainly by drinking at surface water sources. They also obtain some fluid from succulent vegetation. Their minimum daily requirement of water is a volume equal to about 3 percent of their body weight. At moderate temperatures, doves can function for a number of days without water, but in hot desert habitats they must find water daily. Because surface water is scarce in the desert, congregations of one hundred or more doves at a water hole are not uncommon, particularly just before nightfall. At left is a group of white-winged and mourning doves perched next to a water hole on the Kofa Game Range in Arizona. At right are mourning doves about to drink at the edge of the same water hole. Mourning doves normally choose to approach water on bare ground, as shown, but where there is limited slope to the water's edge. Where water is scarce, such choices can be overruled. *Photos by E. P. Hadden; courtesy of the U.S. Fish and Wildlife Service.*

equivalent to 10.8 percent of their body weight (MacMillen 1962). Doves need to drink only a few minutes every day in order to retain a normal water balance.

GRIT

Grit (sand and gravel) is an essential component of the mourning dove diet, but its function is primarily mechanical rather than nutritive. It ranges from fine sand to items the size of small soybeans. Grit is retained in the gizzard (muscular stomach) for hours or days and is used in the grinding action to pulverize hard foods. Such grit, as it becomes abraded by friction, also may supply some dietary mineral requirements.

Some gallinaceous birds use hard seeds as substitutes for a portion of their grit requirements. The volume of gravel in such instances is inversely proportional to that of hard seeds (Beer and Tidyman 1942). Doves eat hard seeds that may supplement grit in the diet. Bobwhite quail have some ability to retain grit in the gizzard when it is in short supply in their daily diet (Nestler 1946), and doves may have a similar ability.

McClure (1943: 405) found the following materials in crops: "Limestone lumps, coal, cinders, chert, quartz grains (rounded to sub-rounded), rose quartz, quartzite (slightly ferruginous), glass fragments, rose quartz (attached to the rounded grain of transparent quartz), lead foil (some slightly scorched), clam shell fragments, plaster (probable origin of some quartz grains and glass fragments), quartz (with ferruginous spots and streaks, subangular sockets still distinct), small white glass bead, vesicular bone tissue, fine rose quartz sandstone (a few grains larger than the matrix are transparent) and bone fragments (quite soft)." In addition to such foreign items as glass, plaster, concrete fragments and lead foil, doves also ingest spent lead shot, apparently for use as grit (Locke and Bagley 1967, Lewis and Legler 1968). Abrading lead within the gizzard leads to lead poisoning. Osborn et al. (1983) fed doves number 8 lead shot and found that, within four weeks, a single pellet caused 24 percent mortality, two pellets caused 60 percent mortality and four pellets caused 52 percent mortality (see also chapter 12).

Grit is readily accessible at almost any feeding site with sandy or glaciated soils but is less so on clay and loess soils. In habitats where grit is not readily available, doves fly to specific sites to acquire grit. Grit frequently is secured along road edges or from any piece of barren ground where small stones are exposed.

After grit is ground to small pieces, usually less than 0.004 inches (1 mm) in diameter, it is excreted with the feces (McClure 1943). Some grit items (including lead pellets) are excreted six to seventeen days after ingestion (McConnell 1967). McClure (1943) found an average of two such tiny particles per dropping beneath night roosts. He reported an adult dove passed thirty to fifty droppings daily, so it would be excreting sixty to one hundred pebbles daily. Thus, the required daily grit ingestion levels would be significant.

SALT

Salt may be important in the mourning dove diet and seems to attract the birds (MacPherson 1897). McClure (1943) theorized that salt may be necessary for proper egg viability.

Salt may be useful to bait doves for trapping (Taber 1926, Reeves et al. 1968). However, in an evaluation of baits useful for trapping doves in Oklahoma, wheat and salt in combination were only one-third as attractive to doves as was wheat alone (Lewis and Morrison 1973).

FEEDING PATTERNS AND FLIGHT DISTANCES

Distances that doves move to feed are important in defining management strategies. The typical daily activity pattern consists of feeding and watering in early morning, followed by resting (Schmid 1965, Slade 1969). Another feeding/watering period occurs in late afternoon. Daily activity and movements also are discussed in chapters 9 and 10.

A three-year radio telemetry study of movements in northcentral Missouri, May through August, indicated mourning doves were quite mobile during the breeding season (Sayre et al. 1980). Males ranged from 0.5 to 4.8 miles (0.8 to 7.7 km) from the nest, and females moved as far as 3.3 miles (5.3 km). Daily movements mainly consisted of flights from the roost or nest to favored feeding and loafing areas. The home range of radio-tagged

Mourning doves often congregate at sites where grit is readily available. Although more important for the mechanics of digestion than for nutritional elements, grit is an essential component of the dove diet. It functions primarily to grind and pulverize hard foods in the gizzard. It also may provide some necessary dietary minerals. *Photo by Ralph E. Mirarchi; courtesy of the Auburn University Department of Zoology and Wildlife Science and the Alabama Agricultural Experiment Station.*

males during a nesting cycle varied from 1,190 to 8,647 acres (482 to 3,500 ha). Unmated males had smaller home ranges of 845 to 2,774 acres (342 to 1,123 ha). By recapture of banded doves, Tomlinson et al. (1960) also studied local movements of mourning doves during summer in Missouri. About 90 percent of all doves were retrapped no farther than 1 mile (1.6 km) from the original capture location. The greatest distance documented was 3.3 miles (5.3 km) moved by an adult male.

Sayre et al. (1980) observed feeding activity of radio-tagged doves during four phases of the nesting cycle: nest site selection; nest building; incubation; and brooding. During nest site selection, feeding occurred at low levels throughout the day within the nesting territory. The nesting territory size of six males ranged from 1.0 to 3.2 acres (0.4 to 1.3 ha) (Sayre et al. 1980). Some feeding activity occurred outside the nesting territory about midday (1:00 to 5:00 P.M.). During the nest building phase, low-level feeding occurred outside the nesting territory from 9:00 A.M. to dusk.

Males generally incubated the eggs from midmorning to late afternoon (Sayre et al. 1980). Their feeding activity was from 7:00 to 9:00 A.M. and again in the evening. During the brooding phase, male doves spent most of the early morning away from the nest. They brooded the young from midmorning until late afternoon, so their feeding again occurred in early morning and late in the day. During incubation and brooding phases, females fed mainly at midday. Unmated males fed mainly in late morning and in evening before going to roost.

Fledglings became independent of the parents by age eighteen to twenty-one days if food was adequate within 55 to 220 yards (50 to 200 m) of the nest tree (Hitchcock and Mirarchi 1984). Thus, survival of fledglings may be influenced by the quality of habitat surrounding the nest tree.

Howe and Flake (1988) studied mourning doves on the northern edge of the Great Basin Desert in Idaho. They placed transmitters on forty-seven adults and monitored their movements from June through August. Maximum distances doves moved from their watering sites averaged 1.9 miles (3.1 km). Maximum distances moved from nest sites to feeding or loafing sites (includes watering sites) averaged 2.3 miles (3.7 km). The farthest a dove was known to travel from its nest site was 3.7 miles (6.0 km). The mean distance from the nest to the nearest watering site was 1.1 miles (1.8 km). The greatest distance any dove was known to feed or loaf from its nearest known watering site was 17.6 miles (28.3 km). Howe and Flake (1988) concluded that dove populations in desert areas would be enhanced by establishing permanent water sites where the distance between existing permanent watering places is more than 3.7 miles (6.0 km).

Lewis et al. (1982) studied the autumn and winter activity of doves in southwestern Oklahoma. Doves were trapped and color-marked so it was possible to monitor movements of individual birds and flocks. Doves present during the September–October hunting season were summer residents and migrants. They formed large feeding flocks of up to a thousand birds, flew about 2.0 to 7.5 miles (3.2 to 12.1 km) from night roosts to feeding sites, and fed in morning and late afternoon. These doves fed in wheat fields when waste grain was available, otherwise they fed on haygrazer (a common sorghum/Sudangrass cross), sunflower and weed seeds. Doves day-roosted in ravines or uplands near the stock ponds where they drank at midday.

In the evening, mourning doves drank at other stock ponds before night-roosting in river bottom or upland trees and thickets (Lewis et al. 1982). Winter residents in smaller flocks (fifteen to three hundred) roosted and watered close to their feeding fields. Wintering doves spent longer periods feeding and did little flying that could be considered unnecessary to acquiring food. Their efforts seemed directed at conserving energy and maximizing food intake. The principal winter food was haygrazer. Habitat components used by winter-resident doves were fields of haygrazer or sorghum close to surface water and roosts.

The studies described above indicate that, during the nesting cycle, adult doves are dependent on feeding habitat within a few kilometers' radius of the nest. As fledglings first become independent of their parents, the feeding habitat qualities within a few hundred meters of the nest tree are the most important. There appears to be a gradual exodus from home sites when doves attain the age of five or six weeks (Hanson and Kossack 1957). Movements increase as the young mature and join flocks of subadults. Roosting and feeding sites may be about 2.0 to 7.5 miles (3.2 to 12.1 km) apart during migration. Doves limit daily movements and often roost beside or in their feeding areas during winter.

FOOD INTAKE AND METABOLIZABLE ENERGY

The metabolic efficiency and nutritional requirements of mourning doves are not well known, and this is a fertile subject area for future research. Weight of foods digested daily by birds was studied by Taber (1928). Twenty-two doves ingested foods equivalent to 7.8 to 24.1 percent of their body

Mourning doves are particularly attracted to sites and fields in which more than one preferred food is available, such as a wheat stubble field with a heavy growth of sunflowers above. Nearby surface water, perching or loafing trees, and a source of grit would make the scene above ideal. *Photo by Ken Gamble; courtesy of the Texas Parks and Wildlife Department.*

weights. Doves daily ate foods equal to just over 16 percent of their body weight (0.7 ounces: 19.4 g), but there appeared to be some seasonal variation. Doves ingested an amount equivalent to 11.7 percent of their weight in spring and summer, compared with 20.4 percent in September and October (Taber 1928).

Energy intake was studied in August and September in North Dakota (Schmid 1965). The average weight of food taken in the morning feeding period was 0.26 ounces (7.37 g) and in the evening 0.29 ounces (8.23 g). Thus, the total daily food intake was 0.57 ounces (16.09 g). Average energy intake for these birds was 71 kilocalories daily per bird, with a range of 66.6 to 75.4. Common flax and charlock had the highest energy content of nine common food plants tested by Schmid (1965); bread wheat and Indian corn had the lowest *(Table 28)*.

The physical condition of doves reflects external environmental conditions, such as food availability and weather, and such physiological demands as egg production, brood rearing, feather molt and migration. Regional weight and fat deposit differences within mourning doves in Illinois were associated with differences in the kinds of foods eaten and their nutritional value, soil fertility, and farming practices. Larger body fat deposits were associated with fertile soils and availability of corn. Birds with little fat deposits were associated with sandy, infertile soils where seeds of noxious weeds and native plants were the primary foods (Hanson and Kossack 1957).

The energy of foods used by or potentially available to mourning doves during winter in Kansas was studied by Shuman et al. (1988). Seeds of twelve plants were evaluated under simulated winter conditions: 41 degrees Fahrenheit (5° C) and 50-

Table 28. Species of seeds eaten by mourning doves in northeastern North Dakota and their energy equivalents.[a]

Seed species	Percentage occurrence in diet		Energy content (Kcal/g)
	by bird	by weight	
Green bristlegrass	83.0	39.8	4.40
Yellow bristlegrass	68.9	21.4	4.70
Bread wheat	58.5	19.6	3.96
Dullseed cornbind	25.5	5.1	4.21
Indian corn	5.7	4.7	4.06
Broomcorn panicum	3.8	3.0	4.29
Common flax	15.1	2.0	6.30
Charlock	24.5	1.6	5.98
Lambsquarters goosefoot	5.1	1.2	4.63

[a] Adapted from Schmid (1965).

percent relative humidity. Eight diets considered acceptable had metabolic efficiencies of 69 to 94 percent. The doves ingested 0.25 to 0.60 ounces (7 to 17 g) per day of the suitable diets (*Table 29*). Seeds with high fat, high fiber and low moisture had lower metabolic efficiency. Doves gained weight on diets of reed canarygrass, broomcorn panicum, common sorghum and thistle ($\bar{x} = 0.028$ ounces [0.8 g] per day) but lost weight ($\bar{x} = 0.06$ ounces [1.7 g] per day) on diets of Indian corn, Maximilian sunflower, common timothy and bread wheat. The high metabolic efficiency of corn (94 percent) may have been an artifact, because the birds' excreta was difficult to collect and analyze.

Illinois bundleflower, wild senna, honeyvine milkweed and common buckwheat were not readily eaten by doves, and the birds lost 22 to 28 percent of their mass during diet trials with these four species. So little of these foods was consumed that metabolic efficiencies could not be calculated.

Broomcorn panicum and common sorghum appear to be good species to plant for doves, but common timothy and Indian corn are poor choices (Shuman et al. 1988). High-energy foods allow doves to maintain their body weight during cold weather, maintain resistance to disease and possibly enter the spring breeding period in better condition. The finding that Indian corn is a poor-quality food raises questions, because corn is known to be the principal winter food in Ohio (Hennessy and Van Camp 1963), Missouri (Chambers 1963) and Ontario (Armstrong and Noakes 1983). Martin et al. (1961) reported that Indian corn comprised 10 to 30 percent of the mourning dove's diet in the Northeast, Southeast and prairie states.

Table 29. Mean energy values and metabolic efficiency of seed species eaten during simulated winter conditions.[a]

Seed species	Energy content[b]	Energy consumption[c]	Percentage metabolic efficiency
Reed canarygrass	4.7	51.1	78.3
Indian corn	4.4	38.3	94.0
Maximilian sunflower	5.6	40.1	68.1
Broomcorn panicum	4.5	80.8	83.7
Common sorghum	4.6	64.8	90.6
Thistle	6.2	46.6	71.7
Common timothy	4.7	37.9	80.2
Bread wheat	4.4	44.3	85.8

[a] Adapted from Shuman et al. (1988).
[b] Kilocalories per gram.
[c] Kilocalories per dram.

DEPREDATIONS BY DOVES

Mourning doves are seldom considered a problem to agricultural crops. Most of the agricultural seeds they eat are spillage left after harvest, livestock feeding or pasturing or around storage buildings. An infrequent exception is depredations by doves feeding on newly sprouted cucumber seeds (Braum as reported in McClure 1943). The dove's only significant negative economic impact seems to be to the forest industry. Their use of coniferous seed species can significantly diminish regeneration in the wild (Burleigh 1938, Abbott 1966) and in seedbeds at commercial nurseries (Rosene 1939, Gresham 1950, Royall and Neff 1961, Schemnitz 1975). Unnatural colors applied to seeds did not provide adequate protection (Royall and Neff 1961). Detrimental dove use can be diminished by coating seeds with Arasan 42S (Abbott 1958) or other powder coatings (Royall and Neff 1961).

A burlap mat used to conserve moisture in seedbeds at the Stuart tree nursery in Louisiana helped protect pine seeds from doves. However, the burlap had to be removed after the seed germinated, and greatest seed loss to birds occurred after the mats were removed. In 1949, ninety-nine doves shot at the nursery contained 75 percent (volume) of slash and longleaf pine seed in their crops. Gresham (1950) suggested the use of some other favored dove food, such as peas planted in strips near pine seedbeds, as a lure crop to diminish depredations on pine seed.

COMPETITION

Davison (1961) studied food competition between gamebirds and nongame birds. Of particular concern were blackbirds, cowbirds, crows, grackles and sparrows that gather in large flocks throughout the Southeast and feed heavily on seeds of agricultural crops and some nonagricultural seed crops (e.g., ragweed, pines and barnyardgrass). Many choice foods of nongame birds also are favored by mourning doves. Davison (1961) concluded that nongame flocking birds pose a serious problem for gamebirds in the Southeast in autumn and winter, but he referred primarily to food competition in plantings made specifically to benefit wildlife.

Dietary overlap, however, does not automatically mean that competition for food exists to a detrimental degree. Competition becomes detrimental only when the food resource is limited. There is little evidence that mourning doves nationwide are experiencing food shortages due to competition with other birds.

Coon (1968) studied food competition between blackbirds (red-winged blackbird, common grackle, brown-headed cowbird and starling) and mourning doves. Doves and blackbirds were collected in Alabama and their food habits compared. The doves' main food volume (82.6 percent) was whole-kernel corn. The blackbirds' main food (85.4 percent) was cracked corn. Only one of the 131 blackbirds contained a whole kernel of corn. Doves left the immediate vicinity of incoming large feeding flocks of blackbirds but did not normally leave the field itself. The blackbirds were attracted to grain cracked and scattered by harvest techniques or livestock. Coon (1968) concluded that some competition may occur on a local basis when large flocks of blackbirds invade small fields. Little evidence was found to substantiate claims of large-scale competition between doves and blackbirds.

Griffing and Davis (1976) studied food competition between scaled quail and mourning doves in the Southwest. They found relatively little overlap in diet. From their observations, it appears there is little opportunity for food competition between the two species.

SUMMARY

Mourning doves are primarily granivorous ground feeders with a diet almost exclusively of plant materials. The grass family is a principal food source and other important families include spurge, composite, buckwheat, pulse, pokeweed, goosefoot and amaranth. Agricultural crops, primarily the cereal grains, comprise a large proportion of the diet in many states. Mechanical harvest practices leave an abundant supply of seeds shattered on the ground and available for bird use. Of particular importance are Indian corn, bread wheat, common sorghum, millets, common rye, sixrow barley and common oats.

Dove populations are strongly influenced by man's agricultural activities. For example, important foods in Texas (Dillon 1961) indicate doves were feeding mainly in or near agriculture. Doves in California obtain most of their foods from lands disturbed by humans, either by cultivation, grazing, ditch and roadbed maintenance, or similar practices that encourage weedy annuals and cultivated plants (Browning 1962).

Many of the most favored dove foods are seeds produced on herbaceous plants found in early successional stages. They are typically referred to as weeds, plants that volunteer on unvegetated soils recently disturbed by man or nature. Native grasses important as dove foods include barnyardgrass, bristlegrasses, canarygrass, crabgrasses, dropseed grass, Johnsongrass, panicums, paspalums and ricegrasses. Other wild plants important as dove foods include crotons, euphorbias, turkey-mullein, goosefoot, saltbushes, sunflowers, ragweeds, common pokeberry, pricklypoppy, pigweed, amaranths, sedges, buckwheats, hemp, redmaids rock-purslane, mustards and pine seeds.

Mourning doves are primarily seed eaters that feed on the ground. Ninety-nine percent of their diet is seeds or plant parts. Nevertheless, their impact on agricultural crops is negligible, and about the only depredations of concern to some people are mourning doves' attraction to bird feeders. The doves shown here are consuming sorghum. *Photo by Larry Ditto.*

Nestling doves are fed crop milk produced by glands in the lateral lobes of the crop of each parent. The crop is a pocket in the esophagus wall used for food storage. Crop milk is formed by desquamation of the proliferating epithelium of the crop wall (Lewis 1957). The milk is rich in fats and proteins. Within a few days after hatching the nestling is being fed significant numbers of seeds. The crop glands of the parents begin regressing by nine days posthatching. Young birds usually are totally independent from the parents by three weeks of age, and their diet is similar to the adults'.

Mourning doves require fresh water for drinking on a regular basis (Elder 1956). They fly to water to drink in morning and evening after feeding (McClure 1943, Slade 1969). Doves will utilize desert habitat but only where they can fly to water every few days. At moderate temperatures (73° F: 23° C) doves can function four or five days without water or succulent foods and suffer no permanent ill effect (Bartholomew and Dawson 1954). The ability to drink some saline solutions of up to 0.15 molar sodium chloride permits them to utilize saline springs in desert areas.

Grit (sand and gravel) is an essential component of the diet, but its function is primarily mechanical rather than nutritive. Doves eat hard seeds, which may supplement grit in the diet.

During the nesting cycle, adult doves are dependent on feeding habitat within a few kilometers' radius of the nest. As fledglings first become independent of their parents, the feeding habitat within a few hundred meters of the nest is the most important. Feeding movements increase as the young mature and join flocks of subadults. Roosting and feeding sites may be 1.9 to 7.5 miles (3 to 12 km) apart during migration. Doves limit their daily movements and often roost beside or in the feeding areas during winter.

One study indicated doves daily ingest foods equivalent to 10 to 20 percent of their body weight (Taber 1928). In North Dakota (August and September), researchers noted that average daily food intake was about 0.56 ounces (16 g), with an average energy intake of 66 to 75 kilocalories (Schmid 1965).

Mourning doves are seldom considered a problem to agricultural crops. Most of the agricultural seeds they eat are spillage left in the fields or around buildings. The doves' only negative economic impact seems to be on the forest industry, where their use of coniferous seeds can diminish regeneration in the wild and at nurseries (Burleigh 1938, Rosene 1939, Gresham 1950, Royall and Neff 1961, Abbott 1966, Schemnitz 1975). Doves utilize many seeds that also are eaten by other birds. However, there is little evidence that mourning doves are experiencing food shortages due to food competition with other birds.

Chapter 12.

Diseases, Parasites and Contaminants

Joseph A. Conti
Southeastern Cooperative Wildlife Disease Study
College of Veterinary Medicine
The University of Georgia
Athens, Georgia

There are many publications on infectious and noninfectious diseases affecting mourning doves, but more baseline and experimental data are necessary to further understand the epizootiology of disease in populations of this species. Although agricultural practices of modern times probably have greatly benefited mourning dove populations, the potential for epizootics has increased. In addition, given the migratory behavior of mourning doves, a highly infectious and lethal disease agent may cause serious population fluctuations on a widespread basis.

PARASITES

Protozoa

Coccidia. An intestinal coccidian protozoan of the genus *Eimeria* has been reported from mourning doves only three times (Boughton and Volk 1938, Barrows and Hayes 1977, Conti and Forrester 1981). Prevalences range from 7 percent in doves examined throughout the southeastern United States (Barrows and Hayes 1977) to 42 percent in doves examined specifically from Florida (Conti and Forrester 1981). *Eimeria* infections probably occur in doves throughout the United States. Barrows and Hayes (1977) found thickened duodenal mucosas in two mourning doves harboring infections of high intensity.

Although the effects of this coccidian parasite on populations of mourning doves are not completely understood, *Eimeria* is generally believed to be pathologically insignificant in free-flying doves (Barrows and Hayes 1977). Young pigeons have been known to succumb to severe infections (Pellerdy 1974). As with many parasites, coccidian infections may become a problem only when continuous reinfection reaches pathogenic levels, especially in young susceptible birds. This could occur if doves were heavily concentrated in certain feeding areas or in captive flocks where infective stages of the parasite could be ingested easily.

The species of *Eimeria* in mourning doves have not yet been determined, and there is evidence that at least one may be new to science (Conti 1980). Because eight species of *Eimeria* and one species of *Isospora* already have been described from only a few species of columbiforms, Varghese (1980) believed that knowledge of coccidian parasites in birds of this order is in its infancy.

Sarcocystis is another coccidian protozoan found in mourning doves. Like *Eimeria*, infective stages of *Sarcocystis* are picked up by doves from contaminated soil and water. Once within the dove's intestine, the infective stages eventually spread to muscle tissue, where they multiply and encapsulate in elongate, usually visible white cysts. The breast muscle is a common place to observe cysts. It should be noted that the cysts may be microscopic in size, requiring the use of specialized

205

techniques to determine their presence (Box and Duszynski 1977). The mourning dove is the intermediate host of *Sarcocystis*, with flesh-eating predators serving as the final host.

Sarcocystis sp. was found in 13 percent of 255 doves examined in a study involving twelve states of the southeastern United States (Barrows and Hayes 1977) and in 8 percent of 455 doves examined in Florida (Conti and Forrester 1981). It probably occurs in mourning doves throughout the United States and generally is considered harmless. To date, no mourning dove has been found with an extreme or fatal infection of *Sarcocystis*.

Although *Sarcocystis* is considered harmless to man, thorough cooking of all dove meat should ensure destruction of the cysts and their infective stages.

Toxoplasma is a protozoan much like the *Sarcocystis* organism. There is only one report of *Toxoplasma* sp. from the mourning dove (Couch 1952). Although reports of this tissue-invading protozoan in the mourning dove are rare, it has been detected in pigeons by other researchers and is known to occur commonly in mammals and birds worldwide (Sanger 1971). *Toxoplasma* infections in most mammals and birds are asymptomatic or uneventful (Sanger 1971).

Blood parasites. The simple technique involved in preparing blood smears (Bennett 1970) from mourning doves has resulted in an abundance of information on the blood parasites harbored by these birds. The blood parasites found include at least eight protozoans and an unknown number of filariids (Levine and Kantor 1959).

The most common blood parasite identified in mourning doves is the protozoan *Haemoproteus columbae (H. maccallumi)*. This parasite lives within the red blood cell and is transmitted by blood-sucking arthropods, such as hippoboscid flies and possibly biting midges of the genus *Culicoides*. Prevalences of *H. columbae* vary greatly throughout the United States; it is not unusual to find more than 90 percent of the doves infected in one area (Shamis and Forrester 1977) and few or none of the doves infected in another (Knisley and Herman 1967).

Transmission of *H. columbae* is influenced by various factors that affect vector activity and abundance. Biologists should be aware of the time of year when blood smears are made, since prevalences of infection may vary seasonally. While determination of the prevalence of blood parasite infection in a population of doves is important, perhaps even more significant is the intensity of infection per individual dove. Finding the ratio of the number of blood parasites per number of blood cells examined provides a clearer picture of the real

or potential impact of the infection on the health of a particular dove. Determination of both the prevalence and intensity of infection may be affected by such factors as time and method of dove collection, site of blood collection from the actual dove, number of blood smears and/or blood cells examined, and manner in which blood smears are examined (Godfrey et al. 1987).

By removal of a few feathers, the brachial vein of a mourning dove can be made accessible for extraction of a few drops of blood necessary for the preparation of blood smears. Veins on the exposed parts of the legs (inner tibia) also can be used. A lancet is used to prick veins and blood is removed with a microcapillary tube. Although the brachial vein is very visible and blood is extracted easily, such extraction may not be advisable because heavy bleeding can occur after pricking. Pressure then would have to be applied to the vein for several minutes after blood extraction to ensure sufficient clotting. Although difficult to see, veins on the inside of the lower legs (tibia) may be preferable extraction sites, since heavy bleeding there usually does not occur. Only a few drops of blood from the microcapillary tube are dropped onto a glass slide for the smear, as usually only ten thousand erythrocytes are necessary in finding avian hematozoa and microfilariae. After methyl alcohol fixation and Giemsa stain, microscopic study of blood smears can reveal prevalence data (number of doves infected with a particular blood parasite in any given population) as well as parasitemia data (number of a particular blood parasite per ten thousand erythrocytes in a single dove). *Photo by Joseph A. Conti; courtesy of the University of Florida Laboratory of Wildlife Disease Research and the Southeastern Cooperative Wildlife Disease Study, University of Georgia.*

Another species of *Haemoproteus, H.sacharovi*, also is found in mourning doves but usually is less common than *H. columbae*. This possibly is due to the fact that *H. sacharovi* disappears from the blood faster than *H. columbae* does, rendering it harder to find in a single blood smear (Greiner 1970).

The other species of blood protozoans reported from doves—*Leucocytozoon marchouxi, Plasmodium elongatum, P. hexamerium, P. polare, P. relictum, P. cathemerium* and *Trypanosoma avium*—rarely are encountered in mourning doves. Microfilariae, or immature forms of adult filariid worms, also are found on occasion in the blood of mourning doves. It is generally believed that the vectors of *Plasmodium* spp. and microfilariae are mosquitoes and that of *L. marchouxi*, black flies; it has not been determined which blood-sucking arthropod is the vector of *T. avium*.

Although the effects of blood parasite infections are not fully understood, no morbidity or mortality in mourning doves has ever been attributed to these infections. However, more studies are needed on the effects of blood parasites concomitant with other disease agents.

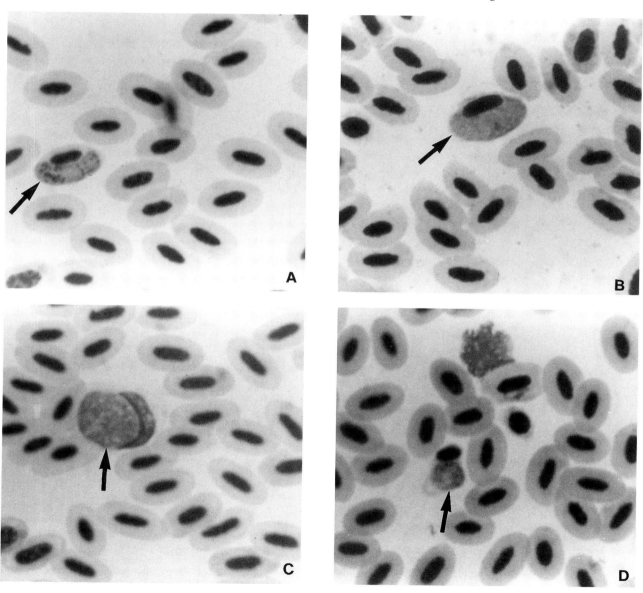

Gametocyte (adult) stages of four intracellular blood protozoans (arrows) in mourning doves: A = *Haemoproteus columbae* (= *maccallumi*) (the most common blood parasite in mourning doves—vectors include hippoboscid flies and biting midges); B = *H. sacharovi* (also common in mourning doves but relatively difficult to detect—vectors are the same as for *H. columbae*); C = *Leucocytozoon marchouxi* (rare in mourning doves— vectors thought to be black flies); and D = *Plasmodium relictum* (also rare—vector possibly mosquitoes). *Photos by Ellis C. Greiner; courtesy of the University of Florida Veterinary School and the Southeastern Cooperative Wildlife Disease Study, University of Georgia.*

Oral flagellates and ciliates. Perhaps the most important disease agent with respect to the health of mourning dove populations throughout North America is *Trichomonas gallinae*. This is a highly motile flagellated protozoan that normally resides in the mouth, esophagus and crop of many species of columbiforms. The organism was first described from a pigeon in Italy in 1878, although it was recognized by falconers hundreds of years earlier as a disease agent in birds of prey that had fed on infected pigeons (Stabler 1954).

It generally is believed that the rock dove, or common pigeon, is the primary host of *T. gallinae* (Kocan and Herman 1971). The organism has been found in this species of pigeon worldwide and was reported in this host for the first time in the United States by Waller (1934) and Cauthen (1934). It probably existed in pigeons in North America long before this date, however, as the pigeon was brought to North America from Europe by the early colonists in the 1600s (Schorger 1952). The first report of *T. gallinae* in mourning doves was from a captive

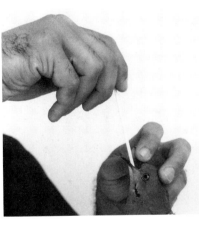

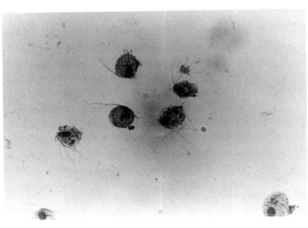

Trichomonas gallinae, a flagellated protozoan (lower right), may be the most significant disease agent impacting mourning dove populations. Facial or esophageal lesions can inhibit the infected bird's sight, breathing or feeding and frequently cause death. Even doves that are exposed but resistant to virulent strains of *T. gallinae* can become carriers of the disease. The common pigeon is the primary host of this highly motile protozoan, so testing of these columbids as well as mourning doves is important in tracking strains and monitoring for outbreaks. A visual check for mouth lesions in columbids can be easily performed with a penlight (top left: pigeon). To examine columbids for *T. gallinae*, the mouth, esophagus and crop are swabbed with a cotton-tipped applicator that was dipped once in normal saline solution (top right and bottom left: mourning dove and white-winged dove, respectively). The trichomonads can be removed by swirling or dabbing the cotton tip in a drop or two of normal saline solution sitting on a glass slide. After a cover slip is applied, the slide can be examined microscopically (100x, 400x) (bottom right). However, light infections can be missed using this technique; therefore, in the case of a negative throat swab, it is best to culture the entire throat swab (reswabbing may be necessary) in a solution called "Diamond's medium" (Diamond 1957). There is no danger of humans becoming infected with *T. gallinae* through handling or consumption of diseased doves. Nevertheless, researchers should be cautious in handling doves infected with *T. gallinae*, especially when checking for the organism, because sloppy technique can lead to infection between doves. If possible, researchers should avoid having their fingers contact doves' mouths in rapid succession. *Photos courtesy of the Southeastern Cooperative Wildlife Disease Study, University of Georgia, and the University of Florida Laboratory of Wildlife Disease Research.*

colony containing infected doves and pigeons in New York (Cauthen 1934). Since then, there have been numerous reports of the infection in mourning doves throughout the United States. It probably is safe to assume that the organism may occur in mourning doves wherever the birds are found.

Trichomonas gallinae is unusual in that it often exists peaceably in the columbiform host, but at other times it causes severe pathological reactions (Kocan and Herman 1971). Cheesy, yellowish growths in the mouth and esophagus are typical lesions produced by *T. gallinae*, although these growths can extend into the crop, lungs and possibly other organs (Kocan and Herman 1971). Mouth lesions often inhibit or prevent feeding, resulting in severe emaciation and eventually death. Lesions sometimes extend all around the beak, sinuses and eyes and can resemble gross lesions of avian pox virus infection (distinguishing characteristics of both diseases are discussed later). Doves infected with a virulent strain of *T. gallinae* usually die about one or two weeks after initial exposure to the organism.

The presence of both avirulent and virulent strains of *T. gallinae* and the devastating effects of virulent strains make this organism one of the most

dangerous pathogens in mourning doves and other native species of columbiforms. To date, it is not clear why there are different strains of *T. gallinae*, although laboratory research indicates that pathogenicity appears to be controlled genetically within the organism itself (Stabler et al. 1964, Honigberg et al. 1971). No one has studied the genetics of the columbiform host to see if there are any differences in resistance to the pathogenic effects of *T. gallinae*.

Although the mechanisms by which strains of *T. gallinae* become virulent in nature are not completely understood, it is known that either an avirulent infection or survival of a virulent one will provide a mourning dove with protective immunity for some time against further exposure to virulent strains (Stabler 1948). For example, in an area of South Carolina where previous outbreaks of apparently virulent strains of *T. gallinae* occurred, Kocan and Amend (1972) challenged wild-caught, trichomonad-free mourning doves with virulent *T. gallinae* and found a high resistance to disease. Resistant doves, however, may harbor virulent strains without developing lesions, thus rendering them carriers of the lethal strains and possible sources of infection to susceptible doves. The ramifications are not to be taken lightly. Mourning dove populations

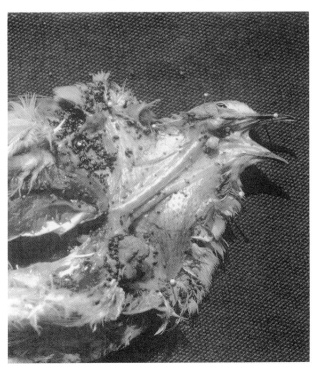

Cheesy, yellowish lesions around the mourning dove's beak or eyes or in the bird's mouth or esophagus are characteristic of *Trichomonas gallinae*. Growths also occur in the crop, lungs, sinuses and elsewhere. Except by clinical examination, such manifestations of *T. gallinae* are indistinguishable from those of avian pox infection. Hunters could help researchers by notifying state wildlife agency officials of diseased doves observed in the field. Delivering fresh or refrigerated specimens within a short period after death may also be helpful for a definitive diagnosis. *Left photo by Russ Reagan, right photo by Glenn Chambers; both courtesy of the Missouri Department of Conservation.*

experienced the ravages of this disease when infections with virulent *T. gallinae* reached epizootic proportions in all the southeastern states in 1950 (Haugen 1952). Extensive investigations during 1950 and 1951 in Alabama alone led to the belief that mortality, primarily among breeding birds, could easily have totaled twenty-five thousand to fifty thousand doves each year (Haugen and Keeler 1952). As carcasses and morbid doves usually are eliminated expeditiously from the environment by scavengers, the mortality may have been grossly underestimated. Further emphasizing the vulnerability of morbid doves, George (1992) reported an instance of snails infesting a live, flightless mourning dove weakened by *T. gallinae*.

The 1950 epizootic made biologists more aware of *T. gallinae*, stimulating much research. Nothing quite as serious has since occurred in mourning doves, although localized die-offs often are reported in the literature. For example, a localized epizootic of trichomoniasis in mourning doves was observed in railroad yards and at a grain elevator in Lincoln, Nebraska, during the summer of 1972 (Greiner and Baxter 1974). The doves (and domestic pigeons) were feeding on spilled grain. A total of 64 dead doves was found in four days in the railroad yards, while 110 dead doves were observed at a grain elevator in one day.

Many reported die-offs have involved poorly maintained backyard feeding and watering stations in conjunction with large concentrations of doves (Rosen 1959). For example, *T. gallinae* is believed to have killed 750 mourning doves associated with bird feeders from April to July, 1985, in Las Cruces, New Mexico (National Wildlife Health Research Center 1985a). Since *T. gallinae* can live for some time on moist grains and, to a limited extent, in water (Kocan 1969), better sanitation methods and dispersal of large flocks of doves in backyard situations should be employed to correct the problem. Other means by which *T. gallinae* is spread between doves are in the billing behavior among mated adults (see chapter 10) and the feeding of young by both parents via regurgitation (see chapters 5 through 7).

Although prevalences of *T. gallinae* in wild mourning dove populations have never been reported to be very high, differences in strain virulence are important enough—as shown by the 1950–51 epizootic in the Southeast—to cause concern. In California, a lethal strain of *T. gallinae* was responsible for the deaths of at least sixteen thousand band-tailed pigeons during February to April 1988 (D. P. Connelly personal communication: 1988). The band-tailed pigeon is another native species of columbiform in which, like the mourning

Biomagnification of virulent strains of *Trichomonas gallinae* is a concern to mourning dove biologists, since the disease already is prevalent to some degree throughout the range of pigeons and doves in the Americas. Birds that prey on doves and pigeons are vulnerable as well. Above are screech owl nest mates, one of which was exposed to the pathogen when it was fed an infected dove or pigeon by its parent. *Photo courtesy of the University of Florida Laboratory of Wildlife Disease Research and the Southeastern Cooperative Wildlife Disease Study, University of Georgia.*

dove, low prevalences of *T. gallinae* normally are found (Stabler 1951, Sileo and Fitzhugh 1969).

Because other columbiforms such as feral domestic pigeons and white-winged doves appear to be excellent reservoir hosts for *T. gallinae*, owing to the high prevalence of the parasite in these birds, the chances may be increased for mourning doves or band-tailed pigeons to contract potentially serious infections of epizootic proportions. At least two studies have shown that *T. gallinae* from white-winged doves was avirulent in susceptible pigeons in Texas (Stabler 1961) and susceptible mourning doves in Florida (Conti et al. 1985). Continued testing of the strains of *T. gallinae* in wild columbiforms must be done in order to give more meaning to the prevalence surveys. Although several drugs can cure doves of the avirulent infection and earlier stages of the disease caused by virulent strains, there are no practical chemical methods to eliminate or control *T. gallinae* directly in the wild. An indirect method of limiting the spread of this organism is to discourage the buildup of large concentrations of doves (more than a few pairs) where they obtain food or water, as at livestock feedlots or, in some instances, bird-feeding stations clustered in suburban neighborhoods.

Besides the flagellate protozoan *T. gallinae*, a ciliate protozoan, *Colpoda steinii*, has been found in the saliva of mourning doves. This large, rapidly moving ciliate was first recognized in 76 (32 percent) of 240 doves in Louisiana, 18 (50 percent) of 36 doves in Florida and 3 (5 percent) of 58 doves in Arizona (Toepfer 1964). Although *C. steinii* has been reported as a facultative parasite of the land snail, *Agriolimax agrestis* (Reynolds 1936), it normally is found in soil and in such freshwater habitats as ponds and ditches where doves presumedly obtained the organism during drinking (Toepfer 1964). However, Kocan (1968) determined that doves and pigeons in captivity obtained *C. steinii* through ingestion of moist grain containing cysts of the ciliate. This mode of acquisition was believed to occur in the wild as well. Because the organism lasted for only two consecutive days in any captive dove or pigeon examined, Kocan (1968) concluded that *C. steinii* was a transient organism rather than a parasite or commensal.

Helminths

The following discussion of internal helminths (nematodes, flukes and tapeworms) is based on three reports, all of which involve mourning doves from the southeastern United States (Barrows and Hayes 1977, Conti and Forrester 1981, Forrester et al.

1983). While these studies are geographically limited, it is very likely that many of the species of helminths reported occur in doves throughout the United States. Only one other reported attempt was made to examine mourning doves for helminths outside of the Southeast, but no parasites were found in fifty doves from Illinois (Hanson et al. 1957).

Nematoda. *Ornithostrongylus quadriradiatus*, a small, threadlike intestinal nematode, probably is the most common helminth of mourning doves. This parasite may be difficult to find, however, because of its extremely small size and the likelihood of its being obscured by intestinal contents. Careful screening of intestinal contents with a number 100 sieve can aid greatly in detecting this worm, which usually is blood red in color. Barrows and Hayes (1977) reported 51 percent of 255 mourning doves examined from twenty-five collection sites in twelve southeastern states to be infected with *O. quadriradiatus*. The majority of infected birds harbored fewer than ten worms (mean = nine), and gross lesions were not observed. Forrester et al. (1983) found 67 percent of 455 mourning doves in Florida harboring *Ornithostrongylus* spp. (predominantly *O. quadriradiatus*) with a mean of thirteen worms per infected dove and with no associated lesions. Another species of *Ornithostrongylus*, *O. iheringi*, was reported in that study and lumped statistically with *O. quadriradiatus* because of its rare occurrence. Although these studies indicated that *Ornithostrongylus* was not a significant pathogen in mourning doves, large numbers of this blood-ingesting parasite have been known to produce a catarrhal enteritis and anemia in domestic pigeons (Cuvillier 1937, Tongson et al. 1975). Since *Ornithostrongylus* has a direct life cycle, severe pathological consequences are possible only if large concentrations of mourning doves continuously use feeding areas that become highly contaminated.

Ascaridia columbae is a robust nematode that lives in the small intestine of columbiforms. Unlike *Ornithostrongylus* it is easily observed because of its large size. Hunters often see these worms moving around in the abdominal cavities of doves whose intestines have been perforated by gunshot pellets.

Ascaridia columbae has been reported only in mourning doves from South Carolina and Florida, but further studies probably would show it to have a much wider geographic occurrence. Although only 2 percent of 255 mourning doves examined from the southeastern United States were infected (Barrows and Hayes 1977), nearly 31 percent of 455 doves harbored *A. columbae* in the Florida study (Forrester et al. 1983). Intensities of infection were high in the former study (mean = forty-eight worms per infected dove) but much lower in the latter (mean = four worms per infected dove). Barrows and Hayes found two doves with 108 and 127 *A. columbae*, respectively; in each bird, portions of the duodenum were distended, accompanied by mucosal hyperemia. Conti (1980) found a similar but milder form of this reaction in mourning and white-winged doves with much smaller intensities of infection, even with as few as five or six ascarids. A large accumulation of ascarids may cause obstruction and rupture of the intestine, leading to either debilitation or death (Wehr 1971). Perforation of the intestine, peritonitis and death have been reported in pigeons infected with large numbers of *A. columbae* (Mozgovoi 1953).

Although infections of *A. columbae* in populations of mourning doves are not considered serious, problems could develop where doves are concentrated since the infective stages of the parasite are picked up directly from contaminated soil, as in the case of *Ornithostrongylus*.

Dispharynx nasuta is a ubiquitous nematode in wild birds. It appears as a stout but somewhat small coiled worm usually found anteriorly embedded in the mucosal wall of the proventriculus. A severe proventriculitis occurs when this worm is present in large numbers, and it has been associated with pathologic changes, illness and/or death in grouse, turkeys and pigeons (Goble and Kutz 1945, Bendell 1955, Hwang et al. 1961, Wehr 1971, Hon et al. 1975). As birds must ingest an intermediate host (probably an isopod such as the sowbug) containing the infective stage of this nematode, it is unlikely that *D. nasuta* could ever become a serious problem in mourning doves since they are predominantly vegetarians.

Studies of mourning doves in the southeastern states have shown generally low prevalences and intensities of infection of this parasite (Barrows and Hayes 1977, Forrester et al. 1983). Although 16 percent of the mourning doves in Florida harbored *D. nasuta*, with a mean of eleven worms per infected dove (Forrester et al. 1983), a specific population of doves in that study showed an elevated prevalence (37 percent) but lower intensity of infection (Conti and Forrester 1981). Doves either are ingesting sowbugs intentionally or mistaking them for seeds, since these invertebrate intermediate hosts form a round ball as a defensive posture. Although little is known regarding the pathology of *D. nasuta* in mourning doves, a few doves with approximately fifteen to twenty-five worms were observed to exhibit a mild reaction in the proventriculus, characterized by hypersecretion of mucus around the clustered group of nematodes (Conti 1980).

Ascardia columbae nematodes frequently are found in the small intestines of columbids, including mourning doves, particularly in the Southeast. Although infestations of this parasite do not appear to impact mourning dove populations adversely to a significant degree, large accumulations of ascarids may be fatal to individual birds by virtue of intestinal blockage or rupture. *Photo by Joseph A. Conti; courtesy of the University of Florida Laboratory of Wildlife Disease Research and the Southeastern Cooperative Wildlife Disease Study, University of Georgia.*

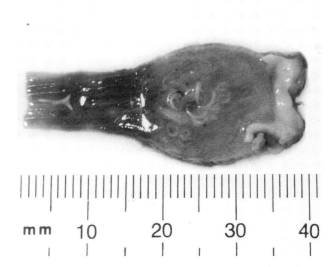

Dispharynx nasuta is a small, coiled nematode found occasionally in the mourning dove proventriculus (the true stomach, situated between the crop and gizzard). The worm probably is introduced in most cases by dove ingestion of sowbugs, one of the parasite's primary intermediate hosts. Mourning doves likely mistake sowbugs for seeds. The pathology of *D. nasuta* in mourning doves is not well understood, but proventriculitis (resulting in illness or death) may occur when large numbers accumulate. *Photo by Joseph A. Conti; courtesy of the University of Florida Laboratory of Wildlife Disease Research and the Southeastern Cooperative Wildlife Disease Study, University of Georgia.*

Aproctella stoddardi is a mosquito-transmitted filarial nematode; adult forms normally reside in the abdominal cavity. The microfilariae (or immature worms) are found in the circulatory system. Several upland gamebirds can harbor infections with *A. stoddardi* (Anderson 1957). In hunter-killed doves with intestinal perforations, hunters can usually distinguish adults of *A. stoddardi* from adults of intestinal-dwelling *Ascaridia columbae* by virtue of the former's much smaller size and relative slenderness. In the Florida study, 10 percent of the mourning doves were infected (mean = six worms per infected dove) (Forrester et al. 1983). This compares favorably with an 8 percent prevalence (mean = nine worms per infected dove) reported in mourning doves from combined areas of the southeastern United States (Barrows and Hayes 1977). Although infections with *A. stoddardi* in mourning doves usually are considered pathologically insignificant, they have resulted in adhesions of the liver and small intestine to the body wall in one dove and a granulomatous pericarditis in another when the parasite occurred in the pericardial sac (Barrows and Hayes 1977).

Only two other nematodes have been reported from mourning doves in North America: *Tetrameres columbicola* and *Capillaria obsignata* (Conti and Forrester 1981, Forrester et al. 1983). Both were reported from Florida, with very low prevalences (4 percent and less than 1 percent, respectively) and intensities (mean = two and six worms per infected dove, respectively) of infection. *Tetrameres columbicola* is found in the proventriculus. Male worms are microscopic in size, while the female worms are much larger and usually observed macroscopically as circular, red-colored foci embedded in the mucosal wall of the proventriculus. *Capillaria obsignata* is a microscopic, long, threadlike nematode found in the small intestine. Both *Tetrameres* and *Capillaria* have been associated with severe lesions when present in large numbers (Wehr 1971), but they are considered unimportant in mourning doves because of their infrequent occurrence in very low numbers.

An accidental infection with larvae of *Baylisascaris* sp. in the brains of two mourning doves from Illinois is of interest (Evans and Tangredi 1985). Both doves exhibited severe ataxia, headtilt, torticollis, anorexia and weight loss. Histologic sections of the brain revealed ascarid larvae, the adult nematodes of which usually occur in the intestines of raccoons and skunks. Evans and Tangredi noted that undigested seeds from dried raccoon and skunk feces sometimes are ingested by ground-feeding birds such as doves and pigeons; they speculated that this may explain the infection of birds by this parasite. The migrating larvae have a predilection for brain tissue in the abnormal host, and only a few larvae are necessary to cause death in birds. The implications of cerebrospinal nematodiasis caused by larvae of *Baylisascaris* sp. on populations of mourning doves are unknown but believed to be minimal. It appears that serious problems could only develop in areas where raccoon densities and *Baylisascaris* sp. infections are high, with a resultant widespread contamination of an environment heavily used by large feeding flocks of mourning doves.

Trematoda and cestoda. Only three flukes and three tapeworms have been reported in mourning doves, and all occur rarely and in very low numbers. The flukes *Echinostoma revolutum, Brachylaima* sp. and *Tanaisia bragai* have all been reported in less than 1 percent of the doves examined (Barrows and Hayes 1977, Forrester et al. 1983). *Echinostoma revolutum* and *Brachylaima* sp. are intestine dwelling, whereas *T. bragai* is found within the urinary tract and kidneys.

The intestinal tapeworms *Killigrewia delafondi, Hymenolepis* sp. and *Raillietina* spp. have been found in less than 2 percent of mourning doves in Florida (Forrester et al. 1983), although prevalences of *K. delafondi* and *Hymenolepis* sp. were slightly higher (4 percent and 5 percent, respectively) when doves were examined from a wide geographical area of the southeastern United States (Barrows and Hayes 1977). Harkema (1942) first reported *K. delafondi* in the mourning dove when he found 16 percent of thirty-one doves from North Carolina infected with from one to three tapeworms.

Ecological aspects of the fauna. Forrester et al. (1983) discussed the ecology of helminth parasitism of 455 mourning doves from Florida. Although 14 species of helminths were found overall, the number of species per infected dove varied from 1 to 5 (mean = 1.5). The total number of helminths per infected host ranged from 1 to 163 (mean = 14). The nematodes *Ornithostrongylus* spp., *Dispharynx nasuta, Ascaridia columbae* and *Aproctella stoddardi* were considered the major components of the helminth fauna. Some analysis performed on a subpopulation of mourning doves during a single year showed peaks in prevalence and intensity in spring and summer months for *Ornithostrongylus* spp., *Dispharynx nasuta* and *Aproctella stoddardi; Ascaridia columbae* showed higher prevalences in the winter months and a relatively stable intensity throughout the year. The helminth fauna of mourning doves from Florida was compared with those of doves from nine other southeastern states and found to be most similar to those from Alabama and Mississippi (Forrester et al. 1983).

Ectoparasites

Only a few researchers have surveyed mourning doves for ectoparasites. The studies by Hanson et al. (1957) in Illinois and by Conti and Forrester (1981) in Florida provide baseline information about the more common species of mites and lice that occur on these birds. A study by Greiner (1975) increased knowledge of the different kinds of blood-sucking diptera that frequent mourning doves. Although the effects of ectoparasitic infestation on mourning doves are unknown, they are believed to be inconsequential. In unusual circumstances, however, large numbers of ectoparasites may directly influence the declining health of an already sick or injured bird. In addition, many ectoparasites indirectly affect mourning doves by introducing other pathogens, as in the case of the blood-sucking diptera.

The two most common mites found on mourning doves are *Diplaegidia* sp. and *Faculifer* sp. Of ninety-six doves examined from Florida, 44 percent and 48 percent, respectively, were infested with low numbers of these feather mites (Conti and Forrester 1981). They also were reported as common on mourning doves from Illinois (Hanson et al. 1957).

A nasal mite, *Tinaminyssus (Neonyssus) zenaidurae*, was found on 6 percent of ninety-six doves from Florida, while 1 percent of the same sample was infested with another feather mite, *Dermoglyphus* sp. Strandtmann (1961) reported 15 percent of seventy-four mourning doves from Texas harboring the nasal mite *T. zenaidurae*. In Oklahoma, 17 percent of 191 mourning doves harbored one to seven (mean = 2.5) *T. zenaidurae* in their nasal sinuses, with no significant difference in the prevalence between mature and immature birds (Powders and Coffey 1983). Pathologic effects were not found. Higher prevalences of *T. zenaidurae* have been reported in other investigations, but these usually involved smaller sample sizes (Powders and Coffey 1983).

Clark (1964) described from the mourning dove a new species of mite, *Syringophilus zenadourae*, which characteristically lives inside the shaft of large flight feathers of the wing, particularly the secondaries.

The only other species of mite reported on mourning doves is *Ornithonyssus (Bdellonyssus, Liponyssus) sylviarum*. This mite was commonly found in the nests of mourning doves from Iowa and Illinois (McClure 1943, Hanson et al. 1957). Although swarming numbers of *O. sylviarum* were observed at times, dove nesting activity apparently was not affected (McClure 1943).

Four species of biting lice were found in the feathers of ninety-six mourning doves from Florida with the following prevalences: *Columbicola macrourae* (35 percent), *Bonomiella columbae* (24 percent), *Physconelloides zenaidurae* (19 percent) and *Hohorstiella paladinella* (1 percent) (Conti and Forrester 1981). In addition to *C. macrourae* and *P. zenaidurae*, *Colpocephalum* sp. was found on mourning doves in Illinois (Hanson et al. 1957). There are many species of *Colpocephalum*, most of which have been reported from domestic pigeons (Emerson 1972). Although identification of the species of lice from mourning doves requires taxonomic expertise, at least one species, *Columbicola macrourae*, can be easily recognized by its long, slender, dark-bodied appearance. *Columbicola macrourae* probably is common in mourning doves throughout the United States and not very host-specific, since many other columbiforms have been infested with this ectoparasite (Emerson 1972). *Bonomiella columbae* and *P. zenaidurae* have been reported previously from the domestic pigeon (Emerson 1972).

Greiner (1975) found a variety of blood-sucking diptera that fed on mourning doves, including the mosquitoes *Culex tarsalis*, *C. pipiens*, *Orthopodomyia signifera* and *Aedes trivitattus*, the biting midges *Culicoides haematopotus* and *C. crepuscularis*, the black fly *Simulium aureum*, and the hippoboscid flies *Stilbometopa podopostyla* and *Microlynchia pusilla*. Other hippoboscid flies reported from mourning doves are *Ornithoica confluenta*, *O. vicinia* and *Lynchia americana* (Herman 1937, Bequaert 1956, Main and Anderson 1970). Blood-sucking larvae of the blowfly *Protocalliphora asiovora* have been reported from nests of mourning doves in California (Sabrosky et al. 1988). There probably are many

Lesions on the leg of an injured mourning dove squab caused by blood-sucking larvae of the blowfly *Protocalliphora*. Although rarely reported in doves and considered nonpathogenic, blowfly larvae occasionally cause death in young birds either outright or by weakening the body's defense system and thereby allowing other debilitating factors to prove fatal. *Photo courtesy of the U.S. National Archives.*

other blood-sucking diptera that feed on mourning doves in other areas of the United States. The importance of these flies with regard to the health of mourning doves lies in their potential as vectors of pathogenic organisms.

VIRUSES

Avian Pox

Avian pox is a viral infection of birds that results in lesions on the skin and/or mucous membranes of the mouth and upper respiratory tract (Karstad 1971). Related strains of the virus have been known for some time to affect a variety of wild and domestic birds (Karstad 1971), and it appears that several strains of pox exist, each with different effects on certain host species. Avian pox was first reported in hunter-killed mourning doves from Illinois (Kossack and Hanson 1954). Since then, numerous reports of the virus infecting mourning doves have been published.

In mourning doves, the pox virus is manifested in two forms—cutaneous and diphtheritic. A mourning dove may have cutaneous pox, diphtheritic pox or both. Cutaneous pox is the most common and noticeable form because it is characterized by variable-sized nodules around the eyes, at the base of the beak, on top of the head and on the legs and feet (Locke et al. 1960a). These nodules range from 0.04- by 0.08-inches (1 by 2 mm) thickenings of the lower eyelid to large growths 0.4 inches (1 cm) in diameter (Locke et al. 1960a). Large, crusty nodules about the eyes and base of the bill are most serious since they may occlude vision, resulting in death through starvation. The lesions also are subject to secondary invasion by bacteria and fungi, which in turn may increase the severity of pox infection. If a mourning dove can survive the initial stages of infection, the nodules eventually will regress and/or drop off after some time, leaving the bird with a degree of protective immunity to further infection (Karstad 1971).

The diphtheritic form of pox is characterized by small, yellowish, diamond-shaped lesions in the back of the mouth, which may eventually develop into larger masses (Locke et al. 1960a). Severe diphtheritic lesions closely resemble the typical lesions caused by virulent forms of *Trichomonas gallinae* and can be equally lethal. Therefore, laboratory procedures are necessary to differentiate diphtheritic pox and virulent *T. gallinae* lesions (Locke et al. 1960b). Avian pox can be confirmed via histological procedures that reveal intracytoplasmic inclusion bodies in the cells of the infected host

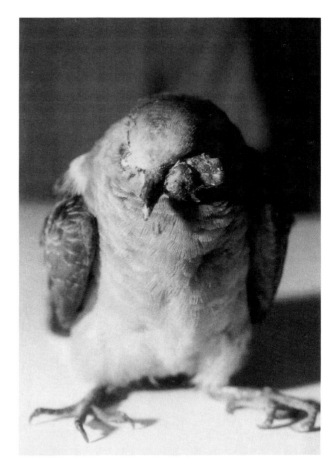

Cutaneous infection is the most common form of the avian pox virus in mourning doves. Lesions are nodules around the eyes, beak, top of the head, legs and feet. The size of the nodule may restrict the bird's movements or senses and thereby reduce its vitality and ability to survive. Such lesions also are prone to secondary bacterial or fungal infections. If the stricken dove can survive these impacts, the nodules eventually regress or drop off. *Photo courtesy of the University of Florida Laboratory of Wildlife Disease Research.*

tissue. Lack of inclusion bodies in a dove with lesions where *T. gallinae* organisms also are present may implicate the flagellate as responsible, but bacteria and fungi must be considered as well. Isolation of the *T. gallinae* organism in pure culture and experimental demonstration of its virulence in known clean birds are suggested to aid in a definitive diagnosis (Kocan and Herman 1971).

Avian pox is highly contagious, and susceptible birds can become infected either through mechanical transmission by mosquitoes, hippoboscid flies or biting midges or from direct or indirect contact with the virus through other infected birds or contaminated objects (Karstad 1971). Although the virus is unable to penetrate unbroken skin, small abrasions due to minor injuries are sufficient to permit infection (Locke et al. 1960b, Karstad 1971).

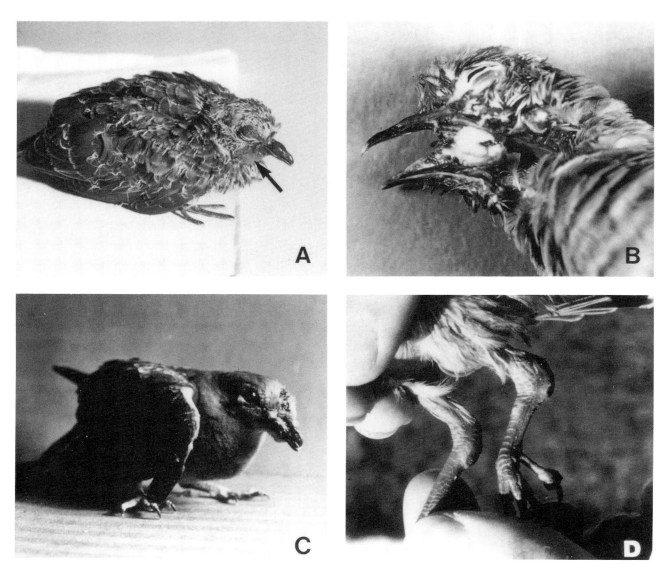

Laboratory investigation, including histological procedures, is needed to differentiate between lesions of virulent *Trichomonas gallinae* and diphtheritic pox. Shown above are a mourning dove nestling (A) and adult (B) with virulent *T. gallinae*. The nestling is in depressed condition, with swelling (arrow) in the upper esophagus. The incised mouth and esophagus of the adult reveal a yellow, cheeselike lesion. Also shown is an adult mourning dove (C) with a severe cutaneous avian pox infection, evidenced by nodules on the lower eyelid and around the base of the beak. A mourning dove's legs and toes (D) also may be affected by avian pox virus. *Photos courtesy of the University of Florida Laboratory of Wildlife Disease Research and the Southeastern Cooperative Wildlife Disease Study, University of Georgia.*

There is some evidence that the peak of infection in wild populations of mourning doves may be in September or October (Winston 1951, Blankenship et al. 1966). Avian pox infections of wild turkeys in Florida have been observed mostly during the months of September through December—a period that also corresponded with population peaks of two species of mosquitoes capable (proven experimentally) of transmitting this virus (Akey et al. 1981). In addition, a study in Michigan showed the population of a species of hippoboscid fly—another potential vector of avian pox—to peak in autumn,

which also corresponded with the peak occurrence of a common blood parasite found in pigeons (Klei and DeGiusti 1975). It could be that the combined autumn factors of highest populations and concentrations of doves, due to both reproduction and migration, and highest peaks of potential vector abundance result in higher rates of transmission and therefore peak infection of avian pox during this time period.

Avian pox infection in mourning doves is geographically widespread and probably occurs throughout a major portion of the species' range.

As Locke (1961: 212) noted, "the occurrence of pox infection has ranged from isolated, infected birds shot by hunters to severe, decimating epizootics, primarily among captive mourning doves." Although effects of this viral disease on populations of mourning doves in the wild may or may not be significant, biologists should continuously monitor the occurrence and severity of these infections to help ascertain their role as a mortality factor.

Other Viruses

Only a few other attempts at identifying viruses from mourning doves are recorded, most of which concern human or domestic animal implications, without mention of the pathologic effects on the doves themselves. Carpenter et al. (1972) tested sera from one hundred doves in Oklahoma for eastern equine, western equine, St. Louis and California group (La Crosse) encephalitis viruses, two strains of Newcastle disease virus, a paramyxovirus (Yucaipa), and three strains of influenza type-A virus. No antibodies were detected and Carpenter et al. concluded that, from a public and animal health viewpoint, the doves were not an important reservoir for these pathogens. Bigler et al. (1975) tested sera from wild mourning doves in Florida for arbovirus antibodies from 1965 to 1974. Everglades and western equine encephalitis virus antibodies were not detected via hemagglutination inhibition (HI) tests of 3,616 and 21 mourning dove serum samples, respectively. Of 3,637 dove serum samples tested for St. Louis encephalitis antibody, 10 were HI reactive, with 5 of those confirmed by serum neutralization (SN) tests. The same number of dove serum samples was tested for eastern equine encephalitis antibody and showed HI reactivity in only 4 samples. In an earlier serosurvey conducted in Florida in 1962, Jennings et al. (1969) found St. Louis encephalitis virus to be fairly common (31 [28 percent] infected of 111 examined) in mourning doves from the Tampa Bay area, where an outbreak in the human population had been observed concurrently. Alexander et al. (1981) isolated five viruses via cloacal swabs of 114 doves from Tennessee in 1975. The five were shown to be a new serologically distinct group of related avian paramyxoviruses and were designated as PMV-7.

BACTERIA

Very little is known about bacterial organisms harbored by mourning doves. Hanson and Kossack (1963) reported paracolon bacteria from the cloacas

of three mourning doves from Illinois. However, there is only one survey—involving one hundred doves from Oklahoma—where extensive microbiological studies were conducted (Carpenter et al. 1972). Cultures were made from the nasal sinuses, tracheae, lungs, air sacs, intestines and cloacas to determine the presence of bacterial pathogens. No organisms were isolated from the respiratory tracts of 15 percent of the birds; however, twelve types of respiratory bacteria were found in the remainder. The greatest frequency of isolation occurred in the tracheae, followed by the lungs. No bacterial growth was found in 71 percent of the nasal sinuses. The most common respiratory bacteria isolated were *Moraxella*-like and *Pasteurella*-like organisms in 47 percent and 37 to 59 percent of the doves, respectively. An unidentified gram-negative rod and a *Herellea*-like organism were the next most common bacteria (28 percent and 25 percent prevalences, respectively). The latter two organisms were considered insignificant in the overall flora of the respiratory tracts of mourning doves. The remaining bacterial types with even lower prevalences were *Mycoplasma* spp. (19 percent), *Micrococcus* spp. (19 percent), *Corynebacterium* spp. (12 percent), *Bacillus* spp. (4 percent) and a few other types of unidentified bacteria with varying degrees of prevalence. It should be noted that none of the organisms was considered pathogenic and that none of the infected doves displayed clinical signs or exhibited gross lesions. However, this does not mean that the organisms are incapable of producing disease. The *Mycoplasma* spp. isolated from 19 percent of the doves were determined serologically to be neither *M. gallisepticum* nor *M. meleagridis*, two species causing much concern in the domestic poultry industry (Yoder et al. 1978).

The cloacal and intestinal swabs from the one hundred doves were cultured to detect *Salmonella* spp. and *Paracolobactrum arizonae* (Carpenter et al. 1972). Although no isolations were found, the authors speculated that transmission of the pathogenic *Salmonella* bacteria by doves would seem possible. Kocan and Locke (1974) reported the first and only instance of *Salmonella typhimurium* var. *copenhagen* in a mourning dove from Maryland. The dove was unable to fly and died in captivity. Postmortem examination revealed an enlarged, pulpy spleen and yellowish liver with small white spots; bacteria were cultured from both organs. *Salmonella* spp. have been isolated from other columbiforms (Kocan and Locke 1974), and one species was considered responsible for a significant white-winged dove die-off in Arizona (Stair 1959). This die-off occurred in a very densely populated white-winged dove nesting area where mourning doves also were abundant. Although mourning doves were unaffected, the *Salmonella meleagridis* organism resulted in a caseous ulcerative enteritis in the white-winged doves, which led to extreme emaciation and death.

RICKETTSIA

Carpenter et al. (1972) also serologically tested the one hundred doves for *Chlamydia*, commonly known as the psittacosis or ornithosis disease agent. Although *Chlamydia* antibodies were not found in the mourning doves, naturally acquired infections in other doves and pigeons do occur (Burkhart and Page 1971). The organism was directly implicated in unusual die-offs of juvenile white-winged doves in the Lower Rio Grande Valley of Texas in 1959 and 1961 (Grimes et al. 1966).

FUNGI

Kocan and Hasenclever (1972) reported several species of mycotic organisms from the upper digestive tract in nine (24 percent) of thirty-seven mourning doves from Maryland and South Carolina. Of

the infected doves, six harbored *Candida albicans* and one each carried *C. tropicalis, C. guilliermondii* and *Geotrichum* sp.

In the same study, five other species of fungi were found in six other species of columbiforms. Pigeons and mourning doves harbored the greatest number of different organisms, and *Candida albicans* was the most frequently encountered species. Most of the species of fungi isolated from columbiforms are capable of producing disease, but they probably remain harmless in healthy birds. Kocan and Hasenclever (1972) reported no evidence of disease in any of the columbiforms they examined that harbored mycotic organisms. They expressed concern over the potential role of urban-dwelling feral pigeons as reservoir hosts in the potential spread of *C. albicans* to humans.

ENVIRONMENTAL CONTAMINANTS

Lead

Lead shot ingestion by various species of waterfowl in North America has received much attention because of the harmful toxic effects and mortality produced in these birds (Bellrose 1959). There are

Where mourning doves are trapped for research purposes, bait sites should be cleaned periodically and rotated frequently to minimize the possibility of establishing specific foci for parasite and disease transmission. Cleaning and rotation times could be every few days or every few weeks, as this is a subjective measure dependent on trapping success and the resulting bait site conditions. In general, any large buildup of dove feces at the bait site is to be avoided. Also, it may help to scrub the wire cages with a strong disinfectant on occasion, especially after capturing doves with open wounds due to trap conditions or those with obvious lesions due to avian pox infection. The bottoms of cages with wire bottoms especially should be scrubbed, since fecal matter can adhere to the wires. *Photo by Don Wooldridge; courtesy of the Missouri Department of Conservation.*

increasing reports of lead shot and lead poisoning in various species of upland gamebirds. For example, lead poisoning was suspected to be responsible for the deaths of some of a group of twenty-five mourning doves that died over a two-day period during 1985 in Las Cruces, New Mexico (National Wildlife Health Research Center 1985b).

One of the earliest reports of lead shot in mourning doves was by McClure (1950b), who observed parent doves feeding lead pellets to nestlings and later found the pellets in the gizzards of the young birds. The first diagnosis of lead poisoning in a mourning dove was made by Locke and Bagley (1967) in Maryland. The dove was extremely emaciated and contained two lead pellets in its gizzard. The concentrations of lead in the liver and tibia were 75 ppm and 187 ppm (wet weight), respectively.

Locke and Bagley (1967) examined the gizzards of sixty-two other hunter-killed mourning doves obtained approximately twenty-five miles (40 km) from where the sick dove was found. Four (6.5 percent) of the gizzards contained one to three lead pellets, although the concentrations of lead in the livers of these birds were low, suggesting recent acquisition of the shot. Overall, concentrations of lead in forty of the sixty-two livers, including the four doves with lead shot, ranged from 0.4 to 14.0 ppm (wet weight). Bagley and Locke (1967) reported concentrations of lead in normal liver tissue of mourning doves as ranging from 0.4 to 7.0 ppm (wet weight). In an extensive study in Tennessee, 1 percent of 1,949 mourning doves contained ingested lead shot in their gizzards (Lewis and Legler 1968). The number of shot ingested generally ranged from one to five, although one dove had ingested twenty-four pellets. Lead concentrations in the gizzards of these birds ranged from 8.9 to 87.0 ppm (wet or dry weight not indicated in text).

Kendall and Scanlon (1979) found that 2.4 percent of 412 mourning doves from mid-Atlantic wildlife management areas had ingested at least one lead shot, although an additional 5 percent had elevated liver lead concentrations with no direct evidence of ingested shot. In a sample of mourning doves from Alabama, 1 percent of 469 contained a single ingested lead pellet in their gizzards (Buerger et al. 1983), but these birds were collected from an area that was hunted lightly. A single ingested lead pellet was found also in the gizzard of only 1 (0.24 percent) of 420 mourning doves examined from southeastern New Mexico, although liver analysis showed 20 (8 percent) of 250 contained concentrations of lead 3 ppm (wet weight) or greater, with 9 (3.6 percent) of those showing concentrations in excess of normal values (more than

7 ppm wet weight) (Best et al. in press).

Attempts to determine the extent of exposure of mourning doves to lead based on the presence of lead shot in the gizzard result only in conservative estimates. Lead pellets often are overlooked during gizzard analysis (Anderson and Havera 1985), and doves may eliminate or completely erode ingested lead shot prior to collection (Kendall 1980). In addition, mourning doves are susceptible to lead ingestion from their utilization of roadside grit contaminated with lead from automobile exhausts (Kendall and Scanlon 1979). Therefore, the reported percentages (range = 1.0 to 6.5 percent) of mourning doves with lead shot in the gizzard represent only minimum values with regard to actual lead exposure.

Experimental work has led to development of a new technique that can produce more accurate results concerning lead exposure in mourning doves. This technique allows researchers to diagnose as well as monitor concentrations of lead without having to kill the bird for either retrieval of lead shot or histological and chemical analyses of tissue. Kendall and Scanlon (1982) found that a sample of blood from a live dove could be assayed for an important enzyme necessary in heme biosynthesis, delta-aminolevulinic acid dehydratase (d-ALAD). Experimentally, they found that d-ALAD activity in the blood decreased as liver lead concentrations increased in lead-poisoned mourning doves. Therefore, deviation from normal d-ALAD activity in the blood could determine the seriousness of lead concentrations in mourning doves. Specifically, inhibition of heme biosynthesis (through decreased d-ALAD activity) greater than 75 percent of normal enzyme activity can result in serious consequences to the avian system (Kendall and Scanlon 1982).

Using pen-reared, lead-free mourning doves, George (1987) determined that 1,100 units represented the lower limit of normal d-ALAD values in mourning doves. When control and lead-treated (one number-8 shot) birds were compared, there were no differences in body weight, hemoglobin concentration or hematocrit; however, d-ALAD values of treated doves were only 8 percent of control birds within twenty-four hours of ingestion. The earliest d-ALAD activity in any treated bird exceeded 1,100 units was nine weeks post-treatment, while mean d-ALAD activity in treated birds exceeded 1,100 units at seventeen weeks post-treatment. In the same study, George (1987) examined free-flying doves in an attempt to correlate d-ALAD activity with femur lead content. Because of a lack of correlation, he suggested that, while d-ALAD activity is a sensitive indicator of relatively recent lead ingestion, it is not a reliable indicator of total body lead burden. Nevertheless, George emphasized the usefulness of this technique in obtaining more accurate results than those obtained from gizzard analysis. Of 102 free-flying doves, 16 percent had d-ALAD activity below 1,100 units, indicating recent lead exposure, as compared with the 1.0- to 6.5-percent range produced by the gizzard analysis studies mentioned previously.

The concern stimulated by findings of lead shot in upland gamebirds has resulted in some experimental studies on the effects of lead poisoning in mourning doves. McConnell (1967) force-fed one to thirty-five lead pellets to thirty-four mourning doves of various ages and sexes. Thirteen (38 percent) of the doves exhibited signs of sickness and eleven (32 percent) died; young doves had a higher mortality rate than did older doves. Doves died with as few as five lead pellets in their gizzards, although one dove survived the ingestion of twenty pellets. The signs of lead poisoning in the experimental doves included loss of weight, weakness, lethargy and in some cases diarrhea. The first signs of sickness occurred on the fourth day, and the first death occurred on the sixth day after the lead pellets were ingested.

Histologically, Kendall et al. (1983) showed that mourning doves poisoned experimentally with lead developed hemosiderosis in the liver and acid-fast intranuclear inclusion bodies in epithelial cells of the proximal convoluted tubules of the kidney. These lesions are typical for other avian species with lead poisoning. The histological findings as reported by Kendall et al. (1983), as well as the concentrations of lead in tissues of the same experimental mourning doves, correspond with the histological findings and toxicologic concentrations in the wild lead-poisoned mourning dove reported by Locke and Bagley (1967). The study by Kendall et al. (1983) also showed that inclusion bodies of the proximal convoluted tubule cells in the kidney were primarily intracytoplasmic several days after lead shot ingestion; they became predominantly intranuclear after several more days. This phenomenon may be important in the diagnosis of lead poisoning in specimens of other avian species that are collected shortly after ingesting lead shot.

Stress and diet may augment the deleterious effects of lead toxicity in mourning doves. In an experimental study, Kendall et al. (1981) reported mortality of five (71 percent) of seven ringed turtledoves that ingested lead shot and were exposed to cold temperatures, whereas lead-treated control doves not exposed to the cold survived despite the occurrence of seizures in several of the birds. Buerger et al. (1986) attributed a high mortality rate (45 percent of seventy-five mourning doves fed one

to four lead shot) in their experimental birds (kept outdoors) to a combination of the stresses of winter and increased gizzard activity possibly associated with increased lead absorption due to the feeding of cracked corn. Marn et al. (1988) found that exposure to cold temperatures had little effect on mortality, body weight or concentration of lead in tissues of mourning doves dosed with lead. However, the type of diet did affect expulsion rates of lead shot as well as tissue concentrations of lead. The mixed seed diet resulted in an increased likelihood of lead shot expulsion, but this phenomenon was offset by nutritional and/or other factors that apparently increased absorption and/or retention of lead in body tissues.

Lead poisoning also may affect the reproductive potential of mourning doves. A histological study of lead-poisoned ringed turtledoves in the laboratory not only showed the typical lesions in the kidney and liver, as noted previously for mourning doves, but also showed lesions in the testes and inhibition of spermatogenesis in the seminiferous tubules (Kendall et al. 1981). In another study, the effects of lead ingestion on the reproductive characteristics of ringed turtledoves showed that lead treatment did not increase the time required to produce eggs, disrupt egg production or lessen the fertility of eggs (Kendall and Scanlon 1981a). However, it was noted that (1) weights of lead-dosed birds generally tended to be below those of the controls, (2) testes weights and spermatozoan numbers were lower in lead-treated males than in controls, and (3) lead was transmitted from adults to juveniles via the egg and probably by feeding of crop milk. Adult females had more than ten times the bone lead concentration of males, which may have been influenced by active bone metabolism during egg laying. Although offspring of lead-treated parents had higher tissue lead concentrations than did controls, packed cell volumes and body weight gains in the juveniles were not affected. Buerger et al. (1986) found no mortality in twenty-five breeding female mourning doves fed one lead pellet each and no significant effects on egg measurements, productivity, fertility or squab weights. However, the hatchability of eggs was affected because of early embryonic mortality of the young of lead-treated doves.

The forementioned experimental studies of ringed turtledoves provided insight into the possible deleterious effects of chronic lead ingestion in breeding populations of mourning doves (Kendall and Scanlon 1981a). Although the data were inconclusive, results of field studies may indicate that lead shot ingestion adversely affected survival of treated doves (Carrington and Mirarchi 1989).

Mourning doves are at risk from ingestion of lead from either contaminated roadside grit or spent lead shot (Kendall and Scanlon 1979, Kendall 1980). In terms of dosage, the ingestion of spent lead shot is far more significant and poses more immediate danger than does the ingestion of contaminated roadside grit (George 1987). In a Tennessee field with an eight-year history of managed public dove shooting, the top 0.37 inches (0.95 cm) of soil contained 10,890 shot per acre (26,909/ha) prehunt and 43,560 shot per acre (107,637/ha) posthunt (Lewis and Legler 1968). In Indiana, where the top 0.5 inches (1.3 cm) of soil from thirteen fields was sampled both before and after the hunting season, shot densities increased by 645 percent "from 3,311 to 24,665 shot/ha" (Castrale 1989: 185). In southeastern New Mexico, estimates of 67,823 and 348,108 lead shot per acre (167,593 and 860,185/ha) in the upper 5.1 inches (13 cm) of soil were reported for August and October, respectively (Best et al. in press).

Discing or plowing a field soon after hunting may reduce the amount of shot available at the surface (see Fredrickson et al. 1977, Castrale 1989), but the substantial accumulation of lead in uncultivated fields as reported in these studies represents a potential threat to populations of mourning doves. There is evidence that steel shot can be just as effective as lead shot in hunting mourning doves (Kringer et al. 1980), and the use of such shot should be encouraged on heavily hunted areas to prevent or correct lead-poisoning hazards for mourning doves and other avian species.

Pesticides and Other Contaminants

Much attention has been given to chemical contamination of the environment, in light of the effects various chemicals can have on domestic animals, wildlife and ultimately humans. Organochlorine insecticides—such as DDT and its metabolites, aldrin, dieldrin, chlordane, benzene hexachloride (lindane), heptachlor and toxaphene—were widely used after World War II. However, their use has declined rapidly since 1970, having been largely replaced by such organophosphates as parathion, malathion, fenthion and diazinon. Polychlorinated biphenyl (PCB) compounds are used in industry but contaminate the environment in the manufacture and disposal process via accidental leakage, spillage and vaporization (Zinkl 1982).

Organophosphates degrade quickly in nature, but both organochlorines and PCBs are very persistent in the environment, where they can remain for years. They can be stored in the body fat of many animals and undergo biomagnification through the food chain, with the highest concentrations then occurring in the summit predators and scavengers (Zinkl 1982). While acute poisoning with organophosphates, organochlorines or PCBs results in neurologic signs, chronic poisoning by the latter two causes degenerative changes in body organs. Trace amounts of pesticides in animal tissues are common.

Organochlorines. Kreitzer (1974) examined samples of breast muscle from 145 mourning doves from fifteen eastern states and found residues of DDT, DDT metabolites and heptachlor epoxide in all of the birds; seventy-three contained dieldrin. Relatively small amounts of residue were found in all doves. Low concentrations of organochlorine insecticides also were reported by Edwards et al. (1983) in 8 mourning doves from Illinois that contained heptachlor epoxide, dieldrin and DDE, but not heptachlor or aldrin.

In a series of experiments, Young et al. (1952) exposed mourning doves to varying dosages of the organochlorine insecticides benzene hexachloride, toxaphene, dieldrin and aldrin under simulated field conditions. Although routine field application of benzene hexachloride and toxaphene did not cause any serious effects in the doves, dieldrin and aldrin were found to be extremely toxic.

In experimental testing of the acute toxicities of certain insecticides, Dahlen and Haugen (1954) found mourning doves to be three times as resistant as were bobwhite quail to any toxicant tested. Medium lethal doses—in milligrams per kilogram—for mourning doves were: aldrin, 15 to 17; dieldrin, 44 to 46; toxaphene, 200 to 250; and lindane, 350 to 400.

Erling (1957) believed that at least fifteen hundred white-winged doves and a much smaller number of mourning doves died after some fields in Arizona were aerially dusted with a mixture of DDT and lindane. Hunt (1966a) reported insignificant effects on the nesting success of mourning doves in California exposed to DDT in a mixture with several organophosphates for pesticide treatment in pear culture. Flickinger and King (1972) reported that, from 1967 to 1971, ten mourning doves from two areas of the Texas Gulf Coast were found dead in or near rice fields treated with aldrin. Analysis of certain tissues from two of these doves revealed concentrations of dieldrin, endrin, and DDT and its metabolites as well (Flickinger and King 1972).

Polychlorinated biphenyls. Kreitzer (1974) found small amounts of PCB residue in samples of breast muscle from 145 mourning doves representing fifteen eastern states. Edwards et al. (1983) reported low concentrations (0.4 ppm) in the fat of 8 mourning doves from Illinois. Tori and Mayer (1981) experimented with the effects of PCBs on the metabolic rates of mourning doves exposed to low ambient temperatures. They attributed PCB-induced reductions of metabolic rates and body temperatures to a possible breakdown in the thermoregulatory ability of doves. This could affect the survival of PCB-exposed doves in periods of inclement winter weather (Tori and Mayer 1981).

Tori and Peterle (1983) found that PCBs significantly altered the courtship behavior and reproductive effort in mourning doves. Doves treated with 10 ppm PCB spent twice as much time in courtship behavior as did control doves and had a 50-percent laying success rate (compared with 100 percent in the controls). Similar results were obtained by Koval et al. (1987), who additionally reported slightly lower plasma progesterone concentrations in PCB-treated doves during the reproductive cycle, as well as delayed oviposition of treated doves following the progesterone peak. Koval et al. concluded that sublethal PCB ingestion by mourning doves resulted in a general decrease in reproductive efficiency.

Organophosphates and carbamates. Organophosphate and carbamate pesticides are potent anticholinesterase substances that have been known to kill large numbers of wild birds (Hill 1988). Based on seven healthy mourning doves, Hill (1988) listed the mean normal whole brain cholinesterase activity for this species to be sixteen (SD = 1.0) micromoles of acetylthiocholine iodide hydrolyzed per minute per gram of tissue, wet weight. The median lethal dosage that produces 50-percent mortality (or LD50) in experimental populations has been determined in mourning doves for two organophosphate insectides (fenthion 2.50 to 2.68 mg/kg and phosphamidon 2.0 to 4.0 mg/kg) and two carbamate insecticides (mexacarbate 2.83 mg/kg, and propoxur 4.20 mg/kg) (Tucker and Crabtree 1970, Hudson et al. 1984).

Hunt (1966a) reported insignificant effects on the nesting success of mourning doves in California exposed to the organophosphates diazinon, azinphosmethyl and parathion in a mixture with the organochlorine DDT. Niethammer and Baskett (1983) found no discernible brain cholinesterase inhibition in five mourning doves from Missouri exposed to the organophosphate methyl parathion mixed with the organochlorine toxaphene, although inhibition was noted in red-winged blackbirds and dickcissels. Stone (1979) reported the deaths of hundreds of birds, mostly mourning doves, in an area where a farmer was suspected of poisoning depredatory birds. Corn in the crops of these birds contained high residues of parathion (142 ppm) and some methyl parathion (0.5 ppm). Mourning dove was one of the principal species involved in the mortality of five hundred birds in Massachusetts due to parathion (National Wildlife Health Research Center 1982). The extremely toxic insecticide parathion has been used to poison pest species of birds. Also, it has been implicated as the causative agent for unintentional wildlife die-offs more often than has any other organophosphate (Smith 1987).

Smith (1987) alluded to an unpublished account of a die-off of mourning doves due to the organophosphate fensulfothion and cited a study where adult and nestling mourning doves in a lemon grove were not poisoned by a ground application (unspecified rate) of phosphamidon (see also Sachsse and Voss 1971). Smith (1987) also reported that monocrotophos was detected in the gastrointestinal tracts of mourning doves that were found dead near an area where chemicals were used to kill birds. In this instance, the brain cholinesterase activity in the doves examined was inhibited 85 to 92 percent. In Texas, mourning doves were among the eleven hundred birds representing twelve species that died from ingestion of rice seed illegally treated with dicrotophos or monocrotophos and placed near rice fields as bait to attract and kill birds (Flickinger et al. 1984).

In another report from Texas, mourning doves were collected by shotgun from six agricultural fields and checked for brain cholinesterase activity after having been exposed to the organophosphates sulprofos, EPN-methyl parathion, azinphos-methyl and monocrotophos (Custer and Mitchell 1987). Mean brain cholinesterase activity of doves was not significantly different from the mean control values following application of sulprofos, EPN-methyl parathion and azinphos-methyl. However, mean brain cholinesterase activity of doves from two of three collections was significantly lower than the mean control values following application of monocrotophos. Custer and Mitchell (1987) reported no observable deaths from application of all these organophosphates but found one immature dove that appeared to be sick, apparently too young to escape during the application of monocrotophos. This dove had a brain cholinesterase inhibition of 81 percent. Monocrotophos also was responsible for the deaths of twenty-five hundred birds in Arizona, most of which were mourning doves (National Wildlife Health Research Center 1980).

With regard to carbamate pesticides, Schafer et al. (1975) found that exposure of mourning doves to methiocarb (sometimes used as a bird repellent) under experimental conditions could result in acute toxicity. However, chronic toxicity appeared to be noncumulative. It would be nearly impossible for doves to consume lethal doses of methiocarb under field conditions, even if minimal alternate food sources were available. Schafer et al. (1975) also determined that methiocarb had no effect on the reproductive parameters of breeding coturnix quail in the laboratory, but it is not known what reproductive effects this carbamate might have on mourning doves. Another carbamate, carbofuran, was responsible for the deaths of more than one hundred birds in New York, including mourning doves, when the victims ingested wheat that was purposely poisoned with this chemical (Stone 1979). Stone reported carbofuran concentrations of 4.6 to 17.0 ppm in the gizzards and 1.7 to 21.0 ppm in the livers of the mourning doves he examined.

Even though mourning doves are reasonably resistant to chemical contamination via pesticides and herbicides, government restriction on certain highly toxic organochlorines certainly has not hurt the species. The fact that chemical residue buildups are not found frequently in mourning doves may very well be correlated with the doves' high annual turnover rate. This is encouraging news for consumers of the birds' flesh. *Photo by Don L. Braithwaite; courtesy of the U.S. Soil Conservation Service.*

Carbofuran also was used illegally to kill birds feeding on newly planted rice seed in Texas, resulting in the deaths of four mourning doves and over one hundred other birds representing ten species (Flickinger et al. 1986). At least three hundred birds, of which the mourning dove was one of the principal species involved, were killed by carbofuran in Illinois (National Wildlife Health Research Center 1984). The carbamate oxamyl killed 186 mourning doves in Tennessee (National Wildlife Health Research Center 1983).

Miscellaneous contaminants. Kreitzer (1974) reported that all 145 mourning doves he examined from fifteen eastern states showed residues of mercury in samples of breast muscle; 8 (5.5 percent) contained residues of mirex. The amount of residue in both instances was considered insignificant. Contrary to this finding, mercury residues above the minimum concentrations established for safe human consumption were reported in samples of tissue from mourning doves collected in an agricultural area of southern Georgia (Browning 1979). Residues of four other major pesticides also were found in doves from this area, where an increase in the use of chemical pesticides had been noted (Browning 1979). Flickinger and King (1972) reported mercury in the kidney of a mourning dove from Texas.

The use of strychnine for bird control was believed responsible for the unintentional poisoning of twenty-six mourning doves in South Dakota (Jonkel 1967) and possibly forty doves in California (Hunt 1966b). Tucker and Crabtree (1970) reported the LD50 for strychnine in mourning doves to be greater than 5.1 mg/kg. A starling and blackbird control program in Arizona, to prevent the spread of coccidiosis among cattle, led to the deaths of more than a thousand mourning doves and possibly many more after the use of Starlicide DRC-1339 (R. E. Tomlinson personal communication: 1986).

Thallium-treated grain to control ground squirrels in California resulted in the deaths of more than three thousand mourning doves (Linsdale 1931). The use of sodium monofluoroacetate, or 1080, also to control ground squirrels in California, apparently had no effect on mourning doves (Hegdal et al. 1986). No effect of this compound on mourning doves was noted earlier by Keyes (1945). The experimentally established LD50 for 1080 in mourning doves is low enough (8.5 to 14.6 mg/kg) to result in losses of doves feeding on 1080-treated bait in the wild (Tucker and Crabtree 1970, Hegdal et al. 1986). However, after finding only a few dead mourning doves following a 1080 baiting, Spencer (1945) observed that the compound often acted as an emetic to mourning doves. This information might help to explain the apparent harmlessness of 1080 to mourning doves alluded to earlier.

Experimental studies with the bird-frightening agent 4-aminopyridine resulted in acute toxicity in mourning doves at certain concentrations, but no cumulative toxicity was noted during long-term exposure (Schafer and Marking 1975). Schafer and Marking felt that the registered application rate of this chemical could not adversely affect populations of mourning doves.

With the advent and development of nuclear facilities, radionuclides have received much attention as potential environmental contaminants. Markham and Halford (1982) reported on concentrations of radionuclides in 252 mourning doves collected near nuclear facilities in Idaho. Cesium-137 was the radionuclide most commonly found in the tissues of doves. Twenty other radionuclides also were detected but with much lower frequencies of occurrence and concentrations. Samples of muscle tissue from all of the 252 doves yielded concentrations of cesium-137 ranging from less than 0.40 pCi/g (the minimum detectable concentration) to 171 pCi/g. Cesium-137 concentrations were highest in doves collected at two particular nuclear facility sites where contamination from atmospheric and liquid sources was very likely. For example, mean concentrations of cesium-137 at these two sites over a four-year period ranged from 0.84 to 15.85 pCi/g as compared to the mean concentrations ranging from 0.44 to 0.75 pCi/g at the control site. Markham and Halford (1982) also determined that the doses received by mourning doves were low compared with results obtained from birds and mammals in other studies, and that the concentrations would not be expected to produce any radiation hazard to doves. Dose rates ranged from less than 0.01 to 3.20 mrad per day, and the highest doses occurred at the two nuclear facility sites noted earlier.

If a human consumed a dove containing the maximum concentration of cesium-137, the potential radiation dose to that individual would be only 0.30 mrem. Since the maximum permissible whole-body dose commitment to individuals in a population is 500 mrem per year, the potential radiation dose to humans from the consumption of doves was considered to be negligible (Markham and Halford 1982). In addition, Markham and Halford reported that the half-life of cesium-137 probably is similar to that in other birds (somewhere between six and eleven days), and that doves may quickly eliminate cesium-137 once they have moved from the contaminated environment.

Isolated instances of acute mortality in mourning doves from chemical application do not pose a serious threat to the continental population. In cases where it does occur, numerous methods of chemical application exist that can circumvent most acute intoxication of nontarget species, such as the use of specific bait, specific placement and safe dilution rates (Schafer and Marking 1975). Since doves have a high annual mortality rate and are migratory in nature, it is difficult to say whether the liberal use of long-lasting insecticides and other chemicals has had or can have any serious effect on the species today. As mentioned previously, doves sampled usually exhibit only trace amounts of residue in their tissues. It should be noted also that eggshell thickness has been used as a measure to determine chronic exposure and toxicity in individual avian species, and the thickness of mourning dove eggs collected in widely distributed states in 1969 and 1970 had not changed significantly from the thickness of eggshells taken during the period 1861–1935 (Kreitzer 1971). Despite these indications, continuing studies are important in order to shed more light on the possible interactions of various concentrations of chemical residues with other aspects of mourning dove biology, such as behavior, reproduction and infectious diseases.

SUMMARY

It is evident that mourning doves are exposed to a wide variety of infectious and noninfectious disease agents. Although deaths from some of these agents are unavoidable, certain management practices may reduce the likelihood of large-scale mortality. Most importantly, large concentrations of doves ought to be discouraged when possible in order to decrease the chances of widespread contamination with any infectious disease agent. This strategy is particularly appropriate for the parasitic disease agents but may be effective in limiting the spread of viruses, bacteria and fungi as well. While apparent difficulties exist in controlling such noninfectious disease agents as lead shot, insecticides and other chemicals, certain common sense measures can be taken to minimize the risks of exposure to these elements.

Finally, continued research is necessary to understand the relationship between disease and mourning dove population levels. This is particularly true for the two disease agents considered to be the most pathogenic for doves—the protozoan *Trichomonas gallinae* and the avian pox virus. The mourning dove does not appear to be a reservoir for serious infectious diseases or chemical contamination transmissible to domestic animals and/or humans.

Chapter 13

Other Natural Mortality

Kenneth C. Sadler
Wildlife Division
Missouri Department of Conservation
Columbia, Missouri

There is no doubt that the mourning dove is the most sought-after and harvested gamebird in the United States. Hunter harvest and crippling loss are estimated to be approximately 70 million birds each year (see chapter 24). Despite this prodigious annual kill, all available evidence indicates that nonhunting mortality is four to five times that attributable to hunting. Included in the list of "natural" causes of mortality are weather, predators and accidents of all types, as well as those related to disease, parasites and poison as discussed in chapter 12.

Unfortunately, there is no way at present to put the various forms of natural mortality into a meaningful order of importance or, indeed, to ameliorate these losses significantly. Most natural mortality factors are beyond the control of even the most advanced scientific management.

Although banding records permit measurement of disappearance rates of banded birds and enable monitoring of overall mortality rates, they are inadequate to determine the relative importance of various causes of natural mortality. The problem results because of (1) very little information about how nonhunting mortality occurs and (2) biases frequently associated with reporting of bands, i.e., whether or not a banded bird is apt to be found and reported. Typically, more banded doves are reported as "found dead," with no explanation of the probable cause, than all those reported with the cause of death known or suspected *(Table 30)*.

Losses of banded mourning doves directly associated with human activities, such as hunting, predation by pets, motor vehicle strikes, etc., are far more likely to be observed and reported than are losses caused by unfavorable weather, disease or parasites. The tabular information in this chapter should be examined with these biases in mind.

Table 30. Sources of band recoveries from mourning doves.[a]

Source	Number	Percentage
Hunter harvest (shot)	46,625	90.302
No explanation (found dead)	2,708	5.245
Accident	944	1.828
Predation	577	1.118
Miscellaneous	528	1.023
Disease, parasites, poison	239	0.463
Illegal kill	11	0.021
Total	51,632	100.000

[a] From records to 1984 of the U.S. Fish and Wildlife Service's Bird Banding Laboratory, Patuxent Wildlife Research Center, Laurel, Maryland. A total of 85,808 bands were recovered to 1984, of which 51,632 included "how obtained" and "present condition" codes.

WINTER WEATHER

In addition to the disruption of nests and nesting activities caused by wind and rainstorms (La-Perriere 1972, Grand et al. 1984, see also chapter 5), severe winter weather also can be extremely damaging to local and even regional mourning dove populations. And by no means are winter losses limited to northern areas of the dove's range. By virtue of their higher winter densities, doves in southern and midlatitude states can be more vulnerable to heavy losses than those wintering in northern states. Severe winter weather of the type that can be fatal to mourning doves is less likely to occur in southern regions, but when these conditions occur, the results can be devastating. During one particularly severe blizzard in late January 1951, mourning doves suffered extensive losses across Arkansas, Kentucky, Tennessee, Alabama, Louisiana and Texas (Alexander 1951, Schultz 1954, Russell 1954, Swank 1955a, Newsom et al. 1957). Losses from the storm in some parts of Louisiana were estimated at 25 to 50 percent of the doves present (Newsom et al. 1953). Schultz (1954) estimated that more than sixty-three thousand dead doves were found in Tennessee after the storm; one can only speculate about the magnitude of unobserved losses. Winter storm-related losses of mourning doves also have been recorded during other years in Tennessee (Schultz 1954), Oklahoma (Sutton 1967, Morrison and Lewis 1975), North Carolina (Anonymous 1943), Iowa (Errington 1935), Ontario (Alison 1976, Armstrong and Noakes 1983) and Missouri (K. C. Sadler unpublished data).

In contrast to nonmigratory gamebirds, such as quail, wild turkey and pheasant, mourning doves are ineffective at scratching out foods covered by snow. Even light snow cover can put an immediate starvation stress on doves. Freezing rain and ice storms create an additional burden because the birds may be deprived of both food and water. Hanson and Kossack (1963) believed that conditions that deprive doves of food and water for a period of four days can cause extremely heavy mortality.

Although mourning doves six to nine days old challenged by 66-degree Fahrenheit (19° C) temperature showed an ability to increase their metabolic rates and maintain body temperatures (Breitenbach and Baskett 1967), fully feathered doves in Illinois responded to lowered temperatures by *reducing* their metabolic rates (Ivacic and Labisky 1973). This reduction in metabolic function resulted in a corresponding reduction in body temperatures. This same reaction to cold by doves was noted earlier by Hudson and Brush (1964). Many resident bird species respond to lowered ambient temperatures by *increasing* their metabolic rates and thereby maintaining body temperatures (Kendeigh 1944a, Seibert 1949, Dawson and Tordoff 1959, Misch 1960, Veghte 1964, Pohl 1969). Under some weather conditions, the lowering of metabolic rates and body temperatures might have survival advantages (i.e., conserving stored energy), provided that temperatures do not reach the critical point where normal body temperatures cannot be restored. Failure to maintain body temperature could explain the torpid condition often observed in doves during and immediately following severe winter weather, and why doves often seek shelter in sheds, in abandoned dwellings and under bridges.

Morrison and Lewis (1975: 75) provided a graphic description of how mourning doves in western Oklahoma reacted to severe winter conditions: "Cold returned at the end of December, a light snow fell on 3 January, then on 5 January a powerful blizzard swept in from the north. High winds brought in sleet which froze into a solid sheet of ice over the ground by 6 January, then about 10 cm of snow covered the ice. Cold temperatures and wind persisted for several days, and thousands of doves died in western Oklahoma. . . . On 5 and 6 January, doves seemed not to feed. A few were seen at cattle feed lots, but most of them sat torpidly in barns, sheds, hedge rows, and under piles of tumbleweeds along fences. Many doves simply sat and died in these shelters."

Rapid drops in temperature, particularly in association with freezing rain or snow, can cause extensive mortality to wintering mourning doves. Because adult doves attempt to overwinter farther north than do juveniles, they can be especially vulnerable during some years. One especially severe blizzard in January 1951 caused widespread losses across Kentucky, Tennessee, Alabama, Louisiana, Arkansas and Texas. Known losses in Tennessee alone exceeded 63,000 mourning doves. *Photo by Glenn D. Chambers; courtesy of the Missouri Conservation Department.*

Ivacic and Labisky (1973) believed that adult mourning doves, perhaps because of their age or size superiority, seemed physiologically better able to withstand the rigors of northern climates than were juveniles, especially juvenile females. Ivacic and Labisky reasoned that age and size advantages might explain wintering flocks of doves in Missouri that favored adults and males (see Chambers et al. 1962), higher autumn migration rates among juveniles in Massachusetts (see Austin 1951) and Missouri (see Tomlinson et al. 1960), greater attachment to northern breeding areas by adults (see Chambers et al. 1962) and greater tendency of males to winter farther north in North Carolina than do female doves (see Quay 1951a). Better resistance to cold temperatures by adults also may explain why mortality rates are higher among juvenile doves than for adults (Atkinson et al. 1982, Dunks et al. 1982).

That mourning doves frequently are subjected to damaging cold stress is further suggested by the number of doves with missing toes (Thompson 1950, Chambers 1961, Hennessy and Van Camp 1963, Nickell 1964, Alison 1976, Armstrong and Noakes 1983). Most reporters of this phenomenon believed that these "natural amputations" resulted from freezing. Brown (1980) observed a live mourning dove with its feet frozen to an icy road.

Mourning doves with missing toes are not uncommon. During the 1970 summer dove-trapping program in Missouri, 26 percent of the adults examined had at least one missing toe. During other years, adult doves with missing toes amounted to only 3 percent. *Photo by Robert A. Montgomery; courtesy of the Max McGraw Wildlife Foundation.*

During 1961 to 1973, records were compiled about the foot condition of adult doves in Missouri during preseason trapping, May through August (K. C. Sadler personal files). From a total of 5,634 adult doves examined (3,681 males and 1,953 females), 420 (11.4 percent) of the males and 143 (7.3 percent) of the females had at least one missing toe. Yearly means of adult doves with lost toes varied from 3 percent in 1966 to 26 percent in 1970.

Precise information is lacking on the magnitude of winter climate-related mortality of mourning doves across their range. There seems little doubt, however, that mourning doves are not physiologically well adapted to prolonged, severe cold temperatures, ice or snow; that they occasionally and perhaps frequently are subjected to conditions that cause the loss of one or more toes; and that widespread, heavy losses are known to have occurred. Tori and Mayer (1981) believed that PCB contamination could further reduce survival in cold-stressed mourning doves. Kreitzer (1974) examined a sample of doves from fifteen states in the eastern United States and found PCBs in all (see chapter 12).

PREDATORS

U.S. Fish and Wildlife Service records show that banded mourning doves reportedly have been killed by a wide variety of predators *(Table 31)*. Unfortunately, efforts to determine the comparative impacts of various predators on mourning doves are clouded by whether or not the acts of predation were witnessed by humans. For example, the number of banded doves recovered as a result of their being "caught by or due to the actions of a cat" places the domestic cat at the head of the predator list. However, domestic cats may have had no more impact on banded doves than raptors, simply because the probabilities of observing these two types

Table 31. Mourning dove band recoveries from predation.[a]

Source	Number	Percentage
Domestic cats	406	70.4
Domestic dogs	80	13.9
Raptors	53	9.2
Miscellaneous animals	29	5.0
Miscellaneous birds	6	1.0
Rodents	2	0.3
Fish	1	0.2
Total	577	100.0

[a] From records to 1984 of the U.S. Fish and Wildlife Service's Bird Banding Laboratory, Patuxent Wildlife Research Center, Laurel, Maryland.

of encounters are widely different. Cats usually remain fairly close to humans; hawks and owls do not. Undoubtedly, too, some bands have been reported when the carcass of a banded dove was found and brought to the owner's house by a well-fed cat. There is not intent here to minimize the losses of doves to predation by domestic cats, only to caution that direct comparisons among predator-related band recoveries—indeed all recoveries—may be misleading.

Of the 51,632 U.S. Fish and Wildlife Service dove bands recovered before 1984 and for which appropriate data were recorded, 577 (1.1 percent) were retrieved as a consequence of predation. Seventy percent of the bands recovered in this category resulted from encounters with domestic cats. Domestic dogs were associated with 80 (13 percent) of the predator-related recoveries. On the surface, at least, domestic cats seem to kill five times more doves than dogs do. Other predator-associated band recoveries were attributed to raptors (9 percent), miscellaneous animals (5 percent), other birds (1 percent), rodents (0.3 percent) and fish (0.1 percent). Some imagination is needed to visualize how a fish and a banded dove got together, to say

nothing of how the band was recovered from the fish.

Grand et al. (1984) provided some insight into the frequencies and causes of mortality of nestling and fledgling mourning doves in Alabama. Losses of these age groups were related to weather (33 percent), predation (30 percent), abandonment (2 percent) and unknown causes (35 percent). In that study, weather ceased to be a factor when the young birds passed two weeks of age. Avian predators accounted for 18 percent of all losses, while reptilian and mammalian predators accounted for 8 and 4 percent, respectively.

The literature also contains references to doves being preyed on by a gray rat snake (Mirarchi and Hitchcock 1982), a loggerhead shrike (Balda 1965), a marsh hawk (George 1951) and an American kestrel (Lesser 1966), and to an unsuccessful attack by a bullfrog (Blair 1967). J. A. Conti (personal communication: 1992) observed a green tree snake attempting to swallow a mourning dove egg.

Raptors and other birds reportedly have accounted for about 10 percent of predation mortality of mourning doves, based on band recoveries from dove carcasses for which cause of death was known. These data, however, do not reflect total predation, because the sampling included only banded birds and would not reflect the relatively high rate of avian predation on eggs and nestlings. At right, a wildlife researcher using radio telemetry tracked and located a radio-collared mourning dove killed by an unknown predator. Such radio transmitters are equipped with motion-sensitive switches that alter their pulse rates when tagged birds are inactive. This enables researchers to get to dead birds as quickly as possible before the carcasses are entirely destroyed. *Left photo by Joseph A. Conti; courtesy of the Southeastern Cooperative Wildlife Disease Study, University of Georgia, and the University of Florida Laboratory of Wildlife Disease Research. Right photo by Robert Ferguson; courtesy of the Missouri Department of Conservation.*

Rat snakes are predators of mourning dove eggs and nestlings in the southeastern United States. They also capture older doves, particularly hatching-year birds and incubating or brooding adults. The conspicuous bulge in the gray rat snake in the left scene represents a radio-tagged fledgling mourning dove. The right scene is the carcass of a mourning dove that a snake (species unidentified) attempted to swallow but could not. *Left photo by Ralph E. Mirarchi; courtesy of the Auburn University Department of Zoology and Wildlife Science and the Alabama Agricultural Experiment Station. Right photo by Ken Gamble; courtesy of the Texas Parks and Wildlife Department.*

ACCIDENTS

Banded mourning doves have been found and reported after their fatal encounters with a wide variety of fixed and moving objects *(Table 32)*. Quite certainly, many additional banded doves met similar fates and were never found or, if found, not reported. Collectively, accidental deaths accounted for 1.8 percent of all bands recovered prior to July 1984. Somewhat more than half of these accident-related recoveries resulted from dove encounters with motor vehicles or were from banded doves found near highways. Automobiles and trucks accounted for an overwhelming majority (97.5 percent) of the vehicle accidents; trains, aircraft and farm machinery contributed 0.7, 0.5 and 0.1 percent, respectively. Overhead wire and tower strikes accounted for 143 (15 percent) and 25 (3 percent), respectively, of recoveries associated with accidents. Injury-producing accidents from unknown causes accounted for 203 (21 percent) of the band recoveries. Other accidents resulted when banded birds were caught in traps (not for banding) (4 percent); became entangled in wire, fishing line, string, etc. (1 percent); or were killed during control operations for other bird species (1 percent).

Cowan (1952) observed the fatal injury of an adult dove that struck a barb on a barbed-wire fence, and Passmore (1980) examined a disabled dove with a sandbur-impacted esophagus.

Mourning doves appear to be no less vulnerable to accidents than most other avian species. Strikes by vehicles, for example, account for most recorded accidental deaths and injuries, but the location and nature of such deaths (frequently visible to humans) may exaggerate their perceived population influence. A mourning dove apparently was attracted to the sheen of tar at the La Brea tar pits in Los Angeles, California, and probably assumed it was landing in or next to water. *Photo courtesy of the George C. Page Museum.*

Table 32. Mourning dove band recoveries from accidents.[a]

Accident cause or source	Number	Percentage
Found near highways	257	27.2
Vehicle impact	255	27.0
Unspecified injury	203	21.5
Stationary object impact	143	15.2
Caught in traps, etc.	39	4.1
Electrical wire strike	25	2.7
Entanglement	9	1.0
Train impact	7	0.7
Aircraft impact	5	0.5
Farm machinery strike	1	0.1
Total	944	100.0

[a] From records to 1984 of the U.S. Fish and Wildlife Service's Bird Banding Laboratory, Patuxent Wildlife Research Center, Laurel, Maryland.

MISCELLANEOUS

Some mourning dove losses do not conveniently fit into any of the aforementioned categories. Collectively, these mortalities accounted for 1 percent of the total bands recovered (*Table 33*). Losses associated with dove trapping (for banding) accounted for 251 (50 percent) of these recoveries. An additional 165 (33 percent) banded doves were taken from the wild for study purposes. These two sets of figures likely are greatly magnified because their reporting rates probably were near 100 percent.

The remaining recoveries in this category are birds that were "dead in buildings" (9 percent) and those "caught by hand" (8 percent). Such circumstances suggest birds that were not in normal health.

Also in the miscellaneous category are such mortality causes as disease, parasites, poison, pesticides, starvation and weather (previously discussed). Despite the fact that large numbers of mourning doves are known to succumb to these factors, the "how obtained" codes for recovered bands still rarely point to them as direct causes of dove losses. Based on the total bands recovered (51,632), disease accounted for 140 (0.27 percent), trichomoniasis for 82 (0.16 percent), poisons for 15 (0.03 percent), weather for 13 (0.025 percent), starvation for 4 (0.008 percent) and pesticides for only 2 (0.004 percent).

It is easy enough to speculate why so few banded doves have been found and reported as having succumbed to these factors. For whatever the reasons, there is substantial disparity between field observations of all forms of dove mortality (except, perhaps, hunter harvest) and estimates based on banding studies. Banding is a useful technique and the most efficient means of assessing certain aspects of mourning dove biology, but it is far from capable of producing statistically precise or even reliable records. Dove biologists are cautioned not to rely too heavily on banding to explain the range and rates of mortality causes for doves. If, as believed, the annual autumn flight is approximately 500 million mourning doves and the annual mortality rate is approximately 52 percent—47.3 percent for adults and 56.2 percent for immatures (Dunks et al. 1982)—through one means or another 260 million mourning doves are lost each year. And if hunting accounts for about 71 million annually (see chapter 24), all other forms of mortality must account for the remaining 189 million. Basically, understanding of the demise of 30 to 40 percent of the annual dove population is, at best, inadequate. In order to manage the species and their habitats better, improved methodologies to assess dove mortality influences and their potentials must be a priority.

Table 33. Mourning dove band recoveries from miscellaneous mortality causes.[a]

Cause	Number	Percentage
Died during trapping or banding	251	32.7
Collected for study	165	21.5
Unknown disease	140	18.3
Trichomoniasis	82	10.7
Found dead in buildings, etc.	45	5.9
Caught by hand	42	5.5
Poison (not pesticides or lead)	15	2.0
Weather	13	1.7
Nontarget bird-control operation	7	0.9
Starvation	4	0.5
Pesticides	2	0.3
Found dead in nest	1	0.1
Total	767	100.0

[a] From records to 1984 of the U.S. Fish and Wildlife Service's Bird Banding Laboratory, Patuxent Wildlife Research Center, Laurel, Maryland.

III.

Population Characteristics and Appraisal

Chapter 14

The Call-count Survey:
Historic Development and Current
Procedures

David D. Dolton
Office of Migratory Bird Management
U.S. Fish and Wildlife Service
Laurel, Maryland

Estimation of size of animal populations is an integral part of wildlife conservation. Management goals for a migratory bird species can be expressed in terms of a desired numerical abundance and, for game species, a desired level of harvest (Martin et al. 1979). With respect to abundance, management may be directed at: (1) reducing population size in areas experiencing undesirable economic problems, such as crop depredation; (2) increasing numbers in areas where a species is declining or persisting at low levels; and (3) maintaining sizes of populations judged to be at desirable levels. For a game species, these abundance-oriented goals must be considered in the context of creating or maintaining a harvest level consistent with recreational interests.

Considerable progress has been made since the early 1900s in the methodologies for measuring wildlife abundance. Since Kendeigh (1944b) reviewed the historical development of surveys for bird populations and evaluated methods in use at the time, many new techniques have been developed (Ralph and Scott 1981).

In the context of mourning dove populations, a survey is employed to determine relative abundance as opposed to a census aimed at ascertaining absolute abundance. The Call-count Survey is an investigation designed specifically for the species.

EVOLUTION OF PROCEDURES

Development of Survey Technique

Development of a survey technique to detect and measure mourning dove population changes was a major objective of a Cooperative Dove Investigation initiated in the southeastern states in 1948 (Southeastern Association of Game and Fish Commissioners 1957). Leonard E. Foote, of the Wildlife Management Institute, was instrumental in originating and providing assistance throughout this study. Key personnel from the U.S. Fish and Wildlife Service included George C. Moore, who coordinated the project, and Harold S. Peters, who assisted in developing and testing field techniques. State project leaders included James Keeler (Alabama), David Donaldson (Arkansas), Frank Winston (Florida), Dan Nelson (Georgia), Dan Russell (Kentucky), John Newsom (Louisiana), St. Clair Thompson (Mississippi), Henry Bobbs (Mississippi), Don Allison (North Carolina), Harold Poole (South Carolina) and Jay Hammond (Tennessee).

Much was known about the mourning dove's life history prior to the project, but additional biological information was needed, including a technique suitable for monitoring breeding populations. Since it was deemed impossible to make a complete count of all doves, a method to develop an index to the population was sought. A variety of approaches was tried for the purpose of formulating an indexing technique that was economical, practical, statistically appropriate (e.g., estimating the same fraction of the population from year to year), permitted area-to-area and time-to-time comparisons, and was of sufficient sensitivity to detect differences within both high and low populations.

Initially, evaluations were made of different methods to provide an index to the level of the posthunting season dove population for comparison with indices at other seasons of the year. Roadside counts were conducted during winter by rural mail carriers, biologists and wardens. Records indicated large numbers of observations of a few birds and a small number of observations of large numbers of birds. This variation necessitated a large sample for desired reliability. Additionally, other deficiencies precluded use of winter road counts as a national survey method. Winter plot counts also were tried, but were disregarded due to variability and time requirements for extensive application.

Year-round random and controlled road counts were found to provide valuable indices for determining average dates of population peaks for hunting regulations if the sample was large and if the data were gathered on a comparable basis from year to year. Breeding season random road counts yielded an index with a fair degree of precision if the sample was large enough and data were collected by trained observers with approximately the same geographic coverage annually.

Ultimately, a Call-count Survey—in which numbers of individual doves heard calling (cooing) are counted along preselected routes—was judged to provide the best index to the population. Data from doves heard were found to be less variable than data from doves seen. Credit for the original idea of adapting an auditory index to doves in the late 1940s is more or less equally shared by George C. Moore, Daniel J. Nelson, Harold S. Peters, Edward Wellein and Leonard E. Foote (Foote and Peters 1952). Foote and Wellein initiated the original discussions for the possible use of an auditory method based on research by McClure (1939), who studied mourning dove calling activity and suggested its use for surveying the birds. He found that cooing was greatest in early morning and least at midday, increasing again in the evening before sundown.

Fieldwork to investigate and develop procedures for using Call-counts began in March 1950, with a three-car, 0.5-mile (0.8 km) interval route (Foote and Peters 1952). Duvall and Robbins experimented with Call-counts at 1.0-mile (1.6 km) stops

in Maryland, Pennsylvania and New York during May and June. Peters followed similar procedures in Ohio in June, July and August of that year. These early studies served to determine the practicality of certain procedures in the Call-count method, particularly the starting time (morning or afternoon), the number of stops (twenty) and the distance between them—1.0 mile (1.6 km) with a driving time of three minutes—and the length of time for counting at each stop (three minutes). Coordinated research was proposed in late 1950 and begun the following spring.

At various times between 1951 and 1954, intensive studies designed to permit biological and statistical evaluation of the Call-count technique were conducted in Wisconsin (Wagner 1952), Tennessee (Kerley 1952), Ohio (Peters 1952), New York, Pennsylvania, Maryland and Virginia (Duvall and Robbins 1952), and Georgia (McGowan 1952, 1953, Lowe 1956). The results of these studies and additional data are reviewed in Southeastern Association of Game and Fish Commissioners (1957).

Similarities were seen in results of these investigations that led to the establishment of additional survey standards for large-scale surveys. In several of these studies, both morning and afternoon surveys were conducted to ascertain the best time of day to run the survey. Early morning counts were found to be consistently higher and less variable than afternoon counts. Mourning dove calling reaches a peak at sunrise and then diminishes gradually over the next hour and a half. To compare survey results from area to area, it was determined that counts should be standardized to start exactly one-half hour before sunrise. Throughout the range of the mourning dove, a plateau period of calling existed from mid-May to mid-June, during which calling levels were relatively stable. Breeding populations were spread more homogeneously throughout the range during this period than at any other season (Foote and Peters 1952). Analyses indicated that the three-minute listening period was the most efficient. Wind had a pronounced effect on one's ability to hear doves calling and, in high velocities, on the intensity of calling itself. Researchers suggested that no counts should be taken when wind velocity exceeded Beaufort 3 (8 to 12 miles per hour: 12.9 to 19.3 km/hr). Calling activity was depressed with light rains and practically ceased during heavy rains. McClure (1939) found that calling was very uniform between 41 and 77 degrees Fahrenheit (5 and 25° C). Doves did not coo as much when the temperature was below freezing or above 77° F (0 to 25° C).

Many intensive studies of cooing performance of penned or individually marked free-flying doves have provided new insights into the validity of mourning dove Call-count Survey procedures (see Baskett et al. 1978, see also chapter 15).

Inception of the Survey

After the initial studies in a few states were concluded in 1950, 133 routes in twenty-two states were established in 1951. Most of these routes were located in eight southeastern states (Alabama, Florida, Georgia, Kentucky, Louisiana, Mississippi, North Carolina and South Carolina), plus Ohio and Texas.

By 1952, 196 routes had been established in thirty-two states. During 1950 to 1952, the routes were surveyed three to ten times at four- to seven-day intervals annually to gather extensive basic data. Data analyses indicated that a more efficient sampling design would result from doubling the number of routes and surveying each route only once (Southeastern Association of Game and Fish Commissioners 1957).

Coverage expanded to a nationwide survey beginning in 1953, with 542 routes in forty-one states. The number was increased to 730 routes in forty-four states in 1954. These routes were surveyed only once each season. In 1959, all forty-eight conterminous states were represented by survey routes. During the past several years, the number of routes has varied between 1,000 and 1,065, as some states added routes for three- to five-year periods for special evaluations and then reduced the number of routes. In 1987, the number of routes was 1,062.

The U.S. Fish and Wildlife Service has coordinated the Call-count Survey from its inception and is responsible for analyzing the data and preparing reports. Personnel from state and federal agencies "run" the survey routes, as do a few specially selected volunteers.

Between 1966 and 1971, cooperators ran their routes from May 20 through June 10. From 1972 to 1976, the official survey period was designated as May 20 to 31. However, a grace period to June 10 was allowed for any person who was unable to complete the survey during the designated time frame. Beginning in 1977 and continuing to present, the official survey period still has an end date of May 31, but the extension has been shortened to June 5. This measure was adopted because of short time constraints between the time data are received and when reports have to be prepared for regulations purposes. Routes run June 5 to 10 were accepted, although the data were not used in the current year's analysis.

Selection of Route Locations

When Call-count Surveys were first initiated, route locations were personally selected, usually by the person making the counts, rather than on a statistically acceptable basis of randomization (Southeastern Association of Game and Fish Commissioners 1957). People may have tended to select routes in the better dove habitats, but this was unknown.

As part of the Cooperative Dove Investigation, Call-count samples for 1953 and 1954 were sorted into life zone, biotic province, soil province and soil association subgroups, and analyses of variance were made. Significant differences were found in dove populations in subgroups for each major classification. Consequently, suggestions were made for refinement of the sampling technique for Call-counts (Southeastern Association of Game and Fish Commissioners 1957). One recommendation was to select routes randomly within geographic sampling areas if tests indicated present sampling was biased.

A test to compare data from randomly located routes with those obtained from nonrandom routes was a high priority in the dove management program (Foote 1957). Subsequent to the Cooperative Dove Investigation, a study was conducted of the efficiency of existing dove Call-counts in seven southeastern states, with particular reference to tests of a random sampling design that would yield more reliable data (Foote et al. 1958). Appropriate sampling would permit area-to-area comparisons and proper weighting of Call-count data from geographic areas. Foote et al. (1958) found that the original route sampling was indeed positively biased, signifying that higher-than-average dove population areas had been sampled. Results also indicated that stratification by ecological zones was a more efficient sampling design than was either stratification by state or completely random sampling. Suggestions were made for revising the nationwide Call-count sampling scheme.

Foote (1959) devised a sampling system for mourning dove Call-counts based on an allocation of routes by geologic areas known as physiographic regions. The various regions were based on a map entitled "Physical Divisions of the United States," prepared by Fenneman (1931) *(Figure 34)*. The boundaries of some regions were modified based on an examination of the survey data and other geographical characteristics. Ruos (1971) made additional minor modifications after examination of more recent ecological studies.

Original, nonrandom routes gradually were replaced by randomly located routes stratified within

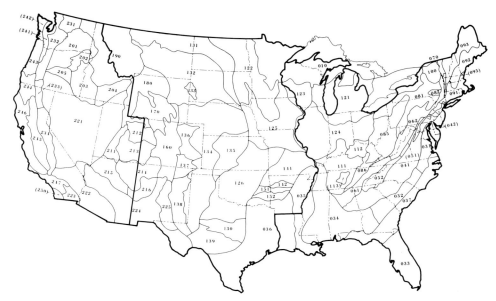

Figure 34. United States physiographic regions used in analyses of mourning dove population data, revised 1970. Based on Fenneman's (1931 [revised 1970]) map featuring physical divisions of the United States. Dark lines outline the three major mourning dove management units.

	Laurentian Upland Division
010	Superior Upland Province
	Atlantic Plain Division
	Coastal Plain Province
031	Embayed section
032	Upper Coastal Plain
033	Floridian section
034	East Gulf Coastal Plain
035	Mississippi Alluvial Plain
036	West Gulf Coastal Plain
037	Lower Coastal Plain
	Appalachian Highlands Division
	Piedmont Province
041	Piedmont Uplands
042	Piedmont Lowlands
	Blue Ridge Province
051	Northern section
052	Southern section
	Valley and Ridge Province
061	Tennessee section
062	Middle and Hudson Valley section
	St. Lawrence Valley Province
070	Champlain and Northern section
	Appalachian Plateaus Province
081	Mohawk and Allegheny section
082	Catskill section
085	Kanawha section
086	Cumberland section
	New England Province
091	Southern section
092	Northern section
093	Mountain section
095	Taconic section
100	Adirondack Province

	Interior Plains Division
	Interior Low Plateaus Province
111	Highland Rim section
112	Lexington Plain
113	Nashville Basin
	Central Lowland Province
121	Eastern Lake section
122	Western Lake section
123	Wisconsin Driftless section
124	Till Plains
125	Dissected Till Plains
126	Osage Plains
	Great Plains Province
130	Central Texas section
131	Missouri Plateau, glaciated
132	Missouri Plateau, unglaciated
133	Black Hills
134	High Plains
135	Plains Border
136	Colorado Piedmont
137	Raton section
138	Pecos Valley
139	Edwards Plateau
	Interior Highlands Division
	Ozark Plateaus Province
141	Springfield-Salem plateaus
142	Boston "Mountains"
	Ouachita Province
151	Arkansas Valley
152	Ouachita Mountains
	Rocky Mountain Division
160	Southern Rocky Mountains Province
170	Wyoming Basin Province
180	Middle Rocky Mountains Province
190	Northern Rocky Mountains Province

	Intermontane Plateaus Division
	Columbia Plateaus Province
201	Walla Walla Plateau
202	Blue Mountain section
203	Payette section
204	Snake River Plain
205	Harney section
	Colorado Plateaus Province
211	High Plateaus of Utah
212	Uinta Basin
213	Canyon Lands
214	Navajo section
215	Grand Canyon section
216	Datil section
	Basin and Range Province
221	Great Basin
222	Sonoran Desert
223	Salton Trough
224	Mexican Highland
225	Sacramento section
	Pacific Mountain Division
	Cascade Sierra Mountains Province
231	Northern Cascade Mountains
232	Middle Cascade Mountains
233	Southern Cascade Mountains
234	Sierra Nevada
	Pacific Border Province
241	Puget Trough
242	Olympic Mountains
243	Oregon Coast Range
244	Klamath Mountains
245	California Trough
246	California Coast Ranges
247	Los Angeles Ranges
250	Lower Californian Province

physiographic regions between 1957 and 1966 in forty-four states. Call-count data were analyzed for the first time by physiographic region in 1966 (Ruos and Tomlinson 1968). Selection of twelve random routes in the remaining four states—Maine, New Hampshire, Rhode Island and Vermont—was completed by 1970.

The procedure for randomly selecting routes was to draw a grid of squares or cells, twenty miles (32.2 km) on a side, on a large map of the United States. Physiographic region boundaries were superimposed on the map. Cells then were numbered by region, excluding those that were substantially covered with open water and those, such as urban areas, that could not be surveyed (Foote et al. 1958, Foote 1959). Routes were allocated to regions proportional to presumed dove populations (mean counts from either 1954–56 or 1956–57 routes, depending on state and weighted by land area).

Mourning dove Call-count surveys were run in Canada between 1961 and 1965. Standard procedures for conducting the survey were followed. However, the routes had been nonrandomly located, as was done initially in the United States. When routes were relocated in the U.S., Canadian authorities decided to discontinue the survey rather than relocate routes in their country. Before terminating the survey, there were seventy-nine routes in Ontario, two each in British Columbia and Manitoba, and one in Alberta. Wight et al. (1964) reported results for 1963–64; Tomlinson (1965) summarized results for 1964–65.

A suggestion was made for a new stratification of routes based on potential natural vegetation (Blankenship et al. 1971). The U.S. Fish and Wildlife Service decided, however, not to change physiographic region boundaries because of discouraging statistical problems in adapting a new stratification to the current one based on regions. (D. MacDonald personal communication: 1988, D. W. Hayne personal communication: 1988). In addition, a considerable amount of historical data would be lost, since the data from earlier years would not be comparable.

Current Procedures

Each Call-count route usually is located on lightly traveled secondary roads and run between May 20 and May 31, with a grace period to June 5. Counts begin one-half hour before sunrise and continue for two hours.

On each route, twenty listening stations are spaced at 1.0-mile (1.6 km) intervals. During a three-minute period at each stop, the number of doves heard calling, the number seen and the level of disturbance (noise) that impairs the observer's ability to hear doves are recorded. Also noted is the number of doves seen during a three-minute drive between stops.

Surveys are not made when wind velocities exceed 12 miles per hour (19.3 km) or when it is raining, as noted earlier.

A U.S. Fish and Wildlife Service biologist conducts a Call-count Survey on a secondary road in central Maryland. Separate records are made of doves heard and seen during a three-minute period at each of twenty listening/observation stations (stops) of 1.0-mile (1.6 km) intervals. Binoculars serve to verify dove observations. *Photo by David Dolton.*

As Call-count Surveys are being conducted, observers record a variety of information on a special form prepared by the U.S. Fish and Wildlife Service's Office of Migratory Bird Management. At the start and conclusion of each survey, wind velocity, temperature and percentage cloud cover are logged. At each stop, the number of individual mourning doves heard calling (cooing), the number of doves seen (singles or in pairs or flocks) and the disturbance level are documented. The number of doves seen during three-minute drives between stops also are recorded. *Photo by David Dolton.*

DATA ANALYSIS

Presentation

Methods of presenting or analyzing the data have changed periodically over the years. Results were mimeographed and distributed in "Mourning Dove Newsletters" from 1949 to 1960 (files of the U.S. Fish and Wildlife Service, Laurel, Maryland). Thereafter, results were presented in mimeographed administrative reports or published as Special Scientific Reports (e.g., Dolton 1977).

Data for doves heard and seen were summarized according to several different types of state groupings over the years. For example, the United States was divided into seven regions based on recoveries of banded doves. These regions also were combined into three larger regions, roughly dividing the U.S. into eastern, central and western units. Other summaries combined the regions into two units, with the Mississippi River as the dividing line between the eastern and western units. This division also roughly separated the eastern and western subspecies of the mourning dove (see chapter 2).

Counts of doves seen were determined to be more variable than counts from doves heard (Southeastern Association of Game and Fish Commissioners 1957). Consequently, data on doves seen were not analyzed between 1958 and 1984. Beginning in 1985, however, results from doves

seen were deemed to be useful with long-term, sophisticated analyses and again were reported solely as supplemental information to doves heard (Dolton 1985).

Analyses of banding data led to the establishment of mourning dove management units in 1960 (see chapter 4) (Kiel 1961). These areas encompass the principal breeding, migration and U.S. wintering areas for largely independent populations. Since that time, management decisions have been made within the boundaries of the Western (WMU), Central (CMU) and Eastern (EMU) management units.

For many years, the EMU and CMU were divided into two groups of states— those permitting dove hunting and those prohibiting hunting—for analysis comparisons. However, hunting status among states, particularly in the CMU, has changed considerably. For example, in 1966, seven of the fourteen CMU states allowed hunting and seven did not. By 1987, twelve CMU states allowed hunting. The situation was further complicated by the fact that both South Dakota and Nebraska allowed hunting in some years but not in others during that overall period. Thus, comparisons between hunting and nonhunting states of the CMU now are impractical.

In different treatments, both the CMU and WMU were divided into separate geographic reference areas adopted by Dunks et al. (1982) and Tomlinson et al. (1988) *(Figure 35)*. These north/south-oriented tiers contain dove populations with

Figure 35. Geographic reference areas in the Western and Central management units.

similar migration patterns. The EMU was not similarly segmented, since a proper division of states has not been determined at this time (however, see chapter 4 for possible subdivisions to be considered). The reference areas are herein referred to as Coastal WMU, Interior WMU, West CMU, Mid-CMU and East CMU. In this analysis, Nevada was grouped with the interior states of the WMU rather than the coastal states as done in the aforementioned publications because of a greater similarity in dove populations with the interior states (Tomlinson et al. 1988).

Analyses

Analytical methods also have changed or evolved over the years to enable better interpretation of Call-count results.

Stratification. Call-count data initially (1956) were stratified by state and weighted by the estimated number of square miles of productive dove habitat in each state to arrive at average Call-count indices for a management unit (see Table 43 for an explanation of weighting). It was recognized, however, that statistically more precise estimates could be obtained with the same effort by collecting and analyzing survey data by ecological stratum rather than by political unit. Foote et al. (1958) suggested a sampling design using physiographic regions as the basis for stratification, and it eventually was adopted. Beginning in 1966, after establishment of randomly located routes, the population index for each state was determined as the mean number of doves heard calling per route, weighted by the land area of each physiographic region (stratum) within the state (Ruos and Tomlinson 1968). Management unit indices were calculated from state indices weighted by the land area of states within the unit.

Variables associated with counts. Since time of day is one of the most important factors affecting dove calling behavior, and therefore the Call-count Survey, Dolton et al. (in preparation) investigated whether an analysis based on doves heard at ten stops (starting at the normal thirty minutes before sunrise) would be as efficient as one using the standard twenty stops. They found that trend estimates on all twenty stops appeared to have about the same precision as the estimates based on the first ten stops but that the twenty-stop analysis was preferred since more doves are counted and little extra effort is required. Accordingly, the twenty-stop standard has been retained.

It was recognized early that observers do not have uniform ability to hear birds (see Bart and Schoultz 1984). When observer changes are made

for Call-count routes, differences in hearing acuity could affect comparisons of data among years. Beginning in 1966, the ability to hear dove calls by different observers was considered in data analysis (Ruos and Tomlinson 1968). Each observer change was evaluated for unexpected differences in count results. Criteria were developed for acceptance or rejection of data following observer changes (Ruos 1974) and retroactively employed for all data from 1966 to 1971. Dolton et al. (in preparation) later evaluated various aspects of data analysis associated with route conditions, including observer change. Models with covariables for wind, temperature, percent cloud cover, disturbance (noise), observer change and different combinations of these covariables were tested to determine the best model. An adjustment for observers was the only factor found to affect Call-count results. The negative findings of the other variables probably resulted from the practice of limiting the counts to times when weather and noise covariables are within narrow bounds, thus effectively removing much of the variability associated with those factors. Baskett et al. (1978) also reported that weather has little effect on Call-counts except at the extremes.

Population trends. The issue of comparability has played a central role in data analyses to determine if a trend in the population is present. For example, if one or more routes from a state were not run in a specific year or they were run by different observers in successive years, the data from those routes were not considered comparable with data for the preceding and succeeding years. Using earlier methods of analysis, the data for those routes were omitted for the two years in question, resulting in the loss of a considerable amount of information throughout the survey. Through 1958, data were summarized by pairs of years. The percentage change for a state or management unit from one year to the next was calculated from comparable routes only. However, data for a series of years could not be compared, since all routes were not necessarily run in all years. To overcome this deficiency, a "base-year" system of analysis was adopted in 1959 and used through 1984. This method employed selection of a specific year (e.g., 1961) as the base year. During the period 1959–66, the average number of mourning doves heard calling on *all* routes for a state or management unit in that specific year (without regard to comparability) was used as the base index. Once the base year was established, percentage changes for preceding and succeeding years were calculated using data from *comparable* routes and applied to the base index. The resulting annual indices then were presented in tabular form for the period of years of data collection. The reader could visually scan these figures and determine if the resulting line was increasing or decreasing.

To obtain a more representative index than had been possible earlier, Ruos and Dolton (1977) selected a new base year (1971) for data analyzed in 1975 and thereafter. As their base index, however, they elected to use an average of comparable route results for a six-year period (1968–73). Since each year consisted of two comparable data sets (1968, for example, had one set to compare with 1967 and one to compare with 1969), a total of twelve data sets were used to obtain the average. This was done to reduce "the influence of a possible atypical year and . . . provide more reliable population indices used in calculation of both long- and short-term trends" (Ruos and Dolton 1977: 3). Trends were estimated by fitting a regression line through indices for a state or management unit. In retrospect, averaging over the six-year period probably served to mask actual low or high counts that occurred in 1971. Percentage changes were thus calculated in many cases from an erroneous starting index (the base year) and trends may have been biased. This factor is thought to have delayed detection of a declining trend in WMU dove populations for several years.

During the late 1970s, it became apparent that the base-year method was not providing the level of precision desired. In addition to the problem noted above, it was discovered that random errors were accumulating over time as indices moved away from the base year, resulting in unreliable trend information (Geissler and Noon 1981). Dolton (1982) calculated new indices using 1977 as the new base year and demonstrated that this treatment more accurately reflected a state's relative dove density during current years than when 1971 was used as the base year. The discrepancy was especially apparent for data from the WMU. This procedure, however, did not solve the inherent problems with the base-year analytical technique. Clearly, an improved method of analysis was needed.

During the early 1980s, statisticians at the Patuxent Wildlife Research Center in Laurel, Maryland, were assigned the task of exploring alternative means of analysis. A route regression method was developed and tested by Geissler (1984) and eventually implemented in 1985. Random errors did not accumulate with this method, and its reliability was demonstrated with computer simulations. For route regression analysis, the trend still is defined as an average rate of change over time, i.e., the ratio of the dove population in an area in year t to the population in year $t-1$. To estimate a trend in

a population for a specific area over a specified period of years, a trend is first estimated for each route through linear regression. The use of log-transformed counts estimates a proportional change per year. For each route, parallel lines are fitted through each observer's counts (i.e., the observer is included as a covariable). This method allows observers to count at different levels of efficiency but still estimates a common slope (trend) among all observers for the route *(Figure 36)*.

The trend for a physiographic region within a state is estimated as the average of the route trends weighted directly by the dove density and inversely by the relative variance of the individual route trends. The relative variance depends on the number of different observers and the number and distribution of years the route was run. For example, the program gives more weight to a route that has been run by a single observer for ten years than one that was run for only two years. More weight also is given to a route run twice, five years apart, than to a route run twice, two years apart. When estimating a trend for a state or management unit, trends for physiographic regions within states are combined in an average that is weighted by the land area of each physiographic region. Variances of state and management unit trends are estimated by a statistical procedure known as "bootstrapping" (Efron 1982).

The route regression method is currently the method employed by the U.S. Fish and Wildlife Service to provide trend information from the nationwide mourning dove Call-count Survey.

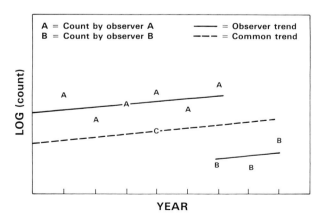

Figure 36. Illustration of a mourning dove population trend calculation for one Call-count route. Point C is an average of the counts and is used as the index of relative abundance of mourning doves on the route. The dash line indicates the common trend for all observers.

Annual indices. From 1959 through 1984, annual indices derived from the base-year analyses for states and management units were presented in annual reports and usually summarized by eleven-year periods. These indices were subject to the same problems as the base-year trends. Geissler (1984) and Sauer and Geissler (1990) developed two different annual index estimates, a linear model approach and a residual-based approach, to complement the trend estimates. Their methods give similar estimates of indices, but the residual indices are easier to compute.

Under this procedure, indices are calculated for the purpose of showing population fluctuations around a fitted line. Estimated indices are determined for an area by finding the average deviation between observed counts on all routes in the area and those predicted on the routes from the area trend estimate. These residuals are averaged on the log scale by year for all routes in an area and added to the fitted trend for the area to produce the annual index of abundance *(Figure 37)*. This method of finding indices superimposes yearly variation in counts on the long-term fitted trend. The indices provide an accurate representation of the fitted trend for areas that are adequately sampled by survey routes (ten or more). Additionally, only data from within an area are incorporated into the area's index. Since indices are adjusted for observer differences and trend, the index for an area may be quite different from actual count in individual years at the ends of a period. The index in midyear, however, is about equal to the average of all counts (raw data) for all years.

Annual indices are designed to show dispersion of actual data around a long-term trend. They are calculated from predicted counts over the entire period of years for which data are available. In contrast, trends are calculated using only data from specified sets of years. Consequently, the percentage change per year estimated from trend analysis may differ due to chance from the percentage change per year calculated directly from breeding population indices. The percentage change estimated from the trend analysis is the appropriate statistic to consider, as statistical significance is assessed from the trend analysis.

INTERPRETATION OF RESULTS

Trends

As a general rule for obtaining trend information, a minimum of ten routes in an area of consideration is required for reasonable confidence intervals. The number of routes used in the Call-count analysis for different time periods can vary as a result of mechanics of the analysis. Normally, there are more routes in the longer time periods, e.g., twenty-two years, since some routes may have been relocated (considered as a new route) and the old routes are included in the analysis. In addition, new routes may be initiated periodically within an area or areas.

The percentage change per year over all time periods may appear exaggerated for those areas with small numbers of routes that have large changes in counts over the years.

A two-year change obtained from the route regression trend analysis may differ from that calculated from index values. With Kansas as an example, the percentage change calculated by hand between 1986 and 1987 from the index values in Table 34 is 10.8 percent. However, the percentage change from the trend analysis in Table 35 for the same two-year period is 36.0 percent. In some instances (e.g., Indiana), the two-year trend *(Table 35)* and the indices for those years *(Table 34)* may appear to be in opposite directions. The trend indicates an increase, while the indices show a decrease. As discussed previously, indices were calculated over the entire twenty-two-year period and are designed to show year-to-year variation in the context of long-term trends. These index values tend to be somewhat smoothed and therefore may not exactly replicate results from the trend analysis over a shorter period, since the trend is calculated using only data from the shorter period. In the case of Indiana, one should note that the percentage

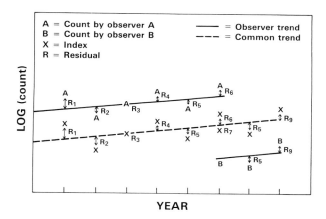

Figure 37. Illustration of mourning dove population index calculations for one Call-count route. The "residual" R_i represents the deviation of the yearly predicted count (based on trend) from the actual data. In this example, observer differences in ability to perceive birds are eliminated by placing the residuals on the predicted (common) trend line.

Table 34. Breeding population indices for mourning doves heard by management unit and state, 1966–87.[a]

Management unit/state	Year													
	1966	1967	1968	1969	1970	1971	1972	1973	1974	1975	1976	1977	1978	1979
EMU														
Alabama	23.5	21.2	19.5	19.9	20.0	16.6	23.8	21.2	16.8	21.2	21.1	23.2	25.7	25.0
Connecticut	2.5	4.0	4.2	2.0	8.4	6.4	6.1	5.2	5.6	10.2	10.9	11.3	14.9	16.1
Delaware	3.1	5.8	4.2	0.0	8.6	5.7	4.1	9.2	9.2	12.4	8.2	4.8	7.9	5.2
Florida	11.0	10.6	9.3	9.9	11.8	9.6	11.1	11.2	12.3	13.0	11.6	12.8	9.3	10.1
Georgia	26.8	21.6	20.5	20.8	26.9	23.4	21.3	22.7	24.5	29.7	24.7	26.0	29.5	26.0
Illinois	21.6	18.9	22.5	19.6	23.1	21.2	21.8	21.9	18.6	26.9	26.5	28.6	22.3	19.6
Indiana	46.9	41.7	41.9	38.4	36.3	47.6	40.4	35.6	33.2	33.7	32.7	36.7	20.3	20.7
Kentucky	28.4	22.6	22.9	23.7	28.8	26.7	22.6	24.6	28.5	21.4	23.0	21.7	25.5	18.6
Louisiana	12.1	12.3	11.5	13.1	9.0	11.9	12.8	10.0	11.4	12.3	12.1	9.9	12.1	9.8
Maine	1.5	1.5	2.8	2.5	1.7	2.2	−0.1	−0.6	0.9	0.9	0.9	7.9	6.8	4.2
Maryland	23.6	26.6	18.3	19.8	24.1	22.5	23.0	21.9	22.8	15.3	19.4	19.8	19.1	19.9
Massachusetts	9.6	18.8	5.8	5.0	12.3	8.1	12.1	14.0	10.8	11.3	7.2	11.2	13.2	8.0
Michigan	12.6	13.2	8.9	9.5	9.0	13.7	13.1	10.1	9.9	9.9	11.2	10.1	10.4	7.2
Mississippi	38.2	33.0	28.3	26.0	28.7	30.1	32.8	29.2	24.3	25.7	26.6	26.7	29.6	25.4
New Hampshire	3.7	2.3	2.4	2.1	3.2	3.4	3.5	5.0	3.8	2.8	3.2	3.5	4.2	3.6
New Jersey	21.4	17.7	23.4	21.2	27.8	25.0	26.7	23.9	20.6	15.5	18.3	20.0	16.1	17.0
New York	7.4	7.2	6.8	6.6	7.9	9.1	7.6	7.6	7.9	13.7	9.0	8.9	8.7	6.5
North Carolina	40.4	32.2	33.4	23.5	32.1	29.9	27.7	34.6	24.5	23.6	23.4	26.7	22.9	21.2
Ohio	25.8	23.2	21.3	23.5	25.1	23.1	24.2	18.8	22.7	29.5	23.5	22.4	11.3	11.2
Pennsylvania	11.9	12.7	12.0	11.4	7.2	7.4	10.7	7.1	10.2	7.1	7.3	6.4	6.8	7.2
Rhode Island	6.5	7.3	6.8	10.3	3.7	10.1	7.8	6.8	8.6	9.3	9.7	6.9	10.8	12.9
South Carolina	33.5	36.3	37.1	37.3	34.5	31.1	27.6	32.3	30.0	29.3	29.0	24.7	31.9	28.3
Tennessee	32.3	22.7	25.0	23.9	29.6	21.5	29.3	21.2	23.2	21.8	21.0	25.2	27.8	19.6
Vermont												4.5	2.8	7.0
Virginia	30.5	25.9	25.0	23.2	28.6	26.1	17.0	19.4	23.5	26.6	24.6	32.9	24.4	23.7
West Virginia	4.9	4.4	4.5	5.3	5.5	4.7	6.3	3.4	3.9	2.2	4.8	4.8	5.9	6.5
Wisconsin	13.1	17.9	16.1	13.1	12.7	16.4	17.9	14.3	13.0	15.1	16.1	17.2	11.3	11.2
Weighted average	21.0	19.4	18.2	17.6	18.8	18.5	19.3	17.8	17.3	18.2	18.2	18.8	16.8	15.0
East CMU														
Arkansas	30.0	28.6	28.2	26.3	25.9	26.3	29.8	27.5	23.0	20.7	24.7	20.2	15.1	12.6
Iowa	36.2	32.4	34.7	29.8	21.6	26.6	32.9	30.5	24.0	22.3	28.0	21.4	24.0	20.4
Minnesota	23.1	22.0	21.0	22.5	16.4	21.7	25.1	20.2	22.5	24.8	24.5	27.8	24.5	27.0
Missouri	46.0	43.2	52.8	31.0	42.7	35.0	47.1	35.7	29.9	33.0	29.0	32.8	21.6	20.5
Mid-CMU														
Nebraska	40.2	36.1	45.9	44.9	43.6	42.0	41.4	40.1	41.1	39.9	44.3	44.4	38.4	39.9
North Dakota	24.1	24.4	33.3	27.0	25.0	27.4	27.5	32.3	32.1	25.7	41.7	35.3	39.0	37.0
Oklahoma	26.7	32.1	39.5	39.8	26.9	24.8	33.5	29.8	30.3	26.4	30.5	39.5	28.5	29.0
South Dakota	49.4	31.4	41.4	37.4	45.6	38.8	39.1	41.7	50.8	43.6	46.9	40.4	44.8	42.5
Texas	25.3	20.1	22.1	19.1	20.3	19.2	25.9	21.3	22.2	20.0	19.9	18.9	19.5	23.6
West CMU														
Colorado	13.6	17.4	13.6	15.8	20.5	15.0	21.4	16.0	22.1	18.0	21.9	24.1	28.6	23.6
Kansas	48.2	47.1	52.6	49.9	46.2	48.2	54.8	47.4	47.0	45.4	50.2	48.3	37.6	52.6
Montana	24.5	21.9	19.1	19.7	16.1	22.6	17.1	12.8	14.5	19.6	15.3	18.6	17.6	18.0
New Mexico	12.5	9.1	13.3	11.1	10.7	10.3	12.8	9.4	11.1	14.7	14.6	13.8	14.3	10.5
Wyoming	18.3	18.7	9.2	16.9	18.5	9.3	12.6	13.7	17.6	15.3	15.1	11.1	14.0	11.2
Weighted average	28.0	25.4	28.3	25.7	25.3	24.8	28.5	24.9	26.0	24.6	26.0	25.1	24.1	24.4
Coastal WMU														
California	31.1	29.6	29.0	25.8	25.9	20.3	24.3	19.2	20.5	18.7	20.8	17.4	14.2	12.3
Oregon	23.7	16.4	17.6	18.6	13.1	11.3	9.8	11.7	15.6	11.8	11.3	12.6	6.2	6.3
Washington	13.0	16.1	15.6	12.3	13.5	14.0	10.9	8.6	9.8	10.1	9.9	10.9	6.7	9.0
Interior WMU														
Arizona	26.3	28.3	24.6	29.1	29.8	19.9	20.7	27.1	23.6	24.0	26.5	22.4	23.0	24.4
Idaho	17.1	17.9	16.2	16.8	16.0	12.7	12.2	13.9	12.0	9.8	15.4	19.0	10.1	10.1
Nevada	9.5	7.8	18.6	13.2	9.3	5.7	6.9	4.9	7.5	4.2	7.1	6.8	4.1	6.3
Utah	18.3	26.7	15.0	14.9	15.6	22.8	12.8	11.5	13.5	15.1	16.8	19.1	8.5	11.2
Weighted average	20.2	20.1	20.0	19.4	18.6	14.8	14.7	14.5	15.4	14.0	16.3	15.5	11.1	11.9
United States	24.1	22.6	22.7	21.6	22.0	20.6	22.0	20.3	20.7	20.3	21.4	21.2	18.7	18.2

[a] Annual indices are defined as the predicted value from the trend analysis plus the deviation from the expected value in a year.

Table 34. (continued)

			Year				
1980	1981	1982	1983	1984	1985	1986	1987
25.6	25.3	26.7	26.2	22.4	27.9	25.6	24.5
13.5	20.1	14.7	12.0	14.9	20.7	42.0	17.2
7.4	8.4	9.0	4.0	10.2	10.3	15.3	12.4
9.1	7.9	9.6	11.3	6.9	9.5	11.1	10.3
25.0	28.5	30.7	27.2	21.0	28.3	26.5	27.1
20.1	23.3	28.5	30.0	24.3	21.0	30.2	31.7
25.7	29.4	20.0	17.3	18.9	16.7	22.2	21.2
15.7	24.3	24.8	17.3	21.4	21.6	20.0	23.5
12.9	11.6	14.3	13.0	12.0	10.6	9.8	14.0
8.0	7.6	8.8	7.8	6.8	9.1	9.7	6.9
17.6	17.6	18.4	14.8	14.5	16.1	18.6	14.9
10.7	11.8	11.1	9.8	9.9	10.6	10.8	9.9
11.9	11.7	10.6	9.0	9.9	10.2	12.9	11.7
23.9	23.5	29.9	25.4	18.9	25.5	25.1	22.6
3.1	5.3	3.4	6.8	3.8	3.7	6.1	5.0
15.6	13.8	14.8	17.1	11.3	12.7	14.1	12.0
11.0	10.7	10.1	9.2	8.5	8.2	6.9	8.1
24.2	21.1	21.6	21.4	21.9	20.9	21.6	22.3
13.5	16.2	15.0	15.6	14.5	13.1	13.5	16.1
10.3	10.3	10.4	9.7	9.2	9.1	9.8	11.2
11.3	11.9	13.8	9.0	7.5	9.2	8.5	11.2
34.4	33.6	35.1	32.4	28.8	29.0	25.2	36.3
21.5	18.9	24.7	18.4	16.0	20.2	15.6	19.1
7.1	8.1	4.1	4.1	6.3	7.5	5.8	7.4
21.6	20.1	20.5	22.2	21.6	19.6	17.4	17.5
7.1	6.1	5.8	5.5	5.5	6.4	6.5	7.0
16.7	19.6	11.6	13.5	12.0	11.8	12.6	11.8
17.0	17.6	17.9	16.8	15.1	16.3	16.4	17.1
20.5	20.3	20.6	16.5	12.9	13.0	12.7	15.0
27.1	29.5	21.3	16.7	21.9	24.3	22.2	20.4
28.1	27.7	21.9	22.8	17.8	20.5	19.6	23.1
29.9	26.1	23.3	22.9	20.4	19.2	19.6	21.3
50.9	48.7	47.0	44.6	42.2	44.3	35.5	36.1
43.1	44.6	43.4	41.5	33.4	43.6	47.0	50.6
28.3	29.0	31.4	30.4	23.0	22.8	25.1	27.0
43.6	38.7	46.7	42.7	44.3	41.4	39.9	36.6
23.0	20.6	20.1	19.0	18.0	19.1	21.1	19.9
29.0	36.2	33.8	21.3	29.3	31.9	29.7	36.0
59.6	54.8	52.5	62.0	48.0	60.4	42.6	47.2
16.8	15.5	18.3	16.0	12.2	15.0	16.1	13.9
16.9	17.4	13.9	18.2	19.9	18.0	20.6	24.4
10.7	12.1	13.4	10.1	8.1	9.8	11.4	9.5
27.5	26.5	25.5	23.9	22.1	23.7	24.0	24.2
17.5	16.2	16.4	10.9	15.2	10.6	12.9	10.0
9.8	7.8	7.5	5.6	6.5	7.7	5.8	5.3
5.8	6.8	6.3	4.9	4.2	5.5	6.3	4.8
20.9	23.3	25.8	20.8	25.5	21.2	22.8	16.7
10.4	11.7	11.6	9.6	11.3	10.6	7.2	10.1
9.1	6.3	3.7	3.2	3.3	4.5	2.9	3.4
13.4	18.1	10.7	10.6	12.9	8.0	12.2	9.8
13.5	13.5	12.5	9.7	11.6	10.3	10.4	9.0
20.7	20.7	20.2	18.4	17.6	18.3	18.5	18.3

change is not significant, the confidence intervals are wide, and the actual trend could be either negative or positive. Additionally, in a population where the trend has been increasing but declines have occurred in counts of the last two years, the indices may not be sensitive to short-term fluctuations.

Confidence intervals about the trend estimates indicate the range of values in which 95 percent of the observations will occur. The smaller the interval, the more precise the point estimate. With wide intervals, little trust can be placed in the actual value (percentage change) presented. However, even in the presence of a wide confidence interval, if it does not overlap zero (meaning the trend is significant), one can conclude that the population is either increasing (positive percentage change) or decreasing (negative percentage change). The numbers are not as important as the direction.

Completed mourning dove Call-count Survey forms are received by the U.S. Fish and Wildlife Service's Office of Migratory Bird Management at Patuxent Wildlife Research Center in Laurel, Maryland. There a mourning dove specialist (biologist) quality checks each form for clarity (above) before having them keypunched for computer entry. After the forms are keypunched and entered in a computer, a biometrician performs the trend analysis and calculates indices by means of a minicomputer. *Photo by Mary Ann McKeough.*

Table 35. Trends (percentage change[a] per year as determined by linear regression) in number of mourning doves heard by management unit and state, 1966–87.

Management unit/state		2-year (1986–87)			5-year (1983–87)		
		N	Change[b]	CI		N	Change[b]	CI
EMU	Alabama	24	−3.7	−19.3	11.8	30	−2.8	−7.7	2.0
	Connecticut	2	−60.6***	−97.4	−23.8	2	22.9	−20.3	66.1
	Delaware	2	−8.9	−53.1	35.4	2	44.9***	32.0	57.7
	Florida	21	−20.8*	−42.9	1.3	22	−3.4	−13.1	6.4
	Georgia	21	−0.7	−15.9	14.4	22	−2.0	−4.9	0.8
	Illinois	15	23.9	−16.0	63.9	20	3.8	−6.0	13.7
	Indiana	12	4.8	−16.4	26.0	15	6.0**	0.0	12.0
	Kentucky	14	14.0	−6.0	34.0	20	3.7	−2.2	9.6
	Louisiana	17	5.7	−11.3	22.6	18	−2.5	−10.0	5.0
	Maine	7	−32.4**	−57.6	−7.2	9	−12.6	−31.9	6.7
	Maryland	11	−31.7***	−55.3	−8.0	13	1.7	−6.5	9.9
	Massachusetts	7	−3.4	−35.2	28.4	16	−1.0	−10.8	8.8
	Michigan	19	−2.9	−25.7	20.0	20	9.0**	0.9	17.1
	Mississippi	22	−15.5**	−27.6	−3.4	22	3.0	−2.7	8.7
	New Hampshire	0	0.0	0.0	0.0	3	−6.2	−14.8	2.4
	New Jersey	11	−8.9	−22.9	5.1	18	−4.8	−11.9	2.2
	New York	9	−4.7	−49.6	40.2	12	−7.1**	−13.2	−1.1
	North Carolina	18	24.0*	−2.2	50.1	21	0.8	−3.0	4.6
	Ohio	16	7.6	−16.9	32.1	37	3.2	−3.0	9.4
	Pennsylvania	13	23.5	−13.2	60.2	15	4.5	−2.2	11.2
	Rhode Island	2	29.1**	2.1	56.1	2	4.9**	0.7	9.2
	South Carolina	17	17.4**	2.8	32.0	20	−1.1	−8.9	6.7
	Tennessee	21	28.1***	16.9	39.2	24	−2.3	−6.2	1.6
	Vermont	18	−3.3	−31.6	25.0	21	−3.3	−8.0	1.4
	Virginia	9	12.0	−31.0	54.9	11	−1.1	−7.0	4.8
	West Virginia	6	45.1	−19.0	109.2	7	9.5	−8.3	27.3
	Wisconsin	15	−27.5***	−47.3	−7.6	20	−0.9	−7.8	6.0
	Weighted average	323	1.6	−3.7	7.0	442	0.3	−1.1	1.7
East CMU	Arkansas	13	−10.4	−31.9	11.1	15	−2.0	−8.0	3.9
	Iowa	14	−16.8	−41.7	8.2	16	1.2	−3.3	5.7
	Minnesota	6	33.7	−25.3	92.8	11	−3.9	−15.6	7.8
	Missouri	20	−7.9	−31.2	15.4	20	−3.8	−10.6	3.0
Mid-CMU	Nebraska	21	3.2	−11.0	17.5	25	−6.1***	−9.3	−2.9
	North Dakota	15	7.1	−12.1	26.3	25	8.3	−2.6	19.3
	Oklahoma	14	26.2	−15.3	67.7	16	−2.9	−8.4	2.5
	South Dakota	15	−10.3	−36.5	15.9	21	−10.3***	−18.0	−2.6
	Texas	107	−11.3**	−20.9	−1.7	133	2.2	−1.0	5.4
West CMU	Colorado	14	25.2	−7.9	58.3	16	−1.5	−7.6	4.6
	Kansas	21	36.0*	−3.3	75.2	25	−5.9*	−12.0	0.1
	Montana	15	−6.4	−27.9	15.0	23	−3.2	−14.2	7.8
	New Mexico	20	25.2*	−5.0	55.4	26	18.5**	2.8	34.2
	Wyoming	14	3.7	−39.8	47.1	16	4.2**	0.6	7.8
	Weighted average	296	4.9	−2.4	12.2	388	−1.7*	−3.7	0.3
Coastal WMU	California	35	−14.4	−36.4	7.6	51	−4.4	−10.7	2.0
	Oregon	10	−23.8***	−34.9	−12.6	17	1.0	−10.9	12.8
	Washington	11	−14.9	−43.8	14.0	15	11.2*	−1.1	23.4
Interior WMU	Arizona	46	−21.8***	−31.5	−11.9	54	−8.1**	−15.9	−0.3
	Idaho	11	25.4	−15.1	66.0	21	0.9	−5.5	7.2
	Nevada	16	−9.4	−85.9	67.0	19	0.3	−13.1	13.6
	Utah	12	−30.0	−70.8	10.9	15	−1.4	−9.6	6.9
	Weighted average	131	−17.4***	−26.3	−8.5	192	−3.5**	−6.9	−0.1
United States		750	0.8	−3.9	5.5	1,022	−1.3*	−2.6	0.1

[a] Mean of route weighted by land area and population density. The estimated count in the next year is (percentage ÷ 100 + 1) times the count in the current year where percentage is the annual change. Note: extrapolating the estimated trend statistic (percentage change per year) over time (e.g., 22 years) may exaggerate the total change over the period.
[b] *$P<0.1$, **$P<0.05$, ***$P<0.01$.

Table 35. (continued)

	10-year (1978–87)			15-year (1973–87)			22-year (1966–87)	
N	Changeᵇ	CI		N	Changeᵇ	CI		N	Changeᵇ	CI
33	−2.4	−5.3	0.5	37	1.8	−0.7	4.3	39	1.4**	0.3	2.5
2	−6.0	−45.8	33.8	2	5.5	−21.5	32.6	2	11.3	−14.0	36.5
3	12.6	−9.7	35.0	3	−0.9	−26.4	24.6	3	3.8	−16.1	23.6
24	−1.4	−6.6	3.9	24	−1.6	−4.2	1.1	27	−0.7	−2.6	1.2
22	0.0	−2.1	2.1	25	0.0	−2.1	2.1	26	1.1	−0.6	2.8
22	4.2**	0.6	7.8	22	1.7	−1.5	5.0	22	1.4	−1.5	4.4
15	−0.8	−2.5	0.9	15	−5.3***	−7.0	−3.6	17	−4.6***	−5.6	−3.5
21	−1.8	−9.8	6.1	23	−2.2	−6.8	2.4	25	−1.5	−4.8	1.8
19	−1.5	−5.3	2.3	19	−1.1	−4.0	1.8	22	−0.1	−2.7	2.5
9	0.5	−6.2	7.3	9	7.5*	−1.2	16.3	11	10.3	−15.4	36.1
14	−2.4	−7.9	3.1	15	−2.6**	−5.3	−0.0	15	−1.7*	−3.7	0.2
18	−0.1	−4.6	4.4	18	0.9	−4.1	5.9	19	−0.2	−4.3	3.8
20	3.0	−1.1	7.2	20	0.2	−4.2	4.7	20	−0.1	−4.7	4.5
23	−1.9**	−3.6	−0.3	24	−0.7	−3.6	2.3	25	−1.9	−5.3	1.5
3	2.1***	2.1	2.1	4	−1.1	−6.1	3.9	8	3.1***	0.9	5.4
18	−2.5	−7.5	2.5	18	−4.0*	−8.9	0.8	19	−3.3	−7.6	1.1
15	−1.7**	−3.0	−0.4	17	−0.4	−2.5	1.6	19	0.3	−1.9	2.4
21	0.8	−0.6	2.3	21	−1.0	−2.9	1.0	21	−2.8***	−4.2	−1.4
52	6.5**	1.4	11.5	52	−3.8**	−6.9	−0.8	54	−3.4***	−5.5	−1.3
15	4.1**	0.6	7.5	16	4.0**	0.3	7.6	16	−0.6	−3.6	2.3
2	−3.0*	−6.0	0.0	2	1.0**	0.2	1.8	5	1.9	−16.3	20.2
23	−1.7	−4.0	0.7	23	−0.4	−4.0	3.1	23	−0.8	−3.3	1.7
24	−3.1**	−5.7	−0.5	27	−1.8	−4.0	0.5	30	−1.8*	−3.6	0.0
21	0.4	−10.4	11.2	21	3.3	−9.3	15.9	23	8.9	−7.9	25.7
11	−2.9*	−6.3	0.5	11	−2.3*	−4.9	0.3	11	−1.6*	−3.5	0.3
8	2.5	−1.4	6.4	10	3.5	−1.8	8.8	11	2.3	−3.2	7.9
21	−1.6	−6.1	3.0	21	−2.6*	−5.4	0.3	21	−1.1	−3.1	0.8
479	−0.5	−1.3	0.3	499	−0.8**	−1.6	−0.1	534	−0.9***	−1.7	−0.2
15	−2.1	−5.7	1.5	15	−4.7***	−8.0	−1.4	16	−3.6***	−5.9	−1.3
17	−2.5***	−3.9	−1.2	17	−1.4***	−2.1	−0.6	17	−2.0***	−2.4	−1.6
12	−5.1*	−10.8	0.6	12	−2.0	−7.5	3.6	13	−0.1	−3.4	3.1
22	−2.6***	−4.3	−0.8	24	−3.4***	−5.0	−1.9	26	−4.0***	−5.8	−2.1
25	−3.1**	−5.6	−0.7	25	−0.3	−1.8	1.1	26	−0.0	−1.1	1.1
26	−0.9	−4.7	2.8	26	1.6	−1.3	4.5	27	3.2***	1.1	5.4
16	−3.7	−9.8	2.5	17	−2.7*	−5.9	0.4	19	−1.0	−3.9	2.0
23	−5.5***	−8.3	−2.8	23	−2.8**	−5.4	−0.1	26	0.1	−2.0	2.2
144	−1.9**	−3.4	−0.3	154	−0.6	−2.0	0.9	183	−0.5	−1.9	0.9
18	−2.9***	−4.8	−1.1	18	3.0*	−0.3	6.4	19	4.4***	2.0	6.9
28	−2.7*	−5.4	0.1	30	0.5	−1.4	2.4	31	0.1	−1.1	1.3
24	−2.9	−11.5	5.7	26	2.4	−2.2	6.9	28	−1.7	−5.9	2.5
28	7.4***	2.5	12.4	30	8.1***	3.1	13.0	30	4.2**	0.8	7.5
18	−1.3	−6.8	4.2	19	−4.2	−12.9	4.4	19	−2.9	−6.5	0.8
416	−2.6***	−3.5	−1.6	436	−0.7*	−1.6	0.1	480	−0.5*	−1.1	0.1
59	−6.5***	−9.8	−3.3	61	−5.3***	−7.9	−2.7	70	−4.9***	−7.3	−2.5
21	−0.5	−3.6	2.6	21	−3.3**	−5.9	−0.6	22	−6.0***	−8.3	−3.7
18	−2.8	−7.5	1.9	19	−6.0***	−10.2	−1.7	20	−6.0***	−9.8	−2.3
55	−2.8**	−5.5	−0.1	58	−1.5	−5.8	2.7	63	−1.1	−4.2	2.0
22	−0.5	−4.4	3.3	22	−2.2	−6.6	2.2	23	−2.3	−5.3	0.8
20	−8.6*	−18.8	1.6	22	−3.1	−9.2	3.0	27	−5.2***	−8.2	−2.1
16	−0.2	−3.1	2.6	16	−4.0	−9.5	1.5	16	−2.8	−6.6	1.0
211	−3.9***	−5.5	−2.2	219	−3.8***	−5.8	−1.9	241	−3.4***	−4.9	−1.9
1,106	−2.1***	−2.7	−1.5	1,154	−1.2***	−1.8	−0.6	1,255	−1.1***	−1.5	−0.6

Indices

The main value of indices is to identify *patterns* of counts that may deviate from the fitted line in some years. They allow the reader to evaluate the consistency of the trend over a selected time interval and to provide a relative measure of the variability of year-to-year changes.

Since indices are meant to represent fluctuations, they may not agree exactly with the magnitude of fluctuations of raw data that are biased by observer differences (Geissler and Noon 1981). The indices are adjusted for periodic variation associated with routes that were not run, changes in observers, disturbance and other factors. Consequently, these adjustments may cause the indices to be different from the mean of actual counts of doves heard or seen (raw data). However, it is important to note that, in some cases, the actual counts may be more misleading because they have not been adjusted.

Any area with a small number of routes and a large but nonsignificant trend may have exaggerated indices. Although indices are computed so that the adjusted value in the middle year of the interval equals the midyear raw data average value, variances associated with the trend line may cause the indices to be greater than the actual numbers of doves present. This exaggeration increases as the index gets farther away from the midyear.

After mourning dove Call-count Survey data are compiled, consolidated by computer program and analyzed, the results are summarized in an annual report completed and distributed prior to a Washington, D.C. public hearing held each June on early hunting season regulations. *Photo courtesy of the U.S. Fish and Wildlife Service, Office of Migratory Bird Management.*

The reader should use indices as a means of examining deviations from long-term trends. However, patterns that are identified by indices should be verified by estimating trends over the selected interval of years. Comparisons of dove density may be made among areas, if done cautiously. Indices are affected by the same biases that raw data are, such as differences in observer ability to hear or see doves among areas. Also, as explained above, indices from one area may be exaggerated while those from another area may not. These problems generally occur only at the state or physiographic region level, rather than for management units that have large sample sizes.

RESULTS: 1966 to 1987

For the purposes of this volume, the latest analyses for annual indices and trends were conducted in 1987 *(tables 34 to 37)*. The route regression method was used to estimate trends for doves *heard* and *seen* for several reference areas (e.g., management unit, submanagement unit and state). Trends were calculated for the most recent two-, five-, ten- and fifteen-year intervals and for the entire twenty-two-year period between 1966 and 1987. Statistical significance is defined as $P < 0.05$, except for the two-year comparison where $P < 0.10$ was used because of the low power of the test. Significance levels were approximate for areas with less than ten routes. Annual indices were calculated over the entire twenty-two-year period. A brief overview of the results is presented in the following discussion. Additional details are discussed in other chapters of this book dealing specifically with each management unit.

Doves Heard

Indices. Indices provide a means to compare breeding densities among areas of the United States *(Figure 38)*. For example, the CMU consistently registers higher population indices of doves heard than do the other two units *(Table 34)*. In 1987, the CMU index was 24.2 doves heard per route compared with 17.1 in the EMU and 9.0 in the WMU. Furthermore, the index from the Mid-CMU (the Great Plains states) registered an index of 31.7 (see Table 56). This high breeding density combined with the large area involved leads to the conclusion that the Mid-CMU is the most important mourning dove-producing area of the nation. In contrast, the Coastal WMU and northeastern sections of the EMU (with indices lower than ten) are

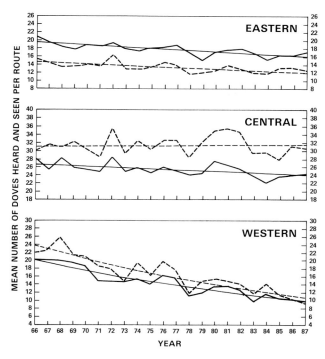

Figure 38. Population indices of breeding mourning doves for the Eastern, Central and Western management units, 1966–87. Heavy solid line = doves heard; heavy dash line = doves seen; light solid and dash lines = predicted trends.

relatively unimportant dove production areas. This aspect will be covered in greater detail in later chapters on the individual management units.

Trends. Lacking a standardized, nationwide harvest survey, breeding dove trend estimates are the primary sources of information in formulating annual hunting regulations and for other management considerations (*Figure 39 and Table 35*). For the

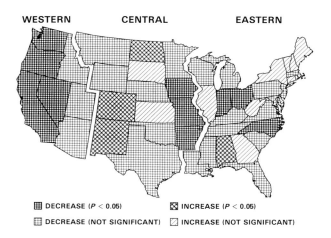

DECREASE (P < 0.05)   INCREASE (P < 0.05)

DECREASE (NOT SIGNIFICANT)   INCREASE (NOT SIGNIFICANT)

Figure 39. Twenty-two-year (1966–87) trends of mourning doves heard in the Western, Central and Eastern management units.

EMU, estimates indicate that small (less than 1 percent per year) but significant downward trends have occurred for the fifteen- and twenty-two-year periods. No trends are noticeable for the more recent time periods, indicating that populations may have stabilized at a lower level in recent years. For the CMU, a downward trend is indicated for the most recent ten years. Although no significant trends ($P < 0.05$) were detected for other time periods, a tendency for a decline ($P < 0.10$) is noted for each time frame. When the CMU is examined by subunit, highly significant downward trends are apparent for the East CMU during the ten-, fifteen- and twenty-two-year periods, whereas populations appear to have been stable for the Mid- and West CMU subunits. For the WMU, highly significant downward trends ($P < 0.01$) are noted in all time periods except for the five-year period (and that at $P < 0.05$). This decline in WMU dove populations was most apparent in the Coastal subunit, where highly significant downward trends are detected for the ten-, fifteen- and twenty-two-year periods.

Doves Seen

Indices. Information for *doves seen* on the nationwide Call-count Survey has been routinely summarized over the years (*Table 36*), but it is used only as supporting data to *doves heard* because of higher variability in the estimates. Nevertheless, when plotted index points are examined by year for both parameters, a close similarity is seen for all three management units (*Figure 38*). However, indices for doves seen in the CMU and WMU have been consistently higher than indices for doves heard in those units, whereas those in the EMU were lower, probably because doves are more visible in the open country of the West than in the more forested regions of the East. Thus, for comparisons among units, the doves-seen index data yield misleading conclusions as to the relative breeding population densities, particularly between the EMU and the other two units. For example, in 1987, the doves-seen index values were CMU 30.7, EMU 12.6 and WMU 9.2 (*Table 36*). It is concluded that only doves-heard data should be used for relative density comparisons among geographical units.

Trends. Trends for doves seen by management unit generally agreed with those for doves heard, although there were some exceptions (*Figure 40 and Table 37*). For the EMU, estimates indicated a downward trend for the entire twenty-two-year period (as for doves heard), but a few inconsistencies occurred within the other time periods (most were insignificant and therefore of no real import for

Table 36. Breeding population indices for mourning doves seen by management unit and state, 1966–87.[a]

Management unit/state	Year													
	1966	1967	1968	1969	1970	1971	1972	1973	1974	1975	1976	1977	1978	1979
EMU														
Alabama	16.9	18.9	15.5	16.2	16.0	14.1	25.4	22.3	14.1	15.3	18.4	16.4	15.9	20.4
Connecticut	3.3	2.9	1.9	2.0	2.7	3.5	10.5	2.7	4.9	5.3	13.1	8.3	11.8	12.1
Delaware	5.2	7.4	4.0	0.1	15.5	7.7	15.8	23.3	30.7	0.9	5.0	8.3	23.4	3.1
Florida	6.4	4.6	5.6	5.7	4.6	3.9	7.3	7.5	6.5	9.5	11.9	7.3	9.7	8.6
Georgia	17.0	14.1	11.7	13.3	15.1	13.0	15.2	12.9	14.5	12.1	12.5	15.0	15.3	17.0
Illinois	17.5	24.3	19.1	21.6	16.6	16.8	20.9	15.8	14.3	14.8	19.1	16.9	13.0	10.2
Indiana	36.1	32.4	30.8	36.0	34.5	28.6	27.4	26.6	33.8	30.8	30.9	25.8	8.7	11.7
Kentucky	21.1	19.5	17.0	18.2	17.9	13.6	17.0	13.4	16.7	14.2	21.2	16.7	14.0	13.7
Louisiana	14.5	12.9	11.2	12.6	10.1	14.0	15.3	11.9	11.5	10.8	9.3	15.3	12.9	11.9
Maine	1.4	1.4	1.6	0.9	1.8	1.6	−0.0	−0.1	1.0	1.0	3.0	4.9	2.9	1.4
Maryland	10.6	17.5	12.0	13.3	18.8	17.1	16.2	13.2	14.9	11.3	21.2	17.9	14.8	15.0
Massachusetts	6.9	8.2	13.3	10.9	19.2	9.7	9.2	10.4	7.2	15.4	5.0	9.8	17.3	8.4
Michigan	9.1	6.6	8.2	4.8	7.0	7.0	7.9	6.1	6.5	8.9	7.3	7.4	5.5	5.1
Mississippi	32.7	28.1	27.2	25.5	24.2	24.3	34.1	23.1	23.2	25.3	19.3	25.8	24.4	25.6
New Hampshire	1.7	1.0	1.1	2.5	3.0	2.4	2.4	3.6	2.6	1.1	1.5	1.5	0.9	2.5
New Jersey	1.6	23.0	19.1	20.4	11.5	23.6	29.5	19.5	8.5	14.8	27.2	21.7	30.3	22.4
New York	3.2	2.5	2.8	4.1	4.4	3.3	3.4	3.2	2.3	4.6	2.8	3.2	3.3	3.4
North Carolina	26.5	23.6	21.8	17.2	23.9	23.2	19.5	19.4	21.6	16.4	20.7	17.2	21.8	20.3
Ohio	13.1	19.1	18.2	22.6	24.1	21.9	22.2	20.1	22.2	26.0	24.0	20.0	10.3	10.7
Pennsylvania	15.0	12.7	11.5	14.2	10.3	10.4	10.7	11.4	14.9	14.0	13.2	6.7	7.5	9.1
Rhode Island	1.7	3.8	12.6	4.5	3.1	3.5	5.1	1.7	3.8	10.1	12.0	8.5	9.5	4.0
South Carolina	22.0	22.9	19.4	22.2	17.2	29.6	25.0	19.0	21.5	27.3	24.5	21.0	27.9	27.8
Tennessee	33.4	25.1	21.2	22.3	24.8	26.5	28.7	18.1	19.6	21.3	22.5	27.2	22.6	22.2
Vermont	2.2	0.5	1.1	1.3	1.3	2.6	0.9	0.9	1.8	0.8	5.3	1.5	2.7	4.3
Virginia	18.1	10.9	11.9	9.4	21.2	12.7	22.0	15.9	15.4	12.7	18.6	18.8	17.3	18.6
West Virginia	3.7	2.2	2.4	1.7	1.7	2.9	2.6	1.5	1.8	2.2	2.3	2.3	2.1	3.5
Wisconsin	3.8	3.7	4.0	3.6	4.6	4.0	7.0	4.2	4.5	5.1	5.3	5.6	3.0	6.2
Weighted average	15.4	14.2	13.3	13.4	13.9	13.5	16.3	12.8	12.7	13.4	14.6	13.7	11.5	12.1
East CMU														
Arkansas	21.0	35.2	25.4	27.7	24.1	20.3	30.1	24.9	23.9	19.3	29.3	19.6	19.9	22.0
Iowa	20.1	21.5	19.5	16.7	13.1	16.3	24.5	16.4	17.0	13.2	16.7	20.8	16.6	13.3
Minnesota	18.9	16.1	15.4	10.3	13.9	17.7	22.3	10.2	13.5	12.6	16.9	22.4	12.3	17.7
Missouri	56.5	53.0	44.0	52.4	43.6	41.0	53.0	39.9	36.3	33.1	27.8	30.6	22.4	25.8
Mid-CMU														
Nebraska	48.8	49.5	55.1	58.4	53.4	57.7	61.4	60.7	65.3	72.7	80.8	80.6	79.1	75.1
North Dakota	15.5	19.2	17.2	19.6	17.6	17.2	19.7	22.8	17.2	18.1	24.7	25.4	22.1	24.5
Oklahoma	50.3	69.4	87.6	81.8	57.3	65.7	85.9	58.5	83.4	75.3	73.1	61.8	102.1	93.3
South Dakota	39.8	31.9	38.5	41.6	43.9	36.6	38.9	42.0	46.4	37.2	48.7	46.9	41.8	45.0
Texas	37.5	29.3	36.4	32.9	34.5	28.4	36.9	29.4	35.2	33.1	32.1	31.7	29.4	39.7
West CMU														
Colorado	18.4	22.0	17.4	18.5	16.5	20.8	20.9	20.2	29.2	13.9	36.9	29.3	28.9	19.1
Kansas	65.5	75.8	53.0	71.8	74.2	67.1	80.0	69.9	70.2	69.1	69.9	75.0	63.3	73.0
Montana	7.4	14.6	10.1	11.9	13.3	9.4	12.2	13.1	13.6	11.9	12.7	18.0	11.6	14.5
New Mexico	13.9	9.9	13.9	12.0	14.0	10.0	21.0	9.7	15.9	17.4	16.2	13.1	10.8	10.8
Wyoming	19.5	18.9	19.2	25.4	16.2	16.9	15.3	17.4	17.0	24.2	17.4	24.1	12.6	15.9
Weighted average	30.1	31.6	31.0	32.3	30.5	28.4	35.5	29.4	32.4	30.3	32.6	32.6	28.3	31.9
Coastal WMU														
California	35.1	31.7	33.1	30.2	27.3	24.9	25.5	20.8	26.7	25.5	25.6	23.0	14.2	18.1
Oregon	12.4	10.7	13.0	11.7	9.7	9.8	11.5	7.6	11.3	8.7	9.5	12.3	7.2	6.8
Washington	14.9	11.8	10.8	10.7	10.9	9.8	13.7	8.5	6.7	7.3	11.1	9.1	5.3	5.8
Interior WMU														
Arizona	36.0	43.4	51.7	38.8	46.2	27.7	26.6	31.2	27.6	25.0	23.4	20.3	20.6	26.3
Idaho	24.6	31.8	20.8	17.7	12.5	18.9	20.6	13.5	16.1	14.8	18.3	17.9	12.3	12.1
Nevada	10.2	8.8	23.9	15.6	9.2	11.7	8.1	6.3	14.6	7.4	24.5	16.1	5.8	12.4
Utah	10.4	15.2	15.3	13.9	24.8	24.3	11.8	6.3	29.3	16.5	28.5	20.0	10.1	14.6
Weighted average	21.9	22.4	25.7	21.3	20.9	18.5	17.8	14.7	19.4	16.3	19.8	17.5	11.7	14.8
United States	23.9	23.6	23.7	23.2	23.1	21.8	25.3	20.7	22.8	22.0	24.5	23.4	19.2	21.5

[a] Annual indices are defined as the predicted value from the trend analysis plus the deviation from the expected value in a year.

Table 36. (continued)

			Year				
1980	1981	1982	1983	1984	1985	1986	1987
19.1	14.5	19.4	17.6	14.5	18.3	20.5	11.4
10.1	14.6	8.9	9.3	9.8	14.4	20.7	19.0
17.2	14.9	8.5	3.9	17.6	33.3	14.3	7.9
9.2	16.0	11.5	9.2	15.1	16.1	14.8	12.9
13.3	16.2	10.9	8.8	12.4	17.4	13.0	13.2
11.1	14.4	11.0	11.6	8.1	13.0	12.9	13.3
15.4	23.6	16.4	15.7	15.2	14.3	16.7	23.0
12.0	19.9	20.9	17.3	13.5	20.8	15.0	21.2
13.7	14.1	13.7	18.2	17.1	10.4	15.2	13.7
2.9	2.1	2.5	2.1	2.2	1.7	2.2	2.4
18.5	16.7	7.8	14.7	20.6	14.8	20.7	17.8
7.7	6.8	7.2	5.2	6.2	11.3	7.6	5.5
6.4	8.5	5.2	5.8	5.2	7.8	8.7	7.6
22.7	20.9	25.7	29.2	20.7	20.9	23.2	18.0
6.1	1.5	3.1	5.9	2.6	3.3	2.9	2.9
14.2	18.0	20.4	16.9	17.2	13.0	19.5	11.3
3.9	4.2	5.0	3.6	2.1	3.6	4.7	4.6
17.6	20.1	15.7	13.9	18.8	18.3	21.2	20.8
12.4	18.7	19.1	16.4	15.7	16.5	18.6	22.0
11.5	9.1	8.9	11.1	8.6	10.0	12.5	9.6
5.1	2.1	9.0	3.7	1.7	6.6	5.1	6.2
24.7	28.3	38.6	23.5	27.4	25.8	23.6	27.6
21.2	22.0	22.4	16.3	19.3	19.4	18.2	21.3
4.3	2.9	2.7	2.8	3.2	5.8	4.6	3.8
17.8	13.3	13.2	14.7	11.5	12.8	8.2	10.7
2.5	3.9	3.6	2.6	5.1	4.8	3.4	3.7
6.5	8.9	5.7	6.7	5.3	4.7	6.9	7.6
12.4	13.8	12.9	11.8	11.6	13.2	13.3	12.6
24.7	23.1	21.0	27.9	15.6	16.5	18.3	17.4
23.5	16.5	18.6	14.8	17.2	15.2	13.4	17.3
15.3	16.0	11.6	14.2	12.3	13.2	11.0	9.0
26.5	32.4	28.3	32.5	21.0	15.3	21.6	24.0
73.8	79.1	81.2	62.5	65.9	66.7	59.8	69.8
25.1	25.7	23.1	20.2	18.9	20.2	22.3	25.4
104.8	82.4	100.6	81.7	70.6	77.8	89.9	81.0
40.4	44.4	42.0	40.0	46.3	39.2	31.0	36.7
35.7	40.7	41.5	34.0	31.7	30.2	37.6	37.4
35.0	35.5	36.8	24.1	34.3	28.9	39.9	34.0
89.1	68.3	75.4	70.7	72.1	62.4	65.7	65.0
15.7	18.6	13.4	10.8	13.7	18.0	14.7	14.5
18.5	17.4	14.9	13.5	24.6	16.7	18.9	14.9
16.2	12.8	17.4	9.7	9.7	9.5	15.0	11.3
34.7	35.5	34.5	29.4	29.7	27.8	31.1	30.7
20.5	21.0	21.8	17.5	17.6	15.6	14.4	13.7
9.3	13.4	9.6	7.1	7.2	6.3	6.8	8.1
5.1	5.9	5.6	3.8	6.8	3.8	4.0	3.3
19.6	13.5	20.2	14.3	14.7	15.1	13.0	8.1
11.7	13.7	15.3	12.2	15.4	9.5	10.1	10.3
17.2	11.7	5.7	8.5	12.5	8.3	5.7	7.9
19.1	27.2	10.5	12.2	28.5	13.4	15.9	13.9
15.3	14.8	13.9	11.5	14.1	11.2	10.4	9.2
22.8	23.9	22.8	20.0	20.7	20.4	21.2	20.2

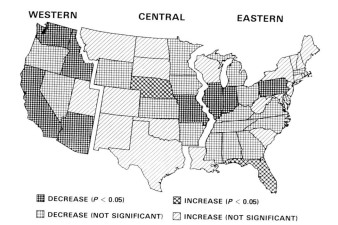

WESTERN   CENTRAL   EASTERN

⊞ DECREASE (*P* < 0.05)   ⊠ INCREASE (*P* < 0.05)
▦ DECREASE (NOT SIGNIFICANT)   ▨ INCREASE (NOT SIGNIFICANT)

Figure 40. Twenty-two-year (1966–87) trends of mourning doves seen in the Western, Central and Eastern management units.

management decisions). For the CMU, downward trends were indicated in the five-, ten- and fifteen-year periods, whereas for doves heard, a downward trend was registered only for the ten-year period. No trend was noted for the twenty-two-year period for doves either seen or heard. For the WMU, highly significant downward trends were indicated for all but the two-year period. This result matched that for doves heard.

Comparison with the North American Breeding Bird Survey

The North American Breeding Bird Survey annually monitors all birds seen and heard, including the mourning dove, along more than two thousand routes in Canada and the United States (Robbins et al. 1986). Whereas this survey was designed to provide trend information for all species of birds encountered, the Call-count Survey was developed to yield annual comparisons and trend information specific to mourning dove populations. Nevertheless, the Breeding Bird Survey provides an independent measure of mourning dove population trends for comparison with the Call-count Survey, despite several differences in timing, methods and results of the two surveys.

Sauer et al. (in preparation) made a detailed comparison of mourning dove population trend estimates from the two surveys for the 1966–88 period. For the United States, both the Call-count Survey data (−0.66 percent per year) and Breeding Bird Survey data (0.05 percent per year) showed no trend (both surveys = *P* > 0.10). Both survey analyses indicated a population decline in the WMU but with differing magnitudes (Call-count Survey, −2.38 percent per year, *P* < 0.05; Breeding Bird

Table 37. Trends (percentage change[a] per year as determined by linear regression) in number of mourning doves seen by management unit and state, 1966–87.

Management unit/state		2-year (1986–87)			5-year (1983–87)		
		N	Change[b]	CI		N	Change[b]	CI	
EMU	Alabama	24	−29.9***	−49.2	−10.5	30	−1.6	−8.0	4.8
	Connecticut	2	0.0	0.0	0.0	2	25.7***	21.9	29.4
	Delaware	2	−66.6**	0.0	−10.7	2	30.8	−36.5	98.2
	Florida	21	0.1	−20.3	20.5	21	1.3	−7.7	10.3
	Georgia	21	13.2	−26.1	52.5	22	−4.2	−19.6	11.2
	Illinois	15	21.4	−14.8	57.6	20	16.0***	5.0	27.1
	Indiana	12	43.2***	20.4	66.0	15	9.6	−2.9	22.2
	Kentucky	14	5.1	−31.0	41.2	20	2.6	−11.0	16.1
	Louisiana	16	−19.6	−51.7	12.6	18	5.6*	−0.4	11.6
	Maine	6	−22.6	0.0	102.3	7	−14.5	−41.2	12.2
	Maryland	10	−20.9*	−43.7	1.8	13	15.7*	−1.9	33.2
	Massachusetts	6	−48.0**	−87.3	−8.6	16	10.5	−11.0	32.1
	Michigan	18	12.0	−28.7	52.8	20	17.8***	5.7	30.0
	Mississippi	22	−22.0**	−43.2	−0.7	22	−1.9	−13.1	9.3
	New Hampshire	0	0.0	0.0	0.0	3	−22.9***	−29.3	−16.3
	New Jersey	10	−43.7***	−60.9	−26.5	18	−5.8	−18.0	6.3
	New York	8	9.9	−45.8	65.5	10	19.1***	5.9	32.3
	North Carolina	18	−19.0	−58.2	20.3	21	5.5***	2.0	9.0
	Ohio	16	18.8	−22.9	60.5	38	15.7***	4.2	27.2
	Pennsylvania	13	11.2	−38.0	60.3	15	12.0	−6.1	30.0
	Rhode Island	2	25.6	−49.9	101.2	2	22.1***	20.8	23.3
	South Carolina	17	−8.8	−24.4	6.8	20	1.0	−5.6	7.6
	Tennessee	21	16.6	−5.5	38.8	24	6.0	−10.8	22.8
	Vermont	16	−28.8*	−58.3	0.7	23	10.3	−7.2	27.8
	Virginia	8	−16.2*	−35.8	3.3	11	−15.6***	−20.8	−10.4
	West Virginia	9	−10.6	−71.1	49.8	10	−7.5	−39.2	24.3
	Wisconsin	15	−12.5	−42.4	17.4	20	9.1***	3.7	14.5
	Weighted average	317	−4.3	−11.6	2.9	443	2.9*	−0.2	5.9
East CMU	Arkansas	13	−4.5	−52.8	43.8	15	−9.9***	−14.7	−5.0
	Iowa	14	2.5	−34.4	39.4	16	6.4*	−0.5	13.4
	Minnesota	6	47.4	−83.9	178.8	11	−12.5	−38.6	13.6
	Missouri	20	20.0	−4.7	44.8	20	1.2	−4.5	6.8
Mid-CMU	Nebraska	21	19.5**	2.0	37.1	25	0.1	−7.1	7.3
	North Dakota	15	11.9	−26.9	50.8	25	2.9	−3.9	9.6
	Oklahoma	14	−8.0	−58.1	42.1	16	−9.7**	−17.5	−1.8
	South Dakota	15	36.8	−12.2	85.8	21	−9.7*	−19.8	0.3
	Texas	107	−5.1	−19.7	9.6	133	1.6	−3.1	6.2
West CMU	Colorado	13	−22.9**	−42.1	−3.6	16	7.6	−4.4	19.7
	Kansas	21	0.0	−21.4	21.5	25	−8.5**	−15.9	−1.2
	Montana	16	2.2	−31.6	36.0	22	−6.4	−19.3	6.3
	New Mexico	20	−33.3**	−63.2	−3.4	26	0.5	−11.9	12.9
	Wyoming	10	1.7	−37.3	40.8	15	−3.9	−25.8	17.9
	Weighted average	292	1.5	−7.1	10.0	386	−3.1**	−6.1	−0.2
Coastal WMU	California	34	6.1	−13.5	25.7	48	−6.5	−14.8	1.7
	Oregon	8	−12.9	−47.3	21.5	15	13.2	−4.6	31.0
	Washington	11	7.4	−41.0	55.7	15	−6.3*	−13.2	0.7
Interior WMU	Arizona	40	−31.3**	−56.3	−6.3	52	−21.4***	−34.2	−8.7
	Idaho	10	91.5	−62.9	245.8	21	2.0	−6.3	10.3
	Nevada	15	71.8	−19.5	163.1	21	−14.5	−37.7	8.6
	Utah	10	−20.2***	−35.8	−4.7	14	0.1	−12.7	13.0
	Weighted average	116	1.5	−12.3	15.4	186	−6.9***	−11.6	−2.1
United States		725	0.2	−6.0	6.4	1,015	−2.2**	−4.4	−0.0

[a] Mean of route weighted by land area and population density. The estimated count in the next year is (percentage ÷ 100 + 1) times the count in the current year where percentage is the annual change. Note: extrapolating the estimated trend statistic (percentage change per year) over time (e.g., 22 years) may exaggerate the total change over the period.
[b] *$P < 0.1$, **$P < 0.05$, ***$P < 0.01$.

Table 37. (continued)

	10-year (1978–87)				15-year (1973–87)				22-year (1966–87)		
N	Change[b]	CI		N	Change[b]	CI		N	Change[b]	CI	
33	−3.0	−7.4	1.3	37	−0.2	−3.6	3.2	39	−0.5	−2.3	1.3
2	−7.6	−32.5	17.2	2	6.0	−2.7	14.6	2	10.6***	9.5	11.7
3	8.3	−33.5	50.1	3	4.9	−17.8	27.7	3	3.2	−21.8	28.3
21	2.6	−1.5	6.6	23	5.8***	3.0	8.5	26	6.4***	4.2	8.6
22	−2.4	−5.8	1.0	25	0.5	−1.3	2.3	26	−0.1	−3.3	3.1
22	2.8*	−0.0	5.7	22	−2.4**	−4.7	−0.1	22	−3.3***	−5.8	−0.9
15	8.0***	3.1	12.9	15	−4.0*	−8.5	0.4	17	−4.4**	−8.3	−0.4
21	4.8	−4.0	13.6	23	2.0**	0.2	3.8	24	−0.2	−3.1	2.8
18	1.8	−1.3	4.9	18	1.8	−1.5	5.1	22	0.9	−3.0	4.8
8	−0.3	−10.4	9.8	8	−0.1	−9.0	8.8	10	2.7	0.0	141.6
14	6.2***	2.8	9.7	15	3.5	−1.2	8.2	15	1.4	−1.3	4.2
18	−3.9	−9.5	1.6	18	−1.8	−6.1	2.4	19	−2.9*	−6.3	0.5
20	4.7	−1.7	11.2	20	1.1	−3.4	5.6	20	−0.4	−4.7	3.9
23	−1.9*	−3.9	0.1	24	0.4	−1.4	2.3	25	−1.4	−3.4	0.7
3	14.1***	9.3	18.9	3	7.5	−2.9	17.9	8	3.2	−9.1	15.4
18	−5.2	−12.0	1.6	18	−2.5	−6.6	1.5	19	0.3	−7.2	7.8
14	−6.0	−14.5	2.5	14	2.0	−3.0	6.9	16	1.6	−4.8	8.0
21	0.3	−1.6	2.3	21	1.5	−0.6	3.7	21	−1.1	−2.6	0.4
52	9.2***	2.8	15.7	52	−1.4	−4.3	1.4	54	−1.3	−3.5	0.8
15	7.2**	0.5	13.8	16	2.0*	−0.0	4.1	16	−3.0**	−5.9	−0.2
2	−4.2	−18.5	10.1	2	−1.6	−4.2	0.9	4	0.9	0.0	297.8
23	0.2	−4.9	5.3	23	1.2	−1.3	3.7	23	1.1	−2.4	4.6
24	−1.0	−6.7	4.6	27	1.5	−3.6	6.6	30	−1.2	−4.5	2.2
23	3.5	−11.4	18.5	23	9.2	−3.4	21.8	25	7.8	−7.1	22.7
11	−8.5***	−12.8	−4.2	11	−5.7***	−8.8	−2.6	11	−1.9	−4.4	0.6
10	5.2***	2.8	7.5	11	9.2***	6.4	12.1	11	3.0	−4.5	10.6
21	3.7	−1.1	8.5	21	2.4	−1.1	5.8	21	2.7*	−0.2	5.5
477	0.4	−0.7	1.6	495	0.2	−0.6	1.1	529	−0.9**	−1.7	−0.1
15	−3.5***	−5.9	−1.1	15	−5.0***	−7.6	−2.5	16	−1.7	−4.5	1.2
17	−0.6	−4.7	3.4	17	0.2	−2.1	2.4	17	−0.5	−2.5	1.5
12	−8.7*	−18.9	1.5	12	−4.7	−11.4	2.0	13	−2.1	−7.4	3.3
22	−2.5**	−4.7	−0.2	24	−3.1***	−4.9	−1.3	26	−4.8***	−7.4	−2.3
25	−3.7***	−5.9	−1.5	25	−1.5*	−3.1	0.1	26	1.5***	0.5	2.5
26	−7.3***	−11.1	−3.6	26	−2.2	−6.3	1.8	27	1.6	−0.6	3.9
16	−10.4***	−17.3	−3.6	17	0.2	−2.2	2.7	19	1.6	−0.8	4.0
23	−6.7***	−11.3	−2.1	23	−3.9**	−7.5	−0.3	26	0.0	−3.9	3.9
145	−1.2	−3.7	1.3	155	0.9	−0.8	2.6	183	0.5	−1.2	2.3
18	−0.3	−3.3	2.7	18	4.4***	1.6	7.2	19	3.9*	−0.1	7.9
28	−4.0***	−6.7	−1.3	30	−1.6	−3.6	0.4	31	−0.1	−2.2	2.0
25	−1.4	−9.7	6.8	26	−0.8	−7.1	5.6	28	2.0	−3.7	7.7
27	4.6	−4.9	14.2	30	6.0	−3.4	15.3	30	2.0	−0.8	4.8
17	−4.6	−14.8	5.6	18	−8.6*	−17.3	0.0	18	−2.5	−6.3	1.3
416	−4.7***	−6.6	−2.7	436	−1.0**	−1.8	−0.2	479	0.1	−0.7	0.9
58	−3.9*	−7.9	0.1	61	−5.4***	−8.3	−2.5	70	−4.0***	−5.6	−2.3
18	2.0	−1.4	5.3	19	−1.5*	−3.2	0.2	20	−2.4	−6.3	1.5
16	−3.6	−11.9	4.6	18	−7.6**	−13.5	−1.6	19	−6.1**	−11.2	−1.1
54	−12.0***	−18.8	−5.1	58	−7.8***	−13.4	−2.1	63	−6.7***	−10.4	−3.0
22	0.3	−6.6	7.3	22	0.5	−3.9	5.0	23	−3.3**	−6.4	−0.1
21	−6.0	−16.5	4.5	22	−0.2	−13.6	13.2	26	−0.8	−8.2	6.5
16	8.5***	2.0	14.9	16	1.2	−5.0	7.3	16	0.2	−3.4	3.7
205	−3.9***	−6.6	−1.2	216	−4.1***	−6.2	−2.0	237	−3.3***	−5.0	−2.5
1,098	−3.6***	−5.1	−2.1	1,147	−1.1***	−1.7	−0.4	1,245	−0.6*	−1.2	0.0

Survey, -2.35 percent per year, $P < 0.01$). For the CMU, neither survey analysis detected a significant trend (Call-count Survey, -0.43 percent per year; Breeding Bird Survey, -0.4 percent per year; both $= P > 0.10$). In the EMU, the point estimates of trend differed in magnitude: the Call-count Survey indicated a possible negative population change (-0.34 percent per year), whereas the Breeding Bird Survey data showed an increasing population trend ($+0.58$ percent per year). However, neither trend was significantly different from zero ($P > 0.10$). Interpretation of results for the EMU are discussed in greater detail in chapter 17.

A comparison of results from the two surveys by state revealed significant differences in trend estimates for eleven (23 percent) of the forty-eight states sampled. Many of the discrepancies were associated with differences in strata used in each survey, as well as with large differences in the sample sizes (number of routes) associated with many states in each survey. Generally, the Breeding Bird Survey exhibited smaller variances than did the Call-count Survey among states in the EMU and WMU where the former's sample sizes were greater. Variances were especially greater for Call-count Survey estimates among northeastern and mid-Atlantic states where sampling was perceptibly lower. Sauer et al. (in preparation) concluded that the greater sample sizes associated with the Breeding Bird Survey appeared to provide more precise trend estimates than did those of the Call-count Survey in the EMU and WMU. On the other hand, the Call-count Survey appeared to yield estimates with about equal precision in the CMU.

The merits of maintaining two surveys that collect similar information on mourning doves recently were reviewed in 1989 by the U.S. Fish and Wildlife Service. It was decided to retain and rely on the Call-count Survey for management decisions because:

1. The Migratory Bird Treaty Act specifies that, when adopting hunting regulations, the Secretary of the Interior give *due regard* to, among other considerations, the distribution, abundance and flight lines of migratory birds. These considerations—especially abundance—can change from year to year, so it has been logical from the beginning to develop hunting regulations annually. The Call-count Survey is the *only* survey program designed to monitor mourning doves on a national scale and provide status information in time for consideration in the annual harvest regulations-setting process, which begins each June. A yearly assessment of populations helps assure that regulations are appropriate and commensurate with the status of the resource. The Call-count Survey provides timely information needed for regulations development; data from Breeding Bird Survey routes are not available to meet the June deadline.

2. Each survey has its own respective strengths and provides information on different aspects of mourning dove populations. For example, the Breeding Bird Survey presently provides more extensive coverage in the eastern U.S., while the Call-count Survey has better coverage in the western states. The Breeding Bird Survey collectively records doves heard and doves seen and, therefore, can be influenced by the greater variability of doves seen. The Call-count Survey records doves heard and doves seen separately, allowing a more detailed analysis of trends by considering two independent variables. At some locations, increased disturbance can be an important factor in census results. Trends, using disturbance as a covariable, can only be assessed with the Call-count Survey. Consequently, the Call-count Survey provides information that is unavailable from the Breeding Bird Survey.

3. The Call-count Survey was developed specifically as a survey technique for mourning doves, and various assumptions associated with the survey have been reviewed periodically to assure continued reliability of this program. Future use of both surveys' results in mourning dove management will be contingent on a more thorough comparison of survey methods and consideration of other issues, such as comparability to historical data sets and availability of information to meet current timetables for development of hunting regulations.

Chapter 15

Biological Evaluation
of the Call-count Survey

Thomas S. Baskett
Cooperative Fish and Wildlife Research Unit
U.S. Fish and Wildlife Service
The School of Natural Resources
University of Missouri, Columbia, Missouri

In his presentation "Counting Birds for a Relative Measure (Index) of Density," Dawson (1981: 12) provided an excellent perspective for many bird surveys: "Counts of birds from points of transect lines give an index of population density, even when distances have not been accurately estimated. Factors which influence the counts include the species, age, sex or reproductive group of each bird, the season, habitat, time of day, weather, environmental noise, the observer, the number of other birds being recorded and details of the counting technique. If valid deductions about bird densities are to be made, such influences must be standardized, or their effects removed."

Here, attention is focused on a single species, the mourning dove, and primarily with audio, not visual, counts. The preceding chapter dealt with details of the counting technique, including improvements in statistical design and analyses of data, and the consistency of observer performance. In the national Call-count Survey, the season, time of day, allowable limits for weather and habitat all have been standardized. This chapter emphasizes biological considerations of the Call-counts and attempts to answer (1) what a cooing mourning dove is and (2) what influences its cooing rates in ways that might affect the audio counts. Some of these factors pose problems that can be solved through standardization of counting methods, but some

problems cannot.

The "perch coo" is the only vocalization recorded on Call-count Surveys (see chapters 10 and 14). It consists of "five to seven notes; one note, then a higher one and finally three to five lower notes held at a greater length" (McClure 1939: 323). It is the mourning dove's song (Craig 1911). It is uttered chiefly by the male, although the female sometimes sings a faint version (Frankel and Baskett 1961). Perch cooing serves to announce the presence of a male and to attract and court the female. Since perch cooing decreases soon after pair bond formation, mate attraction may be the most important function of dove song (Stone 1966).

Mourning doves of both sexes have another vocalization, which Craig (1911) termed the "nest call" (see also chapter 10). It resembles the first three notes of the perch coo but usually is fainter and variable in volume, length and inflection. It differs in function from the perch coo, for it usually is employed as communication between mates, particularly during courting and nest site selection (Jackson and Baskett 1964). Nest calls and accompanying behavior similar to those of the mourning dove probably are universal among the world's doves and pigeons (Craig 1911, Murton and Isaacson 1962). The nest call is not tallied in the North American Call-count Survey, so observers (listeners) must be able to distinguish it.

The perch coo is the song—the *only* song—of the mourning dove. When singing (perch cooing), the male arches his neck, puffs out his throat, stiffens his body and bobs his tail with each of the five to seven notes. *Photo by Mike Blair; courtesy of the Kansas Department of Wildlife and Parks.*

FACTORS AFFECTING PERCH-COOING RATES

Pairing Status

By far the most important factor affecting perch-cooing activity of male mourning doves is whether they are mated. Frankel and Baskett (1961) noted tenfold increases in perch-cooing frequency among males confined in small pens when their mates were removed. When the females were returned, cooing dropped to previous levels if pair bonds were restored. These findings were substantiated by several field studies of free-flying birds, most of them marked *(Table 38)*. Three-minute perch-cooing rates of unmated males ranged from 6.2 to 20.7 times higher than those of mated males.

Cooing rates were computed as total coos divided by total numbers of three-minute periods each dove was observed. Data reported by Sayre et al. (1980) are the most appropriate for these comparisons because they were provided by radio-tagged doves monitored during the entire two-hour study periods, beginning half an hour before sunrise. In other studies *(Table 38)*, marked mated birds usually were silent and inconspicuous when away from their territories. At such times, they usually would not be included in the database because they were not observed.

For interpretation of Call-count Survey results, the relative probability that mated and unmated males will utter the perch coo during a three-minute period is a more useful figure than is the frequency of cooing. The probability figures *(Table 38)* were derived by dividing numbers of three-minute periods in which each dove perch cooed by the number of periods during which it was observed. Even this more conservative approach (comparing probability instead of frequency of cooing) shows that an unmated dove is 6.3 times more likely to be heard in a given three-minute period than is a mated bird (Sayre et al. 1980).

The combined sample sizes in the four field studies summarized in Table 38 were substantial. At least 65 marked individual doves were involved, and several of them provided data for both the unmated and mated status. Other known but unmarked birds brought the total known individuals to 91. Data were gathered during thousands of three-minute periods during hundreds of hours of observation. The conclusions about the cooing rates of unmated versus mated males were further supported by findings of Stone (1963) in a field study in Colorado.

Table 38. Cooing rates and probabilities of cooing per three-minute period by mated and unmated male mourning doves in four field studies (data for courting unmated males excluded).

Status (N)	Mean coos per three minutes	Ratio of cooing rates unmated/mated	Probability of cooing during three-minute periods	Number of three-minute periods	Location	Source
Unmated (8)	8.40	13.3	0.93	820	Missouri	Jackson and Baskett (1964)
Mated (6)	0.63		0.23	820		
Unmated (12)[a]	8.19	6.8	0.94	[b]	Arizona	Irby (1964)
Mated (25)	1.21		0.31	[b]		
Unmated (20)	8.88	6.2	0.95	3,543	South Carolina	Sayre et al. (1978)
Mated (6)	1.44		0.42	321		
Unmated (5)	8.68	20.7	0.94	952	Missouri	Sayre et al. (1980)
Mated (14)	0.42		0.15	2,546		

[a] Includes 5 males studied both as unmated and mated.
[b] Numerical bases for means not given; 488 total hours of observation.

Results of several studies of confined doves also have confirmed the lower perch-cooing rates for mated than for unmated males. However, overall rates for both groups generally are lower in pens than in the wild because doves in pens are silent for longer periods (Armbruster 1983).

During courtship, males (some of which never establish pair bonds) perch coo at rates intermediate between those of unmated and mated males (Irby 1964, Sayre et al. 1980). Despite this complication, the decrease in perch-cooing rates of males as they become mated is sufficiently dramatic and consistent to be used as a measure of mating status in various experiments with penned doves (Frankel and Baskett 1963, Goforth and Baskett 1965, Sayre et al. 1981, Armbruster 1983).

The potential impact of cooing by unmated male doves on the outcome of Call-count Surveys still has not been considered sufficiently. The problem extends to many other avian species, reviewed by Thorpe (1961), who noted that it is very unusual for a mated male to sing (perch coo) more frequently than any unmated bird, which is a considerable understatement. Species in which singing is at least partially suspended after mating include bobwhite quail (Stoddard 1931), song sparrow (Nice 1943), English robin (Lack 1946), pied flycatcher (von Haartman 1956), chaffinch (Thorpe 1961), field sparrow (Best 1975), Cassin's finch (Samson 1978), house wren (Wilson and Bart 1985) and others.

For the mourning dove, evidence is overwhelming that unmated males have higher rates and probabilities of perch cooing than do mated males. The effect of pairing status on cooing is so great that it must be considered in any analysis of other factors influencing cooing rates. The most important question is how differential cooing performance of unmated and mated males affects results of the mourning dove Call-count Survey (discussed later).

Position in the Nesting Cycle

Cooing performance of mated male doves also is affected by the stage of the nesting cycle, as suggested by Craig (1911) and Webb (1949). Quantitative studies of the relationships between perch cooing and nesting status have produced some contrary results (see Stone 1966, Baskett et al. 1978). Possible reasons for the apparent contradictions include differences in categorizing nesting cycle stages, sample sizes, penning effects and different subspecies of doves.

Frankel and Baskett (1961) noted small numerical differences in perch-cooing rates of three penned mourning doves according to nesting stages. These differences were not consistent among individuals nor statistically significant ($P > 0.05$). Frankel and Baskett concluded that any small differences in cooing rates at different nesting stages were overshadowed by the high rates of cooing of unmated males. In a study of six marked, mated, free-flying doves, Jackson (1963) and Jackson and Baskett (1964) reached the same conclusion, but Jackson's (1963) data showed numerical (not statistically significant) differences in cooing rates related to nesting stages that agreed with results of later, more complete data sets (Table 39). Mackey's (1965) observations of one mated, unconfined male during parts of five nesting cycles produced similar results (Table 39). Yet another study produced somewhat analogous numerical results, but cooing rates did not differ significantly according to stage of nesting (LaPerriere and Haugen 1972b).

Irby's (1964) two-year study involving 32 individually marked male mourning doves and numerous unmarked males provided data that clearly showed patterns of perch cooing that differed statistically according to stage of the nesting cycle. Irby's study, conducted in Arizona, also provided a framework for the three-year field study by Sayre et

Table 39. Mean perch-cooing rates per three-minute period for male mourning doves, related to phase in the nesting cycle, as determined in four studies of marked, free-flying, mated males.

Source	Nesting cycle phase						
	Selecting nest site	Building nest	Laying eggs	Incubating	Brooding young	After successful nesting	After nest disrupted
Jackson (1963)	a	0.59		0.65	0.52	0.75c	
Irby (1964)	0.19	0.21	1.41	1.53	0.37	2.11	2.64
Mackey (1965)[b]				1.32	0.26	3.56c	
Sayre et al. (1980)	0.42	0.48	0.85	0.70	0.24	1.12	0.47

[a] No data.
[b] Rates computed from Mackey's Table 2.
[c] From listings as "between nestings" by both Jackson (1963) and Mackey (1965).

al. (1980) in Missouri, in which 19 male doves were monitored by radio telemetry.

In both of these studies, perch-cooing rates and probability of cooing were low during nest site selection and nest building *(Table 39 and Figure 41)*, requiring one to three days and two to four days, respectively. Cooing increased during laying (two to three days) and during the fourteen-day incubation period, then dropped markedly during the ten to fourteen days when the adults brooded the young. Both Irby (1964) and Sayre et al. (1980) showed cooing rates and probabilities rising between nestings. In Irby's study, cooing rates did not differ significantly ($P > 0.05$) when the doves were singing after successful and unsuccessful nestings. In the Sayre et al. study, however, singing (perch-cooing) rates were dramatically and significantly ($P < 0.05$) higher following successful nestings than were those following unsuccessful nestings *(Table 39 and Figure 41)*.

Perch-cooing rates of mated males in different phases of the nesting cycle are related in complex ways to other behavioral traits, particularly the apportionment of the birds' time in different locations. Mated males coo principally when within their nesting territories (Jackson and Baskett 1964, Irby 1964, Sayre et al. 1980) but often perch coo briefly before leaving the roost. Other off-territory cooing is minimal *(Table 40)*.

The amount of time the male spends in the nesting territory generally decreases as each cycle progresses (Sayre et al. 1980). During the early phases (nest site selection, building and laying) nesting males spent much of the observation

Table 40. Mean perch-cooing rates per three-minute period, in relation to location, by mated male mourning doves observed from 30 minutes before to 90 minutes after sunrise (from Sayre et al. 1980).

Location	Cooing rate (mean ± 1 SE)	Number of three-minute periods
On territory	1.02 ± 0.06	1,242
Off territory	0.01 ± 0.00	1,046
Roost	0.41 ± 0.08	258

period in the vicinity of the nest. During the laying period the perch-cooing rate is quite high, reflecting a particularly active cooing period as well as prolonged presence near the nest.

During incubation and brooding, males spent considerable portions of the morning observation period away from nests. During incubation, perch-cooing rates remained high regardless of this fact, but then fell to a minimum during brooding *(Figure 41)*. Also during this stage, audibility of perch coos may be greatly reduced through interference from the crop when engorged with crop milk and seeds (M. J. Armbruster personal communication: 1987). Moreover, brooding males often do not come to nesting territories each morning until after the two-hour observation period (Sayre et al. 1980). When off territory, these males, mostly silent, may be as far as 5 miles (8 km) from nesting territories. (Many of the birds, even though marked, could not have been included properly in the database for cooing performance without having been found and located periodically through radio tracking.)

The considerable differences in perch-cooing rates according to stage in the nesting cycle, particularly the disparity between cooing rates of brooding males and males between nestings, were the basis for Irby's (1964) concern about the validity of Call-count data under certain circumstances. He thought that storms might disrupt large numbers of nests, which would be followed by synchronous renesting. Resulting waves of high then low cooing rates related to position of mated males in the nesting cycle, depending on timing of the Call-count Survey, might produce misleading indices. It seems unlikely, however, that such a high degree of nesting synchronization would occur over the large areas sampled in the Call-count Survey. Even on a local basis, T. S. Baskett and R. P. Breitenbach (unpublished data) found no evidence of synchronous renesting following a severe thunderstorm that destroyed known nests in two islands of nesting habitat in central Missouri.

Clearly, stage of the nesting cycle does affect perch-cooing rates, but the mated male is never a match in cooing performance for his unmated

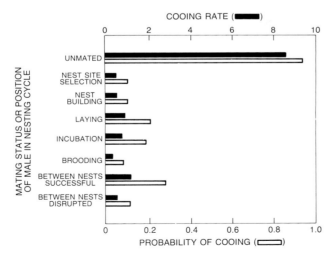

Figure 41. Mean perch-cooing rates and probabilities of cooing in three-minute intervals by radio-tagged, unconfined male mourning doves in Missouri, related to position in the nesting cycle (based on data from Sayre et al. 1980).

counterpart, as shown dramatically in *Figure 41*. We doubt that varying rates of cooing by mated males in different positions of the nesting cycle could affect Call-count Survey results seriously on more than a very local basis.

Age

Armbruster (1983) was the first researcher to investigate possible effects of age on perch-cooing performance of confined male mourning doves. He compared cooing rates and probabilities of cooing within three-minute intervals by confined yearling and older (at least two years old) males. Samples were 25 unmated and 25 mated males observed during 501 periods between thirty minutes before and ninety minutes after sunrise, the period used in Call-count Surveys.

Older unmated males cooed about 1.4 times more frequently per three-minute interval during the entire two-hour periods than did unmated yearling males. Probability of cooing by unmated males in a three-minute interval was about 1.3 times that of mated males.

However, no significant age-related differences in perch-cooing rates or probabilities of cooing were found among mated males of the two age groups. Thus, changes in age composition of the population do not seem likely to affect seriously the interpretation of Call-count Survey results.

Time of Day

Most early studies (Duvall and Robbins 1952, McGowan 1952, Peters 1952, Cohen et al. 1960) showed that perch cooing by male mourning doves is more frequent during early portions than during late portions of the two-hour morning observation period formally adopted in 1953 in the national Call-count Survey. However, Robbins (1981) found little difference in mourning doves detected by sound and sight in the first and second hours of the nationwide Breeding Bird Survey, 1965–79. McGowan (1952) noted that fewer were heard at the end of the route than at the beginning, even if the population at the end equaled that at the beginning.

Later, Frankel and Baskett (1961) and Jackson and Baskett (1964) showed that daily time patterns of cooing by mated and unmated males differ markedly. These findings were confirmed and elaborated with substantial data in field studies of individually marked birds in Arizona (Irby 1964) and South Carolina (Sayre et al. 1978) and with radio-

tagged doves in Missouri (Sayre et al. 1980). The same general tendencies were evident in results of all three studies. Unmated males cooed at high rates throughout the entire two-hour period. Rates of mated males were much lower and patterned very differently in time than those of unmated birds. Mated males cooed at their highest rates just before sunrise, then the rates dropped and steadied at a low level by about forty-five to fifty minutes after sunrise.

Data from Sayre et al. (1980) offered the most complete picture of cooing patterns related to time *(Figure 42)* because, as explained earlier, the males in that study were monitored by radio telemetry even when they were off territory. Mean cooing rates of unmated males computed for the first and second hours (8.6 versus 8.5 coos per three-minute interval) were not significantly different ($P > 0.05$, *t*-test). In contrast, mated males cooed about three times as much per three-minute interval during the first hour as during the second (0.76 versus 0.25 coos per three-minute interval, $P < 0.05$, *t*-test). Mean cooing rates and probabilities for mated males were highest in the fifteen minutes preceding sunrise. Rates dropped gradually during the remainder of the first hour, then dropped markedly during the last forty-five minutes of the observation period *(Figure 42)*. Time-related trends (cooing patterns) were similar for mated males regardless of position in the nesting cycle (Sayre et al. 1980).

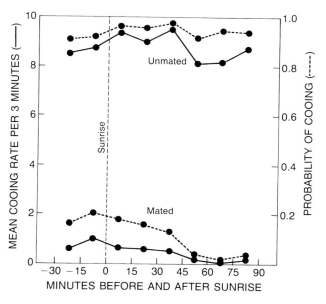

Figure 42. Mean perch-cooing rates and probabilities of cooing by mated and unmated male mourning doves during three-minute intervals within fifteen-minute segments of the morning survey period (after Sayre et al. 1980).

Radio tagging and telemetry have helped to show that unmated male mourning doves perch coo at a much greater rate than do mated males. Since the perch coo is the vocalization basis of the Call-count Survey and unmated males do most perch cooing, the Call-counts can serve as a measure of relative dove abundance in large areas and from one time to another, where ratios of mated to unmated males are relatively stable. Call-count data do not serve well as indicators of numbers of nesting doves on small, intensively studied areas. *Photo courtesy of the Missouri Cooperative Fish and Wildlife Research Unit.*

The probabilities of cooing within three-minute periods, which actually determine the numbers of doves tallied on Call-count routes, showed time patterns similar to those of calling rates *(Figure 42)*. Thus, the cooing of mated males that sing mostly before and soon after sunrise "is superimposed upon the cooing of unmated males which coo at a high rate throughout the morning period" (Frankel and Baskett 1961: 379). The early cooing activity of mated birds probably accounts for the greater numbers of doves tallied during the first hour of the survey than during the second hour. As noted by Baskett et al. (1978), differences in daily cooing patterns doubtless produce a very different mix of mated and unmated males in the tallies made during the first and second hours of the survey.

In many types of avian surveys, effects of daily time differences must be recognized (Shields 1977). A study in Ontario by Weber and Theberge (1977) well illustrates the potential problem. They used standard Breeding Bird Survey procedures (see Robbins and Van Velzen 1969) requiring more stops, longer routes and more time than the mourning dove Call-count Survey. Habitat for mourning doves was much better near the eastern end than the western end of one route. When Weber and Theberge ran this route from east to west, they tallied nearly three times as many singing male doves (mean = 12.4 doves per one hundred stops) as when they ran the route from west to east (4.3 per hundred stops). This finding emphasizes the necessity to run mourning dove Call-count routes in the same compass direction in consecutive years, as is customary.

If the mourning dove Call-count Survey could be restricted to the first hour, with other routes added to compensate for the reduced sample, the following advantages might be realized, as spelled out by Baskett et al. (1978: 169):

"1. More doves per stop would be tallied, and the sampling would be more representative for an entire route.
2. The statistical frame would probably be better, according to the findings of Gates et al. (1975) whose paper showed that for the Texas call-count survey, more routes with fewer stops would reduce the variance of the overall mean.
3. The number of mated males tallied per stop would be higher, as would their ratio to unmated males."

Population Density

Information about effects of population density on cooing is contradictory. Duvall and Robbins (1952), Southeastern Association of Game and Fish Commissioners (1957) and Cohen et al. (1960) all found that doves coo more frequently when their densities are high than when they are low. (The breeding status of the doves was not taken into account.

Irby (1964) reported cooing rates of mated males about 1.5 times higher in dense populations (three pairs of breeding doves per acre: 7.4/ha) than in sparse populations (one pair per acre: 2.5/ha). He had additional evidence from cooing rates of individual doves reinforcing his belief that mated birds coo more frequently when in sight or sound contact with other doves. Irby noted, however, that cooing by unmated males was unaffected by density—they cooed at high rates whether or not they were in sight or sound contact with other males.

LaPerriere and Haugen (1972b) compared mean cooing rates per bird during three-minute intervals according to numbers of other male doves heard; pairing status of the birds was not determined. Cooing rates were significantly ($P < 0.001$) higher when two doves were cooing than when only one was heard. No significantly elevated rates were found in means of the small samples when more than two birds were heard *(Table 41)*.

Table 41. Mean perch-cooing rates in relation to the number of cooing mourning doves present, as reported by LaPerriere and Haugen (1972b) and Sayre et al. (1978).

	LaPerriere and Haugen		Sayre et al.	
Number of cooing doves	Mean coos per three minutes[a]	Number of three-minute periods	Mean coos per minute[b]	Number of one-minute periods
1	5.08	376	2.68	2,614
2	7.36	61	2.99	3,417
3	9.07	9	2.99	2,375
4	8.13	2	2.95	1,142
5+			2.89	374

[a] Pairing status of males not specified.
[b] Coos issued by unmated males.

Sayre et al. (1978) studied the effects of density on perch cooing of marked unmated and mated males separately. For unmated males, the mean rate of perch cooing per one-minute interval was significantly ($P<0.05$) higher when two or more were cooing than when only one was heard (*Table 41*). There were no significant ($P>0.05$) increases in mean cooing rates if more than two were cooing.

Data of this type for mated doves did not suffice for analysis in the study by Sayre et al. (1978). Infrequency of calling periods for mated males argues against any direct relationship between densities and calling rates on a short-term (one-minute) basis. However, on numerous occasions during the study, mated males were observed issuing a brief series of perch coos following territorial disputes (Sayre 1976). Thus, density might be a contributing factor in the total amount of cooing of a mated male over an extended period.

Sayre et al. (1978) also separately analyzed cooing rates of mated and unmated doves on two study areas with vastly different densities of cooing doves, based on local Call-count Survey data. Nearly 2.5 times as many males were tallied on one area as on the other. Cooing rates of neither mated nor unmated doves differed significantly by area. In fact, raw data for mated males on the high-density area defied the expected trend, for the birds cooed somewhat less frequently than did their low-density counterparts (*Table 42*).

Disagreements regarding effects of density on cooing rate in the literature may arise from the researchers' failure to distinguish between mated and unmated males in their data collection and analyses. Pairing status influences perch-cooing performance so powerfully that it cannot be overlooked in collection or analysis of data used to evaluate other factors influencing cooing performance.

In conclusion, perch cooing of individual mated males over an extended period may be affected somewhat by density (Irby 1964, Sayre 1976). Density can affect cooing rates of unmated males by a factor of about 1.1 (Sayre et al. 1978, see also *Table 41*). These small differences probably would have little effect on reliability of the Call-count Survey. Moreover, the findings of Sayre et al. (1978)—that area differences in population density did not markedly change calling rates or probabilities of calling within three-minute periods for either mated or unmated males—reinforces the belief that population density is not a serious problem in interpreting Call-count Survey data.

Weather

Well before the preliminary nationwide Call-count procedures were established in 1953, and continuing thereafter, numerous investigators

Table 42. Comparison of mean cooing rates per three-minute period for mated and unmated mourning doves in two areas of South Carolina with differing dove densities (from Sayre et al. 1978).

	Low density		High density	
Pairing status	Cooing rate (mean ± SD)	Number of observations[a]	Cooing rate (mean ± SD)	Number of observations[a]
Unmated	8.88 ± 2.16	138	8.75 ± 1.31	29
Mated	1.64 ± 1.01	13	0.82 ± 0.40	4

[a] Observations of individual birds lasting 30 minutes or more.

studied the influence of temperature, humidity, barometric pressure, cloud cover and wind velocity on mourning dove cooing activity (McClure 1939, Duvall and Robbins 1952, McGowan 1952, Davey 1953, Wimmer 1953, Mackey 1954, Southeastern Association of Game and Fish Commissioners 1957, Frankel 1961, Frankel and Baskett 1961, Irby 1964). The broad objective of most of these studies was to develop and evaluate methods of determining the abundance of breeding doves (Duvall and Robbins 1952). One facet of special interest concerned establishing or testing limits on weather conditions under which standardized Call-count procedures would give useful and consistent results. Studies of weather factors related to cooing activity made before the mid-1960s were reviewed and analyzed by Stone (1966).

Some early observations were anecdotal. Even when quantitative results were obtained, they were not always treated statistically, and "analyses involving the interaction of two or more influents were seldom made" (Stone 1966: 16). And it was not always clear that only the perch coo was tallied or considered, and changing audibility as well as changing cooing rates may have influenced readings obtained under certain weather conditions.

Nevertheless, reasonable boundaries for weather seem to have been set as a result of the early studies. Call-counts are not recorded during rainfall or if winds exceed Beaufort scale number 3, 12 miles per hour (19.5 km/hr) (see chapter 14). These boundaries conform with the Southeastern Association of Game and Fish Commissioners' (1957) finding that cooing rates are depressed during light rains and with Mackey's (1954) observation that cooing ceases during heavy rains. Mackey also noted that cooing did not diminish as wind velocities rose until winds reached 10 to 12 miles per hour (16.1 to 19.3 km/hr).

Studies made after the mid-1960s dealt with combined effects of many weather variables on cooing and employed multivariate analyses. Gates (1969) studied the effects of temperature, cloud cover, and wind direction and velocity on the number of doves heard on Call-count routes in Texas. The data base was impressive—there were ninety-one routes, each run four times per year for three years. Analyses of covariance indicated that, within the limits of the investigation, weather factors had little or no consistent influence on numbers of cooing doves heard along the routes.

Working in Iowa, LaPerriere and Haugen (1972b) examined the relationship between dove cooing activity (both perch cooing and nest cooing) and climatic factors by employing a principal components factor analysis of twenty-eight variables associated with Call-count data. Results indicated that four synoptic weather situations (conditions occurring simultaneously over broad areas) might influence cooing activity sufficiently to affect Call-count Survey results. These synoptic conditions were linked to position or movement of weather fronts; each of the four had characteristic complex interactions of wind speed and direction, cloud cover, fog, etc.

Finally, Sayre et al. (1978) used a multiple regression model to evaluate relationships between weather and cooing performance of marked, free-flying, unmated male doves in South Carolina. The number of perch coos per minute per day per bird was the dependent variable; independent variables included temperature, increasing and decreasing temperature, barometric pressure, rising or falling pressure, wind speed and direction, cloud cover, two visibility categories of fog, humidity, and frontal passage occurring during the twenty-four-hour period preceding or following an observation. Analyses indicated that, within limits of standard Call-count procedures, weather factors did not significantly affect cooing activities of unmated males.

In a prior review of effects of weather on cooing activity, Baskett et al. (1978) noted that Gates (1969) and Sayre et al. (1978) came to similar conclusions, even though one study was based on analysis of actual field survey data and the other on cooing performance of individual wild birds. Considering their results, and the similar findings of Frankel and Baskett (1961) for penned birds and of Irby (1964) for large numbers of free-flying birds in Arizona, Baskett et al. (1978) concluded that effects of weather on Call-count Survey results were unlikely if survey instructions were followed carefully. That conclusion still seems valid; cooing performance seems profoundly affected by weather only beyond extremes that are excluded from standard Call-count tallies.

Seasonal and Short-term Variability in Cooing

Seasonal patterns of cooing by mourning doves were studied by McGowan (1952, 1953), Duvall and Robbins (1952), Wagner (1952) and Lowe (1956). They described a "plateau" period of cooing, principally in May and June, in localities ranging from Georgia to Tennessee, Ohio and Wisconsin. In some cases, these plateaus coincided with nesting peaks (McGowan 1953, Lowe 1956). Information about the cooing plateau, particularly as related to location or year, was reviewed by the Southeastern Association of Fish and Game Commissioners (1957) and Stone (1966).

Other studies did not substantiate the existence of a seasonal plateau period of cooing (Irby 1964, Clark 1968, Armbruster et al. 1978) or a relationship between doves calling and doves nesting (Armbruster et al. 1978, Olson et al. 1983, Armbruster and Baskett 1985). Call-counts fluctuated throughout the summer months in these studies.

Stone (1966) and Baskett et al. (1978) reexamined earlier data concerning seasonal trends of cooing and agreed that, for considerable periods in late spring and summer, marked fluctuations in cooing activity were apparent but without identifiable trends. Data did not show smooth, steady levels of cooing implied by the word "plateau." A clear example of the jagged pattern was furnished by Olson et al. (1983) in their Colorado study *(Figure 43)*: from late May until mid-July, high but fluctuating numbers of doves were heard on three routes censused every other week.

Causes of these fluctuations in numbers of doves heard on the same routes over short periods probably are complex but must depend on a summation of cooing performance of individual birds. Sayre (1976) found mean cooing rates of marked mated and unmated doves to be quite variable (coefficients of variability were 71.0 and 24.3, respectively). Differences in cooing rates related to position in the nesting cycle, superimposed on individual variation, undoubtedly accounted for the greater overall variability of cooing by mated males. This latter phenomenon was noted earlier by Frankel (1961), whose penned mated males all reached a peak in cooing at a different time. Unmated males, on the other hand, had a steady, high calling rate as long as they were unmated or until the seasonal decline in calling in September. A similar pattern in cooing of marked, unmated, unconfined males was recorded by Sayre (1976). It should be remembered that both the Frankel (1961) and Sayre (1976) data were based on calling frequencies of individual birds, not on total number of doves heard calling along routes, as in the case of other studies discussed (e.g., Olson et al. 1983).

Early cooing peaks (in April or early May), documented in several studies reviewed by Stone (1966) and more recently demonstrated by Best (1981), may be attributable to the presence of numerous unmated males that either migrate onward or remain and later become mated and less vocal as breeding populations stabilize.

Even though there is little evidence of a "plateau" in cooing, debating its existence is largely an academic exercise, because the survey is adequately timed to include periods of fairly high cooing activity when nesting is in full swing and breeding populations should be stabilized (Wight 1962).

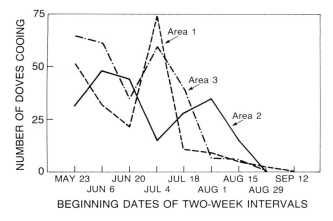

Figure 43. Seasonal perch-cooing patterns of mourning doves in northern Colorado, 1978 (adapted from Olson et al. 1983).

SUITABILITY OF CALL-COUNT DATA FOR INTENSIVE STUDY OF LOCAL BREEDING POPULATIONS

Data collected annually in the Call-count Survey are used primarily as an index to relative densities and long-term population trends in the three management units (groupings of eastern, central and western states) and in the states comprising them (Keeler 1977, Dolton 1987, see also chapter 14).

Modifications of Call-count Survey procedures or related audio-census programs have also been used in intensive studies of mourning dove breeding populations on small areas, e.g., 151 acres (61 ha) as in Lowe (1956). This intensive approach—often with implications of great precision in estimating numbers of breeding doves and nesting densities or even in predicting production of young on the small study areas—has been confused from the beginning (McClure 1939) with the use of Call-count data as indices to population trends and for other broad-scale purposes wherein great accuracy is neither expected nor probably needed.

Prominent among early studies employing coo counts, at least in part to assess breeding parameters on areas of 99 to 284 acres (40 to 115 ha), were those of Kerley (1952), Hopkins and Odum (1953), McGowan (1953) and Lowe (1956). When these studies were made, little was known about differences in cooing behavior of unmated and mated male doves. Hopkins and Odum (1953: 134) wrote that "A bird or pair consistently perched, calling or otherwise associated with a potential nesting site was considered to represent a breeding pair, to be verified by location of an actual nest when possible." These "potential" nests were used in computation of total nesting and production. Many of the males observed may have been unmated, and nesting density probably was overestimated. Only twenty-three of fifty-eight "nests" used by Lowe (1956) to quantify breeding density and nesting effort were actually known nests.

In several of the studies listed above, spot mapping (modified from Williams 1936) was used rather than the Call-count procedures soon to be standardized. Spot mapping to determine breeding bird populations is subject to serious interpretational errors, even when used for highly territorial passerines (Best 1975).

Other workers have not found tallies of cooing male doves to be consistently related to breeding densities, nests or production on small, intensively studied areas (Webb 1949, Caldwell 1955, Jackson 1963, Stone 1963).

Three other studies examined in detail the relationship between calling doves and nesting in areas surrounding listening stops of survey routes. Olson et al. (1983), in Colorado, provided data on cooing activity and nesting along one Call-count Survey and two Breeding Bird Survey routes from late March through October in two years. Numbers of nests found varied from 135 in 1978 to 46 in 1979, despite similar nest-searching effort. There was little evidence that the number of dove nests could be estimated from Call-count data, as is evident in Figure 43. This lack of clear connection was confirmed with regression analyses.

In the other two investigations, both in Missouri, cooing and nesting data were collected for two stops on a Call-count route and the 151-acre (61 ha) area surrounding each. The first of these studies was based on seventy-nine Call-count runs, each followed by intensive nest searches, during two years (Armbruster et al. 1978). As in the Colorado study (Olson et al. 1983), there was great variability in calling birds counted—as much as 50 percent along the entire route on consecutive days (Armbruster 1973). There were no consistent relationships between number of calling males tallied at the two stops and number of nests in each surrounding 151-acre (61 ha) area.

The second Missouri study added five years to the data base on the same study areas (Armbruster and Baskett 1985). During the entire seven years, mean numbers of calling males at one stop were not significantly correlated ($r=0.06$, $P>0.10$) with the numbers of active nests found in the circular plot surrounding it. At the other stop, numbers of calling doves and nests were significantly correlated ($r=0.857$, $P<0.03$), but only one nest was found during the last four of seven years. Results from the entire seven years reinforced the earlier conclusions by Armbruster et al. (1978) and Olson et al. (1983:

335) that there "is little evidence that the number of mourning dove nests in a local area can be estimated from Call-count data."

Similar conclusions were reached by Rappole and Waggerman (1986) in a study of white-winged doves in the Lower Rio Grande Valley of Texas. For nine of ten sites, the number of breeding pairs per hectare estimated by coo counts exceeded nest count estimates by as much as fifteen times.

Possible reasons for the uncertain relationship between calling and nesting are many and include the greater calling rates of unmated compared with those of mated males and differences in calling rates of mated males according to position in the nesting cycle. The considerable mobility of the mourning dove during the breeding season (Hegdal and Gatz 1977, Sayre et al. 1980) also may be a factor. Problems in estimating numbers of breeding birds through counts of singing males are by no means confined to mourning doves, as elucidated by Mayfield (1981). However, his counts of calling doves were only 33 percent "efficient"—i.e., doves were tallied only ten of thirty possible times on an intensively studied area.

Armbruster and Baskett (1985) suggested that numbers of active nests found by direct search are the best available estimators of numbers of breeding pairs of doves on small study areas. Precise linkages, however, among numbers of active nests, breeding pairs and ultimate production of young are unknown. A large-scale effort, similar in scope to the one intended to assess seasonal patterns of nesting and effects of September hunting (U.S. Fish and Wildlife Service 1982), probably would be needed to settle, once and for all, the validity of using Call-count data to assess breeding populations on limited areas and for purposes other than approximating relative densities and trends.

The weak or variable relationships demonstrated between mourning dove Call-counts and nesting or production on small study areas offer little comfort to those using the Call-count Survey for broader purposes. However, the results of these intensive studies are not entirely relevant to and do not disprove the usefulness of the mourning dove Call-count Survey as an index to relative densities of doves or their population trends on a broad scale, such as the mourning dove management units. Nor do they invalidate the approach to dove habitat assessment described by Grue et al. (1976, 1981, 1983). Grue et al. related dove Call-count data to habitat types on 133 15-mile (24 km) transects in ten ecological areas in Texas. Questions remain, however, as to how well their audio data reflect population densities; Grue et al. (1983) considered this problem carefully.

CALL-COUNT SURVEY RESULTS AS INDICES TO DOVE POPULATIONS AND TRENDS

The great importance of the mourning dove as an ecological and recreational resource makes it imperative that attempts continue to be made to refine and improve the only coordinated wide-scale inventory for this species: the Call-count Survey.

In a review of information then available, Baskett et al. (1978) concluded that several factors could influence Call-counts somewhat but posed no major problems within limits of then-current Call-count Survey procedures. These factors were position in the nesting cycle, population density and weather. To this list, age of the males (yearling or older) now can be added. Survey procedures probably would be more sound biologically (tallying higher numbers of doves and higher proportions of mated males), and statistically as well, if the number of three-minute stops were halved and the number of routes increased.

Importance of Pairing Status

As emphasized throughout this chapter, the principal factor influencing cooing rates of male doves and the probability that they will issue the perch coo in any three-minute period is whether they are mated. The effect of this factor on Call-count Survey results remains unknown, but it has the potential to affect survey results from area to area and year to year. Unfortunately, mated and unmated males cannot be distinguished by cooing rates at such short periods as the three-minute stop in Call-count Surveys, because mated males may coo as frequently as their unmated counterparts during bursts of singing, then fall silent for long periods.

To evaluate the effects of unmated males on survey results, it must be determined (1) whether those males exist in substantial numbers, and (2) more importantly, whether ratios of unmated to mated males change substantially from place to place or year to year.

When a pair bond is attained by an adult male and adult female, the male's perch cooing dramatically declines. This indicates that the primary purpose of this distinctive vocalization is mate attraction. Perch cooing by mated males likely serves as a territory advertisement. *Photo by Jim Rathert; courtesy of the Missouri Department of Conservation.*

Presence of Unmated Males in Breeding Populations

In four field studies, 45 of 91 male doves, whose pairing status was known over long periods, were unmated, as discussed earlier. The proportion of unmated birds (49 percent) does not reflect the true condition in the field because of the much greater ease in finding and observing unmated males, and perhaps greater ease in trapping them for marking. However, the numbers of unmated males observed in the studies mentioned show that unmated males in the wild are readily available for study (see also Stone 1963).

The presence of highly vocal, unmated, male passerine birds during the breeding season has been well documented (e.g., Kendeigh 1944b, Enemar et al. 1976). The potential for tallying unmated males in audio surveys of "breeding" birds is attested to by Best's (1975) finding that 67 percent of the singing observations of field sparrows were of marked males known to be unmated at the time. "Floating populations" of both males and females (surplus nonbreeders that can breed if resources become available) for many other species have been reported by other authors (see Stutchberry and Robertson 1985).

Variation in Ratios of Unmated and Mated Males

Ratios of mated to unmated male mourning doves still have not been accurately determined. Therefore, the crucial information about changes in these ratios from large area to area or year to year is not available. The potential for varying sex ratios certainly is present, based on differential wintering tendencies of the sexes; males winter farther northward than do females (Quay 1951a, Chambers et al. 1962, see also chapter 3). Thus, severe winter conditions over parts of the wintering range might cause disproportionate losses of birds of either sex, with resultant changes in adult sex ratios during the subsequent breeding season.

Using hypothetical models, Wight (1964) asserted that changes in ratios of unmated to mated males will not significantly affect results of the Call-count Survey in which sex ratios of adults approach equality. Preliminary calculations suggested that the adult sex ratio should stabilize at about 110 males per 100 females. Wight claimed that, within this range, changes would have little influence on survey results.

From a later perspective, one weakness in Wight's computations was that he used figures provided by Jackson (1963) and Jackson and Baskett (1964) for probabilities of hearing mated (0.23) and unmated (0.93) doves perch coo during survey hours. If more accurate probabilities provided later by Sayre et al. (1980)—0.15 for mated and 0.94 for unmated doves—had been used, Wight's model would have shown the contributions of unmated birds to be of greater importance than he judged them to be.

Another problem with Wight's approach is the lack of unbiased data on adult sex ratios (unmated males presumably being the excess left after all females are mated). Much evidence suggests an excess of males in most dove populations. Hanson and Kossack (1963) found a great preponderance of males among nestling doves in Illinois—158:100, based on sixty broods. However, Hanson and Kossack quoted unpublished data supplied by Wight reporting seasonal changes in nestling sex ratios, and the ratio was only 105 males to 100 females, based on 265 nestlings (see also chapter 8.)

Summer trapping data often show a heavy preponderance of male doves, ranging from 161:100, 178:100 (Tomlinson et al. 1960) and 176:100 (Rice and Lovrien 1974) to 241:100 overall (Henry et al. 1976). Many of these data were not available to Wight in 1964. Such ratios are assumed to be greatly biased; the traditional explanation is that daily incubation schedules cause males to feed in hurried and unwary fashion, thus they are vulnerable to trapping. These ratios may indeed reflect bias, but unpublished observations by both M. J. Armbruster and M. W. Sayre show very leisurely feeding by mated males, with frequent preening and loafing. Moreover, radio telemetry data confirmed that incubating or brooding males devoted about as much or more time in early morning or late evening to activities other than feeding (e.g., loafing) as to feeding (Sayre et al. 1980).

Sex ratios derived from shot samples also frequently show a predominance of males, but they may be biased because of different migration and wintering habits of males and females (original data presented and literature reviewed by Chambers et al. [1962] and Hanson and Kossack [1963]). Although there were notable exceptions (cf. Pearson and Moore 1941, for example), most studies reviewed in the papers cited above showed great preponderance of males in shot samples in both autumn and winter. Many ratios based on sizable samples ranged over 150 males to 100 females. In their Illinois data, Hanson and Kossack (1963) noted greater preponderance of males among adults than among immatures.

In some studies, survival rates of females banded as adults are significantly ($P<0.05$) lower than those of males. Such a condition was found for doves in the Eastern Management Unit (Hayne 1975) and for adults banded in Missouri, where survival rates of males were 46.7 versus 31.2 percent for females (Atkinson et al. 1982). However, for the entire Central Management Unit, survival rates of adult females (51.0 percent) did not differ from those for males (51.7 percent) (Dunks et al. 1982). In a recent analysis of data from mourning doves banded in the Western Management Unit from 1967 to 1977, there likewise was no significant difference in survival rates by sex (Tomlinson et al. 1988). These analyses, taken together, offer little indication that differential survival by sex might produce the unbalanced sex ratios (favoring males) that are often reported.

It is not known how to interpret the sex ratio data presently available. Variations in trapping methodology obviously can result in biased samples (Henry et al. 1976), and season and geographic location can similarly affect sex (and age) composition of shot samples (Chambers et al. 1962). Nevertheless, most sizable, carefully analyzed samples of adults, both in summer and autumn, show sex ratios unbalanced in favor of males. It is concluded that most breeding populations contain surplus males.

At least some unmated males may be present in populations for long periods before, during and after the Call-count survey period. Irby (1964) observed two marked unmated males for more than a month. Both became mated early in April, well before the Call-count period. Sayre (1976) followed one marked unmated male from April 24 to June 27 (forty-one observations) and another from May 8 to July 30 (twenty-four observations) – thus, both were unmated throughout the Call-count period. M. W. Sayre (personal communication: 1980) followed another male fitted with a radio transmitter; it remained unmated from July 13 to August 22. Sayre et al. (1980) had radio telemetry contact with five unmated males for about one month each before, during and after the Call-count Survey period. The length of time the doves were known to be unmated was limited by transmitter life, not by known change in their pairing status.

Sex ratios may not wholly reflect ratios of unmated to mated male doves. R. E. Mirarchi (personal communication: 1977) estimated that 15 to 20 percent of about 160 female doves force-paired with males in quail breeder batteries failed to breed with the first males presented to them, even when they were kept together from February until June. After June, birds were shuffled and many of them mated. Armbruster (1983), working with doves in large aviaries, also found it necessary to reshuffle birds to ensure their pairing. A few males formed and re-

tained homosexual bonds even though unmated females were present. These failures to pair may be attributable to penning, but there is fragmentary evidence of a "floating" population of unmated female mourning doves in the wild (Taber 1926). Jackson and Baskett (1964) observed remating of a marked nesting male mourning dove within ten days after his mate was destroyed. Irby (1964) documented eight cases in which males found new mates when their females were destroyed or pair bonds were otherwise disrupted. (Some of these "new" females may have become available because their own mates were lost.) The presence of unmated females could be important to Call-count Surveys only if their proportions changed from year to year or place to place, but this information is lacking. In several other avian species, presence of unmated females has been demonstrated or surmised (Brown 1969, Best 1977, Stutchberry and Robertson 1985), but their existence has not been studied as carefully as that of surplus males.

In a review paper, Baskett et al. (1978) noted that an important and still unresolved question about pairing status is whether ratios of unmated to mated males present during the Call-count Survey period vary markedly by year and by locality. There are many gaps in knowledge needed to evaluate survey results with respect to these ratios. Because of these gaps, opinions differ widely as to the validity of Call-count Survey results. Wight (1964) was comfortable with the survey, but information not available to him might have altered his view somewhat. Gates and Smith (1972: 357) wrote: "Differential calling rates of mated and unmated doves may present no particular difficulty as long as the other assumptions are met if their rates do not differ substantially. Should their rates change relative to one another during the survey season the problem could be more severe. It would appear to be fruitless to approach this difficulty analytically unless means are found for distinguishing the calls of mated and unmated males." As with Wight (1964), Gates and Smith did not know then that rates of calling of unmated males may exceed those of mated birds by a factor of twenty or more.

A different view was expressed by Wilson and Bart (1985). They pointed out that applying the three-minute cooing probabilities provided by Sayre et al. (1980) for mated (0.15) and unmated (0.94) males would produce a survey result for a population containing 50 percent mated birds that would be 37 percent higher than for one containing 75 percent mated birds. The difference would be due solely to the difference in average detectability. Wilson and Bart (1985: 69) concluded: "Thus, for Mourning Doves, changes in reproductive status may cause substantial changes in survey results. This finding raises doubts about the effectiveness of these surveys in detecting changes in density."

The conclusions of Wight (1964) and Gates and Smith (1972) concerning probable effects of pairing on Call-count results can reasonably be questioned. If, for example, a population of 100 males, all mated, is distributed along a Call-count route, it can be expected that only 15 of them, on average, will be detected when a Call-count Survey is run. If 45 unmated males are added to the population, it can be expected that 42 new birds (0.92 x 45), plus the 15 mated birds, will be detected, for a total of 57 *(Figure 44)*. Thus, increasing the real population by 45 percent would increase the number detected by 280 percent; the resultant sex ratio would be 145 males to 100 females. This degree of disparity is commonplace in summer samples of adults, as discussed earlier. Even with considerably lesser disparities in true sex ratios, the consequences to Call-counts of adding unmated males are quite dramatic.

Admittedly, changes in dove sex ratios of the magnitudes proposed above are quite unlikely to occur over large areas, and the examples probably put Call-count Survey results in an unrealistically poor scenario. The examples, however, emphasize the need for better sex ratio information and for adequate backup to the Call-count Survey. In this context, Wight (1964) wrote that methods to measure ratios of unmated to mated dove males do not exist, so indirect methods must be used for estimations. Regrettably, little progress has been made in solidifying these indirect methods since 1964.

CONCLUSIONS

Changes in proportions of mated and unmated mourning dove males of the magnitudes suggested in models by Wilson and Bart (1985) and in the reckoning above could occur in local populations, and such changes may lie behind the observed shortcomings of Call-count data when used to predict nesting effort and other breeding parameters of mourning doves in small, intensively studied areas (e.g., Olson et al. 1983, Armbruster and Baskett 1985).

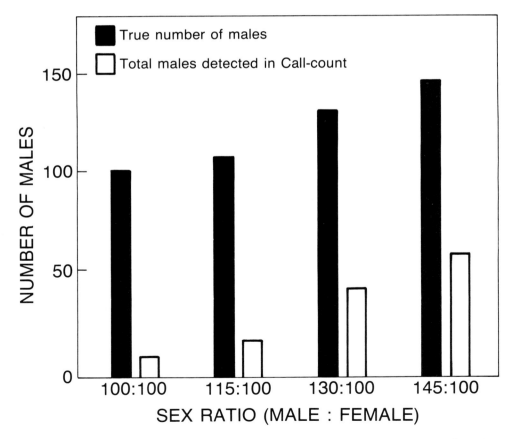

Figure 44. True numbers of male mourning doves versus numbers detected by Call-count procedures in a population of 100 mated males augmented in increments of 15 unmated males each (based on data of Sayre et al. 1980).

It is difficult to imagine, though, that differences in sex ratios (and consequent proportions of unmated males) could pose a comparable threat to the formal Call-count Survey results when only gross comparisons in space and time are needed. Data derived from large samples of Call-count routes (e.g., management units) likely provide reasonable estimates of long-term population trends because any local changes in proportions of unmated males may level out over the larger areas.

Several optimistic notes can be reported. Brown and Smith (1976) found a significant ($r=0.74$, $P<0.01$) correlation between Call-count data and hunting success (numbers of doves bagged per hunter per season) during ten seasons in Arizona. Their approach seems valid, because most direct recoveries of doves in that state are of birds banded within the state or in adjacent localities.

California data for 1966–85 showed significant correlations between Call-count data for that state and total harvest of mourning doves ($r=0.76$, 18 df, $P<0.01$) and mourning doves bagged per hunter ($r=0.52$, 18 df, $P<0.05$). Data for the entire Western Management Unit during 1966–83 also showed significant correlations between Call-counts and total harvest ($r=0.53$, 16 df, $P<0.05$) and between Call-counts and doves bagged per hunter ($r=0.49$, 16 df, $P<0.05$) (R. E. Tomlinson personal communication: 1987). These relationships lend considerable plausibility to Call-count procedures but need further verification on other statewide bases and in the Eastern and Central management units. The need is evident, because in preliminary analyses, some statewide data do not show the expected correlations (R. E. Tomlinson personal communication: 1987).

Visual counts also provide a means of checking Call-count results. In the mourning dove Call-count Survey, numbers of doves seen along the routes are tallied. Resulting data are analyzed as a supplement to Call-count data. Dolton (1987) showed that trends of counts of doves seen on Call-count routes of all three management units, 1966–87, were similar to trends of doves heard. However, in the 1966–90 counts, trends in doves seen and heard diverged with time in the Central Management Unit and converged in the Western Unit (see Dolton 1990).

Both Missouri and North Dakota have conducted long-term roadside counts of doves seen on 20-mile (32 km) routes during summer after Call-count Surveys have been made. For data collected during 1968–85 in Missouri, average numbers of birds seen per route along 111 routes were strongly correlated ($r=71$, 16 df, $P<0.01$) with average numbers of doves heard per route on Call-count Survey routes (R. E. Tomlinson personal communication: 1987). These Missouri counts were made in June and included a few early-hatched immatures. The North Dakota counts were made in July, when many immatures were present. However, immature doves tend to concentrate in fields, not along roads (Henry et al. 1976). The North Dakota data, collected 1966–85, showed even higher correlation ($r=0.82$, 18 df, $P<0.01$) between Call-count data and average numbers of doves seen per route on a total of 1,143 transects (R.E. Tomlinson personal communication: 1987). These findings also lend credibility to the Call-count Survey and its results.

As might be expected for any survey based on data whose validity is affected by many complex biological factors, the mourning dove Call-count Survey needs to be backed up with corroborative information, particularly uniformly gathered harvest figures. The need for a standardized nationwide harvest survey for doves has been discussed for years (e.g., Baskett et al. 1978) and is well advocated in chapters 23, 24 and 29. Both total harvest data and doves bagged per hunter are needed because the former may reflect trends in numbers of hunters, not just numbers of doves available. Such a survey would require an adequate sampling frame that could be provided by a "dove stamp" similar to the present federal duck stamp. Unfortunately, little progress has been made toward establishing uniform harvest surveys for mourning doves.

Another need is sex ratio data that will permit comparisons among years and large areas, such as states. Such data possibly could be gathered by extensive summer trapping programs in which dates, procedures and trapping effort are held in a rigorously similar manner from place to place and year to year. Efforts for uniform gathering of shot samples of doves in autumn would also be valuable. Sex ratio data of these sorts appear to be the only reasonable way to estimate percentages of surplus males in populations and thus permit intelligent surmises as to the effect of the high cooing rate of unmated males.

Although the formal Call-count Survey procedure mandates starting each run precisely one-half hour before sunrise (see chapter 14), there can be "slippage" on this point in operational counts. In those procedures, "close" timing may not be entirely adequate. At Columbia, Missouri, for example, sunrise changes from 4:53 to 4:44 CST between May 20 and June 5. Thus, a "clock time" prescription possibly could produce results at "hot" dove stops on the survey route early in the permissible survey period not comparable to those later in the period. At least, this point may deserve further investigation.

Another point that needs scrutiny and possibly further research is the procedure used in relocating Call-count Survey routes when the traditional routes become dangerous or unsuitable to run owing to highway changes or commercial and suburban developments.

In conclusion, the mourning dove Call-count Survey is a well-managed, well-coordinated and adequately statistically interpreted wildlife survey. Deserving special commendation are early researchers—particularly McClure (1939), who furnished the initial ideas and information—and investigators and administrators of the late 1940s and early 1950s who provided information used to establish ground rules for the survey. Over the years, the survey coordinators have been quick to seek improvements, particularly relating to statistical matters.

The national Call-count Survey clearly should be continued for long-range monitoring of mourning dove populations over large areas. As pointed out by Wilson and Bart (1985: 71), "Investigators using data from surveys such as the Mourning Dove coo-count . . . usually calculate trends on the basis of 10 or more years. It is difficult to see how chance factors could have much effect with so large a sample."

Nevertheless, the great necessity for accurate, reliable population monitoring of a species so important to both hunter and nonhunter demands corroboration of the principal monitoring system. Such corroboration could be provided if there were an adequate base for uniform harvest sampling throughout the hunted range of the mourning dove. This base could be available if a federal "dove stamp" were established to provide a sampling frame. This is a matter of paramount importance. Further comparisons of visual counts with Call-count results and provision of uniformly gathered sex ratio data would be useful adjuncts.

This general methodology was used by Kiel (1959) to delineate the three mourning dove management units in the United States. Derivation probabilities also have been estimated for doves shot in Texas (Dunks 1977), Missouri (Atkinson et al. 1982), the CMU (Dunks et al. 1982) and the WMU (Tomlinson et al. 1988). Hayne and Geissler (1977) used this methodology, in conjunction with dove-harvest estimates based mostly on state surveys, to estimate the actual number of doves from a particular breeding state that were harvested in each state of the United States. Migration chronology of doves arriving in an area also has been investigated by examining derivation of harvest by ten-day periods within the hunting season and by looking at changes in estimated derivation probabilities over time (Dunks 1977, Dunks et al. 1982, Tomlinson et al. 1988).

The conceptual basis is sound for weighting band recoveries to estimate parameters associated with distribution and derivation of the harvest. If inferences about numbers and relative numbers of harvested birds are to be based on band recoveries, it is reasonable to attempt to compensate for geographic differences in banding effort. Area-specific estimates of population size, or at least relative population size, are needed for such compensatory weighting. For mourning doves, a state's relative population size is estimated as the product of its breeding population index (from Call-count Survey data) and its land area. The ratio of this estimate to total population size should be a constant for all states, and for some purposes, for all years included in an analysis. These two conditions may not be met by estimates based on the Call-count Survey (see chapter 14). Even if these conditions are met, Call-count-based estimates likely will translate into large variances for the parameter estimates associated with distribution and derivation of the harvest. Therefore, invoking both caution and common sense is recommended when interpreting these estimates based on weighted band-recovery data.

SURVIVAL AND HARVEST RATES

Banding and band recovery data can be used to estimate total annual survival rates of mourning doves. Table 44 shows a generalized data matrix representing a four-year banding study. The data needed to estimate survival rate are the numbers of birds banded annually, N_i, and the number of recoveries in year j from birds banded in year i, the R_{ij}. Historically, several different types of estimation methods have been applied to data of this

Table 44. Mourning dove band recovery data matrix[a] for a four-year banding study.

Year banded	Number banded	Year of recovery				Row total[b]
		1	2	3	4	
1	N_1	R_{11}	R_{12}	R_{13}	R_{14}	R_1
2	N_2		R_{22}	R_{23}	R_{24}	R_2
3	N_3			R_{33}	R_{34}	R_3
4	N_4				R_{44}	R_4

[a] R_{ij} = number of birds recovered in year j from those banded in year i.

[b] $R_i = \sum_{j=i}^{4} R_{ij}$ = the total number of recoveries obtained from birds banded in year i.

type. For example, life table approaches, such as those described by Hickey (1952), have been used to estimate mourning dove survival rates in several instances (Austin 1951, Southeastern Association of Game and Fish Commissioners 1957, Tomlinson et al. 1960). However, the assumptions required for reasonable performance of these life table methods usually are not met by migratory bird banding and recovery data, and these methods are no longer recommended (see Eberhardt 1972, Seber 1972, Anderson and Burnham 1976, Burnham and Anderson 1979, Anderson et al. 1981). Modern analyses have been based on the models and methods summarized in Brownie et al. (1985), and these form the basis of the following discussion.

For each of the N_1 birds banded in year one of the experiment depicted in Table 44, there is an associated probability of being recovered in year one and thus being included in R_{11}. Similarly, there are probabilities of being recovered in years two (and included in R_{12}), three (R_{13}) and four (R_{14}). Finally, there is a probability that a bird will not be recovered at all during the experiment (the number of these birds is given by $N_1 - \sum_{j=1}^{4} R_{1j}$). The key to building estimation models for data of this type is to express these probabilities in terms of parameters of interest (e.g., survival and recovery rates) and in a way that makes biological sense. Under Model 1 of Brownie et al. (1985) (see also Seber 1970, Robson and Youngs 1971), the probability associated with each entry in the data matrix can be written in terms of survival rates (S_i) and recovery rates (f_i) as shown in Table 45. For example, consider the probability associated with R_{13}, which is written as $S_1 S_2 f_3$ in Table 45. A bird banded in year one and recovered in year three must survive from year one to year two (this event occurs with probability S_1) and from year two to year three (this oc-

Table 45. Probabilities under Model 1 (Brownie et al. 1985) corresponding to each element of the data matrix in Table 44.[a]

Year banded	Number banded	Year of recovery			
		1	2	3	4
1	N_1	f_1	$S_1 f_2$	$S_1 S_2 f_3$	$S_1 S_2 S_3 f_4$
2	N_2		f_2	$S_2 f_3$	$S_2 S_3 f_4$
3	N_3			f_3	$S_3 f_4$
4	N_4				f_4

[a] f_i = recovery rate for year i, and S_i = annual survival rate for year i.

curs with probability S_2), and then must be recovered in the hunting season of year three (this event occurs with probability f_3). The product of these three probabilities yields the probability that a bird banded in year one will be recovered in year three (and appear in R_{13}).

Table 45 defines a probability model for the data in Table 44 and is used to derive estimators for the model parameters, S_i and f_i. The resulting estimators for Model 1 are intuitively reasonable, and this can be seen most easily for f_1 and S_1. The estimator for f_1 is simply R_{11}/N_1—a statistic often called the "direct recovery rate." Thus, the probability of a banded bird alive at the time of banding in year one being recovered during the hunting season of year one is estimated simply as the proportion of birds banded in year one that is recovered that year. The probability of a banded mourning dove surviving between years one and two is estimated as:

$$\hat{S}_1 = [(R_1 - R_{11})/N_1]/(R_2/N_2). \tag{1}$$

The numerator of the estimator (1) is the proportion of birds banded in year one that is recovered in all hunting seasons after year one. The denominator of the estimator is simply the proportion of birds banded in year two that is recovered in all subsequent hunting seasons. So the numerator and denominator include birds recovered in the same hunting seasons (year two until the end of the experiment). Under Model 1, the only reason that these proportions should differ is that doves banded in year one must survive from year one to year two in order to have a chance of being recovered in a subsequent hunting season. The ratio of these two proportions thus estimates that survival probability, S_1. Estimators for survival and recovery rates for years after one are somewhat more complicated but can be shown to have the same intuitive basis as the year one estimators.

Although Model 1 is a reasonable model that has proven useful with many data sets for mourning doves and other bird species, other models also are possible. For example, if annual survival rate is

constant from year to year, each S_i in Table 45 can be replaced with an S. This yields Model 2 of Brownie et al. (1985). Additional models both more and less general than Model 1 are described by Brownie et al. (1985) and implemented in the associated computer program ESTIMATE. Although the models included in ESTIMATE were developed for adult birds, Brownie et al. (1985) also discussed other models developed for cases where birds of more than one age class are banded each year. Program BROWNIE includes several models for use when both young and adult birds are banded. These two computer programs, ESTIMATE and BROWNIE, compute estimates under several different models, as well as goodness-of-fit and between-model test statistics that are used to decide which model should be used for a given data set (Brownie et al. 1985). The methods of Brownie et al. have been used to estimate survival and recovery rates of mourning doves in the EMU (Hayne 1975), CMU (Dunks et al. 1982) and WMU (Tomlinson et al. 1988), as well as in Texas (Dunks 1977) and Missouri (Atkinson et al. 1982).

As with all statistical models, those of Brownie et al. (1985) are based on several assumptions. With regard to estimating survival and recovery rates, nine assumptions are listed by Brownie et al. and discussed by Pollock and Raveling (1982).

The first assumption is that the sample is representative of the target population. This assumption has nothing to do with the statistical model used for estimating survival and recovery rates and is relevant to all inferences from data resulting from banding or any other type of sampling. In the recent CMU and WMU banding programs for mourning doves, efforts were made to distribute the banding effort uniformly throughout the available range, although in practice this was not always possible (Dunks et al. 1982, Tomlinson et al. 1988). The importance of this assumption is dependent on the degree of variation actually present in the estimated quantities. For example, assume that the entire banded sample for some state comes from one particular banding site. If inferences about survival and recovery rates estimated from these bandings are restricted to the site, then no problems exist. If inferences are intended to apply to the entire state, and if survival and recovery rates exhibit little variation from one area to another, then the use of the single site again presents no problems, regardless of how atypical the sampled area may be in other respects (i.e., with respect to characteristics other than survival and recovery rates). However, statewide inferences are inappropriate and may be very misleading if survival and recovery rates do indeed vary from one part of the state to another.

The second assumption is that age and sex of individuals are correctly determined by banders. In this respect, mourning doves present more problems than do many other migratory bird species. Banders often are unable to determine the sex of immature mourning doves because of unreliable plumage characteristics. In addition, immature mourning doves that have hatched early may have lost their diagnostic primary coverts by late summer and sometimes are incorrectly classified as adults by inexperienced banders (Tomlinson et al. 1988, see chapter 21). Implications of aging and sexing problems for survival and recovery rate estimation are discussed under assumption eight.

The third assumption is that there is no band loss. It is likely met for mourning doves in most cases (Dunks et al. 1982). For short-lived species such as the mourning dove, rates of band loss would have to be quite high to cause substantial bias in survival rate estimates (Nelson et al. 1980).

The fourth assumption is that the process of trapping and banding birds does not influence subsequent survival. There is no reason to suspect that this assumption is not met for mourning doves in standard banding operations.

The fifth assumption is that the hunting season of recovery is correctly reported and recorded. Delayed reporting is not believed to be an important problem in most practical applications of band-recovery models (Anderson and Burnham 1980).

The sixth assumption is that the fate of each banded bird is independent of the fate of other banded birds. This assumption likely is not perfectly met for any vertebrate species, but it may be approximately true for mourning doves. For example, Austin (1951: 161) noted that mourning doves "do not remain in close-knit groups either on migration or in winter" and that generally "birds move individually." Lack of independence in fates can result in underestimated variances of survival and recovery rate estimates (Pollock and Raveling 1982).

The seventh assumption is that the fate of a given banded bird is a multinomial random variable. This assumption follows from the assumption of independence.

The final two assumptions relate to model structure (e.g., *Table 45*). Assumption eight is that all banded individuals in an identifiable class (e.g., age or sex) have the same annual survival and recovery rates. Certainly, no two individuals are exactly alike with respect to every characteristic that could potentially affect survival and recovery rates, so this assumption is never met exactly. The degree to which violation of this assumption causes problems in estimation depends on the magnitude of variation among individuals. If individuals within a particular age/sex class exhibit survival rates ranging from 0.45 to 0.50, then bias in survival and recovery rate estimates resulting from treating all individuals as though they had identical survival rates would be very small (Pollock and Raveling 1982, Nichols et al. 1982). However, if survival rates ranged from 0.20 to 0.80, then much larger biases would result. Discussions of this assumption and consequences of its violation are presented by Pollock and Raveling (1982) and Nichols et al. (1982).

The problems associated with aging and sexing mourning doves, as noted in assumption two, may lead to problems with assumption eight. Inability to determine the sex of immature doves leaves the bander with two basic alternatives for analysis. The bander can either omit young doves from any analyses of survival rates (inferences about combined-sex recovery rates still are possible using direct recovery rates) or combine sexes for adult birds also for a combined-sex analysis. Dunks et al. (1982) and Tomlinson et al. (1988) tested for sex-specific variation in survival and recovery rates of adult mourning doves in the CMU and WMU, respectively. Although test results were not clear-cut, Dunks et al. (1982) concluded that no substantial differences in these rates existed between adult male and female mourning doves in the CMU. This conclusion led them to pool data for both sexes in order to estimate survival and recovery rates of young and adult mourning doves. Tomlinson et al. (1988) found evidence that adult male doves in Arizona had higher recovery rates than did adult females but found no other sex-specific differences among adult doves in the WMU. Tomlinson et al. (1988) thus carried out combined-sex analyses for all states except Arizona. This approach of testing for sex specificity among adults and basing decisions about combined-sex analyses on results of these tests seems very reasonable. However, absence of sex specificity among adults does not ensure its absence among young birds. Therefore, it is important to consider results of the model goodness-of-fit tests, which have some ability to detect departures from the assumption of homogeneous survival and recovery rates (Nichols et al. 1982). Incorrect assignment of ages to banded doves also can result in heterogeneity of survival and recovery rates, because young mourning doves tend to have higher recovery rates and lower survival rates than do adults (Dunks et al. 1982, Tomlinson et al. 1988). Evidence of geographic variation in survival and recovery rates of mourning doves also has been found (e.g., Dunks et al. 1982, Tomlinson et al. 1988), so inappropriate combinations of banding sites to form banding reference areas also could lead to problems of heterogeneity.

Records from about 50 million bandings of 890 species of birds and 2.8 million recoveries since the early 1900s have been stored on computer tapes at the BBL (top left). Between 1903 and September 1991 there were 88,482 recoveries from 1,892,486 banded mourning doves. Discrepancies in banding and recovery data are resolved (top right), then a biologist reviews "kickouts" from computer quality checks and handles correspondence (center left). After all checks are made, a computer matches numbers from recovered bands with their banding data. Data on the recovery are sent to the bander, and a Certificate of Appreciation is awarded to the person who reported the recovered band's number (bottom left). The stored banding data provide information for wildlife biologists to assess such biological parameters as survival and harvest rates, the distribution of harvest, and the timing and patterns of migration (bottom right). *Top and center left photos by David Dolton. Bottom photos courtesy of the U.S. Fish and Wildlife Service, Office of Migratory Bird Management.*

The final assumption listed by Brownie et al. (1985) concerns variation in survival and recovery rates by age, sex, area and time. This simply refers to the manner in which the data are pooled and to the actual model selected for estimation purposes. The goodness-of-fit and between-model tests described by Brownie et al. (1985) can be used to decide which specific models and pooling choices are most appropriate for any data set. Past analyses have shown that different models are most appropriate for different dove data sets (see Dunks et al. 1982, Tomlinson et al. 1988) and that there is no single model that can be thought of as "best" for mourning doves.

Hypotheses about geographic, temporal, age-specific, sex-specific and other sources of variation can be tested in either of two general ways using band-recovery models. One general method involves use of between-model tests, such as those described in Brownie et al. (1985). Hypotheses not handled by either program ESTIMATE or BROWNIE still can be tested via likelihood ratio statistics using the more general programs SURVIV (White 1983) and MULT (Conroy and Williams 1984). The other approach to hypothesis testing involves the use of point estimates and their associated variances and covariances to compute z statistics (Brownie et al. 1985) and their general analogs for composite hypotheses (Sauer and Williams 1989). Dunks et al. (1982) and Tomlinson et al. (1988) provided examples of various tests with mourning dove data.

Although the band-recovery models of Brownie et al. (1985) can be used to estimate survival and recovery rates of mourning doves, we note that among hunted species of North American migratory birds, doves are among the least suited for use with these models. The precision of estimates obtained from these models depends heavily on the numbers of banded birds that eventually are recovered (the R_i of Table 44). As can be seen by inspection of Table 45, larger survival and recovery rates result in larger numbers of recoveries. Mourning doves tend to have lower recovery and survival rates than do most species of migratory birds hunted in North America. For example, most of the average survival rate estimates reported by Dunks et al. (1982) and Tomlinson et al. (1988) ranged from 0.40 to 0.60 for adult mourning doves and 0.30 to 0.50 for immature birds. Most of the average recovery rate estimates in these two studies ranged from 0.005 to 0.035 for adult doves and 0.010 to 0.050 for immature doves.

Brownie et al. (1985) provided many useful recommendations for planning banding studies designed to estimate survival and recovery rates using band-recovery models. In addition to providing general guidelines, they provided equations that can be used to compute banded sample sizes needed to achieve specified levels of precision for arithmetic mean annual survival rate estimates. Table 46 lists annual banded sample sizes (number of birds to be banded each year of the banding program) needed to achieve a coefficient of variation of the mean annual survival rate for adult birds of 0.06 $[C\hat{V}(\hat{\bar{S}}) = S\hat{E}(\hat{\bar{S}})/\hat{\bar{S}} = 0.06]$. The survival and recovery rates used in Table 46 are intended to cover a reasonable range of values for adult mourning doves. Required banded sample sizes can be seen to decrease with increasing recovery rates, survival rates and duration of the banding program *(Table 46)*. In any case, the sample sizes in Table 46 provide a general indication of banding requirements for prospective mourning dove banding programs, and the equations of Brownie et al. (1985) and Wilson et al. (1989) can be used with young birds as well as for different values of recovery rate, survival rate and years in the banding program. Finally, similar equations have been derived to compute sample sizes needed to estimate annual survival rate for a particular year, rather than the mean annual survival rate over the entire banding program (Wilson et al. 1989). However, the low recovery and survival rates of mourning doves likely never will permit strong inferences about survival during particular calendar years. Estimation of an average annual survival rate over a number of years probably is the best that can be done for this species.

When band-recovery analyses such as those of Brownie et al. (1985) are based on hunting season recoveries of birds shot and found dead, then recovery rate estimates provide an index to harvest rate. Harvest rate includes banded birds shot but not reported to the Bird Banding Laboratory,

Table 46. Approximate annual banded sample sizes of adult birds needed to obtain $C\hat{V}(\hat{\bar{S}}) = 0.06$[a], for different annual survival rates, recovery rates and years of banding.[b]

Recovery rate	Years of banding	Annual survival rate		
		0.40	0.50	0.60
0.01	5	8,800	6,200	4,800
	10	2,600	1,600	1,100
0.03	5	2,900	2,100	1,600
	10	900	500	400
0.05	5	1,700	1,200	900
	10	500	300	200

[a] $C\hat{V}(\hat{\bar{S}})$ denotes the coefficient of variation of the mean annual survival rate estimate, $C\hat{V}(\hat{\bar{S}}) = S\hat{E}(\hat{\bar{S}})/\hat{\bar{S}}$. $C\hat{V}(\hat{\bar{S}}) = 0.06$ will result in 95-percent confidence intervals approximately ± 0.05–0.07 about the mean annual survival rate.

[b] From Tomlinson et al. (1988).

whereas recovery rate includes only those birds that are reported. As noted above, parameter estimation using the models of Brownie et al. (1985) requires rather large sample sizes (especially for mourning doves), several consecutive years of banding, and bandings of both adult and young birds for estimates of parameters for young. Although survival rate estimation from banding and recovery data requires the use of these models, estimation of recovery rate does not. The Brownie et al. (1985) recovery rate estimators are more efficient (make best use of available data) when complete data matrices are available, but first-year or direct recovery rates (R_{ii}/N_i in the notation of Table 44) also estimate the recovery rate parameter. The direct recovery rate estimator is especially useful for isolated banding years and for cases in which only young birds are banded. Direct recovery rates have been used as indices of harvest rates in several mourning dove studies (e.g., Dunks 1977, Atkinson et al. 1982).

Recovery rate estimates ($\hat{f}$) can be used in conjunction with band-reporting rate estimates ($\hat{\lambda}$) to estimate harvest rate ($\hat{h}$) as:

$$\hat{h} = \hat{f}/\hat{\lambda}. \qquad (2)$$

Potentially the most reliable method of estimating reporting rates is via the use of reward bands. Reward bands are assumed to be reported with probability 1.0. Band-reporting rate can then be estimated as:

$$\hat{\lambda} = \hat{f}_c/\hat{f}_R, \qquad (3)$$

where $\hat{f}_R$ and $\hat{f}_C$ denote recovery rates for reward and control bands, respectively. Note that, if all reward bands are reported, as assumed, then $\hat{f}_R = \hat{h}$. In practice, the estimation of reporting rate from reward band studies often is complicated by band solicitation, geographic stratification, use of recoveries from more than one hunting season, etc., requiring modifications to the simple estimator given above. Methods for estimating reporting rate from data of reward band studies are provided and discussed by Henny and Burnham (1976), Conroy and Blandin (1984) and Conroy (1985).

Reward band studies have been carried out for mourning doves in scattered areas throughout the United States during 1965 and 1966 (Tomlinson 1968) and in the EMU and CMU during 1970 to 1972 (Reeves 1979). Tomlinson (1968) estimated that the reporting rate was 0.66 for three states thought to have been influenced by publicity about the banding program. Reporting rate for states not influenced by publicity was estimated to be 0.32. This latter value agrees reasonably well with estimates obtained by Reeves (1979) for the CMU ($\hat{\lambda} = 0.45$)

and EMU ($\hat{\lambda} = 0.33$). The reporting rate estimate of Tomlinson (1968), $\hat{\lambda} = 0.32$, has been used to estimate harvest rates from recovery rate estimates in recent mourning dove studies (Dunks et al. 1982, Tomlinson et al. 1988). However, a critical assumption that likely was not met in the previous mourning dove reward band studies (indeed, it is doubtful that it has been met in any previous reward band study in North America) is that reporting rate for reward bands is 1.0. Reeves (1979) discussed the probable nonreporting of mourning dove reward bands. If reward bands are reported at probabilities less than 1.0, then reporting rate estimates are positively biased. Conroy and Williams (1981) discussed sources of bias in reward band studies and provided numerical examples of the magnitude of bias resulting from nonreporting of reward bands.

The preceding discussion regarding estimation of survival rates and harvest mortality rates was based on the use of band recoveries obtained during the hunting season. However, mourning doves appear to have relatively strong migrational homing tendencies and can be recaptured at banding sites in successive years (Tomlinson et al. 1960, Harris 1961). In some situations, it may be possible to estimate survival rates of mourning doves using capture history data in conjunction with open-population capture/recapture models (Jolly 1965, 1982, Seber 1965, 1982, Pollock 1981a, Brownie et al. 1986, Pollock et al. 1990). Because these models have not been used with mourning doves, they are not discussed here in detail. Reviews of the use of these models in bird studies are provided by Pollock (1981b) and Nichols et al. (1981), and good general reviews are provided by Seber (1982) and Pollock et al. (1990). If capture probabilities are sufficiently high, then capture/recapture data may provide more precise estimates of survival rate than do band-recovery data.

An important difference between survival estimates obtained using band-recovery versus capture/recapture data is that capture/recapture estimates pertain to a specific sampling area (e.g., a particular trap site or set of trap sites). Survival estimates from capture/recapture data can thus be thought of as representing the product of two probabilities: (1) the probability of surviving from the sampling period in year i to the sampling period in year $i+1$ and (2) the conditional probability of being in the area exposed to sampling efforts, given that the bird is alive in sampling period $i+1$. If this second probability is near 1.0, as might be true for mourning doves on breeding areas (Tomlinson et al. 1960, Harris 1961), then capture/recapture survival estimates would reflect "true" survival—probability (1) above. Survival estimates based on both capture/recapture and band-recovery models can be used to test the hypothesis that homing probability—probability (2) above—is 1.0 and to estimate this probability if it is concluded to be less than 1.0 (see Anderson and Sterling 1974, Hepp et al. 1987). The proportions of birds released in year i and recaptured in year $i+1$ by Tomlinson et al. (1960) and Harris (1961) are large enough to yield capture/recapture survival estimates with reasonably good precision, especially compared with precision of band-recovery model estimates. Thus, it may be worthwhile to consider estimating survival rates of mourning doves using capture/recapture methods in some situations.

POPULATION SIZE AND AGE RATIO

It is possible to estimate both population size and age ratio using banding and recovery data combined with harvest survey estimates. Because there is no standardized nationwide harvest survey for mourning doves, these methods are less useful for doves than for waterfowl species (for which there is a standardized nationwide harvest survey). However, many state harvest surveys include mourning doves, and resulting harvest estimates have been used to estimate population size (Dunks et al. 1982, Tomlinson et al. 1988).

The conceptual basis is fairly simple for estimating population size from banding, recovery and harvest data. The number of birds harvested (shot and retrieved by hunters—denote harvest as H) during a particular hunting season can be written as the product of population size (N) at some time before the hunting season and harvest rate (h), the probability that a bird in this preseason population, N, is harvested during the hunting season. This equation, $H = Nh$, can be used to estimate population size as:

$$\hat{N} = \hat{H}/\hat{h} \qquad (4)$$

provided that H and h can be estimated. As noted earlier, estimates of harvest rate can be obtained as in (2) from recovery rate estimates (obtained from banding data) and reporting rate estimates (obtained from a reward band study). Estimates of H must come from some kind of harvest survey.

Despite the conceptual simplicity of this method for estimating population size, it is likely to yield poor estimates in many real-world situations. It is clear that the method requires good estimates of harvest, $\hat{H}$, and harvest rate, $\hat{h}$. Estimates of total harvest from harvest survey data are notoriously poor (see Wright 1978). Although recovery rate can be estimated reasonably well from particular

banded samples, there is not much confidence in estimates of reporting rate and, hence, harvest rate. Even if harvest survey and reward band methodology provided good estimates of harvest and harvest rate for specific areas, problems associated with geographic variation still would have to be faced. The ideal situation for estimating N using this method is to have a discrete preseason population of birds that are easily banded and that are all harvested in a particular area. In reality, however, banded samples generally are obtained from preseason populations throughout the different management units, and banded doves from these samples usually are shot in many different states and sometimes in more than one management unit. Thus the critical task of matching the harvest rate estimate to the total harvest estimate is extremely difficult. Therefore, efforts to deal with geographic variation must involve attempts to estimate the proportion of birds in each preseason population i that is shot in each harvest area j (distribution of the harvest) and the proportion of the harvest in harvest area j that is derived from preseason population i (derivation of the harvest).

One of the first uses of this general method of estimating population size was to estimate the total number of ducks in the autumn flight in North America (Lincoln 1930). The method has been used to estimate mourning dove population size in Texas (Dunks 1977), the CMU (Dunks et al. 1982) and the WMU (Tomlinson et al. 1988). The computational methods provided in these reports illustrate the problems of dealing with geographic variation and stratification in exercises of this type. Although methods of estimating the variance of $\hat{N}$ are available (Seber 1982), the poor (or nonexistent) estimates of variance for $\hat{H}$ and $\hat{\lambda}$ and the complexities of dealing with geographic variation have discouraged workers from trying to compute it. In addition, the potential sources of bias of $\hat{N}$ are sufficiently numerous and important that degree of confidence in $\hat{N}$ could not be assessed from a variance estimate alone.

In summary, Lincoln-type estimates of population size often provide the only means of estimating numbers of mourning doves. Perhaps this is adequate justification for computing such estimates. However, placing much faith in such estimates is *not* recommended because those estimates invariably are quite imprecise and may be biased.

Banding, recovery and harvest survey data also can be used to estimate population age ratio at the time of banding. Preseason age ratio often is a good index of reproductive rate and is widely used as such for North American waterfowl populations (see Martin et al. 1979, Munro and Kimball 1982).

One way to estimate age ratio is to estimate preseason population size of young and adult birds separately using the above Lincoln estimator. If preseason age ratio (denoted as P) is expressed as young per adult, then this ratio of Lincoln estimators can be written as:

$$\hat{P} = \hat{N}_Y/\hat{N}_A = \frac{(\hat{H}_Y/\hat{h}_Y)}{(\hat{H}_A/\hat{h}_A)} = \frac{(\hat{H}_Y/\hat{H}_A)}{(\hat{h}_Y/\hat{h}_A)} \qquad (5)$$

where the subscripts Y and A denote young and adult, respectively.

Examination of (5) shows that separate estimates of young and adult harvest and harvest rate are not always needed to estimate age ratio. It generally is easier to estimate age ratio in the harvest—denote this estimate $(\widehat{H_Y/H_A})$—than to estimate the actual young and adult harvests, $\hat{H}_Y$ and $\hat{H}_A$. Such estimates can be obtained from representative samples of wings of doves taken during the hunting season. As noted, harvest rate is estimated as the ratio of recovery and reporting rate estimates (2), and past reporting rate estimates for mourning doves are likely biased low. However, if reporting rate is assumed to be the same for young and adult birds $(\lambda_Y = \lambda_A = \lambda)$, then h_Y/h_A, which often is termed differential vulnerability, can be estimated simply as the ratio of young to adult recovery rates:

$$\widehat{h_Y/h_A} = \hat{f}_Y/\hat{f}_A. \qquad (6)$$

Thus, preseason age ratio can be estimated with an estimate of age ratio in the harvest and estimates of young and adult recovery rates:

$$\hat{P} = \frac{\widehat{H_Y/H_A}}{(\hat{f}_Y/\hat{f}_A)}. \qquad (7)$$

The data requirements for (7) are much less stringent that those for (5), and (7) is to be preferred (provided that the assumption of equal reporting rates for young and adult birds is true).

This method of estimating preseason age ratio has not seen much use for mourning doves. Hanson and Kossack (1962) briefly discussed this method and concluded that they did not have sufficient banding data to estimate differential vulnerability well. Dunks et al. (1982) and Tomlinson et al. (1988) estimated differential vulnerability $(\hat{f}_Y/\hat{f}_A)$ for mourning doves as 1.3 for both the CMU and WMU, indicating that young mourning doves have higher probabilities of being shot than do adult doves. Both Dunks et al. (1982) and Tomlinson et al. (1988) noted that their estimates of differential vulnerability could be used in conjunction with harvest age ratio data from state wing collection surveys to estimate preseason age ratio. As was the case for estimating mourning dove population size, geographic variation and the need to match wing age ratios with differential vulnerability estimates make this a difficult task.

Chapter 17

Population Characteristics and Trends in the Eastern Management Unit

Fant W. Martin
Office of Migratory Bird Management
U.S. Fish and Wildlife Service
Arlington, Virginia

John R. Sauer
Patuxent Wildlife Research Center
U.S. Fish and Wildlife Service
Laurel, Maryland

HABITAT DESCRIPTION

The Eastern Management Unit (EMU) includes twenty-seven states and encompasses 30 percent of the land area in the conterminous United States. All of the states in the unit except Louisiana lie east of the Mississippi River (see *Figure 4*). Based on long-term (1966–87) results of the Call-count Survey, some 26 percent of the doves in the lower forty-eight states nest in the EMU (Dolton 1987).

The potential natural vegetation of the EMU is characterized by forested habitats (Küchler 1964). Eastern deciduous forest (Braun 1950) covers the vast majority of the region, and only Florida, Illinois and Louisiana contain substantial naturally unforested areas *(Figure 45)*. Within EMU forests, however, there is great diversity in both tree species and habitat types, ranging from the hemlock/white pine/northern hardwood association in northern states to the oak/chestnut and beech/maple regions in the central states to the southeastern evergreen region. It is beyond the scope of this chapter to discuss these habitats in detail, but it must be noted that potential natural vegetation may bear little resemblance to the vegetation now present. Klopatek et al. (1979) examined the relationships among potential and actual vegetation and determined that

human-induced land-use changes have had major effects on vegetative types in the United States. In EMU states, an estimated average of 56.4 percent of the potential natural vegetation remained as of 1979. Amounts varied from only 11 percent in Illinois to 88 percent in Maine.

Many EMU habitats were manipulated by Native Americans (primarily through burning) before the advent of colonization by Europeans, although the extent of these manipulations is not clear (Myers and Peroni 1983, see also chapter 2). Since settlement by European colonists, agricultural development has been the primary form of land-use modification; by 1900, approximately 378.3 million (65.7 percent) of the 575.8 million acres (153.1 of 233.0 million ha) in the EMU were in farmland. These historical land-use manipulations undoubtedly had positive effects on mourning dove populations, creating a mosaic of fields for feeding and edge habitats for cover and nesting (Keeler 1977). Recently, however, farmland in the EMU has decreased—from approximately 349.4 million acres (141.4 million ha) in 1950 to 223.4 million acres (90.4 million ha) in 1990 (U.S. Department of Agriculture 1951, 1990)—and modern agricultural practices (such as removal of hedgerows, large fields, increased harvesting efficiency that minimizes waste seeds, and use of herbicides) make existing farmland less beneficial to doves. The effects of changes in farming practices on the dove population are discussed later.

Other forms of land use in the EMU also affect dove populations. Urbanization is increasing dramatically (Klopatek et al. 1979) and likely influences mourning doves adversely. However, depending on the prior habitat, certain kinds of development (e.g., suburban housing) may be beneficial.

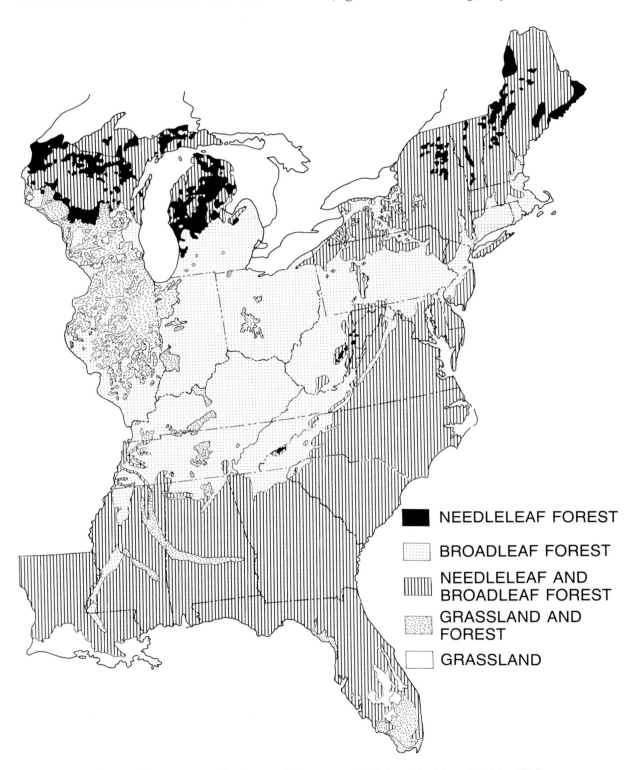

NEEDLELEAF FOREST

BROADLEAF FOREST

NEEDLELEAF AND BROADLEAF FOREST

GRASSLAND AND FOREST

GRASSLAND

Figure 45. Potential natural vegetation in the Eastern Management Unit (modified from Küchler 1964).

Historically, the Eastern Management Unit was heavily forested. Early settlers cut and burned pristine forests to create towns, homesteads and agricultural fields, and the mourning dove benefited from the enhanced "edge" and increased variety of foods. The proliferation of mourning doves under pioneering circumstances took place long before this bird gained popularity as a game species. *Photos by Bluford W. Muir; courtesy of the USDA Forest Service.*

DOVE DISTRIBUTION AND DENSITY

Mourning dove breeding populations are distributed throughout all twenty-seven states encompassing the EMU, but densities vary considerably. Data from the nationwide Call-count Survey can be used to compare relative densities of breeding doves among geographic areas. For the EMU, mean mourning dove densities were derived as follows: the yearly numbers of birds heard calling on each survey route were averaged for the period 1966–87; these route means then were averaged by physiographic region within states and weighted by land area to obtain dove density estimates for each state or physiographic region.

Mourning dove densities in the EMU *(Figure 46)* range from more than 40 birds heard per route in the upper coastal plain in South Carolina and Georgia to less than 4 birds in northern spruce/hardwood habitat in northern Wisconsin. The Cumberland Plateau and Appalachian Mountain habitats ranging from New York to Tennessee also have comparatively low densities, averaging fewer than 10 doves per route. Generally, the highest dove densities occur in the western half of the unit, from Illinois, Indiana and part of Ohio south to eastern Louisiana, Mississippi and Alabama; the lowest densities are in the eastern forests from Maine to Florida. In comparison with the other two units, average density of doves in the EMU is

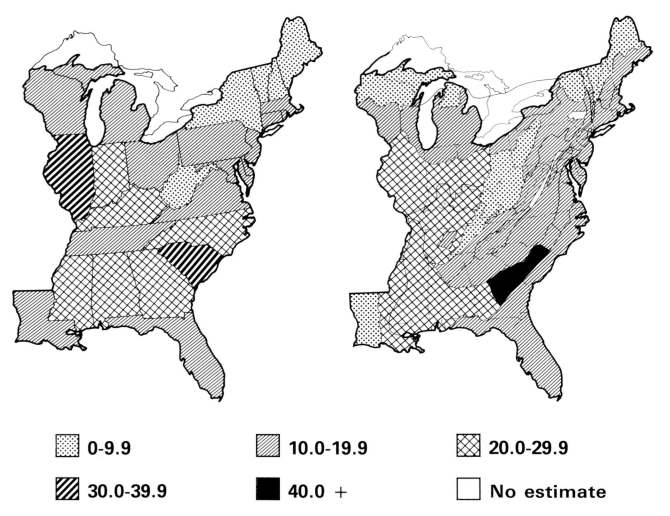

0-9.9   **10.0-19.9**   **20.0-29.9**

30.0-39.9   **40.0 +**   **No estimate**

Figure 46. Comparative densities of mourning doves by state (left) and physiographic region (right) in the Eastern Management Unit, estimated from average number of doves heard per Call-count route, 1966–87.

higher than in the Western Management Unit (WMU) and lower than in the Central Management Unit (CMU).

Although mourning doves breed throughout the EMU, they emigrate in winter from at least the northern parts of their range. Christmas count data indicate that doves winter in every state in the unit (Root 1988), although few remain above 45 degrees north latitude. Mourning doves reach their maximum winter densities in the interior parts of the EMU—namely, in Indiana, Ohio, Illinois, Tennessee and Mississippi.

HUNTING

Federal regulations permit all states to select hunting seasons for doves, but only seventeen of the twenty-seven states in the EMU have chosen to have a dove season in recent years.

The decision of whether or not a state permits dove hunting is based largely on public attitudes. In most northern EMU states, the dove is considered a songbird, and efforts to make it a gamebird have not been successful. In contrast, the mourning dove is hunted in all EMU states south of the Mason-Dixon line as well as in four states north of it (*Figure 47*). The dove is especially popular among hunters in southern states; an average of more than 1.3 million EMU hunters, most of them in southern states, pursued doves during the 1983–87 hunting seasons (see chapters 24 through 26). As pointed out by Newsom et al. (1957), popularity of doves among southern hunters, in addition to the wide distribution and the sporting characteristics of the bird, is chiefly due to two factors: traditionally, dove hunting seasons are the first upland game seasons to open in autumn; and mourning doves can be harvested by the "one-gallus" hunter without expensive equipment or extensive travel.

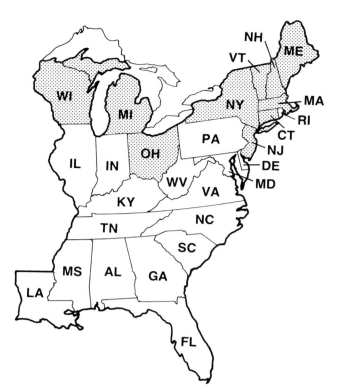

Figure 47. Hunted (clear) and nonhunted (shaded) states of the Eastern Management Unit, 1989.

MOURNING DOVE MANAGEMENT HISTORY

Southeastern Cooperative Dove Study

The major push toward improved management of mourning doves occurred in 1948, when the Southeastern Association of Game and Fish Commissioners (now the Southeastern Association of Fish and Wildlife Agencies) decided to undertake a regionwide dove study under the Federal Aid in Wildlife Restoration Act (also known as the Pittman-Robertson or "P-R" Program). The time was ripe for such a study. State wildlife departments had recently employed eager young biologists, most of them veterans of World War II who had returned home and obtained degrees in the fledgling field of wildlife management. For the first time, both a dependable source of funds and trained biologists were available, and the Southeastern Cooperative Dove Study soon was underway. Ten southeastern states participated in the study, and most fieldwork was completed by 1952. Newsom et al. (1957) described the purpose of the study and summarized major findings, and a final report was published soon after (Southeastern Association of Game and Fish Commissioners 1957, see also chapter 14).

Several important mourning dove studies already had taken place or were underway in the Southeast when the cooperative study was initiated (e.g., Moore and Pearson 1941, Quay 1954), and much had been learned about the species' life history. However, interest in doves and dove hunting had increased greatly since the end of the war, and there was need for information on dove numbers and distribution, productivity and effects of hunting on dove populations. This was a tall order, especially since many of the techniques required to collect the data either had not been developed or were still in their infancy.

One major contribution of the cooperative study was development of the Call-count Survey to obtain annual and long-term indices of the comparative size of the dove breeding population (see chapter 14). This survey continues to be the major means by which dove population status is monitored nationwide. Other techniques that were developed or improved as a result of the study included trapping and banding methods and methods of age determination using plumage characteristics of wings.

Results of the study provided details on monthly nesting activity and timing of autumn emigration as those factors relate to hunting season dates. Analyses of banding data, in particular, showed that EMU doves had a high population turnover and that hunting mortality at the time was low.

The study was cooperative in the fullest sense of the word. Each participating southeastern state assigned a biologist to the study, and assistants, technicians and conservation law enforcement personnel often participated in seasonal activities. Biologists of the U.S. Fish and Wildlife Service and the Wildlife Management Institute participated throughout. At least six hundred people cooperated in the work. Special newsletters kept cooperators informed of progress, suggested methods and new ideas, and helped ensure that the data were collected in a uniform way (Newsom et al. 1957). Names and affiliations of key people in the study are shown in the final report (Southeastern Association of Game and Fish Commissioners 1957).

The contributions of the dedicated professionals in the cooperative dove study afforded other lasting benefits by providing guidance for further research and for ongoing operational banding and survey activities. Also, the recognized importance of the dove and need for continued attention to its management resulted in the formation of a Southeastern Dove Technical Committee, as well as the permanent assignment in the U.S. Fish and Wildlife Service of a biologist whose responsibility was to stimulate and coordinate development of a nationwide dove program. Some states outside of the Southeast already had major dove projects under way, but assignment of a federal biologist proved helpful in increasing nationwide participation in the program by state fish and wildlife agencies and universities. The Missouri Cooperative Wildlife Research Unit and the Missouri Department of Conservation were especially active during this time. Nationally, there was increased emphasis on banding and the Call-count Survey. As a result, the three mourning dove management units were established in 1960 (Kiel 1961); by 1966, the original Call-count routes established in 1953 had been replaced with a more random nationwide system of routes based on results of a pilot study made in the Southeast (Foote et al. 1958).

Experimental Increase in Daily Bag Limits

Mourning dove hunting regulations in eastern states were conservative for more than a decade after World War II. The hunting season usually did not open until mid-September or later, and by the time the EMU was established in 1960, only Louisiana and four northern and midlatitudinal states (Illinois, Kentucky, Pennsylvania and Tennessee) opened their seasons in the first week of September (U.S. Fish and Wildlife Service 1977). There were several reasons for conservative regulations during these years. First, a widespread outbreak of trichomoniasis in 1950 and 1951, along with severe winter weather, caused a substantial mourning dove population decline that persisted until 1955 (Newsom et al. 1957, see also chapter 12). Second, uncertainty remained about the incidence of late nesting, especially in southern states, and the effects that early September hunting had on success of these nests. And third, the effects of different hunting regulations on harvest and dove population status were unclear.

Some biologists believed that the then-current level of hunting pressure had no adverse effect on the dove population and that early September seasons were appropriate because they allowed hunters to harvest doves that otherwise would die from natural causes (Newsom et al. 1953, Winston 1954).

The U.S. Fish and Wildlife Service gradually liberalized mourning dove hunting regulations during the late 1950s and early 1960s, but due to a lack of data, there were strong differences of opinion between state and Service officials over the impacts that hunting (through relaxed hunting regulations) had on doves. Finally, in 1965, in an attempt

to resolve the issue, the Southeastern Association of Fish and Wildlife Agencies and the Service undertook a major study to determine the effects of a change in the daily bag limit on harvest and mourning dove population status. During this cooperative study, the daily bag limit remained at the usual 12 birds during the 1966–68 and 1971 hunting seasons but was increased to 18 during the 1969–70 seasons. Effects of the change were evaluated by means of (1) an annual telephone survey to estimate hunting activity and harvest, (2) bandings to measure recovery rates and survival rates, (3) Call-count Surveys to obtain annual indices of breeding population size and (4) a wing-collection survey to obtain information on annual recruitment. All sixteen EMU states that permitted mourning dove hunting participated in the study, although two (Pennsylvania and West Virginia) elected not to increase the daily bag limit during the experimental years. A number of EMU nonhunting states also participated by banding doves and making Call-count Surveys. Except for an increase in mean number of doves bagged per hunting trip when the bag limit was 18 ($P > 0.10$), the experiment provided no evidence that liberalized bag limits resulted in a change in numbers of hunters, hunting trips, doves harvested, trips per hunter, doves per hunter, first season recovery rates (a measure of shooting pressure), annual survival rates, breeding density index (based on Call-counts) or age composition in the mourning dove population (Hayne 1975).

The bag limit study assessed the effects of increasing the daily limit on harvest and on dove population status, but it did not deal with the more important question of hunting impact on annual survival of doves when the daily limit was 12. Although results did not indicate that the increase in the daily limit from 12 to 18 had an adverse effect, it is possible that the larger bag limit simply made it legal for an unknown but substantial number of hunters to kill about as many birds as they did when the limit was 12. The study probably would have been more informative had the limit been reduced rather than increased. However, there was little interest in conducting the study under restrictive regulations.

Recent Events

In the mid-1960s, primarily through the efforts of the Southeastern Association of Fish and Wildlife Agencies, the Wildlife Management Institute, and other organizations, Congress began appropriating funds for expanded research on mourning doves, American woodcock, and other migratory shore and upland gamebirds. The Accelerated Research Program for Migratory Shore and Upland Game Birds was established in 1967 as the result of this special appropriation. The program was funded at an annual level of $250,000 until it was terminated in 1981. Most of the funds were used to support research by states and universities, but a portion also was reserved for research by the U.S. Fish and Wildlife Service on mourning doves and woodcock. These funds helped to support long-term studies of doves by Service biologists at a field station at the Carolina Sandhills National Wildlife Refuge in South Carolina and later at the University of Georgia. Details of the Accelerated Research Program are discussed in Sanderson (1977), which includes a summary about the mourning dove and a proposed long-term management plan (Keeler 1977). The purposes of that work on migratory shore and upland gamebirds were to provide summaries about the status of mourning doves and other shore and upland species and to identify information gaps and funds needed for effective management.

The Accelerated Research Program received little outside recognition or support and was abolished early in the 1980s. This proved unfortunate because the U.S. Fish and Wildlife Service also terminated its mourning dove research at about the same time. As a consequence, except for a recent nationwide study of effects of September hunting seasons on dove production rates (discussed later), federal and state efforts in recent years have been limited largely to monitoring mourning dove population status in the EMU and other management units.

POPULATION TRENDS

Population Trends Based on the Nationwide Call-count Survey

As discussed in chapter 14, the present system of obtaining annual and long-term indices of mourning dove breeding abundance from the nationwide Call-count Survey was initiated in 1966 and is based on roadside counts made along suitable, randomly established routes located throughout the nation. More than 500 of the nationwide total of ±1,050 routes are in the EMU. From Call-counts made in the EMU from 1966 to 1987, mourning dove population trends are shown for five-, ten-, fifteen- and twenty-two-year intervals *(Table 47)*. Data were segregated by hunting and nonhunting states to compare population trends with differences in hunting regulations, shooting pressure, climatic phenomena and agricultural practices. Long-term trends for combined hunting and nonhunting states and for the entire EMU are represented in *Figure 48*.

Hunting states. For the twenty-two-year period (1966–87), dove population trends were downward for ten hunting states and upward for six, but changes were significant only for North Carolina (−2.8 percent per year, $P < 0.01$), Maryland (−1.8 percent per year, $P < 0.05$) and Alabama (+1.4 percent per year, $P < 0.05$) *(Table 47)*. For combined EMU hunting states, no significant trend was detected (−0.6 percent per year, $P > 0.10$). For 1978–87, however, population indices for combined hunting states have declined at a rate of 0.9 percent per year ($P < 0.05$).

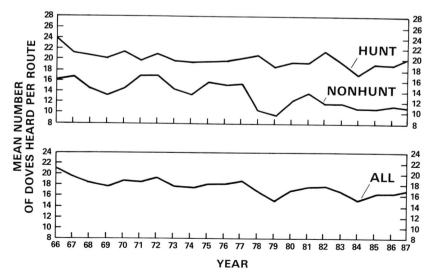

Figure 48. Annual Call-count indices of mourning dove abundance in the Eastern Management Unit, 1966–87. Indices are shown for hunting states and nonhunting states (top) and all states combined (bottom).

Table 47. Trends (percentage change[a] per year as determined by linear regression) in number of mourning doves heard per route by state in the Eastern Management Unit, 1966–87.

State	\multicolumn{4}{c}{5-year (1983–87)}				\multicolumn{4}{c}{10-year (1978–87)}				\multicolumn{2}{c}{15-year (1973–87)}	
	N	Percentage change[b]	95%	C.I.	N	Percentage change[b]	95%	C.I.	N	Percentage change[b]
Hunting										
Alabama	30	−2.7	−7.5	2.0	33	−2.4*	−5.3	0.5	37	1.8
Delaware	2	44.9***	32.8	56.9	3	12.6	−9.9	25.1	3	−0.9
Florida	22	−3.5	−13.2	6.3	24	−1.8	−6.8	3.3	24	−1.7
Georgia	22	−2.0	−4.8	0.9	22	−0.2	−2.4	2.0	25	0.1
Illinois	20	4.5	−4.2	13.3	22	4.2**	0.8	7.6	22	1.8
Kentucky	20	3.3	−2.2	8.8	21	−1.4	−9.2	6.5	23	−2.2
Louisiana	18	−2.7	−9.9	4.6	19	−1.6	−5.2	2.1	19	−1.0
Maryland	13	2.3	−5.7	10.2	14	−2.5	−8.1	3.1	15	−2.7**
Mississippi	22	2.9	−2.8	8.7	23	−2.0**	−3.8	−0.3	24	−0.6
North Carolina	21	0.8	−3.0	4.7	21	0.8	−0.7	2.4	21	−1.0
Pennsylvania	15	4.8	−2.7	12.2	15	4.2**	0.4	8.0	16	3.7*
Rhode Island	2	4.9**	0.5	9.3	2	−3.0*	−6.1	0.1	2	1.0**
South Carolina	20	−1.8	−9.7	6.1	23	−1.9*	−4.1	0.4	23	−0.7
Tennessee	24	−2.2	−6.2	1.8	24	−3.2***	−5.5	−0.8	27	−1.8
Virginia	11	−1.0	−6.8	4.7	11	−2.9*	−6.0	0.3	11	−2.1
West Virginia	7	9.7	−6.2	25.6	8	2.6	−1.7	7.0	10	3.5
Subtotal	269	−0.2	−1.7	1.3	285	−0.9**	−1.7	0.0	302	−0.4
Nonhunting										
Connecticut	2	22.9	−21.5	67.3	2	−6.0	−45.5	33.4	2	5.5
Indiana[c]	15	6.2**	0.1	12.4	15	−1.0	−2.6	0.7	15	5.4***
Massachusetts	16	0.2	−9.8	10.2	18	0.4	−3.5	4.2	18	1.5
Maine	9	−11.8	−31.7	8.2	9	0.0	−6.6	6.7	9	7.7
Michigan	20	9.8**	2.1	17.6	20	3.0	−1.3	7.2	20	0.1
New Hampshire	3	−5.8	−15.4	3.8	3	1.8***	1.8	1.8	4	−1.5
New Jersey	18	−4.9	−11.8	2.0	18	−2.2	−6.9	2.5	18	−4.4*
New York	12	−7.6**	−14.2	−1.1	15	−2.1***	−3.5	−0.7	17	−0.6
Ohio	37	3.3	−2.4	9.1	52	6.5**	1.1	11.9	52	−3.8**
Vermont	21	−3.2	−7.7	1.2	21	0.4	−10.4	11.1	21	3.8
Wisconsin	20	−1.1	−8.0	5.7	21	−1.5	−6.0	3.0	21	−2.7*
Subtotal	173	2.1	−0.4	4.6	194	0.8	−0.6	2.2	197	−2.8***
Total	442	0.2	−1.1	1.6	479	−0.6*	−1.4	0.1	499	−0.9**

[a] Route trend means weighted by land area and population density. The estimated count in the next year is (percentage ÷ 100 + 1) times the count in the current year, where percentage is the annual change.
[b] *$P<0.1$, **$P<0.05$, ***$P<0.01$.
[c] Indiana became a hunting state in 1984.

Nonhunting states. Long-term population trends were downward in four nonhunting states and upward in seven (Table 47). No nonhunting state showed a significantly increasing long-term trend, and only Indiana (−4.5 percent per year, $P<0.01$) and Ohio (−3.5 percent per year, $P<0.01$) exhibited significantly decreasing trends. The long-term trend for combined nonhunting states was downward (−2.2 percent per year, $P<0.01$). However, for 1978–87 no significant trend was detected (+0.8 percent per year, $P>0.10$).

Unitwide. Long-term downward population trends were recorded for fourteen (52 percent) of the twenty-seven EMU states, and for the entire unit, the population declined 0.9 percent per year

($P<0.01$). However, more recently—1978–87 (−0.6 percent per year, $P<0.10$) and 1983–87 (+0.2 percent per year, $P>0.10$)—the EMU trend essentially was stable (Table 47).

Population Trends Based on the North American Breeding Bird Survey

An independent annual survey of breeding birds, the North American Breeding Bird Survey, has been conducted throughout the nation since 1966. Like the Call-count Survey, the Breeding Bird Survey is made along roads, but it differs from the Call-count Survey in several features (see chapters

Table 47. (continued)

15-year (1973–87)		22-year (1966–87)			
95%	C.I.	N	Percentage change[b]	95%	C.I.
−0.8	4.4	39	1.5***	0.4	2.6
−30.6	28.8	3	3.8	−14.1	21.6
−4.3	1.0	27	−0.7	−2.7	1.3
−2.2	2.4	26	1.1	−0.3	2.6
−1.5	5.0	22	1.5	−1.5	4.6
−6.9	2.5	25	−1.4	−4.7	1.9
−3.9	1.9	22	−0.0	−2.7	2.7
−5.2	−0.2	15	−1.8**	−3.6	−0.0
−3.6	2.3	25	−1.9	−5.3	1.6
−3.0	0.9	21	−2.8***	−4.2	−1.3
−0.2	7.6	16	−0.8	−4.1	2.5
0.1	1.9	5	1.9	−12.5	16.3
−4.2	2.7	23	−0.9	−3.3	1.5
−4.2	0.6	30	−1.7*	−3.5	0.1
−4.7	0.5	11	−1.7*	−3.5	0.1
−1.7	8.8	11	2.3	−3.2	7.8
−1.3	0.4	321	−0.6	−1.4	0.2
−22.8	33.9	2	11.3	−13.9	36.4
−6.8	−3.9	17	−4.5***	−5.6	−3.5
−2.8	5.8	19	0.3	−4.1	4.6
−1.9	17.3	11	10.0	−24.8	44.9
−4.0	4.2	20	0.1	−4.6	4.8
−6.7	3.7	8	2.6*	−0.4	5.7
−9.1	0.3	19	−3.2	−7.9	1.5
−2.6	1.5	19	0.1	−2.0	2.2
−6.8	−0.8	54	−3.5***	−5.4	−1.5
−8.7	16.2	23	9.4	−7.0	25.8
−5.4	0.0	21	−1.1	−2.9	0.6
−4.0	−1.7	213	−2.2***	−3.5	−0.8
−1.6	−0.2	534	−0.9***	−1.7	−0.2

14 and 15). Volunteer observers survey fifty stops (listening points) rather than twenty as in the Call-count Survey, and total numbers of birds of all species seen and heard are recorded. In the Call-count Survey, numbers of doves heard and seen are recorded and analyzed separately. The Breeding Bird Survey was designed to monitor the distribution and abundance of all migratory nongame birds. Because of this, there may be more within-route variability for doves than is the case with the Call-count Survey. However, the Breeding Bird Survey is much more extensive in terms of numbers of routes located in the EMU (1,116 routes versus 500 for the Call-count Survey). For this reason, results from this survey were compared with long-term trends estimated from dove Call-counts.

Based on results from 651 Breeding Bird Survey routes in combined EMU *hunting* states during 1966–87, no upward or downward trend was detected ($P > 0.10$). Dove populations increased in the hunting states of Alabama, Delaware, Florida, Pennsylvania and West Virginia ($P < 0.05$) and declined in Illinois ($P < 0.05$). In contrast, populations represented by 461 Breeding Bird Survey routes in combined EMU *nonhunting* states increased 1.3 percent per year ($P < 0.05$). Individual dove populations in Connecticut, Maine, Massachusetts, New Hampshire, New Jersey, New York and Vermont all registered increases. For the entire EMU, Breeding Bird Survey results indicated no significant long-term increases or decreases.

Differences in Population Trends between the Call-count and Breeding Bird Surveys

The Breeding Bird Survey and Call-count Survey showed similar dove population trends in the CMU and WMU (see chapters 18 and 19). However, results of the two surveys differ in many EMU states, and the long-term unitwide decline observed in the Call-count Survey is not evident in the Breeding Bird Survey. Although it is not clear which survey, if either, provides unbiased estimates of EMU dove trends, it should be noted that the latter has more routes in each state. The larger sample sizes permit better estimation of variances and greater precision in annual point estimates of population trend. For these reasons, Breeding Bird Survey results may better represent dove population trends in the EMU, but research is needed on this important question. When the results of the two surveys are considered, the unitwide dove population likely was essentially stable during the 1966–87 period.

HARVEST CHARACTERISTICS

Size, Distribution and Derivation of Harvest

Source of data. Measurements of size, distribution and derivation (origin) of harvest to, from and in the EMU are based largely on data found in Hayne and Geissler (1977). Hayne and Geissler presented 1966–71 dove harvest estimates for states in each management unit (see Table 2.1 in their report), as well as direct (first-year) recoveries from nationwide preseason bandings during the same time span. The recoveries were weighted by Call-count indices and estimates of band-reporting rates and harvest.

Conclusions on distribution and derivation in this chapter were derived from 14,329 direct recoveries, including 11,309 from doves banded as immatures and 3,020 from doves banded as adults. All EMU hunting states except Delaware and West Virginia were well represented by bandings and resulting direct recoveries. However, it was not possible to measure the contribution from all EMU nonhunting states, either because doves were not banded in some of them or the numbers of recoveries from the banded samples were too small.

Size of harvest. The average annual harvest in the EMU during 1966–71 was estimated to be 27.6 million mourning doves *(Table 48)*. By state, the average annual harvests ranged from a low of 30,500 doves in West Virginia to a high of 3.5 million in Georgia. For 1983–87, the estimated unitwide harvest averaged 28.5 million doves, suggesting that the harvest remained rather constant over the years *(Table 48)*. Between 1966 and 1987, EMU states annually accounted for about 60 percent of the nationwide harvest, even though the unit, in 1987, contained only an estimated 28 percent of the nation's dove population (Dolton 1987). Since harvest estimates are derived with differing survey methods among state wildlife agencies, caution must be used in interpreting combined state harvest figures. Nevertheless, it seems clear that EMU

doves are heavily cropped and have been for many years. In chapter 24, the nationwide harvest has been estimated for different sets of years, and findings are discussed in detail.

Distribution of harvest. In initial examination of recoveries to assess harvest distribution from the EMU, data were retained only for states with 50 or more direct band recoveries for an age class. First, it was determined whether the proportional distribution of in-state recoveries differed between adult and immature doves. Dunks et al. (1982) found that there was such a difference in the CMU, as did Tomlinson et al. (1988) in the WMU, and both concluded that either immature doves from the two units emigrated earlier than adults or that some adults did not emigrate.

The proportion of direct recoveries reported in the EMU hunting state where banded ranged from highs of 99.0 and 98.6 percent for Florida immatures and adults, respectively, to lows of 56.3 and 72.4 percent for immatures and adults banded in Illinois *(Table 49)*. In general, a high percentage of recoveries from each group was recovered in-state, and there was no latitudinal or geographic age-specific pattern in distribution. For the entire unit, mean in-state percentages were 89.1 for immatures and 90.4 for adults. Although the difference is statistically significant ($P < 0.05$), adult in-state pro-

Table 48. Estimated mean size of mourning dove harvest in hunting states of the Eastern Management Unit, 1966–71 and 1983–87.[a]

| State | Estimated size and percentage of harvest | | | |
| | 1966–71 | | 1983–87 | |
	Number[b]	Percentage	Number[b]	Percentage
Alabama	2,978.7	10.8	3,029.6	10.6
Delaware	133.5	0.5	102.8	0.4
Florida	2,640.8	9.6	1,635.2	5.7
Georgia	3,540.1	12.8	3,155.5	11.1
Illinois	2,026.2	7.3	1,344.5	4.7
Indiana[c]			162.2	0.6
Kentucky	1,154.0	4.2	1,930.0	6.8
Louisiana	1,720.2	6.2	2,497.0	8.8
Maryland	368.8	1.3	411.8	1.4
Mississippi	1,755.6	6.4	2,933.6	10.3
North Carolina	3,265.4	11.8	2,498.6	8.8
Pennsylvania	565.7	2.1	1,488.0	5.2
Rhode Island	32.9	0.1	10.0	Tr[d]
South Carolina	2,698.9	9.8	3,148.3	11.0
Tennessee	2,988.1	10.8	3,183.7	11.2
Virginia	1,689.1	6.1	931.8	3.3
West Virginia	30.5	0.1	40.3	0.1
Total	27,588.5	99.9	28,502.8	100.0

[a] Data for 1966–71 from Hayne and Geissler (1977), and for 1983–87 from Table 90.
[b] In thousands.
[c] Season closed 1966–71.
[d] Tr = trace = less than 0.1 percent.

Table 49. Chi-square tests of hypothesis that equal percentages of immature and adult mourning doves were directly recovered in Eastern Management Unit states where they were banded.

State	Immature			Adult			X²[a]
	Total	In-state	Percentage	Total	In-state	Percentage	
Alabama	1,372	1,156	84.3	473	415	87.7	3.37*
Florida	688	681	99.0	74	73	98.6	0.07
Georgia	1,221	1,122	91.9	319	303	95.0	3.50
Illinois	277	156	56.3	156	113	72.4	11.02***
Kentucky	263	217	82.5	84	72	85.7	0.47
Louisiana	1,895	1,734	91.5	351	311	88.6	3.06*
Maryland	449	411	91.5	141	119	84.4	5.99**
Mississippi	740	637	86.1	173	165	95.4	11.34***
North Carolina	610	572	93.8	265	256	96.6	2.92
Pennsylvania	292	278	95.2	134	130	97.0	0.74
South Carolina	1,215	1,085	89.3	155	132	85.2	2.37
Tennessee	1,130	1,012	89.6	273	262	96.0	10.83***
Virginia	661	571	86.4	247	221	89.5	1.54
Total/mean	10,813	9,632	89.1	2,845	2,572	90.4	4.16**

[a] X² statistics with 1 df: *$P<0.10$; **$P<0.05$; ***$P<0.01$.

portions were higher than those for young in only nine (69.2 percent) of the thirteen states, indicating considerable heterogeneity. This result was not unexpected because, regardless of age, doves in most southern EMU hunting states either do not migrate or move only short distances. In contrast, doves from many CMU and WMU hunting states migrate through the units into Mexico. Any age differences would be detected more readily in the more migratory populations to the west of the EMU.

The following discussions on distribution and derivation are based on combined direct recoveries of immatures and adult doves. For combined bandings, the mean proportion of in-state recovery was 89 percent for the fourteen states from which there were adequate data. The consistently high percentages among the EMU hunting states indicate that most of the harvest of EMU mourning doves occurs in the same state in which those doves are produced.

Of 14,329 direct recoveries of doves banded in the EMU, 14,041 (98 percent) were reported from within the EMU; 257 (1.8 percent) from eight EMU states were reported from the CMU (184 in Texas); and 31 recoveries (0.2 percent) from five states were reported from Mexico (28) and Central America (3) *(Table 50)*. Most of these distant recoveries originated from Louisiana and Mississippi and from northern and midlatitudinal states, especially Wisconsin. The small proportion of EMU recoveries in Mexico is in marked contrast to the CMU and WMU, where 15 percent and 6 percent, respectively, of recoveries were reported from Mexico and Central America (Dunks et al. 1982, Tomlinson

et al. 1988).

Derivation of harvest. Regarding the origin of doves harvested in EMU hunting states, results are based on weighted direct recoveries from doves banded anywhere and reported as shot or found dead during the hunting season in an EMU state (Hayne and Geissler 1977). Certain regions—such as Canada, Maine, Vermont, New Hampshire and Connecticut—were represented by either small or no banded samples and therefore were not registered as contributing areas. Despite this informational gap, the overall contribution from these areas is believed to have been minimal because their dove populations generally are small, and because the direct recovery rates were low from nonhunting states in which sizable numbers of doves were banded.

The weighted derivation of harvest (in percentages) for each EMU hunting state *(Table 51)* suggests that harvest in some midlatitudinal states came almost entirely from locally produced doves (especially in Kentucky, Pennsylvania, Rhode Island and West Virginia), whereas harvest in southern states came from many other locations. For example, twenty-four or more other states in the EMU and CMU contributed varying numbers of doves to the harvests in Florida, Alabama and Georgia. Thus, states in the southern portion of the EMU derived their harvest from a wider geographic area than did states farther north. Despite the importance of doves from other locations, however, locally produced birds accounted for more than half of the harvest in all southern EMU states except Florida and Louisiana.

Table 50. Percentage distribution of direct recoveries of mourning doves (all ages and sexes combined) banded in the Eastern Management Unit, 1966–71.[a]

Area where harvested	State where banded (production area)										
	AL	FL	GA	IL	IN	KY	LA	MA	MD	MI	MS
Eastern Management Unit											
Alabama	85.1	0.1	3.6	4.4	12.7	0.3	0.4	5.2	0.2	14.3	0.3
Delaware								2.6	0.7		
Florida	2.3	99.0	2.8	9.5	21.3	3.2	0.6	7.8	1.2	31.0	1.8
Georgia	8.8	0.9	92.5	4.8	6.4	0.6	0.1	14.2	2.0	21.3	
Illinois	Tr[b]			62.2	2.1	3.7	Tr				
Kentucky				0.9	36.2	83.2					
Louisiana	0.8			6.9	8.5	2.0	91.1			14.3	6.9
Maryland	Tr							11.7	89.8		
Mississippi	0.6		0.1	1.6	2.1	0.3	1.1			9.5	87.8
North Carolina			0.3	0.7		0.3		14.3	1.9	2.4	
Pennsylvania					2.1			5.2	0.8		
Rhode Island								19.5			
South Carolina			0.3	1.2				9.1	1.9	4.8	
Tennessee	2.3		0.3	0.9		3.2				2.4	0.7
Virginia			0.1	0.2				10.4	1.5		
West Virginia											
Subtotal	100.0	100.0	100.0	93.3	91.4	96.8	93.3	100.0	100.0	100.0	97.5
Central Management Unit	0.0	0.0	0.0	6.2	4.3	3.2	6.4	0.0	0.0	0.0	2.3
Mexico and Central America	0.0	0.0	0.0	0.5	4.3	0.0	0.3	0.0	0.0	0.0	0.2
Total	100.0	100.0	100.0	100.0	100.0	100.0	100.0	100.0	100.0	100.0	100.0
Number of recoveries	1,845	762	1,540	433	47	347	2,246	77	590	42	913

[a] Percentages not shown for states from which there were less than 25 recoveries (Connecticut, Delaware, Maine, New Hampshire and Vermont).
[b] Tr = trace = less than 0.1 percent.

Eleven EMU states derived some of their harvest from the CMU. The relative contributions of these birds varied widely among states, ranging from less than 1 percent of the harvest in Kentucky to 22 percent in Florida to 27 percent in Louisiana *(Table 51)*. Without taking into account the unknown contribution from areas in which doves either were not banded or were not banded in such numbers as to provide at least 25 direct recoveries, the weighted recovery data suggested that some 93 percent of the harvest in the EMU came from doves within the unit and 7 percent from the CMU. Thus, of the estimated mean harvest of 27.6 million doves in the EMU from 1966 to 1971 *(Table 48)*, an estimated 25.6 million came from within the unit.

Harvest within the Hunting Season

During the 1966–71 hunting seasons (corresponding to the banding period reported by Hayne and Geissler [1977]), most EMU states opened their dove hunting seasons on September 1 or soon after. This is the earliest opening date permitted for hunting of migratory gamebirds under federal hunting season frameworks, and most EMU states open dove seasons on or near that date. For example, in the 1987–88 season, fifteen of the seventeen EMU states that permitted dove hunting opened their seasons during the first week of September. An early September opening is selected so that locally produced doves may be hunted before they emigrate (U.S. Fish and Wildlife Service 1977). As discussed previously, the earlier opening is especially important in the northernmost states in the unit, because they derive almost all of their harvest from locally produced doves *(Table 51)*.

Federal frameworks permit EMU states to select as many as three splits in the dove hunting season, either statewide or in zones within the state. During the 1966–71 hunting seasons, Kentucky, Maryland, Tennessee and West Virginia selected splits that extended into January or February. Nevertheless, few out-of-state doves were taken in these

Table 50. (continued)

State where banded (production area)											Eastern Management Unit
NC	NJ	NY	OH	PA	RI	SC	TN	VA	WV	WI	
0.5		5.7	11.8	0.5		0.1	1.1	0.4	3.7	12.1	12.1
	3.6	6.5		0.2							0.1
0.8	3.6	8.4	19.6	0.2	1.2	1.1	1.0	1.5		20.4	7.5
0.3	10.6	14.0	17.6	0.7	1.2	4.1	0.5	3.0	3.7	6.3	12.5
							0.1			3.4	2.0
			2.0				1.8	0.1		1.0	2.4
		4.7	21.6				1.0			17.0	15.6
	14.3	12.1	2.0								3.9
		0.9	7.7	0.5			2.6	0.2		4.4	6.3
94.6	10.7	15.9		0.7	1.1	5.9	0.2	4.5	3.7	2.4	7.1
	28.6	1.9		95.9							3.0
					93.0						0.7
2.5	17.9	17.8	9.8	0.9		88.8	0.2	2.8	3.7	1.5	9.3
	3.6		2.0	0.2	2.3		90.9	0.2	3.7	2.4	9.4
1.3	7.1	12.1		0.2	1.2			87.3		1.0	5.9
									81.5		0.2
100.0	100.0	100.0	94.1	100.0	100.0	100.0	99.4	100.0	100.0	71.9	98.0
0.0	0.0	0.0	5.9	0.0	0.0	0.0	0.6	0.0	0.0	19.4	1.8
0.0	0.0	0.0	0.0	0.0	0.0	0.0	0.0	0.0	0.0	8.7	0.2
100.0	100.0	100.0	100.0	100.0	100.0	100.0	100.0	100.0	100.0	100.0	100.0
875	28	107	51	426	86	1,370	1,403	908	27	206	14,329

states (Table 51). For example, Orr (1973) found that resident doves form most of the harvest in Tennessee and that nearly half of the harvest of doves from other states occurs in the first ten days of September. Several EMU states continue to establish split seasons in which one segment extends well into the winter, even though late-season harvest in most of them likely is small.

Louisiana and Florida both winter and harvest large numbers of out-of-state doves (Table 51). In an analysis of bandings made in Louisiana from 1949 to 1967, Watts (1969) showed that most of the harvest of locally produced birds takes place in September and that most of the harvest of doves from other states occurs in later months. Harvest of migrants is largely in the southern portion of the state. Florida is the only EMU state that has delayed the opening date for the mourning dove hunting season. From 1966 to 1971, for example, the statewide season opened in October and the third and final segment of the split season extended into January. Because of this state's geographic position and late season, out-of-state doves formed 70 percent of the harvest in Florida—the highest percentage in any EMU state during the 1966–1971 seasons (Table 51).

Since 1980, federal regulations have permitted all-day hunting of doves in the EMU, and since 1983, all states in the unit have been given an option of (1) seventy hunting days with daily bag and possession limits of 12 and 24 doves, respectively, or (2) a sixty-day season with daily bag and possession limits of 15 and 30, respectively. The long season, liberal limits, use of zones and split seasons, and relaxation of restrictions on baiting have increased dove hunting opportunities so much that there now is little agitation for further liberalization of regulations in the EMU.

Effects of September Hunting on Annual Production

A major issue concerning dove hunting and dove hunting regulations in recent years has been concern over effects of September hunting on doves still nesting at that time. The fate of eggs and young of nesting adults that are shot in September was of particular concern. Nesting doves feed their

Table 51. Weighted derivation (in percentage) of mourning dove harvest in hunting states of the Eastern Management Unit, 1966–71.[a]

Area where banded	Harvest area														
	AL	FL	GA	IL	KY	LA	MD	MS	NC	PA	RI	SC	TN	VA	WV
Eastern Management Unit															
Alabama	71.4	2.5	6.5	0.1		0.7	0.3	0.5					2.7	0.1	
Florida	Tr[b]	30.3	0.2												
Georgia	3.3	3.1	72.0					Tr	0.4			Tr		0.4	0.1
Illinois	3.0	8.3	2.8	76.9	0.6	5.1		0.9	0.6			0.8		0.9	0.2
Indiana	0.9	1.9	0.4	0.3	2.5	0.6		0.1		0.3					
Kentucky	0.4	4.9	0.6	9.4	94.9	2.6		0.3	0.4				5.0		
Louisiana	0.2	0.3	0.1	Tr		45.0		0.4							
Maryland	Tr	0.2	0.2				87.6		0.3	0.1		0.3		0.3	
Massachusetts	Tr	0.1	0.1				0.7		0.1	0.1	1.9	0.1		0.1	
Michigan	2.7	8.9	2.3			3.7		3.2	0.2			1.1		0.2	
Mississippi	0.4	2.5				7.8		86.8					1.1		
New Jersey		0.1	0.2				1.6		0.2	0.8		0.2	Tr	0.2	
New York	0.4	0.8	0.9			0.3	6.4	0.1	1.3	0.2		1.3		1.3	
North Carolina	0.4	0.8	0.2						84.3			2.0		1.5	
Ohio	0.8	1.2	0.7		0.1	1.2	1.0	0.4				0.6	0.1		
Pennsylvania	0.4	0.2	0.4					0.2	0.5	98.5		0.6		0.2	
Rhode Island	Tr	0.1	0.1						0.1		98.1	0.2		0.2	
South Carolina	0.1	1.3	3.1						6.0			87.1			
Tennessee	0.8	0.9	0.3	Tr	1.2	0.6		1.6	0.2			0.1	86.3		
Virginia	0.4	1.5	2.0			0.1		0.2	3.8			2.1	0.3	95.3	
West Virginia	0.1		0.2						0.5			0.2	0.6		100.0
Wisconsin	4.1	8.4	1.8	2.3	0.3	5.8		1.4	0.9			0.5	1.0	0.5	
Subtotal	89.8	78.3	95.1	89.0	99.6	73.5	97.6	96.1	99.8	100.0	100.0	97.4	98.8	100.0	100.0
Central Management Unit															
Arkansas	1.7	1.9	0.3			2.4		0.3				0.3	0.4		
Iowa	2.6	4.4	1.4	2.0		4.8		0.1				0.9	0.1		
Minnesota	1.0	3.2	0.9			3.8		1.0	0.2						
Missouri	2.8	10.9	2.3	6.5	0.3	7.3	2.4	1.2				1.4	0.7		
North Dakota	1.1					1.6									
Nebraska						0.6		0.6							
Oklahoma						1.4									
South Dakota	0.5	1.3			0.1	2.0		0.3							
Texas	0.5					2.7		0.4							
Wyoming				2.5											
Subtotal	10.2	21.7	4.9	11.0	0.4	26.5	2.4	3.9	0.2	0.0	0.0	2.6	1.2	0.0	0.0
Total	100.0	100.0	100.0	100.0	100.0	100.0	100.0	100.0	100.0	100.0	100.0	100.0	100.0	100.0	100.0

[a] Percentages not shown for states of banding from which there were less than 25 recoveries (Connecticut, Delaware, Maine, New Hampshire and Vermont).

[b] Tr = trace = Less than 0.1 percent.

young with a milklike substance secreted from their crops (see chapter 7), and the incidence of hunter-killed adults with visibly "active" crop glands has been used to assess the nesting underway when September seasons opened (e.g., see Southeastern Association of Game and Fish Commissioners 1957). Largely because of concern about the effects of September hunting on nesting adults and their young, southern states in the EMU did not begin September hunting until well into the 1950s.

Questions about the propriety of September dove hunting surfaced early (see McClure 1944, Pearson and Moore 1939, Quay 1954). The issue arose again when Guynn and Scanlon (1973) found that a substantial proportion of sampled adult doves shot in Virginia in September 1971 and 1972 had active crop glands. Although single parents often are able to rear nestlings successfully if the disruption occurs late in the incubation period (Laub 1956, Haas 1980), there were reasonable grounds for concern, and the U.S. Fish and Wildlife Service (1977) addressed the problem in an environmental assessment. Based on review of the literature and analyses of banding and other records, the Service concluded that September hunting likely did not reduce production to an important degree or affect status of the overall dove population. September dove seasons were continued, but the Service decided to assess the problem more thoroughly. In 1978, the Service and twenty-nine state agencies initiated a two-year study to evaluate the importance of September/October nesting to total annual production and to assess if September hunting seasons had an adverse effect on mourning dove nesting and production. Results of this major study (Geissler et al. 1987) confirmed many of the conclusions reached earlier in the environmental assessment (U.S. Fish and Wildlife Service 1977). Based on 6,950 active nests found during the two years, 4.5 percent of total nationwide dove nesting activity occurred in September and October, and 10.3 percent of all observed fledging was in these months. September hunting was not believed to have a material effect on nesting activity, because incidence of nesting declined before September 1. In a separate part of the study, 688 nests were observed in areas (mostly in the EMU) where hunting early in September was permitted (experimental) and where it was not (control). Daily survival rates of eggs and young averaged 33 percent in closed areas and 26 percent in areas where hunting was allowed. The difference in this measure of fledging rates was not statistically significant, and Geissler et al. (1987) concluded that mourning dove hunting under regulations in place at that time had no substantial impact on recruitment of fledglings into the population.

Although only 4.5 percent of the annual total nesting activity occurred in September and October, this does not mean that only 4.5 percent of all adult doves nested during those months. The proportion of adults that nested then is not known, but it could have been large. For example, in the South EMU, 41 percent as many nests were found in the first week of September as in the second week in June, when the peak number of nests was located (calculated from Geissler et al. 1987). The small contribution of September nests to the cumulative annual total of nesting activity (and productivity) in the South EMU is due to the fact that doves there already have nested a number of times before September, and *not* because few doves nest then. From observations of radio-equipped doves in 1979 and 1980 in Georgia, Haas (no date) found that doves made an average of 7.2 nesting attempts during a lengthy nesting season but that nesting after August accounted for only 5.6 percent of total nesting activity. He determined that September hunting caused the loss of 7.7 percent of the nests that were active at that time, but this loss amounted to less than 1 percent of potential recruitment during the year. Despite the small contribution of late nesting to the total annual nesting activity, 36 percent of the radio-tagged adult doves were associated with

active nests on September 2 to 8, 1979, and 67 percent were associated with nests during August 31 to September 6, 1980 (G. H. Haas personal communication: 1980).

Thus, in at least some EMU locations, a substantial portion of the mourning dove population clearly is nesting when the hunting season begins in September.

POPULATION CHARACTERISTICS

Analysis of Banding Data

Estimates of survival and band-recovery rates were obtained from immature and adult doves banded preseason (June, July and August) and later reported as shot or found dead during the hunting season. Locals (nestlings) were not included in the analysis. Band-recovery models described by Brownie et al. (1985) were used to estimate survival rates of doves from both individual states and combined data sets for various groups of states. When possible, survival rates were estimated as both unweighted and weighted (by population indices and land area) averages of state estimates. Because of small sample sizes, it was not possible to estimate survival rates for doves from individual nonhunting states in the EMU, so banding data were combined from all of these states in the analysis. Sex- and age-specific (immature versus adult) differences in mean survival rates were tested using z-tests suggested by Brownie et al. (1985). The method described by Sauer and Williams (1989) was employed to test homogeneity of survival estimates for groups of states. (See chapter 16 for a discussion of the applicability of band-recovery models to dove-banding data.)

The banding effort from which most of the useful information was obtained occurred during the special study of bag limit changes (Hayne 1975). The range of years for bandings used in the analysis was determined by the volume of banding data available for each state in the unit and generally included the period 1966–73. Also obtained were mean estimates of survival for doves banded in hunting states for time periods prior to (1954–58) and after (1975–83) the bag limit study. The purpose of these additional analyses was to assess whether there may have been a temporal trend in dove survival. The data base for each of these additional time spans was too small to obtain survival estimates for individual hunting states. Therefore, the combined data for all hunting states were utilized in these additional analyses, and age-specific survival rates only were estimated. All banding and recovery records came from the U.S. Fish and Wild-life Service's Bird Banding Laboratory.

Survival Rates

Sex specificity of adult survival rates. Estimates of mean annual survival rates of adult male and female doves were made from bandings accomplished during 1966–73 in all EMU states for which there were adequate data for one or the other sex, and for eight hunting states for which estimates could be made for both sexes *(Table 52)*. Estimates were used only if they fit ($P > 0.05$) one of the models developed by Brownie et al. (1985). Survival estimates for grouped states were found, both as unweighted averages of state estimates and by averages weighted by state Call-count data and land area. In practice, weighting had little effect on the estimates. Unweighted survival estimates for all states with usable data averaged 38.9 ± 1.3 percent (standard error) for adult males (twelve states) and 37.4 ± 1.8 percent for adult females (nine states). Eight hunting states listed in Table 52 banded enough birds to provide separate estimates for each

sex (Illinois, Kentucky, Louisiana, North Carolina, Pennsylvania, South Carolina, Tennessee and Virginia). Unweighted mean estimates in these hunting states averaged about the same as the overall estimates presented above (adult males 37.4 ± 1.4 percent, adult females 36.2 ± 1.8 percent). In both comparisons, there were no statistically significant differences between sexes in mean annual survival rates within or among states. Depending on the group of states used, weighted point estimates of survival ranged from 37.4 to 38.9 percent for adult males and 36.2 to 37.4 percent for adult females. These results thus provide evidence that there is little if any difference in mean annual survival between the sexes of adults from EMU hunting states.

Two studies in other sections of the country can be used for comparison. For the CMU, Dunks et al. (1982) found no difference in mean annual survival rates of adult male (51.7 percent) and adult female doves (51.0 percent). More recently, Tomlinson et al. (1988) found that the unweighted survival rates of adult doves banded between 1964 and 1975 in the WMU averaged 48.0 percent for females and 47.0 percent for males. Thus, although survival rates of adults appear to differ markedly among the three

Table 52. Estimated mean annual survival and recovery rates (in percentage) of adult male and female mourning doves banded preseason in selected hunting states in the Eastern Management Unit, 1966–73.

Sex/state	Years	Model with best fit	Probability of fit test	Survival rate	Standard error	Recovery rate	Standard error
Male							
Alabama	1966–71	M1	42.5	42.4	3.2	3.1	0.2
Georgia	1966–71	M2	26.0	38.5	3.5	3.4	0.3
Illinois	1966–71	M3	97.6	44.5	3.2	2.0	0.2
Kentucky	1966–71	M2	14.6	34.2	7.4	4.8	0.7
Louisiana	1966–71	M2	18.3	37.3	2.8	4.3	0.3
Maryland	1966–71	M2	21.1	40.9	6.2	3.2	0.4
Mississippi	1966–71	M1	10.0	46.3	5.8	3.6	0.4
North Carolina	1966–73	M2	17.2	31.1	2.8	4.2	0.3
Pennsylvania	1966–73	M2	40.8	39.8	5.1	3.4	0.4
South Carolina	1966–71	M3	44.7	40.0	2.7	3.4	0.2
Tennessee	1966–71	M2	39.9	32.7	3.7	4.2	0.3
Virginia	1966–71	M3	8.4	39.3	2.7	2.4	0.2
Mean				38.9[a]	1.3	3.5	0.1
Female							
Florida	1967–69	M3	23.0	46.6	7.2	2.1	0.4
Illinois	1966–71	M3	50.4	39.3	5.3	2.4	0.3
Kentucky	1966–71	M3	21.1	45.1	7.4	4.0	0.8
Louisiana	1966–71	M2	21.1	36.5	4.2	3.8	0.3
North Carolina	1967–73	M2	85.3	31.4	3.7	3.8	0.4
Pennsylvania	1968–73	M3	48.8	28.9	5.5	2.5	1.4
South Carolina	1966–71	M3	18.0	30.6	3.0	3.9	0.3
Tennessee	1966–71	M2	8.5	37.0	3.8	3.9	0.4
Virginia	1966–71	M2	16.2	41.0	5.0	2.2	0.3
Mean				37.4[b]	1.8	3.2	0.1

[a] Test of null hypothesis that mean adult male survival rates are equal: $x^2 = 17.38$, d.f. = 11; $P > 0.05$.
[b] Test of null hypothesis that mean adult female survival rates are equal: $x^2 = 11.18$, d.f. = 8; $P > 0.05$.

management units (with lowest rates in EMU hunting states), there is no indication of a real sex difference in adult survival for any mourning dove population in the nation.

Adult sex ratio. As noted in chapters 5, 15 and 18, the adult population of doves appears to be highly skewed in favor of males when nesting begins in spring. In fact, most of the calling during this time apparently is by unmated males. It is unclear if there are more adult males than females in spring or if the perception of a distorted adult sex ratio is created by the much greater visibility of males. The mean annual survival rates of adult males and females are similar. Therefore, an unbalanced sex ratio in spring could be caused only by higher first-year survival of immature males than of females, by recruitment that favored males more than females or by a combination of the two factors. Because of difficulty in accurate sex determination in preseason banding of immature doves, little is known regarding possible sex differences in first-year survival (Tomlinson et al. 1988). Immature survival rates were estimated from six hunting states in the EMU based on bandings of sexed immatures from 1968 to 1973. Survival estimates varied widely among states, and individual coefficients of variation were large (averaging 38 percent). Across six states (Alabama, Maryland, North Carolina, South Carolina, Tennessee and Virginia) survival rates averaged 32.9 ± 4.3 percent for immature males and 26.6 ± 5.0 percent for immature females. Although estimated mean survival rates are higher for males than for females, the difference is not statistically significant.

Limited evidence exists concerning the sex ratio of nestling doves. Hanson and Kossack (1963) concluded that the sex ratio in nestling doves is influenced by seasonal environmental conditions (mainly temperature) and by physiological conditions associated with the increasing reproductive experience of the adults. The Hanson and Kossack sample of nestlings raised in captivity suggested a preponderance of males. However, a sample of 469 immatures shot early in September showed a sex ratio of 1.05 young males per young female, which is not significantly different from an even sex ratio. In their report, Hanson and Kossack (1963) included data on nestling sex ratios provided by Missouri Conservation Department biologist Howard Wight, who showed that significantly more females than males hatched by June 30 but that the reverse was true after that date. The average sex ratio for the 265 nestlings in Wight's sample was not significantly different from even. There is little evidence to suggest that higher recruitment of fledged males or higher survival of immature males results

in a larger fraction of males in the spring population. The evidence for the unbalanced adult sex ratio itself is circumstantial, however, and more study clearly is needed on this basic question. Since no evidence of between-sex differences in survival was found, data for both sexes were combined in further analyses.

Immature and adult survival rates: Hunting states. Annual survival rates were estimated for both immature and adult doves from bandings made during 1966–71 in nine of the sixteen states (Florida, Georgia, Illinois, Kentucky, Louisiana, Mississippi, North Carolina, Pennsylvania and South Carolina) that permitted dove hunting during the period *(Table 53)*. Valid estimates could not be obtained for the remaining seven states, either because the number of bandings was inadequate or the estimates did not fit any of the available models (Brownie et al. 1985). Data from eight of the nine states with usable records fit program BROWNIE model HO2, whereas H1 tested best for data from the remaining state. For all states, the coefficients of variation for immature and adult survival rates were less than 20 percent. The resulting survival rates from the nine states are deemed representative of the unit, since during the years in question, these states accounted for 70.9 percent of the breeding population index for EMU hunting states and 51.8 percent of the index for the entire unit.

Adult survival rates varied significantly ($P < 0.01$) among the nine states *(Table 53)*. The highest survival rate was from doves banded in Mississippi (45.6 percent) and the lowest from doves in North Carolina (32.3 percent). Immature survival rates ranged from a high of 29.0 percent in Pennsylvania to a low of 18.5 percent in Kentucky, but rates did not differ significantly ($P > 0.05$) among states.

Adult survival was higher ($P < 0.05$) than survival of immatures in all states except Pennsylvania ($P > 0.10$). Unweighted mean survival rates for combined data were 39.4 ± 1.0 percent for adults and 24.0 ± 1.1 percent for immatures, and the difference is highly significant *(Table 53)*. Mean survival rates, weighted by Call-counts and land area, were virtually identical to unweighted rates (adults 39.7 percent, immatures 24.0 percent).

Survival rates estimated from combined banding and recovery data for all thirteen hunting states in the EMU also were almost identical to the means derived from individual state estimates. Used in the combined analysis were 4,405 recoveries from 88,548 adults and 13,080 recoveries from 218,443 immatures banded from 1966 to 1971 in all EMU hunting states. Based on model HO2, adult survival for all hunting states averaged 40.1 percent

Table 53. Estimated mean annual survival and recovery rates (in percentage) of immature and adult mourning doves banded 1966–71 in selected states in the Eastern Management Unit.

Age/state	Years	Model with best fit	Probability of fit test	Survival rate	Standard error	Recovery rate	Standard error
Immature							
Florida	1967–71	H02	7.7	28.6	4.2	3.1	0.1
Georgia	1966–71	H1	45.7	23.2	2.0	5.6	0.2
Illinois	1966–71	H02	50.4	23.4	3.0	2.7	0.2
Kentucky	1966–71	H02	14.4	18.5	3.5	6.1	0.4
Louisiana	1966–71	H02	4.6	22.3	1.6	6.9	0.2
Mississippi	1966–71	H02	30.1	26.6	2.7	4.9	0.2
North Carolina	1966–71	H02	6.6	19.9	2.0	5.5	0.4
Pennsylvania	1966–71	H02	89.1	29.0	5.5	6.1	1.5
South Carolina	1966–71	H02	16.1	24.2	1.8	5.2	0.2
Mean				24.0[a]	1.1	5.1	0.2
Adult							
Florida	1967–71	H02	7.7	42.8	4.0	1.6	0.2
Georgia	1966–71	H1	45.7	35.5	2.2	3.7	0.2
Illinois	1966–71	H02	50.4	42.2	2.7	2.1	0.2
Kentucky	1966–71	H02	14.4	39.4	4.4	4.1	0.4
Louisiana	1966–71	H02	4.6	39.6	1.8	4.0	0.2
Mississippi	1966–71	H02	30.1	45.6	2.7	3.2	0.2
North Carolina	1966–71	H02	6.6	32.3	2.4	5.1	0.5
Pennsylvania	1966–71	H02	89.1	34.7	4.6	4.6	0.6
South Carolina	1966–71	H02	16.1	42.8	2.0	3.4	0.2
Mean				39.4[b]	1.0	3.5	0.1

[a] Test of null hypothesis that there is no difference among states in mean survival of immature age class: $x^2 = 9.46$, df = 8; $P > 0.05$.
[b] Test of null hypothesis that there is no difference among states in mean survival of adult age class: $x^2 = 22.90$, df = 8; $p < 0.01$.

and mean survival of immatures was 25.0 percent. H1 estimates were 38.9 percent for adults and 24.4 percent for immatures.

Although no consistent pattern of deviation emerged from the goodness-of-fit tests, the models selected for data from grouped states in the combined analysis did not fit any of the Brownie et al. (1985) models ($P < 0.05$). Examination of the observed and expected values indicates that this lack of fit probably does not bias the point estimate of survival, but it suggests that the variances are underestimates (Burnham et al. 1987). Nevertheless, because of the poor fit of the model to the combined data, any inferences concerning immature and adult survival rates in hunting states should be based on the mean values obtained from nine states, as discussed above.

Immature and adult survival rates: Nonhunting states. Bandings from 1966 to 1971 in EMU nonhunting states were not sufficient to permit determination of usable age-specific survival estimates for doves in any individual state. As an alternative, age-specific survival estimates were obtained from three different groupings of nonhunting states: (1) all nonhunting EMU states combined; (2) combined eastern nonhunting EMU states (Connecticut, Maine, Massachusetts, New Hampshire, New Jersey, New York and Vermont); and (3) combined

western nonhunting EMU states (Indiana, Michigan, Ohio and Wisconsin). These configurations follow those employed in Hayne's (1975) report on bag limit changes in the unit. For all nonhunting states combined, adult survival rates averaged 50.0 ± 2.9 percent and the mean for immatures was 53.8 ± 5.2 percent. Estimated survival rates in eastern nonhunting states were 49.8 ± 4.4 percent for adults and 61.5 ± 9.1 percent for immatures. For western nonhunting states, the adult survival rate averaged 50.5 ± 3.8 percent and the immature rate was 47.5 ± 6.2 percent. In all cases, BROWNIE model HO2 provided the best fit to the data. The average weighted survival rates for doves banded in eastern and western nonhunting states were 50.3 percent for both immatures and adults.

There were no significant differences apparent in mean survival rates of adults and immatures in any of the three groupings of nonhunting states. However, except for adults in eastern nonhunting states, mean survival rates for doves banded in combined nonhunting states were significantly higher than were overall mean survival rates for birds banded in hunting states in the unit.

Immature and adult survival rates: Unitwide. Unitwide survival rates of mourning doves were derived by weighting estimates calculated for hunting and nonhunting states. For the reasons given above, the weighted means were obtained only for 1966–71. Weighted mean survival rates for this period were 42.4 percent for adults and 31.1 percent for immatures.

Trends in survival rates. To determine if mean annual survival rates differed over time, estimates were obtained for all combined hunting states for three separate chronological periods, 1954–58, 1966–71 and 1975–83. The data base for individual states, combined nonhunting states, and other time periods was not sufficient for comparisons. Furthermore, the sample sizes were relatively small for doves banded during 1954–58 (22,557 immatures and 5,770 adults) and 1975–83 (9,677 immatures and 7,239 adults).

Annual survival rates of immatures banded 1954–58 averaged 21.6 ± 2.1 percent; those banded 1966–71 averaged 24.0 ± 1.1 percent; and those banded 1975–83 averaged 15.9 ± 2.4 percent. For adults, the survival rates averaged 37.4 ± 2.6 percent, 39.4 ± 1.0 percent and 30.2 ± 2.2 percent, respectively. Survival rates for both age classes did not differ between the 1954–58 period and the other two periods, but rates for 1975–83 were significantly lower than those for 1966–71. There is more confidence in the survival rate estimates from the 1966–71 bandings than in those from the other periods because of the larger banded samples resulting from the organized banding program during the bag limit study.

Comment. Results of the Hayne (1975) analysis of dove survival in the EMU, using bandings from 1965 to 1970, generally were consistent with the above analysis using bandings from 1966 to 1971. However, there were some noteworthy dissimilarities. For example, Hayne (1975) found significant sex-specific differences in adult survival; no such differences were found for the 1966–71 period. Similarly, Hayne estimated a survival rate for immatures in nonhunting states (31.2 percent) that was significantly different from our estimate (50.3 percent). Why some results of the two analyses differed is perplexing, since essentially the same data set was used in each. Inconsistencies may represent the different methodologies used to derive the estimates, as Hayne did not have access to the complete set of Brownie et al. (1985) models when he wrote the report.

Productivity Required to Maintain the Population

The production necessary to maintain a stable dove population can be calculated from a simple population model using survival estimates (adult

mortality rate ÷ immature survival rate × 2 = production per pair). With overall mean survival rates of 31.1 percent for immature and 42.4 percent for adult doves in the EMU during 1966–71 (including both hunting and nonhunting states), each adult pair would have had to produce 3.7 young per year to maintain the population. For combined hunting states during the same period of years, the required production was 5.0 young per pair (at 24.0 and 39.4 percent survival rates, respectively, for immatures and adults). During 1975–83, the productivity of doves in hunting states would have required 8.8 young per pair to maintain a stable population because of the lower survival rates, especially for immatures. However, the model used makes assumptions concerning dove population stability that may not have been met. Nevertheless, results are of value because they provide a general measure of productivity needed to maintain stable numbers with observed survival rates.

To obtain productivity information on doves in the EMU, a special wing-collection survey was conducted during the aforementioned bag limit study (Hayne 1975). The survey included all EMU hunting states and was conducted each September from 1967 to 1971. Based on calculations from data in Table 13 of Hayne's (1975) report, an average of 77.4 percent of the wings sampled were from immature doves. When adjusted by the relative band-recovery rates of immatures and adults (to account for age-specific difference in survival and differential vulnerability to shooting), the estimated age ratio in the population averaged 4.8 immatures per pair of adults. This recruitment rate is well above that required to maintain the unitwide dove population (3.7) but slightly lower than the 5.0 production rate needed in hunting states.

Information on recruitment rates of mourning doves is limited. Although many field studies of nesting success have been conducted, few have documented productivity of individual pairs because of difficulty in following multibrooded individuals throughout a nesting season. In 1979 and 1980, Haas (no date) made observations of twenty-five radio-tagged doves in Georgia. During the two nesting seasons, those doves averaged 7.2 nesting attempts and produced an average of 5.7 young per pair per year. It is noteworthy that, in an earlier study that took place in portions of North and South Carolina, Haas (1978) reported an identical production rate (5.7) based on age ratios in the harvest, adjusted by relative band-recovery rates. Similar studies of mourning dove production rates are needed in other parts of the EMU to determine if productivity continues to be adequate to offset mortality.

Band-recovery Rates

Adult males and females. Estimates of mean annual first-season recovery rates of adult males and females were made from the same 1966–73 bandings *(Table 52)* from which survival rates were estimated and are based on the procedures discussed in Brownie et al. (1985).

For hunting states, recovery rates for both adult males and females varied significantly among states. Mean unweighted rates for adult males for the twelve states from which survival rates were obtained averaged 3.5 ± 0.1 percent; for the nine states for which survival rates of adult females were estimated, mean unweighted recovery rates averaged 3.2 ± 0.1 percent *(Table 52)*. The estimates for each sex were precise and not significantly different. There also was no significant difference between direct recovery rates of adult males (3.6 ± 0.1 percent) and adult females (3.3 ± 0.2 percent) from the eight states with adequate data to obtain usable estimates of survival rates for each sex.

Data were not adequate to assess possible differences in recovery rates for sexes of adults in nonhunting states or for other time spans in hunting states. However, the large samples of doves banded 1966–73 in hunting states suggest that recovery rates are essentially the same for adult males and adult females. Hayne (1975) reached the same conclusion from bandings made from 1965 to 1970.

Immatures and adults. Recovery rates of immature and adult mourning doves were estimated for bandings made in EMU hunting states during the same three periods for which age-specific estimates of mean annual survival were obtained (1954–58, 1966–71 and 1975–83). Age-specific recovery rates varied over time, but no pattern was apparent for either age. For example, among adults, mean rates for 1954–58 bandings (4.7 percent) were significantly higher than rates for 1966–71 bandings (3.5 percent), but not for adults banded 1975–83 (3.8 percent). Recovery rates of immature doves differed among all three periods, with the highest mean rates in 1966–71 (5.1 percent) and lowest in 1975–83 (3.2 percent). Mean recovery rates of immatures were significantly higher than such rates for adult bandings in 1966–71 but not in the other two time spans. The recovery rates noted in 1966–71 are believed to be representative of doves from EMU hunting states *(Table 53)*.

Recovery rate estimates for immatures and adults from nonhunting states came from the combined 1966–71 bandings. Recovery rates from bandings in eastern nonhunting states in the EMU averaged 1.1 ± 0.1 percent for immatures and 0.8 ± 0.1 percent for adults. Mean rates from western non-hunting states in the unit were 0.8 ± 0.5 percent for immatures and 0.5 ± 0.1 percent for adults. For eastern and western EMU nonhunting states combined, weighted recovery rates averaged 0.8 percent for immatures and 0.6 percent for adults. In regard to the low recovery rates of doves banded in nonhunting states, two factors are apparent: (1) few banded doves from nonhunting states in the EMU were recovered after they emigrated to states where dove hunting is permitted; and (2) the low rate of recovery explains why the estimated survival rates are so imprecise for doves banded in nonhunting states.

Weighted estimates of overall first-season recovery rates for immatures and adults unitwide in the EMU were calculated only for doves banded during 1966–71 because of inadequate data in other time spans. The best estimates (as determined by tests in Brownie et al. 1985) were 4.0 percent for immatures and 2.7 percent for adults.

Proportion of Dove Population Taken by Hunters

It is standard practice in analyses of banding data to adjust recovery rates by a band-reporting rate and a crippling loss rate to obtain an estimate of the proportion of the population removed by hunting, or kill rate (Dunks et al. 1982, Tomlinson et al. 1988, see chapter 16). A band-reporting rate of 32 percent (Tomlinson 1968) was used in this analysis to adjust recovery rates to harvest rates. Harvest rates then were adjusted by a crippling loss rate of 30 percent, as reported by Haas (1977) and others, to obtain kill rates. Thus, if the direct recovery rate is 5.0 percent, harvest rate is $5.0 \div 0.32 = 15.6$, and the kill rate is $15.6 \div 1.0 - 0.30 = 22.3$ percent.

From 1966–71 bandings in the EMU hunting states, estimated harvest rates averaged 16 percent for immatures and 11 percent for adults. Kill rates averaged 22.9 and 15.8 percent, respectively.

For doves from the EMU's nonhunting states, weighted harvest rates averaged 2.6 percent for immatures and 1.8 percent for adults banded 1966–71. Average kill rates were 3.7 and 2.6 percent, respectively.

From 1966–71 bandings, unitwide harvest rates averaged 12.4 percent for immatures and 8.5 percent for adults. Average kill rates were 17.7 and 12.2 percent, respectively. These figures suggest that hunting mortality accounted for 25.7 percent of the total unitwide mortality rate (68.9 percent) of immatures and 21.2 percent of the mean annual mortality rate of adults (57.6 percent). For hunting states, shooting accounted for an estimated 30.0 percent of the mean annual mortality of immature doves (76.0

percent) and for 26.4 percent of the adult annual mortality (60.6 percent).

For the WMU, Tomlinson et al. (1988) estimated that shooting mortality accounted for 22.0 percent of the mean annual mortality of immatures and 20.8 percent of the mortality of adults, based on bandings from 1967–75. These proportions are roughly similar to estimates for the EMU, but the proportions in both units are much larger than those reported by Dunks et al. (1982) for the CMU (11.2 and 9.9 percent for immatures and adults, respectively). However, estimates for the EMU suggest that hunting mortality accounts for a much higher percentage of the total annual mortality of doves from hunting states than for the unit as a whole. And this percentage was much larger for the EMU hunting states than for states in the other management units, at least during the time span considered here.

CONCLUSIONS AND OUTLOOK

Dove Population Trends

As noted earlier, the Call-count Survey and Breeding Bird Survey yield somewhat contradictory long-term population trend results. The unitwide difference between surveys is not great, however, and it has been concluded that the overall mourning dove population essentially was stable between 1966 and 1987. Nevertheless, conflicting long-term trend results were noted for several individual states in the EMU, and which survey, if either, provides a valid index to long-term population status is unknown. This deficiency warrants prompt investigation, particularly to determine if the conflicting results are due to procedural differences between the surveys or to inadequate sampling by the Call-count Survey in some EMU states.

Since the harvest in most EMU states is derived mainly from locally produced doves, it is important to develop the capability to monitor dove population status in these states and not solely for grouped hunting states. Otherwise, any indicated population declines in the future might necessitate restrictive hunting regulations unitwide rather than for the specific problem areas.

Most conclusions regarding dove survival rates are based on bandings made during the bag limit study that began more than twenty years ago. Although a new unitwide banding program may not be warranted because of high costs and questionable precision of data output in some areas, it would be prudent for mean annual survival rates to be monitored in several key hunting states from

which precise estimates were obtained in earlier years. It also would be desirable for survival estimates to be obtained from one or more EMU nonhunting states. However, in view of the low recovery rates that can be anticipated from such mourning dove bandings, some type of annual recapture method likely will be required to obtain reasonably precise survival estimates, as discussed in chapter 16.

To assess properly the survival of doves in the EMU and elsewhere, reliable estimates of production are needed. Although review of available information suggests that EMU dove productivity is high, especially among birds in southern states, definitive data are lacking. Radio telemetry has proven to be an effective way to measure dove production rates, and this method ought to be employed in the same EMU states that might participate in a new banding program.

Effects of Weather on Population Trends

Major storms that occurred during individual years of the survey period appeared to correlate with population changes in nonhunting states of the EMU. For example, declines in Call-count Survey indices occurred in 1969 and 1973 in nonhunting states, suggesting that dove production was adversely affected and that populations subsequently declined because of heavy rains and winds associated with hurricanes Abbey and Agnes during the summers of 1968 and 1972, respectively. The effects of these storms were less apparent on population indices of hunting states.

Similarly, prolonged freezing weather occurred in the eastern United States during the winters of 1976–77 and 1977–78. Weather conditions during the latter winter were especially severe. The eastern bluebird and the Carolina wren underwent sharp population declines because of the harsh weather conditions, and a number of other species of birds also were affected adversely (Robbins et al. 1986). The severe winters affected bird populations as far south as Kentucky and Tennessee. Mourning dove population indices in the EMU, estimated by both the Call-count Survey and Breeding Bird Survey, declined in spring 1978 following the winter of 1977–78, but a decline was not noted following the less severe winter of 1976–1977. Based on the Call-count Survey, dove populations in nonhunting states generally have increased since 1978, suggesting recovery from the severe winters. Call-count Survey population indices in hunting states declined after 1978 (*Table 47 and Figure 48*). However, as mentioned earlier, Breeding Bird Survey results have shown no significant change in dove numbers in these states.

It is difficult to assess the importance of winter weather on mourning dove populations because of the absence of information regarding the wintering distributions of the breeding populations that are monitored by the Call-count Survey. Winter counts, although not directly tied to breeding populations, provide some insight into the comparative numbers of mourning doves likely to be affected by severe winter weather. Hayne (1982) examined Christmas bird-count survey data from 1959 through 1974 and estimated mean numbers of doves in different physiographic regions of the EMU. Within hunting and nonhunting states, counts varied greatly from year to year but averaged 76.2 per 100 miles (47.4/100 km) for hunting states and 53.9 per 100 miles (33.5/100 km) for nonhunting states. Over the sixteen-year period, these counts showed a significant dove increase in northern nonhunting EMU states. Results thus suggest that substantial numbers of mourning doves winter in northern and midlatitudinal portions of the EMU and that especially severe winter weather could adversely affect populations in some years.

Schultz (1956) documented large losses of mourning doves in Tennessee and other southeastern states due to a severe ice storm in winter 1950–51. He concluded that, even though nesting success was good in 1951, the population did not increase to the 1950 level in the area affected by the storm. Severe weather cannot explain all of the variation in Call-count indices, but comparisons suggest that adverse weather sometimes causes short-term population declines in the EMU. In the other two management units where doves appear more prone to migrate farther south, the probability of winter storm-induced mortality likely is less.

Effects of Agriculture on Population Trends

The ecological character of most of the eastern United States has been altered greatly by humans, beginning with Native Americans long before the first Europeans arrived several hundred years ago (see chapter 2). As noted earlier, agriculture has been the pre-eminent land modification since settlement time. In general, the cutting of forests and development of small farms in the EMU undoubtedly benefited mourning doves by increasing edge habitat and food (especially small grains and weed seeds). Conversely, modern agriculture, with increased emphasis on mechanization and widespread use of herbicides and insecticides, probably is not beneficial and may be detrimental to doves.

The Call-count and Breeding Bird surveys provide data on the extensive geographic scale necessary to examine the effects of agriculture and different agricultural crops on dove numbers. Annual Call-count indices, population trend information from the Call-count Survey and Breeding Bird Survey, and agricultural crop acreage statistics were used to address several questions regarding land use and dove numbers, including: (1) the possible relationship between crop acreage and dove density; (2) the correlation between trends in crop acreages and dove numbers; and (3) the correlation of yearly changes in crop acreages and subsequent annual indices of dove abundance. Data on crops came from annual publications of *Agricultural Statistics* (U.S. Department of Agriculture 1963, 1968, 1973, 1978, 1983, 1984) and included eleven crops—barley, corn, cotton, oats, peanuts, rice, rye, sorghum, soybeans, tobacco and wheat. Total crop acreages discussed in the following relate only to these crops. The named crops were considered beneficial (barley, corn, peanuts, rice, sorghum, tobacco and wheat), neutral (cotton, oats and rye) or perhaps negative (soybeans) to dove populations, based on a general review of the literature on dove food habits.

Relationship of crop acreage to dove density. The proportion of total land area devoted to agricultural crops from 1966 to 1983 varied widely among EMU states, ranging from lows of less than 1 percent in New England states to a high of 60.5 percent in Illinois *(Table 54)*. Most correlations of land area in crops to average densities of doves heard per route for individual states were not significant. Only corn ($P = 0.06$) and tobacco ($P = 0.09$) provided weak evidence of a positive correlation with dove abundance *(Table 55)*. Overall, there is a significant positive relationship among all of the EMU states in dove density (as shown by the Call-count Survey) and the proportion of total land area in crops ($r = 0.50$, $P < 0.01$).

A positive relationship between dove population indices and the proportion of land being farmed could be expected, since lands used for agricultural purposes have always supported varying numbers of doves during the nesting season. The significant correlation does not prove that there is a causal relationship between croplands and dove densities; it merely suggests that the areas that are more extensively farmed tend to have larger numbers of doves. Many factors must influence mourning dove numbers, and few significant correlations have been found between specific crops and dove densities. Consequently, no strong conclusions can be drawn from this particular analysis. For example, doves have higher popu-

Table 54. Proportion of land area devoted to 11 major agricultural crops,[a] and mourning dove densities in the Eastern Management Unit states, 1966–83.

State	Number of crops represented	Percentage of land area	Doves heard per route[b]
Alabama	8	9.3	22.6
Connecticut	2	1.8	9.6
Delaware	6	40.9	7.0
Florida	7	2.5	10.3
Georgia	10	13.0	25.2
Illinois	7	60.5	23.4
Indiana	8	47.7	29.2
Kentucky	9	12.8	22.9
Louisiana	8	12.6	11.7
Massachusetts	2	0.8	10.4
Maryland	7	20.9	19.2
Maine	2	0.5	3.8
Michigan	6	12.3	10.7
Mississippi	8	17.2	26.9
New Hampshire	1	0.4	3.6
New Jersey	6	8.7	17.6
New York	6	5.8	8.4
North Carolina	10	14.9	25.5
Ohio	7	33.2	8.0
Pennsylvania	8	8.8	9.1
Rhode Island	1	0.6	8.8
South Carolina	10	13.8	31.5
Tennessee	9	14.1	22.2
Vermont	2	1.9	4.9
Virginia	10	8.2	22.9
West Virginia	5	1.0	5.2
Wisconsin	7	15.3	14.1

[a] Barley, corn, cotton, oats, peanuts, rice, rye, sorghum, soybeans, tobacco and wheat.
[b] Average numbers of mourning doves heard per route in state, from national Call-count Survey.

lation densities in the South, where most tobacco is grown. Latitude, rather than the particular crop, thus may account for the positive relationship between dove density and tobacco.

Table 55. Correlations between the average proportion of land area devoted to 11 major crops in states of the Eastern Management Unit and the average population indices for those states, 1970–83.

Crop	Correlation (R)	N[a]	P[b]
Wheat	0.294	21	0.20
Corn	0.372	27	0.06
Oats	0.026	23	0.91
Barley	−0.227	17	0.38
Sorghum	0.194	12	0.54
Rice		2	
Rye	−0.227	16	0.40
Cotton	0.209	10	0.56
Tobacco	0.427	17	0.09
Peanuts	−0.084	7	0.86
Soybean	0.333	20	0.15

[a] Number of states in analysis containing measurable acreages of agricultural crop tested.
[b] Probability that no correlation exists.

Trends in dove populations and crops. Using population indices from both surveys, weighted trends were estimated for each state in the EMU, and the combined trend estimates were correlated with trends in crop acreages. Combined dove trend data correlated positively with corn ($P < 0.05$), oats ($P < 0.05$) and soybeans ($P < 0.002$) but negatively with tobacco ($P < 0.0003$) and wheat ($P < 0.07$). These results generally are not consistent with the relationships expected between crops and dove numbers.

Data from the Call-count Survey also were used to assess the relationship between annual indices of dove abundance and yearly changes in crop acreages. This analysis generally indicated that increases in acreages of all crops except soybeans tended to have a positive effect on the next year's dove population index. Increases in soybeans tended to have a negative effect.

All of the aforementioned analyses rely on the assumption that survey routes adequately sample all crop types within a state. Given the current small samples of Call-count Survey routes and the small acreages of many crops in most EMU states, it is likely that analyses of dove trends and crops at the state level will have little power to detect correlations that may exist. Factors such as weather also influence dove numbers and may cause population changes that obscure the importance of changes in crop acreages.

It is possible that crop acreages alone are not adequate measures of the effects of land use on dove numbers, or that other agricultural crops or activities that are important have been overlooked. Perhaps other environmental factors should be considered. For example, Grue et al. (1983) examined the general habitat characteristics on 133 Call-count routes in Texas and related dove numbers with the distribution, abundance and structural features of habitats that met the requirements for dove reproduction and survival (food, water, and resting and nest sites). Analysis suggests that the environments associated with most of the agricultural crops examined in the EMU are beneficial to mourning doves. The fact that doves are found

throughout most of the EMU suggests that many different types of croplands and associated habitats may be acceptable to them.

Soybeans may be an exception, and this is a concern because soybeans are a major crop in many EMU states and, in recent decades, have replaced other crops of value to doves. Plantings of soybeans throughout the EMU rose from 9.5 million acres (3.8 million ha) in 1950 to 36.8 million acres (14.9 million ha) in 1989 (U.S. Department of Agriculture 1951, 1990)—an increase of 287 percent.

Hunting Mortality and Dove Population Status

Definitive information is lacking on the relationship between hunting mortality and total mortality of EMU mourning doves. As discussed earlier, the experimental increase in the daily bag limit from 12 to 18 did not result in decreased dove survival rates. However, it cannot be concluded that shooting mortality at the time had no adverse effects on dove population status, because it is not known if shooting already was having an impact before the daily limit was increased. Whatever the effects of shooting may be, EMU doves from hunting states clearly experience much higher hunting mortality than do doves from nonhunting states. Estimated kill rates for doves banded in hunting states from 1966 to 1971 were more than six times greater than those for doves banded in the unit's nonhunting states.

As shown earlier, survival estimates of mourning doves from nonhunting states were imprecise. Nevertheless, both immature and adult doves from EMU nonhunting states had significantly higher annual survival rates than did doves from EMU hunting states. Therefore, the possibility that the much higher kill rate among doves from hunting states was the reason for the lower annual survival rate of these birds cannot be ruled out. If this premise is true, however, it does not necessarily follow that harvest was excessive. The production rate of EMU doves is thought to be high, especially among southern hunting states, and the unit population and harvest both appear to have been essentially stable for a number of years. Nevertheless, in the future, regulatory action to reduce the hunting mortality rate may be a practical way to increase survival and thus increase the dove population in the event that productivity declines or annual mortality becomes too high for the doves to maintain their numbers. The goal of mourning dove management in the EMU should be to maintain a healthy and productive population—one that can sustain ample hunting opportunity and harvest.

Until recent decades, land-use practices associated with agricultural productivity in the Eastern Management Unit generally enhanced mourning dove habitat. Highly mechanized monotypic and corporate farming, while more efficient and economical, tends to limit benefits to doves. Perhaps more significantly, farming has become more of a competitive industry rather than a lifestyle, and the rural character of the region and human contact with the landscape have been diminished. These factors impinge not only on the amount and diversity of habitat for doves and other wildlife but also on the opportunities for wildlife management. *Photo by O. S. Welch; courtesy of the U.S. Soil Conservation Service.*

Chapter 18

Population Characteristics and Trends in the Central Management Unit

Roy E. Tomlinson
Office of Migratory Bird Management
U.S. Fish and Wildlife Service
Albuquerque, New Mexico

James H. Dunks
Ducks Unlimited, Inc.
Austin, Texas

HABITAT DESCRIPTION

The Central Management Unit (CMU) lies between the eastern boundaries of Idaho, Utah and Arizona to the west and the Mississippi River to the east. It consists of fourteen states *(Figure 49)* with a combined area of about 1.4 million square miles (3.6 million km²), or about 46 percent of the conterminous United States (Dunks et al. 1982). Although the unit contains almost half of the nation's land area, its human population is relatively sparse, constituting only 19 percent of the total (Soukhanov and Ellis 1984). Following the lead of Dunks et al. (1982), the CMU has been divided into three north/south-oriented subunits to facilitate discussion about mourning dove population characteristics that differ somewhat among subunits *(Figure 50)*.

Habitats within the CMU vary greatly because of heterogeneity in elevation, topography and climate. Seven broad, natural vegetation types characterize the unit (Dunks et al. 1982): *needleleaf forests* in upper elevations of the Rocky Mountains and northern Minnesota; *broadleaf forests* restricted to

the East CMU subunit, major riverbottoms and eastern Texas; *mixed needleleaf and broadleaf forests* mainly confined to southeastern Missouri, Arkansas and eastern Texas; *shrub vegetation* generally in conjunction with grasslands in local western areas and a narrow strip along the Rio Grande in Texas; *mixed forests and grasslands* of southern Iowa, northern and western Missouri, eastern Kansas, mideastern Oklahoma, and much of central Texas; *shrub/grassland association* found in southern and west Texas and southern New Mexico; and the vast *grasslands*—referred to as the Great Plains—generally occupying the Mid-CMU subunit, ranging from North Dakota deep into Texas.

Humans have modified the original vegetation to a large extent through urbanization, farming, grazing, lumbering, irrigation, stock pond development, flood control, power generation and other activities. These alterations generally have been beneficial to mourning doves in the CMU. Perhaps the most important habitat change that affected mourning doves was the plowing of grasslands for cereal grain production. During and after harvest, waste grain is important as a food source for mourning doves. In addition, other farming practices have proven favorable for habitation of the species. The planting of field and farmstead shelterbelts and development of stock ponds have provided substantially more nesting habitat and drinking water than was available originally. Additional nesting and roosting habitat was created when trees and shrubs were planted in cities and towns associated with farming communities.

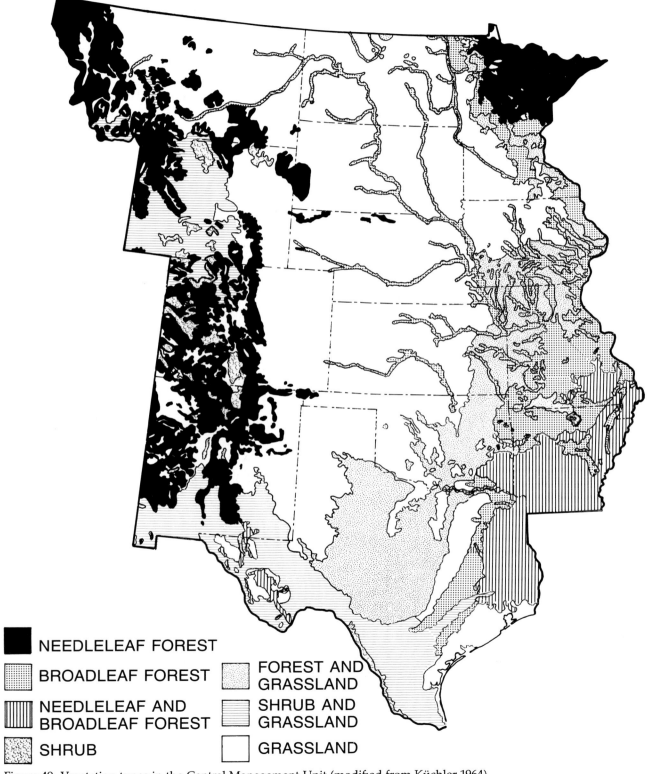

NEEDLELEAF FOREST

BROADLEAF FOREST

NEEDLELEAF AND BROADLEAF FOREST

SHRUB

FOREST AND GRASSLAND

SHRUB AND GRASSLAND

GRASSLAND

Figure 49. Vegetation types in the Central Management Unit (modified from Küchler 1964).

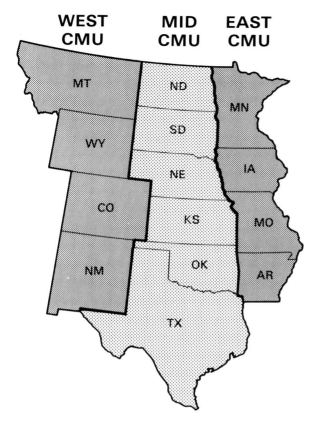

WEST CMU   MID CMU   EAST CMU

Figure 50. Subunits of the Central Management Unit.

Along the southeastern edge of the CMU, lumbering and agricultural practices have increased dove nesting habitat by creating a greater amount of "edge." In the dry West CMU subunit, development of irrigation systems has permitted productive farming of lands otherwise unsuited for intensive agriculture, consequently creating favorable conditions for doves.

Conversely, removal of shrubs and trees throughout the CMU since the 1950s has resulted in the loss of important nesting sites for mourning doves. In the Southwest, programs for brush control and phreatophyte removal have been designed to improve pastures and conserve water. Of particular concern are programs to remove shelterbelts in the Great Plains. Originally planted to reduce wind erosion and to protect buildings and livestock, trees in many shelterbelts are now becoming overmature and dying. Since farmers now desire to put more of their land into direct production of crops, continued maintenance and retention of shelterbelts are not compatible with modern, intensive agricultural practices. It is feared that continued removal of windbreaks could have an adverse effect in future years on soil conservation, wildlife and the general environment (Olson et al. 1991).

Overall, however, the CMU probably provides

the most ideal combination of habitats for mourning dove nesting, feeding, cover and water requirements of any unit. Except for the highest alpine meadows and forests of the Rocky Mountains, doves have adapted to all the CMU habitats, both modified and unmodified. Basically, the mourning dove is a tree-nesting species, although it frequently nests on the ground when trees are not available. It generally shuns deep woods or forest and utilizes open woodlands and "edge" between forest and prairie biomes. It is a seed eater that has adapted readily to small grains such as wheat and sorghum. Thus, diversified farming communities of the CMU have proved to be excellent mourning dove habitat.

ADMINISTRATIVE AND TECHNICAL ORGANIZATION

Management of mourning doves in the United States is primarily a federal responsibility because of migratory bird treaties with various countries, including Canada and Mexico. Historically, however, state conservation agencies have played an important role in supporting and supplementing federal migratory gamebird management programs. In the CMU, federal and state biologists coordinate management functions for mourning doves through the Central Migratory Shore and Upland Game Bird Technical Committee. The committee consists of technical representatives from each of the fourteen states in the CMU and meets each year in March to discuss the status of dove populations and make recommendations for research and management programs, including preliminary proposals for hunting season regulations. Recommendations of the technical committee are presented to the parent Central Flyway Council and, if approved, are submitted to the U.S. Fish and Wildlife Service at the Early Hunting Seasons Regulations hearing in Washington during late June. The Service, in turn, makes final decisions for management based on recommendations from the Council and its own staff through the Service Regulations Committee. This committee is composed of five members of high-ranking Service personnel. Management decisions then are published in the *Federal Register* as a series of documents culminating in Final Hunting Season Regulations.

Although many deliberations of the Central Migratory Shore and Upland Game Bird Technical Committee involve hunting regulations, the committee also plans and implements other actions. For example, it cosponsored (with the Service) a mourning dove banding program between 1967 and 1974, which culminated in data analyses and a better understanding of dove population dynamics in the CMU (Dunks et al. 1982). It participated in a joint federal/state study of September hunting in relation to mourning dove nesting success (Geissler et al. 1987). Recently, it investigated agricultural practices and their possible effects on population trends (George et al. 1987). At present, a comprehensive study has been initiated in Missouri and Iowa to investigate the role of hunting mortality in relation to total mortality and the effects of habitat change on dove production. Close cooperation of states and the U.S. Fish and Wildlife Service has been and continues to be an integral aspect of dove management in the CMU.

BREEDING POPULATION STATUS AND MONITORING

Call-count Routes

The Call-count Survey, conducted annually by the U.S. Fish and Wildlife Service and cooperators,

monitors the status of breeding mourning doves throughout the conterminous United States (see chapter 15). Nearly four hundred Call-count routes are run annually in the CMU (see *Figure 34*). These routes are distributed randomly in thirty-two physiographic regions throughout the unit. Because sample sizes are small in some states and physiographic regions, comparisons of indices (mean number of doves heard per route) among these areas for specific years are imprecise. However, examination of the same data for long-term trends provides useful information for evaluating status of populations. In addition, when state estimates are combined to obtain a management unit index, statistical precision is improved considerably.

Population Trends

Breeding population indices derived from the nationwide Call-count Survey have been calculated for each CMU state since 1966 *(Table 56)*. During the first five years of the survey (1966–70), the number

Table 56. Annual breeding population indices[a] of mourning doves, expressed as the mean number of calling doves heard per route, by states and subunits of the Central Management Unit, 1966–87.

| Year | East CMU | | | | | Mid-CMU | | | | | | |
	MN	IA	MO	AR	Subtotal	ND	SD	NE	KS	OK	TX	Subtotal
1966	23.1	36.2	46.0	30.0	32.4	24.1	49.4	40.2	48.2	26.7	25.3	32.3
1967	22.0	32.4	43.2	28.6	30.6	24.4	31.4	36.1	47.1	32.1	20.1	28.4
1968	21.0	34.7	52.8	28.2	33.5	33.3	41.4	45.9	52.6	39.5	22.1	34.8
1969	22.5	29.8	31.0	26.3	26.9	27.0	37.4	44.9	49.9	39.8	19.1	31.0
1970	16.4	21.6	42.7	25.9	26.2	25.0	45.6	43.6	46.2	26.9	20.3	30.4
1971	21.7	26.6	35.0	26.3	27.5	27.4	38.8	42.0	48.2	24.8	19.2	29.7
1972	25.1	32.9	47.1	29.8	33.7	27.5	39.1	41.4	54.8	33.5	25.9	34.2
1973	20.2	30.5	35.7	27.5	28.6	32.3	41.7	40.1	47.4	29.8	21.3	31.9
1974	22.5	24.0	29.9	23.0	25.0	32.1	50.8	41.1	47.0	30.3	22.2	33.4
1975	24.8	22.3	33.0	20.7	25.0	25.7	43.6	39.9	45.4	26.4	20.0	30.0
1976	24.5	28.0	29.0	24.7	26.5	41.7	46.9	44.3	50.2	30.5	19.9	32.7
1977	27.8	21.4	32.8	20.2	24.9	35.3	40.4	44.4	48.3	39.5	18.9	31.3
1978	24.5	24.0	21.6	15.1	20.7	39.0	44.8	38.4	37.6	28.5	19.5	30.3
1979	27.0	20.4	20.5	12.6	18.9	37.0	42.5	39.9	52.6	29.0	23.6	34.7
1980	28.1	27.1	29.9	20.5	26.6	43.1	43.6	50.9	59.6	28.3	23.0	36.1
1981	27.7	29.5	26.1	20.3	26.0	44.6	38.7	48.7	54.8	29.0	20.6	33.5
1982	21.9	21.3	23.3	20.6	22.4	43.4	46.7	47.0	52.5	31.4	20.1	33.4
1983	22.8	16.7	22.9	16.5	19.7	41.5	42.7	44.6	62.0	30.4	19.0	32.3
1984	17.8	21.9	20.4	12.9	18.4	33.4	44.3	42.2	48.0	23.0	18.0	29.3
1985	20.5	24.3	19.2	13.0	19.1	43.6	41.4	44.3	60.4	22.8	19.1	31.8
1986	19.6	22.2	19.6	12.7	18.5	47.0	39.9	35.5	42.6	25.1	21.1	32.1
1987	23.1	20.4	21.3	15.0	20.1	50.6	36.6	36.1	47.2	27.0	19.9	31.7
Averages												
1966–70	21.0	30.9	35.4	27.8	29.9	26.8	41.0	42.1	48.8	33.0	21.4	31.4
1983–87	20.8	21.1	20.7	14.0	19.2	43.2	41.0	40.5	52.0	25.7	19.4	31.4
1966–87	22.9	25.8	31.0	21.4	25.1	35.4	42.2	42.3	50.1	29.7	20.8	32.1

[a] Annual indices are defined as the predicted value from the trend analysis plus the deviation from the expected value in a year.

of calling doves per route in the CMU averaged 26.5, and during the latest five years (1983–87), the number was 23.6, indicating an 11-percent decline. For the Mid-CMU subunit, the average density remained virtually the same (31.4) for the two periods; in the West CMU, density increased 21 percent (from 15.4 to 18.7 birds per route). In the East CMU subunit, however, density declined 36 percent (from 29.9 to 19.2 birds per route), which accounted for the apparent overall CMU decline. Individual states exhibiting the severest declines were Iowa (32 percent), Missouri (42 percent) and Arkansas (50 percent) in the East CMU, and Montana (28 percent) and Wyoming (40 percent) in the West CMU. Dove populations in all other states appeared to be relatively stable or increasing.

Call-count routes are distributed randomly within eighty-two physiographic regions of the United States. Of the twenty-nine physiographic regions in the CMU with sufficient data for comparison *(Table 57)*, nine exhibited population increases of more than 10 percent between 1966–70 and 1983–87, eleven had decreases of more than 10 percent and nine showed changes (in either direc-

Table 56. (continued)

		West CMU			CMU
MT	WY	CO	NM	Subtotal	Total
24.5	18.3	13.6	12.5	16.2	28.0
21.9	18.7	17.4	9.1	15.3	25.4
19.1	9.2	13.6	13.3	14.2	28.3
19.7	16.9	15.8	11.1	15.4	25.7
16.1	18.5	20.5	10.7	15.6	25.3
22.6	9.3	15.0	10.3	14.4	24.8
17.1	12.6	21.4	12.8	16.1	28.5
12.8	13.7	16.0	9.4	12.5	24.9
14.5	17.6	22.1	11.1	15.6	26.0
19.6	15.3	18.0	14.7	17.1	24.6
15.3	15.1	21.9	14.6	16.6	26.0
18.6	11.1	24.1	13.8	17.0	25.1
17.6	14.0	28.6	14.3	18.1	24.1
18.0	11.2	23.6	10.5	15.2	24.4
16.8	10.7	29.0	16.9	18.2	27.5
15.5	12.1	36.2	17.4	19.1	26.5
18.3	13.4	33.8	13.9	18.7	25.5
16.0	10.1	21.3	18.2	17.1	23.9
12.2	8.1	29.3	19.9	17.0	22.1
15.0	9.8	31.9	18.0	18.4	23.7
16.1	11.4	29.7	20.6	20.7	24.0
13.9	9.5	36.0	24.4	20.5	24.2
20.3	16.3	16.2	11.3	15.4	26.5
14.6	9.8	29.6	20.2	18.7	23.6
17.3	13.0	23.6	14.4	16.8	25.4

tion) of less than 10 percent. Those regions exhibiting *increased* dove populations were distributed mainly in eastern Colorado, New Mexico and west Texas. Those regions with substantial dove *decreases* were distributed in two general areas: from Iowa south through Missouri and Arkansas into south Texas; and western Montana through western Wyoming and western Colorado. The general areas showing dove increases and decreases in the West CMU are associated with regions of the Western Management Unit (WMU) that had similar changes. It appears, then, that West CMU mourning doves west of the Continental Divide and north of New Mexico have experienced severe population declines, whereas those populations west of the Continental Divide in New Mexico are increasing. Dove declines in physiographic regions of the East CMU generally are associated with similar decreases in adjacent regions of the Eastern Management Unit (EMU). Thus, the Mississippi River apparently does *not* act as a major barrier between East CMU and EMU doves, and factors affecting breeding populations on either side of the river appear to be equivalent.

Results of the Call-count Survey for 1966–87 were analyzed by the "route regression" method described by Geissler (1984). Population trends were calculated for the entire twenty-two years as well as for the most recent five-, ten- and fifteen-year periods *(Table 58)*. During that twenty-two-year span, the overall dove population in the CMU fluctuated moderately around a mean of 25.4 doves heard per route, with no upward or downward trend indicated (-0.5 percent per year, $P < 0.10$). The CMU population was relatively stable over the long-term period. Significant downward trends for the most recent five- and ten-year periods for South Dakota, Nebraska, Kansas and Texas might cause initial concern. In each case, however, it is noted that the 1987 indices are no lower than several indices obtained previously *(Table 56)* and approximate the twenty-two-year average. Short-term fluctuations in the past have been noted and must be expected by managers. Thus, these five- and ten-year downward trends can be viewed with guarded optimism.

Conversely, when population indices indicate steady long-term downward trends, managers must determine the cause and implement measures to reverse the trends. It is evident that such a trend is occurring in the East CMU subunit *(Table 58)*. Declines are noted in all four time periods for the subunit as a whole, and significantly in all but the latest five-year period ($P < 0.01$). Individually, each state shows a declining dove population, but Missouri and Arkansas appear to exhibit the great-

Table 57. Annual breeding population indices[a] of mourning doves, expressed as the mean number of calling doves heard per route, by physiographic region of the Central Management Unit, 1966–87.

Physiographic region[b]	Year											
	1966	1967	1968	1969	1970	1971	1972	1973	1974	1975	1976	1977
10	11.7	11.9	11.9	8.4	7.2	15.9	16.8	9.6	11.0	14.8	12.2	16.6
35	46.4	47.9	48.8	41.6	34.8	47.1	40.6	38.1	42.5	38.5	38.5	33.7
36	26.2	24.1	19.8	20.8	19.6	21.5	22.5	18.8	23.2	16.7	19.8	17.9
122	39.0	37.2	44.8	35.9	33.3	39.4	38.4	41.2	41.5	32.1	48.0	40.6
125	49.9	43.0	46.7	39.3	36.1	37.2	46.8	40.3	32.1	38.1	41.7	34.9
126	37.7	43.5	49.5	32.9	37.7	30.9	45.2	41.2	32.6	35.2	41.7	40.0
130	53.2	25.8	38.8	37.0	30.7	27.0	41.2	24.0	42.1	26.4	34.8	32.9
131	27.0	21.8	31.4	30.6	26.4	27.7	34.7	31.9	29.8	29.6	33.5	39.7
132	31.5	25.9	25.3	28.0	24.1	28.7	24.4	23.7	31.9	29.7	27.0	27.4
134	22.1	22.7	27.3	27.5	24.2	26.1	25.8	22.3	26.1	25.2	22.3	27.7
135	46.8	55.3	55.3	59.6	68.8	57.9	58.1	61.1	62.3	55.5	63.1	54.8
136	11.4	18.7	11.6	12.9	20.3	8.7	25.3	16.3	25.9	18.4	22.7	22.8
137	4.1	3.0	5.4	5.8	6.6	7.0	4.1	8.9	14.9	6.9	8.1	11.4
138	42.5	8.4	43.9	13.4	9.6	4.2	22.0	11.1	15.0	32.4	21.8	20.3
139	36.5	18.5	13.1	16.4	23.2	18.8	26.2	31.2	21.6	24.6	19.8	15.6
141	25.7	24.8	29.8	19.4	28.2	21.8	28.4	20.7	18.6	20.0	15.8	20.1
142	3.5	2.6	1.8	3.0	1.6	1.3	5.0	2.0	2.6	1.0	1.3	3.5
151	26.7	21.4	23.1	26.9	15.5	17.9	32.7	22.0	27.2	15.7	19.8	12.3
152	13.5	7.3	16.6	17.3	13.1	17.7	14.0	12.5	4.5	11.1	9.7	7.9
160	10.9	11.8	9.9	17.9	19.1	10.6	19.2	4.3	14.9	6.8	22.2	14.5
170	13.8	17.5	9.8	14.6	18.8	9.6	11.2	13.5	13.5	17.5	16.2	13.1
180	15.1	11.4	10.2	10.0	13.0	9.0	9.8	6.7	11.0	7.3	9.4	11.2
190	12.5	9.6	9.7	8.4	8.2	7.0	6.3	6.7	5.8	4.7	5.8	6.4
212	25.3	55.2	23.9	33.6	13.8	36.2	17.4	19.7	19.7	17.9	25.5	25.3
213	22.4	28.9	21.9	23.2	26.1	25.7	16.3	28.8	24.1	26.0	30.4	30.0
214	11.2	5.8	8.0	8.0	9.8	4.9	8.5	14.7	6.6	13.9	11.2	6.3
216	13.8	11.9	6.8	5.2	18.7	41.3	27.6	9.5	15.6	17.8	15.5	21.6
224	7.5	10.8	8.9	11.4	11.9	9.0	8.6	16.2	13.4	13.8	16.8	13.5
225	23.3	8.3	17.4	17.6	40.7	6.0	9.5	17.9	7.7	13.1	16.9	11.0

[a] Annual indices are defined as the predicted value from the trend analysis plus the deviation from the expected value in a year.
[b] See Figure 34 for explanation of numerical codes.

est decreases. The Missouri Department of Conservation has conducted a long-term annual census of mourning doves seen along roadsides in June. The results of this survey were compared with the federal Call-count Survey results in Missouri by linear regression, and close correlation was obtained ($r = 0.71$, 16 d.f., $P < 0.01$). The independent data sets both suggest that a real population decline is occurring in Missouri and, by inference, in Iowa and Arkansas as well. At present, the cause or causes of the East CMU declines are unknown. The Central Migratory Shore and Upland Game Bird Technical Committee is investigating possible contributing factors, such as changing agricultural practices, loss of nesting habitat and the relationship of hunting mortality to total mortality.

Breeding Bird Survey

Another source of breeding mourning dove population data is the Breeding Bird Survey, also administered by the U.S. Fish and Wildlife Service. This survey has been conducted annually by cooperators in all areas of the United States and in certain areas of Canada since 1966, although some were not established until 1968 (see Robbins et al. 1986, see also chapter 14). Breeding Bird Survey cooperators count all species of birds heard *and* seen that are encountered on about 2,100 50-mile (80.5 km) routes in the United States during June. Several methodological differences between the Breeding Bird and Call-count surveys prohibit direct comparisons (see chapters 15 and 16). For example, the former samples all species of birds and combines numbers of individuals both heard and seen. The Call-count Survey samples only mourning doves and separately summarizes doves heard and seen. Since doves are seen more readily in parts of the Midwest and all of the open West than in the forested East, comparisons of Breeding Bird Survey dove indices geographically are im-

Table 57. (continued)

Year										Averages		
1978	1979	1980	1981	1982	1983	1984	1985	1986	1987	1966–70	1983–87	1966–87
8.7	9.1	14.3	16.7	10.9	9.4	8.1	9.6	10.8	8.1	10.2	9.2	11.5
28.6	26.4	29.2	27.3	35.5	29.9	23.6	26.4	30.6	26.9	43.9	27.5	35.6
19.4	18.1	20.5	18.8	19.9	17.6	17.7	15.5	18.1	16.5	22.1	17.1	19.7
40.6	39.4	46.0	46.2	42.4	39.0	34.1	42.4	37.9	40.9	38.0	38.9	40.0
31.3	32.9	39.6	41.7	32.8	31.2	31.9	33.2	35.4	29.0	43.0	32.1	37.5
35.0	35.7	41.8	35.6	31.6	36.2	27.4	35.0	32.6	33.8	40.3	33.0	36.9
28.5	33.9	39.3	37.7	36.8	36.2	32.7	29.6	34.6	35.4	37.1	33.7	34.5
34.9	34.1	38.7	36.6	40.5	45.9	37.0	32.4	45.8	40.9	27.4	40.4	34.1
28.1	28.0	25.8	27.3	27.8	27.5	22.6	25.6	26.1	24.4	27.0	25.2	26.9
24.0	27.5	29.2	27.2	25.4	29.3	23.8	28.3	24.7	25.8	24.8	26.4	25.7
57.5	58.7	64.4	68.0	60.1	65.1	51.0	70.8	45.6	49.8	57.2	56.5	58.6
42.6	32.2	41.6	44.9	44.7	32.7	52.3	54.0	41.8	82.4	15.0	52.6	31.1
13.8	8.0	13.2	9.6	27.8	9.8	39.8	19.4	24.0	21.7	5.0	22.9	12.4
12.1	20.7	21.9	35.6	14.6	19.4	22.4	25.6	35.8	33.5	23.6	27.3	22.1
21.4	47.9	34.3	22.3	36.1	21.4	26.4	26.4	31.5	26.2	21.5	26.4	25.4
8.3	9.7	17.2	13.9	12.5	11.5	8.4	9.8	8.0	13.5	25.6	10.2	17.6
5.7	4.1	2.7	2.3	3.3	4.0	6.7	7.6	10.4	7.5	2.5	7.2	3.8
15.6	13.8	26.0	18.5	17.5	16.6	15.9	12.2	14.8	18.7	22.7	15.6	19.6
7.8	7.8	9.5	8.9	12.1	7.7	6.2	7.1	4.2	9.8	13.6	7.0	10.3
14.4	9.9	14.6	16.4	11.0	6.5	5.5	9.5	14.2	11.7	13.9	9.5	12.5
11.7	11.0	12.2	14.1	12.4	12.8	15.4	12.5	13.6	14.0	14.9	13.7	13.6
11.3	11.2	7.7	7.2	13.0	6.5	5.6	8.9	8.7	7.7	11.9	7.5	9.6
5.3	4.6	4.1	4.0	5.1	2.8	3.1	3.9	2.2	2.8	9.7	3.0	5.9
14.5	29.6	21.3	40.2	26.6	12.2	15.5	19.4	24.9	22.6	30.4	18.9	24.6
24.1	18.9	23.0	32.7	21.1	22.2	41.0	14.9	21.6	15.3	24.5	23.0	24.5
9.7	8.9	10.5	10.0	9.2	7.8	10.1	10.1	19.0	8.6	8.6	11.1	9.7
18.6	7.9	18.0	28.5	19.5	19.0	39.2	15.6	29.2	25.2	11.3	25.6	19.4
16.9	16.5	20.3	21.0	21.0	22.7	21.2	21.5	19.5	23.8	10.1	21.7	15.7
14.4	13.0	15.4	9.4	17.6	15.6	19.9	22.0	20.6	19.8	21.5	19.6	16.2

practical. Furthermore, the formidable task of counting all species for the Breeding Bird Survey probably results in incomplete coverage of any single species, such as the mourning dove. These and other factors probably serve to render the Breeding Bird Survey less reliable to predict mourning dove population trends than is the Call-count Survey. Nevertheless, the Breeding Bird Survey trend data for mourning doves are presented here as a supplementary source of information.

According to Breeding Bird Survey data for the period 1966–87, the mean number of mourning doves heard and seen in the CMU remained stable, with no trend indicated (+0.01 percent per year, $P > 0.10$). In comparison, the Call-count Survey suggested that a decrease of 0.5 percent per year in number of doves heard throughout the CMU was likely ($P < 0.10$). Considering the three subunits, both surveys detected a highly significant decline in dove populations in the East CMU (Breeding Bird Survey, −1.9 percent per year; Call-count Survey, −2.3 percent per year; both $P < 0.01$) and a stable trend in the Mid-CMU (Breeding Bird Survey, +0.4 percent per year; Call-count Survey, +0.1 percent per year; both $P > 0.10$). For the West CMU, the Breeding Bird Survey indicated a stable population trend (+0.6 percent per year, $P > 0.10$), whereas the Call-count Survey suggested an increasing trend of 1.7 percent per year ($P < 0.10$). Thus, the two surveys independently obtained somewhat similar results for the broad geographic limits of the subunits and the CMU as a whole. However, trends by state differed considerably. In four of the fourteen CMU states, trends were in the opposite direction, depending on survey. And for five of the ten that agreed in direction, the degree of significance was considerably different.

Although physiographic regions incorporated by each survey are different and therefore not directly comparable, results of the two surveys were visually assessed by region on maps. There was some agreement in some broad zones (e.g., the eastern section of the CMU), but there were more zones with opposing trends.

Table 58. Trends (percentage change[a] per year as determined by linear regression) in breeding population indices for mourning doves heard by state in the Central Management Unit, 1966–87.

Location	5-year (1983–87)				10-year (1978–87)			
	N	Percentage change[b]	95%	C.I.	N	Percentage change[b]	95%	C.I.
East CMU								
Minnesota	11	−3.9	−15.6	7.8	12	−5.1*	−10.8	0.6
Iowa	16	1.2	−3.3	5.7	17	−2.5***	−3.9	−1.2
Missouri	20	−3.8	−10.6	3.0	22	−2.6***	−4.3	−0.8
Arkansas	15	−2.0	−8.0	3.9	15	−2.1	−5.7	1.5
Subtotal	62	−2.5	−7.3	2.3	66	−3.3***	−5.3	−1.2
Mid-CMU								
North Dakota	25	8.3	−2.6	19.3	26	−0.9	−4.7	2.8
South Dakota	21	−10.3***	−18.0	−2.6	23	−5.5***	−8.3	−2.8
Nebraska	25	−6.1***	−9.3	−2.9	25	−3.1**	−5.6	−0.7
Kansas	25	−5.9*	−12.0	0.1	28	−2.7*	−5.4	0.1
Oklahoma	16	−2.9	−8.4	2.5	16	−3.7	−9.8	2.5
Texas	133	2.2	−1.0	5.4	144	−1.9**	−3.4	−0.3
Subtotal	245	−3.2***	−5.5	−0.9	262	−2.8**	−4.0	−1.6
West CMU								
Montana	23	−3.2	−14.2	7.8	24	−2.9	−11.5	5.7
Wyoming	16	4.2**	0.6	7.8	18	−1.3	−6.8	4.2
Colorado	16	−1.5	−7.6	4.6	18	−2.9***	−4.8	−1.1
New Mexico	26	18.5**	2.8	34.2	28	7.4***	2.5	12.4
Subtotal	81	2.6	−2.4	7.5	88	−0.4	−2.7	2.0
Total CMU	388	−1.7*	−3.7	0.3	416	−2.6***	−3.5	−1.6

[a] Route trend means weighted by land area and population density. The estimated count in the next year is (percentage ÷ 100 + 1) times the count in the current year where percentage is the annual change.
[b] *$P<0.1$, **$P<0.05$, ***$P<0.01$.

Historically, most human-caused alterations of pristine landscape in the region that now constitutes the Central Management Unit created more favorable conditions for mourning doves. Stock ponds, irrigation systems and reservoirs to benefit livestock and crop production provided wildlife with new and well-distributed sources of water. Shelterbelts and other plantings in agricultural areas, around farmsteads and in communities greatly enhanced nesting cover for doves. But most important was the transformation of vast grasslands to croplands that afforded the birds an abundance of food. *Immediate right photo (New Mexico) courtesy of the U.S. Soil Conservation Service. Center right photo (South Dakota) courtesy of the South Dakota Department of Game, Fish and Parks. Far right photo (Montana) by B. C. McLean; courtesy of the U.S. Soil Conservation Service.*

Table 58. (continued)

	15-year (1973–87)				22-year (1966–87)		
N	Percentage change[b]	95%	C.I.	N	Percentage change[b]	95%	C.I.
12	−2.0	−7.5	3.6	13	−0.1	−3.4	3.1
17	−1.4***	−2.1	−0.6	17	−2.0***	−2.4	−1.6
24	−3.4***	−5.0	−1.9	26	−4.0***	−5.8	−2.1
15	−4.7***	−8.0	−1.4	16	−3.6***	−5.9	−1.3
68	−2.8***	−4.4	−1.2	72	−2.3***	−3.4	−1.2
26	1.6	−1.3	4.5	27	3.2***	1.1	5.4
23	−2.8**	−5.4	−0.1	26	0.1	−2.0	2.2
25	−0.3	−1.8	1.1	26	0.0	−1.1	1.1
30	0.5	−1.4	2.4	31	0.1	−1.1	1.3
17	−2.7*	−5.9	0.4	19	−1.0	−3.9	2.0
154	−0.6	−2.0	0.9	183	−0.5	−1.9	0.9
275	−0.5	−1.5	0.4	312	0.1	−0.6	0.8
26	2.4	−2.2	6.9	28	−1.7	−5.9	2.5
19	−4.2	−12.9	4.4	19	−2.9	−6.5	0.8
18	3.0*	−0.3	6.4	19	4.4***	2.0	6.9
30	8.1***	3.1	13.0	30	4.2**	0.8	7.5
93	2.8*	−0.3	5.9	96	1.7*	0.0	3.4
436	−0.7*	−1.6	0.1	480	−0.5*	−1.1	0.1

Breeding Population Size

How many mourning doves there are in the United States or just in the CMU is not known with certainty. Mourning doves are small, drab and therefore inconspicuous. In addition, during the breeding season they generally are ubiquitous and do not concentrate in confined areas. Therefore, censuses of doves cannot be accomplished as is done for highly visible concentrations of birds, such as waterfowl. However, the Breeding Bird Surveys conducted in the United States and Canada during 1967 and 1968 and again in 1977 indicated that the mourning dove was one of the most abundant bird species in North America (Robbins and Van Velzen 1969, Robbins et al. 1986). Mourning doves counted on the routes were surpassed in numbers only by the robin, starling, house sparrow, red-winged blackbird and common grackle. In the 1987 and 1988 surveys, the dove was exceeded in number only by red-winged blackbirds and brown-headed cowbirds (see chapter 1). The mourning dove clearly is an important component of the nation's bird life.

Using independent harvest and banding data from Texas, the CMU and the WMU, Dunks (1977),

Dunks et al. (1982) and Tomlinson et al. (1988) estimated the autumn flight of mourning doves in the conterminous United States to be 476 million, 350 to 600 million and 470 million birds, respectively. Tomlinson et al. (1988) suggested that 475 million represented a conservative and reasonable estimate of the United States population.

Based on the estimate of 475 million doves for the conterminous United States and the calculation that the CMU contains an average 57 percent of the total population (*Table 59*), the number of doves originating from the CMU during autumn is 271 million. Assuming a stable population, that all adults pair and breed, and a production requirement of 2.2 young per breeding pair (Dunks et al. 1982), the average breeding population in the CMU consists of approximately 129 million mourning doves. This total could be divided further into 25 million for the East CMU, 75 million for the Mid-CMU and 29 million for the West CMU (see also Dunks et al. 1982). However, broad assumptions were made to satisfy conditions of these mathematical derivations, some of which may have been invalid. Thus, the figures are presented here solely to advise of the approximate magnitude of dove populations within the CMU.

Table 59. Relative importance of mourning dove breeding populations in the United States, 1966–87.

Breeding area	Land area weight[a]		Mean number of doves per route	Breeding population index	Importance (percentage)
Western Management Unit					
Coastal WMU					
Washington	43.87		9.3	407.99	1.0
Oregon	62.27		11.0	684.97	1.7
California	101.71		19.0	1,932.49	4.9
Subtotal	207.85	(10.8)		3,025.45	7.6
Interior WMU					
Idaho	54.37		12.8	695.94	1.7
Nevada	71.27		6.7	477.51	1.2
Utah	53.34		14.4	768.10	1.9
Arizona	72.65		23.9	1,736.34	4.4
Subtotal	251.63	(13.1)		3,677.89	9.2
WMU total	459.48	(23.9)		6,703.34	16.8
Central Management Unit					
West CMU					
Montana	94.47		17.3	1,634.33	4.1
Wyoming	62.33		13.0	810.29	2.0
Colorado	67.18		23.6	1,585.45	4.0
New Mexico	77.98		14.4	1,122.91	2.8
Subtotal	301.98	(15.7)		5,152.98	12.9
Mid-CMU					
North Dakota	45.54		35.4	1,612.12	4.0
South Dakota	49.20		42.2	2,076.24	5.2
Nebraska	49.69		42.3	2,101.89	5.3
Kansas	52.43		50.1	2,626.74	6.6
Oklahoma	44.40		29.7	1,318.68	3.3
Texas	170.03		20.8	3,536.62	8.9
Subtotal	411.29	(21.4)		13,272.29	33.3

Table 59. (continued)

Breeding area	Land area weight[a]		Mean number of doves per route	Breeding population index	Importance (percentage)
East CMU					
Minnesota	54.09		22.9	1,238.66	3.1
Iowa	36.15		25.8	932.67	2.3
Missouri	45.10		31.0	1,398.10	3.5
Arkansas	34.37		21.4	735.52	1.8
Subtotal	169.71	(8.8)		4,304.95	10.8
CMU total	882.96	(46.0)		22,730.22	57.1
Eastern Management Unit					
Maine	19.85		4.5	89.33	0.2
Rhode Island	0.67		9.1	6.10	Tr
Massachusetts	5.31		10.6	56.29	0.1
New Hampshire	5.80		3.8	22.04	Tr
Vermont	5.95		5.9	35.11	0.1
New York	30.49		8.5	259.17	0.7
Connecticut	3.23		11.9	38.44	0.1
New Jersey	4.91		18.6	91.33	0.2
Pennsylvania	29.01		9.3	269.79	0.7
Michigan	37.18		10.8	401.54	1.0
Wisconsin	36.07		14.3	515.80	1.3
Illinois	35.09		23.7	831.63	2.1
Indiana	23.36		30.8	719.49	1.8
Ohio	26.42		19.2	507.26	1.3
West Virginia	15.41		5.3	81.67	0.2
Maryland	6.55		19.5	127.73	0.3
Delaware	1.29		7.3	9.42	Tr
Virginia	26.05		23.3	606.97	1.5
Kentucky	26.08		23.1	602.45	1.5
Tennessee	27.07		22.7	614.49	1.5
North Carolina	22.51		26.0	585.26	1.5
South Carolina	19.99		31.7	633.68	1.6
Georgia	37.82		25.4	960.63	2.4
Alabama	33.32		22.9	763.03	1.9
Mississippi	30.63		27.3	836.20	2.1
Louisiana	31.14		11.8	367.45	0.9
Florida	35.82		10.4	372.53	0.9
EMU total	577.02	(30.1)		10,404.83	26.1
United States total	1,919.46 (100.0)			39,838.39	100.0

[a] Percentage in parentheses.

Partial clearing vegetation in many parts of the Central Management Unit has created areas of edge cover that are particularly attractive and beneficial to mourning doves. *Photos courtesy of the U.S. Soil Conservation Service.*

Breeding Population Densities

Although mourning doves breed throughout the United States, the diverse habitats are such that certain areas support larger populations than others. The most favorable areas contain an intermixture of wooded "edge" habitat used by doves for nesting and farmland that produces grain and weed seeds used for food. The least attractive habitat occurs in monotypic forests of the Northeast, Northwest and Rocky Mountains.

By using the average numbers of doves heard calling on the national Call-count routes between 1966 and 1987, respective state mourning dove densities in the CMU can be illustrated *(Figure 51 and Table 56)*. By far the highest densities in the United States occur in the CMU, and particularly in the Mid-CMU subunit. In South Dakota, Nebraska and Kansas, the average numbers of mourning doves heard calling per route exceeded 40; in North Dakota and Oklahoma, the average counts exceeded 29 birds. These states are characterized by fertile soils and a thriving grain farm economy.

The East CMU subunit supported a moderate to high density of about 25 doves heard per route. These states (Minnesota, Iowa, Missouri and Arkansas) also have relatively fertile soils and farming economies, but a larger fraction of the states are forested and thus provide less favorable conditions for nesting.

Dove densities in Montana, Wyoming, Colorado and New Mexico were relatively low (an average 17 doves heard per route) because of the high-altitude forests and ranching economy—conditions not conducive to dove production.

The relative importance of various breeding mourning dove populations can be illustrated further by breeding population indices obtained from each state (see Dunks et al. 1982). The indices were obtained by multiplying the average number of calling birds per route by the geographic size of the area where they are found *(Table 59)*. As expected, the CMU ranks highest in importance as a dove production area. The CMU constitutes 46 percent of the land area and contains 57 percent of the breeding dove population. Although the Mid-CMU makes up only 21 percent of the conterminous United States, it contains about 33 percent of the country's doves (Dunks et al. 1982). The East CMU states comprise 9 percent of the land area and contain 11 percent of the total doves. The Rocky Mountain states of the West CMU account for approximately the same proportion of the country's doves (13 percent) as does the East CMU, but in an area almost twice the size.

BANDING AND POPULATION DYNAMICS

Banding Programs

Banding of mourning doves in what now is designated as the CMU began in the 1930s, mainly as isolated studies in scattered locations (e.g., see McClure 1943). Several of these projects were short-term, and data gathered in most of them were not analyzed or published. Exceptions to this rule were studies conducted in South Dakota, Missouri and Texas. In South Dakota, nearly 45,000 doves were banded by state and federal cooperators from 1917 to 1970, and the results were published by Rice and Lovrien (1974). Missouri's work was initiated by the Department of Conservation in 1952 and continued annually until about 1975. Three comprehensive analyses were made of data obtained from the Missouri bandings (Tomlinson et al. 1960, Henry 1970, Atkinson et al. 1982). The Texas Parks and Wildlife Department also published an analysis of banding data for doves banded and recovered in Texas during 1967–74 (Dunks 1977).

The first coordinated banding effort in the CMU was part of a nationwide program, conducted

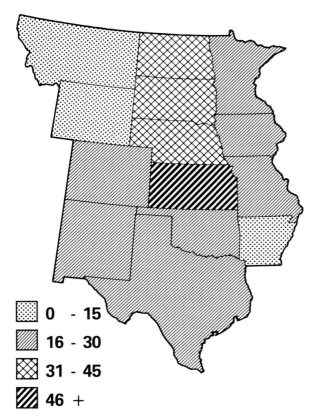

0 - 15
16 - 30
31 - 45
46 +

Figure 51. Mean number of mourning doves heard calling per route in the Central Management Unit, 1983–87.

between 1953 and 1957, to band nestling mourning doves. Nestlings were selected because their exact origins were known. However, it soon was learned that adults and immatures (free-flying young) banded during June through August also represented birds of known origin, and the study eventually included these cohorts as well. Of the nearly 114,000 doves banded during this program, 46,287 were banded in the CMU (Kiel 1959). Recoveries from these bandings provided the first insight into migratory pathways of doves from known areas of origin and enabled Kiel (1959) to delineate the three management units in use today.

In an effort to relate hunting mortality to overall mortality of mourning doves, the U.S. Fish and Wildlife Service advocated a pre- and postseason banding program in the early 1960s. The premise of this banding program was to compare second-year recovery rates of birds banded during summer with first-year recovery rates of birds banded after the hunting season—the difference indicating survival during the hunting season. However, emphasis on this program was discontinued when it became apparent that the pre- and postseason bandings were sampling different mourning dove population segments and that calculated rates therefore were inappropriate.

A nationwide banding program administered by the U.S. Fish and Wildlife Service was conducted during the mid-1960s to the mid-1970s (1967–74 in the CMU). This program sought to obtain bandings of adults and immatures during June through August (preseason) distributed evenly throughout the country. An annual quota of 175,000 banded doves was set for the United States, distributed according to size of each state (Martinson 1969, 1971). State wildlife agencies, the U.S. Fish and Wildlife Service, and private individuals participated. Although not all goals were accomplished, more than 868,000 doves were eventually banded. The CMU segment of the program—in which 332,000 doves were banded from 1967 to 1974—was coordinated through the Central Migratory Shore and Upland Game Bird Technical Committee. Much of the banding effort by state wildlife agencies was supported by contracts issued under the Accelerated Research Program for Migratory Shore and Upland Game Birds (Sandfort 1977) and the Federal Aid to Wildlife Restoration (or Pittman-Robertson) program (Dunks et al. 1982). Analyses of data from this program were published by Hayne and Geissler (1977) for the EMU, by Tomlinson et al. (1988) for the WMU and by Dunks et al. (1982) for the CMU. Much of the following information is based on data obtained from this program and the resulting analysis by Dunks et al. (1982).

Since 1974, no organized mourning dove banding has been conducted in the CMU. Thus, the information provided below represents populations and conditions that existed during the eight years prior to 1975. It can be argued that survival rates, recovery rates and other banding-derived information presented here may be considerably different from current rates and should be viewed in that light. However, the Central Migratory Shore and Upland Game Bird Technical Committee recently considered initiation of a new banding program and decided that the results to be gained from such a program could not justify the increased costs of conducting it. Instead, efforts are being directed toward more cost-efficient projects. Nevertheless, data gained during 1967–74 constitute the best information available and provide valuable insight into mourning dove population dynamics in the CMU.

Preseason Bandings and Recoveries, 1967 to 1976

Banded samples. During 1967–74, 181,975 immature and 150,339 adult mourning doves (totaling 332,314 birds) were banded in the CMU. Bandings were distributed fairly evenly by year and among states. Yearly bandings ranged from a low of about 25,000 in 1968 to a high of 53,000 in 1972. Total bandings by state ranged from a low of about 7,000 in Wyoming to a high of 48,000 in South Dakota. The bandings also were fairly well distributed geographically, although the western part of the unit was sampled less heavily than other areas (Dunks et al. 1982).

Of the 146,000 adults whose sex was determined at banding, the unweighted sex ratio was heavily skewed toward males (187:100). Although it is generally recognized that males outnumber females in wild mourning dove populations (see Baskett et al. 1978, Sayre et al. 1980), the sex ratio in the trapped sample of this program probably was biased toward males because of selectivity in trapping practices (see chapter 20, Dunks et al. 1982). As discussed later, adult males and adult females survive at the same rate in the CMU. Therefore, if adult males really do outnumber adult females, either a differential survival exists among immature doves (in which immature males survive at a higher rate than do immature females) or recruitment at hatching favors males, or both. The limited evidence suggests that the sex ratio at hatching approaches 100:100 and that immatures sampled by hunting in September also exhibit an equal sex ratio (see Hanson and Kossack 1963). Intuitively, then, one would suspect differential survival of immature doves as the factor in the preponderance of adult males. However, because the sex of live immature doves cannot be determined accurately until they reach a primary molt stage of five (i.e., the number-five primary has been replaced by adult plumage), banding cooperators are instructed to list all trapped immatures as unknown sex. As a result, banded samples of immature doves are inadequate to determine survival estimates by sex, and it presently is not possible to determine if these cohorts have different survival characteristics. Thus, the apparent preponderance of adult males in the population is an enigma to managers and bears further investigation.

The overall unweighted age ratio of the banded sample was 121:100, immatures to adults. This ratio is low and probably not representative of the true age ratio of the preseason population, because trapping in many areas was accomplished before substantial numbers of immature doves had been produced.

Recoveries. The analysis incorporated recoveries obtained during 1967–76 from: (1) doves banded in the CMU and recovered anywhere; and (2) doves banded in the EMU and WMU and recovered in the CMU, Mexico and Central America. Because of the limited number of dove bandings in Canada and Mexico, banding data from those countries were not considered in the analysis. Of the 332,314 doves banded in the CMU, 6,972 were recovered in the CMU, 398 in the EMU, 131 in the WMU and 1,590 in Mexico and Central America. The CMU also derived 357 and 24 recoveries, respectively, from doves banded in the EMU and WMU. Recoveries from the first hunting season following banding are called "direct recoveries," whereas those from subsequent hunting seasons are termed "indirect recoveries" (see *Table 43* for definition of terms). For purposes of determining recovery rates and distribution and derivation of the harvest, direct recoveries are better indicators than are indirect or total recoveries. In total, 5,266 direct recoveries in the CMU were obtained from doves banded in the CMU and an additional 262 direct recoveries were from the EMU (249) and WMU (13). In addition, 1,004 direct recoveries were reported in Mexico and Central America from United States bandings (792 from the CMU).

Recovery rates. The recovery rate is the proportion of a banded sample that is taken by hunters or found dead during the hunting season and reported to the U.S. Fish and Wildlife Service's Bird Banding Laboratory in Laurel, Maryland. Recovery rates reflect hunting pressure; the higher the rate, the heavier the pressure.

Direct and indirect recovery rates of doves banded as immatures and adults by banding location are summarized in Table 60. The state estimates were weighted by average breeding population indices (1967–74) and land area to obtain average recovery rates for subunits and the CMU as a whole. However, these estimates were nearly identical to simple arithmetical averages for each geographical reference area. The weighted direct recovery rates for immatures and adults were 1.8 and 1.4 percent, respectively. By dividing the former rate by the latter (relative recovery rate), it is seen that immatures banded in the CMU were about 1.3 times more vulnerable to hunting than were adults, a conclusion also reached by Dunks et al. (1982) using unweighted estimates. In comparison, the relative recovery rates calculated for the EMU and WMU were 1.5 and 1.3 percent, respectively (see chapters 17 and 19). Thus, immatures throughout the United States are uniformly more vulnerable to the gun than adults are.

Recovery rates in hunting versus nonhunting states. Seven CMU states permitted dove hunting throughout the ten-year recovery period (1967–76), five states did not permit hunting and two allowed hunting during some years but not others. To compare hunting pressure among subunits of the CMU, direct recovery rates were grouped by hunting and nonhunting states and weighted to obtain averages for each by subunit *(Table 61)*. As was expected, immature and adult doves banded in hunting states were recovered at a rate 2.6 to 3.2 times that of doves banded in nonhunting states in the CMU. This trend was particularly true for the East CMU and Mid-CMU. For the West CMU, however, doves were recovered at nearly the same rate (hunting states 1.3 times that of nonhunting states). In fact, direct recovery rates for the West CMU hunting states compared favorably with direct recovery rates from nonhunting states in the East CMU and Mid-CMU. This reflects the generally low hunting pressure in Colorado and New Mexico.

Recovery rates among subunits. Among the subunits, the East CMU had the highest direct recovery rate, 2.3 percent, versus 1.7 percent for the Mid-CMU and 0.8 percent for the West CMU *(Table 60)*. For nonhunting states, the differences among subunits were not great (East CMU, 1.0 percent; Mid-CMU, 0.7 percent; West CMU, 0.7 percent) *(Table 61)*. However, for hunting states of the unit, the East CMU had the highest direct recovery rate (3.3 percent), which was 1.6 times that of the Mid-CMU (2.1 percent) and 3.7 times that of the West CMU (0.9 percent).

Recovery rates among management units. Because all states in the WMU permit hunting, comparisons of recovery rates in that unit with those of

Table 60. Direct and indirect band recovery rates for immature, adult and total mourning doves banded in the Central Management Unit, 1967–74.

| | Recovery rates (percentage) | | | | | |
| | Immature | | Adult | | All doves | |
Banding location	Direct	Indirect	Direct	Indirect	Direct	Indirect
East CMU						
Minnesota	1.2	0.6	0.9	0.8	1.1	0.7
Iowa	1.1	0.8	0.7	0.8	0.9	0.8
Missouri	3.6	1.1	2.5	1.7	3.2	1.3
Arkansas	4.2	1.0	2.3	1.4	3.5	1.0
Subtotal[a]	2.6	0.9	1.7	1.2	2.3	1.0
Mid-CMU						
North Dakota	0.9	0.9	0.6	0.8	0.8	0.9
South Dakota	2.0	1.4	1.9	1.7	1.9	1.6
Nebraska	0.7	1.4	0.6	1.2	0.7	1.3
Kansas	1.6	1.4	1.8	1.5	1.7	1.4
Oklahoma	2.0	1.3	1.9	1.2	2.0	1.3
Texas	2.8	1.5	2.2	1.6	2.5	1.5
Subtotal[a]	1.8	1.4	1.6	1.4	1.7	1.4
West CMU						
Montana	0.9	0.7	0.3	0.7	0.7	0.7
Wyoming	0.7	0.5	0.3	0.6	0.6	0.5
Colorado	1.0	0.9	0.9	0.9	1.0	0.9
New Mexico	0.8	0.9	0.7	0.7	0.8	0.8
Subtotal[a]	0.9	0.7	0.5	0.7	0.8	0.7
Total[a]	1.8	1.1	1.4	1.2	1.7	1.2

[a] Subtotals and total weighted by average breeding population indices for 1967–74 and land area by state.

Table 61. Weighted average direct recovery rates of mourning doves by age class for hunting and nonhunting states in the Central Management Unit, 1967–76.

Location	Immature	Adult	All doves
Hunting states[a]			
East CMU	3.8	2.4	3.3
Mid-CMU	2.2	2.0	2.1
West CMU	1.0	0.8	0.9
All hunting states	2.4	1.9	2.2
Nonhunting states[b]			
East CMU	1.2	0.8	1.0
Mid-CMU	0.8	0.6	0.7
West CMU	0.9	0.3	0.7
All nonhunting states	0.9	0.6	0.8
All CMU states[c]			
East CMU	2.6	1.7	2.3
Mid-CMU	1.8	1.6	1.7
West CMU	0.9	0.5	0.8
CMU	1.8	1.4	1.7

[a] Hunting states during 1967–76 were: Missouri and Arkansas (East CMU); Kansas, Oklahoma and Texas (Mid-CMU); Colorado and New Mexico (West CMU).
[b] Nonhunting states during 1967–76 were: Minnesota and Iowa (East CMU); North Dakota and Nebraska (Mid-CMU); Montana (West CMU).
[c] CMU averages include all states; South Dakota and Wyoming permitted hunting during some years but not others.

the other two units were done using data from CMU and EMU hunting states only. The weighted direct recovery rates for immatures and adults banded in CMU hunting states were 2.4 and 1.9 percent, respectively *(Table 61)*. In comparison, direct recovery rates of immatures and adults from EMU hunting states were 5.6 and 3.9 percent, respectively (Hayne 1975), and those from the WMU were 3.4 and 2.7 percent, respectively (see chapter 19). Thus, assuming equal reporting rates in all units, hunters in the EMU harvested doves at a rate more than two times that of the CMU, and hunters in the WMU harvested doves at a rate nearly 1.5 times that of the CMU.

Further comparisons were made among sub-units of the CMU and WMU. The weighted direct recovery rates for immatures and adults, respectively, were 3.8 and 2.4 percent in hunting states of the East CMU, 2.2 and 2.0 percent for hunting states of the Mid-CMU, and 1.0 and 0.8 percent for hunting states of the West CMU *(Table 61)*. Again, it is seen that hunting pressure in the unit decreased from east to west. In comparison, the weighted direct recovery rates for immatures and adults were 4.5 and 3.2 percent in the Coastal WMU and 2.6 and 2.3 percent in the Interior WMU (see chapter 19). Thus, the Coastal WMU recovery rates were about 1.2 times greater than those of the East CMU and about twice those of the Mid-CMU. Interior WMU recovery rates for both age classes were nearly identical to those from hunting states of the

Mid-CMU but more than twice those of the adjacent West CMU. The higher hunting pressure, combined with other factors experienced in the WMU (particularly in the Coastal WMU), may have contributed to the population declines, whereas the lower hunting pressure experienced in the CMU (particularly in the West CMU and Mid-CMU sub-units) was associated with stable or increasing populations. Conversely, the high recovery rates encountered in hunting states of the EMU are associated with a stable dove population. Additional study is needed to understand the relationship of hunting mortality to mourning dove population status.

Distribution of Recoveries

Comparison of band-recovery distribution among CMU geographical areas is difficult because some states allowed hunting during the recovery period and others did not. Lack of in-state recovery for nonhunting states thus skews the distributional proportions. To correct for this problem, recovery rate indices (RRIs) were calculated for each recovery area *(Table 62)*. The recovery rate index is the recovery rate in each area multiplied by ten thousand; each index represents the relative frequency at which an individual dove will be recovered in that area, and comparisons can be made among different banding areas, recovery areas, and age

Table 62. Distribution of direct recovery rate indices[a] for doves banded in the Central Management Unit, 1967–76.

Age class	Banding location	Recovery location						
		East CMU	Mid-CMU	West CMU	EMU	WMU	Mexico	Central America
Immature	East CMU							
	Minnesota	1	46	1	33	2	31	4
	Iowa	1	50	3	36	0	11	6
	Missouri	245	31	0	67	1	10	1
	Arkansas	367	14	0	22	0	5	3
	Subtotal	125	39	1	41	1	17	3
	Mid-CMU							
	North Dakota	0	37	5	7	2	29	9
	South Dakota	<1	140	5	8	1	40	2
	Nebraska	0	23	5	2	0	41	1
	Kansas	0	123	1	0	0	25	10
	Oklahoma	0	159	2	1	0	32	3
	Texas	0	248	<1	3	0	24	3
	Subtotal	<1	142	3	4	1	32	4
	West CMU							
	Montana	0	6	30	0	14	38	0
	Wyoming	0	7	27	2	7	29	0
	Colorado	0	9	48	1	7	36	1
	New Mexico	0	7	48	0	0	28	1
	Subtotal	0	7	41	<1	6	33	<1
	CMU total	34	82	12	13	2	28	3

Table 62. (continued)

Age class	Banding location	Recovery location						
		East CMU	Mid-CMU	West CMU	EMU	WMU	Mexico	Central America
Adult	East CMU							
	Minnesota	0	46	0	16	0	18	4
	Iowa	2	33	0	16	0	13	5
	Missouri	210	16	0	15	0	3	4
	Arkansas	198	22	0	7	0	0	0
	Subtotal	74	31	0	14	0	10	4
	Mid-CMU							
	North Dakota	4	42	2	0	0	9	5
	South Dakota	0	165	3	1	1	14	4
	Nebraska	0	33	1	0	0	18	6
	Kansas	1	164	2	0	0	14	3
	Oklahoma	0	170	0	3	0	16	0
	Texas	0	215	0	0	<1	7	1
	Subtotal	<1	149	1	<1	<1	12	3
	West CMU							
	Montana	0	3	3	0	7	13	3
	Wyoming	0	0	4	0	4	20	0
	Colorado	0	6	66	0	4	15	1
	New Mexico	0	5	53	0	0	10	0
	Subtotal	0	5	51	0	3	14	1
	CMU total	17	93	11	3	1	12	3
All doves	East CMU							
	Minnesota	<1	46	<1	27	2	27	4
	Iowa	2	40	2	25	0	12	5
	Missouri	233	26	0	49	<1	8	2
	Arkansas	304	23	0	17	0	3	2
	Subtotal	105	36	<1	31	1	14	3
	Mid-CMU							
	North Dakota	1	39	4	5	1	22	8
	South Dakota	<1	154	4	4	1	25	3
	Nebraska	0	28	3	1	0	29	4
	Kansas	<1	147	2	0	0	18	6
	Oklahoma	0	161	2	1	0	29	2
	Texas	0	245	0	5	0	8	2
	Subtotal	<1	145	2	2	<1	22	4
	West CMU							
	Montana	0	6	24	0	12	32	1
	Wyoming	0	4	19	1	6	26	0
	Colorado	0	8	58	<1	5	25	1
	New Mexico	0	6	50	0	0	21	<1
	Subtotal	0	7	45	<1	5	25	1
	CMU total	26	87	12	9	1	21	3

[a] Recovery rate index = recovery rate × 10,000; these indices reflect the relative frequencies at which individual doves will be taken in given locations. Example: an immature dove from the East CMU is 10 times as likely to be recovered in the EMU than an immature from the Mid-CMU (41 ÷ 4 = ± 10).

and sex cohorts of the population sampled. For example, the recovery rate indices for immature doves banded in the East CMU, Mid-CMU and West CMU and subsequently recovered in Mexico are 17, 32 and 33, respectively. Therefore, a dove banded in the Mid-CMU or West CMU is about twice as likely to be recovered in Mexico as one banded in the East CMU. Only direct recoveries were used to ensure that the origination area represented the true natal or nesting location of each banded bird. However, if

substantial differences in reporting rate occurred among recovery areas, the following comparisons would be invalid.

Based on recovery rate indices of all doves (immature and adult data combined) originating within the entire CMU *(Table 62)*, an individual dove had a much higher probability of being recovered in the CMU (RRI = 125) than in the EMU (RRI = 9) or the WMU (RRI = 1), and it was five times as likely to be recovered in the CMU than in

Mexico or Central America (RRI = 24). However, a CMU dove was twice as likely to be recovered in Mexico or Central America as in the West CMU (RRI = 12) and about equally as likely to be recovered there as in the East CMU (RRI = 26). Thus, Mexico and Central America were important harvest locations for CMU-banded doves.

A dove banded in the East CMU had little likelihood of being recovered in the West CMU (RRI < 1) or the WMU (RRI = 1) but equal probability of being recovered in the Mid-CMU (RRI = 36) and the EMU (RRI = 31). It is interesting to note that doves banded in Minnesota and Iowa were unlikely to be recovered in Missouri and Arkansas (i.e., directly south). Rather, they were either recovered in the Mid-CMU (RRIs ± 43) or the EMU (RRIs ± 26), indicating a two-pronged migration pattern favoring the Southwest by nearly 2 to 1. Missouri doves also had a bifurcate distribution pattern but were recovered nearly twice as frequently in the EMU (RRI = 49) as in the Mid-CMU (RRI = 26).

Doves banded in the Mid-CMU rarely strayed from that subunit and were many times more likely to be recovered in Mexico and Central America (RRI = 26) than in the East CMU (RRI < 1), the West CMU (RRI = 2), the EMU (RRI = 2) or WMU (RRI < 1). Thus, doves from the Mid-CMU appear to migrate directly south through Texas and into Mexico.

West CMU doves also tended to migrate straight south into Mexico. A dove from this subunit was about four to five times as likely to be recovered in Mexico (RRI = 25) as in the Mid-CMU (RRI = 7) or the WMU (RRI = 5).

In comparing the three subunits, it can be seen that doves from the East CMU tend to disperse in a wide fanlike migration pattern, both to the southwest and southeast (see *Figure 7*). In contrast, doves originating from the Mid-CMU and West CMU subunits migrate straight south through those subunits. Doves from the Mid-CMU and West CMU have equal likelihood of being recovered in Mexico and Central America (RRIs = 26 each) and are about 1.5 times as likely to be recovered there than are doves from the East CMU (RRI = 17). Somewhat surprisingly, the probability of a dove from any of the CMU subunits (and particularly the West CMU) being recovered in the WMU is quite low (RRIs ≤ 1). On the other hand, doves from the East CMU have a relatively high likelihood of being recovered in the EMU.

Distribution patterns were similar for adults and immatures. However, some differences were noted. For doves banded in the East CMU, immatures (RRI = 125) were about 1.7 times as likely as were adults to be recovered in the same subunit

(RRI = 74), and they were three times more likely than adults to be recovered in the EMU (RRIs = 41 and 14, respectively). Likewise, immatures were 1.4 times more likely than were adults to be recovered in Mexico and Central America (RRIs = 20 and 14, respectively). Both age cohorts demonstrated low probability of being recovered in the West CMU and the WMU.

For doves banded in the Mid-CMU, immatures and adults had equal likelihood of being recovered in that subunit (RRIs = 142 and 149, respectively). Although neither age group showed much tendency to go into the adjoining units (West CMU and East CMU), immatures were more likely to do so. The one big difference was that immatures were nearly 2.5 times as likely as adults to be recovered in Mexico and Central America (RRIs = 36 and 14, respectively). These data support the Dunks et al. (1982) conclusion that immatures either begin migration before adults do or that they are more likely to migrate farther than adults.

Similar results were noted for doves banded in the West CMU. Adults (RRI = 51) had a slightly higher tendency to be recovered in the subunit of banding than were immatures (RRI = 41) but had about equally low probability of being recovered in other subunits or units. However, as with doves from the Mid-CMU, immatures from the West CMU were 2.3 times as likely as adults to be recovered in Mexico and Central America (RRIs = 34 and 15, respectively).

In summary, doves that breed or are hatched in the CMU generally migrate south or southwest through the unit into Mexico and Central America. The exception is that a sizable proportion of doves from the East CMU migrates into the EMU. Even in this case, however, doves from the East CMU are nearly five times more likely to be recovered in the CMU than in the EMU (RRIs = 142 and 31, respectively). Thus, the present boundaries of the three management units appear to be well positioned to allow separate management of essentially independent dove populations.

Derivation of Harvest

Band-recovery data can be used to determine various areas of origin for doves reported from designated harvest areas. To achieve this, raw data must be weighted to account for differences in banding efforts among origination areas, as well as for varying sizes of the areas and densities of breeding doves within them. Dunks et al. (1982) calculated harvest derivation in the CMU and Mexico and Central America from direct recoveries of mourning doves banded during 1967–75. The following discussion is based on information modified from Dunks et al. (1982).

During the band-recovery period, eight of the fourteen CMU states permitted hunting and therefore were harvest areas. Of these, two (Missouri and Arkansas) were in the East CMU, four (South Dakota, Kansas, Oklahoma and Texas) were in the Mid-CMU and two (Colorado and New Mexico) were in the West CMU. Nearly 98 percent of all birds (immatures and adults combined) harvested in the CMU originated from within the unit; less than 2 percent were from the EMU, and less than 1 percent were from the WMU *(Table 63)*. This fact

Table 63. Weighted derivation[a] of the harvest (percentage) of mourning doves recovered in the Central Management Unit, 1967–76.

Age class	Recovery location	State of recovery	East CMU	Mid-CMU	West CMU	CMU	EMU	WMU
Immature	East CMU							
	Missouri	94.1	94.8	0.2	0.0	95.0	5.0	0.0
	Arkansas	94.8	96.1	0.0	0.0	96.1	3.9	0.0
	Subtotal	94.4	95.3	0.1	0.0	95.4	4.6	0.0
	Mid-CMU							
	South Dakota	96.2	0.4	99.3	0.0	99.7	0.3	0.0
	Kansas	89.4	6.2	93.0	0.3	99.5	0.5	0.0
	Oklahoma	87.4	4.9	94.2	0.8	99.9	0.1	0.0
	Texas	59.7	8.4	87.2	1.7	97.3	2.1	0.6
	Subtotal	70.3	7.0	89.9	1.3	98.1	1.5	0.4
	West CMU							
	Colorado	51.2	2.6	12.6	82.8	98.0	0.6	1.4
	New Mexico	48.9	1.4	23.4	71.1	95.8	0.0	4.2
	Subtotal	49.9	1.9	18.6	76.3	96.8	0.2	3.0
	CMU total	74.6	27.1	64.8	5.5	97.4	2.1	0.5
Adult	East CMU							
	Missouri	95.4	96.7	2.0	0.0	98.7	1.3	0.0
	Arkansas	95.1	99.0	0.0	0.0	99.0	1.0	0.0
	Subtotal	95.3	97.4	1.4	0.0	98.8	1.2	0.0
	Mid-CMU							
	South Dakota	99.3	0.4	99.3	0.3	100.0	0.0	0.0
	Kansas	95.1	1.1	98.6	0.0	99.7	0.3	0.0
	Oklahoma	94.4	2.5	97.5	0.0	100.0	0.0	0.0
	Texas	58.2	7.6	88.9	1.2	97.7	2.1	0.3
	Subtotal	74.7	4.9	93.1	0.7	98.7	1.2	0.1
	West CMU							
	Colorado	87.8	0.0	7.3	92.7	100.0	0.0	0.0
	New Mexico	75.3	0.0	10.9	89.1	100.0	0.0	0.0
	Subtotal	81.2	0.0	9.2	90.8	100.0	0.0	0.0
	CMU total	78.6	20.8	72.8	5.1	98.7	1.2	0.1
All doves	East CMU							
	Missouri	94.3	95.2	0.9	0.0	96.0	4.0	0.0
	Arkansas	94.4	96.4	0.0	0.0	96.4	3.6	0.0
	Subtotal	94.3	95.6	0.5	0.0	96.2	3.8	0.0
	Mid-CMU							
	South Dakota	97.5	0.4	99.3	0.2	99.8	0.2	0.0
	Kansas	93.7	3.2	96.3	0.1	99.6	0.4	0.0
	Oklahoma	90.4	4.2	95.3	0.5	99.9	0.1	0.0
	Texas	59.2	8.1	87.7	1.6	97.4	2.1	0.5
	Subtotal	72.7	6.0	91.2	1.0	98.3	1.4	0.3
	West CMU							
	Colorado	62.5	1.1	10.6	86.7	98.5	0.4	1.1
	New Mexico	57.5	0.8	17.9	79.0	97.6	0.0	2.4
	Subtotal	59.9	0.9	14.5	82.6	98.0	0.2	1.8
	CMU total	76.5	24.6	67.6	5.6	97.9	1.8	0.3

[a] Raw data were weighted by average breeding population indices (1967–75) and land area to derive estimated percentages for states, subunits and CMU.

reinforces the conclusion (using distribution data) that CMU doves remain within the unit during migration and seldom venture into either of the other management units. However, when examining the data by subunit within the CMU, an interesting phenomenon was discovered. Although most recoveries within a specific subunit originate within that subunit (e.g., 95.6 percent, East CMU; 91.2 percent, Mid-CMU; and 82.6 percent, West CMU), the proportion that originates outside each subunit comes almost entirely from adjacent units or subunits to the *east*. For example, of the 4.3 percent of recoveries that originate from outside the East CMU, 3.8 percent come from the EMU and less than 1 percent come from areas to the west. Thus, it appears that, within the CMU, mourning doves demonstrate a definite tendency to migrate south and southwest before entering Mexico. This phenomenon is consistent with the ultimate wintering location of many doves in western Mexico.

There were few differences in derivation patterns between age cohorts, although adults were more likely to be recovered in the state of banding than were immatures. This appeared to be particularly true for doves banded in the West CMU, where 81 percent of adults originated from the state of banding, whereas only 50 percent of immatures did. As with distribution data, the evidence suggests that immatures are more prone to migrate than are adults.

Of all doves banded in the United States and subsequently recovered in Mexico or Central America, 89 percent were reported from Mexico and 11 percent from Central America (Dunks et al. 1982). The Western Highlands of Mexico (consisting of the states of Jalisco, Michoacan, Guanajuato, Guerrero and Colima) were the predominant recovery location with 70 percent. Other important harvest locations were Mexico's Northwest Coast (9 percent), Central Highlands (5 percent) and Guatemala (5 percent). Thus, the major wintering area for doves from the United States appears to be Mexico's Western Highlands.

A weighted derivation was calculated for recoveries in Mexico and Central America of doves banded in the CMU *(Table 64)*. Of the 695 recoveries in Mexico, 69 percent originated from the Mid-CMU, 21 percent from the West CMU and 10 per-

Table 64. Weighted derivation of recoveries[a] in Latin America of mourning doves banded preseason in the Central Management Unit, 1967–74.

| Contributing area | Recovery area | | | | | |
| | Mexico | | | | | |
	Northwest Coast	Northern Highlands	Northeast Coast	Western Highlands	Central Highlands	Yucatán Peninsula
East CMU						
Minnesota	4 (3.5)	3 (10.6)	1 (4.9)	54 (3.9)	5 (3.9)	
Iowa				21 (2.8)	3 (4.3)	
Missouri		1 (10.6)	1 (14.9)	10 (2.1)	1 (2.4)	
Arkansas				4 (0.7)		
Subtotal	4 (3.5)	4 (21.2)	2 (19.8)	89 (9.4)	9 (10.6)	0 (0.0)
Mid-CMU						
North Dakota	2 (5.9)		1 (16.6)	25 (6.0)	4 (10.6)	
South Dakota	8 (9.3)	2 (9.4)	2 (13.1)	97 (9.2)	5 (5.2)	
Nebraska	2 (5.4)	2 (21.8)	1 (15.3)	63 (13.9)	6 (14.6)	
Kansas	3 (13.9)			32 (12.1)	3 (12.5)	
Oklahoma	3 (16.8)			34 (15.6)	5 (25.2)	
Texas	2 (5.0)	1 (10.1)	2 (28.4)	57 (11.7)	7 (15.8)	
Subtotal	20 (56.3)	5 (41.3)	6 (73.4)	308 (68.5)	30 (83.8)	0 (0.0)
West CMU						
Montana	3 (7.8)			38 (8.0)		
Wyoming	4 (12.9)			14 (3.7)		
Colorado	8 (9.7)	3 (14.7)	1 (6.8)	57 (5.6)	4 (4.3)	
New Mexico	7 (9.9)	4 (22.9)		41 (4.7)	1 (1.3)	
Subtotal	22 (40.2)	7 (37.5)	1 (6.8)	150 (22.1)	5 (5.6)	0 (0.0)
Total	46 (100.0)	16 (100.0)	9 (100.0)	547 (100.0)	44 (100.0)	0 (0.0)

[a] Percentage of total in parentheses.
[b] Includes 15 recoveries from unknown areas in Mexico.

cent from the East CMU. In contrast, of the 97 Central American recoveries, 79 percent originated in the Mid-CMU, only 3 percent from the West CMU and 18 percent from the East CMU. The Mid-CMU (especially Nebraska, Kansas, Oklahoma and Texas) was the most important contributing area for the Mexican and Central American harvest. The West CMU contributed moderately to the Mexican harvest but relatively little to the Central American harvest. This pattern was similar to that determined for the WMU (see chapter 19). It is concluded that doves from the WMU and West CMU migrate to the Western Highlands of Mexico, where they remain for the winter. Doves from the Mid-CMU and East CMU also winter in the Western Highlands but many continue into Central America.

Migration Chronology

Immature mourning doves begin congregating in flocks as early as late June. These flocks, including adults finished with nesting, reach peak numbers in late July and early August and migration

Table 64. (continued)

	Recovery area		
Mexico			
Southern	Mexico total[b]	Central America	Latin America
2 (3.9)	69 (3.9)	10 (3.7)	79 (3.8)
3 (10.9)	29 (3.0)	12 (8.1)	41 (3.7)
2 (11.8)	16 (2.7)	4 (4.4)	20 (2.9)
	4 (0.5)	2 (1.8)	6 (0.7)
7 (26.6)	118 (10.1)	28 (18.0)	146 (11.1)
1 (6.6)	33 (6.2)	12 (14.8)	45 (7.4)
3 (7.8)	121 (9.0)	16 (7.8)	137 (8.8)
2 (12.1)	76 (13.2)	10 (11.4)	86 (12.9)
1 (10.4)	40 (11.8)	13 (25.3)	53 (13.6)
2 (25.2)	47 (16.9)	4 (9.4)	51 (15.9)
2 (11.3)	72 (11.6)	10 (10.5)	82 (11.4)
11 (73.4)	389 (68.6)	65 (79.3)	454 (70.0)
	42 (7.0)	1 (1.1)	43 (6.2)
	18 (3.7)		18 (3.2)
	74 (5.7)	2 (1.0)	76 (5.1)
	54 (4.9)	1 (0.6)	55 (4.3)
0 (0.0)	188 (21.3)	4 (2.7)	192 (18.8)
	695 (100.0)	97 (100.0)	792 (99.9)
18 (100.0)			

begins during mid to late August (Truett 1966, Miles 1976, see also chapter 4). One method to determine the chronology of migration is to measure changes in the origin of doves harvested in a southern area as the season progresses. Dunks (1977) and Dunks et al. (1982) examined recovery dates of banded doves (adults and immatures combined) harvested in Texas. Texas is an area of heavy dove harvest that receives birds from every state in the CMU and several states outside the CMU. A segment of the state, identified as north Texas, was the only area in the CMU having sufficient numbers of recoveries over a wide span of time for which chronological derivations could be examined. The weighted origin of doves harvested in north Texas was calculated for each ten-day period in September and for the entire month of October. Only direct recoveries were used.

September 1–10. During this time, 72 percent of the harvested doves originated from within north Texas. Oklahoma contributed 16 percent, whereas Kansas and south Texas each contributed 3 percent; eleven other areas each contributed less that 1 percent. Although the contribution from areas outside north Texas was low, it is evident that migration had begun by early September.

September 11–20. For this span, 57 percent of the harvest originated from within north Texas, whereas 9 percent came from Oklahoma and 13 percent from Kansas. The twelve remaining CMU states contributed 20 percent of the harvest and the EMU contributed 1 percent. Thus, migration was well underway during mid-September.

September 21–30. For this time frame, the proportion of harvested doves originating from within north Texas declined to 35 percent. Other states from the CMU each contributed a higher proportion of the harvest (e.g., Oklahoma, 15 percent; Kansas, Nebraska and South Dakota, 9 percent each; North Dakota, 8 percent) and the EMU contributed about 1 percent. Migration apparently was in full swing during late September.

October 1–31. During this time period, 27 percent of the harvested doves originated from within north Texas. Oklahoma, Kansas, Nebraska, South Dakota, North Dakota and Iowa each contributed 9 to 10 percent. Minnesota and Missouri contributed 5 and 2 percent, respectively, and 3 percent came from the EMU. October thus represents a period when most doves from more northern CMU states have arrived at staging areas in Texas, either to find wintering areas or to migrate farther into Mexico and Central America.

Dunks et al. (1982) used a series of log likelihood ratio tests (see Sokol and Rohlf 1969) to test the hypothesis that immature and adult mourning doves have similar chronological recovery patterns in north Texas. They found that the patterns were different ($P<0.01$) and that the difference fell mainly within the September 1–10 period (accounting for 77 percent of the total chi-square value). Further testing led the investigators to conclude that immatures from the North arrived earlier in north Texas than did adults. This result provides further evidence that immatures begin migration earlier than adults do.

The chronology of direct recoveries in Mexico for doves banded in the CMU also was examined by Dunks et al. (1982). The arrival of CMU mourning doves in Mexico appeared to be well synchronized. Doves began arriving in Mexico during late September and early October. However, there was a marked increase in recoveries during October 11–20; recoveries during this period were three times that of October 1–10 and were the highest of all ten-day periods.

In summary, mourning doves from nearby states began entering Texas before September; the bulk of the population arrived later in September. Doves from more northern states began entering Texas in mid-September and the peak arrival period occurred in late September and October. Immature doves migrate earlier than adults. In Mexico, doves began arriving on wintering areas during September, but peak arrival dates were during mid-October.

Survival Estimates

Basic to understanding mourning dove population dynamics is survival rate—the probability (in percentage) that a banded bird will survive one calendar year. It is estimated using a set of stochastic computer models developed by Brownie et al. (1978) (see chapter 16). Dunks et al. (1982) calculated mourning dove survival rates for all CMU states that had sufficient data.

The unweighted average survival rate for adult females in the CMU was 51.0 percent; for adult males, it was 51.7 percent. Statistical tests indicated no difference in survival between the two sex cohorts, and the data were pooled. Although there was considerable variation among states (e.g., 65.1 percent for New Mexico and 31.5 percent for Arkansas) *(Figure 52)*, the unweighted average adult survival rate was 52.1 percent. Because there were no differences by sex for adults, it was assumed that no sex difference occurred for immatures as well (although, as discussed earlier, this assumption may be in error); therefore, data for all immatures also were pooled *(Figure 52)*. The average un-

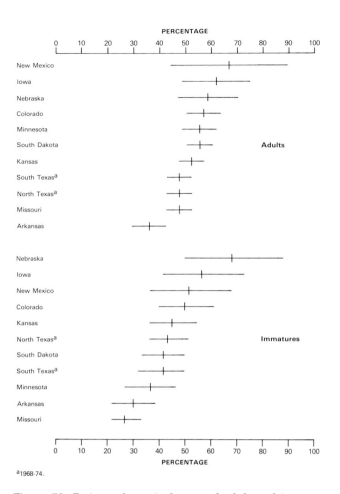

Figure 52. Estimated survival rates of adult and immature mourning doves banded in the Central Management Unit, 1967–74.

weighted immature survival rate in the CMU was 43.8 percent. A composite test indicated that survival rates of adults and immatures differed ($P<0.05$); of the eleven areas used in the test, adults survived at a higher rate than did immatures in all states but Nebraska.

To determine if survival differed among geographical areas of the CMU, survival rates for adults and immatures were examined by state in each subunit. In general, the variability by state in each subunit was so great that pooling the data for statistical analysis was precluded. Nevertheless, the unweighted average survival rates by subunit suggested that subunit differences may exist. For adults, average survival rates were: East CMU, 46.9 percent; Mid-CMU, 52.0 percent; and West CMU, 62.9 percent. For immatures, the average rates were 36.7, 47.1 and 49.7 percent, respectively. For both age cohorts, survival was progressively greater from east to west. Although the similarity may be coincidental, this result is consistent with trends indicated by the Call-count Survey (in which populations are declining in the East CMU, stable in the Mid-CMU and increasing in the West CMU).

Survival rates of adult and immature doves banded in CMU states that permitted hunting (Missouri, Kansas, Colorado, New Mexico, Oklahoma, Arkansas and Texas) were compared with those from the unit's nonhunting states (North Dakota, Minnesota, Nebraska and Iowa) (Dunks et al. 1982). The average survival rates of adult doves were 50.2 percent in hunting states and 58.1 percent in nonhunting states, and the average survival rates of immature doves were 40.2 and 52.9 percent in hunting and nonhunting states, respectively. For both age cohorts, the differences were significant ($P < 0.05$). These data suggest that mourning doves originating in hunting states have a lower survival rate than do doves from nonhunting states. A similar conclusion was reported for doves in the EMU by Hayne (1975). Dunks et al. (1982) cautioned, however, that results may indicate geographical differences in survival rates (north versus south) rather than differences attributable to hunting practices.

Hunting Mortality

Each year, hunting removes a large number of mourning doves from the population. In chapter 24, it is estimated that the average annual hunting harvest of mourning doves in the CMU was about 12.5 million birds during 1983–87. Knowledge of the relationship of hunting loss to total mortality can aid biologists and managers in developing annual harvest strategies. Dunks et al. (1982) employed an indirect method (see Geis 1972) to determine the proportion of the CMU dove population that died as a result of hunting. This method adjusts the direct recovery rate to account for bands that are encountered but not reported (reporting rate) and for birds that are downed by hunters but not retrieved (crippling rate). The resulting kill rate can be compared with annual mortality to determine the proportion of mortality directly attributable to hunting. However, because current knowledge of reporting rate for mourning doves is meager at best, the estimates given below are subject to error. For example, a reporting rate of 45 percent (see Reeves 1979) was used for the CMU exercise, whereas Tomlinson et al. (1988) used a rate of 32 percent (see Tomlinson 1968) for WMU calculations. The former rate is believed to be more suitable for doves in the CMU. But if not, the kill rate values are considerably underestimated.

Estimated kill rates for immature and adult doves banded during 1967–74 were 6.3 and 4.7 percent, respectively *(Table 65)*. Dividing these kill rates by the average estimated mortality rates for each age category, the estimated proportion of total mor-

Table 65. Hunting mortality in relation to total annual mortality of immature and adult mourning doves banded in the Central Management Unit, 1967–74.

Age class	Hunting states			Nonhunting states[d]	CMU total
	East CMU[a]	Mid-CMU[b]	West CMU[c]		
Immature					
Direct recovery rate	4.1	2.2	1.0	1.0	2.0
Harvest rate[e]	9.1	4.9	2.2	2.2	4.4
Kill rate[f]	13.0	7.0	3.1	3.1	6.3
Annual survival rate	27.9	41.9	49.7	52.9	43.8
Annual mortality rate	72.1	58.1	50.3	47.1	56.2
Percentage annual mortality attributed to hunting	18.0	12.0	6.2	6.6	11.2
Adult					
Direct recovery rate	2.2	2.0	0.9	0.7	1.5
Harvest rate[e]	4.9	4.4	2.0	1.6	3.3
Kill rate[f]	7.0	6.3	2.9	2.3	4.7
Annual survival rate	41.1	50.2	61.5	58.1	52.7
Annual mortality rate	58.9	49.8	38.5	41.9	47.3
Percentage annual mortality attributed to hunting	11.9	12.7	7.5	5.5	9.9

[a] Missouri and Arkansas.
[b] South Dakota, Kansas and Texas.
[c] Colorado and New Mexico.
[d] Minnesota, Iowa and Nebraska.
[e] Recovery rate ÷ band reporting rate = harvest rate; band reporting rate ≈ 45 percent (Reeves 1979).
[f] Harvest rate ÷ 1 − crippling rate = kill rate; crippling rate ≈ 30 percent.

tality due to hunting in the CMU was about 11 percent for immatures and 10 percent for adults. This means, of course, that most dove mortality during 1967–74 in the CMU resulted from nonhunting factors, such as weather, disease and predation.

Kill rates and mortality also were examined for doves from hunting states by subunit and for doves from nonhunting states in the CMU *(Table 65)*. For immatures from hunting states, kill rates were highest in the East CMU (13 percent), at midlevel in the Mid-CMU (7 percent) and lowest (3 percent) in the West CMU. The proportions of mortality due to hunting were 18, 12 and 6 percent, respectively. Thus, hunting mortality for immature doves in the East CMU was about 1.5 times greater than for immatures in the Mid-CMU and 3.0 times greater than for immatures in the West CMU. A similar pattern is seen for adult doves—the kill rate was highest in the East CMU (7 percent), next highest in the Mid-CMU (6 percent) and lowest in the West CMU (3 percent). However, for adults, Mid-CMU doves had a slightly higher proportion of mortality (13 percent) due to hunting than did doves in the East CMU (12 percent).

The kill rates for doves banded in nonhunting states of the CMU were 3 percent for immatures and 2 percent for adults. The proportions of annual mortality attributable to hunting were 7 percent for immatures and 6 percent for adults. These rates compare closely with those for doves from the West CMU, where hunting is light. Dunks et al. (1982) concluded that it is difficult to conceive that, given conditions during 1967–76, hunting adversely affected a dove population that sustained a hunting mortality that was only 10 to 12 percent of total mortality. We see no reason to modify that stance, although the situation in the East CMU (lowered population numbers) merits careful monitoring.

Production Required to Maintain Population

Dunks et al. (1982) computed the amount of production needed by each pair of mourning doves in the CMU to compensate for annual mortality and maintain a constant breeding population (average annual mortality rate of adult doves divided by average annual survival rate of immatures, then multiplied by 2). By state, the production requirement ranged from 1.2 (Nebraska) to 4.4 (Arkansas) young per pair of breeding adults and averaged 2.2 for the entire CMU. By subunit, the production rates for hunting states averaged 4.3 for the East CMU, 2.4 for the Mid-CMU and 1.7 for the West CMU, reflecting the differences in survival from east to west. For three nonhunting states (Minnesota, Iowa and Nebraska), the average production rate was 1.7, identical to that for hunting states of the West CMU.

A compilation of seventeen mourning dove nesting studies across the United States (U.S. Fish and Wildlife Service 1977) indicated that the average annual number of fledgings produced per pair of adults was 3.3 in northern latitude states, 4.4 in midlatitude states and 3.7 in southern latitude states. The estimated production required to maintain a stable population in the CMU generally seems to be within the measured capabilities reported in the literature. However, doves in Missouri and Arkansas may be near their upper productive

The Central Management Unit constitutes 46 percent of the coterminous United States. It has been shown to contain about 57 percent of the nation's total mourning dove breeding population. A key to management of the species is sustained productivity balanced against changing land uses, hunter harvest, other mortality factors and such variables as weather. It is a dynamic and sometimes fragile balance. Productivity to maintain stable mourning dove populations in the unit appears to be adequate at present, but more precise indicators and data are needed. *Photo (Rolling Plains of Texas) by Wyman Meinzer.*

capacity to balance the high mortality indicated for those states. Additional mourning dove nesting studies are needed in areas such as the East CMU to provide more precise and up-to-date information.

HUNTING AND HARVEST

Mourning dove hunting is a popular sport in the CMU, particularly in Texas, Oklahoma and Kansas. Dove populations have been high and well distributed within the unit, and hunters normally have little trouble finding large numbers of birds to hunt. In 1990, twelve of the fourteen CMU states permitted dove hunting, with only Minnesota and Iowa remaining as nonhunting states. Seven CMU states (Missouri, Arkansas, Kansas, Oklahoma, Texas, Colorado and New Mexico) have extensive dove hunting traditions, but even those states with shorter traditions now have allowed dove hunting for five years or longer. In some cases, such as in North and South Dakota, the effort of establishing dove seasons was long and arduous because of opposition from antihunting groups and many individuals who believed that doves should be classified as songbirds. In South Dakota, dove seasons were allowed for five years (1968–72), but oppositionists succeeded in blocking the seasons for eight years. Finally, a state referendum was won and dove hunting now has been permitted in South Dakota since 1981. Thus, dove hunting in the CMU is a well-established recreation.

Dove hunting in the CMU is conducted similarly to that in other parts of the country. Participants generally hunt over harvested grainfields and at stock tanks or other water sources. Except in the West CMU, where extensive public landholdings occur, most hunting takes place on privately owned land. Most landowners readily grant permission to hunt on their land when asked in advance by prospective hunters. However, because of negligence and vandalism on the part of some hunters, a growing reluctance to grant permission by some landowners has been noted within the past two decades. This problem appears to be growing and must be countered if mourning dove hunting is to continue as a pleasurable pastime. An increasing practice among landowners, particularly in Texas, is to establish daily or seasonal leases for hunting. Although this practice originated for deer hunting in the 1920s, it has only become common for mourning and white-winged dove hunting during the past twenty years (Teer and Forrest 1968). Fees for daily mourning dove hunting leases in Texas usually range from $15 to $25; in south Texas, where whitewings also are hunted, the daily cost can reach $50 (R. George personal communication: 1991, see chapter 25).

Unfortunately, mourning dove harvest data are not collected in one coordinated and standardized survey; rather, most state wildlife agencies run individual surveys, using highly divergent sampling and analysis procedures. These data were obtained from the individual state agencies and summarized for the United States (see chapter 24) and for the

In or along grain crop fields and in the vicinity of small surface water sources, such as stock tanks and stock ponds, are favored sites to hunt mourning doves in the Central Management Unit. *Photos by Ron George; courtesy of the Texas Parks and Wildlife Department.*

Table 66. Estimated numbers of mourning dove hunters in the Central Management Unit, as measured by state surveys, 1966–87.

	Number of mourning dove hunters							
	East CMU			Mid-CMU				
Year	Missouri	Arkansas	Total East CMU	North Dakota	South Dakota	Nebraska	Kansas	Oklahoma
1966							67,000	40,805
1967	52,885						63,300	50,128
1968	55,474				8,860		66,100	52,536
1969	63,741				11,340		74,500	66,455
1970	66,062				14,300		74,200	71,784
1971	74,030				13,800		81,200	57,728
1972	81,151				14,820		85,900	66,264
1973	79,705						78,200	55,111
1974	81,436						94,300	59,744
1975	84,054					60,667	86,000	53,724
1976	90,495					49,959	89,700	62,729
1977	70,841					43,159	89,200	55,863
1978	67,022					44,467	89,300	69,940
1979	68,967			21,870		42,425	98,700	94,629
1980	70,934			24,845		42,413	104,100	61,772
1981	71,920			23,525	23,720	41,095	103,000	85,915
1982	67,931			24,535	21,530	41,158	107,300	88,960
1983	63,779	52,286	116,065	17,340	20,300		104,900	77,155
1984	61,218	33,549	94,767	17,165	21,260		85,900	67,372
1985	55,576			15,430	14,560	35,987	84,200	78,183
1986	56,333			14,802	15,350	32,500	91,291	73,973[a]
1987	67,600			15,018	10,800	33,197	83,100	78,325[a]
Average:								
1966–87	69,103	42,918	112,020	19,392	15,887	42,457	86,427	66,777
1983–87	60,901	42,918	103,819	15,951	16,454	33,895	89,878	75,002

[a] Change in survey methods.

CMU (*tables 66 to 68*) to obtain a rough estimation of hunting intensity and harvest. Using data for the five-year period 1983–87 (see *Table 90*), an average of 782,000 hunters annually harvested 12.5 million doves in the CMU, compared with 1.3 million hunters and 28.5 million doves in the EMU and 304,000 hunters and 4.6 million doves in the WMU. The average seasonal harvest during 1983–87 was 16.1 doves per hunter in the CMU, 21.2 in the EMU and 15.0 in the WMU. Despite larger dove populations in the CMU, the annual harvest is less than half that attained in the EMU. This is no doubt a reflection of human population size and heavier hunting pressure in the latter unit. On the other hand, Texas, with an average 393,000 dove hunters and a harvest of 5.2 million doves per year, has the largest dove harvest of any single state in the nation.

Because several CMU states did not permit dove hunting continuously between 1966 and 1987, and others did not conduct harvest surveys, hunter and harvest data within the unit were fragmented. Therefore, evaluation of trends by unit or subunit was impossible. To illustrate hunter and harvest

changes over time, four states were selected because of their constancy of data: Missouri in the East CMU; Kansas and Oklahoma in the Mid-CMU; and Colorado in the West CMU. The following discussion assesses these parameters and attempts to relate them to the subunit in which each state lies.

Hunter Numbers

An average of nearly 750,000 hunters participated in dove hunting in the CMU during 1966–87 (*Table 66*). As expected, the largest proportion of dove hunters occurred in the Mid-CMU (77 percent), and particularly in Texas (46 percent). For the unit as a whole, the number of hunters appears to have remained relatively constant throughout the twenty-two-year period.

East CMU. Hunter numbers in Missouri steadily increased from 1967 to 1976 (r = 0.97, 8 d.f., $P < 0.01$), dropped precipitously in 1977 and generally declined thereafter (r = −0.74, 10 d.f., $P < 0.01$) (*Figure 53*). A linear regression analysis was em-

Table 66. (continued)

| | Mid-CMU | | West CMU | | | | | |
	Texas	Total Mid-CMU	Montana	Wyoming	Colorado	New Mexico	Total West CMU	Total CMU
					25,226	17,350		
					24,593	17,025		
					25,186	19,873		
	441,127				25,119	22,966		
	339,178				24,146	23,055		
	318,166				22,033	24,476		
	308,000				33,299	23,093		
	237,854			2,067	31,688	28,269		
	203,274			3,465	41,500	26,804		
				4,182	40,672	28,670		
				4,903	34,321	23,742		
				4,875	33,074	26,635		
				4,085	25,077	24,952		
				5,429	32,295	28,966		
				5,975	31,476	24,034		
	408,866	686,121		6,104	35,744	32,173		
	427,251	710,734		6,216	33,934	11,238		
			175	6,947	35,398	21,276	63,796	
			540	5,975	30,739	17,543[a]	54,797	
			565	5,512	30,218	12,687[a]	48,982	
	389,307	617,223	539	4,956	26,983	18,560[a]	51,038	
	397,210	617,650	563	4,368	26,386			
	347,023	577,963	476	5,004	30,414	22,542	58,437	748,420
	393,259	624,438	476	5,552	29,945	17,517	53,489	781,746

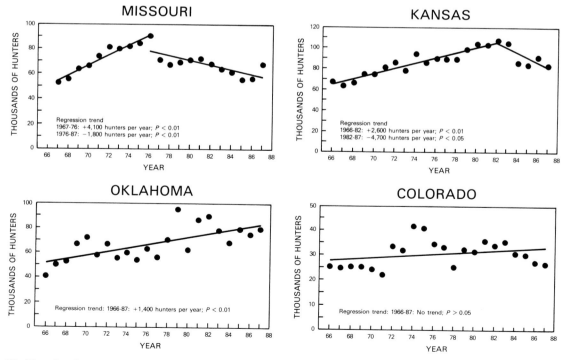

Figure 53. Trends of mourning dove hunters in Missouri, Kansas, Oklahoma and Colorado, based on state harvest surveys, 1966–87.

Table 67. Estimated average annual harvest of mourning doves per hunter in the Central Management Unit, as measured by state surveys, 1966–87.

| | Average number of mourning doves per hunter | | | | | | | |
| | East CMU | | | Mid-CMU | | | | |
Year	Missouri	Arkansas	Average East CMU	North Dakota	South Dakota	Nebraska	Kansas	Oklahoma
1966							20.6	19.7
1967	13.6						16.0	24.7
1968	15.1				11.9		17.9	26.0
1969	17.9				14.1		17.6	20.6
1970	15.4				14.9		17.6	23.7
1971	16.8				14.9		16.8	22.4
1972	17.1				15.3		18.1	26.0
1973	19.0						17.1	25.0
1974	16.9						17.7	24.8
1975	18.2					13.8	16.8	23.8
1976	19.0					17.7	18.9	25.8
1977	16.3					19.4	18.1	22.2
1978	15.1					22.5	19.5	24.6
1979	14.6			4.3		19.7	19.6	23.5
1980	16.2			4.3		19.9	18.4	24.6
1981	16.4			5.2	16.7	21.6	20.5	29.9
1982	16.9			6.4	15.4	17.9	20.6	27.2
1983	17.8	20.3	18.9[a]	4.7	19.7		23.1	25.6
1984	15.1	17.9	15.7[a]	4.8	16.3		19.2	21.7
1985	14.4			4.8	15.1	18.1	18.8	22.9
1986	15.2			6.3	13.5	16.8	18.6	28.0[b]
1987	17.8			5.7	13.7	17.0	18.2	25.1[b]
Average:								
1966–87	16.4	19.1	17.5[a]	5.2	15.1	18.6	18.6	24.4
1983–87	16.1	19.1	17.5[a]	5.3	15.7	17.3	19.6	24.7

[a] Total harvest in unit divided by total number hunters.
[b] Change in survey methods.

ployed to compare the Missouri dove Call-count indices with numbers of hunters over time. From 1967 to 1976, there was a moderate negative correlation between the two parameters (r = −0.65, 8 d.f., $P < 0.05$); from 1976 to 1987, there was a similar positive correlation (r = 0.68, 10 d.f., $P < 0.05$). This is interpreted to mean that, during the early years, despite declining dove populations, hunters in Missouri found sufficient numbers of doves to encourage increased hunting activity. But in 1976, mourning dove populations had decreased such that many hunters discontinued hunting doves. Although the underlying causes for the population decline are unknown, dove hunting appears to have been adversely affected. Lacking data for Arkansas (the only other hunting state in the East CMU), it is assumed that the same factors affected hunter participation there as well.

Mid-CMU. For Kansas, the number of hunters increased from 1966 to 1982 (r = 0.95, 15 d.f., $P < 0.01$) and decreased from 1982 to 1987 (r = −0.81, 4 d.f., $P < 0.05$) *(Figure 53)*. However, the overall trend for the twenty-two-year period was increasing (r = 0.70, 20 d.f., $P < 0.01$). When com-

pared with Call-count data for 1966–87 (excluding 1978, when an abnormally low average Call-count was recorded), there was a positive correlation (r = 0.45, 19 d.f., $P < 0.05$). Thus, the Kansas Call-count Survey can be used with moderate success to predict hunting pressure in any specific year. The large and stable breeding populations in Kansas appear to support the present level of hunting pressure.

In Oklahoma, the numbers of hunters increased from about forty-one thousand to nearly eighty thousand between 1966 and 1987 (r = 0.69, 20 d.f., $P < 0.01$) *(Figure 53)*. During the same period, breeding populations reflected by the Call-count Survey fluctuated widely with a hint of a decline during 1962–87 (−2.7 percent per year, $P < 0.10$). Essentially no correlation was found between the two data sets (r = −0.14, 20 d.f., $P > 0.05$). This is interpreted to mean that the relatively secure breeding population in Oklahoma was able to support increasing hunting pressure over the twenty-two-year period with no apparent difficulty.

Incomplete data from other hunting states of the Mid-CMU indicate that hunter numbers gener-

Table 67. (continued)

Mid-CMU		West CMU					Average CMU
Texas	Average Mid-CMU	Montana	Wyoming	Colorado	New Mexico	Average West CMU	
					12.8		
					11.8		
				12.3	13.3		
21.6				12.9	11.2		
20.4				12.4	12.6		
22.3				13.6	11.4		
16.7				15.4	11.5		
20.6			7.7	15.3	11.1		
23.6			8.8	16.6	12.9		
			10.3	15.7	14.9		
			11.2	14.4	13.1		
			11.7	14.9	12.4		
			10.3	15.4	13.5		
			11.0	14.7	14.5		
16.5	18.7[a]		11.5	15.0	12.1		
16.4	18.1[a]		11.8	15.0	15.2		
			11.2	14.9	15.0		
		2.6	11.0	14.8	14.8	17.2[a]	
		7.4	10.7	12.6	30.9[b]	18.2[a]	
13.1	15.7[a]	8.7	10.1	14.7	31.2[b]	18.4[a]	
13.4	15.5[a]	9.8	9.4	13.3	29.8[b]	18.8[a]	
		11.0	10.2	13.4			
18.5	18.4[a]	7.9	10.5	14.4	15.5	14.4[a]	18.0[a]
13.3	15.6[a]	7.9	10.3	13.8	26.7	18.2[a]	16.1[a]

ally have remained constant or increased over the twenty-two-year period. It is concluded that dove populations were stable in the subunit and the increased hunting pressure had no adverse effects on these populations.

West CMU. Dove hunting in Colorado is a relatively minor pastime. Between 1966 and 1987, the number of dove hunters in Colorado varied widely, from a low of about twenty-two thousand in 1971 to a high of nearly forty-two thousand in 1974, and averaged thirty thousand. No overall increasing or decreasing trend was detected ($r = 0.30$, 20 d.f., $P > 0.05$) *(Figure 53)*. During the same period of time, the breeding population increased significantly (4.4 percent per year, $P < 0.01$). When the two parameters were compared by linear regression, no correlation was obtained ($r = 0.18$, 20 d.f., $P > 0.05$). The increasing dove populations in Colorado apparently were insufficient to lure hunters away from the other hunting opportunities in the state.

In Montana, Wyoming and New Mexico, mourning dove populations and numbers of hunters were generally stable over the twenty-two-year period. As in Colorado, hunting pressure was light. Hunting pressure on doves in the West CMU probably could be increased substantially without affecting the breeding population.

Seasonal Harvest

The seasonal harvest (number of birds harvested per hunter per year) provides an index to hunter success over time. During the period 1966–87, the seasonal harvest in the CMU averaged 18.0 doves per hunter *(Table 67)*. Generally, hunters in the Mid-CMU reported the highest seasonal harvest (e.g., 24.4 in Oklahoma, 18.6 in Kansas and Nebraska, and 18.5 in Texas), whereas those in the West CMU reported the lowest (e.g., 7.9 in Montana and 10.5 in Wyoming). Latitude of hunting locations also was instrumental in hunting success, with less success in northern areas and more success in midlatitudinal and southern areas. For example, North Dakota and Montana exhibited the lowest seasonal bags, whereas Kansas, Oklahoma and Texas exhibited the highest *(Table 67)*. Because mourning doves begin migration during late August, hunting opportunity in northern areas

Table 68. Estimated numbers of mourning doves harvested in the Central Management Unit, as measured by state surveys, 1966–87.

	East CMU			Mid-CMU				
Year	Missouri	Arkansas	Total East CMU	North Dakota	South Dakota	Nebraska	Kansas	Oklahoma
1966							1,378.0	803.2
1967	719.8						1,013.0	1,238.2
1968	837.9				105.6		1,183.0	1,365.9
1969	1,138.3				160.0		1,312.0	1,369.0
1970	1,016.1				213.2		1,304.0	1,701.3
1971	1,243.2				205.4		1,363.0	1,293.1
1972	1,387.3				226.9		1,556.0	1,722.9
1973	1,517.2						1,333.0	1,377.8
1974	1,378.1						1,668.0	1,481.6
1975	1,528.5					839.6	1,448.0	1,278.6
1976	1,716.9					884.8	1,694.0	1,618.4
1977	1,151.0					838.9	1,612.0	1,240.2
1978	1,021.1					1,001.0	1,739.0	1,718.4
1979	1,008.0			93.8		836.0	1,933.0	2,222.1
1980	1,146.5			107.3		842.8	1,916.0	1,521.8
1981	1,181.9			122.1	395.9	886.2	2,115.0	2,568.9
1982	1,147.5			158.0	332.0	735.3	2,208.0	2,416.5
1983	1,134.4	1,061.4	2,195.9	81.0	399.9		2,400.0	1,975.6
1984	922.8	565.1	1,487.9	82.9	346.5		1,647.0	1,461.4
1985	882.6			74.1	219.9	652.0	1,586.0	1,794.1
1986	854.5			93.8	207.2	546.9	1,697.0	2,071.0[a]
1987	1,202.5			85.3	147.7	567.9	1,500.0	1,968.1[a]
Average:								
1966–87	1,149.3	813.3	1,962.6	99.8	246.7	784.7	1,618.4	1,645.8
1983–87	999.4	813.3	1,812.6	83.4	264.2	588.9	1,766.0	1,854.0

[a] Change in survey methods.

essentially is limited to the first ten to fifteen days of September. In southern locales, doves usually are present in numbers throughout the hunting season.

Except for Kansas, which registered an increasing trend in seasonal bag ($r = 0.46$, 20 d.f., $P < 0.05$), states in the CMU demonstrated little evidence of increasing or decreasing trends during the twenty-two-year period *(Figure 54)*. The intermittent data from Texas indicate that hunting success may have declined in that state. Generally, however, seasonal harvest of mourning doves throughout the unit was stable, even in Missouri where dove populations have declined.

Linear regression comparisons of Call-count data and seasonal harvest were made for Missouri, Kansas, Oklahoma and Colorado. For Kansas, the increasing Call-count trends and seasonal harvests (excluding data for 1978) correlated positively ($r = 0.56$, 19 d.f., $P < 0.01$); for the other three states, no correlations were obtained ($P > 0.05$). It is concluded that hunters in the Mid-CMU and West CMU subunits were successful in locating and harvesting doves during the twenty-two-year period and that population numbers were sufficiently high

to support the level of harvest exhibited. For Missouri (representing the East CMU), hunter participation declined during 1967–87, although those hunters who persisted sustained pre-1976 individual hunting success. As previously noted, the long-term decline in Missouri mourning dove populations is assumed to have precipitated the drop in hunter participation. However, because the average seasonal bag remained constant throughout the twenty-two-year period, other factors (e.g., increased costs of hunting and difficulty in attaining access to shooting fields) also may have contributed to the decline in hunter numbers.

Harvest

During 1966–87, hunters in the CMU harvested nearly 13.5 million mourning doves per year *(Table 68)*. Texas hunters were by far the greatest harvesters of doves in the unit with 6.3 million (47 percent), followed by Oklahoma and Kansas with 1.6 million (12 percent) each. With annual harvests of 4,000 (trace) and 53,000 (0.4 percent) mourning doves, Montana and Wyoming hunters, respec-

Table 68. (continued)

Mid-CMU		West CMU					Total CMU
						Number of mourning doves harvested (×1,000)	
Texas	Total Mid-CMU	Montana	Wyoming	Colorado	New Mexico	Total West CMU	Total CMU
					222.5		
					201.4		
				308.9	263.9		
9,541.0				323.8	256.9		
6,931.0				301.6	289.5		
7,106.0				298.8	277.8		
5,154.0				513.9	265.0		
4,902.6			15.9	484.7	312.3		
4,799.1			30.5	688.3	346.3		
			43.2	639.9	247.6		
			54.7	492.9	310.5		
			57.2	493.6	336.4		
			42.2	385.7	337.6		
			59.3	473.6	418.6		
			68.6	473.1	290.4		
6,748.5	12,836.6		72.1	535.2	488.7		
7,010.5	12,860.2		69.7	506.6	168.4		
		0.5	76.5	525.2	493.3	1,095.5	
		4.0	63.7	387.4	541.9[a]	997.0	
		4.9	55.5	446.3	395.6[a]	902.3	
5,087.6	9,703.6	5.3	46.8	358.3	550.9[a]	961.3	
5,327.4	9,596.4	6.2	44.6	354.7			
6,260.8	10,656.2	4.2	53.4	449.6	334.1	841.2	13,460.0
5,207.5	9,764.1	4.2	57.4	414.4	495.4	971.4	12,548.1

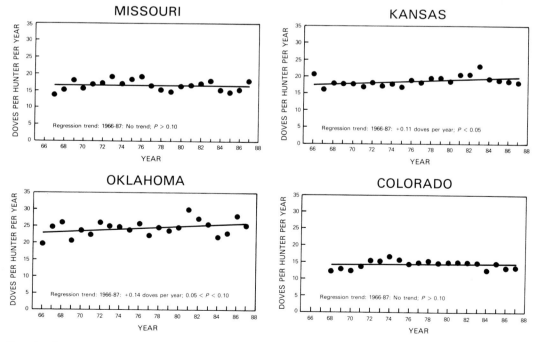

Figure 54. Trends of average number of mourning doves harvested per hunter per year in Missouri, Kansas, Oklahoma and Colorado, based on state harvest surveys, 1966–87.

tively, took the fewest.

Harvest, calculated as the product of the number of hunters and the seasonal harvest, obviously reflects the trends of those statistics. Because seasonal harvests in the CMU (Missouri, Kansas, Oklahoma and Colorado) were essentially stable during 1966–87, overall harvest trends in the CMU were nearly identical to trends in hunter numbers. Thus, prior discussion about hunters also pertains to harvest. Dove harvest in Missouri increased from 1967 to 1976, fell precipitously in 1977, and remained relatively constant at the lower level from 1977 to 1987. The Kansas and Oklahoma dove harvests both increased substantially throughout the twenty-two-year period. However, there appears to have been a general decline in harvest throughout the Mid-CMU between 1981–84, followed by a modest increase since. The Colorado dove harvest varied substantially by year, with no increasing or decreasing trend noted.

Summary

The level of mourning dove hunting pressure varied widely among states within the CMU during 1966–87, with the highest in Mid-CMU states and the lowest in West CMU states. Indications are that numbers of hunters, seasonal harvest and total harvest in the East CMU (as reflected by Missouri data) have declined as a result of decreased dove population numbers. Conversely, increasing or stable dove populations in the Mid-CMU (Kansas and Oklahoma) have resulted in sustained high hunter numbers and harvest during the twenty-two-year period. In the West CMU (Colorado), stable or increasing dove populations have been lightly harvested.

CONCLUSIONS AND OUTLOOK

Mourning doves nest in nearly all habitat types of the vast area that comprises the CMU. For the most part, they have adapted to changes wrought by humans and have maintained their populations at high levels.

As measured by the nationwide Call-count Survey, breeding densities of mourning doves in the CMU are higher than anywhere in the country. The Mid-CMU has the highest densities, averaging 31 doves heard per route and ranging from 19 in Texas to 52 in Kansas. For states in both the East CMU and West CMU, densities average about 19 birds heard per route. An estimated overall mourning dove breeding population of approximately 129 mil-

lion adults annually produces an autumn population of about 271 million birds.

Migration begins during August and concludes in October. Generally, doves produced in the CMU migrate to areas within the unit or to Mexico, and of the doves recovered in the CMU, less than 2 percent originate from outside the unit. Thus, CMU mourning dove populations essentially are independent of those from other units. There are some exceptions to this rule, particularly in the East CMU. Doves from the East CMU have a bifurcate migrational pattern, with most birds going southwest into Texas and Mexico but a sizable segment moving southeast into the Carolinas, Georgia, Florida and Alabama. Mid-CMU doves generally migrate south or southwest into Texas, Mexico and Central America. Most West CMU doves also migrate straight south into Mexico, although a small proportion of the recoveries are reported from the WMU. Major wintering areas for CMU doves are Texas, the Western Highlands of Mexico, and Central America.

The overall status of mourning doves in the CMU is good. Call-count data indicate that the unitwide population was essentially stable during 1966–87 (-0.05 percent per year, $P<0.10$). However, doves in two areas of the unit have experienced a long-term decline: (1) Iowa, Missouri and Arkansas in the East CMU (-2.3 percent per year, $P<0.01$); and (2) portions of Montana, Wyoming and Colorado west of the Continental Divide (probability varies by physiographic region). The indicated declines in western portions of the West CMU appear to be extensions of declines experienced by mourning doves in the WMU, but the annual indices are so variable that it is difficult to tell how severe the declines are. Conversely, decreased mourning dove populations in the East CMU are real and at levels that are cause for concern. At the present time, causes of the declines are unknown, but efforts are underway to identify reasons for this perplexing problem.

Because of the fact that agricultural cropping practices have changed over the years, some preliminary comparisons were made of trends in doves heard calling and crop acreages by year in Missouri during 1966–83 (U.S. Fish and Wildlife Service [Albuquerque, New Mexico] unpublished data). During those eighteen years, Missouri farmers gradually increased soybean production and decreased corn production to meet economic demand. If these changed agricultural practices were responsible for declining dove populations, one would expect a positive correlation of Call-counts with acres of corn harvest (a good dove food source) and a negative correlation with acres of soy-

Center-pivot irrigation is a significant agricultural practice in the Central and Western management units. It has enabled production of grain crops on lands heretofore unsuitable for agriculture and allowed more efficient use of irrigation waters. Shelterbelts along margins are particularly attractive to doves as shelter and for nesting, but plantings as depicted in the photo are fairly uncommon. On the down side, expanded farming operations availed by center-pivot irrigation have contributed to water shortages, water table drawdown and a tenuous economy in many parts of the unit, to the potential detriment of wildlife management in general. *Photo (Nebraska) by E. W. Cole; courtesy of the U.S. Soil Conservation Service.*

In recent decades, brush control and phreophyte eradication programs to improve pastureland for livestock have reduced important nesting habitat for mourning doves in the Central Management Unit. The removal of shelterbelts in the unit, to accommodate increased acreage for cultivation, has had the same consequence for doves. *Photo by Don Domenick; courtesy of the Colorado Division of Wildlife.*

beans harvested (beans not consumed by doves). Indeed, there was a positive correlation of corn harvest and Call-count indices ($r = 0.61$, 15 d.f., $P < 0.05$) and a strong negative correlation of soybean harvest and Call-count indices ($r = -0.70$, 15 d.f., $P < 0.01$). These comparisons suggested that increased production of soybeans and concurrent decreased corn production may have adversely affected mourning dove populations in Missouri.

A more comprehensive comparison of dove Call-count indices and agricultural factors was conducted by a special subcommittee of the Central Shore and Upland Game Bird Technical Committee (George et al. 1987). Trends in acreages of the ten leading crops, size of farms and number of farms were compared with trends in numbers of doves heard calling over a twenty-year period (1966–85) in Minnesota, Iowa, Missouri, Arkansas and Texas. Although correlations of doves heard and corn and soybean production were verified for Missouri, the same comparisons indicated little consistent agreement among other states in the tests. Of all individual agricultural factors considered, the number of farms (positive) and size of farms (negative)

In the Central Management Unit, a trend since the late 1950s toward fewer and larger farms, with associated losses of shelterbelts and weedy fencerows, has been implicated as a causal factor in the unit's decreasing mourning dove population. *Top photo (North Dakota) by B. C. McLean; courtesy of the U.S. Soil Conservation Service. Bottom photo (Nebraska) by W. J. Stuart; courtesy of the U.S. Soil Conservation Service.*

appeared to be correlated most consistently with doves heard over time. The trend to fewer and larger farms, with the attendant loss of shelterbelts and weedy fencerows, almost certainly have had adverse impacts on mourning doves during the past two decades. Other than that, the tests used were unable to isolate any other consistent agricultural factor that may have been responsible for dove declines in the East CMU.

There is a strong dove hunting tradition in the CMU. During 1985–90, twelve of the fourteen states permitted hunting (only Minnesota and Iowa did not). On average, 12.5 million doves were harvested each year in the CMU, of which 5.2 million were in Texas (42 percent), 1.8 million in Oklahoma (14 percent), 1.8 million in Kansas (14 percent) and 1 million in Missouri (8 percent). Only four states in the CMU had sufficient data with which to compare harvest trends. Colorado, in the West CMU, demonstrated a variable but generally stable trend in annual harvest between 1966 and 1987. Harvests in Kansas and Oklahoma (Mid-CMU) increased significantly. For Missouri (East CMU), harvest increased from 1966–76, decreased sharply in 1977 and remained low thereafter.

When long-term population declines are detected, such as that noted in the East CMU, a logical question is whether hunting was a causative factor. For example, survival rates for doves in nonhunting states of the CMU were significantly higher than for doves in hunting states. Since Minnesota and Iowa do not permit hunting, and because doves from neither contribute significantly to the harvests in Missouri and Arkansas, it is unlikely that hunting was responsible for decreasing dove populations in those two states. Unfortunately, dove banding data for Missouri and Arkansas were available only for the first nine to ten years of the 1966–87 period. Nevertheless, these data suggest that hunting cannot be ruled out as a contributing factor, at least during the early years. For these two states, survival rates for adults (41 percent) and immatures (28 percent) were significantly lower than for doves from hunting states of the other two subunits. Furthermore, the kill rates, particularly for immatures, were higher than for doves from other subunits. Although the proportion of mortality attributable to hunting for adult doves (12 percent) from Missouri and Arkansas was about equal to that for the Mid-CMU (13 percent), the same proportion for immatures (18 percent) was 1.5 times that of the Mid-CMU and 3.0 times that of the West CMU.

Regardless of whether hunting has had an effect on dove populations in hunting states of the East CMU, overall mortality was so high during 1967–76 that the production required to counteract it was 4.3 young per pair of breeding adults. This rate compares with 2.4 and 1.7 young per pair in hunting states of the Mid-CMU and West CMU, respectively, and 1.7 for nonhunting states of the unit. The documented nest success determined from nesting studies throughout the United States (four young per pair) indicates that, at least during the period covered, breeding dove populations in Missouri and Arkansas may have failed to balance mortality through production.

The Central Migratory Shore and Upland Game Bird Technical Committee has sponsored a four-year study in Missouri designed to answer some of the questions about decreasing dove populations. The investigation, initiated in 1990, has the objective of developing the tools necessary to: (1) assess the impact of local hunting pressure on subsequent survival rates of adult mourning doves; (2) determine local dove population size; (3) determine the response of the local dove population to exploitation; and (4) obtain estimates on the parameters of annual survival rates, period survival rates, local

harvest rates, annual harvest rates, period population size, annual recruitment rates and nest densities. The studies will be conducted on nonhunted areas as well as on hunted areas. Results and associated costs will be evaluated; if feasible, a further six-year unitwide investigation will be recommended. The preliminary study is unique in that costs are to be shared by several CMU states, a few states from outside the unit, and the U.S. Fish and Wildlife Service. The Wildlife Management Institute will serve as the disbursing agent to the Missouri Department of Conservation for work completed under the project agreement. It is hoped that this study will shed some light on the aforementioned problems.

Agricultural use of pesticides and herbicides has burgeoned during the past twenty-five years. Although DDT was banned in 1972, many substitute substances have since been approved for use. A particularly toxic form of pesticide to songbirds is the family of granular insecticides containing active ingredients of terbufos, carbofuran, fonofos and phorate (Balcomb et al. 1984). The granules are seed-sized (10 to 50 mesh) and produced under names such as Dasinit, Furadan and Temik. These products are used widely on corn, cotton, rice, soybeans, sorghum and other crops in the United States. Field corn is the most heavily treated crop. Although regulations require soil incorporation (covering of granules), currently used farm equipment can leave granules exposed in the field. Because of their size, doves and other small birds feeding in fields could and probably do ingest the granules. Onset of symptoms of anticholinesterase poisoning and death upon ingestion are rapid. Balcomb et al. (1984) found that the carbamates Furadan, Tattoo and Temik caused death within nine to eighteen minutes for house sparrows and red-winged blackbirds. One to five granules were sufficient to cause death to more than 80 percent of the test individuals. Thus, the widespread use of granular pesticides should certainly be investigated as a possible cause for high mortality in mourning doves of the East CMU and other areas.

Diseases such as trichomoniasis can cause epidemic mortality in mourning doves (Haugen and Keeler 1952). However, no widespread trichomoniasis outbreak is known to have been evident in the CMU during the past twenty-five years. It is doubtful that disease has been a major mortality factor for doves in the East CMU.

Loss of nesting habitat through clearing of hedgerows and other forested areas could be responsible for dove declines. As mentioned earlier, the trend to fewer and larger farms correlated positively with dove declines in the East CMU. In 1988, however, an area of intensive dove study in Missouri during the 1950s (Tomlinson et al. 1960) was revisited, and little if any change in the nesting habitat was noted. The Missouri Department of Conservation plans an investigation of habitat changes in conjunction with the survival and production study described above.

Encouraging notes are that: (1) Call-count data for 1985–91 for Iowa, Missouri and Arkansas (1988–91 data not included in *tables 56 to 58*) indicate a modest increasing short-term trend in breeding doves; and (2) harvest in Missouri increased during 1987–89. These facts give rise to cautious optimism about the future of mourning dove populations in the East CMU.

Generally, the density and size of mourning dove populations in the CMU are high and the trend is stable. The number of hunters and the harvest of mourning doves are increasing, but neither appears to be affecting the population adversely, at least for the greater part of the unit. No other major limiting factors have been detected. Thus, the foreseeable future is envisioned as one of continued well-being for the mourning dove in the midsection of the United States.

Chapter 19

Population Characteristics and Trends in the Western Management Unit

Henry M. Reeves
Office of Migratory Bird Management
U.S. Fish and Wildlife Service
Washington, D.C.

Roy E. Tomlinson
Office of Migratory Bird Management
U.S. Fish and Wildlife Service
Albuquerque, New Mexico

James C. Bartonek
Office of Migratory Bird Management
U.S. Fish and Wildlife Service
Portland, Oregon

HABITAT DESCRIPTION

The Western Management Unit (WMU) administratively consists of seven states—Washington, Oregon, Idaho, Utah, Nevada, California and Arizona. It measures about 0.7 million square miles (1.8 million km²), or about 24 percent of the area within the contiguous United States. In addition, most mourning doves breeding in southern Alberta and British Columbia probably winter in or migrate through the WMU. Mourning doves have been recorded as rare migrants to southeastern Alaska and irregular visitors westward to the head of Bristol Bay (Kessel and Gibson 1978), but there is no evidence of their breeding there. Recoveries of doves banded during summer in the WMU have been reported from throughout the unit, western Mexico (including Baja California) and Central America south into Honduras.

The WMU is characterized by a variety of habitats because of its large size, diverse physiography and climate. The WMU in general and California in particular have the most heterogeneous habitats used by mourning doves in the United States. Seasonally, dove habitats occur at elevations from below sea level to timberline. Temperatures vary from very hot in the deserts to frigid in the mountain ranges. Coastal temperatures are moderated by westerly winds off the Pacific Ocean. More variable temperatures occur inland beyond the oceanic influence and according to elevation and latitude. Winter precipitation and summer drought characterize the coastal climates, whereas inland areas receive most of their precipitation during summer. Annual precipitation averages less than 2 inches (5 cm) in some southern deserts but exceeds 128 inches (325 cm) along the western Olympic Peninsula in Washington.

Mourning dove habitats are more diverse in the Western Management Unit than in either of the other two units. Elevations range from deserts below sea level to montane forests and parklands thousands of feet above sea level. *Top photo (California) by Robert B. Branstead; courtesy of the U.S. Soil Conservation Service. Center photo (Washington) by Earl R. Baker; courtesy of the U.S. Soil Conservation Service. Bottom photo (Nevada) courtesy of the U.S. Bureau of Land Management.*

Major Vegetational Zones

Vegetation reflects the various altitudinal, climatic and edaphic conditions found in the WMU. Natural climax vegetation still occurs in limited portions of the unit, but most areas have been significantly modified by human activities, particularly livestock grazing, lumbering, farming (including irrigation and chemical applications), fire suppression, industrialization or urbanization.

Küchler's (1964) national vegetation classification system, later modified by the U.S. Geological Survey (1970), includes 106 vegetation types, 47 of which occur within the WMU. In addition, such local areas as sand dunes, lava flows and lakes are essentially unvegetated. For this chapter, the modified Küchler vegetation types are further consolidated into six major categories plus an unvegetated group *(Figure 55)*. The following briefly describes the major vegetation types.

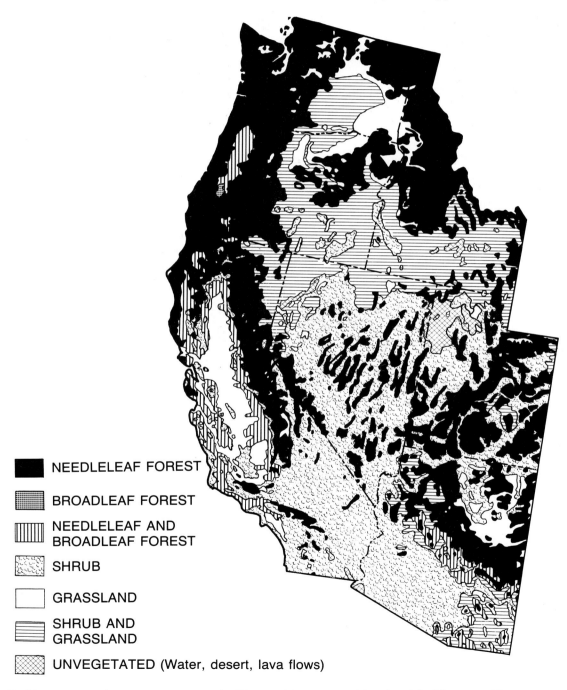

- ■ NEEDLELEAF FOREST
- BROADLEAF FOREST
- NEEDLELEAF AND BROADLEAF FOREST
- SHRUB
- GRASSLAND
- SHRUB AND GRASSLAND
- UNVEGETATED (Water, desert, lava flows)

Figure 55. Major potential vegetation types in the Western Management Unit (modified from Küchler 1964).

Needleleaf forests occupy the upper elevations of the Rocky Mountains, the Sierra Nevada, the Cascade and Coast ranges, and intervening lowlands of western Washington, Oregon and California. The area supports some of the most luxuriant needleleaf forest in the world and consists of dense stands of towering Douglas firs, true firs, spruces, hemlocks, cedars, pines and—locally—redwoods.

Broadleaf forests in the WMU are essentially confined to the Oregon oak woods of the Willamette Valley and to mesquite bosques in southern portions of the unit. Initially, both broadleaf forest types were limited in scope, but ranching and overgrazing have triggered the spread of mesquite in the Southwest.

Mixed needleleaf and broadleaf forests of the WMU are likewise restricted in area and exist chiefly in the foothills of the Central Valley and Coast Range of California and in central and southeastern Arizona. In the first locale, needleleaf forest species are intermixed with oaks. In California, the major tree cover includes oaks, madrone, firs and pines. In southern Arizona, the type is characterized by oaks and junipers.

Shrub dominates vast expanses of the central and southern Great Basin, the Colorado River drainage and the deserts of southern California and southwestern Arizona. The northern shrub zone occupies most of Nevada, adjoining California lowlands and western Utah. Sagebrush is the predominant shrub there, but in the more southerly arid, steeper or more alkaline areas, it is replaced by creosotebush, chaparral, mountainmahogany, saltbush, greasewood, paloverde, cactus shrub and associated species.

Mixed shrub and grasslands characterize the northern Great Basin, Snake River drainage and lower elevations of the Columbia River watershed of Washington and Oregon east of the Cascades. Sagebrush is the dominant vegetation, augmented by many grasses. On steeper terrain, scrub juniper, mountainmahogany and other woody shrubs replace sagebrush.

Grasslands originally occurred over scattered expanses of the WMU. They included the Palouse Prairie of southwestern Washington and adjoining Idaho, the foothills and steppes of northeastern Oregon, and eastcentral Arizona. This type also includes the alpine meadows of the higher mountain ranges. Major grasses include fescues, wheatgrasses, needlegrasses, bluegrasses and gramas. Vast tule (bulrush) marshes once dominated the watercourses and seasonally flooded bottomlands of the Central Valley of California.

Unvegetated areas of the WMU include the extensive salt flats lying west of Great Salt Lake in Utah, lava flows in southeastern Idaho, alkaline sumps in California, Oregon, Nevada and Utah, and extremely arid deserts in southwestern Arizona and southern California.

The mourning dove has adapted as a breeding, migrating or wintering species to nearly all WMU habitats except possibly the high alpine meadows and extensive tracts of climax needleleaf forests. It is predominately a tree- or shrub-nesting species, although it commonly nests on the ground when such sites are unavailable. Doves generally shun deep forests but readily use open woodlands and edges between habitat types. The mourning dove is a seed eater that has readily adapted to cultivated small grains such as wheat.

Land Use

Major changes in land use wrought by humans have altered the original ecology of the mourning dove in the WMU. An important change began with the breaking of grasslands and shrublands for grain production in the mid-1800s, which accelerated during both World Wars. Mechanized harvesting, especially in early years, left large quantities of waste grain in fields for doves and other wildlife.

Among the historically significant changes in land use influencing mourning dove populations in the Western Management Unit was farming of native grasslands. Seed crops diversified the dove's food base. Mechanized harvesting helped make the crop plant seeds available as waste grain. And with successful farming came shelterbelts, homesteads, communities and artificial water sources that accommodated other habitat needs of the readily adaptive dove. *Photo (Idaho) by John D. Massey; courtesy of the U.S. Soil Conservation Service.*

Planting shrubs for field and farmstead shelterbelts created preferred nesting sites and roosting habitat. Maturing fruit and nut orchards also were readily accepted by doves as nesting sites. Farm impoundments, stock ponds, and irrigation canals and ditches provided dependable sources of water.

The Central Valley of California is world-renowned for its production of vegetables, fruits, cereals and nuts for human consumption and of forage and grain used by livestock and poultry. Mourning doves initially adapted well to this farming regime. However, doves no longer benefit from agriculture to the degree they experienced in the past. Many small family farms have yielded to large corporate farms with monocultural cropping practices. Farmers are continually improving yields and efficiency, and these practices have reduced the availability of waste grain and weed seeds sought by the doves as food (see chapter 2).

Mature coniferous forests in the Northwest generally supported few doves. But as lumbering advanced into climax forests, clearings and second growth provided an edge habitat acceptable to doves. Although forest regeneration frequently filled clearings, others were maintained for farms, pastures, towns and roads. Forest fires also created clearings, often vast, that took years to reforest. The resultant habitat diversity led to a modest range expansion and population increase in forested areas once devoid of doves.

Phreatophytes—such as willows, cottonwoods, mesquite and the introduced saltcedar—provide valuable nesting habitat for mourning doves in the arid Southwest. These trees depend on ground-water obtained from extensive taproot systems and compete with cultivated crops for limited soil moisture. For example, Robinson (1965) estimated that a tall, dense stand of saltcedar in a hot, dry climate annually uses more than 9 acre feet of water per acre (27,700 m^3/ha) (see also Kerpez and Smith 1987). Large-scale reclamation projects have been undertaken to eradicate it and other phreatophytes, and their removal has been especially detrimental to mourning and white-winged doves (Wigal 1973, Kerpez and Smith 1987).

Fruit and nut orchards in many areas of the WMU can provide excellent nesting habitat for mourning doves. Doves formerly nested in moderate to high densities in important fruit-producing areas of eastern Washington, Oregon and Idaho. However, the practices of replacing standard-sized fruit trees with semidwarf varieties and the use of elevated sprinkler irrigation have seriously deterred dove nesting and production there (Zeigler 1977). Citrus groves in Arizona, formerly important dove production areas, are rapidly being cleared and replaced with more profitable crops (Wigal 1973).

Forest cutting in the Western Management Unit advanced open areas, second-growth vegetation and edge cover in which the mourning dove was able to prosper. *Photo courtesy of the National Archives.*

Irrigated orchard farming in many parts of the Western Management Unit has been beneficial to mourning doves by providing additional food, shelter and water. However, the trends toward dwarf varieties of fruit and nut trees and elevated sprinkler irrigation have diminished the value of such orchards to nesting doves. *Photo (Washington) by Earl R. Baker; courtesy of the U.S. Soil Conservation Service.*

Livestock grazing can be beneficial to doves because it opens understory in brush or timbered areas and encourages weed seed production. However, chronic overgrazing, prevalent throughout much of the West, causes long-term soil deterioration and eventual loss of grasses and forbs, both important seed producers for doves.

According to agricultural statistics for 1982 (U.S. Department of Agriculture 1982), land use in the WMU was classified as: grasslands and pasture, 40.5 percent; forests, 31.7 percent; special uses (urban, industrial, parks and wildlife refuges, military lands, roads, railroads, ungrazed desert, rock, swamp, and miscelleanous other uses), 10.7 percent; croplands, 6.8 percent; pasture only, 1.0 percent; idle, 0.3 percent; and "other," 9.0 percent.

Major land uses varied markedly among the seven states. Washington led in the proportion of

On open rangelands in the Western Management Unit, early livestock grazing was not particularly beneficial to wildlife, including mourning doves, because it tended to be too intensified, resulting in removal of forbs and grasses and in soil compaction and erosion. When and where livestock grazing has been managed wisely for long-term production, wildlife usually has benefited. The bottom scene depicts the same area as above nearly a half century later; it reveals the vegetative conversion from grassland to grassland/scrub after overgrazing by cattle and subsequent cessation of grazing. The phreophyte (mesquite) invasion provided shelter and nesting cover for mourning doves. *Top photo (southern Arizona) taken about 1900 by D. Griffiths; courtesy of the USDA Forest Service. Bottom photo by Matt Culley; courtesy of the USDA Forest Service.*

its land devoted to crops (18.0 percent), followed by Idaho (11.2 percent) and California (9.5 percent), with Nevada being the least intensively farmed (1.0) percent). Rangelands, consisting of grasslands and pasture, comprised 65.2 percent of Nevada, followed by 57.2 percent of Arizona and 44.2 percent of Utah. Washington, with 18.3 percent, had the least rangeland. Oregon ranked first in proportion of land forested (47.9 percent), followed by Washington (43.6 percent) and California (37.0 percent), with Nevada being the least forested (10.3 percent).

Based on 1983 data, ten major national crops accounted for only 64 percent of the WMU acreage classified as cropland. The remaining cropland acreage was fallow or planted to regionally important crops. Among the ten major crops, hay, cotton and sugar beets are of little use to mourning doves. Crops that provide food for mourning doves are corn, wheat, barley, oats, rice, sorghum and rye. Trends of major crop acreages and their implications are discussed later.

Far more federal land is located in the WMU than in either the Eastern (EMU) or Central (CMU) Management Unit. About half of the land in the western United States is federally owned. In the WMU, the percentage of federal ownership varies by state: Nevada, 85 percent; Idaho, 64 percent; Utah, 64 percent; Oregon, 49 percent; California, 46 percent; Arizona, 44 percent; and Washington, 29 percent (Chadwick 1989). Notably large holdings are administered by the U.S. Bureau of Land Management, Forest Service, National Park Service, Fish and Wildlife Service, Bureau of Reclamation, Department of Defense, and Bureau of Indian Affairs. The individual states also control and manage substantial holdings as state forests, parks and wildlife areas.

TECHNICAL AND ADMINISTRATIVE ORGANIZATIONS

The evolution of federal and state laws and regulations governing the management of migratory gamebirds is summarized in chapter 23. Although the federal government has primary responsibility (exercised through the U.S. Fish and Wildlife Service), mourning dove management is in practice a cooperative effort shared with the states and others.

Early U.S. federal and state wildlife programs for migratory gamebirds, especially waterfowl, focused on harvest regulation. Banding data for waterfowl and mourning doves indicated that migration routes in the United States followed fairly

well-defined longitudinal corridors. Four waterfowl flyways and three mourning dove management units were established in 1948 and 1960, respectively, to aid in administration of hunting regulations for the birds in the United States (see chapter 23).

Kiel (1959) found that 80 percent of the doves banded in states that later would comprise the WMU and reported as shot had been banded in the same state, 16 percent were from other WMU states, and only 4 percent were from bandings outside the WMU. Kiel also demonstrated that 76 percent of the recovered doves were taken in the same state in which they had been banded, 15 percent were taken in other WMU states, 1 percent were taken in another management unit and 8 percent were taken in Mexico and Central America. The WMU has greater integrity than does either of the two other units because a higher proportion of its harvest is derived from its own breeding population and production and fewer of its doves are taken in other management units. The integrity of the WMU as a whole has facilitated the coordination of cooperative dove programs and activities by federal and state wildlife agencies.

WMU Technical Committee

Establishment and evolution. Soon after Kiel's (1959) work, the Pacific Flyway Council (the organization of state wildlife agency representatives in the Pacific Flyway that deals primarily with waterfowl matters) recommended to the Western Association of State Fish and Game Commissioners that a "Dove Technical Committee" be formed to coordinate and oversee dove management and research activities in the seven western states. The Western Association responded to the Council's request in autumn of 1961 by appointing one wildlife technician from each member state to constitute such a committee. Representatives from all member states were present at the first meeting of the Western Mourning Dove Technical Committee, held in Reno, Nevada on March 27 and 28, 1962. The group has met annually since that time. In essence, the Council deals with policy matters, while the Dove Technical Committee formulates and oversees biological studies and makes management recommendations to the Council for consideration and possible adoption.

The purpose of the Western Mourning Dove Technical Committee (1962: i) was identified in its first report as follows: "It was felt that the committee's work will assist the national program and in addition help the individual states by:

1. Focusing more attention on the relative importance of the mourning dove in the Western Management Unit.
2. Gaining support from the Western states to actively participate in the national program.
3. Adding support to the hunting regulations submitted by the individual states to the U.S. Fish and Wildlife Service.
4. Assisting the USFWS [U.S. Fish and Wildlife Service] as a clearing house for information and coordinating the activities of the states in the management of doves."

Initially, the committee worked only with the mourning dove, but over the years it was assigned responsibilities by the Council for other migratory gamebirds. In 1964, the band-tailed pigeon was included; in 1968, the committee was renamed the Western Migratory Upland Game Bird Technical Committee to reflect its broadened scope. Alaska formally became a Committee member in 1981. Canadian federal and provincial officials regularly participate in the committee's meetings, and Mexican representatives sometimes attend.

Among the three management unit technical committees, only the WMU committee formally documents its activities in its annual Western Migratory Upland Game Bird Committee Report. By reviewing these reports, one can readily follow the committee's evolution over the years and the various activities in which it has played a leading role.

Activities. Projects coordinated or implemented through the committee over the years include randomization of Call-count Survey routes; a combination preseason and postseason banding program in the early 1960s; a weekly survey to document progression of autumn migration; standardization of studies of state harvest surveys; a second preseason banding program beginning in the mid-1960s; evaluation of studies proposed for funding under the "Accelerated Research Program for Migratory Shore and Upland Game Birds"; coordination of the WMU portion of a national mourning dove nesting study; analysis of data from the second preseason banding program; and development of species management plans. Additionally, the committee annually makes recommendations to the Pacific Flyway Council on hunting regulations.

Early assessment of the WMU. One of the first undertakings of the Technical Committee was to prepare an assessment of the WMU dove population and factors influencing it (Gallizioli 1961). Call-count Surveys during 1955–60 (not randomized at that time) showed no definite population trend, although the California index increased substantially during the interval. Based on survey responses from member states, the WMU harvest in 1959 was estimated at 3.5 million doves, with California leading with 1.7 million, followed by Arizona with 0.9 million. More doves were harvested in the WMU than any other upland game species. Unit dove hunters totaled 284,000, with California and Arizona together accounting for nearly two-thirds.

Dove hunting interest varied greatly among states, with only 6 percent of Oregon hunters but 33 percent of California hunters participating in dove hunting. Daily harvest success ranged from 4.9 doves per hunter in Nevada to 5.8 in Arizona, whereas hourly success ranged from 1.9 doves per hunter in California to 3.4 in Arizona.

Respondents to that early survey thought that current agricultural practices were more beneficial than detrimental to the mourning dove, except in Arizona where plans were afoot to eradicate riparian brush (saltcedar and mesquite) so valuable to nesting doves. Hunting was not thought to be an important mortality factor and was believed to account for about 5 percent of the autumn population (estimated at about 20 million birds). The future of the mourning dove seemed bright, and arguments were presented for raising the daily bag limit from 10 to 15 doves daily.

That historically important assessment, in retrospect, was overly optimistic, but it set the stage for this review of WMU mourning doves, their abundance, population trends, characteristics and harvest—including an unenviable obligation to explain a long-term downward trend of mourning doves in the WMU since the late 1950s.

POPULATION SIZE AND TREND

Populations of migratory birds are best monitored on their breeding grounds. Many mourning doves winter in Mexico and Central America, and it is not feasible to inventory them there. Further, wintering mourning doves cannot be differentiated from dove populations that reside year-round in Latin America. Finally, breeding population surveys provide the latest population assessment just prior to promulgation of annual hunting regulations.

From a management standpoint, then, it is more practicable to sample the breeding population than the wintering population. Fortunately, mourning dove breeding populations are ubiquitous throughout the conterminous United States and generally occur in areas well traversed by roads. As male mourning doves call frequently during spring and summer, a nationwide Call-count Survey was established in the 1950s to monitor breeding populations (see chapter 14). Call-count information gathered since 1966 provides the basis of current understanding of mourning dove breeding population size, distribution, density and trend in the WMU. The number of doves *heard calling* per survey route serves as the primary annual index to the size of the breeding population present. The Call-count Survey initially was designed to reflect changes in dove populations by management unit; however, with accumulating data over the years, it also provides insight into relative dove population densities and trends by state and physiographic region. Survey participants also routinely record the numbers of doves *seen* per survey route. Information on doves seen generally is not used for management decisions, but it has been useful as an independent parameter to compare with doves *heard*. Trends obtained from both data sets in the WMU are remarkably similar (Dolton 1987). In the following discussion of the WMU population and trend, emphasis is placed on doves heard calling, although data on doves seen also are given for some key discussion topics.

Within the WMU, there are two subunits in which mourning dove populations are essentially independent of each other (see chapter 4). Therefore, in discussions of population trends and other

parameters, these subunits have been designated as the Coastal WMU (Washington, Oregon and California) and the Interior WMU (Idaho, Nevada, Utah and Arizona).

Population Size

Breeding population. The WMU comprises 24 percent of the land area of the United States and, in 1987, contained 12 percent of the nation's mourning dove breeding population (Dolton 1987). In comparison, 61 percent of the nation's dove population was located in the CMU (46 percent of the land area) and 27 percent in the EMU (30 percent of the land area).

Call-count data reflect relative densities of breeding dove populations in the WMU *(Table 69)*. During the first five years of the Call-count Survey (1966–70), the number of calling doves per route averaged 19.7, whereas during a recent five-year period (1983–87), the number averaged 10.2. This population reduction of nearly 50 percent in the WMU is cause for great concern and will be discussed later.

The latest five-year average (1983–87) of 10.2

Table 69. Annual breeding population indices[a] of mourning doves, expressed as the mean number of calling doves heard per route, by states and subunits of the Western Management Unit, 1966–87.

Year	Coastal WMU				Interior WMU					Total WMU
	Washington	Oregon	California	Subtotal	Idaho	Nevada	Utah	Arizona	Subtotal	
1966	13.0	23.7	31.1	24.2	17.1	9.5	18.3	26.3	17.5	20.2
1967	16.1	16.4	29.6	22.9	17.9	7.8	26.7	28.3	18.3	20.1
1968	15.6	17.6	29.0	22.7	16.2	18.6	15.0	24.6	18.3	20.0
1969	12.3	18.6	25.8	20.6	16.8	13.2	14.9	29.1	18.9	19.4
1970	13.5	13.1	25.9	19.4	16.0	9.3	15.6	29.8	18.2	18.6
1971	14.0	11.3	20.3	16.4	12.7	5.7	22.8	19.9	13.7	14.8
1972	10.9	9.8	24.3	16.9	12.2	6.9	12.8	20.7	13.4	14.7
1973	8.6	11.7	19.2	14.9	13.9	4.9	11.5	27.1	14.6	14.5
1974	9.8	15.6	20.5	16.7	12.0	7.5	13.5	23.6	14.5	15.4
1975	10.1	11.8	18.7	14.9	9.8	4.2	15.1	24.0	13.1	14.0
1976	9.9	11.3	20.8	15.7	15.4	7.1	16.8	26.5	16.6	16.3
1977	10.9	12.6	17.4	14.6	19.0	6.8	19.1	22.4	16.1	15.5
1978	6.7	6.2	14.2	10.3	10.1	4.1	8.5	23.0	11.8	11.1
1979	9.0	6.3	12.3	9.9	10.1	6.3	11.2	24.4	13.7	11.9
1980	5.8	9.8	17.5	12.5	10.4	9.1	13.4	20.9	14.2	13.5
1981	6.8	7.8	16.2	11.7	11.7	6.3	18.1	23.3	14.9	13.5
1982	6.3	7.5	16.4	11.6	11.6	3.7	10.7	25.8	13.1	12.5
1983	4.9	5.6	10.9	8.1	9.6	3.2	10.6	20.8	11.2	9.7
1984	4.2	6.5	15.2	10.0	11.3	3.3	12.9	25.5	13.1	11.6
1985	5.5	7.7	10.6	8.8	10.6	4.5	8.0	21.2	11.6	10.3
1986	6.3	5.8	12.9	9.6	7.2	2.9	12.2	22.8	11.1	10.4
1987	4.8	5.3	10.0	7.7	10.1	3.4	9.8	16.7	10.2	9.0
Average										
1966–70	14.1	17.9	28.3	22.0	16.8	11.7	18.1	27.6	18.2	19.7
1983–87	5.1	6.2	11.9	8.8	9.8	3.5	10.7	21.4	11.4	10.2
1966–87	9.3	11.0	19.0	14.6	12.8	6.7	14.4	23.9	14.4	14.4

[a] Annual indices are defined as the predicted value from the trend analysis plus the deviation from the expected value in a year.

doves per route in the WMU compared with 23.6 in the CMU and 16.3 in the EMU. Thus, the density of doves in the WMU was less than half that of the CMU and about two-thirds that of the EMU. Historically lower dove densities in the WMU reflect less favorable nesting habitats provided by the WMU's extensive high, mountainous terrain and Great Basin sagebrush flats. Dove densities during 1983–87 also varied considerably by state within the unit, with the highest in Arizona (21.4) and lowest in Nevada (3.5) *(Figure 56)*. However, population densities have changed dramatically over the twenty-two-year period. During 1966–70, the average number of calls per route in the Coastal WMU (22.0) was greater than in Interior WMU states (18.2). By 1983–87, average density in Coastal states had dropped to 8.8 and in Interior states to 11.4. Although populations have declined in both subunits, doves in the Interior WMU now nest in higher densities than do those in the Coastal WMU. This change reflects the greater rate of decline for doves in Washington, Oregon and California since 1966.

The relative size and importance of dove breeding populations for each state and subunit also

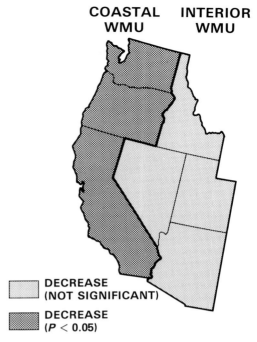

Figure 56. Mean number of mourning doves heard calling per route, by state, in subunits of the Western Management Unit, 1983–87.

Table 70. Annual breeding population indices[a] of mourning doves, expressed as the mean number of calling doves heard per route, by physiographic region[b] in the Western Management Unit, 1966–87.

Year	Physiographic region

Year	190	201	202	203	204	205	211	212	213	214	215	216
1966	20.7	20.2	11.7	14.8	25.0	41.8	4.9	18.9	24.4	34.3	32.3	2.7
1967	16.6	20.5	9.4	20.7	31.2	22.7	18.2	40.7	30.9	18.4	36.1	2.4
1968	16.6	24.3	10.4	22.3	20.4	22.4	6.5	17.3	21.9	22.3	20.3	1.4
1969	14.6	16.9	9.2	23.3	22.4	37.3	2.9	24.4	23.2	22.3	32.2	1.1
1970	14.6	18.8	9.0	14.7	29.4	24.9	10.2	10.0	25.0	23.8	24.5	4.2
1971	13.3	19.8	11.1	14.7	14.1	14.5	15.2	26.1	23.2	10.0	26.8	10.3
1972	11.9	13.3	10.2	15.0	15.4	20.4	12.5	12.5	14.3	15.1	34.0	6.9
1973	13.0	12.3	7.9	12.9	24.7	21.4	1.6	14.0	24.5	25.8	12.5	2.4
1974	12.5	14.0	7.5	16.4	15.6	19.3	1.6	13.9	20.1	11.3	15.2	4.9
1975	10.2	21.6	12.4	10.3	4.7	17.5	2.9	12.6	21.6	20.5	18.1	7.6
1976	13.2	14.5	6.5	12.7	20.2	18.2	4.3	17.9	22.8	16.5	16.0	6.8
1977	14.8	20.6	9.9	9.3	21.4	18.9	6.3	17.7	22.4	8.1	30.4	10.2
1978	12.4	11.1	3.4	7.3	12.5	9.1	1.6	10.0	17.1	11.2	14.8	10.0
1979	10.9	11.2	4.8	8.8	17.7	18.4	1.6	20.3	12.9	9.7	11.2	4.4
1980	10.1	7.1	2.5	12.9	15.8	19.8	4.3	14.5	15.0	10.4	6.3	10.9
1981	10.2	11.1	3.0	7.9	15.2	19.6	7.1	27.2	20.7	10.4	10.9	19.0
1982	13.0	10.2	8.7	9.7	12.6	12.5	4.5	17.8	13.2	8.2	23.6	16.0
1983	7.3	8.4	2.5	8.0	11.8	13.3	4.4	8.1	12.8	5.0	7.0	16.3
1984	8.1	8.0	5.6	10.3	14.8	10.2	11.5	10.3	23.7	6.3	24.2	34.1
1985	10.6	11.1	4.8	8.3	12.5	12.2	4.9	12.8	8.6	5.5	9.6	14.8
1986	6.0	10.9	2.7	10.7	11.8	14.5	3.2	16.4	12.4	10.2	9.0	30.1
1987	7.7	7.0	4.8	10.6	15.7	11.1	2.9	14.8	8.6	4.4	11.9	26.7
Average												
1966–70	16.6	20.1	9.9	19.2	25.7	29.8	8.5	22.2	25.1	24.2	29.1	2.4
1983–87	7.9	9.1	4.1	9.6	13.3	12.3	5.4	12.5	13.2	6.3	12.3	24.4
1966–87	12.2	14.2	7.2	12.8	17.5	19.1	6.1	17.2	19.1	14.1	19.4	11.1

[a] Annual indices are defined as the predicted value from the trend analysis plus the deviation from the expected value in a year.
[b] Modified from Fenneman (1931).

can be illustrated by Breeding Population Indices (Tomlinson et al. 1988). For this purpose, the average numbers of calling birds per route for 1983–87 were weighted by the size of the land area of each state where the birds were located. The Interior WMU contained 61.6 percent of the nesting population, with 32.9 percent in Arizona, 12.1 percent in Utah, 11.3 percent in Idaho and 5.3 percent in Nevada. In the Coastal WMU, 25.6 percent of the doves nested in California, 8.2 percent in Oregon and 4.7 percent in Washington, for a subunit total of 38.5 percent. Nearly 60 percent of the doves in the WMU nested in Arizona and California.

Average Call-count data for 1983–87 also were compiled for physiographic regions within the WMU *(Table 70)*. Each physiographic region (modified from Fenneman 1931) generally encompasses similar climatic, geographic and vegetational characteristics that differ from those of adjacent regions (see Figure 34 for name and number designations of physiographic regions). During the most recent five-year period, five regions in the southern portion of the WMU had densities exceeding 20 mourning doves per route *(Figure 57)*. Of these, only one (the Salton Trough, California, No. 223)

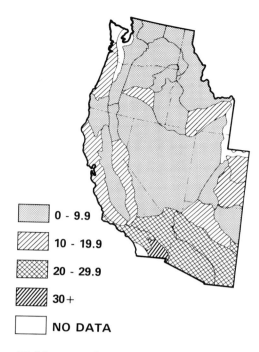

	0 - 9.9
	10 - 19.9
	20 - 29.9
	30+
	NO DATA

Figure 57. Mean number of mourning doves heard calling per route, by physiographic region (see Figure 34), in the Western Management Unit, 1983–87.

Table 70. (continued)

						Physiographic region						
221	222	223	224	231	232	233	234	243	244	245	246	247
18.1	51.1	22.0	15.9	20.7	8.8	6.0	23.3	2.0	6.2	32.4	34.2	78.0
16.4	47.5	23.4	21.8	23.7	8.8	5.9	31.0	0.9	4.0	33.7	25.6	73.5
22.8	46.4	27.6	17.9	26.7	6.2	11.4	19.7	5.3	5.2	34.8	30.5	29.5
19.0	49.8	20.5	22.1	29.3	4.3	8.9	16.7	0.5	4.6	35.2	25.5	66.9
15.8	37.3	28.5	23.3	22.5	3.0	0.0	25.1	1.3	4.4	29.1	23.2	41.2
12.0	22.5	27.3	17.3	28.5	5.8	3.9	16.9	0.9	3.4	27.4	23.5	39.3
10.7	29.5	21.8	16.2	21.6	2.5	17.6	21.0	3.1	2.8	27.2	29.8	22.3
9.5	34.6	24.1	28.8	16.9	3.9	7.4	20.5	0.2	3.3	16.8	19.0	55.4
12.7	35.5	28.8	22.8	14.7	5.9	7.5	30.2	6.7	2.8	9.3	22.3	45.4
8.7	32.0	26.7	23.0	14.4	2.6	11.2	19.3	0.3	7.3	14.1	23.5	13.9
11.6	32.3	34.9	27.1	12.0	3.0	23.6	24.5	4.2	4.5	14.2	20.2	47.0
9.8	25.0	16.2	20.9	11.3	4.6	5.7	24.2	2.0	3.9	14.2	23.2	28.7
6.5	26.4	26.4	25.4	9.5	1.4	10.8	10.4	4.3	2.5	12.2	18.1	24.9
7.2	30.4	34.4	24.4	13.4	3.2	5.4	10.4	4.5	1.0	8.4	23.4	24.1
12.1	28.8	24.5	29.0	8.0	3.9	6.3	15.1	6.7	3.0	11.1	24.4	22.3
8.7	29.3	38.8	29.1	10.4	3.0	0.5	22.2	14.0	4.7	9.8	20.5	19.3
6.2	22.4	35.1	28.5	8.8	1.9	10.0	14.8	20.0	1.7	11.2	20.7	25.3
5.0	27.0	32.6	29.7	7.9	1.5	4.3	12.7	10.4	2.3	5.9	14.9	23.5
5.3	23.3	42.1	26.8	3.4	2.0	15.4	15.9	38.7	2.3	7.8	20.2	26.3
4.9	20.8	33.3	26.8	6.5	3.2	12.7	10.3	10.5	2.7	4.9	17.9	22.9
4.9	17.5	35.0	23.7	6.5	1.7	8.1	13.2	2.5	2.6	5.5	22.6	20.3
4.9	13.2	32.4	28.7	5.6	1.6	6.8	10.3	6.5	1.7	4.3	19.8	18.5
18.4	46.4	24.4	20.2	24.6	6.2	6.4	23.2	2.0	4.9	33.0	27.8	57.8
5.0	20.4	35.1	27.1	6.0	2.0	9.5	12.5	13.7	2.3	5.7	19.1	22.3
10.6	31.0	28.9	24.0	14.7	3.8	8.6	18.5	6.6	3.5	16.8	22.9	34.9

exhibited a density of more than 30 birds per route (35.1). Most of the interior portion of the unit, from the Great Basin (No. 221) to the Northern Cascade Mountains (No. 231), had dove densities of less than 10 per route. On the eastern edge of the unit, four regions (Nos. 204, 212, 213 and 215) supported densities of 10 to 20 doves per route. Similarly, four regions lying mainly within Oregon and California (Nos. 205, 234, 243 and 246) also had dove densities of 10 to 20 per route.

Judging from the foregoing, it is difficult to categorize dove habitat preferences within the WMU. Clearly, mourning doves are most abundant in the southern desert habitats of Arizona and California and least abundant in the Great Basin, Columbia Plateau and Cascade Mountains. Oddly, the Sierra Nevada region appears to support a moderate population density. Doubtlessly, low dove populations (or none) at higher elevations are counterbalanced by high populations in the foothills of this region. The irrigated farmlands of southern Arizona and California provide adequate food and water for dove use, whereas the relatively sterile environment of the Great Basin produces few preferred foods and little available water.

Changes in average dove densities during the twenty-two-year period (1966–70 versus 1983–87) by physiographic region also are depicted in Table 70. Of the twenty-five regions of the WMU, densities increased in only five, three of which were in the south (Nos. 216, 223 and 224). Doves in the Southern Cascades (No. 233) and Oregon Coast Range (No. 243) also registered increases. In all

other regions, dove densities declined substantially (30 to 83 percent). The greatest decline occurred in the California Trough (No. 245), where densities decreased 83 percent, from 33 birds heard per route to 6 per route. Decreases of at least 50 percent were registered in fourteen of the twenty-five regions and at least 40 percent in four others. These declines will be addressed later and in more detail.

Autumn flights. By combining band recovery and harvest information, it is possible to estimate indirectly the size of the population from which the harvest was extracted. This procedure—the Lincoln-Peterson capture/recapture estimator (see chapter 16)—requires acceptance of several assumptions that may not be fully met. Therefore, results must be viewed with caution. However, the estimates portray the relative magnitude of autumn mourning dove populations in management units and the United States. Using average harvest and banding data for the WMU during the period 1967–75, Tomlinson et al. (1988) estimated an autumn flight of 76 million mourning doves in the WMU and 470 million in the United States. Similar procedures, using data from the CMU during the same general period (1967–74), produced an estimate of 91 million mourning doves in the WMU autumn flight and 476 million in the United States (Dunks et al. 1982). Thus, the WMU autumn flight during 1967–75 appears to have been on the order of 75 to 90 million mourning doves, or 16 to 19 percent of the nationwide population. These estimates from data obtained more than a decade ago suggest that the WMU population then comprised

Table 71. Trends (percentage change[a] per year as determined by linear regression) in breeding population indices for mourning doves heard by state in the Western Management Unit, 1966–87.

State	5-year (1983–87)				10-year (1978–87)			
	N	Percentage change[b]	95%	C.I.	N	Percentage change[b]	95%	C.I.
Coastal states								
Washington	15	11.2*	−1.1	23.4	18	−2.8	−7.5	1.9
Oregon	17	1.0	−10.9	12.8	21	−0.5	−3.6	2.6
California	51	−4.4	−10.7	2.0	59	−6.5***	−9.8	−3.3
Subtotal	83	−1.7	−7.1	3.6	98	−5.6***	−8.2	−3.0
Interior states								
Idaho	21	0.9	−5.5	7.2	22	−0.5	−4.4	3.3
Nevada	19	0.3	−13.1	13.6	20	−8.6*	−18.8	1.6
Utah	15	−1.4	−9.6	6.9	16	−0.2	−3.1	2.6
Arizona	54	−8.1**	−15.9	−0.3	55	−2.8**	−5.5	−0.1
Subtotal	109	−4.4*	−9.0	0.2	113	−2.3**	−4.3	−0.3
Total WMU	192	−3.5**	−6.9	0.1	211	−3.9***	−5.5	−2.2

[a] Route trend means weighted by land area and population density. The estimated count in the next year is (percentage ÷ 100 + 1) times the count in the current year where percentage is the annual change.
[b] * = $P < 0.1$, ** = $P < 0.05$, *** = $P < 0.01$.

more of the United States population than current Call-count data suggest it now does—a further demonstration of the unit's dove decline.

Breeding Population Trends

Long-term trends. As explained in chapter 11, the procedure for calculating population trends from Call-count information was changed in 1985 from a base-year to a route-regression method. This method corrected deficiencies associated with the base-year analysis and allowed computation of confidence limits about the trend estimates. In late 1987, the Office of Migratory Bird Management of the U.S Fish and Wildlife Service provided an updated route-regression analysis to incorporate all data from 1966 to 1987. Population trends were determined for four periods: five years (1983–87); ten years (1978–87); fifteen years (1973–87); and the entire twenty-two-year period (1966–87). Table 71 summarizes these trends by state and subunit within the WMU.

The analysis demonstrated that the WMU mourning dove breeding population declined steadily during the twenty-two-year period at a highly significant rate ($P < 0.01$). The downward trend was particularly evident in the Coastal WMU, with highly significant decreases ($P < 0.01$) in each of the three states of the subunit and for the subunit as a whole *(Figure 58)*. The Interior WMU also registered a significant long-term decline ($P < 0.05$), but decreases in Idaho, Utah and Arizona were not significant ($P > 0.05$). Nevada's population declined

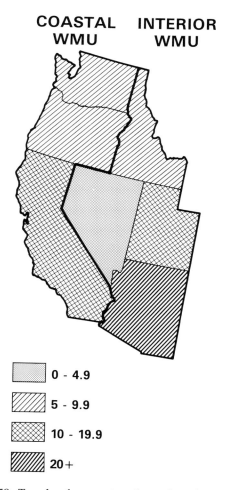

Figure 58. Trends of mourning doves heard calling per route, by state, in subunits of the Western Management Unit, 1966–87.

Table 71. (continued)

	15-year (1973–87)				22-year (1966–87)		
N	Percentage change[b]	95%	C.I.	N	Percentage change[b]	95%	C.I.
19	−6.0***	−10.2	−1.7	20	−6.0***	−9.8	−2.3
21	−3.3**	−5.9	−0.6	22	−6.0***	−8.3	−3.7
61	−5.3***	−7.9	−2.7	70	−4.9***	−7.3	−2.5
101	−5.2***	−7.4	−2.9	112	−5.1***	−7.1	−3.1
22	−2.2	−6.6	2.2	23	−2.3	−5.3	0.8
22	−3.1	−9.2	3.0	27	−5.2***	−8.2	−2.1
16	−4.0	−9.5	1.5	16	−2.8	−6.6	1.0
58	−1.5	−5.8	2.7	63	−1.1	−4.2	2.0
118	−2.3	−5.2	0.5	129	−2.0**	−3.9	0.0
219	−3.8***	−5.8	−1.9	241	−3.4***	−4.9	−1.9

at a highly significant rate ($P<0.01$), which strongly influenced the subunit's population decline.

Data for mourning doves seen along Call-count routes corroborated the declines indicated by doves-heard data. Doves-seen data for 1966–87 suggested that WMU mourning doves declined 3.3 percent per year ($P<0.01$). For individual states, mourning dove populations decreased at a highly significant rate ($P<0.01$) in Arizona and California and at a significant rate ($P<0.05$) in Idaho and Washington. Nevada and Oregon exhibited nonsignificant decreases ($P>0.05$), and Utah registered a small gain ($P>0.05$).

Trends also were computed for physiographic regions within the WMU (*Table 72 and Figure 59*). In thirteen of the twenty-five WMU physiographic regions from which there were sufficient data, dove populations declined significantly ($P<0.05$) over the twenty-two-year period. Eight additional regions registered nonsignificant ($P>0.5$) decreases, and four showed nonsignificant increases. A definite pattern was evident in that the greatest long-term declines occurred in the central portion

of the unit, extending from the far north to the far south (*Figure 59*).

Doves-seen data for 1966–87 by physiographic region yielded similar results. Mourning doves registered highly significant ($P<0.01$) declines in eight regions and significant ($P<0.05$) declines in three others. Nonsignificant decreases were evident in twelve regions and increases were noted in only three regions—one highly significant ($P<0.01$), one significant ($P<0.05$) and one nonsignificant ($P>0.05$).

Mid- and short-term trends and annual rates of change. For the ten- and fifteen-year periods tested (as for the twenty-two-year period), declines were noted for each state of the unit, although they were significant mainly in the Coastal subunit (*Table 71*). By the last five-year period in the Coastal WMU, the annual rate of population decline had slowed substantially (Washington and Oregon even registered nonsignificant increases). This pattern also was noted for doves of the Interior WMU. For Arizona, however, the rate of population decline increased with each succeeding time period and,

Table 72. Trends (percentage change[a] per year as determined by linear regression) in annual breeding population indices of mourning doves, based on the mean number of calling doves heard per route, by physiographic region in the Western Management Unit, 1966–87.

Physiographic region	5-year (1983–87)				10-year (1978–87)			
	N	Percentage change[b]	95%	C.I.	N	Percentage change[b]	95%	C.I.
190	12	0.7	−9.4	10.8	12	−0.7	−6.5	5.1
201	10	7.0	−13.4	27.5	10	−0.1	−4.2	4.0
202	3	27.0***	21.4	32.6	3	6.6	−7.0	20.1
203	8	9.5	−11.6	30.7	9	2.1	−8.3	12.6
204	4	5.1***	1.4	8.7	4	−2.9	−7.3	1.5
205	0	0.0	0.0	0.0	2	39.2	−12.4	90.7
211	2	−17.2	−39.8	5.4	2	16.8***	5.7	27.8
212	2	50.5***	30.3	70.7	2	10.6	−20.6	41.9
213	4	−2.0	−29.0	25.0	5	−3.6	−9.2	2.0
214	6	19.1	−42.4	80.5	6	16.0	−38.7	70.7
215	8	−5.6	−30.7	19.5	8	0.4	−8.7	9.6
216	2	30.4***	13.0	47.9	2	24.0***	18.9	29.2
221	33	−2.0	−10.7	6.7	37	−2.7	−7.3	1.8
222	21	−20.1***	−29.6	−10.6	21	−8.9***	−13.3	−4.4
223	4	−1.2	−7.1	4.8	5	6.1*	−0.1	12.2
224	20	−3.2	−14.9	8.6	21	−3.0	−7.4	1.4
231	4	12.5*	−1.2	26.3	4	−8.8***	−14.5	−3.1
232	3	10.5	0.0	121.7	5	2.6	−10.0	15.2
233	3	6.7	−67.4	80.8	3	6.1***	1.5	10.6
234	11	−7.8*	−16.1	0.5	12	−4.4***	−6.8	−1.9
243	2	−43.2***	−58.6	−27.8	3	−8.0	0.0	141.4
244	3	5.8	−10.5	22.1	5	−3.1	−33.0	26.8
245	8	−11.8**	−22.0	−1.6	9	−9.7***	−16.0	−3.4
246	14	4.0	−5.6	13.5	16	−3.4	−9.5	2.8
247	2	1.8	−2.1	5.8	2	−3.6	−25.1	17.9

[a] Route trend means weighted by land area and population density. The estimated count in the next year is (percentage ÷ 100 + 1) times the count in the current year where percentage is the annual change.
[b] * = $P<0.1$, ** = $P<0.05$, *** = $P<0.01$.

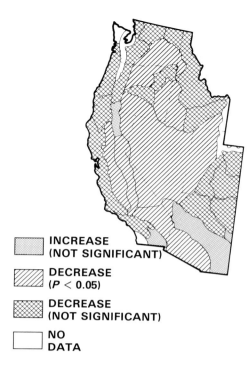

INCREASE
(NOT SIGNIFICANT)

DECREASE
(*P* < 0.05)

DECREASE
(NOT SIGNIFICANT)

NO
DATA

Figure 59. Trends of mourning doves heard calling per route, by physiographic region (see Figure 34), in the Western Management Unit, 1966–87.

Table 72. (continued)

by 1983–87, accounted for the greatest rate of decrease for the unit.

Trends by physiographic region during the 1983–87 period also suggested that doves may have increased in several regions. Although this conclusion must be viewed cautiously because of the small sample sizes over a short period of time, the mere fact that fourteen of the twenty-five WMU regions registered increases (4 significant, $P < 0.05$) gives rise to the hypothesis that the population may have been stabilizing at a lowered, or depressed, level.

Breeding Bird Survey. A secondary source of mourning dove population information is the Breeding Bird Survey (see Robbins et al. 1986), administered by the U.S. Fish and Wildlife Service and conducted annually by cooperators throughout the contiguous United States and southern Canada. Design and procedural differences prohibit direct comparisons between that survey and the annual mourning dove Call-count Survey (see chapter 14). The Breeding Bird Survey attempts to monitor birds of all species, so it probably is less precise as an indicator for mourning doves than is the Call-count Survey, which is specific to that species.

	15-year (1973–87)				22-year (1966–87)		
N	Percentage change[b]	95%	C.I.	N	Percentage change[b]	95%	C.I.
12	−4.7	−13.1	3.7	12	−3.4	−10.1	3.3
10	−2.9*	−6.4	0.5	10	−4.9***	−7.7	−2.1
3	−9.8***	−9.8	−9.8	3	−5.9***	−8.6	−3.1
9	−2.1	−6.6	2.4	10	−3.8**	−7.1	−0.5
4	−1.6	−5.3	2.0	4	−3.2	−10.4	4.1
2	34.9**	3.4	66.4	2	−4.4***	−4.3	−4.3
2	12.5***	8.3	16.6	2	−3.3***	−3.8	−2.8
2	6.1	−4.0	16.3	2	−1.8	−5.1	1.4
5	−8.3***	−12.0	−4.5	5	−4.4*	−9.4	0.6
6	−3.1	−7.3	1.0	7	−7.9	−24.4	8.5
8	−7.1	−23.2	9.0	9	−5.7**	−10.9	−0.4
2	18.3***	9.4	27.3	2	13.4	−15.9	42.7
39	−5.6*	−11.3	0.1	45	−6.4***	−11.4	−1.5
23	−7.8***	−12.7	−2.9	26	−4.4***	−6.4	−2.4
5	5.1	−2.4	12.5	7	2.5	−4.5	9.6
22	1.9	−3.0	6.8	23	2.3	−1.7	6.4
5	−9.3***	−15.6	−2.9	5	−8.7***	−14.7	−2.6
5	1.4	−5.9	8.8	5	−6.5**	−11.8	−1.1
3	−0.2	−5.4	5.0	4	0.8	−12.5	14.1
14	−6.1***	−8.6	−3.5	14	−4.9***	−7.5	−2.4
3	5.8	0.0	127.9	3	−15.0	−42.2	12.2
5	−6.8**	−13.2	−0.3	5	−4.9***	−7.7	−2.1
9	−6.9**	−12.4	−1.5	10	−9.5***	−15.4	−3.6
16	−0.9	−3.6	1.8	19	−1.9	−4.7	0.9
2	−4.5***	−6.5	−2.4	3	−5.1	−13.9	3.7

Long-term (1966–87) Breeding Bird Survey trend data for mourning doves were provided by the U.S. Fish and Wildlife Service. The mean numbers of doves heard *and* seen in the WMU declined 2.1 percent annually ($P < 0.05$), compared with the mourning dove Call-count Survey decline of 3.4 percent per year ($P < 0.01$) for the same period. Declines were evident in each of six states (significant only in Oregon at $P < 0.01$). Utah registered a small upward trend ($+ 0.7$ percent, $P > 0.05$).

The Breeding Bird Survey data also were examined by subunit. Mourning dove populations in the Coastal WMU were estimated to have declined 2.0 percent annually ($P < 0.05$), whereas Call-count data indicated an annual decline of 5.1 percent ($P < 0.01$). Doves in the Interior WMU were estimated to have declined 2.3 percent per year by the Breeding Bird Survey and 2.0 percent per ($P < 0.05$) by the Call-count Survey.

Physiographic regions used by the Breeding Bird Survey differ from those of the Call-count Survey. However, of the twenty-one Breeding Bird Survey regions lying partially or totally within the WMU, nineteen exhibited long-term dove declines (three at $P < 0.01$) and only two showed increases ($P > 0.05$).

Thus, the Breeding Bird Survey results independently corroborated the trends described earlier for the Call-count Survey, although the former's trends were not as strong, particularly by state. Both surveys demonstrated that WMU mourning dove populations declined substantially between 1966 and 1987 and that the greatest decline occurred in the Coastal WMU.

BANDING AND POPULATION DYNAMICS

Banding Programs

Four distinct banding programs have been undertaken in the WMU since the mid-1950s, when mourning dove banding first began in a coordinated manner (see chapter 3). The first was a nestling banding program, initiated in 1953 and continued until about 1957 as part of a nationwide undertaking (Kiel 1959). The goal of this program was to mark flightless young mourning doves clearly associated with known breeding locales. Of the 113,978 doves (60 percent of which were nestlings) banded nationwide, 22,472 were marked in states that eventually were consolidated into the WMU. Recoveries from this program provided the first broad insight into the dispersal and migration of young doves from known production locations

and enabled Kiel (1959) to delineate the three mourning dove management units.

The second major banding effort occurred during the early 1960s when cooperators banded samples of both immature and adult doves on their breeding grounds before the hunting season (preseason) and samples of wintering mourning doves at the conclusion of the hunting season (postseason). This investigation sought to determine the amount of mortality caused by hunting, based on the assumption that both marked samples represented the overall breeding and wintering populations. Despite considerable banding effort, it soon became apparent that the same population segments were not being sampled during both periods. To illustrate, many doves banded preseason in a northern state, such as Idaho, may winter well beyond the United States in Mexico or Central America, where no postseason banding was performed.

The third type of banding undertaken in the unit represents special investigations by individuals pursuing local or special studies. Among those in the WMU were Channing's (1979) banding work in the San Joaquin Valley of California and Leopold and Dedon's (1983) study in Berkeley, California.

In the mid-1960s, the fourth and largest banding program was conducted nationwide by state, federal and private banders. Both immature and adult doves were banded during the preseason period, defined as June through August. By then, improved age- and sex-determination techniques had been developed, and it was possible to ascertain the sex of most adults and some immatures, as well as to differentiate between the two age classes more precisely. The analyses of this large-scale banding program—involving more than 868,000 mourning doves nationally, including more than 88,000 in the WMU—have been published: for the EMU, see Hayne and Geissler (1977); for the CMU, see Dunks et al. (1982); and for the WMU, see Tomlinson et al. (1988). Much of the following information is based on the latter banding program and resultant analyses.

Preseason Banding and Recoveries, 1967–77

Banded samples. During this program 55,917 immature and 32,622 adult doves, totaling 88,539 birds, were banded in the WMU. To the extent possible, the banded sample was evenly distributed throughout the preseason period and geographically over the WMU.

The overall unweighted age ratio of the banded sample was 1.7 immatures per adult, and the adult sex ratio was 1.5 males per female. However, these ratios do not reflect the true age and sex ratios of the wild populations because of recognized biases associated with trapping techniques (see Dunks et al. 1982).

Recovery rates. The recovery rate is the proportion of the banded sample that is taken as a result of hunting and reported to the Bird Banding Laboratory (BBL) in Laurel, Maryland. Recoveries from the first hunting season following banding are called "direct recoveries," while those from subsequent hunting seasons are termed "indirect recoveries" (see *Table 43* for definition of terms). Recovery rates are indicators of hunting pressure—the higher the rate, the higher the hunting pressure.

Direct and indirect recovery rates of doves banded as immatures and adults by banding location are summarized in Table 73. The state estimates were weighted by average breeding population indices for 1967–75 and land area to obtain average recovery rates for the Coastal and Interior subunits and the WMU as a whole. The weighted direct recovery rates for immatures and adults in the WMU were 3.4 and 2.7 percent, respectively. Thus, immatures banded in the WMU were about 1.3 times more vulnerable to hunting than were adults (3.4 divided by 2.7). Dunks et al. (1982) calculated an identical relative recovery rate for the CMU. This phenomenon of higher vulnerability to hunting in immature cohorts is common for both migratory and resident gamebirds.

Weighted direct recovery rates for immatures (4.5 percent) and for adults (3.2 percent) in the Coastal WMU were about 1.5 times greater than those for immatures (2.6 percent) and adults (2.3

percent) in the Interior WMU. Considering that dove populations were declining at a higher rate in Coastal states than in Interior states during the sample period, it is possible that the heavier hunting pressure in the former contributed to the decline. However, it is interesting that indirect recovery rates for both cohorts in Coastal states were only marginally higher than those in Interior states.

Recovery rates also can be calculated by the stochastic models described by Brownie et al. (1978). These rates are derived by complex statistical methods designed for determining survival characteristics from banding data (see chapter 16). Tomlinson et al. (1988) and Dunks et al. (1982) estimated recovery rates using this procedure for mourning doves in the WMU and CMU, respectively. The WMU recovery rates for immatures and adults were 3.2 and 2.2 percent, respectively; these compare favorably with direct recovery rates shown in Table 73. The recovery rates for both age cohorts in the WMU were moderately higher than the rates of 2.0 percent for immatures and 1.5 percent for adults in the CMU, suggesting that hunting pressure is higher in the WMU. Test results provided strong evidence that recovery rates varied age-specifically for doves in both units.

Distribution of recoveries. Band-recovery data have long been used to illustrate the migratory distribution of birds from their breeding and natal areas. Tomlinson et al. (1988) provided information on mourning dove distribution in the WMU from birds banded during 1967–75. The following discussion relies on data modified from that analysis. Only direct recoveries were considered in the comparisons in order to avoid inclusion of data from

Table 73. Direct and indirect band recovery rates for immature, adult and total mourning doves banded in the Western Management Unit, 1967–75.

| | Recovery rates (percentage) | | | | | |
| | Immature | | Adult | | All doves | |
Banding location	Direct	Indirect	Direct	Indirect	Direct	Indirect
Coastal states						
Washington	5.3	2.0	3.4	2.6	4.9	2.1
Oregon	5.8	1.2	3.8	1.6	5.2	1.3
California	3.8	1.4	3.0	2.1	3.6	1.5
Subtotal[a]	4.5	1.4	3.2	2.0	4.2	1.6
Interior states						
Idaho	0.9	0.9	0.9	0.8	0.9	0.8
Nevada	2.1	1.5	1.6	1.8	1.9	1.6
Utah	1.1	0.6	0.9	0.6	1.0	0.6
Arizona	4.0	1.8	3.7	1.9	3.9	1.8
Subtotal[a]	2.6	1.3	2.3	1.4	2.5	1.3
Total WMU[a]	3.4	1.3	2.7	1.6	3.2	1.4

[a] Subtotals and total weighted by average breeding population indices for 1967–75 and land area by state.

banded doves that failed to return to first-year breeding or natal areas in succeeding years (thus, the exact breeding area in subsequent years would be unknown).

Based on direct recovery data of all doves (regardless of age or sex) banded in the WMU, 70 percent were reported from the same state in which they had been banded, and 89 percent were from within the WMU *(Table 74)*. Less than 1 percent of the recoveries were reported in the CMU and about 10 percent were from Latin America. A large proportion (92 percent) of the Latin American recoveries was centered in the Western Highlands (70 percent) and the Northwest Coast (22 percent) regions

of Mexico (Tomlinson et al. 1988) (see *Figure 32*). Of the 178 Latin American recoveries originating in the WMU, only 2 were reported as far south as Central America. Tomlinson et al. (1988) calculated that mourning doves banded in the CMU were thirteen times more likely to be recovered in Central America than were doves banded in the WMU, indicating that WMU doves terminate migration farther north than do CMU doves.

These findings confirm that doves migrating in the WMU follow corridors within the unit to southern Arizona and California and into Mexico. They seldom stray into the adjacent CMU. Furthermore, each state relies heavily on local production for

Table 74. Percentage distribution of direct recoveries of doves banded in the Western Management Unit, 1967–75.

Age class	Banding location	Recovery location				
		State of banding	Other state, same subunit	Other subunit	CMU	Latin America
Immature	Coastal states					
	Washington	81.0	8.6	2.7	0.8	7.0
	Oregon	78.0	13.4	1.8		6.7
	California	89.6		2.9	0.2	7.2
	Subtotal[a]	82.9	7.3	2.5	0.3	7.0
	Interior states					
	Idaho	35.7	7.1	28.5		28.5
	Nevada	47.1	22.1	17.6		13.2
	Utah	39.1	20.3	14.5	5.8	20.3
	Arizona	94.1		0.6	0.6	4.7
	Subtotal[a]	54.0	12.4	15.3	1.6	16.7
	Total WMU[a]	66.4	10.2	9.8	1.1	12.5
Adult	Coastal states					
	Washington	83.9	14.3	1.8		
	Oregon	65.2	23.9	4.3		6.5
	California	93.7		3.0		3.4
	Subtotal[a]	80.9	12.7	3.0		3.3
	Interior states					
	Idaho	38.5	23.1	23.1		15.4
	Nevada	66.7	17.8	11.1	2.2	2.2
	Utah	64.6	23.2			12.2
	Arizona	95.7	0.3	2.8		1.2
	Subtotal[a]	66.4	16.1	9.2	0.6	7.8
	Total WMU[a]	72.6	14.7	6.6	0.3	5.8
All doves	Coastal states					
	Washington	81.4	9.3	2.5	0.7	6.0
	Oregon	75.2	15.7	2.4		6.7
	California	90.5		2.9	0.2	6.4
	Subtotal[a]	82.4	8.3	2.6	0.3	6.4
	Interior states					
	Idaho	37.0	14.8	25.9		22.2
	Nevada	54.9	20.4	15.0	0.9	8.8
	Utah	53.0	21.9	6.6	2.6	15.9
	Arizona	94.7	0.1	1.4	0.4	3.4
	Subtotal[a]	59.9	14.3	12.2	1.0	12.6
	Total WMU[a]	69.5	11.7	8.1	0.7	9.9

[a] Percentages for subunit and WMU are arithmetical means of the recovery location totals.

its hunting harvest. This dependence usually is strongest in northern states. Harvest in southern areas of the unit include both locally produced birds and migrants from more northern production areas.

On a subunit basis, doves banded in the Coastal WMU were recovered within state of banding at an average rate of 82 percent, whereas those banded in the Interior WMU were recovered in-state at a rate of 60 percent (Table 74). Thus, Interior doves were more likely to be recovered away from banding areas than were Coastal doves. Similarly, doves banded in the Interior WMU were twice as likely to be recovered in Latin America as were doves banded in the Coastal WMU (13 versus 6 percent). This suggests either that Interior doves are more likely to migrate or that they begin migration earlier than Coastal doves.

Mourning doves banded in Washington and Oregon were several times more likely to be recovered in California than those banded in Idaho, Utah and Nevada (Tomlinson et al. 1988). Likewise, doves from Utah and Nevada were more apt to be recovered in Arizona than were doves from other WMU states. It is concluded that doves from each subunit migrate generally south or slightly southeast and seldom stray into adjacent units or subunits. However, when they reach Mexico, they winter in the same general region, the Western Highlands (see Tomlinson et al. 1988).

Differences in distribution were noted between immature and adult cohorts, particularly in the Interior WMU (Table 74). For the latter subunit, immature doves were less likely to be recovered in the state of banding (54 percent) than were adults (66 percent), and more likely to be recovered in Latin America (17 versus 8 percent). The same tendency, although weaker, occurred for doves in the Coastal WMU. These data suggest that immature doves, at least in Interior states of the WMU, either begin migration earlier than adults or are more prone to migrate than adults are.

Distribution of recoveries by sex cohort also was examined by Tomlinson et al. (1988). Migratory patterns generally were the same for adult males and females. Tomlinson et al. observed that the proportion of direct recoveries occurring in the state of banding was higher for adult males than for adult females in five of the seven states, but the apparent differences were not statistically significant.

Derivation of the harvest. Derivation of the harvest is the relative importance (in percentage) of the various origination areas for banded doves recovered in specific harvest areas (see chapter 16). Dunks et al. (1982) and Tomlinson et al. (1988) cal-

culated harvest derivation in the CMU and WMU, respectively, by weighting direct recoveries from birds banded during 1967–75. This weighting procedure adjusted the raw data to account for differences in banding efforts among origination areas, as well as for varying sizes of the areas and densities of breeding doves within them. The following discussion is based on the Tomlinson et al. (1988) study for derivation of WMU harvest and on Dunks et al. (1982) for derivation of harvest in Latin America. Mourning doves from breeding populations in British Columbia and Alberta were not banded during the study, so are not considered in the derivation calculations.

With the exception of California and Arizona, hunters in the WMU states harvested doves that primarily nested or were hatched within the state of banding, i.e., less than 10 percent of the harvest originated from other states (Table 75). Because California and Arizona are at the southern end of the unit, it is not surprising that 19 and 11 percent of their respective harvests came from other locations. Of all doves harvested in the WMU, about 98 percent were produced in the unit. Less than 2 percent of the doves came from the CMU and none from the EMU. This was true regardless of age, as both immatures and adults originated mainly within the unit. Thus, the integrity of the unit boundary between the WMU and CMU appears to be justified for management purposes. Furthermore, the Coastal and Interior WMU subunits appear to contain essentially discrete dove populations. Less than 5 percent of the recoveries in each subunit originated in the other subunit.

Of the 902 direct recoveries in Mexico from doves banded in the United States during 1967–75, 23 percent originated in the WMU, 75 percent in the CMU and less than 2 percent in the EMU (Dunks et al. 1982). Similarly, less than 4 percent of Central American recoveries originated in the WMU, whereas 96 percent came from the CMU. Thus, the WMU was considerably less important than the CMU as a contributor to the Mexico and Central America dove harvests.

Of the 175 Mexico and Central America recoveries for doves banded in the WMU, 54 percent originated from the Coastal subunit and 46 percent from the Interior subunit (Tomlinson et al. 1988). California (28 percent) and Arizona (18 percent) were the main WMU origination states, but doves from all states of the unit migrated to Mexico, where they wintered primarily in the Western Highlands.

Chronology of migration. Studies using roadside counts of mourning doves in the WMU documented that dove populations are at peak numbers in late July and early August and initiate migration

Table 75. Weighted derivation[a] of the harvest (in percentage) for mourning doves banded in the Western Management Unit, 1967–75.

Age class	Recovery location	State of recovery	Other state, same subunit	Other subunit	Other management unit
Immature	Coastal states				
	Washington	97.4	2.6		
	Oregon	100.0			
	California	80.5	9.9	7.3	2.3
	Subtotal[a]	88.0	5.9	4.7	1.4
	Interior states				
	Idaho	88.9		2.2	9.0
	Nevada	91.0		9.0	
	Utah	92.2		2.6	5.0
	Arizona	89.3	5.5	3.0	2.2
	Subtotal[a]	89.5	4.8	3.2	2.5
	Total WMU[a]	88.7	5.4	4.0	1.9
Adult	Coastal states				
	Washington	91.8	4.1	4.1	
	Oregon	100.0			
	California	79.8	13.2	6.8	0.1
	Subtotal[a]	85.5	9.3	5.1	0.1
	Interior states				
	Idaho	100.0			
	Nevada	90.2	4.6	5.2	
	Utah	100.0			
	Arizona	88.3	6.1	3.1	2.4
	Subtotal[a]	89.5	5.5	2.9	2.1
	Total WMU[a]	87.6	7.3	4.0	1.1
All doves	Coastal states				
	Washington	96.2	0.9	2.9	
	Oregon	100.0			
	California	81.0	10.8	6.4	1.8
	Subtotal[a]	87.9	6.7	4.4	1.1
	Interior states				
	Idaho	91.5		1.7	6.7
	Nevada	90.6	2.0	7.5	
	Utah	94.9		1.7	3.4
	Arizona	88.9	5.7	3.1	2.2
	Subtotal[a]	89.4	5.1	3.2	2.3
	Total WMU[a]	88.6	5.9	3.8	1.6

[a] Raw data were weighted by average breeding population indices (1967–75) and land area to derive estimated percentages for states, subunits and WMU.

by late August (McClure 1950a, Smith 1970, Miles 1976). To demonstrate further the chronology of migration, Tomlinson et al. (1988) examined dates of band recoveries in California and Arizona. Because these states are located in the southern part of the WMU, the proportion of recoveries by time period within state, in relation to the proportion from other locations, provides an indication of movement through these states.

During the first ten days of the hunting season (September 1–10), hunters in Arizona and California mainly harvested doves that nested or were reared in those states. However, all states in the WMU and several states from the CMU contributed a small proportion of the birds harvested during that time period, suggesting that migration had begun throughout the unit before the hunting season began. By September 11–20, doves originating from Arizona and California became less prevalent, whereas those from northern states contributed proportionately more to the harvest in these two southern states. By September 21–30, doves from Washington and Oregon formed a large proportion of the harvest in California. In Arizona during that

Table 78. Estimated average annual harvest of mourning doves per hunter in the Western Management Unit, as measured by state surveys, 1961–87.

	Average number of mourning doves per hunter									
	Coastal states				Interior states					Total WMU
Year	Washington	Oregon	California	Subtotal	Idaho	Nevada	Utah	Arizona	Subtotal	
1961	15.0	11.0	19.4	18.4	9.2	15.7	8.4	25.4	17.4	18.2
1962	17.4	9.9	21.8	20.7	10.2	15.0	9.9	11.8	11.4	18.6
1963	17.2	11.1	21.6	20.5	10.7	14.0	8.9	29.0	18.2	20.0
1964	15.4	12.0	19.7	18.8	11.7	13.8	9.8	24.6	18.1	18.7
1965	13.7	10.1	19.0	18.0	11.1	12.7	8.7	25.8	17.8	17.9
1966	13.8	12.0	17.0	16.4	10.8	13.5	10.3	28.7	20.3	17.3
1967	11.8	10.4	18.5	17.5	11.7	16.0	10.5	30.5	21.3	18.5
1968	12.1	10.0	16.9	16.0	10.2	12.3	8.3	23.9	18.3	16.7
1969	11.5	10.5	16.5	15.7	10.0	15.4	9.6	22.6	17.8	16.4
1970	11.6	10.4	17.0	16.2	11.3	11.5	9.7	20.2	16.4	16.3
1971	11.4	10.3	17.5	16.5	10.9	10.9	8.7	20.3	15.8	16.2
1972	10.4	10.7	17.0	15.9	10.4	11.8	8.1	19.6	15.3	15.7
1973	11.0	9.9	17.3	16.3	8.7	12.3	11.2	22.2	17.7	16.8
1974	9.4	9.2	17.8	16.6	9.7	11.9	9.0	18.4	15.0	16.0
1975	10.6	11.3	17.5	16.5	9.7	12.1	11.2	20.0	16.2	16.4
1976	8.8	10.9	16.3	15.2	8.4	15.3	9.5	20.8	16.5	15.7
1977	11.0	11.4	16.0	15.2	10.6	12.8	9.9	18.3	15.4	15.3
1978	9.5	10.3[a]	16.7	15.5[a]	8.3	12.0	10.7	22.1	17.2	16.2[a]
1979	9.8	9.5	16.7	15.4	9.6	13.8	10.1	22.9	18.2	16.6
1980	8.1	10.4	15.9	14.8	8.6	12.3	10.5	16.8	14.0	14.5
1981	8.7	11.0	16.2	15.1	10.6	11.9	10.3	19.3	15.8	15.4
1982	8.4	11.0	16.0	15.2	9.3	10.3	8.9	19.4	15.1	15.1
1983	8.8	11.1	15.6	14.8	10.7	13.0	9.6	19.8	15.6	15.1
1984	8.6[b]	11.3[a]	14.7	14.1[a]	10.1[b]	10.5	9.2	20.3	15.7	14.7[a]
1985	8.2	11.5	15.9	15.2	12.5	12.6	9.1	19.7	16.2	15.6
1986	8.0	10.7	14.6	13.8	10.9	11.4	8.5	18.3	15.0	14.4
1987	8.1	11.3	14.4	13.8	11.7	11.5	9.1	16.1	13.9	13.9
Average										
1961–65	15.7	10.8	20.3	19.3	10.6	14.2	9.1	23.3	16.6	18.7
1971–75	10.6	10.3	17.4	16.4	9.9	11.8	9.6	20.1	16.0	16.2
1983–87	8.3	11.2	15.0	14.3	11.2	11.8	9.1	18.8	15.3	14.7

[a] No surveys were conducted in Oregon during 1978 and 1984; harvest per hunter for those years was estimated by averaging data from preceding and following years. Coastal and WMU totals include derived estimates for Oregon.
[b] Washington and Idaho changed survey methods in 1984. Estimates for 1984–87 have been adjusted to maintain comparability with preceding years.

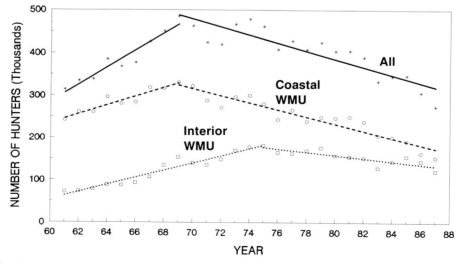

Figure 61. Trends of mourning dove hunters in the Western Management Unit, based on state harvest surveys, 1961–87.

Table 79. Estimated number of mourning doves harvested in the Western Management Unit, as measured by state surveys, 1961–87.

Year	Number of mourning doves harvested ($\times 1,000$)									
	Coastal states				Interior states					Total WMU
	Washington	Oregon	California	Subtotal	Idaho	Nevada	Utah	Arizona	Subtotal	
1961	335.8	202.1	3,906.7	4,444.6	140.0	110.2	128.0	886.6	1,264.8	5,709.4
1962	363.0	164.1	4,864.3	5,391.4	159.7	106.8	144.8	435.4	846.7	6,238.1
1963	398.4	184.0	4,766.3	5,348.7	203.3	121.6	162.8	940.6	1,428.3	6,777.0
1964	460.1	208.5	4,911.8	5,580.4	191.9	91.5	193.5	1,138.2	1,615.1	7,195.5
1965	436.8	163.1	4,451.3	5,051.2	198.0	120.8	164.1	1,075.7	1,558.6	6,609.8
1966	437.7	196.8	4,019.9	4,654.4	182.5	96.1	212.7	1,394.1	1,885.4	6,539.8
1967	288.7	172.4	5,128.3	5,589.4	214.4	155.6	263.9	1,644.4	2,278.3	7,867.7
1968	420.3	186.4	4,461.9	5,068.6	195.6	110.3	207.9	1,944.0	2,457.8	7,526.4
1969	339.2	198.5	4,680.3	5,218.0	220.2	170.4	279.3	2,072.2	2,742.1	7,960.1
1970	300.3	208.6	4,712.2	5,221.1	223.9	131.3	232.5	1,717.6	2,305.3	7,526.4
1971	318.1	180.8	4,248.3	4,747.2	249.3	115.8	226.6	1,552.0	2,143.7	6,890.9
1972	280.0	192.3	3,850.5	4,322.8	251.5	119.5	238.4	1,671.8	2,281.2	6,604.0
1973	316.7	156.9	4,350.2	4,823.8	229.8	130.0	307.1	2,345.8	3,012.7	7,836.5
1974	263.4	161.1	4,551.1	4,975.6	238.3	140.6	306.1	1,984.9	2,669.9	7,645.5
1975	274.6	201.9	4,151.6	4,628.1	246.8	147.2	420.3	2,122.1	2,936.4	7,564.5
1976	212.0	179.8	3,306.1	3,697.9	210.1	146.6	298.5	2,066.2	2,721.4	6,419.3
1977	287.3	206.1	3,543.5	4,036.9	268.4	125.5	267.5	1,833.9	2,495.3	6,532.2
1978	216.6	209.6[a]	3,267.0	3,693.2[a]	192.6	113.0	383.7	2,231.3	2,920.6	6,613.8[a]
1979	223.2	213.1	3,396.4	3,832.7	219.3	125.5	351.2	2,500.9	3,196.9	7,029.6
1980	163.1	215.6	3,262.4	3,641.1	195.7	143.3	343.9	1,527.7	2,210.6	5,851.7
1981	172.5	266.2	3,336.9	3,775.6	243.9	120.4	310.1	1,775.6	2,450.0	6,225.6
1982	121.2	214.3	3,272.6	3,608.1	204.5	112.8	282.2	1,699.1	2,298.6	5,906.7
1983	111.8	191.5	2,738.7	3,042.0	219.8	117.3	273.0	1,402.5	2,012.6	5,054.6
1984	100.6[b]	187.9[a]	2,551.6	2,840.1[a]	247.3[b]	85.5	282.3	1,639.2	2,254.3	5,094.4[a]
1985	84.9	184.2	2,640.6	3,909.7	356.1	81.0	256.0	1,820.2	2,513.3	5,423.0
1986	76.7	160.6	2,018.4	2,255.7	261.0	70.0	227.0	1,606.0	2,164.0	4,419.7
1987	66.0	113.7	1,935.6	2,115.3	212.2	66.3	204.0	1,207.0	1,689.5	3,804.8
Average										
1961–65	398.8	184.4	4,580.1	5,163.3	178.6	110.2	158.6	895.3	1,342.7	6,506.0
1971–75	290.6	178.6	4,230.3	4,699.5	243.1	130.6	299.7	1,935.3	2,608.8	7,308.3
1983–87	88.0	167.6	2,377.0	2,632.6	259.3	84.0	248.5	1,535.0	2,126.7	4,759.3

[a] No surveys were conducted in Oregon during 1978 and 1984; harvest for those years was estimated by averaging data from preceding and following years. Coastal and WMU totals include derived estimates for Oregon.
[b] Washington and Idaho changed survey methods in 1984. Estimates for 1984–87 have been adjusted to maintain comparability with preceding years.

Linear regressions also were used to compare trends in hunter numbers (dependent variable) with trends in mourning dove population (Call-count indices, independent variable) during 1966–87 (Call-count figures were not available prior to 1966). For the Coastal WMU, a strong positive correlation was found between the two variables ($r = 0.85$, $P < 0.01$), suggesting that decreasing dove numbers may have discouraged hunter participation. Consequently, one could predict the number of hunters expected by inspecting the annual Call-count results in the Coastal WMU. For the Interior WMU, however, a weak negative correlation was obtained between the two variables ($r = -0.27$, $P > 0.05$), indicating that predictions of numbers of hunters could not be made for the Interior WMU

for the twenty-two-year period. On the other hand, a moderately positive correlation ($r = 0.62$, $P < 0.05$) was obtained for the twelve-year period 1976–87. Thus, Interior hunters continued to increase during the earlier years, despite declines in the dove population. Perhaps the population decline was insufficient to discourage Interior WMU hunters until the mid-1970s.

Although evidence suggests a cause-and-effect relationship between dove population size and hunter participation in the WMU, such other factors as socioeconomic changes must not be ruled out. Increased costs of hunting and the growing difficulty of gaining access to suitable hunting locations also may have contributed to decreased hunter participation throughout the unit.

Seasonal Harvest

Seasonal harvest is defined here as the average number of doves harvested per hunter per year. During 1961–87, the average seasonal harvest in the WMU varied from a high of 20.0 birds per hunter in 1963 to a low of 13.9 in 1987 *(Table 78)*. Generally, hunters in the major dove hunting states of California and Arizona reported the highest seasonal harvests in the WMU (e.g., 21.6 and 29.0, respectively, in 1963, and 14.4 and 16.1 in 1987). The lowest seasonal harvests were reported in more northern states, such as Idaho and Utah (10.7 and 8.9, respectively, in 1963, and 11.7 and 9.1 in 1987). Because doves rapidly migrate from northern areas in late summer and early autumn, they are less available for hunting than are the doves in more southern areas.

Unlike the numbers of hunters, which increased for a number of years and then declined, seasonal harvest generally declined throughout the unit during the entire twenty-seven-year period (average rate for the WMU = −1.0 percent per year, r = −0.88, P<0.01) *(Figure 62)*. This was true for both the Coastal WMU (−1.2 percent per year, r = −0.87, P<0.01) and the Interior WMU (−0.94 percent per year, r = −0.68, P<0.01). There were exceptions (all nonsignificant) for some states in each subunit: Oregon (+0.11 percent per year, r = 0.13, P>0.05) in the Coastal WMU and Idaho (−0.03 percent per year, r = −0.03, P>0.05) and Utah (+0.06 percent per year, r = 0.06, P>0.05) in the Interior WMU maintained relatively stable seasonal harvest throughout the 1961–87 period.

Linear regression tests revealed strong positive

correlations between seasonal bag and Call-count indices for the period 1966–87 in both the Coastal (r = 0.76, P<0.01) and the Interior (r = 0.62, P< 0.01) subunits. Thus, one could predict seasonal harvest within the subunits by inspection of Call-count results. This information suggests that, as mourning dove populations decreased throughout the unit between 1966 and 1987, hunting success declined proportionately. It is reasonable to assume that lowered dove population numbers adversely affected hunting harvest success.

Harvest

Harvest is the product of the number of hunters and seasonal harvest and therefore reflects the trends of those statistics. It is not surprising, then, that harvest trends in the WMU were similar to those for the other two parameters, but particularly for numbers of hunters. The total WMU harvest ranged from a high of 8.0 million mourning doves in 1969 to a low of 3.8 million in 1987 *(Table 79)*. California and Arizona hunters were the greatest harvesters of doves by far, accounting for about 85 percent of the WMU total throughout the twenty-seven-year (1961–87) period.

Generally, WMU harvest increased between 1961 and 1969 (+3.4 percent per year, r = 0.85, P<0.01) and then decreased between 1969 and 1985 (−3.0 percent per year, r = −0.90, P<0.01) *(Figure 63)*. Only Idaho registered an increase in harvest during the entire 1961–87 period (+1.33 percent per year, r = 0.58, P<0.01). Some interesting distinctions were noted between subunit harvest trends.

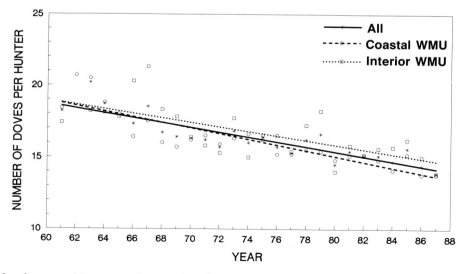

Figure 62. Trends of seasonal harvests of mourning doves in the Western Management Unit, based on state harvest surveys, 1961–87.

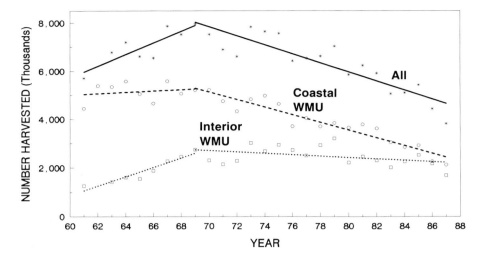

Figure 63. Trends of mourning doves harvested in the Western Management Unit, based on state harvest surveys, 1961–87.

For the Coastal WMU, harvest remained fairly stable with no trend between 1961 and 1970 ($+0.47$ percent per year, r = 0.20, $P > 0.50$) but rapidly declined thereafter (-4.2 percent per year, r = -0.95, $P < 0.01$). Dove harvest in the Interior WMU increased dramatically between 1961 and 1969 ($+9.9$ percent per year, r = 0.96, $P < 0.01$) but since 1969 has remained relatively stable (-1.2 percent per year, r = 0.42, $P > 0.05$). Thus, the decline in harvest since 1969 in the WMU as a whole was mainly due to decreased harvest in the Coastal subunit.

Linear regression tests comparing harvest versus Call-count indices during 1966–87 indicate a strong positive correlation between the two variables for the Coastal WMU (r = 0.86, $P < 0.01$) but no correlation for the Interior WMU (r = -0.15, $P > 0.05$). Thus, harvest has declined substantially in the Coastal WMU commensurate with lower populations but has remained constant in the Interior WMU despite declining population trends. Since seasonal harvest decreased throughout the twenty-seven-year period in both subunits, the continued high level of hunter participation in the Interior WMU has resulted in continued high harvest. It remains to be seen whether this trend will continue.

Harvest distribution within season. Dove hunting activity and harvests normally occur during the early part of the season. For example, 90.8 percent of the 1,042 bands from all doves reported in California (and for which recovery dates were known) were taken during September 1–10, 5.1 percent during September 11–20 and 4.1 percent during the remaining two months of hunting (Tomlinson et al. 1988). Similarly, in Arizona 92.0 percent of 835 recoveries were taken during September 1–10,

6.0 percent during September 11–20 and the remaining 2.0 percent during the following seven weeks of hunting. In more northern states of the unit, dove harvests were even more skewed toward the season opening because dove populations migrate early and are not available to be hunted at later dates.

POSSIBLE FACTORS INFLUENCING POPULATION TRENDS

The long-term downward trend in WMU mourning dove population and harvest is of great concern to wildlife managers. In the following discussion, several factors are examined that may have contributed to this decline.

Current Status Assessment

The first step in identifying factors possibly involved in the WMU mourning dove population decline was a comparison of key population characteristics of the WMU with those of the CMU, where population levels remained stable during the twenty-two-year period 1966–87. A second phase was an analysis of how population characteristics and harvests differed between subunits of the WMU.

WMU and CMU comparisons.
1. Density of breeding doves in the WMU was only 57 percent that of the CMU (average number of doves heard calling per route, 1966–87: WMU, 14.4; CMU, 25.4).
2. Long-term rate of decline for WMU dove popu-

lations was about seven times greater than for CMU doves and was statistically more certain (1966–87 average annual decline: WMU, − 3.4 percent, $P < 0.01$; CMU, − 0.5, $P < 0.10$, NS).

3. Differences were noted in recovery distribution patterns between the two units (Tomlinson et al. 1988). A dove from the WMU was more than twice as likely to be recovered in the unit of banding as was a dove banded in the CMU. However, individual birds banded in the WMU and CMU had equal chances of being recovered in the adjacent unit and in Mexico. In contrast, a dove banded in the CMU was thirteen times more likely to be recovered in Central America than was one banded in the WMU.

4. Each unit was similarly dependent on its own dove populations for its harvest. For both units, about 98 percent of the recoveries originated from within the unit.

5. Average unweighted survival rate estimates for immatures (WMU = 35 percent; CMU = 44 percent) and adults (WMU = 52 percent; CMU = 53 percent) suggest that immature doves in the WMU experienced higher mortality than did immature doves in the CMU.

6. Hunting mortality (kill rate) of WMU doves was greater than that of CMU doves (immatures: WMU = 14 percent, CMU = 6 percent; adults: WMU = 10 percent, CMU = 5 percent).

7. Similarly, the proportion of total annual mortality attributed to hunting was twice as great for WMU doves as for CMU doves (immatures: WMU = 22 percent, CMU = 11 percent; adults: WMU = 22 percent, CMU = 10 percent).

8. Finally, to offset annual mortality and maintain a stable population, WMU breeding adults needed to fledge 2.8 young per pair annually, somewhat more than the 2.2 young per pair required for CMU doves.

In summary, a smaller and sparser population of mourning doves in the WMU was harvested more intensively, experienced higher mortality and had a higher proportion of hunting-induced mortality than did the CMU population. Greater productivity was required to maintain population stability.

Coastal and Interior WMU comparisons.

1. Breeding mourning dove densities were higher in the Coastal WMU than in the Interior WMU during the late 1960s but lower during the late 1980s (1966–70: Coastal WMU = 22.2 doves per route, Interior WMU = 18.8; 1983–87: Coastal WMU = 8.8, Interior WMU = 11.6). Densities declined 60 percent in the Coastal WMU and 38 percent in the Interior WMU between the two periods.

2. The rate of annual decline of doves in the Coastal WMU was 2.5 times greater than in the Interior WMU and had stronger statistical reliability. Average annual decline: Coastal WMU = − 5.1 percent ($P < 0.01$); Interior WMU = − 2.0 percent ($P < 0.05$).

3. Coastal WMU doves were more likely to be recovered in the state of banding (Coastal WMU = 82 percent; Interior WMU = 60 percent) and in the entire unit (Coastal WMU = 93 percent; Interior WMU = 86 percent) but less likely to be recovered in Mexico and Central America (Coastal WMU = 6 percent; Interior WMU = 13 percent) than were Interior WMU doves.

4. Both subunits depended heavily on their own breeding season populations for harvest (Coastal WMU = 88 percent; Interior WMU = 89 percent).

5. Doves from the Coastal WMU exhibited higher kill rates than did doves from the Interior WMU (immatures: Coastal WMU = 20 percent, Interior WMU = 5 percent; adults: Coastal WMU = 15 percent, Interior WMU = 4 percent).

6. Doves banded in the Coastal WMU survived at lower rates than did those in the Interior WMU (immatures: Coastal WMU = 31 percent, Interior WMU = 38 percent; adults: Coastal WMU = 46 percent, Interior WMU = 57 percent).

7. A greater proportion of the total annual mortality of Coastal WMU doves was attributable to hunting loss than was the case for Interior WMU doves (immatures: Coastal WMU = 30 percent, Interior WMU = 9 percent; adults: Coastal WMU = 29 percent, Interior WMU = 11 percent).

8. Production needed to maintain a stable population was greater in the Coastal WMU than in the Interior WMU (3.1 young fledged per pair in the Coastal WMU; 2.1 young per pair in the Interior WMU).

9. Average hunter densities per square mile (2.59 km²) were more than 1.5 times greater in the Coastal WMU than in the Interior WMU during 1983–87 (Coastal WMU = 0.57; Interior WMU = 0.35).

10. Hunter numbers in the Coastal WMU increased 3.6 percent per year between 1961 and 1969 and declined 2.5 percent per year between 1969 and 1987. For the Interior CMU, hunter numbers increased 6.9 percent per year until 1975, then decreased 2.4 percent per year through 1987.

11. Seasonal harvest decreased at about 1.0 percent per year for both subunits during 1961–87.

12. Total harvest in the Coastal WMU remained stable between 1961 and 1970, then declined 4.2 percent per year through 1987. In the Interior WMU, harvest increased 9.9 percent per year between 1961 and 1969 and declined minimally thereafter.

In summary, doves of the Coastal WMU were harvested more intensively, experienced higher annual mortality and required greater production to maintain stable populations than did mourning doves of the Interior WMU.

Nesting and Productivity

A study conducted throughout the United States in 1979 and 1980 (Geissler et al. 1987) provided insight into mourning dove nesting chronology and productivity among the three management units (data from Utah and California represented the WMU). The effective length of the dove nesting season is shorter in the WMU than elsewhere in the country, with the possible exception of northern states in the CMU. The season extends for about 89 days in the WMU, 101 days in the CMU and 138 days in the EMU. Proportionately, more nests are begun, more eggs laid and more young produced in the summer (May through August) in the WMU than in the other two units. Contrarily, fewer nesting activities are associated with spring and autumn in the WMU than in the other two units. In particular, the spring period (February through April) was more important to all phases of nesting activity in the CMU and EMU than in the WMU.

Although daily survival rates were reported, the study did not provide information on the frequency of nesting or the numbers of young produced per pair, so productivity could not be compared among units. However, other conditions being equal, the shorter nesting season in the WMU would require that each nesting attempt be more successful in producing young to compensate for mortality than in other sections of the country. Considering the high production required to maintain a stable population and the long-term downward population trend in the WMU, the ability of doves to counterbalance mortality may have been exceeded during the past twenty-five years. Further studies are needed to determine the productivity of WMU mourning doves.

Environmental Changes

Habitat. Varied mourning dove habitats in the WMU have been adversely affected by changes in agricultural, ranching, water reclamation and land-development practices (Tomlinson et al. 1987, Tomlinson and Dolton 1987). Large acreages of sagebrush in the northern Great Basin have been altered or eradicated to improve range conditions for livestock. In a recent study in southeastern Idaho, virtually all dove nests were situated on the ground under brush, usually sagebrush (Howe and Flake 1989a). This suggests that clearing of sagebrush eliminates formerly suitable nesting habitat in areas where trees already are in short supply. In California, many large live oak trees that previously supported nesting dove populations have been cut and processed for firewood, chipboard and barbecue briquettes. In the San Joaquin Valley of California and elsewhere, many acres of formerly fallow fields or pastures have been converted to cotton and nut or fruit tree production. Weed seeds formerly associated with these fields no doubt have decreased substantially, thus reducing foods available to doves. Autumn plowing and burning of ditch banks and field edges also have reduced natural food supplies. Industrial development and urbanization have eliminated orchards and farmlands once beneficial to doves for nesting and feeding.

The trend to fewer and larger farms and fields has affected doves adversely through elimination of windbreaks and fencerows, as well as from the coincident shift from diversified cropping practices to monocultural farming. For example, vast acreages of vineyards now occupy many areas of Napa, Sonoma and San Joaquin counties of central California. During 1981–82, Tobin and Hothem (1983) conducted studies to determine the species and relative abundance of birds flying into and departing from five vineyards during late July to late September. Not a single mourning dove was seen, although 9,645 individual birds of twenty-eight species were counted during the survey periods. Although inconclusive, these data indicate that vineyards are little used by nesting or migrant doves.

Orchards in Washington and Oregon have been rendered less desirable for dove nesting because of a shift from standard to semidwarf varieties of trees and because of overhead sprinkling systems. Knight et al. (1984) investigated dove nesting in three categories of fruit orchards in northcentral Washington. Preferred nesting trees (6.6 nests per one hundred trees) tended to be twenty to twenty-seven years old and of the standard variety, which typically provide horizontal branching suitable for nest platforms. Younger, semidwarf trees with vertical branching generally were found to be unsuited for dove nesting. This subject is discussed in more detail later.

In Arizona and southern California, many riparian trees, such as saltcedar and mesquite, have been eliminated because of reclamation projects and lowered water tables from irrigation demands. Because of its high evapotranspiration rate, the predominant phreatophyte, saltcedar, is a primary target for removal along southwestern rivers and streams (Kerpez and Smith 1987). Although saltcedar is of varying importance to doves throughout its range, it is used intensively as nesting habitat by mourning doves in some areas. Indeed, most riparian trees are used heavily by mourning doves throughout the year. For example, in a study of bird use of riparian thickets along the Colorado River in Arizona, Anderson and Ohmart (1977) discarded dove data because the overwhelming abundance of doves precluded their analysis of information for less abundant species.

In extensive upland areas of the Southwest, mesquite and other trees and brush often are removed by chaining to improve grass production for livestock grazing. Total elimination of mesquite results in reduced populations of mourning doves, but there is some evidence that reducing the density of mesquite may be beneficial. Studies of three pastures near Tucson, Arizona showed that, where all mesquite had been removed, transect counts averaged 1.6 doves per mile (1.0/km), compared with 1.0 dove per mile (0.6/km) in undisturbed mesquite and 6.1 doves per mile (3.8/km) where mesquite had been partially removed (Germano et al. 1983). Unfortunately, most clearing operations remove all woody vegetation and therefore are detrimental to dove populations.

Clearing of native brush, brush control by fire, and urban/suburban sprawl all have contributed to reducing habitat components for mourning doves in the Western Management Unit. *Top left photo (Utah) by Charles Hart; courtesy of the U.S. Soil Conservation Service. Top right photo (Washington) by Harmon S. Hodgkinson; courtesy of the U.S. Soil Conservation Service. Bottom photo (California) by Daniel Rabey; courtesy of the U.S. Soil Conservation Service.*

Where citrus groves have replaced native vegetation, mourning doves frequently make heavy use of the groves for nesting and roosting. Near Blythe, California, Wells et al. (1979) recorded up to 13.5 doves per acre (33.4/ha) of citrus during the summer. Densities in nearby mesquite, although high, were nonetheless 44 percent below the densities in citrus. During the past twenty-five years, however, many citrus orchards have been cleared, mainly as a result of housing development. For example, Arizona citrus acreage declined from about 20,000 acres (8,100 ha) in the early 1960s to 14,000 acres (5,700 ha) in 1989 (L. True personal communication: 1989). Here, too, doves doubtlessly lost valuable nesting habitat.

Housing developments in native vegetation of the Southwest also result in changes in bird densities and diversity of species. Tweit and Tweit (1986) studied bird densities during winter and early spring in "bajadas" (alluvial fans emanating from adjacent mountains) near Tucson, Arizona. Because of their scenic position overlooking the city, bajadas are highly desired as residential sites and are rapidly being altered by bulldozers. Little change occurred in the avifauna with moderate development (0.8 house per acre: 2/ha) as long as native vegetation remained. When native vegetation was replaced by exotic plants, the avifauna changed dramatically. Mourning dove densities were 28 to 280 birds per square mile (11 to 108/km²) in relatively undisturbed areas but less than 16 per square mile (6.2/km²) in developed areas.

Although it is known that degradation of habitats has occurred in the WMU, assessment of the net effects on mourning doves is difficult because documenting statistics generally are not available. Nevertheless, it can be said with certainty that mourning doves have encountered increasingly unfavorable habitat conditions in the unit at least since the mid-1960s. Certainly, these detrimental habitat modifications have contributed to the dove population decline.

Agriculture. Farming practices also have changed during the past twenty-five years in response to economic demands. Among other factors, the transformation from a small-grain farming economy to one of cotton in Arizona has been identified as a contributing factor in the decline of white-winged doves in that state (P. Smith personal communication: 1988). To determine if trends in cropping practices may have adversely affected mourning dove populations, agricultural data were compared to mourning dove Call-count and harvest data during 1966–83 (Tomlinson et al. 1987, Tomlinson and Dolton 1987).

Of ten principal crops, corn, wheat, rice and sorghum were considered potentially beneficial as food sources; barley, oats and dry beans were considered of little value; and cotton, sugar beets and alfalfa were deemed of no food value. From the mid-1960s to the mid-1980s, wheat acreage increased 31 percent, corn acreage rose 96 percent and rice increased only slightly. Mainly in Arizona and California, sorghum decreased by 77 percent and cotton increased 96 percent. Barley, oats, sugar beets and alfalfa all decreased by varying amounts.

Linear regressions were computed using crop acreages as the independent variables, with Call-count indices, dove harvests, numbers of hunters and seasonal bags as the dependent variables for the eighteen-year period 1966–83 in the WMU. Although strong correlations were exhibited for sorghum ($r = 0.75$, $P < 0.01$), corn (-0.73, $P < 0.01$) and cotton (-0.60, $P < 0.01$) with average seasonal bag (and to a lesser extent with the other parameters), it was concluded that the comparisons were not sufficiently conclusive to infer that specific cropping practices were responsible for mourning dove declines. Too many variables were present (e.g., availability of waste grain to doves, plowing and discing practices, availability of alternate food sources, as well as coincidental trends of the parameters tested) to enable an impartial judgment on cause and effect. However, the strong correlations associated with sorghum, corn and cotton suggest that changing agricultural practices could have had some adverse impacts on dove populations. Additional research is needed.

The most productive agricultural lands in the WMU generally are associated with irrigation. Water for irrigation is obtained either from naturally occurring surface water augmented by a storage and delivery system of reservoirs, canals and ditches, or by pumping from subsurface aquifers. With problems arising regarding both types of water supply, the future of irrigation farming is in doubt. In 1982, for example, irrigation drainwater at Kesterson National Wildlife Refuge in California's San Joaquin Valley was found to contain lethal quantities of the trace element selenium, which has caused a complete shutdown of the refuge (van Schilfgaarde 1989, C. Smith personal communication: 1989). Similar problems have been documented over wide areas of the West. Likewise, depletion of western aquifers threatens the supply and quality of water and increases irrigation costs. The overdraft of groundwater from irrigation pumping is categorized as critical (El-Ashry and Gibbons 1987) in much of central California and southeastern Arizona, both among the most productive agricultural regions of the WMU. Future water management policies in the West likely will include responses to problems of water quantity and quality. The resulting measures can be expected to affect the relationship of agriculture to the mourning dove.

Contaminants and other detrimental factors. Possibly the greatest threat to dove populations, other than habitat destruction and excessive hunting, is the widespread application of many types of chemical pesticides and herbicides. During 1987 alone, an estimated 14.1 million pounds (6.4 million kg) of various pesticides (active ingredients only) were applied to crops, forest lands and industrial/ residential areas of Oregon (Rinehold and Witt 1989). Although not all chemical applications are hazardous to mourning doves, those with adverse impacts apparently have had greater influence than was realized previously, particularly in the WMU. Yet no comprehensive evaluation of their direct and indirect effects on doves has been undertaken.

A thorough review of pesticides and bird populations by Risebrough (1983) provided little information specific to mourning doves (see also chapter 12).

In experiments by Tori and Peterle (1983), courtship periods of mourning doves fed 10 ppm polychlorinated biphenyls (PCBs) were lengthened significantly, and aberrant courtship activity of the treated doves sometimes led to discontinuance of reproductive efforts. Similarly, the period preceding renesting of captive ring doves was extended by 2.5 times when Haegele and Hudson (1973, 1977) introduced DDE into the diets of the experimental cohorts; they also noted marked reduction of courtship behavior of the treated birds.

Certain organophosphate and carbamate pesticides—used widely in the United States at seed-planting time to protect a variety of crops—are formulated as granules. Properly applied, the granules are buried mechanically in the soil, but through spillage or careless procedure, some may remain exposed. As few as one to five granules of some of these pesticides (e.g., Dasanit, Furadan, Temik) can be lethal to house sparrows and red-winged blackbirds (Balcomb et al. 1984), suggesting hazard to doves and other ground-feeding granivorous birds.

More specifically relevant to the WMU, Blus et al. (1983) attributed mourning dove mortality in Washington to endrin, which was then being used as a rodenticide in western orchards. DeWeese et al. (1984), studying organochlorides in thirty-eight avian species collected in eight western states, noted that dichlore diphenyl dichloroethylene (DDE) and PCBs were identified most often and found in the highest concentrations. Although most of these pesticides have been prohibited in

The extensive use of pesticides in the Western Management Unit may have an extremely adverse impact on mourning dove populations via direct contamination and alteration of vegetative communities. The extent of impact is not known but needs to be investigated. *Photo (Oregon) by John L. Rogers; courtesy of the USDA Forest Service.*

the United States, their use continues in Mexico and Central America, where many doves winter. Any study focusing on the effects of agricultural biocides on mourning doves should encompass the year-round range of the species.

Mourning doves also are subject to various diseases. The most notable is trichomoniasis, which is caused by the flagellate protozoan *Trichomonas gallinae* (see chapter 12). This organism is common in doves and pigeons but becomes pathogenic only at certain times. In a recent study of mourning doves collected in California's Central Valley near Fresno, 38 percent of fifty-five doves collected in July and August were found to harbor trichomonads (Rupiper and Harmon 1988). Of nine adults, only one was positive (11 percent), whereas nineteen (42 percent) of forty-five immature doves were infected. The investigators speculated that the higher incidence among immatures, which typically migrate earlier than adults, may indicate a relatively wide origin of infection. However, Rupiper and Harmon believed that the investigated strain may have been avirulent and possibly protective against infection by strains of greater pathogenicity.

Highly virulent stains of *Trichomonas* can cause widespread mortality among mourning doves. A large-scale die-off occurred in Alabama during 1949 and 1950, in which an estimated 50,000 mourning doves were lost (Haugen and Keeler 1952). There are no documented cases of widespread mortality among mourning doves in the WMU, but two local outbreaks occurred in the central Willamette Valley of Oregon in the spring of 1988 (C. J. Henny personal communication: 1989). East of Corvallis, approximately 100 doves were found dead, and another 25 were found between Lebanon and Scio. In both cases, the deaths were associated with "backyard" bird feeding. W. Mathewson (personal communication: 1989) also reported seeing obviously sick doves in his Salem backyard, and his description was indicative of trichomoniasis. Doves are particularly susceptible to the disease when concentrated at these feeders and waterers, and hundreds of birds may succumb unless the source is eliminated.

This fragmentary information suggests that trichomoniasis is endemic among WMU mourning doves, but knowledge of its overall distribution and virulence is poorly defined.

Other mortality associated with hunting. In addition to the hunter harvest, illegal shooting is responsible for several associated forms of mourning dove mortality. Haas (1977) calculated an unretrieved crippling loss of 27 to 41 percent in South Carolina. Managers generally use 30 percent of the legal harvest as an average crippling rate. Baiting and over-bagging (shooting more than the daily bag limit)—two activities frequently uncovered by conservation law enforcement agents—undoubtedly result in additional dove mortality. Unfortunately, the magnitude of the loss to illegal shooting cannot be estimated with certain precision, and its effect on the dove population is unknown.

Several studies have documented deaths of mourning doves from ingestion of lead shot (Locke and Bagley 1967, Lewis and Legler 1968, Kendall and Scanlon 1979, Buerger et al. 1983). Currently, no definitive studies have been attempted to assess the effect of toxic lead ingestion on dove populations. With the steady progression to the use of nontoxic shot for waterfowl hunting and advances in ammunition technology, the day may be close when this form of mortality will vanish.

Local Observations

In the absence of comprehensive information on changes in dove habitat, views were solicited from several competent observers who have lived in specific areas of the WMU for many years. Their judgments are subjective but worthy of consideration.

Turlock, California. The Turlock area is in the California Trough (San Joaquin Valley) Physiographic Region (No. 245). During the 1966–87 period, Call-count indices declined from an average of 33.0 to 5.7 doves per route—an average decline of 9.2 percent per year (r = 0.92, $P < 0.01$). This was the greatest decline registered in any of the regions of the WMU.

Edward Channing, a veteran dove bander and authority on local dove movements, reported that the dove population on his farm near Turlock in 1937 was "fantastic." By 1976, however, he had to drive several hundred miles of local farm roads to locate trappable numbers of doves for his study. Channing attributed the decline in dove populations to deterioration of dove habitat around Turlock. Major changes included more intensified farming, changes in types of crops planted, elimination of eucalyptus trees that had been planted in groves for shade and wind protection, removal of trees and brush along roads and field boundaries as well as in odd, unfarmed areas, and the lining of irrigation canals and ditches with concrete (or entirely piping the water supply system).

On the other hand, as the mourning dove lost ground in the rural areas, it increasingly colonized urban habitats (Channing 1979). In his view, these "urban" doves do not move into the countryside and therefore are exposed to little or no hunting.

Medford, Oregon. Medford is located in the Klamath Mountains Physiographic Region (No. 244). Although never a major dove production area, it has experienced a marked reduction in dove population. During 1966–87, Call-count indices declined an average of 3.9 percent per year (r = − 0.59, $P < 0.01$); during 1987, fewer than 1.7 doves were heard per route in the region.

Robert H. Smith, retired biologist with the U.S. Fish and Wildlife Service, has resided in the upper Rogue River Valley for about forty years. He expressed belief that several agricultural practices have been detrimental to breeding mourning doves and that these, singly or in the aggregate, contributed to the population decline. Especially apparent are changes in maintenance of pear orchards. Once an excellent habitat for nesting mourning doves because of structure and form of the pear trees, these orchards now support a relatively low density of breeding birds. Turbine pesticide sprayers came into local use during the 1950s and have been used since. Turbine spraying begins in the preblossoming period in March and continues at biweekly periods throughout the fruiting period, which

Land-use changes in the Western Management Unit are shown by time-stage aerial photography on the Edward Channing farm, located 4 miles (6.4 km) south of Turlock in Merced County, California. The photograph on the left is dated July 31, 1937; the right scene was taken on June 1, 1987. Major changes on the 120-acre (48.6 ha) farm over the fifty-year span included: (1) elimination of all but one wetland by filling and reduction of seepage; (2) removal of nearly all eucalyptus plantings along roads and elimination of all but one grove; (3) lining of dirt irrigation ditches with concrete; (4) decrease in uncultivated fields and pastures; (5) reduction in shrubs around farmsteads; (6) removal of all vineyards; (7) total conversion of orchards from peaches to almonds; (8) decrease in the extent and diversity of annual weeds by cultivation and herbicides; (9) field plowing immediately after harvest; and (10) increase of paved roads. These changes were detrimental to the amount and quality of mourning dove habitat. Overall, the nine types of land use evident in forty-six units or fields in 1937 was reduced to six types of land use practiced in twenty-two units in 1987. During the interval, the mourning dove changed from an abundant to a scarce breeding species. *Photos courtesy of the National Aerial Photography Program, EROS Data Center, Sioux Falls, South Dakota.*

coincides with the major dove nesting season. Because of the great velocity of the pressurized discharge, repetitive spraying is capable of destroying flimsily constructed mourning dove nests and could virtually decimate all dove nesting attempts. In addition, the direct and indirect effects of the applied pesticides on adult and nestling doves could be devastating.

Eastcentral Washington. Eastern Washington is in the Walla Walla Plateau Physiographic Region (No. 201). It is characterized by extensive apple orchards and wheat fields. During 1966–87, calling doves decreased an average of 4.6 percent per year ($r = -0.81$, $P < 0.01$). Whereas the number of calling

birds per route averaged 20.1 in 1966–70, it now averages only 9.1 birds (1983–87).

Information on the changed status of breeding mourning doves in this region comes from (1) observations of James W. Mullan (U.S. Fish and Wildlife Service biologist) and C. C. "Red" Pittack (agricultural pesticides authority), both long-time residents, and (2) findings from a 1977 unpublished study by Don L. Zeigler of the Washington Department of Game.

Breeding mourning doves once were abundant in the renowned fruit production area of the Wenatchee-Yakima region, with apple trees being the preferred sites for nesting. Two events occurred that reduced the desirability of apple orchards as nesting locations. Severe freezes during the winters of 1964 and 1968 killed many mature "standard" apple trees. The dead and damaged trees in many cases were replaced with better-producing dwarf and semidwarf varieties. Unlike the umbrella-shaped standard apple trees, which had many horizontal limbs, the new varieties were pruned after the central-leader system, resulting in fewer horizontal branches suitable for nest sites. In 1961, dwarf and semidwarf varieties comprised only 7 percent of all apple trees; by 1974, they accounted for 52 percent of the total. Concurrently, irrigation systems were changed from gravity flow ditches, or "rills," to overhead sprinklers with high-pressure, 40-pound-per-square-inch (2.8 kg/cm^2) sprinkler heads.

During Zeigler's (1977) study, few dove nests were found in apple trees less than fifteen years old. Breeding doves preferred to nest in and were more successful in old (twenty-five to thirty-five years) trees that were not overhead irrigated. In one segment of the study, 6 acres (2.4 ha) of standard-sized apple trees that were overhead irrigated had only 0.6 nests per acre (1.5/ha) compared to 3.1 (7.7) and 4.1 (10.1) nests, respectively, for standard apple orchards irrigated by ground sprinklers and rills.

Marked agricultural changes likewise occurred in the vast dryland wheat region of eastern Washington. Early in the 1970s, farmers began routinely applying herbicides, such as 2-4-D, to eliminate annual grasses and forbs. Today, these fields essentially are devoid of all vegetation other than wheat, and the wheat stubble and waste grain often are eliminated by plowing and discing shortly after harvest. Great changes also have occurred in farming practices for lands irrigated from Lake Roosevelt above Grand Coulee Dam. More intensive farming, changes in crops, and broad applications of pesticides and herbicides are thought to be responsible for the much reduced mourning dove populations in this area.

Conclusions

The foregoing examples illustrate the marked changes that have occurred throughout the WMU during the past two to three decades. No single factor can be isolated as the cause for mourning dove declines. The WMU's decreasing dove populations are the result of a combination of factors that includes loss of nesting habitat, agricultural changes that degraded many habitats, pesticides, disease and mortality from hunting. But knowing both the identity and importance of each factor working for and against the mourning dove is insufficient, because it is the net effect of these that is vital. It is foreseen that, with ongoing changes in agricultural technology, the species' environment will be unpredictable in the years ahead. Initial efforts must be aimed at halting the dove's long-term population decline, followed by efforts to rebuild the population to former levels. Managers are faced with a formidable task to identify and counter limiting factors in order to restore stable, self-sustaining mourning dove populations in the WMU.

IV.

Research and Management

Chapter 20

Capturing, Banding, Marking and Radio-tagging Techniques

Thomas S. Baskett
Cooperative Fish and Wildlife Research Unit
U.S. Fish and Wildlife Service
The School of Natural Resources
University of Missouri
Columbia, Missouri

Much of the study of mourning doves, whether for enhancing basic knowledge or for improving management strategies, is based on effective techniques for capturing, banding, marking and tracking the birds. These techniques may be central to the success of both field and pen studies and sometimes even laboratory studies. They underlie accurate recognition of individual doves or cohorts, alive or in hunters' bags.

CAPTURING

Capturing birds for banding, marking or penning is the obvious first step in many modern studies of mourning doves. Traps and other equipment for capturing doves are well described in the U.S. Fish and Wildlife Service *Special Scientific Report—Wildlife No. 117* (Reeves et al. 1968). For details of construction and capture procedures involving traps and other devices, the reader is referred to that publication.

The purpose of this chapter is to summarize and update information about contrivances and procedures used to capture mourning doves and to evaluate their effectiveness, particularly with respect to biases inherent in their use, as revealed in studies during the last two or three decades.

Portable Bait Traps

Reeves et al. (1968) asserted that more mourning doves have been captured in bait traps than in any other devices; this statement undoubtedly still applies. Bait traps of small or moderate size, usually made of galvanized welded wire or hardware cloth, can be transported easily and placed, set and serviced by one person. Some types can be collapsed for easier transport and storage.

Traps of this group are self-operating. Doves enter baited cells through wire funnels, through openings guarded by hinged doors that close outward when the prop-wires are moved by doves brushing trip wires or strings in the baited spaces, or through openings provided with short, stiff wire bobs that swing inward, then return to the vertical position, blocking exits once the doves are inside the trap. These traps range from about 24 to 36 inches (61 to 91 cm) long and from 8 to 12 inches (20 to 30 cm) tall. Welded wire of 1- by 2-inch (2.5 by 5 cm) mesh is often used to construct them. Commonly used small to medium-sized bait traps include the following.

Thompson two-cell trap. The Thompson trap has a hinged door at each end that swings shut when doves in the baited cell brush a tripping thread *(Figure 64)*. The door of each cell functions

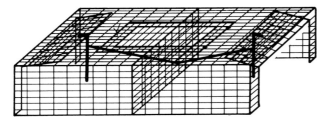

Figure 64. Diagram of a Thompson two-cell trap. *Illustration by C. Baysinger-Daniel; courtesy of the Missouri Cooperative Fish and Wildlife Research Unit.*

independently, and doves often enter one cell after the door to the other cell has been tripped.

Potter two-cell trap. The end doors of the Potter trap drop vertically when tripped by the weight of a dove on a pedal whose movement releases the door catch through a wire linkage. Mechanisms for the two compartments function independently as with the Thompson two-cell trap.

Stoddard collapsible swing-wire trap. The Stoddard trap has only one entrance door, guarded by inwardly swinging wire bobs. Reeves et al. (1968) pointed out that these wires must be spaced close enough to prevent the doves from escaping by pushing the wires aside. Because the wires are not as "safe" as a rigid door, Reeves et al. (1968) suggested that these traps be placed so that the trapper can approach from the entrance side and securely block the entrance with a board, rock or brick before moving to the side with the door used to remove the doves.

Modified shorebird trap. This funnel trap was developed to capture shorebirds but has been successfully modified for dove trapping. In the version described by Reeves et al. (1968), heavy hardware cloth or welded-wire fencing material 12 inches (30.5 cm) wide is shaped to form sides that describe an imperfect figure eight in plan view. The "dimples," which are not directly opposite each other, are open, forming funnel entrances. The trap proper is about 36 inches (91 cm) long but has a rectangular, transportable "gathering cage" attached to one end when in operation.

Kniffin modified funnel trap. The Kniffin trap—one of the most popular among dove banders—is similar to several earlier funnel traps, notably the rectangular, "basic" rigid funnel trap described by Reeves et al. (1968) *(Figure 65)*. Advantages of the Kniffin include its moderate size—24 inches (61 cm) square when viewed from above, and 8 inches (20 cm) high. The trap has two wire funnels located on opposite sides (but not directly opposite each other). The material is 1- by 2-inch (2.5 by 5.0 cm) galvanized welded wire. Several other features—e.g., side walls, with the 1-inch (2.5

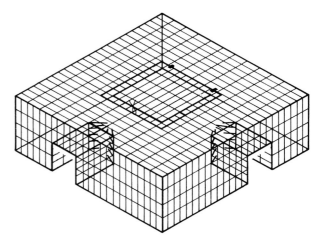

Figure 65. Diagram of a Kniffin modified funnel trap. *Illustration by C. Baysinger-Daniel; courtesy of the Missouri Cooperative Fish and Wildlife Research Unit.*

cm) spaced wires positioned vertically rather than horizontally—used in construction of the modified trap may help reduce trap injuries and make Kniffin traps easier to transport or service. The Kniffin trap has been modified further by investigators to serve specific needs of their studies.

The Kniffin modified funnel trap is preferred by many mourning dove banders because it is moderate in size, portable, self-operating, relatively safe for captured birds and modifiable to individual trapping circumstances. *Photo by Charles W. Schwartz.*

Other portable funnel traps. Other funnel traps have been used to capture mourning doves. The "Pinkham modified funnel trap," a collapsible trap similar to the basic rigid funnel trap, was developed to facilitate storage and transporting. According to Reeves et al. (1968), two or three dozen Pinkham traps can be nested to fit in an automobile trunk.

A two-cell derivative of the three-leaved "cloverleaf trap" was developed to be collapsible and easily transported (Keeler and Winston 1951). Other funnel traps of various shapes have been developed and used, including circular, kidney-shaped and heart-shaped designs.

Comparative Capture Success

Four types of commonly used portable bait traps were tested for comparative trapping success in western Oklahoma during 1969–70 (Lewis and Morrison 1973). The trapping localities were mixed-grass eroded plain (Duck and Fletcher 1944) with sparsely wooded ravines and mesquite/grassland. Traps were placed along the edges of wheat fields where they bordered mesquite thickets, Osage-orange hedgerows and shelterbelts in which doves nested.

The traps tested (all collapsible) were Kniffin modified funnel, Thompson two-cell (hinged door), heart-shaped funnel and Stoddard swing-wire. The Kniffin and Thompson traps were constructed as described by Reeves et al. (1968). The Stoddard swing-wire trap was similar to that described by Reeves et al. (1968) but substantially smaller—8 by 24 by 24 inches (20 by 61 by 61 cm) versus 12 by 36 by 36 inches (30.5 by 91 by 91 cm). The heart-shaped funnel trap had an entrance 2.5 inches (6.3 cm) wide in the indentation of the "heart."

Experimental design was rigorously planned to permit statistical evaluation of trap type, bait type, single or paired deployment and use of artificial decoys.

In the first year (1969) of the Lewis and Morrison (1973) study, data about relative capture success according to types of traps were provided by 1,998 doves captured during 20,037 trap days. The Kniffin and Thompson traps, whether deployed singly or in pairs, were far superior ($P<0.005$) to the other traps, requiring 5.8 and 6.3 trap days, respectively, per dove captured. The heart-shaped and Stoddard traps required 22.9 and 42.0 trap days per dove, respectively. In general, average catch per trap was higher with a single trap than with two traps per site.

The Pinkham collapsible funnel trap was widely used in mourning dove capture/banding programs because it was easy to store and transport. Also, its "hinged" side walls allowed for prebaiting trials. *Photo courtesy of the Texas Parks and Wildlife Department.*

Researchers bait a heart-shaped trap to capture mourning doves in western Oklahoma. This design, with entrance at the heart indentation, takes advantage of the mourning dove's propensity, when approaching a trap, to walk first along its sides. The trap's curvature "leads" the dove to the opening. *Photo courtesy of U.S. Fish and Wildlife Service.*

In the second study year, Lewis and Morrison further tested capture rates for the Kniffin and Thompson traps only, using exclusively white proso millet, the leading bait in the previous year's tests. They captured 1,561 doves in 9,797 trap days in this experiment; the two types of traps produced similar rates of capture ($P > 0.05$).

Another set of experiments for evaluation of trap types was conducted during two years by Amend and Kniffin (1970) in southern Indiana. In total, 6,956 captures were made; the results were presented at the Midwest Wildlife Conference but never formally published. In their first year's experiment, Amend and Kniffin tallied more than 30.5 percent of all mourning dove catches in modified shorebird traps similar to the type described by Reeves et al. (1968). Catches in a two-cell drop door (Thompson-type) trap (28 percent) did not differ significantly from those in the shorebird trap, but both differed from catches in "standard" funnel traps (17 percent) and Kniffin modified funnel traps (16 percent). In the first experiment, all four types caught many more doves than did a readily collapsible "Ruos" trap with funnel entrances.

In the second year's experiment, 42 percent of the catches were in four-cell drop-door traps, differing significantly from percentages of catches in shorebird traps (19 percent), Kniffin traps (18 percent) and Ruos traps with wire bobs (18 percent). Results of an ancillary experiment by Amend and Kniffin (1970) showed no significant difference between proportions of catches in Kniffin funnel traps constructed as described by Reeves et al. (1978) and those in similar traps with 2.25 times the floor area.

Amend and Kniffin (1970) noticed that, when approaching a trap, mourning doves often walk around the perimeter. They suggested that this behavior pattern is capitalized on by the rounded shape of the shorebird trap (their version did not have a rectangular gathering cage attached to an end) and by the wide, unrestricted opening of drop-door traps. Although the shorebird trap performed well in the Amend and Kniffin experiments, the authors found it particularly time-consuming to set up and not easily transported.

Baits

The lists of bait seeds used with some success to trap mourning doves are quite lengthy. As Reeves et al. (1968: 38) observed, "The best type of bait to use creates debate whenever dove banders assemble." Keeler and Winston (1951: 177), who banded doves in the Southeast, favored scratch feed consisting of cracked corn and wheat, but they noted that mixtures of sorghum, buckwheat, rye and other cereal grains also were used successfully. They concluded: "The [dove] trapper must use his own judgment on baits, weighing local conditions and the availability and price of the various grains which can be used."

In a twenty-one-year dove research program on Cape Cod, Massachusetts, Low (1935) and Austin (1951: 149) banded 2,690 mourning doves, using "a standard chicken scratch feed for bulk, [supplemented with] smaller quantities of millet . . . buckwheat, and sunflower seed to increase its attractiveness."

In addition to the grains named above, Reeves et al. (1968) listed rye, whole-grain corn, and both milo and hegari (varieties of grain sorghum) as proven dove baits. They noted that a bait preferred by doves in one region may be rejected elsewhere. As examples, they stated that proso—a white millet—is much preferred to wheat in South Dakota, but evidently not in Maryland. Moreover, they wrote, in South Dakota and Minnesota, proso millet is preferred to brown or Japanese millet.

The well-designed field experiments conducted by Lewis and Morrison (1973) in western Oklahoma evidently included the best quantitative evaluation of bait preferences available in the published literature. In the relevant experiment, they captured 396 mourning doves during 3,117 trap days. White proso millet was the most effective bait tested; traps containing proso captured doves at a significantly greater rate ($P < 0.005$) than did those baited with sorghum, the second-ranking bait. Wheat used alone was a poor third, and wheat mixed with table salt (sometimes suggested to prevent sprouting of grain baits) required nearly 4.5 times as many trap days per bird caught as did wheat alone (see Table 3 in Lewis and Morrison 1973). White proso millet was the only bait used in the very successful dove trapping experiments conducted in Indiana by Amend and Kniffin (1970).

The diversity of bait preferences reported by various dove researchers prompted R. E. Tomlinson (personal communication: 1989) to suggest that mixtures of proven baits such as proso, wheat, cracked corn and sorghum be used in new trapping operations. Bait offerings then can be modified as appropriate to the selections by the local doves.

Procedural Tips for Bait Trapping

Successful programs involving capture of mourning doves (or most other wild animals) often owe much to procedural "tricks of the trade" known to investigators and passed on by word of mouth, or alluded to in publications, without quantitative proof of efficacy. In the case of the mourning dove, capture success depends, at least in part, on baiting procedures. Much of the intuitive wisdom about baiting doves for capture is based on experience gained through use of the adaptable portable bait traps described above, but good procedural advice came from earlier studies using semipermanent bait traps, as well. This advice may be appropriate, also, in use of other capture devices described below.

Most dove banders would agree that bait must be presented on bare surfaces for effective trapping. In the Southeast, "Doves . . . are attracted easily to cleared areas baited with scratch food" (Keeler and Winston 1951: 177). In Arkansas, Booth et al. (1975, 1976) mentioned trapping doves on gravelly areas with sparse vegetation and cutting weeds to make the area suitable for feeding by doves. In Missouri, Tomlinson (1959) cleared roadside trap sites—each about 3 by 6 feet (1 by 2 m)—by hoeing; Henry et al. (1976) similarly cleared field sites. Bivings and Silvy (1979) described very successful trapping of urban mourning doves on gravel-topped roofs of buildings on the Texas A&M University campus. Amend and Kniffin (1970) successfully deployed traps on an abandoned concrete-surfaced airport runway and taxiway in Indiana.

Prebaiting trap sites before the traps are in place or open has been recommended or practiced in some instances. Keeler and Winston (1951) deemed it useful to prebait in compact areas within fields having very little waste grain, because the practice tends to concentrate the doves and thus facilitate trapping. In Arkansas, Booth et al. (1975) prebaited trap sites for almost one month and placed Kniffin traps upside down at the sites during the period in an attempt to familiarize the doves with them. The following year, Booth et al. (1976) prebaited for nearly two months and placed the traps on stilts during the last week of prebaiting to allow the birds to become accustomed to feeding under them before removing the stilts. The lag time between normal positioning of the traps and first captures was reduced by ten to twenty days in the second year. Bivings and Silvy (1979) prebaited prospective trap sites on rooftops of buildings for two weeks before trapping; this practice, especially when mixed grain was exposed, possibly helped the doves locate the future trap sites. It should be noted that published accounts of many successful dove trapping projects do not mention prebaiting.

According to Reeves et al. (1968), live doves trapped in one cell of either the Thompson or Potter trap may decoy additional doves to the still-open

Prebaiting mourning dove trapping sites for at least several weeks prior to initiation of a trapping effort is recommended to concentrate and condition doves. The type of bait to be used depends largely on the locality's principal grain crop, but as a rule, millet, sorghum, wheat and cracked corn or mixed grains are effective. *Photo by David Dolton.*

second compartment. In the field, it is easy to surmise that feeding doves often attract others. However, Lewis and Morrison (1973) tested the influence of artificial decoys on rates of capture by placing one papier-mâché dove hunting decoy in a feeding position in each of forty-two traps, matched by an equal number of controls without decoys. More doves actually were caught in the control traps than in experimental ones, but the difference was not significant ($P > 0.05$).

Prominent among the problems encountered in bait trapping for mourning doves is the intrusion of nontarget birds and such mammals as ground squirrels and cottontail rabbits. These animals can diminish dove-trapping efficiency by prematurely tripping drop-door traps or exhausting bait supplies and, through their attempts to escape, can frighten off doves and attract predators. Nontarget avian species frequently mentioned include cowbirds, common grackles, house sparrows and feral pigeons (Reeves et al. 1968). The interference, particularly in triggered traps, of many species of seed-eating birds was mentioned by Keeler and Winston (1951) in the Southeast. They listed cardinals, red-winged blackbirds and "sparrows" as frequent culprits. They found "steady repeater" individuals to be particularly troublesome. In their rooftop trapping program in Texas, Bivings and Silvy (1979) found feral pigeons and great-tailed and common grackles to be principal nuisance birds.

In the published literature, suggested solutions to problems brought about by nontarget species are considerably fewer than laments. Reeves et al. (1968) noted that changing the composition of bait mixtures may be helpful. In Maryland, for example, not using cracked corn, millet and milo was suggested for lessening problems with grackles, cowbirds and feral pigeons, respectively. Reeves et al. also mentioned that California banders, plagued by capture of small nontarget birds, lessened the problem by providing exits through which these small birds, but not doves, could escape. To direct ground squirrels away from baited dove traps, Reeves et al. suggested routinely sprinkling small amounts of bait near their burrow entrances. Perhaps the most universally appropriate way to reduce interference from nontarget species is to step up the frequency of attending the dove traps.

Predators are attracted to concentrations of feeding doves and may frighten many doves from baited sites before they can be captured. Predators also can cause problems after doves are captured by disturbing or actually attacking the captured birds. In North Carolina, M. H. Taylor identified three species of hawks as particularly disruptive to a dove-trapping program—Cooper's hawk, American kestrel and northern harrier (Quay 1951a). Sometimes, the hawks entered the traps, killed and partly consumed the doves, then were unable to escape. Keeler and Winston (1951) listed these same three hawks as well as dogs, house cats and raccoons as troublesome to dove trapping in the Southeast. R. E. Tomlinson (personal communication: 1989) found human disturbance and vandalism to be a significant problem in his Missouri roadside trapping program.

In some instances, it may be possible to capture the offending wild predators and transport them considerable distances before release. Dogs and cats may be confined if the owners can be identified and persuaded to do so.

Timing and frequency of operators' visits may be keys to the success of well-designed dove-trapping programs. Keeler and Winston (1951) wrote that bait traps should be visited at least twice daily and suggested midmorning and "dark" as logical times because they coincided with the ends of dove feeding periods. Under no circumstances should doves be left in traps overnight, they said, because of danger of predation. They also favored attending traps every two hours during periods of midsummer heat—a precaution strongly endorsed by R. E. Mirarchi (personal communication: 1989) based on dove-trapping experiences in Alabama. Reeves et al. (1968) suggested 1.5-hour frequency of trap checks during snowy weather.

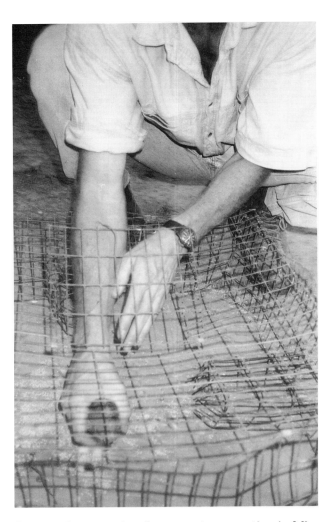

As part of a mourning dove trapping operation in Missouri, a researcher removes a dove from a funnel trap baited with proso millet. The trap (and others) were checked every thirty to sixty minutes from late afternoon until after sunset to minimize capture stress and predation. *Photo by Mary McGary; courtesy of the Missouri Department of Conservation.*

Much of the published advice about techniques for dove trapping seemingly is based on the premise that the primary or sole purpose of the program is to catch large numbers of doves for banding. When this indeed is the case, a few large traps or clusters of smaller ones can be placed in promising locations selected in part to facilitate trap attendance. This idea was exploited effectively in the trapping scheme described by Bivings and Silvy (1979). They caught 1,648 doves in one year on rooftops of buildings at Texas A&M University, with a minimum investment of professional time and at an estimated cost (aside from salaries) of thirty-one cents per dove banded. Obviously, one advantage was great flexibility in trap-checking frequency according to need.

Clustering traps to capture mourning doves minimizes the time and effort of monitoring and attending to the traps and site. For such clustering, careful site selection is mandatory and prebaiting advisable. *Photo courtesy of the Missouri Department of Conservation.*

When mourning doves are trapped for research purposes, bait sites should be cleaned periodically and rotated frequently to minimize the possibility of establishing specific foci for parasite and disease transmission. This scene shows a Kniffin modified funnel trap successfully baited with cracked corn. *Photo by Joseph A. Conti; courtesy of the Southeastern Cooperative Wildlife Disease Study, University of Georgia, Athens.*

In contrast, the roadside trapping programs described by Tomlinson et al. (1960) resulted in 1,444 doves banded in two summers, but to satisfy the research objectives, the authors opted for a trap-deployment scheme that required driving 20 miles (32 km) per run, with stops at each of fifty-five traps. Traps were checked four or five times daily according to need. Research objectives were well satisfied, but there was little opportunity for flexibility in the daily schedule.

In publications reporting dove-trapping programs, authors (e.g., Booth et al. 1975) often mentioned positioning bait sites so that doves are attracted by access to bait, water and "protective perches" in nearby trees or power lines.

Reeves et al. (1968: 44) offered advice particularly relevant to long-range, large-scale banding operations: "In the future . . . emphasis should be placed on purposeful development of perennial trapping sites, especially on national wildlife refuges and state management areas where land is under public control, agricultural equipment is usually available, human disturbance can be controlled, and personnel are usually available for . . . trapping. Also grain baits can be produced locally."

Semipermanent Bait Traps

For appropriate research objectives, and where surroundings warrant, large bait traps semipermanently situated have been found quite useful. Semipermanent traps were used extensively in early studies to determine migratory pathways of mourning doves, accuracy of migratory homing, population turnover rates and other demographic information. For example, Austin (1951: 149) used "house" traps "located semi-permanently in fixed positions" on the research station grounds during his twenty-one-year study of mourning doves on Cape Cod, Massachusetts. Initial captures of doves totaled 2,690, and total dove captures (including recaptured birds) were 6,870. In this instance, other upland bird species were targeted for study as well, and the house traps served investigators well for all these species.

House trap. This trap, as described by Lincoln (1947), is a large structure—6 feet (1.8 m) tall with 5- by 5-foot (1.5 by 1.5 m) sides. The outer shell is made (in place) with wooden uprights joined by horizontal members at the top and is covered on sides and top with woven wire of mesh size 0.75 inches (1.9 cm) or less. A doorway large enough to admit the operator is fashioned at one corner. Inside, a braced woven-wire wall, fitted with narrow, hinged doors, separates the main compartment from the vestibule. Birds are led by bait trails through the outer doorway, the vestibule and the partly closed inner doors into the main compartment. After entering and closing the outer door, the operator gains access to the main compartment through the inner doors.

Three-leaf clover trap. Lincoln (1947) described the cloverleaf trap, developed for the capture of mourning doves, as very useful at banding stations. The trap was made of 0.75-inch (1.9 cm) poultry wire in either 18- or 24-inch (46 or 61 cm) widths cut into three pieces each about 54 inches (137 cm) long and placed on edge in the ground to form a cloverleaf outline. These sides were held in the ground by pegs, spaced so that the ends were far enough apart to act as funnels. A cover of poultry netting was provided.

As Lincoln (1947) pointed out, the three entrances to this trap are advantageous, permitting doves to approach an opening from any direction; however, his view of the three-leaf clover trap as "readily portable" was not widely shared (cf. Keeler and Winston 1951).

Other Capture Devices

Cannon nets. During 1967–74, Texas Parks and Wildlife Department employees captured and banded about 83,400 mourning doves in a statewide research project. According to information furnished by T. L. Clark (personal communication: 1989), about 74,000 of the birds were captured in baited wire-funnel traps, the standard instruments of the project. However, a need was perceived for devices that were more effective where very large numbers of doves were concentrated or where food was so abundant that the birds seemed reluctant to enter funnel traps. These conditions sometimes prevailed at livestock feeding sites or near watering sites, especially during the posthunting-season dove-banding period. Drop nets were helpful

Cannon netting is an efficient method of capturing mourning doves where the birds are heavily concentrated and not easily baited to traps. Prebaiting the site, camouflaging the netting, adequate explosive charge and projectile trajectory are important preparatory logistical considerations. Well planned and executed operations can net one hundred or more doves per shot. *Top right photo by Ken Gamble; courtesy of the Texas Parks and Wildlife Department. Top left photo by T. L. Clark; courtesy of the Texas Parks and Wildlife Department. Bottom photo (at the Imperial National Wildlife Refuge in California), showing 134 doves trapped by a single shot, courtesy of the U.S. Fish and Wildlife Service.*

under these conditions, but cannon nets were more productive. About 7,300 mourning doves were caught with cannon nets during the study and 100 or more were commonly taken per cannon shot.

The Texas investigators found that the cannon net apparatus developed by Dill and Thornsberry (1950) for capturing Canada geese and other waterfowl required considerable modification for good results with mourning doves. Greater velocity for the leading edge of the net in a low trajectory was essential. This, in turn, required increased propellant charges and cannons constructed of seamless aircraft tubing with very high tensile strength for safe and effective operation. Because of the rapid acceleration of the projectiles, it was necessary to link them to the net with high-tensile chains. Bait placement, as described and diagrammed by Clark et al. (1969), was critical. The effectiveness of the

cannon net as modified in the Texas project is attested by the capture of 237 mourning doves in one firing (T. L. Clark personal communication: 1989).

Drop nets. Personnel of the Texas Parks and Wildlife Department have used drop nets as an alternative to cannon nets for capturing doves where the clear area suitable for mass capture was smaller than that required for cannon net deployment (about 30 feet [9.1 m] per side for the drop net versus 75 feet [22.9 m] for cannon netting). About 1,800 mourning doves were caught in drop nets during 1967–74 (T. L. Clark personal communication: 1989).

Rocket nets. Nets projected by rockets have been used successfully for capturing several kinds of birds, e.g., geese in England by Peter Scott (see Dill and Thornsberry 1950) and shorebirds (Thompson and DeLong 1967) in North America.

Drop nets released (dropped) from corner posts by remote detonation of blasting caps embedded in the braided nylon ski ropes used for attachment can be effective in capturing large numbers of doves. Such nets suspended over bait are more obtrusive and less portable than cannon nets but require less flat, clean space and less ballistic precision. Drop nets are regarded as less potentially hazardous to personnel than are cannon nets, so they require less supervisory talent and time. Cannon netting, however, can produce much larger captures. *Top photo by Ken Gamble; courtesy of the Texas Parks and Wildlife Department. Bottom photo—a moment after release by detonation—by T. L. Clark; courtesy of the Texas Parks and Wildlife Department.*

Because of their great acceleration and lack of recoil, rockets have been suggested as superior propellants for small-mesh, lightweight nets to capture doves (Reeves et al. 1968, R. Reynolds personal communication: 1989). However, rocket nets are not known to have been used extensively to capture mourning doves. T. L. Clark (personal communication: 1989) experimented with rocket nets as a means of capturing mourning doves in Texas and found that the initial sound of rocket ignition flushed the doves before the net reached them. (Persons using rocket nets for bird capture must have a cooperative agreement with the U.S. Fish and Wildlife Service.)

Mist nets. Mist nets, developed hundreds of years ago in Japan to capture birds for food, are made of very fine strands of netting and "supported in sections (shelves) by cross lines (trammels), strung between two poles and attached with loops" (Keyes and Grue (1982: 1). Birds fly into the nets from either side and become entangled in pockets of netting supported by the tighter cross lines. When used for capturing large numbers of doves, mist nets 40 to 60 feet (12 to 18 m) long by 7 feet (2.1 m) high have been used successfully in Maryland and Utah (Reeves et al. 1968). These nets had four shelves; mesh sizes useful for capture of doves generally ranged from 2.5 to 4 inches (6.3 to 10 cm) when stretched.

Mist nets with dimensions similar to those described above have been effective for capturing doves from concentrations that were not susceptible to bait trapping; abundance of natural food frequently was a factor (Reeves et al. 1968). Under such conditions, two nets often were deployed end-to-end and attached to three poles of light electrical conduit.

Mist nets also have been used to capture individual doves known to be associated with certain nests, thereby permitting intensive study of their behavior relative to position in the nesting cycle, their renesting patterns, etc. Harris and Morse (1958) used nets made from nylon gill netting (for fish) dyed black and strung on nylon fishing line. In twenty-five hours of trapping in Minnesota, they made 51 captures of 42 adult birds at thirty-six nests. Their net was 33 feet (10 m) long and 6 feet (1.8 m) deep. Their method required three people—two held the net poles with the net in front of the nest tree while the third person (the "panic man") approached the nest from the side opposite the net and flushed the nesting dove into the net.

An adaptation of this technique was developed by Blockstein (1985), who used a shorter 20-foot (6 m) net. The system required only two people. The trappers opened the net about 165 feet (50 m) from the nest tree and surrounded it with the net. To do so, the lead net carrier stepped in front of the nesting bird while extending the net toward it, and the other person wrapped the rest of the net around the tree and then flushed the dove. Overall, Blockstein reported about 60-percent success in capture attempts and found the technique especially effective for nests less than 5.5 feet (3 m) high in spruce trees with dense foliage and for those in isolated trees.

Mist netting requires special precautions, and it is necessary to obtain special permission to use this technique for bird banding in the United States. (The banding permit must show specifically that mist netting is allowed.) Removal of large numbers of birds from mist nets is very time-consuming yet must be done as quickly as possible. This technique often results in damage to the nest because of entanglement of the net in vegetation when the operators wrap the nest trees (see Blockstein 1985).

Nest traps. Swank (1952) developed and used a trap that could be installed at active dove nests and was useful in capturing nesting adults. Best results were obtained when nests contained squabs four to eight days old, because in that interval there was less disruption to nest contents (eggs or young) and squabs could not yet leave the nests and remove the incentive for adults to return to them.

The Swank nest trap itself was made of 1- by 2-inch (2.5 by 5.1 cm) mesh, galvanized, welded wire bent to form an inverted U 12 inches (30.5 cm) long, 7 inches (18 cm) across the flat top and 7 inches (18 cm) tall. This body was fitted with slides at the ends to accommodate drop doors held in open position by pins released simultaneously by an operator pulling a cable. The trap was held in place by attaching cloth netting placed under the nest limb to the open (bottom) ends of the inverted U sides. Further details of construction and placement of the trap can be found in Swank (1952), Reeves et al. (1968) and Day et al. (1980). One disadvantage of the trap is that it requires at least 14 inches (35 cm) of vertical clearance above the nest to accommodate the door slides.

Age and Sex Selectivity of Capture Procedures

Type of capturing device, trap deployment or other procedural nuances may influence age or sex composition of the catch. These possibilities must be considered in designing studies wherein age and sex ratios of mourning doves captured are important elements. Several investigators have noted that adults seem more wary of traps than do immatures. Amend and Kniffin (1970) asserted that traps that captured doves readily, without eliciting avoidance behavior, captured high proportions of adults. In the experiments by Lewis and Morrison (1973), the two-cell Thompson traps captured significantly more adults than did other trap types, with doves evidently entering the wide entrance of the drop-door trap more readily.

Henry et al. (1976: 122) reviewed earlier papers showing "that increasing percentages of immatures in the summer catch generally reflect recruitment of young as the breeding season progresses." However, they reminded us that the accuracy with which recruitment is reflected is affected by several factors, including greater ease of capture of adults in June than later in the summer, and time of day, as shown by Lewis and Morrison (1973).

The study by Henry et al. (1976) was prompted in part by findings of Tomlinson et al. (1960) that catches in roadside traps did not appear to sample adequately the large flocks of immature doves feeding in grainfields during late summer. To test this possibility, Henry et al. (1976) repeated the roadside trapping regimen established earlier by Tomlinson et al. (1960). In the new study, conducted during 1963–69, the investigators set traps about 433 yards (396 m) apart at fifty to fifty-five sites each year along secondary roadsides. In addition, fifty field traps were placed in clusters of two to four in cleared-off portions of wheat stubble fields, cornfields or pastures. With a few exceptions, Thompson two-cell drop-door traps were used.

Adults comprised 81 percent of the catch in roadside traps versus 34 percent in field traps. Differences by month and by year were statistically significant. The percentages of immatures, June through August, increased much more rapidly in field than in roadside catches. Among adults, males comprised about 71 percent of the catch in roadside traps versus 61 percent in field traps; these differences were highly significant when either years or months were used as replicates.

From the results, Henry et al. (1976: 122) concluded: "Trapping techniques must be considered carefully if inferences about age and sex composition of dove populations are to be drawn from capture data, or if investigators wish to concentrate banding efforts on a specific age or sex group of mourning doves." Their general conclusion is strongly reinforced by information from others (e.g., Amend and Kniffin 1970, Lewis and Morrison 1973) who noted that capture of adults could be facilitated by limiting trapping to time of day or season when more adults can be caught. Lewis and Morrison (1973) made 66 percent of their total catch on their evening trap run, but 80 percent of their

catch of adults was made on that run. Trapping of adults at nests, whether by Swank nest traps or by mist nets, would of course produce catches with very different sex compositions, depending on timing of the operation in relation to incubation schedules of males and females. For example, Swank (1952: 89) reported that males were taken almost exclusively when nest traps were sprung between 3:30 and 5:00 P.M.

BANDING

Numbered metal bands of sizes 3A and 3B are designated for use on mourning doves in North America (U.S. Fish and Wildlife Service and Canadian Wildlife Service 1984). The 3A band—larger than 3B—accommodates the tarsus size of doves in the range of the eastern subspecies, *Zenaida macroura carolinensis* (see chapter 3); the 3B band is more appropriate to birds in the range of the western subspecies, *Z. m. marginella*. In the zone of overlap, extending from the Lake States south-southwestward into parts of Iowa, Missouri, Arkansas, Louisiana and portions of states immediately west of those named (see *Figure 3*), the wiser strategy is to use the larger 3A band.

Since the western subspecies of mourning dove is somewhat smaller than the eastern subspecies, banders can use 3B bands for the former and 3A bands for the latter. For banding operations in zones of overlap or in cases of uncertainty, the larger 3A band should be chosen. *Photo courtesy of the New Jersey Division of Fish, Game and Wildlife.*

Sizes of bands used for adult and immature mourning doves have had a convoluted history, as recounted by Kaczynski and Kiel (1963). Before 1936, banders used either size 4 (too large) or size 3 bands. During 1936–39, size 4 bands only were recommended, although some banders trimmed the ends to reduce the diameter when closed. During 1939–49, size 3 bands were specified. In 1949, size 3A bands, with a diameter of 7/32 inches (5.6 mm), were introduced specifically for mourning doves because of concerns that the size 3 bands with diameters of 6/32 inches (4.8 mm) were too snug for eastern mourning doves (see Blake 1956).

Special Banding Pliers

Large-scale banding operations, as in numerous mourning dove projects, may dictate rapid banding and release of many birds. Use of conventional banding pliers under such conditions can result in "overcrimping" or other imperfect closure of bands on the doves' legs. Besides danger of injury to the birds, flawed crimping is difficult and time-consuming to rectify. To facilitate correct band closure, H. M. Wight (R. E. Tomlinson personal communication: 1989) and others (e.g., Larsen 1968) developed banding pliers that close bands accurately around birds' legs in a single clamping motion. The key feature is a hole drilled through the base of the closed jaws, into which a band of the desired size fits exactly when closed. Presently (1992), pliers sized for mourning dove bands are available commercially from the following:

- Gey Band and Tag Company
  P. O. Box 363
  Norristown, PA 19404
  (3A or 3B bands)
- Roger McDonald
  850 Main Street
  Lynnfield, MA 01940
  (3A or 3B bands; pliers have "nipples" to aid in opening bands)
- National Band and Tag Company
  721 York Street
  Newport, KY 41072
  (3A bands only)

At left, a researcher records data from a trapped mourning dove prior to banding with specially designed banding pliers that prevent imperfect band closures, which can injure or eventually debilitate the banded birds. At right, the dove banding pliers features a top hole for 3A and 3B mourning dove bands. The bottom hole is for size 4 bands used on white-winged doves. *Left photo courtesy of the New Jersey Division of Fish, Game and Wildlife. Right photo by David Dolton.*

Banding Nestlings

Determination of the relationships of production areas to harvest areas obviously requires precise knowledge of the locations of both. Because mourning doves trapped as immatures might not have been produced locally, nestling banding programs were developed. In a cooperative state/federal program, about 70,000 nestlings were banded during 1953–57 (Kiel 1959). Unfortunately, first-season recoveries of birds banded as nestlings were too few to permit solid conclusions, but they did provide a basis for statistical assurance that data from the nestling banding could be combined with other banding data to describe migratory pathways linking production and harvest areas. Thus, data from banded nestlings helped Kiel (1959) to delineate the three mourning dove management units.

Banding nestlings presents special problems because "Bands of a size suitable for adult birds are too large to be retained by the very young birds" (Kaczynski and Kiel 1963: 272). Kossack (1952) found that band retention on young nestlings could be improved significantly by affixing the too-large aluminum bands to the nestlings' legs with Dalzoflex elastic tape cut to lengths that permitted generous overlap of the ends when applied around the closed bands on the nestlings' legs. About half the width of the tape was affixed to the band and the other half to the upper leg. Kossack (1952: 29) asserted that, on captive doves, the tape worked loose from the legs in about nine to twelve days "without ill effects upon the bird," and from the band in about twenty-five days.

To test band retention, Kaczynski and Kiel (1963) banded 597 nestlings, aged four through nine days, during June through August 1960 in Mississippi. Depending on age at banding, the nestlings were checked when nine through twelve days old. Band sizes were 3 or 3A—the latter with or without securing with Dalzoflex tape. In the four- to six-day age groups, only 7.7 percent of the size 3 bands that could be checked were lost, whereas 66.3 percent of the 3A bands without tape were lost—a statistically significant difference. No taped bands were known to be lost, but predators ate a significantly larger proportion (13.8 versus 0.8 percent) of nestlings with taped bands than those with untaped bands.

Kaczynski and Kiel (1963: 277) suggested six days as the minimum age for banding nestlings with size 3 bands, eight days for 3A bands, and four days or less for tape-assisted bands. Because 10 percent of the eleven-day-old nestlings were "lost" (escaped) by flushing from the nests, Kaczynski and Kiel concluded that attempting to band

Important to management of mourning doves is an understanding of the species' movements, including the geographic relationship of dove production to harvest areas. By banding nestlings, researchers can be more certain that the banding sample represents birds originating in the area, region or unit in question. Most nestlings are banded between the ages of six and eleven days; for these doves, band sizes appropriate for adults (3A or 3B) should be used. *Photo by Ron George; courtesy of the Texas Parks and Wildlife Department.*

nestlings older than eleven days was impractical. They acknowledged that, despite the earlier "security" of size 3 bands without tape applied to nestlings, it was questionable whether these bands would be large enough when the nestlings grew to adulthood.

In a study designed to provide information on age and growth of mourning doves in Texas, Morrow et al. (1987) found it convenient to flush nine- to ten-day-old mourning dove fledglings from the nests with the aid of a mirror pole, capture and band them, and return them to the nests. The return operation was aided by use of a device fashioned from galvanized tin flashing cut into pieces serving as a top, flap and body. The device was attached to a section of rigid conduit and hoisted to the nest site in the shut position, then opened by a pull rope and tilted to spill the nestlings into the nest. Morrow et al. reported a loss rate of 2 percent when using this device to return 971 nestlings to their nests.

A telescoping mirror pole can be used to flush nestling mourning doves from their nests so they can be banded. It amounts to a painter's extender with a bicycle mirror attached by a hose clamp. The same sort of device is used to examine incubating eggs. If a pole is used in a banding operation, the researchers must be able to return the squabs safely to the nest. A separate pole mechanism for this purpose is noted in the text. *Left photo by Robert Ferguson; courtesy of the Missouri Cooperative Fish and Wildlife Research Unit. Right photo by David Dolton.*

Reward Banding

Band-recovery data can be very useful in answering basic biological questions and attacking management problems for avian species such as the mourning dove. Statistical treatment of these data, however, requires accurate estimates of band-reporting rates (the percentages of bands recovered that are reported to the U.S. Fish and Wildlife Service's Bird Banding Laboratory). An approach to determining band-reporting rates is "reward banding" performed in conjunction with regular banding activities.

In a program reported by Tomlinson (1968), each immature dove of an experimental cohort was provided with a band on each leg. On one leg, the band was a size 3A regular numbered band; on the other was a band inscribed only with the word "Reward." Controls were immature doves banded with regular bands only and released at the same banding stations as the experimentals. Reports from fifteen widely separated sections of the United States showed considerable variation in recovery rates of mourning doves, both with and without reward bands. "The overall percentages of banded doves . . . reported as recovered were 9.69 percent for those with reward bands and 3.83 percent for controls" (Tomlinson 1968: 6), yielding an estimated reporting rate of 39.5 percent (3.83 divided by 9.69). However, when data from states prominently publicizing the reward band program were

excluded, the estimated reporting rate was 32 percent—a figure widely used in analyses of dove banding data.

In a follow-up study, Reeves (1979) examined the reported recoveries of reward and control bands placed on immature mourning doves in the Eastern and Central management units (EMU and CMU). The estimated reporting rates for EMU-banded immature doves were 31 percent for direct (first season) and 44 percent for indirect (later season) recoveries. Corresponding rates for CMU-banded doves were 38 and 65 percent. Reeves suggested that high reporting rates of regular bands from Mexico and Central America contributed to the greater CMU reporting.

As in Tomlinson's (1968) study, these estimates of reporting rates were derived by dividing the percentage of regular bands applied that were reported by the similar proportion of reward bands. The estimates were based on the unproven assumption that *all* reward bands recovered were reported to the Bird Banding Laboratory.

Reeves (1979: 42) concluded in part that "Future efforts to obtain more precise or corroborating estimates of band reporting rates for dove bands in the United States seem dependent upon the initiation of uniform nationwide surveys of dove hunters and harvests." This important conclusion—that nationwide uniform hunter and harvest surveys are needed—appears in several other contexts in this book.

MARKING

Most of the schemes devised for color-marking birds have been tried, with mixed success, on mourning doves. Sometimes the marking techniques have not been appropriate to the objectives or conditions of the study. Results may have been affected by aberrant behavioral responses of the marked doves' mates or other associates. Increased predation rates on marked doves may have been a factor in some field studies.

In other instances, the marking device may not have been sufficiently evident to be helpful. Colored and coiled plastic bands, for example, apparently have had little use in field studies of mourning doves. As Mackey (1954) observed, the dove's body is held so low, even on the ground, that breast feathers almost cover the feet. However, R. E. Mirarchi (personal communication: 1989) has found colored bands helpful for ready identification of individual penned doves (see chapter 22).

Color-marking Plumage

Swank (1952) used Testor's model airplane dope to mark adult mourning doves trapped on their nests in southeastern Texas. Objectives of the study included determining the permanence of pair bonds during a breeding season and numbers of young fledged per female. Swank applied the airplane dope with a small brush onto the large feathers of wings and tails. White and yellow, painted in distinct solid lines, were the most satisfactory combinations to "read" under field conditions. Because it was important for the birds to carry their distinguishing marks until the end of the nesting season, Swank was careful to include the outer primaries in the marking scheme; these feathers usually are not molted until October by breeding adults in southeastern Texas. Feathers of wings and tails were spread when the dope was applied and held in that position for a few minutes until it had dried; then the birds were released. Swank (1955a) followed seven marked pairs through the nesting season; five pairs produced seven young each to fledging, and the remaining two marked pairs produced six. He mentioned no ill effects of the color marks or the procedure.

In their experimental studies of the effects of pairing on cooing performance of penned mourning doves, Frankel and Baskett (1963) found that marking the heads of paired females copiously with Testor's yellow airplane dope had adverse effects on pair bonds. In one example, the female of a mated pair was removed from the pen. The male responded as expected, with increased perch cooing. The head of this female was marked copiously with yellow airplane dope (to facilitate identification during twilight observation periods) before she was returned to the pen, nine days after removal. The pair bond was obviously not reestablished, and perch-cooing rates of the male remained high. After five days, the marked female was removed from the pen and replaced with a different, unmarked female. A pair bond was quickly established, and the perch-cooing rate of the male dropped dramatically, while the nest-cooing rate increased. Similar behavioral aberrations occurred in other experiments as well when the females' heads were marked with yellow airplane dope. As one colleague put it, "No wonder. You made those females look like yellow-headed blackbirds."

Airplane dope (orange or red) was used by Mackey (1965) on the upper mandibles of two pairs of wild mourning doves, and on tips of tails and wings, without noticeable alteration of behavior. Mourning doves in Florida were dyed by rolling trapped birds in shallow pans containing dye solution, "taking care that no dye got into the doves' eyes" (Winston 1952: 8). Doves were kept in carrying cases overnight to dry and released the next morning. The dye used in the Florida program was an orange aniline mixed with water, grain alcohol and acetic acid (Winston 1954).

The purpose of color-marking programs in Florida and other southeastern states involving dyed doves was to improve recovery rates of standard, numbered bands during the hunting season. Extensive publicity about the dyed birds ("flying oranges" in Florida) did create interest, and when the recovered, numbered bands were reported, they helped delineate migratory pathways. Of course, recovery data thus obtained would pose special problems in demographic analyses. In the early Florida program, "flying oranges" were shot near Miami, 450 air miles (724 km) from the banding site, as few as three days after release.

In a similar program in Tennessee, autumn-trapped birds were banded and dyed crimson, but no dyed bird ever was seen more than a few miles from its banding station (Hammond 1956).

Dyeing doves with aniline dye solutions according to the methods described by Winston (1954) proved to be a useful supplement to trap/band/retrap procedures in the study reported by Tomlinson et al. (1960). During four summers, at least 95 percent of the banded immature doves recaptured in roadside traps were not caught more than two weeks after the banding date. Banded adults, however, were recaptured throughout the summer trapping period.

During two summers, immature doves were both banded and dyed a distinctive color during each summer month. None of the dyed immatures was sighted on the study area or vicinity after about two weeks. "Control" adults dyed differently during July 1957 were sighted repeatedly throughout August. Thus, the inference drawn from the recapture data—that immatures (whether produced locally or not) left their natal areas soon after fledging—was reinforced by data that could not be attributed to some peculiarity of the trapping system. (More precise information on development of fledglings' mobility has become available through radiotelemetry [see Hitchcock and Mirarchi 1986].)

Tagging

Head tags. Colored plastic tags were used on heads of penned mourning doves in experiments reported by Goforth and Baskett (1965) and intended principally to expand and clarify the earlier findings of Frankel and Baskett (1963) about head-marking. The tags were made of Scotch pressure-sensitive tape cut in rectangular pieces 1.125 by 0.5 inches (2.9 by 1.3 cm), stuck directly to the crown feathers and extending posteriorly from the culmen to cover the crown.

Yellow markers placed on heads of mated females while in their pens during the pairs' first incubation attempts of the season disrupted pair bonds, as evidenced by abandonment of nests and abrupt increases in perch-cooing rates by males. Controls in which females were handled similarly in their pens but not marked brought about no such disruptions. Bonds of other pairs that were in their second nesting cycles were not disrupted by marking the females' heads with yellow tags while in the pens. However, when pair bonds were broken by removing females and their squabs or eggs, and yellow head tags were added before the females were returned to their erstwhile mates a few days later, pair bonds were not reestablished. Unmarked "control" females were accepted readily by their former mates. Marking females with red, green or white head tags did not prevent reestablishment of bonds between mates that had been separated and then reunited after a successful nesting. No behavioral aberrations were detected when males were marked even with yellow head tags under similar conditions.

Head-marking has been a useful technique in some studies of penned mourning doves but has not been important in field studies. The principal contribution of head-marking experiments with doves probably has been to alert investigators about the need to check out possible behavioral and other aberrations of the target species before mass application of marking devices.

Back tags. Colored plastic back tags, often with designs permitting recognition of individual birds, have been used frequently and successfully in field studies of mourning doves. It is comforting to researchers that back tags—even yellow ones, such as placed on female doves by Goforth and Baskett (1965)—did not elicit the behavioral aberrations seen when yellow head tags were used.

For mourning doves, Mackey (1965) modified a tag assembly first described by Taber (1949) for use with ring-necked pheasants. Mackey's tag measured 2.25 by 0.75 inches (5.7 by 1.9 cm). It was fastened to a snap that was soldered to a silver safety pin inserted through the skin at the base of the dove's neck. The linkage permitted the tag to assume positions favorable to "reading" by the observer when the dove was on the ground, flushed or even sometimes on the nest. Tags had bold designs involving combinations of white, red and yellow. Mackey noted no departures from normal nesting behavior by tagged doves of either sex or their mates, and the tags fulfilled their purpose in his interesting study of dove behavior and reproduction on the Columbus campus of Ohio State University. The only serious difficulty he noted was the loss of five of forty markers due to tearing of the skin, but fourteen doves carried their tags for two to six months before passing from observation. One dove, tagged in February 1953, was captured a year later with the tag intact.

A back tag developed by Blank and Ash (1956) for study of gray partridges has proved useful, when modified, in mourning dove research. The Blank and Ash device consisted of a plastic tab, distinctly marked, lying flat on the bird's back and held in position with a soft leather harness. In Jackson's (1963) modification, a strip of vinyl upholstery plastic measuring 3 by 1 inches (7.6 by 2.5 cm) was fastened with wire staples to two loops of sewing elastic that were slipped over the dove's wings into position next to the body. Plastic designs in contrasting colors were stapled to the tag. These tags were individually identifiable with binoculars at seventy yards (64 m). In preliminary tests, the tags remained intact for nine months on penned doves and for at least a year on some wild doves. Tagged wild doves nested repeatedly in the study by Jackson and Baskett (1964) on the University of Missouri campus. A version similar to Jackson's (1963) tag also was used successfully in one phase of the pen study by Goforth and Baskett (1965).

Colored plastic back tags similar to the Blank and Ash (1956) devices but made of Saflag plastic-covered nylon (available from Safety Flag Company of Pawtucket, Rhode Island) were used by Irby and Blankenship (1966) in their Tucson, Arizona study. The tags were useful in their determination that some hatching-year mourning doves breed in the wild; marked doves, both adult and immature, were observed nesting and calling. Details of the tag's attachment were not published.

Wing tags. Hewitt and Austin-Smith (1966) developed a marker easily fastened to the wings of small birds; after preliminary tests on captive European starlings, American robins and catbirds, they field-marked 1,365 birds of five species. Performance of the tag, both in pen and field trials, was good; no evidence of behavioral or reproductive problems was perceived.

The tag material was Saflag. Brilliant pink, orange and green were useful colors in the field. The tag was cut as one piece, with a large dorsal rectangle connected by a narrow isthmus ("humerus strap") to a small ventral tab. The tag was attached by passing the strap around the base of the humerus and fastening the small ventral tab to the large dorsal one with a metal staple or rivet. Sizes of all parts of the tag were easily made suitable for the bird.

This tag, sized appropriately, was used successfully as one method of color-marking 1,065 mourning doves in a study in South Carolina (Sayre et al. 1978). Twenty-six of the wild marked males were studied intensively from April through early August to appraise factors affecting perch-cooing rates.

The Hewitt and Austin-Smith wing tag was an adjunct to radio telemetry in the Alabama study by Hitchcock and Mirarchi (1984) wherein the duration of dependence of fledgling mourning doves on the parents was studied. The authors suspected that certain bright tag colors (e.g., white) ultimately led to higher rates of predation on the wing-tagged fledglings compared with their radio-tagged siblings. Consequently, wing tags were not used in follow-up studies (R. E. Mirarchi personal communication: 1989).

Radio Tagging

Radio telemetry is an exciting and often effective tool for study of behavior, habitat use, mobility and other aspects of biology of wild mourning doves, particularly during the breeding season. The following studies illustrate the value of radio telemetry in dove research and reveal some associated technical problems and the need to anticipate them.

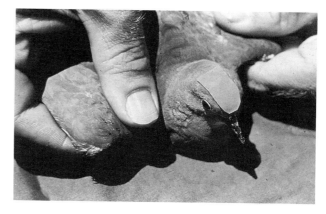

Wildlife researchers primarily use three types of tags—head, back and wing—to mark and monitor individual mourning doves. Head tags (top) are useful for some studies of captive doves but not for field studies of free-flying wild doves. Back tags (center) have been used with good success in the field. Wing tags (bottom) have proven effective for study of both penned and wild mourning doves. *Photos courtesy of the Missouri Cooperative Fish and Wildlife Research Unit.*

Radio-tagging effects and breeding biology of doves in Missouri. In two closely related studies of both captive and free-flying doves during three breeding seasons, Sayre et al. (1980, 1981) radio-tagged 48 doves of both sexes. The 24 radio-tagged captive doves were used in experiments requiring the presence of 25 additional unmarked doves as controls or potential mates for the radio-tagged birds. In the field study, 19 males and 5 females wore transmitters.

The radio package used throughout these studies was an SM1 transmitter, 565-HG battery, and a 6- or 12-inch (15.2 or 30.4 cm) antenna supplied by AVM Instrument Company of Champaign, Illinois. A small oval-shaped piece of latex rubber was glued to the transmitter package base to provide a bonding surface. Total weight was less than 5 percent of the dove's body weight. The package was attached to the dove by trimming feathers of the lower middle back to about 0.4 inches (1 cm) and gluing the package to the trimmed area with a cyanoacrylate glue (Sayre et al. 1981: 430).

In the pen studies (Sayre et al. 1981), perch-cooing rates of unmated males decreased markedly for two days following radio tagging. In four of seven trials, the rates returned to prior levels by the third day; in the other three trials they did not, but reversal of dominance between radio-tagged and control birds in the pens was a factor. In twelve experimental trials with captive doves, and based on observations of 24 free-flying doves (both sexes), radio tagging did not affect previously established pair bonds.

In the field study (Sayre et al. 1980), radio tagging made possible acquisition of the most precise information yet available about cooing rates of wild mourning doves in relation to their breeding status. Moreover, data acquired through use of radio telemetry filled gaps in knowledge of other aspects of doves' breeding biology in northern Missouri habitats to an extent probably impossible without this technique.

Duration of parental care of fledglings. In their two-year field study in Alabama, Hitchcock and Mirarchi (1984) equipped the older nestling/ fledgling at each of thirty-five nests with a radio transmitter. They also marked the younger nest mate at thirty-four of these nests with a colored wing tag of the Hewitt and Austin-Smith (1966) design. The older squabs were radio-tagged at seven or eight days of age; they left the nests about fifteen days after hatching and were observed for another twelve days with aid of radio tracking. The epoxy-coated backpack consisted of a transmitter weighing 0.08 ounces (2.5 g) and a 1.5-volt battery, from Wildlife Materials, Inc., of Carbondale, Illinois. Completing the assembly were a harness of surgical tubing, an antenna 6 inches (15 cm) long and a small polyurethane pad glued to the underside of the package to reduce irritation to the bird.

Hitchcock and Mirarchi's interesting findings about interactions between mourning dove parents and young after the latter had left the nests and

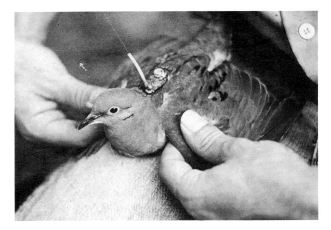

A miniature radio transmitter can be attached to a mourning dove's back by gluing the radio base to a small piece of latex rubber, which in turn is bonded to the bird's back (feathers trimmed) with a cyanoacrylate glue. The adhesiveness is satisfactory, and the radio package does not significantly impair the subject's movements or alter its behavior. *Photos by Mark W. Sayre.*

interactions between fledged siblings obviously were highly dependent on radio telemetry. The authors stated that the "parent doves were not marked because of the likelihood of nest abandonment" (Hitchcock and Mirarchi 1984: 100). Parents were identified, instead, by other distinctive characteristics of plumage and vocalization.

Subsequently, Grand and Mirarchi (1988) successfully used the telemetry devices and procedures employed by Hitchcock and Mirarchi (1984) to quantify habitat use by 28 recently fledged mourning doves radio-tagged in eastcentral Alabama. In another interesting product of the Alabama program, Mirarchi and Hitchcock (1982) described radio-tracking a gray rat snake near a dove roost; when captured and held for observation, it expelled in its feces a radio transmitter and some remains of the fledgling dove to which the transmitter had been attached.

Dove mobility during the breeding season in southeastern Idaho. In a two-summer study by Howe and Flake (1988), 41 adult mourning doves were fitted with radio transmitters to determine extent of movement from man-made watering sites (some of which were radioactive leaching ponds) within the Idaho National Engineering Laboratory grounds to their nests or feeding areas. Radio transmitters were attached to clipped back feathers. The transmitters had a range of 0.6 miles (1 km) and a battery life of twenty days, and total package weight was 0.09 ounces (2.5 g). Radio locations were made from aircraft and from the ground, with five-element Yagi antennas attached to a mobile ground-tracking unit.

Howe and Flake (1988) found small likelihood of doves transporting radionuclides outside of the Idaho National Engineering Laboratory grounds during the breeding season, but they suggested likely enhancement of dove breeding populations in the desert if additional permanent watering sites were established. Once again, radio telemetry seemed crucial to the success of this research.

Attachment of transmitters to doves. Perry et al. (1981) evaluated transmitter attachment techniques for mourning doves, both in pens in Maryland and in the field in South Carolina. In the pen studies, three major attachment techniques were tested on a total of 28 wild-trapped mourning doves, and some preliminary tests of adhesives were conducted on captive ringed turtledoves and feral pigeons as well. In all tests, the transmitter unit, including battery, weighed about 0.2 ounces (6 g), and a 6-inch (15 cm) antenna projected vertically from the encapsulated unit.

Surgical implantation under the skin of the back, with the antenna protruding through the skin, was not a suitable technique. The relatively large size of the transmitter, compared with the small potential subcutaneous space of the surgical site, resulted in disruption of blood supply, and the sutures broke loose following necrosis of the skin. Moreover, the antennas sometimes lodged under the wings, creating problems when the birds walked or flapped their wings. Antennas frequently were pulled by doves, as if they were trying to remove the transmitters. The doves also seemed reluctant to fly.

Harnesses also proved unsuitable in these experiments. One type, employing a double loop, was lost from the doves within two days. The other, a wing-loop harness, appeared to hinder the birds' flight, at least at first. The investigators did suggest further harness testing, however.

Perry et al. (1981) found that gluing the radio package to the back feathers, clipped or not, with a commercial product containing cyanoacetate was the most satisfactory technique in the pen studies. This technique also was used on 48 mourning doves in field experiments and proved useful in determining habitat use, movement patterns and nesting activity (including incubation and brood rearing by radio-tagged doves of both sexes) at the South Carolina study area. The successful adhesives, known popularly as instant bonding glues, were Krazy Glue (Krazy Glue, Inc., of Chicago, Illinois), Super Glue (Woodhill Permater of Cleveland, Ohio) and Eastman 910 (Eastman Chemical Products, Inc., of Kingsport, Tennessee). According to Perry et al., these products were equally effective. Retention time was longest if the glue was applied in an amount sufficient for the transmitter package to bond both to feathers and underlying skin.

Use of a suitable restraining device can greatly expedite marking live mourning doves with contrivances as diverse as standard leg bands or radio-transmitter backpacks.

DISCUSSION

Much of modern understanding of mourning dove biology and related management problems and solutions can be attributed to improved techniques of the types described above. Nevertheless, biologists should not be complacent either about knowledge of the bird's biology or "state-of-the-art" means to advance that knowledge.

Techniques used for trapping and conventional banding (with numbered metal bands) seem entirely adequate if practiced judiciously. Indeed, where would management be without them, in terms of understanding mourning dove population dynamics and migratory pathways? (Unfortunately, rising costs of large-scale trapping and banding programs have led to their abandonment since about 1975. The ability to explain and deal with the long-term population decline, particularly in the Western Management Unit, is thus reduced.)

Color-marking may be tricky, although colored back tags based on the Blank and Ash (1956) device and colored wing tags of the type described by Hewitt and Austin-Smith (1966) were both useful when modified for doves. Colored tags, in order to be useful to the observer, must be obtrusive. If easily noticed by the human observer, why not by keen-eyed avian predators? Could increased predation, or the attraction of predators, affect the results of the study?

There is good documentation in the literature of the "signal" value of certain small, natural color

A simple restraining device, modified from use with northern bobwhite quail (DeMaso and Peoples in press), enables one person to attach leg bands and/or radio transmitters to mourning doves. Made of 2.54-centimeter (1.0 in) pine or plywood, the device is 30.5 centimeters long, 12.7 centimeters wide and 30.5 centimeters high (12 by 5 by 12 in). A dove can be positioned so that its legs fit through a 2.54-centimeter (1.0 in) hole in the top board. Several inches beneath the board is a parallel rubber band extended between eye bolts. Paper clips attached to the rubber band are hooked to the halux of each leg (left), with enough pressure to keep the dove motionless. During a 1992 mourning dove study in the Central Management Unit, more than 300 doves were banded and marked using the restraining device. *Photos by Craig Haskell; courtesy of the Missouri Department of Conservation.*

markings on birds in eliciting reactions by their associates. An example is the importance of the moustache mark on male flickers in sex recognition, reported by Noble (1936), and the confusion resulting if the mark is experimentally hidden. Another illustration is the interference with recognition and pairing in four species of gulls resulting from alterations in eye-ring color (Smith 1967).

It is incorrect to assume that colored markings applied safely to one part of a bird's body will not bring unwanted results when applied elsewhere. A striking example is seen in the long-term effects of wing tags applied to ring-billed gulls at a breeding colony in Michigan (Kinkel 1989). Compared with color-banded gulls, fewer wing-tagged birds returned to the colony in spring; wing-tagged birds that did return arrived later; fewer females mated; and pair bonds were more easily broken.

To some extent, field studies involving radio-tagged mourning doves can be "policed" more easily than those in which other marking devices are used, because radio-tagged doves can be monitored much more consistently. However, data gathered through use of other techniques have provided valuable supplements to or control checks for telemetry results (e.g., Sayre et al. 1980, Hitchcock and Mirarchi 1984); this possibility should not be overlooked in project design.

Despite the excellent advantages afforded by telemetry techniques, those techniques are not infallible. Gessaman and Nagy (1988), for example, showed differences in flight times of homing pigeons that flew 66 or 198 miles (90 or 320 km) with no radio packages versus those with dummy packages weighing either 2.5 or 5.0 percent of the pigeon's body weight. On longer flights, the heavier packages slowed the birds' time by more than 31 percent, and birds produced 85 to 100 percent more carbon dioxide (a measure of metabolic energy used) than did the unencumbered controls. Results with the lighter transmitter package did not differ appreciably from those with the heavier one, indicating that pigeons were slowed more by air drag than by additional mass. As Cochran (1980) pointed out, there is nothing sacred about the 4 percent of body weight seemingly tolerated in telemetry packages by many species of birds. Moreover, Gessaman and Nagy (1988) advised that flight speeds of their high-performance homing pigeons may have magnified the perceived effects of radio burdens beyond expectations for birds flying at more efficient speeds.

In another example arguing for cautious approaches to radio telemetry, Massey et al. (1988) abandoned the technique as a means of determining foraging patterns of least terns in California because of behavioral aberrations of radio-marked birds and their harassment by predators. They concluded that the only proven marking technique for least terns was leg bands. This study and that of Gessaman and Nagy (1988) by no means argue against using radio telemetry for mourning doves. They do, however, add to arguments for careful checking of techniques for unwanted side effects.

Chapter 21

Aging, Sexing and Miscellaneous Research Techniques

Ralph E. Mirarchi
*Department of Zoology and Wildlife Science
and
Alabama Agricultural Experiment Station
Auburn University, Alabama*

Accurate methods of determining the age and sex of mourning doves are vitally important to the proper management of dove populations. When data obtained by those techniques are combined with data provided by intensive banding programs, biologists can obtain information on the population dynamics of the species on state, regional and national bases. They then can use this information to recommend prudent hunting regulations. Many of the techniques used to age and sex mourning doves are based on an understanding of the birds' molting processes and their nesting patterns in different parts of the continent (see chapters 8 and 5, respectively).

AGE CHARACTERISTICS

Embryos (one to fourteen days postlaying)

The embryological development of mourning doves has been well documented, and laboratory aging techniques that use photographs, gross de-scriptions and measurements have been described by Muller et al. (1984) (see also chapter 8).

Embryos also can be aged in the field by use of candling techniques, photographs and gross descriptions (Hanson 1954, Hanson and Kossack 1957). The small egg size and translucent eggshells of mourning doves are particularly suited to candling. A portable egg candler, or high-intensity flashlight, is used to view the eggs; the presence or absence of an embryo or the shape, position and size of the embryo are key characteristics with which to determine the stage of incubation (*Figure 66*) (see also Hanson and Kossack 1957, 1963).

Nestlings (one to fifteen days posthatching)

The growth and development of mourning dove nestlings has been well described and pictured previously (Hanson and Kossack 1957, 1963, Cheney and Cheney 1967, Holcomb and Jaeger 1978). These developmental stages also are summarized in chapter 8.

Day 1

Day 3

Day 6

Day 9

Day 12

Day 14

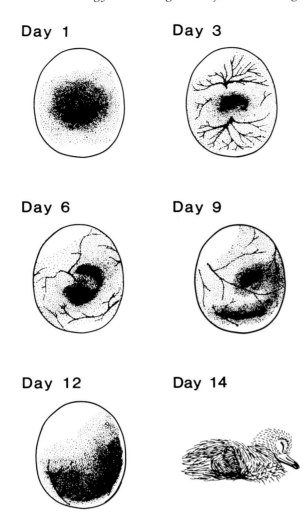

Figure 66. Selected stages of embryonic development as revealed by egg candling (drawn from photographs in Hanson and Kossack 1963).

Immature Doves—Alive

Plumage pattern and wear. Many mourning doves can be classified easily as immatures by noting whether they have one or more light-tipped (buff to white) primary wing coverts present *(Figure 67)* (Pearson and Moore 1940). This aging method becomes unreliable once the wing molt proceeds to primary eight, because the molt of the primary coverts precedes that of the corresponding primaries (Wight et al. 1967). Thus, immature doves molting primaries eight through ten usually do not retain any light-tipped coverts and appear to be adult birds.

If no light-tipped primary wing coverts are present, the primary wing feathers must be checked carefully. The presence of a buff-colored fringe on the trailing edge of primaries nine and ten indicates an immature bird (Wight et al. 1967). The fringe is visible when the wing is viewed against a dark background. Buff-colored fringes are found on primaries of immature and adult doves, but adult doves molt their primary wing feathers only once a year during the breeding season and early autumn. During late summer, primaries nine and ten are about one year old in adults but only about five months old in immature birds. This difference in

An immature mourning dove (right) usually is distinguishable from an adult (left) by the presence on the former of light-tipped (white or buff-colored) primary wing coverts. *Photos by Ron George; courtesy of the Texas Parks and Wildlife Department.*

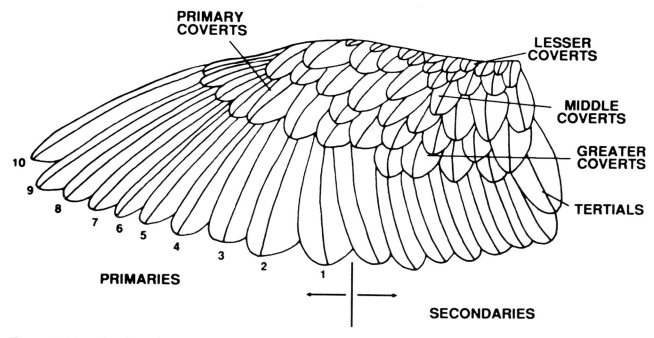

Figure 67. Mourning doves have ten primary wing feathers. Molt begins with the innermost primary (1) and progresses outwardly until the final primary (10) is molted (from Reeves and Amend 1970).

age results in more wear on the primaries of the adult birds and causes the buff-colored fringe to be worn away. The technique is virtually 100-percent accurate for doves from the eastern and midwestern United States, but it is not as reliable for those from the Southwest. Apparently, additional feather wear from harsh vegetation and soil conditions there causes the decrease in reliability (Wight et al. 1967).

Molt pattern. Fairly accurate age classes (within a few days) can be delineated by observing the molting pattern of the primary wing feathers in immature birds. This aging technique was developed primarily from study of captive doves in Georgia (Jenkins 1955) and Texas (Swank 1955b) and was later substantiated for wild doves in Indiana (Allen 1963). Morrow (1983) noted that ages predicted by molt of immature primaries in Texas *(Table 80)* were less than those traditionally used by most biologists (Swank 1952, 1955b). Morrow also recommended against using primaries nine and ten to predict age in immature mourning doves because of the wide variation in ages when these primaries are molted.

In early studies of wing molt, it was noted that captive doves molted more slowly than wild doves (Southeastern Association of Game and Fish Commissioners 1957), presumably as a result of dietary deficiencies (Payne 1972) or other "malfunction, disease, or injury" (Swank 1955b: 414). In wild doves, the primary feather "molt proceeds at a

Table 80. Mean observed postjuvenal primary molt age (days) for known-age hatching-year mourning doves in central Texas (from Morrow 1983).

Primary	Mean age	n	Standard deviation	Minimum	Maximum
1	30.1	21	5.5	22.0	45.0
2	35.5	18	4.3	29.0	47.0
3	39.9	9	4.9	34.0	47.0
4	50.4	7	8.0	42.0	64.0
5	61.2	9	10.5	49.0	82.0
6	74.0	5	15.8	59.0	101.0
7	87.0	5	9.2	79.0	102.0
8	107.5	2	19.1	94.0	121.0
9	123.0	6	18.9	109.0	157.0
10	157.8	6	36.6	128.0	222.0

rather constant rate from one primary to another within a single season, but the interval does vary from year to year" (Johnson 1989: 661). This primary wing molt can be delayed by severe winter weather and associated food shortages (Ault et al. 1976). Between-year variation in molting rate also might occur because of "differences in condition due to the stresses of breeding and raising young" (Johnson 1989: 661). Morrow (1983) also observed that the rate of molt recorded in immatures hatched early and late in the nesting season differed from those hatched during the middle portion of the season *(Figure 68)*.

An intensive study of wing molt patterns of immature doves in North and South Carolina

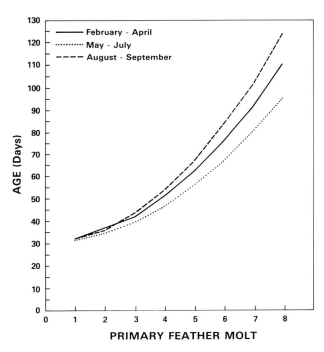

Figure 68. Predicted age of postjuvenal primary feather molt of known-age mourning doves relative to hatching period (from Morrow 1983).

(Haas and Amend 1976), when compared with results from the Indiana study (Allen 1963), indicated no statistically significant differences in molting rate between the two geographic areas and habitat types. Consequently, Haas and Amend concluded that their aging method could be used throughout the Eastern Management Unit (EMU). The median age (days) at which the primaries (P) were molted in the Carolinas was: P1 = 38 days; P2 = 43; P3 = 52; P4 = 60; P5 = 70; P6 = 80; P7 = 93; P8 = 112; P9 = 122; and P10 = 131. Johnson (1989) used a least-squares method of estimating the rate at which the doves in the Haas and Amend study molted their primaries and found that the onset of their molt averaged about May 11; the estimated interval between molts of their primary feathers was thirteen to fourteen days.

Biologists would be well advised to become familiar with all of the aforementioned studies and use the molt/age schedules most appropriate to their region of the country. In addition, care should be taken to adjust the schedules in accordance with the stage of the breeding season.

Aging keys. The age class designations used herein are taken from the *Bird Banding Manual* (U.S. Fish and Wildlife Service and Canadian Wildlife Service 1977) and are based on the calendar year. These designations should be mastered by those who regularly band mourning doves.

Fortunately, there are only a few different age

designations for doves and they are rather simple. Each time a bird passes December 31, it moves into the next higher year class. For example, if the age of a dove born in August is determined during the same calendar year as it is hatched, it is referred to as a hatching-year bird. The same bird aged after December 31 is considered a second-year bird (even though it is only five months old), because it passed December 31 *but* still contained plumage characteristics of the hatching-year bird. Both hatching-year and second-year doves are considered immatures because the difference is based solely on calendar time. It is impossible to age doves beyond the second year because they acquire adult characteristics that do not change from year to year. They are then referred to as after-hatching-year birds.

The key from the *Bird Banding Manual* uses the information described previously, together with information on timing of the autumn molt of immature and adult doves analyzed by Sadler et al. (1970) in Missouri. Unfortunately, the key "contains ambiguities and inaccuracies" that can cause errors in differentiating between hatching-year and after-hatching-year doves (Cannell 1984: 112), and it probably will not be updated for some time (R. E. Tomlinson personal communication: 1989). One problem is that the timing of molt in mourning doves is now known to vary geographically (discussed later). Another problem results from incorrect usage of the word "molt." Cannell (1984) emphasized that interpreting "molt" to mean dropping, losing or shedding feathers *without* considering replacement of the feathers could cause a key user to classify incorrectly hatching-year birds that are replacing their outer primaries as do after-hatching-year birds. Molt should be used to indicate *both* the loss and replacement of plumage. A simple loss of feathers should be indicated by terms such as "dropped," "shed" or "lost."

The new key proposed by Cannell (1984) minimizes these problems and should be used by dove banders (*Figure 69*). It is possible that dove banders in the western United States and western Canada will age some doves incorrectly because of possible differences in molting rates of the western and eastern subspecies (Bivings and Silvy 1980). However, little more can be done until information about primary molt is collected at additional localities, thereby allowing keys to be refined further.

Immature Doves—Dead

Bursa of Fabricius. Another aging technique is available to separate immature from adult doves

1A. One or more primary coverts with white to buff edging .... See 5
1B. No primary coverts with white to buff edgings .... See 2
   2A. Summer/Fall primary loss complete (replacement
      may be in process or completed) .... See 3
   2B. Some (or all) outer primaries have not yet been
      dropped (as part of summer/fall molt) .... See 4
3A. May 15-August 31 .... HY (See 7)
3B. September 1-Dec. 31 .... U (See 7)
3C. January 1-May 14 .... AHY (See 7)
   4A. Outermost primaries, not yet dropped, have
      smooth light-colored inner edges and tips .... See 5
   4B. Outermost primaries, not yet dropped, have dark
      frayed inner margins and tips .... AHY (See 7)
5A. Latest primary (P) dropped on or before the following
   date: none, Jan. 29; P1, Feb. 1; P2, Feb. 5; P3, Feb. 14;
   P4, Feb. 23; P5, Mar. 4; P6, Mar. 13; P7, Mar. 26; P8,
   Apr. 12; and P9, May 7 .... SY (See 6)
5B. Latest primary dropped after corresponding date in 5A .... HY (See 6)
   6A. HY/SY with latest primary dropped 0-7 .... Unknown sex
   6B. HY/SY with latest primary dropped 8-10 .... See 7
7A. Crown and nape blue or blue-gray and breast and throat
   clearly washed with pink or rose .... Male
7B. Crown and nape brown or grayish-brown and breast and
   throat tan .... Female
7C. Not as above (5% to 20% will be intermediate between
   7A and 7B depending upon age, time of year, and
   experience of bander) .... Unknown sex

Figure 69. Revised aging and sexing key for mourning doves (from Cannell 1984).

that have proceeded beyond the eighth primary feather molt. The technique, which can be used in the field or laboratory when large numbers of dead mourning doves are available, involves determining whether the bursa of Fabricius is present (Wight 1956). The dove is held on its back, and heavy scissors or shears are placed immediately behind the posterior lip of the vent. A transverse cut is made completely through the tail and the pygostyle, as close to the vent as possible without cutting into the cloaca. If present, the bursa is found immediately dorsal to the vent *(Figure 70)*. It is pink or yellow and has fine vermiculations throughout. It can vary in size but usually is 0.39 to 0.47 inches (10 to 12 mm) long and 0.24 to 0.31 inches (6 to 8 mm) wide.

The bursa also can be probed (cf. Petrides 1950) and used as an aging technique by locating its

opening on the dorsal edge of the cloaca (Wight 1956). The procedure can be conducted routinely in the laboratory, but it is too time-consuming for rapid use in the field.

Other. Van Soest and Van Utrecht (1971) described a method of age determination in birds based on the presence of annual deposits in the periosteal zone of bones. The most pronounced layering was present in bones bearing the most mechanical load or tension. Since then, columbid biologists and researchers have expressed an interest in using this technique. Manikowski and Walasz (1980) tested the method on homing (domestic) pigeons of known age and found the technique unreliable in that species. No known research on wild columbids has been conducted to test this technique. This lead should be explored for potential use with mourning doves.

Adult Doves—Alive

Plumage pattern and color. The plumage of adult mourning doves supposedly is definitive, i.e., the basic plumage patterns and colors in both sexes are the same each year and usually do not change with age. However, there is some suspicion that the plumage of some older females may tend to resemble that of adult males (K. C. Sadler personal communication: 1989). This suspicion probably should be examined more closely through well-designed research.

The principal differences in adult and immature plumages involving patterns and color have been described previously. However, a secondary criterion sometimes is helpful in verifying age.

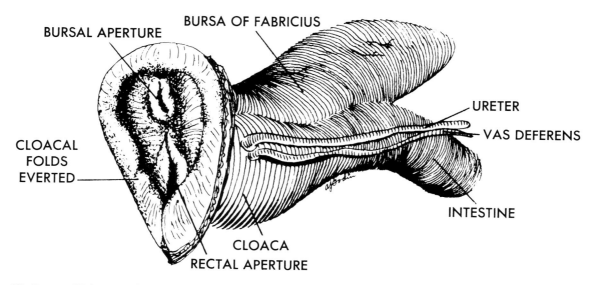

Figure 70. Bursa of Fabricius (from Larson and Taber 1980). *Illustration by A. J. Godin.*

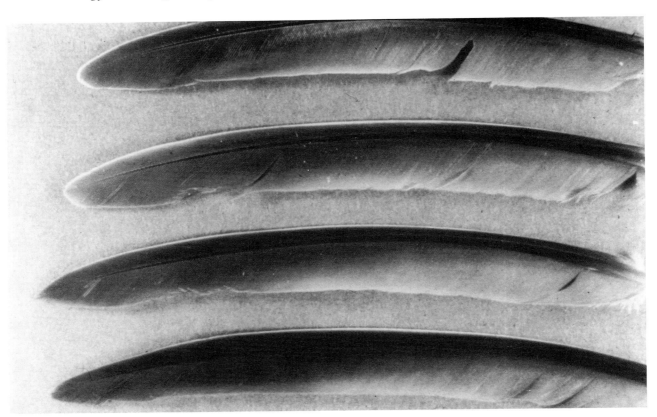

A secondary distinction between primary feathers of immature mourning doves (top two) and those of adults (lower two) is that the latter show more wear and less white on the trailing edge near the tip as a result of more use. *Photo courtesy of the U.S. Fish and Wildlife Service.*

Adult doves often have badly frayed tertial wing feathers (those closest to the body) because of their greater age (Reeves and Amend 1970). This criterion should be used only in conjunction with the principal plumage characteristics and should not be relied on in the absence of other more definitive wing characteristics.

Molt pattern. The primary feather molt of adult mourning doves differs geographically. For example, in the Carolinas, 56 percent of the adult population has begun the primary molt by the first week of June, and 7.5 percent has completed primary molt by the first week of September (Haas and Amend 1979). They shed their primaries at the rate of one per 14 days. In Missouri, 50 percent of the adults have begun primary molt by the first week of June, and 2.5 percent of the adult population has completed primary molt before October (Sadler et al. 1970). They shed their primaries at a rate of one per 16.5 days for males and one per 15.5 days for females. Haas and Amend (1979) believed these data indicated a north-to-south gradient of molt completion. They also believed it could prove useful in correcting age ratio data collected from wing surveys in states at the same latitude as from those where studies had been completed. How-

ever, Bivings and Silvy (1980) found that adult mourning doves in Texas molted at a rate similar (fewer than 1 percent had completed the molt by September 1) to those in Missouri, and they did not believe a significant north-to-south gradient existed. Bivings and Silvy suggested that an east-west gradient, due to differences between the eastern and western mourning dove subspecies, was more likely. Obviously, additional research is needed on adult dove molting rates at other latitudes and longitudes.

Aging keys. Information on aging keys for adult mourning doves was presented previously.

Other. Additional secondary criteria sometimes are helpful in verifying age. Adult mourning doves, like adult zenaida doves (Garrigues et al. 1989), generally have legs that are deep red in color, whereas the legs of immatures are grayish pink (Reeves and Amend 1970). Also, because they often overwinter in northern areas, they may lose toes from frostbite. Thus, well-healed wounds associated with missing toes suggest that the dove is an adult (Reeves and Amend 1970). As mentioned previously, these criteria should be used in conjunction with the principal wing characteristics and not be relied on in their absence.

Adult Doves—Dead

Bursa of Fabricius. The absence of the bursa in specimens examined in laboratory or field is indicative of adult birds (Wight 1956), although some adults may carry small remnants—0.08 to 0.12 inches (2 to 3 mm) long—of the bursa for some time.

SEXUAL CHARACTERISTICS

Immature Doves—Alive

Plumage color. Immature doves replacing primary feathers six through ten can be sexed properly, particularly by experienced personnel, by using plumage color characteristics of adult birds (Reeves et al. 1968). Only about half of those replacing primary feathers four and five can be sexed correctly, and very few of those replacing primary feathers three, two or one can be.

Immature Doves—Dead

Even when dead doves are available for dissection, determination of sex is not always easy, particularly with younger birds. The easiest way to verify the bird's sex is to lay it on its back and remove the breast. This can be accomplished quickly and easily by plucking the feathers away from the tip of the breast bone, inserting the thumb firmly under its tip, and pushing firmly inward and pulling upward at the same time. The breast will pull free of the rest of the carcass and be attached only by the ribs and the bone and muscle connections to the wings. These connections can be detached easily with heavy scissors. Once the breast is removed, the gizzard and the attached viscera are pulled up and away from the backbone. This can be accomplished without detaching them, and the backbone and the kidneys are thus exposed.

The reproductive organs are located approximately in the middle of the back just below the bright pink tissue of the lungs (see *Figure 19*). The testes of the male are small, beanlike structures on either side of the backbone. They can vary in size from approximately 0.08 to 0.4 inches (2 to 10 mm) and range from reddish pink to white in color. Testes of the older birds become larger in size and whiter in color as they approach puberty. The ovary of the female normally becomes aligned at about a 25- to 30-degree angle to the backbone. In very young females, it is approximately 0.12 to 0.16 inches (3 to 4 mm) long and virtually translucent.

Some fine, grainlike speckling (rudimentary follicles) also may be visible on the surface. In older females, the surface begins to resemble a miniature cluster of pink grapes as follicles develop. The oviduct is difficult to see in very young birds but becomes visible as a pinkish white strand leading to the cloaca as the bird ages. (See chapter 9 for more detailed coverage of reproductive anatomy and physiology.)

Adult Doves—Alive

Plumage color. The breeding (alternate) plumage of adult male mourning doves consists of a distinctive blue cap and nape and pinkish rosy hue over the face, throat and breast (Petrides 1950). The neck feathers are tinged with a pink iridescence, and the eye rings are sky blue. The alternate plumage of the adult female is much more drab and consists of a gray cap and nape, olive-brown face and throat, and tan breast. Females occasionally have a tinge of pink on the breast but still possess other female characters (Reeves et al. 1968). The neck feathers usually are tinged with an olive-green iridescence, although some pink iridescence occasionally occurs. The eye rings are turquoise-green. The winter (basic) plumage is essentially the same, but it is much more drab and the sexes are not as easily distinguished. Any sexual differences in plumage should be used together rather than individually to minimize potential errors in determining sex (Menasco and Perry 1978).

Whiteness of tips of the outer three tail feathers also can help distinguish sex (Reeves et al. 1968). White tips on the outer three tail feathers indicate males, whereas white tips on only one or two of these feathers (other tips being gray) indicate females. This criterion should be used only in conjunction with the principal plumage characters.

Other. Experienced personnel can sex live mourning dove adults by means of a human nasal speculum that is inserted into the cloaca (Miller and Wagner 1955). The vasa deferentia of the male terminate in conical papillae that are visible on each side of the cloaca; these are absent in females, but the left oviductal opening is present and visible. The technique is more than 95 percent accurate and might prove useful in conjunction with the use of plumage characters, particularly during winter months.

Male mourning doves also tend to have flatter crowns and less rounded heads than do females (Reeves and Amend 1970). This subtle difference should be used only to help verify the more prominent differences in sexual characteristics.

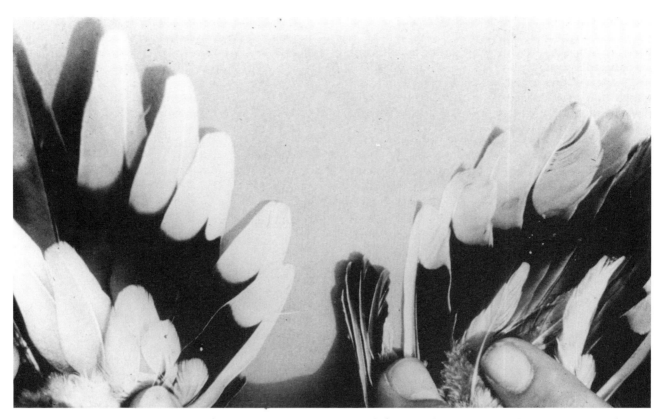

A mourning dove's outer three tail feathers sometimes can be helpful in indicating the bird's sex. The tips of these feathers tend to have a whitish cast in the male (left) and a grayish hue in the female. *Photo courtesy of the U.S. Fish and Wildlife Service.*

The crown and nape of the adult male mourning dove (top) tends to be slightly lighter colored and the head less rounded than those of the adult female (bottom). *Photo courtesy of the Missouri Cooperative Fish and Wildlife Research Unit.*

Adult Doves—Dead

Adult doves can be sexed rather easily using the procedures described previously for immature doves. Gonads of adult birds are larger than those of immatures during the breeding season. During the nonbreeding season, they shrink and look very much like the gonads of older immatures (see chapter 9).

MISCELLANEOUS RESEARCH TECHNIQUES AND CONSIDERATIONS

Many of the techniques used in research on mourning doves have been described in the individual chapters on their life history, management and propagation. However, some techniques that are infrequently used, are very specialized or have not been covered in detail elsewhere are described here.

Activity Budgets

No intensive time-activity studies have been conducted on mourning doves until recently. This probably resulted from an inability of researchers to overcome visibility biases that often enter studies of species such as mourning doves that spend at least some of their time in dense habitats. Also, investigators often were stymied by sampling constraints that cause data variability (e.g., what to do if the bird of the species being sampled flies out of view).

Using radio-tagged mourning doves to guide investigators to experimental dove flocks, Losito et al. (1989) developed some new time-activity techniques that alleviated many of these problems. "Focal-switch sampling" allowed investigators to switch from one bird in a flock to another as the initial bird being sampled became obstructed by vegetation. Focal-switch sampling included a formula that weighted habitat use, tested for restrictions of habitat structure on behavior and had a standard waiting period to decide when to end sampling or continue pursuit of lost flocks. These techniques reduced observer bias, increased research efficiency by 12 percent and saved 24 percent of sampling periods from premature termination. Losito et al. recommended using focal-switch sampling in conjunction with focal-animal sampling (Altmann 1974) when sampling mourning doves in view-restricted habitats.

Nesting Studies

Use of artificial nesting substrates. Mourning doves readily use old nests of other birds (e.g., Nice 1922) and occasionally use man-made structures such as ledges, eaves and bridge girders (McClure 1946) as platforms on which to construct their nests. This tendency has stimulated interest in providing artificial nesting substrates as a means of enhancing mourning dove production or concentrating dove nests in areas where they can be easily studied.

Calhoun (1948) initiated research in this area and used roofing paper cut and formed into cone shapes as nesting platforms. They were nailed to suitable crotches and forks of trees on a study area in Ohio. Practically all (11 of 13 pairs: 85 percent) of the doves in the area utilized the platforms during the breeding season, but nesting success was only about 39 percent. Cowan (1959) provided similar platforms constructed of hardware cloth for mourning doves in California. He observed a high rate of utilization (27 of 37 pairs observed: 73 percent), but did not present information on nesting success.

Nelson (1976) compared nesting success in artificial and natural nests of mourning doves on a study area in central Minnesota. He also used hardware cloth as a nesting substrate and observed a 34-percent rate of utilization (69 attempts on 59 of 203 artificial substrates). Although this rate of utilization was lower than in previous studies, nesting success in nests on artificial substrates was high (60.9 percent) and significantly greater than in natural nests (44.2 percent).

Mourning doves obviously accept artificial nesting substrates on which to build their nests in different regions of the United States. Utilization of and nesting success when using such substrates can be high. Consequently, mourning dove researchers may want to consider use of artificial nesting substrates when designing experiments that require concentrated nestings in selected areas.

Effects of observer visitation. A great deal of time, money and effort has been expended on nesting studies involving mourning doves (see chapter 5). Such studies generally have sought to determine nesting success rates in different regions of the continent, in different types of habitats, at different times of the year and under different treatment regimes. Inherent in many of these studies was the idea that nest visitation by an observer did not influence outcome of the nesting. Little concern was expressed that an observer could possibly influence nesting success by pinpointing the location of a nest to a variety of potential predators.

Bart (1977) first questioned the advisability of such an assumption when he concluded that daily mortality rates of mourning dove nestlings were higher the first day after a nest visit than on subsequent days during the nestling period. Later, Bart and Robson (1982) concluded that these earlier observations may actually have been an artifact of sampling methods. However, Morrow and Silvy (1982) noted that, on at least twelve different occasions during a nesting study in eastern Texas, blue jays attempted to steal contents of mourning dove nests while the investigators were checking them. Nichols et al. (1984) provided the most comprehensive information on the effects of nest visitation on nesting success. Based on intensive study in Maryland, they concluded that predators did not respond differently to nests visited at daily and weekly intervals; consequently, success rates of such nests were similar when checked at daily and weekly intervals.

Based on these somewhat inconsistent findings, it would be prudent for mourning dove researchers to keep nest visitations to a predetermined minimum, as dictated by the needs of the study. Morrow and Silvy (1983: 22) indicated that "statistically equivalent data on nesting success of mourning doves can be obtained with a minimum of disturbance if only the fate of the nest is known." In most cases (e.g., if information is needed by nestling age class) this would involve flushing the adult from the nest only once. If information is needed only on fledging success, then the adult would never need to be flushed. Certainly, more research on this subject is warranted in different regions of the country and in different habitat types within regions.

To minimize nest disturbance and allow researchers quick access to low nests, a mirror mounted on a telescoping pole is useful. *Photo by David Dolton.*

Calculating nesting success. For mourning dove studies in which nesting success has been calculated, active nests are visited regularly until they are destroyed or abandoned or until the eggs hatch and the young fledge. Typically, active nests first encountered after incubation has begun and nests that fail often are of unknown age, whereas successful nests are back-aged afterward. Biologists usually have calculated the survival time of such nests from the first encounter by using the Mayfield method (Mayfield 1961, 1975) or variations thereof. Nest days are assumed to be independent events and have a constant probability of survival. This method does not use information on the age at discovery of successful nests, and it combines information from nests of widely differing ages.

A new discrete survival model has been developed using mourning dove data (Pollock and Cornelius 1988). It allows estimation of survival distribution from the time of nest initiation rather than from the time of first encounter as used in other models. The researchers believed their model was a serious competitor with the Mayfield model because precision of the estimate of overall probability of nest success was very similar and they were able to use more of the information available in their data. Dove researchers would be well advised to consult this paper prior to initiating similar nesting studies.

Estimating Hatching Dates

Hatching dates of mourning doves regularly have been estimated by back-dating specimens whose ages have been ascertained by primary feather molt. These hatching dates often have been calculated from the aging table presented for mourning doves in the *Wildlife Management Techniques Manual* (Larson and Taber 1980), which is based primarily on the work of Swank (1955b). However, investigators should be aware that substantially changing sampling intensity over time and sampling during restricted periods of the year (e.g., hunting seasons) can drastically affect predicted hatching distributions (Morrow et al. 1985). Such potential biases should be considered in the design of similar studies.

Chapter 22

Care and Propagation of Captive Mourning Doves

Ralph E. Mirarchi
Department of Zoology and Wildlife Science
and
Alabama Agricultural Experiment Station
Auburn University, Alabama

Captive flocks of mourning doves are valuable research tools. Captive breeding studies have been used to delineate specific anatomical (Mirarchi and Scanlon 1980, Books-Blenden et al. 1984, Muller et al. 1984), physiological (Mirarchi and Scanlon 1981, Mirarchi et al. 1982) and behavioral (Armbruster 1983) processes crucial to understanding of the species. Controlled studies of captive flocks have provided valuable comparisons to companion or subsequent field studies, e.g., Buerger et al. (1986) followed by Carrington and Mirarchi (1989), and Frankel and Baskett (1961) followed by Jackson and Baskett (1964). The potential of captive mourning dove colonies (flocks held indoors) for studies on the effects of environmental contaminants on survival (Buerger et al. 1986, Marn et al. 1988), reproduction (Buerger et al. 1986, Koval et al. 1987) and behavior (Tori and Peterle 1983, Koval et al. 1987) has been realized only recently.

Attempts at captive propagation of mourning doves have met with varied success because of differences in types of facilities in which the birds were housed and problems associated with feeds, mate selection, predation and acclimatization of wild doves to captivity. Increased success with captive dove flocks will occur as facilities, care and techniques involved with their propagation become proven and standardized.

Anyone planning to develop captive flocks of mourning doves for research purposes should purchase and become familiar with the overview of the management of wild birds in captivity provided by the Institute of Laboratory Animal Resources (1977), and with guidelines for the use of wild birds in research provided by the American Ornithologists' Union (1988). Also warranted is careful reading of federal guidelines on the welfare of captive animals (Animal Welfare Act of 1966 {P.L. 89–544} as amended by the Animal Welfare Act of 1970 {P.L. 91–579}, the 1976 Amendments to the Animal Welfare Act {P.L. 94–279} and the 1985 Amendments {P.L. 99–198}). These acts and amendments are designed to ensure that animals used in research receive humane care and treatment. They are regulated by the U.S. Department of Agriculture (USDA) and implemented by the USDA's Animal and Plant Health Inspection Service (APHIS). Copies of the rules and regulations pertaining to implementation can be obtained from the Deputy Administrator, USDA, APHIS-VS, Federal Building, 6505 Belcrest Road, Hyattsville, Maryland 20782.

In addition, researchers interested in developing captive mourning dove flocks should become familiar with the husbandry techniques developed for domestic pigeons (see Levi 1977, Whitney 1968, Schrag et al. 1977). Many of the techniques described in the following sections are modifications of suggestions from all of these literature sources. Others were developed from a combination of experience, common sense and humane considerations.

PROCUREMENT AND POSSESSION PROCEDURES

Statutory Restrictions

The capture, transportation and possession of mourning doves and their eggs are regulated by federal and state laws and require special permits to be held by those involved. All federal and state regulations must be strictly followed to prevent statutory violations and to allow the continued use of captive mourning doves for research. Because the mourning dove status (i.e., gamebird versus songbird) differs among states, and because as migratory birds these doves are under federal jurisdiction, investigators contemplating the use of mourning doves in captivity should contact their state conservation agency and the Special Agent in Charge, U.S. Fish and Wildlife Service, at the appropriate federal regional office for guidelines to obtain the necessary permits.

Trapping, Inspection and Transport

Trapping of wild doves for introduction into the captive flock can be skewed toward specific age and sex groups using trap placement, as described in chapter 21. Of course, the types of traps used should be selected to minimize the likelihood of injury to the birds and checked frequently to minimize stress. Timing of trapping should be arranged according to the proposed use of the captive flock. If hatching-year doves are required, trapping is best in July and August, when hatching-year flocks are large and can be concentrated before grain harvest. If after-hatching-year birds are required, the best time for trapping usually occurs in late winter/early spring, about the time of spring "green-up."

All doves should be inspected at the trap site for injuries or signs of disease that would preclude their use in the captive flock. Doves with abnormalities that would interfere with proposed experiments should be released at the trap site. Some of the birds may suffer abrasions on the front edge of the wing and on the cere if welded wire traps are used. These birds still can be used in the captive flock. Abrasions should be treated with an antiseptic ointment on arrival at the holding facility.

All doves must be examined for signs of disease, particularly lesions indicative of trichomoniasis or avian pox, after removal from the trap. Such lesions often can be detected upon close inspection (see chapter 12). The handler should wear disposable gloves and the dove's mouth should be opened and examined for cheeselike lesions (signs of either trichomoniasis or diphtheritic form of avian pox) in the oral cavity or esophagus. If lesions are present, the bird should be euthanized to prevent its suffering and spread of the disease. A new set of gloves should be used to examine subsequent birds if such lesions are detected. After the mouth is examined, the mandibles, eyes, legs and feet, and the frontal edge of each wing should be examined for the wartlike lesions indicative of avian pox. These lesions can be as small as a pinhead or larger than a pencil eraser. These birds should be released immediately because the disease will spread rapidly among the captive flock, particularly when abrasions are present. In the wild, they usually will recover from the disease if it does not enter the eyes

All wild mourning doves trapped for captive flocks must be screened carefully for lesions indicating avian pox (pictured) and trichomoniasis. Doves exhibiting cheeselike lesions in the mouth or wartlike lesions around the eyes should be euthanized. *Photo by Ralph E. Mirarchi; courtesy of the Auburn University Department of Zoology and Wildlife Science and the Alabama Agricultural Experiment Station.*

or mouth (Karstad 1971). If the eyes or mouth is involved, the bird should be euthanized for humane reasons.

Temporary holding of doves at a trap site and the transporting of those birds to a captive holding facility should be brief and conducted so they are protected from injury, can assume a normal posture (standing or crouching) and are uncrowded. Clean burlap sacks (from feed stores) or dark-colored bird-holding bags (see Reisinger 1968) work well in such situations. These materials allow air exchange and are soft enough to prevent injury and dark enough (particularly the burlap) to keep the doves quiet. No more than three or four doves should be transported in the smaller bags, and no more than ten doves should be transported in the burlap sacks at one time. This prevents heat stress as a result of overcrowding on hot, humid days. All doves should be transported to the holding facilities as quickly as possible and should never be kept in hot temperatures (greater than 85 degrees Fahrenheit: 29.4° C) for more than ten minutes.

Receiving Procedures

Doves should be sexed and aged in the holding area, marked with identifying bands to ensure individual recognition and assigned to appropriate cages. U.S. Fish and Wildlife Service metal bands should not be used unless the birds are being held for a short time only before release. These bands are for use only on free-ranging populations. Plastic (Bandette) and metal (Aluminum Butt End) leg bands of various colors are available (e.g., National Band and Tag Co. of Newport, Kentucky) and have been used successfully. The 0.22- to 0.25-inch (5.6 to 6.3 mm) metal leg bands seem to give the best results because they are inflexible and do not slip over the foot as often as plastic bands do. The band should fit close to the dove's leg yet move freely around it. Banded birds should be checked in hand after one week to ensure that the bands fit correctly; they should be checked monthly thereafter to ensure that bands allow sufficient room for growth. This is particularly important in hatching-year doves. It is also advisable to dust all incoming birds with an appropriate pesticide (e.g., pyrethrin powder) to eliminate feather parasites (American Ornithologists' Union 1988).

Records should be maintained that include date and place of capture, age, sex, band number, cage number, health records, experimental history, therapy and final disposition. Other types of information can be added depending on projected uses of the doves.

Quarantine Procedures

Recently captured doves must be placed in quarantine for at least four weeks (and preferably six) prior to introduction into the captive flock. Quarantine ensures that diseases such as trichomoniasis or avian pox that are not yet demonstrating visible lesions will not develop in the recently captured birds and spread into the remainder of the flock. All personnel working regularly with doves should learn to recognize common signs of sickness and disease and be able to respond accordingly. Personnel also should have access to standard references on the subject, e.g., Davis et al. (1971), Institute of Laboratory Animal Resources (1977), Petrak (1982), Friend (1987), and Davidson and Nettles (1988).

Acclimatization Procedures

Quarantine. During this period, doves should be kept in small cages to minimize injuries that occur from trying to escape. Battery breeding pens (G. Q. F. Manufacturing Co. of Savannah, Georgia) have been used with excellent results and should be filled as birds are received. Two doves are placed in each cage after completing the receiving procedures. Each dove, in turn, should be offered the opportunity to drink at this time. This can be accomplished by holding the bird firmly around the body and introducing it to the water trough at the back of the cage by entering through the front cage door. The dove's head is forced through the back of the cage, and its bill is immersed in the water by placing downward pressure on the back of its head with the index finger. A large number of mourning doves drink heavily when given this opportunity, probably as a result of dehydration while in the traps and during transport. This procedure also helps the captive doves learn the location of the watering trough.

Special care must be taken to help recently captured mourning doves adjust to captivity. Lighting and temperature regimes should approximate ambient conditions—same day length and temperature (±10 degrees Fahrenheit)—until experimentation begins. Handlers should keep noise to a minimum when in the same room, and all movements and activities should be conducted as subtly as possible. The doves should be "visited" several times daily, if possible, so they become accustomed to the handlers. Captive mourning doves that are seldom visited may remain very "wild" and sensitive to disturbance (Institute of Laboratory Animal Resources 1977).

Battery breeding pens have been used successfully to house large numbers—2 per cage, 48 per unit (six cages per row)— of captive mourning doves in relatively small indoor areas. Vital to the well-being of mourning doves in captivity are temperature control, exposure to light, sanitation, minimal stress, protection from predation and continual supplies of food and water. *Photo by Wanda L. McKenzie; courtesy of the Auburn University Department of Zoology and Wildlife Science and the Alabama Agricultural Experiment Station.*

Two doves should be placed in each cage to increase the speed at which they learn how to obtain feed and water. Care should be taken when pairing doves in cages at this time. Hatching-year birds should be paired with birds of similar age (± twenty days), and after-hatching-year birds should be paired with members of the opposite sex. These procedures minimize problems of incompatibility.

All recent arrivals must be monitored closely to detect adjustment problems, incompatibility with cage mates, injuries or symptoms of disease. Caretakers should visually, without handling, inspect the doves in each cage and the excrement under each cage daily. They should look for lesions indicative of avian pox, immobility with "fluffed-out" feathers, abnormal posture or behavior, the absence of plumage from back of head and nape of neck, reduced feed intake and abnormally colored or textured feces. Abnormal posture or behavior

indicates injury, disease or deterioration of physical condition because of lack of food or water. Absence or disruption of plumage on the head, neck or back indicates an overly aggressive cage mate. Abnormally colored feces, particularly dark green in color, indicate at least one of the cage mates is not feeding and is beginning to break down its body tissues. This may be symptomatic of a failure to acclimate or its displacement from food and water by an overly aggressive cage mate.

Acclimatization problems must be handled quickly. Injured, diseased or abnormally behaving doves should be immediately removed, examined and treated by a veterinarian if necessary and isolated with individual food and water supplies. If the bird does not begin feeding from the troughs within two days, food and water can be introduced directly into the cage in separate small bowls. If the bird refuses to eat or drink from these dishes, it probably will never acclimate to captivity. Force-feeding rarely works in these instances. Consequently, the bird should be set free if still strong enough to fly or euthanized if in a weakened state. Up to 8 percent of captured doves fail to acclimate to the captivity (R. E. Mirarchi personal files).

Recently captured doves should be acclimated to new diets gradually, starting with foods as close to natural as possible and ending with those on which they will be maintained. Wild birdseed mixes (e.g., Purina Wild Bird Seed Mix of the Ralston Purina Co. of St. Louis, Missouri) supplemented with grit work well as initial food sources because of the variety of seeds present. Each week the seed mix should be reduced by at least 20 percent and replaced with the diet on which the doves ultimately will be maintained. This should continue until only the new diet is being fed. If soft or pelleted diets are fed for extended periods, grit may no longer be necessary (Kendall and Scanlon 1981b). Doves should be acclimated to diets at least one month before data are collected, unless responses to changes in diet are part of the experimental design.

Breeding. Wild adult mourning doves once were thought unsuitable for captive breeding because of the injuries they inflicted on themselves after being introduced into wire enclosures (Quay 1951a). These problems have been resolved by allowing recently captured doves to acclimate to captivity for a minimum of three months before being used for breeding purposes. Better success in breeding experiments is achieved when doves are captured during late summer and overwintered

prior to breeding the next spring. Breeding success improves as the length of confinement increases. Best breeding success occurs when mourning doves are raised in captivity.

Breeding pairs that have been moved from indoor (e.g., battery breeding pens) to outdoor cages should be allowed to acclimate for two to three weeks before they can be expected to begin a normal nesting cycle. This permits the pair to replace missing feathers, allows the female to discard eggs currently in the oviduct and provides the pair the opportunity to select a nest site and procure nesting materials. It is common for the female to lay one or two clutches of eggs on the cage floor until she becomes acclimated to the new surroundings. If this behavior persists beyond the third clutch, however, it usually indicates the female is injured and cannot reach the nesting platforms or that she has not acclimated to the captive situation. In such situations, she should be replaced with a new female, and the pair should be watched closely for signs of incompatibility.

HOLDING, QUARANTINE AND EXPERIMENTAL FACILITIES

For the sake of expedience, the holding, quarantine and experimental facilities for the captive mourning dove flock should be combined into one complex, as long as the potential for disease transmission is given proper consideration (*Figure 71*). The entire complex should be located in an area free from human disturbance.

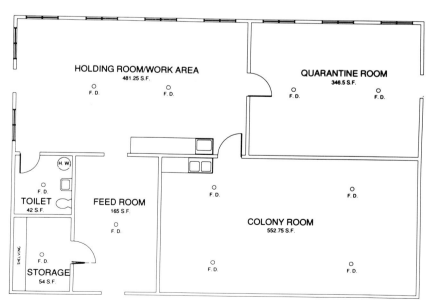

Figure 71. Schematic diagram of indoor facility designed for proper care and propagation of captive mourning doves (S. F. = square feet; F. D. = floor drain).

Indoor facilities for receiving, quarantining and holding mourning doves should be combined into one complex located away (≥150 feet: 45.7 m) from human disturbances. *Photo by Theodore T. Buerger; courtesy of the Auburn University Department of Zoology and Wildlife Science and the Alabama Agricultural Experiment Station.*

Holding

The holding area should be of a size that can adequately serve as a central location for record keeping, lab procedures and storage of lab materials (antiseptics, syringes, etc.) and equipment (incubators, hatchers, candlers, balances, etc.). It should have storage shelves and cabinets, a sink, lab benches, dissection table, and desk. It should be well lit and maintained at room temperature. Normally, the holding area is one of transit or for use in certain experimental procedures. Consequently, doves are kept there only for short periods.

Quarantine

The size of the quarantine area depends on the number of doves to be housed, but a 400-square-foot (37.2 m²) room can easily accommodate 200 birds. Large numbers of doves can be housed safely and efficiently in battery breeding pens that consist of four stacked rows of six cages 19 by 13 by 9 inches (48 by 33 by 23 cm) each. Feed and water troughs run the length of the front and back, respectively, of each row. Dropping paper is dispensed beneath the cages from rolls attached at the end of each row.

This area must be kept separate from the remainder of the facility. Optimally, it should have internal air circulation, venting to the outside, and separate lighting and temperature controls. The lighting should be fluorescent and recessed into the ceiling to prevent accumulations of dust or debris that could hold disease organisms. Special wide-spectrum fluorescent lamps are commercially available that approximate daylight more closely than do those normally used (Institute of Laboratory Animal Resources 1977). The walls should be constructed of a washable material (e.g., tile) or a substrate such as cinder block that can be painted with a slick, washable, oil- or epoxy-based paint. The floors also should be constructed of material similar to the walls or have a smooth concrete finish that allows washing. They should be sloped toward recessed floor drains running around the perimeter of the room or several drains equally spaced over the floor. Floor drains should lead to an easily accessible trap that allows heavy materials such as grain and droppings to settle out prior to going into the septic system. This allows regular cleaning and prevents blockage of sewage or septic system lines (see also Institute of Laboratory Animal Resources 1977, 1985).

Experimental Breeding

The objectives of breeding experiments must be well defined before the exact type of facility needed for the experiments is constructed. In certain instances, a variety of breeding facilities may need to be included within the complex. Mourning doves generally will not breed successfully and consistently if more than one pair is confined per cage (unless extremely large), due to territorial conflicts (Hanson and Kossack 1963). Also, single pairs confined to cages that are too small lay heavily but have few hatches (Hanson and Kossack 1963, R. E. Mirarchi personal files).

Indoor. Mourning doves will successfully court, mate and lay eggs indoors at regular intervals throughout the breeding season. The use of battery breeding pens facilitates these activities and allows large numbers of doves to be involved at one time. The colony room should be of a size necessary to accommodate a large number of birds at 2.0 square feet per bird (0.19 m²). The room should be constructed of materials and in the manner (lighting, climate control, internal air circulation, etc.) described for the quarantine facilities. In addition to natural lighting and recessed fluorescent ceiling lights, strips of fluorescent lights can be mounted vertically on the walls of the facility to distribute the light more evenly (Kendall and Scanlon 1981b, Buerger et al. 1986). Indoors, breeding doves should be maintained under thermostatically controlled temperature conditions (72 ± 5 degrees Fahrenheit: 22 ± ° C) and under lighting that approximates the natural photoperiod. Breeding seasons can be extended through artificial lighting if necessary to achieve experimental objectives, but doves should be allowed to undergo refractory periods each year to allow other physiological processes (e.g., molt) to occur.

Eggs obtained from breeding mourning doves in battery breeding pens can be artificially incubated, hatched and the squabs raised by foster parents or by hand (discussed later) if necessary. Mourning dove pairs have nested and raised young in modified indoor rabbit cages (5.9 by 2.3 by 1.6 feet: 1.8 by 0.7 by 0.5 m), but success was low and nesting was erratic (Mirarchi 1978). Apparently, cages of this size just barely meet minimum space requirements for breeding in this species. If young need to be consistently raised, larger indoor (or outdoor) breeding facilities are needed.

Outdoor. Mourning doves have successfully raised young in a variety of facilities of different shapes and sizes *(Table 81)*. The optimum-sized and

A variety of indoor (left) and outdoor (top right) cage complexes has been used to raise young mourning doves to fledging, but large, outdoor breeding cages (bottom right) have provided the most consistent success. *Photos by Ralph E. Mirarchi; courtesy of the Auburn University Department of Zoology and Wildlife Science and the Alabama Agricultural Experiment Station.*

Table 81. Shapes and sizes of outdoor cages used successfully to breed and raise mourning doves in captivity.[a]

Dimensions	Special characteristics	Source
5 by 5 by 6 feet (1.52 by 1.52 by 1.82m)	Top covered with roofing paper	Hanson and Kossack (1963)
8 by 6 by 6 feet (2.44 by 1.82 by 1.82m)	Wooden frame Poultry mesh with soft netting on top	W. R. Goforth (personal communication: 1975)
6.56 by 3.28 by 6.56 feet (2 by 1 by 2m)	Wooden frame with poultry netting	Mirarchi (1978)
8.85 by 6 by 6 feet (2.7 by 1.8 by 1.8m)	Wooden frame with welded wire	Mirarchi (1978)
4 by 6 by 6 feet (1.2 by 1.8 by 1.8m)	Wooden frame with welded wire	R. E. Mirarchi (personal files)

[a] One pair of birds per cage.

most cost-effective facility appears to be a complex of twenty (or more) wooden-framed cages 8 by 6 by 6 feet (2.4 by 1.8 by 1.8 m), made of 1- by 2-inch (2.5 by 5.1 cm) welded wire. Each cage has a 0.25- by 0.25-inch (6.3 by 6.3 mm) hardware cloth bottom that extends 1 foot (0.3 m) up the side of the cage and contains two horizontal perches 4.5 feet (1.4 m) from the cage bottom. Wooden paneling or translucent fiberglass 1 foot high (0.3 m) runs around the perimeter of the base of each cage and around the end of each perch to provide a visual barrier between cages at locations where territorial disputes are most likely to occur. A portion of the upper rear of each cage is shielded from the elements on three sides and contains two nesting platforms (one in each corner). Pine straw is placed on the bottom of each cage to cover the exposed hardware cloth floor and provide nesting material. Food and water are provided via automatic waterers and gamebird feeders (e.g., Sears, Roebuck and Co. of Chicago, Illinois). The entire facility is on stilts and encompassed by two strands of electric fencing to provide protection from mammalian and reptilian predators. Sliding doors should be used if possible.

A complex (bottom left) of twenty outdoor cages (ten per side) for captive mourning doves to breed and raise young appears to be most cost efficient. Hardware cloth is used to surround the base of each elevated cage, and electric wires (white insulators) are effective mammalian predator deterrents. Each cage has several doors (top right) to facilitate easy and safe access for various housekeeping or handling functions. Sliding doors are preferable. Nesting platforms, perches and a portion of each cage shielded from adverse weather (bottom right) are important cage features. *Photos by Theodore T. Buerger; courtesy of the Auburn University Department of Zoology and Wildlife Science and the Alabama Agricultural Experiment Station.*

Experimental—Other

Outdoor. Large (1 acre: 0.4 ha) outdoor flight pens have been used to confine free-flying experimental dove populations in Missouri. These pens were modified from existing rabbit pens described previously (Malecki et al. 1974) and are described herein as per Armbruster (1983). Poultry netting (buried 6 inches: 15 cm) formed the base of four sides (5 feet high: 1.5 m), and gamefarm netting covered the remaining sides and roof of each enclosure. Penta-treated poles 16 feet (4.9 m) long were buried 3 feet (0.9 m) deep at 25-foot (7.5 m) intervals, to support a network of #9 construction wire. A roof of gamefarm netting was constructed over this network. At completion, each enclosure was 13 feet (4 m) high. A single electric fence wire was positioned along the poultry netting 4 feet (1.2 m) above the ground. The gamefarm netting was not recommended by its manufacturer for construction of pen sides, but no problems were encountered during Armbruster's study when netting was used as described. No attempt was made to exclude small mammals or reptiles from the enclosures.

Armbruster (1983) attempted to simulate natural conditions in a confined situation. Nesting structures consisted of 0.25-inch (0.6 cm) hardware cloth fashioned into a cone (Cowan 1959) supported by a loop of #9 construction wire attached to various poles within each enclosure. Eastern red cedar boughs were placed over nest cones to supply shade and protection from rain. Perches of cedar limbs were attached to various poles so that doves

using them would be clearly visible from an elevated (3 feet: 0.9 m) 6- by 7.5-foot (1.7 by 2.3 m) observation blind centrally located at the eastern end of each enclosure. Trees were left or cedars and shortleaf pines transplanted in each enclosure. An area approximately 23 feet (7 m) wide and 151 feet (46 m) long was disced in each enclosure and maintained as bare soil. Feeders and waterers were located on these disced areas. Feeders were covered with a 4- by 4-foot (0.37 m²) square of sheet metal to limit their attractiveness to cowbirds that were able to enter enclosures through the netting. Enclosures were routinely mowed to facilitate observation of ground activity and supply potential nest material.

Other Facilities

Storage. A separate room is needed to store feed, grit and other materials to maintain the captive mourning dove flock. A 200-square foot (18.6 m²) room with an adjacent 60-square-foot (5.6 m²) storage closet should prove satisfactory. A small supply of feed and any bait used to trap doves can be stored there in large pest-proof containers for short periods of time (less than ten days). Grit can be stored in such containers indefinitely. Bags of feed to be stored for extended periods should be stacked on benches or racks off the floor. The small storage room can be used for paper towels, light bulbs, trapping equipment, etc. These rooms should have regular lighting and be maintained at room temperature.

Large (1.0 acre: 0.4 ha) outdoor flight pens have been used successfully for behavioral studies of captive mourning doves. The "house" in the center of this scene is an observation station. *Photo courtesy of the Missouri Cooperative Fish and Wildlife Research Unit.*

NUTRITION

Foodstuff and Diet Mixtures

Feed mixtures for captive mourning dove flocks have changed over time. Obviously, diets that allow the birds to conduct routine activities, including reproduction, are necessary. Early on, captive flocks were maintained on commercial feed mixtures for domestic pigeons, which included hemp, kafir corn, milo, millet, hard wheat, vetch, buckwheat, field peas and whole corn fortified with 0.86 ounces (24.5 ml) of cod liver oil per pound (0.45 kg) of feed (Hanson and Kossack 1963). Specialized "health" grits were furnished, consisting of granite, calcium iodide, cobalt calcium carbonate, bone meal, sodium chloride, anise and oyster shell (Hanson and Kossack 1963). Poultry scratch also was used (W. R. Goforth personal communication: 1975).

The need for well-balanced diets arose when research on captive doves increased and the use of captive breeding flocks became important. Quail layer rations (mash consistency) were first used to ensure a diet complete in vitamins, minerals, amino acids, etc., necessary for breeding doves (Mirarchi 1978). Although doves found the layer ration palatable, much of the food was wasted because the mash consistency allowed the doves to sling it out of the feed troughs as they searched for choice particles (R. E. Mirarchi personal files).

A complete, well-rounded feed mixture that has a consistency palatable to doves and discourages wastage is now available in pelleted form (e.g., Purina Pigeon Chow Checkers of the Ralston Purina Co.). This feed has proved satisfactory for use with laboratory ringed turtledoves (Kendall and Scanlon 1981b) and mourning doves (Buerger et al. 1986, Marn et al. 1988). Recent developments in commercial feed mixtures and systems for domestic pigeons (e.g., NutriBlend of the Ralston Purina Co.) offer the opportunity to regulate protein and carbohydrate intake rather easily. Such systems should be readily adaptable to captive colonies of mourning doves and offer a variety of new research opportunities. Researchers should follow strict acclimatization procedures whenever new feed mixtures or diets are introduced to the captive dove flock. Feed mixtures should be stored in large pest-proof cans just outside colony or experimental rooms.

Water use presents fewer problems for captive dove flocks because mourning doves readily accept and thrive on regular tap water. However, researchers should determine if regular tap water will confound experimental results before introducing it to the flock. Tap water contains certain additives (e.g., chlorine and fluorine) and contaminants (e.g., lead) that may preclude its use. In such instances, distilled or deionized water can be used instead (Buerger et al. 1986). Distilled or deionized water can be stored in large carboys just outside colony or experimental rooms.

Feeding and Watering Systems

Several feeding and watering systems are available for use with captive dove flocks and colonies. Commercial chicken feeders of various sorts and sizes, including feed and water troughs associated with battery breeding pens, have been used effectively (Hanson and Kossack 1963). Automatic watering systems are available with battery breeding pens; these save time and manpower, eliminate the possibility of experimental complications caused by failure to water the birds and reduce disturbance to them. A modification of small-mammal watering bottles has been successfully used for ringed turtledoves (Kendall and Scanlon 1980) and could prove useful for work with captive mourning doves housed individually. The advantages of such a device include ready quantification of water consumption, minimal disturbance to the birds when changing or refilling, lessened chances of disease being spread among birds and easy administration of treatments and medication (Kendall and Scanlon 1980).

Outdoor pens pose some additional problems for delivery of feed and water. Commercially made plastic automatic waterers and metal gamebird feeders have been used with certain modifications (Buerger et al. 1986). Automatic watering systems that operate from city water pressure are available for pigeons and will dispense water into a cup fount that is attached to each cage (e.g., Edstrom System of Stromberg's Chicks and Pets Unlimited of Pine River, Minnesota). Such systems can be easily modified for use with mourning doves. Researchers must ensure that water lines do not freeze (i.e., use water heaters or heat tape), making water unavailable to the birds for extended periods during cold weather. Additionally, metal gamebird feeders function fine with heavy seed mixes but tend to become clogged when mash or pelleted foods are used in humid or wet weather (R. E. Mirarchi personal files). These feeders work best when they are shielded from the elements on all sides. Researchers should be aware that the type of device used to dispense feed or water also may confound experimental results because of potential contamination. Special precautions (e.g., use of stainless steel watering troughs [Buerger et al. 1986]) have been used to prevent problems such as lead contamination from soldered trough joints.

GENERAL MAINTENANCE

Routine Health Care: Doves

In addition to routine daily inspection of captive mourning doves, as described earlier, each bird should receive a close-up, in-the-hand examination twice yearly (excluding experimental periods). A small checklist can be maintained for each dove (see Institute of Laboratory Animal Resources 1977). The oral cavity, eyes, plumage, feet and cloaca should be examined closely for abnormal appearance indicative of injury or disease. This in-hand examination rarely detects injuries or disease not observed during the routine daily inspection, but it adds a check to the system and allows for routine care of the plumage and nails. If the birds are held in wire cages, such as the battery breeding pens previously described, their nails will grow abnormally long because of the lack of abrasion on a hard surface. They should be trimmed with nail clippers back to normal length. Care should be taken not to clip nails too short because this will result in profuse bleeding. Clip the nails a little at a time until the normal nail length is attained. If a blood vessel is ruptured, apply firm pressure on the toe behind the nail and apply a silver nitrate stick to the nail tip (Leonard 1969). Bleeding should stop quickly. Occasionally, the upper mandible of the bill will have to be treated similarly.

Doves generally will take care of their plumage with little need of outside assistance. While birds are being held on wire, such as in battery breeding pens, the tips of the outer primaries and the central tail feathers will become broken and frayed. These feathers can be left alone, unless they are causing the bird discomfort. Once the doves are introduced to outdoor flight pens, the central two or three tail feathers should be removed to promote regrowth. The doves do reasonably well in the flight pens without them, and these feathers regrow rapidly to give them a more normal appearance.

Routine Health Care: Personnel

Approximately thirty-five diseases and parasites reported for humans involve birds as alternate hosts, with two or three (psittacosis, histoplasmosis, toxoplasmosis) likely to involve columbids (Herman 1982). All personnel working with doves should be made aware of the symptoms of zoonoses common to birds and people and report persistent symptoms to a doctor.

High standards of hygiene among personnel are essential in protecting themselves and the doves under their care. The size, location and function of a captive dove flock should determine the intensity of procedures involved with hygiene. Certainly, where infectious agents are involved in experimentation, maximum precautions are required (see Institute of Laboratory Animal Resources 1977). In such instances, personnel should pass through a locker/washroom in which they don lab clothing and wash their hands with a germicidal soap before entering work areas where birds, bird feed or related items are kept. When passing into the work area, they also should step through a germicidal footwear bath. The reverse procedures should be followed when leaving the area. If exceptionally dirty work is involved, such as cleaning cages or aviaries, a shower also should be required.

Less intensive care can be taken when captive dove flocks are used for less sensitive work. Common sense dictates in such situations. Lab clothing should be worn when entering quarantine and colony areas and removed prior to leaving. Hands should be washed immediately after leaving such areas. Personnel should never move directly from the quarantine area into colony or experimental rooms without changing lab clothing and/or washing hands. Shoes should be brushed free of debris prior to leaving the quarantine room.

Occasionally, personnel working with captive dove flocks have (or develop) allergies to the powder down (waterproofing agent), bird dander (flakes of epithelial tissue), excrement or dust associated with large concentrations of doves. Minor allergic symptoms usually can be prevented or reduced by wearing lab clothing and a surgical mask designed for allergy sufferers. Prescribed antihistamines should be taken prior to working with the captive flock. Washing hands and face after leaving the work area also helps. In rare situations, allergies or asthmatic attacks caused by the above may be so severe that it precludes an individual from working with the captive flock. Handlers also should be aware that pigeon breeders and fanciers occasionally develop an allergic pulmonary disease ("bird fancier's lung") caused by inhalation of the antigens in avian excreta (Hargreave et al. 1966).

Sanitary Measures

Sanitary procedures with captive dove flocks vary according to flock size, type of caging, whether indoors or outdoors, and the purpose for holding the birds in captivity. Doves held indoors in battery breeding pens require regular sanitary maintenance. During normal holding periods, dropping paper should be changed weekly after any excessive dropping buildups are removed from the cages. Used dropping paper and other refuse from the facility should be deposited in pest-proof containers in the holding area until removal from the facility.

Water and feed troughs should be disinfected with Lysol (Sterling Drug, Inc., of Montvale, New Jersey) or Micro-phene (Oxford Chemicals of Atlanta, Georgia) and rinsed thoroughly every two weeks. The frequency of this schedule should be decreased to biweekly changes of paper and monthly disinfection of feed and water troughs to minimize disturbance when the captive doves are being used in breeding experiments. Frequency of the disinfection procedure should be increased if any diseases are diagnosed.

The entire battery cage complex should be scrubbed clean and disinfected between experiments, or every six months if it does not interfere with experimentation. Floors should be swept as necessary to prevent food and dust accumulations, and floors and walls should be washed and disinfected as described previously for the battery cage complex. Only one or two individuals should clean the cages at any time to minimize disturbance to the doves. If two individuals are involved, they should never position themselves on opposite sides of the battery breeding pens. This frightens the doves considerably and inevitably leads to injuries.

Doves kept in outdoor breeding facilities, large flight pens or large indoor rooms need less stringent sanitation procedures. Adequate substrates (e.g., coarse sand or fine gravel) may make it possible to reduce cleaning to once or twice a year (Institute of Laboratory Animal Resources 1977). Dried excrement, feathers and buildup of dried food can be removed by occasional raking of the substrate. Large enclosures or flight rooms should be cleaned entirely at least once a year, including perches, nestboxes, etc., and sprayed with some type of disinfectant. The birds should be removed during spraying and not reintroduced for at least one week.

Nesting material (e.g., pine needles) should be autoclaved prior to introduction of doves to the breeding facilities, whether indoors or outdoors, to prevent the spread of such diseases as avian pox. Development of a sterile yet satisfactory substitute for pine needles as nesting material would save a great deal of time and energy and warrants investigation.

Prophylaxis

The use of prophylactic drugs and immunizations generally is not necessary to maintain healthy captive mourning dove flocks as long as adequate standards of nutrition, housing and sanitation are practiced. Indeed, attempts to immunize captive mourning doves against avian pox using a pigeon pox vaccine have proved unsuccessful in our program. Apparently, the strain used was too virulent for mourning doves, because all those treated contracted the disease. Emtryl (Salisbury Laboratory of Charles City, Iowa) has been successfully used in drinking water (1 gram per 0.95 liters of tap water) of hatching-year doves for five continuous days after capture and for five days prior to experimentation to prevent trichomoniasis (Armbruster 1983). A variety of vitamin supplements (e.g., Pigeon Builders, Avitron), antibiotics (e.g., Aureomycin), coccidial treatments (e.g., NFZ, Merck Aprol), wormers (e.g., Piperzine) and louse powders (e.g., Featherkleen) are available for pigeons and possibly could be used for mourning doves if necessary.

ANIMAL DAMAGE CONTROL

Indoor Facilities

Captive dove colonies must remain free of nuisance pests and potential predators to ensure their health and safety. Insects such as mosquitoes, flies and roaches are unsightly as well as being potential vectors of disease. All windows of the captive holding facility should be screened to exclude airborne insects. Airborne insects that accidentally enter the facility through the opening of doors, etc., can be effectively controlled using fly tape (Aeroxon Products, Inc., of New Rochelle, New York). Roach populations inevitably grow as a result of food, water, and breeding and hiding substrates available to them in any indoor aviary. They can be controlled by keeping the facility as clean as possible and using approved insecticides (e.g., Dursban LO of Dow Chemical Co. of Midland, Michigan, and Roach-Prufe of Copper Brite, Inc., of Los Angeles, California) on a regular basis. If such insecticides are used, researchers must make certain they are safe to use in the presence of the doves and will not confound results of ongoing experiments.

Avian and mammalian pests and predators are fairly easily excluded from indoor facilities. As long as the building is structurally sound, and windows and any window flight cages associated with the facility are enclosed with small-mesh screening, there is little opportunity for entrance of nuisance birds and mammals. Rats rarely cause problems in a sound building as long as it and the surrounding grounds are kept free of trash and the immediate area surrounding the facility is mowed regularly. Occasionally, house mice or field and woodland mice may work their way into the facility by enlarging a wall seam, gnawing a hole, etc. They can be removed easily. First, make sure their source of entry to the facility is closed. Second, make sure all feed is secure in pest-proof cans and the floors are swept clean of spilled feed. Then set appropriately sized snap traps, with a piece of corn impaled on the trigger, in each corner of the facility. Check daily. Mice populations are usually eliminated in a matter of days using these procedures.

Snakes, particularly rat snakes, will readily enter indoor facilities through the smallest openings in search of prey. One rat snake climbed more than 3.3 feet (1.0 m) straight up a cinder-block wall to enter a building through a small hole in a screened window. It climbed to the top row of cages in a battery breeding pen complex, entered a cage, and killed and consumed two fledgling doves (R. E. Mirarchi personal files). The doves' disappearance would have been a mystery had the snake not been discovered in the cage the next morning unable to squeeze back through the cage bars with its evening meal. Such occurrences obviously can disrupt important experiments and need to be prevented. Regular examination of the entire building for potential entry sources and closing such openings should exclude reptilian predators.

Outdoor Facilities

As with indoor facilities, outdoor aviaries must be protected from predators to ensure the safety of experimental birds and provide an atmosphere conducive to normal behavior. Insect control outdoors is a complex problem, with few remedies short of total screening of cages. Such a proposition would be expensive and also might alter normal behavior of the enclosed doves. In most instances, insects do not appear to affect captive birds adversely in outdoor pens as long as the pen area undergoes regular sanitary maintenance. However, young (twenty-five to thirty days old) fledglings raised in outdoor enclosures in Alabama did contract avian pox at a high rate (more than 50 percent), possibly as a result of transmission of the disease by insect vectors (R. E. Mirarchi personal files). Close monitoring for such disease developments and research in this area are warranted.

Avian predators, particularly sharp-shinned and Cooper's hawks, will attempt to kill doves held in outdoor cages. They are easier to exclude than mammalian or reptilian predators. Avian attacks can be deterred by protecting nesting platforms, perches, feeders and waterers with wooden paneling placed on the outside of the cages, or simply by placing these structures away from cage sides and tops. Perches kept under a roof or cover should be made available in each cage to offer a retreat to birds under attack. After a few unsuccessful attempts at capture, the avian predator usually will move on. If the predator continues to harass the birds for a period of days, it may be necessary to scare it off or trap and relocate it some distance away.

With a minor investment of time and money, mammalian predators can be excluded from outdoor facilities. Early attempts to exclude stray cats and dogs from outdoor dove cages included building the cages on stilts and surrounding the area with fencing (Hanson and Kossack 1963). All outdoor facilities should be surrounded by a chain-link-type fence with a concrete footing or one buried in the ground to a depth of 1 foot (0.3 m). This will deter feral and free-ranging cats and dogs that could disturb the captive doves. However, the cages themselves must have additional protection against wild predators that climb over (e.g., raccoons) or go through (e.g., snakes and weasels) the outer fencing. If the cages are built directly on the ground, the cage fencing must be buried in the ground at least 6 inches (15.2 cm) (Armbruster 1983). Also, the base of the cages for a height of at least 12 to 14 inches (30.5 to 35.6 cm) should consist of 0.25- by 0.25-inch (6.3 by 6.3 mm) hardware cloth (R. E. Mirarchi personal files) and be surrounded by two strands of electric fencing (Armbruster 1983). This prevents mammalian predators, particularly raccoons, from grasping birds through the wire and pulling them through. If cages are built on stilts, the bottoms as well as the sides to the aforementioned height should be built of 0.25- by 0.25-inch (6.3 by 6.3 mm) hardware cloth. Two electric wires at heights of 12 inches (30.5 cm) and 36 inches (91.4 cm) from the base of cage should surround each cage or the entire cage complex.

Reptilian predators, particularly rat snakes, pose the greatest exclusion problems for outdoor pens. They easily climb stilts, avoid electric fencing, enter cages of all but the smallest mesh and are very successful at catching doves in cages. Some success has been achieved by using electric wire strung so close to the cage that a snake can crawl neither over nor under without touching it; however, snakes still occasionally enter cages (R. E. Mirarchi personal files). The most foolproof (and most expensive) way to exclude snakes is to surround the entire complex with a snake-proof fence (Byford

1983). Glue boards (e.g., Victor Holdfast Glue-board Traps of the Woodstream Corp. of Lititz, Pennsylvania [see Knight 1986]) on the stilts of the cage complex may effectively capture foraging snakes, and chemical repellents (e.g., Tack Trap from Animal Repellents, Inc., of Griffin, Georgia [see Johnson 1983]) may serve as deterrents. Both techniques should be tested. Predator guards installed on the stilts, like those used on wood duck nest boxes, also might work and should be tested.

REPRODUCTION IN CONFINEMENT

Mate Selection

Mate selection by doves in captivity usually is influenced by the researcher to a certain degree. Hanson and Kossack (1963) picked birds at random and removed them to outdoor cages between March 15 and April 1. If the male and female were compatible, courtship began in approximately five days (range = zero to fourteen), nest building in about ten days (range = one to twenty) and egg laying in about eleven days (range = two to twenty-three). When male/female associations were incompatible, they were terminated, and new birds were introduced as possible mates. Mackey (1954) isolated pairs in breeding pens no later than January and switched females to different males if they did not associate. The female plays the deciding role in mate selection by either permitting or rejecting the male's advances (Armbruster 1983, R. E. Mirarchi personal files). However, yellow head marks on female mourning doves disrupt recently formed pair bonds and prevent reestablishment of well-developed pair bonds when the female is separated from her mate and returned after a few days (Goforth and Baskett 1965, see chapter 21). Other marker locations and areas tested have no such effects, nor does marking the heads of males with yellow.

Mourning doves can be stimulated to breed through force-pairings, and unless otherwise noted, the following observations are based on experiences in my program. Female doves should be introduced to the cages of prospective mates a minimum of two weeks before the breeding season begins. If possible, prospective pairs should be overwintered together. Some mourning dove females (15 to 20 percent of 160) have been housed with males for three to four months during the breeding season with no indication of pairing. Once these females were introduced to cages of new males, many of them immediately began laying, while a few had to be introduced to several males before

pairing. Obviously, females are selective about mates, and it may be necessary to try various combinations of males and females when attempting force-pairings. If a force-pairing does not result in egg laying in two to three weeks during the normal breeding season, females should be introduced to new males. Handlers must pay close attention to the condition of both doves during this time. Overly aggressive males, in particular, will pluck feathers from or scalp cage mates that do not submit to their advances and occasionally will kill the female if they are not separated. Sometimes, aggressive females will harass subordinate males similarly, although they never have been observed to kill one. Shuffling individuals so that the most aggressive males and females and the least aggressive males and females are housed together often results in successful pairings.

Nesting and the Nest Cycle

Suitable nesting sites and nesting materials must be provided to ensure successful and continuous breeding. Goforth and Baskett (1971b) provided a cone-shaped piece of tar paper secured to a wire loop, similar to that described by Calhoun (1948), as a nesting structure. The wire holding the cone was attached to a board and nailed to the corner of the breeding pen. Pine needles were placed on the ground for nesting material. For nesting platforms, Hanson and Kossack (1963) used coffee cans with screening soldered on top. Needles from white pine and Austrian pine proved to be the most successful nesting material. Armbruster (1983) used a shallow cone constructed from 0.25-inch (6.3 mm) hardware cloth as a nesting substrate. Similarly designed artificial nesting cones had a 34-percent rate of utilization and resulted in greater nesting success than did natural nests when tested on wild dove populations in Minnesota (Nelson 1976). Armbruster's cones were supported by attaching them to posts with a loop of #9 construction wire. A few pine needles from longleaved species then were added to the nesting cones. Nest sites were provided with some type of shade during the day. Pine needles from loblolly, longleaf and shortleaf pines all have been used successfully as nest material (R. E. Mirarchi personal files). Any pine needles of this approximate size and consistency should be satisfactory.

Woodward (1929) noted that captive mourning doves were engaged in nesting for approximately eight months in southern California. Jenkins (1955) reported a nesting cycle of captive doves comparable to that of free-ranging doves. The entire cycle required thirty to thirty-eight days for completion, with seven days used for courtship and nest preparation, two to three days for laying eggs, and fourteen days for incubation. The young remained with the parents for about twelve days, with several females beginning new nests immediately after the young had left the nest. Captive mourning doves had a tendency to abandon the first nest of the season.

Egg-laying Characteristics

A captive mourning dove colony was studied during the breeding season for two consecutive years in Virginia (Mirarchi and Scanlon 1978). Paired birds held in battery breeding pens were checked daily at 5:00 P.M., and the number of eggs laid by each pair was recorded. Egg laying generally began during the last week of February. Eggs were removed shortly after laying. Egg-laying intervals (mean ± SE) between the first and second and between the second and the third clutches were 9.8 ± 0.6 days and 8.8 ± 1.1 days, respectively. There was no difference in intervals between the first and second or the second and third clutches of eggs (*Table 82*).

Measurements of the greatest length and greatest width of each egg were recorded (*Table 83*), as were mean monthly egg lengths and widths (*Table 84*). No consistent differences between egg measurements in each clutch were found within months, although there were differences in egg length between eggs of each clutch over all months. Differences in length of eggs also were found between the first and second egg laid within both the first and second clutches, and also over all clutches. This information correlates well with what has been observed in the wild and indicates that confinement has little effect on the egg-laying characteristics of the species.

The nesting cycle and behavior of captive mourning doves closely approximates that of their wild, free-ranging counterparts, although captive adult breeders showed a greater tendency to abandon their first nest of the season. *Photo of adult feeding an advanced nestling courtesy of the Missouri Cooperative Fish and Wildlife Research Unit.*

Table 83. Mean measurements of eggs laid in battery breeding cages by captive mourning doves (Mirarchi 1978).

Egg number	Clutch number	Number of eggs	Egg measurement in centimeters (Mean ± S.E.)	
			Length	Width
First	1	92	2.76 ± 0.01^{ad}	2.14 ± 0.01^{ac}
Second	1	86	2.85 ± 0.02^{b}	2.16 ± 0.01^{b}
First	2	34	2.79 ± 0.02^{d}	2.15 ± 0.02^{c}
Second	2	36	2.88 ± 0.02	2.17 ± 0.01
First	3	12	2.79 ± 0.05^{c}	2.17 ± 0.01^{c}
Second	3	12	2.89 ± 0.04	2.17 ± 0.02
First	All	138	2.77 ± 0.01^{e}	2.15 ± 0.01^{c}
Second	All	134	2.86 ± 0.01	2.16 ± 0.01
All	All	272	2.82 ± 0.00	2.15 ± 0.01

[a] No difference ($P > 0.05$) between first eggs laid over all clutches.
[b] No difference ($P > 0.05$) between second eggs laid over all clutches.
[c] No difference ($P > 0.05$) between eggs laid within clutches.
[d] Difference ($P < 0.001$) between eggs laid within clutches.
[e] Difference ($P < 0.001$) between eggs laid over all clutches.

Table 82. Egg-laying intervals of captive mourning doves held in battery breeding cages (Mirarchi 1978).[a]

Intervals between clutches[b]	Number of females	Time period in days (Mean ± S.E.)
1	37	9.8 ± 0.6^{c}
2	12	8.8 ± 1.1
All	49	9.5 ± 0.3

[a] Doves were checked daily at 5:00 P.M.
[b] Number of days between oviposition of first egg of one clutch and first egg of the next clutch.
[c] Not different ($P > 0.05$) from the second laying interval.

Table 84. Monthly mean measurements of eggs laid by captive mourning doves held in battery breeding cages (Mirarchi 1978).

Clutch number	Month	Egg number	Number of eggs	Egg measurement in centimeters (Mean ± S.E.)	
				Length	Width
1	3	First	3	2.68 ± 0.06[ac]	2.14 ± 0.02[ac]
		Second	2	2.79 ± 0.13[b]	2.10 ± 0.04[b]
	4	First	24	2.77 ± 0.02	2.17 ± 0.02
		Second	24	2.85 ± 0.04	2.18 ± 0.02
	5	First	22	2.74 ± 0.03	2.11 ± 0.02
		Second	21	2.79 ± 0.03	2.13 ± 0.02
	6	First	27	2.79 ± 0.03	2.15 ± 0.01
		Second	25	2.87 ± 0.03	2.18 ± 0.01
	7	First	11	2.78 ± 0.05	2.15 ± 0.02
		Second	9	2.89 ± 0.06	2.17 ± 0.02
	8	First	5	2.75 ± 0.03[d]	2.16 ± 0.02
		Second	5	2.90 ± 0.05	2.18 ± 0.03
1	All	First	92	2.76 ± 0.01[g]	2.14 ± 0.01
		Second	86	2.85 ± 0.02	2.16 ± 0.01
2	3	First	1	2.57	2.12
		Second	1	2.84	2.13
	4	First	3	2.84 ± 0.02[ac]	2.15 ± 0.02[ac]
		Second	4	2.92 ± 0.04[b]	2.12 ± 0.04[b]
	5	First	6	2.72 ± 0.02[e]	2.07 ± 0.03
		Second	6	2.87 ± 0.03	2.12 ± 0.01
	6	First	16	2.82 ± 0.05	2.17 ± 0.03
		Second	17	2.88 ± 0.04	2.16 ± 0.01
	7	First	6	2.76 ± 0.04	2.16 ± 0.02
		Second	6	2.84 ± 0.05	2.17 ± 0.02
	8	First	2	2.78 ± 0.01	2.16 ± 0.06
		Second	2	2.91 ± 0.05	2.24 ± 0.05
2	All	First	34	2.79 ± 0.03[f]	2.15 ± 0.02
		Second	36	2.88 ± 0.02	2.17 ± 0.01
3	5	First	1	2.81	2.17
		Second	1	2.89	2.19
	6	First	8	2.79 ± 0.07[ac]	2.17 ± 0.02[ac]
		Second	8	2.90 ± 0.06[b]	2.14 ± 0.02
	7	First	3	2.79 ± 0.09	2.19 ± 0.02
		Second	3	2.82 ± 0.05	2.21 ± 0.05
3	All	First	12	2.79 ± 0.05	2.17 ± 0.01
		Second	12	2.89 ± 0.04	2.17 ± 0.02

[a] No size difference (P > 0.05) between first eggs laid within clutch across months, unless otherwise specified.
[b] No size difference (P > 0.05) between second eggs laid within clutch across months, unless otherwise specified.
[c] No size difference (P > 0.05) between first and second egg laid within clutches within months, unless otherwise specified.
[d] Size difference (P < 0.05) between first and second egg laid within clutches within months.
[e] Size difference (P < 0.01) between first and second egg laid within clutches within months.
[f] Size difference (P < 0.05) between first and second egg laid within clutches across months.
[g] Size difference (P < 0.001) between first and second egg laid within clutches across months.

ARTIFICIAL INCUBATION, HATCHING AND FOSTERING

Incubators and Hatchers

Good incubation and hatching results can be obtained by using artificial incubators and hatchers, although hatching success always is lower (50 percent is good) than what would normally be observed in the wild (Institute of Laboratory Animal Resources 1977).

Eggs laid in battery breeding pens should be collected at a consistent time each day and measurements taken, if necessary. They should *never* be washed and should be identified on the side with a blunt, soft-lead pencil. Covering the blunt, rounded end of the egg, particularly with oily or waxy markers, reduces gas exchange and hatchability (Institute of Laboratory Animal Resources 1977). Mourning dove eggs usually are incubated immediately (e.g., see Buerger et al. 1986), but incubation of fertilized eggs of other species normally can be delayed (preincubation holding) if incubation facilities are not immediately available or to assure a particular hatching date. Freshly laid, unwashed eggs of several species can be maintained for one to two weeks at temperatures of 57±5 degrees Fahrenheit (14±3° C) and at 70-percent relative humidity (Institute of Laboratory Animal Resources 1977). This has not been tested with mourning dove eggs, but it should be.

Mourning dove eggs have been artificially incubated and hatched in different devices and under different temperature and humidity regimes (Graber 1955, Wetherbee and Wetherbee 1961). The most natural incubation periods obtained from the largest sample of eggs, however, indicate that they should be incubated in commercial incubators (e.g., Humidaire Incubator, Model 25 from The Humidaire Incubator Co. of New Madison, Ohio) at an average temperature of 99.5±0.5 degrees Fahrenheit (37.5±0.3° C), a hygrometer reading of 85° F (29.4° C) (approximately 55.5-percent relative humidity) and an ambient room temperature of 70 to 75° F (21.1 to 23.9° C) (Buerger 1984). Eggs are automatically turned at regular intervals in commercial incubators. Candling with a high-intensity light source can be used to determine fertility after three or four days of incubation. Fertile eggs then can be returned to the incubator and nonfertile eggs discarded. If embryonic development is obviously behind the normal developmental state, the egg can be opened and the age of the embryo at death can be determined (Muller et al. 1984).

After fourteen days of incubation, eggs should be placed in a hatcher (e.g., Humidaire Hatcher, Model 20 from The Humidaire Incubator Co. of New Madison, Ohio) with an average temperature of 99.5±0.5° F (37.5±0.3° C), a hygrometer reading of 89° F (31.7° C) (approximately 65.5-percent relative humidity) and the same room temperature previously described (Buerger 1984). The hatcher should be checked daily, and newly hatched squabs can be assigned to foster parents, hand-reared or euthanized as appropriate for the ongoing experiments. If eggs do not hatch after three days in the hatcher, they should be removed.

Foster Parents

Foster parenting of birds during incubation has been accomplished using domestic chickens and canaries (Institute of Laboratory Animal Resources

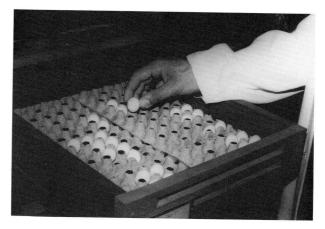

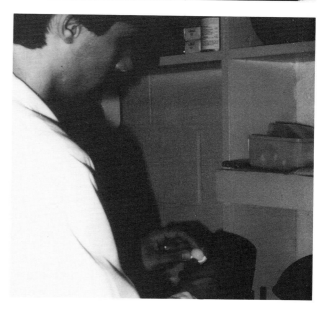

Large numbers of eggs produced by paired mourning doves in battery breeding pens can be incubated successfully (top) and hatched (center) in commercial incubators and hatchers. Fertility and development can be determined by candling (bottom) using a high-intensity light source. *Photos by Wanda L. McKenzie; courtesy of the Auburn University Department of Zoology and Wildlife Science and the Alabama Agricultural Experiment Station.*

1977). Occasionally, pigeon and dove breeders use foster parents to incubate eggs and raise young squabs of birds that abandon nests, die or are lost (Delacour 1980). However, timing is critical in such situations because the hormonal condition of foster parents must be aligned closely with the required stage of incubation or brooding to ensure satisfactory results.

No published reports are known regarding successful foster parenting of mourning doves in captivity. The best chances of success probably would occur if a captive breeding colony of ringed turtle-doves (Kendall and Scanlon 1981b) were available to act as surrogates when necessary. They are slightly larger than mourning doves and have slightly different incubation and brooding periods, but they are the domesticated species that comes closest to the brooding and incubation periods of the mourning dove. Interestingly, Hanson and Kossack (1963) attempted propagation of mourning doves by using ring doves to incubate their eggs. The ring doves incubated and hatched the eggs but would not feed the squabs. Obviously, more research is needed to determine if this was an unusual occurrence or a consistent pattern that would prevent use of ring doves as foster parents. Certainly, if techniques for successful preincubation holding of mourning dove eggs were developed, the use of such fostering techniques would be simplified. Theoretically, mourning dove eggs then could be held until the proper time was reached in the incubation cycle of the foster parents, and the eggs of the foster parents could be replaced by mourning dove eggs.

Hand-rearing Squabs

Mourning dove squabs can be hand-reared from about seven to eight days of age by feeding them a slurry of pelleted ration and wild bird mix (e.g., Purina Pigeon Chow Checkers and Wild Bird Seed Mix of the Ralston Purina Co.). The slurry can be fed to the squab by pursing the fingers, grasping the bill of the young bird with the fingertips and rhythmically pumping the food into the bird's open bill. A large syringe with a piece of plastic tubing inserted where the needle normally is seated is even more efficient. Initially, bills of the squabs may have to be forced open and the food or tube inserted until they readily accept it. They should be fed until the crop is full and regularly thereafter as the crop empties. After a while, hungry squabs often will beg vociferously as handlers approach. Once the young are sixteen days old, small amounts of seed should be made available to the young in their holding pen. Hand-feedings should

be gradually reduced during this time as the young birds begin to experiment with the available seeds. They should be capable of feeding entirely by themselves by twenty-seven days of age. Hand-feedings can be used to supplement self-feeding anytime the doves are not feeding well enough on their own.

Hand-rearing mourning dove squabs less than six days of age presents some unique problems. Slurry mixtures of pelleted ration normally fed to adults were accepted by birds this young, but birds thus fed did not grow normally and developed into runts (R. E. Mirarchi personal files). Apparently they suffered from protein deficiencies in the feed mixture. Young ring dove squabs have been reared successfully on pediatric formulas and slurries of chicken starter feed (Fisher 1972). Diets for hand-feeding pigeon squabs from hatching to twenty-eight days of age have been administered successfully via a syringe-tube device and tested (Yang and Vohra 1987). The optimal diet for the first seven days contained 53.3 percent crude protein and 3,675 kilocalories of metabolizable energy per kilogram, whereas the optimal diet for the remainder of the growth period contained 20 percent crude protein and 3,200 kilocalories of metabolizable energy per kilogram. Obviously, a high protein/high energy slurry of this type administered by eye dropper, pipette or syringe-tube should be tested on young mourning dove squabs.

Squabs should be kept in a moderately lit environment during normal daylight hours to prevent retinal degeneration (Institute of Laboratory Animal Resources 1977). Young squabs (less than twelve days of age) must be kept for various periods in controlled environments with temperatures near those required for incubation. Although a heating pad or lamp will help in this regard, it may be necessary to keep doves one to four days old in artificial nests with heating (e.g., see Lanyon and Lanyon 1969) to maintain proper body temperatures.

SURGICAL PROCEDURES

Restraint

Any type of surgical procedure on mourning doves involves restraint. A small proportion (less than 1 percent) of mourning doves will die, apparently from stress or shock, while being handled. They can be held safely and firmly for short periods by grasping their head and neck firmly between the index and middle finger, extending the legs toward the tail, and folding the hands and fingers over the wings and legs, respectively. This prevents the dove from pushing off with its legs and leaving the handler with just a handful of feathers. Additionally, by simply turning the hand palm up one can hold the bird firmly with little struggling and examine, treat or bleed it from a variety of sites, particularly if the handler has an assistant (Donovan 1958). Care must be taken not to constrict the abdominal region, as such constriction may interfere with normal respiratory mechanics and result in respiratory stress or death (Institute of Laboratory Animal Resources 1977).

If doves need to be restrained for longer than a few minutes, they can be held motionless by placing them in the bottom of a small bird-holding bag (Reisinger 1968) and wrapping them with the remainder. Other inexpensive, easily constructed holders of various types are available (Donovan 1958, Nelson and Peck 1964) depending on the type and extent of restraint needed.

Blood Collection

Blood can be collected, by venipuncture or from ruptured veins of mourning doves, without harming the birds. Cardiac puncture results in high mortality in nestlings (Sooter 1954) and higher than acceptable mortality in adults (R. E. Mirarchi personal files) and should be avoided. Blood samples should not exceed 20 percent of the total blood volume, which equates to approximately 7 percent of the body weight (Institute of Laboratory Animal Resources 1977).

Venipuncture. The wing veins (brachial or cutaneous ulnar) of mourning doves have been successfully used to collect blood for a variety of research purposes (Sooter 1954, Bigler et al. 1977, George 1987). Blood can be either collected in capillary tubes after the wing vein has been pierced with a 26-gauge needle (George 1987) or withdrawn using a 25-gauge, 0.5-cubic-centimeter syringe (Bigler et al. 1977). Up to 0.5 cubic centimeters of blood (approximately 6 to 10 percent of a mourning dove's blood volume) can be removed without adverse effects (Bigler et al. 1977). After removal of the needle, pressure should be applied to staunch the flow of blood and prevent formation of a hematoma.

The median metatarsal and jugular veins have been used to extract blood from birds, but no specific results are available that quantify how satisfactory the process is for mourning doves. Use of the right (larger) jugular vein may be satisfactory because it has been used successfully in living birds as small as one-day-old tree sparrows and as large as black-crowned herons (McClure and Cedeno

1955). However, repeated sampling from this area may cause problems (Kerlin 1964). Blood collection usually involves at least two people, but a restraining device is available for use with waterfowl that allows one person to conduct blood extractions (e.g., see Bolen et al. 1977). Such a device could be modified easily for use with mourning doves.

Ruptured veins. Blood also can be obtained from mourning doves by clipping a toenail until a blood vessel is broken. The blood can be collected via pipette, capillary tube or syringe. This procedure has proved successful in other species (Leonard 1969). Blood flow can be controlled by applying pressure to the toe with the thumb and forefinger, and it can be stopped by applying additional pressure and then cauterizing the surface of the nail with a silver nitrate applicator stick, as discussed earlier (Leonard 1969).

Anesthesia

Anesthetics are used as analgesics (produce insensitivity to pain), chemical restraining devices, agents to remove fear of prolonged handling, and muscle relaxants. Several local and general (inhalation, parenteral, per os) anesthetics are available for use with birds (see Institute of Laboratory Animal Resources 1977 and American Ornithologists' Union 1988 for tabular summaries). Although no known studies on mourning doves have used anesthetics other than for capture (e.g., see Williams and Phillips 1972), those used successfully on closely related species (e.g., domestic pigeon [Bree and Gross 1969]) should prove safe and effective for mourning doves. Prior to beginning mourning dove experiments, researchers who anticipate the use of anesthetics should delineate their specific needs, investigate appropriate literature sources and consult with a veterinarian who has experience with anesthetization of birds.

Surgery

Numerous therapeutic surgical procedures have been performed on birds (e.g., cecal ablation, cropectomy, cyst and tumor removal). Surgical procedures for experimental purposes include caponization, surgery for gonadal examination, implantation of electrodes and a variety of others. All have been described in detail and are summarized by the Institute of Laboratory Animal Resources (1977). Generally, all procedures involved minimizing blood loss, maintaining body temperature during surgery and recovery, and turning the bird from

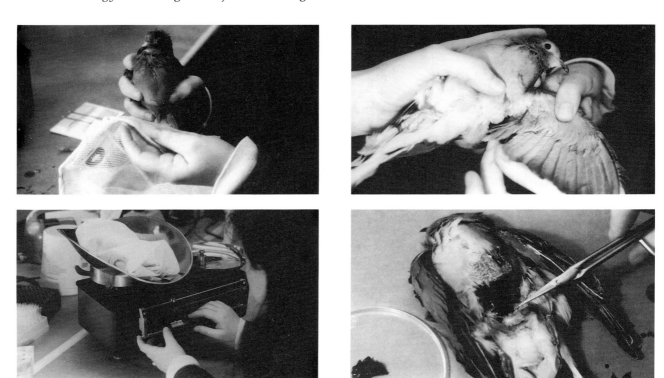

Captive mourning doves can be restrained for short periods by firmly holding the wings and legs against the body (top left). Thereafter, blood samples can be drawn easily from the wing veins (top right). Doves can be restrained for longer periods when placed in a holding bag (bottom left). Tissues from euthanized captive mourning doves (bottom right) provide valuable information on interactions with environmental contaminants. *Photos by Carolyn M. Marn; courtesy of the Auburn University Department of Zoology and Wildlife Science and the Alabama Agricultural Experiment Station.*

side to side at thirty-minute intervals during recovery. Few of these procedures have been attempted on mourning doves, and more research in this area is warranted.

Euthanasia

Whenever animals are killed during experiments, humane techniques that ensure euthanasia (a quiet, painless death) but do not interfere with data interpretation must be used (Institute of Laboratory Animal Resources 1977). Satisfactory methods of euthanasia in birds have been described (Jones 1965, Breazile and Kitchell 1969) and should be used as guidelines in experiments involving mourning doves. Intravenous administration of an overdose (three to five times anesthetic doses) of sodium pentobarbital is the best method of euthanasia for birds large enough for easy venipuncture. If data collection will be confounded by drugs that produce euthanasia, crushing the cervical vertebrae at the base of the skull between the handles of a pair of large scissors results in quick death (R. E. Mirarchi personal files). For mourning dove squabs, an inhalation agent may have to be used for

euthanasia. Chloroform has been used (Buerger et al. 1986), but neither it nor ether produces euthanasia because their vapors irritate mucous membranes and cause considerable excitement before loss of consciousness (Institute of Laboratory Animal Resources 1977). T-61 (veterinary euthanasia compound) may be the safest, gentlest and most rapid euthanasia agent, but it is expensive (American Ornithologists' Union 1988).

Captive mourning doves can and should eventually be released back to the wild (except those used in toxicology or disease experiments). They first should be allowed freedom in fairly large outdoor flight pens for at least a month to regain full flight capability. Broken flight and tail feathers should be plucked prior to this time to allow for proper replacement of the crucial plumage. All individual markers (e.g., colored leg bands) should be removed before release of the birds to the wild. Mourning doves that do not exhibit normal flight capability after a month in the flight pen should be euthanized.

Carcass disposal must follow specifications outlined in state and federal permits. Most permits provide for proper disposal through incineration or preparation for museum specimens.

Chapter 23

Mourning Dove Hunting Regulations

Henry M. Reeves
Office of Migratory Bird Management
U.S. Fish and Wildlife Service
Washington, D.C.

During the eighteenth and early nineteenth centuries, the mourning dove was perceived both as a species to be hunted and one to be fully protected. In some northern states, where populations were relatively sparse, it was seldom regarded as a gamebird. Elsewhere, particularly in the Southeast, it was avidly sought for recreational hunting.

The unique sporting values and status of the species often were overlooked because of its resemblance to the passenger pigeon, a species then plummeting to extinction. But the two species differed greatly in many ways—one could thrive under changing conditions, the other could not (see chapter 2). Moreover, the abundance of other hunted species temporarily obscured the qualities of the mourning dove as game.

Although some strong opposition to dove hunting lingers (see chapters 1 and 2), the bird's popularity among hunters steadily increased over the years to the point where it now solidly ranks among America's premier gamebirds.

The mourning dove's wide distribution, abundance and adaptability to human activities and works have tempered concerns for its future. Consequently, few comprehensive management programs, other than the setting of hunting regulations by federal and state authorities, have been implemented for the mourning dove. In fact, the setting of these annual regulations still is the primary management tool employed by wildlife managers, even though questions persist about the efficacy of those regulations.

This chapter reviews the complex genesis and development of the major laws and ensuing regulations that determine whether, when, where and how mourning doves may be hunted. Also, it summarizes the development of specific hunting regulations that have been in effect since 1918, when the Migratory Bird Treaty Act was implemented in the United States, and touches on hunting regulations applicable in other nations frequented by the mourning dove.

EARLY STATE LAWS AND REGULATIONS

Before the United States government's assumption of primary responsibility for migratory birds, state entities had enacted a variety of laws or issued regulations concerning their harvest. Laws passed by state legislatures generally were the first to appear; when specific conservation agencies were created, they were usually given regulatory authority for hunting. For many years, state hunting regulations were compiled annually by the U.S. Bureau of Biological Survey (predecessor of the U.S. Fish and Wildlife Service) and published in *Farmer's Bulletins* of the federal Department of Agriculture.

Early in the 1900s T. S. Palmer (1912), then chief law enforcement officer of the Bureau, summarized the early state provisions in his *Chronology and Index of the More Important Events in American Game Protection, 1776–1911*. Palmer noted that state hunting restrictions before 1912 for the mourning dove included complete protection in Connecticut and New Jersey in 1850, prohibition of baiting in Georgia in 1898 and outlawing of ground shooting in Ohio in 1904. Minnesota, in 1897, was the first to impose a bag limit. Palmer reported that in 1910 forty-four states afforded some degree of protection to the mourning dove and that, in twenty of these, there was no open (hunting) season.

One of the most informative early publications on gamebirds, including their management, is *The Game Birds of California* (Grinnell et al. 1918). The authors described in detail the development of mourning dove hunting regulations in California and difficulties encountered in setting seasons satisfactory to both the hunting public and the species' welfare. In California the first statewide law protecting doves was passed in 1880, when the open season was made to extend from July 1 until January 1. Since 1880, they noted, there seemed to have been constant dissatisfaction on the part of hunters, with resulting readjustment of open and closed seasons. There were eleven different legislative enactments on the subject during the next thirty-five years. The 1915 California regulations for hunting mourning doves furnished a lucid explanation of problems besetting the regulatory process for hunting this species in much of the United States and continuing to this day: "The present (1915) law . . . will be . . . the most conservative of any yet enacted in California. Two opposing conditions make the regulation of the dove season here extremely difficult, namely, the late nesting, and the rather early migration in the northern part of the state. Birds in the region surrounding the head of the Sacramento Valley are nesting almost up to the time that they begin to leave for the south, so that if hunters in this section are to be allowed to shoot the birds at all, the open season will have to include the later part of the nesting period and be rather short at best. Opening the season on September 1 will not prevent shooting while some nesting is still in progress, yet it will allow the great majority of the young birds to be fully fledged before hunters take the field" (Grinnell et al. 1918: 599).

Because the continental mourning dove population is so abundant, widespread, migratory and adaptable to a wide range of habitats, comprehensive management is difficult to implement or measure. To date, the most direct form of management has been hunter harvest regulation. Such regulations obviously pertain mostly to the dove's annual mortality. On the other hand, devising, refining and encouraging implementation of conservation practices in broad-scale agricultural, forestry, water and other resource programs—on public and private lands—are vital management investments for all wildlife, including mourning doves. Hunters certainly are beneficiaries of such investments, but more importantly, so are dove populations. *Photo by Charles H. Dickey.*

Despite admirable intentions of some early state efforts to afford greater protection to mourning doves, such efforts were ineffective simply because of the species' migratory nature. An individual mourning dove in its regular annual movements might appear in upward of five or six states and as many countries (e.g., doves banded in North Dakota have been recovered in Nicaragua). Clearly needed was a more comprehensive management strategy extending across both state and national boundaries.

FEDERAL LEGISLATION AND THE MIGRATORY BIRD TREATY ACT

The earliest federal game laws did not address the need for coordination of state regulations affecting migratory birds. Federal game laws date back to 1832, when Congress prohibited the capture of game in the Indian Territory by any person other than Indians, except for subsistence purposes (Palmer 1912). The first federal game law specifically including birds was enacted June 15, 1878 for the District of Columbia (Coues and Prentiss 1883). This law specified which birds could be hunted and when; no mention was made of the mourning dove. Coues and Prentiss (1883: 91) noted that the mourning dove was a permanent resident of the District but not very common there, and added that "Sometimes . . . Doves collect in large flocks in the fall, when they frequent corn and buckwheat fields." Thus, it appears that the lack of mourning doves was not the reason for excluding the species from the list of the District's gamebirds.

The genesis of formal efforts to provide nationwide federal protection specifically to migratory birds dates back to 1904. In that year, Congressman George Shiras III introduced legislation entitled "An Act to Protect the Migratory Game Birds of the United States." Although the bill did not become law, it constituted the original legislative expression of a principle destined to become law a few years later. The bill's preamble stated that experience had shown that laws passed by states and territories of the United States to protect gamebirds within their respective geographic boundaries had proved ineffective in protecting those that were migratory in nature and that nested and hatched their young in states other than those through which they passed during the usual hunting season. The bill was to require that all migratory gamebirds that did not remain year-round within the borders of any state or territory would be deemed to be within custody of the United States government. The mourning dove was not specifically mentioned.

Continued deterioration in the status of many migratory birds, notably waterfowl, and increased public concern for these birds culminated in passage in 1913 of the Weeks-McLean bill—a virtual reiteration of the Shiras bill (routinely reintroduced since 1904)—as a rider to the Agricultural Appropriations Act of that year. This legislation proclaimed all migratory game and insectivorous birds to be within the custody and protection of national authority. When complimented by a sportsman friend for signing the conservation legislation, President William Howard Taft reportedly replied that he would have vetoed the entire appropriation act had he been aware of the rider (Trefethen 1961).

A congressional act in itself could not address the needs of a resource that crossed national boundaries during its annual migrations. Sympathetic legislators soon recognized that nearly indisputable protection could be afforded the migratory bird resource by negotiating a treaty with a neighboring nation sharing that resource. Canada was the logical partner because it "produced" many of the migratory birds, notably waterfowl, that eventually flew into the United States. Moreover, Canadians were likewise concerned about reduced numbers of migratory birds that returned annually to nest in their country.

Negotiations between the two nations eventually materialized in signing the Convention between the United States and Great Britain for the Protection of Migratory Birds (hereinafter "U.S./Canada Convention") in 1916. In legal parlance, the terms "convention" and "treaty" are synonymous. Because Canada at that time could not independently formalize a treaty with a foreign power, the convention's preamble noted (Anonymous 1916): "The United States of America and His Majesty the King of the United Kingdom of Great Britain and Ireland and of the British Dominions beyond the Seas, Emperor of India, being desirous of saving from indiscriminate slaughter and of insuring the preservation of such migratory birds as are either useful to man or harmless, have resolved to adopt some uniform system of protection which shall effectively accomplish such objectives." President Woodrow Wilson proclaimed the U.S./Canada Convention on December 7, 1916.

The U.S./Canada Convention is a succinctly worded document containing ten articles. Article I specifies that birds of the family Columbidae (doves and pigeons) were specifically designated as migratory gamebirds. Article II established a closed season on migratory gamebirds between March 10 and September 1 and provided that the hunting period not exceed three and one-half months "as the high contracting powers may deem appropriate and define by law or regulation."

The U.S./Canada Convention was implemented by the United States in 1918 with passage of the Migratory Bird Treaty Act (Anonymous 1918) and by Canada with the Migratory Birds Convention Act (Anonymous 1917). These acts gave broad protection to the defined migratory birds and prohibited their hunting, taking, killing, etc., except as permitted by regulations. Section 3 of the Migratory Bird Treaty Act directed the Secretary of Agriculture "to determine when, to what extent, if at all, and by what means, it is compatible with the terms of the convention to allow hunting, taking, capture . . . and . . . to adopt suitable regulations . . . [to] become effective when approved by the President."

Section 7 of the Act stated that nothing in it "shall be construed" to prevent the states and territories from making or enforcing laws or regulations consistent with its provisions, or from making or enforcing laws or regulations giving further protection to migratory birds.

More mourning doves are harvested annually in North America than any other gamebird. Statutory authority for federal management of mourning doves in North America is vested by the Migratory Bird Treaty Act of 1918 (U.S.), the Migratory Birds Convention Act (Canada) and the 1936 U.S./Mexico Convention. These provide the basis for annual hunting regulations that determine if, how, where, when and to what extent doves may be hunted. *Photo by Glenn D. Chambers; courtesy of the Missouri Department of Conservation.*

The constitutionality of the U.S./Canada Convention and Migratory Bird Treaty Act was promptly challenged but was sustained by the United States Supreme Court in 1920 in Missouri v. Holland. The validity of the Convention and the enabling Canadian legislation was similarly challenged but also upheld in 1920 by the Supreme Court of Prince Edward Island in King v. Russel C. Clark.

OTHER MIGRATORY BIRD TREATIES

The Migratory Bird Treaty Act also has served as the enabling legislation for subsequent migratory bird treaties signed with Mexico in 1936, Japan in 1972 and the Soviet Union in 1976.

In general, the three latter treaties added little to the basic provisions of the U.S./Canada Convention insofar as the mourning dove is concerned. However, the U.S./Mexico Convention provides that hunting seasons be set to avoid the main nesting period of the species, and the U.S./Japan Convention includes a requirement for maintaining migratory birds at "optimum" population levels. Neither of these provisions has been specifically defined or interpreted, and both have been subjected to litigation, with the government's position prevailing.

THE DOVE MANAGEMENT UNIT CONCEPT

In early years following passage of the Migratory Bird Treaty Act, administrators and biologists sought to identify workable concepts for establishing annual hunting regulations. Because of the precarious state of waterfowl, that group of birds received major emphasis. Since relatively little was known then about the migration patterns and population dynamics of the mourning dove, management principles developed for waterfowl simply were extended to mourning doves. More Game Birds in America Foundation—predecessor to Ducks Unlimited, Inc.—promoted the concept of latitudinal zones across the United States as the basis for setting waterfowl hunting seasons, with earliest seasons in the northernmost states and latest seasons in the southernmost states.

One of the most significant uses of banding data was Frederick C. Lincoln's (1935) identification of four flyways—the Atlantic, Mississippi, Central and Pacific—later used as the basis for setting waterfowl hunting seasons. Lincoln described migration routes as the individual lanes of avian travel from breeding grounds to winter quarters, and flyways as broader areas into which certain migration routes blend or come together in a definite geographical region. Thus, each waterfowl flyway consists of the composite routes of all ducks, geese and swans that share common breeding, migration and wintering locales. Although adjustments of the original flyway boundaries sometimes were necessary, the flyway concept has served since 1948, principally for cooperative administrative purposes, as the foundation for waterfowl hunting regulations.

In general, the development of regulatory concepts for setting annual hunting regulations for mourning doves followed advances in understanding of waterfowl migration patterns and population dynamics. This was natural, since waterfowl biologists had available an impressive body of banding information and, later, breeding ground and winter survey data and information on harvest magnitude, species, and age and sex composition by area and time period. Further, the sale of federal Migratory Bird Hunting and Conservation Stamps ("duck stamps"), required of all waterfowl hunters sixteen years of age or older, gave insight into the annual number of hunters and their geographical distribution. In contrast, dove biologists had relatively little banding data available until the mid-1960s and no nationwide population data until implementation of the national Call-count Surveys a few years later (see chapter 14). Good information on the national dove harvest and the number of participating hunters still is lacking—a matter discussed in chapter 24.

Mourning dove hunting seasons from 1918 through 1950 generally followed the latitudinal approach advanced by the More Game Birds in American Foundation. The season openings essentially coincided with the progress of autumn migration.

Beginning in 1951, three years after implementation of the flyway concept by the U.S. Fish and Wildlife Service for waterfowl regulations, dove hunting seasons were established by flyway units. Some regulatory differences were apparent among the flyways. For example, 8 mourning doves could be taken daily and possessed by each hunter in the Atlantic and Mississippi flyways that year, but 10 were permitted in states of the Central and Pacific flyways.

In 1954, H. M. Wight, working in Missouri, presented data showing the mourning dove migration patterns differed from those of waterfowl (Wight 1954a). Although Missouri was located in the Mississippi Flyway, Wight's data showed that most out-of-state recoveries of doves banded in

Missouri occurred in Texas, a Central Flyway state. Of 33 out-of-state recoveries, 25 were from the Central Flyway, 5 from the Mississippi Flyway and 3 from the Atlantic Flyway. Wight also demonstrated that, for the most part, dove recoveries from bandings in Minnesota, Iowa, Missouri, Arkansas and Louisiana were located to the southwest, often crossing the boundary between the Mississippi and Central flyways (Wight 1954b). Wisconsin and Illinois band recoveries revealed a nearly even division between southeasterly and southwesterly migrations, while banded doves of the remaining states of the Mississippi Flyway exhibited a strong southeasterly migration pattern.

Wight (1954a) concluded that the waterfowl flyways were inadequate as divisions for management of doves in the Mississippi Flyway. He recommended that a new pattern for mourning doves be developed in order that management be based on evidence at hand for the species, not on migrational patterns of waterfowl. (Data provided later by Atkinson et al. [1982] showed that 62 percent of 187 Missouri-banded doves recovered out-of-state had crossed the traditional waterfowl flyway boundaries.)

Wight's concern coincided with the nationwide mourning dove nestling banding program (see chapters 14 and 16). By the end of 1957, 113,978 doves had been banded, from which 3,543 recoveries had accumulated. The resultant data were analyzed by Kiel (1959). On the basis of an analysis of bandings during the 1953–57 period, Kiel outlined three tentative management units—Eastern (EMU), Central (CMU) and Western (WMU). He claimed that each most nearly met the criteria of an ideal management unit: a geographical area that produces the doves it harvests and does not produce doves that are harvested by other units. As an average for the three management units, Kiel wrote, 95 percent of a unit's hunting kill is produced within the unit and 96 percent of a unit's harvested production is shot inside the unit or in Mexico or Central America. Hence, he concluded, the three units are "practically" independent of each other.

Although tens of thousands of additional dove band recoveries have materialized since Kiel's (1959) pioneering work, his original three management units have remained intact (see chapter 4).

As for waterfowl management, it has been found that the Continental Divide is a somewhat better natural boundary with respect to mourning dove management than is the political line separating Montana, Wyoming, Colorado and New Mexico from Idaho, Utah and Arizona. Braun (1979) showed that doves banded west of the Continental Divide in Colorado, Montana, New Mexico and

Wyoming tended to migrate into the WMU rather than remain in the CMU, to which those states were assigned. However, dove populations in this relatively narrow north/south zone are comparatively low, as is hunting pressure, and doves migrate early from the area. Consequently, little interest has been expressed in changing the boundary between the two management units.

MOURNING DOVE HUNTING REGULATIONS IN THE UNITED STATES

Annually in the *Federal Register*, the U.S. Fish and Wildlife Service states the objectives of its proposed hunting regulations. Those particularly relevant to mourning dove management are as follows: to provide an opportunity to harvest a proportion of certain migratory gamebird populations by establishing legal hunting seasons; to limit harvest of migratory gamebirds to levels compatible with their ability to maintain their populations; and to provide equitable hunting opportunity in various parts of the country within limits imposed by abundance, migration and distribution patterns of migratory gamebirds.

Federal hunting provisions are of two types: (1) the "basic" regulations defining the means by which migratory birds may be taken, possessed, transported, imported and exported; and (2) the "annual" regulations prescribing whether, where and when hunting is permitted and the number of birds of particular species or populations that may be taken and held in possession daily. Specific hunting seasons are identified by the year in which they commenced, even though some continue into the following calendar year.

Basic Regulations

The basic regulations, all of which apply to mourning doves as well as other migratory gamebirds, prohibit the use of: guns other than shotguns of 10 gauge or smaller bore (since 1919) holding more than three shells (since 1935); live decoys to attract birds (since 1935); motorized conveyances (since 1918); bait to attract birds to hunters (1931); and electronic calls (1957). Of the basic regulations, those relating to baiting (including use of salt) and the identification requirements for bagged birds merit special attention here.

Baiting. The most significant and controversial basic regulation relating to doves has been the prohibition of baiting—attracting birds to hunting

locales by artificially distributing food or other defined substances, including salt. Mourning doves are notoriously opportunistic in finding choice feeding locations, particularly newly harvested grainfields during late summer and autumn. They often return to these fields despite heavy hunting pressure. The practice of baiting capitalizes on this habit and renders doves more vulnerable to hunting.

Efforts over the years to write effective and understandable regulations prohibiting baiting often have ended in a quagmire of semantics. Sustained attempts by federal and state officials, lawyers and several special task forces and "blue ribbon" committees have been only partially successful in protecting mourning doves and waterfowl from baiting. Indeed, efforts to define "baiting" have been difficult because of regional differences in crops grown, planting, cultivation and harvesting practices, advances in farming technology, and local and regional hunter practices and sentiments.

Federal hunting regulations first addressed the baiting problem in 1931 by declaring: "provided . . . that the hunting, killing, or taking of mourning doves is not permitted on or over, at or near, any area which has been baited with salt, corn, wheat, or other grains or other foods placed or scattered thereon" (U.S. Bureau of Biological Survey 1931: 2). It is noteworthy that the 1931 baiting regulations did not apply to waterfowl. Further, no definition was offered for "baiting." These initial baiting restrictions were followed by many other versions.

In 1932, the baiting regulations prohibited the taking of mourning doves "within 100 yards of bait distributed by the hunter himself or to his knowledge" (U.S. Bureau of Biological Survey 1932: 2). This relaxation presented conservation law enforcement officers with the responsibility to prove who actually did the baiting. In 1934, for the first time, a formal definition of bait was provided: "Corn, wheat, oats, or other grain, or products thereof, salt, or any kind of feed, by whomsoever placed, deposited, distributed, scattered, or otherwise put out, whereby mourning doves are lured, attracted, or enticed" (U.S. Bureau of Biological Survey 1934: 2).

The 1935 regulations interjected the concept of "direct or indirect use" of food for baiting (U.S. Bureau of Biological Survey 1935: 2).

In 1939, recognition was given to the attraction of unharvested crops to doves: "it is not intended to forbid the taking of such birds attracted by growing or standing crops of grain or by harvested grainfields so long as such crops are not manipulated on such fields or have not been harvested by man or his agencies so as to cause such grain to be placed, deposited, scattered, or otherwise put out" (U.S. Bureau of Biological Survey 1939: 2).

In further clarification, the 1944 regulations excepted as bait "grains found solely as a result of agricultural harvesting" (U.S. Fish and Wildlife Service 1944b: 2).

In 1950 the term "normal" was inserted so that the wording read "normal agricultural harvesting" (U.S. Fish and Wildlife Service 1950: 2).

The 1951 regulations incorporated a distance and time clause by providing that migratory gamebirds may not be taken "within one-half mile of any place" where feed or salt had been deposited (U.S. Fish and Wildlife Service 1951: 2). In recognition that some crops are normally planted in autumn, the 1954 regulations excluded as bait those grains found "scattered solely as a result of normal agricultural planting or harvesting" (U.S. Fish and Wildlife Service 1954: 2).

Beginning in 1956, federal regulations attempted to facilitate the understanding of baiting by separately describing both permitted and prohibited methods. The 1964 regulations provided: "nothing . . . shall prohibit . . . the taking of all migratory game birds, except waterfowl, on or over any lands where shelled, shucked, or unshucked corn, wheat or other grain, salt or other feed has been distributed or scattered solely as the result of valid agricultural operations or procedures" (U.S. Fish and Wildlife Service 1964: 4).

In 1973 the regulations permitted hunting over feed resulting from: "agricultural operations or procedures, or as a result of a crop or other feed on the land where grown for wildlife management purposes: Provided, that manipulation for wildlife management practices does not include the distributing or scattering of grain or other feed once it has been removed from or stored in the field where grown" (U.S. Fish and Wildlife Service 1973: 4).

In essence, the still-effective 1973 wording allows crops to be planted and manipulated (e.g., disced or dragged upon maturing, without harvesting) to attract doves, provided that, once the grain has been harvested and removed, it is not redistributed on the fields. Thus, forbidding the redistribution of harvested grains in the fields remains a key element in the present dove-baiting regulations.

Unfortunately, few quantitative data are available to measure the effects of baiting and crop manipulation on dove hunting success. One study, however, was made in conjunction with a change in the basic hunting regulations whereby it was permissible to hunt doves over feed made available by "normal agricultural operations" (Smith 1961). Enforcement officers in twelve southeastern states contacted 20,864 dove hunters to determine hunt-

ing success under various agricultural situations. They found that the highest hunting success, measured as doves bagged per hunting hour, occurred over baited fields (Russell 1961, Smith 1961). A 1987 survey showed that thirty-two of thirty-six state dove biologists did not regard dove baiting as a significant problem in their (hunted) states (see chapter 28).

Salt is a noteworthy item listed among the baits prohibited by the regulations reviewed above; it is known to attract many columbids. A ready salt supply of some sort may be essential for successful rearing of mourning doves (McClure 1943) and, in fact, most columbids (see Schorger 1955). Moreover, doves and pigeons seek salt sources during nonbreeding periods as well. Attraction of mourning doves to salty soil areas may be useful in trapping/banding programs (Taber 1926, Reeves et al. 1968), but the addition of salt to wheat bait clearly reduced success in an Oklahoma dove trapping experiment (Lewis and Morrison 1973, see also chapters 11 and 20).

Although incidental attraction of columbids to salt has been noted (Schorger 1955, Taber 1926) and salt metabolism by mourning doves (and other columbids) has been investigated (e.g., Bartholomew and MacMillen 1960, Smyth and Bartholomew 1966), there is no comprehensive study known concerning the attraction that salt has for doves in the wild, nor has there been any comprehensive study of the illegal use of salt for baiting doves. Both are promising fields for research.

Species identification requirement. Various federal regulations regarding species identification of bagged migratory gamebirds have caused confusion and controversy since 1948. This discussion is confined to identification of mourning doves possessed, transported or shipped within the United States. Although importation and exportation of such carcasses are beyond its scope, it should be noted that additional identification requirements apply because of U.S. Department of Agriculture regulations, as well as laws or regulations of other nations.

Before 1948, federal regulations did not require the retention of any physical character on the carcass so that species identification remained possible. Conservation law enforcement officers were required to prove to the court that the dressed bird carcass was of an illegal species. Although ornithologists sometimes were called on to make positive species identifications from avian parts as small as a single bone or feather, such procedure was costly and inefficient. The logical solution lay in a new regulation requiring that some part of the bird, diagnostic of species, be retained on each carcass.

Beginning in 1948, federal regulations required hunters to retain the head, head plumage and feet on dressed migratory gamebirds. However, many thought the regulation unnecessary and cumbersome for dove hunters. Thus, during 1959 through 1963, mourning doves and white-winged doves were expressly excluded. With development of criteria for determining species, age and sex based on wing plumage characters of many migratory gamebirds, the 1964 regulations substituted "one fully feathered wing" for the head, head plumage and feet provision. The requirement again applied to all migratory gamebirds.

This action renewed concern among some wildlife administrators and sportsmen that insufficient justification existed for reimposing the species identification requirement on doves taken by hunters. Some argued that dressed doves were unlikely to be confused with carcasses of other birds (unlike carcasses of various similar species of ducks). Others maintained that, because dove feathers shed easily, dove carcasses became untidy, if not unsanitary. Further, some persons argued that retention of the wing deterred prompt cooling of the bird, particularly in warm, southern hunting areas. In 1967, in consideration of these concerns, the U.S. Fish and Wildlife Service specifically excluded mourning dove hunters (and, in 1975, hunters of the band-tailed pigeon) from the fully feathered wing requirement. The exclusion continued into the 1990s. Nevertheless, several states—notably Arizona and Texas—require hunters to retain a fully feathered wing or head on doves shot or imported until taken to the shooter's personal abode.

Annual Hunting Regulations

Interestingly, early federal and state hunting regulations frequently used the term "turtle dove" synonymously with "mourning dove"—a recognition of the name popularly but erroneously given the species in parts of the United States. In 1955, the wording used was "mourning doves (turtle doves)." No reference to "turtle doves" has appeared in subsequent years.

Major divisions of the annual hunting regulations include if, where and when mourning doves may be hunted and the number that may be taken daily and held in possession by each hunter. In fulfilling its legal obligations, the U.S. Fish and Wildlife Service established outer limits or "frameworks" from which state wildlife agencies could select specific mourning dove hunting seasons and other offered options.

States allowing mourning dove hunting. States have the option of deciding whether they wish to set seasons for mourning dove hunting. Since 1918, the first year of regulations established under the Migratory Bird Treaty Act, only seven of the conterminous forty-eight states have elected never to hunt mourning doves. Six of these—Maine, New Hampshire, Vermont, Massachusetts, New York and New Jersey—are located in the Northeast or Upper Middle Atlantic region. The other, Wisconsin, is a northcentral state. In contrast, twenty-one states have set seasons consistently since advent of the Act *(Table 85)*. Generally, these states are in southern or middle latitudes or in the West. In the EMU, they are Delaware, Maryland, Virginia, Illinois, Kentucky, Tennessee, North Carolina, South Carolina, Georgia, Alabama, Mississippi, Louisiana and Florida. In the CMU, they include Missouri, Oklahoma, New Mexico and Texas. Idaho, Nevada, California and Arizona of the WMU also have hunted doves continuously. Participation among the remaining states has varied among years.

In 1918, twenty-three states selected seasons. Apparently, some other states had difficulty meeting the new federal requirements the first year; in 1919 the number increased to twenty-nine. Through 1973, the number varied from twenty-five to thirty-one. Thereafter, participation gradually increased to thirty-six states (excluding Hawaii) selecting seasons in 1984. No clear rationale for the recent increase in dove hunting is evident, but the trend clearly coincided with intensified dove research and management programs—both at state and federal levels (often cooperatively)—and greater appreciation of the sporting qualities of the species.

With few exceptions, once states decide to allow mourning dove hunting, seasons are established on a statewide basis. Examples of states allowing hunting only in designated areas include Idaho (1949–53), Montana (1950) and Utah (1951).

Season lengths and limits. In addition to the fundamental questions of if, where and when to allow hunting, decisions on the number of allowable hunting days and birds to be permitted round out the most important regulatory factors addressed annually. Historically, in the event of perceived significant changes in migratory bird populations, changes in season lengths and limits have been implemented simultaneously. This dual approach theoretically distributes the effects of relaxations or restrictions more equitably among hunters than does the changing of number of hunting days or bag limits separately. However, few hunters avail themselves of all the hunting days provided, and most do not attain the bag limit every hunting trip.

Table 85. Types of mourning dove seasons, 1918–87, by states and management units, as instituted in 1960 (C = continuous season; S = split season; Z = state divided into two or more zones; ZS = split season in at least one zone).[a]

Management unit/state	Year and season types
Eastern Management Unit	
Alabama	1918–27 (C); 1928 (S); 1929–40 (ZS); 1941–43 (C); 1944–46 (S); 1947–51 (C); 1952–72 (S); 1973–87 (ZS)
Connecticut	1962 (C)
Delaware	1918–36 (C); 1937–38 (S); 1939–55 (C); 1956–61 (S); 1962 (C); 1963–64 (S); 1965 (C); 1966–67 (S); 1968 (C); 1969 (S); 1970 (C); 1971–87 (S)
Florida	1918–27 (C); 1928–29 (S); 1930–34 (Z); 1935 (S); 1936–40 (Z); 1941–43 (C); 1944–51 (Z); 1952–58 (S); 1959–60 (ZS); 1961–87 (S)
Georgia	1918–28 (C); 1929–35 (S); 1936–40 (ZS); 1941–43 (C); 1944–45 (S); 1946 (Z); 1947–48 (C); 1949 (S); 1950 (C); 1951–72 (S); 1973–74 (ZS); 1975–76 (S); 1977–87 (ZS)
Illinois	1918–87 (C)
Indiana	1919–29 (C); 1984 (C); 1985–87 (S)
Kentucky	1918–59 (C); 1960–87 (S)
Louisiana	1918–27 (C); 1928–33 (S); 1934–36 (C); 1937 (S); 1938–43 (C); 1944–46 (S); 1947 (C); 1948 (S); 1949–55 (C); 1956–72 (S); 1973–85 (ZS); 1986–87 (S)
Maryland	1918–35 (C); 1936–40 (S); 1941–51 (C); 1952–53 (S); 1954 (C); 1955 (S); 1956 (C); 1957–87 (S)
Mississippi	1918–27 (C); 1928–35 (S); 1936 (ZS); 1937 (S); 1938–39 (ZS); 1940 (S); 1941–43 (C); 1944–50 (S); 1951 (C); 1952–72 (S); 1973–79 (ZS); 1980–87 (S)
North Carolina	1918–30 (C); 1931–34 (S); 1935 (C); 1936–39 (S); 1940–44 (C); 1945–87 (S)
Ohio	1919–29 (C); 1975–76 (S)
Pennsylvania	1945–81 (C); 1982–87 (S)
Rhode Island	1957–61 (C); 1962–72 (S); 1973–77 (C); 1978–82 (ZS); 1983–87 (S)
South Carolina	1918–27 (C); 1928–34 (S); 1935 (C); 1936–40 (ZS); 1941–43 (C); 1944–87 (S)
Tennessee	1918–49 (C); 1950–54 (S); 1955 (C); 1956–87 (S)
Virginia	1918–39 (C); 1940 (S); 1941–51 (C); 1952–56 (S); 1957 (C); 1958 (S); 1959–61 (C); 1962–87 (S)

Table 85. (continued)

Management unit/state	Year and season types
Eastern Management Unit (continued)	
West Virginia	1955–64 (C); 1965–67 (S); 1968 (C); 1969–73 (S); 1974–76 (C); 1977–87 (S)
Central Management Unit	
Arkansas	1919–43 (C); 1944–46 (S); 1947–56 (C); 1957–87 (S)
Colorado	1918–29 (C); 1943–87 (C)
Iowa	1977 (C)
Kansas	1919–87 (C)
Minnesota	1920–46 (C)
Missouri	1918–55 (C); 1956–67 (S); 1968–87 (C)
Montana	1949–50 (C); 1983–87 (C)
Nebraska	1919–35 (C); 1937 (C); 1947 (C); 1949–52 (C); 1975–87 (C)
New Mexico	1918–55 (C); 1956–57 (S); 1958–64 (C); 1965–67 (S); 1968 (C); 1969–75 (S); 1976 (C); 1977–87 (S)
North Dakota	1963–64 (C); 1979–87 (C)
Oklahoma	1918–65 (C); 1966 (S); 1967–76 (C); 1977 (S); 1978–87 (C)
South Dakota	1935 (C); 1967–72 (C); 1981–87 (C)
Texas	1918–22 (C); 1923–43 (Z); 1944–53 (ZS); 1954–56 (Z); 1957–62 (ZS); 1963 (Z); 1964–87 (ZS)
Wyoming	1956 (C); 1973–87 (C)
Western Management Unit	
Arizona	1918–54 (C); 1955–79 (S); 1980 (ZS); 1981–87 (S)
California	1918–34 (C); 1935 (Z); 1936–46 (C); 1947–48 (Z); 1949–64 (C); 1965–66 (S); 1967 (Z); 1968–86 (S); 1987 (C)
Idaho	1918–87 (C)
Nevada	1918–87 (C)
Oregon	1918–37 (C); 1941–57 (C); 1958 (Z); 1959–66 (C); 1967–68 (S); 1969–87 (C)
Utah	1919–37 (C); 1951–87 (C)
Washington	1952–78 (C); 1979 (Z); 1980–87 (C)

[a] Number of states open to dove hunting: 1918 (23); 1919 (29); 1920–29 (30); 1930–34 (27); 1935 (28); 1936 (26); 1937 (27); 1938–40 (24); 1941–42 (25); 1943–44 (26); 1945–47 (27); 1948 (26); 1949–51 (28); 1952 (29); 1953–54 (28); 1955 (29); 1956–61 (30); 1962–64 (31); 1965–66 (30); 1967–74 (31); 1975–77 (33); 1978 (32); 1979–80 (33); 1981–82 (34); 1983 (35); 1984–87 (36).

Nonetheless, because season lengths and limits usually change concurrently, they are discussed here together. In general, the frameworks (outermost dates) for mourning dove seasons have been September 1 and January 15.

From 1918 through 1947, mourning dove seasons and bag/possession limits were listed narratively by state in the federal regulations. Beginning in 1948, the states were grouped by waterfowl flyway headings and, in 1960, by mourning dove management units, with all states within each management unit being offered the same number of hunting days and limits.

To illustrate changes in the number of hunting days allowed since 1918, four representative mid-latitude states were selected in the EMU, four in the CMU and two in the WMU *(Table 86)*. Consideration in this selection was given to states that usually chose to hunt doves and did not usually go beyond the federal restrictions. However, some eastern states have "blue laws" that prohibit Sunday hunting; thus, the numbers of *actual* legal

hunting days in these states were somewhat fewer than permitted by the federal regulations.

From 1918 through 1935, the federal framework for season lengths approximated the full three and a half months maximum permitted by the U.S./Canada Convention. Bag limits were 25 doves during 1918–31, 18 during 1932–34 and 20 during 1935–46 *(Table 87)*. Shortened seasons of about seventy-six days during the remainder of the 1930s and 1940 coincided with a perceived general deterioration of wildlife and aroused public concern (Lincoln 1945). Limits were reduced to 15 in 1937 and to 12 in 1940.

In 1941, the season was curtailed to forty-two days and, in 1942 and 1943, further cut in eastern states to thirty days. The daily bag limit was reduced to 10 birds nationwide in 1942. The latter restrictions were in response to severe weather in southern states during January 1940. The 1940 situation precipitated the first of two periods of drastically restricted dove hunting regulations. Reasons leading to the 1940 restrictions were described in

Table 86. Numbers of hunting days in selected states, 1918–59, and by management unit, 1960–81, and nationally, 1982–87 (except in Western Management Unit in 1987). States sometimes further restricted numbers of hunting days from those offered by federal regulations.

	Eastern Management Unit				Central Management Unit				Western Management Unit	
Year	Virginia	N. Carolina	Tennessee	Kentucky	Missouri	Arkansas	Kansas	Oklahoma	Nevada	Arizona
1918	106	106	106	106	106			106	106	106
1919–28	106	106	106	106	106	106	106	106	106	106
1929–30	106	63	106	106	106	106	106	106	106	106
1931–34	106	103	106	106	106	106	106	106	106	106
1935	86	107	86	86	106	86	106	86	106	107
1936	76	73	76	76	76	76	76	76	76	76
1937	76	74	76	76	76	76	76	76	76	76
1938	76	73	76	61	76	76	76	76	76	76
1939	76	73	76	61	76	77	76	76	76	76
1940	72	77	77	61	76	77	76	76	76	76
1941	42	42	42	42	42	42	42	42	42	42
1942–43	30	30	30	30	30	30	42	42	42	42
1944	40	57	57	55	55	57	55	42	42	55
1945–46	46	60	60	55	60	60	60	60	42	60
1947	46	46	60	60	60	60	60	30	42	60
1948	45	40	45	60	60	45	60	30	42	60
1949–51	30	30	30	30	30	30	30	30	30	45
1952–53	30	30	30	30	30	30	30	30	30	42
1954	40	40	40	40	35	40	40	40	40	40
1955	45	45	45	45	45	45	45	45	45	45
1956	55	55	55	55	50	55	50	50	50	50
1957	60	60	60	60	50	60	50	50	50	50
1958–59	65	65	65	65	50	65	50	50	50	50
1960–80	——— 70 ———				——— 60 ———				——— 50 ———	
1981	——— 70 ———				——— 45–60[a] ———				——— 50 ———	
1982	————————————— 45–70[a] —————————————									
1983–86	————————————— 60–70[a] —————————————									
1987	——————— 60–70[a] ———————								——— 30–45 ———	

[a]Combination season length/daily bag and possession limits offered as options.

The Status of Migratory Game Birds: 1939–40 (U.S. Bureau of Biological Survey 1940: 19): "Studies of the movements of the species show that, while large numbers of western mourning doves regularly migrate well into Mexico, the eastern form does not leave the United States in winter but is heavily concentrated in the Southeastern States . . . these birds were particularly vulnerable when the severe weather conditions of January (1940) struck deep into the South . . . thousands of dead doves were found, apparently victims of starvation and cold. Field personnel were accordingly instructed to survey and report on the situation in their respective districts. The study was nationwide in scope. . . . As expected, [reports] . . . showed the greatest losses to be in the Atlantic and Mississippi Flyways. . . . The situation in the Central and Pacific Flyways (western subspecies) was much better, the populations being about normal."

Despite the foregoing concerns, season lengths in 1940 were unchanged, but there was a nationwide reduction in limits from 15 to 12 doves.

The next year, the U.S. Fish and Wildlife Service (1941: 24) reported: "The full significance of [the storm of January 1940] . . . was not fully appreciated at the time. . . . While regulatory action was taken to reduce the kill during the hunting season, it now appears that more drastic measures would have been justified. . . . The situation in the western states is not so serious but even in that region the evidence indicates that there has been a steady and progressive decline in the numerical strength of the mourning dove. The apparent reason is excessive shooting through long seasons."

In response to general alarm about the dove's status, hunting seasons in 1941 were drastically curtailed nationally to forty-two days and the limit cut to 10 doves daily.

The status of the mourning dove in 1942 apparently continued to worsen, as evidenced by excerpts from *The Status of Migratory Game Birds: 1941–42* (U.S. Fish and Wildlife Service 1942: 7–8): "The mourning dove situation has continued to be a matter of grave concern particularly as it affects

Table 87. Daily bag and possession limits for mourning doves in the United States, 1918–87, by management unit.[a]

Year	Eastern Management Unit		Central Management Unit		Western Management Unit	
	Bag	Possession	Bag	Possession	Bag	Possession
1918–31	25	25	25	25	25	25
1932–34	18	18	18	18	18	18
1935–36	20	20	20	20	20	20
1937–39[b]	15	15	15	15	15	15
1940–41[b]	12	12	12	12	12	12
1942–47[b]	10	10	10	10	10	10
1948–54	10	10	10	10	10	10
1955–56	8	8	10	10	10	10
1957–59	10	20	10	20	10	20
1960–61	12	24	15	30	10	20
1962	12	24	12	24	10	20
1963	10	20	10	20	10	20
1964–67	12	24	12	24	12	24
1968	12	24	12	24	10	20
1969–70	18[c]	36[c]	10	20	10	20
1971–80	12	24	10	20	10	20
1981	12	24	12/24 with 60 days or 15/30 with 45 days		10	20
1982	12/24 with 70 days or 15/30 with 45 days		12/24 with 70 days or 15/30 with 45 days		12/24 with 70 days or 15/30 with 45 days	
1983–86	12/24 with 70 days or 15/30 with 60 days		12/24 with 70 days or 15/30 with 60 days		12/24 with 70 days or 15/30 with 60 days	
1987	12/24 with 70 days or 15/30 with 60 days		12/24 with 70 days or 15/30 with 60 days		10/20 with 30 or 45 days depending upon season timing	

[a] A few states sometimes restricted limits further than those permitted by the U.S. Fish and Wildlife Service. Aggregate bag and possession limits of mourning doves, white-winged doves and white-tipped doves often were selected in states or portions thereof where and when hunting of these doves was allowed.
[b] During 1937–47, the limits included white-winged doves on a nationwide basis.
[c] More liberal limits allowed in conjunction with Eastern Management Unit hunting regulations experiment.

the eastern subspecies. . . . In States along the south Atlantic and Gulf coasts, the situation was continuously bad. Reports of 20 to 25 percent decreased [sic] from 1940 were frequent."

In the West, the situation was not so acute, the report confirmed, although material reductions in populations were recorded in four southwestern states.

No improvement in the status of mourning doves seemed apparent in 1942 (U.S. Fish and Wildlife Service 1943). Thus, the season length was reduced further to thirty days in eastern states of the Atlantic and Mississippi flyways. Forty-two-day seasons were retained in the Central and Pacific flyways, and the daily bag limit nationwide was held to 10 doves.

Improvement in the overall status of mourning doves finally seemed apparent in 1943, as reported by the U.S. Fish and Wildlife Service (1944a: 9): "Reports on the 1943 spring migration of mourning doves indicated a gratifying improvement in numerical status. . . . Considering the dangerously low point in the population of this species only 3 years ago, this is considered as indicating a most satisfactory recovery toward normal numbers. . . . The results of these and other special investigations in the Southeastern States followed by a similar nationwide study showed that the mourning dove had experienced another good breeding season and that shortage of ammunition and other war-induced causes had resulted in a very light kill despite the fact that the regulations had been amended to permit increased hunting later in the season."

Although the initial regulations were unchanged from 1943, some relaxations evidently were made after the season was underway.

For 1944, continued improvement in the mourning dove's numerical status was reported generally throughout its breeding range (U.S. Fish and Wildlife Service 1945). The 1944 hunting regulations reflected the improvement by permitting fifty-seven days of hunting, though bag limits were retained at 10 birds daily.

The status of mourning doves continued to improve from 1945 through 1948, with the season lengths being sixty days in most eastern and some western states. The limit remained 10 birds.

Unfortunately, mourning doves in the Southeast experienced a second period of decline. The U.S. Fish and Wildlife Service (1949) reported that the number of birds had steadily decreased after 1944 and the total number using that region was below the level left after the storm of January 1940. It appeared that the principal reason for the decline was increased hunting pressure, particularly at times when too many adult birds still had unfledged young in the nest. The Service's report called for drastic action, with one alternative being short seasons in the entire Southeast, to open well after most of the nesting was known to have ceased.

Although 1948 saw reductions in season lengths in eastern states, it was not until 1949 that seasons nearly nationwide were cut to thirty days. A severe outbreak of trichomoniasis (see chapter 12) caused widespread mourning dove mortality in the Southeast in 1950 (Stabler and Herman 1951, Haugen 1952). The situation was aggravated by low temperatures and ice during a severe storm in late January and early February 1951, causing untold dove deaths in Alabama, Louisiana, Mississippi and Tennessee. A second major outbreak of trichomoniasis occurred during the summer of 1951 (Haugen and Keeler 1952).

During this second period of greatly restricted regulations, the daily bag limit was kept at 10 doves, except in the East where it was further cut to 8 doves during 1955. After 1953, season lengths were increased to forty days in 1954, then gradually to forty-five full days or sixty-five half days in the Southeast in 1958. From 1956 through 1959, season lengths in the central and western states held steady at fifty days. During this period, the limits remained at 10 birds. But in 1958 and thereafter, the possession limit was set at twice the daily bag limit.

Reported dove population declines of the early 1940s and 1950s should be viewed with some reservations, as no means existed for objective evaluations of population losses. The Call-count Survey did not become operational until 1953, and there still are no means of reliably estimating winter population sizes. Furthermore, because uniform dove harvest surveys were (and are) lacking, it was impossible to evaluate the effects of restrictive regulations on mourning dove harvests or populations.

Beginning in 1960, mourning dove regulations were established by the three mourning dove management units. For the period 1960 through 1980, the EMU states were offered seventy half days, the CMU states sixty full days and the WMU states fifty full days of hunting. Although the numbers of hunting days were stabilized, daily bag and possession limits occasionally were altered to reflect apparent breeding population trends based on several years of data from Call-count Surveys. With but one exception, the limits nationally varied only from 10 to 12 doves daily, with corresponding changes in possession limits. The exception was in hunting states of the EMU during 1969 and 1970, when an 18-dove daily bag and 36-bird possession limit were offered as part of a cooperative federal/ state study aimed at determining the effects, if any, of hunting on dove harvests and populations (Hayne 1975, see also chapter 17).

Regulation modifications in consideration of other species. Migratory gamebird regulations sometimes reflect special considerations when two or more species are hunted simultaneously in the same area. Thus mourning dove seasons and limits sometimes differ when white-winged doves or other doves are being hunted. Because whitewings usually migrate early in September from their breeding ranges in New Mexico, Arizona, Nevada and California, their hunting seasons traditionally open on September 1. In South Texas, mourning dove hunting is allowed during the brief early September season set for a special white-winged dove hunting area. In 1987, the season was four half days (September 5, 6, 12 and 13), with the remainder of the mourning dove season delayed until late September.

When concurrent whitewing and mourning dove seasons occur, aggregate bag and possession limits usually are permitted. Aggregate limits were first implemented for the two species of doves in 1937 in Arizona and Texas. Limits vary among states, depending on the population levels and management objectives for the respective species. For example, each Arizona hunter in 1984 was permitted to take 12 mourning and white-winged doves daily in the aggregate, but no more than 6 of these could be white-winged doves. These regulations were designed to shift hunting pressure from whitewings, whose numbers had declined in recent years, to the more abundant mourning doves. In the special whitewing area of South Texas, each hunter in 1984 was permitted to take 10 white-winged, mourning and white-tipped doves, but not more than 2 of each could be mourning doves or white-tipped doves. These regulations were devised to allow the incidental taking of the two latter species during the season established primarily for white-winged doves.

Uniformity of regulations frameworks. In 1981, the Central Flyway Council recommended that the U.S. Fish and Wildlife Service allow member states the options of a sixty-day mourning dove season with daily bag and possession limits of 12 and 24 doves, respectively, or a forty-five-day mourning dove season with respective limits of 15 and 30 birds. The request aimed to permit slightly higher limits in those states that had huntable dove populations only during the first few days or weeks of the seasons. In fact, mourning dove migration from northern areas is underway well before the earliest permissible hunting date, September 1. The

request was implemented for CMU states that autumn, with three states selecting the shorter-season/larger-limit option.

In 1982, states in all management units were offered the option of a season of seventy days with daily bag and possession limits of 12 and 24, respectively, or a season of forty-five days with respective limits of 15 and 30 doves. The latter option was selected by Illinois in the EMU, five states in the CMU and five in the WMU. Several WMU states seldom set seasons as long as the frameworks permitted. In 1983, the number of hunting days associated with the second option was extended to sixty days nationally. The same options were offered during 1984–86.

The concept of national uniformity of hunting regulations frameworks was abandoned by the U.S. Fish and Wildlife Service in 1987, when special restrictions were imposed in the WMU. This action was in response to a national analysis of long-term breeding population trends as indicated by Call-count Survey data since 1966 (D. Dolton personal communication: 1988). That analysis showed that the WMU population had declined at a statistically highly significant rate (see chapter 19). In announcing the reduction, the Service indicated that a combination of factors, including the loss of nesting habitat, agricultural changes and overharvest, was thought to be responsible for the population decline. Accordingly, states in the WMU were offered season length options of not more than thirty consecutive days (between September 1, 1987 and January 15, 1988) or forty-five days to be split between two periods (September 1–15, 1987 and anytime from November 1, 1987 to January 15, 1988). The latter option was designed to distribute hunting pressure better over time and among dove subpopulations. Under both options, the daily bag and possession limits were reduced to 10 and 20 birds, respectively.

Zoning. In its simplest form, zoning is the setting of differing hunting seasons in different parts of a state. One form of zoning occurs when states select shortened seasons (from those offered in federal frameworks) for different areas. To illustrate, if federal frameworks offer a sixty-day season, a state could select a thirty-day season in a north zone followed by a thirty-day season in a south zone. Such an arrangement theoretically reduces the state harvest from that likely under a statewide sixty-day season having the same opening and closing dates. This form of zoning is not common, although some northern and western states do not avail themselves of the full number of hunting days offered in the federal frameworks.

A second form of zoning, more popular and

of far more management consequence, treats each zone as a "state" for the purpose of setting seasons. To illustrate, under the aforementioned offering, a state would select different sixty-day seasons in each of the north and south zones. This sort of zoning enables seasons to coincide better with dove abundance, thus contributing to greater harvest opportunity and hunter satisfaction. It also enables hunters to hunt longer within the state if they wish to travel to different zones when seasons are open. This form of zoning is most justifiable in large states or states having diverse physiographic regions and habitats.

From 1918 through 1922, all dove hunting seasons were set on a statewide basis *(Table 85)*. Beginning in 1923, Texas was permitted to set seasons by north and south zones, in recognition of the large size of the state and its patterns of dove abundance and distribution. Other early zoning authorizations included Alabama in 1929, Florida in 1930, California in 1935 (but not thereafter until 1947), and South Carolina, Georgia and Mississippi in 1936. Beginning in 1973, federal frameworks allowed four southeastern states (Alabama, Georgia, Louisiana and Mississippi) the option to establish north and south zones, providing that the season opening in the south zone was delayed until September 30. The latter provision was in consideration of late nesting by resident doves.

It is not possible to evaluate objectively the consequence of zoning on dove harvests because of the absence of an annual uniform national survey of dove hunting and harvest, as noted earlier.

Split seasons. Season splitting is the practice of dividing seasons into segments with an intervening period or periods when no hunting is allowed. When season splitting is employed for doves, the early segment usually is directed to the harvest of local doves, while the later segment(s) principally is (are) aimed at harvest of migrant doves. Like zoning, season splitting allows administrators better distribution of hunting opportunity—in this instance, by time periods rather than by areas. Season splitting was first employed in 1928 when South Carolina, Alabama, Mississippi and Florida divided their seasons into two periods. It became progressively more popular, and in 1940, six states split seasons. In 1960, fifteen had such seasons, and in 1980, nineteen states split seasons into two or three segments.

Combination zoning and season splitting. The greatest flexibility in setting seasons occurs when a state uses *both* zoning and season splitting. The first instance of this occurred in Alabama in 1929, when a split season was chosen in one zone of the state. South Carolina, Georgia and Mississippi adopted the practice in 1936. Combination zoning and season splitting has been standard in three or four southeastern states and Texas for many years.

Shooting hours. The time of day when dove hunting is permitted has varied considerably among years and by geographical locations *(Table 88)*. Unlike season lengths and limits, which generally reflect perceived changes in dove populations,

Table 88. Daily hunting periods for mourning doves by management unit, state and year, 1918–87 (FD = full day; HD = half day, noon to sunset).

Management unit/state	Year and daily periods
Eastern	
Alabama	1918–47[a] (FD); 1948–54 (HD); 1955 (FD); 1956–79 (HD); 1980 (FD); 1981 (N. Zone, part, FD first season segment, HD thereafter; remainder of N. Zone, HD; S. Zone, HD first season segment, FD thereafter); 1982–83 (N. Zone, part, FD; remainder of N. Zone, HD; S. Zone, FD); 1984 (N. Zone, part, HD; remainder of N. Zone, HD first season segment, FD thereafter; S. Zone, FD); 1985 (N. Zone, HD first season segment, FD thereafter; S. Zone, HD); 1986 (N. Zone, HD on opening day, FD thereafter; S. Zone, FD first season segment, HD thereafter); 1987 (N. Zone, HD on opening day, FD thereafter; S. Zone, FD first two season segments, HD thereafter)
Connecticut	1962 (HD)
Delaware	1918–50 (FD); 1951–87 (HD)
Florida	1918–47 (FD); 1948–80 (HD); 1981–87 (HD first season segment, FD thereafter)
Georgia	1918–47 (FD); 1948–55 (HD); 1956–57 (FD); 1958–79 (HD); 1980–83 (FD); 1984–85 (HD first season segment, FD thereafter); 1986–87 (HD on opening day, FD thereafter)
Illinois	1918–51 (FD); 1952 (HD); 1953–57 (FD); 1958–87 (HD)
Indiana	1919–29 (FD); 1984–86 (HD); 1987 (HD first season segment, FD thereafter)
Kentucky	1918–47 (FD); 1948–79 (HD); 1980 (FD); 1981–82 (HD); 1983 (FD); 1984 (11 A.M. to sunset); 1985–87 (11 A.M. to sunset, first season segment; sunrise to sunset thereafter)

Table 88. (continued)

Management unit/state	Year and daily periods
Eastern (continued)	
Louisiana	1918–47 (FD); 1948–79 (HD); 1980-83 (FD); 1984–86 (HD); 1986 (HD first two days of each season segment, FD thereafter)
Maryland	1918–48 (FD); 1949–82 (HD); 1983 (FD); 1984–87 (HD first season segment, FD thereafter)
Mississippi	1918–47 (FD); 1948–49 (HD); 1980–87 (FD)
North Carolina	1918–47 (FD); 1948–79 (HD); 1980 (FD); 1981 (HD on opening day, FD thereafter); 1982–84 (HD first season segment, FD thereafter); 1985–87 (FD)
Ohio	1919–29 (FD); 1975–76 (HD)
Pennsylvania	1945–50 (FD); 1951–53 (HD); 1954–57 (FD); 1958–81 (HD); 1982–83 (HD first season segment, 9 A.M. to sunset on opening day of second season segment, FD thereafter); 1984–87 (HD first season segment, FD thereafter)
Rhode Island	1957 (FD); 1958-82 (HD); 1983 (FD); 1984 (HD first season segment, FD thereafter); 1985–87 (HD first season segment, sunrise to sunset thereafter)
South Carolina	1918–47 (FD); 1948–79 (HD); 1980–87 (FD)
Tennessee	1918–46 (FD); 1947–79 (HD); 1980 (FD); 1981–86 (HD on opening day, FD thereafter); 1987 (FD)
Virginia	1918–47 (FD); 1948–80 (HD); 1981–87 (HD first season segment, FD thereafter)
West Virginia	1955–57 (FD); 1958–79 (HD); 1980–83 (FD); 1984–87 (HD first season segment, FD therafter)
Central	
Arkansas	1919–47 (FD); 1948–59 (HD); 1960–87 (FD)
Colorado	1918–29 (FD); 1943–87 (FD)
Iowa	1977 (FD)
Kansas	1919–87 (FD)
Minnesota	1920–46 (FD)
Missouri	1918–51 (FD); 1952 (HD); 1953–87 (FD)
Montana	1949–50 (FD); 1983–87 (FD)
Nebraska	1919–35 (FD); 1937 (FD); 1947 (FD); 1949–52 (FD); 1975–87 (FD)
New Mexico	1918–48 (FD); 1949–53 (HD on opening day, FD thereafter); 1954–87 (FD)
North Dakota	1963–64 (FD); 1979–87 (FD)
Oklahoma	1918–87 (FD)
South Dakota	1935 (FD); 1967–72 (FD); 1981–87 (FD)
Texas[b]	1918–50 (FD); 1951–81 (HD); 1982–87 (FD)
Wyoming	1956 (FD); 1973–87 (FD)
Western	
Arizona	1918–87 (FD)
California	1918–52 (FD); 1953–54 (HD on opening day, FD thereafter); 1955–87 (FD)
Idaho	1918–87 (FD)
Nevada	1918–87 (FD)
Oregon	1918–37 (FD); 1941–87 (FD)
Utah	1919–37 (FD); 1951–87 (FD)
Washington	1952–87 (FD)

[a] Full day in 1918, 1931 (except opening day, when hunting began at noon), 1932–33, and 1943–87: one-half hour before sunrise to sunset; 1934 and 1940–42: sunrise to sunset; 1935–39: 7 A.M. to sunset.

[b] In Texas, when the mourning dove season coincided with the white-winged dove season, the daily hunting periods were as follows: 1944–45 (noon to sunset); 1946–53 (4 P.M. to sunset); 1958–64 (2 P.M. to sunset); 1965–83 (noon to sunset); 1984–87 (full day).

shooting hour variations usually arise from regional hunting customs, efforts to distribute hunting pressure better, consideration of time when other game species are hunted or as a means of improving the enforcement of daily bag regulations.

From 1918 through 1947, federal regulations provided for full-day dove hunting nationally. Historically, dove hunting in the central and western states usually was on a full-day basis (commonly one-half hour before sunrise to sunset). However, eastern states, particularly those in the South, often have limited hunting to half days (e.g., afternoon or noon to sunset). This practice was followed from 1948 through 1979. Beginning in 1981, some southeastern states choosing split seasons selected half-day hunting during the first segment and full-day hunting during the remaining season.

Hawaii. In Hawaii, where the mourning dove has been successfully introduced on part of the island of Hawaii, the hunting season extends from the first Saturday in November through the third Sunday in January, with hunting allowed only on Saturdays, Sundays and state holidays. Daily bag and possession limits may include 10 mourning doves, singly or in the aggregate with two other species of gamebirds.

PROCEDURES FOR SETTING REGULATIONS

As described earlier, federal hunting regulations for migratory gamebirds are divided into two major categories, "basic" and "annual." Basic regulations normally change little from year to year. In contrast, the annual hunting regulations often change, usually in response to some biological condition, ecological event or modified management objective(s).

Similar requirements and procedures apply to establishing both the basic and annual regulations. However, before detailed annual hunting regulations are developed, it is administratively necessary to interpret or more precisely define the relatively broad provisions of the various conventions and the Migratory Bird Treaty Act.

Each year, the initial federal regulations define the frameworks within which state conservation agencies may select the actual hunting season dates, hours, limits, areas, etc. After state selections are received, the U.S. Fish and Wildlife Service then makes the regulations final by publishing the state decisions in the *Federal Register*.

The three and a half month limit on length of the migratory gamebird hunting season has been

Reduction of harvest or hunting pressure on mourning doves can be achieved at least in part by instituting half-day hunting, typically from noon to sunset. Mourning doves provide lively shooting late in the day as they move from feeding or watering sites to roosts. Nevertheless, since these doves, when downed, can be difficult to locate in dense vegetation, hunters without retrieving dogs are advised to cease shooting prior to loss of adequate daylight. *Photo by Ron George; courtesy of the Texas Parks and Wildlife Department.*

administratively interpreted to be 107 days, which may be implemented on a species and area basis. This interpretation was sustained in court in 1974.

Legal and Administrative Constraints

Various federal laws and executive orders impose requirements or considerations on federal agencies responsible for developing or promulgating regulations. Those affecting the formulation of migratory bird hunting regulations are as follows.

Administrative Procedure Act. This 1967 law provides overall procedural guidance to regulations-setting agencies. It requires that the developmental procedure be orderly, provides for public involvement in the process and requires publication of proposed and final rules (regulations) in the *Federal Register*.

Endangered Species Act. This 1973 statute, as amended, requires that federal agencies consider the effects of federal programs on designated endangered or threatened species and their critical habitats. Consequently, the U.S. Fish and Wildlife Service undertakes extensive studies each year to ensure that the proposed hunting regulations, if implemented, are not likely to jeopardize any listed species or its critical habitat.

National Environmental Policy Act. This 1969 law mandates that federal agencies consider the likely impacts of their programs on the nation's environment. In fulfilling its responsibilities under this act, the U.S. Fish and Wildlife Service issued in 1975 the *Final Environmental Statement for the Issuance of Annual Regulations Permitting the Sport Hunting of Migratory Birds*. Part of this document is related to mourning dove hunting regulations. From time to time, the Service has updated its Final Environmental Statement by issuing supplemental statements. One addressing the September hunting of mourning doves was issued in July 1977. It concluded that mourning dove hunting in September had no major impact on the welfare of the overall dove population. Only a small proportion of doves still nesting then and their offspring experienced mortality. The initial Final Environmental Statement was updated in 1988 by a supplemental statement bearing the same title.

Regulatory Flexibility Act and Executive Order 12291. These related guidelines define "major" rules (regulations) and require that agencies undertake regulatory impact analyses of such rules as they affect various segments of the economy. Since hunting regulations stem chiefly from biological (population and habitat) conditions—as is mandated in various conventions and the Migratory Bird Treaty Act—little latitude exists for considering economic factors.

Miscellaneous considerations. Additional considerations influencing the annual regulatory schedule include the necessity to obtain, analyze and distribute biological information to the public, including state agencies, and the need to publish the final regulations so that hunters and others can be made aware of their content. Because the North American migratory bird management program is highly cooperative, it is essential that adequate opportunity is afforded state wildlife agencies and the public to comment on federal proposals. Furthermore, considerable time is needed for states to formalize migratory bird hunting seasons within federal frameworks and according to the state's own legal and administrative laws or guidelines.

Typical Schedule
for Setting Annual Hunting Regulations

Development of annual federal hunting regulations (including those for mourning doves) follows a schedule of nearly a year's duration. Preliminary steps begin in late January, when the last of the previous year's seasons are just drawing to a close. For illustrative purposes, the schedule for a typical year (1987) is used. Times in this example pertain to an "early" season, i.e., one opening as early as September 1, as is the case for the mourning dove.

Late January. The annual cycle commences with the first meeting of the U.S. Fish and Wildlife Service's Regulations Committee. This group is comprised of Service officials having primary responsibilities for or special expertise with migratory gamebirds. At this initial meeting, highlights of the past year are reviewed, and fundamental, broad objectives and initial proposals are developed for the current year.

March. The Service publishes in the *Federal Register* its intent to establish hunting regulations for the current year and its proposed initial frameworks. The document also describes various factors to be considered in the regulatory process, objectives of the proposed regulations and the schedule of the annual process. Also, it opens a public comment period, during which citizens may express their views in writing and provide additional pertinent information.

June. A supplemental, proposed rule-making is published in the *Federal Register*. It reflects modifications or further defines the regulations being contemplated. The Service's Regulations Committee convenes toward the end of the month to review the latest biological information, consider public comments and develop regulations frameworks to be presented at a public hearing. On the following day, a public hearing conducted by an administrative law judge is held in the Interior Building in Washington, D.C. The latest biological information is presented, management objectives outlined and proposed frameworks released for discussion. Verbal comments and written statements are received for Service consideration. Later that day, the Regulations Committee reconvenes to consider these comments and refines the frameworks for review by the Service's Director and the Secretary of the Interior.

Early July. Frameworks agreed on by the Director and the Secretary are published in the *Federal Register* for final public comments.

Early August. After consideration of final public comments, the Service publishes the final frameworks in the *Federal Register* as a final rule (regulation). From these frameworks, each state wildlife agency selects season dates and other offered options and informs the Service of those selections.

Late August. State selections are published in the *Federal Register* as a second final rule (rule-making). They also formally appear in the "Code of Federal Regulations." In the meantime, state conservation agencies fulfill their own legal and administrative obligations by setting corresponding state hunting regulations. Both the Service and the states develop, publish and distribute regulatory information in leaflets and news releases for use by media, hunters and the public.

Federal regulatory procedures provide for modifying or even rescinding established hunting seasons (e.g., in response to catastrophic mortality from severe weather, starvation or disease), but with respect to the harvest of mourning doves, this authority has seldom been exercised.

REGULATIONS IN OTHER WESTERN HEMISPHERE COUNTRIES

Canada

In Canada, the Canadian Wildlife Service is the federal agency relegated the responsibility for promulgating annual "Migratory Birds Regulations" (R. Lalonde personal communication: 1991). Final regulations are published in the *Canada Gazette*. The Canadian Wildlife Service works closely with the various provincial wildlife agencies in developing annual regulations. The Annual Federal-Provincial Wildlife Conferences, which began in 1922, constitute the major discussion forums.

Although mourning doves are accorded game-bird status in Canada, no provinces chose to hunt them until 1955. That year, Ontario set seasons for north, central and south districts opening September 15, 17 and October 1, respectively, running through December 15. The season was quite unpopular and fewer than 300 doves were thought to have been harvested (Anonymous 1956). No season has been set in Ontario since then.

Beginning in 1960, mourning dove seasons have been set in portions of British Columbia. That first year, September 3–30 seasons were proclaimed for two zones, with 6 doves allowed daily and 12 permitted in possession. Since 1978, hunting was allowed in only one zone under a September 1 through November 30 season. The regulations in 1991 allowed each hunter to take 10 doves daily and to possess 20.

Mexico

Hunting regulations in Mexico are set annually by the Ministry of Urban Development and Ecology (Secretaría de Desarrollo Urbano y Ecología) through the Mexican Wildlife Service (Dirección General de Conservación Ecológica de Recursos Naturales) as amendments to the Federal Hunting Law (Ley Federal de Caza). Regulations are formulated in midsummer and published in the "Official Daily Register" *(Diario Oficial)* (R. E. Tomlinson personal communication: 1991). The mourning dove is identified by the common name in the regulations as "paloma huilota" (see Birkenstein and Tomlinson [1981] for other names given the mourning dove in Mexico).

Mourning dove season times, season lengths, and daily bag and possession limits typically vary from year to year. Since 1980, hunting regulations have been set by states and often by zones within states; previously, they were established by much broader faunal regions. For purposes of illustration, the following information was summarized from regulations for the 1987–88 season. Mourning dove hunting was allowed in twenty-eight states, with no hunting being permitted in two other states (Quintana Roo and Yucatan, both situated in the Yucatan Peninsula, where the mourning dove is extremely scarce, if not absent). Statewide seasons were set in eighteen states, but in the other ten hunting was not permitted in certain zones. Seasons were uniformly set within each state, except in Michoacan, where the two zones had differing seasons.

Variations in season times, season lengths and limits among the hunting states presumably reflect local populations, habitat conditions and local sentiments. The earliest seasons opened on August 7 in Coahuila and August 14 in Tamaulipas (both in conjunction with the opening of the white-winged dove seasons), and the latest season, in Sinaloa, closed on March 13. In general, early seasons were the rule in northern and lower-elevation areas, whereas late seasons were set in southern, higher-elevation regions. Most seasons opened in October or November and closed in late January to early February.

In sixteen states, dove hunting was permitted for 122 days; elsewhere, seasons ranged from 81 days in part of Michoacan to 136 days in Colima (where bag and possession limits were greatly curtailed). Daily bag and possession limits varied from 5 and 15 doves, respectively, in Chiapas and Colima, to 20 and 60, respectively, in Sonora and Zacatecas. However, most states (fourteen) had limits of 10 to 30 doves or 15 and 45 doves (eight states). In all states, the possession limit was triple the daily limit.

Mexico is not bound to the prohibited hunting period from March 10 to September 1 or the three and a half month maximum hunting period, as is the United States. These restrictions appear in the U.S./Canada Convention but not in the U.S./Mexico Convention. Although the latter agreement does include a four-month-long hunting season limitation, it applies only to waterfowl.

Central America

Mourning doves nest in Central America only in relatively small numbers in localized areas. However, during the November to April period, many doves from the United States and Mexico winter there. Until the late 1970s, both mourning doves and white-winged doves were traditionally hunted in most countries, either for subsistence or recreation. Where the two species occur together, the larger white-winged dove is the preferred quarry. El Salvador, Honduras and Nicaragua had a thriving tourist hunting trade prior to the advent of political unrest (Dunks et al. 1982). Many hunters journeyed from the United States, Canada and Jamaica specifically to hunt doves.

Despite the lucrative tourist trade, hunting laws and regulations among most Central American countries generally were inadequate to protect hunted species. Doves simply were hunted during the time that they were present, usually from November into March. Nicaragua had no limits on doves in 1977–78 (Estrada 1978). In 1977, Honduras imposed a daily bag limit of 50 doves, in the aggregate of all species (Purdy 1978a, Fuller and Swift 1984). Since about 1977, El Salvador prohibited foreigners from hunting doves, but local subsistence was uncontrolled (F. Serrano personal communication to R. E. Tomlinson: 1987). Guatemala had no annual dove hunting regulations. In 1984, Costa

Dove hunters from the United States and a native guide in Tamaulipas, Mexico, during a lull in the action. Hunting seasons in most states and zones within states of Mexico where dove hunting is permitted are lengthy and have relatively liberal daily and/or possession bag limits. Mourning dove hunting is not incidental, but the major attraction in Mexico to U.S. dove hunters is the whitewing. *Photo by Ron George; courtesy of the Texas Parks and Wildlife Department.*

U.S. residents who visit Mexico and Central American countries to hunt doves must declare the number of birds in their possession upon reentry to the United States. In recent years, political turmoil in Central America has restricted tourist hunting trips, complicated the transport of sporting firearms and ammunition and undermined already nominal wildlife management programs. Hopefully, eventual resumption of sport hunting will support enlarged conservation programs that will ensure perpetuation of the migratory gamebird resource. *Photo by Ron George; courtesy of the Texas Parks and Wildlife Department.*

Rica enacted a law governing the taking of animals, including mourning doves, for sport (Fuller and Swift 1984).

Since the late 1970s and early 1980s, civil war and political unrest have had a devastating effect on recreational hunting by foreigners in several Central American countries. El Salvador prohibited all recreational hunting (A. Sermeño personal communication: 1987), and in Honduras, which still lacks a general wildlife law, little hunting persists in the south, where dove hunting was so popular in the 1960s and 1970s (S. Cornelius personal communication: 1987). No dove hunting regulations have been issued to date in Guatemala; in 1986, a decree temporarily suspended all hunting. As one veteran observer noted, it is neither prudent nor safe in recent times for a nonuniformed, armed individual to be afield in much of Central America. However, it can be expected that dove hunting will once again become a popular recreation once peace, political stability and tourism return to troubled areas of Central America. Hopefully, adequate wildlife laws, regulations and means of enforcement will then be in place.

West Indies

In the Caribbean, the mourning dove is largely restricted to the Greater Antilles (Cuba, Hispaniola, Puerto Rico and Jamaica). Although no population surveys are undertaken, the species clearly is less abundant than such other columbids as the zenaida dove, white-winged dove, scaly-naped pigeon and white-crowned pigeon. In Puerto Rico, hunting in 1987 was limited to September 5 through November 2, with all-day (one-half hour before sunrise to sunset) hunting permitted. Aggregate daily bag and possession limits of 10 doves and pigeons of the above species except white-crowned pigeons were allowed. Elsewhere in the Greater Antilles, the mourning dove is of minor importance as a gamebird. No mourning dove hunting is permitted in the U.S. Virgin Islands.

Chapter 24.

Mourning Dove Harvest

Kenneth C. Sadler
Wildlife Division
Missouri Department of Conservation
Columbia, Missouri

In hunted species, such as the mourning dove, reliable harvest data are important for a number of reasons. For instance: (1) changes in harvest success often reflect local and regional population density changes; (2) harvest data can provide a valuable means of comparison with census data; and (3) although hunter kill may account for only a small portion of total mortality, recreational hunting is often the only form of mortality over which the manager can exercise significant control, i.e., through regulations.

MEANS OF GATHERING HARVEST DATA

Most state wildlife agencies use information gleaned from mail questionnaires to estimate harvest and to assess hunting pressure. Fundamental to using mail surveys to estimate harvest, hunter numbers, days afield, daily bag and other information is the acquisition of names and addresses of currently licensed hunters. With a complete and current sampling frame of hunters, and by following moderately rigorous sampling procedures, agency biologists can make reliable harvest estimates across broad geographic areas. Care is required to ensure that hunters return the completed

questionnaires and that nonresponse biases are within acceptable limits (Filion 1978, Dillman 1978). If an inadequate sampling frame is used or if hunter response rates are low, it is possible to derive poor harvest estimates from the survey. Hence, it is essential that those who hunt a particular species have an equal chance of being included in the sample and that those contacted respond appropriately, regardless of their hunting success. The accuracy of harvest estimates will be determined largely by how well these two criteria are met.

Sampling frames can be seriously flawed in a number of ways, a few of which are discussed here. If only licensed hunters are contacted, those who hunt but are exempt from license requirements (e.g., because of age or hunting on one's own land, within one's county of residence) will not be on the mailing list and, therefore, will be excluded from the survey. If many hunters are unlicensed, damaging omissions can occur. Problems also arise if the lists of survey participants were developed from other than the current year's licenses. This happens when license vendors do not promptly submit required sales records. When delays occur as survey mailing deadlines near, those conducting the survey have no recourse but to use an earlier year's list of hunters. As a result, persons with permits to hunt the previous year are mailed questionnaires and those with valid permits for the current year, but not the previous one, may not be. This situation worsens if the turnover rate among license buyers is relatively high.

There are other important survey considerations, such as: (1) questions must be clear; (2) instructions must be easily understood and followed; (3) there must be a means of assuring that the respondent is the addressee; and (4) survey procedures must be carefully planned and executed to ensure maximum participation (Filion 1978).

Annual dove harvest and hunting pressure data presently come from two principal sources: (1) all dove hunting states independently gather some form of harvest data; and (2) the U.S. Fish and Wildlife Service obtains harvest information annually from a nationwide sample of Migratory Bird Hunting and Conservation Stamp ("duck stamp") buyers. Any attempt to estimate state, management unit or national dove harvests must use one or perhaps both of these two sources of information.

It is unknown how well state and federal survey results included in this chapter met the sampling criteria noted above.

STATE MOURNING DOVE HARVEST SURVEYS

Harvest in 1982

From inquiries sent in 1984 to each of the contiguous states in the United States, it was learned that twenty-eight of the thirty-four states that permitted dove hunting during the 1982 season gathered dove harvest and hunting pressure data for that season. Five of the remaining six states also conducted harvest surveys intermittently, but the 1982 season was an "off year." In these instances, the data shown in Table 89 are from an earlier year. The sixth state (Arkansas) used a subjective field bag-check method, which seeks only to determine whether the hunting and harvest pressures are higher or lower than the previous year.

From all of these sources, it is concluded that the total mourning dove harvest in the United States during the 1982 season was approximately 51 million birds. The total number of dove hunters in the U.S. that season was estimated to be about 2.7 million. These hunters spent an estimated 12.6 million days afield during the 1982 dove season *(Table 89)*.

The reader is cautioned that comparing harvest and hunting pressure data among states—which may use widely divergent survey methods—is tantamount to comparing the proverbial apples and oranges. Also, comparisons among states and years can be confused by differing hunting regulations in effect where and when the data were collected. For example, in 1982 some states selected the option of a seventy-day season, which included daily bag and possession limits of 12 and 24 birds, respectively. Other states chose the forty-five-day season length option, which permitted daily bag and possession limits of 15 and 30 birds, respectively. One might intuitively expect the longer season option to encourage more hunting trips and, conversely, that the more liberal bag limits would encourage a higher average kill per trip.

Despite the obvious pitfalls associated with comparing harvest estimates derived from a variety of survey procedures and, occasionally, comparing estimates from different years, some tentative comparisons are inevitable.

Based on what seems to be the best information available, the leading mourning dove harvest states in the United States during the 1982 season were Texas (7.0 million), South Carolina (4.1 million), Mississippi (3.3 million), California (3.3 million) and Alabama (3.0 million). By adjusting the harvest to account for vast differences in the land area among states, those with the highest harvest per square mile in 1982 were: South Carolina—132 (82.0/km²); Mississippi—70 (43.5/km²); Tennessee—68 (42.3/km²); Louisiana—61 (37.9/km²); and Alabama—58 (36.0/km²).

States with the lowest harvest estimates for the 1982 season were Rhode Island (10,000), West Virginia (48,900), Wyoming (69,700), Delaware (91,769) and Nevada (112,800). Those with the lowest harvest per square mile were: Wyoming—0.7 (0.43/km²); Nevada and New Mexico—1.0 (0.62/km²); and West Virginia and North Dakota—2.0 (1.24/km²).

Notwithstanding the uncertainties associated with these estimates, mourning dove harvest intensity in South Carolina is roughly (and arguably) 180 times that estimated for Wyoming.

States that accommodated the most dove hunters during the 1982 season were Texas (427,251), Pennsylvania (208,700), California (204,970), Mississippi (137,099) and Louisiana (134,000). Those with the fewest hunters were Rhode Island (2,500), Wyoming (6,216), Delaware (6,649), West Virginia (8,824) and Nevada (10,952).

States with the highest average harvests per hunter per season were South Carolina (36), Alabama (32), Oklahoma (27), Arkansas (26) and Georgia (25). The highest average harvests per day, which is perhaps the best measure of hunting success, occurred in South Carolina (6.1), Mississippi (6.0), Tennessee (5.5), Alabama and Arizona (5.0).

Table 89. Mourning dove harvest and hunting activity reported by state agencies, 1982 (unless otherwise specified).

Area[a]	Hunters	Days afield	Doves harvested
Eastern Management Unit			
Alabama	94,375	600,797	3,052,110
Delaware	6,649	33,976	91,769
Florida	123,074	468,216	1,106,830
Georgia	104,053	540,275	2,596,050
Illinois	70,870	382,698	1,276,368
Kentucky	50,500	265,500	1,061,500
Louisiana	134,000	683,400[c]	2,972,000
Maryland	26,404	134,443	380,997
Mississippi	137,099	559,500	3,349,858
North Carolina[b]	118,500	539,200	2,280,000
Pennsylvania[b]	208,700	1,092,800[c]	1,674,000
Rhode Island[b]	2,500	7,500	10,000
South Carolina[b]	113,937	669,353	4,104,913
Tennessee	117,474	516,175	2,864,212
Virginia[b]	90,262	403,872	1,258,700
West Virginia[b]	8,824	44,184	48,900[c]
Subtotal	1,407,221	6,941,889	28,128,207
Central Management Unit			
Arkansas	53,900[c]	258,800[c]	1,403,500[c]
Colorado	33,934	154,703	506,600
Kansas	107,300	542,938	2,208,000
Missouri	67,931	356,929	1,147,500
Nebraska	41,550	241,500	742,300
New Mexico	11,238	71,473	168,400
North Dakota	24,535	88,300[c]	158,000
Oklahoma	88,960	507,072	2,416,500
South Dakota	21,530	90,900	332,000
Texas	427,251	1,749,856	7,010,500
Wyoming	6,216	18,845	69,700
Subtotal	884,345	4,081,316	16,163,000
Western Management Unit			
Arizona	87,000	356,300	1,770,000
California	204,970	871,720	3,272,600
Idaho	21,943	93,118	204,500
Nevada	10,952	31,766	112,800
Oregon	19,548	58,644	214,300
Utah	31,700	107,700	282,000
Washington	18,000	54,000	121,200
Subtotal	394,113	1,573,248	5,977,400
United States total	2,685,679	12,596,453	50,268,607
Other			
British Columbia	270	Unknown	1,000
Costa Rica	Unknown	Unknown	7,100[bd]
El Salvador	Unknown	Unknown	106,300[bd]
Guatemala	Unknown	Unknown	159,500[bd]
Honduras	Unknown	Unknown	42,500[bd]
Mexico	Unknown	Unknown	3,196,900[bd]
Nicaragua	Unknown	Unknown	46,100[bd]
Other total	Unknown	Unknown	3,559,400
Grand total	>2,720,139	>12,596,360	53,828,007

[a] States closed to dove hunting during the 1982 season were Connecticut, Indiana, Maine, Massachusetts, Michigan, New Hampshire, New Jersey, New York, Ohio, Vermont, Wisconsin, Iowa, Minnesota and Montana.
[b] Data from 1981 or earlier.
[c] Estimates calculated from Waterfowl Harvest Survey and adjoining state data.
[d] Estimates calculated from band recovery data (Dunks et al. 1982).

Average Harvest 1983 through 1987

By compiling yearly state harvest estimates for the period 1983 through 1987 (information supplied by D. D. Dolton and R. E. Tomlinson personal communications: 1988), the average annual harvest in the United States during this five-year period was estimated to be 44.8 million mourning doves. The average number of dove hunters during the period was 2.4 million per year, and the average number of dove hunting trips (days afield) per year was about 10.5 million *(Table 90)*.

During this period, 1983 through 1987, the highest average annual mourning dove harvests

Table 90. Average mourning dove harvest and hunting activity in the United States reported by state agencies, 1983–87 (unless otherwise specified).

Area	Number of hunters	Days afield	Doves harvested	Years of data
Eastern Management Unit				
Alabama	98,264	552,992	3,029,572	5
Delaware	6,515	33,483	102,755	5
Florida	107,428	393,656	1,635,199	5
Georgia	107,191	589,025	3,155,452	4
Illinois	70,882	360,658	1,344,502	5
Indiana	15,735	100,316	162,230	4
Kentucky	85,994	438,569	1,930,005	1
Louisiana	110,600	462,777[a]	2,497,000	5
Maryland	26,630	129,138	411,826	5
Mississippi	112,597	485,852	2,933,571	4
North Carolina	116,895	567,481	2,498,555	2
Pennsylvania	161,200	642,585[a]	1,488,000	5
Rhode Island	No data	No data	10,000[b]	1
South Carolina	111,996	552,757	3,148,336	1
Tennessee	139,514	527,907	3,183,702	5
Virginia	62,558	271,467	931,776	2
West Virginia	11,455	44,184[b]	40,304[b]	1
Subtotal	1,345,454	6,152,847	28,502,785	
Central Management Unit				
Arkansas	42,918	201,715[a]	813,251	2
Colorado	29,945	122,658	414,376	5
Kansas	89,878	430,732	1,766,000	5
Missouri	60,901	290,184	999,369	5
Montana	476	2,759	4,162	5
Nebraska	34,510	177,759	588,912	3
New Mexico	17,517	115,221	495,452	4
North Dakota	15,951	52,136	83,418	5
Oklahoma	75,002	431,172	1,854,041	5
South Dakota	16,454	73,344	264,240	5
Texas	393,259	1,370,392	5,207,490	2
Wyoming	4,952	16,410	57,434	5
Subtotal	781,763	3,284,482	12,548,145	
Western Management Unit				
Arizona	81,280	291,127[c]	1,534,980	5
California	157,540	477,462[c]	2,376,980	5
Idaho	7,950	29,850[c]	93,800	5
Nevada	7,100	18,189[c]	84,020	5
Oregon	14,550	44,319[c]	162,500	4
Utah	27,260	88,231[c]	248,460	5
Washington	8,600	20,770[c]	69,375	5
Subtotal	304,280	969,948	4,570,115	
United States total	2,431,497	10,407,277	45,621,045	

[a] Estimated from hunting/harvest data in nearby states.
[b] Estimate from information collected prior to 1983.
[c] Average for 1986 and 1987 only.

were reported from Texas (5.2 million), Georgia (3.2 million), South Carolina (3.1 million), Alabama and Tennessee (3.0 million).

Estimates of the average number of dove hunters per year varied widely among states, ranging from highs in Texas (393,259), Pennsylvania (168,175) and California (157,540) to lows in Montana (476), Wyoming (4,952) and Nevada (7,100).

Indiana and Montana opened their dove seasons during this period.

Harvests 1988 through 1989

Based on compilation of data gathered by state wildlife agencies, mourning dove harvests in the United States during the 1988 and 1989 open seasons were 41.8 million and 41.3 million, respectively (D. D. Dolton and R. E. Tomlinson personal communications: 1990) *(Table 91)*. These figures represent declines of 8.6 and 9.4 percent, respectively, from the 1983–87 average annual harvest. The most significant declines in number of birds harvested were in the Eastern (EMU) and Central (CMU) management units, although the percentage decline for the two-year period was greatest in the Western Management Unit (WMU).

Approximately 2.3 million people hunted mourning doves in the United States during both the 1988 and 1989 seasons *(Table 91)*. Regionally, hunter numbers remained fairly stable in the EMU and CMU. In the WMU in 1988, however, hunter numbers declined by about 20 percent. The next season, 1989, hunter numbers increased in each unit but still were lower—individually and collectively—than the average for 1983–87. Because the WMU accounts for only about 10 percent of total mourning dove hunters in the United States, the changes there for 1988 and 1989 were barely detectable in the national summary.

Previous State Harvest Estimates

Keeler (1977) compiled state dove harvest records for the 1972 season in much the same manner as done here and estimated the total United States dove harvest at 49.4 million doves, total hunters at about 2.3 million and number of dove hunting trips at 11.4 million. Even though three additional states were open to dove hunting during the 1982 season, these two estimates a decade apart show a remarkable similarity in total harvest and hunting pressure. Earlier estimates of the harvest have been 11 million in 1942 (McClure 1943), 15 million in 1949 (Dalrymple 1949), 19 million in 1955 (Peters 1956) and 41 million in 1965 (Ruos and Tomlinson 1968).

MOURNING DOVE HARVEST OUTSIDE THE CONTINENTAL UNITED STATES

Although currently available data indicate that most of the mourning dove harvest occurs in the continental United States, additional harvest is known to occur in other countries. Doves banded in the United States, particularly in the states of the Central Management Unit (CMU), frequently are killed and reported by hunters in Mexico and Central America. In most instances, the only basis on which to calculate the harvest outside the United States is by using band-recovery data. If it is assumed, in the absence of other methods, that reporting rates (i.e., the percentage of band recoveries that are reported) in Latin America are comparable to those in Texas, for example, then gross estimates of the harvest in Latin America can be calculated. These harvest extrapolations compare band recoveries in Mexico and Central America with band recoveries and harvest in Texas (Dunks et al. 1982).

Table 91. Mourning dove harvest and hunter numbers in the United States by management unit for 1988 and 1989 compared with averages for 1983–87.

Management unit	Harvest (×1,000)			Number of hunters (×1,000)		
	1983–87[a]	1988	1989	1983–87[a]	1988	1989
Eastern	28,502.8	27,157.3	26,457.5	1,345.5	1,303.9	1,306.4
Central	12,548.1	11,084.1	10,898.6	781.8	743.6	747.2
Western	4,570.1	3,476.0	3,974.5	304.3	246.0	285.9
Total	45,621.0	41,717.4	41,330.6	2,431.6	2,293.5	2,339.5
Percentage[b]		−8.6	−9.4		−5.7	−3.8

[a] Annual average for period.
[b] Compared with annual average for 1983–87.

Based on these calculations, the annual mourning dove harvest in Mexico during the late 1970s and early 1980s was approximately 3.2 million doves, and the combined annual harvest in Central America was about 360,000.

Mourning doves are one of four species of columbids taken by hunters in Puerto Rico. The mourning dove harvest in 1985 was estimated to be about 3,000.

British Columbia is the only Canadian province open to mourning dove hunting. Authorities in British Columbia estimated recent annual dove harvests to be about 800 birds, taken by sixty hunters.

Mourning doves also are hunted on the Island of Hawaii. However, hunting is limited to a few ranches and the harvest is quite small.

TOTAL MOURNING DOVE HARVEST AND HUNTING PRESSURE

Based on estimates provided by state and provincial wildlife agencies, and by making reasonable allowances for missing information, the range-wide harvest of mourning doves in the early 1980s was estimated to be about 54.5 million birds annually. Assuming that the harvest outside the continental United States remained relatively constant at approximately 6 percent of the continental United States harvest, the estimated average annual range-wide harvest during the mid-1980s was approximately 47.5 million doves. Keeler (1977) estimated the 1972 harvest in the United States at approximately 49.4 million doves and the range-wide harvest at approximately 52.5 million birds. Thus, based on these admittedly cursory estimates, it appears that the mourning dove harvest in the United States was approximately 50 million birds annually in 1972 and 1982 and that the average annual harvest 1983–87 was approximately 45.6 million birds, or about 9 percent below those earlier harvest estimates *(Table 92)*.

During 1982, an estimated 2.7 million hunters spent 12.6 million days afield in pursuit of mourning doves *(tables 93 and 94)*. It should be remembered that the numbers of dove hunters and days afield in Mexico and Central America remain unknown and cannot be estimated.

Estimates of the average nationwide autumn population range from 350 million to 600 million mourning doves (see Dunks et al. 1982). If a midpoint number is accepted—475 million birds—the 1982 United States harvest of 51.0 million doves was about 10.8 percent of the estimated autumn population. Tomlinson et al.'s (1988) nationwide autumn dove population estimates—developed in a similar

Table 92. Mourning dove harvest in the United States during 1972 and 1982 and the average annual harvest 1983–87 as reported by state agencies (numbers in parentheses are percentage of total).

Management unit	1972[a]	1982	1983–87 average
Eastern	29,470,300 (59.7)	28,128,207 (56.0)	28,502,785 (62.5)
Central	13,223,300[b] (26.8)	16,163,000 (32.1)	12,548,145 (27.5)
Western	6,675,900 (13.5)	5,977,400 (11.9)	4,570,115 (10.0)
United States total	49,369,500	50,268,607	45,621,045

[a] From Keeler (1977).
[b] Dunks et al. (1982) estimated the average dove harvest in the Central Management Unit, 1967–76, to be about 13 million doves per year.

Table 93. Mourning dove hunters in the United States during 1972 and 1982 and the average per year 1983–87 as reported by state agencies (numbers in parentheses are percentage of total).

Management unit	1972[a]	1982	1983–87 average
Eastern	1,310,400 (55.8)	1,407,221 (52.4)	1,345,454 (55.3)
Central	639,600 (27.2)	884,345 (32.9)	781,763 (32.2)
Western	398,400 (17.0)	394,113 (14.7)	304,280 (12.5)
United States total	2,348,400	2,685,679	2,431,497

[a] From Keeler (1977).

Table 94. Days afield by mourning dove hunters in the United States during 1972 and 1982 and the average days per year 1983–87 as reported by state agencies (numbers in parentheses are percentage of total).

Management unit	1972[a]	1982	1983–87 average
Eastern	7,233,400 (62.9)	6,941,889 (55.1)	6,152,847 (59.1)
Central	2,669,100 (23.2)	4,081,316 (32.4)	3,284,482 (31.6)
Western	1,602,700 (13.9)	1,573,248 (12.5)	969,948 (9.3)
United States total	11,505,200	12,596,453	10,407,277

[a] From Keeler (1977).

manner but based on banding and recovery data from the WMU—also ranged from 350 million to 600 million birds, with 500 million thought to be a conservative and reasonable estimate. If these population and harvest estimates are close to actuality, and assuming an additional 30 percent crippling loss (see Haas 1977, Tomlinson et al. 1988), the annual hunter kill in the United States is about 66.3 million doves, or approximately 13 percent of the autumn population. With allowance for harvest outside the United States *(Table 89)* plus attendant crippling loss, total continental mortality attributable to hunting may have been 71 million in 1982.

Evaluation of State Survey Procedures and Data

In 1980, an ad hoc committee of the International Association of Fish and Wildlife Agencies was appointed to examine the feasibility of standardizing state survey methods for all migratory gamebirds, including mourning doves. If these survey methods could be standardized, the practice of combining state-generated harvest data would be more nearly justified. In making the attempt, the committee encountered some very formidable problems, including: (1) a bewildering array of license types used by states; (2) the widespread practice of using a previous year's license sales records as the sampling frame; and (3) an unknown percentage of hunters not required to possess a license at all (Dunks 1980). The committee concluded that some improvements could be made if a "unit"—i.e., a person or a team—was available to advise each state concerning ways to upgrade its survey. However, development of standardized survey procedures to be followed each year by all states was considered beyond reasonable expectations. The committee further stated that even if their "unit" recommendation were followed, harvest estimates would only be improved, not perfected, and questions concerning the reliability of regional or national harvest estimates more than likely would remain.

In summary, the committee cautioned against accepting regional or national harvest estimates of any of the migratory shore and upland gamebirds if the estimates were derived from state surveys in use at that time. Because no attempt has been made to standardize the state surveys since the committee reported in 1980, there is no reason to believe the regional or national summaries are more reliable now than they were then. Accordingly, harvest and hunting pressure summaries included in this chapter can be considered only as approximations at best.

DOVE HARVEST ESTIMATES FROM THE WATERFOWL HARVEST SURVEY

For many years, the U.S. Fish and Wildlife Service has conducted a nationwide Waterfowl Harvest Survey to measure the retrieved kill of ducks and geese. Survey participants—a sample of hunters who purchase federal duck stamps—are asked to provide information that allows the Service to estimate annual waterfowl harvest and hunting pressure. Data from the survey are categorized according to the four major flyways. Each year since 1961, this information has been used to help set waterfowl harvest regulations for the ensuing year.

Since 1964, Waterfowl Harvest Survey questionnaires have requested information about activities and success hunting other migratory gamebirds, although duck stamps are not required to hunt these other species. During the period 1964–87, mourning doves were the most frequently mentioned "other" species hunted. About 24 percent of the respondents reported that they hunted doves (Martin 1979). Table 95 summarizes the number of duck stamp buyers participating in the 1982 and 1987 Waterfowl Harvest Surveys and their reported mourning dove harvest (Martin 1988).

The Survey recorded a harvest of 13.2 million mourning doves in the United States during the 1982 hunting season, or about 26 percent of the 50 million doves estimated by state surveys. Based on this federal survey, the leading dove harvest states were Texas (2.3 million), Louisiana (1.6 million), California (0.9 million), South Carolina (0.6 million) and North Carolina (0.5 million). States harvesting the fewest doves were West Virginia (11,600), Rhode Island (13,400), Wyoming (48,000), Washington (64,000) and Delaware (71,700).

States with the highest average seasonal mourning dove harvest per hunter were South Carolina (46), Alabama (45), Georgia (36), Tennessee (35) and Kentucky (35). It is noteworthy that three of these five states (South Carolina, Alabama and Georgia) also were shown by state agencies as having the highest seasonal averages, but the averages reported by duck stamp buyers were substantially (74 percent) higher.

By comparing state estimates of harvest and hunting pressure with estimates from the Waterfowl Harvest Survey, a gross measure of the relative sensitivity of the latter can be obtained *(Table 96)*. Presumably, the Waterfowl Harvest Survey is more reliable in states where high percentages of dove hunters also hunt waterfowl and thereby participate in the Survey, and less reliable in states where low percentages of waterfowl hunters participate.

Table 95. Mourning dove harvest and hunting activity in the United States, from the Waterfowl Harvest Survey for the 1982 and 1987 seasons.[a]

Area	Duck stamp buyers participating		Average doves harvested per hunter		Doves harvested	
	1982	1987	1982	1987	1982	1987
Eastern Management Unit						
Alabama	7,200	6,500	45.4	48.1	325,600	310,700
Delaware	4,300	3,700	16.5	21.1	71,700	77,200
Florida	11,100	8,300	34.1	32.3	379,400	266,900
Georgia	9,000	10,200	36.2	38.6	325,400	393,600
Illinois	20,800	19,500	22.3	19.8	463,800	385,400
Indiana		6,300		30.6		193,700
Kentucky	7,300	6,800	34.8	37.4	255,600	253,500
Louisiana	47,200	35,500	33.4	24.4	1,578,500	865,600
Maryland	13,300	12,900	20.5	21.7	272,100	279,000
Mississippi	14,700	9,700	33.3	36.4	490,400	353,700
North Carolina	18,300	17,100	27.6	32.8	506,000	561,800
Pennsylvania	24,400	18,600	15.6	17.3	383,200	322,000
Rhode Island	1,100	700	11.8	7.8	13,400	5,400
South Carolina	13,900	13,800	45.7	48.0	634,000	664,400
Tennessee	13,300	12,500	35.0	33.6	466,200	419,200
Virginia	10,400	10,100	22.1	27.1	230,200	273,800
West Virginia	1,000	500	11.8	14.8	11,600	8,000
Others[b]	5,100	4,500	15.1	13.5	77,200	60,100
Subtotal and average	222,400	197,100	29.2	28.9	6,484,300	5,694,000
Central Management Unit						
Arkansas	15,000	14,000	23.7	28.5	355,100	399,500
Colorado	17,800	11,900	14.4	13.9	255,700	166,000
Kansas	18,200	14,400	26.6	25.8	484,200	371,000
Missouri	16,300	15,600	20.6	24.3	335,800	379,300
Montana		2,300		12.2		28,300
Nebraska	14,600	13,000	20.4	18.8	298,300	244,900
New Mexico	4,500	2,700	31.8	27.9	141,700	75,000
North Dakota	15,000	9,800	14.8	13.8	221,400	135,200
Oklahoma	10,200	7,200	33.2	26.7	339,000	192,200
South Dakota	13,100	10,100	19.0	21.0	249,600	212,300
Texas	66,900	48,900	34.6	35.1	2,316,300	1,717,200
Wyoming	3,100	2,300	15.5	11.6	48,000	26,000
Others[b]	2,400	1,500	21.0	22.4	50,400	33,800
Subtotal and average	197,100	153,700	25.9	25.9	5,095,500	3,980,900
Western Management Unit						
Arizona	6,800	5,200	30.4	26.7	205,500	138,600
California	42,900	32,200	20.3	19.3	870,700	620,900
Idaho	10,100	5,900	13.5	10.6	135,700	62,600
Nevada	5,100	3,600	17.8	14.1	90,000	50,000
Oregon	8,500	4,500	12.9	12.6	109,500	56,800
Utah	12,900	7,300	11.5	12.7	149,300	92,800
Washington	6,700	3,500	9.7	10.1	64,400	35,300
Subtotal and average	93,000	62,100	17.5	17.0	1,625,100	1,057,000
United States total and average	512,500	412,900	25.8	26.0	13,204,900	10,731,900

[a] Data provided by the U.S. Fish and Wildlife Service, Washington, D.C.
[b] No open season on mourning doves in state where federal duck stamp was purchased, and no information to assign hunters or doves to state of harvest.

States with relatively high percentages of dove hunter participation in the Waterfowl Harvest Survey were Delaware (65), North Dakota (61), South Dakota (61), Colorado (53), Rhode Island (52), Maryland (51) and Wyoming (50). States with relatively low percentages of hunter participation in the Waterfowl Harvest Survey were Arizona (8), Alabama (8), Georgia (9), Florida (9), West Virginia

Table 96. State agency estimates of mourning dove hunters and harvest compared with federal duck stamp buyers participating in the Waterfowl Harvest Survey and their dove harvest for the 1982 season (unless otherwise specified).

Area	Hunters			Harvest		
	State	Federal	Percentage	State	Federal	Percentage
Eastern Management Unit						
Alabama	94,375	7,200	7.6	3,052,110	325,600	10.7
Delaware	6,649	4,300	64.7	91,769	71,700	78.1
Florida	123,074	11,100	9.0	1,106,830	379,400	20.2
Georgia	104,053	9,000	8.7	2,596,050	325,400	12.5
Illinois	70,870	20,800	29.4	1,276,368	463,800	36.3
Kentucky[a]	50,500	7,300	14.5	1,061,500	255,600	24.1
Louisiana	134,000	47,200	35.2	2,972,000	1,578,500	53.1
Maryland	26,404	13,300	50.4	380,997	272,100	71.4
Mississippi	137,099	14,700	10.7	3,349,858	490,400	14.6
North Carolina[a]	118,500	16,500[b]	13.9	2,280,000	506,000[b]	22.2
Pennsylvania	208,700	25,100[b]	12.0	1,674,000	383,200[b]	22.9
Rhode Island[a]	2,500	1,300[b]	52.0	10,000	13,400[b]	134.0
South Carolina[a]	113,937	13,600[b]	11.9	4,104,913	634,000[b]	15.4
Tennessee	117,474	13,300	11.3	2,864,212	466,200	16.3
Virginia[a]	90,262	10,100[b]	11.2	1,258,700	230,200[b]	18.3
West Virginia[a]	8,824	900[b]	10.2	48,900[c]	11,600[b]	23.7
Others[a]		5,100			77,200	
Subtotal	1,407,221	220,800	15.7	28,128,207	6,484,300	23.1
Central Management Unit						
Arkansas	53,900[d]	15,000	27.8	1,403,500[d]	355,100	25.3
Colorado	33,934	17,800	52.5	506,600	255,700	50.5
Kansas	107,300	18,200	17.0	2,208,000	484,200	21.9
Missouri	67,931	16,300	24.0	1,147,500	335,800	29.3
Nebraska	41,550	14,600	35.1	742,300	298,300	40.2
New Mexico	11,238	4,500	40.0	168,400	141,700	84.1
North Dakota	24,535	15,000	61.1	158,000	221,400	140.1
Oklahoma	88,960	10,200	11.5	2,416,500	339,000	14.0
South Dakota	21,530	13,100	60.8	332,000	249,600	75.2
Texas	427,251	66,900	15.7	7,010,500	2,316,300	33.0
Wyoming	6,216	3,100	50.0	69,700	48,000	68.9
Others[c]		2,400			50,400	
Subtotal	884,345	197,100	22.3	16,163,000	5,095,500	31.5
Western Management Unit						
Arizona	87,000	6,800	7.8	1,770,000	205,500	11.6
California	204,970	42,900	20.9	3,272,600	870,700	26.6
Idaho	21,943	10,100	46.0	204,500	135,700	66.4
Nevada	10,952	5,100	46.6	112,800	90,000	79.8
Oregon	19,548	8,500	43.5	214,300	109,500	51.1
Utah	31,700	12,900	40.7	282,000	149,300	52.9
Washington	18,000	6,700	37.2	121,200	64,400	53.1
Subtotal	394,113	93,000	23.6	5,977,400	1,625,100	27.2

[a] Data from 1981 or earlier.

[b] Data from the Waterfowl Harvest Survey corresponding to the year of the state survey.

[c] No open season on mourning doves in the state where federal duck stamp was purchased, and no information to assign hunters or doves to state of harvest.

[d] Estimates calculated from the Waterfowl Harvest Survey and adjoining state data.

(10), Mississippi (11) and Virginia (11). Unfortunately, the Waterfowl Harvest Survey appears to be least reliable in some of the most important dove harvest states. Of the ten most important dove harvest states—which account for 66 percent of the total United States dove harvest—Louisiana is the only state where the Waterfowl Harvest Survey has access to more than 25 percent of the dove hunters.

MacDonald and Martin (1971) and Martin (1979) speculated about the inconsistency of the relationship between waterfowl hunting and other migratory gamebird hunting and indicated that waterfowl hunters form a poor sampling frame for hunters of other migratory gamebirds. Martin (1979) also stated that the problem is compounded when waterfowl hunters from the various states are combined to produce totals for larger units.

The feasibility of using state-generated migratory bird harvest data (including data for mourning dove harvest) to augment the Waterfowl Harvest Survey has been examined by the U.S. Fish and Wildlife Service (1986). The Service concluded that its work has raised a number of questions concerning the merits of using information from state agencies to adjust the Service's Survey. It pointed to an inability to determine the precision of data from both the Waterfowl Harvest Survey and state surveys. Therefore, until precise estimates can be calculated, the practicality of using either or both of these surveys to estimate the harvest of the shore and upland gamebirds (including mourning doves) cannot be fully assessed.

NECESSITY OF RELIABLE DOVE HARVEST DATA

Until a reliable method can be developed to ascertain regional and range-wide dove harvests, the U.S. Fish and Wildlife Service and state wildlife agencies will be forced to make important decisions affecting mourning doves without knowing with adequate precision how these decisions will impact the harvest. Baskett et al. (1978) put a high priority on the need to verify the relationship between results of the national Call-count Survey and annual harvest and age ratio information. For reasons already discussed, this population size/harvest relationship cannot be accurately determined with the use of harvest data presently available.

From the late 1960s into the early 1980s, repeated attempts were made to initiate a uniform national permit system, similar to the federal duck stamp program, for hunting shore and upland gamebirds. Several proposals were put forth, but central to all was the requirement that all migratory gamebird hunters possess a low-cost ($1) permit. Although permit sales likely would generate some revenue above the cost of production and administration, the compelling justification for the permit was that it would make possible the gathering of accurate harvest and hunting pressure data each year. Because the proposed permit would have been required for all migratory gamebird hunters regardless of the species sought, hunter's age, veteran status, land ownership, etc., a national sampling frame of the first order was within reach. Revenues that exceeded administrative costs were to be targeted for state wildlife agencies as grants to support migratory bird research and management projects.

Enabling federal legislation for the national permit system was proposed in the Congress in 1967. Similar bills also were written for nearly all sessions of Congress through the late 1970s. Every year, the merits of the various proposals were debated by the International Association of Fish and Wildlife Agencies. And although there appeared to be widespread conceptual support among state wildlife agency directors and their staffs, approval of the proposal was never obtained. Without a clear, supportive voice from that Association the enabling federal legislation was either not introduced or, if introduced, not seriously considered.

Supporters saw the permit system as a means of annually acquiring a national list of migratory gamebird hunters and, with it, access to crucial harvest and hunting pressure information. As mentioned earlier, all migratory gamebirds (waterfowl, woodcock, snipe, rails, gallinules, coots, sandhill cranes, doves and band-tailed pigeons) would have come under provisions of the permit. The new sampling frame would also have made it possible to correct some of the weaknesses believed to be inherent in the Waterfowl Harvest Survey.

Opponents of the proposal focused their objection on the view that the cost of the federal permit, and its inevitable increase, actually might discourage hunting, inasmuch as other permit, license and stamp fees and associated expenses have risen dramatically in recent decades. Others were concerned that the new permit would compete for state license revenues badly needed by state wildlife agencies. Still others have contended that the harvest information being sought was an intrusion on hunters and that state harvest surveys were adequate for the purpose. The latter objection was virtually eliminated after the ad hoc committee completed the report discussed earlier. The former two reservations, both legitimate, continue.

Although the debate continued for many years and efforts to find a suitable alternative to the permit have repeatedly been sought, no satisfactory means have been found or adapted to determine regional and national migratory gamebird harvests, especially for shore and upland species.

In view of the failure to combine existing state and federal harvest surveys into a workable system, serious consideration should be given to assembling a national harvest sampling frame (for all migratory gamebirds) either from state lists of small-game hunters or by means of a uniform national permit system. Since 1967, the Canadian Wildlife Service has used a migratory bird harvest survey of the type needed in the U.S. (Cooch et al. 1978).

Recent (1991) events provide some encouragement that a national United States harvest survey for all migratory gamebirds may be at hand.

Chapter 25

Hunting in the Southwest

Ronnie R. George
Migratory Shore and Upland Game Bird Program
Texas Parks and Wildlife Department
Austin, Texas

THE BIG PICTURE

John Madson (1978: 45, 47), who called the mourning dove "North America's favorite game bird," wrote: "Dove hunting is a tough thing to describe to a hunter not living in a traditional dove state. It's hard to compare to anything else. . . . It's sort of like pass shooting quail, only more so. Everything considered, the mourning dove may be the most difficult of all winged targets." The mourning dove's flashing, twisting, darting flight in a strong wind can truly humble even the best wingshots. When G. Hill (1988: 26) asked a friend at a dove shoot how he did, the friend replied, "I started out real good; got six birds with the first box of shells then I lost the hang of it."

Many writers, including Brister (1975, 1976), G. Hill (1988), Madson (1978), Russell (1974), Dickey (1976) and Sasser (1986), have written eloquently about the pleasures and frustrations of dove hunting. Although these writers might disagree about the perfect shotgun for dove hunting, they generally would agree that dove hunters everywhere have much in common. The most successful dove hunters do some preseason scouting to locate the birds. They pick a good shooting spot where they will be able to retrieve downed birds. They use available cover for concealment and try to remain motionless to avoid spooking incoming doves. The best shooters keep their heads down on the stock, swing the barrel with the bird and follow through. Wise hunters carefully mark and retrieve each bird to avoid losses. Most dove hunters know how to take care of their game and prepare a few favorite dove recipes. Above all, dove hunters enjoy dove hunting.

Despite many similarities, there are also some significant variations in the techniques used to attract and bag doves in different regions of the country. Regional differences were clearly illustrated in a 1987 questionnaire survey prepared for this book and answered by state wildlife agency biologists in all thirty-six states that promulgated and managed dove hunting seasons *(Figure 72)*. The survey confirmed dove hunting was very important in all southern states and less important in northern states. Due to greater accessibility, more mourning dove hunters hunted on public land in western states than did hunters in other regions. Water hole shooting was clearly more important in arid western states. Hunting around crop fields was important in many areas but was consistently important in all southeastern states. Pass shooting for mourning doves was generally more important in western states. Shooting hours were legally restricted to half days (afternoons only) for at least part of the season in many eastern states but not in the western states.

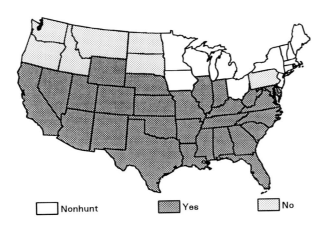

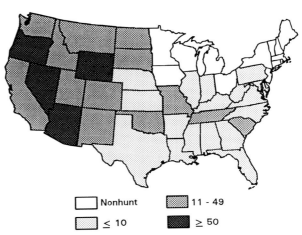

a. Is dove hunting an important event?

b. Percentage dove hunting on public land

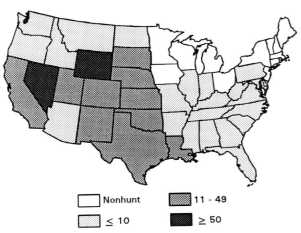

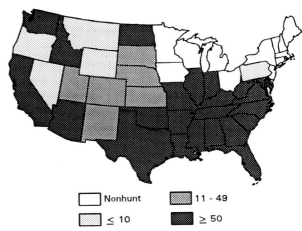

c. Percentage dove hunting around water sources

d. Percentage dove hunting around cropfields

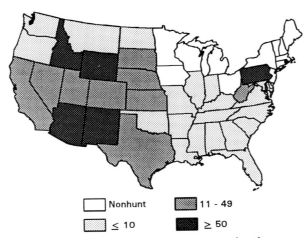

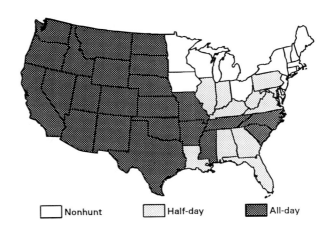

e. Percentage dove hunting involving pass shooting

f. Legal shooting hours for dove hunting

Figure 72. State wildlife agency responses to selected questions from 1987 questionnaire survey about dove hunting activity in each state (Texas Parks and Wildlife Department unpublished data).

"Windmill Shootout," a watercolor painting by well-known Texas wildlife artist John Dearman, typifies the fast action and excitement of a Southwest mourning dove hunt. *Photo from limited-edition print; courtesy of Collector's Covey, Dallas, Texas.*

THE SOUTHWEST

Those distant, bobbing, black specks that suddenly become doves are as eagerly sought by sportsmen in "Cactus Country" as they are in "Dixieland," the "Corn Belt" or any other place where dove hunting is popular (Madson 1978, Brister 1975, Russell 1974) *(Figure 72a)*. The September dove opening is an important date to hunters throughout the southwestern United States, where a dove shoot can be as simple as a youngster with a shotgun down by the stock tank or irrigation ditch after school or as elaborate as a major social event with managed shooting fields, professional staff, dozens of guests and a big barbecue with live music.

Mourning dove hunting around Imperial, California, Casa Grande, Arizona, Deming, New Mexico or Hondo, Texas is similar in many respects to that found in the rest of the country. Southwesterners mostly use 12- or 20-gauge shotguns with light-

load 7½ to 9 shot (but almost any combination of gauge and shot size may be observed). They generally hunt near grainfields, weedy pastures and water holes where birds congregate for food and water, or pass shoot along natural flyways. Southwestern mourning dove hunters usually avoid shooting in the middle of the day, try to stand or sit in the shade where they will not be seen by approaching birds, occasionally use dogs for retrieving and rarely use decoys (Sasser 1986, Brister 1975). In short, southwestern mourning dove hunters use about the same hunting techniques as mourning dove hunters elsewhere do.

However, mourning dove hunting in the Southwest differs in several important ways from that in the rest of the nation. These differences reflect different environmental conditions, local hunting traditions, proximity to Mexico, the presence of doves and pigeons other than mourning doves, and a wide range of public and private hunting access opportunities.

Mourning dove hunters must be sure to secure all required licenses, stamps and permits and carefully scrutinize all pertinent hunting regulations. Pump and semi-automatic shotguns used to hunt mourning doves must be "plugged" to permit no more than three shells in the chamber and magazine. Many experienced dove hunters prefer a short-barreled, lightweight shotgun, with vented rib, open choke and recoil pad. For youngsters, .410 or 28-gauge shotguns may have less "kick" but are not recommended because of their relatively tight shot patterns. Trying to hit doves with these guns is difficult and can prove frustrating and discouraging to the novice hunter. A 20-gauge with recoil pad is both sporting and practical for dove hunting. *Photo by Ron George; courtesy of the Texas Parks and Wildlife Department.*

ENVIRONMENTAL CONDITIONS

The Southwest is famous for sunshine and siestas, but it can also hold surprises for the unwary and the unprepared. Anyone visiting the Southwest for the first time is immediately impressed by stark differences in climate, terrain and vegetation. After inspecting Fort Clark in west Texas in the 1870s, General Sheridan reportedly said, "If I owned both Hell and Texas, I would rent out Texas and live in Hell" (Winfrey 1966: 63). Present-day environmental conditions in the Southwest probably are not quite that severe, but local dove hunters are well aware of the heat, limited surface water, thorny vegetation and myriad creatures that bite or sting.

Nonresidents hunting in the Southwest for the first time may quickly learn the danger of hunting in remote areas without reliable vehicles and adequate drinking water. Bigony (1987) suggested most sportsmen do not adequately prepare for outdoor emergencies, including heat exhaustion and heatstroke. Lightweight, light-colored clothing and a

hat are not an absolute necessity for September dove hunting in the Southwest, but as Brister (1975) noted, proper clothing can certainly contribute to a more enjoyable dove hunt in a region where afternoon temperatures often exceed 100 degrees Fahrenheit (38°C).

Anyone who reads western novels or watches cowboy movies knows that much of the vegetation in the Southwest has thorns or spines. Many of the larger thorny plants, including mesquite, palo-verde, pricklypear, saguaro and Spanish dagger, are used as nesting and roosting cover by desert doves and may provide the only shade available to the desert dove hunter. The very size of these plants makes their thorns fairly easy to see and avoid. It is the less obvious plants, such as sand-burs, catclaw acacia and such smaller cacti as tesa-jillo (pencil cactus), that go unnoticed until they snag the careless hunter. Lechuguilla (a low-growing, sharp-pointed and saw-toothed plant in west Texas and New Mexico) can inflict a severe wound even through leather boots. In Arizona, "teddy-bear" or jumping cholla (another cactus) is a horrible thing to run into. It is especially hard on dogs.

Most mourning dove hunting in the Southwest is done in early morning or late afternoon hours when temperatures are relatively comfortable. Even so, hunters frequently secrete themselves in shade for protection from the sun and to reduce visibility to doves on the wing. Also, shooting generally is easier when sunlight is at an angle rather than overhead. Many southwestern youngsters get their first true exposure to wildlife, wildlands and outdoor recreation ethics on a mourning dove shoot. *Photo by Ron George; courtesy of the Texas Parks and Wildlife Department.*

There is, of course, the distressing possibility of getting stung or bitten by something while dove hunting. The Southwest has a wide variety of creatures that bite or sting, including wasps, ants, spiders, ticks, scorpions, centipedes and poisonous reptiles. Most of these are not life threatening, but tick fever, snakebites and stings inflicted by the yellow slender-tailed Arizona scorpion are not to be taken lightly.

Dove hunters should be especially aware of where they stand or sit and where they reach to retrieve downed birds. Ants quickly cover any birds not retrieved immediately, and snakes can strike an unwary hunter without warning. More than one hunter in the Southwest has reached for a downed dove only to find it being swallowed by a snake. Many sportsmen have completed a dove hunt and found a rattlesnake enjoying the shade beneath the hunters' vehicle. If a mourning dove hunter is careful and reasonably well equipped, however, the snakes, scorpions, thorns, arid climate and other hardships simply add to the mystique, adventure and zest of dove hunting in the Southwest.

HUNTING TRADITIONS

Harsh environmental conditions appear to affect dove shooting in the Southwest in several ways. Leopold (1921) noted that late afternoon and evening water-hole shooting was extremely productive in the Rio Grande Valley of New Mexico. State wildlife biologists reported that the scarcity of surface water in the western states tends to concentrate doves around water holes more than in other regions *(Figure 72c)*.

High afternoon temperatures may alter preferred shooting hours. In much of the nation, mourning dove hunters appear to prefer afternoon shooting. Several eastern states even restrict dove shooting to afternoons only for at least part of their seasons *(Figure 72f)* (U.S. Fish and Wildlife Service 1987a). However, wildlife biologists in Nevada and Utah and other western states reported that searing afternoons have rendered September dove hunting an early morning activity for many of their hunters (Texas Parks and Wildlife Department unpublished data).

Mourning dove hunters in the Southwest wear a variety of "gear," but veteran hunters usually select light, loose clothing of drab or camouflage color. Footwear ranges from tennis shoes to heavy leather boots, depending primarily on the terrain. Snake leggings commonly are worn in some areas, as are sunglasses and baseball-type caps or western hats that protect against the sun and help shield facial features. Wise is the dove hunter who carefully checks where he or she sits and reaches before downed doves are picked up. *Photo by Ron George; courtesy of the Texas Parks and Wildlife Department.*

During midday in the Southwest, when mourning dove movements are minimal, some hunters enjoy jump shooting along watercourses or in shrub areas or fields where their movements are not easily detected. "Flushing" mourning doves from a feeding, roosting, loafing, watering or grit site is not unlike jumping quail coveys. *Photo by Ron George; courtesy of the Texas Parks and Wildlife Department.*

Because of its scarcity in the Southwest, virtually any surface water is likely to attract mourning doves and mourning dove hunters. Southwestern mourning dove hunters probably use retrievers less frequently than do dove hunters in other regions of the country because of the hot, dry conditions and the danger of rattlesnakes. But dogs can add to the enjoyment of any hunt, and many a "lost" mourning dove has been recovered by a well-trained retriever. Dogs used in dove hunting should not break to shot, since following flight birds will flare away from motion on the ground. *Photo by Ron George; courtesy of the Texas Parks and Wildlife Department.*

Because of the heat and inactivity of birds in the middle of the day, September dove hunting at that time is rarely attempted. However, conditions occasionally are just right for a midday jump shoot in the open brush country of the Southwest. In other regions, Hanson and Kossack (1962), for example, reported that jump shooting for doves in Illinois corn and stubble fields seldom was very productive because of the doves' tendency to flush out of range. Also, Brister (1975) noted midday jump shooting for doves resting in trees along field borders was difficult since mourning doves usually dive out of the trees to pick up speed, making for an unnatural and extremely difficult shot. However, in the low, open brush country of the Southwest, midday jump shooting for doves can be quite

productive since the "loafing trees" often are about head height and the doves must flush out and away, much like bobwhite quail. Under these conditions, a hunter equipped with an open-bore gun and willing to face the midday heat can have a very atypical but enjoyable hunting and shooting experience.

Later in the season, after early autumn rains have cooled the desert and stimulated new plant growth, midday dove hunting may be more pleasant and productive for both the hunter and his retriever. Unfortunately, snakes can be a problem on warm days even in midwinter. Although Arizona and Texas currently offer late-autumn or winter dove seasons, no more than 20 percent of the dove hunters in these states take advantage of late-season hunts.

Proximity to Mexico also appears to have an effect on dove hunting. Most southwestern dove hunters know at least a few words of Spanish. They take a *siesta* or nap in the heat of the afternoon, hunt along the *arroyo* or dry wash, and eat *enchiladas* or other Mexican food at La Paloma (The Dove) Restaurant. As one gets closer to the border, *Americano* dove hunters are more likely to employ local "bird boys," who retrieve and clean their downed birds. All the hunter needs is *dinero* (money). The proximity to Mexico also means a greater diversity of dove species.

OTHER COLUMBIFORMS

Undoubtedly, one of the greatest differences between dove hunting in the Southwest and that experienced in other areas involves the presence of native columbiforms other than mourning doves. Seven species of native doves and pigeons occur in the Southwest, and hunters in this region may encounter three additional introduced or non-native species. The presence of these closely related but biologically diverse species creates management problems for wildlife agencies, complicates regulations and creates identification problems for hunters, but these species add to the biological diversity of the region and provide enjoyment to hunters and nonhunters alike.

White-winged Doves

No discussion of dove hunting in the Southwest would be complete without reference to the white-winged dove. The whitewing (known in Spanish as *la paloma alas blancas*) is a tropical species that reaches the northern extent of its vast Central and South American range in southwestern Texas and portions of New Mexico, Arizona, Nevada and California (Cottam and Trefethen 1968). Whitewings are slightly larger than mourning doves and have a square tail and a distinctive white band across each wing.

Whitewings usually are colony nesters but resort to isolated nesting behavior when conditions warrant. They nest in native brush, cacti, riparian vegetation (including saltcedar), citrus orchards and residential shade trees. They generally feed in the same types of areas that attract mourning doves (harvested grainfields, weedy pastures, etc.). Unlike mourning doves, whitewings often perch directly on the seedheads of standing grain sorghum and domestic sunflowers and feed on immature seed still in the "dough" stage. This can result in severe crop depredation problems near major nesting colonies and has earned whitewing flocks the name *la plaga* (the plague) among many Mexican farmers.

Prior to migration in late summer and early autumn, whitewings stage in vast flocks near favored feeding and roosting sites. These large and generally predictable feeding flights attract intense hunter interest. Although whitewings often fly higher than mourning doves, their steady, predictable flight path and tendency to congregate in large flocks at known times and locations often render them more vulnerable to hunting pressure than are mourning doves.

Early in the afternoon on opening day of the whitewing season, it is not unusual to watch a flock of fifty or more whitewings as they swing leisurely over a shooting field, see perhaps half the flock brought down by shotgun fire and never observe a missed wingbeat or any of the erratic or evasive flight behavior expected of mourning doves in a similar situation. As the afternoon progresses, however, the shooting further intensifies and the surviving whitewings become more wary and less predictable. Cartwright (1977: 200) described the scene: "The birds are coming in treetop high, not flocking but swarming like fat minnows in heat, eight or nine or more in crazy patterns, as though some genetic gong has sounded, signaling that it's every bird for itself. Dozens and maybe hundreds of shotguns explode almost simultaneously and birdshot literally rains down on the roofs of pickups and vans. There are at least twice as many hunters as there were at noon and they are jammed together like Hell's reunion."

Hunters in the southwestern United States and Mexico are able to pursue a variety of columbids in addition to mourning doves; the most popular of these are white-winged doves. Larger and more gregarious than mourning doves, whitewings can be seen in massive feeding flights at sunrise and sunset in late summer. Under favorable conditions, whitewings provide scenes reminiscent of yesteryear's passenger pigeon flights. *Photo by Bill Reaves; courtesy of the Texas Parks and Wildlife Department.*

Unlike mourning doves, which usually feed on the ground, whitewings readily perch and feed on the seedheads of domestic sunflowers and other grains. Sunflower fields leased by whitewing hunters provide enjoyable recreational opportunities and fast and furious wing shooting for young and old alike. *Photo by Ron George; courtesy of the Texas Parks and Wildlife Department.*

Historically, the greatest whitewing (and whitewing hunter) densities north of the Mexican border have been in the Lower Rio Grande Valley of Texas and along the Gila, Salt and Colorado river drainages in southern Arizona. Whitewing populations increased in both Texas and Arizona following the introduction of irrigation and grain farming in the late 1800s and reached a peak about 1923 in Texas (Saunders 1940, Marsh and Saunders 1942) and around the late 1960s in Arizona (R. Engel-Wilson personal communication: 1987). Whitewing numbers then declined dramatically in both states due to continued agricultural and urban developments (Cottam and Trefethen 1968, Rea 1983, Hastings and Turner 1965).

About twenty thousand hunters still participate in the whitewing shoot in Arizona, and approximately thirty thousand hunters presently take part in the whitewing "fiesta" in the Lower Rio Grande Valley of Texas. Wooters (1979: 22) noted these hunts are "a major source of revenue for area businesses, including those across the border in Mexico. Without reservations well in advance, motel rooms are nonexistent, and there are waiting lines at all the better restaurants . . . if you don't have prior arrangements for a place to shoot, you won't find one when you arrive." Cartwright (1977) captured much of the carnival flavor of a Texas

whitewing hunt, and noted that whitewing hunters travel to the Valley for a variety of reasons besides shooting birds. Approaching hurricanes and the night life in Mexico are just part of the excitement of a whitewing hunt. Cottam and Trefethen (1968) estimated that the two weekends of afternoon shooting in Texas added $3 to $7.5 million annually to the Valley economy. By 1985 this contribution had risen to an estimated $20 million annually (George 1985).

During the late 1980s, the whitewing situation changed again. Whitewings were declining in the Valley and increasing elsewhere. During May 1990, for the first time since records have been kept, more whitewings nested in other parts of south and central Texas than in the Lower Rio Grande Valley. This change in whitewing distribution may represent displacement of Valley birds due to freeze-related loss of citrus nesting habitat, or it may reflect a natural northward expansion of this tropical species (George 1991).

Rapid agricultural development in the Mexican state of Tamaulipas since the mid-1970s resulted in a rapidly expanding whitewing population estimated at 16 to 19 million birds (Ortega M. and Zamora T. 1984). This resource is attracting increasing numbers of American hunters, who currently harvest an estimated 1.0 to 1.4 million whitewings in northeastern Mexico (Tomlinson 1991). Numerous outfitters and guides make their living by guiding *Americanos* on Mexican whitewing hunts, and the Mexican government now requires all nonresident hunters who hunt in Mexico to use the services of a licensed hunting guide while in the field. Bag limits in Mexico (e.g., 25 birds per day in Tamaulipas in the 1980s) are considered very generous by U.S. standards, and hunting regulations often are poorly enforced. Although current whitewing populations in Mexico appear to be able to sustain a harvest of this magnitude, hunting pressure and harvest there should be carefully monitored in the future (Tomlinson 1987). Purdy and Tomlinson (1982) and George (1985) cautioned that continued agricultural development in Mexico could be expected to result eventually in a decline in whitewing numbers (similar to that which occurred in the Lower Rio Grande Valley of Texas in the 1930s) unless steps were taken to preserve adequate nesting habitat. In this regard, the Mexican government, Game Conservation International, Whitewinged Dove Unlimited, and other individuals and organizations currently are working to maintain some of the best remaining native brush habitat in Mexico.

Those anticipating a whitewing hunt in Mexico will need to obtain the services of a licensed hunting guide to assist with gun permits, tourist cards and other logistical arrangements. These arrangements take at least several weeks of advanced planning. Many Mexican hunting guides offer a package deal that includes transportation, lodging, food and ammunition. Burleson and Riskind (1986) offer excellent advice to those planning to travel in rural Mexico.

Band-tailed Pigeons

The band-tailed pigeon probably is the third most abundant native columbiform gamebird in the Southwest. Bandtails are large, stout-bodied birds with a wide, pale gray band bordered with black across the tail. With few exceptions, bandtails are linked closely to pine/oak forest in their distribution, and the abundance of these pigeons varies directly with the supply of mast, berries and other small fruits. Grainfields and orchards provide additional bandtail food sources (and occasional crop depredation and management problems) (Jeffrey et al. 1977).

Bandtails usually nest as widely scattered pairs but concentrate in nomadic, unpredictable flocks in the nonbreeding season. Bent (1963) reported that bandtail flocks perch for long periods in the tops of tall trees, but if approached too closely, they leave,

a few birds at a time, with a loud clapping of wings. Neff (1947) reported that the bandtail attracted both recreational and market hunters in the early part of this century, and extremely heavy hunting pressure—such as occurred in Santa Barbara County, California during the winter of 1911–12—was believed sufficient to threaten whole populations. R. E. Tomlinson (personal communication: 1991) reported that California continues to have the greatest number of bandtail hunters (about 7,000) and the highest bandtail harvest (about 20,000). Oregon has about 1,600 pigeon hunters and an annual harvest of 3,700 birds. Lower numbers are taken in Washington and British Columbia, and the entire harvest from the "four-corners" population in Arizona, New Mexico, Colorado and Utah amounts to less than 5,000 birds.

Bandtails seldom occur in the same type of habitat where mourning doves are hunted. Sportsmen seeking bandtails usually hunt near mineral springs and estuaries (where the birds concentrate for salts), pass shoot on ridges or still-hunt on oak-covered hillsides where the birds come to feed on acorns. Some bandtails are taken incidental to squirrel and turkey hunting in Arizona (R. Engel-Wilson personal communication: 1987).

White-tipped Doves

The white-tipped or "white-fronted" dove is the newest legal gamebird among the native columbiforms in the southwestern United States (Homerstad 1984). This large, square-tailed bird apparently was named for the white coloration on the tip of its tail. However, the name seems a poor choice since mourning doves, whitewings and whitetips all have white on the tips of their tails. The old name "white-fronted dove" referred to the light coloration on the foreheads of only some individuals. The most distinctive coloration on this dove is the cinnamon or rusty red on the undersides of its wings. The deep, soft call of the white-tipped dove is very distinctive and sounds as though someone were blowing into a bottle or a jug, hence another common name, "old jug blower."

The whitetip is a tropical species that reaches the northern extent of its range in extreme southern Texas. Whitetips inhabit dense brush thickets and citrus orchards. They feed on the ground in openings and seem more inclined to walk than fly. The flight is low and direct and usually covers a short distance (Homerstad 1984).

White-tipped doves were considered uncommon in Texas as recently as the 1960s (Oberholser 1974). In the early 1970s, whitetips suddenly began to increase in number and expand their range throughout an eight-county area of south Texas. Sportsmen did not readily distinguish this "new" dove from legal species, and whitetips began to appear regularly in bag checks. Of 403 citations filed by Texas wildlife conservation officers during a 1979 special white-winged dove season, approximately 20 percent were for illegal possession of white-tipped doves (Texas Parks and Wildlife Department records).

Boydstun (1982) conducted an evaluation of the status of the white-fronted (white-tipped) dove in south Texas and found the species was essentially nonmigratory. He also documented good production and nest success greater than 80 percent for two years. Based on Boydstun's work and on survey information collected by Texas biologists, the U.S. Fish and Wildlife Service and the Texas Parks and Wildlife Department modified the daily bag limits for Texas beginning in 1984 to permit the incidental take of up to two whitetips in the bag during both the regular mourning dove season and the special white-winged dove season. Annual white-tipped dove harvest in Texas reportedly has ranged from 4,000 to 20,000 birds (Waggerman 1988, 1989, 1990). Hunters usually encounter white-tipped doves along the edges of citrus orchards and native brush tracts in south Texas and northeastern Mexico. Whitetips do not gather in large concentrations as whitewings and mourning doves do in autumn and usually are seen as low-flying "singles."

Protected Doves

The red-billed pigeon is another large tropical columbiform that reaches the northern extent of its range in south Texas. Oberholser (1974) reported that redbills—also known locally as "blue rocks" for their bluish gray coloration—declined in number following land clearing in the 1920s and the construction of Falcon Reservoir on the Rio Grande in 1953. The reservoir inhibited natural downstream flooding and degraded the redbill's preferred riverbottom habitat. Redbills now are relatively rare in Texas and protected by state and federal laws. They still are a legal game species in Mexico, however, with a daily bag limit of five birds in some areas. In September 1988, I saw more than 1,000 redbills in a single afternoon along the Rio Soto la Marina east of Lake Guerrero in Tamaulipas, Mexico. About 1,000 to 3,000 redbills are declared annually at U.S. ports of entry by American hunters returning from Mexico (Tomlinson 1989, 1990, 1991).

Inca doves and ground doves are petite, sparrow-sized doves with bright rusty red primary wing feathers. Although both species have fairly wide distribution in the Southwest, they are considered too small to be gamebirds and are protected by state and federal laws.

Due to the presence of protected columbiforms and differential bag limits for some of the game species, two southwestern states (Arizona and Texas) require the retention of one fully feathered wing or the head on dressed doves to provide positive identification for conservation law enforcement purposes. Federal law requires a fully feathered wing on dressed doves imported from Mexico.

Unprotected Exotics

Robbins et al. (1983) described three non-native columbiforms that have become established in the United States. Feral rock doves, better known as domestic pigeons, are widely distributed in North American cities, towns and farmyards, where they usually nest in buildings or other man-made structures. Rock doves have a white rump and (except in white birds) a dark terminal tail band.

The spotted dove is a locally common, introduced species that occurs from Santa Barbara to San Diego, California. Spotted doves are similar in appearance to large mourning doves, but adult spotted doves have a "lace-necked" pattern found in no other dove. This species is found in agricultural lands, parks and suburbs.

The ringed turtledove (or ring-necked dove) is a common cage bird, with uniform sandy plumage and black crescent on the back of the neck, that has become established in Los Angeles, California and locally from Baltimore, Maryland to Miami, Florida. I have encountered them around several Texas cities as well.

Rock doves, spotted doves and ringed turtledoves, originally native to Eurasia, Southeast Asia and North Africa, respectively (Goodwin 1983), now are established as breeding populations in several areas including the southwestern United States. All three of these species occasionally are taken by dove hunters but currently are unprotected by any state or federal wildlife laws.

HUNTER ACCESS

Southwestern dove hunters seem to be faced with a greater range of hunting access opportunities and problems than are most hunters in other regions. An estimated 38 percent of all dove hunting in the southwestern United States occurs on public lands *(Figure 72b)*. Millions of acres of U.S.

Bureau of Reclamation, Bureau of Land Management, Forest Service and state school lands from New Mexico to California are open to public dove hunting. Regulations vary with each management agency, but access for dove hunting generally is free. Some public lands are adequately marked; others are not. Mourning dove hunters on public lands are well advised to study a map of the hunting locale and be certain in the field of their location.

Some state wildlife agency lands are managed specifically for doves and other small game and are open to public hunting under various regulations. In addition, a considerable amount of private land in the Southwest still is available for dove hunting if the landowner's permission is sought and secured in advance of the season or hunt. Access/trespass regulations and laws vary from state to state.

One of the most controversial yet most effective hunter access and habitat management systems in the nation is practiced on many private lands in Texas. Because of legal agreements under which the Republic of Texas entered statehood, there is very

There is more recreational hunting opportunity on public lands in the Southwest than in any other area of the continental United States. Nevertheless, mourning dove hunters unfamiliar with hunting on such lands should become familiar with access routes and constraints, particularly regarding inholdings, leases and grazing permits. Dove hunters in the Southwest should have plenty of water on hand and avoid lengthy exposure to the sun during "slow" times of the day. *Photo by Ron George; courtesy of the Texas Parks and Wildlife Department.*

little public land in Texas compared with that of other southwestern states (U.S. Fish and Wildlife Service 1979, U.S. Bureau of Land Management 1981, Adams and Thomas 1983). Since most of Texas is in private ownership, nearly all hunting in Texas occurs on private lands. The now widespread concept of leased hunting rights seems to have originated in the Edwards Plateau of Central Texas in the 1920s. At first, this practice was limited to white-tailed deer hunting (Teer and Forrest 1968), but it gradually extended to other game species and other regions of the state. Because of its widespread availability (hence, limited monetary value), the mourning dove was one of the last major game species to be specifically included under the lease-hunting system in Texas. Day leases for mourning doves currently range from $5 to $25 per day (up to $50 per day for whitewings), but mourning dove hunting often is included among the game species permitted on areas leased for season-long hunting.

Adams and Thomas (1983) reported that 62 percent of a random sample of 2,304 Texas hunters who hunted during the 1981–82 season were able to hunt on leased land without purchasing a lease (i.e., they hunted as guests on land owned or leased by corporations, friends or relatives). Critics of the Texas system of leasing hunting rights argue that the system limits hunting only to those wealthy enough to afford it, interferes with the American tradition and "right" of free hunting and should be stopped before it spreads to other states (Burger and Teer 1981). Conversely, it can be argued that Texas landowners who lease now have a stronger economic incentive for preserving and developing wildlife habitat than those who do not lease (Teer and Forrest 1968). Many Texas landowners now derive more of their income from hunting leases than from livestock operations. These landowners appear to have overcome the problem addressed by MacMullan (1961), who noted that many habitat preservation programs fail because they do not provide the landowner with enough economic incentive to manage for wildlife habitat.

THE SOUTHWESTERN HUNTER

Southwestern dove hunters have several options concerning where, when, how and what to hunt. Most southwestern dove hunters hunt around grainfields or weedy pastures, but waterhole shooting and pass shooting along local flight lines also is popular. Southwestern dove hunters often encounter whitewings and other dove and pigeon species in the field.

Weedy fields and riparian habitat are excellent locations to hunt mourning doves in the Southwest. Because natural seed crops and surface water availability differ from year to year, dove hunters find considerable advantage in preseason scouting of sites frequented by local doves. *Photo by Ron George; courtesy of the Texas Parks and Wildlife Department.*

Many Southwesterners hunt close to home; some literally have good pass shooting in their own backyards. Other hunters travel hundreds of miles to traditional dove shooting "hot spots." Unfortunately, the reputation of these shooting areas can survive longer than the habitat does, and hunters sometimes are amazed to find a shopping center or channelization project where they once hunted. Free dove hunting still is available on many private, state and federal lands in the Southwest, and excellent, low-cost leased hunting is available on private lands in some states.

As previously noted, most dove hunting in the Southwest occurs during early morning or late afternoon, when the birds are most active and temperatures relatively moderate. From a seasonal standpoint, most of the hunting takes place during the first two weeks of the season, even though most states offer a much longer season and may even provide for late autumn or winter dove shooting.

Veteran southwestern dove hunters generally are well prepared for the harsh environment. They usually wear a hat with a wide brim or bill and may use tinted shooting glasses. Southwesterners usually wear tough, lightweight clothing of a color that blends with the environment. They often carry a stool or folding chair for additional comfort or may simply shoot from the tailgate of a pickup truck. Besides toting drinking water and other refreshments, many hunters also bring a small ice chest specifically for their dressed birds. Wise hunters remember to get all the required licenses and stamps, check the current hunting regulations, buy plenty of shells and watch where they sit.

Mourning dove hunting is the art of pass shooting. The hunter in a good location must have a good field of vision, solid footing, a smooth barrel swing and plenty of shells. *Photo by Roy Tomlinson.*

Dove shoots in the Southwest often are important social events organized in conjunction with picnics or barbecues or as family or business outings. A typical schedule for a big shoot often includes a generous noon meal at a hunting lodge or temporary camp, a lazy afternoon of visiting with friends with an occasional check outside to see if the birds are flying, followed by the real hunting in mid to late afternoon. *Photo by Ron George; courtesy of the Texas Parks and Wildlife Department.*

CARE AND COOKING

As for any wild game, proper care and reasonable skill in cooking and serving mourning doves can make the difference between a gourmet meal proudly served to any dinner guest and one that is an epicurean disaster.

Field Dressing

The first step in preparing a great mourning dove dish begins in the field. Downed doves should be retrieved immediately and cooled down as soon as possible. To avoid spoilage, warm, freshly killed doves should never be placed in a plastic bag or left in a hunting vest longer than absolutely necessary. A paper bag that absorbs moisture and allows air circulation is a good temporary field container for doves. Some southwestern dove hunters cool their birds by hanging them in the shade or placing them in the tray of an ice chest until they can be dressed. Care should be taken to place harvested doves out of the reach of ants.

The decision to dress doves by picking, skinning or breasting-out is a matter of personal choice and largely depends on the recipe(s) in which the dove meat will be used. Picking is the most time-consuming method, since all body, wing and tail feathers must be carefully and completely removed. Feathers can be plucked most easily when the carcass is still warm. Picking is recommended for any method of cooking that is likely to dry out the meat (e.g. baking, roasting or grilling). It is the most versatile method of dressing because picked doves can be skinned or filleted later if the planned method of cooking changes.

Skinning is much quicker then picking, and skinned doves can be used in most dove recipes, particularly if the birds are cooked in sauces or wrapped in bacon or foil to prevent the meat from drying out. Both the picking and skinning methods are completed by removing the crop, entrails, feet, head and tail. The oil gland at the base of the tail also should be removed.

Breasting-out is the fastest method of dressing doves and works well with most recipes that call for dove breasts or fillets. Breasting-out starts with removal of the wings, followed by quick skinning of the breast and back, then two quick, deep parallel cuts between the shoulder blades and spine. A quick pull on the head and the front of the breast then separates the breast from the rest of the bird.

If the planned recipe calls for giblet gravy, mourning dove gizzards, livers and hearts can be saved and used for this purpose.

From 1948 to 1967, mourning dove hunters were required by federal law to retain at least one fully feathered wing on harvested birds transported or in possession. The requirement was eliminated in 1967 in response to reasonable arguments that retaining feathers or other distinguishing body parts inhibited carcass cooling and was unsanitary in some circumstances. Some states still have such a requirement, however, and doves shot or imported must comply with those regulations. In any case, hunters are encouraged to dispose of feathers and inedible body parts of field-dressed doves in a thorough, hygienic and inconspicuous manner. *Photo by R. E. McCabe; courtesy of the Wildlife Management Institute.*

In response to the apparent but unexplained downward trend of autumn flight doves, federal regulations required Arizona and southern California to reduce daily bag limits of mourning doves. The revised limits (10 birds per day) still provided hunters with ample opportunity for hunting and shooting. Evidence indicates that mourning dove hunters in those states, recognizing the need to reduce shooting pressure temporarily, have accepted and complied with the regulation. Certain southwestern plants, such as barrel cacti, provide handy places to cool freshly killed doves. *Photo by Ron George; courtesy of the Texas Parks and Wildlife Department.*

Although dove feathers and entrails are biodegradable, they are unsightly if left on the shooting field or around parking areas. Conscientious dove hunters either bury their refuse or use a feather bag that can be disposed of properly at a later time. (Incidently, dove entrails make excellent catfish bait.)

Transportation and Storage

Once doves have been field dressed and thoroughly cooled, they can be placed in plastic bags and transported home in the tray of an ice chest. An option for transporting doves is to place the dressed birds in an ice chest that is half filled with water and crushed ice. The birds will be thoroughly chilled, and agitation by the sloshing ice water will remove all remaining blood; this option is not for purists, but it works. Doves should be thoroughly washed either in the field or at first opportunity to remove any remaining feathers or blood.

As with almost all foods, mourning doves are best when eaten fresh. However, dressed doves can be kept safely in a refrigerator for several days or in a freezer for several months. Doves placed in a refrigerator should be wrapped or covered to prevent them from drying out. Doves placed in a freezer should be carefully double-wrapped in a freezer paper or placed in water in a semirigid plastic container (a milk carton will do) and frozen as a solid block. Since water expands about 10 percent in volume as it freezes, the container should not be completely filled. Once the container is frozen solid, it should be wrapped or covered. Dressed doves should never be just dropped in a plastic bag and frozen because they will freezer burn rapidly. The flavor of dressed doves deteriorates if they are frozen more than a year. Containers or packages of doves frozen for later consumption should be marked to indicate the species, number of birds in the package and date placed in the freezer.

Table Fare

Gaida and Marchello (1987) reported that mourning dove meat is rich and wholesome and compares favorably in nutrient and mineral contents with other domestic and wild meats. They found dove meat to be only slightly higher in fat than is domestic turkey and lower in cholesterol than is venison *(Table 97)*. It also is better than venison or chicken in terms of mineral content *(Table 98)*.

Like most gamebirds capable of long-distance flight, mourning doves have dark meat. They can taste quite mild or very "gamey" depending on preparation and cooking. Many southwesterners

relish this stronger flavor. Marinating and seasoning provides an excellent means of altering or enhancing the flavor of doves (and other meats) to suit the individual palate. Most marinating methods involve soaking the meat in a blend of various herbs and spices for several minutes or several hours (refrigeration is recommended for doves marinated more than one hour). Southwestern recipes call for a variety of seasonings and marinades, including salt, black pepper, cumin, coriander, cilantro, chopped onion, chopped tomato, chopped jalapeño or serrano pepper, hot sauce, Worcestershire sauce, barbecue sauce, soy sauce, Italian salad dressing, pickle juice, olive oil, fresh milk and buttermilk.

Some of the most popular cooking methods in the Southwest are frying, deep frying, baking, stewing, pressure cooking, crockpot cooking, and grilling over mesquite, huisache, oak or desert ironwood coals. Stewing, baking and crockpot cooking are likely to retain the gamey flavor of doves (for better or worse, depending on personal preference), particularly if the birds have not been skinned. Doves that have been skinned, marinated, and then deep fried or grilled usually have a milder flavor than those cooked in their own juices.

Table 97. Nutrient content of lean tissue from domestic and game meats (from Gaida and Marchello 1987).[a]

Species	Nutrient				
	Moisture (g/100g)	Protein (g/100g)	Fat (g/100g)	Cholesterol (mg/100g)	Energy[b] (Kcal/100g)
Beef (USDA Choice)	70.2	22.0	6.5	72	180
Beef (USDA STD)	73.2	22.7	2.0	69	152
Pork	71.9	22.3	4.9	71	165
Bison	74.5	21.7	1.9	62	138
White-tailed deer	73.5	23.6	1.4	116	149
Mule deer	73.4	23.7	1.3	107	145
Elk	74.8	22.8	0.9	67	137
Moose	75.8	22.1	0.5	71	130
Pronghorn	73.9	22.5	0.9	112	144
Squirrel	73.8	21.4	3.2	83	149
Cottontail	74.5	21.8	2.4	77	144
Jackrabbit	73.8	21.9	2.4	131	153
Chicken	75.7	23.6	0.7	62	135
Turkey (domestic)	73.8	23.5	1.5	60	146
Wild turkey	71.7	25.7	1.1	55	163
Pheasant (domestic)	74.0	23.9	0.8	71	144
Wild pheasant	72.4	25.7	0.6	52	148
Gray partridge	72.1	25.6	0.7	85	151
Sharp-tailed grouse	74.2	23.8	0.7	105	142
Sage grouse	74.3	23.7	1.1	101	140
Mourning dove	73.6	22.9	1.8	94	145
Sandhill crane	73.2	21.7	2.4	123	153
Snow goose	71.1	22.7	3.6	142	121
Mallard	73.2	23.1	2.0	140	152
Wigeon	73.5	22.6	2.1	131	153

[a] Mammal samples = longissimus muscle; avian samples = breast muscle.
[b] Determined by bomb calorimeter.

Table 98. Mineral content of lean tissue from domestic and game meats (from Gaida and Marchello 1987).[a]

Species	Mineral (mg/100g)								
	K	P	Na	Ca	Cu	Fe	Mg	Mn	Zn
Beef	366	172	52	4.2	0.13	1.8	23	.013	3.4
Bison	315	177	52	5.5	0.07	2.5	23	.003	2.4
Mule deer	305	166	54	3.3	0.14	2.7	25	.017	1.4
White-tailed deer	284	212	51	3.8	0.28	3.6	23	.041	2.0
Elk	312	161	58	3.8	0.12	2.7	23	.012	2.4
Pronghorn	339	180	49	3.2	0.17	3.1	26	.019	1.2
Moose	316	149	65	3.6	0.07	3.0	22	.008	2.8
Mourning dove[b]	323 (6)	252 (1)	64 (3)	5.3 (2)	0.32 (1)	4.3 (2)	31 (3)	.043 (2)	0.64 (11)
Chicken	297	180	42	4.7	0.01	0.6	28	.002	0.52
Pheasant	334	219	50	5.1	0.04	1.2	32	.048	0.64
Sharp-tailed grouse	279	200	67	7.2	0.26	4.8	29	.040	0.73
Sage grouse	349	226	57	5.3	0.21	4.1	31	.035	0.71
Gray partridge	364	223	43	4.7	0.17	2.7	32	.031	0.66

[a] Mammal samples = longissimus muscle; avian samples = breast muscle.
[b] Numbers in parentheses represent rank among the 13 meat animals listed.

Whatever the cooking method, the more care you take in preparing doves, the better they will taste. In addition, a careful selection of appropriate, well-prepared, eye-pleasing side dishes served in a pleasant setting will greatly enhance the dove dining experience. Two to four doves is an average serving (more in a hunting camp).

SOUTHWESTERN DOVE RECIPES

Deep-fried Doves

A favorite at south Texas hunting camps (contributed by Horace Gore of Austin, Texas). Pick, dress and rinse whole doves. Cut a 1-inch (2.5-cm) slice in dove breast lengthwise on both sides of breastbone. Shake two or three drops of hot sauce in cuts. Let doves marinate 30 minutes. Roll in flour, salt and pepper. Deep fry in vegetable oil until dove floats. Drain and serve with hot bread, cream gravy, pinto beans and cold beverage.

Brochet de Palomas

A favorite at Mexican hunting lodges (contributed by Bob Tonkin of Brownsville, Texas). Skin, fillet and rinse dove breasts. Marinate fillets in sweet pickle juice (or Italian salad dressing) in refrigerator for several hours. Place a slice of Monterey Jack cheese (or Swiss cheese) on fillet. Wrap fillet and cheese tightly with bacon strip and pin with stainless steel skewer. Skewer fresh or pickled jalapeño pepper slice. Skewer fresh onion slice. Repeat this sequence until all fillets are used. Grill slowly over mesquite coals until bacon is crispy brown. Serve with hot bread, salad and cold beverage.

Doves Stroganoff

The best all-around way to serve doves (contributed by Ron Engel-Wilson of Phoenix, Arizona). Skin, fillet and rinse 24 dove breasts. Pat fillets dry, shake in flour and brown in pan with very little oil. Add 2 tablespoons of flour and brown. Add ½ cup of milk to pan; stir. Add 2 cups of sliced onions; stir. Cover and reduce heat. When onions are soft, add 1 pint of sour cream; salt and pepper to taste. Cover; simmer 30 to 60 minutes. Add more milk if it gets too thick; stir to keep from sticking. Serve over rice, biscuits or bread.

Stewed Doves in Giblet Gravy

For a country breakfast treat (contributed by Herb Kothmann of Austin, Texas), place 12 picked and cleaned mourning doves, along with hearts, livers and gizzards, in a deep saucepan. Cover with water and add 1 large onion (chopped) and 3 sticks of celery (chopped). Bring to a boil on medium heat; then add 1 stick of margarine and season liberally with salt and black pepper. Cover and cook on low heat for 2 hours or until the meat separates from the breastbone. Serve in a shallow bowl, with plenty of bread for sopping gravy. This dish lends itself well to refrigeration and reheating.

Chapter 26

Hunting in the South

Dan M. Russell
Division of Wildlife
Kentucky Department of Fish and Wildlife Resources
Frankfort, Kentucky

"Opening week of the dove season in southern states is a blend of family reunion, lodge picnic, an old-style barbecue, and a Juarez election" (Madson 1978: 46).

EARLY YEARS OF DOVE HUNTING

I saw only the last traces of old-time dove shooting, but I heard a lot about it. Big shoots were a tradition in the South, with few laws governing the season or bag limit. For that matter, no laws governed the method either, though custom as well as necessity dictated the use of shotguns. The take was limited only by the number of shells on hand or how long one could keep shooting before his arm got too sore. "Mostly it depended on the latter—how much bruising the arm could take—because only the fairly well-to-do could afford this kind of shooting" (Russell 1974: 95).

George Moore (personal communication: 1986), a native of the Deep South and former dove biologist with the Alabama Department of Conservation, recalled many aspects of dove shooting in the old days. According to his recollections, there was little grain grown in the Deep South prior to the late 1940s. Most corn was hand picked, and livestock were turned into the fields to glean any waste grain, leaving very little feed in the fields for doves. Following the harvest, landowners (mostly absentee) had their farmhands plant small patches of caraway or bene (sesame) to attract doves for shooting. Mourning doves were attracted to these

food patches despite the shooting because they represented the only food available. Moore also recalled shooting over peanuts, and in small isolated areas of the coastal plain, burned-over fields of volunteer bullgrass attracted large numbers of doves.

In the upper South where I worked, I heard tales of the large flocks of doves that came into the fields of hemp, or marijuana as it is better known now. Before its drug effects were widely known, hemp was grown for the manufacture of rope. The doves did not disappear with the hemp but simply took advantage of other food sources in the region. Dove shoots occurred over harvested wheat fields, cornfields cut for silage, or millet/soybean fields cut for hay.

A dove shoot in those days (pre-1950s) was often the main event for a social gathering and not an everyday affair. For this kind of shooting, most hunters took a case of shells and a farmhand to load one gun while the gunner shot another. It was quite common to find a shoot with fifty to a hundred hunters in the field. The number of doves taken during some of the larger of these affairs seems incredible when compared with the dove shooting of today. G. Moore (personal communication: 1986) recalled hearing of one shoot where more than 10,000 doves were killed in one day. He reported another shoot near Mobile, Alabama, where the low shooter killed 110 doves and shot one case and four boxes of shells. In the biggest shoot I recall, more than 3,000 doves were killed by some three hundred hunters in the course of a day.

The fabled big shoots for mourning doves in the Deep South were changed forever by an expansion of grain farming, which served to disperse the dove population, and by bag limits based on scientific data. Mass production of the pump shotgun in particular and improved shot shell technology also put the expense of recreational shooting within the means of more than just the wealthy. Nevertheless, much of mourning dove hunting in the South remains steeped in tradition, both social and recreational. Modern hunts often are preceded by or concluded with some type of feast, such as a barbecue. *Left illustration by A. Lassell Ripley; photo courtesy of the Library of Congress. Right photo by Ralph E. Mirarchi; courtesy of the Auburn University Department of Zoology and Wildlife Science and the Alabama Agricultural Experiment Station.*

PRESENT-DAY DOVE HUNTING

In the late 1940s, state and federal wildlife agencies began or accelerated formal studies of mourning dove biology and management. Knowledge of this species has improved considerably over the years as more sophisticated techniques of monitoring population levels were developed and implemented. Season lengths and bag limits now are based on sound biological data, and hunting is more closely regulated. Compliance with regulations also has improved. In a two-year study based on clandestine observations of 112 mourning dove hunters on two public hunting areas in Virginia, Bromley et al. (1989) reported safety was a problem but legal violations were rare.

Land-use practices throughout the South also began to change during the late 1940s and early '50s. Farms and fields became larger and fewer as farm acreage was consolidated to provide more land for the more efficient farming methods and machinery being developed. Changes in farming practices and land use altered certain hunting traditions and fostered new attitudes toward the sport. It was no longer a normal or necessarily welcomed part of the sequence following the agricultural harvest. Open invitations to come to the farm and hunt began fading out. Leasing land for shooting and fee hunting are increasingly common practices throughout the South.

THE DOVE HUNT

Mourning dove shooting does not seem to have changed much since I wrote on the subject nearly twenty years ago (Russell 1974). The opening day of dove season still is a time-honored tradition in most southern states. Somewhere around the first of September, carloads of dove hunters will be heading into the country despite afternoon temperatures that may approach 100 degrees Fahrenheit (38° C). Favored shooting areas in early September are harvested small grainfields and farm ponds. Hayfields or other fields where standing crops are interspersed with seed-bearing weeds, ponds, creeks, rivers and sloughs also will attract doves and dove hunters. The size of the area chosen and number of hunters in a party is a matter of personal preference. It is quite common, especially early in the season, to find fields with fifty or more shooters participating in a dove shoot; it is equally as common to find a lone shooter or a pair at the edge of a field or pond taking doves passing over or coming to water.

Shooting over Feeding Fields

Once a flock of mourning doves begins feeding in a field of wheat stubble, sorghum, millet or corn cut for silage, the birds will continue to use the field until shooting pressure or a sudden snap of cooler weather causes them to move on. Most hunters are aware of the possibility of overshooting a field and try to alternate shooting sites to provide the doves a respite—and thereby extend shooting. Doves usually will gather on telephone wires, power lines or trees near a feeding field before they begin feeding. An observant hunter uses such gathering places to locate feeding fields before opening day.

Doves usually feed in the morning and "lay up" in the woods and thickets during the hot part of the day. Sometime during mid to late afternoon (3:00 to 4:00 P.M.), doves will fly out to feed again. After feeding, doves often go to water before heading for roosting sites in late evening.

Dove hunters will station themselves in the fencerows, under trees or even in the middle of a field, using whatever cover is available. A few corn-

The tailgate of a vehicle can provide a convenient "station" from which to hunt mourning doves, since the vehicle provides a degree of obscurity, and shot shells, drinking water, snacks and other equipment can be stored close at hand. However, tailgate shooting necessitates an extra degree of caution in handling firearms, and most states do not allow loaded guns in the vehicle at any time (even between lulls in shooting). Also, for safety and legal reasons, mourning doves should never be hunted from a vehicle parked on a public road. *Photo courtesy of Remington Farms, Chestertown, Maryland.*

stalks or tall horseweeds pulled together will work as a makeshift blind. A simple rule for the hunter to follow is to break up his outline and not move until the bird is within range. If the hunter can restrain himself, watching the doves flying and "working" the field for a few minutes before entering the field to shoot can work to his advantage. The hunter should select a spot with the sun at his back and use some cover but not such that it deters visibility and reasonable shooting motion.

Blinds for mourning dove hunting can be makeshift or elaborate in the manner of a duck blind depending on the shooting site, extent of natural cover and the primary direction (flight lane) from which the doves will approach. The ideal blind allows for hunter visibility in all directions, obscures the hunter's outline and is at least partially shaded. "Staking" a blind is a good practice. It involves setting out flags or stakes at regular intervals (e.g., every 90 degrees) and 35 to 40 yards (32 to 36.6 m) from the blind to serve as reference points of shot range and benchmarks for marking downed birds. Like most other gamebirds, mourning doves get progressively warier during the hunting season, so the hunter who is well camouflaged and motionless is likely to get the most shooting opportunities. *Photos by Charley Dickey.*

The hunter also should mark out an effective shooting distance and keep shots within that range. Once he is situated, the hunter should sit still—doves pay limited heed to a motionless human form.

Water Hole Shooting

Almost any water that has a weed- or grass-free rim or bank may be used by doves. In late summer, farm ponds usually have a low water level and mud-flat perimeter and are preferred watering sites for mourning doves. A rim of small dove feathers at the edge of water is a telltale sign that doves are using a particular watering hole. "Doves seem to prefer scummy, dirty-looking ponds and brackish water" (Russell 1974: 108), but clean, bare ground to land on and walk to the water.

Roost Shooting

When doves head for the roost, daylight is fading, and a "sunset" quitting time by the clock on a cloudy day makes it very near dark. It is dark enough, anyway, to see the fire out of the end of the gun barrel and dark enough to make a shooter duck down to see the dove above the skyline. The poor visibility and frantic shooting at this time result in a high crippling rate and many of the doves that fall dead are never found. Doves become confused when cut off from their usual roost site, and darkness often prevents them from going elsewhere to roost. If forced to roost on the ground or in an unfamiliar site, doves are more vulnerable to predators than they would normally be.

I only mention roost shooting to emphasize the waste. It is a poor sport and not good management to allow it. In all fairness to dove hunters, I have noted that many pass up roost shooting, preferring to leave a little daylight for the doves to get to their roosts. Most of the dove hunters I have questioned prefer to stop shooting a half hour before sunset rather than wait out those last few minutes before legal quitting time.

Pass Shooting

Some of the best dove shooting is with birds on the move to and from feeding fields or watering sites. Doves loaf a lot, but when they fly, they move fast and often erratically. Add a bit of wind and a few random shots and doves can provide a true test of wingshooting ability. I recall once shooting at

Water hole shooting for mourning doves is very popular in the South. Note in this scene (1) the well-constructed blind, (2) the water hole with gradually sloped sides and bare bank, (3) the open retrieval area around the blind and (4) decoys placed in a bare tree, near the water's edge and on the bank. *Photo by Charley Dickey.*

Most shooting at mourning doves involves head-on overhead or angled passing shots, and the speed of doves at those angles is difficult to judge, especially in windy conditions. Shooting is best and safest when the sun is at the hunter's back. A common mistake is for dove hunters to wait until the quarry is too close, restricting barrel swing. This forces an awkward swing and sighting and minimizes the shot pattern. On the other hand, commitment of the hunter too soon may cause the bird to flare before a reasonable shot is possible. Shotgunners who learn to swing through their targets typically have the best success with mourning doves. (Incidentally, if the hunter on the left drops doves in the dwarf palmetto, he is going to have difficulty finding them.) *Photos by Charley Dickey.*

high birds in a high wind. With what I thought was a proper lead, I pulled on the first bird and knocked down the third dove in line, at least 20 yards (18.3 m) behind the bird I was shooting at. Which brings up the question of leading. What is the proper lead to use on mourning doves? That is as debatable as the questions of best gun type, shot size and barrel length. The old-time dove hunters who say "swing and follow through" are the most consistently proficient shooters I have watched.

Identifying Doves in Flight

Hunters can learn quickly to identify mourning doves in flight. Doves appear gray or gray-brown on bright days, but they can look almost black in poor light. The wings appear darker than the body. The dove is much slimmer than a pigeon, with narrower wings and a long, tapered tail. Dove hunters are familiar with the soft whistle of air through the primary feathers when a dove flushes or flies by. The mourning dove carries itself with steady, powerful and rhythmic wingbeats. Although the wingbeats are steady, the flight path is often erratic, twisting and evasive. The speed and agility of this species always is amazing to a new dove hunter, especially one who has observed only the hesitant, timid movements of doves nesting in the backyard. Wild-flying doves in a good stiff wind power-diving through a cordon of shooters are aptly called "gray bullets"—they present a challenge even to the most adept wingshooters.

During the excitement of a dove hunt, wing-shooters should never forget that there may be other similar-sized birds on or over a dove shooting field. Every year the media carries stories about American kestrels and other nongame birds shot by careless dove hunters. The best advice is: if it doesn't fly like a mourning dove or otherwise look exactly like a mourning dove, it probably isn't a mourning dove. All hunters have legal, ethical and moral obligations to be certain of their targets *before* they shoot, not just because of possible legal ramifications or because of triggering media or public misperceptions of hunters and hunting, but primarily because such shooting damages valuable nongame resources.

Guns, Shells and Shot

Any make and model of shotgun can be used to hunt doves in the South. Single-shots, over-and-unders, doubles, semiautomatics and pumps in all gauges and barrel lengths, with chokes from open cylinder to full, can be found with hunters at the shooting fields and water holes. Some hunters prefer single-shot shotguns, claiming they (the hunters) perform better knowing they have only one shot at a bird. A single-shot shotgun often is given to youngsters and beginning shooters for safety and to develop shooting skills. Various shot sizes are used too—from #9 skeet loads to high-brass 4s. For youngsters and others just taking up shooting, good results come with light loads in any gun choked to throw a wide pattern. Such shells produce better success and less shoulder bruising.

Average success of five to nine shots per bagged bird attests to the difficulty and amount of shooting common to a mourning dove hunt. Accordingly, the hunter should use a gun that "fits" in terms of its stock length, comb or drop, weight, trigger pull, barrel length, recoil (gauge) and sight field. A gun that slides on a dove hunter's shoulder or is otherwise uncomfortable invariably produces colorful bruises but few birds in the bag. *Photo by Charley Dickey.*

The most rational discussion on dove shooting that I ever listened to focused on how to select shots—knowing where the dove is in relation to the capability of your gun. A shooter with a more open-choked gun should let his doves come into close range; a shooter with a tight-patterning gun must learn how to lead birds at a distance. Some dove hunters seem never to miss; others hardly ever hit. There is a knack to fast-paced wingshooting—some learn it the first trip out, while others never catch on. Reading the advice of shooting experts is helpful, but practice is the best teacher. And where, other than while mourning dove hunting, can one try out all types of wingshooting, shotguns and shot shells in a single afternoon?

Clothing, Decoys and Retrievers

For mourning dove hunting, it is best to wear something drab—khaki, dark green or almost anything dark. Use of camouflage hats, suits, jackets and netting is helpful. This type of clothing and sitting still until the dove is within range are a productive combination.

Decoys do work, whether they are hand-cut, tar-paper silhouettes or the high-priced commercial versions available in sporting goods stores. Years ago, when I first heard about dove decoys, I could not see much point in trying to decoy birds that naturally drifted in over the shooters anyway. In most situations, decoys are unnecessary. But if a hunter wants to get by himself away from a crowded field or pull doves in off a flyway or make them circle over a position at the end of a field or pond, then decoys are reasonably effective. Decoys work when placed in trees and on fencerows or the ground. They are particularly valuable late in the season and may attract birds that normally would remain out of range.

Dogs can be used to hunt mourning doves if the hunter takes precautions to keep the dogs (especially long-haired breeds) cool and well watered. Most bird-dog breeds will retrieve doves, though some owners claim their dogs cannot stand the feathers, which come out very easily. Dogs often get a mouthful when picking up a dove and then have trouble spitting out all the feathers. Some dogs will not fetch game other than the type on which they were trained, and there are dogs (with and without pedigrees) that simply refuse to pick up a dove. A big shoot on a hot day can be rough on a retriever that is apt to get excited with all the shooting and birds in the air. Dogs should be kept under reasonable control, cool and provided with adequate water during the shoot. Good dogs can find a lot of "lost" doves and should be used more than they are.

Mourning doves are gregarious birds and can be drawn to or toward lifelike decoys or silhouettes strategically placed on fences, bare branches, open ground adjacent to feeding fields or mud flats next to water holes. *Photos by Charley Dickey.*

The sometimes frenetic pace of shooting and numerous opportunities for retrievals make mourning dove hunting ideal for working with and enjoying a canine companion. Careful attention to field care of dogs during mourning dove hunts in the South is essential. Handlers should be especially cognizant of the dog's susceptibility to spiked vegetation, snakes, ticks and dehydration. *Photo by Charley Dickey.*

Care of Doves Bagged

Some hunters field dress their doves, or at least eviscerate them, before leaving the field. In the case of a badly gut-shot bird, this early care can prevent the edible portions of the dove from being tainted by the contents of the entrails and other internal organs. The main purpose of on-the-spot field dressing is to promote cooling of the meat. How important this is depends, obviously, on the day's temperature, how the bagged birds are kept in the field and how quickly they are dressed and refrigerated.

Hunters may be required by law in some states to leave the head or wings intact on their doves, but this need not prevent immediate field dressing. Field dressing can be done quickly by making a cut through the skin at the rear of the breastbone, inserting fingers or a bird-knife hook to pull out the entrails, and then removing the crop. This process lets air circulate through the body cavity for relatively rapid cooling and ensures removal of the contaminating portions of the carcass. Some hunters

simply draw and skin their birds. Others claim that doves are tastier when cooked with the skin and the underlying fat left on. I prefer to pluck my doves if time allows. Still another way to dress doves is to remove the wings (as permitted) and shuck out the breast. Regardless of the method used to dress the bird for cooking, care in the field is essential. *And the birds must be kept cool.* Harvested doves should be kept in the shade or, better still, on ice in a cooler—but not in the water. Water removes the natural protection against bacteria and blanches and softens the meat (cf. chapter 25).

A practical and considerate technique of field dressing is to put the feathers and viscera in a sealed plastic bag and dispose of them properly after leaving the field.

Some hunters make the mistake of putting the birds or dressed meat in a plastic bag or airtight bag. This produces a "greenhouse effect"—cutting off air circulation, intensifying heat and holding in moisture. Under these conditions, the meat gets "ripe" in a big hurry, and such doves are understandably not welcome in the kitchen. If birds have to be carried in a bag, a brown paper bag that will allow air circulation and absorb moisture is recommended. Given proper care in the field and on the way home, mourning doves provide a rich, delicious meat for the table.

VALUES OF MOURNING DOVE HUNTING

What one person gets out of dove hunting is difficult for another to evaluate. How can one put a dollar value on the experience and satisfactions of a mourning dove hunt, regardless of the bag? What is it worth to take a shooting stand in a harvested grainfield alongside a special canine friend or with several other dove hunters, sharing the camaraderie, anticipation, excitement and splendor of a clear autumn day? Obviously, there is much more for the hunter than the handful of doves he or she may take home. If all the hunter departs with is a limit of doves, then he or she has missed the most and best that mourning dove hunting in the South—or anywhere—is about.

Neither the shooting nor the bag makes a hunt complete. A true hunter will recall, just as vividly as his shooting, how he sat back in a fencerow and watched a hot-weather whirlwind spin across the field and dissipate, releasing its load to float slowly back to the ground. Or he may recall how he became so absorbed in a squirrel and blue jay squabble going on in a nearby oak that he let several doves slip by him . . . there is always something.

For most hunters, the success of a mourning dove hunt is measured at least as much by fulfillment of intangible satisfactions as by shots fired or birds bagged. The companionship, antics, enthusiasm and skill of a hunting dog are hard to beat on any hunting trip. *Photo by Glenn D. Chambers.*

Later in the evening, when the shooting has tapered off, he may remain at his stand savoring the close of the day. In the quiet, he can sit and look up at the pink-bottomed clouds and the sky becoming a deeper blue. As the sun drops below the tree line, the hunter can feel the first chill in the evening breeze. A lone dove finishes feeding, picks up out of the field and comes winging over. The up-slanting rays of the sun spotlight its buff-gold breast and glisten off the underwings. The hunter watches the bird on its way to water hole or roost until it disappears from sight. It figured to be an older, wiser bird that waited to feed late. And it is wished well. It may be a contradiction, under such circumstances, after shooting at his kin all afternoon, that the late flyer is held in special regard and admiration. Perhaps it is just a symbol of the whole elusive, enthralling outdoor experience. And how can we measure that in terms of dollars and cents?

SOUTHERN AND SOUTHEASTERN DOVE RECIPES

General Kelley's Doves

A quick, no-mess, no-nonsense way to fix doves (contributed by Charles D. Kelley of Montgomery, Alabama). Pick, clean and rinse 6 to 8 doves. Put about a teaspoon of butter or margarine in the body cavity. Place doves breast up on a sheet of aluminum foil large enough to contain the birds with the edges turned up to hold liquids yet with enough foil to bend the ends back and form a tent over the doves. Add a generous amount of

Worcestershire sauce, soy sauce, lemon juice, salt and pepper. Completely close and seal the "tent" so that the roof is at least 2 inches (5 cm) above the dove breasts. Place in preheated oven and bake at 350° F (133° C) for 45 minutes or until fork-tender. This dish can be prepared in the morning, refrigerated, then baked in the evening for convenience. It should be served with rice, hot rolls or biscuits, vegetable and green salad.

Dove Breast Champignon

By Justin Wilson of Lacombe, Louisiana (Wilson 1990).

½ cup all-purpose flour
   salt to taste
   cayenne pepper (ground) to taste
10 dove breasts (well cleaned)
½ cup oil
1 cup onion (chopped)
½ cup fresh parsley (chopped)
1 cup red wine
1 T garlic (chopped)
1 cup mushrooms (chopped)
1 cup milk
   Louisiana hot sauce or cayenne pepper (ground) to taste
2 T strawberry, plum, blueberry or muscadine jelly or fresh berries

Season the flour with salt and pepper. In a large, high-walled frying pan, heat the oil over a medium heat. Dredge the breasts in the flour and fry each for 10 minutes or until golden brown, turning while frying. Remove the breasts to a plate when they are done frying. Stir the leftover flour into the frying pan and make a small brown roux. This whole process should take about 30 minutes. Once the roux is brown, stir in the onions and parsley, and cook until the onions are tender. Stir in the wine until a paste is formed. Add the garlic and mushrooms. Cook for 10 minutes. Stir in the milk and hot sauce to taste. Return the breasts to the frying pan, lower the heat and cover. Simmer, stirring occasionally, for 1 hour. Remove the lid and stir in the jelly. Serve over rice, mashed potatoes or pasta.

Dove À La Plaquemine

A south Louisiana favorite by Marian "Pie" Pendley of Baton Rouge, Louisiana (courtesy of Hugh A. Bateman).

14 to 16 doves
 1 clove garlic (chopped)
 4 ribs celery (chopped)
 5 medium onions (chopped)
 4 shallots (chopped)
 ½ bunch parsley (chopped)
 1 bay leaf
 1 can consommé
 2 sticks butter
7 to 8 slices bacon
 2 large cans mushrooms (with juice)
   salt, pepper and cayenne pepper (coarsely ground)
   gravy flour

In a large pot, put chopped celery, onions, garlic, shallots, parsley and butter. While ingredients are simmering over low fire, salt, pepper and cayenne the doves. Stuff each dove with a half slice bacon. Place doves in pot. Add both cans of mushrooms with juice, the can of consommé and bay leaf. Cover and cook on a low fire for 1¾ hours. Additional seasonings may be added as desired. Remove cover and thicken gravy with flour. Serve over wild rice.

Dove Pastry

Courtesy of Elizabeth Bolen of Wilmington, North Carolina.

 2 dove breasts
 4 T onion (chopped)
 4 T celery (chopped)
 2 T butter
 1 package refrigerator biscuits
 1 t Worcestershire sauce
 2 t mayonnaise
 ½ t salt
 ½ t pepper
   garlic powder

Bone breasts, giving four fillets. Sauté in butter with onion and celery; sprinkle in salt, pepper and garlic powder. Cook for 10 minutes. Set aside vegetables with drippings. On a cutting board, chop cooked fillets. Place in a mixing bowl with vegetables, drippings, Worcestershire sauce and mayonnaise.

On a lightly floured surface, roll out four biscuits into oval shapes ⅛ inch (0.3 cm) thick. Place one-quarter of mixture on lower half of one biscuit, fold over top half and seal edges closed (with a fork). Prick holes on the top. Repeat for other pastries. Place on a greased baking sheet and bake at 475° F (246° C) for 10 minutes or until golden brown. Serves four.

Mary Draper's Doves

By Georgia H. Hart of Columbia, South Carolina (Lumpkin and Coleman 1982).

12 doves
   salt and pepper
 ¾ stick butter
 1 T Worcestershire sauce
 1 cup water
 2 rounded T flour
   Kitchen Bouquet

Pick and clean doves. Salt and pepper and place breast down in heavy iron frying pan. Add butter, Worcestershire sauce and water. Cook covered over medium heat for 30 minutes and then turn to low heat for about 1½ hours or until tender. Lift doves out and place breast up in Pyrex serving dish, then slip under broiler to brown slightly.

To make thickening for gravy, add a little water at a time to flour in a teacup, stirring until you have a smooth, thin paste. Add thickening to liquid in frying pan to make gravy, using a small amount of Kitchen Bouquet, if necessary, to give color.

Dove/Broccoli Casserole

By Billy and Renee McCord of Charleston, South Carolina (Lumpkin and Coleman 1982).

 8 to 10 dove breasts
 2 pkg. frozen broccoli, chopped
 1 can (10¾ oz.) cream of mushroom soup
 ⅔ cup mayonnaise
 ½ cup milk
 ½ cup shredded Cheddar cheese
 1 T lemon juice
 1 t curry powder
 1 cup cracker crumbs
   salt and pepper

Boil dove breasts and remove meat from bones. Cook broccoli by package directions and drain well. Place broccoli in lightly greased 1½-quart casserole dish and cover with dove meat. Combine remaining ingredients except cracker crumbs, salt and pepper. Stir well and spoon mixture over dove and broccoli. Salt and pepper to taste and top with cracker crumbs. Bake at 350° F for 30 minutes. Serves six.

Chapter 27

Hunting in the Midwest

Richard K. Baskett
Wildlife Division
Missouri Department of Conservation
Columbia, Missouri

The family reunion, "ya'll come," southern-style dove hunting described by Russell (1974) and Madson (1978) leaks across state lines and into the Midwest. In Missouri's southeastern "bootheel," these southern-style openings certainly exist. The season opening is accompanied by considerable anticipation, and hunts are organized by families, communities and corporations. Shooting fields sometimes are leased. Hunts might include barbecues and cocktail parties. Motels in many bootheel towns are filled. In the last decade, with restrictive waterfowl seasons, several old-time (70- to 120-year-old) duck clubs in eastern Missouri have added managed dove hunting to traditional waterfowl hunting and plantation-style social amenities. However, such fanfare generally is not associated with the mourning dove season in Missouri north of the bootheel and is very rare elsewhere in the Midwest.

REGIONAL IMPORTANCE OF DOVE HUNTING

Regional differences in the importance of mourning dove hunting are tough to measure, but there is considerable evidence that regional trends occur (see *Figure 72*). Keeler (1977) reported that no midwestern or northern state estimated that its hunters averaged more than five mourning dove hunts per season, but the southern states estimated an average of more than five dove hunts per hunter per season.

Reduced interest in dove hunting as one goes farther north was reported by Madson (1978), who further noted that all the nonhunting states were in the North. Only about half of the northern states are open to dove hunting. In a 1987 survey (Texas Parks and Wildlife Department unpublished data), state dove biologists in all states that currently hunted doves were asked if dove hunting was considered a "warm-up" for later seasons or if dove hunting was an important activity in its own right. Only nine northern states reported dove hunting to be an important activity (*Figure 72a*). This means that in less than a third of the northern states, dove hunting is both allowed and considered an important hunting activity in its own right. In contrast, mourning doves were hunted in all southern states, and the activity was considered by all states to be important (*Figure 72a*). Seven midwestern states permit dove hunting, and biologists from only four of those states reported that mourning dove hunting was important.

Generally, mourning dove hunting in the Midwest does not approach its popularity in the South or Southwest, because not all Midwest states have seasons or their seasons are shorter, and seasons for other gamebirds—such as pheasants, quail, grouse, woodcock and waterfowl—tend to dilute interest. Where dove hunting is permissible in the Midwest, it is quite popular, although some hunters participate ostensibly to hone their "shooting eye" for later upland bird seasons. *Photo courtesy of the U.S. Soil Conservation Service.*

PLACES DOVES ARE HUNTED

It makes sense that dove hunters in the more arid West would tend to hunt over rangeland or near watering sites where doves concentrate to drink *(Figure 72c)*. Crop fields seem to be important dove hunting habitat in many areas but especially in the Southeast, where the states reported that more than 80 percent of their hunting occurred in crop fields *(Figure 72d)*. In the Southwest, the increased importance of water-hole hunting reduces the dominance of cropfield hunting. Midwestern biologists reported something in between.

The transition from cropfield hunting in the East to a combination of water-hole, rangeland and cropfield hunting in the West is apparent even within the midwestern states. The eastern half of the Midwest seems to hunt mostly crop fields (as in the South and East), and states in the western reaches of the Midwest hunt combinations of water holes, rangeland and crop fields in a pattern much like the western states.

The woodlots, pastures and croplands of the Midwest provide a vast mosaic of habitats used by mourning doves. Most of these habitats are on private agricultural lands, so much of the dove hunting occurs there as well. Crop fields, shelterbelts, and riparian and forest edges—as in other parts of the country—are favored sites for Midwest dove shooting. *Photo courtesy of the Missouri Department of Conservation.*

LAND, DOVES AND WEATHER

Midwest land use is dominated by agriculture, but there also is a diversity of habitat—cropland, range, hedgerows, prairies, riparian and upland forests, timbered draws, and cedar glades. In this mixture of cover types, doves have found an acceptable home. Some of the highest dove breeding densities in North America occur in the Midwest (Keeler 1977, Dolton 1989). The combination of excellent breeding habitat, high breeding densities and various cropland components attracts staging and wintering doves (Madson 1978, Chambers 1963) and creates the *potential* for good dove hunting.

Then there is the weather. For the first eighteen years of my life, I suspected some law set the mourning dove season to open on the first weekend after the first autumn cold front had moved all the doves out of the country. Madson (1978) suggested one explanation for the less-established dove hunting tradition in northern Illinois, namely, the doves' tendency to leave northern areas early in the season. Perhaps it is the potential for finding premigration concentrations of doves that has created a midwestern interest in dove hunting, and perhaps it is the frequent experience of losing these concentrations before the season opens that has restricted the development of a strong midwestern dove hunting tradition.

PRESEASON ACTIVITIES

In the South, many fields are managed for mourning dove hunting and hunts tend to be well organized (Russell 1974). This is less common in most of the Midwest, where dove hunting often is an opportunistic byproduct of agricultural practices. For midwestern dove hunters to find fields where doves are concentrated, they must scout. They begin scouting anytime from a month to a few days before the hunting season opening date. Fields attract the first attention. In the Midwest, these fields can be wheat stubble, sunflowers, cornfields cut for silage, ground tilled for winter wheat or perhaps early-harvested corn or soybean fields. These may be the most likely places to look, but every serious dove hunter has a story of an odd exception—the feedlot, land idled by harsh economic circumstances or federal farm programs, vegetable fields, and many more. I have even seen hunters jump shoot doves from watermelon fields in the Missouri bootheel, where doves were feeding on seeds left behind in melons broken during harvest. (Mourning doves make a distinctive

"thump" as they fly out of hollow Charleston gray watermelons.)

Scouting is what the name suggests: driving around or walking through likely fields and looking for doves in the field, in trees, in the air, and on wires and fences. There is no real trick or secret to scouting—anyone can do it. Madson (1978) suggested that early morning and late evening, when doves are most active, are the logical times to scout. I suggest that scouting is a good time to renew relationships with hunting buddies and landowners and to obtain permission to hunt discovered "hot spots."

For some, scouting may be their only preseason activity. For others, scouting is just part of the preliminaries. Some hunters consider dove hunting a warm-up for later seasons and other game, but many mourning dove hunters consider skeet, trap, sporting clays or just busting clay birds a warm-up for the dove season. I like this attitude. Not only are these hunters prepared for the dove season, but the philosophy of preparing for a season that is a prelude to later seasons can provide the hunter with about 11.5 months of hunting excuse per year. Madson (1978) suggested skeet shooting as the best dove hunting practice because the variety of shots involved most simulates a real hunt. Sporting clays may be even better. In any case, anything that gets the gun out of the closet and on the hunter's shoulder will help.

Another preseason activity often linked to shooting is reloading. Avid dove hunters, especially those who warm up on clay targets, realize that given the amount of shooting these activities provide, reloading is economical. Some reloaders go beyond mere economics and search for the perfect load.

Shooting clay pigeons before dove season may have started as a way to shoot better during the season, and reloading may have economic roots, but all the preseason activities—scouting, target shooting, reloading and others, such as dog training, reading about dove biology, involvement in conservation organizations, etc.—have become part of midwestern dove hunting. Many consider these preseason activities an integral part of the total hunting experience, but each can be an enjoyable pastime in its own right.

PUBLIC LANDS

Across the country, a great deal of mourning dove hunting opportunity is provided on public lands. The amount and type of dove hunting that occurs on public lands varies regionally, from state to state, and probably even within states. In 1987, wildlife biologists from each state indicated there was relatively little use of public land in southern states, heavy use in the western states and something intermediate for the midwestern states *(Figure 72b)*. Of course, there is more public land in the West, so it makes sense that use of public land there would be higher.

Sprinkled throughout the Midwest are locations that are good for dove hunting. There, and in marginally "good" land where managers plant and manipulate a wide variety of crops and natural foods to attract doves, excellent dove hunting fields are established. The intensity of this management and success of the effort dictate just how much hunting pressure occurs. I am sure that these techniques are used to some extent in many states, but there seems to be a concerted effort in the Midwest. I have seen exceptionally productive dove shooting fields in Kansas, Illinois and Missouri. I have also witnessed the tremendous public use these intensively managed areas can provide.

Although most midwestern dove hunting occurs on private land *(Figure 72b)*, much of this relates to opportunity. Those public areas in the Midwest that provide dove habitat and hunting opportunity year after year develop more consistent dove concentrations and hunting pressure. This use of public (generally state-managed) wildlife areas for dove hunting is not unique to the Midwest, but it may be more common in this region than in others.

PRIVATE LANDS AND LANDOWNER RELATIONSHIPS

The relationship between hunters and landowners is an especially important component of Midwest mourning dove hunting. Most Midwest dove hunting is on private land *(Figure 72b)*, but seldom is it associated with organized shooting systems so common in the South. The key to Midwest dove hunting, therefore, may be the establishment and maintenance of good relationships with private landowners.

As good landowner relationships represent the key to Midwest dove hunting, respect is the key to those relationships. This respect begins with making sure that you obtain permission to be on the land. The agreement that allows access can be viewed as a contract. Make sure that both parties clearly understand the contract. Does it include the entire farm, the entire season, other hunters (friends), where to park? These are examples of possible points of conflict that should be discussed

in advance. Advising a consenting landowner of arrival and departure times and giving a description of the vehicle(s) used are simple but important information to convey. At the very least, it is a courtesy due the landowner.

Once on the farm, all property should be respected. Don't litter, including with shell cases. It may not matter as much if you shoot once at a turkey or a half dozen times at quail. But if you shoot a couple boxes at mourning doves, it is important. Livestock, fences and gates, as well as buildings, farm equipment and crops, should be considered. An open gate or damaged tractor is an easy way to end a dove hunter/landowner relationship. The relationship with landowners can be a very rewarding part of hunting; if the privilege is abused the landowner can and likely will end the relationship, and the hunter will be out of a hunting spot. More importantly, a landowner may react by closing his property to all hunters, and the entire sport suffers as a consequence.

Each year in the Midwest, hundreds of thousands of acres are closed to hunting through the negligence and insensitivity of a very few hunters. Landowners are well within their rights and, given liability statutes, are justified to be cautious about allowing recreational access. Even the threat of potential trespass or damage can cause some landowners to restrict or eliminate hunter access. It behooves all hunters to conduct themselves on private land as they would wish others to treat their valued property. Such behavior is common sense, and while it is good for the resource, it is essential to the continuation of the sport of mourning dove hunting in many areas, not just in the Midwest.

THE MIDWEST HUNTER

Removed from the field and away from the vegetation and geography of the Midwest, midwestern mourning dove hunters are similar to those from other regions. They wear much the same clothing, own the same models and gauges of guns and types of shells, possess similar folding stools or buckets—and many yell universal commands and castigations at their dogs.

Shuffled and returned to dove hunting in other regions of the country, midwestern dove hunters would easily recognize their sport. The basics of pass shooting, jump shooting or still-hunting near food, water or roost sites are the same. In shooting fields, these hunters would see some variety in crops, but the essential characteristics of the fields (abundant small seeds scattered on relatively bare ground) are the same. Although habitats differ

Virtually all hunting techniques employed to hunt mourning doves in other regions also are used in the Midwest, but midwestern dove hunters seem to have a slightly greater proclivity for jump shooting than do hunters elsewhere. This may be due to a relative lack of dove hunting tradition, weather more conducive to midday ambling and greater game species overlap. *Top left photo courtesy of the Illinois Department of Conservation. Top right and lower left photos by Craig Bihrle; courtesy of the North Dakota Game and Fish Department. Lower right photo by R. A. Montgomery; courtesy of the Max McGraw Wildlife Foundation.*

from region to region, if a dove hunter sits on a cactus in the Southwest, a sandbur in the South or a honey locust in the Midwest, the results are pretty much the same.

The midwestern dove hunter is no less avid than dove hunters anywhere else. Wherever mourning doves and dove hunters concentrate, there is enjoyable hunting, and midwestern dove hunting is more like dove hunting in the South or Southwest than it is different.

DOVES AND THE YOUNG HUNTER

Mourning dove hunting is a great activity for young people. It can combine lots of action with weather that is not as bitter and habitats not as brushy as with some later seasons. Youngsters can practice shooting skills with moving targets and reinforce good sportsmanship training, such things as marking down birds, controlling dogs, courtesy to other hunters and gun-handling safety.

Approved hunter education courses provide the best preparation for all young hunters. Now required in most states, these courses not only teach young people the safe way to handle a firearm but also provide background in conservation, respect for wildlife, and hunter responsibilities to the environment, landowners and other sportsmen. Required or not, a hunter education course should be viewed as an absolute necessity for all young persons being introduced to hunting of any kind.

Much ado is made by veteran hunters about the best type of shotgun for mourning dove hunting, the best choke and the best shot load. In the end, the choice is a matter of personal preference tempered by economics. For beginning or young dove hunters, these same determinations are somewhat less arbitrary.

As noted in chapter 25, most novice hunters advisedly should begin with a 20-gauge. A .410 or 28-gauge has less recoil, but their shot patterns tend to be too restrictive, and constant missing may prove discouraging. Lower gauges (16 or 12) may have too much recoil or be more heavy than comfortable.

Single-shot shotguns are satisfactory for dove shooting by young hunters. As a youngster, I struggled with a single-shot; its external hammer scared me considerably. The young hunter needs always to be conscious of safety but need not be distracted by it. My fear of that firearm was not unjustified—about 80 percent of self-inflicted gunshot wounds by Missouri hunters involve open-hammered guns (R. D. Staton, Jr. personal communication: 1990). Single-shot shotguns, of course, permit only one shot, and this too can be a learning liability. With the option of a second shot, the inexperienced hunter can better learn to follow through on the swing at a flighted dove. It also enables a follow-up shot at a wounded bird that otherwise might escape. The two main benefits of a single-shot firearm for mourning dove hunting by novices are safety (except with external hammers) and necessary optimal shot selection.

Many of the best wingshots and proficient hunters I know were first exposed to shooting (under hunting circumstances) by being permitted only a single shot, either in the chamber or magazine, regardless of the type of shotgun. The objectives of teaching safety and optimal shot selection are convincingly learned in this manner. As young hunters gain experience, they can progress to multiple-shot capability.

Today, nearly all the sporting firearms manufacturers produce multishot shotguns (pump, semiautomatic and double-barrel) of standard gauges yet sized for youngsters. The "fit" of a shotgun, in final analysis, is more important than style, gauge and choke for the beginner in terms of safety, shooting success and other enjoyment factors. Shotgun weight and barrel length also are important variables. For youngsters, a shotgun weighing 7.5 pounds (3.4 kg) or less with 26-inch (66 cm) barrels may be most suitable for handling comfort and ease of swing.

It used to be that mourning dove hunters who also hunted waterfowl or pheasants or other upland wildlife needed several shotguns to accommodate different chokes. With the advent of polychoke adapters and screw-in choke tubes, many shotguns are easily converted for different types of shooting. Mourning dove hunters—veterans as well as novices—invariably opt for open chokes, which give the widest possible pattern.

Along with an open choke, a high shot size with low brass (#7½, 8 or 9) provides the best results, because more pellets are used in a relatively wide pattern. Many veterans use 8s or 9s for their initial load(s) and a 7½ or 6 as the final shot. For youngsters, straight 8s or 9s are best. For a good discussion of shot shells and other ballistics considerations, Dalrymple's (1949) chapter appropriately titled "Shooting the Breeze" is a good reference.

Mourning dove hunting lends itself to coaching of a young hunter by an experienced gunner. They can sit together, and between "action" the adult can impart advice and experiences that will benefit the sport's newcomer—such as how and where to sit, how to reload safely and efficiently, how to carry a shotgun in the field, how to lead a passing bird, how to position one's feet for shooting, how best to mark down and search for shot birds, what to look for in terms of safe shooting "field," when to shoot and myriad other pointers. Coaching when doves are in the air is equally valuable: "Sit still. Get your gun up. Stay still. Now release the safety. Lead the bird and swing through. Now!" The closeness enables the coach to correct the student's poor shooting technique or deliver a pat on the back. It introduces the youngster to the sense of camaraderie that is a special and significant bond among most hunters.

Wounded mourning doves have a tendency to secret themselves under vegetation. Because of their markings and earth-tone coloration, even dead doves can be difficult to locate. Crippling losses estimated at about 25 to 30 percent can be reduced to nearly zero by use of trained retrievers. *Left photo by Charley Dickey. Right photo by Charles W. Schwartz.*

Few hunting experiences can provide the novice with better exposure to the "dos" and "don'ts" of shooting, through the attention and example of a veteran hunter, than can a shared dove hunt. And such exposure is a necessary hallmark of the next generation of hunter conservationists.

DOVE HUNTING SAFETY TIPS

The Missouri Department of Conservation's (1984) *Hunter Education Student Manual* contains "Ten Commandments of Firearms Safety."

1. Always keep the muzzle pointed in a safe direction.
2. Treat every firearm as if it were loaded.
3. Always make sure the firearm is unloaded and keep the action open except when actually hunting or preparing to shoot.
4. Be sure the barrel and action are clear of obstruction and that you have proper ammunition for the firearms you are carrying.
5. Be sure of your target before you pull the trigger.
6. Never point a firearm at anything you do not want to shoot. Avoid all horseplay with a firearm.
7. Never climb a fence or tree or jump a ditch with a loaded firearm.
8. Never shoot at a flat, hard surface or water.
9. Store firearms and ammunition separately.
10. Avoid alcohol and other drugs before or during shooting.

These commandments form the basis of safe firearm handling and use and apply to dove hunting as well. There also are special characteristics of dove hunting that deserve attention to keep a dove hunting trip safe. Because doves will concentrate, hunters will too. This potential for being close to other hunters should prompt dove hunters to:

- *Communicate.* Let others know where you are and determine where others are.
- *Plan ahead.* Once you have found "the spot" and determined where other hunters are, determine the swing limits of safe shots *and* what shots should be avoided. Madson (1978) observed that a typical dove load has a danger range of 300 yards (274 m). A shooting angle of about 30 percent inclination produces this maximum range. In most cases, it is simply best to avoid shooting at low-flying birds.
- *Limit movement.* When you find yourself in an area with several others, keep movement to a minimum. Continual movement will cause others to lose track of your location. If you do move, do it in open view or communicate verbally.
- *Keep your distance.* Establish and maintain spacing in the field. Safe spacing also is good sportsmanship.
- *Use safety equipment.* Safety glasses or goggles are a good idea for protection from stray pellets. Shooting can damage hearing. Some shooters who would not think of shooting clay birds without ear plugs will shoot boxes of shells at doves with no such protection. Modern hearing protection is inexpensive and comfortable and should be considered.
- *Prepare for the weather.* It can be hot during dove season. Bring plenty of water for everyone in the party (including the dog), and know and be alert for the signs of heat exhaustion. Protect yourself from the sun; sunscreen is an excellent option.
- *Realize that some traditions need to be broken.* If alcohol consumption is a traditional part of dove hunting for you or those with whom you hunt, perhaps it is time to reconsider the tradition. Mixing alcohol with hunting is a formula for trouble.

The vagaries of Midwest weather during the mourning dove hunting season can be more acute than in other regions of the country. In the Midwest, doves can be hunted in hot, balmy conditions one week and cold, freezing rain or snowy conditions the next. *Photo by Glenn D. Chambers; courtesy of the Missouri Department of Conservation.*

More often than not, a darting mourning dove can turn the hunter into a contortionist. Given the pace of dove shooting and the variety of shots taken, safety of the hunter and others nearby must be a foremost consideration. Hunters should practice their swing and gun balance by preseason trap, skeet and sporting clays shooting. In dove fields or blinds, shooters must determine before the start of a hunt the directions they *cannot* shoot, so as not to endanger other hunters or infringe on their shooting opportunities. *Top left photo by Ron George. Bottom left and top right photos by Charley Dickey.*

MIDWEST DOVE RECIPES

Doves in Mushroom Soup

Contributed by Dick Vaught of Columbia, Missouri.

30 dove breasts (marinated in milk)
 2 (10¾ oz.) cans cream of mushroom soup
 4 soup cans of milk (2-percent or skim)
     Salt and pepper to taste
     Flour for dredging

Marinate dove breasts for about 30 minutes in milk (save milk). Remove doves and, while they are still wet, roll in flour that has been seasoned with salt and pepper. After dredging in flour, set the breasts aside for 10 minutes or so to permit flour to adhere better to doves. Place dove breasts in a large skillet of hot grease (Crisco shortening seems to brown them better). Be sure each breast is fried to a golden brown. Remove the breasts and drain grease, leaving brown cracklings in skillet. Replace dove breasts and cover completely with mushroom soup and milk. Stirring frequently to prevent sticking, let simmer for at least an hour (or until meat slides from bone). When gravy is smooth, ladle over a bed of cooked rice or mashed potatoes.

Dove Jambalaya

Contributed by Jennifer Baskett of Columbia, Missouri.

Rub salt and pepper on 12 doves and brown them for about 10 to 15 minutes in a saucepan. Add 1 or 2 cans of chicken broth and simmer for 30 minutes. Remove doves and store on paper towels. Use broth to cook 2 boxes of brown rice. In a skillet, brown ½ pound of sausage and remove grease. Add ½ cup chopped onion, ½ cup chopped green pepper and a garlic clove. When onions are soft add 1 or 2 bay leaves, 1 tsp. chili powder, a pinch of thyme, ½ to 1 cup diced ham, 1 cup tomatoes and a can of tomato paste. Cook for 10 minutes. Mix rice and skillet contents and bury doves in a large roaster. Cook covered for an hour in an oven at medium heat. Especially good when served with corn bread.

Easy Grilled Doves

Contributed by Steve Young of Columbia, Missouri.

With toothpicks, pin about a third of a strip of bacon around dove breasts. Cook over a cool to medium fire for 20 to 30 minutes, but don't overcook. Sauce is optional.

Barbecued Doves

Contributed by Michael K. McCabe of Omaha, Nebraska.

Double up a large sheet of aluminum foil; turn up sides to create a pan. Put 1½ to 2 cups of barbecue sauce in base. Add spices to sauce as desired (e.g., minced onion, chopped garlic, garlic salt and 1 tsp. pepper). Preheat sauce for 5 minutes on grill over a medium fire of hickory chip coals. Add whole doves or dove breasts, lightly salted, to sauce, and pour ½ to 1 cup of sauce over the meat. Cover with aluminum foil. Grill for 10 to 12 minutes. Turn doves, spoon over sauce, re-cover and grill again for 5 to 10 minutes.

Chapter 28

Shooting Field Management

Richard K. Baskett
Wildlife Division
Missouri Department of Conservation
Columbia, Missouri

At first glance, the places where mourning doves are hunted appear to vary greatly—from peanut and millet fields in the South to cactus patches and irrigation ditches in the Southwest to harvested crop fields of the Midwest *(Figure 73)*. On closer examination, however, good hunting spots are not really that different. Waters (1983) noted the mourning dove has four basic habitat needs: food; cover; water; and gravel or grit. Consequently, mourning dove hunting occurs where doves feed, rest, find water and grit, and travel between these sites. The relative amount of hunting that occurs in each habitat type probably is related to "supply and demand." Water holes, roost sites and grit sources certainly provide hunting opportunities, but the most hunted habitats in most states are feeding fields. Waters (1983) noted there frequently is a shortage of high-quality dove food during autumn and winter, even on areas to be hunted, and the best-known way of attracting mourning doves for hunting is to provide them with an abundance of choice food.

With proper management, practically any dove feeding field can be improved as a shooting field. R. A. Montgomery (personal communication: 1991), for example, observed that mourning dove hunting at the Max McGraw Wildlife Foundation in northcentral Illinois has been a tradition for more than twenty-five years. Prior to 1976, when the

Foundation's crop fields were not managed as "dove fields," hunting was merely attendant to normal cropping systems (i.e., winter wheat stubble, newly seeded wheat, corn silage fields), and the effective shooting days were few. When managed fields were established in 1976, hunter success and harvest "improved markedly," and the effective season length increased to two to three weeks.

FEEDING FIELD CHARACTERISTICS

Fields used heavily by mourning doves are most often characterized by an abundance of small seeds scattered on the surface of relatively bare ground with little horizontal cover. Feeding fields commonly are dominated by wheat, millets, sunflowers, corn or grain sorghum *(Figure 73)*. Peanuts, buckwheat, barley and annual rye also will attract doves. Historically, sesame and hemp fields provided excellent feeding habitat for doves.

Mourning doves are opportunistic feeders and will use a tremendous variety of seeds of both natural and cultivated plants (see chapter 11). Korschgen (1958) identified 218 plant species used by doves in Missouri. Although grain crop seeds predominated, the "top 10"—totaling 90.5 percent by volume in the doves' crops—included weedy plant species, e.g., foxtails, croton and ragweed.

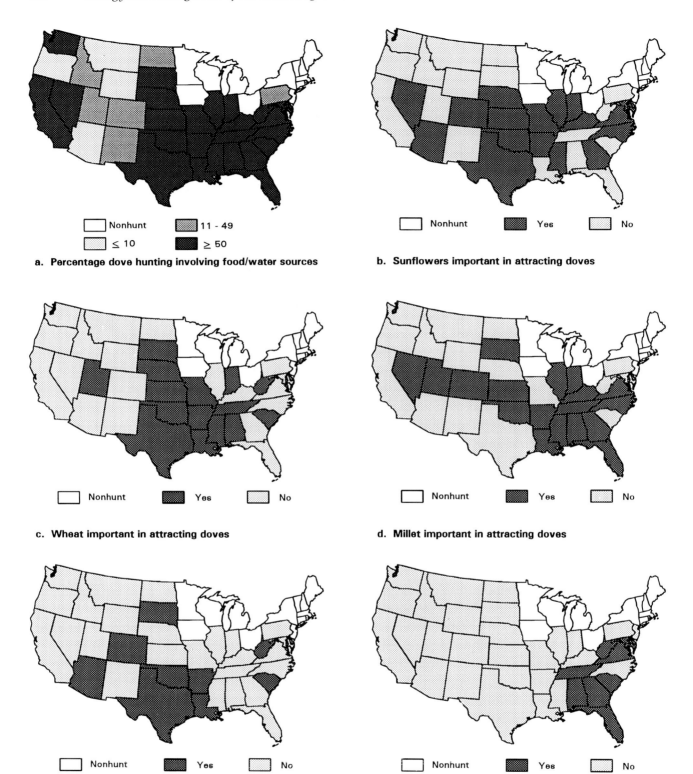

a. **Percentage dove hunting involving food/water sources**

b. **Sunflowers important in attracting doves**

c. **Wheat important in attracting doves**

d. **Millet important in attracting doves**

e. **Grain sorghum important in attracting doves**

f. **Corn important in attracting doves**

Figure 73. State wildlife agency responses to selected questions from 1987 questionnaire survey about the importance of food, water and specific plants grown or managed to attract mourning doves to public or private shooting fields in each state (Texas Parks and Wildlife Department unpublished data).

Historically, sesame fields were planted in small plots in the South to attract doves. In yesteryear, for the most part, sesame was not a commercial crop, because it requires fairly specific soil, temperature and moisture conditions to germinate and produce abundant seeds. However, sesame now is grown commercially on a small scale in parts of the South, particularly Texas. And where such plantings succeed, mourning doves are readily drawn to fields when the seeds are ripe and on the ground. Planting of any crop—whether sesame, corn, millet, wheat, sunflower, safflower or other—primarily for mourning dove feeding/shooting fields can be risky business. A variety of factors, particularly seed ripeness, influences the attraction to mourning doves of any crop. Maximizing seed production, careful timing of crop harvest, providing for bare ground and diversifying the crop plots or fields are the best hedges against crop failure or untimely growth. Agricultural and wildlife extension service agents can provide reliable suggestions on suitable crop types and planting schedules for most areas. *Photo by Ron George; courtesy of the Texas Parks and Wildlife Department.*

With so many food options, the presence of open or bare ground may be as important as availability of specific foods in determining the extent to which mourning doves will use a field for feeding.

Modern agricultural practices tend to provide these conditions in most cultivated fields. Clean cultivation of row crops, harvesting, haying, and grazing or "hogging" (harvesting with livestock) provide at least patches of bare or disturbed ground; shredding or discing of crop residues also provides a bare ground component in managed fields.

Other characteristics of feeding fields are of secondary importance. Doves will use fields of almost any size, although there is probably a minimum size capable of attracting large concentrations of birds; Waters (1983) suggested that management of fields smaller than 2 acres (0.4 ha) is impractical. The proximity of other habitat needs such as water, grit and loafing or roosting sites undoubtedly influences the attractiveness of larger fields to doves.

The key ingredient of feeding fields used by mourning doves is seeds on fairly open ground. The extent of use by doves is strongly influenced by field size, proximity to water, grit and roosting sites. "Loafing" trees near feeding fields also attract mourning doves to the vicinity. *Top photo (grain sorghum field) by Ron George; courtesy of the Texas Parks and Wildlife Department. Bottom photo courtesy of the Illinois Department of Conservation.*

MANAGEMENT OF FIELDS FOR DOVE SHOOTING

In general, shooting field management can be broken down into two major types: (1) fields specifically planted and manipulated to provide dove hunting; and (2) agricultural crop residues managed to provide suitable shooting field conditions *(Table 99)*. Managers of public land and private hunt clubs, farmers and dove hunters have developed methods and techniques to manipulate crop residues and specific plantings to provide the important combination of bare ground and abundant small seeds.

There are numerous plant species that can be used to attract doves. Although the list of the most attractive plants for doves has changed through the years, it has been more stable than the methods used to manipulate plantings. Accordingly, it is important to recognize that any management operation must be in compliance with state and federal regulations regarding baiting. Such regulations and the interpretation of them also have changed somewhat over the years (see also chapter 23).

A mourning dove shooting field typically is a crop field. However, any field that is somehow managed to enhance its attractiveness to doves (other than by illegal baiting) can be considered a shooting field. Such a field must possess at least one of the essential ingredients of dove habitat (food, water, shelter and some open ground) and be in proximity to others. *Right photo by Ray Margo; courtesy of the U.S. Soil Conservation Service. Left photo by Verne E. Davison; courtesy of the U.S. Soil Conservation Service.*

Table 99. Mourning dove shooting field management options with special plantings or manipulation of agricultural crop residues.

	Management options	
Seed crop	Special dove planting	Agricultural crop residue
Corn	Mow, burn, disc	Combine, cut silage, "hog," mow, disc, or burn stalks
Peanuts		Mechanical harvest, "hog"
Wheat	Fresh seed and mow, disc or burn when mature	Combine, burn residue, hay, lightly disc
Browntop, proso and other millet	Clean cultivate in rows, mow or lightly disc if broadcast	Hay, combine
Milo, higera, sorghum	Clean cultivate, mow, disc	Combine, hay, cut silage, shred or burn stalks
Sunflowers	Clean cultivate, mow, lightly disc	Combine
Watermelon		Leave broken melons, mow, disc
Soybeans	Clean cultivate, mow, lightly disc	Combine, hay
Hemp (historically)		Bale for rope
Sesame	Clean cultivate, mow	Harvest
Barley	Mow, lightly disc	Harvest, hay
Annual rye	Mow, lightly disc	Harvest, hay

Federal Baiting Regulations

Federal regulations describe and define baiting in relation to legal management. The *Code of Federal Regulations* (1987) (50 CFR 20 Subpart C Section 20.21 (i)(2)) permits "The taking of all migratory game birds, except waterfowl, on or over any lands where shelled, shucked, or unshucked corn, wheat or other grain, salt or other feed distributed or scattered as the result of bona fide agricultural operations or procedures or as a result of manipulation of a crop or other feed on the land where grown for wildlife management purposes: provided that manipulation for wildlife purposes does not include the distributing or scattering of grain or other feed once it has been removed from or stored on the field where grown."

Although local, state and federal baiting regulations may vary and interpretation of these regulations may be needed for individual situations, it seems that crops planted for wildlife or seeds occurring naturally can be manipulated in any manner on the site where they grew. But once a seed is harvested, it cannot be returned to the field and scattered.

It is the responsibility of the manager, farmer and hunter to be aware of all regulations that govern shooting field management. Some of the potential problems in interpreting baiting regulations are as follows:

1. *Changes in federal regulations.* In 1973, the federal regulations were liberalized to allow more manipulation of plants as part of management for migratory birds other than waterfowl. It is not unreasonable to assume that the regulations may be revised again. In recent decades, several national conservation organizations have promoted standardization of baiting regulations and their interpretation. All those involved in shooting field management should be cognizant of potential changes in existing regulations.
2. *Differences in baiting regulations for waterfowl and other migratory gamebirds.* Because baiting regulations for waterfowl are more restrictive than those for doves, a problem can exist in certain areas where both waterfowl and doves are hunted. The *Code of Federal Regulations* (1987) section describing waterfowl baiting (50 CFR 20 Subpart C Section 20.21 (i)(1)) allows "The taking of all migratory gamebirds, including waterfowl, on or over standing crops, flooded standing crops (including aquatic), flooded harvested croplands, grain crops properly shocked on the field where grown, or grains found scattered solely as the result of normal agricultural plant-

ing or harvesting." Therefore, waterfowl cannot be hunted in fields where crops have been manipulated by methods other than normal harvesting practices. Methods that are legal for dove fields, such as mowing, discing and burning unharvested crops, constitute illegal baiting for waterfowl.

Clearly, baiting regulations, with their potential for change and the differences in regulations for individual species, affect how people can crop, manage and use shooting fields.

Cultivated Crops for Dove Shooting Fields

Within the constraints of federal baiting regulations, raising and manipulating a wide variety of dove foods remains an important management tool. The following techniques and plantings are example of practices used to facilitate shooting field management in different parts of the country (*Table 99*).

Sunflowers in Illinois and Missouri. Illinois has an active dove shooting field management program on public land and on some private clubs as well. Sunflowers are the mainstay of Illinois dove management because they attract and hold doves. Even small patches can be very effective. Just across the Mississippi River, a St. Charles County, Missouri club harvested more than 1,400 doves from a 6.5-acre (2.6 ha) sunflower planting in 1989.

Madson (1978) described the planting method used by some Illinois managers as follows. After tillage and incorporation of 1.5 pints of Treflan per acre (2/ha) and 200 pounds (220 kg) of 12–12–12 fertilizer, managers use corn planters to sow sunflower seeds in rows. Sunflowers should be planted as early as possible after frost at a rate of 5 to 6 pounds per acre (5.6 to 6.7 kg/ha). The variety most often used in Illinois is Peredovick, a small, black-seeded sunflower with a 120-day maturity date. The sunflowers are left standing and doves feed on seeds that shatter on the ground. Several seed companies now have suitable sunflower varieties.

At the Max McGraw Wildlife Foundation in northcentral Illinois, five fields of 2 to 5 acres (0.8 to 2.0 ha) are planted to oil sunflowers (R. A. Montgomery personal communication: 1991). Wheat and millet have been planted in plots and strips, but sunflowers have been more consistent producers of high-quality dove fields. The McGraw fields are fertilized and seedbeds are prepared and sprayed with a pre-emergence herbicide at a minimum rate. Planting is completed by the second week of May. Seeds are drilled in 21- or 28-inch rows (53.3 or 71.1 cm) at rates of 6 to 10 pounds per acre (6.7 to 11.2 kg/ha). The sunflower fields are changed every three or four years, primarily for crop and weed management. Even with annual fertilization, the size of the plants and number of seeds produced declines after two or three years in the same field.

Sunflowers are not harvested at McGraw because the size of the fields does not permit a yield of a profitable crop and because, in a normal year, nongame birds (principally American goldfinch, house finch, blue jay, house sparrow and blackbirds) have consumed most of the seeds by mid-September. This is not considered a problem, since

Sunflower is an excellent and bountiful food plant for mourning doves and is widely used for shooting fields. Different varieties are adapted to the broad range of soil conditions, moisture regimes and growing seasons encompassed by the range of mourning doves. *Top left and bottom photos by Ron George; courtesy of the Texas Parks and Wildlife Department. Top right photo by Charley Dickey.*

the planting is intended for wildlife and income is not sought from the fields beyond that generated by dove shooting.

Missouri managers have had good success harvesting their own seed for sunflower planting the following year. The small area that is combined for seed also provides an area for doves to "pioneer" into the field. Bourne (1991) described a southern Illinois farm that creates bare soil adjacent to sunflowers by alternating twenty-four row strips of sunflowers with a similar width of winter wheat. After the wheat is harvested in summer, the stubble is kept disced. The use of Treflan (or other herbicides) helps maintain the bare ground essential to attracting large numbers of feeding doves. For managers who wish to reduce the use of chemicals on wildlife management areas, mechanical cultivation is an option. If mechanical cultivation fails to provide sufficient bare ground, managers can use mowing or light discing to make weedy sunflower fields more attractive to doves.

Milo, higera and grain sorghum in South Carolina. Milo, higera and other grain sorghums have been used as supplemental plantings to provide late-season shooting in South Carolina cornfields that had been harvested or hogged. Mahan (1978) suggested seeding rates of 6 to 8 pounds per acre (6.7 to 9.0 kg/ha) for milo and 20 to 25 pounds per acre (22.4 to 28.0 kg/ha) for higera and other grain sorghums. He also advised fertilizing with 400 pounds per acre (448 kg/ha) of 3–9–18. Mahan recommended a row spacing of 36 to 42 inches (0.9 to 1.1 meters) for best results. These plants mature in 90 to 120 days and therefore should be seeded sometime from April to June to provide mature seed by the opening of dove season. The crop should be harvested two weeks before the hunting season to permit sufficient time for doves to locate the field. Alternative management techniques include mowing, haying and light discing. A proportional crop harvest that begins before dove season and continues gradually can extend the availability

A 3- to 4-acre (1.2 to 1.6 ha) sunflower field at the Max McGraw Wildlife Foundation managed principally as a mourning dove shooting field. Several weeks before the dove hunting season begins, breaks no larger than 30 feet (9.1 m) are mowed to create strips of sunflowers approximately 100 feet (30.5 m) wide. Every 75 to 100 yards (68.8 to 91.4 m) or so, cross breaks are mowed to produce rectangular blocks of sunflowers. The mowed breaks provide some open and bare ground to attract doves, scatter seed on the ground, help in distribution and visibility of hunters, and primarily assist in marking down and retrieving shot mourning doves. *Photo by Robert A. Montgomery; courtesy of the Max McGraw Wildlife Foundation.*

of seed and subsequent use of the field by doves.

Browntop and proso (dove) millet in Alabama. Browntop and proso millet are two of the most common and universal crops used to attract doves to shooting fields. Waters (1983, 1986) provided excellent and detailed advice for raising these millets (and other crops) for dove management in Alabama. Browntop matures in 60 to 70 days; proso millet requires 70 to 80 days to reach maturity. Planting dates may vary from June 1 to July 15 for browntop and May 22 to July 15 for proso millet. Those dates can be determined with precision in order to provide mature seed two weeks before a field is scheduled to be hunted. Both plants can be broadcast or planted in rows, but rows are recommended because bare ground can be provided by cultivating between the rows. A seeding rate of 8 to 10 pounds per acre (9.0 to 11.2 kg/ha) is appropriate if planted in rows 36 to 42 inches (0.9 to 1.1 m) apart; a rate of 15 to 20 pounds per acre (16.8 to 22.4 kg/ha) is recommended if the millet is broadcast. If planted in rows, doves will use a millet field both before and after harvesting. If the millet is broadcast, some millet harvesting is recommended to provide bare ground conditions in the field. Managers use similar methods with German (foxtail) millet to provide dove feeding habitat in Missouri.

Wheat in Missouri. Wheat is a preferred dove food (Korschgen 1958) and often is used to attract doves for hunting on public land in Missouri. Wheat is unique in that it can provide attractive habitat for doves both when it is planted and after the seed matures the following year. Managers, however, should avoid the temptation to throw a little extra wheat on the surface after planting because this would constitute "baiting." Wheat can be planted in August, although most planting occurs in September. The early plantings provide browse for a variety of wildlife species, such as Canada geese. Dove feeding habitat is provided by discing fields in late July or early August. Wheat is seeded about two weeks prior to the dove season. It can be drilled at 1.5 bushels per acre (0.13 m³/ha) or broadcast at 2.0 to 2.5 bushels per acre (0.18 to 0.22 m³/ha). If broadcast, the wheat usually is covered by light discing or harrowing. Doves are attracted to these fields to feed not only on the uncovered and preferably untreated wheat but also on seeds of weedy annuals scattered by preplanting tillage.

In Missouri, the wheat harvest occurs in June or July. On areas to be used as shooting fields, some of the crop is left unharvested. Portions of the fields are harvested gradually to provide a continual food source for doves until the hunting season opens. Several methods are used to make this unharvested wheat attractive to mourning doves. The Missouri Department of Conservation (1989) uses prescribed burning to remove litter, create bare ground and make the wheat available to doves. If the unharvested wheat is relatively clean, it can be burned standing. If much green weedy vegetation is present, the field should be mowed with a sickle-bar mower and allowed to dry prior to burning. A wheat field should be ringed with a fire line at least 6 feet (1.8 m) wide. Burning can occur anytime from late July to mid-September, but ideal conditions are created if the burn takes place one or two weeks before the opening of the dove season. Burning should be conducted only under appropriate weather conditions, with temperatures of 65 to 80 degrees Fahrenheit (18 to 27° C), relative humidity of 35 to 50 percent and wind speed of 5 to 15 miles per hour (8 to 24 km/hour). Conditions outside these ranges may result in poor burns or slow, hot burns that destroy the seeds. In addition to burning, unharvested wheat can be made available to doves by discing, mowing or haying the field.

Wheat in Texas. Leave it to enterprising Texas cattlemen to figure a way to combine cattle, wheat, wild sunflowers and doves (Bourne 1991). In late autumn, fields of wild sunflowers are tilled. This scatters the sunflower seeds and prepares a seedbed for wheat. The wheat is broadcast in a mixture with fertilizer, and the mixture is worked into the soil. The wheat sprouts quickly and provides six to eight months of good-quality pasture. Sunflowers grow along with the wheat, and when cattle are removed from the pasture in late spring, both wheat and sunflowers are left to produce seeds. In years when grass grows in the wheat and sunflowers, cattle are put back on the pasture to remove some of the grass and scatter out more seeds. Finally, a rotary mower is used to mow all vegetation, scatter seed and uncover bare ground. This system has provided unique supplemental benefits to the farming operation.

Combining crops in Tennessee. Waters (1983) and Mahan (1978) suggested combining crops to improve dove habitat and hunting. This can increase the period of time that doves use a field or complex of fields and may reduce the chance of a complete crop failure that can occur with one crop. Bourne (1991) described a dove management system on a west Tennessee farm that uses millet, corn, sunflowers and winter wheat in the complex. The millet and sunflowers are cultivated specifically to provide dove habitat, and manipulation of the residue of other crops also provides dove habitat as a byproduct of regular farming operations.

Many other crops, including corn, hay, beans, barley and annual rye, are grown specifically for mourning doves. Their manipulation is similar to those described previously. Any of these crops can potentially provide excellent shooting field conditions if properly managed.

Manipulating Crop Residues to Provide Shooting Fields

Much of the mourning dove hunting in North America is done in or adjacent to harvested crop fields, and managing these fields to enhance feeding habitat for doves is a fairly easy and inexpensive proposition. Corn, sorghum, millet, peanuts and soybeans are just some of the crops that can be harvested and still provide excellent shooting opportunities during the dove season. Most harvesting methods, including silage chopping, conventional combining, picking, hogging and haying, all involve provision for open or bare ground with scattered seeds on the surface. Other management considerations that can improve the quality of a field for dove shooting include the following.

Timing of the harvest. Crop harvesting, as noted earlier, should be conducted one or two weeks prior to the opening of dove season to allow sufficient time for doves to locate and begin using the field in large concentrations.

Although sunflower fields at the Max McGraw Wildlife Foundation in Dundee, Illinois, are not harvested per se, as previously noted, the fields are "opened up" two weeks prior to the dove hunting season (R. A. Montgomery personal communication: 1991). Strips 30 to 100 feet (9.1 to 30.5 m) wide are mowed to form blocks of cover. Besides providing for bare ground in places, the strip blocks assist in the marking down and finding of shot doves and in keeping hunters safely spaced.

Scattered seed. The abundance and availability of seeds on the surface of a field is a key factor in the extent to which doves will use a field for feeding. Light discing, hogging or shredding stalks and remaining ears of corn, bean pods, peanut hulls or millet heads improves the potential of the field to attract doves.

Open or bare ground. The same activities that scatter seed can be used to create more open ground within the field. Burning of crop residues also provides the bare ground component important in attracting doves to shooting fields.

The Dollars and Cents of Feeding Field Management

Providing quality dove feeding habitat and dove hunting doesn't have to cost a lot of money.

Natural or artificial water sources can be improved for mourning doves and as dove hunting sites by assuring that there is open ground along portions of the bank and that the bank itself has lengths of shallow grade. *Photo by Craig Bihrle; courtesy of the North Dakota Game and Fish Department.*

Discing or mowing to bare the ground and scatter seed of natural vegetation and crop residues can cost as little as $5 to $10 per acre ($12.36 to $24.71/ha). Once fences and watering facilities are in place, the use of livestock to provide those conditions, locally known as "hogging," costs next to nothing. Burning of fields costs about $2 per acre ($4.94/ha) in Missouri (Missouri Department of Conservation 1989). Harvesting crops, cutting silage and bailing hay crops provide dove habitat with no costs above normal farming operations.

The cost of mourning dove management can be much higher, especially if plantings are for a commercial crop. At best, attempts to estimate the cost of producing commercial crops are subject to a wide variety of economic variables. Each crop has its own production cost associated with seed costs, planting techniques and other considerations. Corn, sunflowers and milo generally cost more to plant than do wheat or millet. But costs for each crop vary regionally and greatly depending on the level of management that is applied. The amount of fertilizer and pesticide used and the number of equipment trips across a field are most responsible for the variability.

As derived from Moore et al. (1988), Ervin et al. (1983) and conversations with farmers and other agribusiness people, ranges of production cost estimates are as follows: corn = $75 to $150 per acre ($185.33 to $370.65/ha); sunflower and milo = $40 to $125 per acre ($98.84 to $308.88/ha); wheat = $35 to $90 per acre ($86.49 to $222.39/ha); and millet = $25 to $55 per acre ($61.78 to $135.91/ha). None of these ranges includes irrigation costs. Fertilizer and seed costs also can change annually. Clearly, these ranges include "food plot" levels of management, with little fertilizer and pesticide and a willingness to accept lower production and weeds. The higher ends of the ranges are tending toward modern "high input/high yield" technology. Most, but not all, dove management costs probably are near or below the midpoint of these ranges.

Those who manage for doves on their own land or belong to hunting clubs know how costly raising crops can be. Those who are fortunate enough to be granted permission to hunt privately owned fields should take just a second to dwell on these costs. Farmers have a lot invested in these crops. They also have substantial investments in equipment and in the land itself, in both money and time. Hunters should recognize that hunting is a privilege. To hunt on private land is a double privilege, for it also involves consented "intrusion" on the owner's property, livelihood and lifestyle.

Management of Natural Vegetation

Fields of natural vegetation, mostly volunteer native annuals, can be managed for improved dove shooting. A short list of native annuals that are readily used by mourning doves and have potential in shooting field management include panicgrass, pigweed (Lewis et al. 1982), Carolina cranesbill, crotons, morningglory (Mahan 1978), barnyardgrass, common ragweed, pokeberry, Texas millet (Waters 1983), foxtails, cane, crabgrass (Korschgen 1958) and wild sunflowers (Bourne 1991). In any field where these or a wide variety of other plant species occur in densities sufficient to provide an abundant seed source, light discing, mowing or burning will attract doves. Soil disturbance prior to or early in the growing season will stimulate production of many seed-producing annuals.

Dove Management and the Farm Act

The 1990 Farm Act (Food and Agriculture Conservation Trade Act) contains both the Acreage Conservation Reserve (ACR), often called "setaside," and the ten-year Conservation Reserve Program (CRP). These programs provide many wildlife benefits. Mourning doves, too, can benefit from management of these "idled" lands—including perhaps 40 million CRP acres (16.2 million ha) and 10 to 30 million ACR acres (4.0 to 12.1 million ha) (E. W. Schenck personal communication: 1991).

Ground-nesting sites certainly occur on properly managed set-aside and on recently established CRP fields. Mourning dove feeding habitat and associated hunting potential can be enhanced where annual weeds and grasses are mowed, disced (on nonerodible soils) or burned in a timely manner after nesting seasons conclude.

Planting small-grain crops on set-aside normally is not allowed, but for landowners considering more intensive dove management, the Farm Act includes provisions for establishing such attractive wildlife food plots on ACR and CRP, although there are limits on the amount of such plantings on both. Using set-aside lands can reduce the cost of providing wildlife benefits, because management is applied to idled land instead of reducing the amount of "money crops." There also are incentives for landowners to establish trees and shrub plantings, including hedgerows and underbrush on CRP lands. These can provide important future dove nesting and roosting habitats.

Participation in these programs varies from state to state and county to county. Interpretations by county Agricultural Stabilization and Conservation Service (ASCS) boards and administrators also vary. Landowners are advised to contact local ASCS officials before instituting management measures to make sure that those actions do not jeopardize involvement in or payments from those valuable conservation programs.

MANAGEMENT OF TOXIC SHOT

Ingestion of spent lead shot by feeding waterfowl is recognized as a significant problem for waterfowl survival and production (Bellrose 1959, 1964, Sanderson and Bellrose 1986). Ingestion of spent lead shot also may be a problem for mourning doves (Locke and Bagley 1967, Lewis and Legler 1968, Buerger et al. 1986, see also chapter 12). Consequently, management of toxic shot may be necessary on some mourning dove shooting fields. Castrale (1989) reported that spent shot accumulated on the surface of the soil rapidly (in one hunting season) and remained until the soil was disturbed. To reduce the likelihood of lead shot ingestion by mourning doves, Castrale (1989) suggested plowing dove fields at the end of the hunting season, establishing postseason vegetation unattractive to doves, designing narrow—less than 165 feet (50 m) wide—shooting fields where spent shot will fall in sites unavailable to feeding doves, and using nontoxic steel shot instead of lead. Kringer et al. (1980) reported that #4 steel shot was effective for taking doves. In any event, care should be taken to prevent hunters from shooting toward each other across narrow fields.

In large fields subjected to heavy shooting over the course of a decade or more, "mining" to reclaim spent lead may be feasible and economical as well as environmentally responsible.

HUNTER MANAGEMENT

Proper shooting field management also involves management of hunts. By regulating hunter pressure, managers often can extend quality dove hunting on an area well into and perhaps throughout the season. Shooting field rotation is a practice used on some southern dove hunting areas. Also, both Mahan (1978) and Waters (1983) suggested that, by limiting shooting on managed fields in the South to once or twice a week, quality dove hunting can be sustained well beyond the initial days of hunting. This technique may not work as well on northern areas where doves tend to migrate early (Madson 1978, R. A. Montgomery personal communication: 1991).

Shooting pressure can be reduced by limiting the hours that fields are hunted each day. Madson (1978) noted that several states have regulations restricting dove hunting to specific times of the day.

Illinois restricts shooting hours during the dove season by enforcing a daily opening of 1:00 P.M. As a result of fifteen years of experience, one successful, privately owned hunting operation in southern Illinois permits dove shooting only between 2:00 and 5:00 P.M. (Bourne 1991). Special regulations on selected management areas in Missouri include afternoon closures.

The desired effect of these practices and regulations is to maintain dove concentrations in an area by allowing doves undisturbed use of managed fields during at least a portion of the day. If resources are expended to prepare and manage dove shooting fields properly, then some level of hunter management may be considered appropriate. It is frustrating to a manager to spend much of a year planning, planting and managing fields for mourning doves only to have them "shot out" in a day or two.

A shooting field manager should not limit his or her concern to maintaining or optimizing harvest, however. High-quality shooting field management must consider shooter safety. Madson (1978: 67) suggested that a dove load has a "danger range" of 300 yards (274 m). This is a reasonable guideline. The shape of a field and other characteristics, such as patterns of vegetation, will determine the safe number and distribution of hunters. On areas with

Proper mourning dove shooting field management involves considerably more than manipulation of crops. Hunter management is essential to assure a safe and quality shooting experience. At the Max McGraw Wildlife Foundation in Illinois, all hunting parties are advised of state and federal regulations, including shooting hours and bag limits (McGraw's daily bag limit is 12, whereas state/federal regulations permit a take of 15; the difference is McGraw's choice not to overshoot the fields and to allow more opportunity for more hunters). In addition, hunting parties are limited to six or seven hunters per field. Hunters are spaced 40 to 50 yards (36.5 to 45.7 m) apart and in single file. At least one guide and a retriever dog are required per party, and birds are to be retrieved as soon as they are downed. Hunter awareness of and compliance with the legalities, ethics and safety practices of mourning dove hunting are requisite to quality dove hunting in all parts of the country and in unmanaged circumstances as well as managed ones. *Photo by Robert A. Montgomery; courtesy of the Max McGraw Wildlife Foundation.*

long, narrow strips of vegetation, one shooting station per 4 acres (1.6 ha) is an acceptable standard for safety. Two or three experienced hunters can shoot safely from each station. For large and open square fields, the aforementioned 300-yard (274 m) "rule" applies, which may limit shooting stations to one per 20 acres (8 ha).

Managers must react promptly to unsafe conditions and careless shooting. Hunters at each station should be advised in advance of constraints on shooting and all other applicable rules and courtesies. Also, alcoholic beverages are not to be consumed before or during a hunt.

Shooting field managers must strive to assure that legal requirements and regulations are carefully observed and followed. Baiting, overshooting limits or legal hours and other violations are not to be tolerated. They damage the resource, foster poor hunter behavior, demean the role and purpose of hunting and eventually may close down hunting on the area altogether.

Also unacceptable is unethical or even unwittingly careless behavior. "Skybusting," shooting doves on the ground, wires or trees, not searching for wounded birds, moving from hunting stations and other actions must not be permitted. The manager has an obligation to inform or remind all shooters of these points.

SUMMARY

Many species of plants that produce small seeds (peanut and corn-size seeds or smaller) can be manipulated by a variety of methods to provide an abundance of seeds on relatively bare ground, the two most important components to successful shooting field management. The dove food resources created by any one plant species or management technique can be enhanced by the introduction of additional plant species and management techniques within the same field or management unit. A diverse field management plan that includes interspersing an early season crop such as millet with a late-season crop such as corn and mechanical manipulation of an idle portion of a field containing pigweed or foxtail can provide quality feeding habitat for doves throughout the year and excellent shooting opportunities during the hunting season.

Few land management practices specifically to enhance game species are more directed toward hunting than are those for mourning doves. Although potential exists to manage land to improve nesting habitat and other needs of doves, most active mourning dove management is focused on harvesting doves. Managers have an obligation to review these priorities and consider year-round needs of doves. Besides, consideration of these needs can pay hunting season benefits. Approximately 93 percent of banded doves harvested in Missouri are banded in Missouri. Immature doves banded in Missouri composed 92 percent of immature banded doves harvested in Missouri (Atkinson et al. 1982). Clearly, hunting success in that state depends on nesting success there, and the same applies to most other states. Even in managed shooting fields, there is mourning dove use when hunters are not present. Before the season opens and, to a lesser extent, after the season closes, managed fields provide habitat for nesting and wintering doves, respectively. It can be argued that a relatively small percentage of doves using a particular shooting field actually are harvested in that field.

Even in the matter of shooting field management, the welfare of the species is the first and foremost interest. Hunting must be conducted on a sustained-yield basis. Implementation of part-day hunting allows doves to use managed fields without disturbance during at least part of the feeding period (*Figure 73f*). Field rotation also helps protect the birds from overharvest. Waters (1983) suggested a small, very early planting of browntop millet in each shooting field complex to provide food for nesting doves. Chambers (1963) found that corn comprised 95 percent of the diet of mourning doves wintering in northern Missouri. He suggested that the availability of corn is the primary factor affecting the survival of wintering doves in the more northerly parts of the winter range. Much of the doves' range features hedgerows and windbreaks. They make excellent cover and shady places from which to hunt doves. Responsible land use should include protection and establishment of these sites. Hedgerows inhibit wind speed, reducing soil erosion and moisture-related stress in crops. They are habitat for many wildlife species and provide important dove nesting and roosting sites. Establishing a food source such as millet or corn for nesting and wintering doves and hedgerows for nesting and roosting doves are sound management practices.

Harvesting mourning doves is a benefit of the species that brings with it responsibilities. If such harvest, along with management of shooting fields, is accomplished with foresight and under promulgated guidelines, laws and regulations, it does not harm the species and does accommodate America's foremost hunting opportunity in terms of man-hours of recreation and total harvest.

Chapter 29

Research and Management Needs

Clait E. Braun
Division of Wildlife
Colorado Department of Natural Resources
Fort Collins, Colorado

Nova J. Silvy
Department of Wildlife and Fisheries Sciences
Texas A&M University
College Station, Texas

Thomas S. Baskett
Cooperative Fish and Wildlife Research Unit
U.S. Fish and Wildlife Service
The School of Natural Resources
University of Missouri
Columbia, Missouri

Roy E. Tomlinson
Office of Migratory Bird Management
U.S. Fish and Wildlife Service
Albuquerque, New Mexico

The mourning dove is among the most studied and inventoried avian species in North America. Yet many gaps in knowledge remain. The most important of these gaps must be filled immediately to allow proper management of this valuable and important renewable resource. In our view, the two most important issues for mourning dove managers today are (1) population declines throughout the Western Management Unit (WMU) and in the eastern tier of the Central Management Unit (CMU), and (2) the lack of a standardized nationwide harvest survey.

The long-term population declines in the eastern CMU and the WMU are not only alarming but puzzling as well, because the underlying causes are uncertain. Studies must be initiated to identify the causative factors and, once they are known, develop and implement measures to combat them. These tasks will be difficult because baseline data generally are not available for conditions prior to the declines, and some factors may not have ready solutions. For example, agricultural practices, whether they encompass pesticide applications or cropping regimes, may be difficult to change. If farmers raise cotton because demand and prices are high, it would be unreasonable to expect them to grow grains that would net them less profit. The same is true of water reclamation projects that destroy nesting habitat. Farmers, ranchers, developers, etc., cannot be expected to change their practices without economic incentive. Thus, unless the reasons for dove declines are simpler than we suspect, it will not be enough to determine what the problems are and make recommendations for change. Resource administrators and managers should be prepared to make substantial economic investments if the downward dove trends are to be reversed.

The need for a uniform nationwide mourning dove harvest survey has been recognized for many years (Tomlinson 1966, Keeler 1977). Although many state wildlife agencies conduct mail surveys to derive harvest estimates of doves and other game populations, these surveys are not done uniformly and estimates are not directly comparable among states. Several states do not conduct dove harvest surveys or do not conduct them annually, leaving gaps in the data. The effects of hunting on mourning doves are difficult to evaluate without standardized harvest data on a nationwide basis.

It is imperative that a sampling frame (such as a nationwide migratory bird hunting permit) be developed to provide information on harvest for mourning doves (and other migratory gamebirds) (Tautin et al. 1989). Reliable mourning dove harvest data then could be compared with trend information from the mourning dove Call-count Survey and evaluated to enable sound management decisions. A foundation for such a permit and sampling system has been developed (Babcock et al. 1990), and the U.S. Fish and Wildlife Service has prepared rules to implement a National Migratory Bird Harvest Information Program (*Federal Register* 56: 28812–28814, June 24, 1991). This proposed permit system would be phased in starting in 1992, with states volunteering for the two-year experimental program. Other states would enter the program in 1994, with full implementation in 1998. However, efforts over the last twenty years to establish such a permit and survey ended in failure. A nationwide harvest survey for mourning doves must be implemented as soon as possible so that the role of hunting of this species can be fully understood.

In addition to these two critical needs (reversing population declines and establishment of a nationwide harvest survey), knowledge is required on other aspects of mourning dove management and biology.

ASSESSMENT OF BREEDING POPULATION STATUS

At present, the only means to assess the status of mourning dove breeding populations are two standardized surveys, the nationwide Call-count Survey and the Breeding Bird Survey, both administered by the U.S. Fish and Wildlife Service. The basic premise—that the number of calling males counted during the Call-count Survey represents the entire population and therefore provides indices to annual population fluctuations—has been extensively studied. Many factors affect rates of perch cooing by males. The most important factor, by far, is whether or not males are mated. If sex ratios in this monogamous species vary significantly each year or by locality, the Call-count Survey may not representatively sample breeding doves. Accurate annual estimates of adult sex ratios by geographic area are necessary to solve this problem.

Call-count Survey data from large areas (e.g., states or management units) probably provide valid estimates of long-term trends, because local and annual changes in proportions of unmated males may average out over larger areas and over time. Comparisons of Call-count Survey data with roadside count data in the CMU and with eyewitness accounts in the WMU tend to substantiate the declining trends in those areas. We believe the Call-count Survey provides accurate trends at least at the management unit level. Unfortunately, standardized harvest survey data are not available to compare trends with those derived from the Call-count Survey. It would be reassuring if trends from the two sets of data corresponded closely; this is all the more reason to press for a nationwide harvest survey.

The Call-count Survey presently does not sample mourning dove breeding populations in Canada, where doves have increased greatly since settlement (Houston 1986), and in Mexico. Because mourning dove populations are interrelated and conditions in Canada and Mexico/Central America could affect the welfare of doves throughout their range, expansion of the Call-count Survey is warranted. Moreover, urban areas of the United States, especially in the Midwest and West, are poorly sampled because large human population centers are avoided in the sampling scheme. The importance of urban areas for breeding mourning doves is suspected to be high, but overall population levels there are not well documented or understood. Within portions of the mourning dove range, some urban populations may be nonmigratory (Leopold and Dedon 1983), and these populations may be unsampled. A method should be designed to include urban populations in the annual assessment. We also recognize the importance of increasing the number of Call-count Survey routes to represent trends better over time by geographic region.

The Breeding Bird Survey also measures population trends of mourning doves (Robbins et al.

1986), and results have been roughly comparable to those of the Call-count Survey. While the former is not specific for mourning doves (all bird species heard and seen are recorded on fifty-stop routes), the larger sample sizes, particularly in the East, yield dove trend estimates with lower variances (Sauer et al. in preparation). It has been suggested that the Call-count Survey be discontinued and reliance placed on the Breeding Bird Survey for management decisions. However, unlike the Call-count Survey, the annual Breeding Bird Survey results are not available prior to the June regulations public hearing when mourning dove seasons are set. In addition, there are enough biological questions about the Breeding Bird Survey (e.g., pooling doves heard and seen, and counting young birds during the later survey period) that it would be unwise to discontinue the long-standing Call-count Survey without a comparative study. We suggest a five-year study in which both Breeding Bird Survey and Call-count Survey routes would be conducted on the same roads using the procedures of each survey during the time period of each survey and by different observers. Sufficient sample routes should be included to yield low-variance trend estimates for comparison. In the meantime, both surveys should be used to assess mourning dove populations, but reliance for management decisions should remain with the Call-count Survey.

To obtain less variable Call-count Survey trend estimates, more routes should be established in certain parts of the country, particularly in the East. In addition, the Call-count Survey presently is stratified according to physiographic regions, some of which are inadequately represented by routes. A redesigned system of stratification should be developed to resolve this shortcoming.

ASSESSMENT OF MORTALITY

Banding has been the primary tool used to estimate mortality. Although it is generally believed that adequate data are available on hunting mortality, closer examination reveals marked differences in harvest rates among areas. Why is mortality attributed to hunting in the WMU (particularly the Coastal subunit) twice as high as that in the CMU? Can mourning doves sustain hunting losses of 21 to 27 percent each year (Reeves 1979, Tomlinson et al. 1988) without such losses being additive? In 1987, hunting regulations in the WMU were restricted because of the long-term decline in that unit. How have dove populations responded to these changes? Answers to these questions might provide some insight into underlying reasons for the

WMU population decline. More emphasis should be placed on understanding hunting mortality as a portion of total mortality experienced by mourning doves. Clearly, well-designed experiments to measure responses of mourning doves to different hunting strategies, regulations and season timing are needed to assess this important mortality factor fully.

Further complicating a better understanding of hunting mortality are questions concerning the magnitude (about 30 percent) of crippling rates (Haas 1977), band-reporting rates, effects of perceived higher losses due to September hunting (Books-Blenden et al. 1984, Olson and Braun 1984), illegal kill and the influences of harvest in Mexico and Central America (particularly in Mexico). More precise estimates of crippling loss and reporting rates in varied geographic areas are needed to derive kill rates from recovery rates of banded birds. The September hunting issue has been investigated fairly well but needs further review, particularly in southern parts of the country. For example, would nesting continue and be significantly more important to total production if hunting seasons were delayed (Giessler et al. 1987)? Multiple bagging (i.e., hunters taking more than one limit per day) and overbagging are reported to occur. Are these factors limiting? In Mexico, intensified participation by U.S. hunters may be increasing the harvest beyond biologically acceptable levels. A banding program combined with measures to determine harvest in Mexico and Central America is needed.

Other types of mortality are even less understood. Considering that annual mortality rates exceed 50 percent and the nationwide population estimate is 475 million mourning doves (Tomlinson et al. 1988), more than 200 million die each year. Approximately 70 percent of the deaths result from causes other than hunting (Dunks et al. 1982, Tomlinson et al. 1988). Apparent important sources of this mortality include trichomoniasis, avian pox, lead poisoning, accidents, winter weather and pesticides. Nevertheless, we know little about the timing and magnitude of nonhunting mortality. Some factors, such as disease, directly affect individual doves and populations (Conti et al. 1985, Harmon et al. 1987), whereas others, such as environmental contaminants, may affect doves both directly and indirectly (Carrington and Mirarchi 1989). Studies are urgently needed to determine the effects of biocides on mourning dove populations, particularly in the WMU, the eastern portion of the CMU, and in Mexico and Central America. In addition, banding studies could be designed to examine all forms of nonhunting mortality in a variety of habitats and areas.

ASSESSMENT OF PRODUCTIVITY

To maintain stable populations, mourning doves must be able to balance high mortality with equally high production. In portions of the CMU and WMU, production may not have equaled mortality in recent years; in the EMU, where mortality is high, production appears to have compensated well. Why do such differences occur among management units and subunits? Are these differences due to differing lengths of the nesting period, dove behavior and adaptation, climate (wet versus arid), recent changes in habitats or some other factor(s)? Are differences year- and site-specific?

Little information is available on the average number of young produced per pair of mourning dove adults in representative areas. Comprehensive studies (involving radio-marked nesting adults, for example) are needed to provide baseline production figures by states and regions. Standardized wing collections from hunter-harvested doves could be an important method to assess annual productivity by state and management unit. However, such studies should be done in conjunction with banding programs. More than fifteen years have elapsed since a coordinated, comprehensive national banding program was conducted. A well-designed and implemented banding program would provide estimates not only of current mortality (survival) but also of differential recovery between age classes with which to correct age ratios derived from wing collections. Because of the considerable cost involved, we suggest these measures be undertaken only in areas where population declines are evident.

The available evidence suggests that adult male doves outnumber adult females by a substantial margin. Since no differences have been detected in estimated survival rates between adult males and females, the reason for the disparity of males is unclear. It is possible that sex ratios at hatch favor males or that immature females experience higher mortality than do males. Although past studies indicate the average sex ratio at hatch is about one to one, this subject is poorly understood (Edmunds and Ankney 1987) and needs additional emphasis. If the proportion of adult females could be increased through management, more production might be achieved with no increase in overall size of the breeding population.

RELATIONSHIPS WITH HABITAT

Mourning doves are a product of the land, and breeding densities generally reflect land capability and diversity (Tomlinson and Dolton 1987). Densities appear to be highest in subclimax ecotones (where productive nest sites are abundant) in association with disturbed areas with abundant food (grain and/or weed seeds) (Armbruster 1983). Other variables, such as vegetation density, height of vegetation and even ready access to nesting material, also appear to affect breeding densities (Goforth and Baskett 1971b, Armbruster 1983). Thus, such large monotypic areas as even-aged forest stands, fields of row crops, and nut- and fruit-producing trees are not attractive to doves throughout much of the year. Houston (1986) suggested that doves markedly increased in prairie Canada because of tree plantings, fire control that allowed trees and shrubs to grow taller, and production of a variety of grain crops with weedy field borders. Dove nesting densities in trees and shrubs usually are high, especially in areas where woody growth is limited, but ground nesting by doves occurs throughout large expanses of their range. Densities of ground-nesting doves may be low, but nest success normally is high. Thus, the importance of ground nests to overall productivity may be significant in many areas (Olson et al. 1991).

Mourning dove nesting and roosting habitats have been systematically destroyed during the past twenty-five to fifty years through urban development, agricultural practices, water reclamation projects and other activities associated with human population growth and development of the country. Studies should be initiated to measure the extent of these losses and recommend ways to counter them. Managers should work more closely with agricultural extension agents and landowners to encourage maintenance of woody fencerows and windbreaks and to discourage autumn plowing and clear-cut forestry practices on private lands.

Significant positive relationships in the EMU have been reported between dove density as measured by the Call-count Survey and the proportion of land in crops, especially corn, oats and soybeans (see chapter 17). Similar relationships exist in the CMU and WMU (see chapters 18 and 19). More definitive studies are needed to delineate these relationships for better management decisions.

Studies are needed to assess habitat needs and productivity. Increased effort should be placed on understanding local and regional relationships of breeding density and productivity with areas of different habitat types, including crops (by type), forest or brushland, other "waste" habitats, urban areas, and farmsteads. Experimental manipulations of dove breeding habitat involving known attractive nesting substrates, bare or sparsely vegetated grounds, and food should be undertaken and evaluated on public lands where high nesting densities can be encouraged and protected. Emphasis should be placed on understanding how dove densities and productivity are interrelated in habitats that support both high and low population densities over time. Changes in habitat types undoubtedly have affected dove populations either positively or negatively. Research should be conducted to understand fully the effects of larger field size, more efficient crop-harvesting machines (leaving less waste grain for food), use of herbicides to control weeds, timing of cultivation, changes in irrigation practices, and use of pesticides to improve or enhance crop yields on mourning dove breeding densities, productivity and survival.

BIOLOGY

The biology of mourning doves is understood reasonably well, but much research remains to be accomplished. A firmer understanding of vocalizations (in relation to adult sex ratios, production of young and geographic differences) is important. Additional information is needed on migration, fidelity to breeding and wintering areas, preparation (fat deposition) for migration, energetic demands, factors that trigger migration and cues used for navigation. Studies are needed to gain insight into energy needs of mourning doves under different environmental conditions. Determination of metabolizable energy in the foods consumed is needed to evaluate energetic consequences of habitat manipulations. Knowledge of general nutrient requirements (vitamins, minerals and micronutrients) also is needed to interpret population/habitat interactions. Further work is needed on understanding energy requirements for nesting and crop milk production, because the amount of crop milk produced affects nestling survival (see chapters 7 and 9). Research indicates that the dependency period of immature doves is longer (up to twenty-seven days posthatching) than was earlier believed and that "reference areas" are important postfledging use sites (see chapters 5 and 6). This shows that research on specific questions can lead to important contributions to better understanding of dove biology. Even molt patterns of adult doves need additional investigation and clarification, as does taxonomy.

Accidental lethal and sublethal poisonings of doves have been documented, but little is known about the long-term effects on dove populations. Are mourning doves being negatively impacted through decreased breeding fitness, productivity and survival? We suspect they are, at least in certain areas such as the Central Valley of California. Little is known about the effects of sublethal amounts of contaminants—such as lead (Marn et al. 1988, Carrington and Mirarchi 1989) and PCBs (Koval et al. 1987)—on dove productivity, indirect mortality and susceptibility to diseases. Biocides banned in the United States (such as DDT) still are being used in Mexico and Central America; what impact does this practice have on wintering mourning doves? Experiments are needed immediately to investigate, understand and counter the effects of these environmental contaminants.

Few investigations to date have probed beyond the incidence of diseases. The importance of trichomoniasis and avian pox virus is evident (see chapter 12), but studies on transmission of *Trichomonas gallinae* and pox virus in the wild are nonexistent. Stabler (1948) reported that exposure to *Trichomonas* provides some immunity (see also Stabler and Braun 1979) and that trichomoniasis can be cured in individual birds by use of drugs (Stabler and Kitzmiller 1967, Stabler and Braun 1979). Field experiments to control or reduce the incidence of this disease have not been conducted. Surely, controlled field experiments in areas with recurring outbreaks of trichomoniasis would increase knowledge of how to control or prevent widespread mourning dove die-offs. The same undoubtedly is true for avian pox virus.

Do techniques used in management and research studies adversely affect doves in terms of short- and long-term survival? Some field biologists hypothesize that capture and banding of doves significantly alter dove survival. If true, many population attributes derived from banding analyses may be incorrect. Although behavioral responses of mourning doves to color marking and radio tagging have been investigated in depth (Sayre et al. 1981), physiological responses to capture, handling and marking are poorly understood. Additional research is needed to evaluate techniques currently used in the study of mourning doves.

HARVEST MANAGEMENT

In many areas of the country, hunters are finding it increasingly difficult to locate areas to hunt doves. Basically, this has evolved because of two factors. The first involves the continuing changes in agricultural practices. The trend toward fewer and larger farms has encouraged destruction of shelterbelts and woody fencerows in which doves nest and roost. In many areas, farmers now grow fewer grain crops (e.g., wheat, sorghum and corn) where doves normally congregate during autumn for food. These practices may not have been instrumental in reducing dove populations, but they certainly have been responsible for changing feeding patterns of doves in autumn, dispersing the birds and possibly causing earlier migration. Second, landowners have been increasingly reluctant to permit dove hunting. This development has occurred because hunters in some cases were negligent in hunting practices or even vandalized property. In addition, there has been poor communication between landowners and hunters, and the sheer number of hunters in many areas tends to discourage landowners from allowing access.

Managers must develop methods to solve these problems if dove hunting is to be sustained into the future. Since most dove hunting is on private land, managers will have to work with landowners to make areas more attractive to doves (e.g., providing grain foods and roosting habitats). Also, they will have to persuade landowners to permit public hunting. This will require considerable effort to improve public relations and probably economic incentives to overcome access/trespass liability concerns. Some ranchers and farmers may want to lease hunting rights on a daily or seasonal basis. Inevitably, the hunter will have to cover the cost of increased landowner cooperation.

Many states have wildlife management areas that easily can be managed for dove hunting. Properly managed shooting areas can ensure that hunters have recreational opportunities available in autumn. Manipulation of crops and tree/shrub habitats not only will provide more hunting opportunity but also will benefit mourning doves by providing additional food and cover. More reliable food sources, particularly in more northern wintering areas, are especially necessary for survival. Managed shooting areas can satisfy some of this need following the hunting season.

ACCOMPLISHING THE GOALS

More attention needs to be focused on the mourning dove at state, regional, national and international levels. An international symposium should be convened to focus attention on mourning doves and initiate preparation of a comprehensive management plan. Such a plan should result in a clearly defined list of priorities for mourning dove research and management. The research and management objectives identified undoubtedly will require substantial funding to accomplish. Even when many of the more important questions are answered, the recommended management procedures must be financed on an operational basis.

Some of these—such as economic incentives to ranchers and farmers to implement beneficial agricultural practices—will require large capital outlays.

Despite the fact that the mourning dove is the most actively hunted and heavily harvested gamebird in North America, the species is not perceived by hunters or the general public as being as "glamorous" as ruffed grouse, quail, pheasants, wild turkeys and waterfowl. Unlike some other gamebirds, the mourning dove has no national or international private organization rallying financial and political support for its improved management. Perhaps for the same reasons, federal and state wildlife agencies appear to be less prone to support mourning dove research and management. Nevertheless, for the mourning dove to remain an important ecological entity and recreational/aesthetic resource, establishment of dedicated funding sources is essential to ensure that needed research and management are both undertaken and continued.

Between 1967 and 1982, the Accelerated Research Program for Migratory Shore and Upland Game Birds was funded within the U.S. Fish and Wildlife Service at an annual level of $250,000. This money was used to support research on this group of gamebirds (including mourning doves) by states and universities. During the nearly two decades of its existence, the Accelerated Research Program funded research studies of doves, pigeons, rails, cranes, woodcock and other species and resulted in nearly 250 publications. The Accelerated Research Program was hugely successful, but due to financial constraints, the U.S. Fish and Wildlife Service discontinued the program in 1982, and funding for work on these species has been severely restricted. Considering the long-term declines of doves and some other "webless" species, a similar federal program at a higher funding level is urgently needed.

Another means to raise funds is to establish state mourning dove stamps required of hunters annually. Nearly all states now require such stamps for waterfowl hunting and many require them for other species, such as turkeys. The Texas Parks and Wildlife Department requires a special stamp to hunt white-winged doves, and the program generates nearly $250,000 annually. This money is used to purchase habitat or finance research. Stamps such as these also could be required of mourning dove hunters to finance dove research and management projects.

Whatever the means, money will be necessary for research and management on a continuing basis to ensure that mourning doves remain an important component of the American scene. We believe that the importance of healthy populations of mourning doves has been clearly identified throughout this book. We further believe it is important to ensure that the mourning dove remains an abundant and widely distributed species, to the benefit and enjoyment of our future generations.

Common and Scientific Names of Plants Cited in the Text

Plants are listed alphabetically by common name(s). A plant may be listed under a variety of different common names used in the text. Scientific names of plant species have been standardized according to the various sources indicated. If a scientific name was not located in the first source, the next source was searched, etc., until the name was located.

Sources: Scott and Wasser (1980), Subcommittee on Standardization of Common and Botanical Names of Weeds (1966), Fernald (1970) and citations from literature sources.

Acacia, catclaw: *Acacia greggii*
Alfalfa: *Medicago sativa*
Alyce clover: *Alysicarpus vaginalis*
Amaranth, redroot: *Amaranthus retroflexus*
Amaranth, slim: *A. hybridus*
Amaranth, tumbleweed: *A. graecizans*
Apple: *Malus*
Apple, common: *M. pumila*
Arborvitae, oriental: *Thuja orientalis*
Ash, green (red): *Fraxinus pennsylvanica*

Barley: *Hordeum*
Barley, sixrow: *H. vulgare*
Barnyardgrass: *Echinochloa*
Barnyardgrass, common: *E. crusgalli*
Beakrush, horned: *Rhynchospora corniculata*
Bean: *Phaseolus*
Bean, mung: *P. aureus*
Bean, Tennessee black: *Glycine soja*
Beech, American: *Fagus grandifolia*
Beeplant, spiny: *Cleome spinosa*
Beet, sugar: *Beta vulgaris*
Bene: *Sesamum indicum*
Bluegrass: *Poa*
Bluegrass, annual: *P. annua*
Bluestem, big: *Andropogon gerardi*
Bluestem, little: *A. scoparius*
Boxelder: *Acer negundo*
Bristlegrass (pigeongrass): *Setaria*
Bristlegrass, Faber: *S. faberi*
Bristlegrass, foxtail: *S. italica*

Bristlegrass, glaucous: *S. glauca*
Bristlegrass, green: *S. viridis*
Bristlegrass, knotroot: *S. geniculata*
Bristlegrass, yellow: *S. lutescens*
Brome, California: *Bromus carinatus*
Brome, rescue: *B. catharticus*
Brome, soft: *B. mollis*
Buckthorn: *Amsinckia douglasiana*
Buckwheat, common: *F. sagittatum*
Buckwheat, common: *F. sagittatum = esculentum*
Bullgrass: *Paspalum boscianum*
Bullnettle: *Cnidoscolus stimulosus*
Bulrush, salt-marsh: *Scirpus robustus*
Bulrush, tule: *S. acutus*
Bundleflower, Illinois: *Desmanthus illinoensis*
Burnet: *Sanguisorba*
Buttercup: *Ranunculus*

Cactus, barrel: *Ferocactus wislizenii*
Cactus, pricklypear: *Opuntia sp.*
Cactus, saguaro: *Cereus giganteus*
Caltrop: *Kallstoemia*
Camellia, wild: *Stewartia (Stuartia)*
Canarygrass: *Phalaris canariensis*
Canarygrass, reed: *P. arundinacea*
Cane: *Sorghum*
Caperonia, bird's-eye: *Caperonia castaneaefolia*
Caraway: *Carum carvi*
Carpetgrass: *Axonopus*
Castorbean, common: *Ricinus communis*
Cedar, arbovitae: *Thuja*
Cedar, eastern red: *Juniperus virginiana*
Chaparral: *Ceanothus* spp.
Charlock: *Bassica kaber*
Chinaberry: *Melia azedarach*
Cholla, teddybear: *Opuntia bigelovii*
Citrus: *Citrus*
Clover: *Trifolium*
Clover, crimson: *Trifolium incarnatum*
Clover, hairy canary: *Dorycnium hirsutum*
Colima: *Zanthoxylum fagara*
Collomia: *Collomia*
Copperleaf: *Acalypha*

Copperleaf, hophornbean: *Acalypha ostryifolia*
Corn: *Zea*
Corn, chicken: *Sorghum vulgare drummondii*
Corn, Indian: *Zea mays*
Corn, kafir: *Sorghum vulgare caffrorum*
Cornbind, dullseed: *Polygonum convolvulus*
Cotton, American upland: *Gossypium hirsutum*
Cottonwood: *Populus*
Cowpea, common: *Vigna sinensis*
Crabgrass: *Digitaria*
Crabgrass, hairy: *D. sanguinalis*
Cranesbill, Carolina: *Geranium carolinianum*
Creosotebush: *Larrea tridentata*
Croton: *Croton*
Croton, broadleaf: *C. glandulosus*
Croton, Gulf: *C. punctatus*
Croton, Lindheimer: *C. lindheimerianus*
Croton, prairie-tea: *C. monanthogynus*
Croton, Texas: *C. texensis*
Croton, woolly: *C. capitatus*
Crownvetch, common: *Coronilla varia*
Cucumber: *Cucumis sativus*
Cupgrass: *Eriochloa*

Dayflower: *Commelina*
Deervetch, Spanishclover: *Lotus americanus*
Devil's-claw: *Proboscidea louisianica*
Dropseed, sand: *Sporobolus cryptandrus*

Elm: *Ulmus*
Elm, American: *U. americana*
Elm, slippery: *U. rubra*
Eucalyptus: *Eucalyptus*
Euphorbia, bent: *Euphorbia geniculata*
Euphorbia, cupped: *E. cyathophora*
Euphorbia, eyed: *E. ocellata*
Euphorbia, painted: *E. heterophylla*
Euphorbia, red: *E. preslii*
Euphorbia, snow-on-the-mountain: *E. marginata*
Euphorbia, spotted: *E. maculata*
Euphorbia, toothed: *E. dentata*
Eveningprimrose, cutleaf: *Oenothera laciniata*

Fescue: *Festuca*
Fescue, tall: *F. arundinacea*
Fig: *Ficus*
Fir: *Abies*
Fir, Douglas: *Pseudotsuga menziesii*
Flatsedge, chufa: *Cyperus esculentus*
Flax, common: *Linum usitatissimum*
Flower of the Holy Ghost: *Peristera elata*

Gama grass, eastern: *Tripsacum dactyloides*
Geranium, Carolina: *Geranium carolinianum*
Goosefoot, lambsquarters: *Chenopodium album*
Goosegrass, ragimillet: *Eleusine coracana*
Grama: *Bouteloua spp.*
Grape: *Vitis sp.*
Grapefruit: *Citrus paradisi*
Greasewood: *Sarcobatus*

Hackberry: *Celtis*
Halogeton, common: *Halogeton glomeratus*
Harding grass: *Phalaris tuberosa stenoptera*
Hawthorn: *Crataegus*
Haygrazer: *Sorghum vulgare x Sorghum sudanense*
Hegari: *Sorghum*
Hemlock: *Tsuga*
Hemp (marijuana): *Cannabis sativa*
Hickory, pecan: *Carya illinoensis*
Higera (common sorghum): *Sorghum vulgare*
Hilaria, tobosa (grass): *Hilaria mutica*
Honeysuckle: *Lonicera*
Horse-purslane, desert: *Trianthema portulacastrum*
Horseweed: *Erigeron canadensis = Conyza canadensis*
Huisache: *Acacia farnesiana*

Indiangrass, yellow: *Sorghastrum nutans*
Indigo, Carolina: *Indigofera caroliniana*
Indigo, hairy: *I. hirsuta*
Ironwood: *Olneya tesota*

Japonica: *Lespedeza japonica*
Johnsongrass: *Sorghum halepense*
Juniper: *Juniperus*

Leaf flower, Carolina: *Phyllanthus caroliniensis*
Lechuguilla: *Agave lechuguilla*
Lespedeza, Kobe: *Lespedeza striata*
Lespedeza, Korean: *L. stipulaceae*
Lespedeza, shrub: *L. bicolor*
Locust: *Robinia*
Locust, black: *R. pseudoacacia*
Locust, honey: *Gleditsia triacanthos*
Lupine, bicolor: *Lupinus bicolor*

Madrone: *Arbutus*
Mallow, high: *Malva sylvestris*
Manzanita (bearberry): *Arctostaphylos*
Maple: *Acer*
Maple, Norway: *A. platanoides*
Maple, silver: *A. saccharinum*
Mayapple, common: *Podophyllum peltatum*
Medic, black: *Medicago lupulina*
Mesquite: *Prosopis*
Mesquite, common: *P. juliflora*
Mesquite, honey: *P. glandulosa*
Milkvetch (poison vetch): *Astragalus*
Milkweed, honeyvine: *Ampelamus albidus*
Millet: *Panicum*
Millet, browntop: *P. ramosum*
Millet, foxtail (German): *Setaria italica*
Millet, Japanese: *Echinochloa crusgalli frumentacea*
Millet, proso: *P. miliaceum*
Millet, Texas: *Panicum texanum*
Milo: *Sorghum vulgare*
Morningglory: *Ipomoea*
Mountainmahogany: *Cercocarpus montanus*
Mulberry: *Morus*
Mulberry, red: *M. rubra*
Muskmelon: *Cucumis melo*
Mustard: *Brassica*

Mustard, black: *B. nigra*

Needlegrass: *Stipa*
Noseburn: *Tragia*
Nutgrass: *Cyperus rotundus*

Oak: *Quercus*
Oak, blackjack: *Q. marilandica*
Oak, live: *Q. virginiana*
Oat: *Avena*
Oat, common: *A. sativa*
Okra: *Hibiscus esculentus*
Orange, common: *Citrus sinensis*
Osage-orange: *Maclura pomifera*
Oxalis, common yellow: *Oxalis stricta*

Palmetto, dwarf: *Sabal minor*
Palms: *Areca* or *Phoenix*
Paloverde: *Cercidium*
Panicgrass: *Panicum*
Panicum: *Panicum*
Panicum, beaked: *P. anceps*
Panicum, blue: *P. antidotale*
Panicum, broomcorn: *P. miliaceum*
Panicum, browntop: *P. fasiculatum*
Panicum, deertongue: *P. clandestinum*
Panicum, Dominican: *P. adspersum*
Panicum, fall: *P. dichotomiflorum*
Panicum, shoredune: *P. amarulum*
Panicum, switchgrass: *P. virgatum*
Panicum, Texas: *P. texanum*
Panicum, witchgrass: *P. capillare*
Partridgepea, senna: *Cassia fasciculata*
Paspalum, bahiagrass: *Paspalum notatum*
Paspalum, bull: *P. boscianum*
Paspalum, dallisgrass: *P. dilatatum*
Paspalum, fringeleaf: *P. ciliatifolium*
Paspalum, giant: *P. giganteum*
Paspalum, ribbed: *P. malacophyllum*
Paspalum, thin: *P. setaceum*
Patata: *Monolepis nuttalliana*
Pea, field (cowpea): *Vigna sinensis*
Pea, garden: *Pisum sativum*
Peach: *Prunus persica*
Peanut: *Arachis hypogaea*
Pear: *Pyrus*
Pear, common: *P. communis*
Peavine, rough: *Lathyrus hirsutus*
Pecan: *Carya illinoensis*
Pennisetum, pearlmillet: *Pennisetum glaucum*
Pepper tree, California: *Schinus molle*
Pigweed: *Amaranthus*
Pine: *Pinus*
Pine, Austrian: *P. nigra*
Pine, jack: *P. banksiana*
Pine, loblolly: *P. taeda*
Pine, lodgepole: *P. contorta*
Pine, longleaf: *P. palustris*
Pine, ponderosa: *P. ponderosa*
Pine, red: *P. resinosa*
Pine, Scotch: *P. sylvestris*

Pine, shortleaf: *P. echinata*
Pine, slash: *P. elliotti*
Pine, Virginia: *P. virginiana*
Pine, white: *P. strobus*
Pink, windmill: *Silene gallica*
Plantain: *Plantago*
Plum, wild: *Prunus*
Pokeberry: *Phytolacca*
Pokeberry, common: *P. americana*
Pokeberry, stiff: *P. rigida*
Poppy, California: *Eschscholtzia californica*
Pricklyash: *Zanthoxylum*
Prickly pear: *Opuntia*
Prickly pear, Arizona jumping: *O. bigelovii*
Pricklypoppy: *Argemone*
Pricklypoppy, Mexican: *A. mexicana*
Pricklypoppy, rough: *A. squarrosa*
Pricklypoppy, white: *A. alba*
Proso, dove: *Panicum miliaceum*

Rabbit brush: *Chrysothamnus*
Ragweed: *Ambrosia*
Ragweed, common: *A. artemisiifolia*
Ragweed, giant: *A. trifida*
Rape, winter: *Brassica napus*
Redweed, common: *Melochia corchorifolia*
Redwood: *Sequoia sempervirens*
Rice, cultivated: *Oryza sativa*
Ricegrass, Indian: *Oryzopsis hymenoides*
Rock cress: *Arabis*
Rockpurslane, redmaids: *Calandrinia ciliata*
Rose: *Rosa*
Rose, multiflora: *R. multiflora*
Rushfoil: *Crotonopsis*
Russian olive: *Elaeagnus angustifolia*
Rye: *Secale*
Rye, common (annual): *S. cereale*
Ryegrass, dalmatian: *Lolium subulatum*
Ryegrass, Italian: *L. multiflorum*

Safflower, common: *Carthamus tinctorius*
Sage, lyre-leaf: *Salvia lyrata*
Sagebrush: *Artemisia*
Sagebrush, big: *A. tridentata*
Saltbush: *Atriplex*
Saltbush, four-wing: *A. canescens*
Sandbur: *Cenchrus*
Senna, wild: *Cassia marilandica*
Sesame, oriental: *Sesamum indicum*
Sesbania, long-pod: *Sesbania macrocarpa*
Signalgrass, broadleaf: *Brachiaria platyphylla*
Smartweed, Pennsylvania: *Polygonum pennsylvanicum*
Sorghum: *Sorghum*
Sorghum, almum: *S. almum*
Sorghum, common (grain): *S. vulgare*
Sorgo: *Sorghum vulgare saccharatum*
Sorrel, sheep: *Rumex acetosella*
Soybean: *Glycine*
Soybean, common: *G. max*
Soybean, reseeding: *G. usuriensis*
Spanish dagger: *Yucca carnerosana*

Spider-flower: *Cleome spinosa*
Spiderwort: *Tradescantia*
Spruce: *Picea*
Spruce, blue: *P. pungens*
Spruce, Norway: *P. abies*
Spruce, white: *P. glauca*
Spurge: *Euphorbia*
Spurge, leafy: *E. esula*
Starwort, chickweed: *Stellaria media*
Stillingia: *Stillingia*
Sudangrass: *Sorghum sudanense*
Sudangrass, wild: *S. arundinaceum*
Sumac: *Rhus*
Sumac, smooth: *R. glabra*
Sumpweed, rough: *Iva ciliata*
Sunflower: *Helianthus*
Sunflower, common: *H. annuus*
Sunflower, Maximilian: *H. maximilianii*
Sunflower, prairie: *H. petiolaris*
Sweetgum, American: *Liquidambar styraciflua*

Tallowtree, common: *Sapium sebiferum*
Tamarisk, saltcedar: *Tamarix pentandra*
Teosinte, perennial: *Euchlaena perennis*
Tesajillo: *Opuntia leptocaulis*
Thistle: *Cirsium*

Thistle, milk: *Silybum marianum*
Timothy, common: *Phleum pratense*
Tobacco: *Nicotiana*
Turkey-mullein: *Ereomocarpus setigerus*

Vetch: *Vicia*
Vetch, common: *V. sativa*
Vetch, hairy: *V. villosa*
Vetch, narbonne: *V. narborensis*
Vetch, narrowleaf: *V. angustifolia*
Vetch, showy: *V. grandiflora*
Vetch, woollypod: *V. dasycarpa*
Vetch, yellow: *V. lutea*
Violet: *Viola*

Watermelon: *Citrullus vulgaris*
Waxmyrtle, southern: *Myrica cerifera*
Wheat: *Triticum*
Wheat, bread: *T. aestivum*
Wheatgrass: *Agropyron*
Wildbean, smooth-seeded: *Strophostyles leiosperma*
Wildbean, trailing: *S. helvola*
Wildrye, creeping: *Elymus triticoides*
Willow: *Salix*

Yew: *Taxus*

Common and Scientific Names of Animals Cited in the Text

Animals are listed alphabetically by common name(s). An animal may be listed under a variety of different common names used in the text. Scientific names of animal species have been standardized according to the various sources indicated. If a scientific name was not found in the first source, the next source was searched, etc., until the name was located.

BIRDS

Sources: American Ornithologists' Union (1983), Goodwin (1983), Gill (1990).

Blackbird, red-winged: *Agelaius phoeniceus*
Blackbird, yellow-headed: *Xanthocephalus xanthocephalus*
Black-throated blue warbler: *Dendroica caerulescens*
Bluebird, eastern: *Sialia sialis*
Bobwhite, northern: *Colinus virginianus*
Canary, common: *Serinus canaria*
Cardinal, northern: *Cardinalis cardinalis*
Catbird, gray: *Dumetella carolinensis*
Chaffinch, common: *Fringilla coelebs*
Chicken: *Gallus gallus*
Coot, American: *Fulica americana*
Cowbird, brown-headed: *Molothrus ater*
Crane, sandhill: *Grus canadensis*
Crow, American: *Corvus brachyrhynchos*
Dickcissel: *Spiza americana*
Dove, common (rock): *Columba livia*
Dove, common ground: *Columbina passerina*
Dove, eared: *Zenaida auriculata*
Dove, fruit: *Ptilinopus*
Dove, Galapagos: *Z. galapagoensis*
Dove, Grayson's: *Zenaida graysoni*
Dove, Inca: *Columbina inca*
Dove, Indian ring: *Streptopelia decaocto*

Dove, mourning: *Zenaida macroura*
Dove, mourning, Clarion Island: *Z. m. clarionensis*
Dove, mourning, eastern: *Z. m. carolinensis*
Dove, mourning, Panamanian: *Z. m. turturilla*
Dove, mourning, western: *Z. m. marginella*
Dove, mourning, West Indian: *Z. m. macroura*
Dove, ringed turtle- (ring): *Streptopelia risoria*
Dove, Socorro: *Zenaida graysoni*
Dove, spotted: *Streptopelia chinensis*
Dove, stock: *Columba oenas*
Dove, turtle-: *Streptopelia turtur*
Dove, white-tipped: *Leptotila verreauxi*
Dove, white-winged: *Zenaida asiatica*
Dove, zenaida: *Z. aurita*
Duck, wood: *Aix sponsa*
Eagles: Family Accipitridae
Falcons: Family Falconidae
Finch: *Carduelis*
Finch, Cassin's: *Carpodacus cassinii*
Finch, house: *C. mexicanus*
Flicker, northern: *Colaptes auratus*
Flycatcher, pied: *Ficedula hypoleuca*
Gallinules: Family Rallidae
Goldfinch, American: *Carduelis tristis*
Goose, Canada: *Branta canadensis*
Goose, snow: *Chen caerulescens*
Grackle, common: *Quiscalus quiscula*
Grackle, great-tailed: *Q. mexicanus*
Grouse, ruffed: *Bonasa umbellus*
Grouse, sage: *Centrocercus urophasianus*
Gull, ring-billed: *Larus delawarensis*
Harrier, northern: *Circus cyaneus*
Hawk, Cooper's: *Accipiter cooperii*
Hawk, marsh: *Circus cyaneus*
Hawk, sharp-shinned: *Accipiter striatus*
Hermit thrush: *Catharus guttatus*
Heron, black-crowned night: *Nycticorax nycticorax*

Hummingbirds: Family Trochilidae
Jay, blue: *Cyanocitta cristata*
Kestrel, American: *Falco sparverius*
Magpie, black-billed: *Pica pica*
Mallard: *Anas platyrhynchos*
Mockingbird, northern: *Mimus polyglottos*
Parrots: Family Psittacidae
Partridge, gray: *Perdix perdix*
Petrel: *Pterodroma spp.*
Phalarope: *Phalaropus*
Pheasant, ring-necked: *Phasianus colchicus*
Pigeon, band-tailed: *Columba fasciata*
Pigeon, common (rock; feral; domestic): *C. livia*
Pigeon, crowned: *Goura*
Pigeon, flock: *Phaps histrionica*
Pigeon, green: *Treron*
Pigeon, passenger: *Ectopistes migratorius*
Pigeon, pheasant: *Otidiphaps nobilis*
Pigeon, red-billed: *Columba flavirostris*
Pigeon, scaly-naped: *C. squamosa*
Pigeon, snow: *C. leuconota*
Pigeon, thick-billed ground: *Trugon terrestris*
Pigeon, white-crowned: *Columba leucocephala*
Pigeon, wood: *C. palumbus*
Quail, Japanese: *Coturnix japonica*
Quail, scaled: *Callipepla squamata*
Rails: Family Rallidae
Raven, common: *Corvus corax*
Robin, American: *Turdus migratorius*
Robin, English: *Erithacus rubecula*
Screech owl, eastern: *Otus asio*
Shrike, loggerhead: *Lanius ludovicianus*
Snipe, common: *Gallinago gallinago*
Sparrow, field: *Spizella pusilla*
Sparrow, house: *Passer domesticus*
Sparrow, song: *Melospiza melodia*
Sparrow, tree: *Spizella arborea*
Starling, European: *Sturnus vulgaris*
Tern, least: *Sterna antillarum*
Turkey, wild: *Meleagris gallopavo*
Veery: *Catharus fuscescens*
Wigeon, American: *Anas americana*
Wigeon, Eurasian: *A. penelope*
Woodcock: *Scolopax*
Woodcock, American: *S. minor*
Wren, Carolina: *Thryothorus ludovicianus*
Wren, house: *Troglodytes aedon*

MAMMALS

Sources: Hall (1981), Honacki et al. (1982), Stock (1972) and citations from literature sources.

Bear, short-faced: *Tremarctotherium simum*
Bison, American: *Bison bison, B. antiguus* (ancient)
Camel: *Camelops* sp., *Tanupolama mirifica*
Caribou: *Rangifer tarandus*
Cat, domestic (feral): *Felis catus*
Cat, saber-toothed: *Smilodon californicus*
Cattle, domestic: *Bos taurus*

Cottontail (rabbit): *Sylvilagus* spp.
Deer, mule: *Odocoileus hemionus*
Deer, red: *Cervus elaphus*
Deer, white-tailed: *Odocoileus virginianus*
Dog, domestic (feral): *Canis familiaris*
Elk, Eurasian (moose): *Alces alces*
Elk, North American: *Cervus elaphus*
Goat: *Oreamnos americanus*
Horse: *Equus*
Human: *Homo sapiens*
Jackrabbit: *Lepus*
Lion, American: *Panthera atrox*
Mammoth, emperor: *Mammothus imperator*
Mastodon, American: *Mammut americanus*
Moose: *Alces alces*
Mouse, field: *Peromyscus*
Mouse, house: *Mus musculus*
Mouse, woodland: *Peromyscus*
Pig (hog): *Sus*
Prairie dog: *Cynomys*
Pronghorn: *Antilocapra americana, Breameryx minor* (ancient), *Stockoceros conkling* (ancient)
Raccoon: *Procyon lotor*
Rat: *Rattus*
Rat, wood: *Neotoma*
Reindeer: *Rangifer tarandus*
Sheep, domestic: *Ovis aries*
Skunk, striped: *Mephitis mephitis*
Sloth, ground: *Paramylodon harlani, Nothrotherium shastense*
Squirrel: *Sciurus*
Squirrel, fox: *S. niger*
Squirrel, gray: *S. carolinensis*
Squirrel, ground: *Spermophilus*
Squirrel, red: *Tamiasciurus hudsonicus*
Swine: *Sus scrofa*
Tapir: *Tapirus*
Weasel: *Mustela*
Wolf, dire: *Canis (Aenocyon) dirus*

OTHERS

Sources: Borror and White (1970), Behler and King (1974).

Ants: Order Hymenoptera, Family Formicidae
Beetles: Order Coleoptera
Blowfly: *Protocalliphora*
Bullfrog: *Rana catesbeiana*
Catfish: *Ictalurus*
Chewing lice: Order Mallophaga
Clover seed chalcids: Order Hymenoptera, Superfamily Chalcidoidae
Coachwhip, western: *Masticophis flagellum testaceus*
Flies: Order Diptera
Grasshopper: Order Orthoptera
Rattlesnake: *Crotalus*
Roaches: Order Orthoptera, Family Blattidae
Salmon: *Oncorhynchus*
Scale insects: Order Homoptera, Superfamily Coccoidea

Scorpion, yellow slender-tailed: *Centruroides sculpturatus*
Snail, land: *Agriolimax agrestis*
Snake, gray rat: *Elaphe obsoleta spiloides*

Snake, green: *Opheodrys*
Snake, rat: *Elaphe obsoleta*
Sow bugs: Class Crustacea, Order Isopoda

References Cited

Abbott, H. G. 1958. Application of avian repellents to eastern white pine seed. J. Wildl. Manage. 22(2): 304–306.

———. 1966. Mourning doves feed on white pine seed. J. For. 64(3):199–200.

Abbott, U. K. and G. W. Yee. 1975. Avian genetics. Pages 151–200 *in* R. C. King, ed., Handbook of genetics. Vol. 4: Vertebrates of genetic interest. Plenum Press, New York. 631 pp.

Abs, M. 1983. Ontogeny and juvenile development. Pages 3–18 *in* M. Abs, ed., Physiology and behavior of the pigeon. Academic Press, New York. 360 pp.

Adams, C. E. and J. K. Thomas. 1983. Characteristics and opinions of Texas hunters. Proc. Ann. Conf. Southeast. Assoc. Fish and Wildl. Agencies 37:244–251.

Akey, B. L., J. K. Nayar, and D. J. Forrester. 1981. Avian pox in Florida wild turkeys: *Culex nigripalpus* and *Wyeomyia vanduzeei* as experimental vectors. J. Wildl. Dis. 17(4):597–599.

Alcorn, G. D. 1949. Nesting of the mourning dove near Tacoma, Washington. Murrelet 30(3):59.

Aldrich, J. W. 1952. The source of migrant mourning doves in southern Florida. J. Wildl. Manage. 16(4): 447–456.

Aldrich, J. W. and A. J. Duvall. 1958. Distribution and migration of races of the mourning dove. Condor 60(2):108–128.

Aldrich, J. W., A. J. Duvall, and A. D. Geis. 1958. Racial determination of origin of mourning doves in hunters' bags. J. Wildl. Manage. 22(1):71–75.

Alexander, D. J., V. S. Hinshaw, and M. S. Collins. 1981. Characterization of viruses from doves representing a new serotype of avian paramyxoviruses. Arch. Virol. 68(3/4):265–269.

Alexander, H. E. 1951. Mourning dove study project 24-R-3. Arkansas Game and Fish Commiss., Little Rock. Mimeo. 69 pp.

Alison, R. M. 1976. Mourning doves wintering in Ontario. Canadian Field-Naturalist 90(2):174–176.

Allen, D. L. 1962. Our wildlife legacy. Rev. ed. Funk and Wagnalls Co., Inc., New York. 422 pp.

Allen, E. G. 1951. The history of American ornithology before Audubon. Trans. Amer. Philosoph. Soc. (New Series) 41(3):387–591.

Allen, G. M. 1909. Fauna of New England. List of the Aves. Occasional Paper. Boston Soc. Natur. Hist. VII. 230 pp.

Allen, J. M. 1963. Primary feather molt rate of wild immature doves in Indiana. Circ. 4, Indiana Dept. Conserv., Indianapolis. 5 pp.

———. Undated. Mourning dove investigation: Mourning dove banding recoveries and returns, 1960–1962. Unpublished rept. Indiana Div. Fish and Game, Indianapolis. 39 pp.

Allin, A. E. 1959. The Canadian lakehead. Flicker 31(3):77–81.

Altmann, J. 1974. Observation study of behaviour: Sampling methods. Behaviour 49(3–4):227–267.

Amend, S. R. 1969. Progress report on Carolina Sandhills mourning dove studies. Proc. Ann. Conf. Southeast. Assoc. Game and Fish Commiss. 23:191–201.

Amend, S. R. and F. C. Kniffin. 1970. Improvements in mourning dove trapping techniques, emphasizing trap design. Midwest Wildl. Conf. 32. 34 pp. [Typescript.]

American Ornithologists' Union. 1957. Check-list of North American birds. 5th ed. Port City Press, Baltimore. 691 pp.

———. 1983. Check-list of North American birds. 6th ed. Allen Press, Lawrence, Kansas. 877 pp.

Anderson, B. W. and R. D. Ohmart. 1977. Vegetation structure and bird use in the Lower Colorado River Valley. Pages 23–34 *in* Importance, preservation and management of riparian habitat: A symposium. Gen. Tech. Rep. RM-43. U.S. Forest Service, Washington, D.C. 217 pp.

Anderson, D. R. and K. P. Burnham. 1976. Population ecology of the mallard. VI. The effect of exploitation on survival. Resour. Publ. 128. U.S. Fish and Wildlife Service, Washington, D.C. 66 pp.

———. 1980. Effect of delayed reporting of band recoveries on survival estimates. J. Field Ornithol. 51(3): 244–247.

Anderson, D. R. and C. J. Henny. 1972. Population ecology of the mallard. I. A review of previous studies and the distribution and migration from breeding areas. Resour. Publ. 105. U.S. Fish and Wildl. Serv., Washington, D.C. 166 pp.

Anderson, D. R. and R. T. Sterling. 1974. Population dynamics of molting pintail drakes banded in south-central Saskatchewan. J. Wildl. Manage. 38(2):266–274.

Anderson, D. R., A. P. Wywialowski, and K. P. Burnham. 1981. Tests of the assumptions underlying life table methods for estimating parameters from cohort data. Ecology 62(4):1,121–1,124.

Anderson, L. and S. P. Havera. 1985. Blood lead, protoporphyrin and ingested shot for detecting lead poisoning in waterfowl. Wildl. Soc. Bull. 13(1):26–31.

Anderson, R. C. 1957. Taxonomic studies on the genera *Aproctella* Cram, 1931 and *Carinema* Pereira and Vaz, 1933 with a proposal for a new genus *Pseudaproctella* n. gen. Canadian J. Zool. 35(1):25–33.

Anderson, T. R., D. S. Pitts, and C. S. Nicoll. 1984. Prolactin's mitogenic action on the pigeon crop-sac mucosal epithelium involves direct and indirect mechanisms. Gen. Comp. Endocr. 54(2):236–246.

Andersson, M. C., G. Wiklund, and H. Rundgren. 1980. Parental defense of offspring: A model and an example. Anim. Behav. 28(2):536–542.

Andrews, E. A. 1925. Birds' nests at home. Auk 42(2):217–230.

Ankney, C. D. 1982. Sex ratio varies with egg sequence in lesser snow geese. Auk 99(4):662–666.

Anonymous. 1883. A complete pronouncing gazetter or geographical dictionare of the world. . . . J. B. Lippincott, Philadelphia. 2,680 pp.

———. 1889. A complete list of the birds of North America. Oologist 6(11):213–218.

———. 1890. A complete list of the birds of North America. Oologist 7(2):31–36.

———. 1916. Convention between the United States and Great Britain (for Canada) for the protection of migratory birds.

———. 1917. Migratory Birds Convention Act (by Canada).

———. 1918. Migratory Bird Treaty Act of 1918, as amended (by the United States).

———. 1936. Convention between the United States of America and the United Mexican States for the protection of migratory birds and game mammals, as amended.

———. 1943. Committee on bird protection, A.O.U. Auk 60(1):152–162.

———. 1956. The mourning dove question. Blue Bill 3(1):3–4.

———. 1957. Mourning dove investigations 1948–1956. Southeast. Assoc. Game and Fish Commiss. Tech. Bull. 1. 166 pp.

———. 1974. Convention between the government of the United States of America and the government of Japan for the protection of migratory birds and birds in danger of extinction, and their environment.

———. 1976. Convention between the United States of America and the Union of Soviet Socialist Republics concerning the conservation of migratory birds and their environment.

Arendt, W. J., T. A. Vargas Mora, and J. W. Wiley. 1979. White-crowned pigeon: Status rangewide and in the Dominican Republic. Proc. Ann. Conf. Southeast. Assoc. Fish and Wildl. Agencies 33:111–122.

Armbruster, M. J. 1973. Evaluation of the mourning dove Call-count as a reliable index to population levels in the field. M.A. thesis, Univ. Missouri, Columbia. 94 pp.

———. 1983. Analysis of behavior in various components of breeding mourning dove populations. Ph.D. dissertation, Univ. Missouri, Columbia. 73 pp.

Armbruster, M. J. and T. S. Baskett. 1985. A seven-year study of mourning dove Call-counts and nesting activity in central Missouri. Trans. Missouri Acad. Sci. 19:23–30.

Armbruster, M. J., T. S. Baskett, K. C. Sadler, and W. R. Goforth. 1978. Evaluating Call-count procedures for measuring local mourning dove populations. Trans. Missouri Acad. Sci. 12:75–90.

Armstrong, E. A. 1975. The life and lore of the bird in nature, art, myth and literature. Crown Publishers, Inc., New York. 250 pp. +

Armstrong, E. R. 1977. Reproductive biology and ecology of the mourning dove in southern Ontario. M.S. thesis. Univ. Guelph, Ontario. 140 pp.

Armstrong, E. R. and D. L. G. Noakes. 1977a. Albino mourning dove sightings in Ontario. Auk 94(1):158.

———. 1977b. Precocial testicular maturation in the mourning dove, *Zenaida macroura*. Canadian J. Zool. 55(12):2,065–2,066.

———. 1981. Food habits of mourning doves in southern Ontario. J. Wildl. Manage. 45(1):222–227.

———. 1983. Wintering biology of mourning doves, *Zenaida macroura*, in Ontario. Canadian Field Naturalist 97(4):434–438.

Atherton, N. W., M. E. Morrow, A. E. Bivings IV, and N. J. Silvy. 1982. Shrinkage of spiral plastic leg bands with resulting leg damage to mourning doves. Proc. Ann. Conf. Southeast. Assoc. Fish and Wildl. Agencies 36:666–670.

Atkinson, R. D., T. S. Baskett, and K. C. Sadler. 1982. Population dynamics of mourning doves banded in Missouri. Spec. Sci. Rept.—Wildl. 250. U.S. Fish and Wildl. Serv., Washington, D.C. 20 pp.

Audubon, J. J. 1827–1838. The birds of America; from original drawings. Published for the author, London. 435 color plates, elephant folio.

———. 1831. Ornithological biography. The passenger pigeon. Vol. 1:319–327. Reprinted *in* The passenger pigeon. Part II:417–424. Smithson. Instit. Ann. Rept., 1911. U.S. Govt. Print. Off., Washington, D.C.

———. 1840–1844. The birds of America, from drawings made in the United States and their territories. 7 vols. J. B. Chevalier, Philadelphia.

Ault, J. W. III, V. J. Heller, J. C. Lewis, and J. A. Morrison. 1976. Delayed molt of primary feathers of mourning doves during winter. J. Wildl. Manage. 40(1):184–187.

Austin, O. L., Jr. 1951. The mourning dove on Cape Cod. Bird-Banding 22(4):149–174.

Babcock, K. M., E. G. Hunt, and P. S. Duncan. 1990. Waterfowl breeding ground surveys and migratory bird harvest surveys. Unpublished ad hoc committee report to the Intern. Assoc. Fish and Wildl. Agencies. Jefferson City, Missouri. 27 pp.

Bagley, G. E. and L. N. Locke. 1967. The occurrence of lead in tissues of wild birds. Bull. Environ. Contam. Toxicol. 2(5):297–305.

Bailey, H. H. 1923. A new dove from Florida—*Zenaidura macroura peninsulari* (Florida mourning dove). Wilson Bull. 35(2):100.

Bailey, R. G. 1983. Delineation of ecosystem regions. Environ. Manage. 7(4):365–373.

Bailey, R. G. and C. T. Cushwa. 1981. Ecoregions of North America. FWS/OBS, 81/29. U.S. Fish and Wildl. Serv., Washington, D.C. 1 pp. [Map.]

Bailey, R. W. 1941. Climate and the settlement of the arid region. Pages 188–196 *in* Climate and man. U.S. Dept. of Agriculture. U.S. Govt. Print. Off., Washington, D.C. 1,248 pp.

Baird, S. F. 1855. Memoranda in reference to the natural history operations. Pages 9–10 *in* I. I. Stevens, Report of explorations for a route for the Pacific Railroad, near the forty-seventh and forty-ninth parallels of north latitude, from St. Paul to Puget Sound. Vol. I: Report of explorations and surveys for a railroad route from the Mississippi River to the Pacific Ocean. U.S. War Dept. A. O. P. Nicholson, Washington, D.C. 651 pp.

Baird, S. F., T. M. Brewer, and R. Ridgway. 1874. A history of North American birds. Land birds. 3 vols. Little, Brown, and Co., Boston.

Baker, R. R. 1978. The evolutionary ecology of animal migration. Holmes and Meier, New York. 1,012 pp.

———. 1984. Bird navigation: The solution of a mystery? Hodder and Stoughton, Toronto. 256 pp.

Balcomb, R., R. Stevens, and C. Bowen II. 1984. Toxicity of 16 granular insecticides to wild caught songbirds. Bull. Environ. Contam. Toxicol. 33(3):302–307.

Balda, R. P. 1965. Loggerhead shrike kills mourning dove. Condor 67(4):359.

Baldiccini, N. E., S. Bienvenuti, V. Fiaschi, P. Ioale, and F. Papi. 1982. Pigeon orientation: Experiments on the role of the olfactory stimuli perceived during the outward journey. Pages 160–169 *in* F. Papi and H. G. Wallraff, eds., Avian navigation. Springer-Verlag, New York. 380 pp.

Baldwin, T. and J. Thomas. 1854. New and complete gazetteer of the United States. . . . Lippincott, Grambo & Co., Philadelphia. 1,364 pp.

Baptista, L. F., W. I. Boarman, and P. Kandianidis. 1983. Behavior and taxonomic status of Grayson's dove. Auk 100(4):907–919.

Barfield, R. J. 1971. Activation of sexual and aggressive behavior by androgen implanted into the male ring dove brain. Endocrinology 89(6):1,470–1,476.

Barkalow, F. S., Jr. 1936. Unusual nesting records of the mourning dove from Cobb County, Georgia. Oriole 1(3):26.

Barnes, J. 1984. The complete works of Aristotle. Rev. Oxford trans. Bollinger Series LXXI 2. Princeton Univ. Press, Princeton, New Jersey. 1,250 pp.

Barrows, P. L. and F. A. Hayes. 1977. Studies on endoparasites of the mourning dove (*Zenaida macroura*) in the southeast United States. J. Wildl. Dis. 13(1):24–28.

Bart, J. 1977. Impact of human visitations on avian nesting success. Living Bird 16:187–192.

Bart, J. and D. S. Robson. 1982. Estimating survivorship when the subjects are visited periodically. Ecology 63(4):1,078–1,090.

Bart, J. and J. D. Schoultz. 1984. Reliability of singing bird surveys: Changes in observer efficiency with avian density. Auk 101(2):307–318.

Bartholomew, G. A., Jr. and W. R. Dawson. 1953. Respiratory water loss in some birds of the southwestern United States. Physiol. Zool. 26(2):162–166.

———. 1954. Body temperature and water requirements in the mourning dove, *Zenaidura macroura marginella*. Ecology 35(2):181–187.

Bartholomew, G. A., Jr. and R. E. MacMillen. 1960. The water requirements of mourning doves and their use of sea water and NaCl solutions. Physiol. Zool. 33(3):171–178.

Bartholomew, G. A., Jr., R. C. Lasiewski, and E. C. Crawford, Jr. 1968. Patterns of panting and gular flutter in cormorants, pelicans, owls, and doves. Condor 70(1):31–34.

Bartlett, R. A. 1962. Great surveys of the American West. Univ. Oklahoma Press, Norman. 410 pp.

Barton, B. S. 1799. Fragments (which are intended to illustrate, in some degree, the natural history of a country . . .). Paper delivered to The Linnaean Society, Philadelphia, April 18, 1799. Pages i–xviii *in* Selected works by eighteenth century naturalists and travellers. 1974 reprint. Arno Press, New York.

Bartram, W. 1791. Travels through North & South Carolina, Georgia, East & West Florida. . . . James & Johnson, Philadelphia. 522 pp.

Baskett, T. S., M. J. Armbruster, and M. W. Sayre. 1978. Biological perspectives for the mourning dove Call-count Survey. Trans. N. Amer. Wildl. and Natur. Resour. Conf. 43:163–180.

Bastin, E. W. 1952. Flight-speed of the mourning dove. Wilson Bull. 64(1):47.

Batschelet, E. 1972. Recent statistical methods for orientation data. Pages 61–91 *in* S. R. Galler, K. Schmidt-Koneig, G. J. Jacobs, and R. E. Belleville, eds., Animal orientation and navigation. Nat. Aero. Space Admin. Symposium. U.S. Govt. Print. Off., Washington, D.C. 606 pp.

———. 1978. Second-order statistical analysis of directions. Pages 3–24 *in* K. Schmidt-Koenig and W. T. Keeton, eds., Animal migration, navigation, and homing. Springer-Verlag, New York. 462 pp.

Beaglehole, E. 1936. Hopi hunting and hunting ritual. Yale Univ. Publ. in Anthro., No. 4. Yale Univ. Press, New Haven, Connecticut. 26 pp.

Beams, H. W. and R. K. Meyer. 1931. The formation of pigeon "milk." Physiol. Zool. 4(3):486–500.

Beckwith, S. L. 1959. Mourning dove foods in Florida during October. J. Wildl. Manage. 23(2):351–354.

Beer, J. and W. Tidyman. 1942. The substitution of hard seeds for grit. J. Wildl. Manage. 6(1):70–82.

Behler, J. L. and F. W. King. 1979. The Audubon Society field guide to North American reptiles and amphibians. Alfred A. Knopf, New York. 719 pp.

Bellrose, F. C. 1959. Lead poisoning as a mortality factor in waterfowl populations. Illinois Nat. Hist. Surv. Bull. 27(3):235–288.

———. 1964. Spent shot and lead poisoning. Pages 479–485 *in* J. P. Linduska, ed., Waterfowl tomorrow. U.S. Fish and Wildl. Serv., Washington, D.C. 770 pp.

———. 1976. Ducks, geese, and swans of North America. Stackpole Books, Harrisburg, Pennsylvania. 544 pp.

Bendell, J. F. 1955. Disease as a control of a population of blue grouse, *Dendragapus obscurus fuliginosus* (Ridgway). Canadian J. Zool. 33(1):195–223.

Bennett, G. F. 1970. Simple techniques for making avian blood smears. Canadian J. Zool. 48(3):585–586.

Bennett, W. C. and R. M. Zingg. 1976. The Tarahumara: An Indian tribe of northern Mexico. The Rio Grande Press, Glorieta, New Mexico. 412 pp.

Bennitt, R. and W. O. Nagel. 1937. A survey of the resident game and furbearers of Missouri. Univ. Missouri Studies 12(2):215 pp.

Bent, A. C. 1932. Life histories of North American gallinaceous birds. U.S. Natl. Mus. Bull. No. 176. Washington, D.C. 506 pp.

———. 1963. Life histories of North American gallinaceous birds. Reprint of 1932 Smithson. Bull. 162. Dover Publications, New York. 489 pp. +

Bequaert, J. C. 1956. The hippoboscidae or louse flies (Diptera) of mammals and birds. Part II. Taxonomy, evolution, and revision of American genera and species (concluded). Ent. Amer. 34, 35, 36:1–611.

Berthold, P. 1975. Migration: Control and metabolic physiology. Pages 77–128 *in* D. S. Farner, J. R. King, and K. C. Parkes, eds., Avian biology. Vol. V. Academic Press, Inc., New York. 523 pp.

Best, L. B. 1975. Interpretational errors in the "mapping method" as a census technique. Auk 93(2):452–460.

———. 1977. Territory quality and mating success in the field sparrow (*Spizella pusilla*). Condor 79(2):192–204.

———. 1981. Seasonal changes in detection of individual bird species. Pages 252–261 *in* C. J. Ralph and J. M. Scott, eds., Estimating numbers of terrestrial birds. Studies in Avian Biol. No. 6, Cooper Ornithol. Soc. 630 pp.

Best, T. L., T. E. Garrison, and C. G. Schmitt. In press. Availability and ingestion of lead shot by mourning doves (*Zenaida macroura*) in southeastern New Mexico. The Southwestern Naturalist.

Bigler, W. J., G. L. Hoff, and L. A. Scribner. 1977. Survival of mourning doves unaffected by withdrawing blood samples. Bird-Banding 48(2):168.

Bigler, W. J., E. Lassing, E. Buff, A. L. Lewis, and G. L. Hoff. 1975. Arbovirus surveillance in Florida: Wild vertebrate studies 1965–1974. J. Wildl. Dis. 11(3):348–356.

Bigony, M. L. 1987. Don't just stand there—do something. Texas Parks and Wildl. 45(10):12–19.

Birkenstein, L. R. and R. E. Tomlinson. 1981. Native names of Mexican birds. Resour. Publ. 139. U.S. Fish and Wildl. Serv., Washington, D.C. 159 pp.

Bivings, A. E. IV. 1980. Breeding ecology of the mourning dove on the Texas A&M University campus. Ph.D. dissertation, Texas A&M Univ., College Station. 64 pp.

Bivings, A. E. IV and N. J. Silvy. 1979. Roof-top trapping of urban mourning doves. Proc. Ann. Conf. Southeast. Assoc. Fish and Wildl. Agencies 33:154–158.

———. 1980. Primary feather molt of adult mourning doves in central Texas. Proc. Ann. Conf. Southeast. Fish and Wildl. Agencies 34:410–414.

———. 1981. Contribution of September mourning dove nesting to total production in central Texas. Proc. Ann. Conf. Southeast. Assoc. Fish and Wildl. Agencies 35:33–37.

Blair, A. P. 1967. Bullfrog attempts to catch dove. Southwestern Naturalist 12(2):201–202.

Blake, C. H. 1956. Leg sizes and band sizes: Second report. Bird-Banding 27(3):76–82.

Blank, T. H. and J. S. Ash. 1956. Marker for game birds. J. Wildl. Manage. 20(3):328–330.

Blankenship, L. H. and H. M. Reeves. 1970. Mourning dove recoveries from Mexico. Spec. Sci. Rept.—Wildl. 135. U.S. Fish and Wildl. Serv., Washington, D.C. 25 pp.

Blankenship, L. H., A. B. Humphrey, and D. MacDonald. 1971. A new stratification for mourning dove Call–count routes. J. Wildl. Manage. 35(2):319–326.

Blankenship, L. H., R. E. Reed, and H. D. Irby. 1966. Pox in mourning doves and Gambel's quail in southern Arizona. J. Wildl. Manage. 30(2):253–257.

Blankenship, L. H., R. E. Tomlinson, and R. C. Kufeld. 1967. Arizona dove wing survey, 1964. Spec. Sci. Rept.—Wildl. 116. U. S. Fish and Wildl. Serv., Washington, D.C. 34 pp.

Blockstein, D. E. 1982. Nesting behavior of mourning doves (*Zenaida macroura*) in Minnesota. M.S. thesis, Univ. Minnesota, Minneapolis. 66 pp.

———. 1985. Active netting to capture nesting mourning doves. N. Amer. Bird Bander 10(4):117–118.

———. 1986a. Reproductive behavior and parental investment of mourning doves. Ph.D. dissertation, Univ. Minnesota, Minneapolis. 222 pp.

———. 1986b. Nesting trios of mourning doves. Wilson Bull. 98(2):309–311.

———. 1989. Crop-milk and clutch size in mourning doves. Wilson Bull. 101(1):11–25.

Blockstein, D. E. and H. B. Tordoff. 1985. Gone forever: A contemporary look at the ecology and extinction of the passenger pigeon. Amer. Birds. 39(5):845–851.

Blockstein, D. E., B. D. Maxwell, and P. K. Fay. 1987. Dispersal of leafy spurge seeds (*Euphorbia esula*) by mourning doves (*Zenaida macroura*). Weed Science 35(2):160–162.

Blus, L. J., C. J. Henny, T. E. Kaiser, and R. A. Grove. 1983. Effects on wildlife from use of endrin in Washington state orchards. Trans. N. Amer. Wildl. and Natur. Resour. Conf. 48:159–174.

Board, R. G. 1974. Microstructure, water resistance and water repellency of the pigeon egg shell. British. Poult. Sci. 15(4):415–419.

Boldt, W. J. and G. O. Hendrickson. 1952. Mourning dove production in North Dakota shelterbelts, 1950. J. Wildl. Manage. 16(2):187–191.

Bolen, E. G., J. S. Loven, and B. W. Cain. 1977. A holding sleeve for waterfowl. J. Wildl. Manage. 41(4):789–790.

Bonaparte, C. L. J. L. 1825–1833. American ornithology; or, the natural history of birds inhabiting the United States, not given by Wilson. 4 vols. Samuel Augustus Mitchell, and Carey & Lea, Philadelphia.

———. 1838. Geographical and comparative list of birds of Europe and North America. Van Voorst, London. 67 pp.

———. 1855. Coup d'oeil sur l'ordre des pigeons. Extrait des comptes rendus des séances de l'Académie des sciences Tomes 39 et 40. Mallet-Bachelier, Paris. 59 pp.

Bond, J. 1971. Birds of the West Indies. 2nd ed. Houghton Mifflin Co., Boston. 256 pp.

Bookhout, T. A. 1958. The availability of plant seeds to bobwhite quail in southern Illinois. Ecology 39(4): 671–681.

Books–Blenden, P., T. S. Baskett, and E. M. Brown. 1984a. Histologic cycle of the mourning dove crop. Trans. Missouri Acad. Sci. 18:41–53.

Books–Blenden, P., T. S. Baskett, and M. W. Sayre. 1984b. Crop gland activity vs. nesting records for assessing September nesting of mourning doves. Wildl. Soc. Bull. 12(4):376–381.

Booth, E. S. 1945. Mourning doves wintering in southeastern Washington and northeastern Oregon. Murrelet 26(2):26.

Booth, T., F. Burnside, and P. R. Dorris. 1976. A continuation of mourning dove studies in Clark County, Arkansas, with emphasis on cyclical behavior patterns. Arkansas Acad. Sci. Proc. 30:19–21.

Booth, T., P. R. Dorrie, W. N. Hunter, and B. Mays. 1975. Preliminary dove banding studies in Clark County, Arkansas. Arkansas Acad. Sci. Proc. 29:22–23.

Borror, D. J. and R. E. White. 1970. A field guide to the insects of America north of Mexico. Houghton Mifflin Co., Boston. 404 pp.

Boughton, D. C. and J. J. Volk. 1938. Avian hosts of Eimerian coccidia. Bird–Banding 9(3):139–153.

Bourne, W. 1991. The art and science of dove-field management. Southern Outdoors 39(5):48–49, 51–53.

Bowser, C. W. 1957. Introduction and spread of the undesirable tamarisks in the Pacific southwestern section of the United States and comments regarding the plants' influence upon indigenous vegetation. Pages 12–17 *in* Symposium on phreatophytes. Phreatophyte Subcommittee of Pacific Inter-Agency Committee, American Geophysical Union, Sacramento, California. 52 pp.

Box, E. D. and D. W. Duszynski. 1977. Survey for *Sarcocystis* in the brown–headed cowbird (*Molothrus ater*): A comparision of macroscopic, microscopic and digestion techniques. J. Wildl. Dis. 13(4):356–359.

Boydstun, C. 1982. Evaluation of current status of white-fronted doves in South Texas. M.S. thesis. Texas A & I Univ., Kingsville. 68 pp.

Brackbill, H. 1970. New light on the mourning dove. Maryland magazine (Spring): 8–11.

Braun, C. E. 1979. Albinism in mourning doves. Southwestern Naturalist 24(1):198–200.

———. 1979. Migration routes of mourning doves west of the continental divide in the Central Management Unit. Wildl. Soc. Bull. 7(2):94–97.

Braun, E. L. 1950. Deciduous forest of eastern North America. Blakiston, Philadelphia. 596 pp.

Breazile, J. E. and R. L. Kitchell. 1969. Euthanasia for laboratory animals. Fed. Proc. 28(4):1,577–1,579.

Bree, M. M. and N. B. Gross. 1969. Anesthesia of pigeons with CI 581 (Ketamine) and pentobarbital. Lab. Anim. Care 19(4):500–502.

Breitenbach, R. P. and T. S. Baskett. 1961. Brooding behavior of mourning doves. Quart. Rept. Missouri Coop. Wildl. Res. Unit, Univ. Missouri, Columbia. Oct.–Dec. 1961:3–8.

———. 1967. Ontogeny of thermoregulation in the mourning dove. Physiol. Zool. 40(3):207–217.

Brereton, J. 1602. A briefe and true relation of the discoverie of the north part of Virginia. . . . Geor. Bishop, London. 48 pp.

Brewer, T. M. 1840. Wilson's American ornithology. . . . Otis, Broaders, and Co., Boston. 746 pp.

Brigham, E. M., Jr. 1943. The mourning dove's nest. Jack-Pine Warbler 21(2):55.

Brisbin, I. L., Jr. 1968. A determination of the caloric density and major body components of large birds. Ecology 49(4):792–794.

———. 1969. Bioenergetics of the breeding cycle of the ring dove. Auk 86(1):54–74.

Brister, B. 1975. Dove hunting. Pages 108–133 *in* D. E. Petzal, ed., The experts' book of upland and waterfowl hunting. Simon and Schuster, New York. 315 pp.

———. 1976. Shotgunning, the art and science. Winchester Press, New York. 315 pp.

Brodkorb, P. 1957. New passerine birds from the Pleistocene of Reddick, Florida. J. Paleon. 31(1):129–138.

———. 1959. The Pleistocene avifauna of Arredondo, Florida. Bull. Florida St. Mus. 4(9):269–291.

———. 1963. Two doves in the Pleistocene of Veracruz, Mexico. Condor 65(4):334.

———. 1971. Catalogue of fossil birds. Part 4. Bull. Florida St. Mus. 15(4):163–266.

Bromley, P. T., E. L. Hampton, and L. D. Wellman. 1989. A study of ethical and safe behavior by dove hunters in Virginia. Wildl. Soc. Bull. 17(4):450–459.

Brooks, S. C. 1943. Speed of flight of mourning doves. Condor 45(3):119.

Brown, D. E. and R. H. Smith. 1976. Predicting hunting success from Call-counts of mourning and white-winged doves. J. Wildl. Manage. 40(4):743–749.

Brown, J. L. 1969. Territorial behavior and population regulation in birds: A review and re-evaluation. Wilson Bull. 81(3):292–329.

Brown, R. L. 1967. The extent of breeding by immature mourning doves (*Zenaida macroura marginella*) in southern Arizona. M.S. thesis, Univ. Arizona, Tucson. 56 pp.

Brown, W. H. 1980. Mourning dove frozen to ground. Kentucky Warbler 56(1):23.

Brownie, C., D. R. Anderson, K. P. Burnham, and D. S. Robson. 1978. Statistical inference from band recovery data—a handbook. Resource Pub. 131. U.S. Fish and Wildl. Serv., Washington, D.C. 212 pp.

———. 1985. Statistical inference from band recovery data—a handbook. Resource Pub. 156. 2nd. ed. U.S. Fish and Wildl. Serv., Washington, D.C. 305 pp.

Brownie, C., J. E. Hines, and J. D. Nichols. 1986. Constant-parameter capture-recapture models. Biometrics 42(3):561–574.

Browning, A. 1979. Mercury and pesticide accumulation in tissues of the eastern mourning dove *Zenaidura macroura carolinensis* (Linnaeus). Georgia. J. Sci. 37(2):67–68.

Browning, B. M. 1959. An ecological study of the food habits of the mourning dove. California Fish and Game 45(4):313–331.

———. 1962. Food habits of the mourning dove in California. California Fish and Game 48(2):91–115.

Bryant, H. C. 1934. The first recorded lists of birds in the United States. Auk 51(4):451–453.

Bucher, E. H. 1982. Colonial breeding of the eared dove *(Zenaida auriculata)* in northeastern Brazil. Biotropica 14(4):255–261.

Bucher, E. H. and A. Orueta. 1977. Ecologia de la reproduccion de la paloma *Zenaida auriculata*. II. Epoca de cria, suceso y productividad en las colonias de nidificacion de Cordoba. Ecosur, Argentina 4(8):157–185.

Buerger, T. T. 1984. Effect of lead shot ingestion on captive mourning dove survivability and reproduction. M.S. thesis, Auburn Univ., Auburn, Alabama. 50 pp.

Buerger, T. T., R. E. Mirarchi, and M. E. Lisano. 1986. Effects of lead shot ingestion on captive mourning dove survivability and reproduction. J. Wildl. Manage. 50(1):1–8.

Buerger, T. T., L. I. Muller, R. E. Mirarchi, and M. E. Lisano. 1983. Lead shot ingestion in a sample of Alabama mourning doves. J. Alabama Acad. Sci. 54:119.

Bull, J. J. 1980. Sex determination of reptiles. Quart. Rev. Biol. 55:3–21.

Bullis, H. R., Jr. and F. C. Lincoln. 1952. A trans-Gulf migration. Auk 69(1):34–39.

Buntin, J. D. 1977. Stimulus requirements for squab induced crop sac growth and nest occupation in ring doves, *Streptopelia risoria*. J. Comp. Physiol. Psychol. 91(1):17–28.

Buntin, J. D. and I. A. Forsyth. 1979. Measurements of pituitary prolactin levels in breeding pigeons by crop sac radioreceptor assay. Gen. Compar. Endocr. 37(1):57–63.

Buntin, J. D. and E. Ruzycki. 1987. Characteristics of prolactin binding sites in the brain of the ring dove *(Streptopelia risoria)*. Gen. Compar. Endocr. 65(2):243–253.

Buntin, J. D. and D. Tesch. 1985. Effects of intracranial prolactin administration on maintenance of incubation readiness, ingestive behavior and gonadal condition in the ring dove. Horm. Behav. 19(2):188–203.

Buntin, J. D., M.-F. Cheng, and E. W. Hansen. 1977. Effect of parental feeding activity on squab induced crop sac growth in ring doves, *Streptopelia risoria*. Horm. Behav. 8(3):297–309.

Burger, G. V. and J. G. Teer. 1981. Economic and socioeconomic issues influencing wildlife management on private land. Pages 252–278 *in* R. T. Dumke, G. V. Burger, and J. R. March, eds., Proc. Symp: Wildl. Manage. on Priv. Lands. Wisconsin Chapt., The Wildl. Soc. La Crosse Print. Co., La Crosse, Wisconsin. 568 pp.

Burger, J., M. Gochfeld, J. E. Saliva, D. Gochfeld, and H. Morales. 1989. Antipredator behaviour in nesting zenaida doves *(Zenaida aurita)*: Parental investment or offspring vulnerability. Behaviour 111(1–4):127–143.

Burkhart, R. L. and L. A. Page. 1971. Chlamydiosis (ornithosis-psittacosis). Pages 118–140 *in* J. W. Davis, R. C. Anderson, L. Karstad, and D. O. Trainer, eds., Infectious and parasitic diseases of wild birds. Iowa St. Univ. Press, Ames. 344 pp.

Burleigh, T. D. 1938. The relation of birds to the establishment of longleaf pine seedlings in southern Mississippi. Occasional paper 75. Southern Forest Exp. Stn. New Orleans, Louisiana. 6 pp.

Burleson, B. and D. H. Riskind. 1986. Backcountry Mexico—a traveler's guide and phrase book. Univ. Texas Press, Austin. 311 pp.

Burley, N. 1980. Clutch overlap and clutch size: Alternative and complementary reproductive tactics. Amer. Natur. 115(2):223–246.

Burnham, K. P. and D. R. Anderson. 1979. The composite dynamic method as evidence for age-specific waterfowl mortality. J. Wildl. Manage. 43(2):356–366.

Burnham, K. P., D. R. Anderson, G. C. White, C. Brownie, and K. H. Pollock. 1987. Design and analysis methods for fish survival experiments based on release-recapture. Amer. Fisheries Soc. Manage. No. 5. Bethesda, Maryland. 437 pp.

Burrage, H. S., ed. 1906. Early English and French voyages, chiefly from Hakluyt, 1534–1608. Charles Scribner's Sons, New York. 453 pp.

Buskirk, W. 1986. The Western Apache. Univ. Oklahoma Press, Norman. 273 pp.

Byford, J. L. 1983. Non-poisonous snakes. Pages F7–F13 *in* R. M. Timm, ed., Prevention and control of wildlife damage. Great Plains Agric. Counc. and Nebraska Coop. Ext. Serv., Univ. Nebraska, Lincoln. Unnumbered.

Cade, T. J. 1965. Relations between raptors and columbiform birds at a desert water hole. Wilson Bull. 77(4):340–345.

Cadman, M. D., P. F. J. Eagles, and F. M. Helleiner, comps. 1987. Atlas of the breeding birds of Ontario. Univ. Waterloo Press, Waterloo, Ontario. 617 pp.

Cadow, G. 1933. Magen und Darm der Fruchtaubben. J. für Orn. 81:236–252.

Caldwell, L. D. 1955. A nesting study of the mourning dove in Kalamazoo County, Michigan. M.S. thesis, Michigan St. Univ., East Lansing. 44 pp.

———. 1964. Dove production and nest selection in southern Michigan. J. Wildl. Manage. 28(4):732–738.

Calhoun, J. B. 1948. Utilization of artificial nesting substrate by doves and robins. J. Wildl. Manage. 12(2):136–142.

Campbell, R. W., N. K. Dawe, I. MacTaggert-Cowan, J. M. Cooper, G. W. Kaiser, and M. C. E. McNall. 1990. The birds of British Columbia. Vol. II. Nonpasserines. Royal British Columbia Mus., Victoria. 635 pp.

Cannell, P. F. 1984. A revised age/sex key for mourning doves, with comments on the definition of molt. J. Field Ornithol. 55(1):112–114.

Cantwell, R. 1961. Alexander Wilson, naturalist and pioneer. J. B. Lippincott Co., Philadelphia. 319 pp.

Carey, C., H. Rahn, and P. Parisi. 1980. Calories, water, lipid and yolk in avian eggs. Condor 82(3):335–343.

Carpenter, J. W. 1970. Nesting of the mourning dove in northwest Oklahoma. Proc. Oklahoma Acad. Sci. 49:163–169.

———. 1971. Food habits of the mourning dove in northwest Oklahoma. J. Wildl. Manage. 35(2):327–331.

Carpenter, J. W., R. E. Corstvet, J. P. Thilsted, J. C. Lewis, and J. A. Morrison. 1972. A bacteriologic survey of the respiratory tract of mourning doves in Oklahoma and a serologic survey of those doves for antibodies to certain pathogens. Avian Dis. 16(3):671–670.

Carr, R. H. and C. M. James. 1931. Synthesis of adequate protein in the glands of the pigeon crop. Amer. J. Physiol. 97(1):227–231.

Carrington, M. E. and R. E. Mirarchi. 1989. Effects of lead shot ingestion on free-ranging mourning doves. Bull. Environ. Contam. Toxicol. 43(2):173–179.

Cartwright, G. 1977. On the wings of a dove. Texas Monthly (11):132–199.

Castelli, P. M. 1988. Mourning dove nesting success and chronology in New Jersey. M.S. thesis, Rutgers Univ., New Brunswick, New Jersey. 34 pp.

Castetter, E. F. and M. E. Opler. 1936. The ethnobiology of the Chiricahua and Mescalero Apache. Part III. Univ. New Mexico Bull. 297. Univ. New Mexico Press, Albuquerque. 63 pp.

Castrale, J. S. 1989. Availability of spent lead shot in fields managed for mourning dove hunting. Wildl. Soc. Bull. 17(2):184–189.

Catesby, M. 1731. The natural history of Carolina, Florida and the Bahama Islands. Vol. 1. Published for the author. London. 170 pp.

———. 1731–1743. The natural history of Carolina, Florida and the Bahama Islands. . . . 2 vols. Published for the author. London.

Cauthen, G. 1934. Localization of *Trichomonas columbae* in the domestic pigeon, ring dove and mourning dove. Proc. Helminthol. Soc. Washington 1(1):22.

Cayouette, R. 1947. The mourning dove in Levis County, Quebec. Auk 64(4):631–632.

Chadwick, A. 1983. Endocrinology of reproduction. Pages 55–72 *in* M. Abs, ed., Physiology and behavior of the pigeon. Academic Press, New York. 300 pp.

———. 1983. Introduction. Pages 1–2 *in* M. Abs, ed., Physiology and behavior of the pigeon. Academic Press, New York. 300 pp.

Chadwick, D. H. 1989. Sagebrush country: America's outback. Nat. Geog. 175(1):52–83.

Chamberlain, J. L. 1965. Fall foods of mourning dove in central Virginia. Wilson Bull. 77(1):84–86.

Chambers, G. D. 1961. A survey of wintering flocks of mourning doves in Missouri. M.A. thesis, Univ. Missouri, Columbia. 86 pp.

———. 1963. Corn a staple food of doves wintering in northern Missouri. J. Wildl. Manage. 27(3):486–488.

Chambers, G. D., H. M. Wight, and T. S. Baskett. 1962. Characteristics of wintering flocks of mourning doves in Missouri. J. Wildl. Manage. 26(2):155–159.

Champy, C. and D. Colle. 1919. Sur une correlation entre la glande du jabot de pigeon et les glandes genitales. C. R. Soc. Biol. (Paris) 82:818–819.

Channing, E. 1979. Movements of banded mourning doves near Turlock, California. California Fish and Game 65(1):23–35.

Chapman, F. M. 1937. Handbook of birds of eastern North America with introductory chapters on the study of birds in nature. 2nd rev. ed. D. Appleton-Century Co., New York. 581 pp. +

Cheney, S. and P. W. Cheney. 1967. Growth rate of nestling doves. Murrelet 48(1):14–16.

Cheng, M.-F. 1973a. Effect of ovariectomy on the reproductive behavior of female ring doves *(Streptopelia risoria)*. J. Comp. Physiol. Psychol. 83(2):221–233.

———. 1973b. Effect of estrogen on behavior of ovariectomized ring doves *(Streptopelia risoria)*. J. Comp. Physiol. Psychol. 83(2):234–239.

———. 1974. Ovarian development in the female ring dove in response to stimulation by intact and castrated male ring doves. J. Endocr. 63(1):43–53.

———. 1975. Induction of incubation behaviour in male ring doves *(Streptopelia risoria)*: A behavioural analysis. J. Reprod. Fert. 42(2):267–276.

———. 1979. Progress and prospects in ring dove research: A personal view. Pages 97–129 *in* J. S. Rosenblatt, R. A. Hinde, C. Beer, and M. C. Busnel, eds., Advances in the study of behavior. Academic Press, New York. 282 pp.

———. 1983. Does behavior influence hormone actions? Acad. Psychol. Bull. 5:473–485.

———. 1986. Female cooing promotes ovarian development in ring doves. Physiol. Behav. 37(2):371–374.

Cheng, M.-F. and W. H. Burke. 1983. Serum prolactin levels and crop sac development in ring doves *(Streptopelia risoria)* during a breeding cycle. Horm. Behav. 17(1):54–65.

Cheng, M.-F. and R. Silver. 1975. Estrogen-progesterone regulation of nest building and incubation behavior in ovariectomized ring doves *(Streptopelia risoria)*. J. Comp. Physiol. Psych. 88(1):256–263.

Cheng, M.-F., C. Desiderio, M. Havens, and A. Johnson. 1988. Behavioral stimulation of ovarian growth. Horm. Behav. 22(1):388–401.

Cheng, M.-F., T. Klint, and A. L. Johnson. 1986. Breeding experience modulating androgen dependent courtship behaviour in male ring doves *(Streptopelia risoria)*. Physiol. Behav. 36(4):625–630.

Cheng, M.-F., M. Porter, and G. Ball. 1981. Do ring doves copulate more than necessary for fertilization? Physiol. Behav. 27(4):659–662.

Clapp, R. B., M. K. Klimkiewicz, and A. G. Futcher. 1983. Longevity records of North American birds: Columbidae through Paridae. J. Field Ornithol. 54(2):123–137.

Clark, G. M. 1964. The acarine genus *Syringogphilus* in North American birds. Acarologia 6(4):77–92.

Clark, N. B. and K. Simkiss. 1980. Time, targets and triggers: A study of calcium regulation in the bird. Pages 191–208 *in* A. Epple and M. H. Stetson, eds., Avian endocrinology. Academic Press, New York. 577 pp.

Clark, T. L. 1968. State-wide mourning dove research. Job No. 2: Nesting and production. Rept. on Fed. Aid Proj. W-95-2. Texas Parks and Wildl. Dept., Austin. 9 pp.

Clark, T. L., K. E. Gamble, C. R. Wilkins, and J. T. Roberts. 1969. Mourning dove banding manual. Texas Parks and Wildl. Dept., Austin. 16 pp.

Cochran, W. W. 1980. Wildlife telemetry. Pages 507–520 *in* S. D. Schemnitz, ed., Wildlife management techniques manual. The Wildl. Soc., Washington, D.C. 606 pp.

Code of Federal Regulations. 1987. Wildlife and fisheries—50 CFR 20 Subpart C Section 20.21, Off. of Fed. Regist., Washington, D.C.

Cohen, A., H. S. Peters, and L. E. Foote. 1960. Calling behavior of mourning doves in two Midwest life zones. J. Wildl. Manage. 24(2):203–212.

Cohen, J. 1981. Olfaction and parental behavior in ring doves, *Streptopelia risoria*. Biochem. Syst. Ecol. 9(4):351–354.

Cole, L. J. 1933. The relation of light periodicity to the reproductive cycle, migration, and distribution of the mourning dove *(Zenaidura macroura carolinensis)*. Auk 50(3):284–296.

Conder, P. J. 1949. Individual distance. Ibis 91(4):649–655.

Conroy, M. J. 1985. Maximum likelihood methods for investigating reporting rates of rings on hunter–shot birds. Pages 215–241 *in* B. J. T. Morgan and P. M. North, eds., Statistics in ornithology. Springer-Verlag, New York. 418 pp.

Conroy, M. J. and W. Blandin. 1984. Geographic and temporal differences in band reporting rates for American black ducks. J. Wildl. Manage. 48(1):23–36.

Conroy, M. J. and B. K. Williams. 1981. Sensitivity of band reporting-rate estimates to violations of assumptions. J. Wildl. Manage. 45(3):789–792.

———. 1984. A general methodology for maximum likelihood inference from band-recovery data. Biometrics 40(3):739–748.

Conti, J. A. 1980. Interrelationships of parasites of white-winged doves and mourning doves in Florida. M.S. thesis, Univ. Florida, Gainesville. 69 pp.

Conti, J. A. and D. J. Forrester. 1981. Interrelationships of parasites of white-winged doves and mourning doves in Florida. J. Wildl. Dis. 17(4):529–536.

Conti, J. A., R. K. Frohlich, and D. J. Forrester. 1985. Experimental transfer of *Trichomonas gallinae* (Rivolta, 1878) from white-winged doves to mourning doves. J. Wildl. Dis. 21(3):229–232.

Cooch, F. G., S. Wendt, G. E. J. Smith, and G. Butler. 1978. The Canada migratory game bird hunting permit and associated surveys. Pages 8–39 *in* H. Boyd and G. Finney, eds., Migratory game bird hunting in Canada. Canadian Wildl. Service Rept. Series No. 43. Ottawa. 127 pp.

Cooke, W. W. 1888. Report on bird migration in the Mississippi Valley in the years 1884 and 1885. Bull. No. 2. Div. Econ. Ornithol. U.S. Dept. Agriculture. Washington, D.C. 313 pp.

Coon, D. W. 1968. An evaluation of field competition between the mourning dove and blackbirds for available grain. M.S. thesis, Auburn Univ., Auburn, Alabama. 62 pp.

Coon, R. A., J. D. Nichols, and H. F. Percival. 1981. Importance of structural stability to success of mourning dove nests. Auk 98(2):389–391.

Cooper, J. G. 1860. Explorations and surveys for a railroad route from the Mississippi River to the Pacific Ocean. Zool. Rept. No. 3, Report upon the birds collected on the survey. Vol. 12, Book 2, Chapter 1, Land birds. Pages 140–287. First House ed. Washington, D.C.

Cooper, J. G. and G. Suckley. 1859. The natural history of Washington Territory. . . . Bailliere Brothers, New York. 399 pp.

Corbusier, W. H. 1886. Apache-Yumas and Apache-Mojaves. Part II. Amer. Antiquity and Oriental J. 8(6): 325–329.

Cottam, C. 1948. The mourning dove in Alaska. Wilson Bull. 60(3):188–189.

Cottam, C. and J. B. Trefethen. 1968. Whitewings—The life history, status, and management of the white-winged dove. D. Van Nostrand, Princeton. 348 pp.

Couch, A. B., Jr. 1952. Blood parasites of some common Texas birds. Field and Lab. 20(4):146–154.

Coues, E. 1874. Birds of the northwest. U.S. Govt. Print. Off., Washington, D.C. 791 pp.

———, ed. 1893. The history of the Lewis and Clark Expedition. 4 vols. Francis P. Harper, New York.

———. 1903. Key to North American birds. . . . 5th ed. Two vols. Dana Estes and Co., Boston.

Coues, E. and D. W. Prentiss. 1883. Avifauna Columbiana: being a list of birds ascertained to inhabit the District of Columbia. 2nd ed. U.S. Nat. Mus., Bull. No. 26. Washington, D.C. 133 pp.

Cowan, J. B. 1952. Life history and productivity of a population of western mourning doves in California. California Fish and Game 38(4):505–521.

———. 1959. "Pre-fab" wire mesh cones give doves better nests than they can build themselves. Outdoor California 20(1):10–11.

Cowardin, L. M. 1977. Analysis and machine mapping of the distribution of band recoveries. Spec. Sci. Rept.—Wildl. 198. U.S. Fish and Wildl. Serv. Washington, D.C. 8 pp.

Cowles, G. S. and D. Goodwin. 1959. Seed digestion by fruit-eating pigeons, *Treron*. Ibis 101(2):253–254.

Craig, W. 1911. The expressions of emotion in the pigeons. II. The mourning dove *(Zenaidura macroura* Linn.). Auk 28(4):398–407.

Crawford, R. D. 1969. Foods and age ratios of hunter-bagged mourning doves in northwest Missouri. Iowa Bird Life 39(4):71–73.

Crissey, W. F. 1955. The use of banding data in determining waterfowl migration and distribution. J. Wildl. Manage. 19(1):75–84.

Culler, R. C. 1970. Objectives, methods, and environment—Gila River phreatophyte project, Graham County, Arizona. Geol. Surv. Prof. Pap. 655-A. U.S. Govt. Print. Off., Washington, D.C. 25 pp.

Cummings, E. G. and T. L. Quay. 1953. Food habits of the mourning dove in North Carolina. J. Elisha Mitchell Sci. Soc. 69(2):142–149.

Cunningham, S. C. 1986. The comparative feeding and nesting ecology of mourning and white-winged doves in the Buckeye-Arlington Valley area of Arizona. Contract Rept. to Arizona Game and Fish Dept. 161 pp.

Custer, T. W. and C. A. Mitchell. 1987. Exposure to insecticides of brushland wildlife within the lower Rio Grande Valley, Texas, USA. Environ. Pollut. 45(3): 207–220.

Cuthbert, N. L. 1945. The ovarian cycle of the ring dove *(Streptopelia risoria)*. J. Morph. 77(3):351–377.

Cutts, E. 1954. Mourning dove: Nesting data. Chat 18(4):103.

Cuvillier, E. 1937. The nematode, *Ornithostrongylus quadriradiatus*, a parasite of the domesticated pigeon. U.S. Dept. Agric. Tech. Bull. No. 569. 36 pp.

Dahlen, J. H. and A. O. Haugen. 1954. Acute toxicity of certain insecticides to the bobwhite quail and mourning dove. J. Wildl. Manage. 18(4):477–481.

Dahlgren, R. B. 1955. Factors affecting mourning dove populations in Utah. M.S. thesis, Utah St. Agric. Coll., Logan. 93 pp.

Dalrymple, B. W. 1949. Doves and dove shooting. P. G. Putnam's Sons, New York. 243 pp.

Davenport, D. A. 1977. Computerized tabulation and display of band recovery data. Spec. Sci. Rep.—Wildl. 199. U.S. Fish and Wildl. Serv., Washington, D.C. 7 pp.

Davey, P. 1953. A study of the mourning dove in southern Michigan. M.S. thesis. Univ. Michigan, Ann Arbor. 47 pp.

Davidson, W. R. and V. F. Nettles. 1988. Field manual of wildlife diseases in the southeastern United States. Southeast. Coop. Wildl. Disease Study, Athens, Georgia. 309 pp.

Davies, W. L. 1939. CIX. The composition of the crop milk of pigeons. Biochem. J. 33(1):898–901.

Davis, C. A. and M. W. Anderson. 1973. Seasonal food use by mourning doves in the Mesilla Valley, south-central New Mexico. Agri. Exp. Stn. Bull. 612, New Mexico St. Univ. 21 pp.

Davis, J. W., R. C. Anderson, L. Karstad, and D. O. Trainer. 1971. Infectious and parasitic diseases of wild birds. Iowa St. Univ. Press, Ames. 344 pp.

Davis, R. M. 1976. Great Plains windbreak history: An overview. Pages 8–11 *in* R. W. Titus, ed., Shelterbelts on the Great Plains. Great Plains Agric. Council Publ. No. 78.

Davison, V. E. 1961. Food competition between game and non-game birds. Trans. N. Amer. Wildl. and Natur. Resour. Conf. 26:239–246.

Davison, V. E. and E. G. Sullivan. 1963. Mourning doves' selection of foods. J. Wildl. Manage. 27(3):373–383.

Dawson, D. G. 1981. Counting birds for a relative measure (index) of density. Pages 12–16 *in* C. J. Ralph and J. M. Scott, eds., Estimating numbers of terrestrial birds. Studies in Avian Biol. No. 6, Cooper Ornith. Soc. 630 pp.

Dawson, W. L. 1909. The birds of Washington. Vol. 2. The Occidental Publishing Co., Seattle. 997 pp.

Dawson, W. R. and H. B. Tordoff. 1959. Relation of oxygen consumption to temperature in the evening grosbeak. Condor 61(6):388–396.

Day, A. M. 1959. North American waterfowl. The Stackpole Co., Harrisburg, Pennsylvania. 363 pp.

Day, G. L., S. D. Schemnitz, and R. D. Taber. 1980. Capturing and marking wild animals. Pages 61–88 *in* S. D. Schemnitz, ed., Wildlife management techniques manual. The Wildl. Soc., Washington, D.C. 606 pp.

Day, G. M. 1953. The Indian as an ecological factor in northeastern forests. Ecology 34(2):329–346.

de Gayangos, D. P. 1866. Cartas y relaciones de Hernan Cortez al Emperor Carlos V. Imprenta Central de los Ferro-Carilles, Paris. 575 pp.

DeGraaf, R. M. and C. W. Stihler. 1979. Nesting habitats of five common suburban bird species. Trans. Northeast. Sec. Wildl. Soc. 36:52–59.

Delacour, J. 1980. Wild pigeons and doves. T. F. H. Publications, Inc., Neptune, New Jersey. 189 pp.

de Lys, C. 1948. A treasury of American superstitions. The Philosophical Library, New York. 494 pp.

DeMaso, S. J. and A. D. Peoples. In press. A restraining device for handling northern bobwhites. Wildl. Soc. Bull.

DeMay, I. S. 1941. Pleistocene bird life of the Carpinteria asphalt, California. Publ. No. 530:61–80. Carnegie Inst. Washington, Washington, D.C.

———. 1942. An avifauna from Indian kitchen middens at Buena Vista Lake, California. Condor 44(5):228–230.

Desmeth, M. 1980. Lipid composition of pigeon crop milk. II. Fatty acids. Comp. Biochem. Physiol. 66B(1): 135–138.

Desmeth, M. and J. Vandeputte-Poma. 1980. Lipid composition of pigeon milk. I. Total lipids and lipid classes. Comp. Biochem. Physiol. 66B(1):129–133.

De Voe, T. F. 1862. The market book, a history of the public markets of the city of New York. Printed for the author. New York. 621 pp.

DeVoto, B. 1947. Across the wide Missouri. Houghton Mifflin Co., Boston. 454 pp.

DeWeese, L. R., L. C. McEwen, G. L. Hensler, and B. E. Peterson. 1984. Pesticide and PCB contamination in migratory birds of the western United States. Abstract. Bull. Ecol. Soc. America 65(2):235.

Diamond, L. S. 1957. The establishment of various trichomonads of animals and man in axenic cultures. J. Parasitol. 43:488–490.

Dice, L. R. 1955. Natural communities. Univ. Michigan Press, Ann Arbor. 547 pp.

Dill, H. H. and W. H. Thornsberry. 1950. A cannon-projected net trap for capturing waterfowl. J. Wildl. Manage. 14(2):132–137.

Dillman, D. A. 1978. Mail and telephone surveys. John Wiley Sons, New York. 325 pp.

Dillon, O. W., Jr. 1961. Mourning dove foods in Texas during September and October. J. Wildl. Manage. 25(3):334–336.

Dodson, M. M. 1955. Oklahoma migratory game bird study. 1949–53 P-R W-32-R. Oklahoma Game and Fish Dept., Norman. 51 pp.

Dolton, D. D. 1977. Mourning dove status report, 1976. Spec. Sci. Rept.—Wildl. 208. U.S. Fish and Wildl. Serv., Washington, D.C. 27 pp.

———. 1981. 1981 mourning dove breeding population status. U.S. Fish and Wildl. Serv., Adm. Rept. Laurel, Maryland. 23 pp.

———. 1982. 1982 mourning dove breeding population status. U.S. Fish and Wildl. Serv., Adm. Rept. Laurel, Maryland. 19 pp.

———. 1985. 1985 mourning dove breeding population status. U.S. Fish and Wildl. Serv., Adm. Rept. Laurel, Maryland. 11 pp.

———. 1987. Mourning dove breeding population status, 1987. U.S. Fish and Wildl. Serv., Laurel, Maryland. 10 pp.

———. 1989. Mourning dove breeding population status, 1989. U.S. Fish and Wildl. Serv., Laurel, Maryland. 12 pp.

———. 1990. Mourning dove breeding population status, 1990. U.S. Fish and Wildl. Serv., Laurel, Maryland. 12 pp.

Dolton, D. D., P. H. Geissler, and J. R. Sauer. In preparation. Mourning dove breeding population status, 1987. U.S. Fish and Wildl. Serv. Tech. Rept. Washington, D.C.

Donovan, C. A. 1958. Restraint and anesthesia of caged birds. Vet. Med. 53(10):541–543.

Downing, R. L. 1959. Significance of ground nesting by mourning doves in northwestern Oklahoma. J. Wildl. Manage. 23(1):117–118.

Downs, T. 1954. Pleistocene birds from the Jones fauna of Kansas. Condor 56(4):207–221.

Drewien, R. C. and R. D. Sparrowe. 1966. Nesting and production of the mourning dove in eastern South Dakota. South Dakota Bird Notes 18:33–44.

Droege, S. and J. R. Sauer. 1989. North American breeding bird survey annual summary 1988. Biol. Rept. 89(13). U.S. Fish and Wildl. Serv., Washington, D.C. 16 pp.

Droege, S. and J. R. Sauer. 1990. North American breeding bird survey annual summary 1989. Biol. Rept. 90(8). U.S. Fish and Wildl. Serv., Washington, D.C. 22 pp.

Duck, L. G. and J. B. Fletcher. 1944. A survey of the game and furbearing animals of Oklahoma. Div. Wildl. Restor. and Res., Oklahoma Game and Fish Commiss. Bull. 3. 144 pp.

Dumont, J. N. 1965. Prolactin-induced cytological changes in the mucosa of the pigeon crop during crop "milk" formation. Z. Zellforsch. u. Mikr. Anat. 68(4):755–782.

Dunks, J. H. 1977. Texas mourning dove band recovery analysis, 1967–1974. Fed. Aid Rept. Ser. No. 14. Texas Parks and Wildl. Dept., Austin. 94 pp.

———, chairman. 1980. Report to the national program planning group from national hunter-harvest survey subcommittee. Unpublished rept. Intern. Assoc. Fish and Wildl. Agencies, Washington, D.C. 5 pp.

Dunks, J. H., R. E. Tomlinson, H. M. Reeves, D. D. Dolton, C. E. Braun, and T. P. Zapatka. 1982. Migration, harvest, and population dynamics of mourning doves banded in the Central Management Unit, 1967–77. Spec. Sci. Rept.—Wildl. 249. U.S. Fish and Wildl. Serv., Washington, D.C. 128 pp.

Durant, M. and M. Harwood. 1980. On the road with John James Audubon. Dodd, Mead & Co., New York. 639 pp.

Duvall, A. J. and C. S. Robbins. 1952. Investigations of methods of determining abundance of breeding mourning doves in certain eastern states. Pages 15–34 *in* Spec. Sci. Rept.—Wildl. No. 17. U.S. Fish and Wildl. Serv., Washington, D.C. 53 pp.

Eberhardt, L. L. 1972. Some problems in estimating survival from banding data. Pages 153–171 *in* Population ecology of migratory birds: A symposium. Wildl. Res. Rept. 2. U.S. Fish and Wildl. Serv., Washington, D.C. 278 pp.

Ebling, W. 1979. The fruited plain, the story of American agriculture. Univ. California Press, Berkeley. 433 pp.

Edminster, F. C. 1954. American game birds of field and forest, their habits, ecology and management. Charles Scribner and Sons, New York. 409 pp.

Edmunds, S. R. and C. D. Ankney. 1987. Sex ratios of hatchling mourning doves. Canadian J. Zool. 65(4):871–874.

Edwards, G. 1743. A natural history of uncommon birds, and of some other rare and undescribed animals. Vol. 1. Printed for author. London. 52 pp.

———. 1743–1751. A natural history of uncommon birds. . . . 4 vols. Published for the author. London.

Edwards, W. R., R. E. Duzan, and R. J. Siemers. 1983. Organochloride insecticide residues and PCBs in tissues of woodcock, mourning doves, and robins from east-central Illinois, 1978–79. Bull. Environ. Contam. Toxicol. 31(4):407–414.

Efron, B. 1982. The jackknife, the bootstrap and other resampling plans. Soc. for Indust. Appl. Math., Philadelphia. 92 pp.

El-Ashry, M. and D. C. Gibbons. 1987. Managing the West's water. J. Soil and Water Conserv. 42(1):8–13.

Elder, J. B. 1956. Watering patterns of some desert game animals. J. Wildl. Manage. 20(4):368–378.

Emerson, K. C. 1972. Checklist of the Mallophaga of North America (north of Mexico). Part IV. Bird host list. Deseret Test Center, Dugway, Utah. 216 pp.

Emlen, S. T. 1975. Migration: Orientation and navigation. Pages 129–210 *in* D. S. Farner, J. R. King, and K. C. Parkes, eds., Avian biology. Vol. V. Academic Press, Inc., New York. 523 pp.

Enemar, A., S-G. Hojman, P. Klaesson, and L. Nilsson. 1976. The relationship between census results and the breeding populations of birds in subalpine birch forests. Ornis Fennica 53:1–8.

Eng, R. L. 1986. Upland game birds. Pages 407–428 *in* A. Y. Cooperrider, R. J. Boyd, and H. R. Stuart, eds., Inventory and monitoring of wildlife habitat. U.S. Bur. Land Manage., Denver, Colorado. 858 pp.

Erickson, C. J. and R. L. Morris. 1972. Effects of mate familiarity on the courtship and reproductive success of ring doves (*Streptopelia risoria*). Anim. Behav. 20(2): 341–344.

Erickson, C. J. and P. G. Zenone. 1976. Courtship differences in male ring doves: avoidance of cuckoldry? Science 192(4,246):1,353–1,354.

Erling, H. 1957. Identification of diseases and parasites of game animals. Proj. W-78-R-1. Arizona Game and Fish Dept., Phoenix. 7 pp.

Errington, P. L. 1935. Winter-killing of mourning doves in central Iowa. Wilson Bull. 47(2):159–160.

Ervin, D. E., C. G. McNabb, and M. D. Bennett. 1983. Conservation tillage and returns. Agric. Guide 350. Univ. Missouri Ext. Div., Columbia. 4pp.

Estrada, O. S. 1978. Estudio sobre el aprovechamiento de palomas migratorias en Nicaragua. Unpubl. rept. M.A. thesis. DIGERENARE, Dpto. de Vida Silv., Managua, Nicaragua. 63 pp.

Evans, R. H. and B. Tangredi. 1985. Cerebrospinal nematodiasis in free-ranging birds. J. Amer. Vet. Med. Assoc. 187(11):1,213–1,214.

Faaborg, J. R. 1988. Ornithology: An ecological approach. Prentice-Hall, Englewood Cliffs, New Jersey. 470 pp.

Farner, D. S. 1945. Age groups and longevity in the American robin. Wilson Bull. 57(1):56–74.

———. 1955. The annual stimulus for migration: Experimental and physiological aspects. Pages 198–237 *in* A. Wolfson, ed., Recent studies in avian biology. Univ. Illinois Press, Urbana. 479 pp.

Fechner, J. H., Jr. and J. D. Buntin. 1989. Localization of prolactin binding sites in ring dove brain by quantitative autoradiography. Brain Res. 487(2):245–254.

Feder, H. H., A. Storey, D. Goodwin, C. Reboulleau, and R. Silver. 1977. Testosterone and "5a—dihydrotestosterone" levels in peripheral plasma of male and female ring doves (*Streptopelia risoria*) during the reproductive cycle. Biol. Reprod. 16(5):666–677.

Feduccia, A., ed. 1985. Catesby's birds of colonial America. Univ. North Carolina Press, Chapel Hill. 176 pp.

Fenneman, N. M. 1931. Physiography of western United States. McGraw Hill Book Co., New York. 534 pp.

Fernald, M. L. 1970. Gray's manual of botany. 8th ed. D. Van Nostrand Co., New York. 1,632 pp.

Ferrando, R., R. Wolter, C. Fourlon, and M. Morice. 1971. Le lait de pigeon. Ann. Nutr. Aliment. 25(5):241–251.

Ferris, R. G. 1968. Explorers and settlers. . . . U.S. National Park Serv. U.S. Govt. Print. Off., Washington, D.C. 506 pp.

Fessler, F. R. 1960. Managing woolly croton for doves and bobwhites. Proc. Ann. Conf. Southeast. Assoc. Game and Fish Commiss. 14:74–77.

Fichter, E. 1959. Mourning dove production in four Idaho orchards and some possible implications. J. Wildl. Manage. 23(4):438–447.

Filion, F. L. 1978. Increasing the effectiveness of mail surveys. Wildl. Soc. Bull. 6(3):135–141.

Fisher, A. K. 1893. Report on the ornithology. . . . Pages 7–158 *in* The Death Valley Expedition: A biological survey of parts of California, Nevada, Arizona, and Utah. N. Amer. Fauna, No. 7. U.S. Bur. Biol. Survey. U.S. Govt. Print. Off., Washington, D.C. 393 pp.

Fisher, H. 1972. The nutrition of birds. Pages 431–469 *in* D.S. Farner and J. R. King, eds., Avian biology, Vol. II. Academic Press, New York. 612 pp.

Fisher, V. and O. L. Holmes. 1968. Gold rushes and mining camps of the early American West. The Caxton Publishers, Caldwell, Idaho. 466 pp.

Fitzgerald, K. 1967. Weathervanes and whirligigs. Clarkson N. Potter, Inc., New York. 186 pp.

Flickinger, E. L. and K. A. King. 1972. Some effects of aldrin-treated rice on Gulf Coast wildlife. J. Wildl. Manage. 36(3):706–727.

Flickinger, E. L., C. A. Mitchell, D. H. White, and E. J. Kolbe. 1986. Bird poisoning from misuse of the carbamate Furadan in a Texas rice field. Wildl. Soc. Bull. 14(1):59–62.

Flickinger, E. L., D. H. White, C. A. Mitchell, and T. G. Lamont. 1984. Monocrotophos and dicrotophos residues in birds as a result of misuse of organophosphates in Matagorda County, Texas. J. Assoc. Off. Anal. Chem. 67(4):827–828.

Foote, L. E. 1957. Suggestions for a mourning dove management program. Unpubl. mimeo. rept. originally presented at the Southeast. Wildl. Conf., Oct. 1953, Chattanooga, Tennessee. On file at Migratory Bird Manage. Off., U.S. Fish and Wildl. Serv., Laurel, Maryland. 14 pp.

———. 1959. A sampling design for mourning dove call counts. Unpubl. rept. to the Bur. Sport Fish. and Wildl. U.S. Fish and Wildl. Serv. from the Wildl. Manage. Instit. 47 pp. +

Foote, L.E. and H. S. Peters. 1952. Introduction. Spec. Sci. Rept. – Wildl. 17:1–3. U.S. Fish and Wildl. Serv., Washington, D.C. 53 pp.

Foote, L.E., H. S. Peters, and A. L. Finkner. 1958. Design tests for mourning dove Call-count sampling in seven southeastern states. J. Wildl. Manage. 22(4):402–408.

Forbes, C. B. 1959. The mourning dove in Maine. Maine Field Natur. 15(2):30–45.

Forbush, E. H. 1927. Birds of Massachusetts and other New England states. Part II. Land birds from bobwhites to grackles. Massachusetts Dept. Agric. Norwood Press, Norwood, Massachusetts. 461 pp.

Forrester, D. J., J. A. Conti, J. D. Shamis, W. J. Bigler, and G. L. Hoff. 1983. Ecology of helminth parasitism of mourning doves in Florida. Proc. Helminthol. Soc. Washington 50(1):143–152.

Forshaw, J. M. 1978. Parrots of the world. 2nd ed. Lansdowne Editions, Melbourne, Australia. 584 pp.

Frankel, A. I. 1961. An analysis of the song and other behavioral aspects of penned mourning doves. M.S. thesis. Univ. Missouri, Columbia. 145 pp.

Frankel, A. I. and T. S. Baskett. 1961. The effect of pairing on cooing of penned mourning doves. J. Wildl. Manage. 25(4):372–384.

———. 1963. Color marking disrupts pair bonds of captive mourning doves. J. Wildl. Manage. 27(1):124–127.

Franks, E. C. 1967. The responses of incubating ringed turtle doves *(Streptopelia risoria)* to manipulated egg temperatures. Condor 69(2):268–276.

Frates, J. E. 1963. A production study of mourning doves in a shelter belt. Nebraska Bird Rev. 31(2):18–24.

Fredrickson, L. H. 1970. A nylon belt for holding birds. Bird-Banding 41(3):242–243.

Fredrickson, L. H. and T. S. Taylor. 1982. Management of seasonally flooded impoundments for wildlife. Resour. Publ. 148. U.S. Fish and Wildl. Serv., Washington, D.C. 28 pp.

Fredrickson, L. H., T. S. Baskett, G. K. Brakhage, and V. C. Cravens. 1977. Evaluating cultivation near duck blinds to reduce lead poisoning hazard. J. Wildl. Manage. 41(4):624–631.

French, N. R. 1954. Notes on the breeding activities and on gular sacs in the pine grosbeak. Condor 56(2):83–85.

Fretwell, S. 1980. Evolution of migration in relation to factors regulating bird numbers. Pages 517–527 *in* A. Keast and E. S. Morton, eds., Migrant birds in the neotropics: Ecology, behavior, distribution, and conservation. Smithson. Instit. Press, Washington, D.C. 576 pp.

Friedmann, H., L. Griscom, and R. T. Moore. 1950. Distributional check-list of the birds of Mexico. Pac. Coast Avif. 29. 202 pp.

Friend, M., ed. 1987. Field guide to wildlife diseases. Vol. 1. General field procedures and diseases of migratory birds. Resour. Publ. 167. U.S. Fish and Wildl. Serv., Washington, D.C. 225 pp.

Frith, H. J. 1977. Some display postures of Australian pigeons. Ibis 119(2):167–182.

———. 1982. Pigeons and doves of Australia. Rigby, Adelaide, Australia. 304 pp.

Fuemmeler, W. J. 1992. Evaluation of techniques for estimating mourning dove nesting parameters in Missouri. M.S. thesis. Univ. Missouri, Columbia. 95 pp.

Fuller, K. S. and B. Swift. 1984. Latin American wildlife trade laws (Leyes del comercio de vida silvestre en America Latina). World Wildl. Fund, Washington, D.C. 354 pp.

Funk, H. D. 1965. Mourning dove migration in Colorado. Game Info. Leafl. 26. Colorado Div. Game, Fish and Parks, Denver. 2 pp.

———. 1977. Mourning dove migration in Colorado. Outdoor Facts, Game Info. Leafl. 26 (rev.). Colorado Div. Game, Fish, and Parks, Denver. 2 pp.

Gabrielson, I. N. 1941. Wildlife conservation. The Macmillan Co., New York. 250 pp.

Gabrielson, I. N. and F. C. Lincoln. 1959. The birds of Alaska. The Stackpole Co., Harrisburg, Pennsylvania. 922 pp.

Gaida, U. and M. J. Marchello. 1987. Going wild: A guide to field dressing, butchering, sausage making and cooking. Watab Marketing, Inc., Sartell, Minnesota. 239 pp.

Gallizioli, S. 1961. The current status and management of the mourning dove in the Western Management Unit. Trans. N. Amer. Wildl. and Natur. Resour. Conf. 26:395–403.

Gardner, L. L. 1930. On the body temperature of nestling altricial birds. Auk 47(3):367–379.

Garrigues, R., Y. Ferrand, M. Anselme, and G. Tayalay. 1989. La couleur des pattes: Un critere d'age chez la tourterelle a queue carree. Gibier Faune Sauvage 6 (Sept.):315–319.

Gates, C. E. 1969. Statistical evaluation of the June 1966–February 1969 mourning dove data of the Texas Parks and Wildlife Department. Final rept. under interagency contract (68–69)–292. Texas A&M Univ., College Station. 116 pp.

Gates, C. E. and W. B. Smith. 1972. Estimation of density of mourning doves from aural information. Biometrics 28(2):345–349.

Gates, C. E., T. L. Clark, and K. E. Gamble. 1975. Optimizing mourning dove breeding population surveys in Texas. J. Wildl. Manage. 39(2):237–242.

Gauthreaux, S. A., Jr. 1982. The ecology and evolution of avian migration systems. Pages 93–168 *in* D. S. Farner, J. R. King, and K. C. Parkes, eds., Avian biology. Vol. VI. Academic Press, Inc., New York. 490 pp.

———. 1985. Migration. Pages 232–258 *in* O. S. Pettingill, Jr., ed., Ornithology in laboratory and field. 5th ed. Academic Press, Inc., New York. 403 pp.

Geis, A. D. 1972a. Role of banding data in migratory bird population studies. Pages 213–228 *in* Population ecology in migratory birds: A symposium. Wildl. Res. Rept. 2. U.S. Fish and Wildl. Serv., Washington, D.C. 278 pp.

———. 1972b. Use of banding data in migratory game bird research and management. Spec. Sci. Rept.—Wildl. 154. U.S. Fish and Wildl. Serv., Washington, D.C. 47 pp.

Geissler, P. H. 1984. Estimation of animal population trends and annual indices from a survey of Call-counts or other indications. Pages 472–477 *in* Proc. 1984 Amer. Statis. Assoc., Sec. on Surv. Res. Methods. Amer. Statis. Assoc., Washington, D.C. 830 pp.

Geissler, P. H. and B. R. Noon. 1981. Estimates of avian population trends from the North American Breeding Bird Survey. Pages 42–50 *in* C. J. Ralph and J. M. Scott, eds., Estimating numbers of terrestrial birds. Studies in Avian Biol. No. 6, Cooper Ornith. Soc. 630 pp.

Geissler, P. H., D. D. Dolton, R. Field, R. A. Coon, H. F. Percival, D. W. Hayne, L. D. Soileau, R. R. George, J. H. Dunks, and S. D. Bunnell. 1987. Mourning dove nesting: Seasonal patterns and effects of September hunting. Resour. Publ. 168. U.S. Fish and Wildl. Serv., Washington, D.C. 33 pp.

George, A. L. III. 1987. Effects of lead shot ingestion on several blood variables and bodyweight in mourning doves. M.S. thesis, Auburn Univ., Auburn, Alabama. 49 pp.

George, J. L. 1951. Marsh hawk catching a mourning dove. Wilson Bull. 63(2):112.

George, R. R. 1985. White-winged dove management in Texas with implications for northeastern Mexico. Unpubl. Rept. First Reg. Conf. on Parks and Wildl. of the Rio Grande Border States. Laredo, Texas. 9 pp.

———. 1986. Mourning dove nesting chronology. Fed. Aid Proj. No. W-115-R-3 Job No. 4. Texas Parks and Wildl. Dept., Austin. 62 pp.

———. 1988. Mourning doves in Texas. Texas Parks and Wildl. Dept., Austin. 18 pp.

———. 1991. The adaptable whitewing. Texas Parks and Wildl. 49(9):10–15.

———. 1992. Mourning dove density, distribution and harvest. Fed. Aid Proj. No. W-128-R Job No. 1. Texas Parks and Wildl. Dept. Austin. 26 pp.

George, R. R. and J. B. Wooley, Jr. 1980. Mourning dove nesting studies. Iowa Conserv. Mag. (April):10.

George, R. R., A. L. Farris, C. C. Schwartz, D. D. Humburg, and J. C. Coffey. 1979. Native prairie grass pastures as nest cover for upland birds. Wildl. Soc. Bull. 7(1):4–9.

George, R. R., R. E. Tomlinson, D. L. Hallett, S. C. Yaich, W. J. Suchy, and A. H. Berner. 1987. Effects of agricultural changes on mourning dove call-count data in the eastern tier states of the Central Management Unit. Unpubl. final rept. to the Central Migratory Shore and Upland Game Bird Technical Committee. Texas Parks and Wildl. Dept., Austin. 4 pp.

Germano, D. J., R. Hungerford, and S. C. Martin. 1983. Responses of selected wildlife species to the removal of mesquite from desert grasslands. J. Range Manage. 36(3):309–311.

Gessaman, J. A. and K. A. Nagy. 1988. Transmitter loads affect the flight speed and metabolism of homing pigeons. Condor 90(3):662–668.

Gifford, E. W. 1909. The mourning dove *(Zenaidura carolinensis)* in captivity. Condor 11(3):84–85.

———. 1940. Cultural element distributions: Apache-Pueblo Anthropological Records, Vol. 4, Part XII. Berkeley, California. 207 pp.

Gill, F. B. 1990. Ornithology. W. H. Freeman and Co., New York. 660 pp.

Ginn, W. E. 1950. Migration tendencies of the mourning dove in Indiana. J. Wildl. Manage. 14(4):378–382.

Goble, F. C. and H. L. Kutz. 1945. The genus *Dispharynx* (Nematoda: Acuariidea) in galliform and passeriform birds. J. Parasitol. 31(5):323–331.

Godfrey, R. D., Jr., A. M. Fedynich, and D. B. Pence. 1987. Quantification of hematozoa in blood smears. J. Wildl. Dis. 23(4):558–565.

Godfrey, W. E. 1966. The birds of Canada. Bull. 203. Biol. Ser. 73. Nat. Mus. Canada. Bull. 203. Queen's Printer and Controller of Stationery, Ottawa, Canada. 428 pp.

Godin, A. J. 1960. A compilation of diagnostic characteristics used in aging and sexing game birds and mammals. M.S. thesis, Univ. Massachusetts, Amherst. 160 pp.

Godish, T. 1985. [Letter to the editor.] Audubon 87(4):98.

Goforth, W. R. 1964. Male mourning dove rears young unaided. Auk 81(2):233.

———. 1971. The three-bird chase in mourning doves. Wilson Bull. 83(4):419–424.

Goforth, W. R. and T. S. Baskett. 1965. Effects of experimental color marking on pairing of captive mourning doves. J. Wildl. Manage. 29(3):543–553.

———. 1971a. Effects of colored backgrounds on food selection by penned mourning doves *(Zenaidura macroura)*. Auk 88(2):256–263.

———. 1971b. Social organization of penned mourning doves. Auk 88(3):528–542.

Goldsmith, A. R., C. Edwards, M. Koprucu, and R. Silver. 1981. Concentrations of prolactin and luteinizing hormone in plasma of doves in relation to incubation and development of the crop gland. J. Endocr. 90(3):437–443.

Goode, G. B. 1897. The beginnings of natural history in America. . . . Address delivered at the Biolog. Soc. of Washington, Feb. 6, 1886. Rept. of U.S. Nat. Mus. 1897:357–466.

Goodridge, A. G. and E. G. Ball. 1967. The effect of prolactin on lipogenesis in the pigeon, *in vitro* studies. Biochem. 6(8):2,335–2,343.

Goodwin, D. 1983. Pigeons and doves of the world. 3rd ed. Cornell Univ. Press, Ithaca, New York. 363 pp.

Gowaty, P. A. 1985. Multiple parentage and apparent monogamy in birds. Pages 11–21 *in* P. A. Gowaty and D. W. Mock, eds., Avian monogamy. Ornithol. Mongr. 37. 121 pp.

Graber, R. R. 1955. Artificial incubation of some non-galliform eggs. Wilson Bull. 67(2):100–109.

Graber, R. R. and J. W. Graber. 1963. A comparative study of bird populations in Illinois, 1906–1909 and 1956–1958. Bull. Illinois Nat. Hist. Surv., Vol. 28, Art. 3:383–518.

Graefe, C. F. and W. F. Hollander. 1945. A pale mutant mourning dove. Auk 62(2):300.

Grand, J. B. and R. E. Mirarchi. 1988. Habitat use by recently fledged mourning doves in eastcentral Alabama. J. Wildl. Manage. 52(1):153–157.

Grand, J. B., R. R. Hitchcock, and R. E. Mirarchi. 1984. Mortality of nestling and fledgling mourning doves in east central Alabama. J. Alabama Acad. Sci. 55(3):131.

Grau, G. A. 1979. Crow predation on attended mourning dove eggs. Jack-Pine Warbler 57(3):169.

Greiner, E. C. 1970. Epizootiological studies on *Haemoproteus* in Nebraska mourning doves *(Zenaidura macroura)*. J. Parasitol. 56 (1):187–188.

———. 1975. Prevalence and potential vectors of *Haemoproteus* in Nebraska mourning doves. J. Wildl. Dis. 11(2):150–156.

Greiner, E. C. and W. L. Baxter. 1974. A localized epizootic of trichomoniasis in mourning doves. J. Wildl. Dis. 10(2):104–106.

Gresham, C. H. 1950. The mourning dove in East Baton Rouge Parish, Louisiana, and vicinity. M.S. thesis, Louisiana St. Univ., Baton Rouge. 80 pp.

Griffin, D. R. 1964. Bird migration. The Natural History Press, Garden City, New York. 180 pp.

Griffing, J. P. and C. A. Davis. 1974. Mourning dove foods in an uncultivated area of New Mexico. J. Wildl. Manage. 38(2):375–376.

————. 1976. Comparative foods of sympatric scaled quail and mourning doves. Southwestern Naturalist. 21(2): 248–249.

————. 1978. Feeding diversity and specific search image of mourning doves in southern New Mexico. Southwestern Naturalist. 23(4):702–704.

Griffith, P. W. 1976. Introduction of the problem. Pages 3–7 *in* R. W. Tinus, ed., Shelterbelts on the Great Plains. Great Plains Agric. Council Publ. No. 78. Lincoln, Nebraska. 218 pp.

Grimes, J. E., T. D. Sullivan, and J. V. Irons. 1966. Recovery of ornithosis agent from naturally infected white-winged doves. J. Wildl. Manage. 30(3):594–598.

Griminger, P. 1983. Digestive system and nutrition. Pages 19–39 *in* M. Abs, ed., Physiology and behavior of the pigeon. Academic Press, New York. 360 pp.

Grinnell, G. B. 1962. Blackfoot lodge tales: The story of a prairie people. Bison Book series. Univ. Nebraska Press, Lincoln. 327 pp

Grinnell, J., H. C. Bryant, and T. I. Storer. 1918. The game birds of California. Univ. California Press, Berkeley. 642 pp.

Gross, A. O. 1958. Birds observed at sea. Maine Field Natur. 14(4):70–73.

————. 1965. The incidence of albinism in North American birds. Bird-Banding 36(2):67–71.

Grue, C. E., R. R. Reid, and N. J. Silvy. 1976. A technique for evaluating the breeding habitat of mourning doves using Call-count transects. Proc. Ann. Conf. Southeast. Assoc. Fish and Wildl. Agencies 30:667–673.

————. 1981. A windshield and multivariate approach to the classification, inventory, and evaluation of wildlife habitat, an exploratory study. Pages 124–149 *in* D. E. Capen, ed., The use of multivariate statistics in studies of wildlife habitat. USDA Forest Serv. Gen. Tech. Rept. RM-87. 249 pp.

————. 1983. Correlation of habitat variables with mourning dove call counts in Texas. J. Wildl. Manage. 47(1): 186–195.

Gutierrez, R. J., C. E. Braun, and T. P. Zapatka. 1975. Reproductive biology of the band-tailed pigeon in Colorado and New Mexico. Auk 92(4):665–677.

Guynn, D. E. and P. F. Scanlon. 1973. Crop-gland activity in mourning doves during hunting seasons in Virginia. Proc. Ann. Conf. Southeast. Assoc. Game and Fish Commiss. 27:36–42.

Haas, G. H. 1977. Unretrieved shooting loss of mourning doves in north-central South Carolina. Wildl. Soc. Bull. 5(3):123–125.

————. 1978. Mourning dove harvest characteristics, survival, and population trend in North and South Carolina. Proc. Ann. Conf. Southeast. Assoc. Fish and Wildl. Agencies 32:280–290.

————. 1980. Success of single-parent mourning dove nests. Proc. Ann. Conf. Southeast. Assoc. Fish and Wildl. Agencies 34:426–429.

————. No date. A preliminary summary of findings on effects of September hunting upon mourning dove populations. Southeast Mourning Dove Station, U.S. Fish and Wildl. Serv., Univ. Georgia, Athens. 14 pp.

Haas, G. H. and S. R. Amend. 1976. Aging immature mourning doves by primary feather molt. J. Wildl. Manage. 40(3):575–578.

————. 1979. Primary feather molt of adult mourning doves in North and South Carolina. J. Wildl. Manage 43(1):202–207.

Haase, E., E. Paulke, and P. J. Sharp. 1976. Effects of seasonal and social factors on testicular activity and hormone levels in domestic pigeons. J. Exper. Zool. 197(1):81–88.

Haegele, M. A. and R. H. Hudson. 1973. DDE effects on reproduction of ring doves. Environ. Pollut. 4(1):53–57.

————. 1977. Reduction of courtship behavior induced by DDE in male ringed turtle doves. Wilson Bull. 89(4): 593–601.

Hailman, J. P. 1989. Common grounddove's injury-feigning distracts Florida scrub jay. Auk 106(4):742.

Hakluyt, R. 1582. Divers voyages touching the discoverie of America, and the lands adjacent unto the same. . . . Thomas Woodcocke, London. Unnumbered.

Hall, E. R. 1981. The mammals of North America. 2nd ed. Two vols. John Wiley and Sons, Inc., New York. 1,181 pp.

Hammond, J. W. Undated [1956]. The mourning dove in Tennessee. Final Proj. Rept. W-11-R, Tennessee St. Game and Fish Commiss., Nashville. 39 pp.

Hamor, Ralphe, the Younger. 1615. A true discourse of the present estate of Virginia. . . . Printed by John Beale for William Welby, London. 69 pp.

Handley, R. B. and W. R. Edwards. 1958. Mourning dove nesting studies in Mississippi. Proc. Ann. Conf. Southeast. Assoc. Game and Fish Commiss. 11:38–45.

Hanson, H. C. 1954. Apparatus for the study of incubated bird eggs. J. Wildl. Manage. 18(2):191–198.

Hanson, H. C. and C. W. Kossack. 1957a. Methods and criteria for aging incubated eggs and nestlings of the mourning dove. Wilson Bull. 69(1):91–101.

————. 1957b. Weight and body-fat relationships of mourning doves in Illinois. J. Wildl. Manage. 21(2): 169–181.

————. 1963. The mourning dove in Illinois. Illinois Dept. Conserv. Tech. Bull. No. 2, Southern Illinois Univ. Press, Carbondale. 133 pp.

Hanson, H. C., N. D. Levine, C. W. Kossack, S. Kantor, and L. J. Stannard. 1957. Parasites of the mourning dove *(Zenaidura macroura carolinensis)* in Illinois. J. Parasitol. 43(2):186–193.

Hargrave, L. L. 1939. Bird bones from abandoned Indian dwellings in Arizona and Utah. Condor 41(5):206–210.

Hargreave, F. E., J. Pepys, J. L. Longbottom, and D. G. Wraith. 1966. Bird breeder's (fancier's) lung. Lancet 1:445–449.

Hariot, T. 1590. A briefe and true report of the new found land of Virginia. . . . Johann Wechel, Frankfort a/M. 33 pp. +

Harkema, R. 1942. The mourning dove, a new host of the anoplocephalid tapeworm, *Aporina delafondi* (Railliet). J. Parasitol. 28(6):495.

Harmon, W. M., W. A. Clark, A. C. Hawbecker, and M. Stafford. 1987. *Trichomonas gallinae* in columbiform birds from the Galapagos Islands. J. Wildl. Dis. 23(3): 492–494.

Harris, S. W. 1961. Migrational homing in mourning doves. J. Wildl. Manage. 25(1):61–65.

Harris, S. W. and M. A. Morse. 1958. The use of mist nets for capturing nesting mourning doves. J. Wildl. Manage. 22(3):306–309.

Harris, S. W., M. A. Morse, and W. H. Longley. 1963. Nesting and production of the mourning dove in Minnesota. Amer. Midl. Natur. 69(1):150–172.

Harrison, C. J. O. 1963. Grey and fawn variant plumages. Bird Study 10:219–233.

Hastings, J. R. and R. M. Turner. 1965. The changing mile. Univ. Arizona Press, Tucson. 317 pp.

Hatch, P. L. 1892. Notes on the birds of Minnesota. First report of the state zoologist. Geol., Natur. Hist. Surv. of Minnesota. Harrison & Smith, Publishers, Minneapolis. 487 pp.

Hatton, J. H. 1935. A review of early tree-planting activities in the Plains region. Pages 51–57 in Possibilities of shelterbelt planting in the Plains region. USDA Forest Serv. U.S. Govt. Print. Off., Washington, D.C.

Haugen, A. O. 1952. Trichomoniasis in Alabama mourning doves. J. Wildl. Manage. 16(2):164–169.

Haugen, A. O. and J. E. Keeler. 1952. Mortality of mourning doves from trichomoniasis in Alabama during 1951. Trans. N. Amer. Wildl. Conf. 17:141–151.

Hayne, D. W. 1975. Experimental increase of mourning dove bag limit in Eastern Management Unit, 1965–1972. Southeast. Assoc. Game and Fish Commiss. Tech. Bull. 2. 56 pp.

———. 1982. Christmas bird count records of mourning dove abundance in the Eastern Management Unit, 1959–1974. Unpubl. rept. Institute of Statistics, North Carolina St. Univ., Raleigh. 18 pp.

Hayne, D. W. and P. H. Geissler. 1977. Hunted segments of the mourning dove population: Movement and importance. Southeast. Assoc. Game and Fish Commiss. Tech. Bull. 3. 152 pp.

Hegdal, P. L. and T. A. Gatz. 1977. Hazards to seed eating birds and other wildlife associated with surface strychnine baiting for Richardson's ground squirrels. Final rept. by U.S. Fish and Wildl. Serv., Denver Wildl. Res. Ctr., to U.S. Environ. Protect. Agency under interagency agreement EPA-IAG D4-0449. 48 pp. +

Hegdal, P. L., K. A. Fagerstone, T. A. Gatz, J. F. Glahn, and G. H. Matschke. 1986. Hazards to wildlife associated with 1080 baiting for California ground squirrels. Wildl. Soc. Bull. 14(1):11–21.

Hegde, S. N. 1972. Composition of pigeon milk and its effect on growth in chicks. Indiana J. Exp. Biol. 11(3): 238–239.

Hennessy, T. E. and L. Van Camp. 1963. Wintering mourning doves in northern Ohio. J. Wildl. Manage. 27(3):367–373.

Henny, C. J. and K. P. Burnham. 1976. A reward band study of mallards to estimate band reporting rates. J. Wildl. Manage. 40(1):1–14.

Henry, D. L. 1970. Population dynamics and migration of Missouri doves. M.A. thesis. Univ. Missouri, Columbia. 104 pp.

Henry, D. L., T. S. Baskett, K. C. Sadler, and W. R. Goforth. 1976. Age and sex selectivity of trapping procedures for mourning doves. J. Wildl. Manage. 40(1):122–125.

Henshaw, H. W. [1875]. Report upon the ornithological collections made in portions of Nevada, Utah, California, Colorado, New Mexico, and Arizona during the years 1871, 1872, 1873, and 1874. Vol V–Zoology, chapter 3 in Report upon geographical and geological explorations and surveys west of the one hundredth meridian. . . . U.S. Govt. Print. Off., Washington, D.C.

Henson, R. C. 1956. A dove nesting study in the Roselawn Cemetery, Baton Rouge, Louisiana. M.S. thesis, Louisiana St. Univ., Baton Rouge. 19 pp.

Hepp, G. R., R. T. Hoppe, and R. A. Kennamer. 1987. Population parameters and philopatry of breeding female wood ducks. J. Wildl. Manage. 51(2):401–404.

Herbert, H. W. 1858. Frank Forester's field sports of the United States, and British Provinces of North America. Two vols. W. A. Townsend, New York.

Herman, C. M. 1937. Notes on hippoboscid flies. Bird-Banding 8(4):161–166.

———. 1982. Bird-borne diseases in man. Pages 653–657 in M. Petrak, ed., Diseases of cage and aviary birds. Lea and Febiger, Philadelphia. 680 pp.

Heusmann, H. W. 1979. Current status and mortality rates of Massachusetts mourning doves. Bird-Banding 50(3):256–262.

Hewitt, O. J. and P. J. Austin-Smith. 1966. A simple wing tag for field-marking birds. J. Wildl. Manage. 30(3): 625–627.

Hickey, J. J. 1943. A guide to bird watching. Oxford Univ. Press, New York. 264 pp.

———. 1951. Mortality records as indices of migration in the mallard. Condor 53(6):284–297.

———. 1952. Survival studies of banded birds. Spec. Sci. Rept.–Wildl. 15. U.S. Fish and Wildl. Serv., Washington, D.C. 177 pp.

Hill, E. F. 1988. Brain cholinesterase activity of apparently normal wild birds. J. Wildl. Dis. 24(1):51–61.

Hill, G. 1988. Shotgunner's notebook. Gun Dog 7(6): 25–26.

Hinde, R. A. 1964. The biological significance of the territories of birds. Ibis 98(3):340–369.

Hitchcock, R. R. 1982. Duration of dependence of wild fledgling mourning doves upon parental care. M.S. thesis, Auburn Univ., Auburn, Alabama. 63 pp.

———. 1986. Recognition of male parent vocalizations by nestling mourning doves and fledgling dispersal from nest sites. Ph.D. dissertation, Auburn Univ., Auburn, Alabama. 56 pp.

Hitchcock, R. R. and R. E. Mirarchi. 1984a. Duration of dependence of wild fledgling mourning doves on parental care. J. Wildl. Manage. 48(1):99–108.

———. 1984b. Comparison between single-parent and normal mourning dove nestings during the post-fledging period. Wilson Bull. 96(3):494–495.

———. 1985. Surrogate feeding and adoptive behavior in mourning doves. J. Wildl. Manage. 49(2):502–504.

———. 1986. Dispersal of recently fledged mourning doves from nest sites. Wilson Bull. 98(4):581–585.

Hitchcock, R. R., R. E. Mirarchi, and R. S. Lishak. 1989. Recognition of individual male parent vocalizations by nestling mourning doves. Anim. Behav. 37(3):517–520.

Hodge, F. W., ed. 1907a. The narrative of Alvar Nunez Cabeca de Vaca. Pages 1–126 *in* Spanish explorers in the southern United States, 1528–1543. Charles Scribner's Sons, New York. 411 pp.

———. 1907b. The narrative of the expedition of Coronado, by Pedro de Casteneda. Pages 273–387 *in* Spanish explorers in the southern United States, 1528–1543. Charles Scribner's Sons, New York. 411 pp.

———. 1907c. Handbook of North American Indians north of Mexico. Vol. 1. Smithson. Instit. Bur. Ethnol. Bull. 30. Washington, D.C. 981 pp.

Holbrook, S. H. 1960. Burning an empire: The story of American forest fires. The MacMillan Co., New York. 229 pp.

Holcomb, L. C. and M. Jaeger. 1978. Growth and calculation of age in mourning dove nestlings. J. Wildl. Manage. 42(4):843–852.

Homerstad, G. 1984. White-tipped dove, Texas's newest game birds. Texas Parks and Wildl. 42(9):8–11.

Hon, L. T., D. J. Forrester, and L. E. Williams, Jr. 1975. Helminths of wild turkeys in Florida. Proc. Helminthol. Soc. Washington. 42(2):119–127.

Hon, W. H. 1956. The status of a ground nesting population of eastern mourning doves in coastal North Carolina. M.S. thesis, North Carolina St. Coll., Raleigh. 57 pp.

Honacki, J. H., K. E. Kinman, and J. W. Koeppl. 1982. Mammal species of the world: A taxonomic and geographic reference. Allen Press, Inc. and Assoc. of System. Collections. 694 pp.

Honigberg, B. M., M. C. Livingston, and R. M. Stabler. 1971. Pathogenicity transformation of *Trichomonas gallinae* 1. Effects of homogenates and of mixtures of DNA and RNA from a virulent strain on pathogenicity of an avirulent strain. J. Parasitol. 57(5):929–938.

Hopkins, M. N. and E. P. Odum. 1953. Some aspects of the population ecology of breeding mourning doves in Georgia. J. Wildl. Manage. 17(2):132–143.

Hornaday, W. T. 1931. Thirty years war for wild life. Permanent Wild Life Protection Fund, Stamford, Connecticut. 292 pp.

Hosford, H. J. 1955. Nesting and migration of the mourning dove in northern Indiana. Indiana Audubon Quart. 33(1):3–10.

Houston, C. S. 1986. Mourning dove numbers explode on the Canadian prairies. Amer. Birds 40(1):52–54.

Howard, H. 1937. A Pleistocene record of the passenger pigeon in California. Condor 39(1):12–14.

———. 1952. The prehistoric fauna of Smith Creek Cave, Nevada, with a description of a new gigantic raptor. Bull. Southern California Acad. Sci. 51(2):50–54.

Howard, H. and A. H. Miller. 1933. Bird remains from cave deposits in New Mexico. Condor 35(1):15–18.

Howarth, R. C. 1954. A study of the mourning dove in Centre County, Pennsylvania. M.S. thesis, Pennsylvania St. Univ., College Park. 45 pp.

Howe, F. P. and L. D. Flake. 1988. Mourning dove movements during the reproductive season in southeastern Idaho. J. Wildl. Manage. 52(3):477–480.

———. 1989a. Nesting ecology of mourning doves in a cold desert ecosystem. Wilson Bull. 101(3): 467–472.

———. 1989b. Mourning dove use of man-made ponds in a cold desert ecosystem in Idaho. Great Basin Natur. 49(4):627–631.

Hubbard, J. P. and R. C. Banks. 1970. The types and taxa of Harold H. Bailey. Proc. Biol. Soc. Washington. 83(30):321–332.

Hudson, J. W. and A. H. Brush. 1964. A comparative study of the cardiac and metabolic performance of the dove *Zenaidura macroura*, and the quail *Lophortyx californicus*. Comp. Biochem. and Physiol. 12(2):157–170.

Hudson, R. H., R. K. Tucker, and M. A. Haegele. 1984. Handbook of toxicity of pesticides to wildlife. 2nd. ed. Resour. Publ. 153. U.S. Fish and Wildl. Serv., Washington, D.C. 90 pp.

Huggins, R. A. 1941. Egg temperatures of wild birds under natural conditions. Ecology 22(2):148–157.

Hultkrantz, A. 1974. The Shoshones in the Rocky Mountain area. Pages 175–214 *in* D. A. Horr, ed., Shoshone Indians. Garland Publishing, Inc., New York. 320 pp.

Hume, E. E. 1942. Ornithologists of the United States Army Medical Corps. The Johns Hopkins Press, Baltimore. 583 pp.

Humphrey, P. S. and K. C. Parkes. 1959. An approach to the study of molts and plumages. Auk 76(1):1–31.

Hunt, E. G. 1966a. Surveillance of pesticide programs. Effects of pesticides used in pear culture on nesting doves. Project FW-1-R-3. California Dept. Fish and Game, Sacramento. 4 pp.

———. 1966b. Surveillance of pesticide programs. Detection and investigation of fish and wildlife losses caused by pesticides. Project FW-1-R-3. California Dept. Fish and Game, Sacramento. 6 pp.

Hutchison, J. B. 1970. Influence of gonadal hormones on the hypothalamic integration of courtship behavior in the Barbary dove. J. Reprod. Fert. Suppl. 11:15–41.

Hutt, F. B. and L. Ball. 1938. Number of feathers and body size in passerine birds. Auk 45(4):651–657.

Hwang, J. C., N. Tolgay, W. T. Shalkop, and D. S. Jacquette. 1961. Case report—*Dispharynx nasuta* causing severe proventriculitis in pigeons. Avian Dis. 5(1): 60–65.

Immelman, K. 1971. Ecological aspects of periodic reproduction. Pages 342–389 *in* D. S. Farner and J. R. King, eds., Avian biology. Vol. 1. Academic Press, New York. 586 pp.

Ingersoll, E. 1923. Birds in legend, fable and folklore. Longmans, Green and Co., London. 292 pp.

Institute of Laboratory Animal Resources (ILAR). 1977. Laboratory animal management. Wild birds. Nat. Acad. Sciences, National Resource Council, Committee on Birds, Washington, D.C. 166 pp.

———. 1985. Guide for the care and use of laboratory animals. Nat. Res. Council, Committee on Care and Use of Laboratory Animals, National Institutes of Health. Publ. No. 85-23. 83 pp.

Irby, H. D. 1964. The relationship of calling behavior to mourning dove populations and production in southern Arizona. Ph.D. dissertation, Univ. Arizona, Tucson. 100 pp.

Irby, H. D. and L. H. Blankenship. 1966. Breeding behavior of immature mourning doves. J. Wildl. Manage. 30(3):598–604.

Ivacic, D. L. and R. F. Labisky. 1973. Metabolic responses of mourning doves to short-term food and temperature stresses in winter. Wilson Bull. 85(2):182–196.

Jackson, A. S. 1940. The mourning dove in Throckmorton County, Texas. M.S. thesis, North Texas St. Univ., Denton. 122 pp.

Jackson, G. L. 1963. The breeding behavior of wild mourning doves *(Zenaidura macroura)*. M.A. thesis, Univ. Missouri, Columbia. 96 pp.

Jackson, G. L. and T. S. Baskett. 1964. Perch-cooing and other aspects of breeding behavior of mourning doves. J. Wildl. Manage. 28(2):293–307.

Jefferson, T. 1781. Notes on the state of Virginia. 1955. W. Peden, ed. Univ. North Carolina Press, Chapel Hill. 315 pp.

Jeffrey, R. G., C. E. Braun, D. E. Brown, D. R. Halladay, P. M. Howard, C. E. Kebbe, D. H. Nish, W. A. Smith, and T. P. Zapatka. 1977. Band-tailed pigeon. Pages 210–245 *in* G. C. Sanderson, ed., Management of migratory shore and upland game birds in North America. Intern. Assoc. of Fish and Wildl. Agencies, Washington, D.C. 358 pp.

Jenkins, J. H. 1955. A contribution to the physiological ecology of the mourning dove, *Zenaidura macroura carolinensis* (Linnaeus): A study of age and seasonal changes in feathers, gonads, weight, and lipid deposition. Ph.D. dissertation, Univ. Georgia, Athens. 100 pp.

Jennings, W. L., W. G. Winkler, D. D. Stamm, P. H. Coleman, and A. L. Lewis. 1969. Pages 118–125 *in* Serologic studies of possible avian or mammalian reservoirs of St. Louis encephalitis virus in Florida. Florida St. Bd. Health Monog. Series No. 12. Jacksonville. 125 pp.

Jewett, S. G., W. P. Taylor, W. T. Shaw, and J. W. Aldrich. 1953. Birds of Washington state. Univ. Washington Press, Seattle. 767 pp.

Johnson, D. H. 1989. Least squares estimation of avian molt rates. Biometrics 45(2):657–661.

Johnson, T. W. 1983. Repelling rat snakes from wood duck boxes with chemical barriers. Proc. Ann. Conf. Southeast. Assoc. Fish and Wildl. Agencies 37:49–55.

Johnston, R. F. 1961. The genera of American ground doves. Auk 78(3):372–378.

Jolly, G. M. 1965. Explicit estimates from capture-recapture data with both death and immigration-stochastic model. Biometrika 52(1–2):225–247.

———. 1982. Mark-recapture models with parameters constant in time. Biometrics 38(2):301–321.

Jones, L. M. 1965. Euthanasia. Pages 987–993 *in* Veterinary pharmacology and therapeutics. 3rd ed. Iowa St. Univ. Press, Ames. 1,037 pp.

Jonkel, G. 1967. Mourning dove poisoning violation results in conviction. South Dakota Bird Notes 19(2):42–43.

Jumber, J. F., E. L. Kozicky, and D. L. Carter. 1956. Factors influencing mourning dove production at Lewis, Iowa, 1955. Iowa Bird Life 26(3):59–61.

Kaczynski, C. F. and W. H. Kiel, Jr. 1963. Band loss by nestling mourning doves. J. Wildl. Manage. 27(2):271–279.

Kalm, P. 1751. Observations on the inhabitants, climate, soil, rivers, productions, animals, and other matters worthy of notice made by Mr. John Bartram. . . . J. Whiston and B. White, London. 94 pp.

———. 1759. A description of the wild pigeons which visit the southern English colonies of North America. . . . Reprinted *in* The passenger pigeon. Part I:407–417. Smithson. Instit. Ann. Rept., 1911. U.S. Govt. Print. Off., Washington, D.C.

Kalmbach, E. R. and J. F. Welch. 1946. Colored rodent baits and their value in safeguarding birds. J. Wildl. Manage. 10(4):353–360.

Karstad, L. 1971. Pox. Pages 34–41 *in* J. W. Davis, R. C. Anderson, L. Karstad, and D. O. Trainer, eds., Infectious and parasitic diseases of wild birds. Iowa St. Univ. Press, Ames. 344 pp.

Keast, A. 1980. Synthesis: Ecological basis and evolution of the nearctic-neotropical bird migration system. Pages 559–576 *in* A. Keast and E. S. Morton, eds., Migrant birds in the neotropics: Ecology, behavior, distribution, and conservation. Smithson. Instit. Press, Washington, D.C. 576 pp.

Keast, A. and E. S. Morton. 1980. Migrant birds in the neotropics: Ecology, behavior, distribution, and conservation. Smithson. Instit. Press, Washington, D.C. 576 pp.

Keeler, J. E. 1953. The mourning dove study, 1948–1952. Alabama Dept. Conserv., Montgomery. 66 pp.

———, chair. 1977. Mourning dove *(Zenaida macroura)*. Pages 274–298 *in* G. C. Sanderson, ed., Management of migratory shore and upland game birds in North America. Intern. Assoc. Fish and Wildl. Agencies, Washington, D.C. 358 pp.

Keeler, J. E. and F. Winston. 1951. Mourning dove trapping in the Southeast. Bird-Banding 22(4):174–179.

Keeton, W. T. 1972. Effects of magnets on pigeon homing. Pages 579–594 *in* S. R. Galler, K. Schmidt-Koenig, G. J. Jacobs, and R. E. Bellville, eds., Animal orientation and navigation, SP-262. Nat. Aeron. Space Admin., Washington, D.C. 606 pp.

———. 1974. The orientation and navigational basis of homing in birds. Pages 47–132 *in* D. Lehrman, J. S. Rosenblatt, R. A. Hinds, and E. Shaw, eds., Advances in the study of behavior. Vol. 5. Academic Press, London. 279 pp.

Kendall, R. J. 1980. The toxicology of lead shot and environmental lead ingestion in avian species with emphasis on the biological significance in mourning dove populations. Ph.D. dissertation, Virginia Polytech. Instit. and St. Univ., Blacksburg. 316 pp.

Kendall, R. J. and P. F. Scanlon. 1979. Lead concentrations in mourning doves collected from middle Atlantic game management areas. Proc. Ann. Conf. Southeast. Assoc. Fish and Wildl. Agencies 33:165–172.

———. 1980. A water bottle modified for avians. Poult. Sci. 59(1):177–178.

———. 1981a. Effects of chronic lead ingestion on reproductive characteristics of ringed turtle doves (*Streptopelia risoria*) and on tissue lead concentrations of adults and their progeny. Environ. Pollut. 26(3):203–213.

———. 1981b. Propagation of a laboratory ringed turtle dove colony. Poult. Sci. 60(12):2,728–2,730.

———. 1982. Tissue lead concentrations and blood characteristics of mourning doves from southwestern Virginia. Arch. Environ. Contam. Toxicol. 11(3):269–272.

Kendall, R. J., P. F. Scanlon, and H. P. Veit. 1983. Histologic and ultrastructural lesions of mourning doves (*Zenaida macroura*) poisoned by lead shot. Poult. Sci. 62(9):952–956.

Kendall, R. J., H. P. Veit, and P. F. Scanlon. 1981. Histologic effects and lead concentrations in tissues of adult male ringed turtle doves that ingested lead shot. J. Toxicol. and Environ. Hlth. 8(4):649–658.

Kendeigh, S. C. 1941a. Length of day and energy requirements for gonad development and egg-laying in birds. Ecology 22(3):237–248.

———. 1941b. Territorial and mating behavior in house wrens. Illinois Biol. Monogr. 18(3):13–20.

———. 1942. Analysis of losses in nesting birds. J. Wildl. Manage. 6(1):19–26.

———. 1944a. Effect of air temperature on the rate of energy metabolism in the English sparrow. J. Exper. Zool. 96(1):1–16.

———. 1944b. Measurement of bird populations. Ecol. Monogr. 14(1):67–106.

———. 1952. Parental care and its evolution in birds. Illinois Biol. Monogr. 22:1–356.

Kennard, J. H. and L. L. Kennard. 1967. Notes on the range extension of mourning doves in New Hampshire. New Hampshire Audubon Quart. 20(4):136–137.

Kennedy, R. J. 1969. Sunbathing behaviour of birds. British Birds 62(7):249–258.

Kerley, C. 1952. The call-road count as an index to breeding populations of the mourning dove in east Tennessee. Pages 8–14 in Spec. Sci. Rept.—Wildl. No. 17. U.S. Fish and Wildl. Serv., Washington, D.C. 53 pp.

Kerlin, R. E. 1964. Venipuncture of small birds. J. Amer. Vet. Assoc. 144(8):870–874.

Kerpez, T. A. and N. S. Smith. 1987. Saltcedar control for wildlife habitat improvement in the southwestern United States. Resour. Publ. 169. U.S. Fish and Wildl. Serv., Washington, D.C. 16 pp.

Kessel, B. and D. D. Gibson. 1978. Status and distribution of Alaska birds. Studies in Avian Biol. No. 1, Cooper Ornith. Soc. 100 pp.

Ketterson, E. D. and V. Nolan. 1976. Geographic variation and its climatic correlations in the sex ratio of eastern-wintering dark-eyed juncos (*Junco hyemalis hyemalis*). Ecology 57(4):679–693.

———. 1983. The evolution of differential migration. Current Ornithol. 1:357–402.

Keyes, B. E. and C. E. Grue. 1982. Capturing birds with mist nets: A review. N. Amer. Bird Bander 17(1):2–14.

Keyes, J. 1945. Compound 1080 as a rodenticide. Control Methods Res. U.S. Fish and Wildl. Serv., Washington, D.C. 9 pp.

Kiel, W. H., Jr. 1959. Mourning dove management units—a progress report. Spec. Sci. Rept.—Wildl. No. 42. U.S. Fish and Wildl. Serv., Washington, D.C. 24 pp.

———. 1961. The mourning dove program for the future. Trans. N. Amer. Wildl. and Natur. Resour. Conf. 26: 418–435.

King, J. R. 1973. Energetics of reproduction in birds. Pages 78–107 in D. S. Farner, ed., Breeding biology of birds. Proceedings of a symposium on breeding behavior and reproductive physiology in birds. Nat. Acad. Sciences, Washington, D.C. 515 pp.

Kinkel, L. K. 1989. Lasting effects of wing tags on ring-billed gulls. Auk 106(4):619–624.

Kitchen, E. A. 1949. Birds of the Olympic Peninsula. Olympic Stationers, Port Angeles, Washington. 262 pp.

Klapp, H. M., ed. 1853. Krider's sporting anecdotes. . . . A. Hart, Philadelphia. 292 pp.

Klei, T. R. and D. L. DeGiusti. 1975. Seasonal occurrence of *Heamoproteus columbae* Kruse and its vector *Pseudolynchia canariensis* Bequaert. J. Wildl. Dis. 11(1):130–135.

Klinghammer, E. and E. H. Hess. 1964. Parental feeding in ring doves (*Streptopelia roseogrisea*): Innate or learned? Z. Tierpsychol. 21(2):338–347.

Klopatek, J. M., R. L. Olson, C. J. Emerson, and J. L. Jones. 1979. Land-use conflicts with natural vegetation in the United States. Environ. Conser. 6(3):191–199.

Knappen, P. 1938. Preliminary report of some of the important foods of the mourning dove in the southeastern United States. Trans. N. Amer. Wildl. Conf. 3:776–781.

Knight, J. E. 1986. A humane method for removing snakes from dwellings. Wildl. Soc. Bull. 14(3):301–303.

Knight, R. L., D. G. Smith, D. M. Gaudet, and A. W. Erickson. 1984. Nesting ecology of mourning doves in fruit orchards in north central Washington. Northwest Sci. 58(3):230–236.

Knisley, J. O., Jr. and C. M. Herman. 1967. *Haemoproteus*, a blood parasite, in domestic pigeons and mourning doves in Maryland. Chesapeake Sci. 8(3):200–202.

Kocan, R. M. 1968. Probable origin of ciliates seen in oral swabbings of doves and pigeons. J. Parasitol. 54(5): 1,033.

———. 1969. Various grains and liquid as potential vehicles of transmission for *Trichomonas gallinae*. J. Wildl. Dis. 5(3):148–149.

Kocan, R. M. and S. R. Amend. 1972. Immunologic status of mourning doves following an epizootic of trichomoniasis. J. Wildl. Dis. 8(2):176–180.

Kocan, R. M. and H. F. Hasenclever. 1972. Normal yeast flora of the upper digestive tract of some wild columbids. J. Wildl. Dis. 8(4):365–368.

Kocan, R. M. and C. M. Herman. 1971. Trichomoniasis. Pages 282–290 *in* J. W. Davis, R. C. Anderson, L. Karstad, and D. O. Trainer, eds., Infectious and parasitic diseases of wild birds. Iowa St. Univ. Press, Ames. 344 pp.

Kocan, R. M. and L. N. Locke. 1974. *Salmonella typhimurium* from a Maryland mourning dove. Condor 76(3): 349.

Komarek, E. V. 1964. The natural history of lightning. Proc. Tall Timbers Fire Ecol. Conf. 3:139–183

Korenbrot, C. C., D. W. Schomberg, and C. J. Erickson. 1974. Radioimmunoassay of plasma estradiol during the breeding cycle of ring doves *(Streptopelia risoria)*. Endocrinology 94(4):1,126–1,132.

Korschgen, L. J. 1955. A study of the food habits of Missouri doves. P-R Series 12, Missouri Fish and Game Div., Jefferson City. 31 pp.

———. 1958. Food habits of the mourning dove in Missouri. J. Wildl. Manage. 22(1):9–16.

Kossack, C. W. 1952. Banding nestling mourning doves. Bird-Banding 23(1):28–29.

Kossack, C. W. and H. C. Hanson. 1953. Unisexual broods of the mourning dove. J. Wildl. Manage. 17(4): 541.

———. 1954. Fowlpox in the mourning dove. J. Amer. Vet. Med. Assoc. 124(924):199–201.

Koval, P. J., T. J. Peterle, and J. D. Harder. 1987. Effects of polychlorinated biphenyls on mourning dove reproduction and circulating progesterone levels. Bull. Environ. Contam. Toxicol. 39(4):663–670.

Kreitzer, J. F. 1971. Eggshell thickness in mourning dove populations. J. Wildl. Manage. 35(3):563–564.

———. 1974. Residues of organochlorine pesticides, mercury, and PCBs in mourning doves from eastern United States–1970–71. Pestic. Monit. J. 7(3/4):195–199.

Kringer, F., W. L. Anderson, and J. A. Ellis. 1980. Effectiveness of steel shot in 2¾ inch 12 gauge shells for hunting mourning doves. Manage. Notes No. 3, Illinois Dept. Conserv., Springfield. 16 pp.

Küchler, A. W. 1964. Potential natural vegetation of the conterminous United States. Amer. Geog. Soc. Spec. Publ. 36. 38 pp.

Kufeld, R. C. 1963. Summary and analysis of data for mourning and white-winged doves banded in Arizona. Spec. Rept., Fed. Aid. Proj. W-53-R-13. Arizona Game and Fish Dept., Phoenix. 9 pp.

Kumaran, J. D. S. and C. W. Turner. 1949a. The endocrinology of spermatogenesis in birds. I. Effect of estrogen and androgen. Poult. Sci. 28(4):593–602.

———. 1949b. The endocrinology of spermatogenesis in birds. II. Effect of estrogen and androgen. Poult. Sci. 28(5):739–746.

Kurland, J. A. and S. J. C. Gaulain. 1984. The evolution of male parental investment: Effects of genetic relatedness and feeding ecology on the allocation of reproductive effort. Pages 259–309 *in* D. M. Taub, ed., Primate paternalism. Van Nostrand Reinhold, New York. 441 pp.

Lack, D. 1944. The problem of partial migration. Brit. Birds 37(7):122–130; 37(8):143–150.

———. 1946. The life of the robin. Rev. ed. N. F. and G. Witherby, Ltd., London. 224 pp.

———. 1953. The life of the robin. 3rd ed. Pelican Books, Harmondsworth, England. 240 pp.

———. 1954. The natural regulation of animal numbers. Clarendon Press, Oxford. 343 pp.

———. 1968. Ecological adaptations for breeding birds. Chapman and Hall, London. 409 pp.

———. 1976. Island biology: Illustrated by the land birds of Jamaica. Univ. California Press, Berkeley. 445 pp.

Lamm, D. W. 1956. Mourning dove and dickcissel on the Atlantic Ocean. Auk 73(2):290.

Lang, R. W. and A. H. Harris. 1984. The faunal remains from Arroyo Hondo Pueblo, New Mexico. Vol. 5. Arroyo Hondo Archeol. Series. School of American Research Press. 316 pp.

Lanyon, L. E. and V. H. Lanyon. 1969. A technique for rearing passerine birds from the egg. Living Bird 8:81–93.

LaPerriere, A. J. 1972. Seasonal precipitation influence on mourning dove breeding populations in Iowa. J. Wildl. Manage. 36(3):979–981.

LaPerriere, A. J. and A. O. Haugen. 1972a. Trends of mourning dove populations in Boone County, Iowa farm groves. Iowa St. J. Sci. 46(3):417–424.

———. 1972b. Some factors influencing calling activity of wild mourning doves. J. Wildl. Manage. 36(4): 1,193–1,198.

LaPointe, D. F. 1958. Mourning dove production in a central Nebraska shelterbelt. J. Wildl. Manage. 22(4): 439–440.

Larsen, K. H. 1968. Banding pliers for pre-opened bands. J. Wildl. Manage. 32(2):425–426.

Larson, J. S. and R. D. Taber. 1980. Criteria of sex and age. Pages 143–202 *in* S. D. Schemnitz, ed., Wildlife management techniques manual. 4th ed. The Wildl. Soc., Washington, D.C. 686 pp.

Laub, K. W. 1956. The relation of parental care and the condition of the glandular crop to the successful rearing of young mourning doves, *Zenaidura macroura* (L.) M.S. thesis, Ohio St. Univ., Columbus. 68 pp.

Lawrence, G. N. (Baird M.S.) 1871. Descriptions of new species of birds from Mexico, Central America and South America, with a note on *Rallus longirostris*. Ann. Lyc. Nat. Hist. New York. 10:1–21.

Lawson, J. 1709. A new voyage to Carolina. . . . 1967 reprint. H. T. Lefler, ed. Univ. North Carolina Press, Chapel Hill. 305 pp.

Lea, R. W. and D. M. Vowles. 1985. The control of prolactin secretion and nest defence in the ring dove *(Streptopelia risoria)*. Boll. Zoo. 52(3/4):323–329.

Lea, R. W., D. M. Vowles, and H. R. Dick. 1986. Factors affecting prolactin secretion during the breeding cycle of the ring dove *(Streptopelia risoria)* and its possible role in incubation. J. Endocr. 110(3):447–458.

Leach, M., ed. 1949. Dictionary of folklore, mythology and legend. Part 1. Funk & Wagnalls Co., New York. 531 pp.

Leash, A. M., J. Liebman, A. Taylor, and R. Limbert. 1971. An analysis of the crop contents of white Carneaux pigeons (*Columba livia*), days one through twenty-seven. Lab. Anim. Sci. 21(1):86–90.

Leffingwell, W. B. 1890. Shooting on upland, marsh and stream. Rand, McNally & Co., Chicago. 473 pp.

Lehner, P. N. 1964. Ecology of the mourning dove in Tompkins County, New York. M.S. thesis, Cornell Univ., Ithaca, New York. 71 pp.

Lehninger, A. L. 1982. Principles of biochemistry. Worth Publishers, Inc., New York. 1,011 pp.

Lehrman, D. S. 1955. The physiological basis of parental feeding behavior in the ring dove (*Streptopelia risoria*). Behavior 7(4):241–286.

———. 1958. Induction of broodiness by participation in courtship and nest building in the ring dove (*Streptopelia risoria*). J. Comp. Physiol. Psychol. 51:32–36.

———. 1964. The reproductive behavior of ring doves. Sci. Amer. 211(5):48–54.

Lehrman, D. S. and P. N. Brody. 1961. Does prolactin induce incubation behavior in the ring dove? J. Endocr. 22(3):269–275.

Lehrman, D. S. and M. Friedman. 1969. Auditory stimulation of ovarian activity in the ring dove (*Streptopelia risoria*). Anim. Behav. 17(3):494–497.

Lehrman, D. S. and R. P. Wortis. 1960. Previous breeding experience and hormone induced incubation behavior in the ring dove. Science 132(3440):1,667–1,668.

———. 1967. Breeding experience and breeding efficiency in the ring dove. Anim. Behav. 15(2–3):223–228.

Lehrman, D. S., P. N. Brody, and R. P. Wortis. 1961. The presence of the mate and of nesting material as stimuli for the development of incubation behavior and for gonadotropin secretion in the ring dove (*Streptopelia risoria*). Endocrinology 68(3):507–516.

Leighly, J. 1941. Settlement and cultivation of summer-dry climates. Pages 197–204 *in* Climate and man. U. S. Dept. Agric. U.S. Govt. Print. Off., Washington, D.C. 1,248 pp.

Leonard, J. L. 1969. Clinical laboratory examinations. Pages 189–215 *in* M. L. Petrak, ed., Diseases of cage and aviary birds. Lea and Febiger, Philadelphia. 528 pp.

Leopold, A. 1921. A hunter's notes on doves in the Rio Grande Valley. Condor 23(1):19–21.

———. 1931. Report on a game survey of the North Central States. Amer. Game Assoc., Madison, Wisconsin. 299 pp.

———. 1933. Game management. Charles Scribner's Sons, New York. 481 pp.

———. 1947. On a monument to the pigeon. Pages 3–5 *in* Silent wings: A memorial to the passenger pigeon. Wisconsin Soc. Ornith., Milwaukee, Wisconsin.

Leopold, A. S. 1943. Autumn feeding and flocking habits of the mourning dove in southern Missouri. Wilson Bull. 55(3):151–154.

———. 1959. Wildlife of Mexico, the game birds and mammals. Univ. California Press, Berkeley. 568 pp.

Leopold, A. S. and M. F. Dedon. 1983. Resident mourning doves in Berkeley, California. J. Wildl. Manage. 47(3):780–789.

Leopold, A. S., R. J. Gutierrez, and M. T. Bronson. 1981. North American game birds and mammals. Charles Scribner's Sons, New York. 198 pp.

Lesser, C. A. 1966. Record of mourning dove killed by American kestrel. Wilson Bull. 78(2):228–229.

Levi, W. M. 1977. The pigeon. Levi Publ. Co., Sumter, South Carolina. 667 pp.

Levine, N. D. and S. Kantor. 1959. Check-list of blood parasites of birds of the order Columbiformes. Wildl. Dis. 1:1–38.

Levy, R. 1978. Coastanoan. Pages 485–495 *in* California handbook of North American Indians. Vol. 8. Smithson. Instit. Press, Washington, D.C.

Lewis, J. C. and E. Legler, Jr. 1968. Lead shot ingestion by mourning doves and incidence in soil. J. Wildl. Manage. 32(3):476–482.

Lewis, J. C. and J. A. Morrison. 1973. Efficiency of traps and baits for capturing mourning doves. Wildl. Soc. Bull. 1(3):131–138.

Lewis, J. C., J. A. Morrison, V. J. Heller, and J. W. Ault. 1982. Fall-winter habitat use and food habits of doves in southwestern Oklahoma. Proc. Ann. Conf. Southeast. Assoc. Fish and Wildl. Agencies 36:678–690.

Lewis, T. H., Jr. 1907. The narrative of the expedition of Hernando de Soto, by the Gentleman of Elvas. Pages 127–272 *in* Spanish explorers in the southern United States, 1528–1543. Charles Scribner's Sons, New York. 411 pp.

Ligon, J. S. 1961. New Mexico birds and where to find them. Univ. New Mexico Press, Albuquerque. 360 pp.

Lincoln, F. C. 1930. Calculating waterfowl abundance on the basis of banding returns. Circ. 118. U.S. Dept. Agric., Washington, D.C. 4 pp.

———. 1933. Eastern mourning dove migrating to Cuba? Auk 50(2):218.

———. 1935. The waterfowl flyways of North America. Circ. 363. U.S. Dept. Agric., Washington D.C. 12 pp.

———. 1937. Eastern mourning dove in Cuba. Auk 54(3):391.

———. 1941. Mourning doves of southern Florida and the Greater Antilles. Auk 58(3):406–407.

———. 1945. The mourning dove as a game bird. Circ. 10. U.S. Fish and Wildl. Serv., Washington, D.C. 8 pp.

———. 1947. Manual for bird banders. U.S. Fish and Wildl. Serv., Washington, D.C. 116 pp.

Lincoln, F. C., S. R. Peterson, and P. A. Anastasi. 1979. Migration of birds. Rev. ed. Circ. 16. U.S. Fish and Wildl. Serv., Washington, D.C. 119 pp.

Linnaeus, (Linnaei), C. 1758. Systema naturae. Regnum animale. Vol. 1, 10th ed. Photographic facsimile reprinted by the British Mus. (Natural History), London. 824 pp.

———. 1766. Systema naturae. Regnum animale. Vol. 1, 12th ed. Photographic facsimile reprinted by the British Mus. (Natural History), London. 532 pp.

Linsdale, J. M. 1931. Facts concerning the use of thallium in California to poison rodents—its destructiveness to game birds, song birds, and other valuable wild life. Condor 33(3):92–106

———. 1933. The nesting season of birds in Doniphan County, Kansas. Condor 35(4):155–160.

Lisano, M. E. and J. E. Kennamer. 1977. Values for several blood parameters in eastern wild turkeys. Poult. Sci. 56(1):157–166.

Litwer, G. 1926. Die histologischen Veräderungen der Kropfwandung bei Tauben, zur Zeit der Bebruütung und Ausfütterung ihrer Jungen. Z. Zellforsch. u. Mikr. Anat. 3(4):695–722.

Locke, L. N. 1961. Pox in mourning doves in the United States. J. Wildl. Manage. 25(2):211–212.

Locke, L. N. and G. E. Bagley. 1967. Lead poisoning in a sample of Maryland doves. J. Wildl. Manage. 31(3):515–518.

Locke, L. N., C. M. Herman, and E. S. King, Jr. 1960a. Case report—pox in the mourning dove in Maryland. Avian Dis. 4(2):198–202.

———. 1960b. The need for differentiation of trichomoniasis and pox infections in doves. J. Wildl. Manage. 24(3):348.

Lofts, B. and R. K. Murton. 1968. Photoperiodic and physiological adaptations regulating avian breeding cycles and their ecological significance. J. Zool. 155(3): 327–394.

———. 1973. Reproduction in birds. Pages 1–107 in D. S. Turner and J. R. King, eds., Avian biology. Vol III. Academic Press, New York. 573 pp.

Lofts, B., R. K. Murton, and N. J. Westwood. 1966. Gonadal cycles and the evolution of the breeding seasons in British Columbidae. J. Zool. 150(2):249–272.

Lord, K. J. 1984. The zooarcheology of Hinds Cave (41 VV 456). Ph.D. dissertation. Univ. Texas, Austin. 310 pp.

Losito, M. P. 1988. Activity budgets, habitat use, and local movements of hatching-year mourning doves in northern Alabama. M.S. thesis, Auburn Univ., Auburn, Alabama. 115 pp.

Losito, M. P. and R. E. Mirarchi. 1991. Summertime habitat use and movements of hatching-year mourning doves in northern Alabama. J. Wildl. Manage. 55(1): 137–146.

Losito, M. P., R. E. Mirarchi, and G. A. Baldassarre. 1989. New techniques for time-activity studies of avian flocks in view-restricted habitats. J. Field Ornithol. 60(3): 388–396.

———. 1990. Summertime activity budgets of hatching-year mourning doves. Auk 107(1):18–24.

Lott, D., S. D. Scholz, and D. S. Lehrman. 1967. Exteroceptive stimulation of the reproductive system of the female ring dove (Streptopelia risoria) by the mate and by the colony milieu. Anim. Behav. 15(4):433–437.

Low, S. H. 1935. Notes on the survival, winter distribution, and migration speed of eastern mourning doves. Bird-Banding 6(2):61–65.

Lowe, J. I. 1956. Breeding density and productivity of mourning doves on a county-wide basis in Georgia. J. Wildl. Manage. 20(4):428–433.

Lumpkin, J. and N. A. Coleman. 1982. The South Carolina wildlife cookbook. 2nd ed. South Carolina Wildl. and Marine Resour. Dept., Columbia. 246 pp.

Lumpkin, S. 1983. Female manipulation of male avoidance of cuckoldry behavior in ring doves. Pages 91–110 in S. K. Wasser, ed., Social behavior of female vertebrates. Academic Press, New York. 399 pp.

Lumpkin, S., K. Kessel, P. G. Zenone, and C. J. Erickson. 1982. Proximity between the sexes in ring doves: Social bonds or surveillance? Anim. Behav. 30(2):506–513.

Lund, J. V. 1952. Nesting activities of the eastern mourning dove in southern Michigan. M.S. thesis. Michigan St. Coll., East Lansing. 54 pp.

Luomala, K. 1978. Tipai-Ipai. Pages 592–609 in California. Handbook of North American Indians. Vol. 8. Smithson. Instit. Press, Washington, D.C.

Luther, D. M. 1979. An intensive study of parental behavior in the mourning dove. Indiana Aud. Quart. 57(4):209–232.

MacDonald, D. and E. M. Martin. 1971. Trends in harvest of migratory game birds other than waterfowl, 1964–65 to 1968–69. Spec. Sci. Rept.—Wildl. 142. U.S. Fish and Wildl. Serv., Washington, D.C. 29 pp.

Macgregor, W. G. 1958. Non-unisexual broods in the mourning dove. J. Wildl. Manage. 22(1):103.

Mackey, J. P. 1954. Some aspects of mourning dove behavior related to reproduction. M.S. thesis. Ohio St. Univ., Columbus. 101 pp.

———. 1965. Cooing frequency and permanence of pairing of mourning doves. J. Wildl. Manage. 29(4): 824–829.

MacMillen, R. E. 1962. The minimum water requirements of mourning doves. Condor 64(2):165–166.

MacMullan, R. A. 1961. Ring-necked pheasant habitat management in the United States. Trans. N. Amer. Wildl. and Natur. Resour. Conf. 26:268–272.

MacPherson, H. A. 1897. A history of fowling, being an account of the many curious devices by which birds are or have been captured in different parts of the world. David Douglas, Edinburgh, England. 511 pp.

Madson, J. 1978. The mourning dove. Winchester Press, East Alton, Illinois. 114 pp.

Mahan, W. 1978. The mourning dove. Pages 3–15 in Game on your land. Part 1—Small game and wood duck. South Carolina Wildl. and Marine Resour. Dept., Columbia. 174 pp.

Main, A. J. and K. S. Anderson. 1970. The genera Ornithoica, Ornithomya, and Ornithoctona in Massachusetts (Diptera: Hippoboscidae). Bird-Banding 41(4): 300–306.

Malecki, R. A., S. H. Allen, J. O. Elliston, K. C. Sadler, W. R. Goforth, and T. S. Baskett. 1974. Cottontail reproduction related to dieldrin exposure. U.S. Bur. Sport Fish. and Wildl. Spec. Sci. Rept. No. 177. 61 pp.

Maltby, H. T. 1958. Banded mourning dove recovered in South America. Bird-Banding 29(1):42.

Manikowski, S. and K. Walasz. 1980. An attempt to age pigeons using layered structure of tibia. Ornis Scandinavica 11(1):73–74.

Manning, A. 1972. An introduction to animal behavior. 2nd ed. Addison-Wesley Publishing, Reading, Massachusetts. 294 pp.

March, G. L. and B. A. McKeown. 1973. Serum and pituitary prolactin changes in the band-tailed pigeon (Columba fasciata) in relation to the reproductive cycle. Canadian J. Physiol. Pharmacol. 51(8):583–589.

———. 1977. Diurnal variations in plasma calcium parathormone and calcitonin levels and crop gland activity in the pigeon. Exper. Endocr. 11(4):263–270.

March, G. L. and R. M. F. S. Sadleir. 1970. Studies on the band-tailed pigeon (*Columba fasciata*) in British Columbia. I. Seasonal changes in gonadal development and crop gland activity. Canadian J. Zool. 48(6):1,353–1,357.

———. 1975. Studies on the band-tailed pigeon (*Columba fasciata*) in British Columbia. III. Seasonal changes in body weight and calcium distribution. Physiol. Zool. 48(1):49–56.

March, G. L., B. A. McKeown, T. M. John, and J. C. George. 1978. Diurnal variation in circulating levels of free fatty acids and growth hormone during crop gland activity in the pigeon (*Columba livia*). Comp. Biochem. Physiol. 59B(2):143–145.

Marder, J. and J. Ben-Asher. 1983. Cutaneous water evaporation I. Its significance in heat stressed birds. Comp. Biochem. Physiol. A. Comp. Physiol. 75(3):425–431.

Mardia, K. V. 1967. A non-parametric test for the bivariate two-sample location problem. J. Royal Stat. Soc., Ser. B. 29:320–342.

———. 1972. Statistics of directional data. Academic Press, New York. 357 pp.

Maridon, B. and L. C. Holcomb. 1971. No evidence for incubation patch changes in mourning doves throughout reproduction. Condor 73(3):374–375.

Marion, W. R. and M. S. Schnoes. 1982. Seasonality of mourning dove nesting in Florida. Proc. Ann. Conf. Southeast. Assoc. Fish and Wildl. Agencies 36:543–551.

Marion, W. R., T. E. O'Meara, and L. D. Harris. 1981. Characteristics of the mourning dove harvest in Florida. J. Wildl. Manage. 45(4):1,062–1,066.

Markham, F. 1975. The Bonapartes. Taplinger Publishing Co., New York. 224 pp.

Markham, O. D. and D. K. Halford. 1982. Radionuclides in mourning doves near a nuclear facility complex in southeastern Idaho. Wilson Bull. 94(2):185–197.

Markham, O. D. and C. H. Trost. 1986. Summer foods of mourning doves in southeastern Idaho. Murrelet 67(2):60–62.

Marn, C. M., R. E. Mirarchi, and M. E. Lisano. 1988. Effects of diet and cold exposure on captive female mourning doves dosed with lead shot. Arch. Environ. Contam. Toxicol. 17(5):589–594.

Marsden, L. 1986. The first landfall of Columbus. Nat. Geog. 170(5):572–577.

Marsh, E. G. and G. B. Saunders. 1942. The status of the white-winged dove in Texas. Wilson Bull. 54(2):145–146.

Martin, A. C., H. S. Zim, and A. L. Nelson. 1961. American wildlife and plants, a guide to wildlife food plants. Dover Publ., New York. 500 pp.

Martin, E. M. 1979. Hunting and harvest trends for migratory birds other than waterfowl: 1964–76. Spec. Sci. Rept.–Wildl. 218. U.S. Fish and Wildl. Serv., Washington, D.C. 37 pp.

———. 1988. Trends in harvest and hunting activity for migratory game birds other than waterfowl and coots: 1987 update. Unpubl. rept. U.S. Fish and Wildl. Serv., Laurel, Maryland. 12 pp.

Martin, F. W., R. S. Pospahala, and J. D. Nichols. 1979. Assessment and population management of North American migratory birds. Pages 187–239 *in* J. J. Cairns, G. P. Patil, and W. E. Waters, eds., Environmental biomonitoring, assessment, prediction, and management—certain case studies and related quantitative issues. Intern. Coop. Publishing House, Fairland, Maryland. 438 pp.

Martinez-Vargas, M. C. 1973. The induction of nest building in the ring dove (*Streptopelia risoria*): Hormonal and social factors. Ph.D. dissertation. Duke Univ., Durham, North Carolina. 66 pp.

Martinson, R. K. 1969. Migratory bird banding needs—January 1, 1969. Unpubl. rept. U.S. Fish and Wildl. Serv., Washington, D.C. 35 pp.

———. 1971. Migratory bird banding needs—January 1, 1971. Unpubl. rept. U.S. Fish and Wildl. Serv., Washington, D.C. 45 pp.

Massey, B. W., K. Keane, and C. Boardman. 1988. Adverse effects of radio transmitters on the behavior of nesting least terns. Condor 90(4):945–947.

Masure, R. H. and W. C. Allee. 1934. The social order in flocks of the common chicken and the pigeon. Auk 51(3):306–327.

Mathiak, H. A. 1953. A mourning dove banding project. Passenger Pigeon 15(1):7–9.

Matthews, G. V. T. 1968. Bird navigation. 2nd ed. Cambridge Univ. Press, London. 197 pp.

Mayer, A. M. 1883. Sport with gun and rod in American woods and waters. The Century Co., New York. 888 pp.

Mayfield, H. 1961. Nesting success calculated from exposure. Wilson Bull. 73(3):255–261.

———. 1975. Suggestions for calculating nest success. Wilson Bull. 87(4):456–466.

———. 1981. Problems in estimating population size through counts of singing males. Pages 220–224 *in* C. J. Ralph and J. M. Scott, eds., Estimating numbers of terrestrial birds. Studies in Avian Biol. No. 6, Cooper Ornith. Soc. 630 pp.

Mayr, E. 1935. Bernard Altum and the territory theory. Proc. Linn. Soc. of New York 45–46:24–38.

McCabe, R. E. 1982. Elk and Indians: Historical values and perspectives. Pages 60–123 *in* J. W. Thomas and D. E. Toweill, eds., Elk of North America: Ecology and management. Stackpole Books, Harrisburg, Pennsylvania. 698 pp.

McCabe, R. E. and T. R. McCabe. 1984. Of slings and arrrows: An historical retrospection. Pages 19–72 *in* L. K. Halls, ed., White-tailed deer: Ecology and management. Stackpole Books, Harrisburg, Pennsylvania. 870 pp.

McClure, H. E. 1939. Cooing activity and censusing of the mourning dove. J. Wildl. Manage. 3(4):323–328.

———. 1941a. Ecology and management of the mourning dove, *Zenaidura macroura* (Linn.), in southwest Iowa. Iowa St. Coll. J. Sci. 16(1):93–95.

————. 1941b. Ecology and management of the mourning dove, *Zenaidura macroura* (Linn.), in Cass County, Iowa. Ph.D. dissertation, Iowa St. Coll., Ames. 366 pp.

————. 1942. Mourning dove production in southwestern Iowa. Auk 59(1):64–75.

————. 1943. Ecology and management of the mourning dove, *Zenaidura macroura* (Linn.) in Cass County, Iowa. Iowa Agric. Exper. Sta. Res. Bull. 310:335–415.

————. 1944. Mourning dove management. J. Wildl. Manage. 8(2):129–134.

————. 1946. Mourning doves in Nebraska and the West. Auk 63(1):24–42.

————. 1950a. An eleven-year summary of mourning dove observations in the west. Trans. N. Amer. Wildl. Conf. 15:335–346.

————. 1950b. Discussions. Trans. N. Amer. Wildl. Conf. 15:169.

————. 1991. Whistling wings. The Boxwood Press, Pacific Grove, California. 99 pp.

McClure, H. E. and R. Cedeno. 1955. Techniques for taking blood samples from living birds. J. Wildl. Manage. 19(4):477–478.

McConnell, C. A. 1967. Experimental lead poisoning of bobwhite quail and mourning doves. Proc. Ann. Conf. Southeast. Assoc. Game and Fish Agencies 21:208–219.

McDonald, M. R. and O. Riddle. 1945. The effect of reproduction and estrogen administration on partition of calcium, phosphorus, and nitrogen in pigeon plasma. J. Biol. Chem. 159(2):445–464.

McGowan, T. A. 1952. An intensive study of the call count as a census method for mourning doves on the Georgia Piedmont. Pages 4–7 *in* Spec. Sci. Rept.—Wildl. 17. U.S. Fish and Wildl. Serv., Washington, D.C. 53 pp.

————. 1953. The call count as a census method for breeding mourning doves in Georgia. J. Wildl. Manage. 17(4):437–445.

McLean, D. D. 1959. O'er deserts and mountains, band returns trace doves. Outdoor California. 20(1):3,7.

McMurtry, L. 1985. Lonesome dove. Simon and Schuster, New York. 945 pp.

McNabb, F. M. A. and M.-F. Cheng. 1985. Thyroid development in altricial ring doves, *Streptopelia risoria*. Gen. Comp. Endocr. 58(2):243–251.

McNabb, F. M. A. and R. A. McNabb. 1977. Thyroid development in precocial and altricial avian embryos. Auk 94(4):736–742.

McNabb, F. M. A., L. J. Lyons, and T. E. Hughes. 1984a. Free thyroid hormones in altricial (ring doves) versus precocial (Japanese quail) development. Endocrinology 115(6):2,133–2,136.

McNabb, F. M. A., F. W. Stanton, and S. G. Dicken. 1984b. Post-hatching thyroid development and body growth in precocial vs. altricial birds. Comp. Biochem. Physiol. 78A(4):629–635.

McNutt, F. A., ed. 1908. Fernando Cortes—his five letters to the Emperor Charles V. Vol. I. The Arthur H. Clark Co., Cleveland. 354 pp.

Meier, A. H. and J. T. Burns. 1976. Circadian hormone rhythms in lipid regulation. Amer. Zool. 16:649–659.

Meier, A. H. and D. S. Farner. 1964. A possible endocrine basis for premigratory fattening in the white-crowned sparrow, *Zonotrichia leucophrys gambelii*. Gen. Comp. Endocr. 4(4):584–595.

Meier, A. H., J. T. Burns, and J. W. Dusseau. 1968. Seasonal variation in the diurnal rhythm of pituitary prolactin content in the white-throated sparrow, *Zonotrichia albicollis*. Gen. Comp. Endocr. 12(2):282–289.

Meier, A. H., D. S. Farner, and J. R. King. 1965. A possible endocrine basis for migratory behavior in the white-crowned sparrow, *Zonotrichia leucophrys gambelii*. Anim. Behav. 13(4):453–465.

Menasco, K. A. and H. R. Perry, Jr. 1978. Errors from determining sex of mourning doves by plumage characteristics. Proc. Ann. Conf. Southeast. Assoc. Fish and Wildl. Agencies 32:224–227.

Merriam, C. H. 1873. Report on the mammals and birds of the expedition. *In* F. V. Hayden, ed., Sixth ann. rept., U.S. Geological Survey of the Territories. Washington, D.C. 844 pp.

Merriam, C. H. and R. F. Heizer. 1879. Indian names for plants and animals among Californian and other western North American tribes. Ballena Press, Socorro, New Mexico. 296 pp.

Michel, G. F. and C. L. Moore. 1985. Contribution of nesting experience to progesterone-induced incubation in ring doves (*Streptopelia risoria*). J. Compar. Psych. 99(3):259–265.

Miles, A. K. 1976. Fall migration of mourning doves in the Western Management Unit. M.S. thesis. Oregon St. Univ., Corvallis. 85 pp.

Miller, A. H. 1941. The buccal food-carrying pouches of the rosy finch. Condor 43(1):72–73.

Miller, A. H. and I. S. DeMay. 1942. Fossil birds of California. Univ. California Publ. Zool. 47(4):47–142.

Miller, L. 1925. Avifauna of the McKittrick Pleistocene. Univ. California Publ. Geol. Sci. XV(9):307–326.

————. 1943. The Pleistocene birds of San Josecito Cavern, Mexico. Univ. California Publ. Zool. 47(5):143–168.

Miller, R. A. and O. Riddle. 1943. Effects of prolactin and cortical hormones on body weight and food intake of adrenalectomized pigeons. Proc. Soc. Exper. Biol. Med. 52:231–233.

Miller, W. J. and F. H. Wagner. 1955. Sexing mature Columbiformes by cloacal characters. Auk 72(3):279–285.

Millikin, D. D. 1955. Bonaparte, Charles Lucien Jules Laurent. Pages 567–568 *in* Collier's Encyclopedia Vol. 3. P. F. Collier and Son, New York.

Minot, H. D. 1895. The land-birds and game-birds of New England. . . . Houghton, Mifflin and Co., Boston. 492 pp.

Mirarchi, R. E. 1978. Crop gland persistence, parental care, and reproductive physiology of the mourning dove in Virginia. Ph.D. dissertation, Virginia Polytech. Instit. and St. Univ., Blacksburg. 249 pp.

Mirarchi, R. E. and R. R. Hitchcock. 1982. Radio-instrumented mourning dove preyed upon by gray rat snake. Auk 99(3):583.

Mirarchi, R. E. and K. Hudson. 1981. Late season production of mourning doves in Alabama. Highlights of Agric. Res. 28(3):10.

Mirarchi, R. E. and P. F. Scanlon. 1978. Egg-laying characteristics of a captive mourning dove colony. Virginia J. Sci. 29:66.

———. 1980. Duration of mourning dove crop gland activity during the nesting cycle. J. Wildl. Manage. 44(1):209–213.

———. 1981. Effects of orphaning on captive fledgling mourning doves. J. Wildl. Manage. 45(1):218–222.

———. 1982. Evaluating mourning dove crop gland activity associated with crop milk production. Alabama Agric. Exper. Sta. Bull. No. 545. 11 pp.

Mirarchi, R. E., D. R. Jensen, and P. F. Scanlon. 1986. Classification of mourning dove crop gland activity phases by discriminant function analysis. J. Environ. Manage. 23(2):149–156.

Mirarchi, R. E., P. F. Scanlon, F. C. Gwazdauskas, and R. L. Kirkpatrick. 1980. Gonadal and hormonal characteristics of juvenile female mourning doves in Virginia. Proc. Ann. Conf. Southeast. Assoc. Fish and Wildl. Agencies. 34:415–425.

———. 1982. Gonadal and hormonal characteristics of captive adult mourning doves during the nesting cycle. Theriogenology 18(6):683–695.

Mirarchi, R. E., P. F. Scanlon, and N. L. Schauer. 1978. Field techniques for detection and evaluation of crop gland activity in mourning doves. Proc. Ann. Conf. Southeast. Assoc. Fish and Wildl. Agencies 32:75–81.

Misch, M. S. 1960. Heat regulation in the northern blue jay, *Cyanocitta cristata bromia* Oberholser. Physiol. Zool. 33(4):252–259.

Missouri Department of Conservation. 1989. Prescribed fire manual. Jefferson City, Missouri. 111 pp.

———. 1984. Hunter education student manual. Compiled by R. D. Stanton, Jr. Education Section. Missouri Dept. Conserv., Columbia. 106 pp.

Monk, H. C. 1949. Nesting of mourning doves in Nashville. Migrant 20:1–9.

Moore, C. L. 1976a. The transition from sitting on eggs to sitting on young in ring doves, *Streptopelia risoria*: Squab-egg preferences during the normal cycle. Anim. Behav. 24(1):36–45.

———. 1976b. Experiential and hormonal conditions affect squab egg choice in ring doves, *Streptopelia risoria*. J. Comp. Physiol. Psychol. 90(6):583–589.

Moore, G. C. 1940. The nesting habits and juvenile development of the mourning dove in Alabama. M.S. thesis, Alabama Polytech. Instit., Auburn. 65 pp.

Moore, G. C. and A. M. Pearson. 1941. The mourning dove in Alabama. Bull. Alabama Dept. Conserv., Montgomery. 37 pp.

Moore, K. C., S. K. Taylor, R. K. Rooel, and G. M. Ehlman. 1988. 1987 Missouri Farm Service custom rates. Agric. Guide 302 (revised). Univ. Missouri Ext. Div., Columbia. 6 pp.

Mori, J. G. and J. C. George. 1978. Seasonal changes in serum levels of certain metabolites, uric acid, and calcium in the migratory Canada goose *(Branta canadensis interior)*. Comp. Biochem. Physiol. 59B(3):263–269.

Morison, S. E., ed. 1963. Journals and other documents on the life and voyages of Christopher Columbus. Heritage Press, New York. 417 pp.

Morrison, J. A. and J. C. Lewis. 1975. Ecology of overwintering mourning doves in Oklahoma. Fed. Aid Proj. 14-16-0008-694. Oklahoma Dept. of Wildl. Conserv. and Oklahoma Coop. Wildl. Res. Unit, Stillwater. Mimeo. 119 pp.

Morrow, M. E. 1983. Primary feather molt of juvenile mourning doves in Texas. M.S. thesis, Texas A&M Univ., College Station. 44 pp.

Morrow, M. E. and N. J. Silvy. 1982. Nesting mortality of mourning doves in central Texas. Proc. Ann. Conf. Southeast Assoc. Fish and Wildl. Agencies 37:19–22.

———. 1983. A comparison of individual and nest survival of mourning doves and implications to nesting studies. Proc. Ann. Conf. Southeast. Assoc. Fish and Wildl. Agencies 37:19–22.

Morrow, M. E., N. W. Atherton, and N. J. Silvy. 1987. A device for returning nestling birds to their nests. J. Wildl. Manage. 51(1):202–204.

Morrow, M. E., A. E. Bivings IV, and N. J. Silvy. 1985. Feather replacement for predicting hatching phenologies of mourning doves. Proc. Ann. Conf. Southeast. Assoc. Fish and Wildl. Agencies 39:499–505.

Morse, F. C. 1922. Birds of the Moree district. Emu 22(1):24–36.

Morton, E. S. 1973. On the evolutionary advantages and disadvantages of fruit eating in tropical birds. Amer. Natur. 107(1):8–22.

Morton, T. 1637. New English Canaan or New Canaan. . . . Jacob Fredrick Stam, Amsterdam. 188 pp.

Mozgovoi, A. A. 1953. Ascaridata of animals and man and the diseases caused by them. Pages 238–243 *in* K. I. Skryabin, ed., Essentials of nematology. Vol. II, Part 1. Israel Program for Scientific Translations, Ltd. Jerusalem. 390 pp.

Mueller, C. D. and F. B. Hutt. 1941. Genetics in fowl: 12-sex-linked, imperfect albinism. J. Hered. 32(2):71–80.

Muller, L. I. 1984. Reproductive capability of wild, hatching-year mourning doves in Alabama. M.S. thesis, Auburn Univ., Auburn, Alabama. 44 pp.

Muller, L. I., T. T. Buerger, and R. E. Mirarchi. 1984. Guide for age determination of mourning dove embryos. Circ. 272. Alabama Agric. Exper. Sta., Auburn. 11 pp.

Munro, R. E. and C. F. Kimball. 1982. Population ecology of the mallard. VII. Distribution and derivation of the harvest. Resour. Publ. 147. U.S. Fish and Wildl. Serv., Washington, D.C. 127 pp.

Murray, B. G., Jr. 1979. Population dynamics. Academic Press, New York. 212 pp.

Murry, R. E. 1952. A food habits study of the mourning dove in Louisiana. M.S. thesis, Louisiana St. Univ., Baton Rouge. 49 pp.

Murton, R. K. 1964. Pigeon milk. Pages 472–473 *in* A. L. Thompson, ed., A new dictionary of birds. McGraw-Hill, New York. 928 pp.

———. 1965. The wood pigeon. Collins, London. 256 pp.

Murton, R. K. and A. J. Isaacson. 1962. The functional basis of some behavior in the wood pigeon *(Columba palumbus)*. Ibis 104(4):503–521.

Murton, R. K. and N. J. Westwood. 1977. Avian breeding cycles. Clarendon, Oxford. 594 pp.

Murton, R. K., E. H. Bucher, M. Nores, E. Gomez, and J. Reartes. 1974a. The ecology of the eared dove (*Zenaida auriculata*) in Argentina. Condor 76(1):80–88.

Murton, R. K., A. J. Isaacson, and N. J. Westwood. 1963. The food and growth of nestling wood pigeons in relation to the breeding season. Proc. Zool. Soc. London 141:747–782.

Murton, R. K., N. J. Westwood, and A. J. Isaacson. 1974b. Factors affecting egg weight, body weight, and moult of the woodpigeon (*Columba palumbus*). Ibis 116(1): 52–73.

Myers, R. L. and P. A. Peroni. 1983. Approaches to determining aboriginal fire use and its impact on vegetation. Ecol. Soc. Bull. 64(3):217–218.

National Research Council. 1970. Land use and wildlife resources. Nat. Acad. Sci., Washington, D.C. 262 pp.

National Wildlife Health Research Center. 1980. Azodrin: Epizootic No. 80–101, Case No. 2183. U.S. Fish and Wildl. Serv., Nat. Wildl. Hlth. Res. Ctr., Madison, Wisconsin.

———. 1982. Parathion: Epizootic No. 82–090, Case Nos. 3033, 3046.

———. 1983. Oxamyl: Epizootic No. 83–150, Case No. 2786.

———. 1984. Carbofuran: Epizootic No. 84–030, Case No. 3623.

———. 1985a. Trichomoniasis: Epizootic No. 85–091, Case No. 5775.

———. 1985b. Lead poisoning: Epizootic No. 85–006, Case No. 5143.

Neff, J. A. 1945. Foster parentage of a mourning dove in the wild. Condor 47(1):39–40.

———. 1947. Habits, food and economic status of the band-tailed pigeon. N. Amer. Fauna No. 58. U.S. Fish and Wildl. Serv., Washington, D.C. 76 pp.

Nelson, A. L. and A. C. Martin. 1953. Gamebird weights. J. Wildl. Manage. 17(1):36–42.

Nelson, G. 1976. Mourning dove nesting success in artificial and natural nests in central Minnesota. Proc. Iowa Acad. Sci. 83(3):112–115.

Nelson, L. J., D. R. Anderson, and K. P. Burnham. 1980. The effect of band loss on estimates of annual survival. J. Field Ornithol. 51(1):263–271.

Nelson, T. E. and L. B. Peck. 1964. An easily constructed economical holder for restraining pigeons. Amer. J. Vet. Res. 25(105):567–568.

Nestler, R. B. 1946. The mechanical value of grit for bobwhite quail in east Texas. J. Wildl. Manage. 9(4): 279–289.

Newsom, J. D., J. B. Kidd, and R. E. Murry. 1953. Mourning dove management in Louisiana. Louisiana Conservationist 5(8):16–18.

Newsom, J. D., D. M. Russell, F. A. Winston, L. E. Foote, and H. S. Peters. 1957. A summary of mourning dove investigations—1948–1956. Trans. N. Amer. Wildl. Conf. 22:360–379.

Newton, I. 1972. Finches. Collins, London. 282 pp.

Nice, M. M. 1922. A study of the nesting of mourning doves. Part 1. Auk 39(4):457–474.

———. 1923. A study of the nesting of mourning doves. Part 2. Auk 40(1):37–58.

———. 1926. Nesting of mourning doves during September, 1925, in Norman, Oklahoma. Auk 43(1):94–95.

———. 1933. Migratory behavior in song sparrows. Condor 35(6):219–224.

———. 1937. Studies in the life history of the song sparrow I. Trans. Linn. Soc. New York 4:1–247.

———. 1938. Notes on two nests of the eastern mourning dove. Auk 55(1):95–97.

———. 1941. The role of territory in bird life. Amer. Midl. Natur. 26(3):441–487.

———. 1943. Studies in the life history of the song sparrow. II. The behavior of the song sparrow and other passerines. Trans. Linn. Soc. New York 6:1–328.

———. 1962. Development of behavior in precocial birds. Trans. Linn. Soc. New York 8:1–211.

Nichols, J. D. and G. M. Haramis. 1980. Sex-specific differences in winter distribution patterns of canvasbacks. Condor 82(4):406–416.

Nichols, J. D. and J. E. Hines. 1987. Population ecology of the mallard. VIII. Winter distribution patterns and survival rates of winter-banded mallards. Resour. Publ. 162. U.S. Fish and Wildl. Serv., Washington, D.C. 154 pp.

Nichols, J. D., B. R. Noon, S. L. Stokes, and J. E. Hines. 1981. Remarks on the use of mark-recapture methodology in estimating avian population size. Pages 121–136 *in* C. J. Ralph and J. M. Scott, eds., Estimating numbers of terrestrial birds. Studies in Avian Biol. No. 6, Cooper Ornith. Soc. 630 pp.

Nichols, J. D., H. F. Percival, R. A. Coon, M. J. Conroy, G. L. Hensler, and J. E. Hines. 1984. Observer visitation frequency and success of mourning dove nests: A field experiment. Auk 101(2):398–402.

Nichols, J. D., K. J. Reinecke, and J. E. Hines. 1983. Factors affecting the distribution of mallards wintering in the Mississippi Alluvial Valley. Auk 100(4):932–946.

Nichols, J. D., S. L. Stokes, J. D. Hines, and M. J. Conroy. 1982. Additional comments on the assumption of homogeneous survival rates in modern bird banding estimation models. J. Wildl. Manage. 46(4):953–962.

Nickell, W. P. 1964. The effects of probable frostbite on the feet of mourning doves wintering in southern Michigan. Wilson Bull. 76(1):94–96.

Niethammer, K. R. and T. S. Baskett. 1983. Cholinesterase inhibition of birds inhabiting wheat fields treated with methyl parathion and toxaphene. Arch. Environ. Contam. Toxicol. 12(4):471–475.

Noble, G. K. 1936. Courtship and sexual selection of the flicker (*Colaptes auratus luteus*). Auk 53(3):269–282.

Normile, J. H. and R. A. Barraco. 1984. Relation between food and water intake in the pigeon (*Columba livia*). J. Compar. Psych. 98(1):76–90.

Nuttall, T. 1832. A manual of the ornithology of the United States and of Canada. Hilliard and Brown, Cambridge. 683 pp.

Oberheu, J. C. 1956. Late summer and early fall foods of the mourning dove, *Zenaidura macroura*, in Illinois. M.S. thesis, Southern Illinois Univ., Carbondale. 54 pp.

Oberheu, J. C. and W. D. Klimstra. 1961. Late summer and early fall foods of the mourning dove in Illinois. Trans. Ill. St. Acad. Sci. 54(3/4):115–120.

Oberholser, H. C. 1974. Bird life of Texas. Univ. Texas Press, Austin. 1,069 pp.

O'Connell, M. E., C. Reboulleau, H. H. Feder, and R. Silver. 1981. Social interactions and androgen levels in birds. I. Female characteristics associated with increased plasma androgen levels in the male ring dove (*Streptopelia risoria*). Gen. Comp. Endocr. 44(4): 454–463.

O'Connor, R. J. 1984. The growth and development of birds. John Wiley and Sons, New York. 315 pp.

Odum, E. P., S. G. Marshall, and T. G. Marples. 1965. The caloric content of migrating birds. Ecology 46(6): 901–904.

Oldys, H. 1911. The game market of to-day. Pages 243–254 *in* Yearbook of U.S. Dept. Agric. for 1910. U.S. Govt. Print. Off., Washington, D.C.

Olson, D. S. 1935. The proposed tree plantations—their establishment and management. Pages 15–17 *in* Possibilities of shelterbelt planting in the Plains region. USDA Forest Service. U.S. Govt. Print. Off., Washington, D.C.

Olson, T. E. and C. E. Braun. 1984. Mourning dove nesting and crop gland activity during September in eastern Colorado. J. Wildl. Manage. 48(3):1,035–1,041.

Olson, T. E., C. E. Braun, and R. A. Ryder. 1983. Cooing activity and nesting of mourning doves in northeastern Colorado. Southwestern Naturalist 28(3):335–340.

———. 1991. Agricultural land use and mourning doves in eastern Colorado: Implications for nesting and production in the Great Plains. Prairie Natur. 23(1):1–10.

Oppenheim, R. W. 1972. Prehatching and hatching behaviour in birds: A comparative study of altricial and precocial species. Anim. Behav. 20(4):644–655.

Oring, L. W., and D. B. Lank. 1984. Breeding area fidelity, natal philopatry, and the social systems of sandpipers. Pages 125–147 *in* J. Burger and B. L. Olla, eds., Shorebirds: Breeding behavior and populations. Plenum Press, New York. 437 pp.

Orr, D. H. 1973. Population characteristics and dynamics of the mourning dove in Tennessee. M.S. thesis. Louisiana St. Univ., Baton Rouge. 124 pp.

Ortega Melendez, H. and H. V. Zamora Treviño. 1984. Study of white-winged dove in Tamaulipas, 1984. Unpubl. rept. (in Spanish). Fifth Latin American Workshop on Function and Manage. of National Wildl. Refuges. Santa Ana Nat. Wildl. Refuge, Alamo, Texas. 10 pp.

Osborn, D., W. J. Eney, and K. R. Bull. 1983. The toxicity of trialkyl lead compounds to birds. Environ. Pollut. 31A:261–275.

Ouellet, H. 1970. Changes in the bird fauna of the Montreal region, Canada. Canadian Field-Natur. 84(1): 27–34.

Pace, D. M., P. A. Landolt, and F. E. Mussehl. 1952. The effect of pigeon crop-milk on growth in chickens. Growth 16(4):279–285.

Palmer, R. S. 1949. Maine birds. Bull. Mus. Comp. Zool. 12. Harvard College, Cambridge, Massachusetts. 656 pp.

Palmer, T. S. 1900. Legislation for the protection of birds other than game birds. U.S. Div. Biol. Surv. Bull. No. 12. Washington, D.C. 94 pp.

———. 1912. Chronology and index of the more important events in American game protection, 1776–1911. Biol. Surv. Bull. 41. U.S. Dept. Agric., Washington, D.C. 62 pp.

Palmer, T. S. and H. W. Olds [sic: Oldys]. 1900. Laws regulating the transportation and sale of game. U.S. Biol. Surv. Bull. No. 12. U.S. Govt. Print. Off., Washington, D.C. 89 pp.

Palmer, W. and J. H. Riley. 1902. Descriptions of three new birds from Cuba and the Bahamas. Proc. Biol. Soc. Washington. 15:33–34.

Passmore, M. F. 1980. Blockage of mourning dove esophagus by an impacted sandbur. Southwestern Naturalist. 25(3):428–429.

———. 1981. Population biology of the common ground dove and ecological relationships with mourning and white-winged doves in south Texas. Ph.D. dissertation, Texas A&M Univ., College Station. 109 pp.

Patel, M. D. 1936. The physiology of the formation of "pigeon's milk." Physiol. Zool. 9(2):129–152.

Payne, R. B. 1972. Mechanisms and control of molt. Pages 103–155 *in* D. S. Farner and J. R. King, eds., Avian biology. Vol. II. Academic Press, New York. 612 pp.

Pearson, A. M. and G. C. Moore. 1939. Nesting habits of the mourning dove in Alabama. Trans. N. Amer. Wildl. Conf. 4:468–473.

———. 1940. Feathers may reveal age of mourning doves. Alabama Conserv. 1(Nov.):9–10.

———. 1941. Dove sex ratio found almost equally divided. Alabama Conserv. 1(7):8.

Pearson, A. M. and W. Rosene, Jr. 1938. Observations on the breeding season of the mourning dove in the south. Trans. N. Amer. Wildl. Conf. 3:865–868.

Pellerdy, L. P. 1974. Coccidia and coccidiosis. Akademiai Nyomda, Budapest, Hungary. 959 pp.

Perdeck, A. C. and C. Clason. 1982. Flyways of Anatidae ringed in the Netherlands—an analysis based on ringing recoveries. Proc. Tech. Meeting on Western Palearctic Migratory Bird Manage. 2:65–88.

———. 1983. Sexual differences in migration and winter quarters of ducks ringed in the Netherlands. Wildfowl 34:137–143.

Perry, M. C., G. H. Haas, and J. W. Carpenter. 1981. Radio transmitters for mourning doves: A comparison of attachment techniques. J. Wildl. Manage. 45(2): 524–527.

Peters, H. S. 1952. A summary of mourning dove call count investigations in Ohio. Pages 35–46 *in* Spec. Sci. Rept.—Wildl. No. 17. U.S. Fish and Wildl. Serv., Washington, D.C. 53 pp.

———. 1956a. 19 million doves. Southern Outdoors 4(6):9.

——. 1956b. Banding—a key to dove management. Trans. N. Amer. Wildl. and Natur. Resour. Conf. 21:365–375.

——. 1961. The past status and management of the mourning dove. Trans. N. Amer. Wildl. and Natur. Resour. Conf. 26:371–374.

Peters, H. S. and T. D. Burleigh. 1951. The birds of Newfoundland. Newfoundland Dept. Nat. Resour., St. John's. 431 pp.

Peters, J. L. 1961. Check-list of birds of the world. Vol. 3. Harvard Univ. Press, Cambridge, Massachusetts. 177 pp.

Peterson, R. T. 1941. How many birds are there? Audubon Mag. XLIII(2):179–187.

Petrak, M. L., ed. 1982. Diseases of cage and aviary birds. Lea and Febiger, Philadelphia. 680 pp.

Petrides, G. A. 1950. Notes on determination of sex and age in the woodcock and mourning dove. Auk 67(3): 357–360.

Pettingill, O. S., Jr. 1985. Ornithology in laboratory and field. Academic Press, New York. 403 pp.

Phreatophyte Subcommittee of Pacific Southwest Inter-Agency Committee. 1958. Symposium on phreatophytes. Sacramento, California. 52 pp.

Picman, J. 1987. Territory establishment size and tenacity by male red-winged blackbirds. Auk 104(3):405–412.

Pike, Z. M. 1810. An account of expeditions to the sources of the Mississippi, and through the western parts of Louisiana . . . performed . . . during the years 1805, 1806, and 1807. . . . C. & A. Conrad & Co., Philadelphia. 356 pp.

Pohl, H. 1969. Some factors influencing the metabolic response to cold in birds. Federation Proc. 28: 1,059–1,064.

Pollock, K. H. 1981a. Capture-recapture models allowing for age-dependent survival and capture rates. Biometrics 37(3):521–529.

——. 1981b. Capture-recapture models: A review of current methods, assumptions, and experimental design. Pages 426–435 *in* C. J. Ralph and J. M. Scott, eds., Estimating numbers of terrestrial birds. Studies in Avian Biol. No. 6, Cooper Ornith. Soc. 630 pp.

Pollock, K. H. and W. L. Cornelius. 1988. A distribution-free nest survival model. Biometrics 44(2):397–404.

Pollock, K. H. and D. G. Raveling. 1982. Assumptions of modern band-recovery models, with emphasis on heterogeneous survival rates. J. Wildl. Manage. 46(1): 88–98.

Pollock, K. H., J. D. Nichols, C. Brownie, and J. E. Hines. 1990. Statistical inference for capture-recapture experiments. Wildl. Monogr. 107:1–97.

Pond, C. M. 1977. The significance of lactation in the evolution of mammals. Evolution 31(1):177–199.

Powders, V. N. and T. Coffey. 1983. Prevalence of the nasal mite, *Tinaminyssus zenaidurae* (Acarina: Dermanyssidae), in mourning doves, *Zenaidura macroura*, from northwestern Oklahoma. Proc. Oklahoma Acad. Sci. 63:107–108.

Preacher, J. W. 1978. Deterioration rates of 35 bobwhite quail foods and their preferential use. Proc. Ann. Conf. Southeast. Assoc. Fish and Wildl. Agencies 32:356–363.

Preston, F. W. and R. T. Norris. 1947. Nesting heights of breeding birds. Ecology 28(3):241–273.

Purdy, P. C. 1978a. La Paloma migratoria en Honduras. Unpubl. rept. DIGERENARE, Dpto. de Vida Silv. y Recursos Ambientales, Tegucigalpa, Honduras. 14 pp.

——. 1978b. Palomas migratorias en Honduras. Tegucigalpa, Honduras: Direccion General de Recursos Renovables Naturales, Depto. de Vida Silv. y Recursos Ambientales. 17 pp.

Purdy, P. C. and R. E. Tomlinson. 1982. Agricultural development in relation to the eastern white-winged dove. Unpubl. rept. Tamaulipan Biotic Province Symp. Corpus Christi, Texas. 20 pp.

Putera, J. A., A. Woolf, and W. D. Klimstra. 1985. Mourning dove use of orchards in southern Illinois. Wildl. Soc. Bull. 13(4):496–501.

Quay, T. L. 1951a. Mourning dove studies in North Carolina. North Carolina Wildl. Resources Commiss., Raleigh. 90 pp.

——. 1951b. Mourning dove studies in North Carolina. Rept. on Fed. Aid Proj. 2-R and 26-R. North Carolina Wildl. Resour. Commiss., Raleigh. 210 pp.

——. 1954. Mourning dove populations in North Carolina. North Carolina Wildl. Resour. Commiss., Raleigh. 46 pp.

Rackham, H. 1947. Pliny: Natural history. Vol. III. Harvard Univ. Press, Cambridge, Massachusetts. 1,250 pp.

Rahn, H. and A. Ar. 1974. The avian egg: Incubation time and water loss. Condor 76(2):147–152.

Rahn, H., C. V. Paganelli, and A. Ar. 1975. Relation of avian egg weight to body weight. Auk 92(4):750–765.

Ralph, C. J. and J. M. Scott. 1981. Estimating numbers of terrestrial birds. Studies in Avian Biol. No. 6, Cooper Ornith. Soc. 630 pp.

Rana, B. D. 1975. Breeding biology of the Indian ring dove in the Rajasthan desert. Auk 92(2):322–332.

Randall, R. N. 1955. Mourning dove production in south central North Dakota. J. Wildl. Manage. 19(1):157–159.

Rappole, J. H. and G. Waggerman. 1986. Calling males as an index of density for breeding white-wing doves. Wildl. Soc. Bull. 14(2):151–155.

Rappole, J. H., E. S. Morton, T. E. Lovejoy III, and J. L. Ruos. 1983. Nearctic avian migrants in the neotropics. U.S. Fish and Wildl. Serv., Washington, D.C. 646 pp.

Rea, A. M. 1983. Once a river. Univ. Arizona Press, Tucson. 285 pp.

Reed, L. L., L. B. Mendel, and H. B. Vickery. 1932. The preparation, identification and assay of prolactin—a hormone of the anterior pituitary. Amer. J. Phys. 105(1):191–216.

Reeves, H. M. 1979. Estimates of reporting rates for mourning dove bands. J. Wildl. Manage. 43(1):36–42.

Reeves, H. M. and S. R. Amend. 1970. External age and sex determination of mourning doves during the preseason banding period. U.S. Fish and Wildl. Serv., Washington, D.C. Mimeo. 5 pp.

Reeves, H. M., A. D. Geis, and F. C. Kniffin. 1968. Mourning dove capture and banding. Spec. Sci. Rept. 117. U.S. Fish and Wildl. Serv., Washington, D.C. 63 pp.

Reisinger, J. H. 1968. Bird bags and mist net bags. Inland Bird-Banding News 40:204–205.

Rensel, J. A. 1952. The life history, ecology and productivity of the mourning dove in central Pennsylvania. M.S. thesis. Pennsylvania St. Coll., University Park. 88 pp.

Revoil, B. H. 1874. Chasses dans l'Amerique du Nord. Transl. by W. H. Davenport in 1874 as The hunter and trapper in North America; or romantic adventures in field and forest. T. Nelson & Sons, London. 393 pp.

Reynolds, B. D. 1936. *Colpoda steinii*, a facultative parasite of the land slug, *Agriolimax agrestis*. J. Parasitol. 22(1): 48–53.

Rice, L. A. and H. Lovrien. 1974. Analysis of mourning dove banding in South Dakota. J. Wildl. Manage. 38(4):743–750.

Ricklefs, R. E. 1968. Patterns of growth in birds. Ibis 110(4):419–451.

———. 1969. An analysis of nesting mortality in birds. Smithsonian Contrib. Zool. No. 9. 48 pp.

———. 1974. Energetics of reproduction in birds. Pages 152–297 *in* R. A. Paynter, ed., Avian energetics. Nuttall Ornithol. Club Publ. No. 15. 334 pp.

———. 1977. Composition of eggs of several bird species. Auk 94(2):350–356.

Riddle, O. 1916a. Studies on the physiology of reproduction in birds. I. The occurrence and measurement of a sudden change in the rate of growth of avian ova. Amer. J. Physiol. 41(3):387–396.

———. 1916b. Sex control and known correlations in pigeons. Amer. Nat. 50(595):385–410.

———. 1917a. The theory of sex as stated in terms of results of studies on pigeons. Science (New Series) 46(1,175):19–24.

———. 1917b. The control of sex ratio. J. Wash. Acad. Sci. 7(11):319–356.

———. 1920. Differential survival of male and female dove embryos in increased and decreased pressures of oxygen: A test of the metabolic theory of sex. Proc. Soc. Exp. Biol. and Med. 18(11):88–91.

———. 1928. Studies on the physiology of reproduction in birds. XXIII. Growth of the gonads and bursa Fabricii in doves, with data for body growth and age at maturity. Amer. J. Physiol. 86(2):248–265.

———. 1931. Factors in the development of sex and secondary sexual characteristics. Phys. Rev. 11(1):63–106.

Riddle, O. and R. W. Bates. 1939. The preparation, assay and actions of lactogenic hormone. Pages 1,088–1,117 *in* E. Allen, C. Danforth, and E. Dorsy, eds., Sex and internal secretions. 2nd ed. Williams and Wilkins, Baltimore. 1,346 pp.

Riddle, O. and E. H. Behre. 1921. Studies on the physiology of reproduction in birds. IX. On the relation of stale sperm to fertility and sex in ring-doves. Amer. J. Physiol. 57(2):228–249.

Riddle, O. and P. F. Braucher. 1934. Studies on the physiology of reproduction in birds. XXXIII. Body size changes in doves and pigeons incident to stages of the reproductive cycle. Amer. J. Physiol. 107(2):343–347.

Riddle, O. and W. H. Reinhart. 1926. Studies on the physiology of reproduction in birds. XXI. Blood calcium changes in the reproductive cycle. Amer. J. Physiol. 76(3):660–676.

Riddle, O., R. W. Bates, and S. W. Dykshorn. 1933. The preparation, identification and assay of prolactin—a hormone of the anterior pituitary. Amer. J. Physiol. 105(1):191–216.

Riddle, O., G. C. Smith, and F. G. Benedict. 1932. The basal metabolism of the mourning dove and some of its hybrids. Amer. J. Physiol. 101(2):260–267.

Ridgway, R. 1915. Descriptions of some new forms of American cuckoos, parrots and pigeons. Proc. Biol. Soc. Washington. 28(18):105–107.

———. 1916. The birds of North and Middle America. U.S. Nat. Mus. Bull. No. 50, Part VII, Washington, D.C. 543 pp.

Rinehold, J. and J. Witt. 1989. Oregon pesticide use estimates for 1987. Spec. Rept. 843, Dept. Agric. Chem., Oregon St. Univ., Corvallis. 75 pp.

Rintamäki, H., R. Hissa, R. J. Etches, C. G. Scanes, J. Balthazart, and S. Saarela. 1986. Seasonal changes in some plasma hormones in pigeons: Diurnal variation under natural photoperiods with constant or seasonably changing ambient temperature. Comp. Biochem. Physiol. 84A(1):33–38.

Risebrough, R. W. 1983. Pesticides and bird populations. Current Ornith. 3:397–427.

Ristow, W. W. 1966. A covey of names. Pages 68–77 *in* A. Stefferud and A. L. Nelson, eds., Birds in our lives. U.S. Fish and Wildl. Serv., U.S. Govt. Print. Off., Washington, D. C. 561 pp.

Robbins, C. S. 1981. Effect of time of day on bird activity. Pages 275–286 *in* C. J. Ralph and J. M. Scott, eds., Estimating numbers of terrestrial birds. Studies in Avian Biol. No. 6, Cooper Ornith. Soc. 630 pp.

Robbins, C. S. and W. T. Van Velzen. 1969. The breeding bird survey 1967 and 1968. Spec. Sci. Rept.—Wildl. No. 124. U.S. Fish and Wildl. Serv., Washington, D.C. 107 pp.

Robbins, C. S., B. Bruun, and H. S. Zim. 1983. A guide to field identification—birds of North America. Golden Press, New York. 360 pp.

Robbins, C. S., D. Bystrak, and P. H. Geissler. 1986. The breeding bird survey: Its first fifteen years, 1965–1979. Resour. Publ. 157. U. S. Fish and Wildl. Serv., Washington, D.C. 196 pp.

Robel, R. J. and N. A. Slade. 1965. The availability of sunflower and ragweed seeds during fall and winter. J. Wildl. Manage. 29(1):202–206.

Roberts, T. S. 1932. The birds of Minnesota. Vol. 1. Univ. Minnesota Press, Minneapolis. 691 pp.

Robertson, P. B. and A. F. Schnapf. 1987. Pyramiding behavior in the Inca dove: Adaptive aspects of day-night differences. Condor 89(1):185–187.

Robinson, L. H. 1972. "Dove" proso millet—new mourning dove food? Proc. Ann. Conf. Southeast. Assoc. Game and Fish Commiss. 25:137–140.

Robinson, T. W. 1965. Introduction, spread, and areal extent of saltcedar (*Tamarix*) in the western states. Professional paper 491-A. U.S. Geological Survey, Washington, D.C. 12 pp.

Robrock, D. P., ed. 1992. Missouri '49ers: The journal of William W. Hunter on the southern gold trail. Univ. New Mexico Press, Albuquerque. 299 pp.

Robson, D. S. and W. D. Youngs. 1971. Statistical analysis of reported tag-recaptures in the harvest from an exploited population. BU-369-M. Cornell Univ. Biometrics Unit, Ithaca, New York. 15 pp.

Roca, P., F. Sainz, M. Gonzalez, and M. Alemany. 1982. Energetic components in the unincubated egg fractions of several avian species. Comp. Biochem. Physiol. 72 B(3):439–444.

Rodgers, R. D. 1983. Reducing wildlife losses to tillage in fallow wheat fields. Wildl. Soc. Bull. 11(1):31–38.

Roest, A. I. 1947. Offshore records of mourning dove and hermit warbler from Baja California. Condor 49(3):130.

Roosevelt, R. B. 1866. The game-birds of the coasts and lakes of the northern states of America. Carlton Publisher, New York. 336 pp.

Root, T. 1988. Atlas of wintering North American birds. Univ. Chicago Press. 336 pp.

Rosen, M. N. 1959. Killing them with kindness. Outdoor California. 20(1):12–13.

Rosene, W., Jr. 1939. A preliminary investigation of the food habits of the mourning dove in Alabama. U.S. Fish and Wildl. Serv. Wildl. Res. and Manage. Leafl. BS-133. 10 pp.

———. 1950. Nesting doves in Iowa. Iowa Bird Life 20(2):34–37.

Rosier, J. 1605. A true relation of the most prosperous voyage made this present yeere 1605. . . . Geor. Bishop, London. Unpaged.

Ross, C. C. 1963. Albinism in North American birds. Cassinia 47:2–21.

Roth, J., and C. Grunfeld. 1981. Endocrine system: Mechanisms of disease, target cells, receptors. Pages 15–72 in R. H. Williams, ed., Textbook of endocrinology. W. B. Saunders Co., Philadelphia. 1,270 pp.

Rowan, M. K. 1983. The doves, parrots, louries and cuckoos of southern Africa. David Philip, Cape Town, South Africa. 429 pp.

Rowan, W. 1931. The riddle of migration. Williams and Williams Co., Baltimore. 151 pp.

Rowland, B. 1978. Birds with human souls: A guide to bird symbolism. Univ. Tennessee Press, Knoxville. 213 pp.

Royall, W. C., Jr. and J. A. Neff. 1961. Bird repellents for pine seeds in the mid-southern states. Trans. N. Amer. Wildl. and Nat. Resour. Conf. 26:234–238.

Royama, T. 1966. Factors governing feed rate, food requirement and brood size of nestling great tits, *Parus major*. Ibis 108(3):313–347.

Ruos, J. L. 1971. Mourning dove status report, 1970. Spec. Sci. Rept.–Wildl. 141. U.S. Fish and Wildl. Serv., Washington, D.C. 36 pp.

———. 1974. Mourning dove status report, 1973. Spec. Sci. Rept.–Wildl. 186. U.S. Fish and Wildl. Serv., Washington, D.C. 36 pp.

Ruos, J. L. and D. D. Dolton. 1977. Mourning dove status report, 1975. Spec. Sci. Rep.–Wildl. 207. U. S. Fish and Wildl. Serv., Washington, D.C. 27 pp.

Ruos, J. L. and R. E. Tomlinson. 1968. Mourning dove status report, 1966. Spec. Sci. Rept.–Wildl. 115. U.S. Bur. Sport Fisher. and Wildl., Washington, D.C. 49 pp.

Rupiper, D. J. and W. M. Harmon. 1988. Prevalence of *Trichomonas gallinae* in central California mourning doves. California Fish and Game 74(4):239–240.

Russell, D. M. 1954. Mourning dove investigations in Kentucky: A four year progress report. Fed. Aid Proj. Kentucky Dept. Fish and Wildl. Resour., Frankfort, Kentucky. 90 pp.

———. 1955. Do we really shoot migrant doves? Proc. Ann. Conf. Southeast. Assoc. Game and Fish Commiss. 9:69–74.

———. 1961. Present status and management of the mourning dove in the Eastern Management Unit. Trans. N. Amer. Wildl. and Nat. Resour. Conf. 26: 375–385.

———. 1974. The dove shooter's handbook. Winchester Press, New York. 256 pp.

Russell, H. S. 1976. A long, deep furrow. Three centuries of farming in New England. Univ. Press of New England, Hanover, New Hampshire. 672 pp.

Ryder, J. P. 1983. Sex ratio and egg sequence in ring-billed gulls. Auk 100(3):726–728.

Saarela, S., R. Hissa, R. Etches, J. Balthazart, and H. Rintamäki. 1986. Seasonal changes in some plasma hormones of pigeons from different environments. Comp. Biochem. Physiol. 84A(1):25–31.

Sabrosky, C. W., G. F. Bennett, and T. L. Whitworth. 1989. Bird blowflies (*Protocalliphora*) in North America. (Diptera: Calliphoridae), with notes on the Palearctic species. Smithson. Instit. Press, Washington, D.C. 312 pp.

Sachsse, K. R. and G. Voss. 1971. Toxicology of phosphamidon. Pages 61–88 in F. A. Gunther, ed., Residue reviews. Vol. 37. Springer-Verlag, New York. 202 pp.

Sadler, K. C., R. E. Tomlinson, and H. M. Wight. 1970. Progress of primary feather molt of adult mourning doves in Missouri. J. Wildl. Manage. 34(4):783–788.

Sahagún, Fr. B. de. 1963–1982 [1559–1569]. General history of the things of New Spain. 13 Vols. J. O. Anderson and C. E. Dibble, translators. School of Amer. Res. and The Univ. Utah, Santa Fe.

Salt, W. R. and J. R. Salt. 1976. The birds of Alberta. Hurtis Publishers, Edmonton, Alberta, Canada. 498 pp.

Samson, F. B. 1978. Vocalizations of Cassin's finch in northern Utah. Condor 80(2):203–210.

Sanderson, G. C., ed. 1977. Management of migratory shore and upland game birds in North America. Intern. Assoc. Fish and Wildl. Agencies, Washington, D.C. 358 pp.

Sanderson, G. C. and F. C. Bellrose. 1986. A review of the problem of lead poisoning in waterfowl. Illinois Natur. Hist. Surv. Spec. Publ. 4. 3 pp.

Sandfort, W. W. 1977. Introduction. Pages 1–3 *in* G. C. Sanderson, ed., Management of migratory shore and upland game birds in North America. Intern. Assoc. Fish and Wildl. Agencies, Washington, D.C. 358 pp.

Sanger, V. L. 1971. Toxoplasmosis. Pages 313–316 *in* J. W. Davis, R. C. Anderson, L. Karstad, and D. O. Trainer, eds., Infectious and parasitic diseases of wild birds. Iowa St. Univ. Press, Ames. 344 pp.

Sasser, R. 1986. Texas mourning doves. Wing and Shot 1(1):52–55.

Sauer, C. O. 1941. The settlement of the humid east. Pages 157–166 *in* Climate and man. U.S. Dept. Agric. U.S. Govt. Print. Off., Washington, D.C. 1,248 pp.

Sauer, J. R. and P. H. Geissler. 1990. Estimation of annual indices from roadside surveys. Pages 58–62 *in* J. R. Sauer and S. Droege, eds., Survey designs and statistical methods for the estimation of avian population trends. Biol. Rept. 90(1). U.S. Fish and Wildl. Serv., Washington, D.C. 166 pp.

Sauer, J. R. and B. K. Williams. 1989. Generalized procedures for testing hypotheses about survival or recovery rates. J. Wildl. Manage. 53(1):137–142.

Sauer, J. R., S. Droege, and D. D. Dolton. In preparation. A comparison of mourning dove population trend estimates from the mourning dove Call-count and North American Breeding Bird Surveys.

Saunders, G. B. 1940. Eastern white-winged dove *(Melopelia asiatica)* in southeastern Texas. Unpubl. rept. U.S. Fish and Wildl. Serv., Washington, D.C. 132 pp.

Sayre, M. W. 1976. Calling behavior of mourning doves related to the Call-count Survey. M.S. thesis. Univ. Missouri, Columbia. 81 pp.

Sayre, M. W., R. D. Atkinson, T. S. Baskett, and G. H. Haas. 1978. Reappraising factors affecting mourning dove perch cooing. J. Wildl. Manage. 42(4):884–889.

Sayre, M. W., T. S. Baskett, and P. J. Books-Blenden. 1981. Effects of radio-tagging on breeding behavior of mourning doves. J. Wildl. Manage. 45(2):428–434.

Sayre, M. W., T. S. Baskett, and K. C. Sadler. 1980. Radio-telemetry studies of the mourning dove in Missouri. Terrestrial Ser. No. 9. Missouri Dept. Conserv., Jefferson City. 17 pp.

Scanes, C. G. and J. Balthazart. 1981. Circulating concentrations of growth hormone during growth maturation and reproductive cycles in ring doves. Gen. Comp. Endocr. 45(3):381–385.

Schafer, E. W., Jr. and L. L. Marking. 1975. Long-term effects of 4-aminopyridine exposure to birds and fish. J. Wildl. Manage. 39(4):807–811.

Schafer, E. W., Jr., R. B. Brunton, N. F. Lockyer, and D. J. Cunningham. 1975. The chronic toxicity of methiocarb to grackles, doves, and quail and reproductive effects in quail. Bull. Environ. Contam. Toxicol. 14(6):641–647.

Schemnitz, S. D. 1975. Food habits and body measurements of mourning doves in southwestern Maine. Life Sci. Agric. Exper. Stn. Tech. Bull. 78. Univ. Maine, Orono. 7 pp.

Schjeide, O. A. and M. R. Urist. 1956. Proteins and calcium in serums of estrogen-treated roosters. Science 124(3,234):1,242–1,244.

Schmid, W. D. 1965. Energy intake of the mourning dove, *Zenaidura macroura marginella*. Science 150(3,700): 1,171–1,172.

Schnell, G. D. and J. J. Hellack. 1978. Flight speeds of brown pelicans, chimney swifts and other birds. Bird-Banding 49(2):108–112.

Schorger, A. W. 1955. Introduction of the domestic pigeon. Auk 69(4):462–463.

———. 1955. The passenger pigeon: Its natural history and extinction. Univ. Wisconsin Press, Madison. 424 pp.

Schrag, L., H. Enz, and H. Klette. 1977. Healthy pigeons. Verlag L. Schober, Hengersberg, West Germany. 198 pp.

Schroeder, M. H. 1970. Mourning dove production in a Kansas Osage orange planting. J. Wildl. Manage. 34(2):344–348.

Schultz, V. 1954. The effects of a severe snow and ice storm on game populations in Tennessee. J. Tennessee Acad. Sci. 29(1):24–35.

———. 1956. A study of mourning dove mortality in the southeast. J. Tennessee Acad. Sci. 31(4):275–286.

Scott, J. M., S. Mountainspring, F. L. Ramsey, and C. B. Kepler. 1986. Forest bird communities of the Hawaiian Islands: Their dynamics, ecology, and conservation. Studies in Avian Biol. No. 9, Cooper Ornith. Soc. 431 pp.

Scott, T. G. and C. H. Wasser. 1980. Checklist of North American plants for wildlife biologists. The Wildl. Soc., Washington, D.C. 58 pp.

Seber, G. A. F. 1965. A note on the multiple-recapture census. Biometrika 52(1–2):249–259.

———. 1970. Estimating time-specific survival and reporting rates for adult birds from band returns. Biometrika 57(2):313–318.

———. 1972. Estimating survival rates from bird-band returns. J. Wildl. Manage. 36(2):405–413.

———. 1982. The estimation of animal abundance and related parameters. 2nd ed. MacMillan Publishing Co., Inc., New York. 654 pp.

Seibert, H. C. 1949. Differences between migrant and non-migrant birds in food and water intake at various temperatures and photoperiods. Auk 66(2):128–153.

Selander, R. K. 1966. Sexual dimorphism and differential niche utilization in birds. Condor 68(2):113–151.

Semenchuck, G., ed. In preparation. The breeding birds of Alberta. Fed. Alberta Natur., Edmonton.

Semmes, T., Jr. 1907. The mourning dove. Oologist 24(1): 8–9.

Sendroy, J., Jr., M. Mackenzie, and A. H. Collison. 1961. Serum protein and calcium of pigeons during the reproductive cycle. Proc. Soc. Exper. Biol. and Med. 108(3):641–645.

Shamis, J. D. and D. J. Forrester. 1977. Haematozoan parasites of mourning doves in Florida. J. Wildl. Dis. 13(4):349–355.

Shani, J., J. Applebaum, and G. Goldhaber. 1977. Movement and localization of prolactin in the pigeon crop sac, an autoradiographic study. J. Endocr. 72(3): 397–398.

Shannon, F. A. 1934. Economic history of the people of the United States. The MacMillan Co., New York. 942 pp.

Sheldon, H. L. 1957. Population and productivity of the mourning dove in central Pennsylvania. M.S. thesis, Pennsylvania St. Univ., College Park. 97 pp.

Shields, W. M. 1977. The effect of time of day on avian census results. Auk 94(2):380–383.

Shotwell, J. A., ed. 1972. [Loye Miller's] Journal of first trip of University of California to John Day beds of eastern Oregon. Bull. 19, Mus. Natur. Hist. Univ. Oregon, Eugene. 21 pp.

Shuman, T. W., R. J. Robel, A. D. Dayton, and J. L. Zimmerman. 1988. Apparent metabolizable energy content of foods used by mourning doves. J. Wildl. Manage. 52(3):481–483.

Siebanaler, J. B. 1954. Notes on autumnal trans-Gulf migration of birds. Condor 56(1):43–48.

Sileo, L., Jr. and E. L. Fitzhugh. 1969. Incidence of trichomoniasis in the band-tailed pigeons of southern Arizona. J. Wildl. Dis. 5(3):146.

Silver, R. 1977. Effect of cyproterone acetate on reproduction in the male and female ring dove *(Streptopelia risoria)*. Horm. Behav. 8(1):8–21.

———. 1978. The parental behavior of ring doves. Amer. Scientist 66(2):209–215.

———. 1983. Biparental care. Hormonal and nonhormonal control mechanisms. Pages 145–171 *in* L. A. Rosenblum and H. Moltz, eds., Symbiosis in parent-offspring interactions. Plenum Press, New York. 284 pp.

Silver, R. and J. Buntin. 1973. Role of adrenal hormones in incubation behavior of male ring doves *(Streptopelia risoria)*. J. Comp. Physiol. Psychol. 84(3):453–463.

Silver, R. and M. J. Gibson. 1980. Termination of incubation in doves: Influence of egg fertility and absence of mate. Horm. Behav. 14(2):93–106.

Silver, R., C. Reboulleau, D. S. Lehrman, and H. H. Feder. 1974. Radioimmunoassay of plasma progesterone during the reproductive cycle of male and female ring doves *(Streptopelia risoria)*. Endocrinology 94(6): 1,547–1,554.

Simkiss, K. 1961. Calcium metabolism and avian reproduction. Biol. Rev. Cambridge Philos. Soc. 36(3): 321–367.

Sims, M. E., G. F. Ball, and M.-F. Cheng. 1987. Sperm competition after sequential mating in the ringed turtle dove. Condor 89(1):112–116.

Sinclair, A. R. E. 1983. The function of distance movements in vertebrates. Pages 240–258 *in* I. R. Swingland and P. J. Greenwood, eds., The ecology of animal movement. Clarendon Press, Oxford. 311 pp.

Sitgreaves, L. 1854. Report of an expedition down the Zuni and Colorado rivers. Senate Report, 53rd Congress, 1st Session. Beverly Tucker, Senate Printer, Washington, D.C. 198 pp.

Skutch, A. F. 1949. Do tropical birds rear as many young as they can nourish? Ibis 91(3):430–455.

———. 1991. Life of the pigeon. Cornell Univ. Press, Ithaca, New York. 130 pp.

Slade, N. A. 1969. Factors affecting mourning dove use of water in artificial catchment basins in a dryland farming area of Utah. M.S. thesis, Utah St. Univ., Logan. 61 pp.

Slipp, J. W. 1941. Notes on the mourning dove in the Northwest. Murrelet 22(3):59–60.

Smith, A. R. and C. Adam. In press. An atlas of Saskatchewan birds. Saskatchewan Natur. Hist. Soc., Regina.

Smith, G. J. 1987. Pesticide use and toxicology in relation to wildlife: organophosphorus and carbamate compounds. U.S. Fish and Wildl. Serv. Resour. Publ. 170. 171 pp.

Smith, J. 1624. The generall historie of Virginia, New England & the Summer Isles. . . . 6 books printed as 1. Printed by I. D. and I. H. for Michael Sparkes, London. *In* Phillip L. Barbour, ed., 1986, The complete works of Captain John Smith. 3 vols. Univ. North Carolina Press, Chapel Hill.

Smith, M., comp. 1979. Chronological landmarks in American agriculture. Agric. Info. Bull. 425. U.S. Dept. Agric., Washington, D. C. 103 pp.

Smith, N. G. 1967. Visual isolation in gulls. Sci. Amer. 214(4):94–102.

Smith, P. B. 1961. Mourning dove harvest by hunting field types. Proc. Ann. Conf. Southeast. Assoc. Game and Fish Commiss. 15:74–77.

Smith, W. A. 1968. The band-tailed pigeon in California. California Fish and Game 54(1):4–16.

———. 1970. Mourning dove and jacksnipe population surveys and management studies, 1969–70. Unpub. rept. Fed. Aid Proj. W-47-R-18. California Dept. Fish and Game, Sacramento. 13 pp.

Smyth, M. and G. A. Bartholomew. 1966. Effects of water deprivation and sodium chloride on the blood and urine of the mourning dove. Auk 83(4):597–602.

Soileau, L. D. 1960. Eastern mourning dove production in Roselawn Cemetery, Baton Rouge, Louisiana. M.S. thesis, Louisiana State Univ., Baton Rouge. 38 pp.

Sokol, R. R. and F. J. Rohlf. 1969. Biometry. W. H. Freeman and Co., San Francisco. 776 pp.

Sooter, C. A. 1954. A technique for bleeding nestling birds by cardiac puncture for viral studies. J. Wildl. Manage 8(3):409–410.

Soukhanov, A. H. and K. Ellis. 1984. Webster's II. New Riverside University Dictionary. Houghton Mifflin Co., Boston. 1536 pp.

Southeastern Association of Game and Fish Commissioners. 1957. Mourning dove investigations 1948–1956. Southeast. Assoc. Game and Fish Commiss. Tech. Bull. 1. 166 pp.

Soutiere, E. C. and E. G. Bolen. 1972. Role of fire in mourning dove nesting ecology. Proc. Ann. Tall Timbers Fire Ecol. Conf. 12:277–288.

———. 1976. Mourning dove nesting on tobosa grassmesquite rangeland sprayed with herbicides and burned. J. Range Manage. 29(3):226–231.

Sparkman, P. S. 1908. The culture of the Luiseño Indians. Univ. California Publ. in Amer. Archeol. and Ethnol. 8(4):187–234.

Speck, F. G. 1946. Bird nomenclature and song interpretations of the Canadian Delaware: An essay in ethnoornithology. J. Washington Acad. Sci. 36(8):249–256.

Spencer, D. A. 1945. Compound 1080, sodium fluoroacetate, as a control agent for field rodents. Nat. Res. Council Insect Control Comm. Rept. 161. Partial Interim Rept. 22 pp.

Sprunt, A., IV. 1951. The seasonal population and nesting success of the mourning dove in Virginia. M.S. thesis, Virginia Polytechnic Institute and State Univ., Blacksburg. 60 pp.

Squires, W. A. 1960. Recent changes in the abundance of certain species of birds in New Brunswick. Maine Field Natur. 16(4):70–76.

Stabler, R. M. 1948. Protection in pigeons against virulent *Trichomonas gallinae* acquired by infection with milder strains. J. Parasitol. 34(2):150–153.

———. 1951. A survey of Colorado band-tailed pigeons, mourning doves, and wild common pigeons for *Trichomonas gallinae*. J. Parasitol. 37(5):471–472.

———. 1954. *Trichomonas gallinae*: A review. Exper. Parasitol. 3(4):368–402.

———. 1961. A parasitological survey of fifty-one eastern white-winged doves. J. Parasitol. 47(2):309–311.

Stabler, R. M. and C. E. Braun. 1979. Effects of a California-derived strain of *Trichomonas gallinae* on Colorado bandtailed pigeons. California Fish and Game 65(1): 56–58.

Stabler, R. M. and C. M. Herman. 1951. Upper digestive tract trichomoniasis in mourning doves and other birds. Trans. N. Amer. Wildl. Conf. 18:145–163.

Stabler, R. M. and N. J. Kitzmiller. 1967. Emtryl in the treatment of trichomoniasis in pigeons and hawks. J. N. Amer. Falconer's Assoc. 6(1):47–49.

Stabler, R. M., B. M. Honigberg, and V. M. King. 1964. Effect of certain laboratory procedures on virulence of the Jones' Barn strain of *Trichomonas gallinae* for pigeons. J. Parasitol. 50(1):36–41.

Stair, J. L. 1959. White-winged dove die-off at Maricopa. Project W-53-R-9. Arizona Game and Fish Dept., Phoenix. 8 pp.

Stevenson, H. M. 1957. The relative magnitude of the trans-Gulf and circum-Gulf spring migrations. Wilson Bull. 69(1):39–77.

Stewart, O. C. 1951. Burning and natural vegetation of the United States. Georgia Rev. 41:317–330.

Stewart, P. A. and J. P. Mackey, Jr. 1954. A pair of mourning doves occupies same nest two successive years. Bird-Banding 24(1):16.

Stickney, H. W. 1967. Preferences exhibited by the mourning dove and blackbirds for 19 kinds of seeds. M.S. thesis, Auburn Univ., Auburn, Alabama. 61 pp.

Stock, C. 1972. Rancho La Brea: A record of Pleistocene life in California. Los Angeles Co. Mus. Natur. Hist. Sci. Ser. No. 20. Paleont. No. 11. 81 pp.

Stockard, C. R. 1905. Nesting habits of birds in Mississippi. Auk 22(2):146–158.

Stoddard, H. L. 1931. The bobwhite quail. Charles Scribner's Sons, New York. 559 pp.

Stone, C. P. 1963. Use of the coo-count census for mourning doves in Larimer County, Colorado. M.S. thesis, Colorado St. Univ., Fort Collins. 102 pp.

———. 1966. A literature review on mourning dove song as related to the coo-count census. Spec. Rept. No. 11, Colorado Dept. Game, Fish and Parks, and Coop. Wildl. Res. Unit, Fort Collins. 29 pp.

Stone, W. 1937. Bird studies at Old Cape Way. Pages 615–618 *in* Vol. 2. Philadelphia Acad. Natur. Sci. No. 521. 941 pp.

Stone, W. B. 1979. Poisoning of wild birds by organophosphate and carbamate pesticides. New York Fish and Game J. 26(1):37–47.

Strandtmann, R. W. 1961. *Neonyssus triangulus* n. sp., nasal mite (Acarina: Mesostigmata) from the white-winged dove (Aves: Columbiformes) and key to the species of the genus *Neonyssus*. J. Parasitol. 47(2): 323–328.

Sturkie, P. D. and W. J. Mueller. 1976. Reproduction in the female and egg production. Pages 302–330 *in* P. D. Sturkie, ed., Avian physiology. 3rd ed. Springer-Verlag, New York. 400 pp.

Sturkie, P. D. and H. Opel. 1976. Reproduction in the male, fertilization, and early development. Pages 331–347 *in* P. D. Sturkie, ed., Avian physiology. 3rd ed. Springer-Verlag, New York. 400 pp.

Stutchberry, B. J. and R. J. Robertson. 1985. Floating populations of female tree swallows. Auk 102(3):651–654.

Subcommittee on Standardization of Common and Botanical Names of Weeds. 1966. Standardized names of weeds. Weeds 14(4):347–386.

Sutton, G. M. 1967. Oklahoma birds. Univ. Oklahoma Press, Norman. 674 pp.

Swank, W. G. 1952. Contributions to the knowledge of the life history and ecology of the mourning dove in Texas. Ph.D. dissertation, Texas A&M Coll., College Station. 157 pp.

———. 1952. Trapping and marking adult nesting doves. J. Wildl. Manage. 16(1):87–90.

———. 1955a. Nesting and production of the mourning dove in Texas. Ecology 36(3):495–505.

———. 1955b. Feather molt as an aging technique for mourning doves. J. Wildl. Manage. 19(3):412–414.

Swift, E. and C. H. Lawrence. 1966. Laws that protect. Pages 468–475 *in* A. Stefferud and A. Nelson, eds., Birds in our lives. U.S. Fish and Wildl. Serv. U.S. Govt. Print. Off., Washington, D.C. 561 pp.

Taber, R. D. 1949. A new marker for game birds. J. Wildl. Manage. 13(2):228–231.

Taber, W. B., Jr. 1926. Special studies of mourning doves by the bird banding method. Wilson Bull. 38(3):172–174.

————. 1928. A method to determine the weight of food digested daily by birds. Auk 45(3):339–341.

————. 1930. The fall migration of mourning doves. Wilson Bull. 42(1):17–28.

Tarboten, W. 1976. Meyer's parrots at the nest. Bokmakierie 28(1):44.

Tautin, J., S. M. Carney, and J. B. Bortner. 1989. A national migratory game bird harvest survey: A continuing need. Trans. N. Amer. Wildl. and Natur. Resour. Conf. 54:545–551.

Taylor, M. H. 1941. Breeding and nesting activities of the eastern mourning dove in North Carolina. M.S. thesis, North Carolina St. Coll., Raleigh. 81 pp.

Teer, J. G. and N. K. Forrest. 1968. Bionomic and ethical implications of commercial game harvest programs. Trans. N. Amer. Wildl. and Natur. Resour. Conf. 33:193–204.

Terres, J. K. 1980. The Audubon Society encyclopedia of North American birds. Alfred A. Knopf, Inc., New York. 1,109 pp.

Thomforde, L. L. 1972. Migration and mortality of banded mourning doves. J. Minn. Acad. Sci. 38(2/3):72–76.

Thompson, A. L. 1936. Bird migration. Witherby Limited, London. 192 pp.

Thompson, D. R. 1950. Foot-freezing and arrestment of post-juvenal wing molt in the mourning dove. Wilson Bull. 62(4):212–213.

Thompson, M. C. and R. L. DeLong. 1967. The use of cannon and rocket-projected nets for trapping shorebirds. Bird-Banding 38(3):214–218.

Thornwaite, C. W. 1941. Climate and settlement in the Great Plains. Pages 177–187 *in* Climate and man. U.S. Dept. Agric. U.S. Govt. Print. Off, Washington, D.C. 1,248 pp.

Thorpe, D. H. 1961. Bird song: The biology of vocal communication and expression in birds. Cambridge Univ. Press, England. 143 pp.

Thwaites, R. G., ed. 1905. Original journals of the Lewis and Clark Expedition, 1804–1806. 7 vols. plus atlas. Dodd, Mead & Co., New York.

————. 1906. Maximilian, Prince of Wied's, travels in the interior of North America, 1832–1834. Part 1. *In* Early western travels, 1748–1846. . . . Vol. XXII. The Arthur H. Clark Co., Cleveland. 393 pp.

Tobin, M. E. and R. L. Hothem. 1983. Diurnal and seasonal abundance patterns of birds in vineyards. Proc. Bird Control Sem. 9:143–149.

Tobler, S. L. and J. C. Lewis. 1981. Bobwhite foods in six Oklahoma habitats. Proc. Ann. Conf. Southeast. Assoc. Fish and Wildl. Agencies 34:430–441.

Todd, W. E. C. 1940. Birds of western Pennsylvania. Univ. Pittsburgh Press, Pittsburgh. 710 pp.

Toepfer, E. W. 1964. *Colpoda steinii* in oral swabbings from mourning doves (*Zenaidura macroura* L.). J. Parasitol. 50(5):703.

Tomback, D. F. 1975. An emetic technique to investigate food preferences. Auk 92(3):581–583.

Tomlinson, R. E. 1959. Migrational homing and local movements of mourning doves. M.A. thesis, Univ. Missouri, Columbia. 86 pp.

————. 1965. Mourning dove status report, 1965. Spec. Sci. Rept. – Wildl. 91. U.S. Fish and Wildl. Serv. Washington, D.C. 37 pp.

————. 1966. A long-range research and management program for mourning doves. Unpubl. rept. U.S. Fish and Wildl. Serv., Laurel, Maryland. 48 pp.

————. 1968. Reward banding to determine reporting rate of recovered mourning dove bands. J. Wildl. Manage. 32(1):6–11.

————. 1988, 1989, 1990. Hunter declarations at border ports of doves and pigeons bagged in Mexico. Unpubl. repts. U.S. Fish and Wildl. Serv., Albuquerque, New Mexico. 12, 13, 14 pp.

Tomlinson, R. E. and D. D. Dolton. 1987. Current status of the mourning dove in the Western Management Unit. Proc. Ann. Conf. West. Assoc. Fish and Wildl. Agencies. 67:119–133.

Tomlinson, R. E., D. D. Dolton, H. M. Reeves, J. D. Nichols, and L. A. McKibben. 1988. Migration, harvest, and population characteristics of mourning doves banded in the Western Management Unit, 1964–77. Fish and Wildl. Tech. Rept. 13. U.S. Fish and Wildl. Serv., Washington, D.C. 101 pp.

Tomlinson, R. E., P. Smith, and L. A. McKibben. 1987. Agricultural practices and their possible effects on mourning dove populations in the Western Management Unit. Unpubl. rept. to the Western Migratory Upland Game Bird Comm. 9 pp. +

Tomlinson, R. E., H. M. Wight, and T. S. Baskett. 1960. Migrational homing, local movement, and mortality of mourning doves in Missouri. Trans. N. Amer. Wildl. and Natur. Resour. Conf. 25:253–267.

Tongson, M. S., V. Sicam, and V. Trovela. 1975. *Ornithostrongylus quadriradiatus* (Stevenson, 1904)—a hitherto unreported helminth of domestic pigeons in the Philippines. Philadelphia J. Vet. Med. 14(1):144–150.

Tori, G. M. and L. P. Mayer. 1981. Effects of polychlorinated biphenyls on the metabolic rates of mourning doves exposed to low ambient temperatures. Bull. Environ. Contam. Toxicol. 27(5):678–682.

Tori, G. M. and T. J. Peterle. 1983. Effects of PCBs on mourning dove courtship behavior. Bull. Environ. Contam. Toxicol. 30(1):44–49.

Townsend, C. W. 1890. Scientific results of explorations by the U.S. Fish Commission steamer Albatross. No. XIV. Birds from the coasts of western North America and adjacent islands, collected in 1888–89, with descriptions of new species. Proc. U.S. Nat. Mus. 13(799):131–142.

Trautman, M. B. 1940. The birds of Buckeye Lake, Ohio. Univ. Michigan Press, Ann Arbor. 466 pp.

Trefethen, J. B. 1961. Crusade for wildlife. Boone and Crockett Club. Winchester Press, New York. 377 pp.

Trewartha, G. T. 1941. Climate and settlement of the subhumid lands. Pages 167–176 *in* Climate and man. U.S. Dept. Agric. U.S. Govt. Print. Off., Washington, D.C. 1,248 pp.

Trippensee, R. G. 1948. Wildlife management: Upland game birds and general principles. McGraw-Hill Book Co., New York. 479 pp.

Trivers, R. L. 1972. Parental investment and sexual selection. Pages 136–179 *in* B. Campbell, ed., Sexual selection and the descent of man, 1871–1971. Aldine-Atherton, Chicago. 378 pp.

Truett, J. C. 1966. Movements of immature mourning doves in southern Arizona. M.S. thesis, Univ. Arizona, Tucson. 60 pp.

Trumbull, G. 1888. Names and portraits of birds which interest gunners, with descriptions in languages understood of the people. Harper and Brothers, New York. 221 pp.

Tucker, R. K. and D. G. Crabtree. 1970. Handbook of toxicity of pesticides to wildlife. Resour. Publ. 84. U.S. Fish and Wildl. Serv., Washington, D.C. 131 pp.

Tufts, R. W. 1961. The birds of Nova Scotia. Nova Scotia Mus., Halifax. 481 pp.

Tweit, R. C. and J. C. Tweit. 1986. Urban development effects on the abundance of some common resident birds of the Tucson area of Arizona. Amer. Birds 40(3):431–436.

Tyler, H. A. 1979. Pueblo birds and myths. Univ. Oklahoma Press, Norman. 308 pp.

Tyler, J. D. and G. L. Jenkins. 1979. Notes on some fall foods of mourning doves in southwestern Oklahoma. Proc. Oklahoma Acad. Sci. 59:82–84.

U.S. Bureau of Biological Survey. 1931. Migratory-bird treaty act regulations and text of federal laws relating to game and birds. U.S. Dept. Agric., Washington, D.C. 18 pp.

———. 1932. Migratory-bird treaty act regulations and text of federal laws relating to game and birds. U.S. Dept. Agric., Washington, D.C. 20 pp.

———. 1934. Migratory bird treaty act regulations and text of federal laws relating to game and birds. U.S. Dept. Agric., Washington, D.C. 21 pp.

———. 1935. Migratory bird treaty act regulations: 1935. U.S. Dept. Agric., Washington, D.C. 7 pp.

———. 1939. Regulations pertaining to migratory birds and certain game mammals: 1939. Wildl. Circul. U.S. Dept. Agric., Washington, D.C. 13 pp.

———. 1940. The status of migratory game birds: 1939–40. Wildl. Leafl. BS-165. U.S. Dept. Agric., Washington, D.C. 22 pp.

U.S. Bureau of Land Management. 1981. Public land statistics. U.S. Govt. Print. Off., Washington, D.C. 194 pp.

U.S. Bureau of Sport Fisheries and Wildlife. 1973. Federal regulations governing the hunting seasons, limits, and shooting hour schedules of mourning and white-winged doves, wild pigeons, rails, woodcock, snipe, sea ducks, and gallinules in the contiguous United States and in Hawaii and of waterfowl, coots, snipe, and cranes in Alaska. Hunting Regulations No. 91, 1973–74. U.S. Dept. Interior, Washington, D.C. 5 pp.

U.S. Department of Agriculture. 1949. Agricultural statistics 1948. U.S. Govt. Print. Off., Washington, D.C. 752 pp.

———. 1951. Agricultural statistics 1951. U.S. Govt. Print. Off., Washington, D.C. 742 pp.

———. 1961. Seeds, the yearbook of agriculture 1961. U.S. Dept. Agric., Washington, D.C. 591 pp.

———. 1963. Agricultural statistics 1963. U.S. Govt. Print. Off., Washington, D.C. 635 pp.

———. 1968. Agricultural statistics 1968. U.S. Govt. Print. Off., Washington, D.C. 645 pp.

———. 1973. Agricultural statistics 1973. U.S. Govt. Print. Off., Washington, D.C. 617 pp.

———. 1978. Agricultural statistics 1978. U.S. Govt. Print. Off., Washington, D.C. 605 pp.

———. 1981. Agricultural statistics 1981. U.S. Govt. Print. Off., Washington, D.C. 601 pp.

———. 1982. Agricultural statistics 1982. U.S. Govt. Print. Off., Washington, D.C. 566 pp.

———. 1983. Agricultural statistics 1983. U.S. Govt. Print. Off., Washington, D.C. 558 pp.

———. 1984. Agricultural statistics 1984. U.S. Govt. Print. Off., Washington, D.C. 558 pp.

———. 1990. Agricultural statistics 1990. U.S. Govt. Print. Off., Washington, D.C. 517 pp.

U.S. Fish and Wildlife Service. 1941. The status of migratory game birds: 1940–41. Wildl. Leafl. BS-196. Washington, D.C. 28 pp.

———. 1942. The status of migratory game birds: 1941–42. Wildl. Leafl. 225. Washington, D.C. 9 pp.

———. 1943. The status of migratory game birds: 1942–43. Wildl. Leafl. 250. Washington, D.C. 11 pp.

———. 1944. The status of migratory game birds: 1943–44. Wildl. Leafl. 261. Washington, D.C. 100 pp.

———. 1945. The status of migratory game birds: 1944–45. Wildl. Leafl. 274. Washington, D.C. 10 pp.

———. 1949. The status of migratory game birds: 1948–49. Unpubl. admin. rept. Washington, D.C. 20 pp. +

———. 1950. Regulations relating to migratory birds and certain game mammals: 1950. Regulatory Announcement 30. U.S. Dept. Interior, Washington, D.C. 15 pp.

———. 1951. Regulations relating to migratory birds and certain game mammals: 1951. Regulatory Announcement 33. U.S. Dept. Interior, Washington, D.C. 15 pp.

———. 1954. Regulations relating to migratory birds and certain game mammals: 1954. Regulatory Announcement 44. U.S. Dept. Interior, Washington, D.C. 15 pp.

———. 1964. Federal regulations governing the hunting–possession–transportation–importation of mourning and white-winged doves, wild pigeons, rails, gallinules, woodcock, and Wilson's snipe and of waterfowl, coots, and cranes in Alaska. Regulatory Announcement 72. U.S. Dept. Interior, Washington, D.C. 11 pp.

———. 1972. Bird banding: The hows and whys. Serv. Conserv. Note 5. U.S. Dept. Interior, Washington, D.C. 7 pp.

———. 1977. Proposal for continuation of September hunting of mourning doves. Unpubl. environ. assess. U.S. Fish and Wildl. Serv., Washington, D.C. 42 pp.

———. 1979. Unique wildlife ecosystems of Texas. U. S. Fish and Wildl. Serv., Albuquerque, New Mexico. 164 pp.

———. 1981. The Platte River Ecology Study. Spec. Res. Rept. Northern Prairie Wildl. Res. Ctr., Jamestown, North Dakota. 187 pp.

———. 1982. Mourning dove nesting: Seasonal patterns and effects of September hunting [cooperative study]. Patuxent Wildl. Res. Center, Laurel, Maryland. 201 + 58 pp.

———. 1986. Preliminary results of cooperative study to develop a harvest survey for migratory shore and upland game birds. Unpubl. rept. Washington, D.C. 11 pp.

———. 1987a. Summary of federal hunting regulations 1987–88. U.S. Dept. Interior, Washington, D.C. 6 pp.

———. 1987b. The sport hunting of migratory birds. Draft SEIS 87. U.S. Dept. Interior, Washington, D.C. 250 pp.

———. 1988. 1985 national survey of fishing, hunting, and wildlife associated recreation. U.S. Dept. Interior, Washington, D.C. 167 pp.

U.S. Fish and Wildlife Service and Canadian Wildlife Service. 1977. Bird banding manual, Vol. II. Bird banding techniques. Population and Survey Division, Canadian Wildl. Serv. Unnumbered.

———. 1984. North American bird banding manual. Washington, D.C.

U.S. Forest Service. 1948. Woody-plant seed manual. Forest Serv., U.S. Dept. Agric. Misc. Publ. 654, Washington, D.C. 416 pp.

U.S. Geological Survey. 1970. The national atlas of the United States of America. Washington, D.C. 332 maps.

———. 1984. National water summary 1983—hydrologic events and issues. Water-Supply Paper 2250. U.S. Govt. Print. Off., Washington, D.C. 243 pp.

U.S. Senate Select Committee. 1960. Water resource activities in the United States. Evapo-transpiration reduction. Print No. 21. U.S. Govt. Print. Off., Washington, D.C. 11 pp.

Vandeputte-Poma, J. 1968. Quelques donnes sur la composition du "lait de pigeon". Z. vgl. Physiol. 58(4): 356–363.

———. 1980. Feeding, growth, and metabolism of the pigeon, *Columba livia domestica*: Duration and role of crop milk feeding. J. Comp. Physiol. 135(1):97–99.

Vandeputte–Poma, J. and G. van Grembergen. 1959. Freie Aminosaure in der Kropfmilch der Taube. Naturwissenschaften 76(9):329.

Van Dyke, T. S. 1895. Game birds at home. Fords, Howard & Hulbert, New York. 219 pp.

van Schilfgaarde, J., Comm. chair. 1989. Irrigation-induced water quality problems. Nat. Res. Coun. Nat. Acad. Press, Washington, D.C. 157 pp.

Van Soest, R. W. M. and W. L. Van Utrecht. 1971. The layered structure of bones of birds as a possible indication of age. Bijdr. Dierk. 41(1):61–65.

Van Tyne, J. and A. J. Berger. 1976. Fundamentals of ornithology. 2nd ed. John Wiley and Sons, Inc., New York. 808 pp.

Varghese, T. 1980. Coccidian parasites of birds of the avian order Columbiformes with a description of two new species of *Eimeria*. Parasitol. 80(1):183–187.

Veghte, J. H. 1964. Thermal and metabolic responses of the gray jay to cold stress. Physiol. Zool. 37(3):316–328.

Voitkevich, A. A. 1966. The feathers and plumage of birds. Sidgwick and Jackson, London. 365 pp.

von Haartman, L. 1949. Der Trauerfliegenschnäpper. I. Orstreue und Rassenbildung. Acta Zool. Fenn. 56: 1–104.

———. 1956. Territory in the pied flycatcher *Musicapa hypoleuca*. Ibis 98(3):460–475.

von Ihering, R. 1935. La paloma *Zenaida auriculata* en el noreste del Brazil. Hornero 6(1):37–47.

Waggerman, G. 1985, 1986, 1987. White-winged dove density, distribution, movement, and harvest. Texas Fed. Aid Perform. Reps. Proj. No. W-115-R. Job. 2. Texas Parks and Wildl. Dept., Austin. 22, 15, 18 pp.

Wagner, F. H. 1952. Preliminary investigations on mourning dove index and survey methods in Wisconsin. Pages 47–53 *in* Spec. Sci. Rep.—Wildl. No. 17. U. S. Fish and Wildlife Serv., Washington, D.C. 53 pp.

———. 1978. Livestock grazing and the livestock industry. Pages 121–145 *in* H. P. Brokaw, ed., Wildlife and America. Council on Environmental Quality. Govt. Print. Off., Washington, D.C. 532 pp.

Walcott, C., and A. J. Lednor. 1983. Bird navigation. Pages 513–542 *in* A. H. Brush and G. A. Clark, Jr., eds., Perspectives in ornithology. Cambridge Univ. Press, Cambridge, United Kingdom. 560 pp.

Walkinshaw, L. H. 1962. Mourning doves raise eight young in the same nest. Wilson Bull. 74(1):101.

Waller, E. F. 1934. A preliminary report on trichomoniasis of pigeons. J. Amer. Vet. Med. Assoc. 84(4):596–602.

Wallman, J., M. Grabon, and R. Silver. 1979. What determines the pattern of sharing of incubation and brooding in ring doves? J. Comp. Physiol. Psychol. 93(3): 481–492.

Walsberg, G. E. 1983. Avian ecological energetics. Pages 160–220 *in* D. S. Farner, J. R. King, and K. C. Parks, eds. Avian biology. Vol. 7. Academic Press, New York. 542 pp.

———. 1985. A test for regulation of egg dehydration by control of shell conductance in mourning doves. Physiol. Zool. 58(4):473–477.

Walsberg, G. E., and K. A. Voss-Roberts. 1983. Incubation in desert nesting doves: mechanisms for egg cooling. Physiol. Zool. 56(1):88–93.

Ward, A. L. 1964. Foods of the mourning dove in eastern Colorado. J. Wildl. Manage. 28(1):152–157.

Warner, R. E., S. P. Havera, and L. M. David. 1985. Effects of autumn tillage systems on corn and soybean harvest residues in Illinois. J. Wildl. Manage. 49(1): 185–190.

Waters, R. E. 1983. How to attract doves for hunting. U.S. Soil Conservation Service, Auburn, Alabama. 16 pp.

———. 1986. Developing dove habitat. Alabama's Treasured Forests 5(2):26–27.

Watts, K. N. 1969. Population dynamics of the mourning dove in Louisiana. M.S. thesis. Louisiana State University, Baton Rouge. 262 pp.

Weatherhead, P. J. 1985. Sex ratios of red-winged blackbirds by egg size and laying sequence. Auk 102(2): 298–304.

Webb, L. G. 1949. The life history and status of the mourning dove, *Zenaidura macroura carolinensis* (L.) in Ohio. Ph.D. dissertation, Ohio State University, Columbus. 147 pp.

Webb, W. P. 1931. The Great Plains. Grosset & Dunlap, New York. 525 pp.

Weber, W. L., and J. B. Theberge. 1977. Breeding bird survey counts as related to habitat and date. Wilson Bull. 89(4):543–561.

Webster, M. D., and M. H. Bernstein. 1987. Ventilated capsule measurements of cutaneous evaporation in mourning doves. Condor 89(4):863–868.

Weeks, H. P., Jr. 1980. Unusual egg deposition in mourning doves. Wilson Bull. 92(2):258–260.

Wehr, E. E. 1971. Nematodes. Pages 185–233 *in* J. W. Davis, R. C. Anderson, L. Karstad, and D. O. Trainer, eds., Infectious and parasitic diseases of wild birds. Iowa State Univ. Press, Ames. 344 pp.

Weigel, R. D. 1967. Fossil birds from Miller's Cave, Llano Co., Texas. Texas J. Sci. XIX(1):107–109.

Wells, D., B. W. Anderson, and R. D. Ohmart. 1979. Comparative avian use of southwestern citrus orchards and riparian communities. J. Ariz.-Nev. Acad. Sci. 14(1):52–58.

Welty, J. C. 1983. The life of birds. 3rd ed. Saunders College Publishing, Philadelphia. 754 pp.

Westmoreland, D. 1986. The significance of clutch size, egg coloration, and other reproductive traits of mourning doves. Ph.D. dissertation, Iowa State University, Ames. 76 pp.

———. 1989. Offspring age and nest defence in mourning doves: a test of two hypotheses. Anim. Behav. 38(6):1,062–1,066.

Westmoreland, D., and L. B. Best. 1985. Effects of researcher disturbance on mourning dove nesting success. Auk 102(4):774–780.

———. 1986. Incubation continuity and the advantage of cryptic egg coloration in mourning doves. Wilson Bull. 98(2):297–300.

———. 1987. What limits mourning doves to a clutch of two eggs? Condor 89(3):486–493.

Westmoreland, D., L. B. Best, and D. E. Blockstein. 1986. Multiple brooding as a reproductive strategy: Time conserving adaptations in mourning doves. Auk 103(1):196–203.

Wetherbee, D. K., and N. S. Wetherbee. 1961. Artificial incubation of eggs of various bird species and some attributes of neonates. Bird–Banding 32(3):141–150.

Wetmore, A. 1931. The avifauna of the Pleistocene in Florida. Smithsonian Misc. Coll. 85(2):1–41.

———. 1956. Additional forms of birds from Panama and Colombia. Proc. Biol. Soc. Wash. 69(13):123–126.

———. 1968. The birds of the Republic of Panama. Pt. 2. Smithsonian Misc. Collect. 150(2):1–605.

Wetmore, A., and B. H. Swales. 1931. The birds of Haiti and the Dominican Republic. Bull. U.S. Nat. Mus. 155:1–482.

White, G. C. 1983. Numerical estimation of survival rates from band-recovery and biotelemetry data. J. Wildl. Manage. 47(3):716–728.

White, L. M., R. E. Mirarchi, and M. E. Lisano. 1987. Reproductive capability of wild hatching-year mourning doves in Alabama. J. Wildl. Manage. 51(1):204–211.

White, S. J. 1975. Effects of stimuli emanating from the nest on the reproductive cycle in the ring dove. III: Building in the post-laying period and effects on the success of the cycle. Anim. Behav. 23(4):883–888.

Whitman, C. O. 1919. Posthumous works of Charles Otis Whitman III. The behavior of pigeons. Carnegie Institute of Washington, Washington, D.C. 161 pp.

Whitney, L. F. 1968. Keep your pigeons flying. P. S. Erickson, Inc., New York. 240 pp.

Wigal, D. D. 1973. A survey of nesting habitats of the white-winged dove in Arizona. Spec. Rep. 2. Arizona Game and Fish Department, Phoenix. 37 pp.

Wight, H. M. 1954a. Doves, bands and flyways. Mo. Conserv. 15(3):10–11.

———. 1954b. Needed: a dove flyway concept. Proc. Ann. Conf. Southeast. Assoc. Game and Fish Comm. 8:78–80.

———. 1956. A field technique for bursal inspection of mourning doves. J. Wildl. Manage. 20(1):94–95.

———. 1962. Mourning dove status report 1962. Spec. Sci. Rep.–Wildl. No. 70. U.S. Fish and Wildlife Serv., Washington, D.C. 33 pp.

———. 1964. Matedness in the mourning dove and its effect on the nationwide dove-call census. Trans. N. Amer. Wildl. and Natur. Resour. Conf. 29:270–281.

Wight, H. M., E. B. Baysinger, and R. E. Tomlinson. 1964. Mourning dove status report, 1964. Spec. Sci. Rep.–Wildl. 87. U.S. Fish and Wildlife Service, Washington, D.C. 38 pp.

Wight, H. M., L. H. Blankenship, and R. E. Tomlinson. 1967. Aging mourning doves by outer primary wear. J. Wildl. Manage 31(4):832–835.

Wiley, J. W., and B. N. Wiley. 1979. The biology of the white-crowned pigeon. Wildl. Monogr. No. 64. 54 pp.

Williams, A. B. 1936. The composition and dynamics of a beech-maple climax community. Ecol. Monogr. 6:317–408.

Williams, L. E., Jr., and R. W. Phillips. 1972. Tests of oral anesthetics to capture mourning doves and bobwhites. J. Wildl. Manage. 36(3):968–971.

Williams, R. 1643. A key into the language of America. Gregory Dexter, London. 97 pp.

Williams, T. 1985. The quick metamorphosis of Indiana's doves. Audubon 87(2):38–45.

Williams-Dean, G. J. 1978. Ethnobotany and cultural ecology of prehistoric man in southwest Texas. Unpubl. Ph.D. dissertation. Texas A&M Univ., College Station. 302 pp.

Willoughby, E. J., and C. T. Krebs. 1986. Adaptability of parental behavior in the mourning dove. J. Field Ornith. 57(3):288–239.

Wilson, D. M., and J. Bart. 1985. Reliability of singing bird surveys: effects of some phenology during the breeding season. Condor 87(1):69–73.

Wilson, K. R., J. D. Nichols, and J. E. Hines. 1989. A computer program for sample size computations for banding studies. Fish and Wildl. Tech. Rep. 23. U.S. Fish and Wildlife Service, Washington, D.C. 19 pp.

Wimmer, R. B. 1953. An ecological study of the mourning dove in Emporia, Kansas, 1953. M.S. thesis. Kansas State Teachers College, Emporia. 111 pp.

Wineland, M. J., and B. C. Wentworth. 1975. Peripheral serum levels of 17B estradiol in growing turkey hens. Poul. Sci. 54(2):381–387.

Winfrey, D. H. 1966. Fort Clark. Pages 63–83 *in* Frontier forts in Texas. R. N. Conger, ed. Texian Press, Waco. 190 pp.

Wingate, D. B. 1973. A checklist and guide to the birds of Bermuda. Island Press, Bermuda. 36 pp.

Winston, F. A. 1951. Mourning dove study. Pittman-Robertson Project 22-R. Florida Game and Fresh Water Fish Comm. 7 pp.

———. 1952. "Flying oranges." Florida Wildl. 13(5):7–8, 50.

———. 1954. Status, movement and management of the mourning dove in Florida. Tech. Bull. No. 2. Florida Game and Fresh Water Fish Comm., Tallahassee. 86 pp.

Wittenberger, J. F. 1979. The evolution of mating systems in birds and mammals. Pages 271–349 *in* P. Marler and J. Vandengergh, eds., Handbook of behavioral neurobiology: social behavior and communication. Vol. 3. Plenum Press, New York. 411 pp.

Wittenberger, J. F., and R. L. Tilson. 1980. The evolution of monogamy: hypotheses and evidence. Ann. Rev. Ecol. Syst. 11:197–232.

Wood, H. B. 1951. Nine-year-old nest of mourning dove. Bird-Banding 22(3):126.

Wood, W. 1634. New Englands prospect. . . . New York: Tho. Cotes. 98 pp + vocabulary.

Woodhouse, S. W. 1852. Description of a new species of *Ectopistes*. Proc. Acad. Nat. Sci. Phila. 6:104–105.

Woodward, C. H. 1929. Long breeding period in captive mourning doves. Condor 31(3):125–126.

Woolfenden, G. E., and S. A. Rohwer. 1969. Breeding birds in a Florida suburb. Bull. Florida State Mus. 13(1):1–83.

Wooters, J. 1979. A guide to hunting in Texas. Pacesetter Press, Houston. 109 pp.

Wright, J. T. 1959. Desert wildlife. Ariz. Game and Fish Depart., Phoenix. 78 pp.

Wright, V. L. 1978. Causes and effects of biases on waterfowl harvest estimates. J. Wildl. Manage. 42(2): 251–262.

Yahner, R. H. 1982. Avian nest densities and nest-site selection in farmstead shelterbelts. Wilson Bull. 94(2):156–175.

———. 1983. Seasonal dynamics, habitat relationships, and management of avifauna in farmstead shelterbelts. J. Wildl. Manage. 47(1):85–104.

Yang, M.-C., and P. Vohra. 1987. Protein and metabolizable energy requirements of hand-fed squabs from hatching to 28 days of age. Poul. Sci. 66(12): 2,017–2,023.

Yoder, H. W., Jr., R. Yamamoto, and N. O. Olson. 1978. Avian mycoplasmosis. Pages 233–270 *in* M. S. Hofstad, B. W. Calnek, C. F. Helmboldt, W. M. Reid, and H. W. Yoder, Jr., eds., Diseases of poultry, 6th ed. Iowa State Univ. Press, Ames. 949 pp.

Young, H. 1948. A comparative study of nesting birds in a five-acre park. Wilson Bull. 61(1):36–47.

Young, H., A. Hulsey, and R. Moe. 1952. Effects of certain insecticides on the mourning dove. Proc. Ark. Acad. Sci. pp. 43–45.

Young, W. C. 1964. The hormones and behavior. Pages 201–254 *in* M. Florkin and H. S. Mason, eds., Comparative biochemistry Vol. VII. Academic Press, New York. 512 pp.

Zeigler, D. L. 1971. Crop milk cycles in band-tailed pigeons and losses of squabs due to hunting pigeons in September. M.S. thesis, Oregon State University, Corvallis. 48 pp.

———. [1977]. Evaluation of the breeding habitat of the mourning dove in eastern Washington. Unpublished rept. Washington Game Department, Olympia. 23 pp.

Zenone, P. G., E. M. Sims, and C. J. Erickson. 1979. Male ring dove behavior and the defense of genetic paternity. Amer. Nat. 114(5):615–626.

Zilker, A. 1976. A study of the productivity and summer and fall ecology of the mourning dove in southeastern Pennsylvania. M.S. thesis, Pennsylvania State University, College Park. 67 pp.

Zinkl, J. G. 1982. Polychlorinated biphenyl (PCB) compounds. Pages 31–37 *in* G. L. Hoff and J. W. Davis, eds., Noninfectious diseases of wildlife. Iowa State Univ. Press, Ames. 174 pp.

Index